THE SCIENCE, TREATMENT, AND PREVENTION OF ANTISOCIAL BEHAVIORS

APPLICATION TO THE CRIMINAL JUSTICE SYSTEM

Edited by
Diana H. Fishbein, Ph.D.

Civic Research Institute
4490 U.S. Route 27 • P.O. Box 585 • Kingston, NJ 08528

Copyright © 2000

By Civic Research Institute, Inc.
Kingston, New Jersey 08528

The information in this book is not intended to replace the services of a trained legal, health or other professional. Civic Research Institute, Inc. provides this information without advocating the use of or endorsing the issues, theories, precedent, guidance, resources, practical materials or programs discussed herein. Any application of the issues, theories, precedent, guidance, resources, practical materials or programs set forth in this book is at the reader's sole discretion and risk. The authors, editors, contributors and Civic Research Institute, Inc. specifically disclaim any liability, loss or risk, personal or otherwise, which is incurred as a consequence, directly or indirectly, of the use and application of any of the contents of this book.

All rights reserved. This book may not be reproduced in part or in whole by any process without written permission from the publisher.

Printed in the United States of America

Library of Congress Cataloging in Publication Data
The science, treatment, and prevention of antisocial behaviors: Application to the criminal justice system/ Diana H. Fishbein

ISBN 1-887554-12-2

Library of Congress Catalog Card Number 99-76750

Acknowledgments

I would like to express my deepest appreciation to Director Tom Carr and the Washington/Baltimore HIDTA Program for being patient with me while editing this book and for supporting my drug abuse prevention efforts. I would also like to thank Deanna Perez and Christine DeStefano for their editorial assistance. And finally, my gratitude and appreciation goes to all those who struggle every day to prevent and treat drug abuse by improving the quality of life for children living under high risk conditions.

About the Authors

Ernest S. Barratt, Ph.D., is the Marie B. Gale Centennial Professor of Psychiatry at the University of Texas, Medical Branch, where he has been on the faculty since 1962. He formerly taught at the University of Delaware and Texas Christian University, and was a special NIH fellow at the Brain Research Institute at the University of California at Los Angeles. His research since the mid-1950s has focused on impulsivity and impulse control disorders. He was a co-founder and past president of the International Society for the Study of Individual Differences. He is currently chief of the Cognitive Neuroscience Laboratory and Psychodiagnostic Service.

Fred S. Berlin, M.D., Ph.D., received his education at a variety of centers, including McGill University in Canada and the Maudsley Institute in England. He is currently an associate professor in the Department of Psychiatry and Behavioral Sciences at The Johns Hopkins University School of Medicine and the Director of the National Institute for the Study, Prevention and Treatment of Sexual Trauma. This program has been designated by the U.S. Department of Justice as a national resource site. Dr. Berlin has addressed a White House Conference on Childhood Sexual Abuse, the Juvenile Justice Subcommittee of the United States Senate, and Colleges of Judges in several states. He has also provided consultation to the National Conference of Catholic Bishops and the European Parliament. He has performed peer reviews for numerous professional journals, including the *Journal of the American Medical Association* and the *American Journal of Psychiatry*. He has been the recipient of a contract from the National Institute of Mental Health to prepare an annotated bibliography on sex offender etiology and treatment, and of a grant from the Guggenheim Foundation to study the activity of brain neurotransmitters during sexual arousal.

Robert J. Blatchley, Ph.D., received his doctorate in human development from the University of Maryland in 1974. He is a licensed psychologist who works with children and adults in private practice and is a research scientist with the Social Research Unit of Friends Research Institute. Dr. Blatchley's major research interest is in the social developmental characteristics of addicts, their families and their children. Currently Dr. Blatchley is clinical supervisor for a major prevention research project involving addict mothers and their preadolescent children.

Don R. Cherek, Ph.D., received his doctorate from the University of Minnesota in 1972 after graduating from Creighton University. He held a research fellowship in the United State Public Health Service Psychopharmacology Training Program at Minnesota. Currently, he is a professor in the Department of Psychiatry and Behavioral Sciences at the University of Texas Health Science Center at Houston. Dr. Cherek has an international reputation for the development of various paradigms for human laboratory research studies. His research is supported by grants DA03166, DA10592, and DA10552 from the National Institute on Drug Abuse.

Diana D. Coates, M.A., L.P.C., is Director of the Youthful Offender Program, Clemens Unit, Texas Department of Criminal Justice. She previously was an associate clinical psychologist with TDCJ and worked as a psychological assistant at the Dallas County Juvenile Department and at the Mexia (Texas) State School. She is a graduate of Baylor University and the University of North Texas.

Emil F. Coccaro, M.D., is a graduate of the New York University School of Medicine, with psychiatric training at the Mt. Sinai School of Medicine. He has authored over 120 publications and is the principal investigator on several National Institute of Mental Health, NIH grants on the biology and treatment of aggression. He has perfected techniques to study central neurotransmitter systems in relation to personality disorders. Currently he is a professor in the Department of Psychiatry, the Pritzker School of Medicine at the University of Chicago.

David E. Comings, M.D., is Director of the Department of Medical Genetics, City of Hope Medical Center, Duarte, California. He is the author of over 400 papers, abstracts, and books on genetics in general, and in the past twenty years on the genetics and molecular genetics of a range of human behavior disorders. He directs a clinic where he has treated over 3,500 individuals with Tourette's syndrome, attention deficit hyperactivity disorder, and conduct and other disorders. He is past president of the American Society of Human Genetics and past editor of the *American Journal of Human Genetics*.

Stephen H. Dinwiddie, M.D., received his medical degree from Eastern Virginia Medical School in 1982 and completed a residency in psychiatry at the Washington University School of Medicine in St. Louis, Missouri. He is board certified in general, forensic, and addiction psychiatry. He is currently Professor of Psychiatry at Finch University of Health Sciences/The Chicago Medical School and Medical Director, Elgin Mental Health Center.

Frank A. Elliott, M.D., is an emeritus professor of neurology at the University of Pennsylvania, and retired Chief of Neurology at the Pennsylvania Hospital. He undertook training at the National Hospital for Nervous Diseases at Queen Square in London. In 1959, he accepted an invitation to organize a Department of Neurology at Pennsylvania Hospital. Dr. Elliott published two textbooks and many chapters and papers on neurological subjects; between 1965 and 1993, he focused on the part played by covert developmental and acquired neurological and neuropsychiatric defects in recurrently violent individuals.

Maurizio Fava, M.D., is associate professor of psychiatry at Harvard Medical School and Director of the Depression Clinical and Research Program at the Massachusetts General Hospital in Boston. He obtained his medical degree from the University of Padua School of Medicine, where he also completed residency training in endocrinology. After moving to the United States, he completed residency training in psychiatry at the Massachusetts General Hospital. He worked as a staff psychiatrist in the Clinical Psychopharmacology Unit for two years and then became Director of the Depression Clinical and Research Program in 1990. Over the past few years, Dr. Fava has been Principal and Co-Principal Investigator in many industry- and National Institutes of Mental Health-supported clinical research studies. His major research interest has been the development of effective short-term and long-term strategies in the treatment of depression and depressive subtypes. Dr. Fava has conducted a number of clinical investigations on a particular depressive subtype characterized by the presence of anger attacks and high levels of irritability and hostility. His contributions to the study of treatment-resistant depression have also been significant, and he was Principal Investigator of the first published study on the pharmacological management of depressive relapses during long-term treatment with antidepressants. Dr. Fava has published more than 120 manuscripts in refereed journals and has edited two books. He has received several awards during his career and is on the editorial board of three international medical journals.

Alan Felthous, M.D., received his medical degree at the University of Louisville School of Medicine and completed his residency training in psychiatry at McLean Hospital and Harvard Medical School. He is Professor of Clinical Psychiatry and Director of Forensic Psychiatry Service, Department of Psychiatry, Southern Illinois University School of Medicine, and Medical Director of the Chester Mental Health Center in Chester, Illinois. Dr. Felthous is Chair of the Psychiatry and Behavioral Science Section, American Academy of Forensic Services, co-editor of *Behavioral Sciences and the Law*, and co-editor of the Forensic Psychiatry Section, *Current Opinion in Psychiatry*.

Carol S. Ferreira, Ph.D., is both a licensed clinical psychologist and an advanced registered nurse practitioner. She received her doctorate in clinical psychology from Kent State University and her master's of science degree in nursing from Wichita State University. Dr. Ferreira completed a postdoctoral fellowship in HIV/AIDS at the University of California at Los Angeles and has an extensive background of practical experience working in rehabilitation settings with persons who have suffered brain damage. Currently, she is a clinical assistant professor in the School of Nursing at East Carolina University. Previously, she was an assistant professor of Community Health Nursing at Washburn University in Topeka, Kansas, where she supervised students in a correctional health care setting. She is active in presenting classes, training seminars, and conference programs focused on both the medical and psychological aspects of crime and corrections.

Diana H. Fishbein, Ph.D., has a joint Ph.D. in psychobiology and criminology from Florida State University. She currently directs the Transdisciplinary Behavioral Science Program for the Research Triangle Institute. Previously, she was Prevention Coordinator and Evaluator at the HIDTA Research Program centered at the University of Maryland and funded by the Office of National Drug Control Policy. Dr. Fishbein began her career as professor of criminology at the University of Baltimore and as a staff scientist first at the University of Maryland School of Medicine and subsequently at the National Institute on Drug Abuse, where she directed neurobiological studies on disruptive behavioral disorders and substance abuse. She then became a senior researcher with the U.S. Department of Justice to develop and evaluate crime prevention programs. Dr. Fishbein consults regularly to federal, state, and local agencies for purposes of expert witnessing in criminal court, training, technical assistance, scientific peer reviews and development of research protocols. In addition to policy papers, her publications include chapters, monographs, and scientific articles on antisocial and violent behavior and drug abuse. She is the primary author of a textbook entitled *The Dynamics of Drug Abuse.*

Wanda D. Foglia, J.D., Ph.D., received both her juris doctorate and her doctorate in criminology from the University of Pennsylvania. She is currently Chair of the Law and Justice Studies Department at Rowan University in Glassboro, New Jersey, where she teaches criminological theory and corrections courses. She is the principal investigator for the Pennsylvania segment of the Capital Jury Project, and her major research interests include cognition and crime, law-related education, and perceptual deterrence.

Peter R. Giancola, Ph.D., received his bachelor's degree in psychology from McGill University and his master's degree and doctorate in clinical psychology from the University of Georgia. He did his clinical internship at the Western Psychiatric Institute and Clinic at the University of Pittsburgh School of Medicine. Dr. Giancola is currently an assistant professor of psychology at the University of Kentucky. His program of research focuses on neuropsychological correlates of aggression and the relation between acute alcohol consumption and aggressive behavior. Dr. Giancola's research is currently funded by the National Institute on Alcoholism and Alcohol Abuse.

David Goldman, M.D., has been Chief of the Laboratory of Neurogenetics of intramural NIAAA/NIH since creation of that laboratory in 1991. Dr. Goldman graduated from Yale University in 1974, received his medical degree from the University of Texas Medical Branch in 1978, and trained as an NIMH Clinical Associate prior to joining NIAAA. His main research interests are the identification of alleles (genetic differences) that influence behavior and the understanding of the mechanisms by which genotype influences behavior. His current work includes studies on the genetics of alcoholism and related psychopathology through the study of population isolates, particularly Native Americans, and the study of families with characteristic phenotypes such as EEG variants and low serotonin turnover. Dr. Goldman has also been an adjunct professor in the Department of Biological Sciences at George Washington University since 1987.

Thomas E. Hanlon, Ph.D., is a research associate professor in the Department of Psychiatry, University of Maryland School of Medicine, Baltimore. He has background training and experience in clinical psychology and in designing and instituting treatment implementation studies, and he has worked for the past several years in the area of substance abuse research and correctional interventions. He has been an author or co-author in approximately twelve published articles in the behavioral sciences, most of which have involved treatment evaluations.

James J. Hennessy, Ph.D., is a professor and past chairman in the Division of Psychological and Educational Services in the Graduate School of Education, Fordham University at Lincoln Center in New York City. He received his doctorate in counseling psychology from New York University, where he specialized in psychological measurement and psychometrics. He serves as a consultant to municipal and other public agencies on program design and evaluation, and has a particular interest in psychometric modeling of crime-rate data. He is co-author, with N. J. Pallone, of *Criminal Behavior: A Process Psychology Analysis* and *Tinder-Box Criminal Aggression: Neuropsychology, Demography, Phenomenology,* among numerous other books and research articles in the field.

Richard J. Kavoussi, M.D., is a graduate of the New York Medical College, with psychiatric training at the New York State Psychiatric Institute. He has authored over fifty publications. Currently, he is the medical director in the CNS Division of Parke Davis Pharmaceuticals.

Tom Kelley, M.S., Ph.D. (cand.), received his master's degree in criminology from Florida State University in Tallahassee. He is currently a doctoral candidate in the Department of Criminology and Criminal Justice at Florida State, where he teaches classes in criminal and delinquent behavior and juvenile justice. He has worked as a Medical Disability Examiner for the Social Security Administration while satisfying the academic requirements for Ph.D. completion.

Thomas A. Kent, M.D., is an associate professor in the Departments of Neurology, Pharmacology and Toxicology, and Psychiatry and Behavioral Sciences at the University of Texas Medical Branch at Galveston, and he is Director of Research there in the Department of Neurology. He completed his residency training in psychiatry at the University of Kansas School of Medicine, and in neurology at the University of Texas Medical Branch. He completed a basic and clinical psychopharmacology fellowship under Sheldon H. Preskorn, M.D. and is board certified in both neurology and psychiatry. He has received funding from a number of peer-review organizations, including the National Institutes of Health, and is the author of over 150 journal articles, chapters in books, and scientific abstracts and presentations.

Scott D. Lane, Ph.D., received his doctorate in experimental psychology from Auburn University. He completed his postdoctoral training in psychopharmacology at the University of Texas Health Science Center at Houston under a fellowship from the National Institute on Drug Abuse. He is currently a member of the Human Psychopharmacology Laboratory in the Department of Psychiatry and Behavioral Sciences at the University of Texas Health Science Center at Houston. His research interests include laboratory measurement of variables related to pathological behavior, including risk taking, aggression, and impulsivity. Relevant research projects are supported by NIDA grants DA 10592 and DA 10552.

Michele J. Liebman, B.S., is a graduate student in psychology at the University of Houston at Clear Lake. She is the chief research technician in the Cognitive Neuroscience Laboratory at the University of Texas Medical Branch, Galveston. Her interests include psychometrics, neuropsychology, and learning theory.

Dwaine McCallon, M.D., is a board-certified pediatrician with a lifelong interest in child development and learning problems. He is the medical director of a 1,000-bed medium security prison and supervises the medical care in a boot camp as well as three honor work camps of inmates. He began the first treatment study for attention deficit disorder in prison populations ten years ago. His present research has extended into Tourette's syndrome, obsessive thinking including the fantasies of sex offenders, and determining behavioral warning signs for future violent crime in adolescents and children. Having presented his work at several national meetings, he is collaborating on an extensive work with Dr. Comings to be titled *Treatable Criminal Minds*.

Brian McNamee, M.D., is currently in the private practice of radiology and the practice of law in greater Metro Cleveland.

David N. Nurco, D.S.W., research professor in the Department of Psychiatry, University of Maryland School of Medicine, Baltimore, has been a prominent contributor to national substance abuse policy and research for the past thirty-five years. His expertise focused on the area of narcotic addiction and in examining the connection between drug use and crime. He served as principal investigator for numerous federally funded studies dealing with the treatment of drug abusing offenders and drug abuse prevention efforts involving inner-city youth. Sadly, Dr. Nurco died in December, 1998. He will be sorely missed by his friends, colleagues, and others in the field.

Richard L. Nygaard, U.S.C.J., has been a judge for eighteen years and is on the U.S. Court of Appeals for the Third Circuit. He received his juris doctorate from the University of Michigan and an LL.D., *honoris causa,* from Edinboro University of Pennsylvania. He has written and lectured extensively on penal philosophy, to promote both research into the genetics of criminal misbehavior and a more humane treatment of rehabilitable miscreants. He is a lecturer in law at Pennsylvania State University at Erie and sits on its Masters in Psychology Advisory Board.

Kevin O'Grady, Ph.D., is an associate professor in the Department of Psychology, University of Maryland at College Park. Having a background of training and experience in clinical psychology, he specializes in data processing and statistical analysis in the medical and behavioral science areas, serving as a consultant and collaborator in substance abuse prevention and treatment research. He has numerous technical and clinical publications.

Nathaniel J. Pallone, Ph.D., is University Distinguished Professor of Psychology at The State University of New Jersey at Rutgers, where he previously served as dean and as academic vice president. He had earlier served at the University of Notre Dame and at New York University and, on leave from Rutgers, as a visiting professor in the Department of Legal Medicine at Harvard's School of Public Health and as Hill Foundation Distinguished Visiting Professor at the University of Minnesota in Duluth. His clinical experience includes twenty-two years as chairperson of the Classification Review Board for Sex Offenders in the New Jersey Department of Corrections. He also served as a consulting psychologist to the New York State Narcotics Addiction Control Commission, the Connecticut Commission on Criminal Administration, and the Criminal Justice Research Center in Albany, New York, and to social service agencies in the northeast and midwest. His current research interests focus on the psychobiology of risk taking, both pro- and antisocial. His recent books include *Altruism, Narcissism, Comity: Research Perspectives from Current Psychology* (1999); *Tinder-Box Criminal Aggression: Neuropsychology, Demography, Phenomenology* (1996); *Fraud and Fallible Judgment: Varieties of Deception in the Social and Behavioral Sciences* (1995); and *Criminal Behavior: A Process Psychology Analysis* (1992, 1994). Earlier notable books include *Rehabilitating Criminal Sexual Psychopaths: Legislative Mandates, Clinical Quandaries* (1990) and *On the Social Utility of Psychopathology: A Deviant Majority and Its Keepers?* (1986). Dr. Pallone presently serves as executive editor of *Current Psychology,* an international research quarterly, and as editor-in-chief of the *Journal of Offender Rehabilitation,* which specializes in correctional psychology.

Roy W. Pickens, Ph.D., has a doctoral degree in experimental psychology from the University of Mississippi (1965) and received postdoctoral training in psychopharmacology from the University of Minnesota (1965–1966). In 1966 he was appointed to the faculty in the Departments of Psychiatry and Psychology at the University of Minnesota, where he taught, conducted research, and provided clinical service. In 1985 Dr. Pickens was appointed Director of the Division of Clinical Research at the National Institute of Drug Abuse in Rockville, Maryland. In 1986 his duties at NIDA were extended to include associate directorship for AIDS. In 1989 he was appointed Scientific Director of the NIDA Intramural Research Program (Addiction Research Center) in Baltimore. He held this position until 1994, when he returned to the laboratory as Chief, Clinical Neurogenetics Section and Associate Director for Training and Education. In July 1999, he accepted the position of Associate Vice President for Research and Director of Research and professor in the Department of Psychiatry at Virginia Commonwealth University.

Wendy Richardson, M.A., L.M.F.C.C., is a Licensed Marriage, Family, Child, Counselor and Certified Addictions Specialist who has been working in the mental health field for twenty-two years. Ms. Richardson is nationally recognized as an expert on ADHD and co-occurring addictions, eating disorders, and relationship issues. She provides training for criminal justice personnel, teaches graduate level courses, and trains professionals on ADHD in America and abroad. Ms. Richardson's new book, *The Link Between ADD and Addiction: Getting the Help You Deserve,* is the first book that sensitively addresses the problems of ADD and co-related addictions, eating disorders, and behavioral addictions; it offers practical solutions in a reader friendly format that people can use to actively address their problems.

Ty A. Ridenour, Ph.D., M.P.E., received his doctorate in school psychology in 1996 from Ball State University in Indiana and his masters in psychiatric epidemiology in 1998 from Washington University School of Medicine. Presently, he is an NIMH postdoctoral fellow in biostatistics and epidemiology at Washington University School of Medicine (grant MH17104). Dr. Ridenour's research interest in the epidemiology and development of antisocial behavior grew out of his four years of counseling and assessment of juvenile delinquents at an Indiana county Boy's Residential Unit and in school settings. His current area of research interest is the etiology of antisocial behavior and substance misuse.

Matthew Robinson, Ph.D., received his doctorate from the Florida State University School of Criminology and Criminal Justice in Tallahassee and is an assistant professor of criminal justice at Appalachian State University in North Carolina. His research focuses primarily on criminological theory, criminal victimization, crime prevention, and criminal justice education. His most recent publications appear in the *British Journal of Criminology, Journal of Crime and Justice*, the *Advances in Criminological Theory* series, *Journal of Security Administration, International Journal of Risk, Security, and Crime Prevention,* and *Environment and Behavior.*

Dace S. Svikis, Ph.D., received her doctorate in clinical psychology from the University of Minnesota in 1989. After completing a postdoctoral fellowship and internship, she became Director of the Center for Pregnancy and Addiction (CAP) at Johns Hopkins Bayview Medical Center in Baltimore in 1992. In addition to her CAP administrative activities, she engages in clinical practice, teaching, and research and has consultantships with several large state and national organizations. She is currently an associate professor in the Department of Psychiatry and Behavioral Sciences and also has an appointment in the Department of Obstetrics and Gynecology at the Johns Hopkins University School of Medicine. Her research interests are primarily in the development and evaluation of interventions to reduce licit and illicit drug use by pregnant women.

Ralph E. Tarter, Ph.D., obtained his doctorate in biological psychology from the University of Oklahoma in 1971. Since then his research has focused on the causes, correlates, and consequences of alcohol and drug abuse. On these topics he has edited or co-edited ten books and authored over 250 articles and book chapters. Currently he is Director of the Center for Education and Drug Abuse Research; this is a NIDA-funded multidisciplinary prospective investigation of 1,000 youth and their families.

Hans Toch, Ph.D., obtained his doctorate in psychology at Princeton University. He is affiliated with the School of Criminal Justice, University, State University of New York at Albany. Among his books are *Violent Men: An Inquiry into the Psychology of Violence, Living in Prison: The Ecology of Survival, Mosaic of Despair: Human Breakdowns in Prison,* and *The Psychology of Crime and Criminal Justice.*

Marianne B. M. van den Bree, Ph.D., received a master's degree in experimental psychology from the Vrije Universiteit in the Netherlands in 1988. She received a doctorate in human genetics from Virginia Commonwealth University in Richmond in 1994. She is currently employed as a research scientist by Hopkins Bayview Medical Center in Baltimore, and works at the National Institute on Drug Abuse in the same city. She is also an adjunct assistant clinical professor in the Department of Human Genetics at Virginia Commonwealth University. She has published scientific articles on headaches in school children and the genetics of sports participation, heart rate and blood pressure, and diet. Since working at NIDA, she has focused on substance abuse and has published books and articles on genetic aspects of alcoholism, drug use, and drug abuse/dependence.

Michael M. Vanyukov, Ph.D., is Director of Genetics Module at the Center for Education and Drug Abuse Research (CEDAR) and assistant professor of psychiatry and human genetics at the University of Pittsburgh. Dr. Vanyukov graduated from Moscow State University in 1978 and received his Ph.D. from the Institute of Medical Genetics, USSR Academy of Medical Sciences, in 1984. In December 1990, he emigrated to the United States and received his postdoctoral training in psychiatry at the Western Psychiatric Institute and Clinic at the University of Pittsburgh. His main research interest is in the genetic studies of substance abuse and antisociality and the search for both genetic and environmental factors influencing variation in human behavior. His current work includes studies of substance abuse and antisociality and the search for both genetic and environmental factors influencing variation in human behavior. His current work includes studies on the association of candidate genes and environmental characteristics with the risk for substance abuse as well as childhood and adult behavioral traits in families and populations.

Cathy Spatz Widom, Ph.D., received her doctorate in psychology from Brandeis University in Waltham, Massachusetts, with a specialization in personality and psychopathology. She taught previously at both Harvard and Indiana University and currently is professor of criminal justice and psychology at the State University of New York at Albany. She is a fellow of the American Psychological Association (Division 41, Law and Psychology) and the American Psychopathological Association. She has published extensively on topics including child abuse and neglect, juvenile delinquency, violence, psychopathy, female criminality, and prostitution. Dr. Widom has received numerous awards for her research. Her recent research focuses on the intergenerational transmission of violence and she is currently engaged in a large study to determine the long-term consequences of early childhood abuse (physical and sexual) and neglect. She serves on the Committee on Law and Justice at the Commission on Behavioral and Social Sciences at the National Research Council.

Table of Contents

Acknowledgments iii
About the Authors v

PART 1: INTEGRATIVE RESEARCH—TOWARD A BETTER UNDERSTANDING OF ANTISOCIAL BEHAVIOR

Chapter 1: Introduction
Relevance of Empirical Findings 1-1
The Past 1-1
Overview of This Volume 1-2
Communication Disconnect Between Disciplines 1-3
Working Toward a Neutral Interdisciplinary Model 1-4
What Are We Doing Wrong? 1-5
Accountability 1-6
Public Health Implications 1-7
The Future 1-7
Summary 1-8

Chapter 2: Alcoholism—A Developmental Disorder
Alcoholism: A Developmental Disorder 2-2
    Variability in Age of Onset 2-3
    Developmental Context of Alcoholism 2-4
        Developmental Disorders 2-4
        Home Environment 2-5
        Peer Group 2-5
    Nonstable Liability Phenotype 2-5
Temperament Phenotypes Associated With Elevated Risk 2-6
    Behavior Activity Level 2-7
    Emotionality 2-8
    Soothability 2-8
    Attention Span-Persistence 2-8
    Sociability 2-9
    Summary 2-9
Alcoholism Phenotype 2-10
Phenotypic Heterogeneity 2-10

Phenotype-Environment Interactions 2-11
    High Behavioral Activity Level 2-12
    Interaction With Environment 2-13
Epigenetic Model 2-14
    Difficult Temperament 2-14
    Interaction With Environment 2-15
Implications of the Developmental-Behavior-Genetic Perspective 2-16
Prevention of Alcoholism 2-16
Treatment of Alcoholism 2-17
Editor's Note 2-18

Chapter 3: The Contribution of Psychology to Criminal Justice Education
Introduction—The Role of Psychology 3-2
Psychological Theories of Criminal Behavior 3-3
    Behavior Theory 3-3
    Social Learning Theory 3-4
    Cognitive Social Learning Theory 3-5
    Attachment Theory 3-6
    Social Control Theory 3-6
New Perspectives or Models of Delinquent and Criminal Behavior 3-7
    Stability of Aggressiveness: Early Problem Behaviors
        Predict Later Problem Behaviors 3-7
    Bidirectionality of Influences and Transactional Models 3-7
    Protective Factors 3-8
    The Importance of Temperament 3-9
    Cognition and Motivation 3-10
Early Childhood Intervention as a Preventive Strategy for Delinquency 3-10
    Risk and Protective Factors 3-11
    Multidimensional Approach 3-11
Psychological and Mental Disorders 3-12
    Link to Crime and Violence? 3-12
Disaggregation and Classification 3-13
Conclusion 3-14

PART 2: BIOLOGICAL UNDERPINNINGS OF ANTISOCIAL BEHAVIOR—RESEARCH APPROACHES AND FINDINGS

Chapter 4: Criterion Measures of Aggression—Impulsive Versus Premeditated Aggression
Criterion Measures of Aggression: Selected Examples 4-2
Comparison of Relationships of Several Biosocial

    Measures to Selected Criterion Measures 4-3
        Overview of Study From Which Data Were Obtained 4-3
        Criterion Measures 4-3
        Social Predictor Measures 4-4
        Personality Measures 4-5
        Biological Predictor Measures 4-5
        Interrelationships of Criterion Measures 4-5
        Family and Social Measures Related to Criterion Measures 4-6
        Personality Traits Related to Criterion Measures of Aggression 4-7
        Biological Measures Related to Aggression Criterion
            Measures 4-7
        Summary of Relevance of Criteria Measures 4-9
    Status of Our Procedures for Classifying Aggression as Impulsive,
        Premeditated, or Other 4-9
        Phenytoin Use 4-9
        Exploratory Studies 4-10
        Identifying the Subjects 4-10
        Outpatient Studies 4-11
        General Population Studies 4-12
        Operational Definitions of "Impulsive" vs. "Premeditated" 4-14
    Summary 4-15
    Editor's Note 4-15

Chapter 5: Biological and Behavioral Investigation of Aggression and Impulsivity

Introduction 5-1
Definition and Measurement of Aggression 5-2
    Rating Scales 5-2
    Laboratory Measurement 5-2
Biological Studies of Aggression 5-4
    Measurement and Manipulation of Serotonin Function 5-4
    Relation of Lowered Serotonin Function to Aggression 5-5
    Tryptophan Manipulation 5-6
    Current Work 5-7
Definition and Measurement of Impulsivity 5-9
    Rating Scales 5-9
    Laboratory Measurements 5-10
Biological Studies of Impulsivity 5-11
    Relation of Lowered Serotonin to Impulsivity 5-11
    Laboratory Measurements 5-12
Conclusions 5-14

      Possible Genetic Links 5-14
      Environmental Factors 5-15
Editor's Note 5-15

Chapter 6: Central Neurotransmitter Function in Criminal Aggression

Introduction 6-2
The Many Faces of Aggression 6-2
Faulty Brakes: Serotonin Systems in Aggression 6-3
      Impulsive Aggression 6-3
      Abnormalities in the Serotonin Synapse 6-4
      Stimulating Serotonin Activity: Pharmaco-Challenge Studies 6-5
Catecholamine Neurotransmitters: The Fuel for Behavior 6-6
      Norepinephrine Activity 6-6
      Dopamine Receptor Sensitivity 6-6
Other Biological Mediators in the Study of Impulsive Aggression 6-7
      Glucose 6-7
      Testosterone 6-7
      Vasopressin Activity 6-7
      Low Serum Cholesterol Levels 6-8
Genetic Vulnerabilities 6-8
Treatment Implications 6-9
Case Study 6-10
Conclusions 6-13
      Genetic Influences 6-13
      Environment 6-13

PART 3: GENETIC STUDIES OF ANTISOCIAL BEHAVIOR

Chapter 7: Genetic Epidemiology of Antisocial Behavior

Introduction 7-2
Approaches to Studying Genotype-Behavior Relationships 7-2
      Animal Studies 7-2
      Relative Risk in Known Genetic Disorders 7-3
      Association and Linkage Studies 7-4
Genetic Epidemiology 7-4
      Twin Studies 7-4
      Adoption Studies 7-5
      Twin and Adoption Study Findings 7-6
          Data Pertaining to Criminal Behavior 7-6
          Estimations 7-6
          Environmental Influences 7-8

Genotype-Environment Correlations and Interactions 7-12
    Biological Parents' Background 7-13
    Adoptive Home Environment 7-13
    Genotype/Environment Interaction 7-13
Discussion—Overlap of Antisocial/Other Phenotypes and
  Other Influences 7-14
    Risks of Twin Birth Complications 7-14
    Age and Assessment Differences in Twin vs. Adoption Studies 7-15
    Implications for Crime Control 7-16
        "Career Criminals" 7-16
        Alcoholism 7-16
        Impulsivity 7-17
        Number of Environmental Stressors Bearing on Risk 7-17

Chapter 8: Antisocial Personality and Drug Use Disorders—Are They Genetically Related?
Introduction 8-1
Common Etiology of APD and SUD 8-2
Methods for Studying Genetic Influences 8-3
    Family Studies 8-3
    Adoption Studies 8-3
    Twin Studies 8-4
Genetic Influences in SUD 8-4
    Adoption Studies 8-5
    Twin Studies 8-5
Genetic Influences in APD 8-6
    Adoption Studies 8-6
    Twin Studies 8-8
APD and SUD Comorbidity 8-10
    Adoption Studies 8-10
    Twin Studies 8-11
Discussion—Etiology, Familial Comorbidity, Future Directions 8-12
    Diagnostic Problems 8-12
    Behavior Genetics Issues 8-13
    Future Directions 8-13

Chapter 9: Genetic Bases for Impulsive and Antisocial Behaviors—Can Their Course Be Altered?
Introduction 9-2
Recent Discoveries 9-3
Basic Terminology, Concepts, and Mechanisms 9-3

   Gene-Environment Interactions 9-3
    Genotype 9-3
    Phenotype 9-4
   Chemicals in the Brain and Their Actions 9-4
    Neurotransmitters 9-4
    Enzymes 9-4
    Hormones 9-4
    Receptors 9-4
   Concepts Unique to Genetics 9-5
    Alleles 9-5
    Cloning 9-5
   Measuring the Extent to Which Traits Are Genetically
   Transmitted 9-5
    Heritability 9-5
    Vulnerability Levels 9-5
 Heritability of Impulsive Behavioral Disorders 9-6
 How to Assess and Evaluate Genetic Effects 9-6
   Linkage Analysis 9-7
   DNA Sequence Scanning 9-7
 Genes and Behavioral Variation 9-8
   Dopamine and Aggression 9-8
   Serotonin and Impulsive Behavior 9-9
    Alcohol-Induced Behaviors 9-10
    Genetic Variants 9-11
   Monoamine Oxidase (MAO) and Criminality 9-11
 Implications for Criminal Justice and Public Health Policy 9-12
   Impact of Environment on Heritable Behaviors 9-13
   A Move to a Public Health Response 9-13
Conclusions 9-14

PART 4: RELATIONSHIPS BETWEEN COGNITIVE DEFICITS, BRAIN DYSFUNCTION, AND AGGRESSION

Chapter 10: Adding an Explicit Focus on Cognition to Criminological Theory

Introduction 10-2
Reasons for the Lack of Emphasis on Cognition in Criminological Theory 10-3
   Sociological/Behavioral Explanations 10-3
   Methodological Problems 10-4
Cognition and Crime 10-5
   Interpersonal and Impersonal Cognition 10-5

Social Perspective-Taking 10-6
    Measuring Social Perspective-Taking 10-7
    Affective Empathy 10-7
Problem-Solving Ability 10-8
    Measuring Problem-Solving Ability 10-9
    Skills vs. Perception of Skills 10-10
Locus of Control 10-10
    Measuring Locus of Control 10-11
    Development of Locus of Control 10-12
Summary 10-12
Cognition in Current Criminological Theory, Research, and Practice 10-12
    The Implicit Role of Cognition in Prominent Criminological
    Theories 10-13
        Social Learning Theory 10-13
        Social Bonding Theory 10-14
        General Strain Theory 10-14
        A General Theory of Crime 10-15
        Summary 10-15
    Integrating Cognition Into Criminological Theory 10-16
    Something Works: The Effectiveness of Cognitive Corrections 10-18
        Cognitive Intervention Modalities 10-18
        Education, Not Simply Therapy 10-19
Conclusion: An Explicit Focus on Cognition Will Enhance
Understanding and Interventions 10-19

Chapter 11: Neuropsychological Functioning and Antisocial Behavior—Implications for Etiology and Prevention

Introduction 11-1
    A Neuropsychological Perspective 11-2
    Cognitive Tests 11-2
Review of the Literature 11-3
    Studies With Preadolescent Boys 11-3
        ECF and Antisocial Behavior 11-3
        ECF as Predictor of Reactive Aggression 11-4
        ECF With Social Disadvantage 11-4
        Summary 11-6
    Studies With Adolescent Females 11-6
        ECF and Antisocial Behavior 11-6
        ECF and Difficult Temperament 11-7
        ECF and Language Skills 11-9
    Laboratory Studies 11-10

A Brief Hypothetical Explanation 11-11
Implications for Prevention 11-12
    Early Skills Development 11-12
    Use of Team Specialists 11-12
    Interactive Interventions 11-13
    Summary 11-13

Chapter 12: The Identification of Neurological Correlates of Brain Dysfunction in Offenders by Probation Officers

Introduction 12-2
    Basic Premises of the Research 12-2
    Primary Purpose of the Research 12-3
Brain Dysfunction and Violent Behavior 12-3
    Frontal and Temporal Lobe Impairment 12-3
    Cognitive and Neurological Defects 12-4
        Speech Processes 12-4
        Neuropsychological Impairments 12-4
Sources of Neurological Dysfunction 12-5
    Head Injuries 12-5
    Dietary Conditions 12-6
        Neuronal Synthesis 12-6
        Hypoglycemia 12-6
    Environmental Toxins 12-7
    Birth Complications/Maternal Drug Use 12-7
    Summary 12-8
Research Methodology 12-8
Findings and Interpretations 12-10
Discussion and Conclusion 12-14
    Effective and Adequate Correctional Programming 12-14
    Primary Goal—Prevention 12-15
Neuropsychological Impairment Screening Worksheet 12-16

PART 5: SUBTYPES AND SYNDROMES OF DELINQUENCY AND CRIMINALITY

Chapter 13: Subtyping of Injecting Drug Users

Introduction 13-1
    Classifying Illicit Drug Users 13-1
    Prognosis/Specific Treatment 13-2
Health Consequences of IDU 13-3

Psychiatric Comorbidity in Drug Injectors 13-3
    Comorbid Substance Use and Dependence 13-3
    Antisocial Personality 13-4
    Depressive Disorders 13-6
    Summary 13-6
Subclassification of Drug Injectors 13-7
Conclusion 13-9

Chapter 14: Childhood Sexual Abuse Among Female Addicts and Changes in Parenting Across Two Generations

Introduction 14-2
    CSA and Female Addicts 14-3
    Methodology and CSA Studies 14-3
The Present Analyses 14-3
    Background 14-4
    Findings of the Statistical Analyses 14-4
        Course of Addiction 14-4
        Family Dynamics 14-5
        Addicts' Self-Report of Parenting Behaviors 14-6
        Addicts' Home Atmosphere—Past and Present 14-7
        Addicts' Psychological Status 14-7
General Impressions 14-8
    CSA and Addiction Careers 14-10
    CSA and Parental Substance Use 14-10
    CSA and Adult Psychological Symptoms 14-10
CSA, Parenting, and Home Atmosphere 14-11
Treatment and Prevention Approaches 14-12

Chapter 15: Serial Killers—Victims of Compulsion or Masters of Control?

Introduction 15-1
Brief Overview of Current Conceptual Models of Serial Killing 15-2
The Question of Sanity and Serial Killing 15-4
    A Legal Definition of Insanity 15-5
    Diagnostic Classifications of Mental Disease 15-5
Can Serial Killers Truly Be Sane? 15-7
    Etiology of Necrophilia 15-7
    The Sanity Consensus 15-8
The Antisocial and Narcissistic Personality Disorders 15-8
    Psychological and Circumstantial Traits 15-9
    Malignant Narcissism 15-10

Are Serial Killers "Driven" to Act? 15-11
    Obsessive-Compulsive Disorder 15-11
    Obsessive-Compulsive Personality Disorder 15-12
    Alienation and Isolation 15-13
Do We Really Believe that Serial Killers Are Sane and Acting Volitionally? ... 15-14
    Free Will and Responsibility 15-14
    Violence—Disease or Man's Dark Side? 15-15
Conclusion 15-15
Editor's Note 15-16

PART 6: ATTENTION DEFICIT HYPERACTIVITY DISORDER AND CRIME—IDENTIFYING GENETIC, ADDICTIVE AND FAMILIAL LINKS TO REDUCE PRISON TERMS AND RECIDIVISM

Chapter 16: The Role of Genetics in ADHD and Conduct Disorder—Relevance to the Treatment of Recidivistic Antisocial Behavior

Introduction 16-2
Genetics of ADHD and Conduct Disorder 16-3
    ADHD as a Genetic Disorder 16-3
    Conduct Disorder Comorbid With ADHD 16-3
    Conduct Disorder as a Genetic Disorder 16-3
ADHD and CD as Predictors of Adult Antisocial Behavior 16-4
Molecular Genetics of ADHD, CD, and Aggression 16-5
    Dopamine Genes 16-6
        DRD2 Gene 16-6
        DRD4 Gene 16-7
        DRD5 Gene 16-8
        DRD1 Gene 16-9
        DAT1 Gene 16-9
    Serotonin Genes 16-9
        HTR1B Gene 16-9
        HTR2A Gene 16-9
        HTR1DA Gene 16-10
        TDO2 Gene 16-10
    Adrenergic Genes 16-10
        DBH Gene 16-10
        ADRA2A and *ADRA2C* Genes 16-10
    Monoamine Oxidase Genes 16-11
    Gamma-Aminobutyric Acid Genes—*GABRB3* Receptor Gene 16-12

　　　　Androgen Receptor Gene 16-12
　　　　Other Genes 16-12
Polygenic Inheritance 16-13
Multivariate Analysis of Associations (MAA) 16-13
Relevance to Treatment 16-17
　　　　Treatment Before Prison 16-17
　　　　Treatment in Prison 16-17
　　　　Ethical Considerations 16-18

Chapter 17: Diagnosing and Treating ADHD in a Men's Prison

Introduction 17-2
Evolution of a Program 17-3
　　　　Initial Interview 17-3
　　　　Follow-Up 17-4
　　　　Relation to Corrections Program 17-5
　　　　ADHD Training Group 17-5
Methods and Goals of Group Training 17-7
Program Results 17-9
Underlying Mechanisms in Behavioral Disorders 17-10
　　　　Justification for Considering Medical Treatment 17-10
　　　　Concerns Regarding Use of Medication in Prison 17-10
Medications for Disorders Commonly Seen in Prisons 17-11
　　　　Attention Deficit and Impulsive Distractibility 17-11
　　　　Marked Hyperactivity and Tics in Tourette's Syndrome 17-12
　　　　Use of Stimulants in the Presence of Tourette's
　　　　　　Syndrome 17-12
　　　　Emotional Leveling 17-12
　　　　Obsessive-Compulsive Behavior 17-13
　　　　Bipolar Disorder 17-13
Unexpected Results of Program 17-14
　　　　The Education of Corrections Officers 17-14
　　　　The Challenge of Prison Medicine 17-15
Differential Diagnoses 17-16
　　　　Atypical Seizures 17-16
　　　　Bipolar Disorder 17-16
　　　　Encephalopathy ("Organic Brain Disorder"), Drug Abuse,
　　　　　　Head Trauma, and Child Abuse 17-17
　　　　Hallucinations and Delusions 17-17
　　　　Psychopathy or Antisocial Personality Disorder 17-17
　　　　An Example of True ADD/ADHD 17-18
The Hidden Costs of Missed Diagnoses 17-19

Chapter 18: Criminal Behavior Fueled by Attention Deficit/Hyperactivity Disorder and Addiction

Introduction 18-2
Neurobiological Aspects of Criminal Behavior 18-2
Characterizing ADHD 18-3
    Impulse Dyscontrol 18-3
    Activity Level 18-4
    Enhanced Sensitivity 18-5
    Rage and Violence 18-5
    Addiction to High Levels of Stimulation 18-5
    Acquired ADHD 18-6
Crime in the Blink of an Eye: The Connection Between Crime and ADHD 18-6
The Offender With ADHD 18-7
Formulating an Accurate Diagnosis 18-8
Differentiating Antisocial Personality Disorder From ADHD 18-9
Comprehensive Treatment 18-9
    Medication 18-10
    Repatterning 18-11
        Therapy 18-11
        Social Responding 18-11
        Anger Management 18-11
ADHD and Co-Occurring Addictions 18-12
    Assessment 18-12
    Treatment 18-12
        Finding Symptoms Dating to Childhood 18-13
        Self-Motivation 18-13
    Potential Controversy 18-13
Alternative Sentencing 18-14
Conclusion 18-14

PART 7: MEDICAL APPROACHES TO UNDERSTANDING AND TREATING ANTISOCIAL BEHAVIOR

Chapter 19: A Neurological Perspective of Violent Behavior

A Neurological Perspective 19-2
A Neurologic Typology 19-2
    Predatory Violence 19-2
    Adolescent Psychopathy 19-4
Affective Aggression 19-4
    Intermittent Explosive Disorder 19-4
    Single-Episode Rage 19-5

      Over-Controlled Personalities 19-6
      Organic Obsessional Pathologies 19-6
      Sleeping Disorders 19-7
Epilepsy and Violence 19-8
Anatomical and Chemical Substrates of Violence 19-9
      Damage to Structural Inhibitors 19-9
      Neurochemical Activators 19-9
      Testosterone and PMS Syndrome 19-10
      Hypoglycemia 19-10
      Other Variables 19-11
Neurophysiological Correlates of Violent Behavior 19-11
      Age 19-11
      Sex 19-12
      Genetics 19-12
Neuropathological Correlates of Criminal Violence 19-12
The Clinical Evolution of Violence 19-13
Neuropathology in Murderers 19-15
Conclusions 19-15

Chapter 20: Drug Treatment of Pathologic Aggression
Introduction 20-2
Assessment Instruments 20-3
      Clinician-Rated Instruments 20-3
      Self-Report Instruments 20-4
Drug Treatments 20-5
Dementia 20-6
Huntington's Disease 20-8
Brain Injury and Organic Brain Syndrome 20-8
Seizure Disorder 20-9
Mentally Handicapped and Retarded Patients 20-9
Children and Adolescents With Aggressive Conduct Disorder
    or Attention Deficit Disorder 20-10
      Psychostimulants 20-10
      Lithium and Neuroleptic Medications 20-11
      Anticonvulsants 20-11
      Other Agents 20-12
Autism 20-12
Schizophrenia and Other Psychoses 20-12
      Antipsychotic Medications 20-12
      Anticonvulsants 20-13
      Serotonergic Agents 20-13

Psychoactive Substance Intoxication or Withdrawal 20-14
Unipolar Depression 20-14
Bipolar Disorder 20-15
Posttraumatic Stress Disorder 20-15
Premenstrual Dysphoric Disorder 20-15
Personality Disorders 20-16
    Antisocial Personality 20-16
    Borderline Personality 20-16
Summary 20-17

Chapter 21: The Etiology and Treatment of Sexual Offending

Introduction 21-1
Assessment 21-2
    Paraphilic Disorders Defined 21-3
    Biologically Based Drives 21-5
    Distinguishing Abnormal Sexual Makeup From Bad Behaviors 21-5
Etiology 21-6
    Sexual Orientation and Affectional Interests 21-6
    Childhood Sexual Abuse 21-7
    Biological Abnormalities 21-7
Rationale for Treatment 21-8
Treatment Approaches 21-8
    Craving Disorder Defined 21-8
    Psychotherapy 21-9
    Behavior Therapy 21-9
    Surgery 21-10
    Medication 21-11
    Medication Plus Counseling 21-12
Concluding Comments 21-13
Editor's Note 21-14

PART 8: APPLICATION OF THE BEHAVIORAL SCIENCES TO THE LAW AND CRIMINAL JUSTICE SYSTEM

Chapter 22: Indifferent Communication Between Social Science and Neuroscience—The Case of "Biological Brain-Proneness" for Criminal Aggression

Introduction 22-1
Knowledge Explosion in the Neurosciences 22-2

Biological Brain-Proneness to Violence, Meet the Skeptics 22-3
False Positives, While Big Brother Watches 22-3
Animal Models and Analogical Reasoning 22-4
ICD-9 and Frontal Lobe Syndrome 22-5
Brain Damage Among Peaceable Rats 22-5
Correlated Variables: But Which Governs Which? 22-6
Nonaccidental Correlates 22-7
Neuropathology–An Important Contributor to Criminal Aggression . . . 22-9
Conceptual and Clinical Cross-Fertilization 22-10
Benefits to the Social Sciences 22-10
Bridging the Gap 22-11

Chapter 23: The Dawn of Therapeutic Justice
Introduction 23-1
A Vision for the Criminal Justice System 23-2
Public Safety Issue 23-3
Kansas v. Hendricks 23-3
History 23-3
The Kansas Sexually Violent Predator Act 23-4
Procedural Issues 23-5
State's Reversal of Ruling 23-5
The United States Supreme Court's Reasoning 23-6
Civil vs. Criminal Commitment 23-6
A Wider Net for "Mental Illness" 23-7
Effect on Legislative Branch of Government 23-7
Summary 23-8
Penal Implications of *Hendricks* Decision 23-9
Therapeutic Justice 23-11
Culpability 23-12
Crime as Antisocial Act, Not Pathology 23-13
"Traditional" Rehabilitation vs. Therapeutic Justice 23-13
The "War" on Drugs 23-14
Conclusion 23-15

Chapter 24: Biological Causes of Criminality and Expert Testimony—Some Cautionary Thoughts
Introduction: Heritable Factors in Criminality 24-1
Nature and Nurture 24-1
Adoption Studies 24-2
Twin Studies 24-3

Implications for Legal Policy 24-4
    Morality vs. Science 24-4
    The Problem With the Paradigm Shift 24-5
Implications for Experts 24-6
    The Legal System vs. Science 24-6
    Role of the Mental Health Scientist 24-7

PART 9: IMPLICATIONS FOR THE PREVENTION AND TREATMENT OF ANTISOCIAL BEHAVIORS

Chapter 25: How Can Neurobiological Research Inform Prevention Strategies?

Introduction 25-2
Structuring the Environment to Minimize Risk Factors 25-2
    Does Neurobiological Research Assume Behavior Is Predestined? 25-3
    Traumatic Experiences 25-4
The Respective Roles of Genetic and Biological Traits and
    Environmental Conditions 25-4
    Concepts Essential to a Prevention Effort 25-4
    A Heuristic Biosocial Model of Antisocial Behavior 25-5
    Examples of the Nature-Nurture Interaction 25-6
        Serotonin Activity 25-6
        Temperament 25-6
        Drugs and Alcohol 25-6
        Cognitive Differences Between Males and Females 25-7
Environmentally Induced Biological Aspects of Antisocial Behaviors 25-7
    "Stress" Defined 25-7
    Prenatal Influences 25-8
        Minor Physical Anomalies 25-8
        Prenatal Drug Exposure 25-9
        Nicotine Exposure 25-10
        Cocaine Effects 25-11
        Social Environment During Pregnancy 25-12
    Perinatal Complications 25-12
    The Social Environment and Its Stressors 25-13
    Environmental Stimulation Needs 25-13
    Caregiver-Child Interactions 25-14
    Child Abuse and Other Traumatic Experiences 25-15
        Abnormal Hormonal Development 25-15
        Brain Cell Death 25-15
    Interactions Between Prenatal Conditions and Parenting 25-16

    Trauma During Adolescence and Adulthood 25-16
    Observing Violence: The Impact of Television Violence 25-17
Implications for Prevention Strategies 25-18
    Neurobiological Processes Affecting Behavior 25-18
    Prevention Techniques to Increase Resiliency and Minimize the
        Impact of Risk Factors 25-19
    Future Research Agenda 25-21

Chapter 26: Prospects for a Public Health Model to Prevent and Treat Antisocial Behaviors

Assessing the Relevance and Significance of Research 26-1
    Estimate the Risk Factors in the Offender Population 26-2
    Identify the Environmental Risk Factors 26-2
    Assess the Dynamic Relationship of Scientific and
        Environmental Factors 26-3
    Determine Whether Intervention Actually Changes Behavior 26-4
Prospective Applications 26-4
    Drug Abuse and Addiction 26-4
    Legal Considerations 26-5
    Public Health Approach 26-5
    Civil Liberty Issues 26-6
Conclusion 26-7

Chapter 27: Violence and the Family—Promoting Violence-Free Families

Past and Present Approaches to Family Violence 27-2
What Is Needed to Stop the Violence? 27-3
Developing Effective Prevention Programs 27-3
    An Epidemiological Perspective 27-3
    The Identification of Risk and Protection Factors 27-3
    Attention to Developmental Processes 27-4
    Environmental Context 27-4
The Effects of Gender Role Socialization 27-4
Developmental Processes and Risk Factors 27-5
The Promise of Empowerment 27-5
The Role of Health Promotion Programs in Preventing
    Violence 27-6
Universal Interventions 27-6
    Interventions for Changing the Social Conditions That Breed
        Violence 27-6
    Interventions for Changing the Attitudes and Behaviors of a
        Whole Population 27-6

    Interventions for Changing the Attitudes and Behaviors of a
     Specific Class of People 27-6
Targeted Interventions—For Changing the Attitudes and Behavior of
 Special At-Risk Groups 27-7
Advantages and Potential Limitations of Universal and Targeted
 Interventions 27-7
    Universal Interventions—Advantages 27-7
    Universal Interventions—Potential Limitations 27-8
    Targeted Interventions—Advantages 27-8
    Targeted Interventions—Potential Limitations 27-8
Promising Approaches to Prevention 27-9
The Importance of Community-Wide Efforts 27-10
The Economic Benefits of Violence Prevention 27-11
What Can Communities and Psychologists Do Together? 27-11
Building Bridges: Mental Health Professionals and Family Violence
 Advocates 27-12
Key Points 27-14
Recommendations 27-14
    Recommendations for Public Policy and Intervention 27-15
    Recommendation for Prevention and Public Education 27-18

Appendices

Appendix 1, Selected Excerpts From the Diagnostic and Statistical Manual of
 Mental Disorders, Fourth Edition A-1
Appendix 2, Glossary A-6
Appendix 3, Bibliography A-12

Table of Acronyms T-1

Index I-1

Part 1

Integrative Research—Toward a Better Understanding of Antisocial Behavior

In recent years, biological aspects of antisocial behavior have been investigated by numerous behavioral scientists employing a multidisciplinary approach that promises to enhance substantially the rigor of the findings and practical applications. Scientists in such fields as genetics, biochemistry, endocrinology, neuroscience, immunology, and psychophysiology have been intensively studying aspects of human behavior that are relevant to the study of antisocial behavior, and to the academicians who examine it and the practitioners who work to manage it. Due to the highly technical and field-specific language of much of this research, the findings generated are not usually included in the literature reviews of criminologists or the practices of criminal justice professionals. The relative lack of interdisciplinary communication has resulted in a lack of awareness of data pertinent to the study of crime and criminal behavior. This book is a first step in an attempt to rectify this situation and fill in the gaps.

In the first, introductory chapter, Diana Fishbein presents an argument for incorporating other mainstream behavioral sciences in the study and management of antisocial behavior. In doing so, social and environmental perspectives are not ignored or downplayed, but they are seen as relative influences that work in concert with biological and genetic factors to affect risk status. Dr. Fishbein presents the advantages to both the investigator and the practitioner of using this integrated approach, and she gives a brief overview of the relevant biological research. Once acquainted with the parameters and findings of biological research, professionals focusing on antisocial behavior may begin to incorporate reliable and comprehensive information into their theoretical and applied frameworks. Although this book provides the reader with only a taste of the research given the vast amount of work accomplished in the behavioral sciences, it will contribute to the development of a sound, scientific, and pragmatic approach for future research and application with an integrative orientation.

In the second chapter, Ralph Tarter and Michael Vanyukov present a contemporary and comprehensive model for studying the etiology of alcoholism from a developmental-behavioral-genetic perspective, which applies directly to the modern study of many forms of antisocial behavior. From birth, temperamental characteristics, through their continuous and reciprocal interaction with the social environment, shape the course of behavioral development. The behavioral characteristics successively acquired during development can be viewed as vectors, or carriers, which determine individual development from conception throughout the lifespan and which culminate ultimately in the clinical disorder of alcoholism. The temperament features that appear to be associated with a heightened risk for alcoholism and related behaviors are examined. Their interactions with the environment during the course of development are considered within a genetic but constantly evolving framework and, as discussed, have important ramifications for improving the prevention and treatment of alcoholism, in addition to related disorders such as antisocial behavior.

Many of the temperamental and personality characteristics considered to be liability traits for alcoholism also appear with respect to other forms of drug abuse and antisocial behaviors, which makes implications for this chapter quite far-reaching, extending beyond application only to alcoholism risk. Drs. Tarter and Vanyukov provide a conceptual framework for a better understanding of the interactions between environmental and genetic forces that ultimately influence the behavioral outcome. Thus, this chapter sheds light on the findings and recommendations of subsequent chapters throughout this book by illustrating how no trait, whether it originated from genetic or environmental conditions or both, is immutable. All traits that relate to human behaviors are fluid and can be altered to some degree during the lifespan.

The implications of the research cited by Tarter and Vanyukov for prevention and treatment strategies are outlined toward the end of the chapter. The authors point out that there is a dire need to implement prevention programs that are tailored to one or more of the following objectives: changing the psychological characteristics of the individual; changing the environment; or changing the quality of interactions between the person and the environment. Specific examples of each are presented. With respect to the treatment of alcoholism and its related disorders, the authors propose that the approach requires modification of factors that have contributed to the final expression of the behaviors of alcoholism or antisocial conduct. Treatment programs should account for individuality in the etiology or causes and the natural history of the disorder. In short, the treatment approach should be well suited to the individual's unique condition and experiences.

In the third chapter, Cathy Spatz Widom and Hans Toch discuss contributions from the field of psychology that enhance understanding of the various forms of antisocial behavior. Psychological traits that increase vulnerability to antisocial behavior form the functional bridge between biological status and the behavioral outcome. In other words, psychological traits such as impulsivity, extroversion, and shyness are rooted in our biological constitution from birth and interact in dynamic ways with the social environment to predict final but fluid behavioral outcomes. Widom and Toch's chapter provides that essential link by emphasizing the need to focus theories of antisocial behavior on the individual. For this book to be whole, the mediating role of psychological traits must be considered. Importantly, temperamental and personality features that comprise our psychological constitution should be the focus of treatment and prevention strategies: (1) they are readily measurable; (2) they are reflective of biological processes; (3) they predict with acceptable reliability a range of behavioral outcomes; and (4) their manipulation can lead to changes in future behaviors. Thus, by examining the unique psychological and biological mechanisms underlying an individual's behavior and identifying their interactive relationships with the external environment, we come one step closer to understanding our subject and developing management techniques. Widom and Toch highlight theories relevant to the study of antisocial behavior, identify significant psychological traits that play a role in its development or expression, and directly address ways in which this research leads us toward specific intervention and education strategies. (Chapter 25 in Part 9 on implications of the neurosciences to the science of prevention provides further synthesis by showing how environmental and social interventions can directly alter psychological expressions and biological processes.)

Chapter 1

Introduction

by Diana H. Fishbein, Ph.D.

Relevance of Empirical Findings 1-1
The Past 1-1
Overview of This Volume 1-2
Communication Disconnect Between Disciplines 1-3
Working Toward a Neutral Interdisciplinary Model 1-4
What Are We Doing Wrong? 1-5
Accountability 1-6
Public Health Implications 1-7
The Future 1-7
Summary 1-8

RELEVANCE OF EMPIRICAL FINDINGS

The practical fields of criminology, criminal justice, drug abuse, and others that deal directly with behavioral disorders have not traditionally incorporated biological or genetic perspectives. There is, however, growing interest in enhancing the rigor of criminal justice practices by basing them on scientific findings and in increasing multidisciplinary representation within research on various dimensions of antisocial behavior. Because practitioners in these fields are instrumental in the design and implementation of criminal justice practices and policies, their involvement, familiarity, and scrutiny are critical.

THE PAST

While the development of particular criminal justice practices is often a response to present funding priorities or simply trial and error, practices are also at times based on the research of criminologists. The implication of this reality is that common criminal justice practices typically arise from unidisciplinary theories of human behavior that disregard the continuous, dynamic interaction between social and biological conditions that contribute to antisocial behavior. A combination of social and political events, methodological flaws, and theoretical reductionism in the history of criminological research led to the eventual discredit of relevant biological research. As a result, feedback between scientific disciplines became circumscribed and, in some cases, nonexistent. Thus, rather than integrating research from various relevant fields, a fear arose within the field of criminology that incorporating research from the biological sciences would circumvent the important role of social factors.

Sociological perspectives subsequently took center stage and have predominated the field, both in theory and practice. Social factors in antisocial behavior have been studied extensively during this century and we now have a consensual knowledge of which social factors increase risk. There are two unfortunate results of this narrow view, however. One is that despite our knowledge, society has allowed effective and necessary social programs designed to reduce risk and increase resiliency to be dismantled over the past twenty years. The second is that we remain ignorant of how social factors interact with the unique brains of those exposed to these influences to affect behavior. The field has yet to answer several essential questions: Why doesn't everyone react similarly to similar social conditions? Why is it that individuals who are socially "protected" (i.e., low social risk) from antisocial outcomes still become antisocial? And why do most individuals exposed to many social risk factors remain law-abiding? Although there are many systemic contributions to these scenarios (e.g., racism, economic disparity, political neglect, and lack of social programs), an understanding of individual, biological differences will help to identify who is most likely to fall victim to these social circumstances.

The present director of the National Institute on Drug Abuse, Dr. Alan Leschner, maintains that "science must replace ideology" before drug abuse can be fully understood, treated, and prevented. The same is true for the study of antisocial behavior in general. Science must inform ideology as a basis for criminological inquiry and for the development of treatment, prevention, and policy strategies. A focus on individual differences, their origins, modulators and interactions with social variables, is paramount. We need to be more creative, innovative, and scientific than approaches used in the past. To date, criminology is the only field devoted to the study of human behavior which has yet to incorporate findings of the other behavioral sciences.

OVERVIEW OF THIS VOLUME

The investigators who contributed to this work represent the wide range of mainstream behavioral sciences that explore linkages between social, psychological, and biological factors in the production of human behavior. Despite the obvious relevance of their research, it remains largely unfamiliar to criminology and criminal justice scholars and practitioners. Each chapter highlights specific research of the contributors and delineates ways in which their findings can be applied and can affect criminal justice policy. Readers will discover the immediate relevance of this research to the study and management of antisocial behaviors; this book is designed to generate interest in the behavioral sciences in practitioners, students, and researchers who devote their careers to studying and controlling antisocial human behavior.

To resolve the controversies at hand, it is important to obtain a basic familiarity with the current research and distinguish it from theories of the past. While a complete description of the research is provided in each individual chapter, an attempt is made in this introductory piece to synthesize the current findings. Chapters provide evidence for individual vulnerability to various dimensions of antisocial behavior from several disciplines, including molecular and behavioral genetics, neurobiology, physiology, psychology, cognitive science, endocrinology, and forensic psychiatry. The vast array of reported studies on vulnerability to antisocial personality disorder, violence, and drug abuse may seem unintelligible at first, but several consistencies across findings reveal a pattern that may characterize vulnerable individuals. Studies indicate that vulnerability to antisocial behavior is partially a function of genetic and biological make-up that manifests during childhood as particular behavioral, cognitive, and psychological traits (e.g., impulsivity, attention deficits, or conduct disorder) and are measurable in physiological and biochemical responses (e.g., heart rate, hormone levels, and electroencephalogram, or EEG, recordings). Instead of viewing evidence from these various disciplines as independent sources of biological and social dysfunction, these sources of evidence should be seen as a continuous, developmental sequence of interacting factors. That is, basic genetic or acquired biological traits contribute to measurable biochemical and physiological conditions that predispose individuals to a constellation of particular behavioral and temperamental outcomes.

Specifically, evidence is mounting to implicate dysfunctions of several chemical systems in the brain in sensation-seeking, impulsivity, negative affect, and other cognitive and behavioral correlates of antisocial behavior. Alterations in function of these brain chemicals, either genetic or acquired, influence activities within brain structures responsible for motivation and experiences of pleasure to perturb nervous system activity levels. Manifestations of these neurobiological aberrations can be measured in physiological and biochemical processes that serve to mediate these behavioral and psychological outcomes. Biological vulnerabilities are, in turn, influenced by socioenvironmental factors that act as triggers, offering one explanation for the disproportionate number of residents prone to antisocial behavior in lower income neighborhoods where triggers are more prevalent. Put simply, abnormalities in certain neurobiological mechanisms heighten sensitivity to adverse environmental circumstances, increasing the risk for an antisocial outcome.

The resulting integration of research findings from various disciplines has direct import to criminological inquiry, informing ideology with science, which should appeal to social scientists who pervade the field with widely divergent views. This research compels the reader to acknowledge several decades of serious scientific criminology research in psychology, psychiatry, and the bio-behavioral sciences. Findings account for both intrapsychic and extrapsychic variables in their emphasis on the recent explosion of genetic and biological evidence that neurobiological conditions often underlie violent and impulsive behaviors by sensitizing the actor to adverse social stimuli.

COMMUNICATION DISCONNECT BETWEEN DISCIPLINES

Despite this revolution in the behavioral sciences, there is a notable absence in criminology studies and criminal justice departments of courses in their curriculum on biological perspectives. Even more disturbing, the overwhelming majority of criminology theory textbooks exclude a contemporary or accurate review of these behavioral sciences. Examination of these books reveals numerous misinterpretations, inaccuracies, and significantly outdated reviews that continue to focus on the archaic theories of Lombroso, the Gluecks, and XYY genotypes. The result of this glaring neglect is resistance to interdisciplinary perspectives; unfortunately, in this case, *lack of familiarity breeds contempt*. For example, concerns that genetic studies will encourage racism can be quelled with an understanding of genetic analytic techniques, which are incapable of producing interracial comparisons, only intraracial ones. Moreover, interindividual differences are so great that they overshadow the significance of any possible interracial ones.

One of the primary reasons for the lack of communication among disciplines is that biological and genetic research employs a highly technical language with field-specific terms and references to techniques that are difficult for the nonbiologist to interpret. Unfamiliarity with terminology, biological and genetic methodology, and underlying biological mechanisms impedes exchange between social and biological researchers. As a result, there have been only a few attempts to integrate these disciplines for an eventual comprehensive understanding of the origins of human behavior generally, and antisocial behavior specifically. That often means we are comfortable with only one-half of the equation, the social or the biological/genetic contributions. Dissection and interpretation of this important research domain is essential for practitioners, academicians, policy-makers, and social scientists who would greatly benefit from its knowledge.

WORKING TOWARD A NEUTRAL INTERDISCIPLINARY MODEL

Dr. Ernest Barratt, a longstanding forerunner in integrated research on impulsive disorders, persuasively argues that there is a profound need for a *neutral interdisciplinary model* for studies on aggression and other correlates of criminal behavior. Development of such a model is critical if we are ever to communicate effectively with other behavioral researchers and to understand interactions and relative contributions of social and biological factors. Foremost among the steps necessary to achieve this goal is the creation of adequate and accurate assessments of behavioral phenotypes under study. Controversies over measurement techniques and the behaviors of interest pervade both social and biological research. For social scientists who study antisocial behavior, the controversy often revolves around whether we are actually studying behavior of the individual, the criminal justice system, or society-at-large. For biological scientists, the question is whether we are measuring the behavioral phenotype, the underlying biological response, or the stimulus. An interdisciplinary model would potentially lead to agreed-upon techniques that enable investigators to examine all of these interacting variables with clear definitions of what is being studied and what role each variable plays in a total social and biological environment.

To create a neutral model for understanding antisocial behavior, identification of the appropriate target behaviors for study is critical. The focus should not be on "crime" per se. Crime is a legal abstraction, not a behavioral reality. The study of crime is the study of the criminal justice system's response to behavior; the criminal justice system defines, labels, and proscribes behaviors in ways that can fluctuate over time and differ cross-culturally. Thus, no behavior is inherently criminal as there are significant legal and social contributions to its definition. Some behaviors are simply more likely to attract the attention of the criminal justice system than others at any given time and in any given culture. Emphasis should be placed instead on the phenotypes or components of antisocial behavior that are measurable, stable, and consistent across cultures, such as aggression, impulsivity, or hostility. In many cases, crime, is secondary to these and other underlying problems that remain unheeded when left unstudied.

WHAT ARE WE DOING WRONG?

Unlike other disciplines, results of research on offenders have direct import to the management and control of antisocial individuals and those at high risk for offending. There are concerns in the field that findings of biological studies could lead to inappropriate or involuntary medical treatment in the criminal justice system and the possibility that individuals who are at high risk but who have not yet engaged in criminal behavior may be prematurely targeted for these control measures. Hypocritically, however, we do not question tactics of the present criminal justice system, which routinely incarcerates the mentally ill and drug addicts who are desperately in need of treatment, not incarceration. Studies have shown that both voluntary and mandatory treatment produces improvements in these populations. Moreover, rather than intervening in cases in which children's rights are visibly being violated (e.g., abuse or neglect) or special needs remain unattended (learning disabilities)—conditions known to increase risk for delinquency—we customarily wait until their problems are compounded and they are old enough to incarcerate. Dr. Fred Berlin, a neuroendocrinologist and psychiatrist, has argued that treatment of offenders by the criminal justice system is archaic and certainly insufficient. On the other hand, treatment of individuals with similar behavior problems in a clinical setting demonstrates that effective methods are available in many cases. As Dr. Mohammed Alam, a forensic psychiatrist, has pointed out, it is medical malpractice to withhold effective treatment in the medical field, which is a dictate in marked contrast to practices of the criminal justice system.

Fears are partially fueled by the notion that biological research will lead to the mass medication of individuals under duress. There are no studies to date suggesting that most offenders are in need of medication. In fact, several strategies, including cognitive-behavioral therapy, therapeutic communities, and early behavioral interventions, are demonstrated to be highly effective in subgroups of offenders without the use of drug treatments. Notwithstanding this, Dr. David Comings, a molecular geneticist and clinician, has consistently shown that the use of pharmacotherapy when medically indicated can produce tremendous improvements in behavior when used in conjunction with traditional therapies, increasing individual self-control rather than requiring the external restraints of the criminal justice system. Consent to treatment must be voluntary, according to Dr. Comings, without implicit sanctions. And once again, the availability of accurate assessments and classifications of human behavior is a prerequisite, not only to identify effective treatments, but to identify appropriate individuals in need of treatment.

Tactics that we rely on presently, however, are based on the assumption that individuals who engage in serious criminal activity are considered to be worthy of punishment and are incarcerated, sometimes even executed. The conditions of prisons are not conducive to positive behavioral or attitudinal change, and they often worsen the prognosis. Some protest that the conditions of most prisons are cruel and inhumane and cannot be justified on the basis of crimes that most offenders commit, particularly in light of their increased risk for offending after imprisonment. Eventually, offenders are nearly always released back into the community in this worsened state and many are destined to commit new offenses; recidivism rates are astronomical. Do we ask offenders if they want to be imprisoned or executed? No. The argument could be made that we also need not ask if they want to be treated. Perhaps we owe it to society to examine the issues and consider the medical treatment of certain offenders under appropriate conditions and with proper regulations intact. The bottom line question is, which is more effective, more justifiable, and more protective of public safety—imprisonment or treatment? Further scientific and policy research must be conducted before an informed opinion can be shaped.

ACCOUNTABILITY

Invariably, the question arises as to whether humans are able to make free decisions if behavior is influenced by biological processes. Although some behavioral scientists are deterministic in their views, attributing behavior to everything from socioeconomic conditions to neurochemical events, most individuals prefer to credit their own free will for their behavior. There is, however, a compromise reflecting a more accurate position on the forces behind human behavior that is widely accepted, the theory of "conditional free will."

Conditional free will theory is based on the laws of probability in which numerous factors interplay in a dynamic fashion, increasing the likelihood of a particular behavior. It is rarely the case that a behavior can be associated with only one cause; an ever-changing interaction of causes is responsible for the final result. Indeed, social human behavior is contingent on a countless number of possible decisions from among which the individual may choose. Not all of those decisions are feasible, nor are the resources available that are required to act on them. Choosing a course of action, therefore, is limited by preset boundaries, which narrow the range of possibilities substantially. Decision-limiting factors include current circumstances and opportunities, learning experiences, physiological abilities, and genetic predispositions. Each one of these conditions collaborates physically and environmentally to produce a final action. The behavioral result is thus restricted to options available within these limitations, yet behavior still cannot be precisely predicted. Nevertheless, stable individuals generally behave with some degree of expectability; certain patterns of behavior are more probable than others in a given situation in a given individual.

The principle of conditional free will postulates that when conditions are suitable for rational thought, we are accountable for our actions. Given "rational" thought processes, calculation of risks versus the benefits, and the ability to judge the realities that exist, the result is likely to be an adaptive response; that is, the behavior will be beneficial for the individual and the surrounding environment. On the other hand, if one or more conditions to which the individual is exposed are disturbed or irregular, the individual is more likely to choose a disturbed or irregular course of action. Thus, the risk of such a response increases as a function of the number of deleterious conditions.

Knowledge of biological factors in antisocial behavior does not, therefore, completely undermine the concept of free will in our society, which is the basis for criminal justice proceedings. Certain adverse sociological conditions are already known to substantially influence propensity to antisocial behavior, but their presence in an individual's life does not excuse their behavior. Defenses such as the "urban stress syndrome" have been tried and debated in criminal court but have not proven successful. There are numerous implications of this research for a variety of criminal justice processes that have yet to be adequately addressed and resolved. Nevertheless, if we do not begin to develop an understanding of underlying precursors of antisocial behavior, sanctions we presently employ will continue to be ineffective. Our criminal justice system operates largely on the notions of vengeance and "just deserts." Research presented in this book suggests that there may be more efficacious and humane responses to antisocial behaviors, including treatment and prevention.

PUBLIC HEALTH IMPLICATIONS

Although a medical approach is believed to be the only implication of this research, that is far from the reality. Instead, interdisciplinary research emphasizes the critical role of universal prevention approaches. No matter what the origins of behavior, we have amassed a substantial knowledge of what conditions trigger antisocial behavior (e.g., deprivation, child abuse/neglect, racism, lead exposure, drug and crime infested neighborhoods, prenatal drug exposure, poor parenting techniques, head injury, and many more social and biological stimuli). While antisocial responses to these triggers will be differentially rather than equally distributed throughout our society by virtue of both individual and environmental differences, structuring the environment in ways that are responsive to basic human needs will provide insulation against such behavioral outcomes. Thus, rather than solely identifying underlying mechanisms, biological research highlights the profound impact of environmental conditions on human biological systems to either increase or decrease risk for antisocial behavior.

THE FUTURE

The implications of this research for the law and criminal justice system are many and varied. But first, several needs for the promising future of interdisciplinary studies must be noted. First and foremost, a consensus on focus, methodology, and modeling must be forged in the field among investigators from various disciplinary backgrounds. As mentioned above, Dr. Barratt emphasizes the need for a neutral interdisciplinary model to accomplish this goal. Second, investigations of the links between the environment, biology, and genetics must integrate perspectives. So-called interdisciplinary studies often merely control for social variables rather than examine their interactive and relative effects. Instead, future studies should manipulate biological and social factors and examine their respective influences on each other and on the behavioral outcome. Third, studies of biological mechanisms in antisocial behavior conducted to date must be replicated. While there are recurrent underlying themes emerging from research results, precision and consistency in measurement is necessary to reduce the number of discrepant findings and increase specificity in terms of biological mechanisms and social contexts involved. And fourth, once our confidence in these results is established and a consensus is reached, an educational campaign directed toward the public, scholars, and policy-makers must ensue. Familiarity with the methods, interpretations, and implications of this research will quell many of the fears evolved over the past century as a result of historically unicausal, naïve, and culturally insensitive investigations.

SUMMARY

In summary, the research presented in this book leads to the following conclusions:

1. All human behavior has a genetic component.
2. There are no genes for specific behaviors. Instead, genes help to design our temperament and personality, and they provide an orientation or predisposition to behave according to certain patterns.
3. The expression of genetic and biological traits can be modified by the environment. No one is predestined to behave in a certain way or to commit crime.
4. On a global level, social deprivation and abuse leads to antisocial behavior. Deterioration of inner cities and dissolution of resources that have protective effects are substantially contributory. Because social influences are known, effective interventions can be implemented now.
5. Vulnerabilities to antisocial behavior cross all boundaries, but will be most abundant where the social risks are highest.

Whether or not criminologists and criminal justice professionals are interested in this research, it will proceed. The unfortunate reality of that situation is that neglect for 50 percent of the human behavior equation will continue, and research on antisocial behavior and criminality will never truly be interdisciplinary or substantially explanatory. Moreover, those who are best qualified to critique the methods and regulate the consequences of interdisciplinary research will remain unfamiliar and uninvolved. The view conveyed in this book is that the presence and participation of criminologists and criminal justice professionals are critical for the behavioral sciences to be whole, to provide a comprehensive understanding of a fundamental dimension of human behavior, that of antisocial or criminal conduct.

Chapter 2

Alcoholism—A Developmental Disorder

by Ralph E. Tarter, Ph.D. and Michael Vanyukov, Ph.D.

Alcoholism: A Developmental Disorder 2-2
    Variability in Age of Onset 2-3
    Developmental Context of Alcoholism 2-4
        Developmental Disorders 2-4
        Home Environment 2-5
        Peer Group 2-5
    Nonstable Liability Phenotype 2-5
Temperament Phenotypes Associated With Elevated Risk 2-6
    Behavior Activity Level 2-7
    Emotionality 2-8
    Soothability 2-8
    Attention Span-Persistence 2-8
    Sociability 2-9
    Summary 2-9
Alcoholism Phenotype 2-10
Phenotypic Heterogeneity 2-10
Phenotype-Environment Interactions 2-11
    High Behavioral Activity Level 2-12
    Interaction With Environment 2-13
Epigenetic Model 2-14
    Difficult Temperament 2-14
    Interaction With Environment 2-15
Implications of the Developmental-Behavior-Genetic Perspective 2-16
Prevention of Alcoholism 2-16
Treatment of Alcoholism 2-17
Editor's Note 2-18

Copyright © 1994 by the American Psychological Association. *Journal of Consulting and Clinical Psychology, 62*, 1096–1107. Adapted with permission. Funding for this work was supported by grants AA-08746 and DA-05605 from the National Institute on Drug Abuse.

ALCOHOLISM: A DEVELOPMENTAL DISORDER

Alcoholism, or its more precise taxonomic designation, Psychoactive Substance Use Disorder-alcohol abuse or dependence (American Psychiatric Association, 1987), can be displayed at any age between early adolescence and late life. Its manifestation is commonly preceded by certain deviant psychological features that are exhibited since childhood (Tarter et al., 1985). However, because the presence of psychological disturbances do not invariably predict an alcoholism outcome, a facilitating environment is also required.

Figure 2.1 schematically illustrates the etiology of alcoholism considered from a developmental-behavior-genetic perspective. The Gaussian (normal bell) curve at the top of the figure depicts the distribution of phenotypes for temperament traits in the population. Certain temperament phenotypes, as will be discussed, appear to be associated with the increased liability to alcoholism. Because temperament traits are measurable in neonates and infants and have significant heritability, they can be viewed as the primary characteristics from which more complex psychological traits develop concomitant to continuous and reciprocal interactions with the environment.

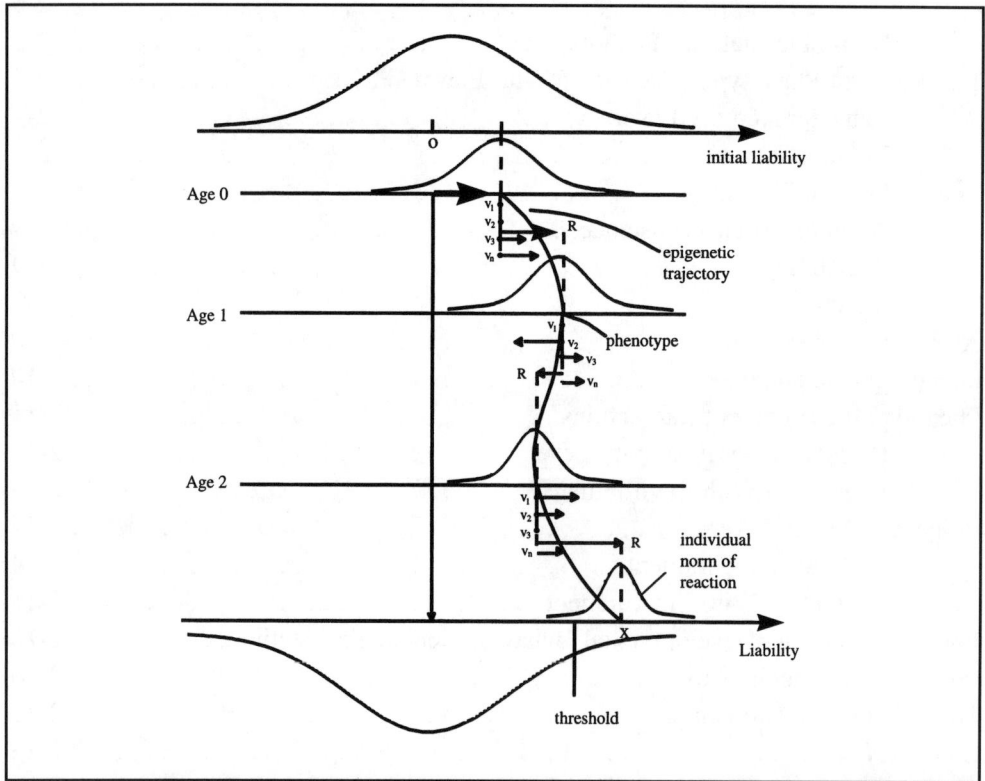

Figure 2.1. Development of Alcoholism. Deviation in temperament comprises a vector which, in combination with other vectors, biases the person toward or away from a threshold of alcoholism. In this figure, the liability is shown to shift with age because the constituent vectors fluctuate throughout life.

The liability to alcoholism is determined by genetic and nongenetic components. This liability can be conceptualized as a trait which, as depicted at the bottom of Figure 2.1, is normally distributed in the population. Importantly, the liability trait is in a state of flux throughout the lifespan due to unfolding ontogenetic (i.e., from conception to adulthood) processes.

Consistent with the multifactorial model of inheritance (Falconer, 1965; Kendler & Eaves, 1986), alcoholism is the label for conditions that are manifest when the individual's liability phenotype surpasses a threshold of severity. The region in the Gaussian distribution at the bottom of Figure 2.1 (right side of the figure) encompasses the segment of the population who manifest the "beyond the threshold" condition—the population who qualify for the diagnosis of alcoholism. Although developmental-behavior-genetic methods are appropriate for understanding the etiology of the full range of alcohol consumption behaviors under the distribution, the discussion here is confined to only the segment of the population who surpass the liability threshold, qualifying for a diagnosis of alcoholism.

Variability in Age of Onset

From the developmental-behavior-genetic perspective, the cardinal task for understanding the etiology of alcoholism is to clarify how phenotypic differences in temperament and developing personality traits, comprising the basis of psychological individuality in the population, culminate eventually in alcoholism for some individuals and not others. This process can be understood as a developmental trajectory. The quality of interaction with the environment, regulated in large part by a child's behavior, determines the force and direction of the trajectory. Consequent to interactions with the environment during development, behaviors are successively established that increase the risk for an alcoholism outcome.

In this fashion, behavior, considered in relation to the outcome phenotype of alcoholism, can be conceptualized as a vector such that it influences the acquisition of subsequent behaviors during ontogeny; this process is referred to as epigenesis. As shown in Figure 2.1, the first vector is presumed to be the temperament phenotype since this is the earliest form of reliably measured behavior after birth. The magnitude of the vector is determined at the outset by the deviation from the population mean in either the positive or negative direction. A central thesis is that temperament deviations in infants and young children negatively affect the quality of the parent-child relationship such that the ensuing behavior disposition of the child increases the risk for alcoholism. These behavior dispositions, comprising vectors, are represented in Figure 2.2 (see p. 2-12) such that their combined influence defines the overall vector (R). It can be seen that the position of R varies, depending on the interactions among the constituent vectors across age. Hence, successive vectors during the life span, consisting of all genetic and nongenetic influences, determine a person's position on the liability trait for alcoholism at any given time. In Figure 2.1, the hypothetical individual develops the affected condition of alcoholism; however, the same conceptual framework applies to cases in which a person does not develop alcoholism. Furthermore, depending on the changing constituents of R, it can be seen how both "spontaneous" remission as well as rapid development of dependence can occur.

A final point with regard to the developmental process pertains to the concept of "norm of reaction." As shown in Figure 2.1, this is the range of potential change for the particular phenotype. In other words, limits are attached to the capacity to influence the magnitude of change that can be expected for a given individual. For example, for a child with Down's syndrome, environmental stimulation has limitations with respect to augmenting intellectual ability. In the same manner, with respect to the alcoholism phenotype, there are limits regarding the magnitude of change that can be accomplished. Hence, it may not be possible to shift the liability phenotype into the normative range for some individuals, for example, those persons at the extreme end of the distribution of affected cases.

The developmental trajectory to an alcoholism outcome can have a short or long duration and can occur anytime between early adolescence and late adulthood (Helzer et al., 1991). Importantly, outcome among young abusers has been shown to be determined by the number of risk factors (Bry et al., 1982) and by how their dynamic interplay over time influences the direction of the developmental trajectory (Labouvie et al., 1991). Existing evidence suggests that higher genetic predisposition leads to earlier age onset alcoholism (Cloninger et al., 1981; McGue et al., 1992). Hence, large deviation in temperament trait expression would be expected to be associated with the risk for an earlier age of onset of alcoholism, whereas later age of onset would be expected to be associated with more normative temperament phenotypes and greater adverse environmental circumstances. Consistent with this proposition, behavioral deviancy in childhood is more common in early-age onset alcoholism, whereas less genetic influence is present in later age onset alcoholism (Cloninger et al., 1981).

Developmental Context of Alcoholism

The discussion up to this point argues for a process-oriented approach to understanding the etiology of early-age onset alcoholism. Central to this perspective is the position that alcoholism is a multidimensional endpoint phenotype that is preceded by a succession of intermediary phenotypes of which the first are detectable relatively early in life in the form of temperament deviations. These phenotypic traits are also predisposing to various antisocial behaviors, explaining the close association between alcoholism and antisociality. Within the life span perspective, a person's phenotype, through reciprocal interactions with multiple environments, can propel the person toward or protect him from problematic involvement with alcohol. Importantly, in this context, problematic involvement develops over time, however short or long the interval.

Developmental Disorders. This approach to understanding alcoholism etiology has several parallels with other, more accepted developmental disorders. Specifically, alcoholism, like more traditionally accepted developmental disorders, shares the common feature of suboptimal acquisition of age-appropriate cognitive, emotional, or behavioral skills. For example, individuals at high risk for alcoholism have been found to be impaired on measures of cognitive capacity, particularly involving attentional and visuospatial ability, compared to children at low risk (Pihl et al., 1990). Attention deficit disorder and conduct disorder commonly precede the onset of alcoholism (Robins & Rutter, 1990). It can be concluded from these findings that for many individuals, especially where the alcoholism outcome is first manifest early in life, alcoholism is one culmination of a developmental disorder, as well as antisocial behaviors such as criminality and violence.

Home Environment. From the developmental perspective, adverse interactions in the home such as physical abuse, parental absenteeism, and poor discipline practices augment a child's liability to alcoholism. Emerging evidence points to the importance of family interaction patterns in shaping the trajectory by inculcating behaviors in the child that promote the likelihood of alcohol (and other drug) initiation. For example, greater mutual dissatisfaction between parent and child (Tarter, Blackson et al., 1993b) and less effective discipline practices (Tarter et al., 1993a) have been observed in families in which there is substance abuse. Moreover, in families in which there is substance abuse, there is a stronger association between parent-child dissatisfaction and ineffective discipline with externalizing and internalizing tendencies in the children compared to normal families. Significantly, association with peers promoting drug use has been found to be related to the combined influence of negative affect and deficient parental monitoring (Chassin et al., 1993). These findings indicate how, among high risk individuals, adverse interactions with the familial environmen, can orient the child toward enhanced risk for a negative outcome.

Peer Group. Concomitant as well as subsequent to parental interaction, the peer reference group influences the child's position on the liability trait. This latter influence can be either positive or negative and has the effect of deflecting the child toward the normative range or toward the affected range. For example, an adverse home environment has been shown to propel a child to affiliations with nonnormative peers (Wills, 1990). This in turn fosters acceptance of or at least tolerance of deviance (Jessor et al., 1991), which in turn is well-recognized to predispose to alcohol use. Viewed within an ontogenetic perspective, it can be seen why alcohol use and abuse among adolescents is also commonly intertwined with other behavioral deviations such as school truancy, risk taking, gang affiliation, and the like. However, the main point is that the person's phenotype on the liability trait for alcoholism is not static. Rather, concomitant to developmental processes and changing circumstances at home and in the social environment, the phenotype, and by definition, the risk for alcoholism, fluctuates over time.

Nonstable Liability Phenotype

From the standpoint of alcoholism prevention and treatment, the practical task is straightforward, albeit difficult. Namely, the many components of the liability trait for alcoholism need to be disaggregated (or separated) such that interventions can be implemented that effectively shift the phenotype toward normality. The same general principle applies to the treatment of alcoholics. Indeed, the observation that a substantial proportion of alcoholics change to nonalcoholic status without receiving an intervention points to instability of the multidimensional phenotype labeled "alcoholism" (Hasin et al., 1990). This instability of the liability phenotype is also starkly illustrated by the common observation that heavy drinking by young adults does not invariably lead to exceeding the threshold for clinical alcoholism. The factors responsible for these phenomena have not been intensively studied, perhaps because they are not congruent with the generally held conception about the etiology and natural history of alcoholism as a progressive disorder. Nonetheless, from the practical standpoint, recognizing the instability of the liability phenotype indicates that the design and implementation of effective interventions could directly affect alcoholism risk, as well as risk for antisocial behavior.

In summary, the liability to alcoholism is conceptualized as a latent trait consisting of genetic and nongenetic factors. The components of the trait vary between individuals in the population due to unique genetic constitution and idiosyncratic environmental experiences. Furthermore, the components of the liability trait change over time within an individual concomitant to changing biological maturation and aging and quality of interactions with the environment. Considered from a developmental perspective, it would appear essential that prevention and treatment interventions have an individual focus in which the main objective is to first decompose the factors comprising the liability phenotype and then apply procedures that effectively shift the phenotype toward the normal or subthreshold segment of the liability trait. The ensuing discussion examines the outset liability as it appears to be manifest early in life from a behavior-genetic framework and concludes with brief discussion of the ramifications of this approach for prevention, treatment, and diagnosis.

TEMPERAMENT PHENOTYPES ASSOCIATED WITH ELEVATED RISK

Allport (1961) provides a definition that captures the meaning of temperament:

[Temperament reflects] the characteristic phenomena of an individual's nature, including his susceptibility to emotional stimulation, his customary strength and speed of response, the quality of his prevailing mood, and all the peculiarities of fluctuation and intensity of mood, these being phenomena regarded as dependent on constitutional makeup, and therefore largely hereditary in origin. (p. 34)

Although there is uncertainty regarding the exact complement of temperament traits or dimensions, strong empirical evidence nonetheless implicates significant heritability (contribution of genotypic variation on phenotypic variation in the population) for several traits. The following discussion examines the evidence for temperament deviations as risk factors for alcoholism according to the dimensions reported by Rowe and Plomin (1977). These authors identified six dimensions upon integration and analysis of the traits investigated in the New York Longitudinal Study (Thomas & Chess, 1984) and Colorado Adoption project (Plomin & DeFries, 1983). These two investigations comprise the most comprehensive effort aimed at determining the impact of temperament on psychological development and psychosocial adjustment. Significantly, a genetic influence has been documented for the traits investigated in these two investigative programs (Cyphers et al., 1990). Hence, the complement of temperament traits proposed by Rowe and Plomin (1977) is the most parsimonious and empirically based description of temperament. The traits identified are:

- Behavior activity level
- Attention span-persistence
- Emotionality
- Soothability
- Sociability
- Reaction to food

The following discussion succinctly reviews the evidence implicating an association between risk for alcoholism and deviation on these traits, with the exception of the trait *reaction to food,* which has not received empirical study. For more detailed reviews of the association between temperament phenotypes and alcoholism risk, the reader is referred to Tarter and Edwards (1988) and Tarter (1988).

Behavior Activity Level

Behavior activity level is an extensively researched temperament dimension. It has also been hypothesized to consist of two components, vigor and tempo (Buss & Plomin, 1975). Rapid behavioral tempo has been implicated to be associated with an increased risk for alcoholism (Vaillant, 1983); however, no research has been conducted regarding the influence of vigor on alcoholism risk.

Evidence from diverse sources indicates that high activity level is associated with a heightened risk for alcoholism. Although not emanating from temperament theory, longitudinal (Jones, 1968; McCord & McCord, 1960; Robins, 1966), adoption (Goodwin et al., 1975; Cantwell, 1972), and retrospective studies (Tarter, McBride et al., 1977) point to an association between alcoholism and high behavioral activity level in childhood. It has been estimated that up to 40 percent of male alcoholics have childhood histories of hyperactivity (Wood et al., 1983).

In addition, sons of alcoholic men score higher on ratings of behavioral activity level than sons of nonalcoholics (Tarter et al., 1990). The possibility is thus raised that the phenotype of high behavioral activity level is a risk factor for alcoholism inasmuch as male offspring of alcoholics are at high risk to also develop this disorder.

With the exception of one study (Moss et al., 1992), behavioral activity level has been measured using rating scales. In the recently completed study by Moss et al. (1992), activity level was directly measured in sons of drug and alcohol abusers and compared to offspring of normal men using an actigraph attached to the subject's wrist. Measurements were taken while the youngster was in a resting position and also during performance on two tasks requiring behavioral suppression and sustained attention. It was found that the boys in the experimental group demonstrated higher behavioral activity level than the children of normal fathers while performing the tasks but not while resting. These findings provide objective evidence for an association between heightened risk status for alcohol and drug abuse and the behavioral phenotype of high activity level. It is also noteworthy that the higher behavioral activity level found in the children of substance abusers was not concomitant to a conduct disorder. Hence, it can be tentatively concluded that this behavioral phenotype, although commonly aggregating with conduct disorder, is related to the risk for alcoholism and probably also to other types of drug abuse.

Emotionality

The temperament trait of emotionality refers to the propensity to be easily and intensely aroused. Children of alcoholics report greater emotional reactivity measured by scores on the neuroticism trait than offspring of nonalcoholics (Sher et al., 1991). It is noteworthy that negative affect and anxiety are common features of youth who consume alcohol (Mezzich et al., 1993) and of the offspring of alcoholics (Chassin et al., 1991); however, these findings are not consistent across all studies (Windle, 1990). Somatic and behavioral symptoms of anxiety are commonly present among boys who develop alcoholism early in life (Gomberg, 1982). In a Swedish cohort of older teenagers and young adults reporting for mandatory military registration, it was observed that susceptibility to emotional distress was associated with quantity of alcohol consumed (Rydelius, 1983a, 1983b). Significantly, in children of alcoholics it has been found that scores on the temperament trait of emotionality covaried with negative affect, which in combination with stress and parental rearing skill, promoted affiliation with negative peer influences (Chassin et al., 1993). Susceptibility to autonomic nervous system arousal among individuals at high risk for alcoholism has also been reported (Finn et al., 1990). Taken together, the psychological and psychophysiological findings point to the likelihood that high emotionality is a phenotype for alcoholism risk.

Soothability

The trait of soothability characterizes the individual's rapidity in returning to baseline level following emotional arousal. To date, no direct examination of this temperament trait has been undertaken. However, indirect evidence, marshaled from several studies, suggests that young men who are at a high risk for alcoholism experience a greater stress dampening effect from ethanol than subjects who are at low risk (Sher & Levenson, 1982). One interpretation of these results is that alcohol consumption by high-risk young men facilitates an otherwise deficient homeostasis. Consequently, they experience a stronger reinforcing effect from alcohol consumption. Thus, even though the evidence is still tenuous, there is indication that the phenotype of low soothability may be associated with an increased risk for alcoholism.

Attention Span-Persistence

Up to 40 percent of male alcoholics have been reported to qualify for an attention deficit disorder—residual type (Wood et al., 1983). Research findings employing neurocognitive tests, rating scales, and structured interviews confirm the high prevalence of attentional disturbances among children and young adults who, as a group, are at high risk for alcoholism (Tarter, Hegedus et al., 1984; Alterman & Tarter, 1983). Also, young alcoholics are inferior to older alcoholics on tasks requiring motor persistence (Alterman et al., 1984); this finding is contrary to what would be expected if the deficit was only the consequence of an alcoholism history and suggests that poor task persistence antedates the alcoholism. It is also noteworthy that neurophysiological investigations reveal deviations on the P300 wave component of event-related potentials (Begleiter et al., 1984). The P300 wave, measured with an electroencephalograph, is widely recognized to reflect attentional mechanisms. Thus, based on the limited available evidence, it appears that attentional limitations and goal impersistence are associated with the risk for alcoholism. Significantly, the findings pointing to low attentional capacity in high-risk individuals are based on a variety of different types of measurements evaluating different components of attention. Research has yet to be undertaken directed to delineating the particular facets of attention that are specifically associated with heightened risk.

Sociability

Systematic research on sociability has not been conducted with respect to the risk for alcoholism. Some evidence has been presented indicating that high scores on the personality trait of extraversion are more common among alcoholics (Barnes, 1983); however, these findings are limited by the fact that the scores could have been confounded by the established chronic course of the alcoholism. The trait "inhibition to the unfamiliar" closely approximates sociability and has been shown to have important developmental ramifications (Kagan & Saidman, 1991); however, its relevance to alcoholism etiology has not been studied.

It appears that many alcoholics present as sociable when in fact the behavior comprises a disinhibited interpersonal style. Hence, even though overtly facile and having an extroverted quality, the behavior is actually reflective of a poor self-control or dysregulation. This conclusion is buttressed by the observation that an antisocial personality disorder is a common comorbid condition of alcoholism.

It is also noteworthy that studies of alcoholics and individuals at high risk, and prospective studies of individuals who subsequently became alcoholic, have frequently documented such features as aggressivity (Kellam et al., 1980), sensation seeking (Zuckerman, 1972), impulsivity (McCord, 1972), and social nonconformity (Robins, 1966). These characteristics represent not the attributes of normative sociability, but rather of behavioral disinhibition.

Complementing this conclusion are the results of several studies indicating that individuals who obtain a low sociability score on the California Psychological Inventory, in conjunction with high behavioral disinhibition score measured by the Minnesota Multiphasic Personality Inventory (MMPI) MacAndrew Scale, obtain a greater stress-dampening effect from alcohol compared to individuals whose scores are more normative (Sher & Levenson, 1982). Because alcohol is more reinforcing among individuals who score low on the trait of sociability, the possibility is raised that habitual alcohol consumption is more likely to occur. In effect, pharmacological disposition may covary with temperament phenotype. Germane to the present discussion, however, is the conclusion that the phenotype predisposing to alcoholism appears to be low sociability, even though at first glance the individual may present as extraverted. This conclusion concurs with the recent finding that parental alcoholism was unrelated to sociability in offspring (Chassin et al., 1993).

Summary

Based on published results, the behavior-genetic approach appears to be a heuristic strategy for determining the psychological characteristics associated with the risk for alcoholism. As noted above, certain temperament phenotypes appear to be associated with a high risk for alcoholism. The temperament phenotypes which to date have been most implicative are high activity level, high emotionality, low sociability, low attention span-persistence, and low soothability. It is emphasized, however, that an alcoholism outcome is not determined directly by temperament phenotype. Rather, as depicted in Figure 2.1, this outcome is the culmination of the epigenetic process. The outset point, temperament phenotype, interacts with the social environment throughout the lifespan to determine risk status. Furthermore, it should be emphasized that factors in addition to temperament deviation (e.g., biochemical, physiological) may also affect the risk for alcoholism. Finally, it is important to note that a temperament deviation is not a necessary condition to predispose to an alcoholism outcome; Figure 2.1 shows that a normative temperament phenotype in the context of either adverse biological or environmental circumstances also can culminate in this outcome. Following a brief examination of issues surrounding the need to concisely define the outcome, namely alcoholism, the focus of the discussion now turns to how temperament-environment interactions underlie the developmental trajectory to alcoholism.

ALCOHOLISM PHENOTYPE

Research into etiology has been hampered by a lack of consensus regarding the taxonomic criteria for defining alcoholism, that is, an objective quantifiable description of the threshold on the continuum. The necessary or defining attribute for alcoholism has yet to be specified. Not surprisingly, therefore, consensus regarding the denotative meaning of this clinical condition remains elusive (Tarter et al., 1992). In the American Psychiatric Association classification system, alcoholism is a multidimensional phenotype applied to individuals who exceed an arbitrary number of adverse consequences concomitant to alcohol consumption behavior. Hence, not surprisingly, the population who is labeled "alcoholic" is very heterogeneous with respect to clinical presentation and natural history. Without a clear specification of the outcome phenotype, alcoholism, it is not possible to elucidate specific etiologic mechanisms and associated developmental pathways. For example, there are numerous permutations of symptoms that could qualify an individual for a diagnosis of alcoholism (Tarter et al., 1987). Thus, to clarify the etiology of alcoholism, the end-point multidimensional phenotype needs to be specified better than currently practiced. Research focusing on particular phenotypic features of alcoholism comprises important progress in this direction for improving our understanding of the interaction between genetic and environmental influences on producing specific outcomes (Heath et al., 1991).

PHENOTYPIC HETEROGENEITY

Recently, a first step in documenting phenotypic heterogeneity was undertaken by proposing a method for quantifying ten endpoints according to their severity (Tarter, 1990). This approach contradicts current efforts to identify pure alcoholic subtypes based on the dimensions of personality, comorbid psychiatric disorder, familial transmission patterns, or natural history. Referring again to Figure 2.1, it is apparent that the pathway to alcoholism is unique for each individual. Hence, efforts to cluster alcoholics into distinct groups are unlikely to be successful, particularly if numerous dimensions relevant to treatment intervention are considered. Tarter (1990) proposed ten salient dimensions that are integral to both etiology and maintenance of problems with alcohol consumption. Thus, rather than assigning this heterogeneous population with the one label of "alcoholism," outcome is instead quantified across ten domains. These ten dimensions, evaluated by the Drug Use Screening Inventory, are: substance abuse, psychiatric disorder, behavior problems, work problems, school maladjustment, peer relations, health disturbances, social skill deficits, family problems, and leisure and recreation.

By ranking severity of alcohol and drug involvement using the DUSI across ten dimensions, it should be possible to more effectively target interventions to specific areas of disturbance and possibly calibrate the intensity of a particular intervention (e.g., inpatient, day hospital, outpatient) to the measured level of severity of disorder. However, it can be readily appreciated that when alcoholism is considered as a multidimensional phenotype, the development trajectory is influenced by numerous factors unique to each person. From the standpoint of treatment, this conclusion underscores the need for individualized intervention rather than a program in which each person receives the same type and intensity of intervention. From the standpoint of etiology, this conclusion buttresses recent findings pointing to the importance of the unshared environment (Reiss et al., 1991). And from the standpoint of taxonomy, this conclusion calls into question the validity of the *Diagnostic and Statistical Manual of Mental Disorders* (DSM) system in general and the value of using labels like alcoholism and alcohol dependence (Tarter et al., 1992). Hence, by improving precision in the measurement of specific dimensions, the developmental trajectory, linking predisposing temperament phenotypes to particular consequences of alcohol consumption, can be better understood.

In summary, for research into alcoholism etiology to progress, concerted effort must be directed to elucidating the characteristics predisposing to specific phenotypic features encompassed within the multidimensional category of alcoholism. For example, the factors underlying pharmacological tolerance, craving, drinking pattern, and the biomedical consequences of drinking (e.g., cirrhosis) are, in all probability, very diverse. Whereas the research conducted to date has typically specified the outcome variable to be dichotomous (alcoholic vs. nonalcoholic), this clinically diagnosed endpoint of alcoholism itself encompasses very heterogeneous populations with respect to etiologic determinants, natural history, and behavioral presentation. Increased precision of measurement and greater specificity of end-point phenotypes are thus necessary in order to further an understanding of alcoholism etiology.

PHENOTYPE-ENVIRONMENT INTERACTIONS

The developmental approach is based on the premise that primordial behavioral characteristics (e.g., temperament phenotypes), modified during the course of ontogeny, establish the psychological propensities associated with a high risk for alcoholism. This developmental trajectory occurs via interaction between the individual and the environment. In effect, the individual seeks out as well as reacts uniquely to the social environment. The person's psychological disposition and others in the social environment thus are mutually influenced by the quality of these interactions. For example, peers commonly cluster on the same behaviors, particularly for substance use and social deviancy (Kandel et al., 1990). Also, it is well established that individuals respond to environmental stimuli according to their particular psychological characteristics. Thus, the person's psychological makeup mediates the quality of interaction with the environment to shape the developmental process; this iterative process has been referred to as the *organismic specificity hypothesis* (Wachs & Gandour, 1983). This framework for elucidating etiology is heuristic for investigating behavior epigenesis, that is, the successive acquisition of phenotypes according to the characteristics of prior phenotypes. Antecedent behavior probablistically affects the expression of subsequent behavior to orient the person toward or away from an alcoholism outcome.

High Behavioral Activity Level

To illustrate this developmental model, Figure 2.2 and the discussion below provides an example of one hypothetical trajectory to an alcoholism outcome. The temperament phenotype, high behavioral activity level, predisposes to a series of outcomes that ultimately manifests as alcoholism. It is noteworthy that each of the processes depicted in Figure 2.2 that are implicated to influence behavioral development has been documented in the empirical literature; however, to date investigations

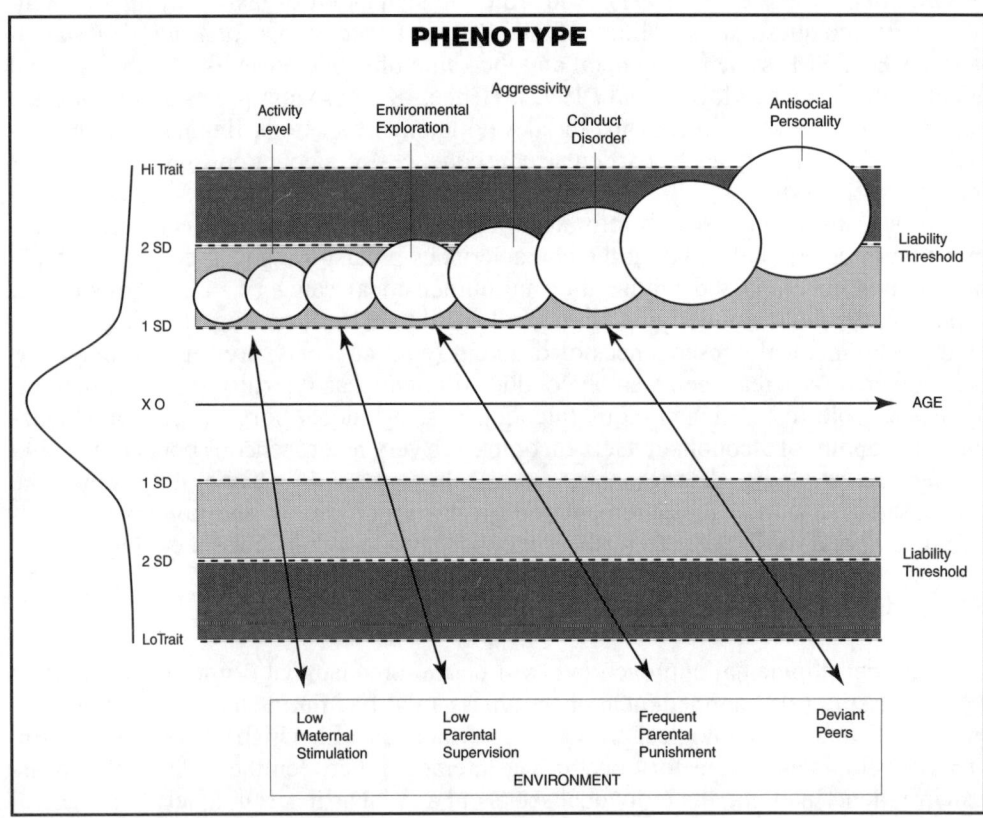

Figure 2.2. Hypothetical Developmental Trajectory to Alcoholism

of alcoholism have not been conducted to encompass the chaining of the behavioral trajectory in a prospective study of alcoholism etiology.

Based on studies of animals and humans, substantial evidence has been accrued demonstrating that variability in behavioral activity level in the population is influenced strongly by genotypic differences. The variation of this trait can be theoretically described within a Gaussian (normal) distribution consisting of infinite phenotypes. Infants manifesting a high behavioral activity level are prone to exchanges with the social environment that promote the development of conduct problems and deviancy. Available evidence indicates that high behavioral activity level in early childhood is associated with a propensity for extensive environmental exploration (Gandour, 1989); notably, this propensity, characterized as a sensation-seeking motivational style, is common among adolescent alcohol and drug abusers (Zuckerman, 1972). Unrestricted exploration of the environment can be associated with ineffective parental supervision; this factor has also been shown to be characteristic of youth at risk for substance abuse (Tarter et al., 1993b) and conduct problems (Patterson et al., 1989). In addition, free ranging access to the environment potentially sets the stage for conflict with caretakers. Children having a high behavioral activity level experience more severe punishment than other children (Webster-Stratton & Eyberg, 1982) and, in this regard, it is noteworthy that children at high risk for substance abuse are subjected to more severe and inconsistent disciplinary practices than other children (Tarter et al., 1993a) and that there is also greater mutual dissatisfaction between parent and child (Tarter et al., 1993b). Thus, the temperament phenotype of high activity level, expressed in early childhood, predisposes to interactions with the environment that promote social maladjustment.

Interaction With Environment

However, as pointed out by Thomas and Chess (1984), an effective environment in responding to the child's behavior can mitigate deviancy and maladjustment. Particularly, a mismatch between the child and caretakers with respect to behavioral and affective disposition has been hypothesized to be a critical factor. In a longitudinal research study conducted at the Center for Education and Drug Abuse Research in Pittsburgh, Pennsylvania, preliminary evidence has been accrued indicating that the similarity between substance abusing fathers and 10- to 12-year-old sons with respect to a composite trait of "difficult affective temperament" is related to magnitude of behavior problems in the child (Blackson et al., 1993). Other research has shown that high behavioral activity of children can promote drinking behavior in adults who have a family history of alcoholism even though they are not alcoholic themselves (Pelham et al., unpublished). The point to be made is that the interactions between the child and caretaker are mutually influential so as to affect the course of the child's psychological development.

A distressed home environment and disruptive behavior by the child in that environment do not necessarily result in problems that come to the attention of professionals. Thus, problems may remain unnoticed until the child enters school where normative behavior patterns are essential for adjustment. Thus, while aggressive and oppositional behavior in the home can be tolerated, even if not effectively managed, such behavior in the school environment is problematic. These types of conduct problems are common among children at high risk for substance abuse (Mezzich et al., unpublished) and predispose to conflicts with teachers as well as social marginalization by normative behaving deviant peers. In reaction to this situation, the child is likely to select and affiliate with similar behaving peers. Hence, behavior disturbances, observable before entering school, become more firmly established such that a suprathreshold phenotype of conduct disorder is eventually manifest. By adolescence, this conduct disorder almost invariably includes alcohol and drug use.

In this developmental scenario, alcohol and drug use are intertwined with conduct problems and ultimately a conduct disorder, which carries a risk of about 0.5 for developing into an antisocial personality disorder in adulthood (Farrington, 1991). Hence, the age at which the person first qualifies for a suprathreshold diagnosis of alcoholism (or other substance abuse) is variable; this disorder can occur at any time following the onset of conduct problems in childhood when the person initiates consumption as part of a generalized pattern of deviancy.

Evidence for the interaction between environmental conditions such as child rearing and genetically influenced temperamental traits provides support for the adoption of empirically based programs and policies. Because we can reliably identify children at high risk for antisocial behavior on the basis of these factors, programs can both treat and prevent this development by considering scientific evidence. Behavioral parenting skills training, in which parents learn to increase their praise and reward and provide more mild, nonabusive consequences for problem behavior, will bring about improvements in parenting and reductions in children's aggressive behavior and risk for alcoholism simultaneously. There are other related family interventions that combine behavioral parenting training with family systems theory which may serve to reduce the impact of existing liability traits.

In summary, alcoholism etiology cannot be understood in the context of a specific cause-effect relationship. The above described scenario, by illustrating one hypothetical developmental pathway to alcoholism, demonstrates how a temperament phenotype early in life develops into successive behavioral phenotypes that eventually place the person onto a trajectory for this adverse outcome. Because the interactions between each child's phenotype and the environment are unique, it follows that every person in the population who develops alcoholism has an idiosyncratic etiology and natural history that can be altered.

EPIGENETIC MODEL

The preceding discussion examined a developmental pathway to alcoholism based on a deviation in only one temperament trait, activity level. It is ultimately necessary to delineate the unique configuration of each person's temperament, involving conjointly all trait dimensions, to understand the etiology of alcoholism. Even within a framework of five temperament traits, as discussed herein, and the theoretically infinite number of phenotypes for each trait, it becomes apparent why every person in the population has a distinctive temperament makeup.

Difficult Temperament

One configuration of phenotype that has received substantial interest is the difficult temperament. Individuals characterized as having a difficult temperament are featured by negative mood, high social withdrawal, high rigidity, high behavioral activity level, irregular eating patterns, sleep and daily activity, and low task orientation (Thomas & Chess, 1977). Significantly, a difficult temperament in early childhood is associated with an increased risk for both internalizing and externalizing behavior disorder by late childhood and adolescence (Maziade et al., 1990).

An association between difficult temperament in childhood and subsequent alcohol and drug use has been reported (Lerner & Vicary, 1984). In addition, children of alcohol and drug abusers have been shown to score higher than offspring of normal parents on the difficult temperament index, derived from the revised Dimensions of Temperament Scale (Tarter et al., 1990; Tarter et al., 1993a, 1993b). Furthermore, it has been observed that a difficult temperament displayed in late childhood mediates the effects of parental history of substance abuse on the child's expression of behavior disturbance (Blackson et al., 1993).

Interaction With Environment

Little is known regarding the mechanisms by which difficult temperament in childhood influences psychological development and initiation subsequently of alcohol and drug use. In one study, it was observed that there is greater mutual dissatisfaction between mother and son in families where the father is a substance abuser (Tarter et al., 1993b) and that the magnitude of dissatisfaction correlates negatively with family cohesion and organization. This finding suggests that the environmental context combined with a suboptimal temperament predisposes to maladjustment, including hyperactivity, aggressiveness, and delinquency in the offspring. It is also noteworthy that male offspring of substance abusers experience more severe and less consistent disciplinary practices than children of normal parents (Tarter et al., 1993a). Taken together, these results indicate that children displaying a difficult temperament, especially if living in a family where there is parental substance abuse, manifest behavioral features that have been frequently observed to predispose to substance abuse. Furthermore, the magnitude of expression of these latter behavioral features in the child is related to assortative mating (partners with similar traits) for these characteristics by the child's parents (Vanyukov et al., 1993).

The epigenetic approach to alcoholism etiology is directed to delineating how behavioral phenotypes successively emerge concomitant to person-environment interaction patterns. The quality of these interactions, as previously discussed, is determined by the conjoint characteristics of the individual and the social environment. In one preliminary examination of the heuristic value of the epigenetic approach, an analysis was conducted on a sample of forty-eight adolescents who qualified for a diagnosis of Psychoactive Substance Use Disorder (Tarter, Kirisci et al., 1994). It was found that a difficult temperament in childhood was present in 35 percent of the sample. Within this subsample, a number of different psychiatric disorders subsequently emerged of which conduct disorder, attention deficit disorder, and anxiety disorder were most prevalent. Alcohol or another drug abuse disorder next emanated from one of these disorders. The implications of these findings are twofold. First, the pathways linking temperament to substance abuse are variable. Second, the breadth of intermediary outcomes ultimately produces a population of alcoholics having limitless heterogeneity.

In summary, an epigenetic paradigm is heuristic for uncovering the developmental pathways to alcoholism and other variations of drug abuse. These pathways are determined by the unique quality of person-environment interactions, which in turn determines the acquisition of successive behavioral phenotypes. This temporal organization and patterning of behavior comprises the developmental trajectory that orients the person toward or away from an alcoholism outcome.

IMPLICATIONS OF THE DEVELOPMENTAL-BEHAVIOR-GENETIC PERSPECTIVE

The extent to which temperamental traits vary is a function of many gene effects (Buss & Plomin, 1984; Plomin, 1990). Therefore, interindividual differences in the liability to alcoholism, as the developmental product of these traits, also has a polygenic basis. Emerging methods in molecular genetics potentially afford the opportunity to delineate how multiple genes located on different chromosomes underlie variation in behavior phenotypes such as temperament. Particularly, quantitative trait loci (QTL) methods of analysis are being developed to elucidate the genetic underpinnings of behavior that could potentially have important applications for understanding alcoholism etiology (see Goldman & Fishbein, Chapter 9). For example, research with rodents has shown that QTL technology can inform about the genetic basis underlying variation in alcohol tolerance (McClearn et al., 1991). As noted previously, different aspects of alcoholism topology may have different underlying mechanisms; however, research to date has not attempted to clarify the various behavioral phenotypes that may contribute to the liability to alcoholism using QTL methods.

PREVENTION OF ALCOHOLISM

Although the greatest period of risk for the onset of alcoholism is in the first half of life, the developmental-behavior-genetic perspective encompasses the whole life span. The life span applicability of the behavior-genetic perspective stems mainly from the premise that it is the quality of interaction between (1) the person having a particular psychological disposition and (2) the social environment that determines the behavior response patterns and emotional reactions. These in turn define, to a large degree, initiation of habitual consumption of alcoholic beverages. At an age when alcohol is accessible and known by the consumer to have desired psychoactive effects (this usually occurs by late childhood), it is possible anytime thereafter for alcoholism to develop.

The model presented in Figure 2.1 conceptualizes how prevention research can be undertaken within the developmental-behavior-genetic perspective. The psychological (temperament) disposition, as discussed earlier, is a vector that orients the person toward or away from alcoholism or a drug abuse outcome. However, myriad environmental factors affect both the force and directional components of the vector. For example, the child's family could exercise a negative impact on the child and thus enhance the risk for an adverse outcome. Offsetting this influence, other influences in the environment can potentially reduce the risk. Thus, risk at any time is determined by the aggregate of environmental factors, positive and negative, interacting with psychological disposition. By disaggregating these factors with the aim of bolstering the positive ones and attenuating the negative ones, the risk for an alcoholism outcome can be diminished.

The implications of this approach to prevention are substantial. Specifically, it underscores the need to implement preventions tailored to one or more of the following objectives: changing the psychological characteristics of the individual, changing the environment, or changing the quality of interactions between the person and the environment. With respect to changing the person, the armamentarium of strategies ranging from pharmacologic to behavior modification methods may be effective in reducing risk status by shifting behavior toward the more normative range. However, because psychological interventions are less intrusive, they are arguably preferred to biological interventions for modifying the liability. Normative behavior, once established, is then a vector for further normative development. Changing the environment could also reduce risk by shifting the person toward normative behavior. For example, reducing accessibility to alcohol and drugs and preventing tobacco use in public places has the effect of forcing compliance with normative behavior. Placing the person in a social context or subculture that redefines normative behavior such that habitual alcohol use is negatively sanctioned comprises another potentially effective environmental manipulation. Common observation of the radical behavioral and attitudinal changes that occur among individuals who join certain religious subcultures underscores the potency of environmental intervention.

Finally, prevention interventions should be implemented that modify the quality of person-environment interaction patterns that are identifiable developmental vectors for future maladjustment. In this regard, interventions may be effective when targeted to interaction patterns in particular environmental contexts (e.g., family, school, job), such that the individual's behavior is modified toward normality. As discussed previously, there appears to be a complex relationship between a child's difficult temperament, quality of parental rearing, and the disruptive behavior in children of substance abusing parents. Improving the parenting quality for children who display a difficult temperament may thus promote normative development and ultimately reduce the risk for alcoholism and substance abuse.

In summary, prevention research can make a substantive contribution to reducing alcohol and drug abuse in society on adopting a developmental-behavior-genetic perspective. By delineating the behaviors comprising vectors for the adverse outcome, it is then possible to identify those individuals who are at high risk to whom tailored interventions should be targeted.

TREATMENT OF ALCOHOLISM

Paralleling the strategy for prevention, the approach to treatment requires modification of factors that have contributed to the suprathreshold diagnosis of drug abuse or alcoholism. The objective of treatment intervention is to disaggregate the factors contributing to severe problem involvement with drugs or alcohol (defined by surpassing the diagnostic threshold) and then to implement interventions that could shift the person toward the normative ranges. As shown in Figure 2.1, this would involve shifting the person's phenotype as an affected condition of alcoholism (shaded area) to the normative area under the curve. Because the person's position on the liability trait is uniquely determined by genetic predisposition, in conjunction with shared and unshared environmental experiences, it is clear that interventions need to be targeted to those specific components that are liability enhancing. Consequently, standardized treatment programs that do not account for individuality in etiology and natural history are likely to be less successful than interventions tailored to specific components of the liability. This approach to treatment emphasizes the development of intervention resources and the implementation of intervention modality on a case by case basis that addresses etiologic determinants occurring through development and current clinical presentation.

As pointed out previously, there are many factors which could trigger problem involvement with drugs and alcohol. The *DUSI* (Gordian Group, 1991; Tarter & Hegedus, 1992) is one efficient method for quantifying severity of alcohol and drug related problems across ten domains of health and psychiatric and psychosocial functioning so that areas in need of intervention can be efficiently detected. The goal of treatment is to deflect the person away from the severe end of the continuum in those domains responsible for maintaining problem involvement with drugs or alcohol. As with prevention intervention, there are three basic strategies in which the person can be deflected from the suprathreshold, or clinically affected range, to the normative range. These include (1) changing the person's dispositional behavior pattern; (2) changing the person's environment; or (3) changing the quality of interaction between the person and the environment. Thus, whether the intervention is directed toward prevention or treatment, the task is to disaggregate the factors, psychological and environmental, that underlie the problem behavior.

Editor's Note

Implications for the Treatment of Criminal Behavior. This chapter provides support for the application of interdisciplinary principles and methodologies in the treatment of offenders. Given that temperament phenotypes set the stage for an adverse outcome such as alcoholism or antisocial behavior, early interventions and treatments to establish a trend toward normality in these traits are likely to redirect the outcome. Dr. Tarter aptly points out that it is first necessary to disaggregate, or isolate, the individual traits underlying the behavioral outcome in order to address the several dimensions of the disorder. Thus, in the presence of a cognitive deficit affecting executive function (see Giancola, Chapter 11), a high activity level and a negative affect, various components of a treatment program should focus on each separately and then as they interact. Strategies may include those that enhance executive function (e.g., psychoeducational methods or speech and language therapy), relieve negative moods and anger (e.g., anger management), and direct activities in constructive ways (e.g., cognitive-behavioral therapy). In some cases, pharmacotherapy may also be indicated.

Juveniles who attract the attention of the legal system can, theoretically, be provided with treatment services more readily. The juvenile justice system is mandated to provide treatment to those who are amenable. In practice, however, most juveniles do not receive treatment services. It is the responsibility of the individual facility and clinician to see that services are provided when indicated. A comprehensive assessment of the aforementioned phenotypes, in addition to the environmental contributions, will lead the practitioner to the appropriate methods. Once the generators of the behavioral disorder have been identified, juvenile justice staff should work with treatment providers, schools, families, and neighborhood support services (e.g., boys' and girls' clubs, community centers, and others) to ensure a targeted and comprehensive approach to their multidimensional problems.

Integrated Services. In the criminal justice system, there is a high incidence of offenders with liability phenotypes. The criminal justice practitioner must coordinate efforts with an integrated network of treatment providers and other supportive services. A "seamless" system between criminal justice practitioners and treatment providers is necessary to build this bridge. The challenge of providing integrated services has received increased attention over the past five years. There is no end to the potential number of services to be considered, as they are intended to be based on client need. The goal of integration is to provide more comprehensive and better coordinated services as well as to improve client outcomes through several elements that have been deemed as essential to integrating services and systems. These include: Cross Training, Information Sharing, Joint Case Management, Joint Tasks, Linkages, Memorandums of Understanding, Shared Assessments, Shared Policies, Shared Procedures, Shared Resources, Staffing, and Targeting. While this seems a daunting task, many states are moving in this direction. Evolution of such a seamless system may be gradual, but will be facilitated by the support and active participation, even initiation, of correctional staff and treatment providers.

References

Allport, G. (1961). *Pattern and growth in personality.* New York: Holt, Rinehart & Winston.

Alterman, A. & Tarter, R. (1983). The transmission of psychological vulnerability. Implications for alcoholism etiology. *Journal of Nervous and Mental Disease, 171,* 147–154.

Alterman, A., Tarter, R., Petrarulo, E. & Baughman, T. (1984). Evidence for impersistence in young male alcoholics. *Alcoholism: Clinical and Experimental Research, 8,* 448–450.

American Psychiatric Association (1987). *Diagnostic and statistical manual of mental disorders* (3d ed. rev.). Washington, DC: American Psychiatric Association.

Barnes, G. (1983). Clinical and prealcoholic personality characteristics. In B. Kissin & H. Begleiter (Eds.), *The pathogenesis of alcoholism*, vol. 6. New York: Plenum Press, 113–195.

Begleiter, H., Porjesz, B. & Kissin, B. (1984). Event-related brain potentials in children at risk for alcoholism. *Science, 225,* 1493–1495.

Blackson, R., Tarter, R., Martin, C. & Moss, H. (1993). Temperament mediates the effects of family history of substance abuse on externalizing and internalizing child behavior. *American Journal of Orthopsychiatry, 64,* 280–292.

Bry, B. H., McKeon, P. & Pandina, R. J. (1982). Extent of drug use as a function of number of risk factors. *Journal of Abnormal Psychology, 91,* 273–279.

Buss, A. & Plomin, R. (1975). *A temperament theory of personality development.* New York: John Wiley & Sons.

Buss, A. & Plomin, R. (1984). *Temperament: Early developing personality traits.* Hillsdale, NJ: Erlbaum.

Cantwell, D. P. (1972). Psychiatric illness in the families of hyperactive children. *Archives of General Psychiatry, 27,* 414–417.

Chassin, L., Pillow, D., Curran, P., Molina, B. & Barrera, M. (1993). Relation of parental alcoholism to early adolescent substance use: A test of three mediating mechanisms. *Journal of Abnormal Psychology, 102,* 3–19.

Chassin, L., Rogush, F. & Barrera, M. (1991). Substance use and symptomatology among adolescent children of alcoholics. *Journal of Abnormal Psychology, 100,* 449–463.

Cloninger, C., Bohman, M. & Sigvardssen, S. (1981). Inheritance of alcohol abuse: Cross fostering analyses of adopted men. *Archives of General Psychiatry, 38,* 861–868.

Cyphers, L., Phillips, K., Fulker, D. & Mrazek, D. (1990). Twin temperament during the transition from infancy to early childhood. *Journal of the American Academy of Child Psychiatry, 29,* 392–397.

Falconer, D. (1965). The inheritance of liability to certain diseases estimated from the incidence among relatives. *Annals of Human Genetics, 29,* 51–86.

Farrington, D. (1991). Antisocial personality from childhood to adulthood. *The Psychologist, 4,* 389–394.

Finn, P., Zeitouni, N. & Pihl, R. (1990). Effects of alcohol on psychophysiological hyperactivity to nonaversive and aversive stimuli in men at high risk for alcoholism. *Journal of Abnormal Psychology, 99,* 79–85.

Gandour, M. (1989). Activity level as a dimension of temperament in toddlers: Its relevance for the organismic specificity hypothesis. *Child Development, 60,* 1092–1098.

Gomberg, E. (1982). The young male alcoholic: A pilot study. *Journal of Studies on Alcohol, 43,* 683–701.

Goodwin, D., Schulsinger, F., Hermansen, L., Guze, S. & Winokur, G. (1975). Alcoholism and the hyperactive child syndrome. *Journal of Nervous and Mental Disease, 160,* 349–353.

Gordian Group (1991). *Drug Use Screening Inventory,* P.O. Box 1587, Hartsville, SC 29550.

Hasin, D., Grant, B. & Endicott, J. (1990). The natural history of alcohol abuse: Implications for definitions of alcohol use disorders. *American Journal of Psychiatry, 147,* 1537–1541.

Heath, A., Meyer, J., Jardine, R. & Martin, N. (1991). The inheritance of alcohol consumption in a general population twin study: II Determinants of consumption frequency and quantity consumed. *Journal of Studies on Alcohol, 52,* 425–433.

Helzer, J., Burman, A. & McEvoy, L. (1991). Alcohol abuse dependence. In L. Robins & D. Regier (Eds.), *Psychiatric disorders in America,* New York, Free Press, 81–115.

Jessor, R., Donovan, J. & Costa, F. (1991). *Beyond adolescence. Problem behavior and young adult development.* New York: Cambridge University Press.

Jones, M. (1968). Personality correlates and antecedents of drinking patterns in adult males. *Journal of Consulting and Clinical Psychiatry, 32,* 2–12.

Kagan, J. & Saidman, N. (1991). Infarct predictors of inhibited and uninhibited profiles. *Psychological Science, 2,* 40–44.

Kandel, D., Davies, M. & Baydar, N. (1990). The creation of interpersonal contexts: Homophily in dyadic relationships in adolescence and young adulthood. In L. Robins & M. Rutter (Eds.), *Straight and devious pathways from childhood to adulthood.* New York: Cambridge University Press, 221–241.

Kellam, S., Ersminger, M. & Simon, M. (1980). Mental health in first grade and teenage drug, alcohol, and cigarette use. *Drug and Alcohol Dependence, 5,* 273–304.

Kendler, K. & Eaves, L. (1986). Models for the joint effect of genotype and environment on liability to psychiatric illness. *American Journal of Psychiatry, 14,* 279–289.

Labouvie, E., Pandina, R. & Johnson, V. (1991). Developmental trajectories of substance use in adolescence. Difference and predictors. *International Journal of Behavioral Development, 14,* 305–328.

Lerner, J. & Vicary, J. (1984). Difficult temperament and drug use: Analysis from the New York Longitudinal Study. *Journal of Drug Education, 14,* 1–8.

Maziade, M., Caron, C., Cote, R., Merrette, C., Bernier, H., Laplante, B., Boutin, P. & Thivierge, J. (1990). Psychiatric status of adolescents who had extreme temperaments at age 7. *American Journal of Psychiatry, 147,* 1531–1537.

McClearn, G., Plomin, R., Gora-Maslak, G. & Crabbe, J. (1991). The gene chase in behavioral science. *Psychiatry and Science, 2,* 222–229.

McCord, J. (1972). Etiological factors in alcoholism: Family and personal characteristics. *Quarterly Journal of Studies on Alcohol, 33,* 1020–1027.

McCord, W. & McCord, J. (1960). *Origins of alcoholism.* Palo Alto, CA: Stanford University Press.

McGue, M., Pickens, R. & Svikis, D. (1992). Sex and age effects on the inheritance of alcohol problems: A twin study. *Journal of Abnormal Psychology, 101,* 3–17.

Mezzich, A., Tarter, R., Kirisci, L., Clark, D., Bukstein, O. & Martin, C. (1993). Subtypes of early age onset alcoholism. *Alcoholism in Clinical and Experimental Research, 17,* 767–770.

Mezzich, A., Tarter, R., Moss, H. & Hsieh, Y. *Substance abuse vulnerability in three groups of prepubertal children of substance abusing fathers.* Unpublished manuscript, University of Pittsburgh, Department of Psychiatry.

Moss, H., Blackson,T., Martin, C. & Tarter, R. (1992). Heightened motor activity level in male offspring of substance abusing fathers: Association with temperament, behavior, and psychiatric diagnosis. *Biological Psychiatry, 32,* 1135–1147.

Patterson, G., DeBaryshe, B. & Ramsey, E. (1989). A developmental perspective on antisocial behavior. *American Psychologist, 44,* 329–335.

Pelham, W., Lang, A., Atkeson, B., Murphy, D., Gnagy, E. & Greiner, A. *Stress induced alcohol consumption in parents interacting with confederate children: Effects of child behavior, offspring psychopathology, and family history of alcohol problems.* Unpublished manuscript, University of Pittsburgh, Department of Psychiatry.

Pihl, R., Peterson, J. & Finn, P. (1990). Inherited predisposition to alcoholism: Characteristics of sons of male alcoholics. *Journal of Abnormal Psychology, 99,* 291–301.

Plomin, R. (1990). The role of inheritance in behavior. *Science, 248,* 183–188.

Plomin, R. & DeFries, J. C. (1983). The Colorado adoption project. *Child Development, 54,* 276–289.

Reiss, D., Plomin, R. & Hetherington, M. (1991). Genetics and psychiatry: An unheralded window on the environment. *American Journal of Psychiatry, 148,* 283–291.

Robins, L. N. (1966). *Deviant children grown up. A sociological and psychiatric study of sociopathic personality.* Baltimore: Williams & Wilkins.

Robins, L. & Rutter, M. (1990). *Straight and devious pathways from childhood to adulthood.* New York: Cambridge University Press.

Rowe, D. & Plomin, R. (1977). Temperament in early childhood. *Journal of Personality Assessment, 41,* 150–156.

Rydelius, P. A. (1983a). Alcohol-abusing teenage boys: Testing a hypothesis on the relationship between alcohol abuse and social background factors, criminality and personality in teenage boys. *Acta Psychiatrica Scandinavica, 68,* 368–380.

Rydelius, P. A. (1983b). Alcohol-abusing teenage boys: Testing a hypothesis on alcohol abuse and personality factors using a personality inventory. *Acta Psychiatrica Scandinavica, 68,* 381–385.

Sher, K. & Levenson, R. (1982). Risk for alcoholism and individual differences in the stress-response-dampening effect of alcohol. *Journal of Abnormal Psychology, 19,* 350–367.

Sher, K., Walitzer, K., Wood, P. & Brent, E. (1991). Characteristics of children of alcoholics: Putative risk factors, substance use and abuse, and psychopathology. *Journal of Abnormal Psychology, 100,* 427–488.

Tarter, R. (1988). Are there inherited behavioral traits which predispose to substance abuse? *Journal of Consulting and Clinical Psychology, 56,* 189–196.

Tarter, R. (1990). Evaluation and treatment of adolescent substance abuse: A decision tree method. *American Journal of Drug and Alcohol Abuse, 61,* 1–46.

Tarter, R., Alterman, A. & Edwards, K. (1985). Vulnerability to alcoholism in men. A behavior-genetic perspective. *Journal of Studies on Alcohol, 46,* 329–356.

Tarter, R., Arria, A., Moss, H., Edwards, K. & Van Thiel, D. (1987). DSM-III criteria for alcohol abuse. Association with alcohol consumption behavior. *Alcoholism: Clinical and Experimental Research, 11,* 541–543.

Tarter, R., Blackson, T., Martin, C., Loeber, R. & Moss, H. (1993a). Characteristics and correlates of child discipline practices in substance abuse and normal families. *American Journal on Addiction, 2*, 18–25.

Tarter, R., Blackson, T., Martin, C., Seilhamer, R., Pelham, W. & Loeber, R. (1993b). Mutual dissatisfaction between mother and son in substance abuse and normal families. Association with child behavior problems. *American Journal on Addiction, 2*, 1–10.

Tarter, R. & Edwards, K., (1988). Psychological factors associated with the risk for alcoholism. *Alcoholism: Clinical and Experimental Research, 12*, 471–480.

Tarter, R. & Hegedus, A. (1992). The drug use screening inventory. Its application in the evaluation and treatment of alcohol and drug abuse. *Alcohol, Health and Research World,15*, 65–75.

Tarter, R., Hegedus, A., Goldstein, G., Shelly, C. & Alterman, A. (1984). Adolescent sons of alcoholics: Neuropsychological and personality characteristics. *Alcoholism: Clinical and Experimental Research, 8*, 216–222.

Tarter, R., Kabene, M., Escallier, E., Laird, S. & Jacob, T. (1990). Temperament deviation and risk for alcoholism. *Alcoholism: Clinical and Experimental Research, 14*, 380–382.

Tarter, R., Kirisci, L., Hegedus, A., Mezzich, A. & Vanyukov, M. (1994). Heterogeneity of adolescent alcoholism. *Annals of the New York Academy of Science, 708*, 102–107.

Tarter, R., McBride, H., Buonpane, N. & Schneider, D. (1977). Differentiation of alcoholics: Childhood history of minimal brain dysfunction, family history, and drinking pattern. *Archives of General Psychiatry, 34*, 761–768.

Tarter, R., Moss, H., Arria, A. & Mezzich, A. (1992). Psychiatric diagnosis of alcoholism: Critique and reformulation. *Alcoholism: Clinical and Experimental Research, 16*, 106–116.

Tarter, R., Moss, H. & Vanyukov, M. (1995). Behavior-genetic perspective of alcoholism etiology. In H. Begleiter & B. Kissin (Eds.), *Alcohol and alcoholism.* New York: Oxford University Press.

Thomas, A. & Chess, S. (1977). *Temperament and development.* New York: Brunner/Mazel.

Thomas, A. & Chess, S. (1984). Genesis and evolution of behavioral disorders. From infancy to early adult life. *American Journal of Psychiatry, 141*, 1–9.

Vaillant, G. (1983). *The natural history of alcoholism.* Cambridge, MA: Harvard University Press.

Vanyukov, M., Moss, H., Plail, J., Blackson, T., Mezzich, A. & Tarter, R. (1993). Antisocial symptoms in preadolescent boys and their parents: Association with cortisol. *Psychiatric Research, 46*, 9–17.

Wachs, T. & Gandour, M. (1983). Temperament, environment, and six-month cognitive-intellectual development: A test of the organismic specificity hypothesis. *International Journal of Behavioral Development, 6*, 135–152.

Webster-Stratton, C. & Eyberg, S. (1982). Child temperament: Relationship with child behavior problems and parent-child interactions. *Journal of Clinical Child Psychology, 11*, 123.

Wills, T. (1990). Multiple networks and substance use. *Journal of Social and Clinical Psychology, 9*, 78–90.

Windle, M. (1990). Temperament and personality attributes of children of alcoholics. In M. Windle & J. Searles (Eds.), *Children of alcoholics: A critical review of the literature.* New York: Guilford Press, 129–167.

Wood, D., Wender, P. & Reimherr, F. (1983). The prevalence of attention deficit disorder, residual type, or minimal brain dysfunction in a population of male alcoholic patients. *American Journal of Psychiatry, 140*, 95–98.

Zuckerman, M. (1972). Drug usage as one manifestation of a "sensation seeking" trait. In E. Keup (Ed.), *Drug abuse: Current concepts and research.* Springfield, IL: C. C.Thomas, 154.

Chapter 3

The Contribution of Psychology to Criminal Justice Education

by Cathy Spatz Widom, Ph.D. and Hans Toch, Ph.D.

Introduction—The Role of Psychology 3-2
Psychological Theories of Criminal Behavior 3-3
    Behavior Theory 3-3
    Social Learning Theory 3-4
    Cognitive Social Learning Theory 3-5
    Attachment Theory 3-6
    Social Control Theory 3-6
New Perspectives or Models of Delinquent and Criminal Behavior 3-7
    Stability of Aggressiveness: Early Problem Behaviors
        Predict Later Problem Behaviors 3-7
    Bidirectionality of Influences and Transactional Models 3-7
    Protective Factors 3-8
    The Importance of Temperament 3-9
    Cognition and Motivation 3-10
Early Childhood Intervention as a Preventive Strategy for Delinquency . 3-10
    Risk and Protective Factors 3-11
    Multidimensional Approach 3-11
Psychological and Mental Disorders 3-12
    Link to Crime and Violence? 3-12
Disaggregation and Classification 3-13
Conclusion 3-14

Reprinted with Permission of the Academy of Criminal Justice Sciences. Adapted from Cathy Spatz Widom and Hans Toch, 1993 "The Contribution of Psychology to Criminal Justice Education." *Journal of Criminal Justice Education* 4(2):251–272.

INTRODUCTION—THE ROLE OF PSYCHOLOGY

The fields of criminology and criminal justice are inherently multidisciplinary. Historically, this means that the stream of knowledge that now falls under the heading "criminal justice" or "criminology" is a composite of tributaries that formerly carried other labels such as "sociology," "psychology," "behavioral science," "political science," and "jurisprudence." Today, as the fields of criminal justice and criminology continue to evolve, much of their substance can be cross-listed under disciplinary headings. New discoveries and new lines of research in traditional disciplines often become contributions to criminal justice and criminology theory and knowledge, and are taught in criminal justice and criminology courses.

One can slice the criminal justice/criminology pie in many ways after being introduced to the field in standard survey courses, which are judiciously sampled portions. One such approach is to capture contributions to the discipline through courses such as "The Sociology of Crime," "Psychological Approaches to Crime," "Biological Approaches to Antisocial Behavior," or "Political Perspectives in Criminal Justice." One advantage of this approach is that it offers a coherent theoretical basis for examining crime-related problems. Another advantage is that it enables criminal justice students to cross disciplinary boundaries without abandoning their concerns with crime and responses to crime.

How would a psychology-centered course in criminal justice or criminology look? Would it be a course about the work of psychologists who are interested in crime problems? If so, it would be incomplete because it would exclude the work of criminologists and individuals from other disciplines who are interested in psychological questions. The course instead would have to be defined in terms of the questions asked and the approach taken to answering the questions. It would have to be based on a definition of the concerns of psychology as a discipline.

Psychology has made and continues to make important contributions to criminology and criminal justice. Early psychological explanations focused on personality disturbances and on psychopathology; discussions of the contribution of psychology to criminology emphasized the treatment of offenders. Typically, what was taught in criminal justice or criminology courses as representing the psychological approach was Freudian or psychoanalytic theory (Abrahamsen 1944; Freud [1916], 1946), Lombroso's ideas (Ferrero-Lombroso, 1911), or Sheldon's (1949) work on body types. In this paper we call attention to more recent developments that we believe represent information necessary for educating criminal justice and criminology students and scholars. In doing so, we focus primarily on the etiology and description of criminal and violent behavior. We omit discussion of psychology as a tool in treating offenders because this would broaden the scope beyond the length limits. Treatment approaches are presented in other chapters within this book.

In focusing on the contribution of one discipline or approach, such as that of psychology, one often is tempted to relegate other approaches to a lesser position. That is not our goal, but neither do we concede that the approach we describe here is expendable. In our opinion, even the best-developed sociological, historical, or biological theories by themselves do not provide an adequate understanding of crime and criminal justice problems. Explanations without references to individuals are not satisfactory. For example, differential association theory delineates social conditions in which crime can flourish, and attempts to explain processes by which individuals become criminal. Among individuals who grow up in similar criminogenic conditions, however, some adopt criminal attitudes and behaviors and others do not. It is equally obvious that poverty is an important causal factor in explaining criminal behavior. Yet, if one were to consider one thousand individuals living in poverty, fewer than one hundred would become criminals. Among the remainder, ten may commit suicide, fifty may end up in psychiatric hospitals, and eight to nine hundred may be noncriminals and not emotionally disturbed.

Even among individuals severely stressed by economic hardship, racial discrimination, or other problems, the majority do not become delinquent, criminal, violent, or abusive (Strauss & Gelles, 1990; Widom, 1989). Although economic and social stressors must be considered in any full account of child abuse, for example, the majority of the most economically and socially stressed parents do not physically abuse their children, whereas parents raised in advantaged circumstances can become abusers. Such statistics underscore the role of the individual or psychological analysis, although they suggest that these phenomena operate in a larger sociocultural context. Even in the most complicated and most thorough social structural models, some portion of the variance is not explained. It follows that a more complete model of criminal behavior must allow for the contribution of psychological variables.

What does it mean to take a psychological approach to problems of criminal justice? What constitutes a psychological theory? The simplest answer is that *theories are psychological insofar as they focus on the individual as the unit of analysis*. Thus any theory regarding the behavior of individual offenders or referring to forces or dynamics that motivate individuals to commit crimes would be considered to have a psychological component. For example, explanations of family violence (including child abuse) that consider the role of impulse control, anger control, conditioned emotional arousal, weak personality development, or inadequate coping mechanisms are using psychological constructs. Similarly, any view of the drug-crime problem that includes concerns about addiction has a salient psychological focus because addiction is an individual psychological process.

A number of contemporary explanations of delinquent and criminal behavior are explicitly psychological or are derived from past psychological theories. We consider five major theoretical approaches to crime and delinquency, and then call attention to recent developments in the field.

PSYCHOLOGICAL THEORIES OF CRIMINAL BEHAVIOR

Behavior Theory

Extrapolating from the broad principles underlying a "science of behavior" outlined by Skinner (1938), researchers over the years have derived and developed explanations for delinquency and criminal behavior. At the heart of behavior theory is the notion that behavior is determined by environmental consequences produced for the individual concerned. Behavior that leads to positive (desirable) consequences for the individual will become more frequent. In such instances, the behavior is said to be reinforced. Behavior that leads to negative (or aversive) consequences will become less frequent, and is said to be punished. In this formulation, any behavior is operant behavior; that is, the behavior operates on the environment to produce changes that are reinforced or punished. Because the consequences of a person's behavior are found in the environment in which the behavior occurs, the determinants of behavior would lie outside the person—not within the person, as in other theories.

According to behaviorally oriented criminologists, the principles that are applicable to nondeviant behavior also apply to criminal and delinquent behavior and reflect an individual's response to environmental contingencies. Individuals can become offenders because they receive tangible rewards (positive reinforcement) for engaging in delinquent and criminal behavior, particularly when no other attractive alternative is available. For example, a female may find that she can support herself on income derived from engaging in illegal behavior (e.g., prostitution). When punishment (if any) of such conduct is neither swift, sure, nor severe, the behavior continues.

An individual may respond to nontangible as well as to tangible rewards for delinquent or criminal behavior, such as approval by a group, social status among peers, or attention from a parent. Such nontangible but nevertheless direct rewards would reinforce this behavior.

Using behavioral principles and applying them to individuals from a variety of backgrounds, one could explain the acquisition and maintenance of all sorts of criminal or delinquent behavior. Once a person has engaged in such behavior, both the promise of future rewards and the threat of future punishment are present. Yet because the probability of being caught (arrested) generally is low and because intermittent reinforcement maintains the behavior, the criminality of delinquency is likely to persist.

As Hollin (1989) noted, violence can be reinforced by the consequences it produces, such as by removing some unwanted element (e.g., a victim who resists being mugged). Crime also can have aversive consequences such as being arrested, being sent to prison, having an intrusive probation officer, or suffering family problems, all of which exercise a direct or indirect punishing effect. "In the final analysis," Hollin writes, "it is the balance of reinforcement and punishment in an individual's learning history which will dictate the present or absence of criminal behavior" (p. 42).

Social Learning Theory

Formulated by Rotter (1954) and developed by Bandura (1969) and others, social learning theory is based on the assumption that behavior can be adopted because it is seen to be functional through observing other people's actions. Observation of behavior is particularly potent when the model observed is successful or of high status. When the opportunity is given to engage in the behavior, it may be practiced and refined. Once learned, behavior can be reinforced or punished (internally or externally) by consequences; such consequences in turn can lead to the future enactment or inhibition of the behavior.

One phenomenon that can be explained in these terms is the *cycle of violence* (Widom, 1989). From a social learning perspective, it is understandable that successive generations of parents can abuse their children, because we assume that physical aggression between family members is likely to serve as a model for learning aggressive behavior as well as for the appropriateness of such behavior within the family (Bandura, 1973; Feshbach, 1980). All children learn behavior at least in part by imitating someone else's behavior. Thus children learn to be aggressive by observing aggression in their families and in the surrounding society. According to this view, "each generation learns to be violent by being a participant in a violent family" (Straus et al., 1980, p. 121).

Unfortunately, social learning theory is not a fully comprehensive explanatory model. Although early laboratory studies demonstrated that children and young adults imitated the behavior of aggressive models in experimental situations (Bandura, 1973; Bandura et al., 1963), these studies did not address the long-term consequences of such modeling. Questions have been raised about the generalizability of aggressive play in the laboratory to assaultive behavior in the street, and of observations of primarily middle-class nursery school children to children of different backgrounds growing up in violent households.

More recent work has included large-scale self-report surveys of exposure to violence and of adult approval of violence or marital violence (Kalmuss, 1984), studies of children of battered women (Rosenbaum & O'Leary, 1981; Wolfe et al., 1985), and studies of television violence and aggressive behavior (Friedrick-Cofer & Huston, 1986). In general, these studies support the notion that observing violence leads to increased risk of further aggression and violence; this is true even of exposure to television violence. In a ten-year follow-up of more than 200 children (Lefkowitz et al., 1972), the amount of violent television watched at age nine was the strongest single predictor of juvenile offenses involving aggression at age nineteen. The mechanisms underlying this linkage, however, are not yet understood fully.

In addition, the simple hypothesis that children model their parents' behavior and thus learn violent behavior is not an adequate explanation of adult violence. By itself, this explanation can not explain why females rarely commit sexual abuse as adults, although girls are more likely to be sexually abused than boys.

Cognitive Social Learning Theory

More recent versions of social learning theory are being revised to allow for cognitions that override reinforcement, and for extrinsic motivational orientations that result from what ordinarily would be considered successful reinforcement. Examples of such theories have been applied to the etiology and maintenance of antisocial behavior (Hawkins et al., 1986; Patterson et al., 1989).

In recent work, Patterson and his colleagues (Patterson et al., 1989) distinguished between early- and late-starter pathways to antisocial behavior, recognizing that both processes involve deficits in family management skills. The early-starter model begins with a troublesome child and/or with parents who lack firmness and skills in discipline; this situation leads to coercive cycles of interaction during early childhood (approximately ages four to nine). The troublesome child cycles are thought to begin with hyperactivity or other conditions that produce irritability in the child, to which the parent responds aversively but ineffectively. This response in turn rewards and reinforces the child's aggressive and aversive behavior, and a stable pattern of mutually coercive styles of interaction is built up from regular daily interactions during childhood. Increased aggressiveness by the child and increasing ineffectiveness on the part of the parent lead to ugly, destructive escalations. In later childhood, the child spends more time unsupervised by parents; they know less about the child's relationships with peers and teachers and are less likely to monitor the child's behavior. Failure in school and contact with deviant peers are likely outcomes.

This theory places primary emphasis on family interactions during early childhood; teachers and peers become more important as the child's world expands. In this sequence, problems in the home or hyperactivity in the child effect the subsequent development of antisocial behavior. Indeed, considerable empirical support for the hypothesized relationships has been reported (Patterson et al., 1991).

Attachment Theory

The precursor to contemporary attachment explanations of delinquent behavior is the work of Bowlby (1944), a British psychiatrist. In a study of forty-four juvenile thieves referred to a child guidance clinic, Bowlby observed that many of these children had experienced an early maternal separation during the first five years of life. From these clinical observations, Bowlby (1951) developed a theory about the importance of separation from and rejection by the mother to explain the most intractable cases of delinquency. He argued that a warm, close, unbroken relationship between child and mother (or permanent mother substitute) was essential for the child's mental health.

The core of Bowlby's theory is that infants become attached to a mother or primary caregiver if this individual is regularly available to interact with them. The infant's role is to signal its needs and to remain close to the caregiver, but differences in the quality of attachments[1] are a function of the caregiver's sensitivity and level of care. Infants develop an "internal working model" that functions as a framework for further interaction with the physical and interpersonal environment. This model involves expectations about the way the world functions, based on the early interactions with caregivers. Secure, attached infants perceive the world as a safe place, responsive to their needs and their personal requirements. Attachment provides a secure base from which to explore, develop, and solve problems. In contrast, rejection or inconsistent, haphazard care can create an insecure-avoidant child, who is likely to interpret neutral or even friendly behavior as hostile and who may show inappropriate aggressive behavior.

Despite criticism of Bowlby's theory and recognition that it may explain only a portion of delinquent behavior, this perspective has stimulated a great deal of research and further theory (Cairns, 1979; Coie, 1990; Dodge, 1980; Sroufe, 1983). For example, Dodge et al. (1990) have suggested that physical abuse is associated with chronic aggressive behavior through the "acquisition of a set of biased and deficient patterns of processing socially provocative information" (p. 1679). In line with their theory, Dodge et al. (1990) found that physically harmed four-year-old children showed deviant patterns of processing social information at age five, and that these patterns were related to aggressive behavior.

Social Control Theory

According to Hirschi's (1969) social control theory, antisocial children do not internalize parental norms because they do not relate positively to their parents. This theory emphasizes a deficit of self-control in the child, which is attributed to the child's failure to form an attachment to his or her parents during early development.

This failure not only causes the child to ignore the injunctions of its parents but also leads to the lack of attachment to other conventional individuals and activities, and to a subsequent nonacceptance of conventional norms and values of society.[2]

In a more recent statement of Hirschi's social control theory, Gottfredson and Hirschi (1990) hardly mention the child's attachment to its parents. Instead, this version of the theory focuses on characteristics of the child that presumably result from its bonding (or lack thereof). This recent version attributes lack of control to lack of parental concern for the child's welfare and behavior (as manifested in hostility and lack of warmth toward the child). Gottfredson and Hirschi argue that parents not only must be concerned about their child, but also must act on their concern through supervision of the child's behavior. The goal of parental supervision is to change the child's behavior from dependence on external control to internal (or self) control.

NEW PERSPECTIVES OR MODELS OF DELINQUENT AND CRIMINAL BEHAVIOR

Stability of Aggressiveness: Early Problem Behaviors Predict Later Problem Behaviors

Research on delinquency and criminality has identified a number of developmental precursors to later antisocial and delinquent behavior. One of the most consistent findings is that childhood behavior is the strongest predictor of adolescent and adult problem behavior. Specifically, longitudinal studies provide fairly conclusive evidence linking early disruptive or aggressive behavior to later aggressive, delinquent, or antisocial behavior (Farrington, 1991; Huesmann et al., 1984; McCord, 1983; Pulkkinen, 1983; Stattin & Magnusson, 1989; Tremblay et al., 1992).

There is growing evidence that problem behavior in small children predicts with reasonable accuracy delinquency later (Loeber, 1991; Loeber & Dishion, 1983). Huesmann et al. (1984) found stability of aggressive behavior across time, as measured by peer nominations at age eight and arrest for violence by age thirty. Farrington (1987) cites several studies showing that teachers' ratings of problem behavior in kindergarten or first grade were related strongly to number of police contacts and serious chronic offenses in the middle and late teens. Patterson et al. (1989) point out that "for many children, stable manifestations of antisocial behavior begin as early as elementary school grades" (p. 329). Loeber (1991) observed that antisocial and disruptive behavior patterns become more stable with age; his finding suggests that such behaviors become less malleable as children grow older. In sum, a substantial body of research suggests that early childhood problems, particularly aggressive behavior, are very likely to lead to later problems of delinquency and adult criminality.

Bidirectionality of Influences and Transactional Models

Reviews of family factors have revealed the importance of parental supervision, and of parental rejection and lack of parental involvement with a child, in predicting antisocial behavior (Loeber & Stouthammer-Loeber, 1986). Researchers studying socialization within developmental psychology, however, have long recognized the limitations of models based on unidirectional influences on behavior (Bell & Harper, 1977) and have called attention to the need to consider the reciprocal nature of relationships and influences. They believe that correlations between parents' and children's behaviors should not necessarily be interpreted as evidence of parental influence on a child's behavior. Lytton (1990), among others, makes a case for the proposition that a child's characteristics must be considered and may have a stronger influence than those of the parent.

Other researchers argue for the usefulness of a transactional perspective on behavior (Campbell & Gibbs, 1986; Sameroff, 1991), which acknowledges the continual interplay between parent and child and that the behaviors that emerge are not attributable to either parent or child alone. From this perspective, a parent's response serves as a stimulus to the child; the child's response, in turn, serves as a further stimulus to the parent. The work of Reid and Patterson (1989) illustrates how such parent-child relationships can develop into coercive cycles of interaction, depending on the techniques used by parents.

The transactional view points to the importance of interactive sequences. It highlights the notion that early patterns of adaptation or maladaptation (Toch et al., 1989) influence later adaptation, but not necessarily in a simple, linear manner. Thus, a disordered pattern of adaptation may lie dormant, only to become manifest in times of increased stress or in particular circumstances (Sroufe & Rutter, 1984). For example, early experiences may lead to the development of impulsive behavioral styles, which are translated in turn into deficiencies in problem-solving skills or inadequate school performance. These shortcomings, in their turn, predispose alienated students toward delinquency or adult criminality. Adaptations that may be functional at one point in a young person's development may later compromise that person's ability to draw on the environment in a more adaptive and more flexible way, or may leave him or her open to victimization.

Protective Factors

Not all children who grow up in poverty or in violent homes become criminal or violent adults. In a large-scale longitudinal study of abused and/or neglected children (Widom, 1989), most of the children did not have official arrest records for delinquency, criminality, or violent criminal behavior, although their risk of arrest was greater than that of a matched control group. Similarly, in another study (McCord, 1983), a number of men appeared to be relatively invulnerable to the adverse effects of parental abuse and neglect. Certainly a wide variety of environmental stresses, potential triggering mechanisms, and other factors are involved in the learning process. Nevertheless, many children appear not to succumb to the adverse effects of earlier childhood experiences or family conditions. Researchers have pointed to the need to determine why children can surmount such conditions and what protects certain children from suffering negative consequences of destructive upbringing. We need studies that examine the role of "protective factors" (Garmezy, 1981)—those dispositional attributes, environmental conditions, biological predispositions, and positive events that can act to mitigate early negative conditions.

For example, it appears that *intelligence* may operate as a protective influence mediating other factors such as school performance, problem-solving skills, or levels of self-esteem, which may affect the likelihood of involvement in delinquency and ultimately in adult criminality. Evidence suggests that lower levels of intelligence are related to higher rates of delinquency and criminality (Wilson & Herrnstein, 1985). Some observers interpret this relationship as an example of the problems experienced by children from educationally deprived backgrounds. Moffit et al. (1981), however, found a negative relationship between IQ and delinquency while controlling for socioeconomic status. They suggest that low-IQ children may be prone to engage in delinquent behavior because poor verbal abilities limit their opportunities to obtain rewards at school. Werner (1983), in a longitudinal study of almost 700 children in Hawaii, found that resilient children were those with high infant intelligence and high verbal skills, among other characteristics.

Other writers have raised questions about the role of cultural biases associated with intelligence tests (McLoyd, 1990). Furthermore, precise mechanisms whereby academic failure can promote delinquency have not been determined. Hirschi and Hindelang (1977) believe that the mechanism lies in scholastic performance and attitudes toward school. The notion is that low IQ leads to poor school performance, which leads to a negative attitude toward school, which leads in turn to delinquency. Despite fairly consistent evidence that delinquents show deficiencies in academic performance and display unreceptive or negative attitudes toward school, the direction of the relationship is not clear. Indeed, some scholars have suggested that antisocial behavior may precede school failure; some researchers claim that schools react differently to children with differing IQs (Menard & Morse, 1984). Rutter and Giller (1984) also point out that lower IQ has been associated with troublesome behavior in early childhood. Thus, lower IQ may be associated with general behavior problems rather than with delinquency per se. To some observers this idea suggests that certain types of temperament may predispose an individual to both educational failure and antisocial behavior.

The Importance of Temperament

Despite problems with the concept and measurement of *temperament* (Bates, 1980), evidence exists that infants and young children have varying temperaments and that some temperaments may protect the child, whereas others may place the child at risk because of their negative effects on parent-child interactions (see Patterson et al., 1989). Certain types of temperaments (impulsive, aggressive, and/or extroverted) have been associated with delinquency and criminality. In her longitudinal study of children in Kanai, Werner (1987) found that children with "difficult temperaments" could become predisposed to delinquency in certain circumstances. Regardless of socioeconomic status, difficult children raised by distressed, unsupportive caregivers in disorganized, unstable families had a greater chance of becoming delinquent than children growing up in supportive homes with nurturant caregivers.

Farrington et al. (1988) concluded that temperament (e.g., being neurotic at age ten) was one of the characteristics predicting success in men (i.e., absence of convictions and other deviant behavior, good adjustment and employment history). These findings are consistent with those of Olweus (1980), who reported that temperament was one of four factors that explained a considerable amount of variance in his sample of Norwegian boys' habitual levels of aggression. The more negative the childhood conditions to which the boys were exposed, and the more active and hotheaded their temperament, the more likely they were to exhibit aggressive behavior in adolescence. In Widom's (1991) analysis of characteristics associated with the avoidance of delinquency in abused and/or neglected children, a small group of children (6.6 percent) whose records contained indications of early behavior problems[3] were more likely to have extensive criminal histories as adolescents than were other abused and/or neglected children, and were more than eight times as likely to be arrested.

The notion is that more impulsive youths are more likely to have difficulties in school. Indeed, a recent National Academy of Sciences report states that "early temperament may well constitute a risk factor for later aggressive and violent behavior" (Reiss & Roth, 1993, p. 365).

Cognition and Motivation

The findings of many studies suggest that a person's cognitive appraisal of events strongly influences his or her response to these events (Lazarus & Launier, 1978). The same event may be perceived by different individuals as irrelevant, benign, positive, or threatening and harmful. Zimrin (1986) studied abused children who survived the traumas of their childhood and grew up to be well-adjusted individuals, and compared them with nonsurvivor children who showed a high degree of psychosocial pathology. She concluded, "The perception of the S (survivor) group of their good personal resources, intellectual potential, good self-image and hope, coupled with relatively sound external resources (support or external responsibility) in the course of cognitive appraisal" (p. 347) tipped the scales in favor of these children's personal resources when they negotiated severe stress.

Older approaches to delinquency and criminality described aspects of motivation, but it may be time to revisit motivational variables. Haynes et al. (1988), for example, administered to a sample of 146 male and female African-American high school students the Learning and Study Strategy Inventory, which measures learning style on ten dimensions: motivation, information processing, study aids, self-testing, scheduling, anxiety, concentration, test strategies, main ideas, and attitude. The authors found that motivation was the strongest predictor of achievement for both males and females.

EARLY CHILDHOOD INTERVENTION AS A PREVENTIVE STRATEGY FOR DELINQUENCY

As noted by Loeber and LeBlanc (1990), most theories in criminology do not adopt a developmental perspective, or one that considers the study of individual change over time. However, this approach is particularly useful in criminology because it can provide knowledge of the processes involved in the emergence of antisocial or delinquent behavior. Such knowledge contributes not only to the study of antisocial and delinquent behavior, but also to the ultimate goal of preventing such behavior in its early stages. Among others, Bell (1986) believes that the most defensible basis for intervention is a clearly understood delineation of the developmental paths to the behavior one is trying to prevent, including changes in family and other contexts that affect the developmental course.

Risk and Protective Factors

While many interventions address current symptoms (i.e., antisocial or delinquent behavior), they ignore the processes that led to the behavior. Muehrer and Koretz (1992) note that there is a critical need to describe the processes that lead to the development of the outcomes to be prevented (in this case, antisocial and delinquent behavior). In suggesting the benefits to be gained from preventive interventions, these authors describe the need to identify risk and protective factors; to find causal, not simply correlational, factors; to decide which combinations of risk and protective factors exercise influence on the outcomes; and, finally, to decide which factors might be modified most effectively through intervention.

Zigler et al. (1992) concluded that "programs to reduce or prevent juvenile delinquency have been generally unsuccessful. Apparently the risk factors that make a child prone to delinquency are based in too many systems—including the individual, family, and community networks—to make isolated treatment methods effective" (p. 997). With some exceptions, programs designed to prevent delinquency have not shown long-term evidence of success. Counseling and casework programs have not proved particularly effective, perhaps in part because they are offered too late. By the time children are treated, often after referral by court personnel (Hawkins & Weis, 1985), they typically have been involved in a long history of antisocial behavior and conduct problems that are not reversed easily (Hawkins & Lam, 1987).

Multidimensional Approach

Early intervention programs that appear to be effective have adopted a multidimensional approach with a variety of components, including health care and services to parents (Berrueta-Clement et al., 1984; Price et al., 1988). Longitudinal studies suggest that such programs may help to reduce future delinquency. The general approach is based on an *ecological* view of child development (Belsky, 1981; Bronfenbrenner, 1977), which calls for the treatment of the child in the context of the child's broader environment rather than through an isolated intervention. This approach assumes that the first important influence on the child is the family, but also that children and families are interacting members of a larger social system that includes schools and communities. The programs attempt to promote social competence in the child by modifying the contextual factors surrounding the child. Not engaging in criminal acts is one indicator of competence that is related to others, such as success in school and in personal relationships. Schweinhart and Weikart (1988) argue that early childhood is an opportune time for intervention because it is a critical juncture in the child's physical, social, and emotional or mental development.

One ecology-based program is the Perry Preschool Project, designed for preschool children at risk of impaired intellectual functioning and eventual school failure (Berrueta-Clement et al., 1984). In this project, low-income, black three- and four-year-olds were assigned randomly to preschool and control conditions. Children in the experimental group received high-quality, cognitively oriented early childhood education for one to two academic years; teachers made weekly home visits and held monthly meetings with parents.

Longitudinal follow-up data on the children up to age nineteen reveal a number of positive outcomes. Compared to children with no preschool, the Perry Preschool children showed more positive attitudes toward school, lower rates of placement in special education classes, less retention in grade, better performance on standard measures of achievement, and higher high school graduation rates. At age nineteen, the former preschool children had higher rates of literacy, social competence and employment, lower rates of welfare assistance, and fewer arrests on criminal charges. Official record searches show that 51 percent of the nonpreschool group were arrested or charged at least once, compared to 31 percent for the preschool group (Berrueta-Clement et al., 1987).

The researchers interpreted these findings to mean that the preschool program influenced the children's school readiness, which in turn resulted in a more positive reaction by kindergarten teachers. This reaction led to a stronger commitment to school on the children's part, followed by better school performance in later grades. Furthermore, the researchers suggested that the enhanced school attitudes, participation, and performance resulted in lower rates of delinquency (Berrueta-Clement et al., 1987).

Zigler et al. (1992) stress that it is not yet known why early childhood programs appear to have an effect on delinquency. They suggest, however, that one common characteristic of the successful programs is that they begin early in a child's life—typically before school entry, and sometimes even before birth. It follows that "the need to begin training at young ages also makes sense for delinquency prevention efforts. Data on the predelinquency programs . . . show that, for the short term, at least, they appear to be more effective than those initiated after delinquent habits have emerged" (p. 1003).

PSYCHOLOGICAL AND MENTAL DISORDERS

Link to Crime and Violence?

Violence and mental disorder have been linked in the minds of the public as well as of some professionals. Relatively recent studies cast doubt on this relationship (Monahan & Splane, 1980), but the controversy has continued and recently has intensified. Although the perception remains that the mentally ill are prone to violence (Monahan, 1992; Steadman & Cocozza, 1978), the empirical support is not overwhelming. Some studies report a relationship between mental disorder and violence (Lindquist & Allebeck, 1990; Swanson et al., 1990), although mental disorder does not appear to represent a major risk factor for violence (Monahan, 1992; Swanson et al., 1990). Other researchers have found that the relationship disappears with appropriate demographic controls (Steadman et al., 1978).

Teplin (1984) has described how police interact with individuals they perceive to be mentally disordered. In more recent work (Teplin, 1990), she demonstrates the prevalence of mental disorder in urban jail populations and calls attention to the need for mental health services for these populations. Although this work is relevant for criminal justice practitioners and policy makers, it also illustrates the need for familiarity with psychiatric diagnoses (schizophrenia, major affective disorders), substance abuse (alcohol and other drugs), and psychotic symptomatology (hallucinations and delusions) as well as with the interview instruments used to determine these diagnoses, such as the National Institute of Mental Health Diagnostic Interview Schedule (Robins et al., 1981).

Estimates of prevalence of mental illness are reached through surveys in which respondents are asked to describe themselves and to state whether they have experienced any of a standard set of symptoms in their lifetime or in the recent past. The symptoms later are grouped into diagnostic categories, based on those which appear in the *Diagnostic and Statistical Manual of Mental Disorders* (DSM) published by the American Psychiatric Association. The DSM diagnoses were formulated by consensus among a group of recognized experts, clinical professionals who work primarily with civilian hospital patients or with persons who are seen in private practice.

Among the kinds of individuals treated by the average clinician, offense-related behavior (such as delinquency or addiction) may signal problems that call for clinical attention. This behavior can be considered "disturbed," though the same conduct may be "normal" for offenders. Although this distinction does not matter in surveying a population that consists largely of nonoffenders, it becomes problematic when we infer, on the basis of differences in these interview responses, that the offenders are sicker than other people. A similar problem arises when we rely solely on personality tests (such as the Minnesota Multiphasic Personality Inventory) that were normed on hospital populations. Such tests may include statements that an offender could make simply because he has been arrested and sent to prison, and therefore feels trapped, isolated, and despondent (Hanley, 1961).

Another difficulty in thinking about disturbed offenders is that offense behavior and symptoms distribute themselves over time, so that a person can be disturbed and law-abiding at one juncture, and nondisturbed and antisocial at another. On the other hand, mental patients who are apt to reoffend tend to have been involved with both the criminal justice and the mental health systems; thus the question arises whether such persons, in the aggregate, in fact are patients who offend at times, or offenders who occasionally gravitate to mental hospitals.

Where symptoms and criminal justice involvements coincide, it does not follow that the two are related causally or in any other particular way. An offender may be caught because his pathology makes him inept, or his symptomatology may create a public nuisance, or he may break down once arrested. The crucial links between symptoms and criminality may not be those which are salient in public stereotypes of crazed homicidal maniacs, but those which denote lower-order relationships such as the coping problems of institutionalized patients, the tendency of offenders to be intoxicated when they offend, or the traumas of vulnerable young offenders in pretrial detention.

For a number of reasons, one must be cautious in making aggregate statements about mental disorder and crime. These reasons include the heterogeneity of offense behavior and the difficulty of generalizing about the relationship between personal problems and violations of law. None of these reasons, however, prevent us from studying relationships between mental disorder and crime or violence, once we can specify which conditions we are relating to which behavior.

Disaggregation and Classification

One possible approach to studying the relationship between mental disorders and crime and violence is disaggregation, in which people are sorted into homogeneous groups or "types." Disaggregation is a way of moving from a sociological to a psychological analysis because attending to smaller groups brings us closer to the individual. Examples of typologies include taxonomies of robbers (Conklin, 1972), rapists (Groth, 1979; Prentky et al., 1985), and repetitively violent men (Toch, 1992).

A disaggregated analysis of disturbed violent offenders was attempted by Toch and Adams (1989), who began with all offenders entering New York state prisons in 1985. The study centered on violent offenders who had received mental health services before confinement, particularly those who had been hospitalized. It dealt separately with offenders who had been hospitalized for drug-related problems. The authors grouped offenders in terms of their mental health and offense histories, and in terms of the type and seriousness of their violence. The clusters that emerged range from extreme violence linked with serious pathology to self-destructive behavior associated with marginal coping. Examples of types include young explosive robbers, disturbed sex offenders, skid row exploders, and multiproblem robbers. Some of the offenders appeared to be in prison by default, while other types stood in need of long-term confinement and posed continuing problems in the prison.

Many individuals defied preclassification solely on the basis of information about their mental health status. The authors point out that "disturbed persons are often capable of committing offenses that are indistinguishable from those perpetrated by nondisturbed offenders. The other side of the coin is that many of the offenses of ostensibly sturdy offenders can reflect nonsturdy motives such as loss of control or impulsivity" (Toch & Adams, 1989, p. 121). Criminal justice clients who have mental health problems are the domain of psychology, but they cannot define this domain because lines between disturbed and nondisturbed offenders are not hard and fast. It is also obvious that the motives of nondisturbed offenders are as interesting as those of disturbed offenders, and equally worthy of study.

Whereas psychologists who work as practitioners are often invoked when mental disorder is at issue, psychologists who are scientists are concerned with offenders' motivation in general. Criminologists come to engage in psychological analysis whenever they move from the study of crime to the study of criminals, or of persons who engage in crime. Psychology thus is not only a separate discipline but also an inextricable branch of criminology, which is the science of the etiology of crime.

CONCLUSION

What does psychology contribute to criminal justice students' understanding of the causation of crime? It tells them that offenders are made, not born, and that they are products of their upbringing and of pressures, temptations, and learning experiences to which they are subjected from an early age. It tells them that the family is the crucible of social learning and of socialization and that other influences are superimposed cumulatively on critical early experiences. It tells them that socialization is interactive or transactional in the sense that reactions to some experiences invite or incite other fateful experiences or pressures, to which one reacts, in turn, thus generating new formative experiences. It tells them that learning is both cognitive and emotional, and that it includes ways of perceiving people and situations and modes of responding to them. It tells them that at some point these ways of perceiving and reacting become remarkably consistent and stable, and therefore obdurate and difficult to change. This means that interventions which make a difference must occur early, before habitual responses are established, and must be comprehensive, to cover diverse areas of experience.

In documenting these lessons, we have used violence—particularly family violence—as our prime example of how the process works. We have done so because the importance of early experience is especially clear in this area, and because effects of socialization can be traced directly. Also, we have emphasized longitudinal research because it lends itself most readily to conclusions about cause-and-effect relationships between experience and conduct. Even so, the conclusions we have relayed here are not hard-and-fast, because knowledge in this area is evolving and new discoveries are made continuously. This fact also benefits students because it tells them that they are entering a field which is dynamic, alive, and exciting, and which offers opportunities for gaining new knowledge and influencing offenders' lives constructively.

Footnotes

[1] In the developmental literature (Shaw & Bell, 1992), the term "attachment" refers to the social behaviors of an infant in relation to a mother or primary caretaker, generally between the ages of twelve and eighteen months. Later behaviors that are thought to emerge from the attachment process usually are known as correlates or manifestations of attachment.

[2] One cannot help noticing the similarity between this version of social control theory and the earlier psychodynamic theories, which attributed delinquency to a failure to develop a superego.

[3] Behavior problems refer to notations in the juvenile probation department records or in the original case material that the child engaged in chronic fighting, fire setting, destructiveness, or defiance of authority; had severe temper tantrums, uncontrolled anger, or sadistic tendencies (as in aggressiveness toward weaker children); or was extremely difficult to control.

References

Abrahamsen, D. (1944). *Crime and the human mind.* New York: Columbia University Press.

Bandura, A. (1969). *Principles of behavior modification.* New York: Holt, Rinehart & Winston.

Bandura, A. (1973). *Aggression: A social learning analysis.* Englewood Cliffs, NJ: Prentice-Hall.

Bandura, A., Ross, D. & Ross, S. (1963). Imitation of film-mediated aggressive models. *Journal of Abnormal and Social Psychology, 66,* 3–11.

Bates, H. E. (1980). The concept of difficult temperament. *Merrill-Palmer Quarterly, 26,* 299–319.

Bell, R. Q. (1986). Age specific manifestations in changing psychosocial risk. In D. C. Farren & J. D. McKinney (Eds.), *The concept of risk in intellectual and psychosocial development.* New York: Academic Press.

Bell, R. Q. & Harper, L. V. (1977). *Child effects on adults.* Hillsdale, NJ: Erlbaum.

Belsky, J. (1981). Child maltreatment: An ecological integration. *American Psychologist, 35,* 320–335.

Berrueta-Clement, J. R., Schweinhart, L. J., Barnett, W. S., Epstein, A. S. & Weikart, D. P. (1984). *Changed lives: The effects of the Perry preschool programs on youths through age 19.* Ypsilanti, MI: High/Scope Press.

Berrueta-Clement, J. R., Schweinhart, L. J., Barnett, W. S., Epstein, A. S. & Weikart, D. P. (1987). The effect of early educational interventions on crime and delinquency in adolescence and early adulthood. In J. D. Burchard & S. N. Burchard (Eds.), *Primary prevention of psychopathology,* vol. 10, *Prevention of delinquent behavior.* Newbury Park, CA: Sage, 220–240.

Bowlby, J. (1944). Forty-four juvenile thieves. *International Journal of Psychoanalysis, 25,* 107–128.

Bowlby, J. (1951). *Maternal care and mental health.* Geneva: World Health Organization.

Bronfenbrenner, U. (1977). Toward an experimental ecology of human development. *American Psychologist, 32,* 513–531.

Cairns, R. B. (1979). *Social development: The origins and plasticity of interactions.* San Francisco: Freeman.

Campbell, A. & Gibbs, J. J. (Eds.) (1986). *Violent transactions.* Oxford, UK: Blackwell.

Coie, J. D. (1990). Toward a theory of peer rejection. In S. R. Asher & J. D. Coie (Eds.), *Peer rejection in childhood.* New York: Cambridge University Press.

Conklin, J. E. (1972). *Robbery and the criminal justice system.* Philadelphia: Lippincott.

Dodge, K. A. (1980). Social cognition and children's aggressive behavior. *Child Development, 51,* 162–170.

Dodge, K. A., Bates, J. E. & Pettit, G. S. (1990). Mechanisms in the cycle of violence. *Science, 250,* 1678–1683.

Farrington, D. P. (1987). Predicting individual crime rates. In D. M. Gottfredson & M. Tonry (Eds.), *Crime and justice,* vol. 3, *Prediction and classification.* Chicago: University of Chicago Press, 53–101.

Farrington, D. P. (1991). Childhood aggression and adult violence: Early precursors and later life outcomes. In D. J. Pepler & K. H. Rubin (Eds.), *The development and treatment of childhood aggression.* Hillsdale, NJ: Erlbaum, 2–29.

Farrington, D. P., Gallagher, B., Morley, L., St. Ledger, R. J. & West, D. J. (1988). Are there any successful men from criminogenic backgrounds? *Psychiatry, 51,* 116–130.

Ferrero-Lombroso, G. (1911). *Criminal man, according to the classification of Cesare Lombroso.* New York: Putnam's Sons.

Feshbach, S. (1980). Child abuse and the dynamics of human aggression and violence. In J. Gerbner, C. J. Ross & E. Zigler (Eds.), *Child abuse: An agenda for action.* New York: Oxford University Press.

Freud, S. A. (1946). Some character-types met with in psycho-analytic work. In *Collected papers,* vol. 4. London: Hogarth, 318–344.

Friedrick-Cofer, L. & Huston, A. C. (1986). Television violence and aggression: The debate continues. *Psychological Bulletin, 100,* 364–371.

Garmezy, N. (1981). Children under stress: Perspectives on antecedents and correlates of vulnerability and resistance to psychopathology. In A. J. Rabin, J. Aronoff, A. M. Barclay, & R. A. Zucker (Eds.), *Further explorations in personality.* New York: John Wiley & Sons, 196–269.

Gottfredson, M. R. & Hirschi, T. (1990). *A general theory of crime.* Palo Alto, CA: Stanford University Press.

Groth, A. N. (1979). *Men who rape: The psychology of the offender.* New York: Plenum Press.

Hanley, C. (1961). The gauging of criminal predispositions. In H. Toch (Ed.), *Legal and criminal psychology.* New York: Holt, Rinehart & Winston, 213–242.

Hawkins, J. D. & Lam, T. (1987). Teacher practices, social development and delinquency. In J. D. Burchard & S. N. Burchard (Eds.), *Primary prevention of psychopathology,* vol. 10, *The prevention of delinquent behavior.* Newbury Park, CA: Sage, 241–274.

Hawkins, J. D., Lishner, D. M., Catalano, R. F. & Howard, M. O. (1986). Childhood predictors of adolescent substance abuse: Toward an empirically grounded theory. *Journal of Children in Contemporary Society, 18,* 1–65.

Hawkins, J. D. & Weis, J. C. (1985). The social development model: An integrated approach to delinquency prevention. *Journal of Primary Preventions, 6,* 73–97.

Haynes, N. M., Comer, J. P. & Hamilton-Lee, M. (1988). Gender and achievement status differences on learning factors among black high school students. *Journal of Educational Research, 81,* 233–237.

Hirschi, T. (1969). *Causes of delinquency.* Berkeley, CA: University of California Press.

Hirschi, T. & Hindelang, A. (1977). Intelligence and delinquency: A revisionist review. *American Sociological Review, 42,* 371–387.

Hollin, C. R. (1989). *Psychology and crime: An introduction to criminological psychology.* London: Routledge.

Huesmann, L. R., Eron, L. D., Lefkowitz, M. M. & Walder, L. O. (1984). Stability of aggression over time and generations. *Journal of Abnormal Psychology, 20,* 1120–1134.

Kalmuss, D. (1984). The intergenerational transmission of marital aggression. *Journal of Marriage and the Family, 46,* 11–19.

Lazarus, A. & Launier, R. (1978). Stress-related transactions between person and environment. In L. A. Pervin & M. Lewis (Eds.), *Perspectives in interactional psychology.* New York: Plenum Press.

Lefkowitz, M. M., Eron, L. D., Walder, L. D. & Huesmann, L. R. (1972). Television violence and child aggression: A follow-up study. In G. A. Comstock & E. A. Rubinstein (Eds.), *Television and social behavior,* vol. 3. Washington, DC: U.S. Government Printing Office, 35–135.

Lindquist, P. & Allebeck, P. (1990). Schizophrenia and crime: A longitudinal follow-up of 644 schizophrenics in Stockholm. *British Journal of Psychiatry, 157,* 345–350.

Loeber, R. (1991). Questions and advances in the study of developmental pathways. In D. Cicchetti & S. Toth (Eds.), *Models and integration: Rochester symposium on developmental psychopathology.* Rochester, NY: University of Rochester Press, 97–115.

Loeber, R. & Dishion, T. (1983). Early predictors of male delinquency: A review. *Psychological Bulletin, 94,* 68–99.

Loeber, R. & LeBlanc, M. (1990). Toward a developmental criminology. In M. Tonry & N. Morris (Eds.), *Crime and justice: An annual review,* vol. 12. Chicago: University of Chicago Press, 375–473.

Loeber, R. & Stouthammer-Loeber, M. (1986). Family factors as correlates and predictors of juvenile conduct problems and delinquency. In A. Morris & M. Tonry (Eds.), *Crime and justice: An annual review of research,* vol. 7. Chicago: University of Chicago Press.

Lytton, H. (1990). Child and parent effects in boys' conduct disorder: A reinterpretation. *Developmental Psychology, 26,* 683–697.

McCord, J. (1983). A forty year perspective on effects of child abuse and neglect. *Child Abuse and Neglect, 7,* 265–270.

McLoyd, V .C. (1990). The impact of economic hardship on black families and children: psychological distress, parenting, and socio-economic development. *Child Development, 61,* 311–346.

Menard, S. & Morse, B. J. (1984). A structuralist critique of the IQ-delinquency hypothesis: Theory and evidence. *American Journal of Sociology, 89,* 1347–1378.

Moffitt, T. E., Gabrielli, W. F., Mednick, S. A. & Schulsinger, F. (1981). Socioeconomic status, IQ, and delinquency. *Journal of Abnormal Psychology, 90,* 152–156.

Monahan, J. (1992). Mental disorder and violent behavior: Perceptions and evidence. *American Psychologist, 47,* 511–521.

Monahan, J. & Splane, S. (1980). Psychological approaches to criminal behavior. In E. Bittner & S. L. Messinger (Eds.), *Criminology review yearbook,* vol. 2. Newbury Park, CA: Sage, 17–47.

Muehrer, P. & Koretz, D. S. (1992). Issues in preventive intervention research. *Current Directions in Psychological Sciences, 1,* 109–112.

Olweus, D. (1980). Financial and temperamental determinants of aggressive behavior in adolescent boys: A causal analysis. *Developmental Psychology, 16,* 644–660.

Patterson, G. R., Capaldi, D. & Bank, L. (1991). The development and treatment of childhood aggression. In D. Pepler & R. K. Rubin (Eds.), *The development and treatment of childhood aggression.* Hillsdale, NJ: Erlbaum, 139–168.

Patterson, G. R., Debaryshe, B. D. & Ramsey. E. (1989). A developmental perspective on antisocial behavior. *American Psychologist, 44,* 329–335.

Prentky, R., Cohen, M. & Seghorn, T. (1985). Development of a rational taxonomy for the classification of rapists: The Massachusetts Treatment Center system. *Bulletin of the American Academy of Psychiatry and Law, 13,* 39–70.

Price, R. H., Cowen, E. L., Lorion, R. P. & Ramos-McKay, J. (Eds.) (1988). *Fourteen ounces of prevention: A casebook for practitioners.* Washington, DC: American Psychological Association.

Pulkkinen, L. (1983). Search for alternatives to aggression in Finland. In A. P. Goldstein & M. Segal (Eds.), Aggression in global perspective. Elmsford, NY: Pergamon, 104–144.

Reid, J. B. & Patterson, G. R. (1989). The development of antisocial behavior patterns in childhood and adolescence. *European Journal of Personality, 3,* 107–109.

Reiss, A. J. Jr. & Roth, J. A. (Eds.) (1993). *Understanding and preventing violence.* Washington, DC: National Academy Press.

Robins, L. N., Helzer, J. E., Croughan, J. & Ratcliff, K. (1981). National Institute of Mental Health diagnostic interview schedule: Its history, characteristics and validity. *Archives of General Psychiatry, 38,* 381–389.

Rosenbaum, A. & O'Leary, K. D. (1981). Children: The unintended victims of mental violence. *American Journal of Orthopsychiatry, 51,* 692–699.

Rotter, J. B. (1954). Social learning and clinical psychology. Englewood Cliffs, NJ: Prentice-Hall.

Rutter, M. & Giller, H. (1983). *Juvenile delinquency: Trends and perspectives.* New York: Guilford Press.

Sameroff, A. J. (1991). Transactional risk factors and prevention. In J. A. Steinberg & M. M. Silverman (Eds.), *Preventing mental disorders.* Rockville, MD: U.S. Department of Health and Human Services, 74–89.

Schweinhart, L. J. & Weikart, D. B. (1988). The High/Scope Perry Preschool Program. In R. H. Price, E. L Cowen, R. P. Lorion & J. Ramos-McKay (Eds.), *Fourteen ounces of prevention: A casebook for practitioners.* Washington, DC: American Psychological Association, 53-65.

Shaw, D. S. & Bell, R. Q. (1992). Developmental theories of parental contributors to antisocial behavior. Presented at the Conference for Life History Research, Coercion and Punishment in Long-Term Perspectives, Philadelphia, PA.

Sheldon, W. H. (1949). *Varieties of delinquent youth: An introduction to constitutional psychiatry.* New York: Harper.

Skinner, B. F. (1938). *The behavior of organisms: An experimental analysis.* New York: Appleton-Century-Crofts.

Sroufe, L. A. (1983). Infant-caregiver attachment and patterns of adaptation in preschool: The roots of maladaptation and competence. In M. Perlmutter (Ed.), *Minnesota symposium in child psychology,* vol. 16. Hillsdale, NJ: Erlbaum, 41–81.

Sroufe, L. A. & Rutter, M. (1984). The domains of developmental psychology. *Child Development, 55,* 17–29.

Stattin, H. & Magnusson, D. (1989). The role of early aggressive behavior in the frequency, seriousness and types of later crime. *Journal of Consulting and Clinical Psychology, 30,* 23–51.

Steadman, H. & Cocozza, J. J. (1978). Selective reporting and the public's misconceptions of the criminally insane. *Public Opinion Quarterly, 41,* 523–533.

Steadman, H., Cocozza, J. J. & Melick, M. E. (1978). Explaining the increased arrest rate among mental patients: The changing clientele of state hospitals. *American Journal of Psychiatry, 135,* 816–820.

Straus, M. & Gelles, R. J. (Eds.) (1990). *Physical violence in American families: Risk factors and adaptations to violence in 8145 families.* New Brunswick, NJ: Transaction Books.

Straus, M., Gelles, R. J. & Steinmetz, S. A. (1980). *Behind closed doors.* Garden City, NY: Anchor/Doubleday.

Swanson, J., Holzer, C., Ganju, V. & Jono, R. (1990). Violence and psychiatric disorder in the community: Evidence from the epidemiologic catchment area surveys. *Hospital and Community Psychiatry, 41,* 761–770.

Teplin, L. (1984). Criminalizing mental disorder: The comparative arrest rate of the mentally ill. *American Psychologist, 39,* 794–803.

Teplin, L. (1990). The prevalence of severe mental disorder among male urban jail detainees: Comparison with the epidemiologic catchment area program. *American Journal of Public Health, 80,* 663–669.

Toch, H. (1992). *Violent men: An inquiry into the psychology of violence.* Washington, DC: American Psychological Association.

Toch, H. & Adams, K. (1989). *The disturbed violent offender.* New Haven, CT: Yale University Press.

Toch, H., Adams, K. & Grant, J. D. (1989). *Coping: Maladaptation in prisons.* New Brunswick, NJ: Transaction Books.

Tremblay, R. E., Masse, B., Perron, D., LeBlanc, M., Schwartzman, A. E. & Ledingham, J. E. (1992). Early disruptive behavior, poor school achievement, delinquent behavior and delinquent personality: Longitudinal analyses. *Journal of Consulting and Clinical Psychology, 60,* 64–72.

Werner, E. (1983). Vulnerability and resiliency among children at risk for delinquency. Presented at the annual meeting of the American Society of Criminology, Denver, CO.

Werner, E. (1987). Vulnerability and resiliency among children at risk for delinquency: A Longitudinal study from birth to young adulthood. In J. D. Burchard & S. N. Burchard (Eds.)., *Primary prevention of psychopathology,* vol. 10, *Prevention of delinquent behavior.* Newbury Park, CA: Sage, 6–43.

Widom, C. S. (1989). The cycle of violence. *Science, 244,* 160–166.

Widom, C. S. (1991). Avoidance of criminality in abused and neglected children. *Psychiatry, 54,* 62–74.

Wilson, J. Q. & Herrnstein, R. (1985). *Crime and human nature.* New York: Simon & Schuster.

Wolfe, D. A., Jaffe, P., Wilson, S. K. & Zak, L. (1985). Children of battered women: The relation of child behavior to family violence and maternal stress. *Journal of Consulting and Clinical Psychology, 53,* 657–665.

Zigler, E., Taussig, C. & Black, K. (1992). Early childhood intervention: A promising preventative for juvenile delinquency. *American Psychologist, 47,* 997–1006.

Zimrin, H. (1986). A profile of survival. *Child Abuse and Neglect, 10,* 339–349.

Part 2

Biological Underpinnings of Antisocial Behavior—Research Approaches and Findings

Most persons experience feelings of anger and frustration and behave aggressively while coping with everyday life stressors. These aggressive behaviors take many forms, last for varying time periods, occur with different frequencies and levels of intensity, and may or may not lead to adjustment problems. Research is often aimed at defining the risk factors for predicting when anger and aggressive behaviors will be counterproductive in coping with life stressors. Although much research has been done, little progress has been made in defining different types of aggression. Without adequate definitions and measurement techniques, we cannot reliably identify the various forms of antisocial behavior that will respond differentially to particular treatment and prevention approaches. Ernest Barratt and his colleagues propose in Chapter 4 that this lack of progress relates to two major problems: (1) lack of agreement on a *discipline neutral* model that can be used to integrate data from a wide range of discipline specific studies and (2) lack of agreement on the criterion measures of aggression. The authors have discussed the need for a discipline neutral, heuristic model elsewhere; in this this chapter they discuss the criterion problem and review their procedures for classifying aggression.

Barratt et al.'s chapter is divided into three sections: (1) examples of selected criterion measures of aggression; (2) the relationships of biosocial predictors to selected criterion measures of aggression—this section will demonstrate that not only are selected popular criterion measures not highly intercorrelated, but further that measures for predicting aggression have different relationships to the different criteria; and (3) the status of the development of their procedures for classifying aggression as impulsive, premeditated, or "other." Data from past research and research in progress are used to illustrate the importance of making explicit the criterion measures one uses.

In Chapter 5, Drs. Lane and Cherek present an overview of the latest scientific advances in the study of aggression and impulsivity. This chapter provides a thought-provoking discussion of the findings of this research, which in many instances differ substantially from public perceptions about crime, violence, and their causes. As a result of the many myths and misconceptions about aggressive behavior in our society, most techniques to control it have failed miserably. We have also notoriously ignored or underestimated the significance of early warning signs that portend eventual aggressive behavior and have missed many opportunities to intervene effectively and redirect negative outcomes. As with Chapter 4, these authors stress the importance of appropriate definition and measurement of the subject under study. Aggression is not a unitary concept; it is diverse, multidimensional, and has many origins. Thus, in order to focus our energies on the suppression of aggressive acts that endanger others, it is necessary that studies employ a consistent and appropriate methodology to accurately identify its many causes.

Drs. Lane and Cherek are well-known for their contributions to the study of aggression. Rather than study aggression and impulsivity with static and artificial self-report measures, they have developed laboratory instruments that actually provoke these behaviors in subjects who are susceptible, so that the various physiological and biological correlates can be monitored. Under controlled conditions, situations can be introduced that trigger aggressive or impulsive responding in some people. In that way, subjects prone to aggressive responses can be distinguished from those who do not respond with aggression by virtue of their behavior, physiology, biochemistry, learned experiences, and so forth. The methods for this testing are described in sufficient detail for the reader to interpret the findings reported later in the chapter and to stimulate interest in these techniques in both researchers and clinicians who have a need to make such discriminations. The authors further elaborate on other methods that have been used to study aggression and impulsivity (such as those employed by Dr. Coccaro, as presented in Chapter 6) and show how the inclusion of these laboratory techniques can greatly enhance the meaningfulness of findings that show biological involvement.

In Chapter 6, Dr. Coccaro and his colleauges highlight current studies of biochemical mechanisms underlying antisocial behavior that focus on the role of central neurotransmitter systems in modulating impulse control and levels of arousal. Dr. Coccaro and his colleagues focus primarily on the neurotransmitter serotonin, although they also refer to other transmitters, peptides, and hormones involved in problems with impulse control and the modulation or production of aggressive behavior. A deficit in serotonergic activity disinhibits or unleashes neurological and behavioral restraints, resulting in an increased likelihood of antisocial or other excessive and inappropriate behavior. Studies cited in this chapter suggest that serotonin is specifically related to the subtype of aggression that is impulsive, not premeditative or defensive, by nature. Studies that reveal the modulating influence serotonin has in excessive drinking behavior and alcoholism are also noteworthy in light of reports that impulsive and violent individuals have shown low serotonergic activity levels and are prone to antisocial behavior while drinking. A decline in serotonergic activity may be partially responsible for alcohol-induced behavioral and neurological disinhibition, leading to the expression of underlying violent tendencies. Alcoholics believed to be at genetic risk for comorbid alcoholism and aggressiveness/criminality may be the product of a preexisting deficit in serotonergic function.

Dr. Coccaro provides a detailed report of a patient who presented himself with a lifelong history of impulsive-aggressive behavior that led to the murder of his wife and his subsequent death sentence. Several tests conducted to examine neurotransmitter function in this man implicated a deficiency in serotonin activity. This example provides a quite useful description of how this information can be used not only in criminal court, but in the diagnosis and management of patients desiring treatment.

While this particular patient was unable to benefit from an appropriate therapeutic regimen due to his incarceration, the use of drugs that stimulate serotonin activity (agonists) in such cases may be a helpful adjunctive therapy for comorbid drug abuse and impulsive-aggression by reducing (1) co-occurring depression and/or anxiety, (2) alcohol craving, (3) some of the reinforcing properties of alcohol, and (4) aggressiveness. Also, as Dr. Coccaro points out, because serotonin is exquisitely sensitive to the environment, behavioral and social interventions have the potential to alter serotonin levels, contributing to improvements in its functioning.

Chapter 4

Criterion Measures of Aggression—Impulsive Versus Premeditated Aggression

by Ernest S. Barratt, Ph.D., Alan Felthous, M.D.,
Thomas Kent, M.D., Michele J. Liebman, B.S., and
Diana D. Coates, M.A., L.P.C.

Criterion Measures of Aggression: Selected Examples 4-2
Comparison of Relationships of Several Biosocial
    Measures to Selected Criterion Measures 4-3
        Overview of Study From Which Data Were Obtained 4-3
        Criterion Measures 4-3
        Social Predictor Measures 4-4
        Personality Measures 4-5
        Biological Predictor Measures 4-5
        Interrelationships of Criterion Measures 4-5
        Family and Social Measures Related to Criterion Measures 4-6
        Personality Traits Related to Criterion Measures of Aggression 4-7
        Biological Measures Related to Aggression Criterion Measures 4-7
        Summary of Relevance of Criteria Measures 4-9
Status of Our Procedures for Classifying Aggression as Impulsive,
    Premeditated, or Other 4-9
        Phenytoin Use 4-9
        Exploratory Studies 4-10
        Identifying the Subjects 4-10
        Outpatient Studies 4-11
        General Population Studies 4-12
        Operational Definitions of "Impulsive" vs. "Premeditated" 4-14
Summary 4-15
Editor's Note 4-15

CRITERION MEASURES OF AGGRESSION: SELECTED EXAMPLES

How aggression is defined and measured can significantly influence research outcomes and, ultimately, clinical decisions. Even the planning of research studies is influenced by the definition of aggression. For example, Goldman (1996) notes that "the variety of behaviors that may be labeled aggressive is large, and aggression is therefore not a phenotype for genetic analysis" (p. 23). He notes further that "changing the definition of aggressive behavior will obviously change the genes involved" (p. 23). Goldman's observations clearly underscore the importance of considering the nature of the criterion measures of aggression when reviewing or planning studies of aggression.

Accurately defining and assessing criterion measures in general is not a new problem in mental health research. Nor is it an easy problem to solve. Nunnally (1978) noted that "whereas it is easy to talk about correlating a predictor test with its criterion, in actuality obtaining a good criterion measure may be more difficult than obtaining a predictor test" (p. 90). A cursory review of current aggression/violence research reveals a wide range of criterion measures (Bech & Mak, 1995; Volavka, 1995; Webster & Jackson, 1997). It is important in conducting and/or reviewing aggression research to understand the underlying assumptions and measurement properties of the criteria being used.

Selected examples of typical criterion measures of aggression are listed in Table 4.1. The list is far from exhaustive, but it indicates the wide range of criteria used in aggression research.

As often happens in behavioral and personality research, measures of personality constructs involving similar techniques will correlate with each other at least at a modest level, but will not significantly correlate with measures using other techniques. The modest correlations share common variance because of the similarity of techniques. Criterion measures of aggression follow this pattern. For example, Muntaner et al. (1990) reported moderate correlations among self-report aggression

Table 4.1
Examples of Criterion Measures of Aggression

1. Self-Report Questionnaires
    a. Hostility Inventory (Buss & Durkee, 1957)
    b. State-Trait Anger Expression Inventory (Spielberger, 1988)
    c. Aggression Questionnaire (Buss & Perry, 1992)

2. Structured and Semi-Structured Interviews
    a. Life History of Aggression (Coccaro, et al, 1997)
    b. Aggressive Acts Assessments (Barratt & Slaughter, 1998; Barratt et al., 1997a)

3. Observations
    a. Overt Aggression Scale (Yudofsky et al., 1986)
    b. Video Recordings and analyses (Volavka, 1995)

4. Laboratory Measures
    a. Point Subtraction Aggression Paradigm (Cherek et al., 1991)
    b. Aversive Stimulation Aggression Model (Taylor, 1967)

measures, but these aggression measures did not significantly correlate with laboratory aggression measures. However, both types of techniques contributed to predicting selected substance abuse diagnoses.

What criterion measures of aggression are most appropriate for research? There are no universally accepted benchmarks for measuring aggression as noted. Why? Because there are no universally accepted models of persons that are multidisciplinary. That is why a heuristic model of personality that includes the construct of aggression along with other personality dimensions (normal and abnormal) is important. We proposed elsewhere (Barratt & Slaughter, 1998) that this model should be discipline neutral and should involve at least the following four classes of measures in defining personality and aggression: biological (primarily but not exclusively the nervous system), social (environmental), cognitive, and behavioral. Our research defines aggression as behavior. We present some examples below of measures in each of these categories related to different criterion measures of aggression to further illustrate the need to understand the dilemma related to choosing criterion measures of aggression for research, clinical, and social/forensic decisions.

COMPARISON OF RELATIONSHIPS OF SEVERAL BIOSOCIAL MEASURES TO SELECTED CRITERION MEASURES

Three different criterion measures will be interrelated and then related to selected biosocial predictor measures. Two characteristics of the latter relationships will indicate that: (1) the majority of the biosocial measures are not consistently related to all of the criterion measures; (2) there is convergence of data suggesting that a few biosocial measures are related to all three types of criterion measures; and (3) these relationships probably involve robust predictor variables.

Overview of Study From Which Data Were Obtained

The data analyses to be presented in this section are from a study of thirty-seven youthful offenders (YOs) who are incarcerated in a prison within the Texas Department of Criminal Justice. The purpose of the study was to extend our research on impulsivity and aggression among adult inmates (Barratt et al., 1997a) to a younger inmate population to determine whether the relationships between predictor and criterion measures would be similar at younger ages. The YOs in this study were legally certified as adults and are serving sentences in adult prisons. They were between the ages of thirteen and seventeen. All participants signed a consent form approved by the University of Texas Medical Branch (UTMB) Internal Review Board for research. A non-inmate control group matched for age and other relevant variables was also studied. The overall analyses are being prepared for publication elsewhere; the analyses presented herein are for the purposes noted above, namely to note differences in the relationships of the same biosocial measures to different criterion measures of aggression.

Criterion Measures

Three criterion measures are included in these analyses. The first is our procedure for establishing the frequency and intensity of aggressive behavioral acts

(Barratt et al., 1997a; Barratt & Slaughter, 1998); the aggressive acts presented herein are not classified as premeditated or impulsive (as discussed in the next section). The second is the Life History of Aggression Interview (LHA) (Coccaro et al., 1997), and the third is the Buss-Perry Aggression Questionnaire (Buss & Perry, 1992). Our two-step procedure for analyzing *aggressive acts* is discussed in more detail in the next section, as just noted. The aggressive acts analyzed in our research are documented either by the reports of correctional officers for inmates or the "reporters" for outpatients.

The LHA that we used is the Clinician Version Revision (June 1995). This is a semistructured interview with ten items. Each item is rated on a six point scale for frequency of aggressive acts: 0 = no events; 1 = one event; 2 = a couple or few events (2-3); 3 = several or some events (4-9); 4 = "many" or "numerous" (i.e., 10+) events; 5 = "so many events they cannot be counted." The first five items are the primary aggression items, although the sixth item involves suicide. The latter items in the LHA are primarily antisocial and interpersonal items. We scored the first five items separately (LHA, 1-5) and also obtained a total score for the analyses presented herein. Underlying this measure is the assumption that subjects have the ability to accurately recall aggressive events.

The Buss-Perry Aggression Questionnaire (BPAQ) has twenty-nine items, which in a confirmatory factor analysis produced four factors (item examples in parentheses):

1. Physical aggression (If somebody hits me, I hit back.);
2. Verbal aggression (When people annoy me, I may tell them what I think.);
3. Anger (Some of my friends think I am a hothead.);
4. Hostility (I know that friends talk about me behind my back).

Items are answered on the basis of a five-point scale; ratings range from 1, which is "extremely uncharacteristic of me," to 5, which is "extremely characteristic of me."

Social Predictor Measures

The social "predictor" measures included in this study are the Sociability Subscale of the California Psychological Inventory (SO-CPI, Gough, 1987) and the McMaster Family Assessment Device (MFAD) (Epstein et al., 1983). The SO-CPI contains thirty-two items related to social relationships and each item is answered true or false. The MFAD has fifty-two items answered on a four-point scale as they apply to the testee (4 is strongly agree, 1 is strongly disagree). The MFAD contains seven subscales related to family functions (item examples in parentheses):

1. Problem solving—PS (We try to think of different ways to solve problems.);
2. Communication—CM (We are frank with each other.);
3. Roles—RL (We discuss who is to do household jobs.);
4. Affective responsiveness—AR (We cry openly.);
5. Affective involvement—AI (When someone is in trouble, the others become too involved.);
6. Behavior control—BC (You can easily get away with breaking the rules.);
7. General functioning—GF (Individuals are accepted for what they are.).

Personality Measures

Two self-report personality questionnaires were used in the study, the Junior Eysenck Personality Questionnaire (EPQ-Jr.) (Eysenck & Eysenck, 1975) and the Barratt Impulsiveness Scale, 11th ed. (BIS-11) (Patton et al., 1995). The EPQ-Jr. is an eighty-one-item questionnaire that is answered "true" or "false." It contains four sub-tests: (1) Psychoticism, a subscale heavily loaded with impulsiveness items; (2) Neuroticism, which measures emotional stability; (3) Extroversion, which measures sociability and outgoing interpersonal feelings and behaviors; and (4) Lie scale, a validity scale that measures conscious or unconscious malingering.

The BIS-11 is a thirty-item, self-report questionnaire that measures (item examples in parentheses):

1. Motor impulsivity (I act on the spur of the moment.);
2. Attentional impulsiveness, labeled "cognitive impulsiveness" in earlier versions of the BIS and scored in reverse order (I concentrate easily.);
3. Non-planning impulsiveness, also scored in reverse order (I am future oriented.)

Except for the EPQ-Jr., the above scales were developed for use with adults. However, we have successfully used them in studies with adolescents (Harmon-Jones et al., 1997). Because inmates in general have poor verbal skills (including reading), we read the items to both inmates and controls. If they do not understand an item, they are encouraged to ask questions, which are answered to avoid projecting bias to the extent possible.

Biological Predictor Measures

An example of the relationship of biological measures related to the different aggression criteria is the event related potential (ERP) data from a go/no-go visual discrimination task. During this task, subjects are seated in front of a television monitor. The task involves pressing a key with the left hand if an arrow on the screen points left, or with the right hand if an arrow on the screen points right. However, the arrow can be red or green. If it is red, the subjects do not press; if it is green, they do press. Reaction times and errors of omission and commission are recorded. During the performance of the task, the electrical activity of the cortex is recorded from scalp electrodes. The ERP data from the midline frontal (Fz), vertex (Cz) and parietal (Pz) electrodes will be presented here. The latency (time to respond) and peak amplitudes for the N200 wave form recorded during go and no-go conditions will be related to the three criterion measures. Peak amplitudes measure the extent of neural involvement at the different cortical sites related to performance of the task at hand; the higher the amplitude, the more neural resources are brought into play to solve the problem.

Interrelationships of Criterion Measures

The frequency and intensity of aggressive acts committed in prison as we measured them using a modification of the Overt Aggression Scale (OAS) (Yudofsky et

Table 4.2
Interrelationships of Three Criterion Measures

		Aggressive Acts	LHA Total	LHA Items 1-5	Buss-Perry Physical	Buss-Perry Verbal	Buss-Perry Anger	Buss-Perry Hostility	Buss-Perry Total
	Aggressive Acts	-							
LHA	Total	0.41*	-						
LHA	Items 1-5	0.31	0.91**	-					
Buss-Perry	Physical aggression	0.38*	0.49**	0.54**	-				
Buss-Perry	Verbal aggression	0.33*	0.42**	0.44**	0.67**	-			
Buss-Perry	Anger	0.18	0.34*	0.38*	0.33*	0.68**	-		
Buss-Perry	Hostility	0.06	0.35*	0.31	0.17	0.34*	0.62**	-	
Buss-Perry	Total aggression	0.30	0.50**	0.54**	0.70**	0.85**	0.85**	0.71**	-

Note. N = 37; LHA = Life History of Aggression Interview (Clinician Version Revision 6/95).
* Significant at .05. ** Significant at .01.

al., 1986) and the total LHA score were significantly related to each other, as shown in Table 4.2. Further physical and verbal aggression as measured by the BPAQ were significantly related to both the mean level of aggressive acts committed in prison and the LHA. As noted, the latter depends on the accuracy of the subjects' memory, as do the self-report measures of the BPAQ. The LHA measures were more significantly related to the BPAQ measures in general than were the aggressive acts measures, consistent with the observation that both measures rely in part on the same cognitive processes (especially memory) for providing answers to items. They are more similar to each other technique-wise than to the aggressive acts measures.

These results indicate that the three criterion measures had in common measuring physical and verbal aggression. It is also clear that in general, the three criterion measures are not measuring the same construct of aggression.

As noted, the aggressive acts reported here did not involve classifying the acts as impulsive, premeditated, or "other," as discussed later in this chapter. The Ns for the current study were too small to perform statistical analyses using our nosology procedures at this point in data collection. However, the analyses that have been done are consistent with our studies which indicate that impulsive and premeditated aggressive acts involve significantly different behaviors and relate to different "at risk for aggression" predictors.

Family and Social Measures Related to Criterion Measures

The SO-CPI was negatively related to all aggression measures but not significantly related to aggressive acts committed while in prison or to hostility. As Table 4.3 shows, the family variable most significantly related to the criterion aggression measures was behavioral control, which was related to all aggression measures except LHA 1-5 and the BPAQ physical aggression subscale.

These results would suggest that lack of disciplinary measures involving a differential reward system for socially positive and negative behaviors in families is a very

Table 4.3
Family and Social Measures Related to Criterion Measures of Aggression

		SO-CPI	PS	CM	McMaster Family Assessment				
					RL	AR	AI	BC	GF
	Aggressive Acts	-0.12	0.12	-0.04	-0.06	0.46**	0.09	0.45**	0.19
LHA	Total	-0.37*	0.19	0.02	0.28	0.26	0.05	0.41*	0.41*
LHA	Items 1-5	-0.35*	0.11	0.08	0.29	0.15	0.00	0.27	0.36*
Buss-Perry	Physical aggression	-0.39*	0.05	-0.01	0.13	0.21	0.21	0.09	0.26
Buss-Perry	Verbal aggression	-0.43**	0.11	0.06	0.30	0.21	0.12	0.44**	0.32
Buss-Perry	Anger	-0.38*	0.01	0.07	0.40*	0.11	0.17	0.49**	0.26
Buss-Perry	Hostility	-0.27	0.07	-0.09	0.51**	0.18	0.23	0.51**	0.15
Buss-Perry	Total aggression	-0.48**	0.07	0.00	0.44**	0.23	0.24	0.49**	0.31

Note. N= 37; SO-CPI = Social scale, California Psychological Inventory; PS = Problem solving; CM = Communication; RL = Roles; AR = Affective responsiveness; AI = Affective involvement; BC = Behavior control; GF = General functioning.

*Significant at .05. ** Significant at .01.

significant characteristic of families with regard to risk for aggression. This family characteristic involves convergence of data across the criterion measures and as such is probably a robust relationship. Again, however, we must use caution in making inferences because behavioral control on the MFAD is not significantly related to the physical aggression subscale of the BPAQ.

Personality Traits Related to Criterion Measures of Aggression

Table 4.4 shows that the EPQ-Jr. P subscale (psychoticism) was significantly related to all criterion measures of aggression. As noted previously, this subscale is heavily loaded with impulsivity items. However, none of the BIS-11 subscales were significantly related to all of the aggression criteria and none of the BIS-11 items were significantly related to the LHA. Thus, the relationship of the EPQ-Jr. P subscale to aggression is not due to impulsivity per se. The EPQ-Jr. P scale contains a number of items that are consistent with a borderline personality disorder in the *Diagnostic and Statistical Manual of Mental Disorders,* 4th ed. (DSM-IV). It is probable that the borderline items and impulsiveness combine to account for the overall relationships between P and the various aggression criteria.

Biological Measures Related to Aggression Criterion Measures

The midline ERPs overall had fewer significant relationships with the criterion measures than did the social and personality measures. These relationships, shown in Table 4.5, involve different types of measures, and as discussed earlier, it is more dif-

Table 4.4
Personality Traits Related to Criterion Measures of Aggression

		EPQ-Jr.				BIS-11			
		P	E	N	L	Inp	Im	Ic	Itotal
	Aggressive Acts	-0.12	0.12	-0.04	-0.06	0.46**	0.09	0.45**	0.19
LHA	Total	-0.37*	0.19	0.02	0.28	0.26	0.05	0.41*	0.41*
LHA	Items 1-5	-0.35*	0.11	0.08	0.29	0.15	0.00	0.27	0.36*
Buss-Perry	Physical aggression	-0.39*	0.05	-0.01	0.13	0.21	0.21	0.09	0.26
Buss-Perry	Verbal aggression	-0.43**	0.11	0.06	0.30	0.21	0.12	0.44**	0.32
Buss-Perry	Anger	-0.38*	0.01	0.07	0.40*	0.11	0.17	0.49**	0.26
Buss-Perry	Hostility	-0.27	0.07	-0.09	0.51**	0.18	0.23	0.51**	0.15
Buss-Perry	Total aggression	-0.48**	0.07	0.00	0.44**	0.23	0.24	0.49**	0.31

Note. N=37; EPQ = Eysenck Personality Questionnaire; BIS-11 = Barratt Impulsiveness Scale; P = Psychoticism; Inp = Nonplanning impulsivity; E = Extraversion; Im = Motor impulsivity; N = Neuroticism; Ic = Cognitive impulsivity; L = Lies; Itotal = Total impulsivity.
*Significant at .05. ** Significant at .01.

Table 4.5
Event Related Potentials (ERP's[a]) Recorded During a Go/No-Go Task Related to Aggression Criterion Measures

		Go						No-Go					
		Amplitude			Latency			Amplitude			Latency		
		Fz	Cz	Pz	Fz	Cz	Pz	Fz	Cz	Pz	Fz	Cz	Pz
	Prison Behavioral Acts	-0.01	-0.06	-0.15	0.18	0.23	0.17	0.39*	0.49**	0.26	0.27	0.2	0.27
	LHA Total	-0.34*	-0.26	-0.18	0.42**	0.49**	-0.06	0.19	0.36*	0.38*	0.28	.35*	0.11
Buss-Perry	Physical aggression	-0.09	±0.00	0.09	0.22	0.27	0.21	±0.00	0.17	0.34*	0.11	.37*	0.32
Buss-Perry	Verbal aggression	-0.09	-0.09	0.05	0.26	0.22	0.33*	0.23	0.29	0.38*	0.25	.45**	0.23
Buss-Perry	Anger	-0.39*	-0.44**	-0.17	0.13	0.18	0.39*	0.2	0.09	0.31	-0.03	0.13	0.01
Buss-Perry	Hostility	-0.48**	-0.46**	-0.36*	0.21	0.16	0.13	-0.04	-0.09	0.02	±0.00	0.07	-0.13
Buss-Perry	Total aggression	-0.37*	-0.34*	-0.15	0.27	0.27	0.34*	0.11	0.13	0.34*	0.09	.32*	0.13

Note. N = 37.
* Significant at .05. ** Significant at .01.
[a] N200.

ficult to obtain significant relationships among measures using different techniques. The results also indicate that biological and social predictor measures are often independent. The peak N200 amplitudes recorded during the no-go task were significantly related to both aggressive acts and the total LHA criterion measures, but not to any of BPAQ subscales. The no-go task involves errors of commission, that is, an error involves responding when you should not respond. This would be consistent with displaying inappropriate aggressive behaviors because of the lack of behavioral inhibition, which probably relates to both frontal and parietal lobe behavioral control centers. In general, we could tentatively conclude that aggression relates to cortical activity levels in the frontal-parietal areas during the performance of a task that involves withholding a response. However, the results again are not consistent across all criterion measures.

Summary of Relevance of Criteria Measures

The goal of this section is to demonstrate the importance of considering the meaning of criterion measures of aggression in research. Which of the three criterion measures discussed above is most representative of aggression? Although the criterion measures are significantly correlated, the correlations are modest. It is also obvious that there are some rather robust relationships between social, personality, and to some extent, biological predictor measures and the three criterion measures. For example, the EPQ-Jr. P scale is significantly related to all of the aggression criterion measures.

These data are currently being prepared along with data from a control group for publication. However, the data presented herein demonstrate the need for caution in making generalizions from aggression studies to applied decisions. It is our opinion that not enough attention has been given to the nature of different criteria when generalizing across aggression studies or from research studies to applied decisions.

STATUS OF OUR PROCEDURES FOR CLASSIFYING AGGRESSION AS IMPULSIVE, PREMEDITATED, OR OTHER

This section briefly reviews the status of our procedures for classifying aggressive acts as premeditated, impulsive, or medically related. We have demonstrated that this classification procedure makes a difference in the predictor profiles of aggression (Barratt et al., 1997a) and in interventions to reduce the frequency and intensity of aggressive acts (Barratt et al., 1997b). To better understand why this classification makes a difference, we will clarify the procedures we have developed to date and consider selected theoretical points.

Phenytoin Use

Our main interventions to date involve the use of anticonvulsants. We have presented the rationale for our use of anticonvulsants, especially phenytoin, in controlling aggressive behaviors elsewhere:

> [P]henytoin significantly reduced the *frequency* of impulsive aggressive acts in a placebo-controlled, double-blind, crossover study (Barratt, et al., 1991). The research reported here is a replication and extension of that study to a comparison of the effects of phenytoin on impulsive and nonimpulsive aggression.
>
> It has been speculated that impulsiveness and impulse control disorders may be associated with sub-seizure states that are related to many of the neural mechanisms proposed as bases for seizure disorders (Barratt, 1972). These

speculations were based in part on studies of brain physiology related to impulse control behaviors (Barratt, 1963; 1967; Barratt & Pray, 1954; Russell et al., 1968) that demonstrated the role of the amygdala in behavioral variability, which was hypothetically linked to impulsiveness (Barratt, 1983; Barratt et al., 1981; Turner, 1967). Phenytoin was reported to be effective in controlling nonepileptic emotional disorders (Turner, 1967) and was suggested to be a potential medication for controlling impulse control disorders (Barratt, 1967). The general rationale for the use of anticonvulsants in the study of aggression was based on the role of the frequency-amplitude and voltage-dependent activity of nerve cells in changing the information processing characteristics of the cortex and subcortical structures. It is well known that phenytoin is use-and-frequency dependent in its action on the nervous system (Yaari et al., 1986). It affects the firing rate of neurons by prolonging the recovery of voltage-dependent sodium channels from inactivation, thus reducing the rate at which neurons can fire action potentials repetitively (Schachter, 1995). As such, there is a high probability that phenytoin can alter impulsive aggressive behavior. (Barratt et al., 1997b)

Exploratory Studies

Based in part on the above rationale, we conducted several *exploratory* studies of the effects of phenytoin on aggression, with equivocal results. Some participants had significant reductions in the frequency and intensity of their aggressive acts, and some did not. In reviewing the cases with positive and negative results, it appeared that the positive effects were found among participants who exhibited what we later described as impulsive aggression and that the negative cases involved other behaviors (primarily planned acts). Based on these case analyses, we arrived at a classification of aggression as impulsive, premeditated, and medically related (Barratt, 1991). We developed over a course of time a semistructured interview for classifying aggressive acts using this schema. The procedure was reliable; it resulted in identifying neuropsychology, cognitive psychophysiological, and "personality" differences between persons with impulsive versus premeditated profiles when medically related aggression was held constant (Barratt et al., 1997a). It was also shown that phenytoin reduces the frequency and intensity of impulsive aggressive acts, but not of premeditated aggressive acts (Barratt, et al. 1997b). It is important to understand that potential participants with medically related disorders were eliminated from these studies, as were persons using any medication. We started with a large number of aggressive inmates and excluded 309 based on chart review alone. Table 4.6 indicates the number of subjects who were eliminated at the various steps in the selection process for the inmate study (Barratt et al., 1997a).

Identifying the Subjects

The primary goal in the selection process was to identify subjects who primarily committed either impulsive aggressive or premeditated aggressive acts. This was an attempt to get our "foot in the door" in classifying aggressive acts. That is, could we develop a nosology that reliably classified aggression for some subjects if not all? The first step in subject selection, as noted above, was to eliminate potential subjects who

Table 4.6.
Classifying Inmates for Participation in Aggression Study

Step		Number of Inmates	
1.	Review of disciplinary records	566	
2.	Eliminated by chart screening	309	
3.	Available for screening interview	257	
4.	Did not volunteer for screening interview	102	
5.	Initial screening interview	155	
6.	Eliminated at initial interview	17	
7.	Entered into study	138	
8.	Eliminated by data screening	12	
9.	Data analyzed	126	
10.	Nosology:		
	a. Impulsive aggressive	127	(21%)
	b. Premeditated aggressive	30	(24%)
	c. Mixed or can't classify	58	(46%)
	d. PDI-R screening	11	(9%)
	(Additional Psychiatric Disorders)		

had any type of medical disorder, including DSM-III-R, Axis I and selected Axis II disorders. The 309 subjects who were initially eliminated by chart screening fell in this category. For example, if a potential subject was on "psychiatry call" within the last year, he was eliminated. Of the remaining 257 who met the aggression criteria, 102 did not volunteer for the initial interview for the study. Of the 155 who did volunteer, 17 were eliminated at the initial interview because they did not meet all of the criteria for entry into the study. Twelve more were eliminated during data analyses (e.g., all left handed subjects were eliminated). Of the remaining 126 subjects, 21 percent were classified as impulsive aggressive, 24 percent as premeditated aggressive, and the remaining either had a psychiatric problem (PDI-R, 9 percent) or could not be classified. Parenthetically, among our YOs who were described above, the percentages in the impulsive and premeditated categories are about the same. Thus, of the subjects who met the inclusion criteria, approximately 45 percent committed aggressive acts that were primarily impulsive or premeditated. We feel we had our foot in the door for the beginning of the development of a nosology of aggression.

Classifying aggressive acts as impulsive or premeditated is not new (Barratt, 1991; Barratt et al., 1997a). For example, Dodge and Schwartz (1997) differentiated between reactive and proactive aggression. Reactive aggression is similar to our construct of impulsive aggression, while proactive aggression is similar to premeditated or planned aggression. Dodge and Schwartz (1997) discuss these two types of aggression primarily using a "social information processing" model of aggression.

Outpatient Studies

All of the inmates who were screened for this study had disciplinary problems because of aggressive behavior, as noted. Although we are presenting data here involving incarcerated persons, we are also studying outpatients, and the results with them to date are similar to what we have presented here. Outpatient research is more difficult than studying inmates because we analyze *each* aggressive act over a predetermined time period and reporters are necessary to document the aggressive acts. This documentation is rather routine among inmates. We are currently interested in studying aggression among the large number of subjects who have a psychiatric disorder and are also aggressive.

General Population Studies

We have noted that the classification of aggressive acts described above was based on structured interviews. Because the classification did make a difference in the relationship of predictor to criterion measures, we wondered whether the constructs of premeditated and impulsive aggression existed in the general population as measurable dimensions. To broach this question, we developed a self-report Aggressive Acts Questionnaire (AAQ) based on the items we used in our semistructured interview (Barratt & Slaughter, 1998). The items in the structured interview had been gleaned from the work of other investigators and represented a good cross-section of the characteristics of impulsive aggression. We wrote twenty-two items for the AAQ based on the elements in our structured interview. In answering the AAQ, subjects first estimate the number of aggressive acts they have committed within the last six months. An aggressive act is defined as "hitting and/or verbally insulting another person or breaking objects because you are angry or frustrated." Subjects are then instructed to list the four most extreme acts they can remember during the six months, including the date, duration, and time of day for each act. They then answer the twenty-two questions to describe each act they have listed, up to four acts.

Some subjects listed four acts, others listed only one, and six listed no acts. Each item on the AAQ is rated on a five-point scale. For example, the first item is "Act was planned." The response choices are "definitely yes," "yes," "cannot decide," "no," and "definitely no." A high score indicates impulsive-aggressive tendencies. Thus, "definitely yes" is scored "1" for the first item. Using this format, we have administered this questionnaire along with selected personality questionnaires to over 200 college students. The total data set are published elsewhere (Barratt, Stanford et al., in press). The data presented herein were selected to answer the question, "Can persons discriminate in their daily lives between premeditated and aggressive behaviors?" Further, if they can reliably make this distinction, what are the characteristics of these acts?

The first analysis involved an item-total score analysis for responses to the first act reported. Of the twenty-two items on the AAQ, twelve items were significantly correlated with the total score, as Table 4.7 shows. These twelve items were then factor analyzed using principal component analyses, which resulted in the identification of four factors that were Procrustes rotated to identify four factors as shown in Table 4.8. Factor 1 is labeled "impulsive aggression" (items 9, 16, 18, 19), Factor 2 "mood on the day the act occurred" (items 8, 12, 21), Factor 3 "premeditated aggression" (items 1, 13, 14), and Factor 4 "agitation" (items 5, 7). Second order factors are less clearly defined (see Table 4.9), although the second order Factor 2 appeared to make sense in clearly combining agitation with impulsive aggression.

We interpret these analyses as indicating that impulsive versus premeditated

Table 4.7
AAQ Items Significantly Correlated With Total AAQ Score Less Item Being Analyzed

1. Act was planned.
5. I became agitated and emotionally upset during the act.
7. My aggressive behavior led to poor social interactions during the incident.
8. The day the act occurred I was having a bad day in general.
9. I lacked self-control.
12. I was feeling more aggressive than usual the day of the act.
13. I profited financially from the act.
14. The act led to power over others or improved social status for me.
16. I felt guilty following the act.
18. I now consider the act to have been impulsive.
19. My behavior was too extreme for the level of provocation.
21. I was in a good mood before the act occurred.

Table 4.8
AAQ: First Order Factor Structure (Procrustes Rotation of Principal Components Solution)

Item	Factor 1	Factor 2	Factor 3	Factor 4
1.	0.24	-0.22	*0.66	0.02
5.	0.00	0.02	0.32	*0.78
7.	0.32	0.15	-0.03	*0.77
8.	0.13	*0.89	0.06	0.07
9.	*0.66	0.10	0.14	0.28
12.	0.19	*0.71	-0.31	0.37
13.	0.11	0.13	*0.57	0.25
14.	0.12	0.12	*0.78	0.07
16.	*0.71	0.2	0.17	0.25
18.	*0.79	0.04	0.23	0.08
19.	*0.81	0.22	-0.01	-0.02
21.	-0.17	*-0.86	-0.11	-0.02

Note. Factor 1—Labeled "impulsive aggression"; Factor 2—Labeled "mood on the day the act occurred"; Factor 3—Labeled "premeditated aggression"; Factor 4—Labeled "agitation."

Table 4.9
AAQ: Second Order Factors

	Factor 1	Factor 2
Factor 1	0.45352	0.75057
Factor 2	0.75220	0.07327
Factor 3	-0.67870	0.11846
Factor 4	0.41002	-0.76852

aggression are constructs that exist in the population at large and that can be described reliably. Further, aggressive acts among "normal" college students occurred much more frequently than we expected. A total of 583 acts was reported. As noted, the details of these analyses, including validity data, are published elsewhere.

Operational Definitions of "Impulsive" vs. "Premeditated"

Of what value are these data? While the validity data are not all gathered to date, one other analysis may shed some light on the value of this research beyond indicating that premeditated and impulsive aggression are constructs present in a nonclinical population. We scored the four factors as separate dimensions and converted the scores for each factor to T scores. We then obtained the ratio of the T scores for Factor 1 (impulsive aggression) to the T scores for Factor 3 (premeditated aggression) for the 583 acts. Figure 4.1 is a plot distribution of the ratios of these two T scores showing a relatively normal distribution. Scores at one end of the distribution represent primarily impulsive aggression, while scores at the other end represent premeditated aggression. We are currently gathering validity data to arrive at cut-off scores to help identify those persons who commit primarily impulsive versus premeditated aggressive acts. This will provide operational definitions of these two types of aggression as we have defined them.

In subject selection for our research, we will continue to use the structured interview as well as the AAQ as developed to date. Subjects in selected populations may

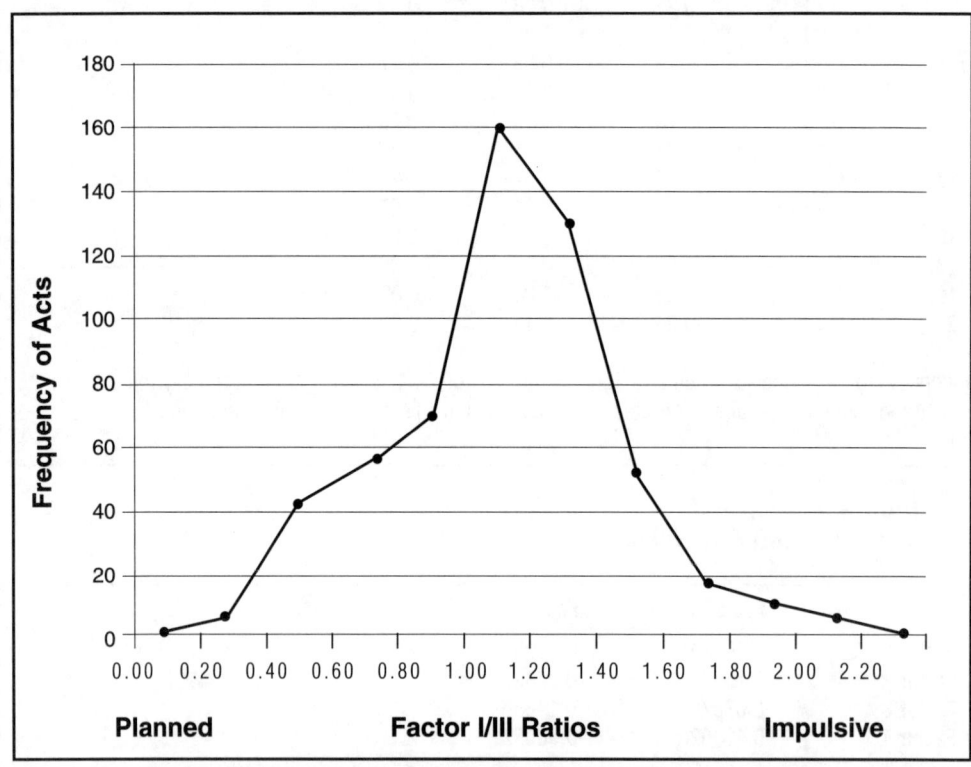

Figure 4.1. A Plot of the Ratio of the AAQ Impulsive and Premeditated Factor T Scores

not be able to meaningfully complete the AAQ. For example, we had to use the AAQ as a structured interview with patients in a state mental hospital.

The intensity and frequency of aggressive acts has to be held constant when comparing subjects with impulsive versus premeditated aggression. The intensity level of aggression was obtained among inmates using a modification of Yudofsky et al.'s (1986) Overt Aggression Scale. The data for YOs discussed earlier involved these data, as noted. Thus, we have a two-step process for classifying aggressive acts (Barratt, Stanford et al., in press). Classifying aggressive acts as impulsive, premeditated, medically related, or other is a beginning, we think, to developing a meaningful nosology of aggression—we do have our "foot in the door." We are currently pursuing this approach with patients who have DSM-IV Axis I disorders.

SUMMARY

This chapter has covered the importance of making explicit the criterion measures in aggression research and of using caution when generalizing across aggression studies that use different criterion measures. It has also provided some evidence for identifying "robust" predictor measures of impulsive aggression. A two-step procedure for classifying aggressive acts as impulsive, premeditated, medically related, or other was also discussed. Data indicating that impulsive and premeditated aggression can be differentiated by the general population in their daily lives was presented. A factor analytic study identified impulsive and premeditated aggression as independent dimensions.

Editor's Note

This chapter has tremendous implications for the treatment of aggressive disorders. It highlights the need to precisely and accurately classify various forms of aggression so that treatment approaches can be tailored to the particular disorder, which is distinguishable based on its manifestations and its underlying generators. As stated by David Goldman, there are most likely different genes involved in different dimensions of aggression. Given that genes involved in aggression code for functions of neurochemical and physiological systems, this may also be true for the biological and behavioral correlates of aggression. Until aggressive disorders are adequately classified, treatment will continue to be primarily trial and error, hit or miss.

Dr. Barratt has, in numerous publications, demonstrated the potential efficacy of pharmacological treatments for aggression based on appropriate classifying information. For example, his interest in the effects of anticonvulsants on impulsive aggression led him to use them on lower primates in his impulsivity research in an attempt to control intraindividual variability of behavior. He and his colleagues had observed that high-impulsive subjects were significantly more variable in performing selected psychomotor tasks that appeared to be related in part to the basolateral nucleus of the amygdala. They had found that phenytoin did decrease the variability of psychomotor responses among squirrel monkeys. For that and other reasons, he and his colleagues decided to explore the use of phenytoin in reducing aggression among humans.

In Dr. Barratt's initial results, phenytoin decreased the frequency and intensity of aggressive acts in a majority of patients. However, phenytoin appeared to work well in controlling aggressive acts with some subjects but did not work at all with others.

Thus, they then compared subjects for whom phenytoin did and did not reduce aggressive acts. They found that two types of aggressive acts in general characterized the two groups: phenytoin reduced impulsive aggression, but did not significantly reduce premeditated or planned aggressive acts. In a follow-up exploratory study using a newly developed classification scheme, Dr. Barratt found that phenytoin did reduce impulsive aggression. On the basis of this study, he and his colleagues have developed an unstructured interview for differentiating between impulsive and premeditated aggressive acts due to the treatment implications.

In addition to the anticonvulsants, Dr. Barratt has reported on Dr. Emil Coccaro's use of medications that enhance serotonin. Given the well-established relationship between the functioning of the serotonin system and impulsive aggression among human subjects as well as other animals, it was hypothesized that pharmacological enhancement of serotonin should be expected to reduce impulsive-aggressive behavior in subjects in whom this behavior is prominent. Fluoxetine was administered to subjects with a history of this behavior, with measures in place to differentiate between aggressive subtypes. Fluoxetine significantly reduced verbal and indirect impulsive aggression (against objects), but did not reduce aggression toward others. Coccaro thus concluded that fluoxetine reduces selected types of impulsive aggression.

In the same vein, it is essential that aggression as related to biological generators is differentiated from aggression primarily due to social causes. Devising and employing well tested classification schemes will facilitate in making these distinctions and lead to more effective treatments across the board.

References

American Psychiatric Association (1994). *Diagnostic and statistical manual of mental disorders* (4th ed.). Washington, DC: American Psychiatric Press.

Barratt, E. S. (1963). Behavioral variability related to stimulation of the cat's amygdala. *Journal of the American Medical Association, 186,* 773–775.

Barratt, E. S. (1967). The effects of thiazesim, LSD-25, and bilateral lesions of the amygdalae on the release of a suppressed response. *Recent Advances in Biological Psychiatry, 9,* 229–240.

Barratt, E. S. (1972). Impulsiveness and anxiety: toward a neuropsychological model. In C. Spielberger (Ed.), *Anxiety: current trends in theory and research.* New York: Academic Press, 195–222.

Barratt, E. S. (1983). The biological basis of impulsiveness: The significance of timing and rhythm disorders. *Personality Individual Differences, 4,* 387–391.

Barratt, E. S. (1991). Measuring and predicting aggression within the context of a personality theory. *Journal of Neuropsychiatry and Clinical Neuroscience, 3,* S35–S39.

Barratt, E. S., Kent, T. A., Bryant, S. G. & Felthous, A. R. (1991). A controlled trial of phenytoin in impulsive aggression. *Journal of Clinical Psychopharmacology, 11,* 388–389.

Barratt, E. S., Patton, J., Olsson, N. G. & Zuker, G. (1981). Impulsivity and paced tapping. *Journal of Motor Behavior, 13,* 286–300.

Barratt, E. S. & Pray, S. L. (1954). Effect of a chemically depressed amygdala on the behavioral manifestations produced in cats by LSD-25. *Experimental Neurology, 12,* 173–178.

Barratt, E. S. & Slaughter, L. (1998). Defining, measuring, and predicting impulsive aggression: A heuristic model. *Behavioral Sciences & the Law, 16,* 285–302.

Barratt, E. S., Stanford, M. S., Dowdy, L., Liebman, M. J. & Kent, T. A. (in press). Impulsive and premeditated aggression: A factor analysis of self-reported acts. *Psychiatry Research.*

Barratt, E. S., Stanford, M. S., Felthous, A. & Kent, T. A. (1997b). The effects of phenytoin on impulsive and premeditated aggression: A controlled study. *Journal of Clinical Psychopharmocology, 17,* 341–349.

Barratt, E. S., Stanford, M. S., Kent, T. A. & Felthous, A. (1997a). Neuropsychological and cognitive psychophysiological substrates of impulsive aggression. *Biological Psychiatry, 41,* 1045–1061.

Bech, P. & Mak, M. (1995). Measurements of impulsivity and aggression. In E. Hollander and D. Stein (Eds.), *Impulsivity and Aggression.* New York: John Wiley & Sons.

Buss, A. H. & Durkee, A. (1957). An inventory for assessing different kinds of hostility. *Journal of Consulting Psychology, 21,* 343–349.

Buss, A. H. & Perry, M. (1992). The aggression questionnaire. *Journal of Personality and Social Psychology, 63,* 452–459.

Cherek, D. R., Spiga, R. Bennett, R. H. & Graboski, J. (1991). Human aggression and escape responding: Effects of provocation frequency. *Psychological Record, 41,* 3–17.

Coccaro, E. F., Berman, M. E. & Kavoussi, R. J. (1997). Assessment of life-history of aggression: Development and psychometric characteristics. *Psychiatry Research, 73,* 147–157.

Dodge, K. A. & Schwartz, D. (1997). Social information processing mechanisms in aggressive behavior. In D. M. Stoff, J. Breiling & J. D. Maser (Eds.), *Handbook of Antisocial Behavior.* New York: John Wiley & Sons.

Epstein, N. B., Baldwin, L. M. & Bishop, D. S. (1983). The McMaster family assessment device. *Journal of Marital and Family Therapy, 9,* 171–180.

Eysenck, H. J. & Eysenck, S. B. (1975). *Eysenck personality questionnaire (junior) manual.* San Diego, CA: Educational & Industrial Testing Service.

Goldman, D. (1996). The search for genetic alleles contributing to self-destructive and aggressive behaviors. In D. M. Stoff & R. B. Cairns (Eds.), *Aggression and Violence: Genetic, Neurobiological, and Biosocial Perspectives.* Hillsdale, NJ: Erlbaum.

Gough, H. G. (1987). *California Psychological Inventory (Administrator's Guide).* Palo Alto, CA: Consulting Psychologists Press.

Harmon-Jones, E., Barratt, E. S. & Wigg, C. (1997). Impulsiveness, aggression, reading, and the P300 of the event related potential. *Personality and Individual Differences, 22,* 439–445.

Muntaner, C., Walter, D., Nagoshi, C., Fishbein, D., Haertzen, C. A. & Jaffe, J. (1990). Self-report vs. laboratory measures of aggression as predictors of substance abuse. *Drug and Alcohol Dependence, 25,* 1–11.

Nunnally, J. C. (1978). *Psychometric theory* (2nd ed.). New York: McGraw-Hill.

Patton, J. H., Stanford, M. S. & Barratt, E. S. (1995). Factor structure of the Barratt impulsiveness scale. *Journal of Clinical Psychology, 51,* 768–774.

Russell, G. C., Barratt, E. S., Deaton, J. M. & Taylor, R. R. (1968). Evoked responses in the putamen and globus pallidus following stimulation of the basolateral amygdala. *Brain Research, 7,* 459–462.

Schachter, S. C. (1995). Review of the mechanisms of action of antiepileptic drugs. *Central Nervous System Drugs, 4,* 469–477.

Spielberger, C. D. (1988). *Manual for the state-trait anger expression inventory (STAXI).* Odessa, FL: Psychological Assessment Resources.

Taylor, S. P. (1967). Aggressive behavior and physiological arousal as a function of provocation and the tendency to inhibit aggression. *Journal of Personality, 35,* 297–310.

Turner, W. J. (1967). The usefulness of diphenylhydantoin in treatment of non-epileptic emotional disorders. *International Journal of Neuropsychiatry, 3,* S8–S20.

Volavka, J. (1995). *Neurobiology of violence.* Washington, DC: American Psychiatric Press.

Webster, C. D. & Jackson, M. A. (1997). *Impulsivity: Theory assessment and treatment.* New York: Guilford Press.

Wistedt, B., Rasmussen, A., Pendersen, L., Malm, U., Traskman-Bendz, L., Wakelin, J. & Bech, P. (1990). The development of an observer-scale for measuring social dysfunction and aggression. *Pharmacopsychiatry, 23,* 249–252.

Yaari, Y., Selzer, M. E. & Pincus, J. H. (1986). Phenytoin: Mechanisms of its anticonvulsant action. *Annals of Neurology, 20,* 171–184.

Yudofsky, S. C., Silver, J. M., Jackson, W., Endicott, J. & Williams, D. (1986). The overt aggression scale for the objective of verbal and physical aggression. *American Journal of Psychiatry, 143,* 35–39.

Chapter 5

Biological and Behavioral Investigation of Aggression and Impulsivity

by Scott D. Lane, Ph.D. and Don R. Cherek, Ph.D.

Introduction 5-1
Definition and Measurement of Aggression 5-2
    Rating Scales 5-2
    Laboratory Measurement 5-2
Biological Studies of Aggression 5-4
    Measurement and Manipulation of Serotonin Function 5-4
    Relation of Lowered Serotonin Function to Aggression 5-5
    Tryptophan Manipulation 5-6
    Current Work 5-7
Definition and Measurement of Impulsivity 5-9
    Rating Scales 5-9
    Laboratory Measurements 5-10
Biological Studies of Impulsivity 5-11
    Relation of Lowered Serotonin to Impulsivity 5-11
    Laboratory Measurements 5-12
Conclusions 5-14
    Possible Genetic Links 5-14
    Environmental Factors 5-15
Editor's Note 5-15

INTRODUCTION

Most mammals exhibit impulsive and aggressive behavior, and at times these behavior patterns serve an adaptive function. However, extreme and persistent forms of human aggression and impulsivity are often indicative of psychopathology (APA, 1994; Martin et al., 1994), especially when they persist beyond adolescence into adulthood

---

Funding for this work was provided by grants DA-03166, DA-10552 and fellowship DA-05774 from the National Institute on Drug Abuse.

(Mealey, 1995; Moffitt, 1993). Maladaptive forms of impulsiveness and aggression have been conceptualized as a fundamental problem in behavioral self-control (Dawes et al., 1997; Patterson & Newman, 1993). In the *Diagnostic and Statistical Manual of Mental Disorders* (DSM-IV), repeated aggressive and impulsive behavior patterns that lead to aversive (unpleasant or detrimental) outcomes constitute diagnostic criteria for several psychiatric disorders, including conduct disorder, antisocial personality disorder, attention deficit hyperactivity disorder, substance abuse, and intermittent explosive disorder. These disorders have long been investigated by scientists in the social and health sciences, but recently public perception of increases in violent and other impulsive criminal activity has escalated to the forefront of public health concerns (Koop & Lundberg, 1992; Robbins, 1995). An overview of scientific advances in the study of aggression and impulsivity is described here, with an emphasis on biological variables. These advances have come from studies of both human and nonhuman behaviors; this chapter will focus primarily on human aggressive and impulsive behavior.

DEFINITION AND MEASUREMENT OF AGGRESSION

Here we will take the perspective that human aggression (1) is a social behavior that involves the interaction at least two people (2) that is intended to harm another person (3) who finds this harm aversive and would act to avoid it (Baron & Richardson, 1994). It is well documented that a social context (i.e., verbal and nonverbal interaction) is a necessary condition for human aggressive behavior. Further, provocation and retaliation, which necessarily require a social context, have been shown to be powerful factors in aggression (Cherek, 1981; Richardson et al., 1986; Taylor, 1967) and are central features of the laboratory procedures described throughout this chapter.

Rating Scales

Measurement of human aggression can be divided into two forms: rating scales and laboratory procedures. Several rating scales have been developed, covering a range of dimensions. These primarily focus on an individual's history of past aggressive acts or on personality and cognitive factors (values, attitudes, and beliefs) that may be related to those aggressive acts. Scales that evaluate the frequency of past aggressive behavior include the Retrospective Overt Aggression Scale (Sorgi et al., 1991), the Life History of Aggression Scale (Coccaro et al., 1997), and the Brown History of Violence Questionnaire (BHVQ) (Brown et al., 1979). Those which evaluate personality/cognitive factors include the Buss-Durkee Hostility Inventory (BDHI) (Buss & Durkee, 1957); Buss-Perry Aggression Questionnaire (Buss & Perry, 1992); and the State Trait Anger Scale (Spielberger et al., 1983). Comprehensive lists of aggression scales can be found in Baron & Richardson (1994) and Bech & Mak (1995).

Laboratory Measurement

Laboratory measurement of aggression provides several advantages. First, physical violence and other forms of aggression are low probability behaviors, are sometimes unpredictable, and can be difficult to identify and measure outside of laboratory settings. Second, experimenters are able to avoid the possibility of physical injury to participants. Third, laboratory methods provide improved precision and manipulation of independent variables, including control over the frequency of presentation of provocative stimuli and subsequent counter attacks. Fourth, drug and alcohol use are known to be important factors in criminal behavior, and assessment of drug and alcohol effects under controlled conditions are made possible.

Laboratory measurement of human aggression has employed a variety of approaches: Buss's Aggression Machine Paradigm (Buss, 1961), the Competitive Reaction Time Task (Taylor, 1967), and the Point Subtraction Aggression Paradigm (PSAP) (Cherek, 1981). In the Buss paradigm, subjects are instructed to "teach" a list of materials to another (confederate) participant by signaling correct responses with a light, and by punishing incorrect responses by ostensibly delivering an electric shock to that (confederate) participant. Aggressive behavior is measured via subjects' selected shock intensity (1 to 10) and duration for which the shock is delivered. In the Competitive Reaction Time Task (Taylor, 1967), subjects compete with a (confederate) participant in a reaction time task in which the loser on each trial receives an electric shock of varying intensity. Win-loss outcomes and shock deliveries to the subject are actually controlled by the experimenter. Aggressive behavior is assessed by measuring the shock levels that the subject selects to ostensibly present to the confederate subject.

The PSAP (Cherek, 1981) is a computer regulated task in which subjects respond on one of several response buttons. Subjects are told that they are paired with other (fictitious) subjects who are linked to their computer. Subjects earn money by responding on a button labeled "A." During the task, subjects are provoked by the subtraction of money they have earned (shown via a running monetary counter on the computer monitor). These subtractions are generated at random times by a computer program, but are attributed to the other (fictitious) subjects. Subjects have the opportunity to retaliate by pressing a button labeled "B" to subtract money from the other (fictitious) subject. Aggressive responding is measured by the number of B responses the subject makes during the task. Responding on the B button also initiates a provocation-free interval during which no point subtractions occur. This provides a reinforcing consequence for aggressive responding which is necessary to maintain aggressive behavior across the experiment.

Each of these three laboratory procedures shares two important common features—(1) a social context in which individuals are interacting in some conflicting manner and (2) aggressive responses that are operationally defined as the ostensible delivery of an aversive stimulus to another person. These features are consistent with the above-noted definition of aggressive behavior. Further, each provides the recognized laboratory advantages of precision in control and measurement. The PSAP offers several additional experimental advantages, including use in a variety of settings (many institutions will not allow use of real or simulated electric shock); use with a variety of subject populations (including children and adolescents); and repeated testing, which affords measurement of behavior across a range of conditions within the same subject. It is currently being used in several laboratories in the United States and Europe.

Several studies have validated the use of these laboratory procedures by showing a relationship between aggressive behavior in the laboratory and (1) self-reported aggression, (2) past violence in natural settings, and (3) alcohol intoxication. For example, aggression on the Taylor Competitive Reaction Time Task has been positively correlated with scores on the assault subscale of the BDHI (Giancola & Zeichner, 1995a), and with acute administration of alcohol (Giancola & Zeichner, 1995b; Taylor & Gammon, 1975). Alcohol-related increases in aggressive responding have also been demonstrated using the PSAP task with normal, healthy males (Cherek et al., 1985) and with individuals who have antisocial personality disorder (Moeller et al., 1998). With the PSAP, positive correlations have been found between scores on the BHVQ, the Overt Aggression Scale (Yudofsky, 1986) and aggressive responding (Cherek et al., 1996). Further, both male and female parolees with a history of violent behavior (and violent offenses) exhibited more aggressive responding on the PSAP than nonviolent parolees (Cherek et al., 1996; 1997; in press). An extensive review of the validity of laboratory aggression paradigms is provided in Giancola and Chermack (1998).

BIOLOGICAL STUDIES OF AGGRESSION

Many studies have sought to locate structures and functions in the central nervous system that might be involved in aggression. One of the most reliably documented biological variables implicated in aggressive behavior is the neurotransmitter serotonin (5-hydroxytryptamine, or 5-HT) (Eichelman, 1990; Van Praag, 1991; Zubieta & Alessi, 1993). Like all neurotransmitters, serotonin functions to send signals throughout the central nervous system by stimulating electrochemical activity in closely connected neurons (brain cells). Behaviorally, serotonin transmission functions in part to regulate mood and sleep, and, importantly, appears to be involved in aggressive and impulsive behavior and in suicide (Åsberg, 1987; Eichelman, 1990; Wilcox & Gonzales, 1995).

A large number of serotonin neurons are located in the brain stem and mid-brain. This is relevant to explanations of aggression proposed by evolutionary biologists and psychologists. Aggression is considered an evolutionarily "primitive" behavior (Daly & Wilson, 1988; McGuire & Raleigh, 1987), and is thus consistent with its anatomical origin in the most primitive area of the brain (the brain stem). Further, mid-brain regions rich in serotonin neurons (the hippocampus, hypothalamus, and limbic system) are believed to regulate emotional behavior in mammals, including aggression (Carlson, 1991; MacDonnell & Flynn, 1966). It should be noted here that any connection between the behavior of an intact organism and the function of a single biological system represents a gross oversimplification of the relevant variables. However, such an approach is germane to science and provides a starting point on which future work can build.

Measurement and Manipulation of Serotonin Function

The data linking serotonin function to aggression has been collected using a number of procedures with both human and nonhuman subjects. A description of these procedures, with emphasis on human subjects, will be provided before describing the relevant data. Generally, the procedures used in this area can be divided into (1) measurement of extant serotonin levels and (2) direct or indirect manipulation of serotonin function. In animals, serotonin function can be observed directly either by measuring concentrations taken from brain slices of sacrificed animals or through microdialysis techniques that allow perfusions of small instruments in the brains of intact animals. A less direct approach involves measuring 5-hydroxyindolacetic acid (5-HIAA) drawn from cerebral spinal fluid (CSF). 5-HIAA is the primary metabolite of serotonin in the central nervous system (CNS) and thus reflects serotonin turnover, or activity (Bloom, 1996). Surgical and chemical lesions provide a means of direct serotonin manipulation. Such procedures typically destroy specific brain regions known to be concentrated with serotonin neurons, which significantly reduces serotonin function (Bloom, 1996).

Practical ethical constraints allow for less precise, more indirect measurement and manipulation of serotonin function in humans. Nonetheless, several techniques have been developed. Some studies have obtained CSF measures of 5-HIAA (Coccaro et al., 1989; Brown et al., 1979), others measure serotonin or serotonin metabolites in the peripheral nervous system through simple blood draws (Modai et al., 1989). Because serotonin is also common outside the CNS (particularly in the gut), techniques that rely on peripheral system measures (e.g., simple blood draws) present problems in experimental control due to uncertainty about the original source of the obtained serotonin metabolites.

Experimental manipulation of serotonin in humans has taken two approaches, neuroendocrine challenge and tryptophan depletion. Neuroendocrine challenge provides a measure of serotonin response to a drug that purportedly has effects on the serotonin system in the CNS. For example, the drugs buspirone, d-fenfluramine, and d,l-fenfluramine are known to exert effects on serotonin (Zubieta & Alessi, 1993). When administered to humans, measurement of serotonin function is assessed through levels of hormone secretion (e.g., prolactin and cortisol) into the peripheral nervous system and can be obtained via simple blood draws. Because serotonin activity in the CNS stimulates neuroendocrine systems, which in turn stimulate the release of these hormones, changes in obtained hormone levels are believed to reflect changes in serotonin transmission (Coccaro et al., 1996; Moss et al., 1990; O'Keane et al., 1992). Thus, administration of drugs such as buspirone and d-fenfluramine that effect serotonin should produce measurable changes in related hormone levels.

Typtophan depletion involves more direct manipulation of the serotonin system. In the CNS, serotonin is synthesized from its precursor tryptophan, a basic dietary amino acid found in many foods. Tryptophan is depleted by providing subjects with a drink containing an abundance of amino acids *other than* tryptophan. These amino acids stimulate the synthesis of new proteins. Since very little tryptophan is in the drink, accumulated body stores of tryptophan are used up during protein synthesis, thus reducing the amount available for serotonin synthesis in the CNS (Cleare & Bond, 1995; Fernstrom, 1993; Wurtman et al., 1981).

Relation of Lowered Serotonin Function to Aggression

The data linking serotonin to aggression have generally employed the procedures described above, with an overall conclusion that levels of serotonin are negatively correlated to aggressive and other antisocial behaviors. In other words, biological studies suggest that lowered serotonin function in the CNS is related to aggressive behavior. Some studies suggest that existing serotonin levels are simply lower in more aggressive humans and nonhumans, while others have shown a blunted or diminished response of the serotonin system following biochemical manipulation. These findings are consistent across both human and nonhuman studies. Lesions to specific brain areas of rats produce both increased aggression (fighting, posturing, etc.) and decreased serotonin levels in the hippocampus, but this effect on aggressive behavior is blocked following high doses of tryptophan (Kantak et al., 1981). Administration of drugs that lower serotonin production in the CNS of rats produces increases in predatory aggression (Gibbons et al., 1978). Rats selectively bred for very low aggressive behavior show higher CNS serotonin and 5-HIAA levels than comparable but more aggressive strains (Popova et al., 1991). Levels of 5-HIAA are negatively correlated with severe and intense forms of aggressive behavior in free ranging rhesus monkeys (Mehlman et al., 1994). Dominant male vervet monkeys have higher serotonin levels than subordinate males and engage in more attack-directed aggression than subordinates. However, when dominant males are removed from the group, subordinates show significant increases in aggression and corresponding increases in serotonin level.

Data from human studies are consistent with the findings from the animal literature, supporting a role for decreased serotonin activity in antisocial behavior. Diminished responsiveness in the serotonin system has been shown in individuals with antisocial personality disorder and comorbid substance abuse (Moss et al., 1990) and in antisocial individuals with a history of violent offenses (O'Keane et al., 1992). Conduct-disordered children have also been found to have decreased serotonin activity (Stoff et al., 1987; 1992). Brown et al. (1979) found a significant negative correlation between CSF 5-HIAA and individual lifetime histories of aggressive behavior. Relatedly, violent offenders with a history of impulsive aggression presented lower CSF 5-HIAA compared to those with nonimpulsive aggressive histories (Linnoila et al., 1983); this outcome was also found in male arsonists (Virkkunen et al., 1987). This collective finding of lower serotonin levels is also common to individuals who direct violent behavior toward themselves. Diminished CSF 5-HIAA was documented in individuals with past suicide attempts (Coccaro et al., 1989), and significantly low serotonin levels were found postmortem in the brains of victims of violent suicide (Coccaro & Astill, 1990). Further, Åsberg et al. (1987) found significantly higher suicide rates among those depressed patients with the lowest CSF 5-HIAA concentrations.

Tryptophan Manipulation

The manipulation of serotonin levels through depletion and supplementation of the serotonin precursor tryptophan (an amino acid used in serotonin synthesis) has provided important data to the study of aggression. As noted above, tryptophan manipulation provides researchers with a systematic means of studying serotonin function in that levels can be directly altered by the experimenter. Studies using tryptophan depletion procedures to reduce serotonin activity have found increases in negative moods. Cleare and Bond (1995) found that males who displayed high trait aggression on the BDHI displayed increases in self-reported measures of anger, aggression, hostility, and annoyance following a tryptophan depletion drink, but improved mood scores following a tryptophan supplement drink. Subjects with low trait aggression showed no changes after either drink. Other studies found increases in irritable and hostile mood in normal, healthy males following tryptophan depletion (Smith et al., 1987; Young et al., 1985).

Importantly, following a tryptophan supplementation, aggressive schizophrenics showed a 30 percent reduction in aggression-related items on a psychiatric checklist (Young et al., 1988). Such results may have implication for treatment.

Under direct laboratory measures of aggressive responding, tryptophan depletion procedures have also produced increases in aggressive responding. In the Taylor Competitive Reaction Time Task, subjects delivered higher shock intensities following tryptophan depletion versus trytophan supplementation (Pihl et al., 1995). This same study also found increased aggression following administration of alcohol and joint administration of alcohol and tryptophan depletion, leading the authors to suggest that low serotonin levels in the CNS may make individuals particularly susceptible to alcohol induced violence. Tryptophan depletion was associated with increases in aggressive responding on the Point Subtraction Aggression Paradigm (Moeller et al., 1996). This study has recently been replicated showing increased aggression following tryptophan depletion, but not after tryptophan supplementation or diet restriction (Bjork et al., 1999).

Current Work

Current work in our laboratory lends support to the general conclusion of previous studies, that serotonin function is related to aggressive behavior. Three aspects of our experimental approach strengthen these conclusions: (1) subject populations (male and female parolees) present a variety of criminal histories (including violent offenses); (2) the procedures employ direct manipulation of the serotonin system; and (3) the procedures use objective laboratory measurement of aggressive behavior (the PSAP task). In a series of experiments, male and female parolees were divided by their criminal history into a violent group (assault, aggravated assault, aggravated robbery) and a nonviolent group (drug possession, forgery, auto theft). A series of experiments demonstrated that the violent history subjects were significantly more aggressive than those with a nonviolent history, as measured by number of aggressive responses on the PSAP.

These data are shown in the top panel of Figure 5.1. In a subsequent experiment, serotonin activity in these same subjects was measured through a neuroendocrine challenge procedure. These subjects received a 0.4 mg/kg dose of buspirone at 9:30 a.m. Buspirone is an antianxiety drug that affects both serotonin and dopamine neurotransmitters. Its activity in the CNS can be estimated through the measurement of prolactin release into the blood stream. Blood draws taken throughout the day recorded serum prolactin levels. The middle panel of Figure 5.2 shows that prolactin release was severely reduced in subjects with a history of violent offenses, suggesting diminished CNS serotonin activity in violent offenders who exhibited more aggressive behavior on the PSAP task.

These results were extended in an ongoing experiment in which the effects of stimulating serotonin activity on aggression were investigated by administering two related drugs. To date, two subjects received doses of placebo and 0.2, 0.4, and 0.85 mg/kg of d,l-fenfluramine, which stimulates the release of both serotonin and dopamine in the CNS (Rowland & Carlton, 1986). Two additional subjects received doses of placebo and 0.1, 0.2, and 0.4 mg/kg of d-fenfluramine, which—in constrast to the d,l-isomer—is selective in its effect on serotonin release. Each dose was administered at approxi-

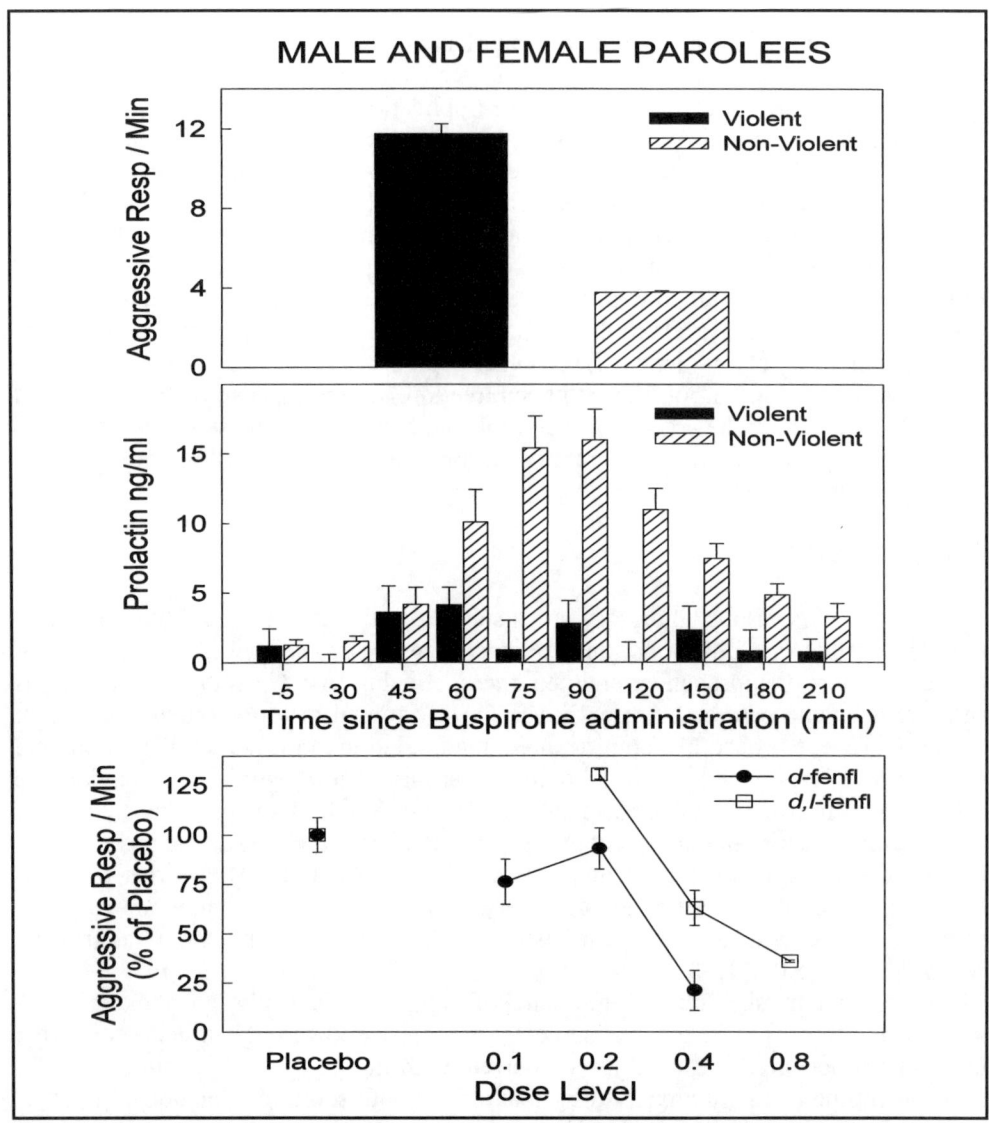

Figure 5.1. Aggressive Responses in Violent Vs. Nonviolent Offenders. The upper panel shows the behavioral responses of violent (■) and nonviolent (▨) male and female parolees (N=60) on the © PSAP task (Cherek, 1981). The Y axis shows the average number of aggressive responses per minute. The middle panel shows the biological response to neuroendocrine challenge with buspirone in violent (■) and nonviolent (▨) male and female parolees (N=48). The Y axis shows the release of prolactin following buspirone administration as a percent of prolactin release on a control day (placebo administration), as measured via blood plasma levels across ten time points. The bottom panel shows the number of aggressive responses on the PSAP task following placebo and three doses of d-fenfluramine (•) and d,l-fenfluramine (□). The Y axis shows aggressive responses per minute as percent of placebo responses.

mately thirty minutes before the first PSAP session of the day, and data were obtained on aggressive responding throughout the remainder of the experimental day (four twenty-five minute sessions). Data for these four subjects are shown in the bottom panel of Figure 5.1. While these data are preliminary, they suggest that, for both drugs and all four subjects, aggressive responding was decreased at high doses.

One collective (albeit tentative) interpretation of this series of studies is that:

- Individuals with violent behavioral histories can be identified as aggressive under laboratory conditions;
- The aggressive behavior is related to diminished serotonin activity; and
- Stimulation of serotonin (or serotonin plus dopamine) produces decreases in aggressive responding.

This interpretation is consistent with the existing literature relating aggression to serotonin function. It should be noted here that causally implicating a single neurotransmitter in a form of behavior as complex and multiply-caused as aggression is an oversimplification, but one which nonetheless provides meaningful scientific information to those interested in its prediction and control.

DEFINITION AND MEASUREMENT OF IMPULSIVITY

Aggressive behavior, especially in the form of human violence, is an acutely salient act that attracts substantial public and political attention. In many contexts, though, aggression can be considered as a type of impulsive behavior. Impulsive behavior may actually take many forms (theft, arson, risky sex and drug use, pathological gambling) that collectively represent larger public health and criminal justice problems than aggression alone. However, measurement and precise definition of impulsive behavior have received less scientific attention than aggression.

Definitions of impulsivity are numerous but closely related. They include a tendency to act hastily without reflection (Barratt & Patton, 1983; Murray, 1938), dysfunctional information-processing (Barkley, 1997; Dickman, 1990), a tendency for risk taking (Barratt & Patton, 1983; Plutchik & Van Praag, 1995), and an inability to sustain attention (Douglas, 1972). While such definitions are clinically useful, they present difficulties in objective measurement. Such difficulties may be overcome by defining impulsivity as a choice (preference) for a less valuable but more immediately available reward over a more valuable reward that is only available after some longer period of time (Ainslie, 1975; Mischel et al., 1989; Logue, 1995; Rachlin & Green, 1972). As an example, consider the chronic drug user who chooses to spend money purchasing drugs on a daily basis rather than to save to pay for housing or food, or the habitual thief who chooses burglary over legal employment. The definition allows for inclusion of many of the theoretical components of impulsivity and also lends well to objective laboratory measurement in which impulsive behavior can be operationally defined.

Rating Scales

Measurement of impulsivity involves both rating scales and laboratory procedures. Many questionnaires exist that either focus specifically on impulsiveness or contain subscales aimed at measuring some dimension of impulsivity. Scales such as the Barratt Impulsiveness Scale, 11th ed. (BIS 11) (Patton et al., 1995), the Eysenck Impulsivity and Venturesomeness Scale (EIVQ) (Eysenck et al., 1985), and the Impulse Control Scale (Plutchik & Van Praag, 1989) concentrate primarily on impulsivity. Other standardized scales such as the Eysenck Extroversion Scale (Eysenck & Eysenck, 1978), the Emotions Profile Index (Plutchik & Kellerman, 1974), the Tridimensional Personality Profile (Cloninger, 1987), and the Wender Utah Rating Scale (Ward et al., 1993) include subscales designed to measure impulsive traits or tendencies. Questionnaires and personality inventories generally treat impulsivity as a personality dimension or attribute, which implies a static, consistent behavioral characteristic. These instruments provide descriptive, diagnostic, and clinical utility.

Laboratory Measurements

Laboratory measures of impulsivity offer researchers several benefits. Like aggression, impulsivity may be difficult to identify and measure in naturalistic settings. Laboratory procedures provide precision and control in manipulating independent variables related to impulsive behavior (including drug effects and other biological manipulations). Further, they provide an operational definition under which impulsive behavior can be plainly identified. One such laboratory procedure is the "go, no-go" task (see Harrison, 1991). In the most common version of this task, subjects learn to respond to certain stimuli (S+, reward) and not others (S-, non-reward or punishment). Then subjects are rapidly presented with both types of stimuli over successive trials. Impulsivity is measured as the frequency of responses and the reaction time in the presence of S- stimuli.

Another procedure involves the use of a differential reinforcement of low rate (DRL) reinforcement schedule (Morse, 1966). In this schedule, subjects are required to wait a given amount of time (N-seconds) before making a specified response. As long as time N-seconds passes between responses, each response produces a reward. Any response less than N results in a resetting of the time, and an additional N-seconds must pass before a response is rewarded. A third procedure is based directly on an operational definition of impulsivity. In this task, subjects are given a choice between a small reward, available immediately or after some short delay, and a larger reward available after a longer delay. Impulsive behavior is defined as the choice of the smaller, immediately available option. For example, a subject may have two choices: selecting choice A provides a $0.05 reward after five seconds and choice B provides $0.15 after fifteen seconds. This task has been extensively used in both human and nonhuman studies of impulsive behavior (see Logue, 1995).

A number of studies have documented a relationship between laboratory-based or psychometric measures of impulsivity and impulsive tendencies in natural settings. Behavioral and psychometric-based studies reveal a relationship between high impulsivity and subsequent delinquent behavior (Mischel, 1989; White et al., 1994). Psychometric ratings of impulsivity show significant correlations with risk for violent and other antisocial behavior (Mealey, 1995; Plutchik et al., 1989). Inmates meeting criteria for antisocial personality disorder (APD) scored significantly higher on the BIS-11 than noninmates without APD (Barratt et al., 1997). In the go, no-go task, diagnosed psychopaths made more responses in the presence of S-(punishment) cues than controls, suggesting a deficiency in withholding responding—a mark of impulsivity (Newman et al., 1990; 1992). Individuals with long drug abuse histories did significantly poorer than non-drug users on a DRL task requiring them to wait at least seconds between responses following an immediate history of high-rate responding (Lane et al., 1998). Among violent and nonviolent parolees, those with a history of violent offenses made significantly more impulsive choices on a small, short-delay versus a large, long-delay impulsivity task (Cherek et al., 1997; Cherek & Lane, in press). Importantly, these data are backed by current theories in criminology which submit that impulsivity may be the primary factor involved in criminal behavior (Gottfredson & Hirschi, 1990).

BIOLOGICAL STUDIES OF IMPULSIVITY

Relation of Lowered Serotonin to Impulsivity

Aggressive behavior occurring in certain contexts can be considered a type of impulsivity, and thus it follows that a major biological variable implicated in impulsive behavior is the neurotransmitter serotonin, or 5-HT. Deficiencies in serotonin function have been associated with several types of impulsive behavior, including several psychiatric disorders marked by symptoms of lack of impulse control (e.g., APD, drug abuse, pathological arson, and gambling). This relationship has been documented in both animal and human studies. In a free ranging population of monkeys, low CSF 5-HIAA was correlated with bouts of impulsive aggression and impulsive risk taking, measured by reaction time, height, and length of jumps in trees (Mehlman, 1994). Rats with lesions to the septum (a procedure that damages brain regions thought to regulate emotion and inhibition of behavior) were behaviorally impaired on tasks requiring delay of gratification or a wait for a reward (Newman et al., 1983). Septal lesions in rats also impaired performance on DRL tasks that require waiting between responses (Ellen et al., 1964) and increased impulsive responding in a version of the go, no-go task (McCleary, 1966). Administration of drugs that block CNS serotonin activity increased impulsive responding on the DRL task, while drugs that stimulate serotonin activity decreased impulsive responding on the same task (Marek et al., 1990). In the small reward, short-delay versus large reward, long-delay task, the frequency of impulsive choices was increased by administration of the stimulant drug d-amphetamine, and decreased by the antianxiety drug diazepam (Valium) (Evenden & Ryan, 1996).

The existing research regarding the biology of impulsive behavior in humans is not extensive, but findings from nonhuman studies are consistent with data collected on human subjects. Individuals with psychiatrically defined impulse control disorders revealed abnormal serotonin functioning (Stein et al., 1993; 1996). Incarcerated, impulsive fire setters and individuals with intermittent explosive personality disorder were found to have lower CFS 5-HIAA concentrations than nonimpulsive offenders and controls (Virkkunen et al., 1989). Linnoila et al. (1983) report that CFS 5-HIAA levels were significantly reduced in violent offenders only when violent acts were of an impulsive nature rather than premeditated. In a study using the neuroendocrine challenge procedure and targeting the serotonin system with the drug *d,l*-fenfluramine, hormone release (a measure of serotonin activity) was correlated with scores on the Barratt Impulsivity Scale, and predicted 47 percent of the variance in impulsivity scores (Fishbein et al., 1989). Relatedly, treatment with the drug fluoxetine (Prozac, which increases serotonin levels) reduced symptoms in patients with kleptomania and bulimia nervosa (McElroy et al., 1989).

Laboratory Measurements

Few studies have examined highly impulsive subjects with criminal histories under laboratory-based conditions (but see Patterson & Newman, 1993). In a series of experiments in our laboratory, Cherek et al. investigated impulsive behavior in these individuals and subsequently examined biological factors that may be involved. The approach taken in these studies mirrors that used to investigate aggressive behavior as described earlier and depicted in Figure 5.1. In the impulsivity experiments, we again divided male and female parolees into violent and nonviolent groups based on their criminal history. An initial study used the small reward, short-delay versus large reward, long-delay task in which subjects were provided with two response options: (*a*) $0.05 available after a five-second delay (defined as an impulsive choice) or (*b*) $0.15 available after a delay that began at fifteen seconds and incremented by two seconds each time that option was selected (defined as nonimpulsive) and decreased by two seconds each time option *a* was selected, down to a lower limit of seven seconds.

Experimental sessions lasted sixty trials, meaning that subjects who selected option *b* on each trial would have to wait as long as 133 seconds before obtaining the $0.15 reward. These data, depicted in the top panel of Figure 5.2, reveal that parolees with a history of violent offenses made significantly more impulsive choices than those who committed nonviolent offenses.

These subjects also participated in the neuroendocrine challenge procedure (identical to that described earlier for the aggression experiments) using the drug buspirone to measure serotonin response in the CNS. In this study, we obtained the serotonin response (as measured by prolactin release into the body) of the fifteen most impulsive and fifteen least impulsive subjects. The middle panel of Figure 5.2 indicates that subjects who made the most impulsive choices on the laboratory task had a significantly blunted prolactin response compared to those who made the least number of impulsive choices. These data are supported by a third study that involved five male subjects who met psychiatric criteria for conduct disorder (CD+) and five male control subjects (CD-). Impulsive responding was measured using the same short- versus long-delay laboratory procedure described above. In addition, the drug *d,l*-fenfluramine, which stimulates the release of serotonin in the CNS, was administered to all subjects in three doses (0.212, 0.425, 0.85 mg/kg), along with placebo. The drug was administered in the morning, and response on the impulsivity task was then measured throughout the day. The bottom panel of Figure 5.2 reveals two important findings. First, during baseline (pre-drug) conditions, CD+ subjects made more impulsive choices than controls. Second, the number of impulsive choices made by CD+ subjects was significantly reduced in a dose-dependent manner by the administration of *d,l*-fenfluramine. No changes occurred in the behavior of control subjects.

Collectively, these studies imply conclusions similar to the aggression experiments completed in our laboratory—specifically, that:

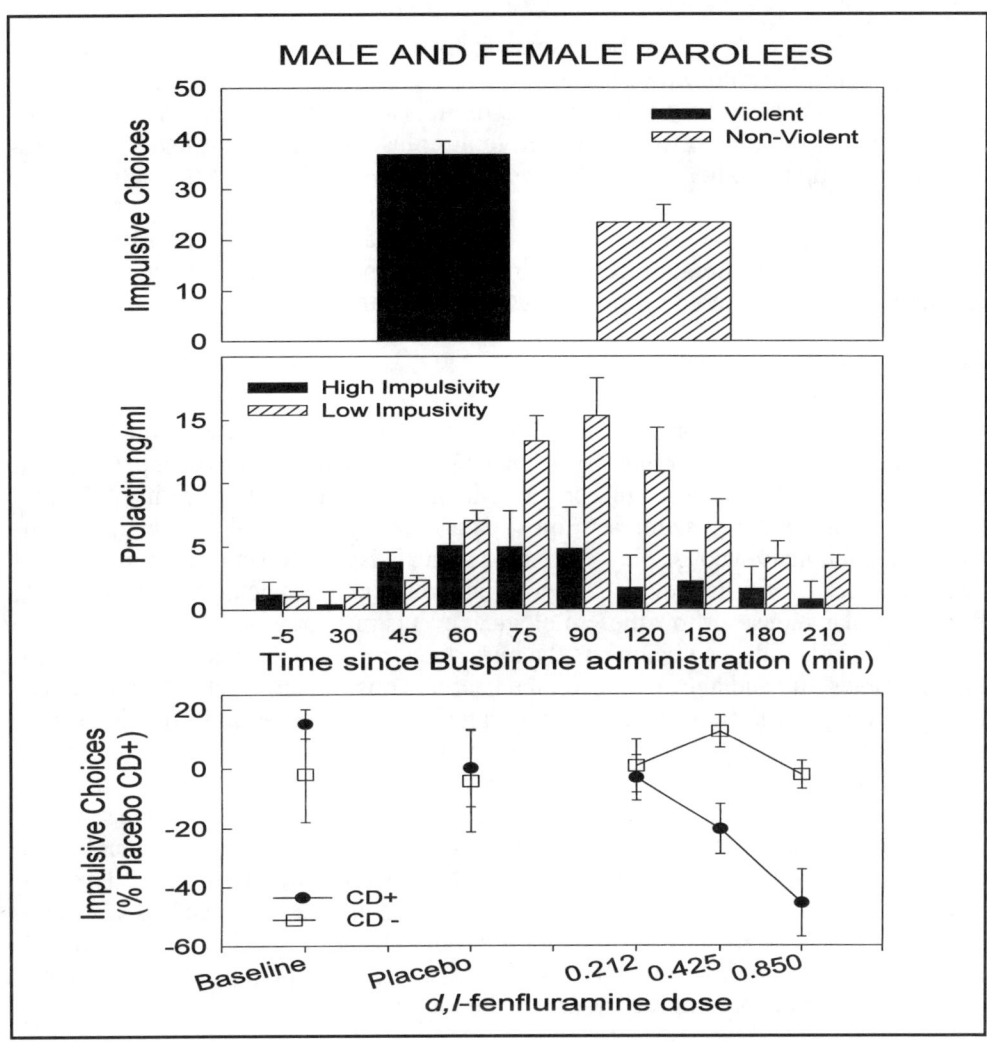

Figure 5.2. Impulsive Responses in Violent Vs. Nonviolent Offenders. The upper panel shows the behavioral responses of violent (■) and nonviolent (▨) male and female parolees on the short-delay, small reward versus long-delay, large reward task. The Y axis shows the average number of impulsive choices per session. The middle panel shows the biological response to neuroendocrine challenge with buspirone in the fifteen most impulsive (■) and fifteen least impulsive subjects (▨) from the upper panel. The Y axis shows the release of prolactin following buspirone administration as a percent of prolactin release on a control day (placebo administration), as measured via blood plasma levels of prolactin across ten time points. The bottom panel shows the number of impulsive choices on the short-delay, small reward versus long-delay, large reward task at baseline, and following placebo and three doses of d,l-fenfluramine in males (N=10) with conduct disorder (•) and without conduct disorder (□). The Y axis shows impulsive choices as a percent of impulsive choices under placebo in subjects with conduct disorder.

- Individuals with violent behavioral histories can be operationally defined as impulsive using laboratory procedures;
- This impulsive behavior is related to diminished serotonin activity; and
- Stimulation of serotonin (or serotonin plus dopamine) systems produces decreases in impulsive behavior in individuals with lowered serotonin function.

While human laboratory data is limited, this explanation of our results is consistent with the current literature relating impulsivity, impulsive aggression, and other criminal activity to lowered serotonin levels in the brain.

CONCLUSIONS

Data from the behavioral and health sciences and from our own laboratory indicate that aggressive and impulsive behavior can be clearly defined and measured under laboratory conditions. Further, there is strong evidence implicating the serotonin neurotransmitter system, with most data indicating that it is somehow diminished in individuals who display extreme and maladaptive forms of impulsive and aggressive behavior. It is, however, appropriate to temper these claims and to provide feasible explanations for how these biological events may arise.

Substantial evidence documents the importance of the serotonin system in pathological impulsivity and aggression, yet the neurochemistry is not well understood. For example, many neurotransmitter systems, including dopamine and norepinephrine, interact with, and in some cases modulate, serotonin function. The influence of these other neurotransmitter systems on aggressive and impulsive behavior may be direct or indirect, and their relationship to serotonin function demands more extensive study. At this point, the strongest conclusions that can be made are that in individuals with extreme aggressive or impulsive behavioral histories, (1) there are lower levels of extant serotonin in the CNS and (2) neurochemical challenges produce less serotonin-related hormonal activity. How and why serotonin levels are lower in these individuals is not known, and this situation creates at least one inherent danger in how the scientific and general communities treat the phenomenon.

Possible Genetic Links

Because many biological systems are modulated by chemical events in the cell nucleus and thus are regulated by genetic coding, one possible interpretation is that aggression and impulsivity are genetically determined and that extreme forms result from genetic aberration (see Mealey, 1995). Given the currently limited understanding of the interplay between biology, aggression, and impulsivity, it would be premature to assume this state of affairs. Perhaps even more significant are the effects of behavioral history and social context. Several studies have established that the consequences for aggressive and impulsive behavior have a major influence on the probability of future aggression and impulsivity. Moreover, changes in serotonin and other significant biochemical systems have been shown to occur in monkeys following changes in successful aggressive activity and ascent in social order (Raleigh et al., 1984), and in mice following repeated defeats in aggressive interactions (Tidey & Miczek, 1996).

Environmental Factors

Environmental factors may result in alterations of behavioral and biological function and thus play a role in resultant pathology. Individuals living in chaotic and unpredictable environments may become more impulsive as a necessary adaptation. Impulsive behavior has utility in an environment in which the availability of long-term rewards is highly variable. Several environmental variables are also known to effect serotonin levels. At least two of these, poor nutrition and head injury, could increase the probability of aggressive and impulsive behavior. It has been well documented that diet has a significant influence on serotonin activity (Fernstrom, 1993; Jacobs & Azmitia, 1992), thus poor nutrition could conceivably lead to lowered serotonin function, increasing the risk for impulsivity and aggression. Further, poor nutrition may create states of deprivation (hunger, sleep disruptions) that effect the likelihood of aggression and impulsivity. To our knowledge, no systematic studies have investigated the contribution of nutrition to aggressive or impulsive behavior. Individuals living in certain environments are also at increased risk for head injury, and head trauma is known to disrupt behavioral and biological functions, creating problems in behavioral self-control (Miller, 1990). These suppositions underscore the importance of focusing research efforts on the interaction of environmental and biological factors. Understanding the interaction of these factors is critically important to the prediction and control of aggression and impulsivity.

Editor's Note

While responses to the drugs described herein reflect experimental conditions and are evoked for research purposes, drugs that stimulate serotonin activity have been shown to be effective in reducing impulsivity and aggressiveness in clinical settings. Pharmacological approaches to treatment intervention, otherwise known as pharmacotherapy, are increasingly used in clinical settings for the modification of behaviors often associated with crime and violence. Several studies provide support for the notion that pharmacotherapy, when combined with conventional psychosocial treatments, produces more favorable treatment outcomes than traditional therapies alone or simple incarceration (Kristiansson, 1995).

While no medications are approved by the Food and Drug Administration specifically for criminal or antisocial behavior, several drugs have been approved for use for patients with behavioral and personality disorders related to criminality (e.g., violence, drug abuse, impulsivity, negative affect, and angry temperament) with significant success (i.e., by improving the disordered behavior of individuals who attract the attention of the criminal justice system) (Nemeroff, 1995). Pharmacologic treatment of certain offenders is predicated on research which finds that violence and aggression, drug addiction, and other excessive and compulsive behaviors are often present in those with underlying disorders of the brain. Medication in these cases may lead to behavioral improvements by stabilizing a neurochemical imbalance or physiological disturbance that would otherwise increase risk for offending behaviors. As a result, the individual becomes more in control of his or her own behavior, minimizing the need for external controls.

Several medications are preferred in the treatment of aggression due to their specific effects on brain processes implicated in aggression and its associated attention deficits and negative mood states. Because a large body of evidence shows that diminished serotonin function in the brain is linked to aggressive behavior, treatments that increase serotonin activity are often used to reduce aggression and impulsivity (Fuller, 1996). Attention deficit hyperactivity disorder (ADHD), which is known to involve neurotransmitter activity and other biologic conditions, is prevalent in the childhood histories of individuals with antisocial behavioral patterns. Various medications with stimulant properties have been used successfully in adult individuals having childhood ADHD to decrease anxiety, impulsiveness, and other untoward symptoms that tend to be otherwise resistant to treatment (Dulcan et al., 1995; Ratey et al., 1991).

While in the past neuroleptics and benzodiazepines have been used extensively to treat aggressiveness, they have grave side effects and unpredictable results. Instead, current approaches with psychiatric patients who exhibit extreme aggressiveness and explosive personality disorders include beta-blockers that have consistently proven to be safer and more effective in enhancing self-control (Ratey et al., 1992; Ratey & Gordon, 1993). Also, a combination of pharmacotherapy and cognitive behavior therapy has shown promising results in psychopathic, criminal men generally considered to be "incurable" (Kristiansson, 1995). Medications are obviously expected to have more efficacy in syndromes that are biologic in origin. Even disorders with social origins, such as histories of severe childhood trauma, may respond to a serotonin agonist given the effects of extreme, chronic stress on the serotonin system (Corrigan et al., 1992; Higley et al., 1991).

Notwithstanding these findings, pharmacotherapy should never be considered in isolation of other approaches. It is critical that a complete assessment be conducted in each individual to determine the underlying generators of the behavioral problem before a treatment can be considered. Situational and circumstantial information must be collected to determine whether the sources of the problem can be ameliorated with lifestyle changes, social skills training, or counseling. Carefully planned manipulations of environmental conditions and insulation from prevalent risk factors can alter behavior via effects on neurotransmitter systems. Pharmacotherapy should only be employed when there is clear evidence and justification for its utility. And even then, it should be accompanied by supportive counseling and other indicated services—no individual should receive only medication when a complex behavioral problem exists. Because antisocial behavior, violence, and substance abuse involve multidimensional manifestations and causes, a comprehensive approach to treatment must be used. As stated previously, research shows that pharmacotherapy is an effective approach when used in combination with other forms of therapy.

References

Ainslie, G. (1975). Specious reward: A behavioral theory of impulsiveness and impulse control. *Psychological Bulletin, 82,* 463–496.

American Psychiatric Association (1994). *Diagnostic and statistical manual of mental disorders* (4th ed.). Washington, DC: American Psychiatric Press.

Åsberg, M., Schalling, D., Träksman-Bendz, L. & Wägner, A. (1987). Psychobiology of suicide, impulsivity, and related phenomenon. In H. Y. Meltzer (Ed.), *Psychopharmacology: The third generation of progress.* New York: Raven, 655–668.

Barkley, R. A. (1997). Behavioral inhibition, sustained attention, and executive functions: Constructing a unifying theory of ADHD. *Psychological Bulletin, 121,* 65–94.

Baron, R. A. & Richardson, D. R. (1994). *Human aggression* (2d ed). New York: Plenum Press.

Barratt, E. S. & Patton, J. H. (1983). Impulsivity: Cognitive, behavioral, and psychophysiological correlates. In M. Zuckerman (Ed.), *Biological bases of sensation seeking, impulsivity and anxiety.* Hillsdale, NJ: Erlbaum, 77–116.

Barratt, E. S., Stanford, M. S., Kent, T. A. & Felthous, A. (1997). Neuropsychological and cognitive psychophysical substrates of impulsive aggression. *Biological Psychiatry, 41,* 1045–1061.

Bech, P. & Mak, M. (1995). Measurements of impulsivity and aggression. In E. Hollander & D. J. Stein (Eds.), *Impulsivity and aggression.* New York: John Wiley & Sons, 25–42.

Bjork, J. M., Dougherty, D. M., Moeller, F. G., Cherek, D. R. & Swann, A. C. (1999). The effects of tryptophan depletion and loading on laboratory aggression in men: Time course and a food restricted control. *Psychopharmacology, 142,* 24–30.

Bloom, F. E. (1996). Neurotransmission and the central nervous system. In L. S. Goodman & L. E. Limbird (Eds.), *Goodman and Gilman's the pharmacological basis of therapeutics* (9th ed.). New York: McGraw-Hill, 267–293.

Brown, G. L., Goodwin, F. K., Ballenger, J. C., Goyer, P. F. & Major, L. F. (1979). Aggression in humans correlates with cerebrospinal fluid amine metabolites. *Psychiatry Research, 1,* 131–139.

Buss, A. H. (1961). The psychology of aggression. New York: John Wiley & Sons.

Buss, A. H. & Durkee, A. (1957). An inventory for assessing different kinds of hostility. *Journal of Consulting and Clinical Psychology, 21,* 343–349.

Buss, A. H. & Perry, M. (1992). The aggression questionnaire. *Journal of Personality and Social Psychology, 63,* 452–459.

Carlson, N. R. (1991). *Physiology of behavior* (4th ed). Boston: Allyn & Bacon.

Cherek, D. R. (1981). Effects of smoking different doses of nicotine on human aggressive behavior. *Psychopharmacology, 75,* 339–349.

Cherek, D. R. & Lane, S. D. (in press). Laboratory and psychometric measurements of impulsivity among female parolees with violent or nonviolent histories. *Biological Psychiatry.*

Cherek, D. R., Lane, S. D. & White, S. (in press). Laboratory and self-report measures of aggression among female parolees with violent or nonviolent histories. *Aggressive Behavior.*

Cherek, D. R., Moeller, F. G., Schnapp, W. & Dougherty, D. M. (1997). Studies of violent and nonviolent male parolees I. Laboratory and psychometric measurements of aggression. *Biological Psychiatry, 41,* 514–522.

Cherek, D. R., Schnapp, W., Moeller, F. G. & Dougherty, D.M. (1996). Laboratory measures of aggressive responding in male parolees with violent and nonviolent histories. *Aggressive Behavior, 22,* 27–36.

Cherek, D. R., Steinberg, J. L. & Manno, B. R. (1985). Effects of alcohol on human aggressive behavior. *Journal of Studies on Alcohol, 46,* 321–328.

Cleare, A. J. & Bond, A. J. (1995). The effect of tryptophan depletion and enhancement on subjective and behavioural aggression in normal male subjects. *Psychopharmacology, 118,* 72–81.

Cloninger, C. R. (1987). A systematic method for clinical description and classification of personality variants: A proposal. *Archives of General Psychiatry, 44,* 573–588.

Coccaro, E. F. & Astill, J. (1990). Central serotonergic function in parasuicide. *Progress in Neuro-Psychopharmacology and Biological Psychiatry, 14,* 663–674.

Coccaro, E. F., Kavoussi, R. J., Cooper, T. B. & Hauger, R. L. (1996). Hormonal responses to *d*- and *d,l*-fenfluramine in healthy human subjects. *Neuropsychopharmacology, 15,* 595–607.

Coccaro, E. F., Berman, M. E. & Kavoussi, R. J. (1997). Assessment of life-history of aggression: Development and psychometric characteristics. *Psychiatry Research , 73,* 147–157.

Coccaro, E. F., Siever, L. J., Klar, H. M., Maurer, G., Cochrane, K. Cooper, T. B., Mohs, R. C. & Davis, K. L. (1989). Serotonergic studies in patients with affective and personality disorders. *Archives of General Psychiatry, 46,* 587–599.

Corrigan, M., Garbutt, J. C., Ekstrom, D. & Golden, R. N. (1992) Serotonergic function in trauma victims. *Biological Psychiatry, 31,* 12.

Daly, M. & Wilson, M. (1988). *Homicide.* Hawthorne, NY: Aldine de Gruyter.

Dawes, M. A., Tarter, R. E. & Kirisci, L. (1997). Behavioral self-regulation: Correlates and 2 year follow-ups for boys at risk for substance abuse. *Drug and Alcohol Dependence, 45,* 165–176.

Dickman, S. J. (1990). Functional and dysfunctional impulsivity: Personality and cognitive correlates. *Journal of Personality and Social Psychology, 58,* 95–102.

Douglas, V. (1972). Stop, look, and listen: The problem of sustained attention and impulse control in hyperactive and normal children. *Canadian Journal of Behavioral Science, 4,* 259–282.

Dulcan, M. K., Bregman, J. D., Weller, E. B. & Weller, R. A. (1995). Treatment of childhood and adolescent disorders. In C. Nemeroff (Ed.), *The American Psychiatric Association textbook of psychopharmacology.* Washington, DC: American Psychiatric Press.

Eichelman, B. S. (1990). Neurochemical and psychopharmacologic aspects of aggressive behavior. *Annual Review of Medicine, 41,* 149–158.

Ellen, P., Wilson, A. S. & Powell, E.W. (1964). Septal inhibition and timing behavior in the rat. *Journal of Comparative Neurology, 10,* 120–132.

Evenden, J. L. & Ryan, C. N. (1996). The pharmacology of impulsive behavior in rats: The effects of drugs on response choice with varying delays of reinforcement. *Psychopharmacology, 128,* 161–170.

Eysenck, S. B. & Eysenk, H. J. (1978). Impulsiveness and venturesomeness: Their position in a dimensional system of personality description. *Psychological Reports, 43,* 1247–1255.

Eysenck, S. B., Pearson, P. R., Easting, G. & Allsopp, J. F. (1985). Age norms for impulsiveness, venturesomeness and empathy in adults. *Personality & Individual Differences, 6,* 613–619.

Fernstrom, J. D. (1993). Role of precursor availability in control of monoamine biosynthesis in the brain. *Physiological Reviews, 63,* 484–546.

Fishbein, D. H., Lozovsky, D. & Jaffe, J. H. (1989). Impulsivity, aggression, and neuroendocrine responses to serotonergic stimulation in substance abusers. *Biological Psychiatry, 25,* 1049–1066.

Fuller, R. W. (1996). The influence of fluoxetine on aggressive behavior. *Neuropsychopharmacology, 14,* 77–81.

Giancola, P. R. & Chermack, S. T. (1998). Construct validity of laboratory aggression paradigms: A response to Tedeschi and Quigley (1996). *Aggression and Violent Behavior, 3,* 237–253.

Giancola, P. R. & Zeichner, A. (1995a). Construct validity of a competitive reaction time aggression paradigm. *Aggressive Behavior, 21,* 199–204.

Giancola, P. R. & Zeichner, A. (1995b). An investigation of gender differences in alcohol-related aggression. *Journal of Studies on Alcohol, 56,* 573–579.

Gibbons, J. L., Barr, G. A. & Bridger, W. H. (1978). Effects of *para*-chlorophenylalanine and 5-hydroxytryptophan on mouse killing behavior in killer rats. *Pharmacology, Biochemistry & Behavior, 9,* 91–98.

Gottfredson, M. R. & Hirschi, T. (1990). *A general theory of crime.* Palo Alto, CA: Stanford University Press.

Harrison, J. M. (1991). Stimulus control. In I. H. Iversen & K. A. Lattal (Eds.), *Experimental analysis of behavior.* Amsterdam: Elsevier.

Higley, J. D., Suomi, S. J. & Linnoila, M. (1991). CSF monoamine metabolite concentrations vary according to age, rearing and sex, and are influenced by the stressor of social separation in rhesus monkeys. *Psychopharmacology, 103,* 551–556.

Jacobs, B. L. & Azmitia, E. C. (1992). Structure and function of the brain serotonin system. *Physiological Reviews, 72,* 165–229.

Kantak, K. M., Hegstrand, L. R. & Eichelman, B. (1981). Dietary tryptophan reversal of septal lesions and 5,7-DHT lesion elicited shock-induced fighting. *Pharamcology, Biochemistry & Behavior, 15,* 343–350.

Koop, C. E. & Lundberg, G. D. (1992). Violence in America: A public health emergency. Time to bite the bullet back. *Journal of the American Medical Association, 267,* 3048–3053.

Kristiansson, M. (1995). Incurable psychopaths? *Bulletin of the American Academy of Psychiatry and Law, 23,* 555–562.

Lane, S. D., Cherek, D. R., Dougherty, D. M. & Moeller, F. G. (1998). Laboratory measurement of adaptive behavior change in humans with a history of substance dependence. *Drug and Alcohol Dependence, 51,* 239–252.

Linnoila, M., Virkkunen, M., Scheinin, M., Nuutila, A., Rimon, R. & Goodwin, F. K. (1983). Low cerebrospinal fluid 5-hydroxyindolacetic acid concentration differentiates impulsive from nonimpulsive violent behavior. *Life Sciences, 33,* 2609–2614.

Logue, A. W. (1995). *Self-control.* Englewood Cliffs, NJ: Prentice-Hall.

MacDonnell, M. F. & Flynn, J. P. (1966). Control of sensory fields by stimulation of hypothalamus. *Science, 152,* 1406–1408.

Marek, G. J., Li, A. A. & Seiden, L. S. (1990). Evidence for involvement of 5-hydroxytryptamine[1] receptors in antidepressant-like drug effects on differential reinforcement of low-rate 72-second schedule. *Journal of Pharmacology & Experimental Therapeutics, 250,* 60–71.

Martin, C. S., Earleywine, M., Blackson, T. C., Vanyukov, M. M., Moss, H. B. & Tarter, R. E. (1994). Aggression, inattention, hyperactivity, and impulsivity in boys at high and low risk for substance abuse. *Journal of Abnormal Child Psychology, 22,* 177–203.

McCleary, R. A. (1966). Response modulating function of the limbic system: Initiation and suppression. In E. Stellar & J. M. Sprague (Eds.), *Progress in physiological psychology,* vol. 1. San Diego, CA: Academic Press, 209–271.

McElroy, S. L., Keck, P. E., Pope, H. G. & Hudson, J. I. (1989). Pharmacological treatment of kleptomania and bulimia nervosa. *Journal of Clinical Psychopharmacology, 9,* 358–360.

McGuire, M. T. & Raleigh, M. J. (1987). Serotonin, social behavior, and aggression in vervet monkeys. In B. Oliver, J. Mos & P. F. Brain (Eds.), *Ethopharmacology of agonistic behavior in animals and humans.* Boston: Martinus Nijhoff, 207–222.

Mealey, L. (1995). The sociobiology of sociopathy: An integrated evolutionary model. *Behavioral & Brain Sciences, 18,* 523–599.

Mehlman, P. T., Higley, J. D., Faucher, I., Lilly, A. A., Taub, D. M., Vickers, J., Suomi, S. J. & Linnoila, M. (1994). Low CSF 5-HIAA concentrations and severe aggression and impaired impulse control in nonhuman primates. *American Journal of Psychiatry, 151,* 1485–1491.

Miller, L. (1990). Major syndromes of aggressive behavior following head injury: An introduction to evaluation and treatment. *Cognitive Rehabilitation, 8,* 14–19.

Mischel, W., Shoda, Y. & Rodriguez, M. L. (1989). Delay of gratification in children. *Science, 244,* 933–938.

Modai, I., Apter, A., Meltzer, M., Tyano, S., Walevski, A. & Jerushalmy, Z. (1989). Serotonin uptake by platelets of suicidal and aggressive adolescent psychiatric inpatients. *Neuropsychobiology, 21,* 9–13.

Moeller, F. G., Dougherty, D. M., Lane, S. D. & Cherek, D. R. (1998). Antisocial personality disorder and alcohol induced aggression. *Alcoholism: Clinical and Experimental Research, 22,* 1898–1902.

Moeller, F. G., Dougherty, D. M., Swann, A. C., Collins, D., Davis, C. M. & Cherek, D. R. (1996). Tryptophan depletion and aggressive responding in healthy males. *Psychopharmacology, 126,* 97–103.

Moffitt, T. E. (1993). Adolescence-limited and life-course-persistent antisocial behavior: A developmental taxonomy. *Psychological Review, 100,* 674–701.

Morse, W. H. (1966). Intermittent reinforcement. In W. K. Honig (Ed.), *Operant behavior: Areas of research and application.* New York: Appleton-Century-Crofts, 52–108.

Moss, H. B., Yao, J. K. & Panzak, G. L. (1990). Serotonergic responsivity and behavioural dimensions in antisocial personality disorder with substance abuse. *Biological Psychiatry, 28,* 325–338.

Murray, H. (1938). *Explorations in personality.* New York: Oxford University Press.

Nemeroff, C. (Ed.) (1995). *The American Psychiatric Association textbook of psychopharmacology.* Washington, DC: American Psychiatric Press.

Newman, J. P., Gorenstein, E. E. & Kelsey, J. E. (1983). Failure to delay gratification following septal lesions in rats: Implications for an animal model of disinhibitory psychopathology. *Personality and Individual Differences, 4,* 147–156.

Newman, J. P., Kosson, D. S. & Patterson, C. M. (1992). Delay of gratification in psychopathic and nonpsychopathic offenders. *Journal of Abnormal Psychology, 101,* 630–636.

Newman, J. P., Patterson, C. M., Howland, E. W. & Nichols, S. L. (1990). Passive avoidance in psychopaths: The effects of reward. *Personality and Individual Differences, 11,* 1101–1114.

O'Keane, V., Moloney, E., O'Neill, H., O'Connor A., Smith, C. & Dinan, T. (1992). Blunted prolactin response to d-fenfluramine in sociopathy. Evidence for subsensitivity of central serotonergic function. *British Journal of Psychiatry, 160,* 643–646.

Patterson, C. M. & Newman, J. P. (1993). Reflectivity and learning from aversive events: Toward a psychological mechanism for the syndromes of disinhibition. *Psychological Review, 100,* 716–736.

Patton, J. H., Stanford, M. S. & Barratt, E. S. (1995). Factor structure of the Barratt impulsiveness scale. *Journal of Clinical Psychology, 51,* 768–774.

Pihl, R. O., Young, S. N., Harden, P., Plotnik, S., Chamberlain, B. & Ervin, F. R. (1995). Acute effect of altered tryptophan levels and alcohol on aggression in normal human males. *Psychopharmacology, 119,* 353–360.

Plutchik, R. & Kellerman, H. (1974). Manual of the Emotions Profile Index. Los Angeles: Western Psychological Services.

Plutchik, R. & Van Praag, H. M. (1995). The nature of impulsivity: Definitions, ontology, genetics, and relations to aggression. In E. Hollander & D. Stein (Eds.), *Impulsivity and aggression.* New York: John Wiley & Sons, 7–24.

Plutchik, R. & Van Praag, H. M. (1989). The measurement of suicidality, aggresivity and impulsivity. *Progress in Neuro-psychopharmacology & Biological Psychiatry, 13,* 523–534.

Plutchik, R., Van Praag, H. M., Conte, H. R. & Picard, S. (1989). Correlates of suicide and violence risk: I. The suicide risk measure. *Comprehensive Psychiatry, 30,* 296–302.

Popova, N. K., Kulikov, A. V., Nikulina, E. M., Kozlachkova, E. Y. & Maslova, G. B. (1991). Serotonin metabolism and serotonergic receptors in Norway rats selected for low aggressiveness towards man. *Aggressive Behavior, 17,* 207–213.

Rachlin, H. & Green, L. (1972). Commitment, choice and self-control. *Journal of the Experimental Analysis of Behavior, 17,* 15–22.

Raleigh, M. J., McGuire, M. T., Brammer, G. L. & Yuwiler, A. (1984). Social and environmental influences on blood serotonin concentrations in monkeys. *Archives of General Psychiatry, 41,* 405–410.

Ratey, J. & Gordon, A. (1993). The psychopharmacology of aggression: Toward a new day. *Psychopharmacology Bulletin, 29,* 65–73.

Ratey, J., Greenberg, M. S. & Lindem, K. J. (1991). Combination of treatments for attention deficit hyperactivity disorder in adults. *Journal of Nervous and Mental Disorders, 179,* 699–701.

Ratey, J., Sorgi, P., O'Driscoll, G. A., Sands, S., Daehler, M. M. L., Fletcher, J. R., Kadish, W., Spruiell, G., Polakoff, S. & Lindem, K. J. (1992). Nadolol to treat aggression and psychiatric symptomatology in chronic psychiatric inpatients: A double-blind, placebo-controlled study. *Journal of Clinical Psychiatry, 53,* 41–46.

Richardson, D. R., Vandenberg, R. J. & Humphries, S. A. (1986). Effect of power to harm on retaliatory aggression among males and females. *Journal of Research in Personality, 20,* 402–419.

Robbins, L. E. (1995). The epidemiology of aggression. In E. Hollander & D. Stein (Eds.), *Impulsivity and aggression.* New York: John Wiley & Sons, 43–58.

Rowland, N. E. & Carlton, J. (1986). Neurobiology of an anorectic drug: fenfluramine. *Progress in Neurobiology, 27,* 13–62.

Smith, S., Pihl, R. O., Young, S. N. & Ervin, F. R. (1987). A test of possible cognitive and environmental influences on the mood lowering effect of tryptophan depletion in normal males. *Psychopharmacology, 91,* 451–457.

Sorgi, P., Ratey, J. J., Knoedler, D. W., Markert, R. J. & Reichman, M. (1991). Rating aggression in the clinical setting: A retrospective adaptation of the overt aggression scale. *Journal of Neuropsychiatry and Clinical Neurosciences, 3,* S52–S56.

Spielberger, C. D., Jacobs, G., Russell, S. & Crane, R. S. (1983). Assessment of anger: The state-trait anger scale. In J. N. Butcher & C. D. Spielberger (Eds.), *Advances in personality assessment,* vol. 2. Hillsdale, NJ: Erlbaum, 159–187.

Stein, D. J., Hollander, E. & Liebowitz, M. R. (1993). Neurobiology of impulsivity and the impulse control disorders. *Journal of Neuropsychiatry and Clinical Neuroscience, 5,* 9–17.

Stein, D. J., Trestman, R. L., Mitropoulou, V. & Coccaro, E. F. (1996). Impulsivity and serotonergic function in compulsive personality disorder. *Journal of Neuropsychiatry & Clinical Neurosciences, 8,* 393–398.

Stoff, D. M., Pastiempo, A. P., Yeung, J. H., Cooper, T. B., Bridger, W. H. & Rabinovich, H. (1992). Neuroendocrine responses to challenge with d,l-fenfluramine and aggression in disruptive behavior disorders of children and adolescents. *Psychiatry Research, 43,* 263–276.

Stoff, D. M., Pollock, L., Vitiello, B., Behar, D. & Bridger, W. H. (1987). Reduction of ^{3}H-imipramine binding sites on platelets of conduct disordered children. *Neuropsychopharmacology, 1,* 55–62.

Taylor, S. P. (1967). Aggressive behavior and physiological arousal as a function of provocation and the tendency to inhibit aggression. *Journal of Personality, 35,* 297–310.

Taylor, S. P. & Gammon, C. (1975). Effects of type and dose of alcohol on human physical aggression. *Journal of Personality & Social Psychology, 32,* 169–175.

Tidey, J. W. & Miczek, K. A. (1996). Social defeat stress selectively alters mesocorticolimbic dopamine release: An in vivo microdialysis study. *Brain Research, 721,* 140–149.

Van Praag, H. M. (1991). Serotonergic dysfunction and aggression control. *Psychological Medicine, 21,* 15–19.

Virkkunen, M., DeJong, J., Bartko, J. & Linnoila, M. (1989). Psychobiological concomitants of history of suicide attempts among violent offenders and impulsive fire setters. *Archives of General Psychiatry, 46,* 604–606.

Virkkunen, M., Nuutila, A., Goodwin, F. K. & Linnoila, M. (1987). Cerebrospinal fluid monoamine metabolite levels in male arsonists. *Archives of General Psychiatry, 44,* 241–247.

Ward, M. F., Wender, P. H. & Reimherr, F. W. (1993). The Wender Utah rating scale: An aid in the retrospective diagnosis of childhood attention deficit hyperactivity disorder. *American Journal of Psychiatry, 150,* 885–890.

White, J. L., Moffitt, T. E., Caspi, A., Bartusch, D. J., Needles, D. J. & Stouthamer-Loeber, M. (1994). Measuring impulsivity and examining its relationship to delinquency. *Journal of Abnormal Psychology, 103,* 192–205.

Wilcox, R. E. & Gonzales, R. A. (1995). Introduction to neurotransmitters, receptors, signal transduction, and second messengers. In A. F. Schatzberg & C. B. Nemeroff (Eds.), *Textbook of psychopharmacology.* Washington, DC: American Psychiatric Press, 3–29.

Wurtman, R. J., Hefti, F. & Melamed, E. (1981). Precursor control of neurotransmitter synthesis. *Pharmacology Review, 32,* 315–335.

Young, S. N., Pihl, R. O. & Ervin, F. R. (1988). The effect of altered tryptophan levels on mood and behavior in normal human males. *Clinical Neuropharmacology, 11,* S207–S215.

Young, S. N., Smith, S. E., Pihl, R. O. & Ervin, F. R. (1985). Tryptophan depletion causes a rapid lowering of mood in normal males. *Psychopharmacology, 87,* 173–177.

Yudofsky, S. C., Silver, J. M., Jackson, W., Endicott, J. & Williams, D. (1986). The overt aggression scale for the objective of verbal and physical aggression. *American Journal of Psychiatry, 143,* 35–39.

Zubieta, J. K. & Alessi, N. E. (1993). Is there a role of serotonin in the disruptive behavior disorders? A literature review. *Journal of Child & Adolescent Psychopharmacology, 3,* 11–35.

Chapter 6

Central Neurotransmitter Function in Criminal Aggression

by Emil F. Coccaro, M.D., Richard J. Kavoussi M.D., and Brian McNamee, M.D.

Introduction	6-2
The Many Faces of Aggression	6-2
Faulty Brakes: Serotonin Systems in Aggression	6-3
Impulsive Aggression	6-3
Abnormalities in the Serotonin Synapse	6-4
Stimulating Serotonin Activity: Pharmaco-Challenge Studies	6-5
Catecholamine Neurotransmitters: The Fuel for Behavior	6-6
Norepinephrine Activity	6-6
Dopamine Receptor Sensitivity	6-6
Other Biological Mediators in the Study of Impulsive Aggression	6-7
Glucose	6-7
Testosterone	6-7
Vasopressin Activity	6-7
Low Serum Cholesterol Levels	6-8
Genetic Vulnerabilities	6-8
Treatment Implications	6-9
Case Study	6-10
Conclusions	6-13
Genetic Influences	6-13
Environment	6-13

Significant portions of this chapter draw on Dr. Coccaro's article entitled "The Biology of Aggression" in *Scientific American: Science and Medicine*, 2, 38–47, and Drs. Coccaro and McNamee's chapter, "Biology of Aggression: Relevance to Crime" in *Psychopathology and Violent Crime* (ed. A. Skodol), APA Press, Washington, D.C., 1998.

INTRODUCTION

A review of the American Psychiatric Association's official psychiatric diagnostic criteria for mental and personality disorders (*Diagnostic and Statistical Manual of Mental Disorders*, or DSM) reveals that psychiatry offers few options in the classification of aggression. This is not surprising. With the exception of aggression arising in the context of psychosis, criminal aggression has not been thought to result from defective mental processes that fall within the rubric of psychiatric study and treatment. Instead, these acts have been thought of as volitional illegal acts unencumbered by aberrant mental or neurobiological processes.

Dealing with criminal aggression through standard psychiatric paradigms, however, is inherently unproductive. First, aggression is not a unitary concept. Aggression can be both premeditated and impulsive. Second, aggression occurs due to a combination of developmental, social, and economic factors. Third, little attention has been paid to the role of innate biological vulnerabilities to aggression. This third issue is extremely important and allows potentially for a paradigm shift in the study of selected criminal behavior in subsets of individuals. Temperament is a person's tendency to view and respond to his or her outer world in a specific and typical fashion. Temperament is dimensional and relatively specific (e.g., extraversion vs. introversion), significantly heritable, noticeable in very early life, and correlated with a variety of biological variables. Character, more complex by contrast, is the expression of a person's value system related to self and others (e.g., conscientiousness vs. non-conscientiousness). It is highly influenced by rearing environment and life experience and less by genetic and biological factors. Accordingly, it is possible that biogenetic temperaments, rather than complex nonbiogenetic character styles, associated with criminal acts could be productive objects for biological study and treatment as they relate to criminal behavior. If certain predisposing temperaments are associated with abnormalities of neurobiological function, it is possible that correction of these abnormalities will reduce or eliminate the potential for criminal behavior.

One reason for the dearth of knowledge about biological predispositions to aggression is the concern that the presence of biological factors will be used to excuse these behaviors, affecting jury verdicts and sentencing decisions. However, the presence of a biological predisposition does not exculpate the perpetrator of a crime. This is because the presence of such factors does not reduce the ability of an individual to understand the difference between right and wrong and the consequences of aggressive behavior. In fact, biologic studies of impulsive aggression have discovered some remarkably consistent evidence of at least some biological predispositions. In turn, these discoveries have led to promising potential treatments to reduce impulsive aggressive behavior. This chapter focuses on the evidence for such biologic predispositions to aggressive behavior. It reviews a case in which these issues arose in a forensic evaluation, and it discusses the implications of these findings in criminal settings.

THE MANY FACES OF AGGRESSION

Before a subject can be studied or discussed in depth, there must be definitions that are descriptive and meaningful. "Aggression" is not particularly descriptive and can refer to almost any hostile action any organism may engage in with any other organism. Aggression can be verbal, directed at inanimate objects, or directed at another living being.

In addition to these forms of assault, aggression can be categorized into a variety of subtypes based on motivating influences. For example, aggression may be called defensive, predatory, or impulsive. Defensive aggression is assaultive behavior that occurs in response to the presence of a real threat to oneself, or to individuals for whom one is responsible. One example of this is aggression in the service of preventing an attack upon oneself or one's family by an armed intruder. Another is the aggression among soldiers in warfare during battle. Aggression in these contexts is usually viewed as justifiable and is not prohibited by society's institutions.

Predatory and impulsive forms of aggression, however, are not considered justifiable by society. Individuals committing acts that fall into either of these two categories are usually held accountable, by society or by persons in the immediate environment. Predatory individuals select their victims and premeditate their attacks, much as an animal predator does with prey. The aggression is merely the instrument by which the aggressor obtains what he or she wants.

Impulsive aggression differs from predatory aggression in that it is not premeditated, but is triggered by the presence of a frustrating or irritating stimulus. There are usually signs of physiologic hyperarousal and anger during episodes of impulsive aggression. Individuals exhibiting affective aggression range from those who simply appear to have a bad temper to those who actually lose control in some circumstances.

Both predatory and impulsive aggression may lead to violent crimes. Studies documenting the prevalence of either of these types of aggression have not been performed among large segments of the criminal population. In general, most data support the idea that impulsive, violent criminal behavior has significant biological underpinnings that might lead to a rationale for pharmacological treatment. These data, as well as related data regarding impulsive aggression in noncriminal populations, are reviewed below.

FAULTY BRAKES: SEROTONIN SYSTEMS IN AGGRESSION

Impulsive Aggression

Most studies point to serotonin as one of the most important central neurotransmitters underlying the modulation of impulsive aggression. Animal studies conducted in the 1970s suggested that there might be an inverse relationship between the activity of the brain neurotransmitter serotonin and aggressive behavior in lower forms of mammals. Specifically, experimental manipulations that lowered brain levels of serotonin increased aggressive responding in various animal models of aggression. Conversely, manipulations that raised serotonin levels decreased aggressive responding. In addition, animals with low brain serotonin activity were aggressive only if an external noxious stimulus was present. Reduced serotonin makes many animal species hyperirritable, thereby lowering the threshold at which an aggressive response might be made. Increased serotonin appears to raise this threshold.

At the same time, psychiatric investigators were beginning to explore the relationship between brain serotonin and violent suicide. For example, depressed people who had attempted suicide were found to have low cerebrospinal fluid (CSF) levels of the major serotonin by-product, 5-hydroxyindolacetic acid (CSF 5-HIAA). The lowest levels were among those who had attempted suicide by violent means, or who had subsequently killed themselves (Åsberg et al., 1976). This finding has been one of the most replicated discoveries in all of biologic psychiatry.

Gregory Brown and colleagues at the National Institute of Mental Health in Bethesda published the first report proposing that CSF 5-HIAA levels were inversely related to a history of aggressive events in male navy recruits having a personality disorder (Brown et al., 1979). Brown found that subjects with a life history of suicide attempts also had low CSF 5-HIAA levels when compared to subjects without this history. In addition, suicidal subjects had greater life histories of aggression. Accordingly, Brown suggested that a threefold relationship existed between low serotonin activity, aggression, and suicidal behavior. Thus, serotonin activity was correlated with aggressive behavior irrespective of whether the behavior was directed at others or at self.

Markku Linnoila and colleagues at the National Institute of Alcohol Abuse and Alcoholism and the University of Helsinki reported similar results in a sample of violent offenders incarcerated in Finland (Linnoila et al., 1983). The importance of this work, however, lay not so much in replication of Åsberg's and Brown's data, but in the finding that low CSF 5-HIAA levels were characteristic of impulsive, rather than of predatory, violent offenders. "Impulsive" offenders (i.e., knew victim less than 24 hours and had no apparent plan) were significantly lower in 5-HIAA than violent offenders whose index crime was classified as "nonimpulsive" (i.e., knew the victim and planned out the crime). These data suggested that reduced serotonin activity was characteristic of "impulsive" aggression rather than premeditated aggression.

Strong support was found for the hypothesis that "impulsiveness" is the key behavioral correlate of reduced serotonin. Virkkunen et al. (1987) reported that lumbar CSF 5-HIAA concentrations of "impulsive" arsonists were reduced to about the same degree as in "impulsive violent offenders." Since lumbar CSF 5-HIAA concentrations in both groups were significantly lower than those observed in a group of normal healthy volunteers, the notion that impulsivity was the critical behavioral correlate of reduced lumbar CSF 5-HIAA concentration was supported. Impulsive arsonists and impulsive violent offenders theoretically had "impulsivity," but not "aggression," in common. However, since subjects were classified by the index crime (i.e., arson vs. homicide/serious assault) it is possible that other factors, including the presence of a more general history of impulsive aggression, could have accounted for similarly lower lumbar CSF 5-HIAA concentrations. Closer examination of similar data from a later report from this investigative group (Virkkunen et al.,1989) reveals that impulsive "arsonists" and impulsive "violent offenders" are similar in a variety of ways that suggest they also share a general history of similar impulsive aggression.

Abnormalities in the Serotonin Synapse

In the early 1980s, Michael Stanley and John Mann at Wayne State and Cornell Universities compared imipramine and spiperone binding sites in the brains of violent suicide and violent accident victims to assess serotonin function (Stanley & Mann, 1983). The data revealed that in the frontal cortex of violent suicide victims, there were fewer presynaptic serotonin transporter sites (proteins responsible for transporting serotonin) and more postsynaptic serotonin-2 binding sites (where serotonin exerts its effects). While little was known about the psychiatric status of the subjects in these studies, the data suggested that in addition to low serotonin turnover in individuals committing violent suicide, there could actually be structural abnormalities in the serotonin synapse itself.

In addition, a variety of studies have discovered reduced numbers of platelet serotonin transporter sites and increased numbers of platelet serotonin-2 receptor sites in individuals who have attempted suicide compared with those lacking a history of suicidal behavior (Coccaro et al., 1996). Although not directly activated by central serotonin neurons, both platelet transporter sites and serotonin-2 receptor sites are essentially identical to the corresponding structures in central serotonin synapses (Cook et al., 1994; Lesch et al., 1993).

Stimulating Serotonin Activity: Pharmaco-Challenge Studies

Another way to study the serotonin system's relationship to impulsive aggression is through the use of psychopharmacologic challenge studies. These studies involve the administration of a small, single dose of a drug that activates a specific neurotransmitter. Activation of the neurotransmitter system sets into motion a cascade of physiological events that result in a hormonal or behavioral response, which is then used as an index of the physiological responsiveness of the neurotransmitter system in question (Coccaro & Kavoussi, 1994). Low responsiveness is indicative of reduced function in that neurotransmitter system.

In order to study involvement of the serotonin system in behavioral and personality disorders, studies using a pharmaco-challenge method often administer fenfluramine, which is an indirect agonist of serotonin. Fenfluramine leads to the release of prolactin, a pituitary hormone, which can be measured in the blood to assess the integrity of serotonin function in the brain. In a study of personality disordered subjects, reduced prolactin response to fenfluramine (PRL[*d,l*-FEN]) was highly correlated with impulsive aggression in personality-disordered patients (Coccaro et al., 1989). This finding has been replicated in most pharmaco-challenge assessments of serotonin activity. All of this evidence suggests that decreased functioning of the serotonin system in the brain can increase an individual's vulnerability to impulsive aggressive behavior.

Findings in children and adolescents provide a somewhat different perspective on the relationship between serotonin and impulsive aggression (Halperin et al., 1994; 1997; Pine et al., 1997). Close examination of several studies suggests that positive relationships between aggression and PRL[*d,l*-FEN] responses are noted only in samples that contain prepubertal, and not older, children. Thus, changes in the serotonin system occurring with development may be having a critical influence on the nature of the serotonin/aggression relationship. According to this model, high PRL[*d,l*-FEN] responses are found in aggressive prepubertal children, there is no relationship in postpubertal children, and low PRL responses are found in aggressive adults. The neurobiological mechanisms possibly underlying this model are unknown at the present time. However, *overexpression* of serotonin early in development can lead to the eventual *downregulation* of the serotonin system later in life in animal models (Whittaker-

Azmita et al., 1994). It is possible that aggressive prepubertal children have an overactive serotonin system early in life that later degrades over time.

CATECHOLAMINE NEUROTRANSMITTERS: THE FUEL FOR BEHAVIOR

Norepinephrine Activity

If serotonin serves as a "brake" on impulsive aggressive behavior, what neurotransmitters might "fuel" this behavior? Based on animal studies, norepinephrine (NE) and dopamine (DA) activity should facilitate aggressive behavior. In support of a NE hypothesis of aggression, Brown et al. (1979) reported a positive correlation between CSF levels of the NE by-product MHPG (3-methoxy-4 hydroxy phenylglycol) and a history of aggression in twelve male personality-disordered subjects. Supporting this finding, Siever and Trestman (1993) reported that plasma NE was modestly, but positively, correlated with self-reported impulsivity in male personality-disordered subjects.

Pharmaco-challenge studies also suggest a positive relationship between NE function and impulsive aggression. For example, there is a positive correlation between the growth hormone response to clonidine, a drug that increases NE activity, and self-reported irritability in male personality-disordered patients and healthy volunteers (Coccaro et al., 1991). A role of NE receptors in aggression has also been suggested by a study in which injection of drugs that increase NE activity into the hypothalamus enhances aggressive responding in the cat (Barrett et al., 1990). In this model, a stimulus that acts on NE mechanisms that are supersensitive in affected individuals could result in an enhancement of the flight-fight response mediated by NE pathways. Accordingly, individuals with a faulty NE apparatus may be primed to "fight" when some minor adverse stimulus (e.g., being insulted) activates a hypersensitive NE system.

Dopamine Receptor Sensitivity

A positive relationship between dopamine function and aggression is suggested by animal studies, but clinical studies in humans are equivocal. Reduced CSF concentrations of homovanillic acid (HVA), the major dopamine by-product, was initially reported among impulsive violent offenders with antisocial personality (but not intermittent explosive disorder only) by Linnoila et al. (1983). While this finding was not replicated in later studies by Virkkunen et al. (1987; 1994), reduced CSF HVA concentration has been reported as a function of recidivism in an offender (Virkkunen et al. 1989) and as a function of violent behavior in the offender's father (Virkkunen et al. 1996). Inverse relationships between CSF HVA and aggression have also been reported in abstinent alcoholics and healthy volunteers (Limson et al., 1991). Interpretation of these findings is complicated by the fact that CSF 5-HIAA and HVA are highly intercorrelated, and CSF HVA may be "driven" by CSF 5-HIAA (Agren et al., 1986). Accordingly, it is possible that CSF HVA findings merely reflect the primary finding with CSF 5-HIAA concentration.

On the other hand, we have also found a significant inverse relationship between

CSF HVA, adjusted for CSF 5-HIAA, and life history of aggression in male and female personality-disordered subjects (Coccaro, 1998). Given a positive relationship between dopamine function and aggression as suggested by animal studies (Coccaro et al., 1996), it is possible that an inverse relationship between CSF HVA concentration and aggression indirectly reflects the positive relationship between dopamine receptor sensitivity and aggression or arousal, which, in turn, can increase the likelihood of aggression under relevant provocative stimuli.

OTHER BIOLOGICAL MEDIATORS IN THE STUDY OF IMPULSIVE AGGRESSION

Glucose

While the serotonin-norepinephrine hypothesis is intriguing, other biological factors have been studied for their involvement in aggressive behavior. For example, glucose is the primary energy source in the brain. Accordingly, significant hypoglycemia, or low blood glucose, might lead to impaired central neuronal function and consequent impairment in cognitive processes and judgment (O'Keefe & Marks, 1977) which can increase the risk for aggressive response to aversive external stimuli. In a series of investigations, Virkkunen and colleagues demonstrated that impulsive violent offenders with antisocial personality disorder (Virkkunen & Huttunen, 1982) or with intermittent explosive disorder (Virkkunen et al., 1994) had a significantly lower blood glucose after glucose challenge compared with normal volunteers. Among violent offenders, the hypoglycemic response to glucose challenge has also been found to be greater among recidivists who have committed new violent crimes (Virkkunen et al., 1989).

Testosterone

Testosterone, the major male hormone, has been examined for a possible relationship with aggression. Animal studies suggest that testosterone facilitates aggression (Archer, 1991). Plasma concentrations of testosterone have been reported to correlate positively with self-rated measures of aggression in some studies of nonpsychiatric subjects and have recently been reported to be higher in alcoholics with a history of repeated episodes of domestic violence (Bergman & Brismar, 1994). Similar relationships have not been found, however, in studies of nonhuman primates (Higley et al., 1992) or of nonalcoholic personality-disordered subjects (Coccaro et al., 1998, unpublished data). In contrast to plasma testosterone data, Virkkunen et al. (1994) have reported higher CSF testosterone concentrations in antisocial impulsive violent offenders, but not in nonantisocial impulsive or nonimpulsive violent offenders, compared with healthy volunteers.

Vasopressin Activity

There is also some data to suggest a positive relationship between aggression and central vasopressin activity, a neuropeptide released by the pituitary gland. Available data indicate that this neuropeptide may facilitate aggression. We recently found a positive correlation between CSF vasopressin concentration and life history of aggression in twenty-six personality-disordered subjects (Coccaro et al., 1998). These findings are consistent with those from animal studies in which drugs that suppress vasopressin activity reduce aggression in golden hamsters, while serotonin reuptake inhibitors increase central serotonin activity and reduce central vasopressin concentration and levels of aggressive behavior in the same species (Ferris & Delville, 1994). If support is found for these findings, it is possible that agents that dampen central vasopressin activity could have the ability to reduce vulnerability to aggression.

Low Serum Cholesterol Levels

An interesting relationship between serum cholesterol and violence has been reported since the late 1970s. Virkkunen (1979) first reported a low serum cholesterol level among antisocial personality-disordered subjects compared with other nonantisocial, personality-disordered subjects. While nearly all the antisocials had committed property crimes, only slightly more than half had committed a violent offense. However, in a second study involving a large group of homicide offenders, Virkkunen (1983) demonstrated that impulsive violent offenders (with either antisocial personality disorder or intermittent explosive disorder) also had lower serum cholesterol levels than nonimpulsive violent offenders. Among all homicide offenders, the presence of a personal history of suicide attempt, self-injurious behavior, and the presence of paternal violence under the influence of alcohol were all associated with lower serum cholesterol levels. It is possible that serum cholesterol bears some relationship with central 5-HT (5-hydroxytryptamine, or serotonin) function. Recent studies performed in the monkey suggest this may be true (Kaplan et al., 1994). In these studies, monkeys were fed low and high cholesterol diets to produce hypo- and hyper-cholesterol bearing monkeys, respectively. As predicted, monkeys very low in cholesterol were more aggressive than monkeys with high cholesterol. In addition, low cholesterol monkeys had lower CSF 5-HIAA concentrations than did high cholesterol monkeys, supporting the hypothesis that serum cholesterol is directly related to central 5-HT system function. Whether these relationships hold in humans is less clear. While one study suggests that there is a relationship between serotonin measures and cholesterol in humans (Terao et al., 1997), another study did not (Delva et al., 1996).

GENETIC VULNERABILITIES

The tendency to behave aggressively in response to provocation or frustration tends to be a lifelong trait. While the frequency, type, or intensity of aggressive behavior may diminish somewhat as one ages, the trait is generally present in the same relative magnitude within a cohort of age-matched contemporaries.

If impulsive-aggressive behavior is mediated by some biological traits of an individual (e.g., serotonin function), it is possible that this biological vulnerability may be under genetic influence. Evidence consistent with a familial-genetic influence on impulsive-aggressive behavior has been reported in a number of studies, using dimensional assessments and categorical descriptors of aggression. Categorical descriptors include delinquency, antisocial behavior, and criminal behavior. Twin studies, including two meta-analyses, estimate the heritability of delinquent behavior in children and criminal behavior in adults to be between 30 and 50 percent. Adoption studies of antisocial and criminal offspring of biological parents with antisocial/criminal behavior demonstrated increased risk of antisocial behavior in males.

One critical observation among the twin and family studies is that the strongest heritability estimates have been found when the aggression variables reflect hostility or irritability, rather than aggression in general. In two studies performed by our laboratory, we found that the behavioral descriptors that have correlated inversely with our pharmaco-challenge studies of brain serotonin activity are indeed heritable in a twin study design. In the two studies, irritability and various forms of aggression appear to have a heritability between 27 and 41 percent. The remainder of the variability in aggression scores appears to be due largely to nonshared environment and reflects the things that make twins different from each other, such as life experience.

Recently, David Nielsen and colleagues from the National Institute of Alcohol Abuse and Alcoholism and the University of Helsinki reported that a DNA variant for a portion of the gene coding for tryptophan hydroxylase (an enzyme that degrades tryptophan, which is an amino acid that helps to synthesize serotonin) and CSF 5-HIAA concentration was associated with suicidal behavior in alcoholic violent offenders (Nielsen et al., 1994). Since tryptophan hydroxylase limits the synthesis of serotonin, DNA variants related to this enzyme constitute good candidates for a specific genetic link between serotonin and impulsive-aggressive behavior.

This is only the beginning of this kind of study in this area. For example, there are known DNA variants for genes related to the serotonin transporter and the serotonin receptor. Since abnormalities in these structures on brain neurons and blood platelets have already been identified, it will be important to examine the relationship between DNA variants of the genes that code for these receptors and the actual function of these receptors as they relate to impulsive aggressive behavior within the same subjects.

TREATMENT IMPLICATIONS

If there is a biological vulnerability to certain types of impulsive-aggressive behavior, it may be possible to reduce the risk of such behavior through the use of certain medications. For example, in the model outlined above, "low" serotonin and "overactive" norepinephrine/dopamine increase the risk of impulsive aggression. Thus, medications that enhance serotonin or block norepinephrine/dopamine should reduce such behavior. Serotonin-enhancing medications have reduced aggression in animal studies (Fuller, 1996), and several selective serotonin reuptake inhibitors have shown promise in the treatment of hostility and aggression in humans. In an open clinical trial, the serotonin reuptake inhibitor sertraline was found to be effective in reducing impulsive-aggressive behavior in a group of eleven patients with a variety of personality disorders (Kavoussi et al., 1994). In a double blind, placebo-controlled trial, fluoxetine (another serotonin reuptake inhibitor) was associated with substantial reductions in overt aggressive behavior and irritability in thirty-nine nondepressed personality-disordered patients with impulsive-aggressive behavior (Coccaro & Kavoussi, 1997). In another double blind study of twenty-one patients with borderline personality disorder, there was a significant decrease in anger among patients receiving fluoxetine, independent of changes in depression (Salzman et al., 1995). In a double blind crossover study, treatment with the serotonin reuptake inhibitor citalopram reduced aggressiveness in chronically violent schizophrenic inpatients (Vartiainen et al., 1995).

Beta noradrenergic blockers appear to be effective in reducing aggressiveness in many different psychiatric conditions. Propranolol and nadolol are effective in reducing aggressive behavior in chronic psychiatric inpatients, independent of psychotic symptoms (Sorgi et al., 1986; Ratey et al., 1992). Propranolol has also been effective in reducing aggressive behavior in adult patients with attention deficit disorder and temper outbursts (Mattes, 1986). Dopamine blocking agents (antipsychotics) have been used to reduce aggression in various psychiatric populations, but their use has been limited by their potential for side effects. The newer, "atypical" antipsychotics (i.e., clozapine, risperidone, olanzapine, sertindole) may be more effective than traditional antipsychotic drugs in aggressive and violent populations. These medicines block serotonin 2 receptors in addition to dopamine receptors. This effect may explain the ability of newer antipsychotic medications to produce a dramatic reduction in aggression and agitation independent of effects on psychotic symptoms (Rabinowitz et al, 1996; Buckley et al., 1995).

Other agents also appear to reduce impulsive aggressive behavior. Michael Sheard et al. (1976) noted that lithium carbonate, an agent used to treat manic depressive disorder, appeared to enhance serotonin brain activity and decrease aggressive responding in animals. He sought to extend that finding to the clinical setting, and he conducted a double blind, placebo-controlled clinical trial of lithium carbonate in prison inmates. The results of his five-month clinical trial were striking. Impulsive-aggressive actions of subjects treated with lithium, as routinely recorded by correctional personnel, were reduced to near zero by the end of the third month. Subjects treated with placebo showed no reduction in these behaviors. Moreover, lithium-treated subjects who were crossed over to placebo in a double blind fashion lost the gains they made during the trial within a month after active lithium treatment had ceased. Of note is that lithium treated only impulsive-aggressive behaviors. Interpersonal behaviors otherwise typical of this population were not affected. This suggests that the tendency toward relatively simple, action-oriented behavior may be modulated by discrete biochemical processes, but that complex behavioral interactions involving cognitive function may be beyond explanation through simple neurochemical mechanisms.

CASE STUDY

At this point, it may be helpful to review a forensic case that illustrates the clinical implications of the above findings. A thirty-year-old, divorced white male (BC) presented for a psychiatric evaluation as part of a criminal defense plea of not guilty by reason of insanity. At the time of his evaluation, BC was incarcerated awaiting trial for the murder of his ex-wife. Until his incarceration, BC worked as an accountant at a small firm in a suburb of a major city.

BC was the oldest of four children. His mother noted early problems with impulsive behavior and anger control. His early school years were noteworthy for hyperactivity and fighting, as well as fire setting, by ages six to seven. Evidence of his impulsive aggressive behavior included an incident in which he severed the tip of his three-year old brother's fifth finger during an altercation, when he himself was age five. He attended a private school from grades 1 through 6 but was asked to leave because of an inability to control his rage. Despite these behaviors his academic performance was always high, with evidence of perfectionist and obsessive tendencies in his school work.

In high school, BC continued to engage in episodic fighting but only when challenged. His academic performance continued to be high. On finishing high school at age seventeen, he had a physical fight with his father, left home, and then joined the Army. He was honorably discharged four years later but recounted a number of violent incidents during his time in the Army.

During his college years, BC began to exhibit identifiable fluctuations in mood. In addition, he seemed to be able to study and do his school work until early hours of the morning, arise after only after a few hours of sleep and attend classes the next day. Alternately he entered periods during which he would isolate himself from others, stay in his room, and not communicate. Throughout this time BC worked regularly, occasionally as a barroom bouncer. BC estimates that he had over one hundred physical fights in his lifetime and had been arrested for fighting on at least twelve occasions.

BC met his ex-wife, with whom he had two children, in the interval between his discharge from the Army and his enrollment in college. Over time, trouble in the marriage led the couple to maintain separate residences. Shortly after his graduation from college, his wife informed him that she desired a divorce. Following divorce, serious problems arose over child visitation issues. After numerous disputes with his ex-wife, the most recent of which led to BC's violation of a restraining order, BC obtained a nine millimeter semiautomatic handgun and started drinking more than usual. BC developed a plan to kill himself in front of his ex-wife. He felt sure that he would be sent to jail for violating her restraining order for a second time. As a consequence, he reasoned that his wife would obtain full custody of the children. Since she had "beaten him," he decided he would kill himself in front of her, leaving his splattered brains on her kitchen wall for her to explain to his children. When BC arrived at his ex-wife's house she ran from the house and went to her neighbor's. As his initial plan went awry, BC instantly became enraged. He followed her to the next house, grabbed her, and killed her with a single shot to the head. Following three weeks of eluding law enforcement authorities, during which time he continued to drink heavily, BC voluntarily presented himself to the local police authorities for prosecution.

The family history was remarkable for impulsive aggression, depression, and alcohol/substance abuse on both the paternal and maternal sides of BC's family. Among the twenty first- and second-degree family members for which information was available, seven had problems with impulsive aggression, five had problems with alcohol/substance abuse, and four had problems with depression.

BC had a cerebrospinal fluid (CSF) level of 5-HIAA (the major metabolite of serotonin) of 92.8 nmol/l. This is in the "normal" range of values reported in studies. His CSF level of HVA (the major metabolite of dopamine) was 107 nmol/l, which would be considered low compared with healthy volunteers (Virkkunen et al., 1994). In addition, BC had a reduced prolactin response to d-fenfluramine (4.15 ng/ml) (Coccaro et al., 1989).

BC is illustrative of the type of impulsive violent offender that has been studied and reported on in the biological psychiatry literature. He meets criteria for intermittent explosive disorder (IED). Impulsive violent offenders usually meet criteria for either IED or antisocial/borderline personality disorder. His act of violence was impulsive in that he committed murder in an impulsive, reactive act of rage after his original plan was "ruined" by his ex-wife's actions (reportedly his plan was to commit suicide, not homicide). While BC's act does not meet a legal definition of non-premeditation (i.e., where there is no conscious thought to kill before the act occurs), there was actually little premeditation or planning in the murder of his ex-wife. BC consciously, but impulsively, altered his plan from suicide to homicide at the scene of the crime. He has a strong family history of impulsive aggressiveness and of alcoholism, particularly on the paternal side of his family.

BC's biological data is generally consistent with that reported in the literature for individuals with high levels of impulsive aggression. He has a reduced prolactin response to fenfluramine, suggesting impairment in serotonin system functioning. He also has a reduced CSF HVA level. While not as consistent a finding as that with the CSF 5-HIAA level, CSF HVA levels have been shown to correlate inversely with measures of aggression (Limson et al., 1990), criminal recidivism (Virkkunen et al., 1989), and paternal violence (Virkkunen et al., 1996).

The presence of these biological abnormalities in BC certainly does not excuse the fact that BC committed a homicide. Rather, it gives insight into the physiological risk factors that may underlie serious violent behavior, particularly if it is relatively impulsive in nature. In the state in which BC's trial took place (and in many other states), a defendant is not guilty by reason of insanity if, as a result of a "defect" or "disease" of the mind, he/she did not know the "wrongfulness" of his/her act. Accordingly, the defense must prove these two elements by a "preponderance of the evidence." In BC's case, the defense attempted to establish the first prong of the insanity defense by introducing evidence that BC was afflicted with an impulse control disorder (IED). Testimony was introduced summarizing his clinical history, which established that he fulfilled criteria for IED. Testimony was also introduced that BC suffered from an untreated form of bipolar disorder. It was the defense's contention that underlying these clinical disorders was evidence of neurochemical abnormalities affecting both serotonin and dopamine pathways, as described above. In the time leading up to the killing, the defense argued that BC was in a state of hypomania which would have increased the risk of an impulsive aggressive outburst typical of BC during his lifetime. This assertion regarding his mood state was corroborated by the testimony of numerous witnesses, including his girlfriend, who described profound symptoms of agitated depression, and at the same time of hypersexuality, just prior to and on the day of the homicide.

In addition, the defense was required to demonstrate that BC did not know the "wrongfulness" of his acts at the time he committed the acts. The presence of an "irresistible impulse," as suggested above, does not satisfy this criterion in the state of BC's trial (nor in most states). The defense's argument was that BC did not intend to kill his ex-wife in the immediate time period preceding the homicide. When his confused planning went awry, BC responded impulsively and aggressively without reflection. Thus, the defense argued, BC was incapable of moral reflection in his uninhibited rage state.

Regardless, the court was not persuaded that BC was not guilty by reason of insanity. BC was found guilty of murder in the first degree. Although the potentially mitigating clinical and biological data were available to the court during the penalty phase of BC's trial, the court rendered a sentence of death.

CONCLUSIONS

Genetic Influences

The evidence from twin, family, and adoption studies clearly suggests that there is an important role for both genetic and environmental influences in mediating impulsive-aggressive behavior in humans. While environment may be more influential in this regard, dismissing the potential significance of biology in the design of intervention strategies for impulsive-aggressive behavior may lead to missing potential avenues to reduce aggression. Further research must examine the long-term efficacy of medications in reducing impulsive-aggressive behavior.

Environment

In addition to medicinal methods to treat neurotransmitter defects in aggressive individuals, there is substantial evidence to indicate that environmental manipulations alter these systems, for better or for worse. Chronic stress, such as in posttraumatic stress disorder, both prenatally and throughout the lifespan, can directly lower serotonin activity in the brain. Improper prenatal care and nutrition or stress in the mother can potentially alter serotonin function in the offspring. Children who are raised in deprived environments, such as those which are drug infested or where violence is observed, can develop serotonin deficiencies as a result.

The converse is also true. Insulation from stressful, traumatic, or neglectful conditions can raise serotonin to increase resiliency and lead to the development of more adaptive coping mechanisms than aggressive responding. Enabling individuals to exert control over their lives rather than to be a victim of their environment can improve neurotransmitter function and behavioral responses. Thus, social and behavioral programs are paramount in the effort to prevent and treat related disorders. Based on our progress to date, a comprehensive biological and environmental understanding of impulsive-aggressive behavior may be in reach within ten to twenty years.

References

Agren, H., Mefford, I. N., Rudorfer, M. V., Linnoila, M. & Potter, W. Z. (1986). Interacting neurotransmitter systems: A non-experimental approach to the 5-HIAA-HVA correllation in human CSF. *Journal of Psychiatry Research, 20,* 175-193.

Archer, J. (1991). The influence of testosterone on human aggression. *British Journal of Psychology, 82,* 1–28.

Åsberg, M., Traksman, L. & Thoren, P. (1976). 5-HIAA in the cerebrospinal fluid: A biochemical suicide predictor? *Archives of General Psychiatry, 33,* 1193–1197.

Barrett, J. A., Edinger, H. & Siegel, A. (1990). Intrahypothalamic injections of norepinephrine facilitate feline affective aggression via alpha-2 adrenoceptors. *Brain Research, 525,* 285–293.

Bergman, B. & Brismar, B. (1994). Characteristics of violent alcoholics. *Alcohol and Alcoholism, 29,* 451-457.

Brown, G. L., Goodwin, F. K., Ballenger, J. C., Goyer, P. F. & Major, L. F. (1979). Aggression in humans correlates with cerebrospinal fluid amine metabolites. *Psychiatry Research, 1,* 131–139.

Buckley, P., Bartell, J., Donenwirth, K., Lee, S., Torigoe, F. & Schulz, S. C. (1995). Violence and schizophrenia: Clozapine as a specific antiaggressive agent. *Bulletin of the American Academy of Psychiatry & the Law, 23,* 607–611.

Coccaro, E. F. (1998). [Unpublished data.] Clinical Neuroscience Research Unit, Department of Psychiatry, MCP at Hanemann School of Medicine, Philadelphia.

Coccaro, E. F. & Kavoussi, R. J. (1994). The neuropsychopharmacologic challenge in biological psychiatry. *Clinical Chemistry, 40,* 319–327.

Coccaro, E. F. & Kavoussi, R. J. (1997). Fluoxetine and impulsive aggressive behavior in personality-disordered subjects. *Archives of General Psychiatry, 54,* 1081–1088.

Coccaro, E. F., Kavoussi, R. J., Hauger, R. L., Cooper, T. B. & Ferris, C. F. (1998). CSF vasopressin: Correlates with indices of aggression and serotonin function in personality-disordered subjects. *Archives of General Psychiatry, 55,* 708–714.

Coccaro, E. F., Kavoussi, R. J., Sheline, Y. I., Lish, J. D. & Csernansky, J. G. (1996). Impulsive aggression in personality disorder: Correlates with H-paroxetine binding in the platelet. *Archives of General Psychiatry, 53,* 531–536.

Coccaro, E. F., Lawrence, T., Trestman, R., Gabriel, S., Klar, H. M. & Siever, L. J. (1991). Growth hormone responses to intravenous clonidine challenge correlates with behavioral irritability in psychiatric patients and in healthy volunteers. *Psychiatry Research, 39,* 129–139.

Coccaro, E. F., Siever, L. J., Klar, H. M., Mourer, G., Cochrane, K. Cooper, T. B., Mohs, R. C. & Davis, K. L. (1989). Serotonergic studies in patients with affective and personality disorders. *Archives of General Psychiatry, 46,* 587–599.

Cook, E. H., Fletcher, K. E., Wainwright, M., Marks, N., Yan, S.Y. & Levanthal, B. L. (1994). Primary structure of the human platelet serotonin 5-HT-2a receptor: Identity with frontal cortex serotonin 5-HT-2a receptor. *Journal of Neurochemistry, 63,* 465–469.

Delva, N. J., Matthews, D. R. & Cowen, P. (1996). Brain serotonin (5-HT) neuroendocrine function in patients taking cholesterol-lowering drugs. *Biological Psychiatry, 39,* 100–106.

Ferris, C. F. & Delville, Y. (1994). Vasopressin and serotonin interactions in the control of agonistic behavior. *Psychoneuroendocrinology, 19,* 593–601.

Fuller, R. W. (1996). The influence of fluoxetine on aggressive behavior. *Neuropsychopharmacology, 14,* 77–81.

Halperin, J. M., Newcorn, J. H., Schwartz, S. T., Sharma, V., Siever, L. J., Koda, V. H. & Gabriel, S. (1997). Age-related changes in the association between serotonergic function and aggression in boys with ADHD. *Biological Psychiatry, 41,* 682-689.

Halperin, J. M., Sharma, V., Siever, L. J., Schwartz, S. T., Matier, K., Wornell, G. & Newcorn, J. H. (1994). Serotonergic function in aggressive and nonaggressive boys with attention deficit hyperactivity disorder. *American Journal of Psychiatry, 151,* 243-248.

Higley, J. D., Mehlman, P. T., Taub, D. M., Higley, S. B., Suomi, S. J., Vickers, J. H. & Linnoila, M. (1992). Cerebrospinal fluid monoamine and adrenal correlates of aggression in free-ranging rhesus monkeys. *Archives of General Psychiatry, 49,* 436–441.

Kaplan, J.R., Shively, C.A., Fontenot, M.B., Morgan, T. M., Howell, S. M., Manuck, S. B., Muldoon, M. F. & Mann, J. J. (1994). Demonstration of an association among dietary cholesterol, central serotonergic activity, and social behavior in monkeys. *Psychosomatic Medicine, 56,* 479–484.

Kavoussi, R. J., Liu, J. & Coccaro, E. F. (1994). An open trial of sertraline in personality disordered patients with impulsive aggression. *Journal of Clinical Psychiatry, 55,* 137–141.

Lesch, K.-P., Wolozin, B. L., Murphy, D. L. & Reiderer, P. (1993). Primary structure of the human platelet serotonin uptake site: Identity with the brain serotonin transporter. *Journal of Neurochemistry, 60,* 2319–2322.

Limson, R., Goldman, D., Roy, A., Lamparski, D., Ravitz, B., Adwoff, B. & Linnoila, M. (1991). Personality and cerebrospinal fluid monoamine metabolites in alcoholics and controls. *Archives of General Psychiatry, 48,* 437–441.

Linnoila, M., Virkkunen, M., Scheinin, M., Nuutila, A., Rimon, R. & Goodwin, F. K. (1983). Low cerebrospinal fluid 5-hydroxyindolacetic acid concentration differentiates impulsive from nonimpulsive violent behavior. *Life Sciences, 33,* 2609–2614.

Mattes, J. A. (1986). Propranolol for adults with temper outbursts and residual attention deficit disorder. *Journal of Clinical Psychopharmacology, 6,* 299–302.

Nielsen, D. A., Goldman, D., Virkkunen M., Tokola, R., Rawlings, R. & Linnoila, M. (1994). Suicidality and 5-hydroxyindoleacetic acid concentration associated with a tryptophan hydroxylase polymorphism. *Archives of General Psychiatry, 51,* 34–38.

O'Keefe, S. & Marks, V. (1977). Lunch time gin and tonic a cause of reactive hypoglycemia. *Lancet, 1,* 1286–1288.

Pine, D. S., Coplan, J. D., Wasserman, G. A., Miller, L. S., Fried, J. E., Davies, M., Cooper, T. B., Greenhill, L., Shaffer, D. & Parsons, B. (1997). Neuroendocrine response to d,l-fenfluramine challenge in boys: Associations with aggressive behavior and adverse rearing. *Archives of General Psychiatry, 54,* 839-846.

Rabinowitz, J., Avnon, M. & Rosenberg, V. (1996). Effect of clozapine on physical and verbal aggression. *Schizophrenia Research, 22,* 249–255.

Ratey, J. J., Sorgi, P., O'Driscoll, G. A., Sands, S., Daehler, M. M. L., Fletcher, J. R., Kadish, W., Spruiell, G., Polakoff, S. & Lindem, K. J. (1992). Nadolol to treat aggression and psychiatric symptomatology in chronic psychiatric inpatients: A double-blind, placebo-controlled study. *Journal of Clinical Psychiatry, 53,* 41-46.

Salzman, C., Wolfson, A. N., Schatzberg, A., Cooper, J., Henke, R., Albanese, M., Schwartz, J. & Miyawaki, E. (1995). Effect of fluoxetine on anger in symptomatic volunteers with borderline personality disorder. *Journal of Clinical Psychopharmacology, 15,* 23–29.

Sheard, M., Marini, J., Bridges, C. & Wapner, A. (1976). The effect of lithium on impulsive aggressive behavior in man. *American Journal of Psychiatry, 133,* 1409–1413.

Siever, L. & Trestman, R. L. (1993). The serotonin system and aggressive personality disorder. *International Clinical Psychopharmacology, 8 (Suppl. 2),* 33–39.

Sorgi, P. J., Ratey, J. J. & Polakoff, S. (1986). Beta-adrenergic blockers for the control of aggressive behaviors in patients with chronic schizophrenia. *American Journal of Psychiatry, 143,* 775–776.

Stanley, M. & Mann, J. (1983). Increased serotonin-2 binding sites in frontal cortex of suicide victims. *Lancet, 1,* 214–216.

Terao, T., Yoshimura, R., Ohmorl, O., Takano, T., Takahashi, N., Iwata, N., Suzuki, T. & Abe, K. (1997). Effect of serum cholesterol levels on meta-chlorophenylpiperazine neuroendocrine responses in healthy subjects. *Biological Psychiatry, 41,* 974–978.

Vartiainen, H., Tiihonen, J., Putkonen, A., Koponen, H., Virkkunen, M., Hakola, P. & Lehto, H. (1995). Citalopram, a selective serotonin reuptake inhibitor, in the treatment of aggression in schizophrenia. *Acta Psychiatrica Scandinavia, 91,* 348–351.

Virkkunen M. (1979). Serum cholesterol in antisocial personality. *Neuropsychobiology, 5,* 27–30.

Virkkunen M. (1983). Serum cholesterol levels in homicidal offenders: A low cholesterol level is connected with a habitually violent tendency under the influence of alcohol. *Neuropsychobiology, 10,* 65–69.

Virkkunen, M., De Jong, J., Bartko, J., Goodwin, F. K. & Linnoila, M. (1989). Relationship of psychobiological variables to recidivism in violent offenders and impulsive fire setters. *Archives of General Psychiatry, 46,* 600–603.

Virkkunen, M., Eggert, M., Rawlins, R. & Linnoila, M. (1996). A prospective follow-up study of alcoholic violent offenders and fire setters. *Archives of General Psychiatry, 53,* 523–529.

Virkkunen, M. & Huttunen, M. O. (1982). Evidence for abnormal glucose tolerance test among violent offenders. *Neuropsychobiology, 8,* 30–34.

Virkkunen, M. & Narvanen, S. (1987). Plasma insulin, tryptophan and serotonin levels during the glucose tolerance test among habitually violent and impulsive offenders. *Neuropsychobiology, 17,* 19–23.

Virkkunen, M., Nuutila, A., Goodwin, F. K. & Linnoila, M. (1987). Cerebrospinal fluid monoamine metabolite levels in male arsonists. *Archives of General Psychiatry, 44,* 241–247.

Virkkunen, M., Rawlins, R., Tokola, R., Poland, R. E., Guidotti, A., Nemeroff, C., Bissette, G., Katoperas, K., Karonen, S. L. & Linnoila, M. (1994). CSF biochemistries, glucose metabolism, and diurnal activity rhythms in alcoholic, violent offenders, fire setters, and healthy volunteers. *Archives of General Psychiatry, 51,* 20–27.

Part 3

Genetic Studies of Antisocial Behavior

For decades, the consistent observation has been made that certain patterns of behavior run in families, including drug abuse and antisocial behavior. There is no question that there is a genetic component. Findings of biological aberrations in youthful users or children at risk by virtue of a substance abusing or antisocial parent and of immutable genetic markers for substance abuse disorders, impulsivity, and aggressiveness suggest that genetics plays a role in these behavioral patterns. Although genes do not code for drug use or antisocial behavior per se, it is likely that genetic susceptibility is reflected in central neurotransmitter dysfunctions and mediated through personality traits, cognitive styles, and psychopathologic conditions that surface in childhood and remain relatively constant throughout the lifespan. Evidence presented in Part 3 suggests that the origins of drug abuse and aggressive disorders are intrinsically linked and cannot be separately studied in a subgroup of the population.

Chapters 7 and 8 provide evidence from twin and adoption studies for a genetic role in antisocial behavior and drug abuse. Dr. Ridenour notes in Chapter 7 that parental antisocial behavior is one of the strongest predictors of children's persistent antisocial behavior. While there are certainly environmental explanations for this relationship, it does not tell the whole story. For example, adoption studies show that even when children are raised by nonaggressive, non-drug-abusing adoptive parents from birth, their eventual behavior more closely resembles that of their biological parents. Similar to the other chapters in this section, Dr. Ridenour argues that rather than directly coding for criminal behavior, genes contribute to biological processes that, in interaction with the prevailing environment, predispose individuals to certain behavioral patterns. Methods for studying these relationships are outlined and the significance of their findings are placed into an environmental context. The concluding portion of Dr. Ridenour's chapter is perhaps the most compelling in its coverage of the implications this research has for the identification, treatment, and prevention of individuals at high risk for offending. Our present criminal justice system has not incorporated findings from the behavioral sciences into its approaches. Rather, there remains a belief that much antisocial behavior is intentional trouble-making; most investigators and practitioners blame systemwide failures on these attitudes. This research leads to the conclusion that society would be better served if we began looking for early warning signs, using a mental and public health approach, and did not rely exclusively on the criminal justice system for behavioral management. Genetic research highlights the role that environment plays in mediating and modulating genetic traits and indicates that behavioral interventions, in addition to medical strategies when indicated, can be highly effective tools in our quest to reduce the incidence of antisocial conduct.

In Chapter 8, Drs. van den Bree, Svikis, and Pickens discuss the association between antisocial personality disorder (APD) and substance use disorder (SUD), which has been frequently observed, although the causes of the comorbidity remain unclear. Adoption and twin studies have found evidence of both genetic and environmental influences in APD and SUD. Therefore, comorbidity between APD and SUD could be the result of shared genetic influences, but also of shared environmental influences, or a combination of the two. Only a limited number of adoption and twin studies have addressed this issue, and the results have not been conclusive. Results of future studies would be easier to interpret if a distinction is made between alcohol and drug abuse, and between juvenile and adult APD symptoms. Twin samples of adequate size would allow use of structural equation analytical methods for estimation of the relative magnitude of genetic and environmental influences shared between the two conditions, as well as influences contributing to each specifically. Results would be highly relevant for the clinical setting as well as for efforts to identify genes involved in either trait.

Because twin and adoption studies do not reveal what exactly is being inherited to increase risk for antisocial behavior, it is necessary to examine the research in molecular genetics, which has very recently become sophisticated enough to elucidate some of these mechanisms. In Chapter 9, Drs. Goldman and Fishbein provide an explanation of the techniques used in molecular genetics to identify potential or candidate genes that influence behavioral disorders. The authors discuss genes considered to be involved in processes that contribute to antisocial behaviors, drug abuse, and alcoholism, along with their genetic function and biological significance. Consistent with studies cited in Part 2 of this book, variants in genes that modulate the activity of the neurotransmitters serotonin and dopamine and the enzyme monoamine oxidase are primary candidates for this involvement. While only one or two genetic defects most often do not produce noticeable impairment or dysfunction, some specific combination of many genetic variants most likely produce the phenotypes of aggression, impulsivity, or drug abuse. The behavioral expression of these genetic traits may be altered through environmental and behavioral interventions, in addition to pharmacotherapy.

Chapter 7

Genetic Epidemiology of Antisocial Behavior

by Ty A. Ridenour, Ph.D.

Introduction 7-2
Approaches to Studying Genotype-Behavior Relationships 7-2
    Animal Studies 7-2
    Relative Risk in Known Genetic Disorders 7-3
    Association and Linkage Studies 7-4
Genetic Epidemiology 7-4
    Twin Studies 7-4
    Adoption Studies 7-5
    Twin and Adoption Study Findings 7-6
        Data Pertaining to Criminal Behavior 7-6
        Estimations 7-6
        Environmental Influences 7-8
Genotype-Environment Correlations and Interactions 7-12
    Biological Parents' Background 7-13
    Adoptive Home Environment 7-13
    Genotype/Environment Interaction 7-13
Discussion—Overlap of Antisocial/Other Phenotypes and
    Other Influences 7-14
    Risks of Twin Birth Complications 7-14
    Age and Assessment Differences in Twin vs. Adoption Studies 7-15
    Implications for Crime Control 7-16
        "Career Criminals" 7-16
        Alcoholism 7-16
        Impulsivity 7-17
        Number of Environmental Stressors Bearing on Risk 7-17

This work was supported by an institutional postdoctoral training grant from the National Institute of Mental Health, MH17104.

INTRODUCTION

The tendency for criminal and antisocial behavior to run in families, referred to as familial aggregation, has been and remains the focus of a considerable amount of research (Glueck & Glueck, 1950; McCord & McCord, 1958; Robins, 1966; West & Farrington, 1973; Kolvin et al., 1988; Earls et al., 1988; Frick et al., 1992; Faraone et al., 1995). Poverty, single-parent homes, immigrant concentrations, parental antisocial behavior and parenting practices, alcohol abuse, brain injury, and gender are all associated with antisocial and violent behavior; exactly how each of these risk factors is associated with antisocial behavior, however, remains unclear (Bohman, 1983; Carey, 1996; Pallone & Hennessy, 1996; Patterson et al., 1992; Sampson & Lauritsen, 1994; Sampson et al., 1997; Rutter & Giller, 1983; Silberg et al., 1996). Parental antisocial behavior is one of the strongest predictors of children's persistent antisocial behavior (e.g., Robins, 1991).

A purely environmental explanation might hypothesize that this relationship is due to a harsh home environment reinforcing antisocial behavior in the children, whereas a purely genetic explanation might posit that the genetic makeup of an antisocial parent is passed on to offspring. Genetic epidemiological researchers recognize that both environmental and genetic mechanisms facilitate (or mediate) the correlation between parental and offspring behavior, and do so interactively (e.g., Rutter, 1997). It is not assumed that a crime gene will be identified; genes do not code for committing crime (which includes antisocial behaviors deemed illegal by a society and detected by the criminal justice system), antisocial personality, or even aggression. Rather, they shape biological underpinnings that predispose persons to some level of risk for antisocial behavior. It is hoped that investigation of genetic influence on antisocial behavior has and will provide data that can improve efforts to curb or even prevent antisocial behavior.

APPROACHES TO STUDYING GENOTYPE-BEHAVIOR RELATIONSHIPS

Several approaches have been used to investigate the influence of genes on antisocial behavior. Three such approaches are described below: animal studies, relative risk studies, and association and linkage studies.

Animal Studies

Perhaps the most powerful method to investigate gene-behavior associations is through animal studies. This approach involves the researcher controlling the genetic makeup of animals through such procedures as controlled matings, "knockout" mutations (in which particular genes are disabled to assess the behavioral consequences), and the development of strains (animals with the same lineage or ancestry that are engineered to have particular characteristics) that differ in levels of a phenotype (an observable trait). For example, a strain of rats that has been bred for aggressive behavior over the course of several generations can be compared with a strain of nonaggressive rats to identify neurochemical or genetic differences between them. The researcher might also control the environment by regulating pre- and postnatal environmental conditions—for example, by manipulating nutrient intake, maternal stress levels, or physical stimulation. However, direct application of animal study results to crime control may not be possible.

Animal research of antisocial behavior has been limited primarily to mouse or rat studies of aggression (Carey, 1994), whereas human criminality encompasses a wide variation of antisocial behaviors such as theft, vandalism and rape, and non-antisocial behaviors such as civil disobedience. Findings from observations of rodents' aggressive behavior may not generalize to human behavior because aggression among other mammals is considered adaptive[1] (Maxson, 1992; Scott, 1989), whereas human aggression is typically considered aberrant. Nevertheless, animal studies provide leads to investigation of human gene-behavior relationships because many associated genes code for equivalent biological functions among rodents and humans (Maxson, 1996).

Animal studies suggest that aggression is influenced genetically, environmentally, and by genotype-environment interactions. Different mouse strains have long been observed to differ with regard to levels of males' aggression (e.g., Brain et al., 1989; Van Oortmerssen & Bakker, 1981), and environmental influence has been suggested by the relationship between neonatal androgens, which are both genetically and environmentally controlled, and later aggression in mice (e.g., Michard-Vanhee, 1988). Observed genotype-environment interactions include variation in patterns of aggression between two members of different strains as a function of environmental variables including time of day, season, duration of exposure to another rodent, and room size (Maxson, 1990).

Relative Risk in Known Genetic Disorders

Comparison of antisocial behavior rates among individuals with known genetic disorders to the general population provides further understanding of gene-antisocial behavior relationships. Carey (1994) conducted a review of research on genetic disorders with known or suspected heritability that have been suggested to generate heightened aggression, including deficiency in the enzyme urokinase, Tourette's syndrome, males' precocious puberty, α-mannosidosis, fragile X syndrome, lipoid proteinosis of Urbach and Wiethe, and deafness-hypogonadism syndrome. Carey concluded that aggression was not characteristic of these disorders except for the last two, which were insufficiently researched to draw a conclusion. Although males having an extra Y sex chromosome were once suspected of heightened capacity for aggression, longitudinal, prospective studies have suggested the mild increase in risk for antisocial behavior is probably secondary to deficits in cognitive and motor skills and in personality (e.g., Bender et al, 1987).

Hence, a single gene, Mendelian mode of inheritance (directly via chromosomes) for antisocial behavior is highly unlikely, and techniques used to investigate genetic influence on antisocial behavior must consider the combined influence of multiple genes at once, which can occur in numerous ways (Plomin et al., 1997). Systems of multiple genes can additively influence a trait; that is, each gene affects antisocial behavior independently and their cumulative genetic influence can be measured as a sum of the influence of individual genes. Nonadditive influence of genes on a trait may result from interactions between genetic mechanisms, such as occurs with the dominant-recessive pattern of eye color inheritance. Dominance refers to the differential influence of forms of an allele (alternative forms of a gene) that are inherited from each parent. A simplified breakdown of the relationship between eye color (brown versus blue) and genotype (individual's combination of alleles) that codes for eye color is that brown eye color is exhibited when one or both of the alleles is the dominant form and blue eye color is exhibited only when both alleles are the recessive form. The genotype is nonadditive because the dominant form of the allele overrides the coding of the recessive allele and having only one "brown eye color" allele does not generate half of the effect as having two such genes. Whereas dominance describes the interaction between alleles at a single locus (place on a chromosome), epistasis describes interlocus interactions in which the genetic effect on a phenotype occurs in a manner other than the sum of individual genes' influence on the phenotype. A single gene that is part of a multi-gene influence on a phenotype is referred to as a quantitative trait locus.

Association and Linkage Studies

Two general analytical techniques have been developed to investigate associations between quantitative trait loci in multiple-gene systems and complex phenotypes. An association study focuses on how antisocial behavior varies as a function of different combinations of genes at one or more specific locations, called candidate genes, that are suspected to influence the phenotype (e.g., Goldman, 1996). The linkage study is more exploratory and examines the relationship between some form of antisocial behavior and genome markers within samples of intergenerational family members (known as pedigrees) in hopes of narrowing the regions on the genome (the complete set of genes) where a gene that influences antisocial behavior might be located (Ott, 1991; Parsian et al., 1991). Because of the high probability of Type I errors (i.e., a statistically significant result that does not occur in reality), particularly in linkage analyses, replicated findings are essential.

Gene-behavior research attempts to answer three questions:

- Is a behavior heritable?
- Where are the genes that influence the behavior located on the genome?
- How do genes influence the behavior? (Maxson, 1996.)

Animal and association and linkage studies provide data regarding the second and third questions. Until the actual genes that influence antisocial behavior are identified, however, the different approaches collectively referred to as genetic epidemiology are used to address the first and third questions.

GENETIC EPIDEMIOLOGY

Twin Studies

Two natural experiments, twinning and adoptions, are typically used by the genetic epidemiologist (behavioral geneticist) to examine the heritability of a trait. The twin study takes advantage of the fact that monozygotic (MZ), or identical, twins share 100 percent of their genetic makeup, and dizygotic (DZ), or fraternal, twins share, on average, half of their genes. If a trait is genetically influenced, monozygotic twin pairs should be more similar with regard to the trait than dizygotic twin pairs. If only additive genetic mechanisms influence a trait, MZ twin pairs' correlation for the trait should equal 1.0, and DZ twin pairs' correlation should equal 0.5. If nonadditive genetic mechanisms influence the trait and no environmental influences occur, then a correlation of less than 0.5 for DZ twin pairs is expected. One complication to interpreting the estimate of genetic influence is that variation due to gene and environment interactions is included in the estimate of genetic influence.

Environmental factors also affect patterns of observed MZ and DZ twin pair associations and are separated into two types: shared and nonshared (or unique). Shared environmental variables include factors that affect phenotypic variation in both twins in the same direction. Shared environmental factors that have been shown to influence antisocial behavior include neighborhood characteristics (Sampson et al., 1997), socio-economic status (Farrington, 1993), and neonatal events (Kandel & Mednick, 1991). However, while both twins experience the same event, each may respond to the event differently, thereby lowering the co-twin correlation. DZ twin pairs' correlation is expected to be greater than half of the MZ correlation if shared environmental factors affect antisocial behavior, because they would cause both types of twin pairs' correlations to increase approximately to the same decrement.

One complication with estimating the strength of influence that the shared environment has on a trait is that while the shared environment decreases the difference in DZ and MZ correlations, nonadditive genetic mechanisms increase the difference in DZ and MZ correlations. Nonadditive genetic mechanisms are more difficult to detect using genetic epidemiological techniques than shared environmental influences, and because the two influences typically cannot both be modeled with the research methods used to date, estimates of shared environmental influence are more common.

Nonshared environmental factors affect each twin uniquely and serve to lower co-twin correlations. Examples of nonshared environmental variables reported to correlate with antisocial behavior include head injuries (Pallone & Hennessy, 1996) and quality of interactions with peers and teachers (Coie & Dodge, 1983; Achenbach et al., 1987). The relative influence of the nonshared environment is estimated from the difference between MZ twins' phenotypic correlation and unity. One complicating factor in interpreting this effect size is that measurement error also is contained in the variance attributed to nonshared environmental influence.

Adoption Studies

The adoption study also is used to investigate the relative influence of genetic and environmental variables on antisocial behavior. Significant phenotypic correlations between biological parents and offspring are attributed to genetic influences because children who have been given up for adoption (adoptees) share only genetic makeup with their biological parents. However, if the environments of biological parents and adoptees are characterized by similar environmental factors, they also may increase phenotypic correlations. Modern researchers attempt to minimize shared environmental effects among biological relatives by including only those adoptee-biological parent pairs that were separated soon after delivery. Despite this complication, a significant association between biological relatives who have been adopted apart is probably due to genetic influences, and significant phenotypic correlations among adoptees and their adoptive parents is interpreted as due to shared environmental influence.

Twin and Adoption Study Findings

Data Pertaining to Criminal Behavior. Tables 7.1 through 7.3 provide a summary of adult and juvenile twin studies and adoption studies that investigated genetic influence on antisocial behavior. Multiple reports have been published from several twin and adoption study databases; however, only those that present unique data, summarize a final dataset (i.e., data collection was complete), and are most relevant to the present discussion are included in this review. Because numerous recent reviews have summarized this literature (e.g., Gottesman & Goldsmith, 1994; Carey, 1996), this discussion is limited to interpretations of the data pertaining to criminal behavior. The questions, "Are the data consistent with a genetic influence on antisocial behavior?" and "Are the data consistent with an environmental influence on antisocial behavior?" are specifically addressed. Results consistent with genetic and/or environmental influences are indicated with "+" and those inconsistent with the effect are indicated with "-". Reasons that data might weakly suggest a particular influence include small effect size and small samples; in this case, a "+/-" was assigned to the genetic and/or environmental effect. Measures with good psychometric properties that have been well-validated were given more leeway in judging the validity of their results with regard to sample size. Probandwise concordance rates, which indicate the probability that a twin is affected given that his or her co-twin is affected, are presented for studies that reported dichotomized assessments of antisocial behavior (e.g., convicted versus not convicted).

Early twin studies of concordance rates of juvenile delinquency and adult criminality have been criticized for small samples, nonrepresentative samples, and poorly defined phenotypes (Slater & Cowie, 1971; Christiansen, 1977). Meta-analyses of these studies have been conducted; however, population prevalence rates must be taken into account when attempting to combine twin study concordance rates to avoid skewed estimates of genetic and environmental influences on a phenotype (Ridenour & Heath, in press). Because we are unable to calculate population prevalences for these phenotypes with a certain degree of accuracy at this time, each study is presented separately.

Estimations. Estimation of the degree to which antisocial behavior is due to genetic and environmental influence was not addressed presently for several reasons. Estimating nonshared environmental influence is difficult because of the unknown contribution of measurement error. The inability to account for genotype by environment interactions in already published datasets is discussed below, but probably renders estimates of genetic and environmental influence to be over-simplified and possibly inaccurate (Rutter, 1996). For many of the sample sizes collected to date, the confidence intervals for genetic and environmental influence are so large that the point estimate of influence provides little information. For example, if the 95 percent confidence limit for genetic influence on antisocial behavior reaches zero, it cannot be concluded that genes have any influence, regardless of the size of the best single estimate. For datasets reporting concordance in antisocial behavior among twin pairs, the liability-threshold model must be assumed to estimate the relative influence of

Table 7.1
Summary of Twin Studies Examining the Genetic Influence on Antisocial Behavior: Adult Twins

Study	Region	Phenotypic Measure/Assessment	Twin Pairs (% pairs affected[A])	Association Probandwise Concordance	r[B]	Consistent with genetic influence?	Consistent with environmental influence?
Gender-Specific Data							
Stumpfl (36)*	Germany	Psychopath Diagnosis	15 (100) M MZ	75%	-	+/-	+
			17 (100) M DZ	58%	-		
Kranz (37)*	Germany	Incarceration	31 (100) M MZ	78%	-	+/-	+
			43 (100) M DZ	70%	-		
Rosanoff, et al. (41)	California	Guilt in Court	38 (100) M MZ	87%	-	+/-	+
			23 (100) M DZ	36%	-		
			7 (100) F MZ	92%	-	+/-	+/-
			4 (100) F DZ	40%	-		
			36 M/F (78) M DZ[C]	27%	-		
			(31) F DZ[D]	11%	-		
Yoshimasu (61)*	Japan	Incarceration	28 (100) M MZ	76%	-	+/-	+
			18 (100) M DZ	20%	-		
Dalgard, et al. (76)	Norway	Criminal record registration	31 (100) M MZ	41%	-	+/-	+
			54 (100) M DZ	26%	-		
Rushton, et al. (86)	United Kingdom	Aggressiveness scale: selected items from the Interpersonal Behavior Survey	90 M MZ	-	.33	+	+
			46 M DZ	-	.16		
			206 F MZ	-	.43	+	+
			133 F DZ	-	.00		
			98 M/F DZ	-	.12		
Centerwall, et al. (89)	United States	Dishonorable discharge from military	5,933 (0.8) M MZ	26%	-	+	+
			7,554 (0.8) M DZ	3%	-		
Carey (92)	Denmark	Penal registration record	365 (20) M MZ	51%	.74[T]	+	+
			700 (21) M DZ	30%	.47		
			347 (4.3) F MZ	33%	.74	+	+
			690 (4.1) F DZ	13%	.46		
			2,073 M/F (9.6) M DZ[C]				
			(1.5) F DZ[D]	13%	.23		
Lyons et al. (96) (95)	United States	Self-reported arrest after 15 years of age	1,774 (26) M MZ	37%	-	+/-	+
			1,452 (28) M DZ	29%	-		
		DSM-III-R antisocial personality sx count	1,774 M MZ	-	.47[P]	+	+
			1,452 M DZ	-	.27		
Taylor, et al. (97)	Minnesota	Delinquent Behavior Inventory	143 M MZ	-	.58	+	+
			72 M DZ	-	.11		
			180 F MZ	-	.46	-	+
			91 F DZ	-	.48		

* Data were obtained and confirmed from secondary sources (Cloninger & Gottesman, 1989; Dalgard & Kringlin, 1976; Hayashi, 1967; Tienari, 1963). A= Percent of pairs in which at least one cotwin was affected in concordance studies. B=Correlations were Pearson product-moments unless otherwise specified. C=Percent of male cotwins affected; concordance of twin pairs given that female cotwin is affected. D=Percent of female cotwins affected; concordance of twin pairs given that male cotwin is affected. M=Male F=Female M/F=Male/Female. MZ=Monozygotic twin pairs. DZ=dizygotic twin pairs. I=intraclass correlation; P=polychoric correlation; T=tetrachoric correlation.

(cont'd on next page)

genes and environment (Falconer & Mackay, 1996; Kendler, 1993; Neale & Cardon, 1992; Pearson, 1901). An essential component in the liability-threshold model is the threshold level of risk, above which antisocial behavior is assumed to be exhibited

Table 7.1 (cont'd)

Study	Region	Phenotypic Measure/Assessment	Twin Pairs (% pairs affected^A)	Association Probandwise Concordance	r^B	Consistent with genetic influence?	Consistent with environmental influence?
Gender-Pooled Data							
Lange (29)*	Germany	Incarceration	13 (100) MZ	87%	-	+/-	+/-
			17 (100) DZ	21%	-		
LeGras (33)*	Netherlands	Incarceration	4 (100) MZ	100%	-	+/-	-
			5 (100) DZ	0%	-		
Borgstrom (39)*	Finland	Incarceration	4 (100) MZ	86%	-	+/-	+/-
			5 (100) DZ	57%	-		
Tienari (63)	Finland	Psychopath diagnosis	201 (13) MZ	57%	-	+	+
Gottesman (63)	Minnesota	MMPI Psychopathic Deviate Scale	34 MZ	-	.57	+/-	+/-
			34 DZ	-	.18		
Gottesman (65) in Gottesman et al.,94)	Boston	MMPI Psychopathic Deviate Scale	80 MZ	-	.46	+	+
			68 DZ	-	.25		
Gottesman et al. (84; in Gottesman et al., 1994)	Minnesota	MMPI Psychopathic Deviate Scale	Reared apart: 51 MZ	-	.64	+	+
			25 DZ	-	.34		
Rose (88; & in Gottesman et al., 1994)	Indiana U.	MMPI Psychopathic Deviate Scale	228 MZ	-	.47	+	+
			182 DZ	-	.23		
Tellegen, et al. (88)	Minnesota	Multidimensional Personality Questionnaire Aggression Scale	Reared together: 217 MZ	-	.43	+	+
			114 DZ	-	.14		
			Reared apart: 44 MZ	-	.46	+	+
			27 DZ	-	.06		
Grove, et al. (90)	Minnesota	DSM-III antisocial personality/sx count	Reared apart: 31 (19) MZ	29%	.28^I	+	+
Coid, et al. (93)	United Kingdom	Conviction	92 (24) MZ	53%	-	-	+
			109 (21) DZ	61%	-		

* Data were obtained and confirmed from secondary sources (Cloninger & Gottesman, 1989; Dalgard & Kringlin, 1976; Hayashi, 1967; Tienari, 1963). A= Percent of pairs in which at least one cotwin was affected in concordance studies. B=Correlations were Pearson product-moments unless otherwise specified. C=Percent of male cotwins affected; concordance of twin pairs given that female cotwin is affected. D=Percent of female cotwins affected; concordance of twin pairs given that male cotwin is affected. M=Male F=Female M/F=Male/Female. MZ=Monozygotic twin pairs. DZ=dizygotic twin pairs. I=intraclass correlation; P=polychoric correlation; T=tetrachoric correlation.

(typically estimated using epidemiological prevalences). Unfortunately, threshold value accuracy is questionable for many studies (e.g., Lange, 1931) because epidemiological estimates of phenotype prevalences are unavailable.

Environmental Influences. Twin study results are generally consistent with both genetic and nonshared environmental contributions to the familial aggregation of antisocial behavior because of the observed higher similarity among pairs of MZ twins versus DZ twins and the lower-than-unity association among MZ twin pairs. The results of many twin studies are inconsistent with shared environmental influences because DZ associations hover around one-half of MZ associations, although

Table 7.2
Summary of Twin Studies Examining the Genetic Influence on Antisocial Behavior: Juvenile Twins

Study	Region	Phenotypic Measure/Assessment	Twin Pairs (% pairs affected[A])	Association Probandwise Concordance	r^B	Consistent with genetic influence?	Consistent with environmental influence?
Gender-Specific Data							
Rosanoff, et al. (41)	California	Guilt in Juvenile Court	29 (100) M MZ	87%	-	+/-	+/-
			17 (100) M DZ	36%	-		
			12 (100) F MZ	92%	-	+/-	-
			9 (100) F DZ	40%	-		
			46 M/F (89) M DZ[C]	72%	-		
			(39) F DZ[D]	32%	-		
Gottesman (66); also see Carey, 1994	Boston	California Personality Inventory-Socialization	34 M MZ	-	.32	+	+
			32 M DZ	-	.06		
			45 F MZ	-	.52	+	+
			36 F DZ	-	.26		
Scarr (66)	Boston	Adjective Check List	24 F MZ	-	.35	+/-	+
			28 F DZ	-	.08		
Hayashi (67)	Japan	Incarceration	15 (100) M MZ	89%	-	-	+
			5 (100) M DZ	86%	-		
Sugamata (67)*	Japan	Incarceration	6 (100) M MZ	91%	-	+/-	
Rowe (85)	Ohio	Antisocial Behavior Scale	61 M MZ	-	.55	-	+
			38 M DZ	-	.76		
			107 F MZ	-	.66	+/-	+
			59 F DZ	-	.47		
Stevenson, et al. (88)	London	Parental behavior ratings	46 (24) M MZ	31%	-	-	+
			48 (31) M DZ	42%	-		
			53 (11) F MZ	50%	-	+	+
			58 (10) F DZ	0%	-		
Lyons, et al. (96) (95)	United States	Self-reported arrest before 15 years of age	1,774 (13) M MZ	47%	-	+/-	+
			1,452 (15) M DZ	41%	-		
		Conduct disorder sx count	1,774 M MZ	-	.39	+/-	+
			1,452 M DZ	-	.33		
Slutske, et al. (97)	Australia	DSM-III-R conduct disorder	396 (25) M MZ	30%	-	+	+
			231 (33) M DZ	18%	-		
			930 (3.6) F MZ	53%	-	+	+
			533 (5.6) F DZ	37%	-		
			592 M/F (19) M DZ[C]	45%	-		
			(3.4) F DZ[D]	8%	-		

(cont'd on next page)

the associations in antisocial behavior among MZ twin pairs reared apart are lower than those found in MZ twin pairs reared together. The only experimental study to examine twin similarity in aggression investigated children's imitation of an adult's aggression toward a Bobo doll; MZ and DZ twin pair associations were consistent with strong shared environmental influences (Plomin et al., 1981; Table 7.2). Data from other twin studies have also suggested imitation of antisocial behavior among twins, but even when imitation is accounted for, the contribution of genetic influence is considerable (Carey, 1992; Rowe, 1983).

Twin studies have been criticized for their assumption of equal environments

Table 7.2 (cont'd)

Study	Region	Phenotypic Measure/Assessment	Twin Pairs (% pairs affected[A])	Association Probandwise Concordance	r[B]	Consistent with genetic influence?	Consistent with environmental influence?
Gender-Pooled Data							
Kranz (37)	Germany	Delinquency	16 (100) MZ 22 (100) DZ	81% 74%	-	+/-	+
Plomin et al. (81)		Observed Bobo doll aggression (median of # of hits, hit intensity, area of hits)	53 MZ 31 DZ	- -	.39[I] .42	-	+
Ghodsian Carpey, et al. (87)	California	Child Behavior Checklist	42 MZ 32 DZ	- -	.78 .31	+	+
Grove, et al. (90)	Minnesota	DSM-III conduct disorder sx count	31 (19) MZ	-	.41[I]	+/-	+
McCartney, et al. (Meta-analysis) (90)		8 studies of aggression published from 67 to 85	not reported MZ not reported DZ	- -	.49 .29	+	+

* Data were obtained and confirmed from secondary sources (Cloninger & Gottesman, 1989; Dalgard & Kringlin, 1976; Hayashi, 1967; Tienari, 1963). A= Percent of pairs in which at least one cotwin was affected in concordance studies. B=Correlations were Pearson product-moments unless otherwise specified. C=Percent of male cotwins affected; concordance of twin pairs given female cotwin is affected. D=Percent of female cotwins affected; concordance of twin pairs given male cotwin is affected. M=Male F=Female M/F=Male/Female. MZ=Monozygotic twin pairs. DZ=dizygotic twin pairs. I=intraclass correlation; P=polychoric correlation; T=tetrachoric correlation.

among MZ and DZ twin pairs based on the reasonable possibility that MZ twins are treated more similarly by other persons than are DZ twins (Carey, 1996; Loehlin & Nichols, 1976). Parental perception of MZ twin pairs' similarity ranges from undifferentiation of the twins at one extreme to that of contrast effects where subtle differences between twins are exaggerated even to the point of mistaken zygosity (i.e., mistaking MZ twins for DZ). If this parental treatment of MZ twins impacts their correlation in antisocial behavior, it is expected that parentally undifferentiated twins should be more similar than twins of parents who use contrast effects; however, this has not been observed (Loehlin & Nichols, 1976; Morris-Yates et al., 1990; Bouchard & Propping, 1993; Kendler et al., 1993).

Moreover, studies of MZ twins reared apart control for confounding effects of parental treatment, and associations among these twin pairs are presumably due in part to genetic similarity. The 1979-1988 Minnesota Study of Twins Reared Apart (Gottesman et al., 1994; Grove et al., 1990; Tellegen et al., 1988) included several measures of antisocial behavior that were also used in other studies, allowing for comparison of twin pair similarity among adopted-away twin pairs and those who were raised by their biological parents. MZ and DZ correlations were similar among studies reporting on the Minnesota Multiphasic Personality Inventory "Psychopathic Deviate Scale" regardless of whether twins grew up in their biological family or were reared apart from other biological relatives (see Table 7.1). Regardless of rearing with or apart from biological families, similar MZ and DZ correlations were also reported in twin studies of conduct disorder symptom counts, adult antisocial personality symptom counts, and other measures of personality (e.g., Multidimensional Personality Questionnaire—Aggression, California Personality Inventory—Socialization; see Gough, 1965, 1987; Tellegen, 1982). Such robust findings provide compelling evidence in favor of a genet-

Table 7.3
Summary of Adoption Studies Examining the Genetic Influence on Antisocial Behavior

Study	Region	Phenotypic Measure/Assessment	# Probands**	Association Probandwise Concordance	r^B	Consistent with genetic influence?	Consistent with environmental influence?
Gender-Specific Data							
Baker, et al. (89)	Denmark	Conviction of property crime					
		(bio. son/father)	3,630 M	28%	-	+	+
		(adoptive son/father)	3,630 M	7%	-		
		(bio. daughter/mom)	3,922 F	12%	-	+	+
		(adoptive daughter/mom)	3,922 F	1%	-		
Bohman et al. (82)	Stockholm	Criminal register entry					
		(biological son/parent)	258	13%	-	-	+
		(adoptive son/parent)	463	10%			
Cadoret, et al. (91)	Iowa	Bio parents' DSM-III APD M childs' aggressivity score	283	64%	-	+	+
Cadoret, et al. (95)	Iowa	Childs' Aggressivity score Bio parents' DSM-III APD	95	54%	-	+	+
Willerman, et al. (92)	Texas	MMPI Pd>69	72 bio mother-child	48%	-	+	+
			72 adopt mother-child	0%	-		
			20 bio-bio sibs	-	-.06		
Gender-Pooled Data							
Zur Nieden (51)	Germany	Social-worker rating of bio. parents' criminal behavior or juvenile offense	148	22%	-	+	+
Crowe (74)	Iowa	Incarceration	41	17%	-	+/-	+
Cunningham, et al. (75)	St. Louis	Parents' DSM-III APD Child's behavior problems	114	40%	-	+	+
Jary, et al. (85)	Iowa	Bio parents' DSM-III APD DSM-III aggressive CD	79	40%	-	+	+
Loehlin, et al. (85)	Texas	California Personality Inventory -Socialization (220 families)	bio father-child	-	.16	+/-	+
			adopt father-child	-	-.03		
			bio mother-child	-	.25	+	+
			adopt mother-child	-	-.04		
		Siblings	76 adopt-adopt sibs	-	.03	-	+
			47 adopt-bio sibs	-	.10		
			15 bio-bio sibs	-	-.01		
(10 year follow-up)		MMPI-Psychopathic Deviate	bio father-child	-	.12	-	+
			adopt father-child	-	.07		
			bio mother-child	-	.07	-	+
			adopt mother-child	-	.01		
		Siblings	44 adopt-adopt sibs	-	.02	-	+
			69 adopt-bio sibs	-	.06		
Parker, 1989 (in Carey, 1994)		Child Behavior Checklist-aggression	45 adoptive sibs (age 4)	-	.54	-	+
			66 natural sibs		.42		

B=Correlations were Pearson product-moments unless otherwise specified. M=Male F=Female M/F=Male/Female. MZ=Monozygotic twin pairs. DZ=dizygotic twin pairs. I=intraclass correlation; P=polychoric correlation; T=tetrachoric correlation.

ic influence on personality measures related to antisocial behavior. Thus, it seems that the relative similarity in MZ and DZ twin pairs' social interactions do not significantly effect the correlations of their antisocial behavior.

Adoption study data generally indicate a moderate association between biological parents and adoptees and a null or small correlation between adoptees and their adoptive parents with respect to antisocial behavior. These findings are consistent with genetic and nonshared environmental influences on antisocial behavior. Generally, the data are inconsistent with adoptees' imitation of other family members' antisocial behavior. One exception is the results reported by Parker (1989, as cited in Carey, 1994), whose findings suggest a shared environmental influence on aggression. Parker's sample of siblings was much younger than sibling samples of other studies (Loehlin et al., 1985; 1987), and the author relied on maternal reports of siblings' antisocial behavior rather than individuals' self-reports. Eaves et al. (1997) illustrates how different estimates of heritability might be derived from different assessments. Thus, it is difficult to determine the extent to which differences in Parker's findings and Loehlin's findings reflect meaningful differences, are due to age or assessment, are otherwise spurious, or are nonsignificant.

GENOTYPE-ENVIRONMENT CORRELATIONS AND INTERACTIONS

Children reared by biological parents who exhibit antisocial behavior are probably at-risk for antisocial behavior genetically and because of the home environment. This is one form of a genotype-environment correlation, which has been described as exposure to an environment as a result of genetic influence (Kendler & Eaves, 1986; Plomin et al., 1977). Another type of genotype-environment correlation is a genetic influence on how individuals shape or actively seek out their environment (e.g., a juvenile with genetic propensity for delinquency might seek out companions with similar tendencies). Although it is difficult to disentangle the relative genetic and environmental influences in genotype-environment correlations, cross-fostering analysis has been used to estimate genotype-environment interactions, which have been described as genetic susceptibility to environments (Plomin et al., 1997).

Cross-fostering analysis is typically used with animal models, but also has been applied to adoption study data and examines adoptees' rate of criminality as a function of risk due to:

- The biological parents' background (genetic risk);
- The adoptive family (environmental risk); or
- Both (interaction effect).

Not surprisingly, in both the Danish and Swedish samples

- The proportion of biological parents who had been convicted of a crime was considerably higher than conviction rates in the general population;
- The adoptees' conviction rate was about the same as the general population; and
- The adoptive parents' conviction rates were considerably lower (Bohman, 1978; 1996; Hodgins et al., 1996; Mednick et al., 1987).

This suggests that adoptive children generally have lower functioning biological parents but higher functioning adoptive parents, a pattern seen in many adoption studies (e.g., see Carey, 1996) that may interfere with their generalizability to the wider population.

Biological Parents' Background

Results from one cross-fostering analysis suggest that if a biological parent of a male adoptee had been convicted of a crime in a Danish court (registered in the Strafferegistrer), the adoptee was more likely to have been convicted (20.5 percent) than a child without the genetic risk (13.6 percent) (Mednick et al., 1987). Of course, there are problems with conviction as a measure, resulting in likely underestimations due to variations in policing procedures and lawyers' skills, and changes in the law. Although the criminal history of adoptive parents did not appear to affect the conviction rates among adoptees whose biological parents were not convicted (14.7 percent if convicted versus 13.5 percent if not convicted), adoptive parents were only permitted to adopt if they had not been involved with the court system during the five years preceding the adoption.[2] Hence, variance in family environments among homes of convicted versus nonconvicted parents is unclear. However, if the biological parent had been convicted, the rate of conviction in adoptees was higher when an adoptive parent had also been convicted (24.5 percent versus 20.0 percent).

Adoptive Home Environment

One correlate of being convicted is membership in a lower social class; evidence for an interaction between a specific genotype and socio-economic status (SES) has been reported (Cadoret, 1985; Farrington, 1993). Cadoret and colleagues (1990) replicated Bohman's (1978; see also Bohman, 1996) findings that low adoptive family SES appeared to increase the risk for antisocial behavior in adoptees only if the adoptees' biological parents had a criminal or juvenile delinquent record. Similar contributions of SES and genetic risks were reported in the Danish sample (Van Dusen et al., 1983), but specific interactions were not reported. Cadoret and colleagues (1995) also replicated these results when adoptive homes were characterized by an "adverse adoptive home environment," defined as the presence of one or more of the following: marital problems, divorce or separation of adoptive parents, legal problems, parental anxiety or depression, or substance abuse or dependence. Hence, one or more of these variables may mediate the genotype by SES interaction.

Genotype/Environment Interaction

Researchers of Stockholm adoptees who were born out of wedlock from 1930 to 1950, assessed criminality risk differently and appeared to better predict risk for petty criminality (Bohman, 1978, 1996; Sigvardsson et al., 1982). Rather than using parental criminality as the risk factor (no adoptive parents were convicted; Bohman, 1996), specific biological parent and adoptive parent risk variables were identified and then used in a cross-fostering analysis to investigate their effect on adoptees' risk for petty criminality (e.g., property offenses). Some risk variables were gender-specific (e.g., females' risk for petty criminality rose with increasing biological father's average months in jail per conviction and males' risk was higher if the biological father had a teenage onset of alcoholism), whereas others affected risk for criminality across genders (e.g., extent of hospital care after birth served as a protective factor; biological father's conviction for a violent crime increased risk).

Although the prevalence of females' criminality was lower than males', gender-specific cross-fostering analyses showed a similar pattern among sexes of a nonadditive genotype/environment interaction. If an adoptee was indicated to be at-risk by biological parent and adoptive family variables, females were twenty-two times as probable, and males thirteen times as probable, to be registered for petty criminality compared to adoptees who were not at-risk. Where only biological parent background indicated risk for adoptees, a fourfold increase in risk for petty criminality was found for both females and males. When adoptees were at-risk for petty criminality by adoptive parents only, the risk in females was sixfold and the risk in males was twice that of adoptees who were not at-risk. These findings are consistent with genetics and environment working in combination to influence antisocial behavior.

Among the males of the Stockholm study, alcohol abuse and criminality were highly correlated. When families with alcohol abusing biological fathers were excluded from the analysis, adoptees with criminal biological fathers (i.e., the fathers were listed in the official register of criminality) were only about twice as likely to have a criminal record than were sons of noncriminal biological fathers (Bohman, 1983). Moreover, alcoholic criminals tended to commit violent offenses, whereas nonalcoholic criminals tended to commit petty offenses (Bohman et al., 1982; Bohman, 1983). Therefore, different etiologies for criminal behavior may occur among alcoholics versus nonalcoholics, including different genetic mechanisms. Findings of similar genetic and environmental influences on both antisocial behavior and alcoholism have been replicated, but further investigation of subtypes of criminal activity as a function of genetic predisposition to alcoholism has not been addressed (e.g., Cadoret, 1985; Cadoret et al., 1990; 1995; Slutske et al., 1998).

Attention deficit hyperactivity disorder (ADHD) appears to aggregate in families independently of conduct disorder and antisocial personality (e.g., Lahey et al., 1988; Stewart et al., 1980). Recent studies, however, suggest a co-occurrence between ADHD, antisocial behavior, and/or alcoholism, at least in a subgroup or in part, due to overlapping genetic etiological contributions (e.g., Biederman et al., 1987; Cadoret & Stewart, 1991; Coccaro et al., 1993; Faraone et al., 1995; Silberg et al., 1996). Thus, ADHD and conduct disordered behavior may reflect early manifestations of underlying genetic mechanisms that place individuals at risk for later antisocial behavior and alcoholism.

DISCUSSION—OVERLAP OF ANTISOCIAL/OTHER PHENOTYPES AND OTHER INFLUENCES

Risks of Twin Birth Complications

Carey (1996) describes potential caveats to the interpretation of twin and adoption studies of antisocial behavior. Equal environments assumes shared environmental factors influence twins identically, although it is possible that twins may respond to these circumstances dissimilarly. The fact that pre- (before) and perinatal (during) birth complications occur more often with twins than with singletons may affect antisocial behavior because of the reported association between brain injury resulting from birth complications and (1) violent behavior (Kandel & Mednick, 1991; Kilby et al., 1994; McNeil et al., 1994; Szatmari et al., 1986), (2) higher rates of behavioral problems, and (3) lower average intelligence scores reported for twins compared to singletons (Gau et al., 1992; Hay et al., 1984; Siminoff, 1992).

If these effects are associated with being a twin, however, the size of shared environmental effects would be inflated and estimates of genetic influence would be reduced. In addressing the present question, "Is there a genetic influence on antisocial behavior?", an affirmative response is evidenced in spite of risks associated with twinning rather than because of those risks. The size of the genetic effect, however, may not generalize directly to singletons.

Estimates of the size of genetic contribution to antisocial behavior derived from twin studies would probably be higher than estimates derived from adoption studies (Carey, 1994). One explanation for the differences in twin and adoption heritability estimates concerns the truncation of samples that occur as a consequence of each study design. Twins who exhibit higher levels of antisocial traits and/or alcoholism are less likely to participate in studies that obtain subjects from the general population (i.e., volunteer or paid subjects; see Rowe, 1986), although some persons with severe pathology do participate. On the other hand, children are more likely to be given up for adoption by parents with problems due to alcohol use or antisocial behavior, and parents with very low levels of antisocial traits or alcoholism rarely give up their children for adoption (Bohman, 1996). The general population twin study sample will therefore represent a wider range of severity in pathology and produce greater variance and larger correlations than do adoption studies.

Age and Assessment Differences in Twin vs. Adoption Studies

The difference in twin and adoption study heritability estimates may also be due, in part, to differences in age and assessments. Twins are assessed at the same age and with the same assessment, whereas adoption studies assess parents and their biological children either using different measures at the same point in time, or using the same measurements (e.g., entry into a criminal register) at different points in time without accounting for possible cohort effects. Because of the lowered correlation resulting from using two measurements or time lapse, a greater estimate of unique environmental influence and a smaller estimate of genetic influence would be detected.

Differences in the size of genetic influence on antisocial behavior may also result from differences in the mislocation of phenotypic variance associated with genotype/environment interaction when it is not accounted for in the study. Phenotypic variance due to interactions between genes and shared environment in studies of twin pairs reared together is confounded with the main effect of additive genetic influences (Heath, 1998; Rutter, 1997). Assuming sizable interactions occur, adoption study estimates of heritability should be lower because the interaction effects would not be included in the adoption study estimates of heritability. Regardless of the reasons for the difference in heritability estimates that would be derived from twin and adoption studies, each points to an important contribution of genetic influences on individual differences in antisocial behavior.

Implications for Crime Control

These results have practical and theoretical implications for crime control strategy. Research indicates that the criminal justice system, which relies on punishment as its primary tactic, is ineffective in deterring crime and that exorbitant amounts of money are being spent to expand the ineffective system in terms of more prisons, high recidivism rates, and a rapidly increasing population of criminals (e.g., Donziger, 1997; Jeffery, in press). Crime control agencies would benefit from research investigating preventive interventions that successfully curb crime and save money in the long term, as well as research identifying subtypes of criminals known to respond unfavorably to their current interventions (e.g., Mulvey et al., 1993; Nygaard, 1996a; Schweinhart, 1987; Seitz et al., 1985; Rice, 1997). Unfortunately, these data and alternative crime control strategies are typically neglected by the criminal justice system (Megargee, 1995; Palmer, 1995; Van Voorhis, 1987).

Genetic epidemiological research provides further compelling evidence that processes other than free will increase the risk for antisocial behavior and provide data that may inform an understanding of the etiology of crime; such research is therefore useful for improving crime control strategies (Nygaard, 1996b; Jeffery, in press). Because twin and adoption studies investigate populations, their results do not inform the determination of the relative contributions of genetic and environmental risk factors for an individual. Phenocopies (i.e., similar phenotypes that are caused by different mechanisms) also interfere with the interpretability of heritability estimates. Moreover, the genetic epidemiology literature has generally neglected to investigate specific mechanisms of genetic and environmental influence on antisocial behavior. However, this body of literature provides consistent, compelling evidence that genetic mechanisms play an important role in the risk for antisocial behavior and crime.

"Career Criminals." It has been argued that the subgroup of criminals who have been labeled "career criminals" or "life-course-persistent" may exhibit antisocial behavior in part due to a unique genetic makeup, since their antisocial behavior persists in spite of harsh punishment of their behavior (e.g., DiLalla & Gottesman, 1989; Farrington et al., 1990; Moffitt, 1993; Nagin et al., 1995; Nagin & Land, 1993). A chronic disease model consisting of early and continuous intervention may be the most promising for this subgroup. Research focusing on identification of this subgroup might eventually enable efficient delivery of early intervention (Fagan et al., 1986; Feldman et al., 1983; Mulvey et al., 1993; Rice, 1997).

Alcoholism. Increasing numbers of studies have examined the overlap in etiology of antisocial behavior and other phenotypes. Application of these behavioral genetic data to inform early interventions may lead to a more efficacious crime control strategy. Emerging literature suggests some degree of overlap in genetic risk for antisocial behavior and alcoholism, which has practical implications in light of the fact that 33 to 60 percent of all crimes involve alcohol consumption (Wilson & Herrnstein, 1985). In approximately 20 percent of all crimes committed by offenders incarcerated in state prisons in the mid-1980s, the offender was under the influence of alcohol, and in approximately 54 percent of the crimes, the offender was under the influence of alcohol and/or another drug (BJS, 1988). The high percentage of crimes committed during intoxication may not be due entirely to physiological changes resulting from alcohol, but also to risk factors common to both alcohol consumption and antisocial behavior.

Investigations of risk and protective factors pertaining to alcohol misuse and assessments of the efficacy of substance abuse intervention programs may also inform crime control strategies. Attempts to decrease risk factors or to increase protective factors associated with alcohol consumption may help lower crime rates. Likewise, future criminal activity in young children who exhibit disruptive behavior might be reduced by administering effective interventions aimed at prevention of substance misuse (Brook et al., 1996). The logic of this strategy is consistent with preschool treatments that failed to accomplish their initial goal of improving intelligence, but lowered rates of delinquency (Farnworth et al., 1985; Mulvey et al., 1993).

Impulsivity. In the same vein, impulsivity, or lack of behavioral inhibition, is consistently associated with antisocial behavior (Coccaro et al., 1993; Gottfredson & Hirschi, 1990). Genetic predisposition plays an important role in individuals' levels of impulsivity, apart from hyperactivity and inattention (Coccaro et al., 1993; Hudziak et al., 1998). Given that high levels of impulsivity might be identified at a young age, treatments implemented early on to reduce impulsivity (or increase behavioral monitoring and inhibition) may subsequently reduce future crime rates among children who would otherwise poorly manage their behavior (Anastopoulos et al., 1991; Newby et al., 1991; Whalen & Henker, 1991).

Number of Environmental Stressors Bearing on Risk. One theoretical conceptualization of the role of genes regarding crime might be derived by generalizing Gottesman's (1991) stress-diathesis model of schizophrenia to antisocial behavior (Hiester et al., 1994). Under this model, individuals are assumed to inherit some level of genetic risk for antisocial behavior and environmental stressors interact with genetic risks to alter the probability that antisocial behavior is exhibited, with additional environmental risks ever increasing that probability (Cicchetti & Lynch, 1993; Pianta & Egeland, 1990; Simmons & Blyth, 1987; Cloninger & Gottesman, 1987). Hence, persons with greater genetic risk for antisocial behavior require fewer environmental risks to exhibit antisocial behavior and vice versa. Such a model implies a very different approach to crime control than a punishment paradigm.

Of course, environmental stressors would be continually in flux and probably would be a focus of intervention (e.g., keeping the number of environmental stressors low; Hiester et al., 1994). Genetic risk is likely to also be at an unstable level as genetic coding "turns on and off," but a within-person average or maximum level of genetic risk for antisocial behavior may be useful for identifying those at greatest risk for criminal activity. Identification facilitates prevention to hinder these individuals from approaching some threshold level of risk for antisocial behavior. An additive model of risk is over-simplified, as demonstrated by the interaction between biological family antisocial behavior and SES. This approach would nevertheless allow for subtypes, fluctuation in risk over age, a variety of developmental pathways into and out of exhibiting antisocial behavior, and gender-specific models, all of which are important components to include in a developmental theory of antisocial behavior and are useful in guiding crime control strategies (Loeber & Stouthamer-Loeber, 1998).

Footnotes

[1] Types of animal aggression include offensive, defensive, infanticide, and predation.

[2] Adults with a criminal record were considered adoption candidates in part because the adoptions took place during 1924 to 1947—a period encompassing the Great Depression and World War II —when persons who were willing to adopt were less prevalent (Mednick et al., 1987).

References

Achenbach, T. M., Edelbrock, C. & Howell, C. (1987). Empirically-based assessment of the behavioral/emotional problems of 2-3 year old children. *Journal of Abnormal Child Psychology, 15,* 629–650.

Anastopoulos, A. D., DuPaul, G. J. & Barkley, R. A. (1991). Stimulant medication and parent training therapies for attention deficit-hyperactivity disorder. *Journal of Learning Disabilities, 24,* 210–217.

Baker, L. A., Mack, W., Moffitt, T. E. & Mednick, S. (1989). Sex differences in property crime in a Danish adoption cohort. *Behavior Genetics, 19,* 355–370.

Bender, B. G., Linden, M. G. & Robinson, A. (1987). Environment and developmental risk in children with sex chromosome abnormalities. *Journal of the American Academy of Child and Adolescent Psychiatry, 26,* 499–503.

Biederman, J., Munir, K. & Knee, D. (1987). Conduct and oppositional disorder in clinically referred children with attention deficit disorder: A controlled family study. *Journal of the American Academy of Child and Adolescent Psychiatry, 26,* 724–727.

Bohman, M. (1978). Some genetic aspects of alcoholism and criminality. A population of adoptees. *Archives of General Psychiatry, 35,* 269–276.

Bohman, M. (1983). Alcoholism and crime: Studies of adoptees. *Substance and alcohol actions/misuse, 4,* 137–147.

Bohman, M. (1996). Predisposition to criminality: Swedish adoption studies in retrospect. In G. R. Bock & J. A. Goode (Eds.), *Genetics of criminal and antisocial behavior.* West Sussex, England: John Wiley & Sons, 99–114.

Bohman, M., Cloninger, C. R., Sigvardsson, S. & von Knorring, A. L. (1982). Predisposition to petty criminality in Swedish adoptees: I. Genetic and environmental heterogeneity. *Archives of General Psychiatry, 39,* 1233–1241.

Bouchard, T. H., Jr. & Propping, P. (Eds.) (1993). *Twins as a tool of behavioral genetics.* New York: John Wiley & Sons.

Brain, P. F., Mainardi, D. & Parmigiani, S. (1989). *House mouse aggression: A model for understanding the evolution of social behavior.* London: Harwood Academic Publishers.

Brook, J. S., Whiteman, M., Finch, S. J. & Cohen, P. (1996). Young adult drug use and delinquency: Childhood antecedents and adolescent mediators. *Journal of American Academy of Child and Adolescent Psychiatry, 35,* 1584–1592.

Bureau of Justice Statistics (BJS) (1988). *Criminal victimization in the United States: Trends.* Washington, DC: U.S. Department of Justice reports.

Cadoret, R. J. (1985). Genes, environment and their interaction in the development of psychopathology. In T. Sakai & T. Tsuboi (Eds.), *Genetic aspects of human behavior.* Tokyo, Japan: Igaku-Shoin.

Cadoret, R. J. & Stewart, M. A. (1991). An adoption study of attention deficit/hyperactivity/aggression and their relationship to adult antisocial personality. *Comprehensive Psychiatry, 32,* 73–82.

Cadoret, R. J., Troughton, E., Bagford, J. & Woodworth, G. (1990). Genetic and environmental factors in adoptee antisocial personality. *European Archives of Psychiatry and Neurological Sciences, 239,* 231–240.

Cadoret, R. J., Yates, W. R., Troughton, E., Woodworth, G. & Stewart, M. A. (1995). Adoption study demonstrating two genetic pathways to drug abuse. *Archives of General Psychiatry, 52,* 42–52.

Carey, G (1992). Twin imitation for antisocial behavior: Implications for genetic and family environment research. *Journal of Abnormal Psychology, 101,* 18–25.

Carey, G. (1994). Genetics and violence. In A. J. Reiss, Jr., K. A. Miczek & J. A. Roth (Eds.), *Understanding and preventing violence,* vol. 2, *Biobehavioral influences.* Washington, DC: National Academy Press, 21–58.

Carey, G. (1996). Family and genetic epidemiology of aggressive and antisocial behavior. In D. M. Stoff & R. B. Cairns (Eds.), Aggression and violence: *Genetic, neurobiological and biosical perspectives.* Hillsdale, NJ: Erlbaum, 3–21.

Centerwall, B. S. & Robinette, C. D. (1989). Twin concordance for dishonorable discharge from the military: With a review of the genetics of antisocial behavior. *Comprehensive Psychiatry, 30,* 442–446.

Christiansen, K. O. (1977). A review of studies of criminality among twins. In S. A. Mednick & K. O. Christiansen (Eds.), *Biosocial bases of criminal behavior.* New York: Gardner Press, 45–88.

Cicchetti, D. & Lynch, M. (1993). Toward an ecological/transactional model of community violence and child maltreatment: Consequences for children's development. *Psychiatry: Interpersonal & Biological Processes, 56,* 96–118.

Cloninger, C. R. & Gottesman, I. I. (1987). Genetic and environmental factors in antisocial behavior disorders. In S. A. Mednick, T. E. Moffitt & S. A. Stack (Eds.), *The causes of crime: New biological approaches.* New York: Cambridge University Press, 92–109.

Coccaro, E. F., Bergeman, C. S. & McClearn, G. E. (1993). Heritability of irritable impulsiveness: A study of twins reared together and apart. *Psychiatry Research, 48,* 229–242.

Coid, B., Lewis, S. W. & Reveley, A. M. (1993). A twin study of psychosis and criminality. *British Journal of Psychiatry, 162,* 87–92.

Coie, J. D. & Dodge, K. A. (1983). Continuities and changes in children's social status: A five-year longitudinal study. *Merrill-Palmer Quarterly, 29,* 261–281.

Crowe, R. R. (1974). An adoption study of antisocial personality. *Archives of General Psychiatry, 31,* 785–791.

Cunningham, L., Cadoret, R. J., Loftus, R. & Edwards, J. E. (1975). Studies of adoptees from psychiatrically disturbed biological parents: Psychiatric conditions in childhood and adolescence. *British Journal of Psychiatry, 126,* 534–549.

Dalgard, O. S. & Kringlen, E. (1976). A Norwegian twin study of criminality. *British Journal of Criminology, 16,* 213–232.

DiLalla, L. F. & Gottesman, I. I. (1989). Heterogeneity of causes for delinquency and criminality: Lifespan perspectives. *Development and Psychopathology, 1,* 339–349.

Donzinger, S. R. (1997). *The real war on crime.* New York: HarperCollins.

Earls, F., Reich, W., Jung, K. G. & Cloninger, C. R. (1988). Psychopathology in children of alcoholic and antisocial parents. *Alcoholism: Clinical and experimental research, 12,* 481–487.

Eaves, L. J., Silberg, J. L., Meyer, J. M., Maes, H. H., Simonoff, E., Pickles, A., Rutter, M., Neale, M. C., Reynolds, C. A., Erikson, M. T., Heath, A. C., Loeber, R., Truett, K. R., Hewitt, J. K. (1997). Genetics and developmental psychopathology: 2. The main effects of genes and environment on behavioral problems in the Virginia twin study of adolescent behavioral development. *Journal of Child Psychology and Psychiatry, 38,* 965–980.

Fagan J., Piper E. & Moore, M. (1986). Violent delinquents and urban youths. *Criminology, 24,* 439–471.

Falconer, D .S. & Mackay, T. F. C. (1996). *Introduction to quantitative genetics.* Essex, England: Longman.

Faraone, S. V., Biederman, J., Chen, W. J., Milberger, S., Warburton, R. & Tsuang, M. T. (1995). Genetic heterogeneity in attention-deficit hyperactivity disorder (ADHD): Gender, psychiatric comorbidity, and maternal ADHD. *Journal of Abnormal Psychology, 104,* 334–345.

Farnworth, M., Schweinhart, L. J. & Berrueta-Clement, J. R. (1985). Preschool intervention, school success and delinquency in a high-risk sample of youth. *American Educational Research Journal, 22,* 445–464.

Farrington, D. P. (1993). Interactions between individual and contextual factors in the development of offending. In R. Silbereisen & E. Todt (Eds.), *Adolescence in context.* New York: Springer-Verlag, 366–389.

Farrington, D. P., Loeber, R. & Van Kammen, W. B. (1990). Long-term criminal outcomes of hyperactivity-impulsivity-attention deficit and conduct problems in childhood. In L. N. Robins & M. Rutter (Eds.), *Straight and devious pathways from childhood to adulthood.* New York: Cambridge University Press, 62–81.

Feldman, R. A., Caplinger, T. E., Wodarski, J. S. (1983). *The St. Louis conundrum: The effective treatment of antisocial youths.* Englewood Cliffs, NJ: Prentice-Hall.

Frick, P. J., Lahey, B. B., Loeber, R., Stouthamer-Loeber, M., Christ, M. A. G. & Hanson, K. (1992). Familial risk factors to oppositional defiant disorder and conduct disorder: Parental psychopathology and maternal parenting. *Journal of Consulting and Clinical Psychology, 60,* 49–55.

Gau, J. S., Silberg, J. L., Erickson, M. T. & Hewitt, J. K. (1992). Childhood behavior problems: A comparison of twin and non-twin samples. *Acta Geneticae Medicae et Gemellologiae, 41,* 53–63.

Ghodsian-Carpey, J. & Baker, L. A. (1987). Genetic and environmental influences on aggression in 4- to 7-year-old twins. *Aggressive Behavior, 13,* 173–186.

Glueck, S. & Glueck, E. (1950). *Unraveling juvenile delinquency.* New York: The Commonwealth Fund.

Goldman, D. (1996). The search for genetic alleles contributing to self-destructive and aggressive behaviors. In D. M. Stoff & R. B. Cairns (Eds.), *Aggression and violence: Genetic, neurobiological, and biological perspectives.* Hillsdale, NJ: Erlbaum, 23–40.

Gottesman, I. I. (1966). Genetic variance in adaptive personality traits. *Journal of Child Psychology and Psychiatry, 7,* 199–208.

Gottesman, I. I. (1991). *Schizophrenia genesis: The origins of madness.* New York: W.H. Freeman.

Gottesman, I. I. & Goldsmith, H. H. (1994). Developmental psychopathology of antisocial behavior: Inserting genes into its ontogenesis and epigenesis. In C. A. Nelson (Ed.), *Threats to optimal development: Integrating biological, psychological, and social risk factors.* Hillsdale, NJ: Erlbaum, 69–104.

Gottfredson, M.R. & Hirschi, T. (1990). *A general theory of crime.* Palo Alto, CA: Stanford University Press.

Gough, H. G. (1965). Conceptual analysis of psychological test scores and other diagnostic variables. *Journal of Abnormal Psychology, 70,* 294–302.

Gough, H. G. (1987). *California Psychological Inventory (Administrator's Guide).* Palo Alto, CA: Consulting Psychologists Press.

Grove, W. M., Eckert, E. D., Heston, L., Bouchard, T. J., Jr., Segal, N. & Lykken, D. T. (1990). Heritability of substance abuse and antisocial behavior: A study of monozygotic twins reared apart. *Biological Psychiatry, 27,* 1293–1304.

Hay, D. A., O'Brien, P. J., Johnston, C. J. & Prior, M. (1984). The high incidence of reading disability in twin boys and its implication for genetic analysis. *Acta Geneticae Medicae et Gemellogiae, 33,* 223–236.

Hayashi, S. (1967). A study of juvenile delinquency in twins. In H. Mitsuda (Ed.), *Clinical genetics in psychiatry.* Tokyo, Japan: Iqaku Shoin, 153–172.

Heath, A. C. (April 20, 1998). Personal communication.

Hiester, M., Ogawa, J. R., Ostoja, E., Susman, A. R. & Weinfield, N. S. (1994). The role of biological and psychosocial risk factors in development: Commentary on Kopp, Musick, and Aber. In C.A. Nelson (Ed.), *Threats to optimal development: Integrating biological, psychological, and social risk factors.* Hillsdale,NJ: Erlbaum, 273–284.

Hodgins, S., Mednick, S. A., Brennan, P. A., Schulsinger, F., & Engberg, M. (1996). Mental disorder and crime. *Archives of General Psychiatry, 53,* 489–496.

Hudziak, J. J., Heath, A. C., Madden, P. A. F., Reich, W., Bucholz, K. K., Slutske, W., Bierut, L. J., Neuman, R. & Todd, R. D. (1998). The latent class and factor analysis of DSM-IV ADHD: A study of female adolescents. *Journal of the American Academy of Child and Adolescent Psychiatry.*

Jeffery, C. R. (1998). Criminology and criminal law: Science vs. policy, and the interaction of science and law. In W. S. Laufer & F. Adler (Eds.), *Advances in criminological theory,* vol. 8. New Brunswick, NJ: Transaction.

Kandel, E. & Mednick, S.A. (1991). Perinatal complications predict violent offending. *Criminology, 29,* 519–530.

Kendler, K. S. (1993). Twin studies of psychiatric illness: Current status and future directions. *Archives of General Psychiatry, 50,* 905–915.

Kendler, K. S. & Eaves, L. J. (1986). Models for the joint effects of genotype and environment on liability to psychiatric illness. *American Journal of Psychiatry, 143,* 279–289.

Kendler, K. S., Neale, M. C., Kessler, R. C., Heath, A. C. & Eaves, L. J. (1993). A test of the equal-environment assumption in twin studies of psychiatric illness. *Behavior Genetics, 23,* 21–27.

Kilby, M. D., Govind, A. & O'Brien, P. M. (1994). Outcome of twin pregnancies complicated by a single intrauterine death: A comparison with viable twin pregnancies. *Obstetrics and Gynecology, 84,* 107–109.

Kolvin, I., Miller, F. J. W., Fleeting, M. & Kolvin, P. A. (1988). Social and parenting factors affecting criminal-offence rates: Findings from the Newcastle Thousand Family Study (1947–1980). *British Journal of Psychiatry, 152,* 80–90.

Lahey, B. B., Piacentini, J. C., McBurnett, K., Stone, P., Hartdagen, S. & Hynd, G. (1988). Psychopathology in the parents of children with conduct disorder and hyperactivity. *Journal of the American Academy of Child and Adolescent Psychiatry, 27,* 163–170.

Lange, J. (1931). *Crime as destiny* (trans. C. Haldene). London: Allen & Unwin.

Loeber, R. & Stouthamer-Loeber, M. (1998). Development of juvenile aggression and violence: Some common misconceptions and controversies. *American Psychologist, 53,* 242–259.

Loehlin, J. C. & Nichols, R. C. (1976). *Heredity, environment and personality: A study of 850 sets of twins.* Austin, TX: University of Texas Press.

Loehlin, J. C., Willerman, L. & Horn, J. M. (1985). Personality resemblances in adoptive families when the children are late-adolescent or adult. *Journal of Personality and Social Psychology, 48,* 376–392.

Loehlin, J. C., Willerman, L. & Horn, J. M. (1987). Personality resemblances in adoptive families: A 10-year follow-up. *Journal of Personality and Social Psychology, 53,* 961–969.

Lyons, M. J. (1996). A twin study of self-reported criminal behavior. In G. R. Bock & J. A. Goode (Eds.), *Genetics of criminal and antisocial behavior.* West Sussex, England: John Wiley & Sons, 61–75.

Lyons, M. J., True, W. R., Eisen, S. A., Goldberg, J., Meyer, J. M., Faraone, S. V., Eaves, L. J. & Tsuang, M. T. (1995). Differential heritability of adult and juvenile antisocial traits. *Archives of General Psychiatry, 52,* 906–915.

Maxson, S. C. (1990). Methodological issues in genetic analyses of an agonistic behavior (offense) in male mice. In D. Goldowitz, R. E. Wimer & D. Wahlsten (Eds.), *Techniques for the genetic analysis of brain and behavior.* Amsterdam: Elsevier Science Publishers.

Maxson, S. C. (1992). Potential genetic models of aggression and violence in males. In P. Driscoll (Ed.), *Genetically defined animal models of neurobehavioral dysfunctions.* Boston, MA: Birkhauser, 174–188.

Maxson, S. C. (1996). Issues in the search for candidate genes in mice as potential animal models of human aggression. In *Genetics of criminal and antisocial behavior.* New York: John Wiley & Sons, 21–35.

McCartney, K., Harris, M. J. & Bernieri, F. (1990). Growing up and growing apart: A developmental meta-analysis of twin studies. *Psychological Bulletin, 107,* 226–237.

McCord, J. & McCord, W. (1958). The effects of parental role model on criminality. *Journal of Social Issues, 14*, 66–75.

McNeil, T. F., Cantor-Graae, E., Torrey, E. F., Sjostrom, K., Bowler, A., Taylor, E., Rawlings, R. & Higgins, E. S. (1994). Obstetric complications in histories of monozygotic twins discordant and concordant for schizophrenia. *Acta Psychiatrica Scandinavia, 89,* 196–204.

Mednick, S. A., Gabrielli, W. F. & Hutchings, B. (1987). Genetic factors in the etiology of criminal behavior. In S. A. Mednick, T. E. Moffitt, S. A. Stack (Eds.), *The causes of crime: New biological approaches.* New York: Cambridge University Press, 74–91.

Megargee, E. I. (1995). Assessment research in correctional settings: Methodological issues and practical problems. *Psychological Assessment, 7,* 359–366.

Michard-Vanhee, C. (1988). Aggressive behavior induced in female mice by an early single dose of testosterone is genotype dependent. *Behavior Genetics, 18,* 1–12.

Moffitt, T. E. (1993). Adolescence-limited and life-course-persistent antisocial behavior: A developmental taxonomy. *Psychological Review, 100,* 674–701.

Moore, M. (1995). Public health and criminal justice approaches to prevention. In M. Tonry & D. Farrington (Eds.), *Building a safer society.* Chicago: University of Chicago Press, 237–262.

Morris-Yates, A., Andrew, G., Howie, P. & Henderson, S. (1990). Twins: A test of the equal environments assumption. *Acta Psychiatrica Scandinavia, 8,* 322–326.

Mulvey, E. P., Arthur, M. W. & Reppucci, N. D. (1993). The prevention and treatment of juvenile delinquency: A review of the research. *Clinical Psychology Review, 13,* 133–167.

Nagin, D. S. Farrington, D. P. & Moffitt, T. E. (1995). Life-course trajectories of different types of offenders. *Criminology, 33,* 111–139.

Nagin, D. S. & Land, K. C. (1993). Age, criminal careers, and population heterogeneity: Specification and estimation of a nonparametric, mixed poisson model. *Criminology, 31,* 327–362.

Neale, M. C. & Cardon, L. R. (1992). *Methodology for genetic studies of twins and families.* Dordrecht, Netherlands: Kluwer.

Newby, R. F., Fischer, M. & Roman, M. A. (1991). Parent training for families of children with ADHD. *School Psychology Review, 20,* 252–265.

Nygaard, R. L. (1996a). On death as punishment. *University of Pittsburg Law Review, 57,* 825–840.

Nygaard, R. L. (1996b). Free will, determinism, penology, and the human genome: Where's a new Leibniz when we really need him? *University of Chicago Law School Roundtable, 3,* 1–40.

Ott, J. (1991). *Analysis of human genetic linkage.* Baltimore: Johns Hopkins University Press.

Pallone, N. J. & Hennessy, J. J. (1996). *Tinder-box criminal aggression: Neuropsychology, demography, phenomenology.* New Brunswick, NJ: Transaction Books.

Palmer, T. (1995). Programmatic and nonprogrammatic aspects of successful intervention: New directions for research. *Crime & Delinquency, 41,* 100–131.

Parsian, A., Todd, R. D., Devor, E. J., O'Malley, K. L., Suarez, B. K., Reich, T. & Cloninger, C. R. (1991). Alcoholism and alleles of the human D2 dopamine receptor locus. *Archives of General Psychiatry, 48,* 655–663.

Patterson, G. R., Crosby, L. & Vuchinish, S. (1992). Predicting risk for early police arrest. *Journal of Quantititative Criminology, 8,* 335–355.

Pearson, K. (1901). Mathematical contributions to the theory of evolution, VII: On the correlation of characters not quantitatively measureable. *Philosophical Transactions of the Royal Society of London, Series A 1901, 195,* 1–47.

Pianta, R. C. & Egeland, B. (1990). Life stress and parenting outcomes in a disadvantaged sample: Results of mother-child interaction project. *Journal of Clinical Child Psychology, 19,* 329–336.

Plomin, R., DeFries, J. C. & Loehlin, J. C. (1977). Genotype-enviornment interaction and correlation in the analysis of human behavior. *Psychological Bulletin, 84,* 309–322.

Plomin, R., DeFries, J. C., McClearn, G. E. & Rutter, M. (1997). *Behavior genetics* (3d ed.). New York: Freeman & Co.

Plomin, R., Foch, T. T. & Rowe, D. C. (1981). Bobo clown aggression in childhood: Environment, not genes. *Journal of Research in Personality, 15,* 331–342.

Rice, M. E. (1997). Violent offender research and implications for the criminal justice system. *American Psychologist, 52,* 414–423.

Ridenour, T. A. & Heath, A. C. (in press). A note on issues in meta-analysis for behavioral genetic studies of non-randomly ascertained samples. *Behavior Genetics.*

Robins, L. N. (1966). *Deviant children grown up. A sociological and psychiatric study of sociopathic personality.* Baltimore: Williams & Wilkins.

Robins, L. N. (1991). Conduct Disorder. *Journal of Child Psychology and Psychiatry, 32,* 193–212.

Rosanoff, A. J., Handy, L. M. & Plesset, I. R. (1941). The etiology of child behavior difficulties, juvenile delinquency and adult criminality with special reference to their occurrence in twins. State of California Department of Institutions Psychiatric Monographs, Serial No. 187.

Rose, R. J. (1988). Genetic and environmental variance in content dimensions of the MMPI. *Journal of Personality and Social Psychology, 55,* 302–311.

Rowe, D. C. (1983). Biometrical genetic models of self-reported delinquent behavior: A twin study. *Behavior Genetics, 13,* 473–489.

Rowe, D. C. (1985). Sibling interaction and self-reported delinquent behavior: A study of 265 twin pairs. *Criminology, 23,* 223–241.

Rowe, D. C. (1986). Genetic and environmental components of antisocial behaivor: A study of 265 twin pairs. *Criminology, 24,* 513–532.

Rushton, J. P., Fulker, D. W., Neale, M. C., Nias, D. K. B. & Eysenck, H. J. (1986). Altruism and aggression: The heritability of individual differences. *Journal of Personality and Social Psychology, 50,* 1192–1198.

Rutter, M. (1997). Nature-nurture integration: The example of antisocial behavior. American Psychologist, 52, 390–398.

Rutter, M. & Giller, H. (1983). *Juvenile delinquency: Trends and perspectives.* New York: Guilford Press.

Sampson, R. J. & Lauritsen, J. (1994). In A. J. Reiss, Jr. & J. Roth (Eds.), *Understanding and preventing violence: Social influences.* Washington, DC: National Academy Press, 1–114.

Sampson, R. J., Raudenbush, S. W. & Earls, F. (1997). Neighborhoods and violent crime: A multilevel study of collective efficacy. *Science, 277,* 918–924.

Scarr, S. (1966). The origins of individual differences in adjective check list scores. *Journal of Consulting Psychology, 30,* 354–357.

Schweinhart, L. J. (1987). Can preschool programs help prevent delinquency? In J. Q. Wilson & G. C. Loury (Eds.), *From children to citizens,* vol. 3, *Families, schools, and delinquency prevention.* New York: Springer-Verlag, 135–153.

Scott, J. P. (1989). *The evolution of social systems.* New York: Gordon & Breach.

Seitz, B., Rosenbaum, L. K. & Apfel, N. H. (1985). Effects of family support intervention: A ten-year follow-up. *Child Development, 56,* 376–391.

Sigvardsson, S., Cloninger, C. R., Bohman, M., & von Knorring, A. L. (1982). Predisposition to petty criminality in Swedish adoptees: III. Sex differences and validation of the male typology. *Archives of General Psychiatry, 39,* 1248–1253.

Silberg, J., Meyer, J., Pickles, A., Simonoff, E., Eaves, L., Hewitt, J., Maes, H. & Rutter, M. (1996). Heterogeneity among juvenile antisocial behaviours: Findings from the Virginia Twin Study of Adolescent Behavioural Development. In G. R. Bock & J. A. Goode (Eds.), *Genetics of criminal and antisocial behavior.* West Sussex, England: John Wiley & Sons, 76–85.

Simmons, R. & Blyth, D. (1987). *Moving into adolescence: The impact of pubertal change and school context.* Hawthorne, New York: Aldine de Gruyter.

Simonoff, E. (1992). A comparison of twins and singletons with child psychiatric disorders: An item sheet study. *Journal of Child Psychology and Psychiatry, 33,* 1319–1332.

Slater, E. & Cowie, V. (1971). *The genetics of mental disorder.* London: Oxford University Press.

Slutske, W. S., Heath, A. C., Dinwiddie, S. H., Madden, P. A. F., Bucholz, K. K., Dunne, M. P., Statham, D. J. & Martin, N. G. (1997). Modeling genetic and environmental influences in the etiology of conduct disorder: A study of 2,682 adult twin pairs. *Journal of Abnormal Psychology, 106,* 266–279.

Slutske, W. S., Heath, A. C., Dinwiddie, S. H., Madden, P. A. F., Bucholz, K. K., Dunne, M. P., Statham, D. J. & Martin, N. G. (1998). Common genetic risk factors for conduct disorder and alcohol dependence. *Journal of Abnormal Psychology, 107,* 363–374.

Stevenson, J. & Graham, P. (1988). Behavioral deviance in 13-year-old twins: An item analysis. *Journal of the American Academy of Child and Adolescent Psychiatry, 27,* 791–797.

Stewart, M. A., deBlois, C. S. & Cummings, C. (1980). Psychiatric disorder in the parents of hyperactive boys and those with conduct disorder. *Journal of Child Psychology and Psychiatry, 21,* 283–292.

Szatmari, P., Reitsma-Street, M. & Offord, D. (1986). Pregnancy and birth complications in antisocial adolescents and their siblings. *Canadian Journal of Psychiatry, 31,* 513–516.

Taylor, J., McGue, M., Iacono, W. G. & Lykken, D. T. (1997). A twin family study of delinquency. Paper presented at the Annual Meeting of the Behavior Genetics Association, Toronto.

Tellegen, A. (1982). Brief manual for the differential personality questionnaire. Unpublished manuscript. Minneapolis, MN: University of Minnesota.

Tellegen, A., Lykken, D. T., Bouchard, T. J., Jr., Wilcox, K. J., Segal, N. L. & Rich, S. (1988). Personality similarity in twins reared apart and together. *Journal of Personality and Social Psychology, 54,* 1031–1039.

Tienari, P. (1963). Psychiatric illnesses in identical twins. *Acta Psychiatrica Scandinavia, 39,* 140–142.

Van Dusen, K. T., Mednick, S. A., Gabrielli, W. F., Jr. & Hutchings, B. (1983). Social class and crime in an adoption cohort. *Journal of Criminal Law and Criminology, 74,* 249–269.

Van Oortmerssen, G. A. & Bakker, T. C. (1981). Artificial selection for short and long attack latencies in wild Mus musculus domesticus. *Behavior Genetics, 11,* 115–126.

Van Voorhis, P. (1987, Mar.). Correctional effectiveness: The high cost of ignoring success. *Federal Probation,* 56–62.

West, D. J. & Farrington, D. P. (1973). *Who becomes delinquent?* London: Heinemann.

Whalen, C. K. & Henker, B. (1991). Therapies for hyperactive children: Comparisons, combinations, and compromises. *Journal of Consulting and Clinical Psychology, 59,* 126–137.

Willerman, L., Loehlin, J. C. & Horn, J. M. (1992). An adoption and a cross-fostering study of the Minnesota Multiphasic Personality Inventory (MMPI) Psychopathic Deviate Scale. *Behavior Genetics, 22,* 515–529.

Wilson, J. Q. & Herrnstein, R. (1985). *Crime and human nature.* New York: Simon & Schuster.

Zur Nieden, M. (1951). The influence of constitution and environment upon the development of adopted children. *The Journal of Psychology, 31,* 91–95.

Chapter 8

Antisocial Personality and Drug Use Disorders—Are They Genetically Related?

by Marianne B.M. van den Bree, Ph.D.,
Dace S. Svikis, Ph.D., and Roy W. Pickens, Ph.D.

Introduction 8-1
Common Etiology of APD and SUD 8-2
Methods for Studying Genetic Influences 8-3
    Family Studies 8-3
    Adoption Studies 8-3
    Twin Studies 8-4
Genetic Influences in SUD 8-4
    Adoption Studies 8-5
    Twin Studies 8-5
Genetic Influences in APD 8-6
    Adoption Studies 8-6
    Twin Studies 8-8
APD and SUD Comorbidity 8-10
    Adoption Studies 8-10
    Twin Studies 8-11
Discussion—Etiology, Familial Comorbidity, Future Directions 8-12
    Diagnostic Problems 8-12
    Behavior Genetics Issues 8-13
    Future Directions 8-13

INTRODUCTION

Drug abusers often have antisocial personality, and individuals with antisocial personality often engage in drug abuse. In the general population, lifetime prevalence ranges between 2.6-3.5 percent for antisocial personality disorder (APD) and 16.7-26.6 percent for substance use disorder (SUD) (7.9-14.1 percent for alcohol dependence, and 3.5-7.5 percent for drug dependence) (Regier et al., 1990; Kessler et al., 1994). However, among individuals with APD, prevalence of SUD is much more common than in the general population. Similarly, APD is more common among individuals with SUD than among those without SUD. Among individuals with any alcohol diagnosis, approximately 14 percent have APD, compared to 18 percent among those with any drug diagnosis (Regier et al., 1990). Approximately 70 percent of individuals with APD have any alcohol diagnosis, and 30 to 40 percent have any drug diagnosis (Lewis et al., 1983; Regier et al., 1990).

Individuals with SUD in combination with APD differ in course, symptoms, and treatment outcome compared to individuals with SUD only. Compared to substance abusers without APD, antisocial substance abusers have more severe use and worse treatment prognosis (Hesselbrock et al., 1984; Woody et al., 1985; Gerstley et al., 1990; Hesselbrock & Hesselbrock, 1994; Brooner et al., 1993, 1997). Intravenous use and sexual behaviors of drug abusers who are comorbid for APD put them at an increased risk for HIV (Gill et al., 1992; Brooner et al., 1993; Compton et al., 1995). Therefore, understanding the association between APD and SUD has clinical as well as public health importance.

Understanding the co-occurrence of APD and SUD is difficult, however, because both are complex clinical syndromes with multiple etiologies. The fourth edition of the *Diagnostic and Statistical Manual of Mental Disorders* (DSM-IV) generally characterizes SUD as a maladaptive pattern of substance use characterized by clinically significant symptoms. Although the disorder may involve a variety of pharmacological agents administered in different ways and for different purposes, symptoms include tolerance, physiological dependence, loss of control over substance use, preoccupation with substance use, and continued substance use despite problems related to use. APD is characterized by a pattern of behavior that indicates a disregard for and violation of the rights of others. The condition has also been referred to as psychopathy, sociopathy, or dyssocial personality disorder. Symptoms include failure to conform to social norms, deceitfulness, impulsivity, irritability and aggressiveness, irresponsibility, and lack of remorse over harming another person (DSM-IV).

COMMON ETIOLOGY OF APD AND SUD

The frequent co-occurrence of SUD and APD has led to speculation about common etiological factors. In one etiological model, both disorders co-occur because one disorder is a risk factor for the other. For example, a person with APD may engage in drug experimentation due to an impulsive personality, which increases the likelihood of the person developing SUD. Alternatively, drug use may directly produce socially deviant behaviors (i.e., intoxication), or may indirectly contribute to socially deviant behavior (i.e., crime to obtain money to purchase drugs). In another etiological model, both disorders co-occur due to a common etiological factor. For example, both alcohol consumption and aggressive behavior may be rewarded in certain societies, thus increasing likelihood of their co-occurrence. Under both etiological models, comorbidity of APD and SUD could be the result of shared genetic and/or environmental influences.

It is unlikely that either APD or SUD is due to a single cause. A large number of putative environmental factors are associated with drug use, including poverty, unemployment, poor quality of education, racial discrimination, ready availability of drugs, family discord, family alcohol and drug use, sexual abuse, lack of family rituals, neuropsychological deficits, childhood aggressiveness, low self-esteem, teenage pregnancy, rebelliousness, delinquency, drug use by peers, mental health problems, and cultural alienation (Pickens et al., 1995). Similarly, a large number of genes are expected to be involved in drug use disorders as well. While to date no specific gene has been found that is associated with drug dependence, as many as sixty genes are believed to be associated with the functioning of a single drug metabolizing system (PYS0) (Nebert, 1997).

In all probability, APD is also determined by multiple factors. Putative environmental factors associated with APD include parental rejection (Jenkins, 1966), physical abuse by a parent (Pollock et al., 1990), broken family background (Sigvardsson et al., 1982; Reich, 1986), parental psychopathology or deviance (Cadoret & Stewart, 1991; Cadoret et al., 1990), low socioeconomic status (Van Dusen et al., 1983; Cadoret & Stewart, 1991; Cadoret et al., 1990), and urbanized environment (Sigvardsson et al., 1982; Robins et al., 1991). Many of these factors also predispose to alcohol and drug use disorders. Also, postnatal influences on antisocial behavior may be different for males and females. For example, low socioeconomic status was reported by Sigvardsson et al. (1982) to be a risk factor only for men.

In this review we examine the role of genetic influences in APD and SUD, although it is recognized that environmental influences may be involved as well. Particular attention is paid to common genetic influences that may contribute to both APD and SUD and be responsible in part for the high rate of comorbidity that is seen between the two disorders.

METHODS FOR STUDYING GENETIC INFLUENCES

Family Studies

Family studies compare the frequency of a disorder in relatives of affected and unaffected probands. If higher rates of the disorder are seen in relatives of affected than unaffected probands, the disorder may be said to "run in families" and thus possibly have a genetic influence. However, since family members share genes as well as a common environment, these types of studies cannot distinguish between the two influences. Adoption and twin studies provide the opportunity for separating genetic and common environmental influences, and therefore have greater meaning for genetic research.

Adoption Studies

In adoption studies, outcomes are compared in adoptees of biological parents with and without the disorder. In addition, outcomes may be compared in adoptees reared by adoptive parents with and without the disorder. By separating biological risk factors (genes) from environmental risk factors (rearing environment), the adoption method makes it possible to establish the significance of each influence separately. If the two adoptee groups are closely matched on all other variables, higher rates of the disorder in adoptees of biological parents with the disorder than in adoptees of biological parents without the disorder indicate a genetic influence. If adoptees having adoptive parents with the disorder are more likely to have the disorder than adoptees having adoptive parents without the disorder, this indicates an environmental influence. Individuals of different genetic backgrounds may respond differently to environmental influences (gene-environment interaction) (see Plomin et al., 1977; Cadoret, 1982). These interactions are evidenced in adoption studies when the effects of biological background are differentially influenced by type of rearing environment.

Twin Studies

In twin studies, information on etiological influences in a disorder is obtained by comparing outcome in monozygotic (MZ) twins (who are genetically identical) and dizygotic (DZ) twins (who share on average 50 percent of their genes). The method assumes that the degree of environmental similarity is approximately the same for both types of twins (equal environment assumption) (Kendler et al., 1993). Since MZ twins share all their genes and their common environment, less than perfect correlation for a disorder in MZ twins must be attributable to unique environmental experiences (a term that also incorporates measurement error). Additive genetic influences are implicated when the correlation for a disorder in DZ twins is approximately half that of MZ twins. A DZ correlation coefficient that is greater than half that for MZ twins is suggestive of common environmental influences.

Heritability (h^2) is the relative contribution of genetic factors to total phenotypic variation (genetic and environmental factors combined) in a trait (see Chapter 9). Similarly, relative contribution of common environmental (c^2) and unique environmental (e^2) influences can be obtained by dividing the variation explained with either factor alone by the total phenotypic variation. A special case of the twin design is the study of MZ twins who are reared apart. Since these twins share their genes but do not have a common environment, the influence of heritable factors can be directly estimated from the MZ correlation coefficient.

For continuous traits, analysis is based on comparison of correlation coefficients, or variance/covariance components for MZ and DZ twin groups. For dichotomous variables (presence or absence of a diagnosis), MZ and DZ resemblance is often expressed in concordance rates, which reflect the percentage of co-twins with the same diagnosis as their previously ascertained pair member (proband) (Gottesman & Shields, 1972). There are two types of concordance rates, depending on ascertainment procedure employed (Allen et al., 1967; Hrubec, 1973). Pairwise concordance represents the proportion of twin pairs in which both members are affected, and varies with ascertainment probability. Probandwise concordance reflects the proportion of affected individuals among the co-twins of proband cases and thus does not depend on ascertainment probability. Liability correlation coefficients can be obtained from twin concordance rates by taking into account prevalence of the trait in the population (threshold models) (Smith, 1974). These models assume that disease liability is normally distributed and that persons whose phenotypic values exceed a certain threshold (defined by prevalence in the population) are affected (see Reich et al., 1979).

GENETIC INFLUENCES IN SUD

Alcoholic probands are more likely than nonalcoholic controls to have relatives with alcohol problems, and the incidence of alcohol problems is higher in relatives of alcoholic probands than in the general population (Schuckit et al., 1972; Merikangas, 1990; Stabenau & Hesselbrock, 1994). Similarly, rates of drug abuse are higher in relatives of drug abusing probands than in the general population (Kosten et al., 1991; Rounsaville et al., 1991; Mirin et al., 1991). While the risk for alcoholism increases with the number of affected biological parents (Merikangas, 1990; McKenna & Pickens, 1981) and males are more likely than females to have SUD (Robins et al., 1984), such familial influences may be due to genetic and/or environmental influences.

Adoption Studies

The majority of adoption studies of substance abuse have focused on alcoholism. For males, four studies have supported a role for genetic influences (Goodwin et al., 1973; Cloninger et al., 1981; Cadoret et al., 1985; 1987). Only one study (Roe, 1944) found no evidence of genetic influences in alcoholism in males. In a recent review, McGue (1994) reported that having an alcohol dependent biological parent placed a male offspring at 1.6 to 3.6 times greater risk for developing alcohol problems than having neither biological parent alcoholic.

The results are less definitive for females, with two adoption studies supporting a role for genetic influences in alcoholism (Cadoret et al., 1986; Bohman et al., 1981) and two studies finding no evidence of genetic influences (Goodwin et al., 1977; Roe, 1944). Some of the heterogeneity in findings with females may be explained by different alcoholism subtypes (Svikis et al., 1994). Cloninger et al. (1981), for example, identified two alcoholism subtypes in an adoption study, with the mild to moderately heritable subtype occurring in both males and females and the highly heritable subtype occurring only in males. These subtypes also differed with regard to sensitivity to postnatal environmental factors, indicating gene-environment interaction. For individuals with the moderately heritable subtype, severity of abuse was predominantly determined by environmental factors, while the postnatal environment had little influence on expression of the highly heritable subtype.

A limited number of adoption studies of drug abuse have been reported. Cadoret and colleagues (1986; 1995b) reported evidence of genetic influences on drug abuse, but also possible heterogeneity in the development of the disorder. A background of alcohol problems in the biological family of adoptees was found to contribute to risk for drug abuse. In addition, APD in biological relatives constituted a second, independent genetic risk factor, suggesting two genetic pathways to drug abuse. In a study of female adoptees only (Cadoret et al., 1996), the second path, but not the first, was replicated, suggesting possible gender hererogeneity in the development of drug abuse. These adoption studies also reported evidence of environmental factors: psychiatric conditions in adoptive families predicted increased APD in the adoptee.

Twin Studies

Twin studies also permit the separation of genetic and environmental influences. Seven twin studies of male alcoholism have been reported. Five studies have supported a role for genetic influences in the development of alcohol dependence (Kaij, 1960; Hrubec & Omenn, 1981; Pickens et al., 1991; Caldwell & Gottesman 1991; McGue et al., 1992), with heritability estimates being relatively consistent and ranging from 0.50-0.60 (McGue, 1994). The remaining two studies (Gurling et al., 1984; Allgulander et al., 1991) found no evidence of genetic influences in alcoholism in males.

For females, twin data are less conclusive. Of six studies reported, only two found evidence for genetic influences in alcoholism in females (Pickens et al., 1991; Kendler et al., 1992). The other four studies (Gurling et al., 1984; Caldwell & Gottesman 1991; Allgulander et al., 1991; McGue et al., 1992) found comparable MZ and DZ concordance rates, with no evidence of genetic liability. Heritability estimates across the six studies for female alcohol dependence ranged from 0 percent to 56 percent (McGue, 1994). Some of the variability may be the result of smaller sample sizes than those used in studies of male alcoholism (Svikis et al., 1994).

Apart from the studies of tobacco use (see Heath & Madden, 1995, for a review), few twin studies have been conducted on other types of drug use. Table 8.1 includes the seven studies that have been published, and considerable methodological differences are evident. Sample characteristics vary across studies. Some of the studies combine results from males and females; others report results separately. Some studies report results for all drugs combined; others report results for separate classes of drugs. Finally, some studies examine only drug use, while others examined the clinical disorder of drug abuse and/or dependence. Methodological differences between studies are likely to be an important contributor to the wide variation in heritability estimates evident from Table 8.1 (range 0-.70).

GENETIC INFLUENCES IN APD

Antisocial behavior encompasses a variety of behavioral problems, including juvenile delinquency and criminality as well as certain personality characteristics. Incidence of APD is consistently higher in males than females, regardless of age or ethnic group (Robins et al., 1991). Rates of APD are higher in relatives of individuals with APD than in the general population (Cloninger & Gottesman, 1987). Although they have lower overall rates of APD, female probands typically have more affected relatives (of both genders) than male probands, suggesting it requires stronger cultural and/or biological influences to become antisocial for women than for men (Cloninger et al., 1975; Cloninger et al., 1978).

Adoption Studies

Adoption studies, as shown in Table 8.2, suggest that individuals with an antisocial biological family background are at increased risk for antisocial behavior, compared to individuals without affected biological family members. For the development of antisocial behavior, biological factors in the family background are of greater importance than environmental circumstances shared by family members. However, the number of studies performed is limited, and the methodological differences are considerable. Some studies use an APD diagnosis; others report on psychopathy or criminal behavior. Some studies use recruited adoptees with antisocial behavior and evaluate symptoms in their relatives; others establish parental antisocial behavior and compare symptoms in their adopted-out offspring and controls. Both male and female subjects participated in some studies, while others were limited to males.

Table 8.1
Twin Studies of Drug Use and Dependence

Investigators	Sample description (# of pairs), gender	Measures*	Category	Genetic influence#					
Pedersen, 1981	Swedish twins, middle-aged (137), M/F	Prescription medication use	Tranquilizers Sleeping pills	.28 0					
Grove et al., 1990	MZ twins only, reared apart (32), M/F	Symptom counts of DSM-III ab/dep, standardized for gender, age, and year of birth	Any drug	.46					
Pickens et al., 1991^	Alcohol/ drug treatment programs (169), M/F	DSM-III ab/dep	Any drug	M .31	F .22				
Gynther et al., 1995	Psychiatric facilities (295), M/F	Five point scale ranging from no use to dep, standardized for race and sex	Any drug	.11					
Jang et al., 1995	Canadian twins (438), M/F	Addictive Behaviors Scale of the DAPP-DQ, standardized for gender and age+	Use Frequent use Interference Rare use	.32 .32 .06 .14					
Tsuang et al., 1996	U.S. military services (3,372), M only	DSM-III-R diagnoses of ab/dep		M					
			Sedatives Opiates Stimulants Cannabis PCP/ Psych Any drug	.38 .43 .44 .33 .25 .34					
van den Bree et al., 1998^	Alcohol/ drug treatment programs (188), M/F	DSM-III diagnoses		Use		Ab/ Dep		Dep	
				M	F	M	F	M	F
			Sedatives	.74	.18	.58	0	.67	0
			Opiates	.67	0	.57	0	.48	0
			Cocaine	.39	0	.74	.42	-	-
			Stimulants	.55	.55	.78	.73	.70	.73
			Cannabis	.17	.53	.68	.53	.78	.58
			Any drug	.16	.23	.79	.47	.74	.31

*Ab/dep: drug abuse and/or dependence; Dep: drug dependence; DSM-III: diagnosis according to the *Diagnostic and Statistical Manual of Mental Disorders* (3d ed.); DSM-III-R: diagnosis according to the revised edition of the DSM-III; DAPP-DQ: Dimensional Assessment of Personality—Differential Questionnaire (Livesley & Jackson, 1995); PCP/Psych: phencyclidine/psychedelics.
^Samples overlapped for the major part, but the 1998 study used analytical methods correcting for treatment status and double ascertainment of twin pairs
- DSM-III does not support a diagnosis of cocaine dependence.
+ Questions were: Used a number of illicit drugs (Use); I used drugs frequently (Freq. use); Drugs have caused me to take time off work or school (Interference); and I rarely use drugs unless prescribed by a doctor (Rare use)

Results of adoption studies are inconclusive about contributions of gene-environment interaction on the development of APD-related behavior. Mednick et al. (1984) found that sons of criminal biological parents who grew up in a criminal adoptive fam-

Table 8.2
Adoption Studies of Antisocial Behavior

Investigators	Sample description (# of pairs), gender	Percentage of disorder in relatives
Schulsinger, 1972	Danish adoptees with psychopathy (P) (57), matched controls (C)(57), M/F	Psychopathic spectrum disorders in: Biological relatives of P, 14.4% Adoptive relatives of P, 7.6% Biological relatives of C, 6.7% Adoptive relatives of C, 5.3%
Crowe, 1974	Adopted-away offspring (P) of incarcerated female offenders (46), matched controls (C)(46), M/F	APD in: P 13% C 2%
Cadoret, 1978	Adoptees with antisocial parents (P)(18), and matched controlod (C)(25), M/F	APD in: P 22% C 0
Mednick et al., 1984; 1987	Danish adoptees with criminal records (6,129), selected from all nonfamilial adoptions in Denmark between 1924 - 1947, and their noncriminal (-) and criminal (+) biological (B) and adoptive (A) parents, M adoptees only	Criminal records in adoptees with: B (-) and A (-) parents 13.5% B (-) and A (+) parents 14.7% B (+) and A (-) parents 20% B (+) and A (+) parents 24.5%
Willerman et al., 1992	Adoptees with high (P) (21) or low (C) (51) MMPI Psychopathic Deviate (Pd) scale scores and their biological (B) mothers, and adoptive (A) parents, M/F adoptees	High Pd scores in: B mothers of P 48% B mothers of C 20% B mothers of P had significantly higher MMPI scores on most clinical scales than B mothers of C. A mothers of P had significantly higher scores on Pd and hypomania scales than A mothers of C. No difference between A fathers of P and C.

ily were at greater risk of becoming involved in criminal activities than were adoptees with a criminal biological background who grew up in a noncriminal adoptive family, a finding that suggests gene-environment interaction. Differences in environmental influences between antisocial adoptees and control adoptees were also reported by Crowe (1974). In contrast, Willerman et al. (1992) found no evidence of gene-environment interaction (although environmental variation was limited because all adoptees were adopted by middle-class families).

Twin Studies

Several studies have examined genetic influences on APD and related behaviors by comparing MZ and DZ twin pair resemblance. DiLalla and Gottesman (1989) reviewed the literature on twin resemblance for criminal acts and obtained a weighted pairwise concordance rate of .87 for MZ and .72 for DZ twins for juvenile delinquency (based on six studies) and of .51 for MZ and .22 for DZ twins for adult criminality (based on nine studies). The differences in MZ and DZ concordance rates suggest heritable influences on both traits, although they appear larger for adult than juvenile samples.

In more recent studies, shown in Table 8.3, comparisons between twin groups are

Table 8.3
Twin Studies of Antisocial Behavior

Investigators	Sample description (# of pairs), gender	Measures	Category	Genetic influence#
Rowe, 1983; 1986*	Adolescents, recruited from high schools and twin clubs (265), M/F	Self-report of delinquent acts committed the previous year	M F	.34 - .45, .41 - .65
Cloninger & Gottesman, 1987	Danish twins (4,175), M/F	Criminal acts as appearing in the National Crime Register	Property crime Violent crime	.78 .50
Grove et al., 1990	MZ twins only, reared apart (32), M/F	Symptom counts of DSM-III APD, standardized for gender, age, and year of birth	Juvenile criteria Adult criteria	.42 .29
Lyons et al., 1995	U.S. military services, (3,226), M only	DSM-III-R diagnoses of APD	Juvenile criteria Adult criteria	.07 .43

*Variance components in 1983 paper were divided by total phenotypic variance to obtain heritability estimates.

based on correlation analysis (or analysis of variance) rather than concordance rates, thus enabling estimation of the magnitude of genetic influences on APD and related behaviors.

These methodologies are quite diverse, however, with a wide range of measures used to establish antisocial behavior. Some of the studies combine results from males and females; others report results separately. Some studies examine delinquent or criminal acts; others examine the clinical disorder of antisocial personality disorder. Some studies distinguish between juvenile and adult symptoms; others do not. Despite the methodological differences, virtually all results indicate that genetic influences play a role in antisocial behavior, with heritability estimates ranging from .07-.65 for juvenile symptoms, and .29-.78 for adult symptoms. Although the ranges suggest that genetic influences may be lower for juvenile than adult behaviors, the evidence is not strong. Juvenile delinquents tend to show lower heritability estimates as a group since many desist in their delinquency once they become adults; only a subgroup persists into adulthood. In addition to genetic influences, most studies also find evidence for both common and unique environmental influences on APD-related behavior.

Antisocial behavior in one twin increases the probability of the same behavior in the other pair member. For example, twins commit criminal acts with one another (Dalgard & Kringlen, 1976; Rowe, 1983). When these sibling effects (Eaves, 1976; Carey, 1986) are taken into account in the analysis of APD, the magnitude of the estimated genetic influences are reduced (Carey, 1992). Rowe (1983) found evidence to suggest the same factors influenced antisocial behavior in both sexes and that the heritability estimates are approximately similar. This finding can be reconciled with higher prevalence rates of APD in males than in females, if it is assumed that females require stronger genetic and/or environmental influences to develop APD (Cloninger et al., 1975, 1978).

APD AND SUD COMORBIDITY

APD and SUD may co-occur because they are influenced by the same genes and/or because they are under similar environmental control. Both conditions tend to occur in the same families (Winokur et al., 1970). It has been suggested, however, that APD and SUD are independent disorders (Reich et al., 1981; Lewis et al., 1983), based on the specificity of their transmission in families. For example, higher rates of alcoholism but not APD have been reported in relatives of probands with alcoholism only, and higher rates of APD but not alcoholism in relatives of probands with APD only. However, relatives of probands with both disorders appear at increased risk for both disorders (Reich et al., 1981). The latter finding indicates some interaction between APD and SUD, which elevates the familial risk for both. Adoption and twin designs also allow separation of the effects of genes and environment in the study of comorbidity of APD and SUD.

In both designs, comorbidity is studied by establishing the influence of one disorder in a proband on the occurrence of the other disorder in a relative. For example, rates of SUD may be compared in adoptees who have biological parents with and without APD. Higher rates of SUD in adoptees with biological parents having APD than in adoptees with biological parents not having APD would suggest common genetic influences in APD and SUD. Similarly, higher rates of SUD in adoptees with adoptive parents having APD than in adoptees with adoptive parents not having APD would suggest environmental influences in APD and SUD.

With the twin method, within-twin and cross-twin correlations are compared to indicate shared associations between two disorders. If two disorders are more highly correlated within the same individual than they are across MZ pair members (who are genetically identical), then environmental influences that are unique to a pair member but shared between APD and SUD are implicated. Since the unique environmental influences contribute to both disorders, the individual who is subjected to them will be more likely to express both disorders. An example would be when one member of a twin pair, but not the other, gets involved with a substance abusing peer group that also commits delinquent acts. This twin pair member will therefore be likely to become involved in both types of activities, while the other member will not.

On the other hand, shared genetic and shared common environmental influences are derived from comparisons of MZ and DZ twin groups. If the DZ cross-person cross-trait correlation is approximately half that for DZ twins, then genetic influences shared by the two disorders are implied. If the cross-person cross-trait correlation in DZ twins is greater than half that for MZ twins, then common environmental influences may be shared between the two disorders. An example of shared common environmental influences is when both members of a twin pair become involved in a peer group that engages in both substance abuse and antisocial activities. Their resemblance for these activities will be increased due to these common environmental influences.

Adoption Studies

Cadoret and colleagues (1985; 1987) found evidence for specificity of inheritance of alcohol abuse and APD. Alcohol problems in the biological family did not increase risk for antisocial behavior in adoptees, nor did antisocial behavior in the biological family increase risk for alcohol problems in adoptees. Alcohol problems in the adoptive family did not increase antisocial behavior in adoptees, suggesting environmental influences were also not shared by alcohol abuse and APD.

In three other adoption studies, Cadoret and co-workers examined the associations between alcohol abuse, drug abuse, and antisocial personality. In one study (Cadoret et al., 1986), log linear model-fitting was used with a sample of male and female adoptees and their adoptive and biological parents. Two mechanisms for genetic inheritance were identified: a direct path leading from alcohol abuse or dependence in the biological parent to drug abuse in the adoptee, and an indirect path from APD in biological relatives to APD in adoptee to adoptee drug abuse. In addition, evidence for a third (environmental) pathway was found, influencing antisocial behavior in adoptees through psychiatric conditions in the adoptive family. Parental drug abuse was not assessed, limiting study findings and not addressing the issue of specificity in genetic transmission of substance use disorders. In a subsequent study (Cadoret et al., 1995b), these results were replicated in a different sample of male adoptees only. However, in a sample of female adoptees only (Cadoret et al., 1996), support for only the indirect path was found, suggesting the possibility of gender-specific biological influences.

Studies of Swedish male and females adoptees (Bohman et al., 1982; Sigvardsson et al., 1982) have suggested genetic and environmental influences in APD-related behavior differ, depending on co-occurrence with alcoholism. Nonalcoholic petty offenders had an excess of biological parents with histories of petty crime, suggesting familial factors in this type of crime. However, crime rate in alcoholic criminals who committed repeated violent acts was uncorrelated with criminality in their biologic parents, but appeared to be primarily symptomatic of the rate of alcoholism in the offender. Environmental factors rather than genetic influences appeared to influence severity of alcoholism (and associated violent crime). Different environmental factors were found to increase risk for the two types of crime. For example, for males, unstable preadoptive placement was found to increase risk for petty crimes, whereas low social status was identified as a risk factor in the development of alcohol-related crimes.

Twin Studies

In a sample of MZ twins who were reared apart, Grove et al. (1990) prepared symptom count scales for DSM-III antisocial personality and alcohol and drug dependence, and estimated genetic associations between the traits. Genetic correlations were higher for childhood APD and drug symptoms ($r_g = .87$) than for childhood APD and alcohol symptoms ($r_g = .54$). In contrast, for adult APD, a higher genetic correlation with alcohol symptoms ($r_g = .75$) than with drug symptoms ($r_g = .53$) was found. Since the sample consisted of MZ twin pairs only, no estimates of common environmental influences shared between APD and drug use could be obtained.

Pickens and colleagues (1995) compared within-twin to cross-MZ and cross-DZ correlations for various DSM-III substance use and mental disorders. In males, the correlation between alcohol dependence and APD within the same individual (.55) was similar to that across MZ twins (.63), suggesting little effect of unique environmental influences on the relationship between alcohol dependence and APD. The correlation between alcohol dependence and APD was significantly higher across MZ (.63) than across DZ (.47) twins, however, suggesting genetic influences. For females, the within-twin correlation between alcohol dependence and APD (.60) was much higher than the cross-MZ correlation (.22), suggesting a role for unique environmental influences. However, the correlation between alcohol dependence and APD across MZ twins (.22) was similar to that for DZ twins (.21), suggesting no shared genetic influences. For both males and females, the two conditions also shared common environmental influences. This study did not estimate the magnitudes of genetic and environmental variation shared between alcohol dependence and APD.

Several publications (DiLalla & Gottesman, 1989; Grove et al., 1990; Lyons et al., 1995) suggest that contributions of genetic and environmental influences change over time. Most results suggest that genetic influences are smaller and that the effect of the common environment is stronger in juveniles than in adults, but this has not been replicated in all studies (Grove et al., 1990).

DISCUSSION—ETIOLOGY, FAMILIAL COMORBIDITY, FUTURE DIRECTIONS

Because SUD and APD frequently co-occur in the same individual, it has been speculated that they share a common etiology. Indeed, the two disorders affect males predominantly, have a number of overlapping clinical features, and tend to run in families. Both also have been separately shown to be heritable.

Apart from these similarities, however, family studies have not found higher rates of alcoholism in relatives of individuals with APD only and vice versa, suggesting independent familial transmission (Reich et al., 1981, Lewis et al., 1983). In addition, adoption studies (Cadoret et al., 1985, 1987) have found no excess of antisocial problems in adoptees who have biological parents with alcohol problems, nor of alcohol problems in adoptees who have biological parents with antisocial problems. Antisocial behavior may be inherited with concomitant drug abuse, however (Cadoret et al., 1986, 1995b). In twin studies, where secular trends in substance use are not so influential and more powerful methodology can be employed, at least some evidence of shared genetic influences between APD and alcohol as well as drug abuse has been reported (Grove et al., 1990; Pickens et al., 1995). The Pickens et al. study found evidence for shared environmental influences in SUD and APD as well. However, contribution of shared genetic and environmental variation may be different for males and females.

Diagnostic Problems

Additional research on the comorbidity of APD and SUD is needed. This research, however, will be difficult for a number of reasons. In the clinical area, problems arise over diagnostic issues related to symptom overlap, where the same symptom may artificially contribute to the diagnosis of both disorders. There are also problems related to diagnostic heterogeneity in both disorders. Because only three DSM-IV symptoms are necessary for diagnosis of either SUD or APD, different individuals may receive the same diagnosis with little symptom overlap. Attention must also be paid to the possibility of subtypes having different etiologies, as the process and prognosis of alcoholism have been found to differ for primary alcoholics and sociopaths with alcoholism (Schuckit, 1973). In addition, there are issues related to subject ascertainment. For example, comorbidity may be increased in treatment-based samples because presence of multiple conditions makes it more likely someone will seek treatment (Kessler et al., 1996).

Behavior Genetics Issues

In the behavior genetics area, the reporting of evidence of gene-environment interaction in both APD and SUD (Dinwiddie & Cloninger, 1991; Crowe, 1974; Cadoret, 1982) complicates genetic and environmental research. In addition, presence of SUD or APD symptoms in an individual may be associated with similar behaviors in his or her spouse (Hall et al., 1983a, 1983b; Vanyukov et al., 1994; Crowe, 1974). This nonrandom selection of mates (assortative mating) is known to influence genetic and environmental estimates derived from twin data (Vanyukov et al., 1996). Reports of reciprocal sibling interaction in APD-related behavior (Carey, 1992) must also be considered in genetic studies. Finally, substance use and subsequent expression of alcohol or drug abuse is dependent on environmental factors such as availability, but also on the attitude of society towards licit and illicit drugs. These factors will influence estimates of genetic and environmental influences as derived from genetic research.

Longitudinal genetic designs could establish possible changes in genetic and environmental influences across time and could estimate whether the same genetic and environmental factors operate across time (Boomsma & Molenaar, 1987). Rather than evidence of shared genetic (and environmental) variation between APD and SUD, it would be helpful to estimate relative magnitude of genetic and environmental variance shared between the traits, as well as variance that is specific to each trait. Given a twin data set of adequate size, this could be achieved with the use of structural equation analytical methods (Neale & Cardon, 1992).

Future Directions

Unfortunately, only limited genetics research has been conducted with SUD other than alcohol, and more research on both SUD and APD in women, in particular, is needed. In addition, several genetic studies have provided evidence that juvenile and adult symptoms of APD are at least partially independent (Grove et al., 1990; Lyons et al., 1995). Future studies of the comorbidity of APD and SUD should make a distinction between the two types of APD symptoms (see also Cacciola et al., 1994).

Recently, we reported evidence of genetic influences in alcohol dependence only in alcoholic twin probands comorbid for other drug or mental disorders; alcoholic twin probands not comorbid for other drug or mental disorders failed to show evidence of genetic influences in alcohol dependence (Pickens et al., 1996). These results suggest comorbidity may be an essential feature of the genetic influence in alcoholism, and that research on the comorbidity between SUD and APD may be a fertile area for future genetic studies.

A better understanding of the comorbidity between APD and SUD could contribute to early identification and treatment of individuals at risk for each disorder. It is useful to know that there is diagnostic overlap and that a diagnosis of one can contribute to the severity, early onset, and resistance to treatment of the other. There is evidence that those with this comorbidity respond better to some treatments (cognitive-behavioral therapy) than others (social skills or counseling), and that certain treatments may actually worsen the prognosis. For purposes of prevention and early intervention, an understanding that these two disorders share several behavioral and psychological dimensions may lead to methods to identify (but not stigmatize) children at high risk by virtue of these characteristics and to incorporate effective teaching and therapeutic strategies into school curricula.

Knowledge of genetic architecture is also important to molecular genetic efforts to identify genes involved in either condition to develop appropriate interventions (see Chapters 9 and 16). If APD and SUD were found to show little genetic overlap, it would be most informative to study subjects who are not comorbid for the conditions to avoid spurious gene-marker associations. On the other hand, if genetic variation in SUD is largely explained by genetic factors in APD, it would be best to conduct studies using subjects with comorbid conditions, as this is the relevant phenotype. Research on the genetics of these disorders is presently at the forefront of the drug abuse and criminological fields and promises to advance our knowledge and practical responses substantially.

References

Allen, G., Harvald, B. & Shields, J. (1967). Measures of twin concordance. *Acta Genetica et Statistica Medica, 17,* 475–481.

Allgulander, C., Nowak, J. & Rice, J. P. (1991). Psychopathology and treatment of 30,344 twins in Sweden. II. Heritability estimates of psychiatric diagnosis and treatment in 12,884 twin pairs. *Acta Psychiatrica Scandinavia, 83,* 12–14.

American Psychiatric Association (1980). *Diagnostic and statistical manual of mental disorders* (3d ed.). Washington, DC: American Psychiatric Press.

American Psychiatric Association (1987). *Diagnostic and statistical manual of mental disorders* (3d ed. rev.). Washington, DC: American Psychiatric Press.

American Psychiatric Association (1994). *Diagnostic and statistical manual of mental disorders* (4th ed.). Washington, DC: American Psychiatric Press.

Bohman, M., Cloninger, C. R., Sigvardsson, S. & von Knorring, A. (1982). Predisposition to petty criminality in Swedish adoptees: I. Genetic and environmental heterogeneity. *Archives of General Psychiatry, 39,* 1233–1241.

Bohman, M., Sigvardsson, S. & Cloninger, C. R. (1981). Maternal inheritance of alcohol abuse: Cross-fostering analysis of adopted women. *Archives of General Psychiatry, 38,* 965–969.

Boomsma, D. I. & Molenaar, P. C. M. (1987). The genetic analysis of repeated measures. I. Simplex models. *Behavior Genetics, 17,* 111–123.

Brooner, R. K., Greenfield, L., Schmidt, C. W. & Bigelow, G. E. (1993). Antisocial personality disorder and HIV infection among intravenous drug abusers. *American Journal of Psychiatry, 150,* 53–58.

Brooner, R. K., King, V. L., Kidorf, M., Schmidt, C. W. & Bigelow, G. E. (1997). Psychiatric and substance use comorbidity among treatment-seeking opioid abusers. *Archives of General Psychiatry, 54,* 71–80.

Cacciola, J. S., Rutherford, M. J., Alterman, A. I. & Snider, E. C. (1994). An examination of the diagnostic criteria for antisocial personality disorder in substance abusers. *Journal of Nervous and Mental Disease, 182,* 517–523.

Cadoret, R. J. (1978). Psychopathology in adopted-away offspring of biologic parents with antisocial behavior. *Archives of General Psychiatry, 35,* 176–184.

Cadoret, R. J. (1982). Genotype-environment interaction in antisocial behaviour. *Psychological Medicine, 12,* 235–239.

Cadoret, R. J., O'Gorman, T. W., Troughton, E. & Heywood, E. (1985). Alcoholism and antisocial personality: Interrelationships, genetic and environmental factors. *Archives of General Psychiatry, 42,* 161–167.

Cadoret, R. J. & Stewart, M. A. (1991). An adoption study of attention deficit/ hyperactivity/ aggression and their relationship to adult antisocial personality. *Comprehensive Psychiatry, 32,* 73–82.

Cadoret, R. J., Troughton, E., Bagford, J. & Woodworth, G. (1990). Genetic and environmental factors in adoptee antisocial personality. *European Archives of Psychiatry and Neurological Sciences, 239,* 231–240.

Cadoret, R. J., Troughton, E. & O'Gorman, T. W. (1987). Genetic and environmental factors in alcohol abuse and antisocial personality. *Journal of Studies on Alcohol, 48,* 1–8.

Cadoret, R. J., Troughton, E., O'Gorman, T. W. & Heywood, E. (1986). An adoption study of genetic and environmental factors in drug abuse. *Archives of General Psychiatry, 43,* 1131–1136.

Cadoret, R. J., Yates, W. R., Troughton, E., Woodworth, G. & Stewart, M. A. (1995a). Genetic-environmental interaction in the genesis of aggressivity and conduct disorders. *Archives of General Psychiatry, 52,* 916–924.

Cadoret, R. J., Yates, W. R., Troughton, E., Woodworth, G. & Stewart, M. A. (1995b). Adoption study demonstrating two genetic pathways to drug abuse. *Archives of General Psychiatry, 52,* 42–52.

Cadoret, R.J., Yates, W.R., Troughton, E., Woodworth, G. & Stewart, M.A. (1996). An adoption study of drug abuse/ dependence in females. *Comprehensive Psychiatry, 37,* 88–94.

Caldwell, C. B. & Gottesman, I. I. (1991). Sex differences in the risk for alcoholism: A twin study. Paper presented at Behavior Genetics Association meeting, St. Louis, MO.

Carey, G. (1986). Sibling imitation and contrast effects. *Behavior Genetics, 16,* 319–341.

Carey, G. (1992). Twin imitation for antisocial behavior: Implications for genetic and family environment research. *Journal of Abnormal Psychology, 101,* 18–25.

Cloninger, C. R., Bohman, M. & Sigvardsson, S. (1981). Inheritance of alcohol abuse: Cross-fostering analysis of adopted men. *Archives of General Psychiatry, 38,* 861–868.

Cloninger, C. R., Christiansen, K. O., Reich, T. & Gottesman, I. I. (1978). Implications of sex differences in the prevalences of antisocial personality, alcoholism & criminality for familial transmission. *Archives of General Psychiatry, 35,* 941–951.

Cloninger, C. R. & Gottesman, I. I. (1987). Genetic and environmental factors in antisocial behavior disorders. In S. A Mednick, T. E. Moffitt & S. A. Stack (Eds.), *The causes of crime: New biological approaches.* New York: Cambridge University Press, 92–109.

Cloninger, C. R., Reich, T. & Guze, S. B. (1975). The multifactorial model of disease transmission: II. Sex differences in the familial transmission of sociopathy (antisocial personality). *British Journal of Psychiatry, 127,* 11–22.

Compton, W. M., Cottler, L. B., Shillington, A. M. & Price, R. K. (1995). Is antisocial personality disorder associated with increased HIV risk behaviors in cocaine users? *Drug and Alcohol Dependence, 37,* 37–44.

Crowe, R. R. (1974). An adoption study of antisocial personality. *Archives of General Psychiatry, 31,* 785–791.

Dalgard, O. S. & Kringlen, E. (1976). A Norwegian twin study of criminality. *British Journal of Criminology, 16,* 213–232.

DiLalla, L. F. & Gottesman, I. I. (1989). Heterogeneity of causes for delinquency and criminality: Lifespan perspectives. *Development and Psychopathology, 1,* 339–349.

Dinwiddie, S. H. & Cloninger, C. R. (1991). Family and adoption studies in alcoholism and drug addiction. *Psychiatric Annals, 21,* 206–214.

Eaves, L. J. (1976). A model for sibling effects in man. *Heredity, 36,* 205–214.

Gerstley, L. J., Alterman, A. I., McLellan, A. T. & Woody, G. E. (1990). Antisocial personality disorder in patients with substance abuse disorders: A problematic diagnosis? *American Journal of Psychiatry, 147,* 173–178.

Gill, K., Nolimal, D. & Crowley, T. (1992). Antisocial personality disorder, HIV risk behavior and retention in methadone maintenance therapy. *Drug and Alcohol Dependence, 30,* 247–252.

Goodwin, D. W., Schulsinger, F., Hermansen, L., Guze, S. B. & Winokur, G. (1973). Alcohol problems in adoptees raised apart from alcoholic biological parents. *Archives of General Psychiatry, 28,* 238–243.

Goodwin, D. W., Schulsinger, F., Knop, J., Mednick, S. & Guze, S. B. (1977). Alcoholism and depression in adopted-out daughters of alcoholics. *Archives of General Psychiatry, 34,* 751–755.

Gottesman, I. I. & Shields, J. (1972). *Schizophrenia and genetics: A twin study vantage point.* New York: Academic Press.

Grove, W. M., Eckert, E. D., Heston, L., Bouchard, T. J., Jr., Segal, N. & Lykken, D. T. (1990). Heritability of substance abuse and antisocial behavior: A study of monozygotic twins reared apart. *Biological Psychiatry, 27,* 1293–1304.

Gurling, H. M. D., Oppenheim, B. E. & Murray, R. M. (1984). Depression, criminality & psychopathology associated with alcoholism: Evidence from a twin study. *Acta Geneticae Medicae et Gemelloligiae, 33,* 333–339.

Gynther, L. M., Carey, G., Gottesman, I. I. & Vogler, G. P. (1995). A twin study of non-alcohol substance abuse. *Psychiatry Research, 56,* 213–220.

Hall, R. L., Hesselbrock, V. M. & Stabenau, J. R. (1983a). Familial distribution of alcohol use: I. Assortative mating in the parents of alcoholics. *Behavior Genetics, 13,* 361–372.

Hall, R. L., Hesselbrock, V. M. & Stabenau, J. R. (1983b). Familial distribution of alcohol use: II. Assortative mating of alcoholic probands. *Behavior Genetics, 13,* 373–382.

Heath, A. C. & Madden, P. A. F. (1995). Genetic influences on smoking behavior. In J. R. Turner, L. R. Cardon & J. K. Hewitt (Eds.), *Behavior genetic approaches in behavioral medicine.* New York: Plenum Press, 45–66.

Hesselbrock, M. N., Hesselbrock, V. M., Babor, T. F., Stabenau, J. R., Meyer, R. E., Weidenman, M., Van Dusen, K. T. & Mednick, S. A. (1984). Antisocial behavior, psychopathology and problem drinking in the natural history of alcoholism. In D. Goodwin (Ed.), *Longitudinal research in alcoholism.* Boston: Kluwer-Nijhoff Publishing Co., 197–214.

Hesselbrock, V. M. & Hesselbrock, M. N. (1994). Alcoholism and subtypes of antisocial personality disorder. *Alcohol and Alcoholism, Supp. 2,* 479–484.

Hrubec, Z. (1973). The effect of diagnostic ascertainment in twins on the assessment of the genetic factor in disease etiology. *American Journal of Human Genetics, 25,* 15–28.

Hrubec, Z. & Omenn, G. S. (1981). Evidence of genetic predisposition to alcoholic cirrhosis and psychosis: Twin concordances for alcoholism and its biological endpoints by zygosity among male veterans. *Alcoholism: Clinical and Experimental Research, 5,* 207–212.

Jang, K. L., Livesley, W. J. & Vernon, P. A. (1995). Alcohol and drug problems: A multivariate behavioural genetic analysis of co-morbidity. *Addiction, 90,* 1213–1221.

Jenkins, R. L. (1966). Psychiatric syndromes in children and their relations to family background. *American Journal of Orthopsychiatry, 36,* 450–457.

Kaij, L. (1960). *Studies on the etiology and sequels of abuse of alcohol.* Lund, Sweden: Almqvist & Wiksell Int'l.

Kendler, K. S., Heath, A. C., Neale, M. C., Kessler, R. C. & Eaves, L. J. (1992). A population-based twin study of alcoholism in women. *Journal of the American Medical Associaton, 268,* 1877–1882.

Kendler K. S., Neale M. C., Kessler R. C., Heath, A. C. & Eaves L. J. (1993). A test of the equal-environment assumption in twin studies of psychiatric illness. *Behavior Genetics, 23,* 21–27.

Kessler, R. C., McGonagle, K. A., Zhao, S., Nelson, C. B., Hughes, M., Eshleman, S., Wittchen, H.-U. & Kendler, K. S. (1994). Lifetime and 12-month prevalence of DSM-III-R psychiatric disorders in the United States. *Archives of General Psychiatry, 51,* 8–19.

Kessler, R. C., Nelson, C. B., McGonagle, K. A., Edlund, M. J., Frank, R. G. & Leaf, P. J. (1996).

The epidemiology of co-occurring addictive and mental disorders: Implications for prevention and service utilization. *American Journal of Orthopsychiatry, 66,* 17–31.

Kosten, T. R., Kosten, T. A. & Rounsaville, B. J. (1991). Alcoholism and depressive disorders in opioid addicts and their family members. *Comprehensive Psychiatry, 32,* 521–527.

LaBuda, M. C., Svikis, D. S. & Pickens, R. W. (1997). Twin closeness and co-twin risk for substance use disorders: Assessing the impact of the equal environment assumption. *Psychiatry Research, 70,* 155–164.

Lewis, C. E., Rice, J. & Helzer, J. E. (1983). Diagnostic interactions: Alcoholism and antisocial personality. *Journal of Nervous and Mental Disease, 171,* 105–113.

Livesley, W. J. & Jackson, D. N. (1995). *Manual for the dimensional assessment of personality pathology.* Port Huron, MI: Research Psychologists Press.

Lyons, M. J., True, W. R., Eisen, S. A., Goldberg, J., Meyer, J. M., Faraone, S. V., Eaves, L. J. & Tsuang, M. T. (1995). Differential heritability of adult and juvenile antisocial traits. *Archives of General Psychiatry, 52,* 906–915.

McGue, M. (1994). Genes, Environment & the Etiology of Alcoholism. National Institute on Alcohol Abuse and Alcoholism, Research Monograph 26. Washington, DC: U.S. Government Printing Office, 1–40.

McGue, M., Pickens, R. W. & Svikis, D. S. (1992). Sex and age effects on the inheritance of alcohol problems: A twin study. *Journal of Abnormal Psychology, 101,* 3–17.

McKenna, T. & Pickens, R. (1981). Alcoholic children of alcoholics. *Journal of Studies on Alcohol, 42,* 1021–1029.

Mednick, S. A., Gabrielli, W. F. & Hutchings, B. (1984). Genetic influences in criminal convictions: Evidence from an adoption cohort. *Science, 224,* 891–894.

Mednick, S. A., Gabrielli, W. F. & Hutchings, B. (1987). Genetic factors in the etiology of criminal behavior. In S. A. Mednick, T. E. Moffitt & S. A. Stack (Eds.), *The causes of crime: New biological approaches.* New York: Cambridge University Press, 74–91.

Merikangas, K. R. (1990). The genetic epidemiology of alcoholism. *Psychology in Medicine, 20,* 11–22.

Mirin, S. M., Weiss, R. D., Griffin, M. L. & Michael, J. L. (1991). Psychopathology in drug abusers and their families. *Comprehensive Psychiatry, 32,* 36–51.

Neale, M. C. & Cardon, L. R. (1992). *Methodology for genetic studies of twins and families.* Dordrecht, Netherlands: Kluwer.

Nebert, D. W. (1997). Polymorphisms in drug-metabolizing enzymes: What is their clinical relevance and why do they exist? *American Journal of Human Genetics, 60,* 265–271.

Pedersen, N. (1981). Twin similarity for usage of common drugs. *Progress in Clinical Biological Research, 69,* 53–59.

Pickens, R. W., Elmer, G. I., LaBuda, M. C. & Uhl, G. R. (1996). Research in the study of drug action and addiction. In C. R. Schuster & M. J. Kuhar (Eds.), *Pharmacological aspects of drug dependence: Towards an integrated neurobehavioral approach.* Berlin: Springer-Verlag, 3–52.

Pickens, R. W. & Svikis, D. S. (1995). Vulnerability as cause of substance abuse: An overview. In J. H. Jaffe, J. C. Anthony, C. Johanson, M. J. Kuhar, M. H. Moore & E. M. Sellers (Eds.), *Encyclopedia of drugs and alcohol.* New York: Macmillan Library Reference, 246–1252.

Pickens, R. W., Svikis, D. S., McGue, M. & LaBuda, M. C. (1995). Common genetic mechanisms in alcohol, drug, and mental disorder comorbidity. *Drug and Alcohol Dependence, 39,* 129–138.

Pickens, R. W., Svikis, D. S., McGue, M., Lykken, D. T., Heston, L. & Clayton, P. J. (1991). Heterogeneity in the inheritance of alcoholism: A study of male and female twins. *Archives of General Psychiatry, 48,* 19–28.

Plomin, R., DeFries, J. C. & Loehlin, J. C. (1977). Genotype-environment interaction and correlation in the analysis of human behavior. *Psychological Bulletin, 84,* 309–322.

Pollock, V. E., Briere, J., Schneider, L., Knop, J., Mednick, S. A. & Goodwin, D. W. (1990). Childhood antecedents of antisocial behavior: Parental alcoholism and physical abusiveness. *American Journal of Psychiatry, 147,* 1290–1293.

Regier, D. A., Farmer, M. E., Rae, D. S., Locke, B. Z., Keith, S. J., Judd, L. L. & Goodwin, F. K. (1990). Comorbidity of mental disorders with alcohol and other drug abuse. *Journal of the American Medical Association, 264,* 2511–2518.

Reich, J. (1986). The relationship between early life events and DSM-III personality disorders. *Hillside Journal of Clinical Psychiatry, 8,* 164–173.

Reich, T., Cloninger, C. R., Lewis, C. & Rice, J. (1981). Some recent findings in the study of genotype-environment interaction in alcoholism. National Institute on Alcohol Abuse and Alcoholism, Research Monograph 5. Washington, DC: U.S. Government Printing Office, 145–165.

Reich, T., Rice, J., Cloninger, C. R., Wette, R. & James, J. (1979). The use of multiple thresholds and segregation analysis in analyzing the phenotypic heterogeneity of multifactorial traits. *Annals of Human Genetics, 42,* 371–389.

Robins, L. N. Helzer, J., Weissman, M. N., Orvascel, H, Gruenberg, E., Burke, J. D. & Reiger, D. A. (1984). Lifetime prevalence of specific psychiatric disorders in three sites. *Archives of General Psychiatry,* 41, 949–958.

Robins, L. N., Tipp, J. & Przybeck, T. R. (1991). Antisocial personality. In L. N. Robins & D. A. Regier (Eds.), *Psychiatric disorders in America: The epidemiologic catchment area study.* New York: The Free Press, 258–290.

Roe, A. (1944). The adult adjustment of children of alcoholic parents raised in foster homes. *Journal of Studies on Alcohol, 5,* 378–393.

Rounsaville, B. J., Kosten, T. R., Weissman, M. M., Prusoff, B., Pauls, D., Anton, S. F. & Merikangas, K. (1991). Psychiatric disorders in relatives of probands with opiate addiction. *Archives of General Psychiatry, 48,* 33–42.

Rowe, D. C. (1983). Biometrical genetic models of self-reported delinquent behavior: A twin study. *Behavior Genetics, 13,* 473–489.

Rowe, D. C. (1986). Genetic and environmental components of antisocial behavior: A study of 265 twin pairs. *Criminology, 24,* 513–532.

Schuckit, M. A. (1973). Alcoholism and sociopathy—diagnostic confusion. *Journal of Studies on Alcohol, 34,* 157–164.

Schuckit, M. A., Goodwin, D. W. & Winokur, G. (1972). A study of alcoholism in half siblings. *American Journal of Psychiatry, 128,* 1132–1136.

Schulsinger, F. (1972). Psychopathy: Heredity and environment. *International Journal of Mental Health, 1,* 190–206.

Sigvardsson, S., Cloninger, C. R., Bohman, M. & von Knorring, A. L. (1982). Predisposition to petty criminality in Swedish adoptees: III. Sex differences and validation of the male typology. *Archives of General Psychiatry, 39,* 1248–1253.

Smith, C. (1974). Concordance in twins: Methods and interpretation. *American Journal of Human Genetics, 26,* 454–466.

Stabenau, J. R. & Hesselbrock, V. M. (1994). *Substance abuse and psychopathology.* Washington, DC: American Psychiatric Association.

Svikis, D. S., Valez, M. & Pickens, R. W. (1994). Genetic aspects of alcohol use and dependence in women. *Alcohol, Health and Research World, 18,* 192–196.

Tsuang, M. T., Lyons, M. J., Eisen, S. A., Goldberg, J., True, W. R., Lin, N., Meyer, J. M., Toomey, R., Faraone, S. V. & Eaves, L. J. (1996). Genetic influences on DSM-III-R drug abuse and dependence: A study of 3372 twin pairs. *American Journal of Medical Genetics, 67,* 473–477.

Van den Bree, M. B. M., Johnson, E. O., Neale, M. C. & Pickens, R. W. (1998). Genetic and environmental influences on drug use and abuse/dependence in male and female twins. *Drug and Alcohol Dependence, 52,* 231–241.

Van Dusen, K. T., Mednick, S. A., Gabrielli, W. F., Jr. & Hutchings, B. (1983). Social class and crime in an adoption cohort. *Journal of Criminal Law and Criminology, 74,* 249–269.

Vanyukov, M. M., Moss, H. B. & Tarter, R. E. (1994). Assortment for the liability to substance abuse and personality traits. *Annals of the New York Academy of Science, 708,* 102–107.

Vanyukov, M. M., Neale, M. C., Moss, H. B. & Tarter, R. E. (1996). Mating assortment and the liability to substance abuse. *Drug and Alcohol Dependence, 42,* 1–10.

Willerman, L., Loehlin, J. C. & Horn, J. M. (1992). An adoption and a cross-fostering study of the Minnesota Multiphasic Personality Inventory (MMPI) Psychopathic Deviate Scale. *Behavior Genetics, 22,* 515–529.

Winokur, G., Reich, T., Rimmer, J. & Pitts, F. N. (1970). Alcoholism III. Diagnosis and familial psychiatric illness in 259 alcoholic probands. *Archives of General Psychiatry, 23,* 104–111.

Woody, G. E., McLellan, A. T., Luborsky, L. & O'Brien, C. P. (1985). Sociopathy and psychotherapy outcome. *Archives of General Psychiatry, 42,* 1081–1086.

Chapter 9

Genetic Bases for Impulsive and Antisocial Behaviors— Can Their Course Be Altered?

by David Goldman, M.D. and Diana H. Fishbein, Ph.D.

Introduction	9-2
Recent Discoveries	9-3
Basic Terminology, Concepts, and Mechanisms	9-3
Gene-Environment Interactions	9-3
Genotype	9-3
Phenotype	9-4
Chemicals in the Brain and Their Actions	9-4
Neurotransmitters	9-4
Enzymes	9-4
Hormones	9-4
Receptors	9-4
Concepts Unique to Genetics	9-5
Alleles	9-5
Cloning	9-5
Measuring the Extent to Which Traits Are Genetically Transmitted	9-5
Heritability	9-5
Vulnerability Levels	9-5
Heritability of Impulsive Behavioral Disorders	9-6
How to Assess and Evaluate Genetic Effects	9-6
Linkage Analysis	9-7
DNA Sequence Scanning	9-7
Genes and Behavioral Variation	9-8
Dopamine and Aggression	9-8
Serotonin and Impulsive Behavior	9-9
Alcohol-Induced Behaviors	9-10

        Genetic Variants 9-11
        Monoamine Oxidase (MAO) and Criminality 9-11
Implications for Criminal Justice and Public Health Policy 9-12
        Impact of Environment on Heritable Behaviors 9-13
        A Move to a Public Health Response 9-13
Conclusions 9-14

INTRODUCTION

Individuals are differentially vulnerable to antisocial behavior. Interactions of genetic and environmental sources of variation underlie these individual differences. The extent of genetic influence is surprisingly high for various behavioral traits, particularly alcoholism, impulsivity, and also for various dimensions of antisocial behavior. One might think that traits such as these would not be measurably influenced by genetic factors because they are, in reality, crudely estimated and strongly influenced by cross-cultural and other environmental factors. However, data from large, methodologically sound twin and adoption studies show traits related to repetitive, aggressive behavior (e.g., impulsivity, negative affect, drug abuse, and cognitive deficits) are significantly heritable. Furthermore, similar findings have been reported for the heritability of personality factors, like extroversion, introversion, cognitive deficits, conduct disorder or anxiety, which may strongly contribute to aggression and associated conditions such as alcoholism. In terms of public policy, treatment, prevention, and research aimed at identifying specific genes in antisocial behavior, the level of heritability is less important than the ability of this science to enhance understanding of the underlying processes, the role of the environment, and particular vulnerabilities and needs of individuals.

Identification of genetic contributions does not reduce behavior to a gene level, but can help explain the origins of behavioral variation in a population. Because the focus of much of the research on deviant behavior is on social and environmental sources, the domain of this chapter is research on the direct detection of genetic vulnerability factors. Genes modulate behaviors that involve impulse control, such as antisocial personality disorder and alcoholism. According to this view, genetic factors help to explain individual vulnerability to certain behavioral patterns or orientations. Nevertheless, other factors such as choice and volition are more important in explaining behavior on a population scale.

Before entering this discussion, two critical points that condition the relationship between genetic traits and behavioral outcomes should be noted. First, there is a genetically determined range of potential responses to environmental inputs by chemical and physiological systems in the brain. Within this range, many environmental influences play a role in determining which behavior will be exhibited from the continuum of behavioral responses. Thus, many behavioral outcomes are possible at any given time; each situation is unique, although consistency in experiences (e.g., adverse or positive) may be cumulative to produce predictable and consistent patterns of behavior. Second, behavior is substantially influenced by environmental factors and is never attributed solely to genotype. The social and physical environment have the potential to significantly alter brain function irrespective of genotypic features; for example, traumatic experiences disrupt neurotransmitter function, hormonal release, and neuropsychological development. Genetically influenced temperament can also alter environmental responses to an individual or an individual's choice of environment, thereby either exacerbating or modulating the behavioral outcome. For example, irritability or negative emotionality in an infant can elicit more severe parenting responses, thereby compounding the child's difficulties (see Moffitt, 1993).

RECENT DISCOVERIES

Application of molecular genetic approaches to studies of impulsive and aggressive behaviors is relatively recent. However, studies are identifying genetic markers (genes associated with a behavior under study) at several gene locations. This has spurred a search for specific genes whose genetic variants (abnormalities) might contribute to differences in behavioral vulnerabilities. Several genetic markers have been identified for neurotransmitter metabolism and activity; these markers are either directly or indirectly associated with the function of certain neurotransmitters. This research suggests that deviations in gene structure and function for these chemicals may be more pervasive in individuals with aggressive and impulsive behaviors. This work implicates genetic deviations in functional markers for the neurotransmitters dopamine and serotonin, and the enzyme monoamine oxidase (MAO) in particular.

Genetic research employs a highly technical language with field-specific terms and references to techniques that may be difficult for the nongeneticist to interpret. Unfamiliarity with terminology, genetic research methodology, and underlying genetic mechanisms impedes interchange between social and genetic researchers. As a result, there have been only a few attempts to integrate genetics with other disciplines (e.g., sociology and psychology) to eventually create a comprehensive understanding of the origins of variation in human behavior. Frequently, that means we are comfortable with only half of the equation—either the sociological or the genetic contribution. Because the purpose of this chapter is to interpret genetic findings relevant to an understanding of impulsive behavioral disorders for the social scientist and practitioner, the authors include a geneticist (Goldman) and a behavioral researcher (Fishbein). The goal is to dissect and interpret this research domain for practitioners, academicians, policy-makers, and social scientists. We begin with a basic explanation of terms and mechanisms for genetic research.

BASIC TERMINOLOGY, CONCEPTS, AND MECHANISMS

Gene-Environment Interactions

Genotype. Genes and the environment interact in the production of human behavior. Even the genotype, which includes the genetic characteristics inherited from parents, is subject to modification, including mutations. Gene expression is modified during gestation and later, and as a result of environmental conditions (e.g., hormonal events, the presence of drugs or alcohol, and other chemical or physiological events).

Phenotype. Phenotype consists of traits that can be directly measured. Behavioral phenotypes most often are appropriate, adaptive responses to particular sets of environmental circumstances (Carey, 1994). Behavioral phenotypes can also be maladaptive in a social context. Maladaptive behaviors resulting in adverse consequences for both the affected individual and society at large are the focus of this chapter.

Two problems accompany the measurement of the behavioral phenotype: accuracy and validity. Concerning accuracy, a diagnosis of antisocial personality is less reliable than certain other psychiatric disorders, for example alcoholism. Concerning validity, many behavioral phenotypes have more meaning in the social context than in the context of genetic studies. Concepts such as criminality or violence are clearly social constructs, rooted in social contexts. They are not independent of the existing social and legal system and, accordingly, are influenced by evolving social processes, laws, judgment, and stigma. Behavioral phenotypes that are more culturally independent (e.g., impulsivity, chronic aggressiveness, negative affect, and cognitive deficits) access this domain of maladaptive behavior and offer an important approach to identifying contributing factors.

Chemicals in the Brain and Their Actions

Neurotransmitters. Genes affect behavior by encoding the structure, building blocks, and regulatory mechanisms of neurobiological systems. Genes lead to behavioral variation by encoding interindividual variation in these processes and structures. A particular emphasis of behavioral research is on neurotransmitters, because these are chemicals in the brain that transmit messages from cell to cell, enabling neural circuits. Neurotransmitter synthesis, metabolism, and receptor function are crucial for most of the brain's functions, including mood, behavior, emotion, cognition, motor movement, sleep cycles, and eating patterns.

Enzymes. The proteins responsible for the degradation or metabolism of other chemicals are called enzymes. The structure, location, and level of expression of enzymes is genetically encoded. Enzymes are partially responsible for both the synthesis and metabolism of neurotransmitters. Genetic variants of enzymes can therefore lead to behavioral differences.

Hormones. Hormones are chemicals released by glands throughout the body and brain, and which act at a distance to elicit responses by other tissues. Examples include prolactin, estrogen, testosterone, and adrenaline. Hormones influence behavior in profound ways. For example, the sexual differentiation of the brain and acquisition of certain male-characteristic and female-characteristic behaviors is dependent on the activation of sex-steroid receptors within key regions of the brain during development.

Receptors. Receptors are proteins, usually located on the cell membrane and oriented toward the extracellular world (external to the cell, but receptive of incoming signals). Receptors specifically bind particular neurotransmitters and hormones, and respond by activating a change in the ion concentration within the cell, or producing a second messenger within the cell, or directly altering gene expression after interaction with the DNA. Concentrations of receptor sites and their functional integrity determine, to a great extent, the adequacy of neurochemical activity. While these neurochemical systems are all influential in human behavior, alterations in their function do not predict particular behavioral outcomes, only predispositions and orientations to environmental conditions.

Concepts Unique to Genetics

Alleles. Most genes come in two copies, one from the mother and one from the father. The individual copies, maternal or paternal, are called alleles. Different forms of the gene in the population are called alleles. Polymorphisms are relatively common (>1%) alleles. A goal of behavioral genetics is to identify alleles that contribute to behavioral variation.

Cloning. Cloning, or duplicating, DNA is often necessary to identify the location, functional significance, and genetic variation of specific genes. When cloned, a segment of DNA is inserted into a vector, for example a virus, which is capable of reproducing. When the vector makes copies of itself, the cloned segment of DNA is also copied so that large quantities become available. Another important method for making many copies of a particular gene without cloning is the chemical synthesis of large quantities of the target gene using the polymerase chain reaction (PCR) method.

Measuring the Extent to Which Traits Are Genetically Transmitted

Heritability. Heritability studies estimate the minimum extent to which interindividual variation in a trait within a particular human population is genetically determined. Because identical twins are genetically identical and fraternal twins are only 50 percent identical, a higher rate of concordance, or similarity, in a behavioral trait between identical twins than fraternal twins is indicative of a genetic influence. Also, the levels and ratios of concordance rates in identical and fraternal twins can be used to estimate heritability. In adoption studies, concordance rates are compared for children and their biological parents relative to children and their adoptive parents. The goal of adoption studies is to separate effects of genotype from the shared environment within the family.

Vulnerability Levels. If a trait is heterogeneous in causation, genetic factors can be present when heritability is low or undetectable. Conversely, a high heritability does not preclude the identification of environmental influences, or effective prevention or treatment, all of which may be facilitated by a genetic finding. In terms of public policy, treatment, prevention or research, what is more important is not the level of heritability, which reflects group data, but the specific genes carried by an individual and the effect of those genes on behavior. For genes involved in behavior, the effects towards behavioral patterns are highly likely to be inclination but not predestination. As genes influencing behavior are identified, it is inevitable that findings relevant to criminality will be generated. The information that is developed can lead to a better understanding of the underlying processes and of the particular vulnerabilities and needs of individuals.

HERITABILITY OF IMPULSIVE BEHAVIORAL DISORDERS

Heritability studies of various dimensions of criminal behavior have most often focused on correlates such as impulsivity, aggressiveness, and antisocial personality. Such correlates are more likely to be genetically influenced than the more complex, socially bound concepts of criminality and violence. Studies on impulsive and aggressive behaviors were reviewed by Coccaro et al. (1993). Six out of twelve twin studies found significant heritability for these traits. Variability in these results are a function of both the measures used, the age of the twins and sampling variation. In children, three out of five studies detected significant heritability for aggressiveness, and the mean was 0.80 (on a scale of .00 to 1.00). Two studies that did not find heritability in children used measures of aggressiveness that may be less strongly influenced genetically (Coccaro et al., 1993). Three out of three studies in adolescents were negative and three out of four studies in adults found significant heritability. In the positive studies, the heritabilities were 0.72 (Rushton et al., 1986), 0.44 (Tellegen et al., 1988), and 0.41 (Coccaro et al., 1993), indicating that impulsivity and aggressiveness are substantially heritable.

A variety of genetically influenced psychiatric disorders are accompanied by increased liabilities for impulsive and aggressive behaviors, including antisocial personality disorder, conduct disorder, and borderline personality disorder. Therefore, identification of genetic factors contributing to these disorders would contribute to an understanding of the antecedents of aggressiveness. Aggressive behavior is frequently triggered by intake of relatively small amounts of alcohol, and more than half of violent crimes may occur under the influence of alcohol (Mark & Ervin, 1970). Thus, alcoholism mediates liability to impulsive and aggressive behaviors. The early-onset subtype of alcoholism, Type II, is itself associated with antisocial behavior and impulsiveness (Cloninger et al., 1981; von Knorring et al., 1987). Other aggression/diagnosis associations include suicide in depression (Tsuang, 1983), schizophrenia and alcoholism (Niskanen & Achte, 1972; Tsuang, 1983), self-directed violence in borderline personality disorder, and self-destructive behaviors in Lesch-Nyhan syndrome and other mental retardation syndromes. Heritability of psychiatric diseases has been reviewed elsewhere—for example, schizophrenia (Gottesman & Shields, 1982), affective illness (Berrettini et al., 1984; Loehlin et al., 1988), alcoholism (Goldman, 1993), and sociopathy (Coccaro et al., 1993).

HOW TO ASSESS AND EVALUATE GENETIC EFFECTS

While twin and adoption studies inform us that genes influencing impulsivity, aggressiveness, and alcoholism exist, a different set of methodologies in genetics, molecular neurobiology, and psychopharmacology is required to identify those genes. The two major genetic methodologies are positional cloning by whole genome linkage and candidate gene analysis; results from both approaches are described below. Progress by either approach has been greatly accelerated by the progress in the complete mapping and sequencing of the human genome and new technologies from genetic analysis.

Linkage Analysis

In linkage analysis, the co-transmission of marker and trait is detected among related individuals in families, or aggregation of genetic marker and trait is detected in a population. Using methods of statistical inference, these studies can detect effects of genetic variation, regardless of whether the gene has been previously identified. Sufficient genetic markers are available to detect effects of genes found anywhere in the genome. The actual genes can be isolated by a series of steps called positional cloning. There are several difficulties in linking genes to common complex traits, and the main problem is the presumed high level of genetic heterogeniety (multiple, individually uncommon genetic causes). A variety of techniques are employed, including the use of biochemical, clinical, and neurophysiological measures to isolate subgroups that are more genetically homogeneous.

Another tactic is to identify large, high density families where a single trait persists (e.g., the Dutch family studied by Brunner et al. for the MAO gene and impulsivity). Use of homogeneous subgroups enables the investigator to study affected individuals who are more likely to carry the same vulnerability alleles. Recently detected linkage "hot spots" for alcoholism found in a whole-genome scan (Long et al., 1988) implicate the dopamine D4 receptor and $GABA_A$ receptors (which bind valium-like drugs) in alcoholism vulnerability. These findings also have implications for the origins of criminality for reasons described herein.

DNA Sequence Scanning

Genes that influence traits can also be detected by directly scanning DNA sequences across many individuals. This is a practical method because of the cloning of numerous candidate genes and the advent of rapid methods for detecting genetic variants and automated sequencing to characterize them. We have recently seen the beginnings of detection of sequence variation within the human genome on a large scale (Cargill et al., 1999). Direct scanning for genetic variants turns the problems of heterogeneity in a population and multiple gene-involvement into advantages, because both "problems" increase the likelihood that analysis of a particular candidate gene will detect an allele that affects function. In this way, the direct scanning of candidate genes has very different advantages as compared with genetic linkage analysis using markers at candidate genes. Also, although it is not possible to evaluate the whole genome by direct scanning, those genes which are excluded from the realm of possible candidates are valid exclusions under realistic models.

Identification of a variant in MAOA, an enzyme involved in the metabolism of dopamine and serotonin, illustrates how gene scanning often follows detection of a gene effect by linkage analysis. The MAOA variant leads to an impulsivity syndrome in one Dutch family (Brunner et al., 1993a). Gene scanning has also detected a series of thyroid hormone receptor variants as a cause of attention deficit hyperactivity disorder (Hauser eet al., 1993), a correlate of impulsive aggression. These findings encourage the conclusion that scanning of additional candidate genes will detect alleles significant for antisocial behaviors. It is important to recognize that the genes expressed in the brain will be scanned and their variants detected independently of any research program specifically directed toward criminality or antisocial personality disorder. As described in this chapter, direct gene analyses have revealed functionally significant genetic variants, many common, at most of the dopamine and serotonin-related genes previously implicated in impulsive behavior.

GENES AND BEHAVIORAL VARIATION

Dopamine and Aggression

Dopamine has been directly implicated in aggressive behavior (reviewed in Brunner et al., 1993b). For example, dopamine metabolism increases when laboratory animals are provoked to behave aggressively (Cases et al., 1995). Among humans, the over-production of dopamine has been associated with psychosis and has been linked to antisocial behavior and violence (Gabel et al., 1995; Tiihonen et al., 1994). Antipsychotic drugs that decrease dopamine levels tend to decrease fighting behaviors (see Raine, 1993). Dopamine is also of interest due to its hypothesized involvement in schizophrenia, affective disorder, and alcoholism, all of which are associated with impulsivity and aggressiveness.

Many genes involved in brain dopamine function have been cloned, including those for dopamine receptors (D1 through D5), the dopamine transporter, the biosynthetic enzymes tyrosine hydroxylase and dopamine ß hydroxylase, and MAOA and B. Polymorphic markers identified within and near these genes permit linkage studies. Several gene structural variants have also been identified that influence the metabolism and activity of dopamine (Gejman et al., 1994; Itokawa et al., 1993; Rietschel et al., 1993). While there are some discrepancies in the literature, several associations between genetic markers for dopamine function have been found for disorders involving impulse dyscontrol, including substance abuse, aggression, and alcoholism (see Goldman et al., 1995).

Genetic defects in dopamine metabolism have been found in excessive and compulsive behaviors of many forms that are often characterized by antisocial behavior, including drug abuse, conduct disorder, Tourette's syndrome, obsessive-compulsive disorder, and posttraumatic stress disorder (see Comings et al., 1996). Nevertheless, genetic association and linkage studies of dopamine-related genes are controversial and some findings are discrepant. To date, gene-behavior relationships have been reported between dopamine transporter and attention deficit hyperactivity disorder (Cook et al., 1995), and D4 and novelty seeking (Benjamin et al., 1996); Ebstein et al., 1996). Findings for a relationship between D2 and alcohol and substance abuse (Blum et al., 1990) were not replicated (see Goldman et al., 1992; Goldman, 1993), thus dampening initial excitement over the possible implications.

Additional studies that focus specifically on the role of dopamine in aggression have also not been replicated. For example, a genetic defect affecting so-called "reward pathways" within the dopamine system has been reported in drug-using subjects exhibiting the most severe drug abuse habits, in addition to having been expelled from school for fighting and having been jailed as an adult for violent crime (Comings et al., 1994). Also, there is some evidence that cocaine addicts with a high incidence of early deviant behaviors and conduct disorder may be genetically susceptible to both drug dependence and aggressiveness due to a defect in the metabolism of dopamine (Noble et al., 1993). Aggressiveness among cocaine users occurs more often in those with a history of the same; however, chronic use increases the likelihood irrespective of a predisposition as a result of disruptions in dopamine activity. Thus, each of the above mentioned disorders may be related by a shared common variable—inheritance of a constellation of alleles at genes involved in dopamine function. Further investigations are needed to clarify the role of dopamine and to more consistently identify particular gene-behavior relationships.

Meta-analyses of dopamine levels in antisocial populations show inconsistencies between studies and no main effects (Raine, 1993). Variations in populations studied and definitions of antisocial conduct employed may explain these discrepancies. Moreover, dopamine function in the brain can be only partially accessed, and interactrions with other neurotransmitter systems have been scarcely considered. While dopamine has a known association with impulsivity and aggressiveness, identification of a role for the dopamine gene variants in behavior may clarify the neurobiology.

Serotonin and Impulsive Behavior

Level of brain serotonergic activity appears to have a profound influence on production of impulsive-aggressive behavior (Muhlbauer, 1985; Soubrie, 1986; van Praag et al., 1987). In rats, lesions of the septal area and other structures dense with serotonergic connections produce rage and attack. Genetic strains of mice with lower serotonergic tone are more aggressive, and intraspecies aggression is suppressed when serotonin metabolism is blocked, resulting in increased serotonergic activation (Cases et al., 1995). The role of serotonin in behavioral inhibition has been reviewed elsewhere (Soubrie, 1986), as have widely replicated observations that a reduction in serotonin activity releases punishment-suppressed behaviors (Linnoila et al., 1983) as well as aggression directed against both self and others (Åsberg et al., 1987).

One of the most widely reproduced findings in neuropsychiatry is that indicators of serotonin activity are lowered in humans characterized as impulsive and violent towards themselves or others (Åsberg et al., 1987; Brown et al., 1979; Coccaro & Murphy, 1991; Fishbein et al., 1989; Linnoila et al., 1983; Virkkunen et al., 1987, 1989). Postmortem studies of the brain have detected serotonergic deficits in individuals who committed violent suicide (e.g., using a gun or knife) as contrasted with individuals who committed "nonviolent" suicide (e.g., using pills or gas) (Brown et al., 1982). Impulsive/violent Finns with exceptionally low concentrations of a serotonin by-product, 5-hydroxindolacetic acid (HIAA), in cerebrospinal fluid (CSF) were almost all alcoholic, and more than half had a history of suicide attempts (Linnoila et al., 1983; Linnoila & Virkkunen, 1992). Impulsive subjects studied by Brown et al. (1979, 1982, 1985) had low CSF 5-HIAA and, although young, were also generally alcoholic. The tendency of alcoholism, suicidal behavior, and impulsive behaviors to aggregate within the same individuals and to be transmitted from parent to offspring (Cloninger et al., 1981, 1985; Bohman, 1978) may indicate a shared underlying serotonergic mechanism. Thus, deficits in brain serotonergic activity produce behavioral disinhibition, resulting in an increased likelihood of impulsive aggressiveness or other excessive and inappropriate behavior.

Alcohol-Induced Behaviors. Studies revealing that serotonin modulates alcohol consumption including excessive drinking are particularly noteworthy in light of reports that impulsive and violent individuals with low serotonergic activity levels and are far more likely to engage in antisocial behaviors while drinking (Ballenger et al., 1979; Coccaro & Murphy, 1991; Linnoila et al., 1994; Roy et al., 1987; Virkkunen & Linnoila, 1990; Virkkunen, 1983). A decline in serotonergic activity may be partially responsible for alcohol-induced behavioral and neurological disinhibition, leading to the expression of underlying violent tendencies (Buydens-Branchey et al., 1989). Alcoholics believed to be at genetic risk for comorbid alcoholism and aggressiveness/criminality (Cloninger, 1987) may be the product of a preexisting deficit in serotonergic function. When drinking, such individuals are more likely to experience dysphoria and display impulsive-aggressive behavior, as alcohol brings serotonergic tone below "the floor" in individuals with preexisting deficiencies in serotonin. As serotonin activity declines during alcohol consumption, compromising impulse control, dopamine activity simultaneously rises, leading to the expression of underlying violent tendencies. It has been suggested that the use of drugs that stimulate serotonin activity (agonists) in such cases may be a helpful adjunctive therapy for comorbid alcoholism and violence by reducing (1) co-occurring depression and/or anxiety, (2) alcohol craving, (3) some of the reinforcing properties of alcohol, and (4) aggressiveness (see Brizer, 1988).

Heritability studies on serotonin are limited by the relative inaccessability of serotonin in the brain. Nevertheless, several studies have found the heritability for 5-HIAA, the major metabolite of serotonin, to be significantly heritable when the 5-HIAA was measured in cerebrospinal fluid (CSF) (Mehlman et al., 1994; Higley et al., 1993; Meltzer & Arora, 1988). Identification of the variant alleles in genes involved in serotonin function has been possible, in part, due to the association of this neurotransmitter with the early-onset form of alcoholism (Type II), which has high heritability. Studies have noted a tendency of alcoholism, suicidal behavior, and impulsive behaviors to occur together, and there is a tendency for alcoholism and impulsive antisocial behavior to be transmitted from parent to offspring (Cloninger et al., 1985; Bohman, 1978). Cloninger has characterized Type II alcoholics as having early-onset, high genetic liability, impulsive behavior, and evidence of lower brain serotonin turnover. These are the alcoholics in whom it would seem most likely that a structural variant of a serotonin candidate gene could be identified.

For Type II alcoholism, a sample of Finnish criminal alcoholics was collected for genetic analysis (Virkkunen et al., 1994). This sample includes families, sibling pairs, and healthy psychiatrically interviewed controls, so that it should be possible to assess the effect of the more abundant serotonin candidate gene structural variants on the Type II alcoholism phenotype. For Type II alcoholism, a large sample of Finnish alcoholic offenders is being systematically studied for the role of genetic variation (Virkkunen & Linnoila, 1990). This sample includes large multiplex families and psychiatrically healthy controls. Finns mostly descend from a small population of founders who settled Finland only eighty to one hundred generations ago. The combination of a genetically isolated population and a high quality health care system with accurate national registers of diseased individuals makes this population close to ideal for genetic studies. The characteristics of these alcoholic violent offenders and healthy volunteers and the assessment methods have been published elsewhere (Virkkunen et al., 1994). A spectrum of other diseases in which serotonin has been implicated have also been analyzed in a search for related alleles, including obsessive compulsive disorder, autism, hereditary myoclonus, schizophrenia, and anorexia nervosa.

A panel of serotonin candidate genes is being scanned for variant alleles across 300–500 Finnish alcoholic offenders and in the other patient populations named above. Due to their roles in serotonin synthesis, neurotransmission, and reuptake, many or most of these genes may alter behavior. The functionally variant alleles may generally be infrequent, requiring efficient screening technology. These genes are being scanned regardless of whether associations or linkages to markers have been reported. A population association was found between a DNA marker at the tryptophan hydroxylase (TPH) gene and suicidal behavior in alcoholic impulsive Finns studied as inpatients at the University of Helsinki (Nielsen et al., 1994). The association of the TPH marker to 5-HIAA concentration was observable only in individuals who, by the nature of their crimes, were impulsive. These findings, which have been replicated in a similar population of Finns (Nielsen et al., 1994), could indicate that functional variants that alter serotonin activity may be present at the TPH gene, but rare in the general population and in nonimpulsive individuals. TPH codes for the rate-limiting enzyme in the synthesis of serotonin and may be a factor influencing serotonin turnover and behaviors controlled by serotonin. Conclusions from this study were that a genetic variant of the TPH gene may influence serotonin metabolism and a predisposition to suicidal and impulsive behaviors in some people.

Genetic Variants. Two rare genetic variants, one functional, were detected in the area of the serotonin 1A receptor gene (Nakhai et al., 1995). Drugs that act at this receptor reduce aggressive and defensive behavior and increase passivity in wild rats in anxiety-provoking situations (Blanchard et al., 1988). Thus, these alleles may be of considerable interest for impulsive behaviors. For another serotonin receptor, 5HT1B, mice in which the serotonin receptor had been "knocked out" show greatly enhanced intruder confrontation aggression (Sadou et al., 1994) without other behavioral or developmental abnormalities, and these knock out mice are alcohol-preferring. In rodents, drugs that both enhance and decrease serotonin 1B activity reduce aggression in intruder confrontation paradigms. Recently, linkage of 5HT1B markers to the human behavior most corresponding to mouse behavior, namely antisocial alcoholism, was detected in two populations (Lappalainen et al., 1998). Abnormal function of the 5HT1B receptor can diminish serotonin turnover and produce low 5-HIAA concentrations such as are seen in impulsive individuals. Still other studies show that genes for the serotonin receptor 2C, which is widely distributed in the brain and is involved in the regulation of hormonal responses, may be implicated in antisocial personality disorder and substance abuse, including alcohol craving (Benkelfat et al., 1991; George et al., 1995; Moss et al., 1990).

Monoamine Oxidase (MAO) and Criminality

Since the early 1980s, deviations in MAO levels have been linked with certain forms of criminality, particularly those involving psychopathy, aggression, and violent behavior (see Ellis, 1991), although these studies did not control for the effect of smoking and other factors known to influence MAO levels. Several studies have related variations in MAO activity to tendencies toward alcoholism, sensation-seeking behavior, and impulsivity (see Hsu et al., 1989). Low platelet MAO levels were found in male student volunteers with histories of psychosocial problems, including convictions for various offenses (Schalling et al., 1987), and among relatives of low-MAO subjects (Buchsbaum et al., 1976). Lidberg et al. (1985) found offenders categorized as psychopaths had lower MAO levels than controls.

One recent study of a large Dutch kindred spanning four generations found fourteen males to be affected by a complex behavioral syndrome that includes borderline mental retardation and impulsive aggressive behavior (Brunner et al., 1993a, 1993b). These fourteen males had a history of shy, withdrawn behaviors, were often without friends, and were chronically prone to unprovoked aggressive outbursts. Low levels of the metabolites for the neurotransmitters dopamine, noradrenaline, and serotonin were detected in their urine. Genetic analyses revealed that affected male members of this family had a variant in the MAOA gene, which is found on the X chromosome. This variant makes the MAOA enzyme inactive, leading to the neurochemical and behavioral abnormalities. Brunner has emphasized that the relationship between a MAO metabolic abnormality and behavioral disturbance is not a simple one (Brunner, 1996). Because this defect has been observed in only one family, it is also incorrect to extrapolate these findings to other families in which impulsive aggression appears prevalent. Nevertheless, it is certain that this Dutch family is not the only family with a gene that positively influences aggression.

IMPLICATIONS FOR CRIMINAL JUSTICE AND PUBLIC HEALTH POLICY

Heritability and molecular genetic studies of behavior are inherently political in their impact and can be personally upsetting. A special implication of genetic findings relevant to criminality is that the heritability or molecular genotype data could be used at either guilt or penalty phases of criminal proceedings.

Concerning heritability, this measure is a group average. Therefore, the precise extent to which a trait is genetically influenced, or indeed whether the trait is measurably heritable, is usually of poor predictive value in any individual case. Many traits are very strongly genetically influenced in particular families, but show nearly zero heritability in a population sample. For example, in a typical Western population, anemia has many causes, including pregnancy, lactation, nutritional deficiencies, and bleeding. The heritability of anemia in most populations would probably be low or, depending on sample size, undetectable. Nevertheless, numerous genetic forms of anemia are known. In particular families and particular populations, the role of a gene in producing a specific anemia is critical and it is quite important to learn about these genes and gain the potential benefits of diagnostic accuracy. On the other hand, highly heritable behavioral traits are strongly determined by environmental factors and individual decisions. These factors should limit the impact in legal settings of data on heritability of behavior.

A genotype is a datum more specific to the individual. A genotype could be highly predictive of behavior; however, it is likely that genotypes will not be highly predictive of particular individuals, including criminal behaviors. It is important that genetic information introduced as mitigating be carefully received and not overvalued due to its novelty or conceptual appeal. Such findings should be interpreted within a well-formed perspective of the complexity of human behavior and its multiple influences. Conversely, it is hoped that effective interventions can be used within the context of punishment and reform of the criminal behavior whenever such interventions are developed based on a better understanding of the origins of behavior.

Impact of Environment on Heritable Behaviors

High heritability of a trait in no way implies that environmental intervention will not modify the trait. Genetic findings can be a necessary prelude to effective intervention. It should be emphasized that heritability studies generally do not fully capture the role of cross-cultural variation and the full impact of the environment in the modern world. Within cultures and at one point in time, antisocial behavior is highly heritable, as shown in studies by Gottesman and others (Gottesman & Shields, 1982; Cloninger & Gottesman, 1987; Rowe, 1986). However, there are large transnational differences in murder rates and levels of other criminal behaviors. In the United States in the post-World War II years, there was a large increase in the murder rate while genotype remained a constant. In the 1990s, murder rates have declined. Heritability studies do not include assessment of the environmental factors that are acting at a whole-society level. The combination of both genetic and social data—increasingly available for criminality and many of the traits known to be related to propensity for violence and criminal behavior, like schizophrenia, alcoholism, and substance abuse—is required.

How might the genetics of vulnerability to a complex behavioral problem or disease enlighten us? Our best understanding is that the common psychiatric, behavioral, and other disorders are complex and multiply determined, which is why these findings constitute not only a very important, but also difficult and refractory, frontier in biomedicine. We anticipate that multiple genes with vulnerability alleles of varying frequencies and effect sizes will be involved. There will be complex interactions between genes and environments, and between genes. And finally, we must allow for the salient ability of humans, as compared to other species, to shape and choose their environments—in effect to use free will—in order to cope with and compensate for their pre-existing vulnerabilities.

A Move to a Public Health Response

We are at the beginning of an evolutionary process in understanding the origins of these complex behavioral problems. Genetic technologies and information can be used in a wise way to develop new tools for treatment and prevention, and to more accurately target them. Neither the brain nor the genome are conveniently compartmentalized by diagnosis. Therefore, increments in our understanding of causation of antisocial behavior, alcoholism, and other psychiatric disorders has enormous implications for the study of criminality and violence, which are frequently a part or accompaniment of other known disorders.

Overall, genetic research is likely to shift the focus of our response to behavioral disorders from the punitive realm and more toward the therapeutic realm. Simple incarceration is notoriously ineffective in dealing with offenders, reducing victimizations, or enhancing public safety. The availability of more effective treatments for various antisocial behaviors will most likely compel the general public and policy-makers to consider alternative official responses to criminal conduct (see Judge Nygaard, Chapter 23 in this book). An understanding of underlying social and biological mechanisms in criminality has the potential to produce more favorable treatment outcomes in offenders and to develop more humane policies that will have preventative effects.

It is reasonable to expect behavioral improvements following a treatment that accounts for both socioenvironmental and genetic conditions. One cannot, however, manipulate genetic conditions and expect behavior to change without attending to other interactive contributions. Once an individual has entered the criminal justice system, behavioral problems are substantially compounded and the treatment of only one condition does not yield adequate therapeutic results. Thus, while findings reported herein have intrinsic clinical significance, there are many social, legal, and ethical issues to be considered, and regulatory safeguards to be instituted, before the implementation of global programmatic and policy changes (see Part 8 of this book for more detailed discussions).

CONCLUSIONS

The following conclusions can be made regarding the genetic bases of impulsive and antisocial behaviors.

1. A multiplicity of genetic and nongenetic variables leads to interindividual variation in the propensity to impulsive and aggressive behaviors.
2. Genetic linkage and direct gene scanning are two general approaches for identifying the genes and alleles. Several of the linkages should be recognized, and publicized, as preliminary but available for the winnowing process of replication.
3. Studies with genetic technologies have already yielded several genes that appear to reliably and specifically contribute to a small fraction of criminal behavior. These findings have little practical importance today but can be taken as a proof of principle that more such genes exist and can be found.
4. Effective use of genetic information will require careful gene/environment interaction studies, a process that will require communication across disciplines and the design of studies appropriate for analyses of the interactions.
5. The potential to improve related behavioral disorders through intervention is great.

References

Åsberg, M., Schalling, D., Traskman-Bendz, L. & Wagner, A. (1987). Psychobiology of suicide, impulsivity and related phenomena. In H. Y. Meltzer (Ed.), *Psychopharmacology: The third generation of progress.* New York: Raven, 655–668.

Ballenger, J. C., Goodwin, F. K., Major, L. F. & Brown, G. L. (1979). Alcohol and central serotonin metabolism in man. *Archives of General Psychiatry, 36,* 224–227.

Benjamin, J., Li, L., Paterson, C., Greenberg, B., Murphy, D. L. & Hamer, D. (1996). Population and familial association between the D4 dopamine receptor gene and measures of novelty seeking. *Nature Genetics, 12,* 81–84.

Benkelfat, C., Murphy, D. L., Hill, J. L., George, D. T., Nutt, D. & Linnoila, M. (1991). Ethanol-like properties of the serotonergic partial agonists meta-chlorophenylpiperazine in chronic alcoholic patients. *Archives of General Psychiatry, 48,* 383.

Berrettini, W. H., Goldin, L. R., Nurnberger, J. I. Jr. & Gershon, E. S. (1984). Genetic factors in affective illness. *Journal of Psychiatry Research, 18,* 329–350.

Bioulac, B., Benezech, M., Renaud, B., Noel, B. & Roche, D. (1980). Serotonergic dysfunction in the 47,XYY syndrome. *Biological Psychiatry, 15,* 917–923.

Blanchard, D., Shepherd, J. K., Rodgers, R. J. & Blanchard, R. J. (1988). Evidence for differential effects of 8-OH-DPAT on male and female rats in the anxiety/defense test battery. *Psychopharmacology Series (Berl), 106,* 531–539.

Blum, K., Noble, E. P., Sheridan, P. J., Montgomery, A., Ritchie, T., Jagadeeswaran, P., Nogami, H., Briggs, A. H. & Cohn, J. B. (1990). Allelic association of human dopamine D2 receptor gene in alcoholism. *Journal of the American Medical Association, 163,* 2055–2060.

Bohman, M. (1978). Some genetic aspects of alcoholism and criminality. A pouplation of adoptees. *Archives of General Psychiatry, 35,* 269–276.

Brizer, D. A. (1988). Psychopharmacology and the management of violent patients. *Psychiatric Clinics of North America, 11,* 551–568.

Brown, G. L., Ebert, M. H., Goyer, P. F., Jimerson, D. C., Klein, W. F., Bunney, W. E. & Goodwin, F. K. (1982). Aggression, suicide and serotonin: Relationships to CSF amine metabolites. *American Journal of Psychiatry, 139,* 741–746.

Brown, G. L., Goodwin, F. K., Ballenger, J. C., Goyer, P. F. & Major, L. F. (1979). Aggression in humans correlates with cerebrospinal fluid amine metabolites. *Psychiatry Research, 1,* 131–139.

Brown, G. L., Kline, W. J., Goyer, P. F., Minichiello, M. D., Kruesi, M. J. P. & Goodwin, F. K. (1985). Relationship of childhood characteristics to cerebrospinal fluid 5-hydroxyindoleacetic acid in aggressive adults. In C. Chagass (Ed.), *Biological psychiatry.* New York: Elsevier, 177–179.

Brunner, H. G. (1996). MAOA deficiency and abnormal behaviour: Perspectives on an association. In Ciba Foundation Symposium, *Genetics of Criminal and Antisocial Behaviour,* Chichester: John Wiley & Sons.

Brunner, H. G., Nelen, M. R., Breakefield, X. O., Ropers, H. H. & van Oost, B. A. (1993a). Abnormal behavior associated with a point mutation in the structural gene for monoamine oxidase A. *Science, 262,* 578–580.

Brunner, H. G., Nelen, M. R., van Zandvoort, P., Abeling, N. G., van Gennip, A. H., Wolters, E. C., Kuiper, M. A., Ropers, H. H. & van Oost, B. A. (1993b). X-linked borderline mental retardation with prominent behavioral disturbance: Phenotype, genetic localization & evidence for disturbed monoamine metabolism. *American Journal of Human Genetics, 52,* 1032–1039.

Buchsbaum, M. S., Coursey, R.D. & Murphy, D. (1976). The biochemical high-risk paradigm: Behavioral and familial correlates of low platelet monoamine oxidase activity. *Science, 194,* 339–341.

Buydens-Branchey, L., Noumair, D. & Lieber, C. S. (1989). Age of alcohol onset: Relationship to susceptibility to serotonin precursor availability. *Archives of General Psychiatry, 46,* 231–236.

Cargill, M., Altshuler, D., Ireland, J., Sklar, P., Ardlie, K., Patil, N., Lane, C. R. Lim, E. P., Kalyanaraman, N., Nemesh, J., Ziagura, L., Friedland, L., Rolfe, A., Warrington, J., Lipshutz, R., Daley, G. Q. & Landers, E. S. (1999). Characterization of single-nucleotide polymorphisms in coding regions of human genes. *Nature Genetics, 22,* 231–238.

Cases, O., Seif, I., Grimsby, J., Gaspar, P., Chen, K., Pournin, S., Muller, U., Aguet, M., Babinet, C., Shih, J. C. & DeMaeyer, E. (1995). Aggressive behavior and altered amounts of brain serotonin and norepinephrine in mice lacking MAOA. *Science, 268,* 1763–1766.

Cloninger, C. R. (1987). Neurogenetic adaptive mechanisms in alcoholism. *Science, 236,* 410–416.

Cloninger, C. R., Bohman, M. & Sigvardsson, S. (1981). Inheritance of alcohol abuse: Cross-fostering analysis of adopted men. *Archives of General Psychiatry, 38,* 861–868.

Cloninger, C. R., Bohman, M., Sigvardsson, S. & von Knorring, A. L. (1985). Psychopathology in adopted-out children of alcoholics. The Stockholm adoption study. *Recent Developments in Alcoholism, 3,* 37–51.

Cloninger, C. R. & Gottesman, I. I. (1987). Genetic and environmental factors in antisocial behavior disorders. In S. A. Mednick, T. E. Moffitt & S. A. Stack (Eds.), *The causes of crime: New biological approaches.* New York: Cambridge University Press, 92–109.

Coccaro, E. F., Bergeman, C. S. & McClearn, G. E. (1993). Heritability of irritable impulsiveness: A study of twins reared together and apart. *Psychiatry Research 48,* 229–242.

Coccaro, E. & Murphy, D. L. (1991). *Serotonin in major psychiatric disorders.* Washington, D. C: American Psychiatric Press.

Comings, D. E. (1996a). *The gene bomb.* Duarte, CA: Hope Press.

Comings, D. E. (1996b). Genetic mechanisms in neuropsychiatric disorders. In K. Blum, E. P. Noble, R. S. Sparks & P. J. Sheridan (Eds.), *Handbook of psychoneurogenetics.* Boca Raton, FL: CRC Press, Inc.

Comings, D. E., Muhleman, D., Ahn, C., Gysin, R. & Glanagan, S. (1994). The dopamine D2 receptor gene: A genetic risk factor in substance abuse. *Drug and Alcohol Dependence, 34,* 1–16.

Cook, E. H. Jr., Stein, M. A., Krasowski, M. D., Cox, N. J., Olkon, D. M., Kieffer, J. E., Leventhal, B. L. (1995). Association of attention-deficit disorder and the dopamine transporter gene. *American Journal of Human Genetics, 56,* 993–998.

Fishbein, D. H., Lozovsky, D. & Jaffe, J. H. (1989). Impulsivity, aggression, and neuroendocrine responses to serotonergic stimulation in substance users. *Biological Psychiatry, 25,* 1049–1066.

Gabel, S., Stadler, J., Bjorn, J., Shindledecker, R. & Bowen, C. J. (1995). Homovanillic acid and monoamine oxidase in sons of substance-abusing fathers: Relationship to conduct disorders. *Journal of Studies on Alcohol, 56,* 135–139.

Gejman, P. V., Ram, A., Gelernter, J., Friedman, E., Cao, Q., Pickar, D., Blum, K., Noble, E. P., Kranzler, H. R. & O'Malley, S. (1994). No structural mutation in the dopamine D2 receptor gene in alcoholism or schizophrenia: Analysis using denaturing gradient gel electrophoresis. *Journal of the American Medical Association, 271,* 204–208.

George, D. T., Benkelfat, C., Rawlings, R. R. Eckardt, M. J., Phillips, M. J., Nutt, D. J., Wynne, D., Murphy, D. L. & Linnoila, M. (1997). Behavioral and neuroendocrine responses to m-chlorophenylpiperazine in subtypes of alcoholics and in healthy comparison subjects. American Journal of Psychiatry, 154, 81–87.

Goldman, D. (1993). Alcoholism: Genetic transmission. *Recent Developments in Alcoholism, 11,* 231–248.

Goldman, D. (1995). Candidate genes in alcoholism. *Clinical Neuroscience, 3,* 174–181.

Goldman, D., Dean, M., Brown, G. L., Bolos, A. M., Tokola, R., Virkkunen, M. & Linnoila, M. (1992). D2 dopamine receptor genotype and cerebrospinal fluid homovanillic acid, 5 hydroxyindoleacetic acid and 3-methoxy-4-hydroxyphenylglycol in alcoholics in Finland and the United States. *Acta Psychiatrica Scandinavia, 86,* 351–357.

Gottesman, I. I. & Shields, J. (1982). *The epigenetic puzzle.* Cambridge: Cambridge University Press.

Hauser, P., Zametkin, A. J., Martinez, P., Vitiello, B., Matochik, J. A., Mixson, A. J. & Weintraub, B. D. (1993) Attention deficit-hyperactivity disorder in people with generalized resistance to thyroid hormone. *New England Journal of Medicine, 328,* 997–1001.

Higley, J. D., Thompson, W. W., Champoux, M., Goldman, D., Hasert, M. F., Kraemer, G. W., Scanlan, J. M., Suomi, S. J. & Linnoila, M. (1993). Paternal and maternal genetic contributions to cerebrospinal fluid monoamine metabolites in rhesus monkeys (Macaca Mulatta). *Archives of General Psychiatry, 50,* 615–623.

Hsu, Y. P., Powell, J. F., Sims, K.B. & Breakefield, X. O. (1989). Molecular genetics of the monoamine oxidases. *Journal of Neurochemistry, 53,* 12–18.

Itokawa, M., Arinami, T., Futamura, N., Hamaguchi, H. & Toru, M. (1993). A structural polymorphism of human dopamine receptor D2 (Ser311-Cys). *Biochemical and Biophysiology Research Community, 196,* 1369–1375.

Lappalainen, J., Long, J. C., Eggert, M., Ozaki, N., Robin, R. W., Brown, G. L., Naukkarinen, H., Virkkunen, M., Linnoila, M. & Goldman, D. (1998). Linkage of antisocial alcoholism to the serotonin 5-HT1B receptor gene in 2 populations. *Archives of General Psychiatry, 55,* 989–994.

Lidberg, L., Modin, I., Oreland, L., Tuck, J. R. & Gillner, A. (1985). Platelet monoamine oxidase activity and psychopathy. *Psychiatry Research, 16,* 339–343.

Linnoila, M. & Virkkunen, M. (1992). Biologic correlates of suicidal risk and aggressive behavioral traits. *Journal of Clinical Psychiatry, 12,* S19–S20.

Linnoila, M., Virkkunen, M., Eckardt, M., Higley, J. D., Nielsen, D. & Goldman, D. (1994). Serotonin, violent behavior and alcohol. *EXS, 71,* 155–163.

Linnoila, M., Virkkunen, M., Scheinin, M., Nuutila, A., Rimon, R. & Goodwin, F. K. (1983). Low cerebrospinal fluid 5-hydroxyindoleacetic acid concentration differentiates impulsive from nonimpulsive violent behavior. *Life Sciences, 33,* 2609–2614.

Loehlin, J. C. Willerman, L. & Horn, J. M. (1988). Human behavior genetics. *Annual Review of Psychology, 39,* 101–233.

Long, J. C., Knowler, W. C., Hanson, R. L., Robin, R. W., Urbanek, M., Moore, E., Bennett, P. H. & Goldman, D. (1998). Evidence for genetic linkage to alcohol dependence on chromosomes 4 and 11 from an autosome-wide scan in an American Indian population. *Neuropsychiatric Genetics, 81,* 216–221.

Mark, V. H. & Ervin, J. F. R. (1970). *Violence and the brain.* New York: Harper & Row.

Mehlman, P. T., Higley, J. D., Faucher I., Lilly, A. A., Taub, D. M., Vickers, J., Suomi, S. J. & Linnoila, M. (1994). Low CSF 5-HIAA concentrations and severe aggression and impaired impulse control in nonhuman primates. *American Journal of Psychiatry, 151,* 1485–1491.

Meltzer, H. M. & Arora, R. C. (1988). Genetic control of serotonin uptake in blood platelets: A twin study. *Psychiatry Research 24,* 263–269.

Moffitt, T. E. (1993). Adolescence-limited and life-course-persistent antisocial behavior: A developmental taxonomy. *Psychological Review, 100,* 674–701.

Moss, H. B., Yao, J. K. & Panzak, G. L. (1990). Serotonergic responsivity and behavioral dimensions in antisocial personality disorder with substance abuse. *Biological Psychiatry, 28,* 325–328.

Muhlbauer, H. D. (1985). Human aggression and the role of central serotonin. *Pharmacopsychiatry 18,* 218–221.

Nakhai, B., Nielsen, D. & Goldman, D. (1995). Two naturally occurring amino acid substitutions in the human 5HT1A receptor: 5HT1A-22>Ser and 5HT1A-28>Val. *Biochemistry and Biophysiology Research Community, 210,* 530–536.

Nielsen, D. A., Goldman, D., Virkkunen, M., Tokola, R., Rawlings, R. & Linnoila, M. (1994). Suicidality and 5-hydroxyindoleacetic acid concentration associated with a tryptophan hydroxylase polymorphism. *Archives of General Psychiatry, 51,* 34–38.

Nielsen, D. A., Lappalainen, J., Eggert, M., Virkkunen, M., Brown, G., Goldman, D. & Linnoila, M. (1998). Alcoholism and suicidality are linked to and associated with tryptophan hydroxylase in Finns. *Archives of General Psychiatry, 55,* 593–602.

Niskanen, P. & Achte, K.A. (1972). The course and prognoses of schizophrenic psychoses in Helsinki: A comparative study of first admissions in 1950, 1960 and 1965. Monograph of Psychiatric Clinics in Helsinki, University Central Hospital.

Noble, E. P., Blum, K., Khalsa, E., Ritchie, T., Montgomery, A., Wood, R. C., Fitch, R. J., Ozkaragoz, T., Sheridan, P. J., Anglin, M. D., Paredes, A., Treiman, L. J. & Sparkes, R. S. (1993). Allelic association of the D2 dopamine receptor gene with cocaine dependence. *Drug and Alcohol Dependence, 33,* 271–285.

Raine, A. (1993). *The psychopathology of crime: Criminal behavior as a clinical disorder.* San Diego, CA: Academic Press.

Rietschel, M., Nothen, M. M., Lannfelt, L., Sokoloff, P., Schwartz, J. C., Lanczik, M., Fritze, J., Cichon, S., Fimmers, R. & Korner, J. (1993). A serine to glycine substitution at position 9 in the extracellular N-terminal part of the doapmine D3 receptor protein: No role in the genetic predisposition to bipolar affect disorder. *Psychiatry Research, 46,* 253–259.

Rowe, D. C. (1986). Genetic and environmental components of antisocial behavior. A study of 265 twin pairs. *Criminology, 24,* 513–532.

Roy, A., Virkkunen, M. & Linnoila, M. (1987). Reduced central serotonin turnover in a subgroup of alcoholics. *Progress in Neuropsychopharmacology and Biological Psychiatry, 11,* 173–177.

Rushton, J. P., Fulker, D. W., Neale, M. C., Nias, N. K. B. & Eysenck, H. J. (1986). Altruism and aggression: The heritability of individual differences. *Journal of Personality and Social Psychology, 50,* 1192–1198.

Saudou, F., Amara, D. A., Dierich, A., LeMeur, M., Ramboz, S., Segu, L., Buhot, M. C. & Hen, R. (1994). Enhanced aggressive behaviour in mice lacking 5-HT1B receptor. *Science, 265,* 1875–1878.

Schalling, D., Åsberg, M., Edman, G. & Oreland, L. (1987). Markers for vulnerability to psychopathology—Temperament traits associated with platelet MAO activity associated with impulsivity and aggressivity. *Acta Psychiatrica Scandinavia, 76,* 172–182.

Soubrie, P. (1986). Reconciling the role of central serotonin neurons in human and animal behavior. *Behavior and Brain Sciences, 9,* 319–364.

Tellegen, A., Lykken, D. T., Bouchard, T. J., Wilcox, K., Seagal, N. & Rich, S. (1988). Personality similarity in twins reared apart and together. *Journal of Personality and Social Psychology, 54,* 1031–1039.

Tiihonen, J., Kuikka, J., Hakola, P., Paanila, J., Airaksinen, J., Eronen, M. & Hallikainen, T. (1994). Acute ethanol-induced changes in cerebral blood flow. *American Journal of Psychiatry, 151,* 1505–1508.

Tsuang, M. T. (1983). Risk of suicide in relatives of schizophrenics, manic depressives and controls. *Journal of Clinical Psychiatry, 44,* 396–400.

Van Praag, H. M., Kahn, R. S., Asnis, G. M., Wetzler, S., Brown, S. L., Bleich, A. & Korn, M. L. (1987). Denosologization of biological psychiatry or the specificity of 5-HT disturbances in psychiatric disorders. *Journal of Affective Disorders, 13,* 1–8.

Virkkunen, M. (1983). Serum cholesterol levels in homicidal offenders: A low cholesterol level is connected with a habitually violent tendency under the influence of alcohol. *Psychophysiology, 10,* 65–69.

Virkkunen, M., De Jong, J., Bartko, J., Goodwin, F. K. & Linnoila, M. (1989). Relationship of psychobiological variables to recidivism in violent offenders and impulsive fire setters. *Archives of General Psychiatry, 46,* 600–603.

Virkkunen, M. & Linnoila., M. (1990). Serotonin in early onset, male alcoholics with violent behaviour. *Annals of Medicine, 22,* 327–331.

Virkkunen, M., Nuutila, A., Goodwin, F. K. & Linnoila, M. (1987). Cerebrospinal fluid monoamine metabolite levels in male arsonists. *Archives of General Psychiatry, 44,* 241–247.

Virkkunen, M., Rawlings, R., Tokola, R., Poland, R. E., Guidotti, A., Nemeroff, C., Bissette, G., Kalogeras, K., Karonen, S. L. & Linnoila, M. (1994). CSF biochemistries, glucose metabolism & diurnal activity rhythms in alcoholic, violent offenders, fire setters and healthy volunteers. *Archives of General Psychiatry, 51,* 20–27.

von Knorring, L., von Knorring, A-L., Smigan, L., Lindberg, U. & Edholm, M. (1987). Personality traits in subtypes of alcoholics. *Journal of Studies on Alcohol, 48,* 523–527.

Part 4

Relationships Between Cognitive Deficits, Brain Dysfunction, and Aggression

Despite a "cognitive revolution" in the field of psychology and breakthroughs in cognitive science in general, currently popular criminological theories generally include little explicit discussion of the role of cognition. In Chapter 10, Dr. Wanda Foglia distinguishes between what she terms "interpersonal" and "impersonal" types of cognition, defining the former as the ability to deal with and understand other people and social interactions, and the latter as the ability to process and appropriately interpret environmental stimuli. Both obviously overlap and are somewhat interdependent; Dr. Foglia addresses interpersonal cognition, while in Chapter 11 Dr. Peter Giancola focuses on impersonal cognition. Dr. Foglia's chapter explains how cognitive deficits make some people more vulnerable to temptation or more likely to choose criminal solutions to problematic situations, and it reviews the literature on associations with crime found for three cognitions: (1) social perspective-taking, (2) problem-solving ability, and (3) locus of control. Implicit assumptions in many criminological theories that thinking influences behavior, examples of successful integrations of these cognitions with social learning and social bonding theories, and the success of cognitive rehabilitation programs also are discussed. Dr. Foglia argues that a more explicit focus on cognition will provide insights into how the environment influences cognition and how cognitive mindsets affect reactions to the environment, as well as enhance prevention and rehabilitation programs.

Dr. Giancola discusses the role of impersonal cognitive skills in the production of antisocial behaviors. Cognitive or neuropsychological deficits have been strongly and consistently associated with the propensity to and incidence of impulsive aggression. Impulsive and aggressive disorders share many of the same biological substrates as substance abuse, given the comorbidity and commonalities in behavioral dimensions such as attention deficits, impulsivity, history of conduct disorder, and other personality disorders and traits. Thus, it comes as no surprise that similar cognitive deficits have been implicated in the development of both substance abuse and aggressive or violent behavior. In particular, there is evidence that both drug abuse and aggressive behavior may be characterized by impairments in ability to assess consequences and act on that assessment, as reflected in the personality trait of impulsivity. Accordingly, it is proposed that the link between brain function abnormality, drug abuse, and antisocial behavior may be mediated by altered cognitive capacities, particularly those involving executive function such as attention, concentration, verbal ability, abstract reasoning, problem solving, and programming and planning goal-oriented behaviors. Dr. Giancola hypothesizes in his chapter that impaired executive cognitive functioning (ECF) compromises the ability to interpret social cues during interpersonal interactions, which may lead to misperceptions of threat or hostility in conflict situations. ECF impairment may further undermine the ability to generate alternative socially adaptive behavioral responses and to execute a sequence of responses necessary to avoid aggressive or stressful interactions. Finally, compromised cognitive control over behavior may permit hostility, negative affective states, and other maladaptive responses (e.g., drug abuse) to dominate.

Studies attempting to localize neural regulatory mechanisms in cognitive impairments that underlie impulsivity and aggression implicate the prefrontal lobes (see also Chaper 19 by Dr. Elliott), which are located in the front of the cortex—the gray matter which is responsible for higher intellectual functioning. Various areas of the limbic system, a primitive portion of the brain responsible for moods, emotions, and many "survival" strategies, may also be involved (e.g., the ventral and dorsal hippocampus, septal area, amygdala, and cingulate gyrus). Studies of substance abusers have reported similar findings. Executive cognitive functioning is believed to be subserved by neural systems located, in part, in the prefrontal cortex. Because particular regions of the prefrontal cortex (e.g., the orbitofrontal and dorsolateral regions) appear to play a role in forethought, behavioral inhibition, and capacity to learn from experience, neuropsychological functions known to be executed by the prefrontal cortex are of particular interest. Many possible sources of damage to the brain may disrupt the ability to assess consequences and to regulate impulses (e.g., head injury, prenatal drug exposure, neurotoxicity, genetic defects, even childhood deprivation or chronic drug use). Thus, treatment of these disorders relies on understanding relationships between brain dysfunction, cognition, impulse control, and propensity for drug abuse and violent behavior. Dr. Giancola outlines several possible remedies for these deficits which would, if used appropriately and rigorously, likely improve cognitive functioning and enhance the ability to self-regulate behavior.

Chapter 12, by Drs. Matthew Robinson and Tom Kelley, highlights the importance of recognizing the role of abnormal brain function in violence in a significant number of offenders. The authors describe a study they conducted within a prison to identify signs of neurological conditions that are believed to increase risk for violent behavior. In an attempt to develop a clinically useful and cost-efficient tool to screen offenders for brain dysfunction, they tested a simple written procedure, called the "Kelley Form," in a correctional setting. The Kelley Form was designed to assess the correlates of brain dysfunction, including evidence of birth complications, family abuse, parental drug use, maternal drug use during pregnancy, persistent physical conditions, abnormal physical conditions, irregular interpersonal characteristics, psychological disturbances, irregular diet, head injury, exposure to environmental toxins, and substance use. After a review of the literature, they describe the results of this study. In sum, there were several "neurological correlates" that significantly differentiated repeat violent offenders from repeat nonviolent offenders and first time offenders. They concluded that the presence of these correlates of brain dysfunction in an offender warrant further medical attention, which could, with proper treatment, lead to behavioral improvements.

Chapter 10

Adding an Explicit Focus on Cognition to Criminological Theory

by Wanda D. Foglia, J.D., Ph.D.

Introduction 10-2
Reasons for the Lack of Emphasis on Cognition in Criminological Theory 10-3
    Sociological/Behavioral Explanations 10-3
    Methodological Problems 10-4
Cognition and Crime 10-5
    Interpersonal and Impersonal Cognition 10-5
    Social Perspective-Taking 10-6
        Measuring Social Perspective-Taking 10-7
        Affective Empathy 10-7
    Problem-Solving Ability 10-8
        Measuring Problem-Solving Ability 10-9
        Skills vs. Perception of Skills 10-10
    Locus of Control 10-10
        Measuring Locus of Control 10-11
        Development of Locus of Control 10-12
    Summary 10-12
Cognition in Current Criminological Theory, Research, and Practice 10-12
    The Implicit Role of Cognition in Prominent Criminological
        Theories 10-13
        Social Learning Theory 10-13
        Social Bonding Theory 10-14
        General Strain Theory 10-14
        A General Theory of Crime 10-15
        Summary 10-15
    Integrating Cognition Into Criminological Theory 10-16
    Something Works: The Effectiveness of Cognitive Corrections 10-18
        Cognitive Intervention Modalities 10-18

Education, Not Simply Therapy 10-19
Conclusion: An Explicit Focus on Cognition Will Enhance
 Understanding and Interventions 10-19

INTRODUCTION

Psychology's recent resurgence of interest in how brain activity relates to mental states and how these cognitive processes influence reactions to environmental stimuli has been called a "cognitive revolution" (Baars, 1986; Sperry, 1993). Cognitive psychology is a subcategory of the broad interdisciplinary field of cognitive science, which also includes developments in biology, anthropology, computer science, linguistics, and philosophy. Researchers in each of these areas are attempting to integrate knowledge from diverse fields to advance our understanding of how the human mind functions. Cognitive scientists all study issues such as how knowledge is represented and acquired, how sensory experiences are organized and given meaning, and how memory works; and cognitive psychologists focus on understanding how processes within the brain relate to thinking, feeling, and behaving. The United States Congress has declared the 1990s the "Decade of the Brain" because of the breakthroughs in understanding cognition (Kellogg, 1995). However, in a discipline closely wedded to sociology, cognition has gotten relatively little explicit attention in the development and testing of theories in the field of criminology.

Psychology's cognitive revolution reflects a shift in emphasis away from the behaviorists' concentration on observable stimuli and responses, to a focus on what happens in a person's mind between the stimulus and the response. Cognitive psychology is concerned with how individuals perceive and process environmental experiences. Although used differently by different social scientists, cognition generally refers to concepts such as belief systems, memory, imagery, intelligence, and reasoning, and it is most widely used as a synonym for thinking (Hollin, 1990).

It is important to stress that psychology's shift in focus is not a return to a mentalistic dualism. Consciousness cannot be separated from a functioning brain, because mental states are "dynamic emergent properties of brain activity" (Sperry, 1993, p. 879). A complete discussion of this paradigm shift, or the vast array of cognitive processes studied by cognitive psychologists, is beyond the scope of this review (see Sperry, 1993 and Baars, 1986 for further information). This chapter focuses on three types of thinking processes that seem especially relevant to explaining criminal behavior and deserving of more explicit attention in criminological theories. These three cognitions which theory and some empirical evidence suggest relate to criminal behavior are:

- Social perspective-taking,
- Problem-solving ability, and
- Locus of control.

The earlier sections of this chapter summarize a few of the primary reasons cognition has received relatively little attention from criminologists. The discussion of cognitions relating to crime provides a general explanation of how cognition theoretically relates to crime and reviews the theory and research on crime and social perspective-taking, problem-solving ability, and locus of control. Later sections discuss the role cognition already plays in criminological theory and practice. These sections present examples of how criminological theories already incorporate cognition to some extent, and they discuss some recent attempts to integrate the three cognitions with currently popular criminological theories. Some empirical evidence of the effectiveness of corrections programs with a cognitive focus is also discussed. The chapter concludes with some ideas for how more emphasis on cognition can enhance theory and practice.

REASONS FOR THE LACK OF EMPHASIS ON COGNITION IN CRIMINOLOGICAL THEORY

Historically, there were but a few criminologists who focused on differences in the thinking of offenders, and many of the currently fashionable theories contain some elements of cognition; but sociological influences have dominated the field and many criminology texts do not even mention cognitive approaches in their discussions of criminological theories. There has been some resistance by criminologists unfamiliar with cognitive theories, but there are also substantive problems with the work on cognition and crime that contribute to the relative neglect. A significant amount of research has been done in correctional settings aimed at revealing cognitive deficits among offenders and evaluating the impact of interventions designed to remediate those deficits, but scattered bits of evidence have not been integrated into a coherent theory. This lack of a systematic approach, along with methodological problems inherent in some of the research, helps explain why cognition has not been more readily embraced by criminologists.

Sociological/Behavioral Explanations

Part of the problem is that when cognitive explanations were first proposed in the 1950s, criminological and sociological theories were dominated by explanations that focused on the social, political, and/or economic status of offenders. Even within psychological circles, cognitive explanations were not warmly received initially because they were inconsistent with the prevailing emphasis on observable behavior. An emphasis on cognitions rather than emotions was also seemingly inconsistent with the medical/psychiatric model that was popular among corrections personnel at the time (Ross & Fabiano, 1985). Even now that the cognitive approach has become a dominant force in psychology, criminological theories still emphasize sociological influences, and discussions of psychology generally are limited to older psychological approaches such as behaviorism, Kohlberg's moral development theory, or personality theories.[1] Criminologists typically have been trained as (or at least by) sociologists, thus they focus more on sociological factors and seem to find it easier to consider the older, more well-established psychological theories rather than the relatively new and less well-understood cognitive approaches.

Research on the connection between cognition and crime can be found in the psychological, sociological, criminological, and educational literature, but this work has been described as consisting of "a number of isolated studies rather than a comprehensive, integrated body of knowledge" (Ross & Fabiano, 1985, p. 32). "Cognition" refers to a variety of functions, and there is a lot of confusion regarding specific terminology. Often, different researchers use disparate terms to refer to what appears to be the same function, or the same label is used to assess what may in fact be different concepts. The lack of coherence in the research in this area is captured by Rotenberg's complaints about the "ambiguity and inconsistency permeating the operational definitions and empirical measures" (1974, p. 1). Similar sentiments were manifest in Ross and Fabiano's more recent review of the literature on cognition and crime (1985):

> [W]e gained the impression that very few researchers in the field are aware that there are others who are active in the same area.... Seldom have there been attempts to study, or even consider, the possible interrelationships among the various specific cognitive functions. (p. 32)

Methodological Problems

Methodological problems with the cognitive approach also have hindered its acceptance. It is more difficult to measure accurately the integrity of a person's thinking process than it is to gauge behavior. Conventional instruments rely on the subject's perception and description, and subjects may deliberately lie or inadvertently create a misleading impression because of differences between the subject's and researcher's interpretations of language. The cognitive approach has also suffered because of its association both with studies that have attempted to identify a criminal personality and have received such mixed reviews (Schuessler & Cressey, 1950; Tennenbaum, 1977; Laufer et al., 1982), and with Yochelson and Samenow's controversial description of "criminal thinking patterns" (1976).[2]

The reliance on institutionalized samples and official measures of delinquency in much of the empirical research on cognition and crime is especially troublesome. Many of the studies compared institutionalized offenders with controls presumed to be nonoffenders, but failed to consider that the cognitive deficits could be a result of institutionalization. Research findings that those incarcerated for longer periods had a more external locus of control underscores the importance of this consideration (Levenson, 1974). People do in fact have less control over their lives when they are incarcerated. A person also may feel hostile, defensive, or rejected when incarcerated, which may make him or her less likely to express empathy for others or to adopt prosocial approaches to problems. Being incarcerated, or even adjudicated delinquent, could easily have an impact on how individuals view the world and their place in it.

Furthermore, using official measures of delinquency implies that only those who get caught and convicted are sampled. These samples may not be representative of delinquents in general. Perhaps the cognitive deficits observed are related to getting caught and failing to negotiate a way out of official processing, rather than committing crime.

In their 1985 review of the literature, Ross and Fabiano complained that there was no research examining cognitions of those who broke the law but have not been caught. In recent years, there have been a few studies that begin to address this concern by examining the relation between cognition and self-reported delinquency in nonclinical samples (Foglia, 1995, 1996; Lau & Leung, 1992; Mak, 1990; Guerra,

1989; DeMore et al., 1988; Dishion et al., 1984). Foglia's sample consisted of inner-city high school students; Lau and Leung's research was focused on Chinese adolescents; Dishion et al.'s involved only white males; DeMore et al.'s was limited to vandalism among college students; and Guerra's focused on differences in consequential thinking. These studies generally support a connection between cognition and crime, but they constitute a very limited amount of evidence compared to the bulk of the research that studies those who have been caught and processed. There is a need for more studies using self-report measures and nonadjudicated samples to separate the impact of cognition on committing crime from any possible effects of institutionalization, differential law-enforcement, or simply not being savvy enough to avoid getting caught or convicted.

Although crime is a social problem and sociological factors play a key role in causation, prevention, and rehabilitation, crimes are committed by individuals oftentimes with distorted perceptions of reality, causal sequences, and consequences. Thus, the functional integrity of their thought processes also must be considered. If criminologists expand their theoretical models to include the cognitions discussed in the next section, they should be able to develop both a more comprehensive understanding of crime causation and more effective interventions.

COGNITION AND CRIME

Cognitive deficits are generally not offered as direct causes of crime, rather they operate like the weak social bonds in Hirschi's social control theory (1969). Similar to people who are weakly bonded to society, people are more likely to succumb to various temptations if they have deficiencies in their beliefs or reasoning. Conversely, prosocial beliefs, like strong social bonds, insulate individuals so that they are less likely to be delinquent (Ross & Fabiano, 1985; Jennings et al., 1983).

Interpersonal and Impersonal Cognition

To understand the focus of the research described in this chapter, it is important to distinguish interpersonal from impersonal cognitions. Interpersonal cognition, sometimes called social cognition, deals with understanding people and social interactions. It includes being able to see the perspective of others, understand social phenomenon (political, economic, legal), solve interpersonal problems, and feel some personal control over social interactions. Aspects of cognition dealing with the processing of information and stimuli from the physical world, including intelligence, are considered impersonal cognitions. These two forms of cognition are not totally independent, but there is a substantial body of research indicating that they are not of the same cognitive dimension (Hollin, 1990; Ross & Fabiano, 1985). There is no evidence that people who solve impersonal problems easily are necessarily as competent when dealing with social problems (Little & Kendall, 1979), and, even when significant, correlations between interpersonal cognitive skills and conventional I.Q. tests are not strong (Spivack et al., 1976).

There is evidence that both impersonal and interpersonal cognitive deficits are associated with offending, but the work on interpersonal cognition is discussed herein. (Impersonal cognitive and neuropsychological deficits are more fully discussed in

Barratt, Chapter 4, and Giancola, Chapter 11.) Deficits in impersonal cognition may place someone at risk for delinquency in a different way, primarily by leading to school failure and difficulties obtaining legitimate opportunities. Interpersonal deficits also can reduce legitimate options, but the focus is on how the inability to understand people and social interactions lead to interpersonal problems that can ultimately result in criminal behavior. The research does not demonstrate that all offenders are deficient in interpersonal cognitive skills, but many are, especially adolescent offenders, substance abusers, and violent offenders.

It is also important to emphasize that the cognitive model does not contradict explanations emphasizing poverty, lack of opportunity, inadequate education, or faulty parenting. These factors are seen as the very conditions that can retard a person's cognitive development. As discussed more thoroughly later in this chapter, integrating cognitions into theories stressing sociological factors will enhance our understanding of how environment affects cognition. A more explicit focus on cognition also may suggest educational interventions aimed at prevention and/or rehabilitation among those who are at risk by virtue of their cognitive deficits.

The following discussions describe the theory and research on (1) social perspective-taking, (2) problem-solving ability, and (3) locus of control. There are numerous types of thinking and many other cognitions that probably are related to crime. These three were chosen because for each, there already exists a substantial body of research showing a connection with crime, yet they have gotten little explicit emphasis in the currently popular criminological theories.

Social Perspective-Taking

One form of cognition repeatedly found to be associated with criminal behavior is difficulty in understanding the perspectives of other people and of social groups (Foglia, 1995, 1996; Mak, 1990, 1991; Chalmers & Townsend, 1990; Chandler, 1973; Rotenberg, 1974; Heilbrun, 1982; also see Ross & Fabiano, 1985, pp. 53–59, for a review of earlier studies finding a relation between delays in developing social-perspective taking skills and antisocial behavior). This construct has been called *social perspective-taking*, *role-taking*, and *empathy* (among other terms), and it has been measured in a variety of ways. Although some researchers have tried to distinguish role-taking and empathy (e.g., Lee & Prentice, 1988), the terms are generally used interchangeably. Chalmers and Townsend's results, which indicate that a role-play program designed to enhance social perspective-taking led to increased scores on tests of empathy, provides empirical support for assuming congruence (1990). The more inclusive term "social perspective-taking" will be used here, because it encompasses an understanding of the "rules, conventions, attitudes, and behavior of social groups" as well as the ability to see and feel for the perspective of others (Ross & Fabiano, 1985, p. 53).

Social perspective-taking involves higher cognitive skills than dealing with the physical environment. It requires making inferences about unobservable psychological and sociological characteristics such as feelings, thoughts, personality traits, social conventions, and rules. This is much more difficult than drawing conclusions from concrete observations (Shantz, 1975). Deficits in this area reflect an egocentric mode of thinking, whereby affected individuals can only see their own needs and viewpoint. Individuals stuck in an egocentric mode of thinking may view rules and laws as arbitrary because they do not recognize or understand their social purpose. They may also antagonize others unintentionally because they do not appreciate the perspective of others (Chandler, 1973).

Chandler's measurement of, and attempt to remediate, social perspective-taking skills among chronic delinquents is a good example of the research supporting the connection between this cognitive deficit and deviance. Initial assessments of forty-five delinquents with lengthy police records and forty-five boys of comparable ages with no known delinquent histories revealed significant differences in social perspective-taking (which he also calls "social egocentrism" and "role-taking ability" at different points in the article). The delinquents were then randomly divided into three groups, one of which was assigned to an experimental program employing drama and the making of videos as a vehicle for enhancing role-taking ability. The remaining groups were assigned to either a placebo or no treatment control conditions. Pre- and post-test comparisons showed that only those in the experimental condition demonstrated significant improvements in social perspective-taking, and an eighteen-month follow-up demonstrated that these improvements were associated with significant reductions in delinquent behavior. (See Ellis, 1982; Megargee, 1972; Kurtines & Hogan, 1972, for similar examples of lower social perspective-taking among adjudicated offenders when compared with allegedly nondelinquent controls).

Measuring Social Perspective-Taking. Not only is the same cognitive skill referred to by different names (often within one article as is the work described in the preceding paragraph), but a wide range of approaches are used to measure what is allegedly the same construct. Rotenberg (1974) should be consulted for a more specific summary of the objections raised regarding various techniques for tapping what he refers to as empathy or role-taking ability, but some examples are helpful here. One common technique is to ask subjects to predict the responses of others on personality inventories or lists of adjectives others would use to describe them. If the subject's predictions correlate highly with the actual responses given by others, the subject is considered empathetic because he or she seems to be able to understand the perspective of others. However, this approach has been criticized as measuring projection or self-conception instead of empathy. Other scales have been faulted for being confounded with measures of opinions, acceptance of rules, and interpersonal effectiveness. Hogan's Empathy Scale (Hogan, 1969) was developed by contrasting responses to a large pool of items taken primarily from the California Personality Inventory (CPI) and the Minnesota Multiphasic Personality Inventory (MMPI) given by subjects who had been independently rated as high versus low in empathetic skill. Although Hogan reports a considerable amount of validity support, Rotenberg argues that although it "might be instrumental in measuring opinion consensus regarding empathic personalities, it appears of little use in measuring actual empathic ability in ongoing interactional situations" (1974, p. 179).

Affective Empathy. A further complication emphasized by several different researchers (e.g., Kaplan & Arbuthnot, 1985; Rotenberg, 1974) is that it might be important to distinguish between *cognitive role-taking* as opposed to *affective empathy*. Chandler's above-described study was more directly measuring cognitive role-taking because it assessed the subject's understanding of what facts were available to third parties. However, Rotenberg, as well as Kaplan and Arbuthnot, suggest that the characteristic that distinguishes offenders may not be the ability to see another's perspective as much as the capacity to care at an affective level about what is perceived. Rotenberg assessed what he called cognitive role-taking and affective role-taking in high school students and incarcerated juveniles. The cognitive measure involved predicting an acquaintance's responses to hypothetical problems, whereas the affective measure determined how much pain the subject was willing to inflict on "volunteers" (actually a confederate of the researchers) to allegedly "teach" them a memory task. In what are described as preliminary results, Rotenberg found that cognitive and affective role-taking were not correlated, and that the delinquents showed significantly less affective role-taking. The differences for cognitive role-taking were not statistically significant in this study, although differences have been found by others using cognitive measures (e.g., Chandler, 1973; Freedman et al., 1978).

The foregoing suggests that cognitive understanding may not be sufficient to guarantee affective understanding. "Confidence men," who cognitively understand their victims' perspectives all too well as they manipulate them, do not seem to empathize on an emotional level (Rotenberg, 1974). Some have speculated that cognitive understanding is not only insufficient, but also unnecessary because people may be able to unconsciously "catch" another person's mood (Perlman & Cozby, 1983, p. 169). The relation between what individuals think and feel is not fully understood, but there is some agreement that the kind of social perspective-taking that inhibits delinquency is strengthened through caring and supportive families, schools, and/or communities in which strong interpersonal bonds are formed with significant others (Buzzell, 1992; Garmezy & Rutter, 1983; Werner & Smith, 1982).

Most of this research has been conducted outside a cognitive developmental framework, but it should be noted that Kohlberg emphasizes role-taking as a key part of the process of moral development. He asserts that "role-taking opportunities" stimulate moral development. The first prerequisite is that the individual be part of a group, which provides opportunities for "the restructuring of modes of role-taking" (1969, p. 399). The family is usually the first group, although Kohlberg emphasizes that it is not unique or indispensable, as interactions in other social contexts can provide the needed experience with relating to the perspective of others.

Although theory and research repeatedly suggest that social perspective-taking is inversely related to delinquency, there is considerable confusion regarding what is being measured and how it should be assessed. In addition, it is unclear that determining whether a subject is cognitively able to understand the perspective of another assures that the subject cares at an affective level about what another experiences. While all offenders do not lack this skill (Ross & Fabiano, 1985), it is not surprising that many offenders do not seem to understand and/or care about the interests of other people or social groups. The reasons for this deficit may be a paucity of social experiences required for the development of cognitive understanding and empathy, and/or a neuropsychological dysfunction, as described in both Giancola's and Barratt's chapters.

Problem-Solving Ability

Another skill considered especially important for adequate social adjustment is the cognitive ability to solve interpersonal problems. This ability has been described to include (1) recognizing potential problems, (2) generating alternative solutions, (3) considering consequences (for self and others), (4) conceptualizing step-by-step means for reaching one's goal, and (5) recognizing cause-and-effect relations between one's action and another's behavior (Spivack et al., 1976). Slaby and Guerra break this skill into similar component parts and add "seeking information, defining the problem, selecting a goal . . . and prioritizing responses" (1988, p. 580). This cognitive skill is related to social perspective-taking, as an understanding of how the perspective of others contributes to how one defines a problem, and a fuller appreciation of consequences that may have an impact on others. The two skills are so closely related that they are sometimes assessed jointly, as in the development of the Adolescent Problems Inventory (API) designed to measure "behavioral role-playing and problem-solving" (Freedman et al., 1978, p. 1448).

Institutionalized offenders have repeatedly been found to score lower on measures of problem-solving ability than controls with no known criminal record (Freedman et al., 1978; Platt et al., 1973). There is also research demonstrating that individuals deficient in interpersonal problem-solving skills tend to be aggressive and impulsive, characteristics that can lead to confrontations with the law (Slaby & Guerra, 1988; Platt et al., 1974; Shure et al., 1971). In addition, problem-solving ability seems to be related to adjustment to institutionalization as several studies find that inmates who are discipline problems score lower than those presenting no major discipline problems (Hains & Herrman, 1989; Higgens & Thies, 1981; Freedman et al., 1978). Johnson and Hunter (1992) found that those who scored at the upper range on problem-solving ability were less likely to violate probation than the rest of the sample.

Measuring Problem-Solving Ability. Again there is a wide variety of approaches to measuring problem-solving ability. The API presents subjects with forty-four hypothetical problems that young people encounter regularly and have difficulty handling. Abstracts of a few sample problems are: "A male, peer stranger deliberately bumps into you on the street," "A friend suggests buying booze illegally," and "You are bored and want some fun" (Freedman et al., 1978, p. 1453). Subjects are asked how they would handle the situation, and responses are rated for competence based on judgments of thirteen advanced psychology students, clinical psychology interns, and professional psychologists. Although only items with a 75 percent consensus among the judges were used and the API did discriminate between groups as expected, the authors themselves emphasize that there are questions regarding whether the judgments of the so-called experts are valid when applied to the life contexts of delinquents. The API responses also did not indicate what the subjects would do if actually confronted with the problem described.

The Means Ends Problem Solving (MEPS) technique was used in the studies by Higgens and Thies (1981) and by Platt, Scura, and Hannon (1973), cited above. This approach consisted of presenting ten "stories" that raise a problem for the protagonist and provide an ending in which the problem was resolved. The subject was asked to fill in the middle with alternatives for reaching the desired resolution and was scored according to how many effective and relevant means he or she produced (Higgens & Thies, 1981). This approach would seem to provide a good indication of the subject's ability to generate alternative solutions, but that is only one component of the myriad of skills necessary for effective problem-solving.

The social problem-solving measure used by Slaby and Guerra (1988) was adapted from the Interpersonal Problem Solving (IPA) analysis developed by Marsh (1982). Subjects were presented with two hypotheticals in which an unknown peer was interfering with what they wanted to do, and were then asked seven questions regarding (1) how they would define the problem, (2) how they would define their goal, (3) what additional facts they would need, (4) how many alternatives they could imagine, (5) what they thought was the best solution, (6) what they thought was the second best solution, and (7) what consequences they anticipated. The total number of nonduplicative responses were tallied for number of facts, number of solutions, and number of consequences, and the remaining responses were scored according to whether they were effective and not violent or hostile. They established test-retest reliabilities ranging from .75 to .93 for the seven measures (Slaby & Guerra, 1988, p. 582). Although the experimenter rating the responses was blind to the status of the subjects, there is still some subjectivity involved in determining what would truly be effective in a real-life context, and the question of whether the verbal responses reflect what the subjects would actually do.

Skill vs. Perception of Skills. The Problem-Solving Inventory (PSI) developed by Heppner (1982) consists of thirty-five items measuring how individuals *believe* they react to personal problems in their daily lives, rather than directly assessing actual problem-solving skills. Sample items are: "I have the ability to solve most problems even though initially no solution is immediately apparent" and "Sometimes I get so charged up emotionally that I am unable to consider many ways of dealing with my problems." Reliability has been established by measures of internal consistency (alpha) equaling .90, and test-retest correlations ranging from .83 to .89. Concurrent, construct, and known-groups validity has also been established (see Corcoran & Fischer, 1987, for additional details). The measure of problem-solving ability in the previously mentioned study by Johnson and Hunter (1992) consisted of seven items from the PSI (with some variation in the wording). This measure does not directly tap actual problem-solving skills but, for subjects with realistic self-perceptions, it may be a better indicator of how they actually handle real-life problems than verbal answers to specific hypotheticals.

However it is measured, there is a wealth of evidence that deficiencies in problem-solving skills are associated with delinquency. Again, not all delinquents have low problem-solving skills (Meltzer et al., 1986), but young people who have not learned to respond effectively to life's problems can be expected to fail repeatedly at legitimate attempts to attain desired goals, and may become frustrated and angry. This hostility can contribute directly to aggression, and repeated failures can prompt resort to illegitimate means of achieving desired ends.

Locus of Control

There is evidence that an external locus of control is associated with antisocial behavior. Individuals can be classified as *internals* or *externals* depending on what they think controls what happens to them (Rotter, 1966). Internals think that they control events in their lives, through their talents or hard work. On the other hand, externals think luck, fate, chance, or powerful others control their destiny (Rotter, 1966, p. 1). Those with an external locus of control are less likely to perceive a connection between their behavior and the consequences that follow (Nowicki & Strickland, 1973; Rotter, 1966). Although it seems logical that those who do not see themselves as responsible would be more likely to engage in delinquency, the empirical evidence is mixed (Ross & Fabiano, 1985).

Comparisons of adjudicated offenders to controls with no known criminal history have found evidence that the offenders perceive themselves as more externally controlled. Graham (1993) compared adult sex offenders with non-sex offenders and a community sample; Parrott and Strongman (1984) compared white and Polynesian delinquent and nondelinquent teens; and Duke and Fenhagen (1975) compared female adolescents in a detention center with nondelinquent controls. Johnson and Hunter (1992) found more probation violations among those who scored high on a measure of powerlessness/fatalism. Although there were no control groups, Cole and Kumchy (1981) and Kumchy and Sayer (1980) found delinquents had a more external locus than the norm for comparable ages. Associations have also been found between an external orientation and self-reported delinquency in student samples (Lau & Leung, 1992, Chinese seventh and eighth graders; DeMore et al., 1988, university students reporting vandalism). However, other studies have found no significant differences between adjudicated delinquents and nonadjudicated adolescents on measures of internal versus external locus of control (Lederer et al., 1985; Valliant et al., 1983).

A recent review of sixteen attitude scales relating to locus of control emphasizes that those exhibiting an external orientation can be further broken down depending on whether they think destiny is controlled by chance or by powerful others (Lefcourt, 1991). This distinction seems especially important when comparing samples under correctional supervision with noncriminal controls (Ross & Fabiano, 1985). It is easy to imagine that those in an institution (or even on probation) could be classified as externals merely because they recognize that their day to day existence is in fact controlled by powerful others. Evidence of such an institutionalization effect is provided by Levenson (1974), who found that those imprisoned more than five years felt more controlled by powerful others than those who had served less than six months, but they did not feel more controlled by chance. Although most of the research focuses on adjudicated offenders, it should be noted that there is some evidence from studies using student samples and self-reported delinquency which would not be subject to this criticism (Lau & Leung, 1992; DeMore et al., 1988; also see Johnson & Hunter, 1992, comparing violation rates between low and high scorers who were all on probation).

Measuring Locus of Control. An example of an assessment technique that is frequently used for adolescent samples is the Nowicki-Strickland Locus of Control Scale (N-SLCS) (Nowicki & Strickland, 1973). Originally designed for children, it has been modified for use with college students and adults. Subjects are asked to answer forty questions, such as "Are you often blamed for things that just aren't your fault?" and "Most of the time, do you feel that you can change what might happen tomorrow by what you do today?". A point is given for each answer indicating an external orientation. The N-SLCS correlates significantly with three other measures of locus of control and is fairly stable with six-week test-retest correlations of .71 for tenth graders (Corcoran & Fischer, 1987).

When measuring locus of control, it is also important to consider the impact of culture, race, gender and/or socioeconomic status (Corcoran & Fischer, 1987; Ross &

Fabiano, 1985). Black inmates have been found to have a more external locus of control orientation than white inmates (Lefcourt & Ludwig, 1965), and people with lower socio-economic status generally exhibit a more external locus (Lefcourt, 1976).

Development of Locus of Control. Werner and Smith (1982) discuss how an internal sense of control develops in *Vulnerable But Invincible: A Longitudinal Study of Resilient Children and Youth*, in which they describe how an internal sense of control is one of the characteristics that distinguish children from high-risk environments who stay out of trouble with the law from those who end up with police records. They used the term "resilient" to refer to those in their sample of children reared in chronic poverty and exposed to above average rates of prematurity and perinatal stress who "managed to develop into competent and autonomous young adults who 'worked well, played well, loved well, and expected well'" (1982, p. 153). Most of the other youths had an external locus of control orientation reflected in feelings that fate, luck, or other factors beyond their control determined what happened to them.

To explain the development of an external locus of control, Werner and Smith used Seligman's work on "learned helplessness" involving subjects who experienced random aversive noise. Seligman found that when there was no connection between the subject's performance and exposure to loud noise, subjects developed a cognitive mindset that their own actions did not effect success or failure. After repeated exposure to the uncontrollable noise, experiences with success did not change their expectations regarding how they would perform, demonstrating "difficulty learning that responses work" (Seligman, 1975, p. 38). Werner and Smith maintained that children repeatedly exposed to adversities beyond their control, such as fewer appropriate caretakers and more family discord, paternal absences, and maternal mental illness, developed an external locus-of-control orientation. In contrast, resilient children had strong attachments to parents or other adults, as well as experiences with supportive, competent role models and opportunities to participate in decisions that impacted their lives.

Summary

The research on social perspective-taking, problem-solving ability, and locus of control suggests that how individuals think influences whether or not they violate the law. Developed independently over the years from diverse sources, the work in this area assumes that behavior is not just a conditioned response to past experience. It involves a reasoned choice based on relevant beliefs and perceptions. The way an individual thinks is influenced by past experiences, but it is the current thinking that is the proximate influence on behavior. Empirical evidence demonstrates that there is less delinquency among those who consider the perspectives of others, who understand how to address interpersonal problems, and who believe they have some control over their fate.

COGNITION IN CURRENT CRIMINOLOGICAL THEORY, RESEARCH, AND PRACTICE

Although the emphasis in criminological theories is on sociological influences, it is difficult to ignore the influence of thinking on behavior. The term cognition traditionally has been used rarely in criminology, but the leading criminological theories do include variables that reflect what individuals are thinking. In addition, there have been a few attempts in recent empirical studies to further integrate cognition into currently popular explanations for criminal behavior. There also has been a significant amount of research in correctional settings aimed at revealing cognitive deficits among offenders and evaluating the impact of cognitive interventions. Those who work with offenders, many of whom have psychology backgrounds, recognize that thinking matters and have designed rehabilitation program that attempt to foster prosocial cognitions. An examination of the role of cognition in prominent criminological theories, recent research on integrated models, and effective rehabilitation programs buttress the argument for a more explicit focus on cognition.

The Implicit Role of Cognition in Prominent Criminological Theories

Some of the early explanations for delinquency assumed that delinquents were impulsive and failed to think about the consequences of behavior (e.g., Loevinger, 1966; Singer, 1955) or had a distinctive concrete mode of thinking that made it difficult to generate alternative solutions to problems (Glueck & Glueck, 1950), but the criminological theories that have dominated the field and generated the most empirical research in recent years have focused primarily on the influence of the social environment. Despite the sociological emphasis, cognition is at least implicit in currently popular theories such as Akers' social learning, Hirschi's social bonding, Agnew's general strain, and Gottfredson and Hirschi's general theories.

Social Learning Theory. Akers' social learning theory focuses on how individuals learn from significant others in their social environment, which inherently involves thinking processes. Along with acting as role models whom a person may imitate, and punishing or rewarding behavior, significant others convey what Akers calls "definitions." These definitions (norms, attitudes, orientations) of behavior as good or bad are described as "verbal or cognitive behavior" (Akers et al., 1979, p. 638).

The role of definitions comes directly from Edwin Sutherland's differential association theory, and Akers presents his social learning theory as the incorporation of behaviorism into Sutherland's sociological approach. Both differential association and social learning theories maintain that people are more likely to engage in criminal behavior if they define it as good or at least justified, or if their conventional belief in its wrongfulness is relatively weak. Defining a criminal behavior as good is often called a delinquent value, and reasoning used to justify the behavior is considered a technique of neutralization (Akers et al., 1979).

As Akers (1990) points out, definitions are analogous to what researchers on deterrence have referred to as internalized norms. Whether it is called a definition or an internalized norm, it is generally assessed by asking individuals how wrong they consider a behavior and reflects what the individual *thinks* about certain behaviors. Tests of social learning theory consistently find that definitions are related to behavior (Akers et al., 1979; Matsueda, 1982; Warr & Stafford, 1991), and several studies of deterrence theory have found that internalized norms are more strongly related to behavior than perceptions regarding the risk of formal punishment or social sanctions (Bishop, 1984; Meier & Johnson, 1977; Paternoster, 1989; Tittle, 1980).

Social Bonding Theory. Hirschi's social bonding theory focuses on how individuals are restrained from committing crime by their bonds or connections to significant others and conventional activities, rather than how they learn crime from others. The emphasis is on *attachment* to others and *commitment* and *involvement* in conventional activity, but one of the four social bonds that inhibit people from committing crime is belief. This bond taps thinking as it measures the "variation in the extent to which people *believe* they should obey the rules of society" (Hirschi, 1969, p. 26—emphasis added). Beliefs are similar to definitions, but Hirschi's construct is limited to how strongly one believes in conventional values such as the wrongfulness of criminal behavior and that laws should be obeyed. He does not think alleged beliefs that criminal behavior is positive (delinquent values) or justifications for delinquency (techniques of neutralization) have causal impact, but sees them as after-the-fact rationalizations (Hirschi, 1969, p. 208). Empirical research suggests that there is a reciprocal effect between beliefs and behavior, indicating that even the strength of one's belief in conventional values is sometimes an after-the-fact rationalization. However, beliefs also are sometimes formed prior to behavior and appear to increase the likelihood of lawbreaking (Agnew, 1985; Thornberry et al., 1994).

General Strain Theory. Agnew uses insights from psychological research on stress, equity/justice, and aggression to reformulate the original strain model developed by Merton (1938), Cohen (1955), and Cloward and Ohlin (1960). Like the original model, general strain theory focuses on negative relationships with other people that lead to delinquency and crime through the strain or negative emotions, especially anger, they sometimes engender. However, this reformulation is more inclusive than the original strain theories because they focused solely on negative relationships in which others prevent someone from achieving positively valued goals. Agnew describes three different types of negative relationships with others. "Other individuals may (1) prevent one from achieving positively valued goals, (2) remove or threaten to remove positively valued stimuli that one possesses, or (3) present or threaten to present one with noxious or negatively valued stimuli" (1992, p. 50). Agnew explains that for each of these, strain can result both from what one actually experiences or from what one anticipates. He also criticizes the other strain theories for focusing solely on the disjunction between aspirations and expectations/actual achievements, and maintains that one also must consider the strain caused by the failure to achieve what one expects or what one considers fair or just.

Both the original strain theory and Agnew's general strain approach emphasize the negative affective states of strain or anger, but cognitive psychologists have long recognized that emotions are influenced by what one thinks (Ellis & Harper, 1976). The cognitive aspect is apparent when one examines the types of relationships that cause strain or anger. Whether a goal or stimuli is positively or negatively valued relates to what one *thinks* of it. Furthermore, strain is caused not only by what one experiences, but also by what one anticipates or *thinks* will happen. Aspirations and opinions regarding fairness or justice reflect what people think they want and what they think is equitable.

The importance of cognition is underlined by the emphasis Agnew places on "cognitive coping strategies." He explains that "several literatures suggest that individuals sometimes cognitively reinterpret objective stressors in ways that minimize their subjective adversity" and that people cope with adversity by telling themselves that "It's not important", "It's not that bad", or "I deserve it" (1992, p. 66). This type of thinking allows some people to minimize their negative emotional reaction to stress and has been offered as an explanation for why the relation between stress and outcome variables is consistent, but weak-to-moderate. Whether stress leads to anger or other negative outcomes depends on one's cognitive interpretation of the experience.

A General Theory of Crime. Gottfredson and Hirschi (1990) maintain in their general theory of crime that low self-control causes crime and that some elements of low self-control relate to what cognitive psychologists call social perspective-taking and problem-solving ability. Self-control is a multifaceted construct. "[T]he self-control construct seems to reflect temperamental, emotional, and cognitive states" (Longshore et al., 1996, p. 210). The self-centeredness and indifference or insensitivity to the pain of others that Gottfredson and Hirschi claim characterize a person with low self-control reflect what others would call low social perspective-taking or low empathy. Questions used to assess self-control that ask how much the individual cares about others are the same types of questions used to tap social perspective-taking (Grasmick et al., 1993; Evans et al., 1997). The tendency to settle conflicts physically rather than verbally is also considered an element of low self-control, and the questions relating to this element are very similar to questions used to tap problem-solving ability. Questions covering the two aspects of self-control that Grasmick et al. describe as impulsivity and a preference for simple tasks ask about tendencies such as acting without thinking, concern for long-term goals, avoiding difficult projects, and quitting when things get difficult. These items relate to problem-solving ability. Low self-control also includes noncognitive elements such as a need for immediate gratification and excitement and a lack of persistence and tolerance for frustration, but it is interesting to note that part of this multifaceted construct includes aspects of thinking that have been found to relate to crime.

Empirical tests of Gottfredson and Hirschi's theory demonstrate that criminal behavior is more frequent among those who measure as having low self-control (Grasmick et al., 1993; Longshore et al., 1996; Evans et al., 1997). Evans et al. cite additional research supporting the general theory of crime, and their research is noteworthy because it finds that the relation between self-control and crime remains even after controlling for a variety of competing sociological factors. A factor analysis of the items used in the research by Grasmick et al. and Longshore et al. identifies five subscales and is not able to separate impulsiveness from self-centeredness. What is particularly interesting from a cognitive perspective is that the composite measure of low self-control was no better at predicting crimes of fraud than the subscale for impulsiveness/self-centeredness.[3] Longshore et al. (1996) can be consulted for further discussion of the question whether the higher order construct of self-control adds anything beyond what we already know about lower order constructs such as impulsivity and self-centeredness.

Summary. As the foregoing illustrates, criminological theories have begun to explore the role of cognition. Whether people define a behavior as good or bad is important in both social learning and social bonding theories. What individuals value, consider noxious, anticipate, aspire to achieve, and consider fair are key to Agnew's strain theory, as are the cognitive interpretations that determine the impact of stressful events. Cognitions described as social perspective-taking and problem-solving ability are aspects of what Gottfredson and Hirschi call self-control. These theories currently dominate the field and have received substantial empirical support. The empirical research often provides evidence that the cognitive components of these theories are especially important. However, the emphasis is still on the sociological factors and there is little explicit discussion of the implications of the relation between thinking and behavior.

Integrating Cognition Into Criminological Theory

There have been a few recent attempts to add cognitive variables discussed here to empirical tests of social learning and social bonding theories. In each of these studies, the addition of cognition enhances the explanatory power of the original theoretical models when it comes to explaining the variance in self-reported delinquency among adolescents. Interrelations among the cognitive variables and the variables used to operationalize the original theories also were explored (Foglia, 1995, 1996; Mak, 1990, 1991).

In a study of self-reported delinquency among 298 high school students from economically depressed neighborhoods in one of the largest cities in northeastern United States, Foglia found that a multiple regression using four cognitive variables explained almost as much of the variance in delinquency as a social learning model (1995, 1996). The cognitive variables included a measure of (1) internalized norms (which is the cognitive portion of the original social learning model), (2) social perspective-taking, (3) sense of personal responsibility (a composite variable derived from factor analysis revealing internal consistency among items originally intended to tap locus of control, problem-solving ability, and belief in techniques of neutralization), and (4) perceived legitimacy of authorities. Combining the cognitive variables with social learning measures (the extent to which youths associated with delinquent peers and expected to be punished for behavior) demonstrated that all of the cognitive variables remained significant except internalized norms, and that the variance explained by this combined model represented a 25 percent improvement over the variance explained by the traditional social learning model.

This research also explored how different types of thinking are interrelated and how they are associated with sociological factors. The need to explore how various cognitions are interrelated is underscored by the results of the factor analysis revealing internal consistency among questions generally used to tap three different constructs: locus of control, problem-solving ability, and techniques of neutralization. All the items loading on the one factor seemed to relate to the degree subjects perceived themselves as personally responsible for their own behavior, and it makes sense that there are associations among the idea that one controls what happens to oneself, a belief in the efficacy of working on problems and learning from past experience, and the rejection of common excuses for denying responsibility. In adddition, the results of a path analysis indicating relations between social learning factors and cognitive constructs discussed herein revealed that those who scored high on social perspective-taking were more likely to expect to get punished for delinquency and to consider delinquency wrong. This research demonstrates the value of considering cognitions along with the sociological variables traditionally stressed by social learning theory, and examining interrelations among the constructs.

Mak added cognitive variables to Hirschi's social bonding theory in two related studies (1990, 1991). She operationalized social bonding theory with measures of attachment to parents, attachment to school, commitment to educational and occupational goals, and belief in the morality of the law. Citing Reiss (1951), Reckless (1967), and Hirschi himself (1969), Mak maintained that adding impulse control and empathy to Hirschi's social bonding theory would increase its ability to predict delinquent behavior. Impulse control and empathy are cognitive measures, which Mak refers to as personal controls, and they are measured by two different scales developed by Eysenck and Eysenck (1978). Impulse control is described as the "ability to appreciate the possible consequences of certain actions and to refrain from acting on the spur of the moment," and some of the items used to tap this construct are similar to questions used to assess social perspective-taking in other studies (Mak, 1990, p. 216). The questions from the empathy scale also are very similar to items others have used to measure social perspective-taking. The importance of these personal controls is not only recognized by Reiss, Reckless, and Hirschi's earlier work, but it is also consistent with the emphasis on self-control in Gottfredson and Hirschi's general theory of crime (1990).

In a sample of 793 Australian secondary school students, Mak found that social control variables, along with background variables (sex, age, home intactness, and father's education as an indicator of socioeconomic status) were able to explain 45 percent of the variance in self-reported delinquency. Adding measures of impulse control and emotional empathy increased the explanatory power to 51 percent (1990). In related research, she compared 103 pairs of official delinquents matched on social background with subjects with no known delinquent history. Again she found support for considering both personal and social controls, as the delinquents not only differed on measures of social control, but were also more impulsive. The expected difference in empathy was found when comparing female delinquents and nondelinquents, although it was not found among males in that study (1991).

Referring to the lack of research considering both personal and social controls simultaneously, Mak asserts that it is necessary to determine whether personal and social controls are independent, or whether they interact. She finds two significant interactions in the study involving Australian secondary school students. There is an interaction between empathy and belief in the moral validity of the law, indicating that empathy is inversely related to delinquency when beliefs are weak, but empathy becomes insignificant for those with strong beliefs in the moral validity of the law. In addition, although neither parental bonds nor empathy were significantly related to delinquency by themselves, there was significantly less delinquency among those who scored high on both parental bonds and empathy.

There also have been examinations of the interaction of sociological variables with moral development level, but these will not be discussed in detail, as moral development level is not a focus of this chapter (Thornberry, 1987; Kohlberg et al., 1972; Higgens et al., 1984; Cohn & White, 1986, 1990). These works, consistent with the research done by Foglia and Mak, conclude that behavior is influenced by an interaction between what is happening within the individual and environmental factors. Considering the evidence that cognitive deficits are related to criminal behavior, it seems they should be included in our theoretical models, as well as in our prevention and rehabilitation programs.

Something Works: The Effectiveness of Cognitive Corrections

Program evaluations have demonstrated that cognitive interventions in correctional settings have been effective. Largely in response to the widespread notion that "nothing works" (see Martinson's review of literature published before 1967 on offender rehabilitation, 1974), Gendreau and Ross reviewed studies published between 1973 and 1987 and found that some programs have been highly successful (1987). One characteristic that almost all the successful programs had in common was that they had some technique that could be expected to affect the offender's thinking: "Effective programs included . . . some techniques which could increase [the offender's] reasoning skills, help him to develop alternative interpretations of social rules and obligations, and help him to comprehend the thoughts and feelings of other people" (Ross, 1992, p. 1). (See also a meta-analysis by Garrett, 1985; Gendreau & Ross, 1987; Ross & Fabiano, 1985; Ross et al., 1988; Andrews et al., 1990).

The efficacy of cognitive interventions was also recognized by the Panel on the Understanding and Control of Violent Behavior (Reiss & Roth, 1993). This panel was created by the National Academy of Sciences at the request of a consortium of federal agencies to review existing research on violence and its implications. They offer "cognitive-behavioral preventive interventions" as one of three promising early intervention strategies (1993, p. 125). This approach, mentioned repeatedly throughout the report, attempts to enhance the interpersonal problem solving skills found important in the research described above.

Cognitive Intervention Modalities. A meta-analysis of studies evaluating programs for adjudicated juvenile delinquents revealed that "programs that included a cognitive component were more than twice as effective as programs that did not" (Izzo & Ross, 1990, p. 138). All the studies published in refereed journals between 1970 and 1985 that included quantitative measures of recidivism from experimental or quasi-experimental designs and that sufficiently reported the data and described the treatment were included (sixty-eight effect size measures). A program was classified as "cognitive" if it included one or more of the following intervention modalities:

- Problem solving
- Negotiation skills training
- Interpersonal skills training
- Rational-emotive therapy
- Role-playing and modeling
- Cognitive behavior modification (1990, p. 139)

The presence of a cognitive component was one of the only two variables, along with treatment setting (treatments were more effective when done in the community rather than in an institution), that could explain the variance in effect size in a multiple regression analysis. Most programs that included a cognitive component lowered recidivism rates (fifteen of sixteen, or 94 percent) whereas most that did not address cognition failed (ten of thirty-four, or 29 percent were effective and 71 percent failed). The importance of the cognitive component confirms a previous qualitative analysis of what distinguishes a successful from an unsuccessful program (Ross, 1980).

Education, Not Simply Therapy. A cognitive model of offender rehabilitation based on an analysis of what was found to be effective in the above described meta-analysis has yielded impressive results. In an experimental test of the efficacy of this program, sixty-two high-risk offenders were randomly assigned to either regular probation, attention control involving life-skill tutoring, or a cognitive group.

> The 80-hour (cognitive) program focused on modifying the impulsive, egocentric, illogical, and rigid thinking of the offenders; developing their social perspective-taking and values; and teaching them to stop and think before acting, consider the consequences of their behavior, conceptualize alternative ways of responding to interpersonal problems, and consider the impact of their behavior on other people (including their victims). (Izzo & Ross, 1990, p. 140)

The reconviction rates after nine months for the regular probation, attention control (life skills), and cognitive groups were 70 percent, 48 percent, and 18 percent and the reincarceration rates were 30 percent, 11 percent, and 0 percent, respectively (Izzo & Ross, 1990).

A wide variety of treatment modalities has been used in effective correctional programs and the cognitive component is more explicitly defined in some than others, but all of these programs reject the medical/disease model that views criminal behavior as a symptom of a pathology that needs to be "cured" through "therapy." In contrast, criminal behavior is viewed as a consequence of various cognitive, as well as social, economic, situational, and behavioral factors. Offenders are not considered sick, but as not having acquired the repertoire of reasoning and problem-solving skills that would enable them to deal adequately with social and economic problems. Thus a comprehensive approach is generally taken that includes modifying antisocial attitudes, correcting faulty thinking or inappropriate social perception, and developing social competence (Hollin, 1990; Ross et al., 1988). When explaining this shift away from a disease model, Ross, Fabiano, and Ross lament that these programs are even referred to as "treatment," because they actually involve more training and education than therapy.

CONCLUSION: AN EXPLICIT FOCUS ON COGNITION WILL ENHANCE UNDERSTANDING AND INTERVENTIONS

A tendency to emphasize sociological influences, combined with incoherence and methodological problems with the work on cognition and crime, has resulted in relatively little attention in the field of criminology to how what people think relates to whether they break the law. Breakthroughs in the cognitive sciences and in cognitive psychology demonstrate that thinking relates to behavior, and it seems inadvisable for criminologists to ignore the role it plays in explaining antisocial behaviors. Leading criminological theories already consider how people define behaviors, what they value, consider noxious, anticipate, aspire to achieve, consider fair and, to some extent, their empathy and problem-solving ability, but there is room for a more explicit focus.

People who see the perspective of others, can solve interpersonal problems, and see themselves as having some control over life events are less likely to succumb to temptations or choose criminal solutions to problematic situations. Research shows that adding these cognitions to traditional criminological models increases their ability to predict deviance. Intervention programs that address these cognitive deficits reduce recidivism. There has been some exploration of how these cognitions relate to one another and to sociological factors, but additional research in this area can enhance our understanding of crime causation and our ability to intervene effectively.

Understanding the interaction between psychological and sociological factors will provide insights into how environmental influences manifest themselves in an individual's thinking, and how cognitive mindsets affect reactions to the environment. Life is a continuous interaction between what is going on inside an individual and environmental influences. What individuals think is influenced both by their environmental experiences and neuropsychological abilities. Empirical investigations that tap thinking and environmental influences simultaneously can help us understand how the environment shapes cognition both on a biological and social level. In turn, thinking based on prior experiences and inherent capacities can influence how one interprets new environmental stimuli. Explorations of how people with different mindsets react differently to the same events can shed light on effective versus counterproductive coping strategies.

The more we understand cognition, the more we can consciously promote prosocial thinking. Understanding the role of cognitions is especially significant because they can be more easily modified than many of the other factors implicated in crime causation. Thinking can be modified to some extent through education. Although changing cognition is not easy, it is a less daunting task than altering biological predispositions, modifying environmental influences, or overhauling the economic structure to provide equal access to opportunities. This is not to say that educating to alter cognitions is a panacea or that these other factors should be ignored. Rather it is to emphasize that cognitions can be addressed immediately in prevention, diversion, and rehabilitation programs; in the existing school system or anywhere education takes place; and by parents, criminal justice personnel, or anyone who wants to reduce the incidence of antisocial behavior. Promoting the understanding of the perspective of others, interpersonal problem-solving skills, or the idea that people have some control over their destiny should help reduce crime.

Footnotes

[1] Kohlberg's moral development theory is one of the earlier cognitive approaches, and there is considerable overlap between some of the personality types and various cognitions that are currently receiving attention. These approaches will not be the focus of this chapter because they have already received attention from criminologists and generated a substantial amount of research.

[2] Yochelson and Samenow identify fifty-two thinking errors that they claim characterize all offenders, based on intensive case studies of criminals in the forensic unit of a hospital. Included among these allegedly distinctive thinking patterns are impulsiveness, concrete thinking, fragmentation,

failure to empathize with others, and irresponsible decision-making. This work has drawn strong criticism because Yochelson and Samenow made generalizations about all criminals based on a sample of 240 chronic offenders, the majority of whom have been found "not guilty by reason of insanity." Furthermore, there was no control group, and the interview used to gather data was not standardized or checked for validity and reliability. They also failed to relate their study to similar work done by other researchers and provided very little explanation for how these faulty thinking patterns develop. Their study epitomizes the problems that plague much of the cognitive research, and some have lamented that because it is so well known, the flaws have not only resulted in the rejection of some valuable insights from this work, but also have weakened the credibility of the entire cognitive approach (Hollin, 1990; Ross & Fabiano, 1985).

[3] Two other subscales, risk seeking and temper, also performed as well as the composite measure of low self-control in some of the analyses (Longshore et al., 1996).

References

Agnew, R. (1985). Social control theory and delinquency: A longitudinal test. *Criminology, 23,* 47-62.

Agnew, R. (1992). Foundations for a general strain theory of crime and delinquency. *Criminology, 30,* 47–87.

Akers, R. L. (1990). Rational choice, deterrence, and social learning theory in criminology: The path not taken. *The Journal of Criminal Law & Criminology, 81,* 653–676.

Akers, R. L., Krohn, M. D., Lanza-Kaduce, L. & Radosevich, M. (1979). Social learning and deviant behavior: A specific test of a general theory. *American Sociological Review, 44,* 636–655.

Andrews, D. A., Zinger, I., Hoge, R. D., Bonta, J., Gendreau, P. & Cullen, F. T. (1990). Does correctional treatment work? A clinically relevant and psychologically informed meta-analysis. *Criminology, 28,* 369–404.

Baars, B. J. (1986). *The cognitive revolution in psychology.* New York: Guilford Press.

Bishop, D. M. (1984). Legal and extralegal barriers to delinquency: A panel analysis. *Criminology, 22,* 403–419.

Buzzell, T. (1992). Using law-related education to foster social development: Towards a cognitive/structural intervention. Report prepared for the Juvenile Justice Initiative of the National Training and Dissemination Project for Law-Related Education, Office of Juvenile Justice and Delinquency Prevention, U.S. Dept. of Justice.

Chalmers, J. B. & Townsend, M. (1990). The effects of training in social perspective taking on socially maladjusted girls. *Child Development, 61,* 178–190.

Chandler, M. J. (1973). Egocentric and antisocial behavior: The assessment and training of social perspective-taking skills. *Developmental Psychology, 9,* 326–332.

Cloward, R. A. & Ohlin, L. E. (1960). *Delinquency and opportunity.* Glencoe, IL: Free Press.

Cohen, A. K. (1955). *Delinquent boys: The Culture of the gang.* Glencoe, IL: Free Press.

Cohn, E. S. & White, S. O. (1986). Cognitive developmental versus social learning approaches to studying legal socialization. *Basic and Applied Social Psychology, 7,* 195–209.

Cohn, E. S. & White, S. O. (1990). *Legal socialization: A study of norms and rules.* New York: Springer-Verlag.

Cole, E. & Kumchy, C. I. (1981). The CPI battery: Identification of depression in a juvenile delinquent population. *Journal of Clinical Psychology, 37,* 880–884.

Corcoran, K. & Fischer, J. (1987). *Measures for clinical practice: A sourcebook.* New York: The Free Press.

DeMore, S. W., Fisher, J. D. & Baron, R. M. (1988). The equity-control model as a predictor of vandalism among college students. *Journal of Applied Social Psychology, 18,* 80–91.

Dishion, T. J., Loeber, R., Stouthamer-Loeber, M. & Patterson, G. R. (1984). Skill deficits and male adolescent delinquency. *Journal of Abnormal Child Psychology, 12,* 37-53.

Duke, M. P. & Fenhagen, E. (1975). Self-parental alienation and locus of control in delinquent girls. *Journal of Genetic Psychology, 127,* 103–107.

Ellis, A. & Harper, R. A. (1976). *A new guide to rational living.* North Hollywood, CA: Wilshire Book Co.

Ellis, P. L. (1982). Empathy: A factor in antisocial behavior. *Journal of Abnormal Child Psychology, 10,* 123–133.

Evans, T. D., Cullen, F. T., Burton, Jr., V. S., Dunaway, R. G. & Benson, M. S. (1997). The social consequences of self-control: Testing the general theory of crime. *Criminology, 35,* 475–504.

Eysenck, S. G. B. & Eysenck, H. J. (1978). Impulsiveness and venturesomeness: Their position in a dimensional system of personality description. *Psychological Reports, 43,* 1247-1255.

Foglia, W. D. (1995). Thinking and experiencing: Adding cognition to a social learning model to enhance understanding of self-reported delinquency among urban youth. Paper presented at the 1995 Annual Meeting of the American Society of Criminology, Boston, MA.

Foglia, W. D. (1996). Exploring the interaction of cognitive and social learning influences to enhance understanding of self-reported delinquency among inner-city youths. Unpublished dissertation, Department of Criminology, University of Pennsylvania, Philadelphia, PA.

Freedman, B. J., Rosenthal, L., Donahoe, Jr., C. P., Schlundt, D. G. & McFall, R. M. (1978). A social-behavioral analysis of skill deficits in delinquent and nondelinquent adolescent boys. *Journal of Consulting and Clinical Psychology, 46,* 1448–1462.

Garmezy, N. & Rutter, M. (1983). *Stress, coping and development in children.* New York: McGraw-Hill.

Garrett, C. J. (1985). Effects of residential treatment on adjudicated delinquents: A meta-analysis. *Journal of Research in Crime and Delinquency, 22,* 287–308.

Gendreau, P. & Ross, R. R. (1987). Revivification of rehabilitation: Evidence from the 1980s. *Justice Quarterly, 4,* 349–408.

Glueck, S. & Glueck, E. (1950). *Unraveling juvenile delinquency.* New York: Commonwealth Fund.

Gottfredson, M. R. & Hirschi, T. (1990). *A general theory of crime.* Palo Alto, CA: Stanford University Press.

Graham, K. R. (1993). Toward a better understanding and treatment of sex offenders. *International Journal of Offender Therapy & Comparative Criminology, 37,* 41–57.

Grasmick, H. G., Tittle, C. R., Bursik, Jr., R. J. & Arneklev, B. J. (1993). Testing the core empirical implications of Gottfredson and Hirschi's general theory of crime. *Journal of Research in Crime and Delinquency, 30,* 5–29.

Guerra, N. G. (1989). Consequential thinking and self-reported delinquency in high-school youth. *Criminal Justice and Behavior, 16,* 440–454.

Hains, A. A. & Herrman, L. P. (1989). Social cognitive skills and behavioral adjustment of delinquent adolescents in treatment. *Journal of Adolescence, 12,* 323–328.

Heilbrun, A. B. Jr. (1982). Cognitive models of criminal violence based upon intelligence and psychopathy levels. *Journal of Consulting and Clinical Psychology, 50,* 546–557.

Heppner, P. P. & Petersen, C. H. (1982). The development and implications of a personal problem-solving inventory. *Journal of Counseling Psychology, 29,* 66-75.

Higgens, J. P. & Thies, A. P. (1981). Social effectiveness and problem-solving thinking of reformatory inmates. *Journal of Offender Counseling Services & Rehabilitation, 5,* 93–98.

Higgins, A., Power, C. & Kohlberg, L. (1984). The relationship of moral atmosphere to judgments of responsibility. In W. M. Kurtines & J. L. Gewirtz (Eds.), *Morality, moral behavior, and moral development.* New York: John Wiley & Sons.

Hirschi, T. (1969). *Causes of delinquency.* Berkeley: University of California Press.

Hogan, R. T. (1969). Development of an empathy scale. *Journal of Consulting & Clinical Psychology, 33,* 307–316.

Hollin, C. R. (1990). *Cognitive-behavioral interventions with young offenders.* Elmsford, NY: Pergamon.

Izzo, R. L. & Ross, R. R. (1990). Meta-analysis of rehabiliatation programs for juvenile delinquents. *Criminal Justice and Behavior: An International Journal, 17,* 134–142.

Jennings, W. S., Kilkenny, R. & Kohlberg, L. (1983). Moral-development theory and practice for youthful and adult offenders. In W. S. Laufer & J. M. Day (Eds.), *Personality theory, moral development, and criminal behavior.* Lexington, MA: Lexington Books.

Johnson, G. & Hunter, R. M. (1987). Using school-based programs to improve students' citizenship in Colorado. Boulder, CO: Action Research Project, University of Colorado.

Johnson, G. & Hunter, R. M. (1992). Evaluation of the specialized drug offender program for the Colorado Judicial Department. Boulder, CO: Action Research Project, University of Colorado.

Kaplan, P. J. & Arbuthnot, J. (1985). Affective empathy and cognitive role-taking in delinquent and nondelinquent youth. *Adolescence, 20,* 323–333.

Kellogg, R. T. (1995). *Cognitive psychology.* Newbury Park, CA: Sage.

Kohlberg, L. (1969). Stage and sequence: The cognitive-developmental approach to socialization. In D. A. Goslin (Ed.), *Handbook of socialization theory.* Chicago: Rand McNally.

Kohlberg, L. E., Scharf, P. & Hickey, J. (1972). The justice structure of the prison: A theory and intervention. *Prison Journal, 51,* 3-14.

Kumchy, C. I., & Sayer, L. A. (1980). Locus of control in a delinquent adolescent population. *Psychological Reports, 46,* 1307–1310.

Kurtines, W. & Hogan, R. (1972). Sources of conformity in unsocialized college students. *Journal of Abnormal Psychology, 80,* 49–51.

Kurtz, R. R. & Grummon, D. L. (1972). Different approaches to the measurement of therapist empathy and their relationship to therapy outcome. *Journal of Consulting and Clinical Psychology, 39,* 105–115.

Lau, S. & Leung, K. (1992). Self-concept, delinquency, relations with parents and school and Chinese adolescents' perception of personal control. *Personality & Individual Differences, 13,* 615–622.

Laufer, W. S., Skoog, D. K. & Day, J. M. (1982). Personality and criminality: A review of the California psychological inventory. *Journal of Clinical Psychology, 38,* 562–573.

Lederer, J. M., Kielhofner, G. & Watts, J. H. (1985). Values, personal causation and skills of delinquents and nondelinquents. *Occupational Therapy in Mental Health, 5,* 59–77.

Lee, M. & Prentice, N. M. (1988). Interrelations of empathy, cognition, and moral reasoning with dimensions of juvenile delinquency. *Journal of Abnormal Child Psychology, 16,* 127–139.

Lefcourt, H. M. (1976). *Locus of control: Current trends in theory and research.* Hillsdale, NJ: Erlbaum.

Lefcourt, H. M. (1991). Locus of control. In J. P. Robinson, P. R. Shaver & L. S. Wrightsman (Eds.), *Measures of personality and social psychological attitudes.* New York: Academic Press.

Lefcourt, H. M. & Ludwig, G. W. (1965). The American Negro: A problem in expectancies. *Journal of Personality and Social Psychology, 1,* 377–380.

Levenson, H. (1974). Multidimensional locus of control in prison inmates. *Personality & Social Psychology Bulletin, 1,* 354–356.

Little, V. L. & Kendall, P. C. (1979). Cognitive-behavioral interventions with delinquents: Problem solving, role-taking, and self-control. In P. C. Kendall & S. D. Holton (Eds.), *Cognitive-behavioral interventions: Theory, research, and procedures.* New York: Academic Press.

Loevinger, J. (1966). The meaning and measurement of ego-development. *American Psychologist, 21,* 195–206.

Longshore, D., Turner, S. & Stein, J. A. (1996). Self-control in a criminal sample: An examination of construct validity. *Criminology, 34,* 209–228.

Mak, A. S. (1990). Testing a psychosocial control theory of delinquency. *Criminal Justice and Behavior, 17,* 215–230.

Mak, A. S. (1991). Psychosocial control characteristics of delinquents and nondelinquents. *Criminal Justice and Behavior, 18,* 287–303.

Marsh, D. T. (1982). The development of interpersonal problem-solving among elementary-school children. *Journal of Genetic Psychology, 140,* 107–118.

Martinson, R. (1974). "What works? Questions and answers about prison reform." *Public Interest,* 35, 22–54.

Matsueda, R. L. (1982). Testing control theory and differential association: A causal modeling approach. *American Sociological Review, 47,* 489–504.

Megargee, E. I. (1972). *The California Psychological Inventory handbook.* San Francisco: Jossey-Bass.

Meier, R. F. & Johnson, W. T. (1977). Deterrence as social control: The legal and extra-legal production of conformity. *American Sociological Review, 42,* 292–304.

Meltzer, L. J., Roditi, B. N. & Fenton, T. (1986). Cognitive and learning profiles of delinquent and learning-disabled adolescents. *Adolescence, 83,* 581–591.

Merton, R. K. (1938). Social structures and anomie. *American Sociological Review, 3,* 672-682.

Nowicki, S., Jr. & Strickland, B. R. (1973). A locus of control scale for children. *Journal of Consulting and Clinical Psychology, 40,* 148–154.

Parrott, C. A. & Strongman, K. T. (1984). Locus of control and delinquency. *Adolescence, 19,* 459–471.

Paternoster, R. (1989). Decisions to participate in and desist from four types of common delinquency: Deterrence and the rational choice perspective. *Law & Society Review, 23,* 7–40.

Perlman, D. & Cozby, P. C. (1983). *Social psychology.* New York: Holt, Rinehart & Winston.

Platt, J. J., Scura, W. & Hannon, J. R. (1973). Problem-solving thinking of youthful incarcerated heroin addicts. *Journal of Community Psychology, 1,* 278–281.

Platt, J. J., Spivack, G., Altman, N., Altman, D. & Peizer, S. B. (1974). Adolescent problem-solving thinking. *Journal of Consulting and Clinical Psychology, 42,* 787–793.

Reckless, W. C. (1967). *The crime problem.* New York: Appleton-Century-Crofts.

Reiss, A. J., Jr. (1951). Delinquency as the failure of personal and social controls. *American Sociological Review, 16,* 196–207.

Reiss, A. J., Jr. & Roth, J. A. (Eds.) (1993). *Understanding and preventing violence.* Washington, DC: National Academy Press.

Ross, R. R. (1980). *Socio-cognitive development in the offender: An external evaluation of the UVIC program at Matsgui Penitentiary.* Ottawa, Canada: Report of the Office of the Solicitor-General.

Ross, R. R. (1992). *Time to think: A cognitive model of delinquency prevention and offender rehabilitation summary.* Ottawa, Canada: University of Ottawa Research Press.

Ross, R. R. & Fabiano, E. A. (1985). *Time to think: A cognitive model of delinquency prevention and offender rehabilitation.* Johnson, TN: Institute of Social Sciences and Arts.

Ross, R. R., Fabiano, E. A. & Ross, R. D. (1988). (Re)Habilitation through education: A cognitive model for corrections. *Journal of Correctional Education, 39,* 44–47.

Rotenberg, M. (1974). Conceptual and methodological notes on affective and cognitive role taking (sympathy and empathy): An illustrative experiment with delinquent and nondelinquent boys. *The Journal of Genetic Psychology, 125,* 177–185.

Rotter, J. B. (1966). Generalized expectancies for internal versus external control of reinforcement. *Psychological Monographs 80,* No. 609.

Schuessler, K. E. & Cressey, D. R. (1950). Personality characteristics of criminals. *American Journal of Sociology, 55,* 476–484.

Seligman, M. E. P. (1975). *Helplessness: On depression, development, and death.* San Francisco, CA: Freeman.

Shantz, C. U. (1975). The development of social cognition. In E. M. Hetherington (Ed.), *Review of child development research,* vol. 5. Chicago: University of Chicago Press.

Shure, M. B., Spivack, G. & Jaeger, M. A. (1971). Problem-solving thinking and adjustment among disadvantaged preschool children. *Child Development, 42,* 1791–1803.

Singer, J. L. (1955). Delayed gratification and ego-development: Implications for clinical and experimental research. *Journal of Consulting Psychology, 19,* 259–266.

Slaby, R. G. & Guerra, N. G. (1988). Cognitive mediators of aggression in adolescent offenders: 1. Assessment. *Developmental Psychology, 24,* 580–588.

Sperry, R. W. (1993). The promise and impact of the cognitive revolution. *American Psychologist, 48,* 878–885.

Spivack, G., Platt, J. J. & Shure, M. B. (1976). *The problem-solving approach to adjustment: A guide to research and intervention.* San Francisco: Jossey-Bass.

Tennenbaum, D. J. (1977). Personality and criminality: A summary and implications of the literature. *Journal of Criminal Justice, 5,* 225–235.

Thornberry, T. P. (1987). Toward an interactional theory of delinquency. *Criminology, 25,* 863–891.

Thornberry, T. P., Lizotte, A. J., Krohn, M. D., Farnworth, M. & Sung, J. J. (1994). Delinquent peers, beliefs, and delinquent behavior: A longitudinal test of interactional theory. *Criminology, 32,* 47-83.

Tittle, C. R. (1980). *Sanctions and social deviance.* New York: Praeger.

Valliant, P. M., Asu, M. E. & Howitt, R. (1983). Cognitive styles of Caucasian and Native Indian juvenile offenders. *Psychological Reports, 52,* 87-92.

Warr, M. & Stafford, M. (1991). The influence of delinquent peers: What they think or what they do? *Criminology, 29,* 851–865.

Werner, E. E. & Smith, R. S. (1982). *Vulnerable but invincible: A longitudinal study of resilient children and youth.* New York: McGraw-Hill.

Yochelson, S. &. Samenow, S. E. (1976). *The criminal personality: A profile for change,* vol. 1. New York: Jason Aronson.

Chapter 11

Neuropsychological Functioning and Antisocial Behavior—Implications for Etiology and Prevention

by Peter R. Giancola, Ph.D.

Introduction 11-1
    A Neuropsychological Perspective 11-2
    Cognitive Tests 11-2
Review of the Literature 11-3
    Studies With Preadolescent Boys 11-3
        ECF and Antisocial Behavior 11-3
        ECF as Predictor of Reactive Aggression 11-4
        ECF With Social Disadvantage 11-4
        Summary 11-6
    Studies With Adolescent Females 11-6
        ECF and Antisocial Behavior 11-6
        ECF and Difficult Temperament 11-7
        ECF and Language Skills 11-9
    Laboratory Studies 11-10
A Brief Hypothetical Explanation 11-11
Implications for Prevention 11-12
    Early Skills Development 11-12
    Use of Team Specialists 11-12
    Interactive Interventions 11-13
    Summary 11-13

INTRODUCTION

Antisocial behavior carries in its wake a legion of devastating physical, psychological, social, and economic consequences. Clearly, there is a serious need for *effective* prevention and treatment interventions. However, the success of any intervention effort, whether it is directed toward the individual or society, is generally dependent upon a full understanding of the etiology of the behavior(s) it is trying to affect.

Factors ranging from genetic influences to disadvantaged familial and social contexts have all been implicated in the expression of antisocial behavior (Farrington, 1989; Mednick et al., 1987). More importantly, these and other factors are known to engender antisociality by interacting, in highly complex ways, over lengthy developmental trajectories (Loeber & Hay, 1997). Our current rudimentary understanding of the causes of antisocial behavior precludes, at the present time, the development of an overarching causal theory. As such, it is important for scientists to conduct theory-based research aimed at constructing working etiological models of antisociality in circumscribed disciplines (e.g., genetics, biochemistry, psychology, sociology, etc.). Ultimately however, achieving a full comprehension of the causal structure of antisocial behavior will require an amalgamation, and further refinement, of these models to form a unifying explanatory theory.

A Neuropsychological Perspective

One scientific discipline that holds much promise for elucidating at least a portion of the causes of antisocial behavior is neuropsychology. Neuropsychology is concerned with brain-behavior relations—that is, the manner in which changes or deviations in brain functioning affect behavior. One neuropsychological factor most recently implicated in the expression of antisocial behavior is executive cognitive functioning (ECF). ECF has been defined as a "higher-order" cognitive construct involved in the planning, initiation, and regulation of goal-directed behavior (Luria, 1980; Milner, 1995). ECF encompasses a number of cognitive abilities including attentional control, strategic goal planning, abstract reasoning, cognitive flexibility, hypothesis generation, temporal response sequencing, and the ability to organize and adaptively use information contained in working memory (Milner & Petrides, 1984; Stuss & Benson, 1984).

Cognitive Tests

ECF is best measured using neuropsychological (i.e., cognitive) tests. Although a review and critique of these tests is beyond the scope of this chapter, some of the most well-established neuropsychological measures of ECF include the Porteus Mazes (Porteus, 1965), the Wisconsin Card Sorting Test (Heaton, 1981), the Tower of Hanoi test (Welsh et al., 1990), the Stroop test (MacLeod, 1991), and various types of word fluency tests (Benton & Hamsher, 1983). For a full description of these and other neuropsychological assessment tools, readers should consult Lezak (1995) and Spreen and Strauss (1991). Pennington and Ozonoff (1996) also provide a useful table of ECF tests (p. 53) and the particular neuropsychological abilities that they assess. From a biological perspective, it has been shown that the prefrontal cortex and some of its subcortical connections (e.g., regions of the basal ganglia) represent the neural substrates *most involved* in subserving ECF.

REVIEW OF THE LITERATURE

A number of empirically-based studies have demonstrated a relation between low ECF and increased antisocial behavior. For example, persons diagnosed with psychiatric disorders characterized by disinhibited or antisocial behavior such as conduct disorder (Moffitt, 1993), attention deficit hyperactivity disorder (Barkley, 1997), antisocial personality disorder (Gorenstein, 1987), psychopathy (Smith et al., 1992), substance use disorders (Giancola & Moss, 1998) and inattention/overactivity difficulties (McBurnett et al., 1993) have all been shown to exhibit poorer performance on neuropsychological measures of ECF compared with controls. Research on violent offenders has also demonstrated lower ECF capacity in these individuals compared with nonviolent offenders (Bryant et al., 1984). On balance, there are some studies that have been conducted on psychopaths (Hare, 1984; Sutker & Allain, 1987) and conduct disordered boys (Appellof & Augustine, 1985) that have not found differences between these groups and controls on tests of ECF. However, it has been suggested that some of these negative findings may be due to methodological differences among studies (see Giancola, 1995). Nevertheless, such mixed findings highlight the need for future research aimed at assessing the relation between low ECF and antisocial behavior.

To help clarify the existence of a relation between low ECF and antisocial behavior, it would be advantageous to conduct studies that are designed: (1) to measure these constructs (i.e., ECF and antisociality) using a variety of different instruments, and (2) to assess their interrelations in both men and women from a variety of different populations. Fortunately, a growing number of recent investigations that have been designed according to these specifications have yielded a wealth of data supporting the proposed relation between low ECF and heightened antisociality. These studies are reviewed below.

Studies With Preadolescent Boys

Children with (FH+) and without (FH-) a family history of a substance use disorder represent one of the many populations in which the relation between low ECF and antisocial behavior has been investigated. FH+ children are an advantageous population in which to study this relation because these individuals tend to display lower ECF capacity and heightened levels of antisocial behavior compared with their FH- counterparts.

ECF and Antisocial Behavior. The first study aimed at assessing the relation between ECF and antisocial behavior in FH+ and FH- children was conducted on 291 10- to 12-year-old boys with ($n = 101$) and without ($n = 190$) a paternal history of substance dependence (Giancola et al., 1996). ECF was indexed by a latent variable comprising five different neuropsychological tests (i.e., Porteus Mazes, Vigilance Task, Forbidden Toy Test, Motor Restraint Test, and Block Design Test). Antisocial behavior was indexed using mother and teacher reports of delinquent and aggressive behavior on the Child Behavior Checklist (Achenbach & Edelbrock, 1983), and mother and self-reports of symptoms of oppositional defiant disorder (e.g., often loses temper, spiteful and vindictive) and conduct disorder (vandalism, often initiates fights) as described in the third revised edition of the *Diagnostic and Statistical Manual of Mental Disorders* (1987).

Another measure of antisocial behavior in this study was a laboratory analogue paradigm of aggression designed for children (Pelham et al., 1991). For this particular task, children competed against a fictitious opponent on a presumed reaction-time task. Depending on the outcome of each trial (i.e., win or lose), subjects either accumulated or lost "points" they could later redeem for prizes. Following a winning trial, subjects gained points by subtracting them from their "opponent"; and following a losing trial, subjects lost points ostensibly subtracted from them by their opponent. Aggression was operationalized as the number of points subjects subtracted from their "opponent" after each winning trial.

Prior to assessing the relations between ECF and the different measures of antisocial behavior, analyses first involved statistically controlling for the effects of socioeconomic status (SES), verbal IQ, and the presence or absence of a family history of a substance use disorder. As Table 11.1 shows, after taking these variables into account, the results indicate that ECF was still significantly related to mother and teacher reports of aggression and delinquency and to responses on the laboratory measure of aggression. The results also demonstrate that the relation between ECF and conduct disorder symptoms was stronger for the FH+ boys compared with the FH- boys (Giancola et al., 1996a).

ECF as Predictor of Reactive Aggression. A follow-up study of 198 of these boys attempted to determine whether ECF measured at ages 10–12 would be useful in predicting reactive aggression two years later (Giancola et al., 1996b). Reactive aggression was defined as an impulsive and hostile aggressive reaction in response to a situational provocation or frustration and was measured using selected items from the Irritability Scale (Caprara et al., 1985) and the Hostility Guilt Inventory (Kazdin et al., 1987) (typical items: "Whoever makes fun of me or my family is asking for a fight."; "Sometimes I shout, hit, and kick to let off steam."). The results indicated that the FH+ boys exhibited significantly lower ECF capacity and significantly higher levels of reactive aggression compared with the FH- controls. Furthermore, after statistically controlling for SES and verbal IQ, the results also demonstrated that ECF predicted reactive aggression in the FH+ boys but not in the FH- boys (Giancola et al., 1996b). These data are displayed in Figure 11.1.

ECF With Social Disadvantage. In addition to the two above investigations, other researchers have also found evidence for an association between low ECF and antisocial behavior in 177 low SES preadolescent boys (Seguin et al., 1995). As with the above studies, ECF was indexed by a latent variable comprising a variety of neuropsychological tests, and antisocial behavior was indexed by teacher reports of fighting in the child. The results indicated that the physically aggressive boys had lower ECF capacity compared with nonaggressive boys, even when controlling for social disadvantage. Seguin et al.'s study also demonstrated that poor performance on tests of ECF is more strongly related to physical aggression than performance on other, non-ECF, neuropsychological tests of verbal learning, spatial learning, and tactile lateralization.

Table 11.1
Relations Between Executive Cognitive Functioning (ECF) and Antisocial Behavior

Step and Measure		R^2	ΔR^2	F for ΔR^2	Final ßs
Mother report on child aggression on the CBCL					
Step 1:	IQ				0.13
	SES	0.028	0.028*	3.8	-0.04
Step 2:	FH	0.052	0.024*	6.7	0.14*
Step 3:	ECF	0.149	0.097***	30.2	0.38***
Step 4:	ECF X FH	0.150	0.001	0.5	0.04
Teacher report on child aggression on the CBCL					
Step 1:	IQ				-0.01
	SES	0.039	0.039**	4.7	-0.05
Step 2:	FH	0.049	0.01	2.4	0.09
Step 3:	ECF	0.083	0.034**	8.6	0.25**
Step 4:	ECF X FH	0.091	0.008	1.9	0.09
Mother report on child delinquency on the CBCL					
Step 1:	IQ				-0.07
	SES	0.079	0.079***	11.6	-0.00
Step 2:	FH	0.118	0.039***	11.8	0.18**
Step 3:	ECF	0.172	0.054***	17.2	0.30***
Step 4:	ECF X FH	0.182	0.01a	3.3	0.11a
a = p = .07					
Oppositional Defiant Disorder Symptoms					
Step 1:	IQ				0.09
	SES	0.017	0.017	2.2	-0.02
Step 2:	FH	0.072	0.055***	15.7	0.26***
Step 3:	ECF	0.083	0.011a	3.1	0.11
Step 4:	ECF X FH	0.085	0.002	0.68	-0.05
a = p =.07					
Conduct Disorder Symptoms					
Step 1:	IQ				-0.10
	SES	0.035	0.035**	5.1	-0.02
Step 2:	FH	0.054	0.019*	5.5	0.12b
Step 3:	ECF	0.059	0.005	1.5	0.11
Step 4:	ECF X FH	0.072	0.013b	3.8	0.12b
b = p = .05					
Aggression Task High Provocation					
Step 1:	IQ				-0.14
	SES	0.048	0.048*	4.5	0.04
Step 2:	FH	0.052	0.004	0.7	-.09
Step 3:	ECF	0.082	0.030*	5.7	0.20*
Step 4:	ECF X FH	0.082	0.000	0.1	-0.03

FH = family history of a substance use disorder; Higher ECF scores represent poorer performance.
*   = p < .05
**   = p < .01
***   = p < .001

Table reprinted with permission from *Journal of Studies on Alcohol, 57*, 352-359, 1996. Copyright by Alcohol Research Documentation, Inc., Rutgers Center of Alcohol Studies, Piscataway, NJ 08854.

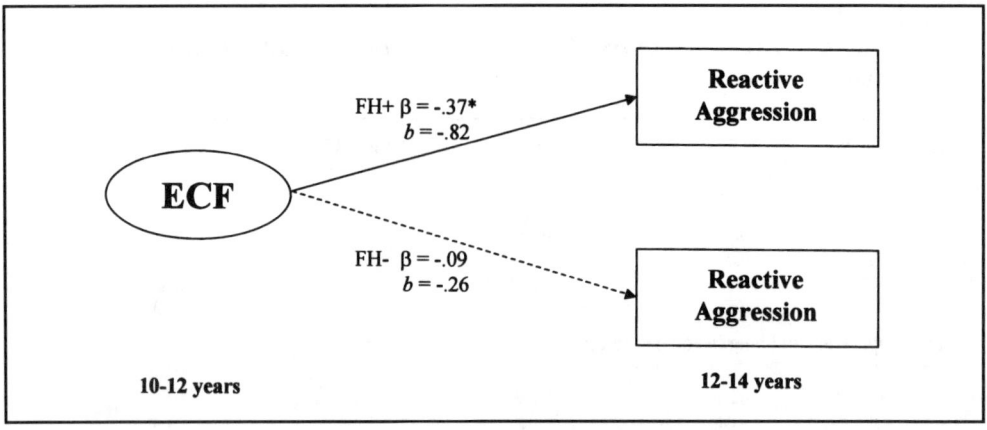

Figure 11.1. Relations Between ECF, Measured at Ages 10–12, and Reactive Aggression, Measured at Ages 12–14, in 198 FH+ and FH- Boys. The values depicted represent final β (standardized) and *b* (nonstandardized) estimates from two *separate* multiple regression equations in which SES and verbal IQ were controlled for statistically. Nonstandardized values are presented for model comparison purposes inasmuch as the two equations were conducted on different subjects.
* = p < .001.

Summary. The three studies just reviewed all report associations between low ECF capacity and different types of antisocial behavior. Clearly however, the participants were male in all cases. The lack of attention paid to the etiology and development of antisocial behavior in females is surprising given that conduct disorder, a psychiatric diagnosis characterized by antisocial behavior, is the second most prevalent psychiatric diagnosis given to female adolescents and is probably one of the most stable (Offord et al., 1987; Robins, 1986).

Studies with Adolescent Females

ECF and Antisocial Behavior. In response to the problem cited above, Giancola and colleagues conducted three investigations on the relation between low ECF and antisocial behavior in adolescent females. The first study involved assessing the relations between ECF and disruptive, delinquent, and physically aggressive forms of behavior in a sample of 283 14- to 18-year-old females with ($n = 188$) and without ($n = 95$) a substance use disorder (Giancola et al., 1998a). Seventy-nine percent of the girls with a substance use disorder also had a comorbid conduct disorder. ECF comprised a latent variable made up of seven neuropsychological tests (i.e., Porteus Mazes, Vigilance Task, Block Design Test, Object Assembly Test, Picture Arrangement Test, Motor Restraint Test, and Stroop Test). Disruptive behavior was indexed by symptoms of oppositional defiant disorder (e.g., often loses temper, spiteful and vindictive); delinquent behavior was indexed by conduct disorder symptoms that did not denote any physical aggression (e.g., truancy, vandalism); and physically aggressive behavior was indexed by conduct disorder symptoms that involved physical aggression (e.g.,

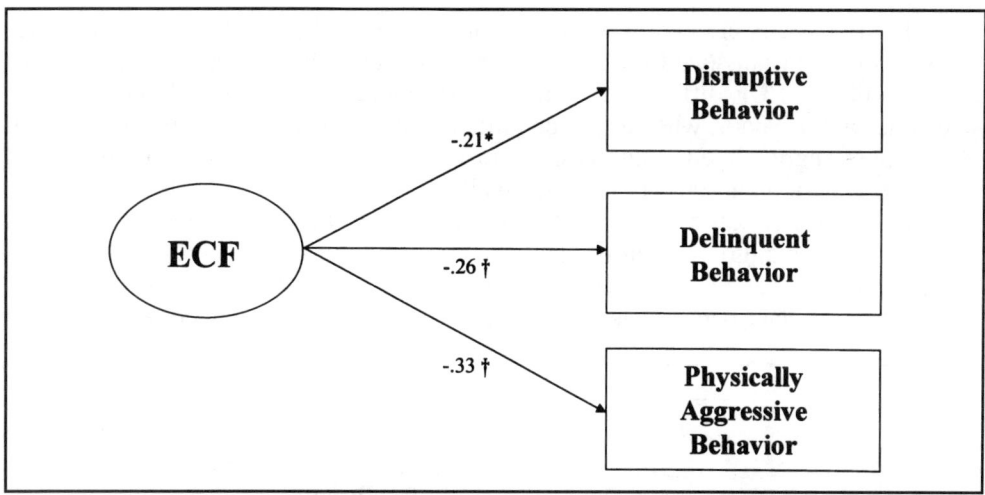

Figure 11.2. Relations Between ECF and Antisociality in Girls Ages 14–18. Relations between ECF and disruptive (oppositional defiant disorder symptoms), delinquent (conduct disorder symptoms that denote no physical aggression), and physically aggressive behavior (conduct disorder symptoms that denote physical aggression) in 283 adolescent females, ages 14–18, with substance use disorder and controls. The values depicted represent final β estimates from three *separate* multiple regression equations in which age, SES, and drug use were controlled for statistically.
† = p < .001; * = p < .05.

using a weapon to hurt someone, initiating fights). The results indicated that even when controlling for age, SES, and drug use, ECF was still significantly related to each of the outcome variables. These data are presented in Figure 11.2.

ECF and Difficult Temperament. The second study examined the relations between low ECF and difficult temperament with aggressive and nonaggressive forms of antisocial behavior in a sample of females similar to the sample in the above study; this investigation assessed 159 conduct-disordered girls and 90 girls with no psychiatric diagnoses (Giancola et al., 1998b). Seventy-five percent of the conduct-disordered group also had a comorbid substance use disorder. ECF was assessed using the same measures employed in the previous study. Temperament was measured using the Dimensions of Temperament Survey—Revised (Windle & Lerner, 1986). A "difficult" temperament denotes behaviors and affective states characterized by irritability, withdrawal from novel stimuli, negative mood, intense reactions to stimuli, low adaptability to change, distractibility, irregularities in biological functions, and poor attention and persistence (Thomas & Chess, 1984; Windle, 1991). Aggressive and nonaggressive antisocial behaviors were indexed using conduct disorder symptoms that denote physically aggressive and nonaggressive behaviors, respectively.

The results indicated that the conduct-disordered group demonstrated lower ECF capacity and a more difficult temperament compared with the control group. Even when statistically controlling for age, SES, crystallized intelligence, and a diagnosis of attention deficit hyperactivity disorder, the combined influence of low ECF capacity and difficult temperament was significantly related to both aggressive and nonaggressive forms of antisocial behavior (in separate equations). Furthermore, in comparison with low ECF, difficult temperament was more strongly related to nonaggressive antisocial behavior, whereas in comparison with difficult temperament, low ECF was more strongly related to aggressive antisocial behavior. These data are presented in Figure 11.3, top and bottom panels. Finally, this study was also able to show that ECF mediated, or in other words, better accounted for, the relation between difficult temperament and aggressive antisocial behavior (see Figure 11.3, bottom panel).

The finding that ECF mediated the relation between difficult temperament and aggressive antisocial behavior is interesting because it has been suggested elsewhere

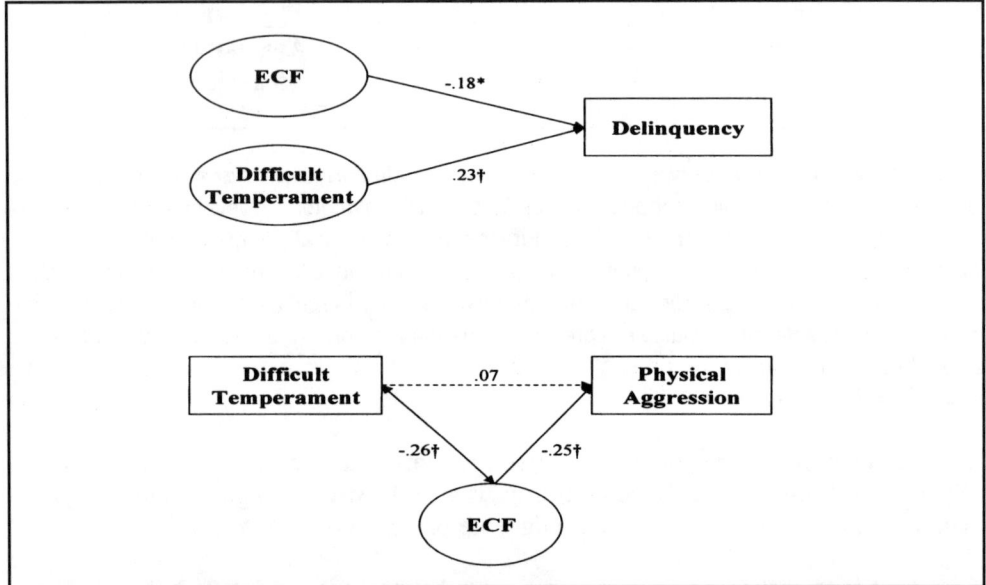

Figure 11.3. Relations Between ECF and Difficult Temperament in Girls Ages 14–18. **Top panel:** Relations between low ECF and difficult temperament with delinquent behavior (conduct disorder symptoms that denote no physical aggression) in 249 14- to 18-year-old adolescent females, with a conduct disorder and controls. The values depicted represent final β estimates from one multiple regression equation in which age, SES, crystallized intelligence, and a diagnosis of attention deficit hyperactivity disorder were controlled for statistically. **Bottom panel:** Model indicating that ECF mediates, or better accounts for, the relation between difficult temperament and physical aggression (conduct disorder symptoms that denote physical aggression) in the same sample of young women. The values depicted represent final β estimates from one multiple regression equation in which age, SES, crystallized intelligence, and a diagnosis of attention deficit hyperactivity disorder were controlled for statistically. The previous β estimate between difficult temperament and physical aggression, prior to entering ECF into the equation, was .12 ($p < .05$). The arrow between difficult temperament and ECF is bidirectional. As such, this model does not suggest that a difficult temperament "leads to" low ECF. It merely illustrates that ECF better accounts for the relation between difficult temperament and physical aggression.
† = $p < .001$; * = $p < .01$ for both panels.

that ECF/the prefrontal cortex is involved in regulating temperament (Tarter et al., 1985). In fact, there are data that show that ECF deficits are related to deviations in temperament (reviewed in Giancola, 1995; Tarter, 1988). Furthermore, it has also been noted that persons with prefrontal cortical damage exhibit a behavioral profile (irritability, impulsivity, labile mood, etc.) similar to non-brain-damaged individuals with a difficult temperament (Starkstein & Robinson, 1991; Stuss et al., 1992). Incidentally, however, the behavioral profile demonstrated by individuals with this type of brain damage is much more severe than that exhibited by individuals with a difficult temperament but no brain damage. Therefore, the finding that ECF mediates the relation between difficult temperament and aggressive antisocial behavior suggests that ECF better accounts, or serves as an underlying mechanism, for this relation.

ECF and Language Skills. The third study in this series sought to determine whether ECF mediated the relations between language skills and five different forms of antisocial behavior in a sample of females similar to those employed in the above two studies. The third investigation assessed 223 conduct-disordered girls and 97 girls with no psychiatric diagnoses (Giancola et al., 1998). Seventy-seven percent of the conduct-disordered group also had a substance use disorder. ECF was measured using the same tests and statistical methods employed in the previous study. Language skills were measured using the Test of Language Competence—Expanded (Wiig & Secord, 1989), a well-established measure of language skills. Five different measures of antisocial behavior were assessed; these included the aggression scale from the Youth Self-Report Inventory (Achenbach, 1991), violent and nonviolent offenses from the Andrew Scale (Andrew, 1974), and violent and nonviolent symptoms of conduct disorder.

The results indicate that language skills were significantly negatively related to all forms of antisocial behavior, even when controlling for age and SES. This is not surprising, as it has previously been shown that language skills are involved in regulating behavior (Luria, 1961, 1980). In addition, this study also demonstrates that ECF mediated the relations between language competence and each of the five outcome variables.

These data, presented in Figure 11.4, support Giancola's hypothesis that the proper development and use of language skills are dependent upon intact ECF (Giancola & Mezzich, in press). Pertinently, Giancola has argued that: proficient language expression is dependent upon the proper organization and sequencing of thoughts and ideas; adept language comprehension requires intact abstract reasoning and attentional skills; the ability to develop a compelling verbal argument is maintained by satisfactory hypothesis generation, planning, and abstract reasoning skills; and the capability to be verbally fluent requires good cognitive flexibility and spontaneity. Finally, it has also been maintained that competent expressive and receptive language functions are dependent upon the proper storage, manipulation, and retrieval of information into and from working memory (Giancola & Mezzich, in press). Indirect support for this hypothesis (i.e., that ECF serves as an underlying foundation for the proper development and use of language skills), comes from Luria's (1961, 1980) determination that the verbal regulation of behavior is governed predominantly by the prefrontal cortex which, as noted earlier, subserves ECF. Thus, based on these arguments and the findings of this study (Giancola & Mezzich, in press), it can be conjectured

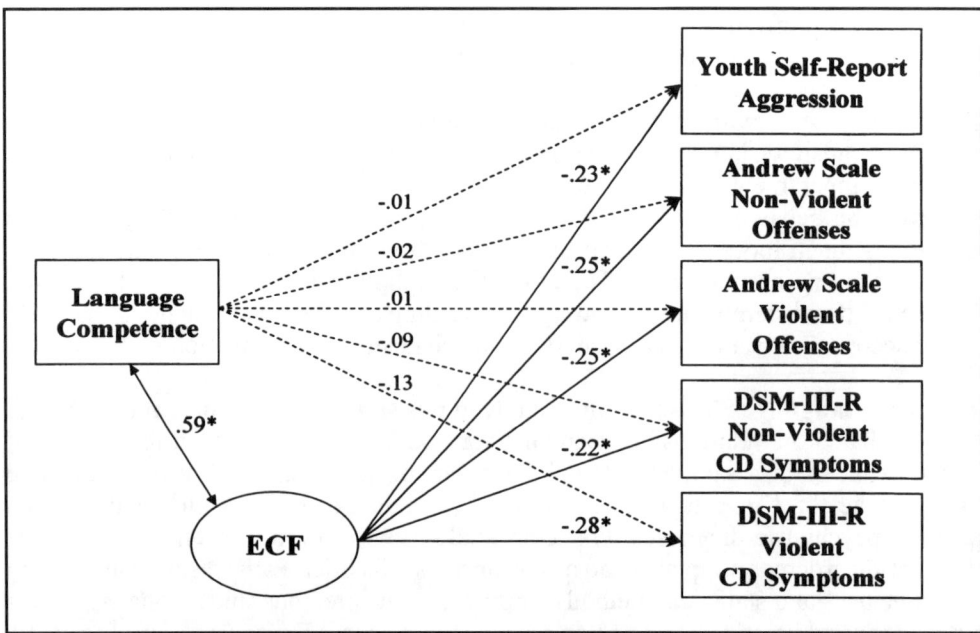

Figure 11.4. Relations Between ECF and Language Skills in Girls Ages 14–18. Model indicates that ECF mediates, or better accounts for, the relations between language competence and five different forms of antisocial behavior in 320 14- to 18-year-old adolescent females with a conduct disorder and controls. The values depicted represent final β estimates from five *separate* multiple regression equations in which age and SES were controlled for statistically. The previous β estimates between language competence and the aggression scale from the Youth Self-Report, nonviolent and violent offences from the Andrew Scale, and nonviolent and violent conduct disorder symptoms, prior to entering ECF into the equation were -.14; -.17; -.14; -.22; -.29, respectively (all p's < .05). The arrow between language competence and ECF is bidirectional. As such, this model does not suggest that poor language competence "leads to" low ECF. It merely illustrates that ECF better accounts for the relation between language competence and the five measures of antisocial behavior.
* = $p < .005$.

that ECF better accounts, or serves as an underlying mechanism, for the relation between language skills and antisocial behavior, as shown in Figure 11.4.

Laboratory Studies

Most of the research reviewed so far in this chapter, either briefly or in depth, has been conducted on clinical, preclinical, or forensic samples. To demonstrate the pervasiveness of the ECF-antisocial behavior relation, however, it is important to show that it also exists in nonclinical and nonforensic populations. Consequently, a number of laboratory-based investigations have examined this relation in normal college and community samples. Laboratory-based research is advantageous over the studies just reviewed because it measures ECF in relation to actual aggressive *behaviors*, not only self-reports of aggression.

The laboratory studies that have examined the relation between low ECF and aggression have used the Taylor Aggression Paradigm (TAP) (Taylor, 1993) to measure physical aggression. Using the TAP, subjects are lead to believe that they are competing against another person, located in a nearby room, on a reaction-time task. They are told that if they win a reaction-time trial, they are allowed to administer a mild electric shock to their opponent. However, they are also told that if they lose a trial, they will receive a shock from this person. In actuality, no opponent exists, a computer program executes the entire protocol, and subjects win and lose a predetermined number of trials. Aggression is operationalized as the average intensity, and sometimes time duration, of the shocks administered by the subject (see Giancola & Chermack, 1998, for a full description of the TAP and other laboratory-based aggression paradigms). Parenthetically, the TAP is a well-established, safe, and valid measure of aggressive behavior.

To date, four published studies have assessed the relation between low ECF and aggressive behavior using the TAP. In each study, subjects were male college students and/or nonclinical/nonforensic community-dwelling individuals. In addition to investigating the ECF-aggression relation, some of these studies had other research aims, such as assessing the effects of alcohol, monetary incentives, and provocation on aggressive behavior. However, despite the addition of these manipulations, each of the four existing studies consistently demonstrated that lower ECF scores were significantly related to higher levels of physical aggression even when statistically controlling for IQ (Giancola & Zeichner, 1994; Hoaken et al., 1998; Lau & Pihl, 1996; Lau et al., 1995).

A BRIEF HYPOTHETICAL EXPLANATION

The above review clearly suggests that there exists a relation between low ECF capacity and heightened antisocial behavior. The studies also indicate that low ECF capacity is associated with varying types of antisocial behavior and that these relations are not restricted only to clinical samples or extreme segments of the population.

However, the fact that a relation may exist between low ECF and antisocial behavior does not explain *why* it exists. Giancola (1995) has theorized that impaired ECF facilitates antisocial behavior due to decreased behavioral inhibition and deficiencies in generating alternative socially appropriate responses in provocative or frustrating situations. Specifically, Giancola hypothesized that impaired self-monitoring, abstract reasoning, and attentional skills may compromise the ability to correctly interpret potentially ambiguous social cues during interpersonal interactions, which may lead to misattributions in the perception of threat or hostility in conflict situations. In addition, ineffectual hypothesis generation, poor concept formation, and cognitive inflexibility, along with poor judgment, may undermine the ability to generate and implement alternative socially adaptive behavioral responses in anger-provoking situations. Moreover, inadequate planning and organization capacities may interfere with the ability to execute a series of responses in the proper sequence and manner in order to avoid an aggressive or argumentative interaction. Finally, compromised cognitive control over behavior may allow hostile cognitions and negative affective states to manifest as overt delinquency or physical aggression. Clearly however, this explanation must be tested and refined before it can be placed within the context of an overarching theory of antisocial behavior.

IMPLICATIONS FOR PREVENTION

The brief model described above stipulates that low ECF capacity, in combination with a provocative or frustrating environment, will contribute to the elicitation of a delinquent or physically aggressive reaction. If this supposition is correct, it could then be argued that in order to decrease the likelihood of such a reaction, ECF skills should be strengthened. It is well known that prevention interventions for antisocial behavior are likely to be more effective when instituted earlier rather than later during the lifespan (Kazdin, 1988). Therefore, for maximum efficacy, the prevention interventions described herein should be targeted at children with low ECF capacity who demonstrate early signs of antisocial behavior (annoying others, bullying, disobedience, stealing, truancy, vandalism, etc.).

Early Skills Development

Fortunately, the same tools that are used to assess ECF skills (i.e., neuropsychological tests) can also be used to strengthen these abilities. For example, the Porteus Maze test (Porteus, 1965) measures planning skills. However, it could be argued that under the proper tutelage, repeated practice on this test could actually improve planning abilities. That is, a child may be taught that successful performance on this test requires good strategic planning, sequencing, and previewing abilities in addition to competency in controlling impulsive behaviors. A trained therapist could then instruct the child on how to invoke these skills. This would then be followed by multiple practice sessions where the child would attempt more challenging mazes as his or her proficiency developed. The therapist would provide helpful corrections and coaching as needed, as the child completed the training.

This type of approach could be used with a number of different tests that cover a variety of ECF skills. However, this idea of strengthening cognitive functioning in order to curtail antisocial behavior is not novel. Barkley (1981, 1997) suggested that children with behavior problems may benefit from intervention techniques aimed at improving ECF abilities. Moreover, Goldman and colleagues demonstrated the efficacy of neuropsychological remediation techniques in alcoholics and also found that in some cases, repeated training on neuropsychological tests generalizes to other tasks requiring similar underlying cognitive demands (Forsberg & Goldman, 1987; Goldman et al., 1985). Nevertheless, critics may correctly argue that whereas such an approach makes intuitive and logical sense, this type of intervention will quickly lead to boredom and, therefore, a lack of treatment compliance. Given this, creative approaches in designing intervention strategies are clearly required.

Use of Team Specialists

Consider combining the skills of a neuropsychologist possessing a keen understanding of the executive cognitive functions, an individual skilled in designing computer games, and a computer programmer. This team of specialists could design a series of computer games that are highly interesting and challenging but that also heavily tax the executive cognitive functions. Children could then graduate from a short, tutor-guided "boring" regimen in which they are introduced and skilled in the rudimentaries of basic ECF abilities to "playing" with fun and exciting computer games. Of course, the computer games would be programmed with a hierarchy of difficulty levels so that the child could play more demanding versions as his or her ECF capacity increased.

There exists empirical support for the use of computer game interventions in strengthening cognitive integrity. Tallal and colleagues (1996) demonstrated that a four-week computer game training program dramatically enhanced receptive speech and language abilities in preadolescent children with language-learning impairments who were lagging behind their normal counterparts by a magnitude of one to three years. Following the training, the childrens' language abilities were found to increase by nearly two years, essentially placing them at par with their age-matched counterparts. Moreover, these gains were maintained six weeks after the end of training, reflecting the lasting effects of the intervention. Thus, the prospect of using computer games to strengthen ECF skills appears highly promising.

Interactive Interventions

Although the computer game approach appears superior to simply engaging in repeated practice on neuropsychological tests, it could be argued that more ecologically valid interventions are also required. Clearly, aggressive behavior is a social phenomenon. Therefore, why restrict interventions to vacuous environments such as those in which computer games are played (i.e., sitting alone at a desk)? Following this line of thought, once ECF skills are adequately improved using the techniques mentioned above (i.e., therapist-assisted practice and computer games), children could then graduate to "live" interactive interventions. In this case, two children could be placed in a prearranged "precarious" situation in which one child provokes the other, and it is the job of the other child to use the ECF skills that he or she has previously learned to diffuse the situation in a nonaggressive manner. Following such interactions, children could then receive feedback and coaching on how to further improve their skills.

Summary

As noted earlier, a large literature based on forensic and clinical samples demonstrates that both males and females, children and adults, characterized by heightened levels of antisocial behavior exhibit low ECF capacity. Furthermore, a number of laboratory studies with normals also indicate that low ECF capacity is related to increased aggression. As such, it can reasonably be argued that low ECF capacity is a likely "risk factor" for antisocial behavior. Thus, given the empirical evidence reviewed in this chapter, it might be useful for researchers interested in violence prevention to consider developing and testing cognitive interventions aimed at strengthening ECF abilities.

References

Achenbach, T. M. (1991). *Manual for the youth self-report and 1991 profile.* Burlington, VT: Department of Psychiatry, University of Vermont.

Achenbach, T. M. & Edelbrock, C. (1983). *Manual for the child behavior checklist and revised child behavior profile.* Burlington VT: University of Vermont.

American Psychiatric Association. (1987). *Diagnostic and statistical manual of mental disorders* (3d ed. rev.). Washington, DC: American Psychiatric Press.

Andrew, J. (1974). Violent crime indices among community-retained delinquents. *Criminal Justice Behavior, 1,* 123–130.

Appellof, E. & Augustine, E. (1985). Prefrontal functions in juvenile delinquents. *Journal of Clinical and Experimental Neuropsychology, 7,* 604.

Barkley, R. A. (1981). *Hyperactive children: A handbook for diagnosis and treatment.* New York: Guilford Press.

Barkley, R. A. (1997). Behavioral inhibition, sustained attention, and executive functions: Constructing a unifying theory of ADHD. *Psychological Bulletin, 121,* 65–94.

Benton, A. & Hamsher, K. (1983). Multilingual aphasia examination. Iowa City: AJA Associates.

Bryant, E., Scott, M., Tori, C. & Golden, C. (1984). Neuropsychological deficits, learning disability, and violent behavior. *Journal of Consulting and Clinical Psychology, 52,* 323–324.

Caprara, G., Cinanni, V., D'Imperio, G., Passerini, S., Renzi, P. & Travaglia, G. (1985). Indicators of impulsive aggression: Present status of research on irritability and emotional susceptibility scales. *Personality and Individual Differences, 6,* 655–674.

Farrington, D. (1989). Early predictors of adolescent aggression and adult violence. *Violence and Victims, 4,* 79–100.

Forsberg, L. & Goldman, M. (1987). Experience-dependent recovery of visuospatial functioning in older alcoholic person. *Journal of Abnormal Psychology, 94,* 519–529.

Giancola, P. (1995). Evidence for dorsolateral and orbital prefrontal cortical involvement in the expression of aggressive behavior. *Aggressive Behavior, 21,* 431–450.

Giancola, P. & Chermack, S. (1998). Construct validity of laboratory aggression paradigms: A response to Tedeschi and Quigley. *Aggression and Violent Behavior, 3,* 237–253.

Giancola, P., Martin, C., Tarter, R., Pelham, W. & Moss, H. (1996a). Executive cognitive functioning and aggressive behavior in preadolescent boys at high risk for substance abuse/dependence. *Journal of Studies on Alcohol, 57,* 352–359.

Giancola, P. & Mezzich, A. (in press). Executive cognitive functioning mediates the relation between language competence and antisocial behavior in conduct disordered females. *Aggressive Behavior.*

Giancola, P. & Mezzich, A. (1998b). Executive cognitive functioning, temperament, and antisocial behavior in conduct disordered adolescent females. *Journal of Abnormal Psychology, 107,* 629–641.

Giancola, P., Mezzich, A. & Tarter, R. (1998a). Disruptive, delinquent, and aggressive behavior in adolescent female substance abusers: Relation to executive cognitive functioning. *Journal of Studies on Alcohol, 59,* 560–567.

Giancola, P. & Moss, H. (1998). Executive cognitive functioning in alcohol use disorders. In M. Galanter (Ed.), *Recent developments in alcoholism,* vol. 14, *The consequences of alcoholism.* New York: Plenum Press, 227–251.

Giancola, P., Moss, H., Martin, C., Kirisci, L. & Tarter, R. (1996b). Executive cognitive functioning predicts reactive aggression in boys at high risk for substance dependence: A prospective study. *Alcoholism: Clinical and Experimenetal Research, 20,* 740–744.

Giancola, P. & Zeichner, A. (1994). Neuropsychological performance on tests of frontal-lobe functioning and aggression in human males. *Journal of Abnormal Psychology, 103,* 832–835.

Goldman, M., Klisz, D. & Williams, D. (1985). Experience-dependent recovery of cognitive functioning in young alcoholics. *Addictive Behaviors, 10,* 169–176.

Gorenstein, E. (1987). Cognitive-perceptual deficit in an alcoholism spectrum disorder. *Journal of Studies on Alcohol, 48,* 310–318.

Hare, R. (1984). Performance of psychopaths on cognitive tasks related to frontal lobe function. *Journal of Abnormal Psychology, 93,* 133–140.

Heaton, R. (1981). *Wisconsin card sorting test manual.* Odessa, FL: Psychological Assessment Resources.

Hoaken, P., Assaad, J. & Pihl, R. (1998). Cognitive functioning and the inhibition of alcohol-induced aggression. *Journal of Studies on Alcohol, 59,* 599–607.

Hoffman, J., Hall, R. & Bartsch, T. (1987). On the relative importance of "psychopathic" personality and alcoholism on neuropsychological measures of frontal lobe dysfunction. *Journal of Abnormal Psychology, 96,* 158–160.

Kazdin, A. (1988). *Child psychotherapy: Developing and identifying effective treatments.* Oxford, England: Pergamon Press.

Kazdin, A., Rodgers, A., Colbus, D. & Siegel, T. (1987). Children's hostility inventory: Measurement of aggression and hostility in psychiatric inpatient children. *Journal of Clinical Child Psychology, 16,* 320–328.

Lau, M. & Pihl, R. (1996). Cognitive performance, monetary incentive, and aggression. *Aggressive Behavior, 22,* 417–430.

Lau, M., Pihl, R. & Peterson, J. (1995). Provocation, acute alcohol intoxication, cognitive performance, and aggression. *Journal of Abnormal Psychology, 104,* 150–155.

Lezak, M. (1995). *Neuropsychological assessment* (3d ed.). New York: Oxford University Press.

Loeber, R. & Hay, D. (1997). Key issues in the development of aggression and violence from childhood to early adulthood. *Annual Review of Psychology, 48,* 371–410.

Luria, A. (1961). *The role of speech in the regulation of normal and abnormal behavior.* New York: Basic Books.

Luria, A. (1980). *Higher cortical functions in man.* New York: Basic Books.

MacLeod, C. (1991). Half a century of research on the Stroop effect: An integrative review. *Psychological Bulletin, 109,* 163–203.

McBurnett, K., Harris, S., Swanson, J., Pfiffner, L., Tamm, L. & Freeland, D. (1993). Neuropsychological and psychophysiological differentiation of inattention/overactivity and aggression/defiance symptom groups. *Journal of Clinical Child Psychology, 22,* 165–171.

Mednick, S. A., Gabrielli, W. F. & Hutchings, B. (1987). Genetic factors in the etiology of criminal behavior. In S. A. Mednick, T. E. Moffitt & S. A. Stack (Eds.), *The causes of crime: New biological approaches.* New York: Cambridge University Press, 74–91.

Milner, B. (1995). Aspects of human frontal lobe function. In H. Jasper, S. Riggio & P. Goldman-Rakic (Eds.), *Epilepsy and the functional anatomy of the frontal lobe.* New York: Raven Press, 67–84.

Milner, B. & Petrides, M. (Nov. 1984). Behavioural effects of frontal-lobe lesions in man. *Trends in Neurosciences,* 403–407.

Moffitt, T. E. (1993). The neuropsychology of conduct disorder. *Development and Psychopathology, 5,* 135–151.

Offord, D., Boyle, M., Szatmari, P., Rae-Grant, N., Links, P., Cadman, D., Byles, J., Crawford, J., Blum, H., Byrne, C., Thomas, H. & Woodward, C. (1987). Ontario Child Health Study. II. Six-month prevalence of disorder rates of service utilization. *Archives of General Psychiatry, 44,* 832–836.

Pelham, W., Milich, R., Cummings, E., Murphy, D., Schaughency, E. & Greiner, A. (1991). Effects of background anger, provocation, and methylphenidate on emotional arousal and aggressive responding in attention-deficit hyperactivity disordered boys with and without concurrent aggressiveness. *Journal of Abnormal Child Psychology, 19,* 407–426.

Pennington, B. & Ozonoff, S. (1996). Executive functions and developmental psychopathology. *Journal of Child Psychology and Psychiatry, 37,* 51–87.

Porteus, S. (1965). *Porteus maze test: Fifty years' application.* Palo Alto, CA: Pacific Books.

Robins, L. (1986). The consequence of conduct disorder in girls. In D. Olweus, J. Block & M. Radke-Yarrow (Eds.), *Development of antisocial and prosocial behavior: Research, theories, and issues*. Orlando, FL: Academic Press, 82–414.

Seguin, J., Pihl, R., Harden, P., Tremblay, R., Boulerice, B. (1995). Cognitive and neuropsychological characteristics of physically aggressive boys. *Journal of Abnormal Psychology, 104*, 614–624.

Smith, S., Arnett, P. & Newman, J. (1992). Neuropsychological differentiation of psychopathic and nonpsychopathic criminal offenders. *Personality and Individual Differences, 13*, 1233–1243.

Spreen, O. & Strauss, E. (1991). *A compendium of neuropsychological tests: Administration, norms, and commentary*. New York: Oxford University Press.

Starkstein, S. & Robinson, R. (1991). The role of the frontal lobes in affective disorder following stroke. In H. Levin, H. Eisenberg & L. Benton (Eds.), *Frontal lobe function and dysfunction*. New York: Oxford University Press, 288–303.

Stuss, D. & Benson, D. (1984). Neuropsychological studies of the frontal lobes. *Psychological Bulletin, 95*, 3–28.

Stuss, D., Gow, C. & Hetherington, C. (1992). "No longer Gage": Frontal lobe dysfunction and emotional changes. *Journal of Consulting and Clinical Psychology, 60*, 349–359.

Sutker, P. & Allain, A. (1987). Cognitive abstraction, shifting, and control: Clinical sample comparisons of psychopaths and nonpsychopaths. *Journal of Abnormal Psychology, 96*, 73–75.

Tallal, P., Miller, S., Bedi, G., Byma, G., Wang, X., Nagarajan, S., Schreiner, C., Jenkins, W. & Merzenich, M. (1996). Language comprehension in language-learning impaired children improved with acoustically modified speech. *Science, 271*, 81–84.

Tarter, R. (1988). Are there inherited behavioral traits that predispose to substance abuse? *Journal of Consulting and Clinical Psychology, 56*, 189–196.

Tarter, R., Alterman, A. & Edwards, K. (1985). Vulnerability to alcoholism in men: A behavior-genetic perspective. *Journal of Studies on Alcohol, 46*, 329–356.

Taylor, S. (1993). Experimental investigation of alcohol-induced aggression in humans. *Alcohol Health and Research World, 17*, 108–112.

Thomas, A. & Chess, S. (1984). Genesis and evolution of behavioral disorders: From infancy to early adult life. *American Journal of Psychiatry, 141*, 1–9.

Welsh, M., Pennington, B., Ozonoff, S., Rouse, B. & McCabe, E. (1990). Neuropsychology of early-treated phenylketonuria: Specific executive function deficits. *Child Development, 61*, 1697–1713.

Wiig, E. & Secord, W. (1989). *Test of language competence* (expanded edition). Psychological Corporation. New York: Harcourt Brace.

Windle, M. (1991). The difficult temperament in adolescence: Associations with substance use, family support, and problem behaviors. *Journal of Clinical Psychology, 47*, 310–315.

Windle, M. & Lerner, R. (1986). Reassessing the dimensions of temperamental individuality across the life span: The revised dimensions of temperament survey (DOTS-R). *Journal of Adolescent Research, 1*, 213–230.

Chapter 12

The Identification of Neurological Correlates of Brain Dysfunction in Offenders by Probation Officers

by Matthew Robinson, Ph.D. and Tom Kelley, Ph.D. (cand.)

Introduction	12-2
Basic Premises of the Research	12-2
Primary Purpose of the Research	12-3
Brain Dysfunction and Violent Behavior	12-3
Frontal and Temporal Lobe Impairment	12-3
Cognitive and Neurological Defects	12-4
Speech Processes	12-4
Neuropsychological Impairments	12-4
Sources of Neurological Dysfunction	12-5
Head Injuries	12-5
Dietary Conditions	12-6
Neuronal Synthesis	12-6
Hypoglycemia	12-6
Environmental Toxins	12-7
Birth Complications/Maternal Drug Use	12-7
Summary	12-8
Research Methodology	12-8
Findings and Interpretations	12-10
Discussion and Conclusion	12-14
Effective and Adequate Correctional Programming	12-14
Primary Goal—Prevention	12-15
Neuropsychological Impairment Screening Worksheet	12-16

INTRODUCTION

All behavior emanates from the brain, and all external environmental influences that may influence behavior must act on the brain before human behavior occurs (Greenfield, 1996). Therefore, studying behavior without either studying the brain or acknowledging the role that the brain plays in human behavior leads to an incomplete understanding of behavior and an inability to prevent or adequately control it. These common sense assertions about human behavior do not amount to biological determinism or reductionism; they simply suggest that brain structure and its processes are important factors in human behavior (Robinson, 1998).

The study of brain-behavior relationships has two objectives (Luria, 1973). The first is to pinpoint areas of the brain associated with specific neurological and psychological disorders, and the second is to promote a greater understanding of the components of brain functions such as learning, problem solving, and memory (also see Greenfield, 1996; Jeffery, 1990).

This chapter does not reflect a study of the brain itself, but attempts to promote a greater understanding of the brain's role in certain pathological dimensions of human behavior, particularly aggressive criminal behavior. The nature and extent of brain dysfunction is examined within a group of known offenders in order to examine and document relationships between different types and degrees of brain dysfunction and offending behaviors. Of particular interest in this study are offenders who have committed violent, particularly repeated violent, offenses against persons, not only because these crimes are considered to be the most serious offenses against society, but also due to extensive evidence that this subgroup is most likely to exhibit biological and genetic vulnerabilities to disruptive behavioral disorders. Conversely, rates of recidivism and serious violent offending are thought to be highest in individuals with underlying neurological defects.

Basic Premises of the Research

This research is grounded by premises emerging from the theoretical and scientific research literature, including the following conclusions:

1. There is an important association between violent behavior and brain dysfunction;
2. There are recognizable personal history and behavioral indicators that constitute correlates or signs of brain dysfunction and that can be observed by non-medically trained professional personnel (e.g., probation officers);
3. Early identification, intervention, and effective remediation of abnormal neurological conditions (as they interact with other biological, psychological, and social factors) are necessary to prevent and control violent behavior, but are not being widely practiced;
4. Routine and systematic procedures for the collection and analysis of data related to brain dysfunction are not well-established uniformly in the correctional process; and
5. Conditions of brain dysfunction are not being adequately addressed in correctional programming for violent offenders.

Primary Purpose of the Research

Proceeding from these premises, the present study was designed and conducted with three primary purposes. The first was to contribute to a fuller understanding of the interactions of biological, psychological, and social factors associated with violent offending by conducting a limited test of premises 1 and 2 above, in comparable samples of violent and nonviolent adult offenders. The second purpose was to test a procedure for screening adult offenders to determine the presence of correlates of brain dysfunction, in order to identify those who are in need of more costly and specialized medical evaluations in conjunction with available social and psychological services. This aspect of the study was aimed at improving circumstances stated in premises 3, 4, and 5 above by facilitating greater specificity in correctional classification of adult offenders so that appropriate programs of treatment services may be provided to those with evidence of brain dysfunctions. Finally, the study tested a screening tool known as the Kelley Form (see the worksheet on page 12-16) which was developed in a previous study of brain dysfunction in juvenile offenders (Kelley, 1997). The Kelley Form arranges recognizable correlates of brain dysfunction into biological, psychological, and social categories so that they can be easily recognized by non-medically trained personnel.

The Kelley Form is not founded on the assumption that brain dysfunctions cause violent behavior; rather, it is based on the conceptual framework of integrated, interactive systems (e.g., see Jeffery, 1990; Miller, 1978). This means that conditions within biological, psychological, and social systems interact to form recognizable patterns of correlates of brain dysfunction, which may influence the propensity for antisocial behavior. The Kelley Form was developed specifically to identify and include for purposes of data collection the appropriate factors at all system levels, so that valid and reliable patterns of brain dysfunction may be discerned.

BRAIN DYSFUNCTION AND VIOLENT BEHAVIOR

Certain forms of brain dysfunction are known to be predisposing to violence by influencing responses to social, psychological, and biological stimuli. A myriad of studies have concluded that there are individual differences in the integrity of brain function within various parts of the brain and that dysfunctions can be identified, in part, by a battery of tests. These tests may expose neurological differences that predispose individuals to commit violent acts. At present, however, these tests are limited because the precise location of brain dysfunctions cannot be specifically identified (Raine, 1993). Nevertheless, structural damage to certain regions of the brain can be detected and to some extent localized by neuropsychological tests of patients with brain lesions. These findings have been informative by elucidating relationships between brain dysfunction and various behavioral disorders.

Frontal and Temporal Lobe Impairment

One of the earliest case studies involving brain dysfunction and antisocial behavior is that of Phineas Gage (Harlow, 1848). Phineas Gage, a dynamite worker for the Great Western Railway, was the victim of a tragic accident; an iron tamping rod 1.25

inches wide by 3.7 feet long was blown through his lower cheek and upper forehead. Gage survived the accident but suffered devastating and dramatic personality changes. Prior to the accident, Gage was a responsible worker and family man without any recorded antisocial behavior. After the accident he became uncontrollably impulsive, profane, and antisocial. His left frontal lobe (in particular, the orbitofrontal cortex) was the portion of the brain that had been damaged, an area that has since been linked to impulsive and aggressive behavior (Raine, 1993).

Brain dysfunctions can be traced to general locations of the brain by recognizing an individual's behavioral responses reflective of function in that region (Yeudall, 1977). For example, damage to the frontal lobe impairs abilities to formulate plans, reduces intellectual functioning involving reasoning and recognizing consequences of actions, impairs ability to sustain concentration and focus for long-term goals, and reduces language processing and foresight needed to regulate behavior. Individuals with frontal lobe damage commonly exhibit periods of distractibility, impulsivity, lack of guilt or shame, periodic affective disorder, and sensitivity to alcohol.

Dysfunction of the left temporal lobe is associated with disturbances in comprehension of written or spoken words, language activities such as reading, writing, spelling, arithmetic, logical and analytical thinking involving sequential processing of information, and hallucinations secondary to verbal processing abnormality. Damage to the right temporal lobe is related to disturbances in processing and recall of information pertaining to visual and kinesthetic spatial abilities and auditory functions involving tone, melody, rhythm, and sound vocalization (Yeudall, 1977).

Cognitive and Neurological Defects

Speech Processes. Studies of recidivistic violent individuals consistently show cognitive abnormalities, for example, less lateralization in the brain for speech processes. Psychopaths, who are frequently characterized by chronic violent behavior and the inability to empathize and develop pain avoidance responses, reportedly use and experience language in unique ways. Cleckley (1982) asserted that deep seated aphasia is characteristic of psychopathy. Other researchers such as Gillstrom and Hare (1988) found that psychopaths make more hand gestures than nonpsychopaths during interviews, and hypothesize that psychopaths misinterpret neutral situations in ways that cause them to misperceive threats. Raine and Venables (1982) found that psychopaths show faster rise time of skin conductance responses to consonant-vowel stimuli than nonpsychopaths. They also show delayed evoked responses to cognitive stimuli. Such studies provide evidence that psychopaths have unusual speech processes, which are under control of the brain.

Neuropsychological Impairments. Other studies demonstrate clear behavioral differences in groups of offenders that are reflective of brain dysfunction. For example, Lewis and colleagues (1986) found in a small study of death row inmates that 100 percent of them suffered from neurological defects. Additionally, Santilla and Haapasalo (1997) compared groups of homicidal offenders, violent offenders, and nonviolent offenders across a set of risk factors that included neurological disorders, early behavioral problems, and traumatic experiences. Results revealed that the onset of alcohol abuse, physical abuse, and histories of drug dependence and cruelty to animals differentiated the homicidal offenders from the other offender groups. Homicidal offenders also tended to have experienced more psychological abuse and to have had more problems with physical and psychological conditions such as hyperactivity, attention deficit, and aggression in later childhood and adolescence. These findings are consistent with other studies (Farrington et al., 1990; Satterfield et al., 1994) and lend further support for the effects of abuse and early behavior problems on later violent behavior.

Other studies by Yeudall (1977) and Flor-Henry (1976) using neuropsychological test batteries to detect brain dysfunction revealed high incidences of neuropsychological impairments within psychiatric, alcoholic, and criminal populations. These studies also provided evidence for the association of brain dysfunction with other psychopathological disorders such as schizophrenia and affective disorders. Critics of these conclusions argue that the subjects chosen for the studies were court referred patients for neuropsychiatric assessment and as such, the samples should be expected to yield higher incidences of brain dysfunctions than the general population. There is a need for such findings to be replicated in independent laboratories (Raine, 1993). As discussed below, the present study uses a sample of nonreferred offenders in order to examine relationships between brain dysfunction and offense behaviors.

SOURCES OF NEUROLOGICAL DYSFUNCTION

Head Injuries

Brain dysfunction can be caused by numerous environmental factors, including dietary deficiencies, exposure to neurotoxins, birth complications, and substance abuse. Genetic factors may also play a substantial role in brain dysfunction, and several defects have already been associated with various dimensions of antisocial behavior (see Chapter 9). One obvious source of brain dysfunction is trauma to the head, as illustrated in the previous example of Phineas Gage. In a study of violent juveniles within a residential treatment center, Kelley (1997) found that of those juveniles in need of complete neurological evaluations, 60 percent had experienced closed head injuries. The effects of head injury on behavior are highlighted in populations with behavioral disturbances, most particularly in offenders who show histories of head injuries more frequently than those in the general population.

Head injury has many origins, but physical child abuse as a source of head trauma is of particular importance in juvenile and adult offenders given its high occurrence in these groups. The effects of physical abuse on children can be drastic and far-reaching. A comprehensive review of studies dealing with the relationship of early physical and sexual abuse and neglect in childhood and later criminal victimization shows that abused and neglected children grow up to commit more crimes than children who have not been abused or neglected (Widom, 1989). Even when age, sex, and race are controlled, the physically abused and neglected groups are found to have higher rates of offending in adulthood. Experiences of abuse or neglect during childhood reportedly increase an individual's risk for criminal behavior as an adult. Kelley's (1997) study showed that 100 percent of those violent juveniles needing complete neurological evaluations had been abused by parents or relatives, either physically or sexually.

Dietary Conditions

Neuronal Synthesis. Another source of brain dysfunction is an irregular or suboptimal diet. Every cell in the human body builds the materials it needs to function normally by converting substances that reach the cells by way of the bloodstream. Nerve cells (neurons) are no exception in that they synthesize many of their neurotransmitters (naturally occurring chemicals that convey signals within the brain) from substances that reach cells by way of the bloodstream. Over one hundred chemicals function as neurotransmitters in the brain and the synthesis of several neurotransmitters relies on substances derived from foods consumed in the diet. Under normal circumstances, the brain maintains relatively constant, or properly regulated, levels of each neurotransmitter. However, if the diet contains a high or low concentration of the precursors (usually amino acids) necessary for making a particular neurotransmitter, the brain may produce a slightly higher or lower than usual amount of that neurotransmitter (Wurtman, 1982, 1983; Wurtman et al., 1981). Although several neurotransmitter systems modulate aggressive behavior (Raine, 1993), studies have consistently implicated low levels of the neurotransmitter serotonin in impulsive and aggressive behavior (see Chapter 6).

Hypoglycemia. The brain's ability to process information and regulate behavior is directly influenced by dietary conditions. For example, hypoglycemia occurs when blood sugar levels (glucose) drop below certain levels and the individual becomes simultaneously symptomatic. When the brain has less than 60-80 mg of glucose per minute, panic, irritability, nervousness, and aggression can result (Marks, 1981). A number of studies have linked hypoglycemia to violent and aggressive behavior. Reactive hypoglycemia can occur two to four hours following a meal and can be exacerbated by drugs such as alcohol. Symptoms of hypoglycemia in prisons are maximal at 11:00 to 11:30 a.m., which expectedly corresponds to assaults on staff and other inmates (Davies, 1982).

The role of hypoglycemia in exacerbating aggressive tendencies has led to the discovery that diet may influence antisocial behavior. Diets that are high in refined carbohydrates and poor in protein and complex carbohydrates can cause unusual fluctuations in blood glucose levels. Highly refined carbohydrates are rapidly absorbed by the body and can lead to sudden surges in glucose within the blood stream. An increase of glucose in the bloodstream elicits secretion of the hormone insulin, which serves to process and store glucose, thus avoiding a glucose overload. In the presence of extreme increases in blood glucose levels, however, the insulin response may be heightened and blood glucose may fall below optimal levels. High levels of circulating insulin and low blood glucose levels, in combination with irregularities in responses to glucose load by several other hormones required to process glucose, have been associated with agitation, irritability, mood swings, and aggression in some individuals. While there is certainly no evidence to indicate that all persons who consume high levels of refined sugars engage in antisocial behavior, there appears to be a subgroup of individuals who are unusually sensitive to the hormonal responses to unusual fluctuations in blood glucose levels and who may react inappropriately to their mood swings.

Through such dietary manipulations, antisocial behavior that is associated with dietary deficiencies may be amenable to identification and management of the contributory conditions. Reducing simple sugars in the diet and increasing fiber intake can help regulate levels of glucose found in the bloodstream (Haber et al., 1977). Schoenthaler (1982) demonstrated over a two-year period on a sample of 12- to 18-year-old delinquents that a planned reduction of refined carbohydrates resulted in a 48 percent reduction in disciplinary offenses, although these findings are highly controversial. Additionally, Fishbein and Thatcher (1982) showed that after a one-month refined carbohydrate-free diet, improvements in conditions of depression and paranoia occurred in a sample of adult male prisoners who were prone to hypoglycemia.

Environmental Toxins

Just as diet affects brain functioning, so do substances in the external, physical environment. For example, sufficient exposure to neurotoxins such as lead can cause brain dysfunction. Studies indicate that lead levels in the environment are related to cognitive, learning, and attention deficits in children (Loeber, 1990; Rutter & Giller, 1983). Lead primarily enters the body through oral absorption, although inhalation is another route. Environmental contamination can occur when water pipes in older homes are allowed to corrode and when paint chips containing lead peel off walls. Although the actual effects of lead and other poisonous chemicals in the environment on violence and criminal behavior are not precisely known, levels of lead, arsenic, mercury, cadmium, and aluminum concentrations found in the hair of children has been related to aggressive behaviors (Marlowe et al., 1985). Needleman and associates (1979, 1990, 1990) specifically demonstrated that children exposed to high levels of lead had lower IQs, more troublesome classroom behavior, and shorter attention spans and long-term learning disabilities than children exposed to less or no lead, controlling for thirty-nine other factors. At a higher level of analysis, Masters (1997) found that high levels of lead and manganese pollution were significantly related to crime rates throughout the United States.

Birth Complications/Maternal Drug Use

Other sources of brain dysfunction include birth complications such as low birth weight and other conditions that can cause reduced oxygen supplies to the brain. Also, maternal drug use during pregnancy and substance abuse during childhood, adolescence, and adulthood are associated with brain dysfunction (Holmes, 1992; see also Farrington et al., 1986; Hawkins, 1996; Jeffery, 1998a, 1998b; Kelley, 1997; Pallone, 1991; Pallone & Hennessy, 1993; Reiss & Roth, 1993; Tonry & Farrington, 1995; Tonry et al., 1991). Kelley's (1997) study of violent juveniles found that of those who most needed complete neurological evaluations, 100 percent had histories of drug use such as marijuana, alcohol, and tobacco. While the relationship between such neurologic dysfunction and drug use is still unclear (i.e., whether the problem exists prior to drug use or is a consequence of it), there is substantial evidence for both causative and consequential relationships.

Each of the environmental factors listed above can have long-term effects on brain development and functioning in individuals and can increase vulnerability to antisocial behavior. Numerous other genetic, congenital, and biological conditions also contribute substantially to impairments in brain functioning to influence propensity for antisocial behavior. Thus, it is critical that brain dysfunction is assessed within offender populations by examining characteristic signs or symptoms. In the presence of conditions such as traumatic head injuries, irregular or deficient diets, exposure to environmental toxins, birth complications, maternal drug use during pregnancy, and chronic substance abuse, brain dysfunction and cognitive deficits may result. These environmental sources of brain damage are amenable to prevention approaches.

Summary

Most recent studies focusing on brain dysfunction in violent offenders have concluded that well-designed and appropriately targeted prevention and early intervention programs are needed to reduce violence. Unfortunately, technologies such as brain imaging techniques, neuropsychological testing, and chemical analyses that can identify brain dysfunctions and cognitive deficits in behaviorally disordered individuals are not readily available, particularly to criminal defendants and offenders. In Kelley's (1997) study of violent juvenile offenders, 21 percent clearly exhibited correlates of brain dysfunction, yet the screening procedures traditionally used by the residential facility had failed to document diagnosis and treatment information for the children and no specific recommendations for specialized programs were made. The result is that past, present, and likely future offenders are left to toil in correctional institutions due to their history of engaging in behaviors that may actually be symptomatic of underlying neurological problems.

RESEARCH METHODOLOGY

The data for the present study were obtained from a group of probation officers in the state of Pennsylvania. Each probation officer was instructed to randomly choose three actual case files from the population of offenders they were responsible for managing. The offender files were grouped into one of three categories of offenders based on both the nature and frequency of their offending behaviors. These categories included: (1) repeat offenders with at least one conviction and adjudication for a violent offense (most serious); (2) repeat offenders with no convictions or adjudications for violent offenses (more serious); and (3) offenders with no prior record of conviction or adjudication for any violent or nonviolent offenses (least serious). A final sample size of fifty-six offenders resulted, including nineteen repeat violent offenders, nineteen repeat nonviolent offenders, and eighteen first-time offenders.

Each student used the Kelley Form for assessing the correlates of brain dysfunction (see page 12-16); these correlates include evidence of birth complications, family abuse, parental drug use, maternal drug use during pregnancy, persistent physical conditions, abnormal physical conditions, abnormal interpersonal characteristics, psychological abnormalities, irregular diet, head injury, exposure to environmental toxins, and offender substance use. Table 12.1 lists the specific indicators associated with each of these categories. Correlates of neurological dysfunction were assessed through screening of all available medical and legal documents accessible to the probation officers, and through interviews conducted by the probation personnel with offenders (when possible).

Table 12.1
Correlates of Neurological Dysfunction

Category	Specific Indicators
Birth complications	Premature birth; problems with delivery; unhealthy baby at birth
Family abuse	Physical abuse; verbal abuse; sexual abuse; witnessed abuse
Parental drug use	Use of any drug (including alcohol and tobacco)
Maternal drug use during pregnancy	Use of any drug by mother while pregnant (including alcohol and tobacco)
Persistent physical conditions	Headaches; breathing problems; seizures; hypertension; hypoglycemia; diabetes; heart problems; sexually transmitted diseases; dizziness
Abnormal physical characteristics	Unusual appearance; emotions; coordination of movement; speech problems; vision problems
Abnormal interpersonal characteristics	Sensitivity to the feelings of others; respect for authority; lying; quick tempered/angered; verbally aggressive; physically aggressive
Psychological abnormalities	Alertness; attention span; confusion; spatial disorientation; memory problems; comprehension; learning problems; judgment; planning; problem solving; psychiatric diagnoses
Irregular diet	Indications of imbalanced meals
Head injury	Indications of trauma to the brain
Exposure to environmental toxins	Indications of exposure to environmental poisons
Offender substance use	Use of any drug (including alcohol and tobacco)

The offenders within each of the three categories described above were compared on the collected indicators of brain dysfunction in order to identify which factors were related to severity and frequency of offending behaviors. It was expected that: (1) repeat offenders with at least one conviction and adjudication for a violent offense (most serious) would have the greatest number of correlates of brain dysfunction and the greatest variation in types of correlates of neurological dysfunction; (2) repeat offenders with no convictions or adjudications for violent offenses (moderately serious) would have fewer correlates of brain dysfunction and less variety in correlates of brain dysfunction than the "most serious" offenders; and (3) both groups would have

Table 12.2
Selected Demographic Characteristics of Offenders in Sample

Group of Offenders	Mean Age	Percent Male	Percent Black
Entire sample (n = 56)	33.2 years	86%	45%
Most serious (n = 19)	33.3	100	58
More serious (n = 19)	33.8	95	37
Least serious (n = 18)	32.5	61	45

more correlates and greater variation in correlates than offenders with no prior record of conviction or adjudication for any violent or nonviolent offenses (least serious).

Selected demographic characteristics are depicted in Table 12.2. Table 12.3 presents these characteristics in the form of a percentage table, showing which groups had the highest percentages of certain neurological correlates, and Table 12.4 presents them in the form of a means table, showing which groups had the highest average levels of certain neurological correlates. No tests for statistical significance were performed, as the study was conducted on a convenience sample of known offenders being managed by a group of probation personnel. Since the sample may not be representative of all offenders, it would not be appropriate to test for statistical significance.

Conclusions are drawn from the data about the relative likelihood that offenders within each of the three groups in this study exhibit signs of possible brain dysfunctions. Thus, the importance of this study is derived from the potential for a relatively simple, convenient, and inexpensive tool to estimate the incidence of neurological deficits in offenders. In addition to its potential research utility, if this instrument is capable of discriminating between offender groups based on nature and severity of offense history, it may also facilitate the identification of offenders in need of treatment.

FINDINGS AND INTERPRETATIONS

Table 12.2 depicts some selected demographic characteristics of the offenders within the sample, including mean age, sex, and race. This table shows that the average age for the entire sample of offenders was 33.2 years and that there were no meaningful differences in average age among any of the groups of offenders. If the average age of the first-time property offenders in this sample had been lower than the repeat property and repeat violent offenders in the sample, one might speculate that the first-time offenders may continue to commit criminal acts and eventually become repeat offenders by the time they reach the same age as the repeat offenders. Since the average age of the offenders in all the offender categories is roughly the same, this scenario is less likely. Instead, we suggest an alternative possibility—that the first-time offenders in our sample are somehow different from the repeat property and violent offenders. Such a difference may help to explain why the first-time offenders in the sample did not commit more crimes and/or why they did not get apprehended and convicted for more criminal acts.

Demographic characteristics may account for some of the differences between the offender groups. Table 12.2 illustrates that the sample of offenders was predominantly male (86 percent) and that males were disproportionately represented among all categories of offenders, but especially in the repeat violent offenders (100 percent) and repeat nonviolent offenders (95 percent). Repeat offenders were more likely to be males than first-time offenders. Table 12.2 also shows that African-Americans are disproportionately represented in the sample of offenders (45 percent) and in all categories of offenders within the sample, especially repeat violent offenders (58 percent).

Table 12.3 illustrates the percentage of offenders within each category of offenders that is characterized by various types of brain dysfunctions. Within the entire sample of offenders (n = 56), the most prominent correlates of brain dysfunction are offender substance abuse, psychological abnormalities, and abnormal interpersonal characteristics. Table 12.3 shows that within the entire sample, 88 percent of all offenders were found to have used some type of illicit substance, while 84 percent suffered from some form of psychological abnormality and 82 percent were characterized by abnormal interpersonal characteristics.

For the repeat violent offenders (most serious), the most significant correlates of brain dysfunction were:

- Abnormal interpersonal characteristics (100 percent)
- Offender substance use (95 percent)
- Psychological abnormalities (90 percent)

For the repeat nonviolent offenders (more serious), the most significant correlates of brain dysfunction were:

- Offender substance use (89 percent)
- Psychological abnormalities (79 percent)
- Abnormal interpersonal characteristics (74 percent)

Finally, for the first-time offenders (least serious), the most significant correlates of brain dysfunction were:

- Psychological abnormalities (83 percent)
- Offender substance use (78 percent)
- Abnormal interpersonal characteristics (72 percent)

Table 12.3 also illustrates other important correlates for brain dysfunction for repeat violent offenders, repeat nonviolent offenders, and first-time offenders, including abnormal physical conditions (68, 58, and 44 percent, respectively), parental drug use (62, 37, and 39 percent, respectively), head injury (58, 26, and 17 percent, respectively), persistent physical conditions (53, 42, and 33 percent, respectively), and fam-

Table 12.3
Presence of Neurological Dysfunction in Sample of Offenders: Percentage of Offenders with Correlates of Each Type of Neurological Dysfunction

Group of Offenders	Correlate											
	1	2	3	4	5	6	7	8	9	10	11	12
Entire sample (n = 56)	14%	39%	48%	20%	43%	57%	82%	84%	25%	34%	25%	88%
Most serious (n = 19)	21	53	62	26	53	68	100	90	26	58	42	95
More serious (n = 19)	10	26	37	26	42	58	74	79	26	26	16	89
Least serious (n = 18)	11	39	39	5	33	44	72	83	22	17	17	78

Note. 1 = Birth complication; 2 = Family abuse; 3 = Parental drug use; 4 = Maternal use of drugs during pregnancy; 5 = Persistent physical conditions; 6 = Abnormal physical conditions; 7 = Abnormal interpersonal conditions; 8 = Psychological abnormalities; 9 = Irregular diet; 10 = Head injury; 11 = Exposure to environmental toxins; 12 = Offender substance use.

ily abuse (53, 26, and 39 percent, respectively). Less than 50 percent of offenders within each offender category were characterized by any of the other correlates for brain dysfunction, although 42 percent of repeat violent offenders were possibly exposed to environmental toxins.

With few exceptions, Table 12.3 demonstrates that a higher percentage of repeat violent offenders are characterized by correlates of brain dysfunction than repeat nonviolent offenders and first-time offenders. This would suggest that in our sample of offenders, brain dysfunction is most associated with repeat violent offending. The correlates that best differentiate repeat violent offenders from repeat nonviolent offenders and first-time offenders include birth complications (21 percent versus 10 and 11 percent, respectively), family abuse (53 percent versus 26 and 39 percent, respectively), head injury (58 percent versus 26 and 17 percent, respectively), parental drug use (62 percent versus 37 and 39 percent, respectively), abnormal interpersonal characteristics (100 percent versus 74 and 72 percent, respectively), and offender substance use (95 percent versus 89 and 78 percent, respectively). Both the repeat violent and the repeat nonviolent offenders can also be differentiated from first-time offenders in terms of maternal drug use during pregnancy (26, 26, and 5 percent, respectively). This would suggest that among our sample of offenders, maternal drug use during pregnancy may be a risk factor for repeat involvement in criminal activity, both violent and nonviolent in nature.

Table 12.4 provides further support for these findings. It shows the average number of correlates of brain dysfunctions of offenders within each category of offenders. Similar to Table 12.3, Table 12.4 demonstrates that within the entire sample of offenders (n = 56), the correlates of brain dysfunction that most stand out are psychological abnormalities, abnormal interpersonal characteristics, and offender substance abuse.

Table 12.4
Presence of Neurobiological Dysfunction in Sample of Offenders: Average Number of Correlates of Each Type of Neurological Dysfunction

Group of Offenders	Correlate											
	1	2	3	4	5	6	7	8	9	10	11	12
Entire sample (n=56)	n/a	0.8	n/a	n/a	1.0	1.2	2.7	4.2	n/a	n/a	0.4	2.7
Most serious (n=19)	n/a	1.2	n/a	n/a	1.6	1.5	4.4	6.1	n/a	n/a	0.6	2.8
More serious (n=19)	n/a	0.5	n/a	n/a	0.6	1.4	2.2	3.9	n/a	n/a	0.3	2.8
Least serious (n=18)	n/a	0.8	n/a	n/a	0.7	0.8	1.3	2.5	n/a	n/a	0.2	2.3

Note. 1 = Birth complication; 2 = Family abuse (average number of type of abuse, including physical, verbal, sexual, and witness of abuse); 3 = Parental drug use; 4 = Maternal use of drugs during pregnancy; 5 = Persistent physical conditions; 6 = Abnormal physical conditions; 7 = Abnormal interpersonal conditions; 8 = Psychological abnormalities; 9 = Irregular diet; 10 = Head injury; 11 = Exposure to environmental toxins (average number of possible exposures); 12 = Offender substance use (average number of substances used); n/a indicates that an average value could not be calculated because it was not an appropriate statistic for this category or because of unavailable or unreliable data.

Table 12.4 shows that within the entire sample, the average number of psychological abnormalities suffered by offenders was 4.2, while the average number of abnormal interpersonal characteristics was 2.7 and the average number of substances used by offenders was 2.7.

For the repeat violent offenders (most serious), the highest average number of correlates of brain dysfunction were:

- Psychological abnormalities (6.1)
- Abnormal interpersonal characteristics (4.4)
- Offender substance use (2.8)

For the repeat nonviolent offenders (more serious), the highest average number of correlates of brain dysfunction were:
- Psychological abnormalities (3.9)
- Offender substance use (2.8)
- Abnormal interpersonal characteristics (2.2)

Finally, for the first-time offenders (least serious), the highest average number of correlates of brain dysfunction were:

- Psychological abnormalities (2.5)
- Offender substance use (2.3)
- Abnormal interpersonal characteristics (1.3)

Table 12.4 also illustrates other important correlates of brain dysfunction for repeat violent offenders, repeat nonviolent offenders, and first-time offenders, including persistent physical conditions (1.6, 0.6, 0.7, respectively), abnormal physical conditions (1.5, 1.4, and 0.8, respectively), and family abuse (1.2, 0.5, and 0.8, respectively). With few exceptions, findings reported in Table 12.4 demonstrate that a higher average number of correlates of brain dysfunction were found in repeat violent offenders than repeat nonviolent offenders and first-time offenders. This would suggest that in our sample of offenders, higher levels of brain dysfunction are most associated with repeat violent offending.

The correlates that best differentiate repeat violent offenders from repeat nonviolent offenders and first-time offenders include persistent physical conditions (1.6 versus 0.6 and 0.7, respectively), abnormal interpersonal characteristics (4.4 versus 2.2 and 1.3, respectively), exposure to environmental toxins (0.6 versus 0.3 and 0.2, respectively), psychological abnormalities (6.1 versus 3.9 and 2.5, respectively), and family abuse (1.2 versus 0.5 and 0.8, respectively). Both the repeat violent and the repeat nonviolent offenders can also be differentiated from first-time offenders in terms of the number of abnormal physical characteristics (1.5, 1.4, and 0.8, respectively). This would suggest that among our sample of offenders, abnormal physical characteristics would appear to be a risk factor for repeat involvement in criminal activity, both violent and nonviolent in nature.

DISCUSSION AND CONCLUSION

Effective and Adequate Correctional Programming

This chapter reports findings from a study of a convenience sample of offenders under the supervision of probation personnel in Pennsylvania. The study had three primary goals: (1) to discover and document the nature of neurological correlates being used by probation personnel to assess brain dysfunction in their clients; (2) to discover and document the nature and amount of brain dysfunctions present in the clients of the probation personnel; and (3) to meaningfully relate correlates of brain dysfunctions to repeat violent offending, repeat nonviolent offending, repeat offending generally, and first-time offending in the probation clients.

Each member of the probation personnel team charged with assessing a group of three offenders for the presence of correlates of brain dysfunction commented on their inability to access vital information needed to adequately assess brain dysfunction in the offenders they managed. For example, reliable data on birth complications was generally not available for most offenders. Information related to other factors such as parental drug use, maternal drug use during pregnancy, and irregular diet were primarily obtained from offender self-reports, not legal or medical documents. Information on possible exposure to environmental toxins was gleaned primarily from the offenders' employment records. Other neurological correlates such as family abuse, persistent physical conditions, abnormal physical characteristics, abnormal interpersonal characteristics, psychological abnormalities, head injury, and offender substance use were more readily apparent based on medical records and previous psychological assessments of the offenders. Perhaps an even larger number of offenders would have been characterized by neurological dysfunction, and even higher average levels of neurological dysfunction would have been found, with more routine and systematic procedures for the collection and analysis of data related to brain dysfunction. Effective methods to address conditions of brain dysfunction in correctional programming for offenders are sorely needed.

Despite the inadequate attention being paid to brain dysfunction and despite poor recordkeeping procedures, this study demonstrates a high incidence of signs of brain dysfunction found among the sample of offenders, with the highest numbers being found among repeat violent offenders. The average number of correlates of brain dysfunction within the total sample of offenders was also high, with the highest number of correlates, once again, found within the repeat violent offender group. Within the sample, correlates of brain dysfunction are pervasive. Thus, there is evidence to suggest that such brain dysfunction may be more characteristic of repeat offending behaviors, particularly repeat violent offending behaviors.

Primary Goal—Prevention

It is possible to reliably identify those individuals who are in need of more costly and specialized medical evaluations in conjunction with available social and psychological services, and to recommend appropriate treatment for those offenders who possess many traits reflective of brain dysfunction. The overriding goal, however, is to prevent conditions conducive to brain damage. A closer examination of each offender's records suggests that a high percentage of the offenders within this study suffered at very early ages from conditions that may have led to neurological impairment. Some damage may have been suffered before birth due to the mothers' drug use habits and birth complications. Others were abused as children by parents, relatives, and guardians, and some suffered head injuries in automobile and sports-related accidents. Still others may have inherited tendencies to develop persistent and abnormal physical and psychological conditions, as the records indicate that many of the offenders in our study came from families with long histories of illnesses, diseases, and psychopathological conditions. Many offenders used illicit and harmful substances and had irregular diets, habits they indicated were formed at early ages by learning from others. Others were employed in potentially hazardous blue collar jobs, which may have increased their exposure to environmental toxins and injuries that adversely affect brain functioning.

Any and all of these potential sources of brain dysfunction can be reduced or even eliminated, suggesting that repeat offending and violent repeat offending behaviors that relate to these conditions may also be reduced or prevented. Proper emphasis must be placed on conditions of brain dysfunction if we hope to deal effectively with behavioral problems related to criminality. This does not mean that other adverse environmental and social factors should be ignored. Many of the correlates of brain dysfunction assessed in this study interact with factors such as conditions of poverty to influence offending behaviors. Virtually all of the repeat offenders in this study grew up in conditions of poverty, suggesting a primary role for environmental deprivation and the possibility that economic rehabilitation programs would exert a preventative effect.

The fact remains that systemic conditions such as poverty and deprivation can increase vulnerability to antisocial behavior through both sociological mechanisms and by increased exposure to conditions that can damage the brain (e.g., trauma, child abuse, neurotoxin exposure, prenatal and perinatal complications, and drug abuse). The successful implementation of crime control policies that focus on underlying mechanisms and preventative techniques will require reprioritization of criminal justice system goals. Emphasis will have to be placed not on the reactive and largely failing mechanisms currently used, but on more proactive measures aimed at reducing brain dysfunction through effective means of early detection and remediation.

Kelley Form

Neuropsychological Impairment Screening Worksheet

Completed by: _____ Date: _____

(use "Addendum" pages to complete responses as needed.)

Birthdate: _____ Current age: _____ Sex: _____ Race: _____

I. MEDICAL HISTORY

A. Regularity of Medical Care:
1. Family physician? (yes/no) _____
2. Frequency of visits? _____
3. Last full physical exam? (date) _____
4. Any abnormal results? _____
5. Any special tests ordered? _____

B. Birth Complications:
1. Premature birth? (If so, by how much?) _____
2. Did mother consume alcohol or other drugs during pregnancy? _____
3. Did mother have serious illness during pregnancy? _____
4. Did mother receive well-baby services (e.g., nutritional assessment)? _____
5. Any problems with birth delivery? _____
6. Infant's health at birth? _____

C. Hospitalization (when, why, length, results): _____

D. Persistent conditions ... (treatments, results?):
1. Headaches? _____
2. Breathing problems (e.g., asthma)? _____
3. Seizures? _____
4. Hypertension [high blood pressure]? _____
5. Hypoglycemia [low blood sugar]? _____
6. Diabetes? _____
7. Heart problems from (e.g., scarlet fever, rheumatic fever, other childhood diseases, blood clots, heart attacks)? _____
8. Sexually transmitted disease? _____
9. Drug use/abuse— including tobacco and alcohol (type, when started, frequency, amount)? _____
10. Any other persistent health problems? _____

E. **Episodes of the following not already noted? (when, treatments, results):**
   1. Head injury? _____
   2. Unconsciousness? _____
   3. Dizziness? _____
   4. High fever? _____
   5. Serious infection? _____
   6. Shortage of breath (e.g., near drowning, suffocation, smoke inhalation—any shortage of oxygen?) _____
   7. Electric shock? _____
   8. Numbness or weakness? _____

II. INDIVIDUAL CHARACTERISTICS

A. **Physical:**
   1. General appearance (neatness, cleanliness)? _____
   2. Scars (how acquired)? _____
   3. Facial expression of emotions? _____
   4. Impaired coordination in movement (walking, reaching, writing)? _____
   5. Tremors or tics? _____
   6. Nervousness (constant movement of hands, feet)? _____
   7. Speech (speed, clarity)? _____
   8. Vision (e.g., holds papers unusually close or far away from eyes, misses details, starts reading in middle of line, sees only half of picture)? _____
   9. Eating habits (e.g., irregular meals, excessive junk foods and/or sweets)? _____

B. **Psychological/Psychiatric**
   1. Alertness (speed of responses)? _____
   2. Attention span? _____
   3. Confusion (inconsistent accounts of events)? _____
   4. Spatial disorientation (confuses left and right, puts things in wrong place, gets lost easily)? _____
   5. Memory (any difficulties in remembering)? _____
   6. Comprehension (difficulties in understanding conversations or directions)? _____
   7. Reading/learning problems (dyslexia, low IQ)? _____
   8. Judgment (difficulties in perception of risk)? _____
   9. Planning (difficulties in organizing and following-through with actions)? _____
   10. Problem solving (difficulties in reasoning and making decisions)? _____
   11. Psychiatric diagnosis of "conversion," "disassociative," or "hysterical" symptoms (when, treatment received, results)? _____
   12. Any other psychological/psychiatric referral for treatment (when, condition, treatment received, results)? _____

C. **Interpersonal:**
   1. Congeniality (e.g., outgoing, friendly, pleasant vs. quiet, reserved, sullen)? _____
   2. Sensitivity to feelings of others? _____
   3. Respect for authority? _____
   4. Lying (habitual, frequent, occasional, seldom)? _____
   5. Quickness of temper/anger? _____
   6. Verbally aggressive (e.g., frequently insults, bullies, makes threats, talks about violence)? _____
   7. Physically aggressive (e.g., frequently shoves, strikes, fights)? _____

III. FAMILY EXPERIENCE

A. Parents, Siblings, and Other Family Members:
1. Major disease (when, type, treatment, results)? _____
2. Mental illness (when, type, treatment, results)? _____
3. Drug use/abuse (including alcohol and medications)? _____
4. Family meal habits and diet? _____

B. Client:
1. Persistently verbally abused? _____
2. Physically abused? _____
3. Witnessed abuse? _____

IV. EXPOSURE TO TOXINS—Home, School, Work

E.g., lead in house paint, asbestos, liquid fuels, cleaning fluids, pet flea powders, lawn chemicals, etc.:

_____
_____
_____

References

Cleckley, H. C. (1982). *The mask of sanity.* St. Louis, MO: Harcourt Health Sciences.

Davies, W. (1982). Violence in prison. In P. Feldman (Ed.), *Developments in the study of criminal behavior.* London: Violence.

Farrington, D. P., Loeber, R. & Van Kammen, W. B. (1990). Long-term criminal outcomes of hyperactivity-impulsivity-attention deficit and conduct problems in childhood. In L. N. Robins & M. Rutter (Eds.), *Straight and devious pathways from childhood to adulthood.* New York: Cambridge University Press, 62–81.

Farrington, D. P., Ohlin, L. E. & Wilson, J. Q. (1986). *Understanding and controlling crime.* New York: Springer-Verlag.

Fishbein, D. H. (1990). Biological perspectives in criminology. *Criminology, 28,* 27–72.

Fishbein, D. H. & Thatcher, R. W. (1982). Nutritional and electrophysiological indices of maladaptive behavior. Paper presented at the MIT Conference on Research Strategies for Assessing the Behavioral Effects and Nutrients. Cambridge, MA.

Flor-Henry, P. (1976). Lateralized temporal-limbic dysfunction and psychopathology. *Annals of the New York Academy of Science, 280,* 777–795.

Gillstrom, B. J. & Hare, R. D. (1988). Language related hand gestures in psychopaths. *Journal of Personality Disorders, 2,* 21–27.

Greenfield, S. A. (1996). *The human mind explained.* New York: Henry Holt & Co.

Haber, G. B., Heaton, K. W. & Murphy, D. (1977). Depletion and disruption of dietary fiber: Effects on society, plasma, glucose and serum insulin. *Lancet, 2,* 679–689.

Harlow, J. M. (1848). Passage of an iron rod through the head. *Boston Medical and Surgical Journal, 39,* 389–393.

Hawkins, J. D. (1996). *Delinquency and crime: Current theories.* New York: Cambridge University Press.

Holmes, C. B. (1992). *Recognizing brain dysfunction.* Brandon, VT: Clinical Psychology Publishing.

Jeffery, C. R. (1990). *Criminology: An interdisciplinary approach.* Englewood Cliffs, NJ: Prentice-Hall.

Jeffery, C. R. (1998a). Criminology and criminal law: Science versus policy and the interaction of science and law. In W. Laufer & F. Adler (Eds.), *Advances in criminological theory,* vol. 8. New Brunswick, NJ: Transaction.

Jeffery, C. R. (1998b). The prevention of juvenile violence. Paper presented at the thirty-fifth annual conference of the Academy of Criminal Justice Sciences, Albuquerque, NM.

Kelley, T. (1997). An integrated systems approach to screening for brain dysfunction in delinquent offenders. Master's thesis. Florida State University, Tallahassee, FL.

Lewis, D. O., Pincus, J. H., Bard, B. & Richardson, E. (1986). Neuropsychiatric, psychoeductional, and family characteristics of 14 juveniles condemned to death in the United States. *American Journal of Psychiatry, 145,* 584–589.

Loeber, R. (1990). Development and risk factors of juvenile antisocial behavior and delinquency. *Clinical Psychology Review, 10,* 1–41.

Luria, A. R. (1973). *The working brain: An introduction to neuropsychology.* New York: Basic Books.

Marks, V. (1981). The regulation of blood glucose. In V. Maker & F.C. Rose (Eds.), *Hypoglycemia.* Oxford, England: Blackwell.

Marlowe, M., Stellern, J., Moon, C. & Errera, J. (1985). Main and interaction effects of metallic toxins on aggressive classroom behavior. *Aggressive Behavior, 11,* 41–48.

Masters, R. (1997). Environmental pollution, neurotoxicity, and criminal violence. In J. Rose (Ed.), *Environmental toxicity.* New York: Gordon & Breach, 1–61.

Miller, J. G. (1978). *The living system.* New York: McGraw Hill.

Needleman, H. & Gatsonis, C. (1990). Low-level lead exposure and the IQ of children. *Journal of the American Medical Association, 263,* 673–678.

Needleman, H., Gunnoe, C., Leviton, A., Reed, P., Peresie, H., Maher, C. & Barrett, P. (1979). Deficits in psychologic and classroom performance of children with elevated dentine lead levels. *New England Journal of Medicine, 300,* 689–695.

Needleman, H., Schell, A., Bellinger, D., Leviton, A. & Alred, E. (1990). The long-term effects of exposure to low doses of lead in children. *New England Journal of Medicine, 322,* 83–88.

Pallone, N. J. (1991). *Mental disorders among prisoners.* New Brunswick, NJ: Transaction.

Pallone, N. J. & Hennessy, J. J. (1993). Tinder-box criminal violence: Neurogenic impulsivity, risk-taking, and the phenomenology of rational choice. In R. V. Clarke & M. Felson (Eds.), *Routine activity and rational choice: Advances in criminological theory.* New Brunswick, NJ: Transaction, 127–158.

Raine, A. (1993). *The psychopathology of crime: Criminal behavior as a clinical disorder.* San Diego, CA: Academic Press.

Raine, A., Roger, D. & Venables, P. H. (1982). Locus of control and socialization. *Journal of Research and Personality, 16,* 147–156.

Reiss, A. & Roth, J. A. (1993). *Understanding and preventing violence.* Washington, DC: National Academy Press.

Robinson, M. B. (1998). The theoretical development of crime prevention through environmental design. In W. Laufer & F. Adler (Eds.), *Advances in criminological theory,* vol. 8. New Brunswick, NJ: Transaction.

Rutter, M. & Giller, H. (1983). *Juvenile delinquency: Trends and perspectives.* New York: Guilford Press.

Santilla, P. & Haapasalo, J. (1997). Neurological and psychological risk factors among young homicidal, violent, and non-violent offenders in Finland. *Homicide, 1,* 1–20.

Satterfield, J. H., Swanson, J., Schell, A. M. & Lee, F. (1994). Prediction of antisocial behavior in attention-deficit hyperactivity disorder boys from aggression deficit scores. *Journal of the American Academy of Child and Adolescent Psychiatry, 33,* 185–190.

Schoenthaler, S. J. (1982). The effect of sugar on the treatment and control of antisocial behavior: A double-blind study of an incarcerated juvenile population. *International Journal of Biosocial Research, 3,* 1–9.

Tonry, M. & Farrington, D. (1995). *Building a safer society.* Chicago: University of Chicago Press.

Tonry, M., Ohlin, L. E. & Farrington, D. P. (1991). *Human development and criminal behavior.* New York: Springer-Verlag.

Widom, C. S. (1989). Does violence beget violence? A critical examination of the literature. *Psychological Bulletin, 106,* 3–28.

Wurtman, R. J. (1982). Nutrients that modify brain function. *Scientific American, 246,* 50–59.

Wurtman, R. J. (1983). Behavioral effects of nutrients. *Lancet, 1*(8334), 1145–1147.

Wurtman, R. J., Hefti, F. & Melamed, E. (1981). Precursor control of neurotransmitter synthesis. *Pharmacological Review, 32,* 315–335.

Yeudall, L. T. (1977). Neuropsychological assessments in forensic disorders. *Canada's Mental Health, 25,* 7–14.

Part 5

Subtypes and Syndromes of Delinquency and Criminality

Individuals exhibiting the cluster of neurobiological and psychological traits described in this book that place them at high risk for antisocial behavior often have a life-long history of learning disabilities, conduct disorder, oppositional defiant disorder, impulsivity, and aggressiveness that present themselves as early warning signs. Irregularities in brain function that characterize those with aggressiveness and substance abuse are more pervasive among affected children than those without. Affected individuals often demonstrate central nervous system instability that prevents proper regulation over processes such as cognitive flexibility, attention, verbal fluency, and problem-solving. These and other skills normally enable an individual to cope, assess consequences, control impulses, make decisions, and mature at a reasonable rate. Thus, antisocial behaviors tend to coexist with a variety of other psychological and behavioral disturbances that often worsens the severity and prognosis of their condition. Interestingly, research also shows that similar traits, or risk factors, are more prevalent among individuals who inject illicit drugs, particularly antisocial personality disorder (APD) and other sensation-seeking conditions. In Chapter 13, Dr. Dinwiddie characterizes the forms of psychopathology that tend to underlie injecting drug use and discusses their implications.

Injecting drug use (IDU), as Chapter 13 points out, is associated with a myriad of adverse health consequences, the most prominent being infection with the human immunodeficiency virus (HIV). As the study of behavioral factors associated with HIV infection has progressed, it has become apparent that in addition to being a direct risk factor due to infection via contaminated needles, *any* lifetime IDU is a marker for elevated risk due to its association with other risk behaviors, possibly because of the relationship between IDU and specific forms of psychopathology, particularly APD. Recent work using latent class analysis, however, indicates that it may be possible to derive more homogeneous, clinically meaningful subgroups of IDUs, which can be shown to differ in baseline risk behaviors, severity of associated psychopathology, and patterns of lifetime substance dependence. Dr. Dinwiddie shows how subclassification of IDUs may lead to better matching of treatment interventions and more precise estimates of HIV risk.

Chapter 14, by Dr. Blatchley and his colleagues, discusses the very critical association between child sexual abuse and risk for later drug abuse. Theories of an intergenerational cycle of addiction and family dysfunction abound in the literature, and there is strong support for a link between parental substance abuse and various forms of psychopathology, including substance abuse, in the parents' children. Many investigators and clinicians believe that this link is to some degree related to the increased incidence of child abuse and neglect in the population of drug-abusing parents. For some reason, however, not all victims of childhood sexual abuse succumb themselves to drug abuse, nor do they all parent their children in similarly dysfunctional ways. This discrepancy in findings has spurred Dr. Blatchley and his colleagues to question whether there are specific events, processes, or traumas in the family of origin that might be key determinants of how addicts function as parents when they undertake responsibility for raising their own children. The answer to this question has crucial implications, both for researchers seeking to identify risk and resiliency factors and for practitioners working to prevent adverse outcomes and treating clients who are either victims or at risk of victimizing their own children. The authors report that sexual abuse occurring in the childhood and in the adolescent years of female addicts is closely related to dysfunction in the family of origin and continues to correlate with aspects of their subjects' adult functioning and adjustment, especially in regard to their ability to parent effectively and to interact in a positive emotional way with their own adolescent children. The authors' findings are consistent with theory relating childhood sexual victimization to substance abuse, depressive disorders, posttraumatic stress, and dissociation. Family support programs and other interventions can effectively treat these dysfunctional family units, ultimately reducing the incidence of substance abuse and poor parenting in the adult victims of sexual child abuse; thus, the intergenerational cycle of addiction and dysfunctional families can be halted. The details of treatment and prevention strategies are provided.

Three-fourths of all serial murderers known to authorities reside within the United States. The last chapter in this section, Chapter 15 by Carol Ferreira, discusses the various generators and characteristics of serial murderers from a psychological vantage point. Unlike other violent offenders, serial murderers engage in methodical, systematic, and patterned killing that is readily distinguished from other sorts of violent predators, most of whom tend to be impulsive rather than premeditative. Serial murderers are primarily white and male, and they exhibit a quest for power over others that is unparalleled, uncontrollable, and insatiable. And although some are clearly "insane" or mentally deranged, most appear to be rational, intelligent, calculating, and "normal" much of the time. They generally know the nature and consequences of their actions and thus are not insane according to legal prescriptions. They are psychopaths, characterized by an inability to experience a normal range of emotions, incapable of intimacy, lacking avoidance responses or feelings of remorse, and incapable of being conditioned by threats of punishment. They are cool, calm, and collected until they are in the throes of some horrendous and unspeakable act. But what is particularly both intriguing and revealing about this subtype of murderers is that their crimes produce tremendous pleasure and excitement for the perpetrator—a pleasure that is highly reinforcing, enticing them to kill again and again for that sensation. There is evidence that their unusual sensation-seeking needs and methods of achieving that heightened level of stimulation is biologically driven by abnormalities within their central nervous system. In combination with the abuse and neglect that most are exposed to throughout childhood, their neurological irregularities may result in bizarre and dangerous behaviors. Only once we understand these biological and psychological generators can we as a society attempt to identify the serial murderer and, more important, to identify ways not to create more.

Chapter 13

Subtyping of Injecting Drug Users

by Stephen H. Dinwiddie, M.D.

Introduction 13-1
    Classifying Illicit Drug Users 13-1
    Prognosis/Specific Treatment 13-2
Health Consequences of IDU 13-3
Psychiatric Comorbidity in Drug Injectors 13-3
    Comorbid Substance Use and Dependence 13-3
    Antisocial Personality 13-4
    Depressive Disorders 13-6
    Summary 13-6
Subclassification of Drug Injectors 13-7
Conclusion 13-9

INTRODUCTION

Classifying Illicit Drug Users

Classification of users of illicit drugs is a daunting task. Such individuals rarely fit into neat categories defined by the pharmacologic class of drug used (those addicted to cannabis, to cocaine, to heroin, and so on). Instead, their life histories are more likely to consist of exposure to multiple drugs over time, often with use of multiple substances during the same time span. Use may wax and wane and may be accompanied by the incidence, remission, and recurrence of a wide variety of symptoms of drug dependence—often, but not always, neatly attributable to a specific drug.

Problematic use is also a powerful marker for coexisting psychiatric illness ("psychiatric comorbidity"), on either a concurrent or a lifetime basis (Regier et al., 1990; Strain et al., 1991), and such comorbidity can dramatically complicate the process of diagnosis both because of symptomologic overlap, as in the case of APD (Dinwiddie & Reich, 1993; Carroll et al., 1993; Dinwiddie & Daw, 1998), and because effects of intoxication or withdrawal can in some cases mimic or perhaps trigger psychotic, mood, or anxiety syndromes (Schuckit, 1985; Schuckit & Hesselbrock, 1994).

Current diagnostic practice consonant with the fourth edition of the *Diagnostic and Statistical Manual of Mental Disorders* (DSM-IV) emphasizes the commonality of manifestations of addiction across substances, dividing problematic use into a presumably milder form, psychoactive substance abuse, or a more severe manifestation, psychoactive substance dependence. However, while the *potential* symptoms of abuse or dependence are consistent across all substances, it is also recognized that specific substances differ in their pharmacologic ability to produce tolerance, stereotypical withdrawal states, and so on. Thus, diagnosis (essential for purposes of prognostication, treatment planning, and, of course, research into epidemiology, etiology, and treatment) merely requires documentation that any three of seven potential manifestations of substance dependence have occurred within the same twelve-month span, without establishing any particular symptom (such as withdrawal or tolerance) as indicative of the disease state. Subclassification of the substance use disorder is then based on severity (abuse versus dependence) and on identification of the specific substance(s) whose use became problematic.

Prognosis/Specific Treatment

Establishing a diagnosis of dependence on a given substance often does not lead to specific treatment, with the exception of a few pharmacological interventions such as methadone maintenance in opioid dependence or prescription of disulfuram (Antabuse) in alcohol dependence (though the past few years have seen substantial advances); more commonly, relatively nonspecific interventions such as twelve-step approaches or relapse prevention techniques, whose use is not restricted to a specific class of drug, are employed as primary modalities of treatment. Given the tremendous heterogeneity of individuals and their symptoms in substance abuse treatment, further ways of subclassifying patients on clinical grounds would be of benefit.

One approach that may have implications for prognosis or treatment matching is to inquire about route of drug administration. In particular, the finding that an individual has, on a lifetime basis, ever injected drugs may prove to be useful information, whether or not he or she is currently injecting. While the association between IDU and HIV infection has raised awareness about one specific health consequence, there are a number of other clinical implications, as discussed herein.

While it is often believed that any IDU is equivalent to heroin use, this perception is not wholly accurate. Although heroin has a high likelihood of being injected, some users avoid this route, preferring to smoke or "snort" the drug. Moreover, while population prevalence of lifetime heroin use has been estimated at 1.5 percent of the population (Anthony et al., 1995) (with approximately 23 percent of those individuals meeting lifetime criteria for dependence), this estimate would not accord well with data from large samples not ascertained directly through drug use in which over 3 percent of subjects (and 5 percent of men) reported injecting drugs at some time in their lives (Dinwiddie, 1997; Turner et al., 1998).

In particular, stimulant drugs, though they appear to have a lower liability for being injected, have been used by a much greater number. In the National Comorbidity Survey, 16.2 percent of the population reported lifetime cocaine use and 15.3 percent use of other stimulants, versus 1.5 percent who reported having used heroin (Anthony et al., 1995). Thus, while the likelihood of a heroin user injecting heroin (as opposed to administering it via another route) appears to be substantially greater than a stimulant user injecting stimulants, the latter class of drugs may actually have been injected by more individuals simply because of the greater number exposed (Dinwiddie et al., 1992a). Such distinctions might appear purely academic, were it not for the observation that cocaine injecting (at least) appears to be associated with greater frequency of needle use and, very likely therefore, exposure to the myriad health risks associated with IDU (Des Jarlais & Friedman, 1988).

HEALTH CONSEQUENCES OF IDU

The most prominent of IDU risks, of course, is HIV exposure. At this time, it is estimated that drug injectors account for approximately one in four new cases of acquired immunodeficiency syndrome (AIDS). However, a wide variety of other adverse health consequences may be seen, including transmission of other diseases (e.g., hepatitis B or C, syphilis, malaria), local infection at the site of injection, and sequelae of unsanitary injecting practices such as endocarditis or brain abscess resulting from bacteremia or the seeding of septic emboli. In addition, the agents used to cut the pure drug may be harmful, potentially causing granulomatous lung disease or central nervous system pathology (Michelson et al., 1986; Stein, 1990; Haverkos & Lange, 1990; O'Connor et al., 1994). Thus, while reduction in needle sharing may decrease risk of HIV infection, injecting drug users remain at substantial risk of other complications.

In addition to being a risk *factor* for HIV infection (by sharing of needles contaminated with blood from an HIV-positive individual), IDU may also be a risk *indicator* due to an association with other HIV-risk behaviors (Kramer et al., 1992; Booth, et al., 1993). Dinwiddie et al. (1996) reported that in a street-outreach sample, those with a lifetime history of IDU, whether or not they were currently injecting, were more likely to report having participated in high-risk sexual behaviors in the six months before their entry into the study, to have engaged in trading money or drugs for sex, and to have had sexual contact with another injecting drug user in the prior six months. There is evidence from other samples as well that IDU appears to be associated with numerous high-risk sexual behaviors such as promiscuity and involvement in prostitution (Watkins et al., 1992; Dinwiddie, 1997).

Of note, in the sample described by Dinwiddie et al. (1996), in a self-rating of perceived HIV risk, only 14 percent of the sample felt themselves to be at high risk, even though two out of three had, in addition to injecting drugs, engaged in more than one high-risk sexual activity, and a quarter had sex within the prior six months had sex with a partner the subject knew to be a drug injector. Consequently, for the majority of the sample, fear of HIV infection did not appear to be a significant motivation for entry into treatment.

PSYCHIATRIC COMORBIDITY IN DRUG INJECTORS

Comorbid Substance Use and Dependence

The above findings might reflect a more pervasive denial of problems associated with drug use among their users. There is evidence to suggest that *any* lifetime IDU conveys substantially increased odds of reporting a variety of physical, social, and psychological problems associated with substance use even when compared to individuals with substantial illicit drug exposure, but who denied any IDU (Dinwiddie et al., 1992b). Indeed, in different non-treatment samples, IDU has been (as might be expected) associated with extremely high rates of lifetime drug exposure with a lifetime diagnosis of dependence on at least one psychoactive substance in 90 to 99 percent of cases (Dinwiddie et al., 1996; Dinwiddie, 1997).

Those who go on to inject drugs also appear to begin substance use quite young. In two samples not derived from individuals seeking treatment for addiction (Dinwiddie et al., 1992a; Dinwiddie, 1997), those with a history of IDU tended to report using substances at an earlier age than those who used such substances but reported no history of IDU. For example, in both samples, drug injectors reported they were approximately one year younger than noninjectors when they first used alcohol (at about age 14 in both samples). Even when restricting comparisons to those who reported use of drugs other than cannabis on at least five occasions, in both samples injecting drug users reported significantly earlier onset of use of stimulants, sedative-hypnotics, and hallucinogens, as well as cannabis. In every case, mean age of onset of substance use among the injectors was below age 21, and typically between ages 17 and 20.

While alcohol and cannabis tend to be the first psychoactive substances used by most, as noted above, such use occurs earlier among those who progress to IDU. Even so, there is evidence to suggest that the average interval between initial use of these substances and initiation of injecting is relatively brief (4.6 years for alcohol, 2.1 for cannabis), while if use of hallucinogens, stimulants, or sedative-hypnotics is ultimately followed by injecting, onset of IDU occurs on average only one year later (Dinwiddie et al., 1992a). In that sample, subjects who reported IDU had an estimated mean age at onset of 18.5 +/- 3.4 years.

Antisocial Personality

In samples derived from drug treatment programs or advertisement, IDU is associated most closely with antisocial personality disorder (APD) and depressive disorders (Brooner et al., 1993; Lipsitz et al., 1994). Similar findings have been reported from a street-outreach sample, with 41 percent of those who reported lifetime IDU meeting the DSM's third revised edition (DSM-III-R) criteria for APD (Dinwiddie et al., 1996), a rate very close to the 44 percent reported by Brooner et al. (1992).

Particularly given the nature of these populations, this association might be ascribed to sampling bias. However, similar results have also been reported from samples more closely resembling the general population. Studying Swedish men conscripted into military service in 1969 and 1970, Stenbacka et al. (1992) found that risk factors for IDU included truancy, solvent abuse, running away, and contact with juvenile authorities, and that injecting drug users were more likely to carry diagnoses of personality or neurotic disorders.

Further evidence that IDU is associated with (and presumably preceded by) significant conduct problems was reported by Tomas et al. (1990). In their sample, 222 self-referred, primarily minority injectors were compared to matched subjects on nine problem behaviors occurring before age 16: running away, fighting, vandalism, school disciplinary problems, truancy, suspension or expulsion, theft, juvenile arrest, and frequent lying. A greater number of these problems were associated with elevated risk for IDU; those having three to six of these conduct difficulties were seven times more likely to become drug injectors, and those with seven or more difficulties were nearly twenty-five times more likely.

Similar findings were reported by Dinwiddie et al. (1992c) using data from relatives derived from the St. Louis Family Study of Alcoholism, probands of which were ascertained either through hospitalized alcoholics, felons, or medical-surgical controls. In that analysis, seven early-onset (before age 15) variables were found to be associated with IDU: fighting, juvenile arrest, cannabis use, truancy, theft, poor parental supervision, and onset of sexual activity. Using these behaviors to construct a seven-point scale, it was found that increasing scores were associated with improvement in positive predictive values (81 percent with a score of five or more), but poor sensitivity (23 percent at a cutoff value of five), suggesting that such a scale would be inefficient if used to screen for high-risk individuals, either over-predicting at-risk cases (using lower cutoff scores) or, at higher cut-off scores, missing the majority of cases.

Further evidence that an association does exist, however, was provided by a partial replication, again using a sample of relatives of alcoholics, this one derived from the Collaborative Study on the Genetics of Alcoholism (COGA). In that study, reported truancy, theft, cannabis use, or sexual activity prior to age 15 approximately doubled the odds of IDU; presence of two of these four behaviors increased odds of IDU by 4.4; three problems led to an increase of 6.3; and presence of all four behaviors increased odds of IDU by a factor of 7.4. Thus, using these four problems with onset before age 15, odds for lifetime IDU increased roughly twofold for each additional symptom reported (Dinwiddie, 1997).

The finding of a relationship between conduct problems, whether or not samples were derived through treatment or self-selection, obviously suggests that IDU might have a particularly close relationship with APD. This would hardly be a surprising finding, given the association between APD and psychoactive substance use disorders in general. However, it is possible that the impulsivity and disregard of consequences so often seen in APD might predispose individuals to riskier drug use practices (such as injecting) as well as to other HIV-risk behaviors.

As mentioned above, such an association has indeed been seen in treatment or volunteer samples. Similar results have also been reported in other samples, however. Dinwiddie et al. (1992d) found that 69 percent of a sample of injecting drug users derived from relatives of hospitalized alcoholics or felons could be diagnosed with APD using the criteria of Feighner et al. (1972). In comparing injectors to individuals who reported (1) no significant drug use, (2) use of cannabis more than five times but no other drug use, or (3) more extensive drug use but who denied ever injecting, odds for a diagnosis of APD were markedly increased, by a factor of 21 relative to individuals with no significant drug use. By contrast, a history of significant use of drugs (greater than five times) other than cannabis was associated with an increase in relative odds for a diagnosis of APD of only 5.3.

Two lines of reasoning suggest that this relationship is more than artifactual, or not merely a complication of severe addiction leading by necessity to involvement in illicit activities. First is the observation that the conduct problems discussed above predate in most cases onset of IDU. This of course does not rule out the possibility that in such individuals early onset of chemical dependency leads both to more severe manifestations (such as IDU) and to consequent involvment in illicit activities.

Secondly, several studies have now indicated that attempting to attribute the cause of individual antisocial symptoms to substance-related problems versus APD markedly decreases diagnostic agreement (Carroll et al., 1993), while simply rating presence or absence of the behavior without attempting to attribute it to substance abuse or APD does not appear to affect commonly accepted indicators of diagnostic validity for the latter diagnosis (Dinwiddie & Reich, 1993) and leads to markedly better temporal stability of diagnosis (Dinwiddie & Daw, 1998).

Depressive Disorders

The only other diagnosis (other than alcoholism or drug dependence) whose prevalence was found to be significantly different between the four groups (no significant drug use, cannabis only, other drug use, and IDU) was depressive illness, found in 34 percent of injecting drug users. However, unlike APD, depression was no more common among injectors than among other drug users (36 percent); for both injectors and other drug users, this represented a three-fold increase in odds for the diagnosis relative to those with no significant drug use history.

Suicide, of course, is widely recognized as a complication of psychiatric illness, particularly depression and dependence on alcohol or other substances. Again as compared to those with no significant drug use, IDU was associated with an eight-fold increase in odds of reporting a history of suicide attempt.

Similar results were obtained from analyses of the COGA sample (Dinwiddie, 1997). APD was not as frequently diagnosed (in 36 percent of injectors), but any lifetime IDU was still associated with an odds ratio of 24 for the diagnosis relative to those with no significant drug use. Using DSM-III-R criteria, major depression was actually less likely to be diagnosed (perhaps because the interview employed by COGA uses a relatively conservative approach to the diagnosis of mood disorders in the setting of significant substance use), though odds for any depressive disorder remained slightly elevated.

As in the prior study, IDU was associated with an eight-fold increase in odds of reporting a prior suicide attempt, though the association was somewhat weakened after accounting for the effects of comorbid APD, alcohol dependence, and major depression.

Finally, using data from a street-outreach program designed to reduce HIV-risk behaviors, Dinwiddie et al. (1996) found, again using DSM-III-R criteria, that 41 percent of those with any lifetime IDU could be diagnosed with APD, versus 30 percent of those who denied IDU. As in the other samples, no other differences in lifetime psychopathology emerged. Of particular note, in this sample, IDU was not associated with any increase in prevalence of mood disorders.

Summary

In summary, in both treatment and non-treatment populations, IDU appears to be powerfully associated with APD. While there is a much weaker association with mood disturbance, this appears more likely due to comorbidity with APD and psychoactive substance dependence, rather than an independent association. Other more severe psychiatric syndromes such as schizophrenia or bipolar illness appear, as in the general population, to be uncommon among lifetime injectors, though odds of suicidal ideation and attempt appear to be elevated four- to eightfold.

SUBCLASSIFICATION OF DRUG INJECTORS

As noted above, IDU appears to be a marker for APD, lifetime use of (and dependence on) multiple psychoactive substances, and to a lesser extent, mood disturbance and suicide attempt. There is, however, evidence to suggest that injecting drug users do not represent a diagnostically homogeneous group.

Dinwiddie et al. (1998) studied results of a street-outreach program, the Effort to Reduce the Spread of AIDS (Cottler et al., 1993), in which subjects in high-risk areas of St. Louis were approached by outreach workers or could present as "walk-ins" to one of two storefront outreach centers. Potential subjects were offered a variety of free health services, and at intake the outreach team obtained information regarding demographics, reason for visit, and use of illicit psychoactive drugs. Subjects reporting regular use within the prior twelve months were invited to participate in the project, one component of which involved free substance abuse treatment.

A unique feature of the project was the inclusion of a comparison group comprised of subjects who declined substance abuse treatment. Both treatment and comparison groups were administered structured diagnostic interviews and assessments of substance abuse and HIV risk behaviors, and were followed up at three, six, nine, twelve, and eighteen months. Almost all (95 percent) of the total intake sample could be located and reinterviewed at eighteen months. Of the total 455 subjects in this sample, 149 reported a lifetime history of IDU. Using latent class analysis (LCA), an attempt was made to subclassify these individuals into groups relatively homogeneous with respect to a given set of characteristics.

Subjects were classified with regard to lifetime diagnoses of APD, any affective disorder, any anxiety disorder, and lifetime dependence on alcohol, tobacco, cannabis, amphetamine, cocaine, sedative-hypnotics, opioids, phencyclidine, or hallucinogens, resulting in the derivation of four latent classes (see Table 13.1). The first group can be broadly characterized as having likelihood of lifetime dependence on a variety of illicit substances and high prevalence of APD (68 percent). Individuals in Class 1 also had the highest probability of receiving a diagnosis of depression (32 percent). Individuals in Classes 2 and 3 had lower probabilities of receiving a diagnosis of APD but very high probabilities of lifetime dependence on cocaine (Class 2) or opioids (Class 3). Individuals in Class 4 were characterized by high likelihood of lifetime dependence on both stimulants (cocaine or amphetamine) and opioids, but by very low probability of a diagnosis of APD.

While the classes did not differ in drug use during the six months prior to entry into the study (an intervention protocol), those from Class 1 were more likely to have used more than one category of drugs. The utility of classification based on *lifetime*, as opposed to current, IDU is further supported by the finding that over 80 percent of those in Classes 1 and 3 reported IDU in the prior six months, as opposed to 40 percent of Class 2 and 60 percent of Class 4. At baseline, the classes also differed in reporting of HIV-risk behaviors prior to entry into the study (see Table 13.2).

Table 13.1
Latent Classes Among Injectors (n = 149)

Variable	Response Probability			
	Class 1 n=41 28%	Class 2 n=33 22%	Class 3 n=49 33%	Class 4 n=26 17%
Alcohol dependence	1.0	0.52	0.60	0.71
Tobacco dependence	0.90	0.57	0.75	0.60
Cannabis dependence	0.92	0.56	0.34	0.64
Amphetamine dependence	0.67	0.00	0.00	1.0
Sedative-hypnotic dependence	0.59	0.10	0.12	0.27
Cocaine dependence	0.82	1.00	0.47	0.96
Opioid dependence	0.97	0.31	0.94	0.88
Phencyclidine dependence	0.23	0.38	0.00	0.14
Hallucinogen dependence	0.58	0.06	0.00	0.27
Antisocial personality disorder	0.68	0.45	0.32	0.00
Any depressive disorder	0.32	0.16	0.00	0.00
Any anxiety disorder	0.33	0.32	0.23	0.60

Table 13.2
High-Risk Behaviors Among Injectors: Baseline*

Behavior	Class				χ^2 (3 df)	P
	1 n=41 n (%)	2 n=33 n (%)	3 n=49 n (%)	4 n=26 n (%)		
Sex with IDU	16(39.0)	4(12.1)	5(10.2)	12(46.2)	19.230	<0.001
≥1 Risky sex behavior	32(78.1)	23(69.7)	27(55.1)	14(53.9)	6.849	0.077
Consistent condom use	5(12.2)	1(3.0)	2(4.1)	1(3.9)	3.815	NS
Trading drugs or money for sex	10(24.4)	7(21.2)	1(2.0)	4(15.4)	10.420	0.015
Trading sex for drugs or money	7(17.1)	9(27.3)	2(4.1)	3(11.5)	9.232	0.026
Sharing works	37(90.2)	21(67.7)	37(75.5)	21(80.8)	5.883	NS
Cleaning works	10(24.4)	2(6.1)	17(34.7)	13(50.0)	15.410	<0.001
Monogamous	24(58.5)	16(48.5)	43(87.8)	16(61.5)	16.185	<0.001

*During six months before entry into study

Thus, at least with regard to lifetime dependence on specific drugs and diagnosis of APD, injecting drug users do not comprise a homogeneous group. Perhaps consequently, the groups also appear to differ in baseline HIV-risk behaviors reported.

CONCLUSION

On a lifetime basis, over 5 percent of men report lifetime IDU. Clinically, this history appears to be a marker for very substantial lifetime involvement in drug use, with consequent problems and thus an increased severity of addiction. Directly conveying risk for HIV infection as well as a host of other health problems, it also appears to be an indicator for high-risk sexual behaviors that independently lead to elevated risk for HIV exposure. Recent evidence that such other high-risk behaviors (e.g., male-to-male sex, prostitution, or sexual contact with injectors) are systematically underreported at least in interview situations (Turner et al., 1998) further underscores the potential clinical usefulness of this historical finding as a marker of elevated medical risk.

Particularly given the high prevalence of APD among injecting drug users, one might speculate that the decision to inject drugs may be related to underlying personality factors that also predispose an individual to engage in a number of other risk-taking behaviors without consideration of possible adverse consequences. However, the LCA results suggest that the picture is more complex, in that the groups identified by LCA differ not only in lifetime psychopathology but in severity of drug use, as reflected in differences in amount of drug use immediately prior to the study, rates of IDU immediately prior to the study, and lifetime substance dependence diagnoses. Perhaps because of such differences, the groups appear to differ as well in their reporting of other HIV-risk behaviors at baseline.

It remains, of course, for further study to determine if such subtyping of injecting drug users has significant clinical utility—predicting, for example, differential response to substance abuse treatment interventions. Nonetheless, use of LCA in this population appears to hold some promise of identifying more clinically homogeneous subgroups among a population characterized by extremely high rates of psychoactive substance dependence, risky behaviors, and psychopathology, particularly APD. If use of this technique proves to be practical in clinical samples, it may ultimately lead to better identification of individuals at high risk for specific complications of addiction and improved prediction of treatment outcome. Such subclassification may also prove to be of use in more precise matching of specific treatment interventions to patient characteristics.

References

American Psychiatric Association (1987). *Diagnostic and statistical manual of mental disorders* (3d ed. rev.). Washington, DC: American Psychiatric Press.

American Psychiatric Association (1994). *Diagnostic and statistical manual of mental disorders* (4th ed.). Washington, DC: American Psychiatric Press.

Anthony, J. C., Arria, A. M. & Johnson, E. O. (1995). Epidemiological and public health issues for tobacco, alcohol, and other drugs. In J. M. Oldham & M. B. Riba (Eds.), *American Psychiatric Press review of psychiatry,* vol. 14. Washington, DC: American Psychiatric Press, 15–49.

Booth, R. E., Watters, J. K. & Chitwood, D. D. (1993). HIV risk-related sex behaviors among injection drug users, crack smokers, and injection drug users who smoke crack. *American Journal of Public Health, 83,* 1144–1148.

Brooner, R. K., Schmidt, C. W., Felch, L. J. & Bigelow, G. E. (1992). Antisocial behavior of intravenous drug abusers: Implications for diagnosis of antisocial personality disorder. *American Journal of Psychiatry, 149,* 482–487.

Brooner, R. K., Greenfield, L., Schmidt, C. W. & Bigelow, G. E. (1993). Antisocial personality disorder and HIV infection among intravenous drug abusers. *American Journal of Psychiatry, 150,* 53–58.

Carroll K.M., Gall, S. A. & Rounsaville, B. J. (1993). A comparison of alternate systems for diagnosing antisocial personality disorder in cocaine abusers. *Journal of Nervous and Mental Disease, 181,* 436–443.

Cottler, L. B., Compton, W. C., Price, R. K., Shillington, A. M., Claverie, D. J., Works, J. E., Mager, D. E., Sharma, D. & Miller, O. (1993). St. Louis' efforts to reduce the spread of AIDS. In J. A. Inciardi, F. Tims & B. Fletcher (Eds.), *Innovative approaches to the treatment of drug abuse, program models and strategies.* Westport, CT: Greenwood Press, 205–218.

Des Jarlais, D. C. & Friedman, S. R. (1988). Intravenous cocaine, crack, and HIV infection. *Journal of the American Medical Association, 259,* 1945–1946.

Dinwiddie, S. H. (1997). Characteristics of injection drug users derived from a large family study of alcoholism. *Comprehensive Psychiatry, 38,* 218–229.

Dinwiddie, S. H., Ben Abdallah, A., Compton, W. & Cottler, L. (1998). Subtypes of injecting drug users: A latent class analysis. Paper presented at the Thirty-fifth Annual Meeting of the Academy of Criminal Justice Sciences, Albuquerque, NM.

Dinwiddie, S. H., Cottler, L., Compton, W. & Ben Abdallah, A. (1996). Psychopathology and HIV risk behaviors among injection drug users in and out of treatment. *Drug and Alcohol Dependence 43,* 1–11.

Dinwiddie, S. H. & Daw, E. W. (1998). Temporal stability of antisocial personality disorder: Blind follow-up study at eight years. *Comprehensive Psychiatry, 39,* 28–34.

Dinwiddie, S. H. & Reich, T. (1993). Attribution of antisocial symptoms in coexistent antisocial personality disorder and substance abuse. *Comprehensive Psychiatry, 34,* 235–242.

Dinwiddie, S. H., Reich, T. & Cloninger, C. R. (1992a). Patterns of lifetime drug use among intravenous drug users. *Journal of Substance Abuse, 4,* 1–11.

Dinwiddie, S. H., Reich, T. & Cloninger, C. R. (1992b). Lifetime complications of drug use in intravenous drug users. *Journal of Substance Abuse, 4,* 13–18.

Dinwiddie, S. H., Reich, T. & Cloninger, C. R. (1992c). Prediction of intravenous drug use. *Comprehensive Psychiatry 33,* 173–179.

Dinwiddie, S. H., Reich, T. & Cloninger, C. R. (1992d) Psychiatric comorbidity and suicidality among intravenous drug users. *Journal of Clinical Psychiatry, 53,* 364–369.

Feighner, J. P., Robins, E., Guze, S. B., Woodruff, R. A., Winokur, G., and Munoz, R. (1972). Diagnostic criteria for use in psychiatric research. *Archives of General Psychiatry, 26,* 57–63.

Haverkos H. W. & Lange, W. R. (1990). Serious infections other than human immunodeficiency virus among intravenous drug abusers. *Journal of Infectious Disease, 161,* 894–902.

Kramer, T. H., Ottomanelli, G. & Bihari, B. (1992). IV versus non-IV drug use and selected patient variables related to AIDS risk behaviors. *International Journal of the Addictions, 27,* 477–485.

Lipsitz, J. D., Williams, J. B. W., Rabkin, J. G., Remien, R. H., Bradbury, M., el Sadr, W., Goetz, R., Sorrell, S. & Gorman, J. M. (1994). Psychopathology in male and female intravenous drug users with and without HIV infection. *American Journal of Psychiatry, 151,* 1662–1668.

Michelson, J. B., Robin, H. S. & Nozik, R. A. (1986). Nonocular manifestations of parental drug abuse. *Survey of Ophthalmology, 30,* 314–320.

O'Connor, P. G., Samet, J. H. & Stein, M. D. (1994). Management of hospitalized intravenous drug users: Role of the internist. *American Journal of Medicine, 96,* 551–558.

Regier D. A., Farmer, M. E., Rae, D. S., Locke, B. Z., Keith, S. J., Judd, L. L. & Goodwin, F. K. (1990). Comorbidity of mental disorders with alcohol and other drug use. *Journal of the American Medical Association, 264,* 2511–2518.

Schnittman, S. M. & Fauci, A. S. (1994). Human immunodeficiency virus and acquired immunodeficiency syndrome: An update. *Advances in Internal Medicine, 39,* 305–355.

Schuckit, M. A. (1985). The clinical implications of primary diagnostic groups among alcoholics. *Archives of General Psychiatry, 42,* 1043–1049.

Schuckit, M. A. & Hesselbrock, V. M.(1994). Alcohol dependence and anxiety disorders: What is the relationship? *American Journal of Psychiatry, 151,* 1723–1734.

Stein, M. D. (1990). Medical complications of intravenous drug use. *Journal of General Internal Medicine, 5,* 249–257.

Stenbacka, M., Allegeck, P., Brandt, L. & Romelsjo, A. (1992). Intravenous drug abuse in young men: Risk factors assessed in a longitudinal perspective. *Scandanavian Journal of Social Medicine, 20,* 94–101.

Strain, E. C., Brooner, R. K. & Bigelow, G. E. (1991). Clustering of multiple substance use and psychiatric diagnoses in opiate addicts. *Drug and Alcohol Dependence, 27,* 127–134.

Tomas, J. M., Vlahov, D. & Anthony, J. C. (1990). Association between intravenous drug use and early misbehavior. *Drug and Alcohol Dependence, 25,* 79–89.

Turner, C. F., Ku, L., Rogers, S. M., Lindberg, L. D., Pleck, J. H. & Sonenstein, F. L. (1998). Adolescent sexual behavior, drug use, and violence: Increased reporting with computer survey technology. *Science, 280,* 867–873.

Watkins, K.E., Metzger, D., Woody, G. & McLellan, A. T. (1992). High-risk sexual behaviors of intravenous drug users in- and out-of-treatment: Implications for the spread of HIV infection. *American Journal of Drug and Alcohol Abuse, 18,* 389-398.

Chapter 14

Childhood Sexual Abuse Among Female Addicts and Changes in Parenting Across Two Generations

by Robert J. Blatchley, Ph.D., Thomas E. Hanlon, Ph.D., David N. Nurco, D.S.W., and Kevin O'Grady, Ph.D.

Introduction 14-2
    CSA and Female Addicts 14-3
    Methodology and CSA Studies 14-3
The Present Analyses 14-3
    Background 14-4
    Findings of the Statistical Analyses 14-4
        Course of Addiction 14-4
        Family Dynamics 14-5
        Addicts' Self-Report of Parenting Behaviors 14-6
        Addicts' Home Atmosphere—Past and Present 14-7
        Addicts' Psychological Status 14-7
General Impressions 14-8
    CSA and Addiction Careers 14-10
    CSA and Parental Substance Use 14-10
    CSA and Adult Psychological Symptoms 14-10
CSA, Parenting, and Home Atmosphere 14-11
Treatment and Prevention Approaches 14-12

This research was supported by grant 5 RO1 DAO 6680 from the National Institute on Drug Abuse and was administered by the Friends Research Institute, Inc. The authors also wish to acknowledge the major contribution of the late Dr. Mitchell B. Balter to this study.

INTRODUCTION

Prior research confirms the fact that a significant number of narcotic addicts, in their retrospective reports, perceive their family of origin as having been dysfunctional in a number of ways (Baer & Corrado, 1974; Eldred et al., 1974; Kaufman, 1981). They report significant differences in parenting skills between their fathers and mothers when both are present in the home, but also report significant positive change in how they parent their own adolescent children (Emmelkamp & Heeres, 1988; Nurco et al., 1998). These findings regarding the addicts' reports of their own parenting skills are interesting in that they differ from those of other investigators (Bauman & Dougherty, 1983; Fiks et al., 1985; Singer, 1974) and are not generally consistent with Bauman and Levine's (1986) theory of an intergenerational cycle of addiction and family dysfunction. This discrepancy in findings leads us to question whether there are specific events, processes, or traumas in the family of origin that might be key determinants of how addicts function as parents when they undertake responsibility for raising their own children.

When analyzing the responses of 248 female narcotic addicts to a detailed interview schedule concerning parent-child relationships experienced in the family of origin and current relationships with their own adolescent children, we noted that 32 percent of these female respondents reported having been sexually abused at some time during their childhood or adolescent years. Of those addicts reporting abuse, 60 percent were victimized by a family member or relative and 40 percent by someone outside the family. Since childhood sexual abuse (CSA) is viewed as a traumatic and influential event in the lives of those victimized (Beitchman et al., 1992; Finkelhor & Browne, 1985; Saunders et al., 1992) and is often associated with later drug and alcohol abuse (Copeland & Hall, 1992; Edwall et al., 1989), we determined to examine CSA as it relates to both the family of origin and the current family status of our addict sample. In this examination we were particularly interested in factors related to parenting and home atmosphere across the three generations involved.

The consequences of CSA as they relate to adolescent and adult development and adjustment are reported to be varied and complex (Briere & Runtz, 1988; Browne & Finkelhor, 1986; Jumper, 1995). In their excellent article examining empirical research findings on child maltreatment, Becker et al. (1995) document CSA-related outcomes, including various degrees of depression, anxiety, low self-esteem, suicidal ideation, sexualized behavior, antisocial behavior, dissociation, and substance abuse. Becker and her colleagues point out, however, that several mediating factors, including perceived family environment as well as specific aspects of the sexual abuse itself, can influence the impact of CSA on the adjustment of adult survivors. In their summary of recommendations for increasing our understanding of the long-term effects of CSA, Becker et al. (1995) emphasize the need for longitudinal studies, as it appears highly probable that various forms of abuse can be transgenerational. Without intervention approaches that use empirical findings from key areas such as mental health, child development, and parenting skills training, it would be difficult to develop effective treatment and prevention approaches to CSA.

CSA and Female Addicts

The association between CSA, adolescent and adult substance abuse, and comorbid disorders is viewed as significant, both in terms of rate of occurrence and lifetime impact, especially among female addicts. In their study of CSA and psychiatric comorbidity in a sample of 180 women with varied histories of substance abuse, Jarvis and Copeland (1997) reviewed prior studies reporting rates of CSA as high as 74 percent for women in alcohol and drug treatment programs. Benward and Densen-Gerber (1975) found that 44 percent of 118 female addicts participating in their study reported some history of CSA. Jarvis and Copeland (1997) cite prior studies linking CSA with depression, anxiety, sleep disturbance, suicidality, dissociation, and post-traumatic stress disorder in substance abusers. Their own findings confirm the relationship of CSA to high levels of dissociation, suicidality, sexual dysfunction, self-harm, and eating disorders. These authors conclude that CSA results in a number of emotional, behavioral, and physical symptoms that demonstrate long-term impact on substance abusers and their treatment and that consequently, CSA must be addressed as a part of any drug treatment program or through other specialist care.

Methodology and CSA Studies

Before proceeding to a presentation of data from our own study of female narcotic addicts both with and without histories of CSA, it seems prudent to note some of the methodological pitfalls that characterize research related to CSA and substance abuse. Arellano (1996) examines many of these issues in her review of child maltreatment and substance abuse. She reviews the conflicting or inconsistent findings of a number of studies that address issues of whether the incidence of CSA is higher in populations with a history of alcohol or drug abuse, and whether CSA is a contributing factor in the addiction process. The author points out that methodological concerns related to sampling, measurement, gender, time frame, and a lack of a sound theoretical framework limit our ability to link childhood victimization to specific outcomes in adolescence and adulthood. In recommending changes, Arellano suggests the use of more representative samples; inclusion of appropriate control groups; the use of standardized measures; the implementation of prospective, longitudinal studies; the institution of controls for the effects of mediating and moderating variables; and the development of a strong theoretical model to guide future research efforts.

THE PRESENT ANALYSES

The data analyses presented and discussed in this chapter address several questions generated from the reports of our sample of 248 female narcotic addicts currently raising adolescent children. These questions are:

1. What is the incidence of CSA reported in this sample?
2. What is the relationship of CSA to the addiction careers of these women?
3. What is the relationship of CSA to parental substance abuse in the family of origin?

4. What is the relationship of CSA to parenting practices and home atmosphere in the family of origin?
5. What is the relationship of CSA to the addicts' current parenting practices with their adolescent children and current home atmosphere?
6. What is the relationship of CSA to the addicts' current psychological status?

While our addict database was not specifically assembled to address questions related to CSA, the overall study was concerned with the intergenerational aspects of substance abuse, parenting skills, and family deviance and dysfunction as they impact adolescent and adult development. Although parenting skills and parent-child bonding are often mentioned as important factors with respect to the effect of CSA in addict populations (Wind & Silvern, 1994), little empirical information is available, especially regarding findings that span the generations. For this reason we feel that the intergenerational data presented here are not only of statistical interest, but also theoretical interest despite methodological limitations that typify research on CSA.

Background

Early in the 1990s, the Social Research Unit of Friends Research Institute undertook a psychoeducational prevention program targeting the adolescent children of narcotic addicts enrolled in methadone maintenance programs in the Baltimore-Washington area. As a part of the development of the intervention for that study, several hundred adult addicts were administered an extensive interview questionnaire concerning a wide variety of self-reported treatment-relevant information on past and present aspects of their lives. One critical question concerned whether the addict parent had been sexually abused by someone older than themselves during their childhood or adolescent years. The current analyses, based on data from a sample of 248 female addicts in the initial survey, detail our findings contrasting the self-reports of those seventy-eight women (31.5 percent) who reported a history of CSA with those 170 women (68.5 percent) who reported no history of such abuse (NA) in childhood or adolescent years. From a demographic point of view, the two groups of women were comparable in age (CSA mean age 36.7; NA mean age 36.8), race (CSA 82 percent African-American, NA 81 percent African-American), and educational achievement (high school graduate or better CSA 42 percent, NA 48 percent).

Findings of the Statistical Analyses

The data presented in Tables 14.1 and 14.3–14.6 were analyzed through the use of one-way analyses of variance, testing differences in means between CSA and NA groups on individual variables using the F ratio test statistic (Cohen, 1977). The data in Table 14.2 were analyzed through the use of the nonparametric chi-square (χ^2) test (Siegel, 1956).

Course of Addiction. We first examined data related to the course of addiction and found both groups to be comparable in terms of their addiction careers, at least as defined by the variables of age at first addiction, total time incarcerated, and total time in drug treatment presented in Table 14.1.

Table 14.1
The Relation of Sexual Abuse to the Course of Addiction

Variable	CSA Subjects		NA Subjects		ANOVA	
	Mean	SD	Mean	SD	F	p
Age first addicted	22.76	6.19	23.49	5.43	0.90	.343
Months incarcerated	4.83	12.92	5.72	18.16	0.15	.697
Months in drug treatment	48.31	52.00	40.04	51.94	1.36	.245

Table 14.2
Parental Alcohol & Drug Abuse Problems in the Addicts' Family of Origin

Problem	Parent	CSA Subjects		NA Subjects		χ^2
		Yes	No	Yes	No	p
Alcohol abuse	Mother	32%	68%	16%	84%	.005
	Father	43%	57%	41%	59%	.839
Narcotic drugs	Mother	0%	100%	2%	98%	.178
	Father	6%	94%	6%	94%	.961

Family Dynamics. In terms of the study's focus on family factors, we were interested in the contrasts between the CSA and NA groups on variables related to parental substance abuse, parenting behavior, and other family dynamics retrospectively reported for the women's families of origin, and contemporaneously reported for the current families in which these female addicts were parenting their own adolescent children. We first examined parental substance abuse in the family of origin. Table 14.2 presents the reported abuse of alcohol or narcotic drugs by the addicts' mothers and fathers.

Parental abuse of alcohol in the family of origin was much more prevalent for all subjects than the use of narcotic drugs. The primary finding, however, is the significant difference in alcohol abuse by the mothers of our CSA subjects (32 percent) compared to the mothers of NA subjects (16 percent). This finding suggests that the abuse of alcohol by the mothers of some of our CSA subjects might have been a contributing factor in creating an environment or set of circumstances in which the abuse took place.

Continuing an examination of the characteristics of the addicts' families of origin, we find that in terms of the parenting behaviors reported, a number of significant differences between CSA and NA groups exist concerning both maternal and paternal behaviors. The following briefly describes the parental behaviors assessed within each dimension, or scale, and briefly addresses the findings related to that particular scale as summarized in Table 14.3. The first scale, Involvement, assessed whether the par-

Table 14.3
Relationship of Sexual Abuse to Retrospectively Reported Parenting Dimensions for Addicts' Family of Origin

Dimension	Parent	CSA Subjects Mean*	SD	NA Subjects Mean*	SD	ANOVA F	p
Involvement	Mothe	5.69	4.26	4.03	3.96	8.70	.004
	Father	7.41	4.11	5.49	3.89	8.59	.004
Attachment	Mother	6.53	4.82	4.36	4.86	10.49	.002
	Father	8.31	7.45	5.55	5.15	7.89	.006
Responsibility	Mother	7.90	6.75	6.18	6.57	3.45	.065
	Father	9.55	6.89	6.59	5.88	8.14	.005
Discipline	Mother	12.99	8.27	9.94	6.93	6.99	.009
	Father	12.11	7.08	9.44	6.41	4.84	.030
Punitive actions	Mother	8.29	4.21	7.38	4.29	1.87	.174
	Father	8.51	4.07	7.27	4.13	2.72	.101

* All scales are constructed so that a lower score reflects healthier, or more effective, parenting behavior.

ent generally knew what the child was doing, talked over problems with the child, paid attention to his or her views, was affectionate toward the child, and communicated clear expectations for the child's behavior. The second, Attachment, assessed the parent-child bond in terms of the child's desire to be like his or her parent and the child's feelings toward the parent regarding issues of trust, love, respect, pride, and approval. The Responsibility scale addressed the parent's ability to meet the child's basic physical, emotional, and other needs, including the ability to maintain a secure family environment. The ability of parents to provide constructive discipline and effective behavioral consequences was measured in the Discipline scale. This scale examined the parent's ability to monitor the child's behavior and to use rewards and punishments in a reasonable, effective, and consistent fashion. The scale Punitive Actions, on the other hand, measured the extent to which parents use shaming, threatening, and ignoring as well as harsh physical and verbal punishment, as methods in their disciplinary efforts. Examining Table 14.3, we see significant differences at the .05 level or better favoring the NA group over the CSA group on three of five variables (Involvement, Attachment, Discipline) for mother's parenting and on four of five variables (Involvement, Attachment, Responsibility, Discipline) for father's parenting in the family of origin when the addicts were ages 12–14.

Addicts' Self-Report of Parenting Behaviors. Table 14.4 presents the self-report data on the same parenting variables for our female addicts regarding their current practices with their adolescent children. These data reveal that those addict mothers

Table 14.4
Relationship of Sexual Abuse to Addicts' Self-Report of Current Parenting Behaviors With Their Adolescent Children

Dimension	CSA Subjects Mean*	SD	NA Subjects Mean*	SD	ANOVA F	p
Involvement	2.67	3.45	1.72	2.28	6.62	.011
Attachment	4.48	3.05	3.19	2.39	9.93	.003
Responsibility	4.94	3.37	4.56	3.15	0.74	.389
Discipline	7.75	4.46	6.79	3.84	2.91	.089
Punitive actions	5.37	2.88	5.88	2.94	1.12	.292

* All scales are constructed so that a lower score reflects healthier or more effective parenting behavior.

who were sexually abused continue to demonstrate the same relative impairment displayed by their parents on the variables of Involvement and Attachment when contrasted with the NA group. This finding is interesting in that these two variables reflect most strongly the interpersonal and emotional relationship existing between parent and child, suggesting that the abuse experienced by CSA victims influences parenting practices intergenerationally, and particularly impacts the interpersonal link between parent and child. Our CSA mothers were able to manage, discipline, and physically care for their children in an acceptable fashion, while the lack of an emotional bond carried over from one generation to the next.

Addicts' Home Atmosphere—Past and Present. In addition to their reporting on parenting behaviors, we asked our subjects to rate both their past and present home environment. These ratings are not made in reference to a specific parent or family member, but reflect the subject's report of the global atmosphere of the home. Ratings address whether the home atmosphere is experienced as being: relaxed or tense, peaceful or violent, happy or gloomy, organized or disorganized, stable or unstable, and physically orderly or physically disorderly. More or less, the general emotional and organizational tone of the home is expressed on this dimension. Examining the Home Atmosphere ratings presented in Table 14.5, we see significant differences between CSA and NA groups on ratings for both family of origin and current family. The data indicate that while both NA and CSA groups rate the atmosphere that their children live in as improved over that which they experienced as children, the ratings of the CSA versus NA group are significantly higher for both retrospective and current assessment of home atmosphere, indicating a less favorable atmosphere in both instances.

Addicts' Psychological Status. Finally, we examined the psychological status cur-

Table 14.5
Relationship of Sexual Abuse to Addicts' Ratings of Home Atmosphere for Family of Origin and Current Family

Dimension	CSA Subjects Mean*	SD	NA Subjects Mean*	SD	ANOVA F	p
Home atmosphere—Family of origin	4.38	3.40	2.67	2.84	25.79	.000
Home atmosphere—Current family	2.96	2.26	2.03	2.14	6.97	.010

* This scale is constructed so that a lower score reflects a healthier or more positive atmosphere.

rently reported by our subjects on a modified form of the Hopkins Symptom Check List (SCL 90) (Derogatis et al., 1974) generating nine symptom scores plus a measure of Global Severity. Analyses reveal a trend for CSA subjects to report more depressive features, including anhedonia, motor retardation, and sad or depressed mood as Table 14.6 reflects. Our CSA group reports significantly greater impairment in cognitive functioning, reflecting problems with memory, decision-making, concentration, and obsessive-compulsive features. Also, we see a significant difference favoring NA subjects on scores for Global Severity, indicating a better overall level of adjustment or emotional stability. Unfortunately, due to the fact that we adopted a modified form of the standard HSCL, we cannot comment on how the groups compare on the basis of adult female norms from either clinical or nonclinical reference groups.

GENERAL IMPRESSIONS

As mentioned earlier, it is important when discussing findings to identify the methodological weaknesses specific to our study. First, our assessment of abuse is limited to a single retrospective inquiry and cannot be adequately evaluated in terms of reliability or validity of response (Finkelhor, 1979). Second, our population is 100 percent narcotic drug-addicted, 100 percent female, 81 percent black, and 100 percent in active treatment, as well as having volunteered for the study—all factors that certainly affect the ability to generalize results. Third, our retrospective approach is subject to both failures of memory and possible deliberate distortion. The cross sectional methodology used leads to interesting associations but cannot establish definitive causative links between abuse, family factors, addiction, and current adjustment. Stronger methodologies, particularly designs that use prospective, longitudinal approaches, are needed to yield more reliable and valid data for future theory building.

Methodological weaknesses acknowledged, it seems fair to say that sexual abuse occurring in the child and adolescent years of our female addicts is closely related to dysfunction in the family of origin and continues to correlate with aspects of our subjects' adult functioning and adjustment, especially in regard to their ability to parent

Table 14.6
Relationship of Sexual Abuse to Addicts' Current SCL Symptom Scores

SCL Symptom Score	CSA Subjects Mean*	SD	NA Subjects Mean*	SD	ANOVA F	p
Somatic anxiety	0.59	0.56	0.52	0.49	1.18	.278
Decreased energy/interest	0.90	0.70	0.73	0.62	3.85	.051
Depressed mood	0.99	0.65	0.84	0.60	3.55	.061
Hostility	0.67	0.59	0.58	0.52	1.35	.247
Anxious mood	0.66	0.50	0.57	0.48	1.74	.188
Panic-Phobia	0.33	0.44	0.24	0.36	2.71	.101
Impaired cognitive function	0.70	0.56	0.49	0.51	8.23	.005
Sleep disturbance	0.83	0.91	0.65	0.80	2.32	.129
Appetite disturbance	0.63	0.67	0.59	0.59	0.22	.638
Global severity score	0.70	0.40	0.57	0.38	5.40	.021

* Higher scores reflect an increased level of self-reported symptomatology.

effectively and to interact in a positive emotional way with their own adolescent children. Our findings are consistent with theory relating childhood sexual victimization to substance abuse, depressive disorders, posttraumatic stress, and reactions of dissociation (Elliott & Briere, 1992; Mullen et al., 1993; Peters, 1988; Pribor & Dinwiddie, 1992). Relationships among these many factors are complex because of the impact of their interaction with other life influences operating over several developmental stages.

Obviously, female addicts who were sexually abused as children and were not subsequently treated need to deal with the consequences of this trauma either as a part of their substance abuse treatment program or in some other therapeutic setting (Briere, 1989; Miller, 1990; Lynskey & Fergusson, 1997). Certainly, a history of CSA and substance abuse needs to be examined in relationship to therapeutic issues of relapse, suicidality, and generally higher rates of psychological distress and personality disorder. It is clear that the findings presented here have implications not only for the addicts but also for their children (Egeland et al., 1987; Mallouh, 1996). If patterns of noninvolvement, neglect, and weak attachment persist from one generation to the next in the context of the parent-child relationship (Miller et al., 1997; Sheridan, 1995), the specter of the children of our sexually abused addicts following in their parents footsteps in some fashion is all too easily imaginable.

CSA and Addiction Careers

Because we began with a population in which all subjects had a history of addiction to narcotics, we are unable to bring any light to bear on the issue of how CSA is related to an initiation into or continuation of substance abuse per se. We can state that within the sample of female addicts studied, there was no relationship between CSA and specific quantifiable aspects of their addiction careers such as age at first addiction, total time in drug treatment, or total time incarcerated. The connection between CSA and the progress of drug use once initiated is an interesting but neglected area of inquiry. Blood and Cornwall (1996) found that adolescents reporting sexual abuse were also more seriously involved with various substances at treatment onset. Both Young (1990) and Copeland and Hall (1992) suggest that CSA can be a factor in relapse during the course of drug and alcohol treatment.

While most studies have focused on CSA as a predictor of substance use or abuse, particularly in the teenage years (Dembo et al., 1987), greater effort needs to be expended on CSA's impact on the progress of substance use, once initiated, with special emphasis on those CSA victims who progress beyond youthful experimentation to adult addiction careers. The implications of such information for both treatment and prevention are clear.

CSA and Parental Substance Use

A number of studies have demonstrated a relationship between an individual's drug abuse and alcohol abuse by one or both parents of drug users. Kaufman (1981) and Stanton and Todd (1982) report that an alcoholic father is present in 50 percent of the families of male drug users. Binion (1980) found that alcohol abuse was reported in 60 percent of the families of female heroin addicts, while Nurco et al. (1998) found that 47 percent of the addicts in a recent study identified parental alcohol abuse as a causal factor in family problems. Jarvis and Copeland (1997) found significant paternal substance abuse in drug- and alcohol-involved female CSA survivors. In a study of women with a history of both CSA and alcohol dependence, Carson (1988) found that this group reported more parental drinking problems than women with either CSA or alcohol dependence alone. The finding of this study reporting maternal alcohol abuse in the CSA group at twice the rate of nonabused addicts deserves further investigation in regard to victims' short- and long-term adjustments. Carson (1988) suggests that the effects of alcohol abuse in the family of origin could contribute to the risk of CSA directly through disinhibitory effects and indirectly through family dysfunction and reduced protection and support of the child.

CSA and Adult Psychological Symptoms

There is a body of literature (Copeland & Hall, 1992; Jarvis & Copeland, 1997) concerned with psychiatric comorbidity in female substance abusers who have been subjected to CSA. Our findings, derived from self-reports using our own modification of the HSCL, indicate that our CSA subjects report significantly greater symptomatology on scales measuring Impaired Cognitive Function and Global Severity. Also evidenced was a statistical trend for our CSA subjects to report higher levels of

Depressed Mood as well as greater presence of Decreased Energy and Interest. The issue of depression in female CSA survivors who have a history of substance abuse is often difficult to evaluate because of the impact of both the use of, and withdrawal from, various substances. The difference between primary and secondary depression needs to be clarified, especially in reference to the population of female substance abusers.

The finding regarding significant differences between CSA and NA groups on Impaired Cognitive Function is interesting from the point of view that this scale's items relate to problems of memory, concentration, and decision-making, which seem to have some overlap with symptoms of dissociation found in the CSA groups examined by Jarvis and Copeland (1997). A possible hypothesis worthy of further investigation concerns the exact cognitive mechanisms which CSA survivors use to cope with the sequela of this trauma as adults. Both Taylor (1983) and Draucker (1995) use conceptual models emphasizing cognitive adaptation, or mediation, as a primary means of coping with the trauma of CSA and thus influencing subsequent adult adjustment. To the degree that this trauma is unresolved, various symptoms or disorders can exist far into adult life. As an example, the average age of our female addicts was 37, indicating that the psychological impact associated with CSA can operate two to three decades after the occurrence of the abuse. Considering this prolonged time frame, even the statistical trends relating CSA to psychiatric symptoms in the present instance are quite remarkable.

CSA, PARENTING, AND HOME ATMOSPHERE

While recognizing that CSA differs from other forms of child maltreatment, Wolfe (1991) sees family support programs as one method of preventing abuse and addressing dysfunctional parent-child relationships. Wolfe and colleagues view dysfunctional parenting as formed in part by learning experiences acquired in childhood years, which may predispose future abusive parental behavior and thus lead to the intergenerational transmission of abuse. We believe that the findings of our study regarding parenting behaviors give strong support to this concept of intergenerational transmission. In particular, our findings demonstrate that CSA is related to deficits in parental involvement and attachment not only in the female addicts' family of origin but also in their own efforts to raise their teenage children. One interpretation of these findings is that the impairment of parental support and concern (involvement) and of the parent-child emotional bond (i.e. attachment) in the family of origin creates a deficit in the functioning of our addicts, who although reported as improved in their own parenting are still left lacking in parental functioning relative to those addict mothers who did not endure CSA.

The same phenomenon is reflected in ratings of home atmosphere. As Becker et al. (1995), Burnam et al. (1988), and Nash et al. (1993) emphasize, negative climate and disorder within the family can increase the occurrence and influence the outcome of CSA. The present data demonstrates that while improvement is reflected in the atmosphere of their current homes, those addicts who experienced CSA are providing a significantly poorer home atmosphere for their children than that provided by those addicts who were not sexually abused. In the process of evaluating the implications of these findings, we must remember that the CSA effects noted were obtained from a sample of female addicts who had all been in methadone treatment and had, therefore, confronted their addiction and related behaviors to varying degrees. One can only assume that addicts who avoid or decline treatment may remain intergenerationally impaired in their parenting and household functioning to an equal, or perhaps even greater, degree than were their parents (Kumpfer, 1987; Sowder & Burt, 1980).

While it is tempting to speculate further on the meaning of findings related to CSA and addiction, we are disinclined to do so because of the methodological limitations discussed earlier. Though there seems to be little doubt that CSA presents formidable challenges to both treatment and prevention efforts with addicts and their families, we need to develop more empirically based knowledge in this important area. As we reported in our paper on family experiences of addicts (Nurco et al., 1998), the final common pathway by which many dysfunctional and/or deviant family characteristics impact and influence children is through the parent-child relationship. Both Sampson and Laub (1993) and Hirschi (1983) reinforce this view and strongly emphasize the influence of parenting deficiencies as determinants in the development of children's current and future dysfunction.

TREATMENT AND PREVENTION APPROACHES

In examining the impact of CSA, we discern a somewhat circular chain of events whereby an impaired parent-child relationship (neglect, lack of bonding or attachment) sets the stage for someone, either within or outside of the family structure, to target the child for sexual abuse. The subsequent impact of that abuse, including whether or not it is revealed, acknowledged, or treated in some way, also appears to be influenced by positive or negative characteristics of both the parent-child dynamics and family atmosphere. As Miller (1990) points out in her article on alcohol, drugs, and family violence:

> Alcohol abuse and sexual abuse are interrelated and the intergenerational aspects of these phenomena cannot be ignored. Parental alcoholism may set the stage for sexual abuse through both environmental and psychological vulnerabilities, while, at the same time, women with sexual abuse experiences appear to be more at risk for the development of alcohol problems. This then sets the stage for the sexual abuse experiences of their own children (a third generation). Further analyses are underway . . . to shape future research about the relationships between childhood sexual abuse and the development of drug abuse problems in women. (p. 199)

In order to break what appears to be an intergenerational cycle of abuse, a number of things have to happen. First, parents must be taught that while discipline and structure are desirable, their involvement with and attachment to their children may well be the strongest protective factor operating to insure the child's safety and healthy development. Second, the current trend to aggressively report, investigate and intervene both legally and therapeutically has to continue to develop. Interventions should ideally center not only on the child, but also on parents and on the family climate, or atmosphere, as it relates to both vulnerability and protective factors. Third, if CSA is not revealed until the victim is an adult, efforts should be made to provide adjunct treatment to any alcohol or drug treatment, with emphasis placed on parenting skills for current and prospective parents. Skills development can focus on a broad range of family issues, but it needs to strongly emphasize the building of positive emotional bonds between parent and child and a continuing commitment on the part of the parent to be closely and consistently involved with the developmental tasks and decisions of their children.

Fostering recognition of the effects of CSA in addicted females and attempting to mitigate these effects on them and their children appears to be a promising strategy for interrupting the intergenerational transmission of both substance abuse and child abuse. From the research literature, we know that in many families these forms of deviance co-occur and thus challenge both prevention and treatment efforts. Hopefully, future prospective research, grounded in sound methodology and diverse sampling, will lead us to effective and efficient interventions directed toward individuals and families dually impacted by CSA and drug or alcohol abuse.

References

Arellano, C. M. (1996). Child maltreatment and substance use: A review of the literature. *Substance Use and Misuse, 31,* 927–935.

Baer, D. & Corrado, J. J. (1974). Heroin addicts' relationships with parents during childhood and early adolescent years. *Journal of Genetic Psychology, 124,* 99–103.

Bauman, P. S. & Dougherty, F. E. (1983). Drug-addicted mothers' parenting and their children's development. *International Journal of the Addictions, 18,* 291–302.

Bauman, P. & Levine, S. A. (1986). The development of children of drug addicts. *International Journal of the Addictions, 21,* 849–863.

Becker, J., Alpert, J. L., BigFoot, D. S., Bonner, B. L., Geddie, L. F., Henggeler, S. W., Kaufman, K. L. & Walker, C. E. (1995). Empirical research on child abuse treatment: Report by the Child Abuse and Neglect Treatment Working Group, APA. *Journal of Clinical Child Psychology, 24,* 23–26.

Beitchman, J. H., Zucker, K. J., Hood, J. E., daCosta, G. A., Akman, D. & Cassavia, E. (1992). A review of the long-term effects of child sexual abuse. *Child Abuse and Neglect, 16,* 101–118.

Benward, J. & Densen-Gerber, J. (1975). Incest as a causative factor in anti-social behavior: An exploratory study. *Contemporary Drug Problems, 4,* 32–55.

Binion, V. J. (1980). A descriptive comparison of the families of origin of women heroin users and abusers. In *Addicted women: Family dynamics, self-perceptions and support systems.* DHEW Publication No. ADM 80-762, National Institute on Drug Abuse, Rockville, MD.

Blood, L. & Cornwall, A. (1996). Childhood sexual victimization as a factor in the treatment of substance abusing adolescents. *Substance Use and Misuse, 31,* 1015–1039.

Briere, J. (1989). *Therapy for adults molested as children: Beyond survival.* New York: Springer.

Briere, J. & Runtz, M. (1988). Symptomatology associated with childhood sexual victimization in a non-clinical adult sample. *Child Abuse and Neglect, 12,* 51–59.

Browne, A. & Finkelhor, D. (1986). Impact of child sexual abuse: A review of the research. *Psychological Bulletin, 99,* 66–77.

Burnam, M. A., Stein, J. A., Golding, J. M., Siegel, J. M., Sorenson, S. B., Forsythe, A. B. & Telles, C. A. (1988). Sexual assault and mental disorders in a community population. *Journal of Consulting Clinical Psychology, 56,* 843–850.

Carson, D. K., Council, J. R. & Volk, M. A. (1988). Temperament, adjustment, and alcoholism in adult female incest victims. *Violence Victims, 3,* 205–216.

Cohen, J. (1977). *Statistical power analysis for the behavioral sciences.* New York: Academic Press.

Copeland, J. & Hall, W. (1992). A comparison of women seeking drug and alcohol treatment in a specialist women's and two traditional mixed-sex treatment services. *British Journal of Addiction, 87,* 65–74.

Dembo, R., Dertke, M., LaVoie, L., Borders, S., Washburn, M. & Schmeidler, J. (1987). Physical abuse, sexual victimization and illicit drug use: A structural analysis among high risk adolescents. *Journal of Adolescence, 10,* 13–33.

Derogatis, L. R., Lipman, R. S., Rickels, K., Uhlenhuth, E. H. & Covi, L. (1974). The Hopkins Symptom Checklist (HSCL): A measure of primary symptom dimensions. In P. Pichot (Ed.), *Psychological measurements in psychopharmacology.* Basel, Switzerland: Karger.

Draucker, C. B. (1995). A coping model for adult survivors of childhood sexual abuse. *Journal of Interpersonal Violence, 10,* 159–175.

Edwall, G. E., Hoffman, N. G. & Harrison, P. A. (1989). Psychological correlates of sexual abuse in adolescent girls in chemical dependency treatment. *Adolescence, 26,* 279–288.

Egeland, B., Jacobvitz, D. & Papatola, K. (1987). Intergenerational continuity of abuse. In R. J. Gelles & J. B. Lancaster (Eds.), *Child abuse and neglect: Biosocial dimensions.* New York: Aldine de Gruyter.

Eldred, C., Brown, B. & Mahabir, C. (1974). Heroin addict clients' description of their families of origin. *International Journal of the Addictions, 9,* 315–320.

Elliott, D. E. & Briere, J. (1992). Sexual abuse trauma among professional women: Validating the Trauma Symptom Checklist (TSC-40). *Child Abuse and Neglect, 16,* 391–398.

Emmelkamp, P. & Heeres, H. (1988). Drug addiction and parental rearing style: A controlled study. *International Journal of the Addictions, 23,* 207–216.

Fiks, K. B., Johnson, H. L. & Rosen, T. S. (1985). Methadone-maintained mothers: Three year follow-up of parental functioning. *International Journal of the Addictions, 20,* 651–660.

Finkelhor, D. (1979). *Sexually victimized children.* New York: The Free Press.

Finkelhor, D. & Browne, A. (1985). The traumatic impact of child sexual abuse: A conceptualization. *American Journal of Orthopsychiatry, 55,* 530–541.

Hirschi, T. (1983). Crime and the family. In James Q. Wilson (Ed.), *Crime and public policy.* San Francisco: Institute for Contemporary Studies.

Jarvis, T. J. & Copeland, J. (1997). Child sexual abuse as a predictor of psychiatric co-morbidity and its implications for drug and alcohol treatment. *Drug and Alcohol Dependence, 49,* 61–69.

Jumper, S. A. (1995). A meta-analysis of the relationship of child sexual abuse to adult psychological adjustment. *Child Abuse and Neglect, 19,* 715–728.

Kaufman, E. (1981). Family structures of narcotic addicts. *International Journal of the Addictions, 16,* 93–112.

Kumpfer, K. (1987). Special populations: Etiology and prevention of vulnerability to chemical dependency in children of substance abusers. In B. S. Brown & A. R. Mills (Eds.), *Youth at risk for substance abuse.* Washington, DC: U.S. Government Printing Office.

Lynskey, M. T. & Fergusson, D. M. (1997). Factors protecting against the development of adjustment difficulties in young adults exposed to childhood sexual abuse. *Child Abuse and Neglect, 21,* 1177–1190.

Mallouh, C. (1996). The effects of dual diagnosis on pregnancy and parenting. *Journal of Psychoactive Drugs, 28,* 367–380.

Miller, B. A. (1990). The interrelationships between alcohol and drugs and family violence. In *Drugs and violence: Causes, correlates, and consequences.* Research Monograph No. 103. Rockville, MD: National Institute on Drug Abuse.

Miller, L., Kramer, R., Warner, V., Wickramaratne, P. & Weissman, M. (1997). Intergenerational transmission of parental bonding among women. *Journal of the American Academy of Child and Adolescent Psychiatry, 36,* 1134–1139.

Mullen, P. E., Martin, J. L., Anderson, J. C., Romans, S. E. & Herbison, P. G. (1993). Childhood sexual abuse and mental health in adult life. *British Journal of Psychiatry, 163,* 721–732.

Nash, M. R., Hulsey, T. L., Sexton, M. D., Harralson, T. L. & Lambert, W. (1993). Perceived family environment, psychopathology, and dissociation. *Journal of Consulting and Clinical Psychology, 61,* 276–283.

Nurco, D. N., Blatchley, R. J., Hanlon, T. E., O'Grady, K. E. & McCarren, M. (1998). The family experiences of narcotic addicts and their subsequent parenting practices. *American Journal of Drug and Alcohol Abuse, 24,* 37–59.

Peters, S. D. (1988). Child sexual abuse and later psychological problems. In G. E. Wyatt & G. J. Powell (Eds.), *Lasting effects of child sexual abuse.* Newbury Park, CA: Sage, 101–117.

Pribor, E. F. & Dinwiddie, S. H. (1992). Psychiatric correlates of incest in childhood. *American Journal of Psychiatry, 149,* 52–56.

Sampson, R. J. & Laub, J. H. (1993). *Crime in the making: Pathways and turning points through life.* Cambridge, MA: Harvard University Press.

Saunders, B. E., Villeponteaux, L. A., Lipovsky, J. A., Kilpatrick, D. G. & Veronen, L. J. (1992). Child sexual assault as a risk factor for mental disorders among women: A community survey. *Journal of Interpersonal Violence, 7,* 189–204.

Sheridan, M. J. (1995). A proposed intergenerational model of substance abuse, family functioning, and abuse/neglect. *Child Abuse and Neglect, 19,* 519–530.

Siegel, S. (1956). *Nonparametric statistics for the behavioral sciences.* New York: McGraw Hill.

Singer, A. (1974). Mothering practices and heroin addiction. *American Journal of Nursing, 74,* 77–82.

Sowder, B. J. & Burt, M. R. (1980). *Children of heroin addicts: An assessment of health, learning, behavioral, and adjustment problems.* Praeger studies in issues and research in substance abuse. New York: Praeger.

Stanton, M. D. & Todd, T. C. (1982). *The family therapy of drug abuse and addiction.* New York: Guilford Press.

Taylor, S. E. (1983). Adjustment to threatening events: A theory of cognitive adaption. *American Psychologist, 38,* 1161–1173.

Wind, T. W. & Silvern, L. (1994). Parenting and family stress as mediators of the long-term effects of child abuse. *Child Abuse and Neglect, 18,* 439–453.

Wolfe, D. A. (1991). Preventing physical and emotional abuse of children. New York: Guilford Press.

Young, E. B. (1990). The role of incest issues in relapse. *Journal of Psychoctive Drugs, 22,* 249–258.

Chapter 15

Serial Killers—Victims of Compulsion or Masters of Control?

by Carol Ferreira, Ph.D., M.S.N., A.R.N.P., C.S.

Introduction	15-1
Brief Overview of Current Conceptual Models of Serial Killing	15-2
The Question of Sanity and Serial Killing	15-4
A Legal Definition of Insanity	15-5
Diagnostic Classifications of Mental Disease	15-5
Can Serial Killers Truly Be Sane?	15-7
Etiology of Necrophilia	15-7
The Sanity Consensus	15-8
The Antisocial and Narcissistic Personality Disorders	15-8
Psychological and Circumstantial Traits	15-9
Malignant Narcissism	15-10
Are Serial Killers "Driven" to Act?	15-11
Obsessive-Compulsive Disorder	15-11
Obsessive-Compulsive Personality Disorder	15-12
Alienation and Isolation	15-13
Do We Really Believe that Serial Killers Are Sane and Acting Volitionally?	15-14
Free Will and Responsibility	15-14
Violence—Disease or Man's Dark Side?	15-15
Conclusion	15-15
Editor's Note	15-16

INTRODUCTION

In the summer of 1991, Jeffrey Dahmer's name became familiar to television viewers, who often watched the evening news in shock and disbelief. Americans across the country were asking, "How could any sane human being commit such acts of cruelty and degradation?" As accounts of his having tortured and murdered at least fifteen boys and men were made public, families in their sitting rooms, people on the street, law enforcement officers in the precincts, mental health professionals in their clinics, and lawyers in the courtroom began debating the sanity of the man who committed these heinous acts. In 1998, long after the courtroom decisions were rendered and after Jeffrey Dahmer himself was murdered, the debates still echo; and in an attitude of mixed repulsion, curiosity and fear, people still ponder the question "How could any human being in his right mind do those horrible things to another human being?"

This chapter will explore issues and perhaps raise more questions than answers regarding the motivating factors that impact human beings who become members of that infamous group we call "serial killers." Discussion will begin with a brief overview of serial killing and Eric Hickey's (1991) conceptual model, the Trauma-Control Model for Serial Murder. The discussion will then address the following issues:

1. Are serial killers insane?
2. Can necrophiles and serial murderers truly be sane?
3. What are antisocial, narcissistic, and malignant narcissistic personality disorders?
4. Are serial killers *driven* to act?
5. Do we really believe that serial killers are sane and acting volitionally?

BRIEF OVERVIEW OF CURRENT CONCEPTUAL MODELS OF SERIAL KILLING

The definitions of serial murder are almost as numerous as the myths and fears surrounding the topic. The phenomenon of serial killing had been frequently referenced as "lust murder" until the early 1980s, when the term "serial murder" came into vogue (Egger, 1998). As pointed out by Drukteinis (1992), Jeffrey Dahmer's actions typify the behaviors of serial killers, whose "similar patterns of sexual sadism, killing and necrophilia have been formally studied for more than 100 years" (p. 532).

For purposes of this discussion, serial murder of a sexual nature will be examined. As Ressler et al. (1988) have reported, serial murder of a sexual nature usually evidences one or more of the following characteristics:

- Clothing is removed or symbolically placed;
- The body is sexually exposed or positioned;
- Body cavities are penetrated with foreign objects; or
- Rape, a substitutive sexual act, or sexual fantasy is enacted.

According to FBI criteria, a serial murderer is someone who commits three or more murders with a cool-down period in between each of the killings (Ressler et al., 1988). Victims and killers are generally unknown to each other, with victims being selected randomly (Ressler et al., 1988). In the majority of cases, serial murders are committed by white males, age 25 to 35, against white females, although males are also often victims. Victims and offenders come from all socioeconomic strata (Hickey, 1997). Although difficult to quantify, estimates for the number of suspected serial killers at large vary from thirty to one-hundred, with most offenders killing thirteen or fewer persons (Holmes & DeBurger, 1990). Typically, the actions of serial killers are seen as well-orchestrated, have some ritualistic component, and most often are focused on attaining dominance, power, and control over victims (Drukteinis, 1992). Dominance over the victim, rather than greed or material gain, has traditionally been thought of as the primary motivating factor (Egger, 1998).

In the Trauma-Control Model for Serial Murder, Hickey (1991) proposes that the desire for power and control over others is the driving force underlying serial murder. Serial murder is conceptualized as the outcome of interactions between a number of factors. Hickey (1991) identified the following as predisposing factors and facilitators that may or may not influence the serial killing process:

- *Trauma events.* These are destabilizing events, such as loss of a parent or sexual abuse, that may occur in the killer's life. Hickey espoused that an individual's inability to cope effectively with such traumatizations may become the "triggering" mechanism that yields feelings of rejection, anxiety, confusion, or distrust in the killer's life. *Rejection* is the most often cited "traumatic event" in interviews with serial killers.

- *Dissociation.* This refers to the psychological "splitting off" or blocking of painful memories or the pain of trauma. This unconscious mechanism for containing the anxiety of events allows the person to temporarily suppress the hurt, fear, anger, or humiliation of the traumatic event(s).

- *Predispositional factors.* These factors include genetic, biological, and psychosocial factors that may influence behavior. History of head injury and familial alcoholism would be examples.

- *Low self-esteem.* As a result of coping poorly with the traumatizations, it is proposed that serial killers may develop feelings of inadequacy, self-doubt, and worthlessness.

- *Facilitators.* These factors include alcohol, drugs, pornography, and material on the occult. (Although it is surmised that facilitators may eventually foster the killing urge, no direct cause and effect relationship between facilitators such as pornography and serial killing is implied).

- *Fantasies.* Many believe that this is the most critical factor in serial murder (Hickey, 1991). As reported by Ressler and colleagues (1988), fantasy is the underlying basis for serial murder. Daydreams and fantasies of inflicting bodily harm to gain total control of victims through sadistic, violent, sexual actions are repetitive and become increasingly violent. The offender practices and refines his killing behavior through fantasy until it becomes "second nature." It is hypothesized that during the actual attack, the offender may reexperience fantasies of the original childhood trauma. Unfortunately fantasies, by their very nature, can never be fully achieved and the underlying anger and lack of self-esteem cannot be remediated by the fantasies of power and domination. Subsequently, as the negative feelings resurface after the murder, the killer again engages in fantasy, which becomes more sadistic, and the killings become repetitive (Hickey, 1997).

The above model for serial murder focuses on the intrinsic, primarily psychological factors that motivate serial killers. In a similar approach, Hale (1994) writes about humiliation being perceived by the offender as an attack on personal worth, a "challenge" the offender feels must be answered. Hale contends that early embarrassment and humiliation become internalized motives for the killings. This sense of humiliation is intensified by the fact that the offender felt powerless in controlling events in his earlier life. Hale asserts that this sense of powerlessness at certain points in life is exacerbated by arrested psychological development, which limits the offender's ability to effectively integrate mastery and social comparison. Consequently, the offender feels the need to correct the humiliation, or "set things right." Because humiliation occurs only in the presence of others, the offender feels an audience is needed to undo the humiliation. Unfortunately, the audience becomes the victim, who is eventually killed. Thus, the killings continue.

Hale (1993) also purports that serial killers act out of the belief that they are behaving logically in response to perceived wrongs. Serial killers, like all people, are motivated to seek approval from parents and others. For various reasons, including maternal deprivation and disrupted bonding with parents, it is postulated that serial killers experience and internalize feelings of frustration when they are blocked from receiving affection, approval, and socialization. This frustration is perceived as humiliation by the killer. If it were possible, the serial killer would probably release the aggression directly upon the person who originally humiliated him. But the killer perceives the humiliator as being "in control" or more powerful than he himself. The emotion of aggression that results from this humiliation is thwarted and eventually becomes displaced onto less threatening persons. In effect, the killer's victims are scapegoats for the person who initially thwarted the killer's drive for affection, approval, and attachment. Hale conceptualizes this process of humiliation, aggression, and displacement within a social learning context and hypothesizes that just as serial killing is a learned response, so can it be "unlearned." As Hale notes, concern has been raised about the application of learning theory to the treatment of serial killers, since "spontaneous recovery" of the killing behavior might be anticipated.

The views discussed thus far serve to define serial killing and illustrate current sociological and psychological approaches to conceptualization of the motivation for serial killing. Biological theories to explain serial killing have been largely neglected; however, several recent findings from studies on psychopaths and repetitively violent offenders have direct import to an understanding of serial murderers. Before exploring further along this line of reasoning, the issues of sanity and insanity in serial killing will be addressed.

THE QUESTION OF SANITY AND SERIAL KILLING

A full discussion of the legalities of criminal responsibility and the insanity defense are beyond the scope of this work. As reported by Palermo and Knudten (1994), the court system has held varying views about intentionality and awareness of the consequences as factors with an impact on responsibility for criminal actions. Although the insanity plea is entered rarely, this issue receives considerable attention from the public, especially when serial killing is discussed (Palermo & Knudten, 1994).

A Legal Definition of Insanity

It should be remembered that "insanity" is a legal term, defined by lawmakers and used to determine criminal responsibility for actions. Although mental health clinicians are often embroiled in the legal controversies surrounding the disposition of violent offenders as "mad or bad," their role is fundamentally to assess and treat mental disorders. While mental illness is now widely known to be the manifestation of both biological and social interactive conditions, within the criminal justice system, mental illness is still viewed as a construct (Nicholi, 1988). This assumption infers that mental illness and disease are defined more by social factors and less by concrete fact. As Nicholi (1988) expressed:

> One basic premise of psychiatry is that there exist feelings, thoughts, and behaviors that are regarded as psychopathological, that is, abnormal: they are deviations from some norm and distressing to the individual and to those around him. Moreover, these behaviors, including the accompanying subjective experience, are profoundly maladaptive for the individual in relationship to his family and social group.
>
> Not all forms of social deviance constitute psychopathology. Thus, for example, under unusual circumstances crime and delinquency are not considered medical problems but social problems that fall within the province of the criminal justice system. Some individuals, however, are both "mad" and "bad" and the conditions under which society is willing to ameliorate its judgment of culpability in view of psychiatric diagnosis is often controversial, particularly when the insanity defense is used for murder and other capital crimes. (p. 74)

Diagnostic Classifications of Mental Disease

Mental health clinicians assess individuals to ascertain whether the person's psychological problems constitute a particular psychiatric disorder (Comer, 1996). Diagnosis is based on a classification system developed by the American Psychiatric Association, *The Diagnostic and Statistical Manual for Mental Disorders* (DSM-IV), which classifies approximately 300 mental disorders. Diseases are divided into two major diagnostic categories, Axis I and Axis II. Diseases in Axis I are clinical syndromes that typically cause more pronounced impairment, such as anxiety, psychosis, and mood disorders. Psychosis, a severe form of mental illness, is an Axis I diagnosis that describes the state in which a person loses touch with reality. The psychotic state is often marked by hallucinations, delusions, and illogical thinking.

Axis II disorders include mental retardation and personality disorders. Personality disorders are more long-standing and less flexible patterns of inner experience and overt behavior that deviate from cultural norms and result in distress and impairment in the person's life (Comer, 1996). Antisocial personality disorder, borderline personality disorder, and narcissistic personality disorder are among the Axis II diagnoses. Persons suffering from only Axis II disorders do not generally experience a break with reality. Persons suffering from antisocial personality disorder (APD), for example, are sometimes referred to as sociopathic or psychopathic. As stated by Egger (1998), people suffering from APD are not considered mentally ill or out of touch with reality, but "unable to experience love or empathy, due to family rejection and needs frustration . . . They lack a sense of moral guilt and are not able to postpone drives for immediate gratification" (p. 7). More recent studies, however, demonstrably show that psychopathy is also associated with various physiologic, biochemical, and genetic markers reflective of central nervous system dysfunction. These findings highlight the role of both nature and nurture in the development of antisocial behaviors. They also bring into question ways in which our criminal justice system responds to all offenders as moral agents rather than as individuals with underlying pathologies.

In an extensive review of serial killers, the editors of Time Life books (1992) reported that only 10 percent of the serial killer population was diagnosed as psychotic. The remaining 90 percent were deemed to be suffering from personality disorders, namely APD. Thus, only one in ten of all serial killers was diagnosed as suffering from a severe form of mental illness that signified a loss of contact with the real world, while the overwhelming majority of serial murderers were considered most likely psychopathic. Both types of disorders are associated with different biological and genetic underpinnings.

The report rendered by one of the expert forensic psychiatrists in the Dahmer case serves to illustrate these concepts. Stating that in his opinion, as a court-appointed nonpartisan expert, Dahmer was legally sane at the time of the offenses, Dr. Palermo wrote:

> [T]o a reasonable degree of medical certainty, this serial killer would best be classified as [having] (1) Personality Disorder Not Otherwise Specified, severe in type, with antisocial, obsessive-compulsive, sadistic, fetishistic, borderline and necrophilic features, and (2) Alcohol Dependence . . . He was thought to be suffering from serious emotional conflicts deeply embedded in his personality structure and not amenable to commonly accepted psychotherapeutic or pharmacological intervention. (Palermo & Knudten, 1994, p. 12)

Dahmer's defense attorney submitted his case to the jury by describing Dahmer as "an insane steamrolling killing machine, whose necrophilia had driven him to slay his victims, and who could not stop killing because of a sickness he discovered, not chose . . . He had to do what he did because he could not stop it" (Drukteinis, 1992, p. 533). Although Dahmer pled not guilty by reason of insanity, the jury found him legally sane.

Despite the court decision regarding his sanity, some nagging questions linger in regard to the *Dahmer* decision. One might ask the following questions: How can any human being in his or her right mind cannibalize another human being? Can necrophilia, the act of having sexual relations with a corpse, be the action of a sane person? Moreover, why is it so difficult for human beings to accept that the brutality and inhumane actions of the Dahmers of the world can be committed by sane people?

Most likely, the classification process employed in the criminal justice system is inadequate and inaccurate.

CAN SERIAL KILLERS TRULY BE SANE?

The Dahmer case serves to illustrate the issues often debated regarding sanity and volition in serial murder. As noted above, Dahmer's defense attorney depicted him as "an insane killing machine whose necrophilia had driven him to slay his victims." As the defense contended, Dahmer was incapable of refraining from his killing behaviors. According to the DSM-IV criteria, necrophilia is listed on Axis I as a "paraphilia, not otherwise specified" within the major category of Sexual and Gender Identity Disorders. Specifically, necrophilia refers to sexual attraction to corpses. Paraphilias are marked by repetitive or preferred sexual fantasies or behaviors involving nonhuman objects, the suffering or degradation of oneself or one's partner, children, or nonconsenting adults. This pattern must occur for a minimum of six months to meet the diagnostic criteria of the DSM-IV.

Etiology of Necrophilia

The etiology of necrophilia is unknown, but theorists have postulated that "paraphilia is created out of the elements of the common chemistry of experience and adaptation" (Kaplan & Sadock, 1985, p. 1066). It is believed that paraphilias may have their onset in childhood or the teen years, become refined in early adulthood, are lifelong, and are recurrent. In the discussion of differential diagnosis of paraphilias in the DSM-IV (1994, p. 525), it is noted that unusual sexual behavior that is often associated with substance intoxication, mania, or schizophrenia can be distinguished from paraphilia by the fact that in the nonparaphilic conditions "unusual sexual behavior is not the individual's preferred or obligatory pattern, the sexual symptoms occur exclusively during the course of these mental disorders and the unusual sexual acts tend to be isolated rather than recurrent and usually have a later age of onset." (See Chapter 21 in this book.)

In their review of necrophilia, Rosman and Resnick (1989) reported that necrophilia is most often motivated by the desire to possess an unrejecting sexual partner. They also noted that psychosis, mental retardation, and sadism are not identified as inherent in necrophilia. As their study of reported cases of necrophilia indicated, 83 percent of necrophiles who killed to obtain a willing partner were diagnosed as suffering from a personality disorder. As they stated, "Although necrophiles have been considered 'crazy' because of the bizarre nature of their acts, only 11 percent of the true necrophiles in the sample were psychotic" (Rosman & Resnick, 1989, p. 159). Similarly, Drukteinis (1992) reported that studies indicate that the majority of necrophiles and lust murderers do not exhibit delusions, hallucinations, or magical thinking, the main features of psychosis.

As the Dahmer prosecution asserted, Jeffrey Dahmer suffered from a personality disorder, not a mental illness (Drukteinis, 1992). As the verdict suggests, the jury apparently believed that Dahmer did have the capacity to appreciate the criminal nature of his actions and could control his behavior (Drukteinis, 1992).

Emphasizing the belief that necrophiles do not suffer psychotic symptoms that preclude them from maintaining contact with reality, Rosman and Resnick (1989) explored the use of alcohol and other drugs as important factors in necrophilia. They reported that some necrophiles use alcohol and drugs to overcome their inhibitions and to reduce the shame, disgust, and morality associated with necrophilia. In other cases, the use of alcohol may have helped reduce inhibitions about the actual killing, rather than about the necrophilic behaviors.

As discussed earlier, humiliation, dehumanization and degradation of the partner are part and parcel of the killer's attempt to have complete control over the victim. Perhaps the following quote by convicted serial killer Edmund Kemper best illustrates this phenomenon:

> I have fantasies about mass murder, whole groups of select women I could get together in one place, get them dead and then make mad passionate love to their dead corpses. Taking life away from them, a living human being, and then having possession of everything that used to be theirs. All that would be mine. Everything. (Drukteinis, 1992, p. 533)

The Sanity Consensus

Legal definitions, psychiatric evaluations and court decisions appear to support the view that serial killers, despite the sadistic and bizarre nature of their actions, are most often deemed to be sane and accountable for their behaviors. Yet, as Drukteinis (1992) related, "Common sense seems to suggest that such outrageous behavior is abnormal" (p. 533). Two questions remain to be addressed: (1) If the actions of convicted serial killers, like Dahmer, are espoused to be the consequence of personality disorders rather than psychotic mental illness, how does such a personality disorder develop? and (2) Why do we, the public, find it so difficult to accept that the sadistic, heinous crimes of serial killers can be committed by sane individuals?

THE ANTISOCIAL AND NARCISSISTIC PERSONALITY DISORDERS

Much scientific investigation has been undertaken to identify and understand the underlying psychic structures, developmental patterns and environmental factors that contribute to the evolution of the serial murderer. Medical evaluations, psychological assessments, intensive interviews and forensic studies have yielded a multitude of varying explanations and theoretical views. Profiles of serial killers have garnered a great deal of interest and are being used in investigations of suspected serial killings.

As Drukteinis (1992) notes, the behavioral patterns of serial killers seem to share some common characteristics, but there appears to be no definitive evidence that serial murder represents a distinct psychological entity. Although sexual sadism is often a trait of the serial murderer, many people engage in varying degrees of sexual sadism without ever acting in a criminal manner. Even more people experience sexually sadistic fantasies without acting them out in any way. Moreover, Drukteinis (1992) points out that aggression, power, dominance, and submission are features of courting and mating behaviors around the world. The factor or factors that push such behavior over the brink into the realm of criminality and brutality remain a mystery.

Psychological and Circumstantial Traits

Research in the area of serial killing has revealed a rather exhaustive list of traits and circumstances that may impact this behavior (Drukteinis, 1992). The following are some of the factors that seem to emerge as characteristics among sexually sadistic criminals (Drukteinis, 1992, p. 534):
- Most often white males
- Family life reflects some "disruption," such as parental divorce or infidelity
- Often educated beyond high school
- History of drug abuse
- History of a homosexual encounter
- History of having been physically or sexually abused during childhood
- History of social isolation and active fantasy life
- Preference for autoerotic activities and/or fetishes
- Feeling "rejected" by society
- History of rebelliousness, aggression, chronic lying, and feeling "entitled"
- Impaired interpersonal and caring relationships
- Arrested psychological development or impaired personality growth

What does this mean in nonpsychiatric jargon? Carlisle (1993) asserts that "The evidence accumulated on serial killers seems to indicate that the individuals were originally good people who went astray, rather than being born evil" (p. 23). According to McKenzie (1995), "It appears that certain factors in the childhood environment act as an "incubator" to enhance and exaggerate childhood behaviors and basic personality tendencies so that when adulthood is reached, in the presence of specific disinhibitors, these already exaggerated tendencies run amok" (p. 3). These speculations, however, ignore evidence that individuals with psychopathy or antisocial personality disorders show differences in their physiology, biochemistry, and genetic make-up early in their childhoods. Thus, their deviance may not have developed simply after exposure to certain environmental conditions. Personality traits that often characterize psychopaths and serial murderers are associated with these biological factors that may be predisposing to severe deviance in combination with social inducements.

McKenzie (1995) analyzed twenty cases of serial murder and categorized twenty-eight personality variables into four groups: childhood environmental incubator, childhood dysfunctional indicators, adult floodgate disinhibitors, and adulthood dysfunctional contributors. Her analysis revealed that the following characteristics occurred in a significant percentage of cases:

- *Childhood environmental incubator:*
  Alcoholic family dysfunction (75 percent)
  Inconsistent parenting and limit setting (93 percent)
  Frequently observed violence in the home (80 percent)

- *Childhood dysfunctional indicators:*
  Bedwetting (50 percent)

Isolation (43 percent)
Arrests (43.8 percent)

- *Floodgate disinhibitors:*
Alcohol or drug abuse (72.2 percent)
Pornography addiction (83.3 percent)

- *Adulthood dysfunctional contributors:*
Feeling of powerlessness (80 percent)
"Zero State" (belief that the entire world sees the person as a nothing and that existence is permanently futile) (85 percent)
Compulsive (a ritualistic approach to various aspects of life) (75 percent)

McKenzie (1995) presents a closely woven tapestry to illustrate how individual characteristics and environmental factors interact to impact childhood in ways that foster emergence of patterns in adulthood. It is hypothesized that problems in childhood lead to poor impulse control, lowered self-esteem, poor sense of oneself, and feelings of rejection and having been wronged (DeHart & Mahoney, 1994; Hale, 1993; McKenzie, 1995). Ultimately, this impairment in development of the personality manifests as antisocial personality disorder, which is characterized by "a lack of empathy, exploitativeness, grandiose sense of self, feelings of entitlement and a need for attention and stimulation" (Myers et al., 1995, p. 435).

Malignant Narcissism

As discussed earlier, it has been estimated that 90 percent of serial killers fall within the diagnostic category of antisocial personality disorder (Time Life, 1992). In his review of celebrated American and British murder cases, Stone (1989) noted that most of the murderers he studied were indeed psychopaths (who are often characterized with antisocial personality disorder), who exhibited insincerity, shamelessness, egocentricity, poor insight, inability to learn from past mistakes, and lack of compassion while appearing to be charming. He suggested that the diagnosis of "malignant narcissism" was, perhaps, more appropriate than the term "antisocial personality disorder." According to the DSM-IV, narcissistic personality disorder is marked by a chronic and pervasive pattern of grandiose self-importance, exaggeration of achievements, feelings of entitlement, need for recognition and admiration, lack of empathy, and inability to sustain stable interpersonal relationships. According to Stone (1989), malignant narcissism might be conceptualized as the "conjunction" of narcissistic personality disorder and antisocial personality disorder. He asserts that this designation better exemplifies the "connotation of evil that necessarily overhangs this domain of personality" (Stone, 1989, p. 649).

As noted by Pollock (1995), Kernberg (1992) depicted malignant narcissism as a form of severe narcissistic and antisocial traits expressed in extremely sadistic and violent behaviors. The malignant narcissist is characterized as someone who exhibits antisocial personality traits combined with unrestrained aggression, lack of conscience, a strong need for power and recognition, distrust of others, and sadism (Kernberg, 1992). Kernberg states that malignant narcissism develops as a defense against feelings of inferiority and rejection. Critical to the development of this disorder are (1) the individual's *perceived* humiliation, (2) disrupted attachments in early childhood, and (3) ineffective coping mechanisms. Cruel and sadistic behaviors serve to create a sense of victory and control over others and to "right past wrongs." The degree to which aggression and violence permeate the personality structure sets malignant narcissism apart from the antisocial and narcissistic personality disorders (Kernberg, 1992).

In his article, "Contributions to Psychiatric Consultation in the Investigation of Serial Murder," Liebert (1985) illustrates the concepts inherent in facilitating communication between law enforcement officials and psychiatrists working jointly on serial murder investigations. As he explains, psychiatrists can be of limited value as members of the team "if investigative personnel believe that a serial murderer is basically a bad person who behaves offensively because he has chosen a particularly nefarious habit" (Liebert, 1985, p. 196). He added that it is important that team members accept the beliefs that (1) sadistic killers commit their offensive acts as a "substitute for normal erotic pleasure;" (2) lust killers, who are often quite intelligent, can present a facade of having interpersonal relationships, but in reality they lack the capacity to experience normal intimate relationships; and (3) lust killers, despite their facades of having normal relationships and high intelligence, *are not* "normal people who have selected a criminal career in life" (Liebert, 1985, p. 197).

In summary, as postulated in the literature, most serial killers are not deemed to be psychotic and are considered to be predisposed to this behavioral pattern as a result of both biological and social forces interacting in complex ways. Moreover, as Pollock (1995) states, "It may be hypothesized that the motivations to commit serial murder emanate from the underlying personality structure and an understanding of the presence of aggression and its integration within the personality is essential in such cases" (p. 259).

ARE SERIAL KILLERS "DRIVEN" TO ACT?

One last issue to be addressed is the role of "compulsion" in serial murder. Are serial killers, as a consequence of abnormalities in personality and biochemistry, "driven" to commit their unspeakable acts?

Obsessive-Compulsive Disorder

Although serial killing is often referred to as "compulsive behavior" and the murderer's actions have been described in the literature as "obsessive-compulsive aggressivity," one should be cautious in interpreting this too literally (Dehart & Mahoney, 1994; Palermo & Knudten, 1994). As defined in the DSM-IV, obsessive-compulsive disorder (OCD) is an Axis I diagnosis, within the category of Anxiety Disorders. The hallmark characteristics are obsessions, which are repetitive thoughts that cause marked anxiety or discomfort, and compulsions, which are behaviors intended to reduce the anxiety. The classic example of OCD depicts compulsive handwashing, which becomes a ritualized behavior designed to reduce anxiety secondary to fears (obsessions) about germ contamination. The compulsions become excessive and disruptive to normal life functioning. The key feature regarding compulsions in regard to serial killing is that in OCD, the goal of the behaviors is "to prevent or reduce anxiety, not to provide pleasure or gratification" (DSM-IV, p. 418). It is this distinction about gratification that is often cited as negating the use of the OCD diagnosis in cases of serial killing (Schneider & Irons, 1996). The DSM-IV further clarifies this issue as follows:

> Some activities, such as eating (e.g., Eating Disorders), sexual behavior (e.g., Paraphilias), gambling (e.g., Pathological Gambling) or substance abuse (e.g., Alcohol Dependence or Abuse) when engaged in excessively, have been referred to as "compulsive." However, these activities are not considered compulsions as defined in this manual because the person usually derives pleasure from the activity and may wish to resist it only because of its deleterious consequences. (DSM-IV, p. 422).

Obsessive-Compulsive Personality Disorder

Obsessive-compulsive personality disorder (OCPD), an Axis II diagnosis, differs from OCD. OCPD is marked by a "preoccupation with orderliness, perfectionism, and mental and interpersonal control, at the expense of flexibility, openness and efficiency" (DSM-IV, p. 669). The features of this disorder are very similar to the characteristics of the "Type A" behavior pattern and it is distinct from OCD, as described earlier. There is no reported relationship between OCPD and serial murder.

Thus, serial killing behaviors do not meet the criteria for OCD or OCPD. Nevertheless, the killing behavior is often described as "compulsive." Is there a relationship between feeling "compelled" to perform an act and freely choosing to perform or inhibit the behavior?

Rotter and Goodman (1993) explored the issue of insight and control in obsessive-compulsive disorder as it pertained to the insanity defense. They reported no significant relationship between control over behaviors and insight into the irrationality and consequences of the behaviors in *nonpsychotic* subjects suffering from OCD. As they note, research in this area is complicated by the fact that there really are no reliable measures to test level of control. In other words, it is difficult to assess the degree to which behaviors are truly volitional. It appears that some behaviors either may be more closely related to impulsivity and lack of forethought or are behaviors over which an individual exerts control but elects to engage in risk-taking behavior. More importantly, as they point out, a "verifiable point at which loss of control reaches a threshold beyond which it is unreasonable to expect a person to control himself has not been identified" (Rotter & Goodman, 1993, p. 247).

As the findings suggest, there were neither positive nor negative correlations between insight and control, or between insight and avoidance and resistance; however, insight was positively correlated with control over *obsessions* (thoughts). As they surmised, "Insight is not totally irrelevant, rather it did not translate into an increased subjective sense of control over *behavior*" (Rotter & Goodman, 1993, p. 250). Moreover, it should be stressed that this work addressed OCD, an anxiety disorder, which is classified on the basis of internal experience of the anxiety and frustrations subjects feel, especially when their rituals are interrupted. Rotter and Goodman caution against viewing anxiety as a pure emotion that compels action, and they emphasize that anxiety is only one of many mental states in which "every system is affected: physiologic, cognitive, motivational, emotional and behavioral" (Rotter & Goodman, 1993, p. 251).

Opponents of the view that serial killers are driven to kill point out that in most instances serial murderers are not deemed psychotic, often demonstrate calculated planning and risk avoidance and, as in the case of Dahmer, tend to act on weekends (Palermo & Knudten, 1994). As Palermo and Knudten (1994) state regarding Dahmer, "There is no doubt that this serial killer understood his feelings, programmed his actions and willfully acted upon them, as he was consciously manipulating his victims—those he killed, those he used, and those to whom he malingered" (p. 15).

Alienation and Isolation

The issue of volition and compulsion is very complex in this matter. As research suggests, serial killers suffer a degree of psychopathology that limits their potential understanding of societal deterrence. Like other criminals, the behavior of serial murderers is governed more by their needs than by social norms and psychological expectations (Palermo & Knudten, 1994). As reviewed by DeHart and Mahoney (1994), developmentalists and learning theorists espouse the view that people learn to anticipate the consequences of misbehavior through the consistent application of punishment. The "conditioned conscience" serves to inhibit aggression. It is postulated that serial killers, like others suffering from antisocial personality disorder, fail to internalize such norms and lack inhibition toward aggression. This lack of normal internalization is seen as being related to the isolation and alienation in the killer's early life. Similarly, containment theory, from the sociological perspective, states that cultural institutions serve to keep individual behavior "in line" by imposing social norms and inhibitions against aggression (Reckless, 1967). Again, serial killers tend to be isolated and, consequently, lack not only internal buffers against aggression but have limited exposure to external (societal) sources of social control (DeHart & Mahoney, 1994; Norris, 1988).

Real and perceived alienation and isolation certainly impact the serial killer's life in many realms. According to Fromm (1973), individuals may respond to alienation by (1) withdrawing completely and minimizing interpersonal contact with others or (2) ritualizing behavior. Basically, ritualization becomes a substitute for socialization and provides a sense of predictability and order in the person's life. As reported earlier, serial murders often reflect compulsive, ritualistic behaviors. Expounding further, Fromm (1973) and Maccoby (1972) demonstrated a relationship between ritualization and necrophilic tendencies that serves to blur the distinctions between the living and the dead. It is purported that this elimination of the distinction between the living and the nonliving and other acts of dehumanization may facilitate commission of the serial killer's deviant behaviors.

As this brief review of the scientific literature reveals, terms such as "compulsive" and "driven" are frequently encountered in the materials written about serial killers. However, little if any scientific research strongly supports the view that *nonpsychotic* serial killers are driven by compulsions to kill and should be absolved of responsibility for their criminal actions due to an inability to refrain from their behaviors. To the contrary, most of the literature reviewed supports the view that "serial murder is a product of extremely primitive emotions" related to an inability to attach with others intimately (Liebert, 1985, p. 188). The interactions of perceived humiliation and maltreatment in the early years, ineffective coping and feelings of rejection and powerlessness combined with unrestrained aggression and lack of conscience are instrumental in the development of the serial killer. As Pollock (1995, p. 261) states, in the case of serial murder, "Malignant Narcissism represents an intermediate form of personality disorder characterized by severe narcissistic and antisocial tendencies, which may be expressed in extreme forms of sadism and violence." Thus, it is postulated that the serial killer's "needs govern his behavior" (Palermo & Knudten, 1994, p. 15) and serial killing becomes a "means to overcome humiliation and lost power" (Hale, 1993, p. 39).

Future investigation of the psychology of serial killers by this author will address research on compulsive sexual behavior and sexual addiction. As Myers (1995) has suggested, the distinction between diagnosed obsessive-compulsives, who perform behaviors to reduce anxiety, and paraphiliacs, who act out of a desire for sexual gratification, may be "arbitrary and unquantifiable." In their article on "Differential Diagnosis of Addictive Sexual Disorders Using DSM-IV, Schneider and Irons (1996) discuss paraphilias and offer recommendations for using current DSM-IV classifications to diagnose behaviors that appear to represent "sexual addiction." Similarly, Blanchard's (1995) report on his prison interviews with lust murderers espouses the view that serial killing may represent a fourth level of sexual addiction.

DO WE REALLY BELIEVE THAT SERIAL KILLERS ARE SANE AND ACTING VOLITIONALLY?

Despite the literature that attempts to explain the motivations and intricacies of the serial killer mind, we—the general public—still question whether the Jeffrey Dahmers of our world can in reality be sane men (and women) who commit the most atrocious acts against other human beings. Moreover, we continue to ponder whether they are compelled, or *driven*, to act so brutally. Why do we struggle so intensely with these issues?

Free Will and Responsibility

First, the question of acting volitionally cannot really be answered with a simple "yes" or "no" statement. Free will is probably better conceptualized as on a continuum than as a categorical variable. As Raine (1993) states:

> [I]t seems much more likely that free will lies on a continuum and that there are differing degrees to which each of us as individuals have a free choice in most of our daily actions as well as those most extreme acts such as killing another individual. While it is true that in most cases a criminal has a choice regarding whether or not to commit a criminal act, the decision is likely to be heavily weighted by a large number of preceding events, including the individual's social history and the presence/absence of both social and biological predispositional influences.
>
> Predispositions clearly place constraints on the individual's free will, though not in the dramatic way as some severe mental disorders such as schizophrenia may place constraints on free will. If we accept that crime is a disorder, acknowledge that there are clear predispositions that form the basis

for recidivistic crime, and acknowledge that in most cases these predispositions are beyond the individual's control, then the implication is that criminal offenders should not be punished as severely as they are currently for their actions. (p. 310)

Yet, when we consider the atrocities committed by serial killers, we tremble to think that such individuals might at some point be released from prison and be allowed to roam our streets. So, we become diligent in demanding that sentencing by the courts is appropriate to the nature of the actions. Nevertheless, many of us may still wonder whether the crimes committed were truly acts of free will. Therein lies the dilemma.

Violence—Disease or Man's Dark Side?

Secondly, if we agree with Hale's (1993) observations that serial killing is not an act committed by a deranged person, but is, in fact, the action of a person who is "behaving in a manner which makes sense and is logical to the killer and is a response to some perceived wrong" (p. 37), then how far removed are we ourselves from being potential murderers? Perhaps it is more reassuring for us to believe that serial killers are flawed human beings who are overcome by violent tendencies—driven to kill. As Drukteinis (1992) notes, in most psychiatric disciplines violence is viewed as a sickness, not as "simply part of the spectrum of human possibility" (p. 537). In perceiving violence as a sickness, we minimize the role of free will and reduce the criminal's responsibility for controlling violent behavior. At the same time, by conceptualizing violence as a disease and character flaw, we hopefully distance ourselves from the possibility that we, the healthy and nonflawed, could ever commit such acts of atrocity. Perhaps it is this fear of the beast within each of us that prompts us to search for the factors that unleash the evil in the behaviors of *other* human beings. The essence of this fear has been poetically captured by Drukteinis (1992) as follows:

The jury in the Dahmer insanity case may have acted reasonably in holding him responsible for not restraining his violence, in spite of the gruesome and sickening behavior of which it consisted. His behavior was simply part of the spectrum of human possibility, a brutal dark side of man, not representing demons or disease. It is only that side of himself which man cannot easily confront that prompts his response of "crazy" to disclosure of Dahmer's brutality. Only by not hiding from his own savagery, only by facing that savagery directly, can man see of what he is capable and then, with full consciousness, truly reinforce restraint. (p. 537)

CONCLUSION

This chapter explores issues regarding the conceptualizations of serial killing and the motivations of serial killers. Discussion about the role of sanity and free will in serial murder, although inconclusive, is presented to encourage future dialogue and investigations into the realm of the minds of serial murderers. Of particular interest for future study is the possibility that sexual serial murder may be reflective of compulsive sexual behavior or sexual addiction. Comments about the nature of violence and the potential for brutality that resides in all human beings have been offered to stimulate discussion and exploration of issues regarding personal responsibility and the role of restraint in preventing heinous crimes against humanity.

Editor's Note

As duly noted in this chapter, much of the literature on serial murdering has been devoted to the social psychology of the killer and his or her childhood. Also described in this chapter is the potential for all humans to commit similar acts of violence. There is ample evidence for these assertions, as the author quite eloquently points out. However, serial killing in general has been largely understudied and neglected, possibly for reasons mentioned herein: that we are so appalled by these behaviors, even though many are intrigued and attracted to the subject matter, that only a few are willing to take an in-depth look into its etiology.

This chapter presents a rationale for serial killing to originate from some unusual combination of psychopathy and OCD. There are elements of OCD in that the perpetrators are obsessed with thoughts about the process of killing to the point that their lives are disrupted. Thus, they engage in compulsive behaviors to alleviate or satisfy these obsessions. There are also elements of psychopathy as manifested by deliberate, planned sequences of action, without remorse and without any signs of conditioned behaviors based on conventional norms. Neither psychopathy nor OCD is considered "normal." Thus, while the legal system contemplates the sanity of serial killing to determine "guilt," the forensic and psychological community views these behaviors as mentally deranged and severely abnormal—which leads us to the conclusion that those of us who function "normally" could not possibly have the propensity to commit these acts. They are deviant and engaged in only by those with noticeable signs of psychopathology.

Because both OCD and psychopathy have been reliably associated with genetic, biochemical and neurological markers, in addition to personality disorders and deleterious childhood experiences, there is a need to incorporate an interdisciplinary approach to the study of serial murdering. Most likely, there is a preexisting psychiatric disorder that in combination with an adverse childhood, culminates in this compulsive pattern of behavior. This pattern is seen in other behavioral disorders, with varying modus operandi and outcomes, that may be instructive in sorting out the generators of serial murdering. For example, an analogy can be made from serial murdering to drug addiction; there are many similarities. In drug addiction, there are sensations of extreme pleasure that cannot be rivaled by satisfying any other basic drive. There is a tendency to increase the dose and frequency of use over time. When the drug is withdrawn, there is craving and, subsequently, withdrawal symptoms that often lead to reuse of the drug. Simply viewing the paraphernalia used to administer the drug can induce craving and relapse. Similarly, in serial murdering, there are sensations of extreme pleasure that cannot be derived by any other behaviors. There is a tendency to increase the intensity of the violence and pursue more powerful victims over time. The frequency with which the act is committed also increases. When the killer is not actively engaged in planning or carrying out the act, there is an experience of craving and even withdrawal, which ultimately leads to plans for another crime—

which in drug addiction is known as relapse. Serial murderers routinely take "paraphernalia" from the crime scene and play with it to relive the sensation, thus, enhancing craving. Because there are particular brain mechanisms involved in propensity to drug addiction (e.g., the neurotransmitter dopamine and prefrontal cortical function), those same mechanisms may be involved in serial killing. In either event, it is likely that serial killers suffer from dysfunctions that have yet to be fully elucidated. In order to enhance our understanding of their behavior and to prevent the formation of future serial murderers, comprehensive study of this population is necessary. The legal system must come to grips with this need and provide access to these individuals for both research and humanitarian purposes.

References

American Psychiatric Association. (1994). *Diagnostic and statistical manual of mental disorders* (4th ed.). Washington, DC: American Psychiatric Press.

Blanchard, G. (1995). Sexually addicted lust murderers. *Sexual Addiction and Compulsivity, 2*, 62–71.

Carlisle, A. (1993). The divided self: Toward an understanding of the dark side of the serial killer. *American Journal of Criminal Justice, 17*, 23–36.

Comer, R. (1996). *Fundamentals of abnormal psychology.* New York: W. H. Freeman.

DeHart, D. & Mahoney, J. (1994). The serial murderer's motivations: An interdisciplinary review. *Omega, 29*, 29–45.

Drukteinis, A. (1992). Serial murder: The heart of darkness. *Psychiatric Annals, 22*, 532–538.

Egger, S. (1998). *The killers among us.* Englewood Cliffs, NJ: Prentice Hall.

Fromm, E. (1973). *The anatomy of human destructiveness.* New York: Holt, Rinehart & Winston.

Hale, R. (1993). The application of learning theory to serial murder. *American Journal of Criminal Justice, 17*, 37–45.

Hale, R. (1994). The role of humiliation and embarrassment in serial murder. *Psychology: A Journal of Human Behavior, 31*, 17–23.

Halpern, A. (1991). The insanity defense in the 21st century. *International Journal of Offender Therapy and Comparative Criminology, 35*, 187–189.

Hickey, E. (1991). *Serial murderers and their victims.* Belmont, CA: Wadsworth Publishing.

Hickey, E. (1997). *Serial murderers and their victims* (2d ed.). Belmont, CA: Wadsworth Publishing.

Holmes, R. & DeBurger, J. (1990). *Serial murder.* Newbury Park, CA: Sage.

Kaplan, H. & Sadock, B. (1985). *Comprehensive textbook of psychiatry.* Baltimore: Williams & Wilkins.

Kernberg, O. (1992). *Severe personality disorders.* New Haven: Yale University Press.

Liebert, J. (1985). Contributions to psychiatric consultation in the investigation of serial murder. *International Journal of Offender Therapy and Comparative Criminology, 29*, 187–200.

Maccoby, M. (1972). Emotional attitudes and political choice. *Politics and Society,* 209–239.

McKenzie, C. (1995). A study of serial murder. *International Journal of Offender Therapy and Comparative Criminology, 39*, 3–10.

Myers, W. (1995, Fall). Addictive sexual behavior. *American Journal of Psychotherapy, 49*, 473–483.

Myers, W., Burket, R. & Harris, E. (1995). Adolescent psychopathy in relation to delinquent behaviors, conduct disorder and personality disorders. *Journal of Forensic Sciences, 40*, 436–440.

Nicholi, A. (Ed.) (1988). *The new Harvard guide to psychiatry.* Cambridge, MA: Harvard University Press.

Norris, J. (1988). *Sexual killers.* New York: Doubleday.

Palermo, G. & Knudten, R. (1994). The insanity plea in the case of a serial killer. *International Journal of Offender Therapy and Comparative Criminology, 38*, 3–16.

Pollock, P. (1995). A case of spree serial murder with suggested diagnostic opinions. *International Journal of Offender Therapy and Comparative Criminology, 39,* 258–268.

Raine, A. (1993). *The psychopathology of crime: Criminal behavior as a clinical disorder.* San Diego, CA: Academic Press.

Reckless, W. C. (1967). *The crime problem.* New York: Appleton-Century-Croft.

Ressler, R. (1985). Violent crimes. *FBI Law Enforcement Bulletin, 54,* 1–31.

Ressler, R., Burgess, A. & Douglas, J. (1988). *Sexual homicide.* Lexington, MA: Lexington Books.

Rosman, J. & Resnick, P. (1989). Sexual attraction to corpses: A psychiatric review of necrophilia. *Bulletin of the American Academy of Psychiatry Law, 17,* 153–161.

Rotter, M. & Goodman, W. (1993). The relationship between insight and control in obsessive-compulsive disorder: Implications for the insanity defense. *Bulletin of the American Academy of Psychiatry Law, 21,* 245–252.

Schneider, J. & Irons, R. (1996). Differential diagnosis of addictive sexual disorders using the DSM-IV. *Sexual Addictions and Compulsivity, 3,* 7–21.

Stone, M. (1989). Murder. *Psychiatric Clinics of North America, 12,* 643–651.

Time Life Editors (1992). *Mass murderers.* New York: Time Life Books.

Part 6

Attention Deficit Hyperactivity Disorder and Crime—Identifying Genetic, Addictive, and Familial Links to Reduce Prison Terms and Recidivism

In his article entitled "Lack of Attention from Loss of Time," Philip Gold states:

The full syndrome of attention deficit hyperactivity disorder (ADHD) imposes a daunting burden, interfering with behaviors and functions that help define our humanity. At the most basic level, individuals with ADHD cannot depend upon themselves to control their own behavior. They are often impulsive, intrusive, and act without apparent regard for the needs of others. Despite unimpaired intellect and high energy levels, they also apparently lack will. Thus they seem unable to persist in the face of temptation, interruption, or frustration. Finally, they show a global deficit in dealing with time. They cannot easily learn from past mistakes, accurately evaluate their present efforts, realistically plan for the future, or organize and execute tasks that require an orderly temporal sequence. It is not surprising that such deficits profoundly interfere with their social, academic, or occupational lives and elicit harsh, if not continuous, criticism. *Science*, 281,1998, p. 1149.

Attention deficit hyperactivity disorder (ADHD) has been cited as a precursor for many forms of antisocial behaviors, including drug abuse and delinquency. While most children with ADHD do not become antisocial, a significant proportion of adults with antisocial behavior demonstrated ADHD in their childhood. The brains of ADHD children often display a paucity of activity in areas responsible for arousal and alertness that may contribute to their stimulation-seeking behaviors. Such a childhood history may predict violent behavior while sober and under the influence of a psychoactive drug; the individual may possess both the susceptibility and the trigger.

In recent years, evidence has accumulated to support the observation of many clinicians that for many people, ADHD doesn't simply disappear in adulthood; the disorder may instead take different forms that often preclude an accurate diagnosis. For example, there may not be motor hyperexcitability or the typical symptoms of what we call hyperactivity. Adults with a childhood history of ADHD who remain symptomatic may primarily display behaviors that are essentially sensation-seeking; they may engage in risky behaviors seemingly without concern for the consequences. They may tend to bore easily, be easily distracted by irrelevant stimuli from their environment, and have difficulty concentrating. Their lifestyles are often complicated by difficulties in maintaining relationships and employment; they may flit from job to job and from relationship to relationship. Routine responsibilities like paying bills, completing tax returns, and attending to paperwork in general may seem like daunting tasks. Often, they may also find drugs of abuse (e.g., alcohol or cocaine) more immediately rewarding than other people; they tend to experiment with drugs at a younger age, become dependent on them more rapidly, and exhibit more aggressive and dysfunctional behaviors while using them.

The neurobiological basis for ADHD is believed to play a role in later behavioral disorders, such as aggressiveness and drug abuse. This section is devoted to discussion of ADHD's genetic and neurochemical underpinnings, and to the ways in which antisocial behaviors can be better treated by addressing these causative mechanisms. Dr. Comings, a molecular geneticist, has made tremendous strides in identifying the many genes associated with ADHD and its behavioral correlates. He presents data in Chapter 16 that implicate genes responsible for metabolism and the activity of several neurotransmitter systems in the disorder, and he highlights ways in which dysfunctions of these systems can contribute to its development. These findings provide practical information for the clinician and criminal justice practitioner who are attempting to treat or manage individuals with antisocial behavior extending from ADHD. The findings are also promising in their relevance to reducing the presently high recidivism rate in offender populations. Dr. Comings provides support for the notion that the combination of ADHD and conduct disorder is particularly insidious, is significantly predictive of criminal propensity, has strong genetic generators, and is related to dysfunction of the neurotransmitters dopamine, serotonin, and norepinephrine. In his discussions of the genetic research, the author refers to several medications that target these neurotransmitters and that have been quite effective in clinical populations. With an eye toward reducing recidivism, Dr. Comings subsequently presents an argument and a method for treating this syndrome within a prison population.

Dr. Comings has recently teamed up with Dr. McCallon, a prison psychiatrist, and Wendy Richardson, a counselor, to provide comprehensive assessment and treatment services to offenders and their families who suffer from ADHD. In Chapter 17, Dr. McCallon continues with a more detailed account of the ADHD syndrome in prison inmates, its manifestations and complications, and the behavioral and pharmacological methods of treatment. Dr. McCallon describes several case examples that typify the offender with ADHD so that the reader can become better acquainted with both the symptomatology and the various obstacles that can arise in its management and treatment. He discusses specific diagnostic and assessment instruments and suggests ways to assemble a team for case management. In addition to several medicinal regimens to control symptoms of ADHD, Dr. McCallon lists several behavioral and psychological interventions that are highly effective when used appropriately with or without medication.

Expounding upon the two preceding chapters, Ms. Richardson further characterizes ADHD in Chapter 18 by describing in great detail the various problems sufferers encounter with their own behavior and the frustrations they bear. She also helps to explain why ADHD individuals are unusually prone to aggression and rage, emotional reactions that often lead to criminal justice involvement. According to Ms. Richardson, criminal activity and substance abuse "medicate" the neurological imbalance that ADHD individuals suffer from by providing heightened levels of stimulation to a brain that is, for either genetic or acquired reasons, underaroused. Coupled with the lack of impulse control that typifies ADHD, the unusual need for emotional and physical stimulation often leads to troublesome behavior that surprises even the perpetrator. Like Dr. McCallon, Ms. Richardson provides treatment suggestions that are both behavioral and medicinal, indicating which types of offenders require which regimen. Importantly, she makes distinctions between ADHD and other syndromes that can mimic or resemble ADHD; without accurate diagnosis, treatment is much less likely to be effective.

Chapter 16

The Role of Genetics in ADHD and Conduct Disorder—Relevance to the Treatment of Recidivistic Antisocial Behavior

by David E. Comings, M.D.

Introduction 16-2
Genetics of ADHD and Conduct Disorder 16-3
    ADHD as a Genetic Disorder 16-3
    Conduct Disorder Comorbid With ADHD 16-3
    Conduct Disorder as a Genetic Disorder 16-3
ADHD and CD as Predictors of Adult Antisocial Behavior 16-4
Molecular Genetics of ADHD, CD, and Aggression 16-5
    Dopamine Genes 16-6
        DRD2 Gene 16-6
        DRD4 Gene 16-7
        DRD5 Gene 16-8
        DRD1 Gene 16-9
        DAT1 Gene 16-9
    Serotonin Genes 16-9
        HTR1B Gene 16-9
        HTR2A Gene 16-9
        HTR1DA Gene 16-10
        TDO2 Gene 16-10

This research was supported in part by grant RO1-DA08417 from the National Institute on Drug Abuse, grant 4RT-0110 from the Tobacco Related Research Disease Program, and by the Gaming Entertainment Research and Education Foundation and the National Center for Responsible Gaming.

Adrenergic Genes 16-10
    DBH Gene 16-10
    ADRA2A and *ADRA2C* Genes 16-10
    Monoamine Oxidase Genes 16-11
    Gamma-Aminobutyric Acid Genes—*GABRB3* Receptor Gene 16-12
    Androgen Receptor Gene 16-12
    Other Genes 16-12
Polygenic Inheritance 16-13
Multivariate Analysis of Associations (MAA) 16-13
Relevance to Treatment 16-17
    Treatment Before Prison 16-17
    Treatment in Prison 16-17
    Ethical Considerations 16-18

INTRODUCTION

One of the most widely recognized characteristics of the present penal system is that for many inmates, imprisonment is largely ineffective and recidivism rates range from 60 to 70 percent. One explanation for repeat criminal activity is that the individuals involved, who characteristically exhibit a lifelong pattern of impulsive and antisocial behavior, may be suffering from genetically or neurologically based behavioral disorders. For these individuals, incarceration with other criminals is not the treatment of choice. Such an approach is known only to worsen their prognosis and teach them new criminal skills (Moffitt, 1993b). A medical approach may provide this subgroup of offenders with an optimal and imminently more effective mode of treatment.

However, a major problem with this potentially more "enlightened" outlook is that it becomes critical to be able to make an accurate diagnosis. This is especially true in a prison system in which evaluators may legitimately be concerned that they could be "conned" into making an incorrect diagnosis. Thus, while highly objective diagnostic criteria for disorders are always valuable, they will be especially critical before a widespread medical approach to criminal behavior is feasible. Since DNA-based genetic tests identify permanent inborn characteristics, are independent of environmental factors such as diet, stress, or the time of day, and cannot be "beaten" like lie detector tests, they represent one of the most objective of all forms of testing. While the role of genetic factors in behavior, especially aggressive and antisocial behavior, has been and probably will remain a controversial subject, the discipline of molecular psychiatry is progressing so rapidly that it is imperative that criminologists and practitioners become aware of how it may have an impact on their field. I address here some of the advances in the study of the molecular genetics of behavior and how these findings may soon play an important role in providing more effective treatment of antisocial behavior and reducing the high recidivism rates.

While a number of disorders such as closed head injury and psychomotor epilepsy have been shown to be associated with aggressive and violent behaviors (Lewis, 1976; Lewis et al., 1982), I will emphasize the role of attention deficit hyperactivity disorder (ADHD) associated with conduct disorder (CD) as a genetic disorder that starts in childhood, often persists for a life time, and has repeatedly been shown to be the single most significant predictor of adult antisocial behavior. Thus, the present chapter is based on the following facts about ADHD and ADHD with motor tics (Tourette's syndrome). These disorders are:

- Common in the general population;
- Frequently associated with other disorders that strongly predict criminal behavior such as childhood CD, drug and alcohol abuse, learning disabilities, poor anger control, and impulsive behavior;
- Common in a prison population;
- Genetic rather than psychosocial disorders;
- Readily responsive to treatment; and
- Amenable to treatment that can result in a dramatic improvement in the success and rate of rehabilitation, and a decrease in recidivism.

GENETICS OF ADHD AND CONDUCT DISORDER

ADHD as a Genetic Disorder

Studies have shown that the frequency of ADHD and other behavioral disorders in the first degree relatives of ADHD children is much higher than in the general population (Morrison & Stewart, 1971; Cantwell, 1972; Biederman et al., 1986; Faraone et al., 1991). While this is consistent with a genetic cause of ADHD, twin studies are better suited to dissecting out the relative role of genetic and environmental factors. Such studies indicate that 75 to 90 percent of ADHD is due to genetic factors (Sherman et al., 1997a, 1997b; Gillis et al., 1992; Stevenson, 1992).

Conduct Disorder Comorbid With ADHD

A number of disorders are very common or comorbid in children and adults with ADHD. These include learning disabilities, dyslexia, drug and alcohol abuse, oppositional defiant disorder, and CD (Biederman et al., 1992; Biederman et al., 1997; August et al., 1983; Loney & Milich, 1982; Kuhne et al., 1997). Each of these disorders has been implicated as a risk factor for adult antisocial behavior (Robins, 1966). While ADHD has also been implicated as a risk factor for adult antisocial behaviors (Farrington et al., 1990) more recent studies have indicated that this holds true only for children with ADHD+CD, and not for those with ADHD only (Satterfield & Schell, 1997; Mannuzza et al., 1989).

Conduct Disorder as a Genetic Disorder

While CD is generally considered to be predominately of psychological and environmental origins, its common association with genetic disorders such as ADHD and Tourette's syndrome (Comings & Comings, 1987; Comings, 1995; Stewart et al., 1981; Biederman et al., 1991; McGee et al., 1984) suggests that genetic factors may also play a role. Thus, is it not surprising that recent twin studies (Slutske et al., 1997) have indicated that genetic factors play just as much of a role in conduct disorder as in ADHD. Twin studies have also shown a strong genetic contribution to adult antisocial behavior (Cloninger & Gottesman, 1986). By contrast, genetic factors play much less of a role in adolescent delinquency. The reason for this potentially confusing finding is that many teenagers engage occasionally in antisocial conduct, but only a subgroup persists in their deviance into adulthood. Thus, an adult population with a chronic, early onset pattern of antisocial behavior is likely to show genetic proclivity.

ADHD AND CD AS PREDICTORS OF ADULT ANTISOCIAL BEHAVIOR

One of the most frequently replicated findings in psychiatry is the persistent course of childhood CD and its role as a strong predictor of adult antisocial and criminal behavior (Robins, 1966; Robins, 1991; Farrington, 1995; Mitchell & Rosa, 1981). In attempting to understand the relationship between childhood CD, adolescent delinquency, and adult criminal behavior, Moffitt (1993b) proposed two types of antisocial behaviors, a life-persistent form characterized by the presence of childhood CD that is present in a small percentage of the population (less than 5 percent) and responsible for a significant proportion of adult criminality; and an adolescent limited form that is very common, resembling a transient right-of-passage type of age-appropriate behavior.

The best way to verify the relationship between some forms of ADHD and criminal behavior would be to determine whether the frequency of ADHD was significantly higher in males in prison than in males in the general population. A single published study of this incidence has been reported. Eyestone and Howell (1994) examined 102 male offenders at the Utah State prison, ages 16 to 64. They found that both ADHD and depression were present in 25.5 percent of inmates. There was a significant association between the presence of ADHD and depression ($p < .001$). They emphasized the need for the diagnosis and treatment of ADHD in a prison setting.

An unpublished study was conducted by Favarino (1988). She collected data on one hundred males in jail and found 28 percent with diagnosable ADHD as children and adults, and 21.3 percent with diagnosable major depression. While not a study of ADHD, Nestor (1992) examined the frequency of a learning disability and childhood CD in a group of subjects charged with murder and other violent crimes. They found that the younger group of subjects had a significantly increased frequency of childhood learning disability and conduct disorder.

A Washington State Life Skills project (Haggerty et al., 1989) for first offender criminals (juvenile as well as adult arrestees) revealed 58 percent had a previously diagnosed or strongly suspected learning disability. The most common disability was ADHD (approximately 80 percent). In the absence of treatment the recidivism rate was 68 percent within two years.

All of the above observations suggest that the life-persistent form of ADHD+CD is largely genetic and analogous to an inborn personality trait, while the adolescence limited form of antisocial behavior is largely nongenetic and transient. This concept is shown in Figure 16.1. Most likely, we can identify the genetic factors associated with childhood ADHD+CD, begin to better understand the cause of the most significant and recidivistic portion of adult criminal offending, and begin to identify truly effective modes of treatment.

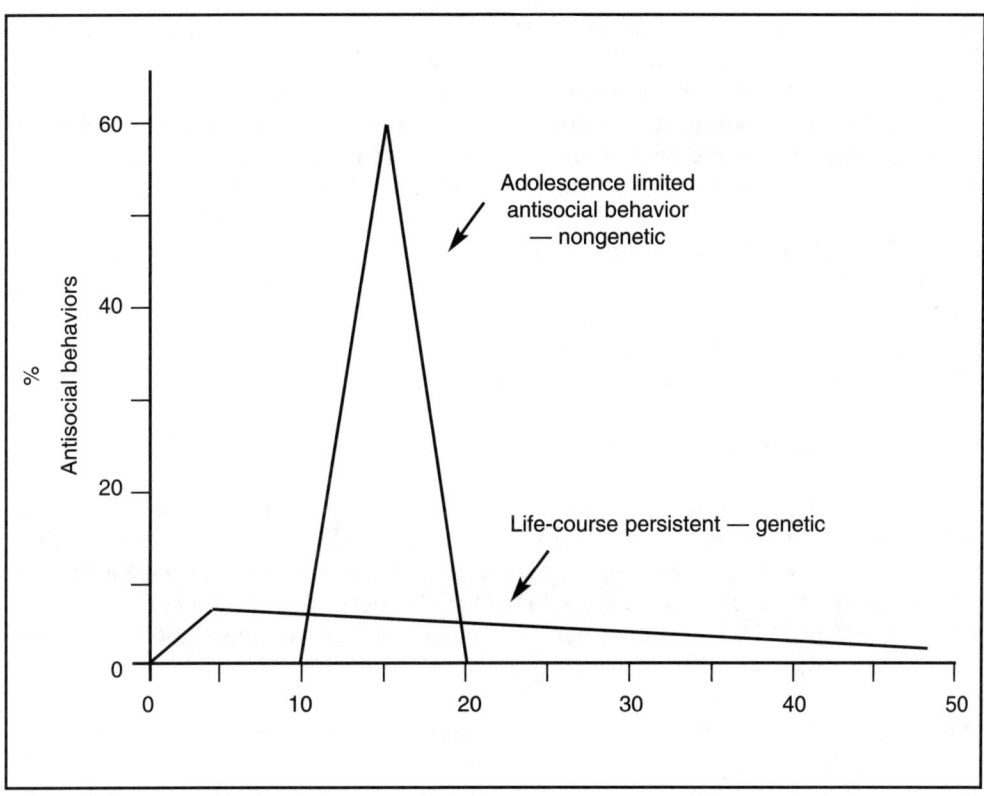

Figure 16.1. Proposed Relationship Between the Adolescence Limited and Life Course Persistent Antisocial Behavior of Moffitt (1993) and Nongenetic vs. Genetic Form of Antisocial Behavior

MOLECULAR GENETICS OF ADHD, CD, AND AGGRESSION

While family and twin studies have provided clear evidence for the important role of genetic factors in ADHD+CD, we can only truly understand, treat, and prevent the negative outcome that often occurs by identifying *which* genes are involved. Despite popular beliefs, genetic traits are not immutable; the chemical imbalances they produce are responsive to appropriate treatments. Although we cannot easily alter behavior on a gene level, knowing which genes are involved in behavioral disorders such as ADHD+CD leads to an understanding of the underlying mechanisms and biological products of the gene action. For example, the identification of particular genes that are associated with a disorder and that regulate neurotransmitter activity enables us to adjust neurotransmitter levels or function either by environmental or pharmacological methods. In the case of ADHD+CD, several genes have been identified, including those that help to regulate activity of the neurotransmitters dopamine, serotonin, and norepinephrine. These neurochemicals are highly sensitive to environmental manipulations; for example, they can be stimulated via appropriately targeted educational curricula or early emotional supports. In others, more effective treatments may necessitate the administration of medications that act on those neurotransmitters to readjust the system and promote optimal brain development and functioning.

In order to fully appreciate the involvement of neurotransmitter function in ADHD+CD, it is important to understand the role of neurotransmitter receptor sites. A receptor site sits on the membrane of a brain cell called a dendrite to receive specific brain chemicals or drugs to produce an effect. Receptors have an affinity to a particular chemical or drug, and when that substance is introduced, the cells' functional properties are altered. When there are too many or too few receptors for a brain chemical, or when the receptor is somehow defective, the activity of cells will become dysfunctional. Thus, in the presence of receptor defects for a neurotransmitter system, the behavioral outcome associated with its function will be less than optimal or disturbed.

Dopamine Genes

Since stimulant medications such as methylphenidate (Ritalin) and dextroamphetamine provide the most effective treatment of ADHD and predominately affect dopamine metabolism, examining the dopamine genes is a reasonable place to start in the search for the genes involved in ADHD+CD. There are five dopamine receptor genes, *DRD1* to *DRD5*. The first gene we examined was the dopamine D_2 receptor gene.

***DRD2* Gene.** The first molecular genetic studies of ADHD were reported in 1991 by Comings et al. (1991). They examined the prevalence of a particular genetic variant (the *Taq* A1 allele) of the *DRD2* gene in range of impulsive, compulsive, addictive behaviors (see Table 16.1). This study showed that in addition to ADHD, the frequency of the A1 allele was significantly elevated in a range of disorders that are often comorbid with ADHD, including autism, alcoholism and drug abuse, CD, posttraumatic stress disorder, and Tourette's syndrome. Since the A1 allele was associated with both ADHD and CD, it is especially likely to be associated with ADHD+CD. These results suggested that genetic variants at the *DRD2* locus played a role in a range of impulsive, compulsive, addictive disorders, including ADHD. The prevalence of the D_2A1 allele in these disorders ranged from 42.3 to 54.5 percent. While it was clear that the *DRD2* was not a major gene causing these conditions since it was usually not even present in half of the cases, it was also clear that the prevalence of the D_2A1 allele was approximately twofold higher than in controls.

In a subsequent study, we also observed a significant increased frequency of the D_2A1 allele (48 percent) in individuals who smoked at least one pack of cigarettes per day and were unable to quit on their own. The prevalence of *Taq* I D_2A1 allele was even higher (51 percent) in a large group of pathological gamblers (Comings et al., 1996d). We also verified the association of the *DRD2* A1 allele with posttraumatic stress disorder (Comings et al., 1996c).

To examine the potential role of the *DRD2* gene in violent behavior, we asked a group of veterans on an addiction treatment unit if they had ever been expelled from school for fighting, as a rough screen for childhood CD (see Table 16.2). Of those who answered yes, 59 percent carried the A1 allele compared to 31 percent of those who answered no (p = .001). We also asked if they had ever been in jail. The frequency of

Table 16.1
Frequency of the A1 Allele of the *Taq*I Polymorphism of the *DRD2* Gene in Impulse Disorders Including ADHD

Diagnosis	N	% 1	c^2	p
Controls	314	24.5		
ADHD	80	46.3	14.64	0.003
ADHD + family Hx TS	24	45.8	5.26	0.02
ADHD Total	104	46.2	17.44	0.0001
Alcoholism ± drug abuse	104	42.3	12.02	0.0009
Autism	33	54.5	13.54	0.0005
Conduct disorder	7	85.7		0.003
Posttraumatic stress disorder	35	45.7	7.23	0.007
Tourette's syndrome	147	44.9	19.43	0.0001
TS relatives with tics	232	49.6	28.90	<0.0001

the A1 allele was not increased in those incarcerated for nonviolent crime such as driving under the influence (DUI) (28.8 percent), but was increased to 53.1 percent in those arrested for violent crimes. If they had been arrested for violent crime and had a history of being expelled from school for fighting, suggesting the presence of childhood CD, the frequency of the A1 allele increased to 69 percent.

These studies show that the A1 allele is present in about one-quarter of normal individuals. This frequency increased to 40 to 60+ percent, but never to 100 percent, in subjects with a range of impulsive, compulsive, aggressive behavioral disorders. These findings are consistent with the notion that the *DRD2* gene may be one of a number of genes contributing to these behaviors—that is, a polygenic (or multiple gene) mode of inheritance (Comings, 1996; Comings, 1998).

***DRD4* Gene.** The *DRD4* gene is the second dopamine receptor gene reported to be associated with ADHD. An important polymorphism of the *DRD4* gene is a 16 amino-acid repeat polymorphism (where a sequence of amino acids occurs repeatedly and is considered to be a genetic variant) within the gene (Van Tol et al., 1992; Lichter et al., 1993). This DNA region is repeated 2 to 8 times, with the most common alleles being the 2, 4, and 7 repeats. The 7 allele demonstrates a blunted response (in terms of intracellular adenyl cyclase inhibition) to dopamine (Asghari et al., 1995), which indicates that dopamine metabolism and/or activity are affected by this polymorphism. Two

Table 16.2
Association of *DRD2* Alleles with Various Behavioral Variables in Subjects with Substance Abuse

	N	A1	(%)A1	A2A2	χ^2	p
A. Expelled from school for fighting?						
Yes	39	23	(59.0)	16		
No	154	48	(31.21)	106	10.35	.001
B. Ever Jailed?						
Substance abuse, never jailed	51	22	(43.1)	29		
Jailed for nonviolent crime						
DUI's only	81	23	(28.4)	58		
Nonviolent crime ± DUI's	30	9	(30.0)	21		
Total	111	32	(28.8)	79		
Jailed for violent crime						
Violent crime not expelled	19	8	(42.1)	11		
Violent crime expelled	13	9	(69.2)	4		
Total	32	17	(53.1)	15		

χ^2—Jailed for nonviolent crime vs. violent crime = 6.51, p = 0.011.
χ^2—Never jailed for violent crime (never jailed + jailed for nonviolent crime) vs. jailed for violent crime = 4.54, p = 0.033

independent laboratories (Benjamin et al., 1995; Novick et al., 1995; Ebstein et al., 1996) have shown an association between the presence of the 7 allele and novelty seeking, a trait associated with impulsivity. Other studies have failed to find such an association (Malhotra et al., 1996; Gelernter et al., 1997).

In a study of thirty-nine children with ADHD compared to thirty-nine controls, LaHoste et al. (1996) reported that 41 percent of the ADHD children carried at least one 7 allele compared to 21 percent of the controls ($p < .01$). In a replication study they found an association only with a subtype of ADHD (Swanson et al., 1998). Grice et al. (1996) reported an association between the 7 allele of the *DRD4* gene and Tourette's syndrome. Sixty-four family trios were examined using the transmission-disequilibrium test (Spielman et al., 1993), twelve from nuclear families and fifty-two from four large kindreds. While there was a significant tendency for transmission of the 7 allele to affected individuals ($p < .001$), the results were most positive in two families, consistent with a lack of genetic uniformity. Van de Wetering did not find an increase in the 7 allele in their Tourette's syndrome probands (cited in Grice et al., 1996). In our own studies of 1,168 controls and 707 patients, we also found an association between the *DRD4* gene and a range of impulsive, addictive behaviors (Comings et al., 1999b).

***DRD5* Gene.** There have been few studies of the *DRD5* gene. However, in our studies of ADHD in subjects with Tourette's syndrome, we found that of the five dopamine receptor genes, the *DRD1*, *DRD2* and *DRD5* contributed the most to the ADHD score (see Figure 16.4).

***DRD1* Gene.** Using a common marker of the *DRD1* gene, we have shown a significant increase in the frequency of a variant in the *DRD1* gene in subjects with a range of addictive behaviors, including varying types of compulsive, addictive behaviors, Tourette's syndrome, smoking, and pathological gambling (Comings et al., 1997).

***DAT1* Gene.** A fifth important dopamine gene is the dopamine transporter gene (*DAT1*). Tansporters are proteins present on the surface of presynaptic neurons that are responsible for transporting a given substance across the membrane. Thus, after dopamine is released into the synapse, the dopamine transporter is responsible for transporting it back into the neuron from which it was released. The *DAT1* is a potentially important gene in ADHD because it is the site of action of methylphenidate (Ritalin), *d*-amphetamine (Dexedrine), pemoline (Cylert), and bupropion (Wellbutrin), the major medications used in the treatment of ADHD. There is a polymorphic 40 base pair repeat in the transcribed part of the gene (Vandenbergh et al., 1992a, 1992b; Giros et al., 1992, 1996). The most common alleles contain 9 or 10 repeats. Comings et al. (1996e), Cook et al. (1995) and Gill et al. (1997) have all independently reported a significant association between the 10 repeat allele and ADHD. Knockout mice missing the dopamine transporter gene are extremely hyperactive (Giros et al., 1996; Caron, 1996). Once again, the implications of these genetic variants are that they occur more frequently in ADHD or related disorders, suggesting a genetic origin, and that dopamine metabolism and/or activity may be altered in these disorders.

Serotonin Genes

Defective central nervous system (CNS) serotonin metabolism has been repeatedly associated with aggressive and violent behavior, including suicide (Brown et al., 1979; Brody, 1970; Lidberg et al., 1984; Linnoila et al., 1983; Roy et al., 1986; van Praag, 1991; Coccaro, 1989; Coccaro et al., 1997; Lidberg et al., 1985). Thus, genes affecting serotonin metabolism should be particularly good candidates for CD and aggressive behavior.

***HTR1B* Gene.** Mice for which the serotonin$_{1B}$ receptor gene has been functionally deleted ("knockout" mice) have been shown to be very aggressive (Saudou et al., 1994). The human $5\text{-}HT_{1B}$ gene has been localized to chromosome 6. Virkkunen et al. (1995) studied polymorphism of this gene with allele frequencies of 0.72 for the G alleles and 0.28 for the C allele (Lappalainen et al., 1995). They found a decrease in the frequency of the C allele in antisocial personality disorder (APD) compare to normals.

***HTR2A* Gene.** We examined a variant polymorphism in the serotonin$_{2A}$ receptor gene in a sample of eighty-six male non-Hispanic Caucasian substance abusers and seventy-eight age- and ethnically-matched controls. On the Addiction Severity Index (which measures the nature and extent of an individual's drug use and related behaviors), this genetic variant was associated with an amount of money spent on drugs (p<.05), a history of rape (p<.05), and a history of shoplifting/vandalism (p<.05). On the Buss-Durkee Hostility Scale, it was associated with elevated scores on the assault (p<.01) and indirect hostility (p<.05) subscales.

HTR1DA Gene. The $5\text{-}HT_{1DA}$ gene has been localized to chromosome 1 and is known to play a role in serotonin metabolism (Glennon et al., 1995). Virkkunen et al. (1995) studied a particular genetic variant that resulted in a silent amino acid substitution. The C variant was significantly more common in adult offenders with APD (10.7 percent), and in childhood CD (33.3 percent) than in normal controls (4.5 percent).

TDO2 Gene. Tryptophan 2,3-dioxygenase (*TDO*) is the enzyme that degrades tryptophan into kynurenine. Since tryptophan in the precursor of serotonin, increased activity of *TDO* is associated with low serotonin levels, a condition known to be associated with aggressive behaviors. Because of its importance, we cloned and sequenced the human *TDO2* gene (Comings et al., 1995) and identified several genetic polymorphisms (Comings et al., 1996e). Several of these were associated with changes in blood serotonin level, alcoholism, drug abuse, ADHD and Tourette's syndrome (Comings et al., 1996e).

Adrenergic Genes

Many studies have suggested an important role for norepinephrine in ADHD (McCracken, 1991; Shekim et al., 1997; Yu-cum & Yu-feng, 1984; Mason, 1980; Halperin et al., 1997; Arnsten et al., 1996). Strong support for such a role comes from the effectiveness of clonidine, an α_2 adrenergic receptor agonist in the treatment of ADHD and CD (Hunt, 1987; Hunt et al., 1985; Comings et al., 1990). Clonidine causes a decrease in synaptic norepinephrine levels (Starke et al., 1974).

DBH Gene. Dopamine ß-hydroxylase is an important enzyme in norepinephrine metabolism because it is responsible for the conversion of dopamine to norepinephrine. In some studies, low blood levels of DBH have been associated with ADHD and CD (Rogeness et al., 1986; Rogeness et al., 1984; Gabel et al., 1993; Rogeness et al., 1989). Based on these studies, Comings et al. (1996e) studied a polymorphism of the *DBH* gene and found a significant association with the 1 allele of the *Taq* I B1 polymorphism and ADHD and learning disabilities in children with Tourette's syndrome. The presence of learning disabilities is consistent with animal studies showing that when rats are given a drug that inhibits DBH, they show impaired maze learning ability (Randrup & Scheel-Kruger, 1966). This is also associated with hyperactivity, aggression, self-stimulation, and stereotypic movements (Randrup & Scheel-Kruger, 1966).

ADRA2A and ADRA2C Genes. Since the primary site of action of clonidine (commonly used to treat ADHD) is on the adrenergic α_{2A} and α_{2C} receptors, these should be particularly good candidate genes for ADHD. This assumption is strengthened by studies of Arnsten and colleagues (Arnsten, 1997; Arnsten et al., 1996; Arnsten &

Goldman-Rakic, 1986) showing that in monkeys, defects in these two receptors can place the frontal lobes "off line." Since most of the symptoms of ADHD can be explained by defective functioning of the frontal lobes (Mattes, 1980; Pontius, 1973; Comings, 1990), any genetic defects that place the frontal lobes off line would be excellent candidate genes for ADHD.

Halperin et al. (1993, 1997) has shown that children with ADHD and cognitive disorders such as reading disabilities had higher plasma norepinephrine levels than ADHD children without reading disabilities. They also showed that children with higher plasma norepinephrine levels had significantly lower average verbal IQ, but normal performance IQ compared to ADHD children with lower norepinephrine levels. This was of particular relevance since many studies have shown low verbal IQ to be a predictor of antisocial behavior (Moffitt, 1993b; Prentice & Kelly, 1963; Miller, 1987). Pliszka et al. (1996) proposed that norepinephrine and adrenergic α_2-receptors played a role in some forms of ADHD through a dysregulation of the posterior cortical attention system (Posner & Peterson, 1990) of the parietal/temporal lobes. This would be distinct from the usual form of ADHD due to defects in the attention centers of the frontal lobes mediated by defective dopamine metabolism. Since the parietal lobes are also the centers for speech and language, and since dyslexia is a defect in word language, abnormalities in these attention centers would more likely be associated with cognitive disorders.

These observations led us to examine the role of three norepinephrine genes, DßH, *ADRA2A* and *ADRA2C* in ADHD, cognitive disorders, and ADHD children with and without cognitive disorders (Comings et al., 1999). There was significant association between quantitative scores for inattention, impulsivity, hyperactivity, learning disorders, grade school academic performance, and oppositional defiant behavior with each of the genes examined. The greatest association ($p = .0003$) was for the additive effect of all three genes. There was a significant increase in the number of variant NA genes, progressing from subjects without ADHD (A-) or learning disorders (LD-), to A+LD-, to A-LD+, to A+LD+ ($p = .0005$), but no comparable effect for dopamine genes. Thus, these genetic studies supported the concept of a parietal form of ADHD preferentially associated with cognitive disorders and defects in norepinephrine genes.

Monoamine Oxidase Genes

Monoamine oxidase (MAO) A and B are two of the enzymes that metabolize dopamine, norepinephrine, and serotonin. When levels of MAO are low, these neurotransmitters become imbalanced. Abnormalities in MAO levels have been implicated in a wide range of psychiatric disorders including alcoholism, ADHD, drug abuse, and impulsive and risk taking behaviors (Wiberg et al., 1977; Gottfries et al., 1975; Devor et al., 1994; von Knorring et al., 1991; Skekim et al., 1982; Buchsbaum et al., 1976; Schooler et al., 1978; Shekim et al., 1989; von Knorring et al., 1984; von Knorring et al., 1991).

Brunner and colleagues (1993) described a family in Holland in which numerous males had a history of aggression, sexual assault, and borderline IQ. Biochemical studies identified a mutation that resulted in inactivation of the *MAOA* gene. Since the *MAOA* gene is X-linked, only males were affected. This is the first description of what is, in effect, a "knockout" study of humans showing that a specific functionally deleted gene could result in aggressive behavior. Goldman and Fishbein, in Chapter 9 in this text, provide further discussion of possible MAO involvement in behavioral disorders.

We examined the alleles of two dinucleotide (CA)n repeat polymorphisms associated with the *MAOA* gene and one dinucleotide repeat polymorphism associated with the *MAOB* gene in 351 Tourette's syndrome patients, relatives, and controls. There was a significant association between the longer base pair (bp) alleles (greater number of repeats) of the *MAOA* gene with various behaviors including ADHD, alcoholism, drug abuse, stuttering, major depressive episode (MDE), conduct, and learning problems (Gade et al., 1998).

Gamma-Aminobutyric Acid Genes—*GABRB3* Receptor Gene

GABA is the most abundant neurotransmitter in the brain and functions as an inhibitor of many different neurons and their activity. Diazepam (or Valium), for example, acts on GABA receptors in the brain to produce its calming effects. Using a microsatellite polymorphism, we found a particularly rich association between those carrying alleles of <188 bp and measures of adult ADHD for subjects on the Veterans Administration Addiction Treatment Unit and controls. Those subjects that carried any <188 bp alleles had the highest scores for the Brown adult ADHD scale (Gade et al., 1996).

Androgen Receptor Gene

The increased frequency of ADHD, CD, oppositional defiant disorder, and learning disorders in males could be due to the involvement of an X-linked gene, or a gene affecting androgen metabolism, or both. Thus, the androgen receptor gene, *AR*, on the X-chromosome would be a reasonable candidate gene for these disorders. The first exon of the *AR* gene contains two trinucleotide repeats, one consisting of GGC and the other of CAG sequences. Both are highly polymorphic with the alleles varying from a few to dozens of repeats (Sleddens et al., 1993; Irvine et al., 1995). Studies have shown that the shorter alleles containing fewer repeats are associated with higher levels of the androgen receptor and with greater androgen effect (Chamberlain et al., 1994). Thus, we tested the hypothesis that individuals carrying the shorter alleles for the GGC repeat would have higher average scores for oppositional defiant disorder and CD. This proved to be the case. Of six different variables including impulsivity, inattention, hyperactivity, CD, oppositional defiant disorder, and learning disorder the *AR* was most significantly associated with CD and oppositional defiant disorder (Comings et al., 1999). Studies of the additive effect of the GGC and CAG polymorphisms and other genes related to androgen metabolism are in progress.

Other Genes

This is just a sampling of a few of the many genes that may play a role in ADHD+CD. Knockout mice missing the nitric oxide (Nelson et al., 1995), estrogen receptor (Ogawa et al., 1996), alpha-calcium-calmodulin kinase II (Chen et al., 1994), serotonin 2B (Ramboz et al., 1996), oxytocin (DeVries et al., 1997), preproenkephalin (Konig et al., 1996), or substance P (DeFelipe et al., 1998) genes show increased or decreased levels of aggression, indicating that they are all candidate genes for CD.

POLYGENIC INHERITANCE

Behavioral disorders such as ADHD, CD, oppositional defiant disorder, depression, and others are polygenically inherited. Polygenic disorders are due to the additive effect of multiple genes. Individuals are affected when they inherit a sufficient number of variant genes to develop clinical symptoms. In our studies of the effect of several dozen genes on a range of behavioral phenotypes, we find that each individual gene accounts for only 0.5 to 7.0 percent of the variance, with the average being less than 1.0 percent (Comings, 1996). Since polygenic disorders are due to the additive effect of multiple genes, we find that the most powerful approach is to study the additive effect of multiple genes. Figure 16.2 shows the results using this approach for three dopamine genes, *DRD2*, *DBH* and *DAT1* on ADHD (Comings et al., 1996b). The ADHD score progressively increased from nonclinical range for those carrying none of the three variants, to borderline range for those carrying one variant, to symptomatic range for those carrying two variants, to high clinical range for those carrying all three variants. In other words, these three genes were additive in their effect on the ADHD score. Figure 16.3 shows the effect of the same three genes on quantitative scores for CD and oppositional defiant disorder in the same set of subjects.

These findings illustrate two features. First, as with the ADHD score, the CD and oppositional defiance scores progressively increased from subclinical to clinical range in subjects carrying 0, 1, 2, or 3 variants. Second, disorders that are comorbid with ADHD, such as CD and oppositional defiance, share genes in common with ADHD. This is presumably the reason they are comorbid; if a given gene contributes to two different behaviors, individuals that inherit such genes are likely to have both disorders.

MULTIVARIATE ANALYSIS OF ASSOCIATIONS (MAA)

Despite the highly significant association between the presence of three dopamine genes, *DRD2*, *DBH* and *DAT1*, and the disorders ADHD, CD and oppositional defiance, and the presence of three norepinephrine genes, *DBH*, *ADR2A2* and *ADR2AC*, with ADHD and learning disorders, in each case they accounted for less than 4 percent of the variance of the respective quantitative scores. If the percent of the variance (r^2) is less than .04, then the predictability, or r, in a regression equation is less than .16.

To attempt to improve predictability, we examined the additive effect of twenty-nine different candidate genes on ADHD and CD (Comings et al., 1998b). This dramatically improved the situation. The final r^2 for twenty of the twenty-nine genes that contributed to the ADHD score was .134. This technique also supported our concept that disorders that are comorbid to ADHD are present because they share genes with ADHD. Thus, a similar analysis of quantitative scores for comorbid disorders showed the following r^2 and p values: oppositional defiant disorder .10, $p < 5.0 \times 10^{-8}$; conduct disorder .075, $p = 5.0 \times 10^{-6}$; tics .062, $p \leq 5.0 \times 10^{-5}$; learning disorders .045, $p \leq 5.0 \times 10^{-4}$; and in adult subjects, alcohol abuse/dependence .14, $p < 8.0 \times 10^{-6}$ and smoking .10, $p \leq 1.0 \times 10^{-4}$. Twenty genes were involved in oppositional defiant disorder, ten in CD, ten in LD, fifteen for alcoholism, and nine for smoking.

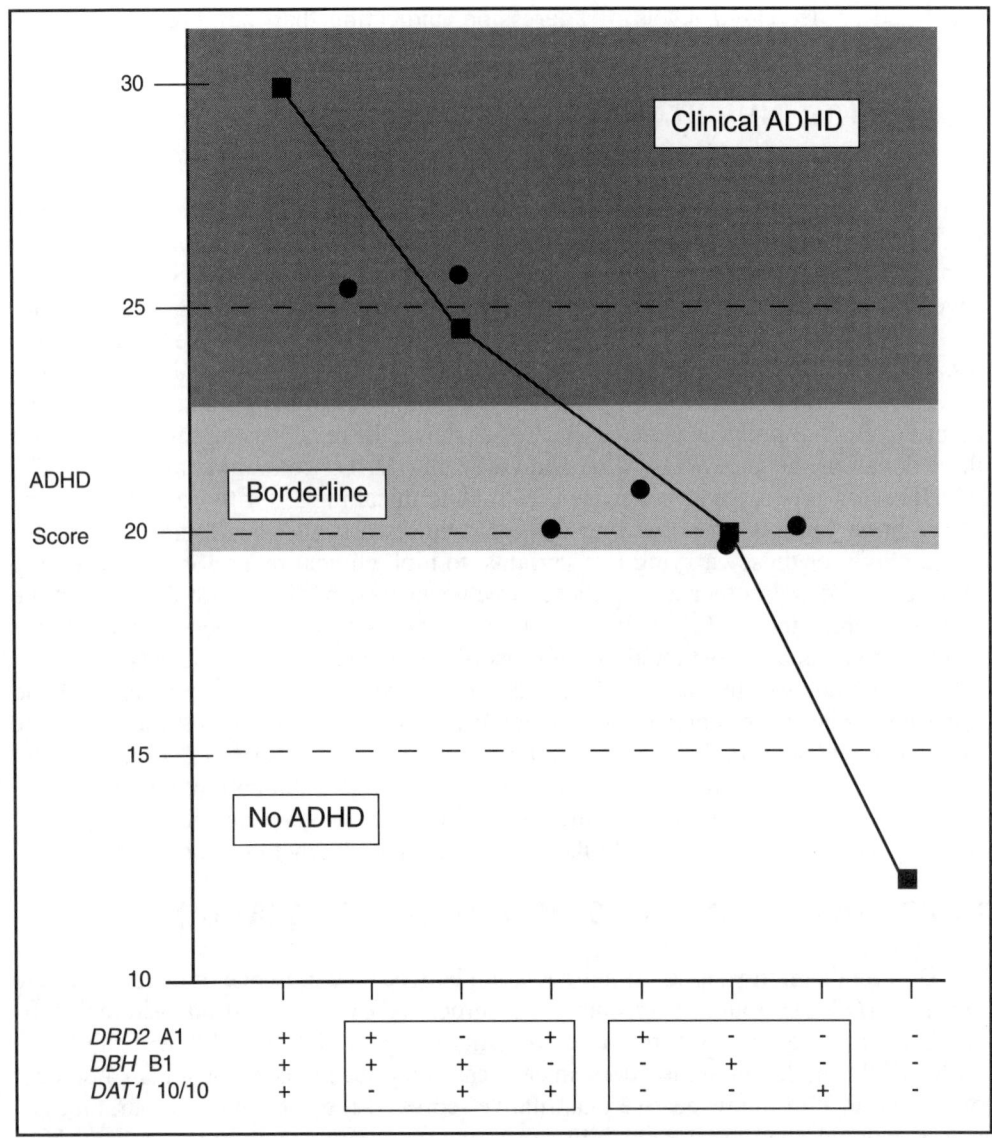

Figure 16.2. Additive Effect of the Three Genes, *DRD2* (*Taq* I A1 Allele), *DBH* (*Taq* I B1 Allele), and *DAT1* (10/10 Genotype), on a Quantitative ADHD Score in 350 Subjects with Tourette's Syndrome and Controls (Comings et al., 1996c)

The MAA technique also allowed the identification of the relative importance of the different genes in different behaviors. Thus, the norepinephrine genes were most important for ADHD. Together the *DBH*, *ADRA2A*, *ADRA2C*, and *NET1* genes accounted for 42 percent of the total r^2 of the ADHD score, while the serotonin genes (*HTT*, *HTR1A*, *HTR1DB*, *HTR2A*, *HTR2C*, and *TDO2*) accounted for only 9.5 percent. This is consistent with the many studies implicating defects in norepinephrine

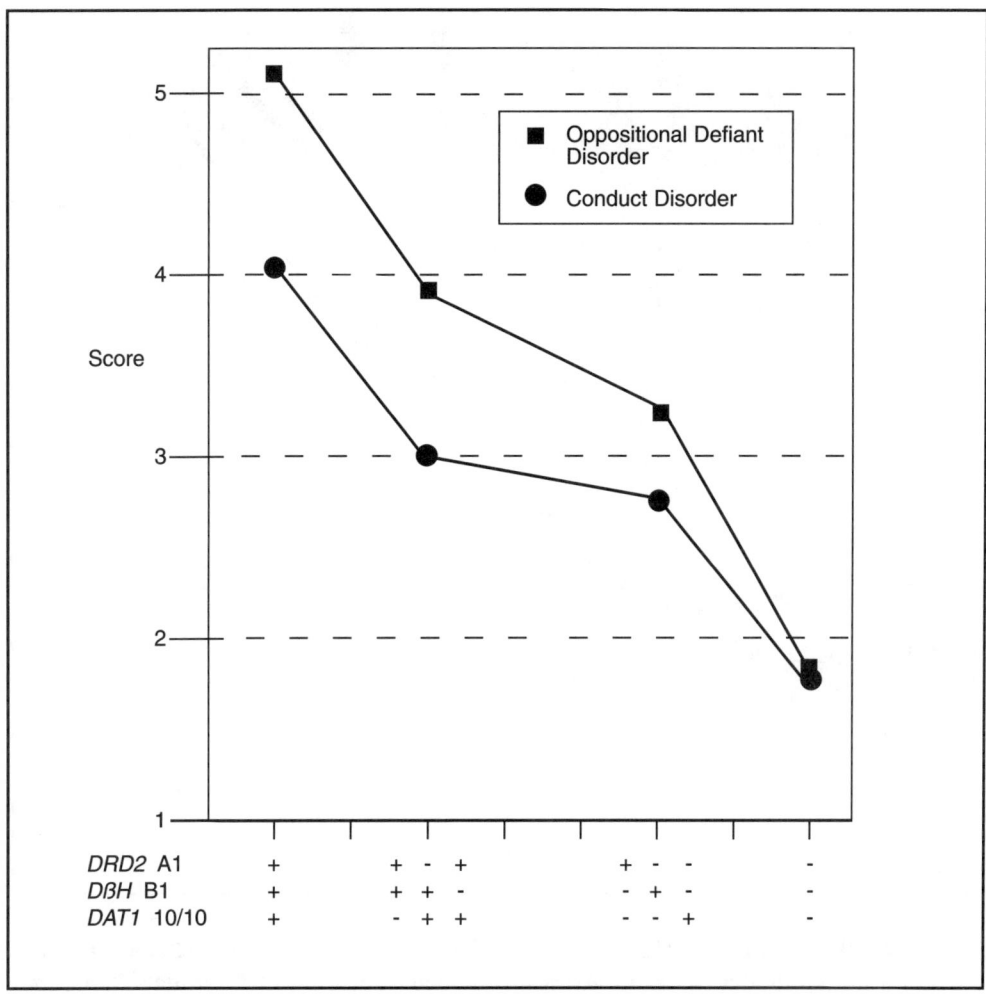

Figure 16.3. Additive Effect of the Three Genes, *DRD2* (*Taq* I A1 Allele), *DBH* (*Taq* I B1 Allele), and *DAT1* (10/10 Genotype), on Quantitative Scores for CD and ADHD in 350 Subjects with Tourette's Syndrome and Controls (Comings et al., 1996c)

metabolism in ADHD. By contrast, the serotonin genes accounted for 34 percent of the variance of the ODD score while the norepinephrine genes accounted for only 13 percent. This is consistent with the many studies cited above implicating abnormalities in serotonin metabolism in ODD.

Figure 16.4 shows the results of using the MAA technique (Comings et al., 1998b) to examine the genes involved in the disorder of special interest here, the combination of ADHD and CD. To examine this, an ADHD+CD score was computed by adding together the scores for the DSM-IV diagnosis of ADHD (range 0–34) and the DSM-IV diagnosis of CD (range adjusted from 0–12 to 0–36 to make it comparable to the ADHD score). Then, the effect on r^2 was examined by progressively adding the scores for the twenty-nine different genes shown at the bottom of the fig-

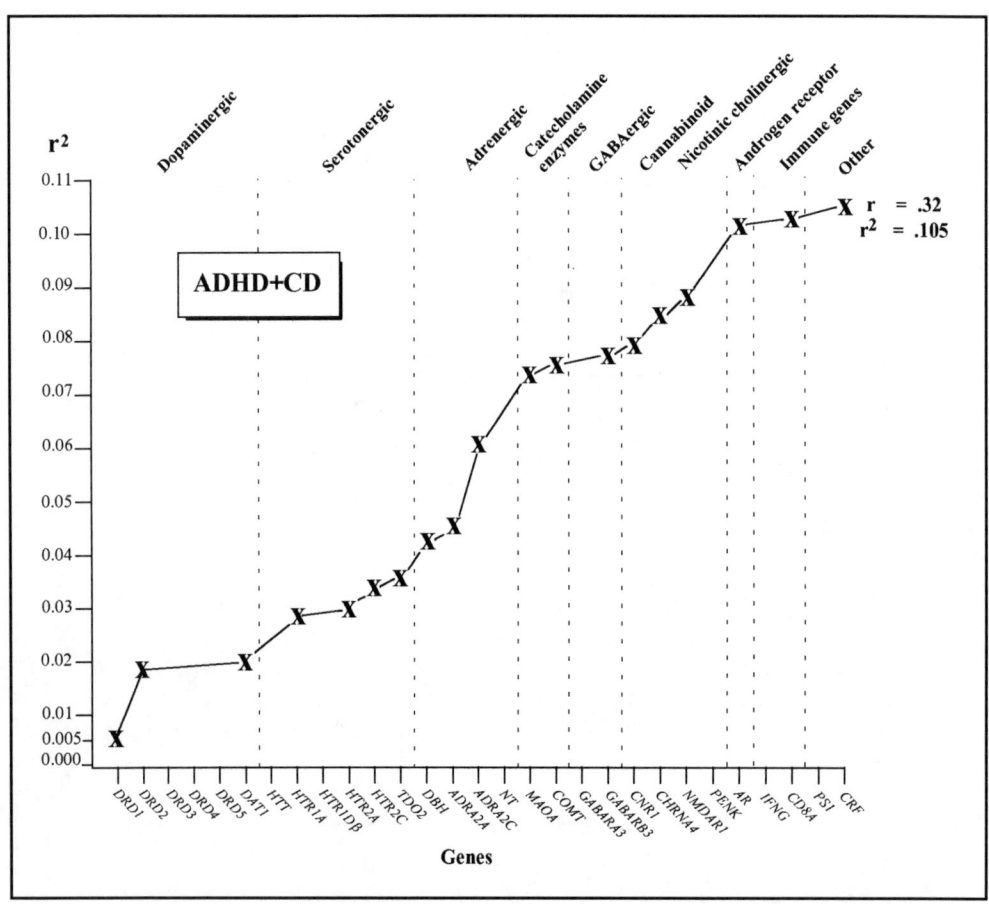

Figure 16.4. Results of the Multiple Additive Associations Technique (Comings et al., 1998c) for a Quantitative Score for ADHD+CD in 336 Subjects with Tourette's Syndrome and Controls

ure. The final r was .324, r^2 = .105, F = 39.21, and p ≤ 1 x 10^{-8}. The genes that were additive in their effect were the genes for the dopamine D_1 and D_2 receptor (*DRD1, DRD2*), the dopamine transporter (*DAT1*), the serotonin 1A, 2A, and 2C receptor (*HTR1A, HTR2A, HTRA2C*), tryptophan 2,3 dioxygenase (*TDO2*), dopamine ß-hydroxylase (*DBH*), the adrenergic 2A and 2C receptor (*ADRA2A, ADRA2C*), monoamine oxidase A (*MAOA*), catechol-o-methyl-transferasc (*COMT*), $GABA_A$ B_3 receptor (*GABRB3*), cannabinoid receptor (*CNR1*), nicotinic cholinergic alpha-4 receptor (*CHRNA4*), NMDA receptor (*NMDAR1*), androgen receptor (*AR*), lymphocyte surface marker C8 (*CD8A*), and corticotropin releasing factor (*CRF*). Those that contributed the most to the r^2 value were the *DRD2, HTR1A, ADRA2C, MAOA*, and *AR* genes.

While these nineteen genes accounted for only 10.5 percent of the ADHD+CD score, the r was .32, indicating that without any clinical information these genes improved the predictability of the ADHD+CD by 32.4 percent. We are presently studying twenty additional genes that when combined with these nineteen, may increase the r to 50+ percent predictability and the r^2 to greater than .25.

RELEVANCE TO TREATMENT

As a whole, these findings implicate genetic causes for ADHD+CD, which is a comorbid condition that often precedes delinquent or criminal behavior, including drug abuse. Although there are well-known environmental and social contributions to these disorders, our ability to predict and treat ADHD+CD based exclusively on this knowledge has been quite limited. This chapter provides support for the notion that also accounting for genetic influences significantly enhances our ability to identify and treat the precursors of behavioral disorders that are often associated with certain types of criminality. Specifically, the identification of genes involved in ADHD+CD implicate dysfunctions within particular neurotransmitter systems that are amenable to both social and medical interventions.

Treatment Before Prison

Our findings are relevant to the question: How can we identify the 4 to 6 percent of children who will be responsible for over 50 percent of the adult crime in time to prevent this outcome? In 1954, Meehl showed that statistical techniques using regression analysis were considerably more accurate in predicting behavioral outcomes than prediction based on clinical interviews or clinical judgment. Based on this method, Duckett (1988) demonstrated the relative accuracy of statistical prediction of future violence based on a few indices of prior violence in adults. Unfortunately, conduct and violent behavior in children and adolescents have a shorter record of prior behavior on which to base predictions. However, when the above genetic data is combined with clinical information and with variables relating to a past history of aggressive and antisocial behavior, it will be possible to identify with considerable accuracy the 4 to 6 percent of the children who may potentially be responsible for over 50 percent of the adult crime. This may allow medical and other therapeutic intervention to alter what otherwise would be an almost inevitable course into adult antisocial behavior.

My clinical experience with the treatment of over 3,000 children with disruptive behavioral disorders, brought to the clinic by their parents, indicates that the use of a small number of medications, including clonidine, fluoxetine, paroxitine, methylphenidate, dexedrine, depakote, molindone, and others (Comings, 1990; Comings, 1996), in association with individualized education plans (IEPs) in the schools and other approaches, can dramatically reverse the course of childhood antisocial behavior. In the presence of such an approach, high-risk children can be treated humanely and appropriately within the medical and mental health systems. In the absence of such an approach, high-risk children are more likely to eventually receive harsh and sometimes inhumane treatment within the criminal justice system.

Treatment in Prison

Genetic tests can also play a valuable role in prisons. As described in this chapter, ADHD is common in prison populations. As described by McCallon in Chapter 17 of this text, the identification and treatment of those inmates with ADHD can result in a dramatic improvement in response to rehabilitation programs and in a decrease in the recidivism rate when the inmates are released. However, one of the potential problems with the widespread implementation of such programs in prisons across the country is assuring prison authorities that the diagnosis of ADHD can be made with a reasonable degree of reliability even where an inmate attempts to "con" the physician into believing he has the disorder and deserves treatment. An important component of these programs is that they should be voluntary. An inmate's wishes to either enter or withdraw from a program should be his free choice. Experience to date indicates that once an inmate experiences how medications improve his attention span, organizational and executive skills, and reduce his anger and impulsivity, he is very motivated to remain in the program.

Ethical Considerations

A number of ethical concerns are often voiced whenever there is a discussion of the role of genetics in identifying those at future risk of antisocial or criminal behavior. One of these concerns is that screening programs will be introduced and individuals with the "wrong" genes will be forced to take "mind numbing" medications against their will. The reality of the situation is that children and adolescents with significant behavioral problems are brought to the clinic for evaluation by their parents. Genetic diagnosis and medical treatment is one of several options to be decided upon by the physician and family. Medication does not bring about a change in behavior because it sedates or numbs the mind. Rather, it brings about a change in behavior because it improves the function of the brain, especially the frontal lobes, toward normal. In the vast majority of cases, this can be accomplished without side effects. Finally, subjects are not identified by population screening. *The behavioral problems preceed the testing.* The use of genetic tests can improve the accuracy of diagnosis, help separate out environmental from genetic causes of the behavior, and improve the accuracy of choosing the appropriate medication. This process is no different than for any other disorder for which parents seek medical help for their children.

A second issue often voiced is that some genes that are identified for violent and aggressive behavior might be found to be present in higher frequency in certain racial groups, and thus the whole concept of using genetic testing in association with antisocial behavior is potentially racist. However, all studies to date on the population frequencies of genes indicate that the genetic variation within races is greater than between races. Equally important, all of these behaviors are polygenic, and there is no such thing as a gene for criminal behavior. Thus, while one gene may be more common in one racial group, another gene is likely to be less common, and over the twenty to fifty genes involved, the frequencies balance out.

The important point is that if a group of individuals with undiagnosed but easily treatable disorders such as ADHD end up in prison because they have never been diagnosed or treated, the identification and treatment of such individuals so they can be rehabilitated and released for treatment outside of a prison, or so they never end up in prison in the first place, benefits all humans, regardless of racial or ethnic background.

These and many other details concerning the treatable criminal mind will presented in more detail elsewhere (McCallon & Comings, 2000).

References

Arnsten, A. F. (1997). Catecholamine regulation of the prefrontal cortex. *Journal of Psychopharmacology, 11,* 151–162.

Arnsten, A. F. & Goldman-Rakic, P. S. (1986). Reversal of stress-induced delayed response deficits in rhesus monkeys by clonidine and naloxone. *Society of Neuroscience Abstacts, 12,* 1464.

Arnsten, A. F., Steere, J. C. & Hunt, R. D. (1996). The contribution of α_2-noradrenergic mechanism to prefrontal cortical cognitive function. Potential significance for attention-deficit hyperactivity disorder. *Archives of General Psychiatry, 53,* 448–455.

Asghari, V., Sanyal, S., Buchwaldt, S., Paterson, A., Jovanovic, V. & Van Tol, H. H. M. (1995). Modulation of interacellular cyclic AMP levels by different human dopamine D4 receptor variants. *Journal of Neurochemistry, 65,* 1157–1165.

August, G. J., Stewart, M. A. & Holmes, C. S. (1983). A four-year follow-up of hyperactive boys with and without conduct disorder. *British Journal of Psychiatry, 143,* 192–198.

Benjamin, J., Li, L., Paterson, C., Greenberg, B. D., Murphy, D. L. & Hamer, D. H. (1995). Population and familial association between the D4 dopamine receptor gene and measures of novelty seeking. *Nature Genetics, 12,* 81–84.

Biederman, J., Faraone, S. V., Keenan, K., Benjamin, J., Krifcher, B., Moore, C., Sprich-Buckminster, S., Ugaglia, K., Jellinek, M. S., Steingard, R., Spencer, T., Norman, D., Kolodny, R., Kraus, I., Perrin, J., Keller, M. B. & Tsuang, M. T. (1992). Further evidence for family-genetic risk factors in attention deficit hyperactivity disorder. *Archives of General Psychiatry, 49,* 728–738.

Biederman, J., Munir, K., Knee, D., Habelow, W., Armentano, M., Autor, S., Hoge, S. K. & Waternaux, C. (1986). A family study of patients with attention deficit disorder and normal controls. *Journal of Psychiatric Research, 20,* 263–274.

Biederman, J., Newcorn, J. & Sprich, S. (1991). Comorbidity of attention deficit hyperactivity disorder with conduct, depressive, anxiety, and other disorders. *American Journal of Psychiatry, 148,* 564–577.

Biederman, J., Wilens, T., Mick, E., Faraone, S.V., Weber, W., Curtis, S., Thornell, A., Pfister, K., Jetton, J. G. & Soriano, J. (1997). Is ADHD a risk factor for psychoactive substance use disorders? Findings from a four-year prospective follow-up study. *Journal of the American Academy of Child and Adolescent Psychiatry, 36,* 21–29.

Brody, J. F. Jr. (1970). Behavioral effects of serotonin depletion and of p-chlorophenylanlanine (a serotonin depletor) in rats. *Psychopharmacologia, 17,* 14–33.

Brown, G. L., Goodwin, F. K., Ballenger, J. C., Goyer, P. F. & Major, L. I. (1979). Aggression in humans correlates with cerebrospinal fluid amine metabolism. *Psychiatry Research, 1,* 131–139.

Brunner, H. G., Nelen, M. R., Breakefield, X. O., Ropers, H. H. & van Oost, B. A. (1993). Abnormal behavior associated with a point mutation in the structural gene for monamine oxidase A. *Science, 262,* 578–580.

Buchsbaum, M. S., Coursey, R. D. & Murphy, D. L. (1976). The biochemical high-risk paradigm: behavioral and familial correlates of low platelet monoamine oxidase activity. *Science, 194,* 339–341.

Cantwell, D.P. (1972). Psychiatric illness in the families of hyperactive children. *Archives of General Psychiatry, 27,* 414–417.

Caron, M. (1996). A mouse knockout. *American Journal of Psychiatry, 153,* 1387.

Chamberlain, N. L., Driver, E. D. & Miesdeld, R. L. (1994). The length and location of CAG trinucleotide repeats in the androgen receptor N-terminal domain affect transactivation function. *Nucleic Acids Research, 22,* 3181–3186.

Chen, C., Rainnie, D. G., Greene, R. W. & Tonegawa, S. (1994). Abnormal fear response and aggressive behavior in mutant mice deficient for alpha-calcium-calmodulin kinase II. *Science, 266,* 291–294.

Cloninger, C. R. & Gottesman, I. I. (1987). Genetic and environmental factors in antisocial behavioral disorders. In S. A. Mednick, T. E. Moffitt & S. A. Stack (Eds.), *The causes of crime: New biological approaches.* New York: Cambridge University Press, 92–109.

Coccaro, E. F. (1989). Central serotonin and impulsive aggression. *British Journal of Psychiatry, 155,* 52–62.

Coccaro, E. F., Kavoussi, R. J., Cooper, T. E. & Hauger, R. L. (1997). Central serotonin activity and aggression: Inverse relationship with prolactin response to d-fenfluramine, but not CSF 5-HIAA concentration, in human subjects. *American Journal of Psychiatry, 154,* 1430–1435.

Comings, D. E. (1990). *Tourette syndrome and human behavior.* Duarte, CA: Hope Press.

Comings, D. E. (1995). The role of genetic factors in conduct disorder based on studies of Tourette syndrome and ADHD probands and their relatives. *Journal of Developmental and Behavioral Pediatrics, 16,* 142–157.

Comings, D. E. (1996). *Search for the Tourette syndrome and human behavior genes.* Duarte, CA: Hope Press.

Comings, D. E. (1998). Why different rules are required for polygenic inheritance: Lessons from studies of the *DRD2* gene. *Alcohol, 16,* 1–10.

Comings, D. E. & Comings, B. G. (1987). A controlled study of Tourette syndrome. II. Conduct. *American Journal of Human Genetics, 41,* 742–760.

Comings, D. E., Comings, B. G., Muhleman, D., Dietz, G., Shahbahrami, B., Tast, D., Knell, E., Kocsis, P., Baumgarten, R., Kovacs, B. W., Levy, D. L., Smith, M., Kane, J. M., Lieberman, J.A., Klein, D. N., MacMurray, J., Tosk, J., Sverd, J., Gysin, R. & Flanagan, S. (1991). The dopamine D2 receptor locus as a modifying gene in neuropsychiatric disorders. *Journal of the American Medical Association, 266,* 1793–1800.

Comings, D. E., Comings, B. G., Tacket, T. & Li, S. (1990). The clonidine patch and behavioral problems. *Journal of the American Academy of Child and Adolescent Psychiatry, 29,* 667–668.

Comings, D. E., Ferry, L., Bradshaw-Robinson, S., Burchette, R., Chiu, C. & Muhleman, D. (1996a). The dopamine D2 receptor (*DRD2*) gene: A genetic risk factor in smoking. *Pharmacogenetics, 6,* 73-79.

Comings, D. E., Gade-Andavolou, R., Gonzalez, N., Blake, H., Wu, S. & MacMurray, J. P. (1999a). Additive effect of three noradrenergic genes (*ADRA2A, ADRA2C, DBH*) on attention deficit hyperactivity disorder and learning disabilities in Tourette syndrome subjects. *Clinical Genetics, 55,* 160–172.

Comings, D. E., Gade-Andavolou, R., Gonzalez, B. S., Wu, S., Dietz, G., Muhleman, D. & MacMurray, J .P. (1998). Multiple additive associations (MMA)—A powerful method of identifying the genes in polygenic disorders: ADHD, ODD, CD, alcoholism and pathological gambling. *American Journal of Human Genetics, 61,* A323.

Comings, D. E., Gade-Andavolou, R., Wu, S., Chiu, C., Dietz, G., Muhleman, D., Saucier, G., Ferry, L., Burchete, R., Johnson, P., Verde, R. & MacMurray, J. P. (1997). Studies of the potential role of the dopamine D1 receptor gene in addictive behaviors. *Molecular Psychiatry, 2,* 44–56.

Comings, D. E., Gonzalez, N., Wu, S., Gade-Andavolou, R., Muhleman, D., Saucier, G., Johnson, P., Verde, R., Rosenthal, R. L., Lesieur, H. R., Rugle, L. J., Miller, W. R. & MacMurray, J .P. (1999b). Studies of the 48 bp repeat of the *DRD4* gene in impulsive-addictive behaviors: Tourette syndrome, ADHD, pathological gambling, and substance abuse. *American Journal of Medical Genetics* (in press).

Comings, D. E., Muhleman, D., Dietz, G., Sherman, M. & Forest, G. (1995). Sequence of human tryptophan 2,3-dioxygenase: Presence of a glucocorticoid response-like element composed of a GTT repeat and an intronic CCCCT repeat. *Genomics, 29,* 390–396.

Comings, D. E., Muhleman, D., Gade, R., Chiu, C., Wu, H., Dietz, G., Winn-Dean, E., Ferry, L., Rosenthal, R. J., Lesieur, H. R., Rugle, L., Sverd, J., Johnson, P. & MacMurray, J. P. (1996b). Exon and intron mutations in the human tryptophan 2,3-dioxygenase gene and their potential association with Tourette syndrome, substance abuse and other psychiatric disorders. *Pharmacogenetics, 6,* 307–318.

Comings, D. E., Muhleman, D. & Gysin, R. (1996c). The dopamine D2 receptor (*DRD2*) gene in posttraumatic stress disorder: A study and replication. *Biological Psychiatry, 40,* 368–372.

Comings, D. E., Rosenthal, R. J., Lesieur, H. R., Rugle, L., Muhleman, D., Chiu, C., Dietz, G. & Gade, R. (1996d). A study of the dopamine D2 receptor gene in pathological gambling. *Pharmacogenetics, 6,* 223–234.

Comings, D. E., Wu, H., Chiu, C., Ring, R. H., Dietz, G. & Muhleman, D. (1996e). Polygenic inheritance of Tourette syndrome, stuttering, ADHD, conduct and oppositional defiant disorder: The additive and subtractive effect of the three dopaminergic genes—DRD2, DBH and DAT1. *American Journal of Medical Genetics (Neuropsychiatric Genetics), 67,* 264–288.

Cook, E. H., Stein, M. A., Krasowski, M. D., Cox, N. J., Olkon, D. M., Kieffer, J. E. & Leventhal, B. L. (1995). Association of attention-deficit disorder and the dopamine transporter gene. *American Journal of Human Genetics, 56,* 993–998.

DeFelipe, C., Herrero, J. F., O'Brien, J. A., Palmer, J. A., Doyle, C. A., Smith, A. J. H., Laird, J. M., Belmonte, C., Cervero, F. & Hunt, S. P. (1998). Altered nociception, analgesia and aggression in mice lacking the receptor for substance P. *Nature, 392,* 394–397.

Devor, E. J., Cloninger, C. R., Hoffman, P. L. & Tabakoff, B. (1994). Association of monoamine oxidase (MAO) activity with alcoholism and alcoholic subtypes. *American Journal of Medical Genetics, 48,* 209–213.

DeVries, A. C., Young, W. S. & Nelson, R. J. (1997). Reduced aggressive behaviour in mice with targeted disruption of the oxytocin gene. *Journal of Neuroendocrinology, 9,* 363–368.

Duckett, J. H. (1988). The prediction of violence. *South African Journal of Psychology, 18,* 10–18.

Ebstein, R. P., Novick, O., Umansky, R., Priel, B., Osher, Y., Blaine, D., Bennett, E.R., Nemanov, L., Katz, M. & Belmaker, R. H. (1996). Dopamine D4 receptor (D4DR) exon III polymorphism associated with the human personality trait of novelty seeking. *Nature Genetics, 12,* 78–80.

Eyestone, L. L. & Howell, R. J. (1994). An epidemiological study of attention deficit hyperactivity disorder and major depression in a male prison population. *Bulletin of the American Academy of Psychiatry and Law, 22,* 181–193.

Faraone, S. V., Biederman, J., Keenan, K. & Tsuang, M. T. (1991). A family-genetic study of girls with DSM-III attention deficit disorder. *American Journal of Psychiatry, 148,* 112–117.

Farrington, D. P. (1995). The development of offending and antisocial behavior from childhood: Key findings from the Cambridge study in delinquency development. *Journal of Child Psycholology and Psychiatry, 360,* 929–964.

Farrington, D. P., Loeber, R. & van Kammen, W. B. (1990). Long-term criminal outcomes of hyperactivity-impulsivity-attention deficit and conduct problems in childhood. In L. N. Robins & M. Rutter (Eds.), *Straight and devious pathways from childhood to adulthood.* New York: Cambridge University Press, 62–81.

Favarino, B. J. (1988). The frequency of depression and attention deficit-hyperactivity disorder in inmates of a county jail. Master's thesis, Brigham Young University.

Gabel, S., Stadler, J., Bjorn, J., Shindledecker, R. & Bowden, C. (1993). Dopamine-beta-hydroxylase in behaviorally disturbed youth. *Biological Psychiatry, 34,* 434–442.

Gade, R., Blake, H., MacMurray, J., Muhleman, D., Johnson, J., Verde, R. & Comings, D. E. (1996). Relationship of the GABRB3 gene to adult ADHD and personality traits in Caucasian and African-American samples. *Psychiatric Genetics, 6,* 164–165.

Gade, R., Muhleman, D., MacMurray, J. & Comings, D. E. (1998). Correlation of length of VNTR alleles at the X-linked MAOA gene and phenotypic effect in Tourette syndrome and drug abuse. *Molecular Psychiatry, 3,* 50–60.

Gelernter, J., Kranzler, H., Coccaro, E., Siever, L., New, A. & Mulgrew, C. L. (1997). D4 dopamine-receptor (*DRD4*) alleles and novelty seeking in substance-dependent, personality-disorder, and control subjects. *American Journal of Medical Genetics, 61,* 1144–1152.

Gill, M., Daly, G., Heron, S., Hawi, Z. & Fitzgerald, M. (1997). Confirmation of association between attention deficit disorder and a dopamine transporter polymorphism. *Molecular Psychiatry, 2,* 311–313.

Gillis, J. J., Gigler, J. W., Pennington, B. F. & DeFries, J. C. (1992). Attention deficit disorder in reading-disabled twins: evidence for a genetic etiology. *Journal of Abnormal and Child Psychology, 20,* 343–348.

Giros, B., El Mestikawy, S., Godinot, N., Zheng, K., Han, H., Yang-Feng, T. & Caron, M. G. (1992). Cloning, pharmacological characterization, and chromosome assignment of the human dopamine transporter. *Molecular Pharmacology, 42,* 383–390.

Giros, B., El Mestikawy, S.R., Wightman, R. M. & Caron, M. G. (1996). Hyperlocomotion and indifference to cocaine and amphetamine in mice lacking dopamine transporter. *Nature, 379,* 606–612.

Glennon, R. A., Dukat, M., Ploom, F. E. & Kupfer, D. J. (1995). Serotonin receptor subtypes. In *Psychopharmacology: The fourth generation.* New York: Raven Press, 415–429.

Gottfries, C. G., Oreland, L., Wiberg, A. & Winblad, B. (1975). Lowered monoamine oxidase activity in brains from alcoholic suicides. *Journal of Neurochemistry, 25,* 667–673.

Grice, D. E., Leckman, J. F., Pauls, D. L., Kurlan, R., Kidd, K. K., Pakstis, A. J., Chang, F. M., Buxbaum, J. D., Cohen, D. J. & Gelernter, J. (1996). Linkage disequilibrium of an allele at the dopamine D4 receptor locus with Tourette's syndrome by TDT. *American Journal of Human Genetics, 59,* 644–652.

Haggerty, K. P., Wells, E. A., Jenson, J. M., Catalano, R. F. & Hawkins, J. D. (1989, summer). Delinquents and drug use: A model program for community reintegration. *Adolescence, 24,* 439–456.

Halperin, J. M., Newcorn, J. H., Koda, V. H., Pick, L., McKay, K. E. & Knott, P. (1997). Noradrenergic mechanisms in ADHD children with and without reading disabilities: A replication and extension. *Journal of the American Academy of Child and Adolescent Psychiatry, 36,* 1688–1696.

Halperin, J. M., Newcorn, J. H., Schwartz, S. T., McKay, K. E., Bedi, G. & Sharma, V. (1993). Plasma catecholamine metabolites in ADHD boys with and without reading disabilities. *Journal of Clinical and Child Psychology, 22,* 219–225.

Hunt, R. D. (1987). Treatment effects of oral and transdermal clonidine in relation to methylphenidate: An open pilot study in ADD-H. *Psychopharmacology Bulletin, 23,* 111–114.

Hunt, R. D., Minderaa, R. B. & Cohen, D. J. (1985). Clonidine benefits children with attention deficit disorder and hyperactivity: Report of a double-blind placebo-crossover therapeutic trial. *Journal of the American Academy of Child Psychiatry, 24,* 617–629.

Irvine, R. A., Yu, M. C., Ross, R. K. & Coetzee, G. A. (1995). The CAG and GGC microsatellites of the androgen receptor gene are in linkage disequilibrium in men with prostate cancer. *Cancer Research, 55,* 1937–1940.

Konig, M., Zimmer, A. M., Steiner, H., Holmes, P. V., Crawley, J. N., Brownstein, M. J. & Zimmer, A. (1996). Pain responses, anxiety and aggression in mice deficient in pre-proenkephalin. *Nature, 383,* 535–538.

Kuhne, M., Schachar, R. & Tannock, R. (1997). Impact of comorbid oppositional or conduct problems on attention-deficit hyperactivity disorder. *Journal of the American Academy of Child and Adolescent Psychiatry, 36,* 1715–1724.

Lahoste, G. J., Swanson, J. M., Wigal, S. B., Glabe, C., Wigal, T., King, N. & Kennedy, J. L. (1996). Dopamine D4 receptor gene polymorphism is associated with attention deficit hyperactivity disorder. *Molecular Psychiatry, 1,* 121–124.

Lappalainen, J., Dean, M., Charbonneau, L., Virkkunen, M., Linnoila, M. & Goldman, D. (1995). Mapping of the serotonin 5-HT1Db autoreceptor gene on chromosome 6 and direct analysis for sequence variants. *American Journal of Medical Genetics (Neuropsychiatric Genetics), 60,* 157–161.

Lewis, D. O. (1976). Delinquency, psychomotor epileptic symptoms, and paranoid ideation: a triad. *American Journal of Psychiatry, 133,* 1395–1398.

Lewis, D. O., Pincus, J. H., Shanok, S. & Glaser, G. H. (1982). Psychomotor epilepsy and violence in a group of incarcerated adolescent boys. *American Journal of Psychiatry, 139,* 882–887.

Lichter, J. B., Barr, C. L., Kennedy, J. L., Van Tol, H. H. M., Kidd, K. K. & Livak, K. J. (1993). A hypervariable segment in the human dopamine receptor (*DRD4*) gene. *Human Molecular Genetics, 2,* 767–773.

Lidberg, L., Tuck, J. R., Åsberg, M., Scalia-Tomba, G. P. & Bertilsson, L. (1985). Homocide, suicide and CSF 5-HIAA. *Acta Psychiatrica Scandinavia, 71,* 230–236.

Lidberg, L., Åsberg, M. & Sundqvist-Stensman, U. B. (1984). 5-hydroxyindole acetic acid levels in attempted suicides who have killed their children. *Lancet, 2,* 928.

Linnoila, M., Virkkunen, M., Scheinin, M., Nuutila, A., Rimon, R. & Goodwin, F. K. (1983). Low cerebrospinal fluid 5-hydroxyindolacetic acid concentration differentiates impulsive from nonimpulsive violent behavior. *Life Sciences, 33,* 2609–2614.

Loney, J. & Milich, R. (1982). Hyperactivity, inattention, and aggression in clinical practice. *Advances in Developmental and Behavioral Pediatrics, 3,* 113–147.

Malhotra, A. K., Virkkunen, M., Rooney, W., Eggert, M., Linnoila, M. & Goldman, D. (1996). The association between the dopamine D4 receptor (*DRD4*) 16 amino acid repeat polymorphisms and novelty seeking. *Molecular Psychiatry, 1,* 388–391.

Mannuzza, S., Klein, R. G., Konig, P. H. & Giampino, T. L. (1989). Hyperactive boys almost grown up. IV. Criminality and its relationship to psychiatric status. *Archives of General Psychiatry, 46,* 1073–1091.

Mason, S. T. (1980). Noradrenaline and selective attention: A review of the model and the evidence. *Life Sciences, 27,* 617–631.

Mattes, J. A. (1980). The role of frontal lobe dysfunction in childhood hyperkinesis. *Comprehensive Psychiatry, 21,* 358–369.

McCallon, D. W. & Comings, D. E. (2000). *The treatable criminal mind.* Duarte, CA: Hope Press.

McCracken, J. T. (1991). A two-part model of stimulant action on attention-deficit hyperactivity disorder in children. *Journal of Neuropsychiatry, 3,* 201–209.

McGee, R., Williams, S. & Silva, P. A. (1984). Behavioral and developmental characteristics of aggressive, hyperactive and aggressive-hyperactive boys. *Journal of the American Academy of Child Psychiatry, 23,* 270–279.

Meehl, P. (1954). *Clinical versus statistical prediction: A theoretical analysis and review of the evidence.* Minneapolis: University of Minnesota Press.

Miller, L. (1987). Neuropsychology of the aggressive psychopath: An integrative review. *Aggressive Behavior, 13,* 119–140.

Mitchell, S. & Rosa, P. (1981). Boyhood behavior problems as precursors of criminality: A fifteen-year follow-up study. *Journal of Child Psychology and Psychiatry, 22,* 19–33.

Moffitt, T. E. (1993a). The neuropsychology of conduct disorder. *Development and Psychopathology, 5,* 135–151.

Moffitt, T. E. (1993b). Adolescence-limited and life-course-persistent antisocial behavior: A developmental taxonomy. *Psychological Review, 10,* 674–701.

Morrison, J. R. & Stewart, M. A. (1971). A family study of the hyperactive child syndrome. *Biological Psychiatry, 3,* 189–195.

Nelson, R. J., Demas, G. E., Huang, P. L., Fishman, M. C., Dawson, V. L., Dawson, T. M. & Snyder, S. H. (1995). Behavioral abnormalities in male mice lacking neuronal nitric oxide synthase. *Nature, 378,* 383–386.

Nestor, P. G. (1992). Neuropsychological and clinical correlates of murder and other forms of extreme violence in a forensic psychiatric population. *Journal of Nervous and Mental Diseases, 180,* 418–423.

Novick, O., Ebstein, R., Umansky, R., Priel, B., Osher, Y. & Belmaker, R. H. (1995). D-4 receptor polymorphism associated with personality variation in normals. *Psychiatric Genetics, 5,* S36.

Ogawa, S., Lubahn, D. B., Korach, K. S. & Pfaff, D. W. (1996). Aggressive behaviors of transgenic estrogen-receptor knockout male mice. *Annals of the New York Academy of Science, 794,* 384–385.

Pliszka, S. R., McCracken, J. T. & Maas, J. W. (1996). Catecholamines in attention-deficit hyperactivity disorder: Current perspectives. *Journal of the American Academy of Child and Adolescent Psychiatry, 35,* 264–272.

Pontius, A. A. (1973). Dysfunction patterns analogous to frontal lobe system and caudate nucleus syndrome in some groups of minimal brain dysfunction. *Journal of the American Medical Women's Association, 26,* 285–292.

Posner, M. I. & Peterson, S. E. (1990). The attention system of the human brain. *Annual Review of Neuroscience, 13,* 25–42.

Prentice, N. M. & Kelly, F. J. (1963). Intelligence and delinquency: A reconsideration. *Journal of Social Psychology, 60,* 327–337.

Ramboz, S., Saudou, F., Amara, D. A., Belzung, C., Segu, L., Misslin, R., Buhot, M. C. & Hen, R. (1996). 5-HT1B receptor knock out—behavioral consequences. *Behavioral Brain Research, 73,* 305–312.

Randrup, A. & Scheel-Kruger, J. (1966). Diethyldithiocarbamate and sterotyped behavior. *Journal of Pharmacy and Pharmacology, 18,* 752.

Robins, L. N. (1966). *Deviant children grown up.* Baltimore: Williams & Wilkins.

Robins, L. N. (1991). Conduct disorder. *Journal of Child Psychology and Psychiatry, 32,* 193–212.

Rogeness, G. A., Hernandez, J. M., Macedo, C. A., Mitchell, E. L., Amrung, S. A. & Harris, W. R. (1984). Clinical characteristics of emotionally disturbed boys with very low activities of dopamine ß-hydroxylase. *Journal of the American Academy of Child and Adolescent Psychiatry, 23,* 203–208.

Rogeness, G. A., Hernandez, J. M., Macedo, C. A., Amrung, S. A. & Hoppe, S. K. (1986). Near-zero plasma dopamine-b-hydroxylase and conduct disorder in emotionally disturbed boys. *Journal of the American Academy of Child Psychiatry, 25,* 521–527.

Rogeness, G. A., Maas, J. W., Javors, M. A., Macedo, C. A., Fischer, C. & Harris, W. R. (1989). Attention deficit disorder symptoms and urine catecholamines. *Psychiatry Research, 27,* 241–251.

Roy, A., Virkkunen, M., Guthrie, S., Poland, R. & Linnoila, M. (1986). Monamines, glucose metabolism, suicidal and aggressive behaviors. *Psychopharmacology Bulletin, 22,* 661–665.

Satterfield, J. H. & Schell, A. (1997). A prospective study of hyperactive boys with conduct problems and normal boys: Adolescent and adult criminality. *Journal of the American Academy of Child and Adolescent Psychiatry, 36,* 1726–1735.

Saudou, F., Amara, D. A., Dierich, A., LeMeur, M., Ramboz, S., Segu, L., Buhot, M-C. & Hen, R. (1994). Enhanced aggressive behavior in mice lacking 5-HT1B receptor. *Science, 265,* 1875–1878.

Schooler, C., Zahn, T. P., Murphy, D. L. & Buchsbaum, M. S. (1978). Psychological correlates of monoamine oxidase acivity in normals. *Journal of Nervous and Mental Diseases, 166,* 177–186.

Shekim, W. O., Bylund, D. B., Frankel, F., Alexson, J., Jones, S. B., Blue, L. O., Kirby, J. & Corchoran, C. (1989). Platelet MAO activity and personality variations in normals. *Psychiatry Research, 27,* 81–88.

Shekim, W. O., Davis, L. G, Bylund, D. B., Brunngraber, E., Fikes, L. & Lanham, J. (1982). Platelet MAO in children with attention deficit disorder and hyperactivty: A pilot study. *American Journal of Psychiatry, 139,* 936–938.

Shekim, W. O., Dekirmenjian, H. & Chapel, J. L. (1997). Urinary MHPG excretion in minimal brain dsyfunction and its modification by d-amphetamine. *American Journal of Psychiatry, 136,* 667–671.

Sherman, D. K., Iacono, W. G. & McGue, M. K. (1997a). Attention-deficit hyperactivity disorder dimensions: A twin study of inattention and impulsivity-hyperactivity. *Journal of the American Academy of Child and Adolescent Psychiatry, 36,* 745–753.

Sherman, D. K., McGure, M. K. & Iacono, W. G. (1997b). Twin concordance for attention deficit hyperactivity disorder: a comparison of teachers' and mothers' reports. *American Journal of Psychiatry, 154,* 532–535.

Sleddens, H. F., Oostra, B. A., Brinkman, A. O. & Trapman, J. (1993). Trinucleotide (GGN) repeat polymorphism in the human androgen receptor (AR) gene. *Human Molecular Genetics, 2,* 493.

Slutske, W. S., Heath, A. C., Dinwiddie, S. H., Madden, P. A., Bucholz, K. K., Dunne, M. P., Statham, D. J. & Martin, N. G. (1997). Modeling genetic and environmental influences in the etiology of conduct disorder: A study of 2,682 adult twin pairs. *Journal of Abnormal Psychology, 106,* 266–279.

Spielman, R. S., McGinnis, R. E. & Ewens, W. J. (1993). Transmission test for linkage disequilibirum: the insulin gene region and insulin-dependent diabetes mellitus (IDDM). *American Journal of Human Genetics, 52,* 506–516.

Starke, K., Montel, H., Gayk, W. & Marker, R. (1974). Comparision of the effects of clonidine on pre-and postsynaptic adrenoceptors in the rabbit pulmonary artery. *Naunyn-Schmiedeberg's Archives of Pharmacology, 285,* 133–150.

Stevenson, J. (1992). Evidence for a genetic etiology in hyperactivity. *Behavioral Genetics, 22,* 337–344.

Stewart, M. A., Cummings, C., Singer, S. & Deblois, C. S. (1981). The overlap between hyperactive and unsocialized aggressive children. *Journal of Child Psychology and Psychiatry, 22,* 35–45.

Swanson, J. M., Sunohara, G. A., Kennedy, J. L., Regino, R., Fineberg, E., Wigal, T., Lerner, M., Williams, L., Lahoste, G. J. & Wigal, S. (1998). Association of the dopamine receptor D4 (*DRD4*) gene with a refined phenotype of attention deficit hyperactivity disorder (ADHD): A family based approach. *Molecular Psychiatry, 3,* 38–41.

Vandenbergh, D. J., Persico, A. M., Hawkins, A. L., Griffin, C. A., Li, X., Jabs, E. W. & Uhl, G. R. (1992a). Human dopamine transporter gene (DAT1) maps to chromosome 5p15.3 and displays a VNTR. *Genomics, 14,* 1866–1868.

Vandenbergh, D. J., Persico, A. M. & Uhl, G. R. (1992b). A human dopamine transporter cDNA predicts reduced glycosylation, displays a novel repetitive element and provides racially-dimorphic Taq I RFLPs. *Molecular Brain Research, 15,* 161–166.

Van Praag, H. M. (1991). Serotonergic dysfunction and aggression control. *Psychological Medicine, 21,* 15–19.

Van Tol, H. H. M., Wu, C. M., Guan, H-C., Ohara, K., Bunzow, J. R., Civelli, O., Kennedy, J., Seeman, P., Niznik, H. B. & Javanovic, V. (1992). Multiple dopamine D4 receptor variants in human population. *Nature, 358,* 149–152.

Virkkunen, M., Goldman, D. & Linnoila, M. (1995). Serotonin in alcoholic violent offenders. In *Genetics of criminal and antisocial behavior*. Chichester, England: John Wiley & Sons, 168–171.

von Knorring, A. L., Hallmann, J., Vonknorring, L. & Oreland, L. (1991). Platelet monoamine oxidase activity in Type-1 and Type-2 alcoholism. *Alcohol, 26,* 409–416.

von Knorring, L., Oreland, L. & Winblad, B. (1984). Personality traits related to monoamine oxidase activity in platelets. *Psychiatry Research, 12,* 11–26.

Wang, S., Detera-Wadleigh, S. D., Coon, H., Sun, C. E., Goldin, L. R., Duffy, D. L., Byerley, W. F., Gershon, E. S. & Diehl, S. R. (1996). Evidence of linkage disequilibrium between schizophrenia and the SCa1 CAG repeat on chromosome 6p23 [letter]. *American Journal of Human Genetics, 59,* 731–736.

Wiberg, A., Gottfries, C. G. & Oreland, L. (1977). Low platelet monoamine oxidase activity in human alcoholics. *Medical Biology, 55,* 181–186.

Yu-cum, S. & Yu-feng, W. (1984). Urinary 3-methoxy-4 hydroxyphenylglycol sulfate excretion in seventy-three schoolchildren with minimal brain dysfunction syndrome. *Biological Psychiatry, 19,* 861–868.

Chapter 17

Diagnosing and Treating ADHD in a Men's Prison

by Dwaine McCallon, M.D.

Introduction 17-2
Evolution of a Program 17-3
    Initial Interview 17-3
    Follow-Up 17-4
    Relation to Corrections Program 17-5
    ADHD Training Group 17-5
Methods and Goals of Group Training 17-7
Program Results 17-9
Underlying Mechanisms in Behavioral Disorders 17-10
    Justification for Considering Medical Treatment 17-10
    Concerns Regarding Use of Medication in Prison 17-10
Medications for Disorders Commonly Seen in Prisons 17-11
    Attention Deficit and Impulsive Distractibility 17-11
    Marked Hyperactivity and Tics in Tourette's Syndrome 17-12
    Use of Stimulants in the Presence of Tourette's Syndrome 17-12
    Emotional Leveling 17-12
    Obsessive-Compulsive Behavior 17-13
    Bipolar Disorder 17-13
Unexpected Results of Program 17-14
    The Education of Corrections Officers 17-14
    The Challenge of Prison Medicine 17-15
Differential Diagnoses 17-16
    Atypical Seizures 17-16
    Bipolar Disorder 17-16
    Encephalopathy ("Organic Brain Disorder"), Drug Abuse,
      Head Trauma, and Child Abuse 17-17
    Hallucinations and Delusions 17-17
    Psychopathy or Antisocial Personality Disorder 17-17

An Example of True ADD/ADHD 17-18
The Hidden Costs of Missed Diagnoses 17-19

INTRODUCTION

In 1990, working part time as a contract physician in a large, medium-security prison for men, I noticed one of our most peculiar inmates carrying a 32-ounce container of black coffee in the corridor. I asked how he could consume so much caffeine and he quickly plead that he had permission from his supervisor in the kitchen to have continuous coffee in large amounts. His growing tic-like movements, apparent distress, distraction and anxiety, as well as an increasing agitated movement, was typical of severe attention deficit hyperactivity disorder (ADHD). I asked him to come to my office late in the afternoon. He missed the appointment, as he was quite paranoid toward anyone in a position of authority over him within the corrections system. I had to call his wing and ask that he be escorted to the clinic.

As a pediatrician with twenty-five years of interest in learning and attentional problems, I had seen many of my learning disabled patients grow into adulthood and develop severe problems with family, employment, education, and even the criminal justice system. In the late 1980s and early 1990s, a large knowledge base regarding attention deficit disorder (ADD) accumulated, enabling clinicians to better diagnose and treat the disorder and its co-occurring symptoms within correctional settings (Cocores et al., 1987; Satterfield et al., 1982). Several findings related to ADD included the possibility that nearly as many females as males may have attention problems, but they are widely underestimated because of an absence of motor overactivity or social acting out in many cases. Thus in females, the same syndrome may differ in its outward manifestations. For boys, on the other hand, the subtypes of ADD, termed "hyperactivity syndrome" or "attention deficit disorder," were considered in the development of three major classifications: ADD with "typical" hyperactivity (ADHD), ADD without this annoying characteristic, and a mixed or combined type with intermittent presence of overactivity symptoms. More important, it was found that many such patients still had significant symptoms into adulthood, even though the obvious symptoms of higher activity and restlessness appeared to diminish.

As I interviewed this coffee-saturated, 34-year-old man, I was stunned at the problems he had experienced with his apparent severe ADHD. He had spent seventeen of his thirty-four years in some sort of lockup. His crimes were nonviolent, often impulsive, involving alcohol, drugs or stealing, often of items he really did not want or need. His reason for drinking two quarts of coffee was to "keep me out of the hole!" He related that he spent much of his time in segregation for missing work lines or forgetting "DLOs" (direct lawful orders from an officer). He was convinced that enough caffeine made it possible for him to remember. Later, on checking with his case manager, I found he had spent between 10 to 15 percent of his time in the hole for continuous minor infractions and "flaky behavior." He appeared to be self medicating his disorder as if he had an intrinsic sense of the benefits of stimulants on his ADHD.

I saw this man, who was nearly illiterate and a fourth-grade runaway, for about six hours over the next ten days. After using several screening tools and carefully administering the Wender Utah Rating Scale (WURS) (Wender, 1985; see also Wender, 1995), I interviewed teachers who had been frustrated with this man, as well as his boss and case managers. Feeling confident of his diagnosis of severe ADHD, I asked a colleague in the mental health clinic to evaluate him independently. He arrived at the same diagnosis.

EVOLUTION OF A PROGRAM

In July 1990, I approached our warden, who was interested in children with special learning needs, as he was the parent of one such child. Explaining what ADHD was and what it was not, I asked him to help me obtain permission not only for special tutoring and counseling, but for stimulant drug therapy with Ritalin, which is commonly used successfully in children with ADHD. He was cautious but willing to approve the administration of a well-controlled trial of medication. The results were remarkable.

Over the next twenty-two months the inmate, who had been expelled from vocational training in the welding shop when he absentmindedly laid down an ignited acetylene torch and nearly burned out the shop, was able to learn to read, to obtain his GED high school equivalent diploma, and to improve his communications ability. Further, he completed a small business management associate's degree, learned basic computer science, mastered five musical instruments, completed a course in radio broadcasting and became the facility in-house radio DJ during the evenings. Most important, he had no further infractions and was paroled about two and one-half years later. It is much more productive to have this intelligent but previously skill-less man now working in a media position for nearly five years and paying taxes rather than using over $25,000 of state tax funds to be incarcerated indefinitely without any hope for rehabilitation.

As we saw this man undergo change, my colleagues and I began looking for signs of ADD/ADHD in our patients. Our prison seemed to be filled with such individuals. I discovered that the characteristics of ADHD (distractability, poor attending, impulsive behavior and resulting poor recall of consequences and poor judgment) may explain many impulsive crimes. Although most persons with ADHD do not end up in prison, prisons house a significant proportion of those with ADD and ADHD. With carefully drawn criteria for accurate diagnosis and tools to determine coexisting or "comorbid" conditions such as depression, bipolar disorder, rage dyscontrol, dyslexia and Tourette's syndrome, we began a small treatment study group to see if appropriate treatment could make a difference.

Early in the study, a charming and handsome man of 32 who found great excitement in burglary blurted out in the training group: "This is my third time down. On the last trips, all of this stuff on mental health crap and especially anger management was a crock; it didn't make sense. Now with the medications, I can understand what they are trying to teach us. Even better, I can remember it more than five minutes!!" This man went on to be a paraprofessional teaching assistant not only in a literacy course but in a basic anger management course. These are only two of many cases that enticed us to continue to learn from each of our carefully selected patients.

Initial Interview

Our present groups are limited to between fifteen and twenty participants. They are now referred by several personnel in education, case management, and even security, as well as from other inmates who have been treated. As we developed this small program with no funding, either my colleagues in mental health, Brooke Pitcock and Diane Godynik-Clements, or I do an initial interview. Then we carefully explain the stringent requirements of being treated in this unique program. The patient is given an elaborate questionnaire that is often very difficult to complete. This instrument was adapted with the permission of Dr. James Lauer, a psychiatrist with many years' experience in diagnosing and treating adult and adolescent ADHD. We inform the referred inmate that other inmates in the library or in our program will help him to complete this extensive history. There are several problems with data collection on this initial screen. Many of these men came from dysfunctional homes and often have a dozen foster homes or youth offender custody sites in their history. School left a bad taste in their mouths of boredom, shame at being dumb, and a humiliation that they bury in their deepest recall. Thus, taking what appears to be a test is not pleasant for them and their memories of various living situations are incomplete.

Follow-Up

During the second visit, we help them to complete the test battery to the extent possible. Often a teacher in the ABE (adult basic education) or literacy course can help us obtain old school records to document early childhood classroom behavior and learning disabilities. Often, however, we cannot obtain this documentation in spite of the "requirements" of the DSM-IV (*Diagnotisic and Statistical Manual of Mental Disorders*, 4th ed.,1994). Our diagnosis may rest on our clinical experience and the appearance of the person as well as his observed and self-reported personal struggles with learning and behavior management. We also administer the Copeland Rating Scale for Adult ADD (Copeland, 1987), which is helpful in establishing an accurate diagnosis. (The differential diagnosis of other, similar-appearing conditions is discussed below.)

Sometimes we do not reach consensus on the diagnosis, particularly in the presence of bipolar symptoms (previously called manic-depression) or past violent behavior. In such cases, we obtain input from educators in contact with the inmate and then make a determination whether to enroll the inmate for a treatment trial. We have found over 50 percent of our ADD/ADHD subjects carry a previous diagnosis of bipolar disorder. A survey in the Utah prison system (Eyestone & Howell, 1994) showing that 25.5 percent of the adult male prisoners studied exhibited very typical adult ADHD by the standards of DSM-III-R (1987) helped explain this finding. This assured us that we were not overdiagnosing this condition of adult ADHD. Additionally, 25.5 percent of the Utah study group exhibited major depression symptoms with a comorbidity rate of 46.1 percent. The implications were that the prison group had an incidence of both depression and ADHD of 50 to 80 percent higher than the general population of similar noncriminal subjects. The presence of one diagnosis or the other predicted a much higher likelihood that the other condition was present (46 percent) beyond what one would expect.

We have found evidence of coexisting bipolar syndrome in four of our subjects so far, in a group of sixty. More important, we have found effective treatments for both conditions, with appropriate medications for each. Two other subjects who appear to have a genetic form of "intermittent explosive rage disorder" also have typical ADHD and we were able to successfully treat these men with gratifying improvement in both syndromes (see later discussion of medication). There is also a surprisingly significant number of cases with Tourette's syndrome, a disorder characterized by facial tics, grunting, uncontrolled vocal noises, eye blinking and other symptoms, and known to involve the neurotransmitters dopamine and serotonin in particular.

Relation to Corrections Program

New patients to this program are informed that the ADD program is not part of the basic medical/mental health care provided in our correctional system and that to enter the program, they must agree to remain in our institution until completion. The time in the program ranges from a minimum of six months to as long as twenty-four months. The maximum possible benefit of this training and treatment program for each individual is determined by the psychologist and myself. The implications of this determination are critical for the inmate. Our correctional department has an excellent incentive program, and with good behavior inmates can not only obtain "good time," which is a shortening of the total mandatory sentence time before meeting parole, but they have other incentives. These include attractive educational and vocational programs and also placement into honor camps with minimally restrictive dormatory living and opportunities to earn part-time college tuition and educational advancement in rural settings with outdoor work.

We admittedly select only highly motivated subjects who wish to control behavior that in many cases has left them depressed over their present situation and imprisonment. On the other hand, for them to sacrifice their chance to advance to a less restrictive facility presents a significant dilemma. This is not a problem with long-term violent or repeat felons, but is a difficult decision for first offenders with fairly short sentences, precisely the inmates who hold the most potential for rehabilitation and change.

We explain to the subjects that medication will not *cure* ADHD or Tourette's syndrome. In the majority of Tourette's cases, however, medication affects the ADHD associated with the disorder, which is often as much or more handicapping than the tics (Comings & Comings, 1984, 1987; Abwender et al., 1996). Patients are taught that part of the treatment for ADHD, Tourette's syndrome, and related conditions is to learn to control their handicapping symptoms, which are largely inherited and can be mastered to a great extent via medication. Such medication may be required for periods as short as six months or for the rest of one's life, depending on the severity of the attentional problems and the other habits, personality problems, and impairments one has acquired or inherited that co-occur with the attentional problem.

ADHD Training Group

The most important component of the program is the ADHD training group. We call this a "training group," as most of the inmate patients are already stigmatized in their own mind about how many "mental health" groups they are required by the state to complete (basic mental health, domestic violence, anger management, and drug and alcohol recovery programs are all mandatory, as well as sex offender and other

Table 17.1
Bibliography of Self-Help and Educational Books and Articles

Books

Amen, D. (1996). *Windows into the ADD mind.* Fairfield, CA: MindWorks Press.

Barkley, R. (1998) *Attention deficit disorder: A handbook for diagnosis and treatment* (2d ed.). New York: Guilford Press.

Comings, D. E. (1990). *Tourette syndrome and human behavior.* Duarte, CA: Hope Press.

Comings, D. E. (1996). *The search for the Tourette and human behavior genes.* Duarte, CA: Hope Press.

Comings, D. E. (1997). *The gene bomb.* Duarte, CA: Hope Press.

Goleman, D. (1997). *Emotional intelligence.* New York: Bantam Books.

Greenfield, S. (Ed.) (1996). *The human mind explained.* New York: Henry Holt & Co.

Hallowell, E. & Ratey, J. (1994). *Driven to distraction: Regcognizing and coping with attention deficit disorder from childhood though adulthood.* New York: Pantheon Books.

Hallowell, E. & Ratey, J. (1996). *Answers to distraction.* New York: Bantam Books.

Hartman, T. (1993). *Attention deficit disorder: A different perception.* Grass Valley, CA: Underwood.

Ledoux, J. (1996). *The emotional brain.* New York: Simon & Schuster.

Ratey, J. & Johnson, C. (1997). *Shadow syndromes.* New York: Pantheon Boos.

Wender, P. (1995). *Attention deficit hyperactivity disorder in adults.* New York: Oxford University Press.

Volavka, J. (1995). *The neurobiology of violence.* Washington, DC: American Psychiatric Press.

Articles

Barkley, R., Fischer, M., Edelbrock, C. & Smallish, L. (1993). Driving related risks and outcomes of attention deficit hyperactivity disorder in adolescents and young adults: A 3–5 year followup survey. *Pediatrics, 92,* 213–219.

Fishbein, D. (1990). Biological perspectives in criminology. *Criminology, 28,* 27–72.

Holman, B. & Devous, M. D., Sr. (1992). Functional brain SPECT: The emergence of a powerful clinical method. *Journal of Nuclear Medicine, 33,* 1888-1904.

Jeffery, C. R. (1994). *Biological and neuropsychiatric approaches to criminal behavior in varieties of criminology: Readings from a dynamic discipline.* New York: Praeger.

Ratey, J., Greenberg, M. & Lindem, K. (1991). Combination of treatments for attention deficit hyperactivity disorder in adults. *Journal of Nervous and Mental Diseases, 179,* 699–701.

Wender, P. & Reimer, F. (1990). Buprorion treatment of attention deficit disorder and hyperactivity disorder in adults. *American Journal of Psychiatry, 141,* 1018–1020.

offense-specific programs). Virtually all of our patients are riddled with shame, depression, and unresolved anger at themselves as well as society, family, and others. Most have had substance abuse problems as an extension of their attempts to self-medicate for their restlessness that is symptomatic of ADD. The training sessions are mandatory in all cases and meet for one or more hours each Friday morning.

It is the responsibility of the inmate to arrange with his boss or teacher to have this training be *first priority* in all cases. The only exceptions are meeting with the parole board, a new job interview, or a special visit for those men who do not have in-state relatives. There are no regular classes at this hour and the work supervisors are very supportive of our ADD program.

Prior to the general group, two or three new enrollees are "mentored" by experienced ADD inmates before joining the sessions. The mentors introduce the new enrollees to several excellent self-help and educational books (see Table 17.1), which are stocked in the library or the mental health clinic. Of great importance, each man is seen individually on a weekly basis for the first month of the program or for the first six to eight weeks if medication is employed. This meeting is to confirm the diagnosis, to monitor progress, and to answer questions and monitor for drug side effects. Each man must progress toward education attainment, find a prison job, and remain free of infraction write-ups or charges during the program. We employ carefully explained contracts for their behavior and progression toward these goals. Disruption, "hot" urines, or contraband selling/trafficking is cause for immediate dismissal from this program. This seldom happens and peer protection is strong within the group (see later discussion of unexpected results).

Because conditions typified by poor short-term and processing memory and impulsive behavior are involved, we allow one or two minor infractions early in the program. In fact, when someone has a hearing for a trivial or "meathead" offense, it becomes "public property" for the group discussion and is used for a group topic.

On completion of the program, the patient-inmate is given a certificate of completion signed by the psychologist and myself to present to future institution employers and, most important, to the parole board (which has become familiarized with our program and ascribes significant weight to this certificate). When a man discharges his sentence or is paroled, he is not simply released; our focus on continuing support and self-progress mandates that we do the following:

1. Provide him with a thirty days' supply of any medication he is taking;
2. Educate his family about his condition;
3. Give him a list of two or three physicians or counselors in his new area of residence who are trained in the diagnosis and treatment of his condition;
4. Give him a summary letter of his case for providers, employers, and other relevant parties;
5. Give him a list of local ADHD support groups and the groups' educational materials;
6. Provide him with a list of national and state support and advocacy groups who have similar materials and other contacts;
7. Remain available to advise him by telephone regarding his case with his mental health or medical providers; and
8. Ask him to report to us for the next one to two years via mail or phone, or via parole officers.

METHODS AND GOALS OF GROUP TRAINING

Early in the program, we found that about half of our subjects had poor communication skills for ordinary social interaction. This was expected; many clinicians have observed "social perceptive deficits" (inability to interpret subtle interpersonal meanings and cues) in young patients, even young adults. Moreover, we observed an equally startling poverty of conventional behavioral values and codes of behavior. For example, some short-term inmates expressed fear and embarrassment of going home and being unable to converse without using the "F" or "MF" words on the street or in their homes. We quickly focused on how to express yourself without using expletives. (One older inmate stated these were the perfect words for prison as they encompassed frustration, being impressed, being pissed off, being in awe, being under stress, responding to threat, explaining life's unfairness, and the like. It was an entomological dissertation on the two perfect words for doing time.)

We then began a training sequence focusing on the inability to clearly state what one means and to instill an understanding of the speaker's feelings. One man began bringing two or three new words each week from the Readers Digest "Word Power" columns along with definitions and proper use in a sentence. We used this and a social-perceptive program beginning with role playing. The first skill was this: how to apologize when you make a mistake or offended someone without losing your self-respect and without misunderstanding your intentions which have gone awry. The inmates initially fumbled and were self-conscious in their efforts. As they developed their communication skills, their pride and confidence grew over the next weeks. This led us to focus part of the group meetings on similar deficits, with many topics. A few of these include:

- How to tell your wife you are wrong and are sorry without losing your "macho-hood"
- How to explain to a friend that you broke something you borrowed
- How to apply for a job, tell the employer you are a parolee, and still convince him to hire you
- How to begin to reconcile with your family whom you feel you have shamed
- How to explain your ADHD, Tourette's syndrome, and other symptoms without using them as an alibi
- How to make a new acquaintance and friendship, especially with a member of the opposite sex
- How to find new settings for making friends
- How to express yourself and your therapeutic progress in a street support group
- How to decline drugs, alcohol, and criminal acts when these are offered to you
- How to say no to illicit offers in a way that places the embarrassment on the other individual and help them understand why their offer is a problem for you

Topics vary from month to month and methods are incorporated to address issues as they arise. Nevertheless, it is important to note that individuals with ADHD or ADD experience great difficulties in ordinary daily functions that others take for granted and find easy to accomplish. As our small, unfunded program has continued over the past five years, the results have been very gratifying in the majority of men who continued until completion. However, the unexpected results were perhaps the most both startling and beneficial for this type of program.

For example, on one occasion the psychologist wrote upon the blackboard: "Is it ever right to kill someone?" After a long and heated discussion, our early group came to the conclusion that killing is not right with the exception of certain circumstances such as: "If a dude messes with your lady, steals your money or takes your stash, then it is probably OK." After a couple of weeks, they discovered that maybe one should refrain from killing in any way possible, not only due to the possible consequences, but because it is likely not the right action to take. Next, we addressed the issues of lying, then stealing, and so on. In spite of occasional outbursts and disagreements, the group opted to continue and alternative modes of action were discussed. With changes in behavior came changes in attitudes that appeared to be enduring.

PROGRAM RESULTS

With our combined experience of over seventy-five years of treating and counseling those with attentional learning disabilities, we have discovered that accurate diagnosis, careful training, and judicious use of appropriate medications could offer focus, social awareness, and the ability to "learn how to learn" in this group of patients. So far, we have had thirty-nine men paroled over twenty-four months, one over twenty-two months, and several more over eighteen months. There have been only one new charge on an inmate and two parole violations, resulting in an unusually low recidivism rate in the period during which most reoffenses take place—the first two years postdischarge. Several of the discharged men stay in touch by mail or telephone. The most stunning finding involves the individual successes and the employment rate. Among the positions obtained are:

- Structural maintenance foreman at a major airport
- Manager of a tire/auto store
- Master auto repair technician for a Big Three auto dealership
- Pipe fitter who is also employed at a horse breeding ranch
- Construction foreman for custom home building firm (owned by a father-in-law who swore he would assault this man if he came near his daughter again; foreman is now reconciled with same daughter, new baby, and happy grandfather)
- Owner of used car dealership
- Sales manager, large Pontiac dealership
- Previous high school dropout, finishing MBA this year
- Automobile paint and body repairman (two)
- Heating and air conditioning technician
- Self-employed jewelry artist making well into five figures

Early in the program, one inmate was paroled back to an area where he experienced severe abuse as a small child in Appalachia. After nearly a year of success after completing the program, he fled to parts unknown. Not understanding this, we asked the group how this could be explained. They were unanimous in their certainty that he had found a lady friend for the first time in his life. Nothing else could explain why he would throw away his future in their view. Later information proved them to be right, and we have discussed the trade-offs of men who have never been certain of love, esteem, or self-worth and who have not absorbed the skills to stay the long course needed for a life change. These inmates find a sense of worthiness in helping other men who enter the program anew and in helping to identify individuals with severe ADHD or Tourette's syndrome who had never been previously diagnosed. Then inmates in the program encourage new inmates to see one of us to seek treatment. The group members often take more pride in the results than the clinicians.

UNDERLYING MECHANISMS IN BEHAVIORAL DISORDERS

Justification for Considering Medical Treatment

Several behavioral disorders share many common symptoms and manifestations; for example, various disorders are characterized by inattention, aggressiveness, or learning disability. Scientists now have a better understanding of their similar underlying mechanisms and recognize that genetic factors are involved in their expression. The concept of overlapping "polygenic" disorders (see Comings, Chapter 16 in this text) helps to explain similarities among disorders and demonstrates their complexity. Very few of these conditions originate from a single dominant gene, particularly when they involve behavior, learning disability, and "personality" inclinations (Comings, 1996). Instead, a constellation of genetic effects is most likely involved in complex behavioral disorders. As an example, a genetic defect involving the function of dopamine D-2 receptors was reported a few years ago when it was found to be highly prevalent in families of severe alcoholics (Blum et al., 1990). This was touted as the gene for alcoholism in the media; however, media reports were overblown and misguided. More accurate studies have recently shown that other dopamine receptor genes have been found in a "polygenic" or multiple gene orchestration to produce many various emotional and behavioral problems. One gene involving D-4 receptor site numbers has been nicknamed the "novelty gene" and has led to an entirely new way of viewing not only obsessive behaviors but the "addictive personality" as well (Blum et al., 1997).

The inability of the brain to regulate restlessness and sensation-seeking behavior, or even craving for rest and quietude, is an important factor in excessive or obsessive thinking and fixations such as drug abuse, which are often inadvertent attempts to "fix" faulty brain function. This understanding offers hope for future treatment of all sorts of excessive and obsessive syndromes (e.g., sexual addictions, substance abuse, pathological gambling, violence). In particular, the strong association between both adolescent and adult "residual" ADD, addictive behaviors and substance abuse is now better understood for its genetic and biological roots. These relationships have been reviewed in an excellent clinical work (Richardson, 1997). Given that they are biologically and oftentimes genetically based disorders, it becomes necessary to consider a more integrated approach to treatment using both behavioral and medical methods in appropriate cases.

Concerns Regarding Use of Medication in Prison

Use of medications to alter brain function in inmates residing in a medium-security prison setting presents several issues that need attention. Offenders often suffer from a multiproblem lifestyle with many social origins and problems. There is not always a primary mental health condition in these cases. Thus, the accurate identification and diagnosis of ADD or ADHD is of the utmost importance in effectively treating these inmates. In some inmates, there may be a co-occurring mental health condition while in others the ADD or ADHD may be primary. For this latter group, the attention deficit often contributes to their social problems and counterproductive lifestyle, and its effects can accumulate over the life span. Thus, it is necessary to assess other underlying and superimposing conditions so that medication is not the sole focus of treatment. As described in previous sections, medication must be used in conjunction with a social skills and training program.

Control over administration of the medications also frequently poses a dilemma. There is always a fear of "cheeking" such medication to barter outside of the medication line in the clinic. In a prison setting drug selling is common, and stimulants like those used to treat ADD exact a high price. In our program, the selling of medication has occurred twice in the past five years to our knowledge; in both cases, other patients in the program immediately reported the offenders to us. Their motivations were expressed simply: "Doc, he may screw up the program entirely and I'll lose the only thing I've found to help me in my entire life!" In these two cases, one inmate was a drug seeking sociopathic person who had manipulated us. This case stimulated us to carefully design a plan to identify such manipulators early (see the discussion of differential diagnoses). The other inmate had severe ADHD and succumbed to the blandishments and threats by others. He was eventually administratively segregated. He was also using street drugs and the other patients witnessed him using a drug intravenously after a visit. They then "fingered" him as an endangerment to our program.

We use Ritalin (methylphenidate) in usual doses, combining it with other case-specific medications for optimum assistance in focusing, anger control, and control over symptoms found commonly in ADHD and Tourette's syndrome. Such symptoms may include oppositional defiance, anger dyscontrol, true bipolar disorder (coexisting in 15 to 31 percent of our population), and seizure disorders from trauma or idiopathic (unknown) psychopathology. In the medication section below, we discuss medication selection for individual patients. It is important to note that Ritalin and pemolin (another stimulant) do not provide an emotional high in ADD patients—only a therapeutic effect when used appropriately.

MEDICATIONS FOR DISORDERS COMMONLY SEEN IN PRISONS

Attention Deficit and Impulsive Distractibility

We have used the following medications with the results as indicated below.

1. *Methylphenidate.* Methylphenidate (Ritalin) is most effective in a prison setting. Given the diagnosis of ADD or Tourette's syndrome, this drug is quite effective in attention focus and very manageable in a corrections setting.

2. *Pemolin.* Pemolin (Cylert) has been discontinued in our program largely because of its less predictable results in adults and because of the occasional myocardial irritation and more common elevation of liver enzymes.

3. *Combined salts of amphetamine.* This medication (Adderal) is proving to be one of the most effective "target drugs" for adult and late adolescent ADD/ADHD. Obviously,

the introduction of a "speed" preparation within prison is beyond consideration due to the explicit risk of abuse and bartering as well as threats and coercion by inmates outside the program. With the permission of the parole officers, we have had a few parolees work with private physicians in using this drug and have had reportedly excellent results. In community corrections, this treatment must be agreed to by the court and the parole office in writing since the parolee will show a positive urine for amphetamine.

Marked Hyperactivity and Tics in Tourette's Syndrome

The most effective and inexpensive approach has been to pretreat the patient with an *alpha agonist*, especially clonidine HCl (Catapres). One effect of an alpha agonist is the smoothing of emotional control and anger. If this treatment is ineffective, newer and more effective *alpha blocker* drugs may be tried such as guanfacine (Tenex).

Use of Stimulants in the Presence of Tourette's Syndrome

Stimulant treatment has had the following effects.

1. *Ritalin*. Many texts still strongly advise that Ritalin not be used nor any other stimulants in the presence of Tourette's syndrome. In actuality, somewhat less than 18 percent of Tourette's syndrome patients will experience an increase in their tics from these agents; on the other hand, about 15 percent will show improvements, and the remainder will not change. These tend to be the results when stimulants are used without a pretreating alpha agonist drug (Comings, personal communication).

2. *Phenothiazines*. Phenothiazines are not used to control tics or marked motor hyperactivity in our patients in this project. While potent agents such as haloperidol may be used to control tics, they may not improve functions like focus, processing memory, and recall, which are often problematic for these patients. We find the trade-off is very negative, indeed negating the progress we seek.

Emotional Leveling

Early in our study of these patients, we observed a very high incidence of anger and oppositional symptoms. In the majority of cases, stimulant treatment facilitated the learning of anger control and management of oppositional symptoms. Patients developed better sensitivity to social cues and nonverbal language. Emotional leveling can be facilitated with the following medications.

1. *Clonidine*. Each patient is cautioned to look for and immediately report any increase in frustration intolerance or anger surges. When these occur, clonidine is started, if not previously prescribed, and we consider the addition of the most useful of our adjunctive medications, the selective serotonin reuptake inhibitors (SSRIs) or bupropion.

2. *Wellbutrin or bupropion*. This has been very effective in our population. Many

patients using this medication have commented that they are better able to act on a decision not to be drawn into prison conflicts. We find this to be a very good adjunctive medication in emotional leveling and also in markedly decreasing the craving for illicit drugs when used in combination with clonidine.

3. *Sertraline.* Sertraline (Zoloft) is preferred if there is significant depression, in the absence of indications of coexisting bipolar disorder and if there are obsessive thoughts or ritualistic behaviors.

4. *Fluoxetine.* Fluoxetine (Prozac) is generally avoided, as some neurologists and researchers believe that the drug does not act on brain structures to inhibit aggressiveness or anger. In view of the occasionally reported rage reactions with this agent, we have used Prozac with the greatest caution in this select group of patients.

5. *Valproate.* With coexisting severe anger or "intermittent dyscontrol" found in violent criminals, our usual drug of choice to initially gain anger control is valproate (Depakote) in modest doses, reaching a serum level of 35-60 rather than the 80-200 mg/dl used for seizure control. If ineffective, then a trial of another anticonvulsant such as carbamazepine (Tegretol) or phenytoin is attempted. Again, serum levels are effective at lower than the usual anticonvulsant therapeutic levels.

Most important, ongoing training, counseling, and group therapy for "anger management" is indispensable. The medication is used to improve focus and increase the inmates' ability to respond to behavioral and psychotherapeutic treatments. These measures are as important in the treatment of emotional control as it is in the development of academic, communication, and vocational skills.

Obsessive-Compulsive Behavior

The most effective drug for the treatment of obsessive-compulsive behavior has proven to be *Zoloft*. If less effective than desired, then *Paxil, Anafranil,* or *Prozac* with *clonidine* may be provided. Once again, in conjunction with the medication, careful training is necessary to teach the patient how to self-monitor his behavior and symptoms and exert self-control. The medication enables him to begin and be receptive to this process.

Bipolar Disorder

As mentioned at the beginning, there is an overlap or "comorbid" diagnosis of bipolar disorder (manic-depression) in over 15 percent of ADD patients. With careful liver and hematologic monitoring, as well as continued awareness of the possibility of myocardial irritability and ECG monitoring, lithium may be employed to control the cyclothymic or bipolar swings. This useful medication works more quickly and more effectively in the presence of an SSRI agent.

The careful and intelligent use of appropriate medication(s), targeted at the particular behavior and learning areas in need of assistance, is of great service to inmates who desire to find some way out of their morass. The doses we employ are very conservative and we seek low therapeutic or even "subtherapeutic" levels that are readily monitored with modern laboratory assays.

UNEXPECTED RESULTS OF PROGRAM

The Education of Corrections Officers

At the beginning of the program, I was approached by a few horrified career correctional officers (COs). One comment will suffice to express their dismay: "You've gotta be outa' your friggin' mind to give speed to inmates, Doc!" Two months later, this third-generation CO came into my office and said, "Doc, I don't know what you're doin' to Louie the Lip, but for God's sake, don't stop!!"

The bane of this officer's existence had been Louie, who was suddenly settling down, compliant, and working well in a prison job. I dared the officer to have lunch with me and learn about ADD/ADHD. He did, and was fascinated as I related the early childhood signs and symptoms of this condition. Two weeks later I evaluated his stepdaughter for her ADHD in my consultative pediatric practice and helped her family physician begin treatment. My skeptical officer became extremely adept at finding such patients among the wards with which he was charged. As word spread, we began receiving referrals from teachers, then crew bosses, then a number of officers, and in many cases, managers. Inmates also began referring disorganized friends to the program.

These discoveries uncovered another phenomenon, the "odd couple factor." ADD inmates tend to find similar friends and then get bunked together in cells or dorms. When we treat the first one of the pair successfully, he finds himself unable to tolerate his cell mate any longer for the very same behaviors that led him to our attention. Some have demanded immediate enrollment of the cell mate whether he wants to or not in an effort to prevent mayhem, even murder, "if he doesn't chill out when I'm trying to study!"

The officers' amazement when they observe inmates undergoing significant behavioral changes is testimony to the appropriateness of this treatment approach. Inmates and officers alike often begin to recognize many symptoms of ADD/ADHD in their family members or even themselves once they are taught about this syndrome. Interestingly, several authors have commented on the choice of professions by intelligent and decisive ADHD persons. I made note of this tendency when I was temporarily associated with special forces in the Army. There appears to be a very high incidence of ADD/ADHD in hazardous occupations such as law enforcement officers, fire fighters, rescue teams, and correctional officers. Risky and dangerous positions initiate the release of catecholamines and adrenalin, stimulating the release of "stress" hormones that can provide some relief (e.g., self-medication) from ADD/ADHD. Such positions are often filled by persons who are capable of quick action to react and handle stressful situations. I have met several trauma surgeons who displayed many of the characteristics of well-trained ADD adults (see Hartmann, 1993).

I have seen and diagnosed these conditions in eleven staff officers and nearly twenty of their children, subsequently referring them to treatment. Three have been promoted several times since then and one recently commented on how the treatment has led him to view inmates much differently: "I used to work in a southern state where if you had a bad hair day, you could get therapy by taking it out on the inmates. I would drink after work to forget. Now when an inmate is angry or depressed or just flaky, I try to find out why he is that way and help!" This same officer attributes the salvage of his marriage and his son's school career to discovering and addressing their family's ADHD.

Other examples include two inmates with textbook cases of severe Tourette's syndrome who had been seen by many medical providers and mental health specialists and diagnosed as anxious and drug seeking. One was transferred to a chronic mental health prison, withdrawn from medications, and sent back with worsened tics, diagnosed with "drug seeking behavior." Another witnessed his mother's suicide with a shotgun at age five. He was labeled as jumpy from the trauma even though the only parents he can recall are the adoptive farm couple who cared for him. His tics disappeared in ten days with medication, and he was paroled to a high stimulus job in a gambling casino. He tells me he can remember nearly one hundred cards at the blackjack table if he is faithful in taking his Tenex and Ritalin. The first time I met Chris, he was doing the "Texas Two Step" with tics, as he termed it, while an officer demanded he remain still so his name tag could be read. The added pressure only worsened his tics and produced animal vocalizations of barking and growling. When I carefully educated the officer, he became a father figure to this inmate as he realized the stigma and shame this young man had endured. He was proud when we regained control over the tics and impulsive behavior. Chris eventually earned his GED.

The Challenge of Prison Medicine

This program has also caused many staff members to be apprehensive about the possibility of being "conned" or manipulated by a felon inmate when making referrals and assisting in the treatment process. Even in private practice, there are many sick or stressed patients who are unable, for whatever reason, to speak the whole truth. One never knows which patients might have this difficulty; thus, it is a challenge to identify them early in the process. In some respects, prison is easier to negotiate for these inmates than a demanding treatment program. The social milieu is conducive to working an angle, an advantage or a special privilege with the people in charge of another person's life. Thus, for both correctional and treatment staff, it is safer to assume that the new inmate in question is most likely not telling the truth during an evaluation.

The challenge of prison medicine, and more so the treatment of these men, is to separate out truth, convince them of your own honesty and evince trust. This accomplishment is most rewarding, as many come from dysfunctional, abusive family backgrounds and are often resistant and lack trust. Their level of shame and self-loathing is significant (as described by Wendy Richardson in Chapter 18). Thus, it is very gratifying when for the first time in their lives they develop positive self-esteem and a belief in their intellectual ability. This approach does not necessitate a "soft on crime" attitude, but instead focuses on the realities of these inmates' lives and their underlying problems so they can remain crime-free. We cannot outbuild the problem of growing inmate populations. No medical and behavioral conditions can be altered without an understanding of the underlying mechanism or cause. This was one of the first aphorisms I learned in medicine. At last, new hope for finding ways to effectively treat these inmates is being discovered in the flood of scientific studies on brain function.

DIFFERENTIAL DIAGNOSES

An axiom in my specialty field of pediatrics is that "not everything that jumps is attention deficit disorder." Several other conditions mimic ADD/ADHD; thus, distinctions in assessment and diagnosis is required. Also, as a result of the tendency of some inmates, particularly the psychopaths, to manipulate staff and even the assessment instruments in an effort to obtain drugs, I have developed a few methods to thwart these attempts.

Atypical Seizures

Inattention is often seen in the fairly common minor motor seizures, petit mal or "absence seizures." However, aside from the daydreamy appearance of the episode, there usually are none of the stigma of true ADD. When an absence spell ceases, the patient with atypical seizures may appear slightly confused for a moment. Conversely, the ADHD/ADD individual who becomes distracted and seemingly "out of it" will regain attention after being verbally redirected and will have a litany of reasons for his or her lack of understanding or recognition. In the absence of confusion and the ability to readily regain focus with verbal direction, atypical seizures involving minor motor impairment should be considered. A sleep deprived electroencephalogram (EEG) with hyperventilation and awakening from drowsiness is recommended to make this distinction.

Bipolar Disorder

Bipolar disorder, previously called manic-depressive illness, is characterized by dramatic mood swings with hyperactive and bizarre euphoria at the high end and plunges into the depths of despondency at the low end of the mood cycle. Cycles may occur as rapidly as one or two in a day or they may develop more slowly, occurring over a period of months. A careful assessment of the behavioral and psychological history will often reveal the extremes of emotions seen with this disorder. The manic phase is very dramatic, often occurring with a feeling of ecstasy involving very insignificant events, such as the giving away of personal belongings (even one's drug stash) or accumulating objects. The depressive side is very pronounced with common thoughts of suicide and hopelessness. ADD/ADHD individuals also suffer from mood swings at times, but they lack the features of bipolar depression. "Situationally depressed" ADD patients can readily discuss their depression and the reasons behind it—for example, they will report "screwing up," facing a hard time, embarrassing their family, or feeling like a "meathead" or unmotivated. The bipolar patient, on the other hand, has more difficulty in identifying particular events or situations responsible for his moods, but rather views depression more as a global sense of hopelessness. Remember that 15 to 38 percent of imprisoned ADD/ADHD patients may also have bipolar depression and both disorders require treatment for behavioral changes to take effect.

Encephalopathy ("Organic Brain Disorder"), Drug Abuse, Head Trauma, and Child Abuse

Severe or repeated closed head injuries, often related to a history of child abuse in this population, and chronic drug abuse are strongly associated with mental dullness, cognitive deficits, distractibility, and poor processing memory. Individuals so affected may appear to suffer from ADD without hyperactivity. A careful historical and neurological examination is necessary to discover previous head trauma or chronic drug abuse, especially involving the so-called designer drugs, which can contribute to attentional problems and cognitive deficits. While an EEG will show diffuse slow wave patterns, a short trial of medication may show no change at all. I am currently treating an inmate with a history of two severe closed head injuries secondary to drunk driving accidents. He had grave difficulty arousing in the morning and tying his shoes took forty-five minutes on a good day. His EEG was totally normal, however, and no seizures were present. Given recent findings that methylphenidate directly arouses the prefrontal cortex (D-2 receptor activity), which is frequently implicated in closed head injuries that impair cognition, I gave him a trial of Ritalin. He takes 20 mg twice daily and has experienced dramatic improvements in behavior and thinking ability. He has now held a job in our laundry for over two years and can even read in the evening. Twice I have stopped his medication, and within ten days he reverted to a slow-of-wit, forgetful, ADD adult.

Hallucinations and Delusions

Patients with active delusions and hallucinations are often hyperactive, but have several distinguishing characteristics. Darting, furtive looks toward unheard sounds as well as an appearance of fearful agitation is a common indication that a patient may suffer from hallucinations. A clinician comfortable with psychotic patients can elicit trust with a warm and supportive posture and voice, and can generally lead them to acknowledge that they hear voices or see faces that are not there. The very disturbed and actively hallucinating patient poses no diagnostic problem due to the obvious bizarre movements, inappropriate answers, and unusually strong feelings of fear. Patients who suffer from hallucinations should be evaluated for schizotypical personality disorder or schizophrenia. Delusional patients should be evaluated for schizophrenia, narcisstic personality disorder, forms of drug-induced psychosis, and other DSM-IV Axis I and II diagnoses.

Psychopathy or Antisocial Personality Disorder

Psychopathy and antisocial personality disorder (APD) are not synonymous, although there is great overlap. Psychopaths, as described by Robert Hare most aptly, comprise a subgroup of those with a diagnosis of APD (Hare, 1993). They are characterized as being manipulative, incapable of deep emotion or empathy, relatively unresponsive to negative sanctions, pathological liars, incapable of feeling remorse, unresponsive to behavioral conditioning strategies, and flat in their affect. Both psychopathy and APD are most prevalent in offender populations and they breed fear and contempt in COs and even experienced prison clinicians due to their ability to "con." Hare's "Psychopathy Checklist" combined with case data and basic work up, as well as a more structured interview, are very helpful in guiding the evaluator to the right diagnosis with these patients (Hare, 1991).

These highly convincing "gamers" in the prison group are usually bright, may or may not have a predatory background, but live without shame or embarrassment for their actions. In an interview, they may attempt to ingratiate and endear themselves to the interviewer. A strategy frequently used by psychopaths is to cause another individual to "relate" to them by identifying common experiences and feelings, even though they are contrived. They often tend to be well read, particularly in the areas of psychology and psychiatry. Many are familiar with DSM criteria and can describe various diagnostic categories. This knowledge may be used to con a clinician or falsify a psychological test to feign mental illness or mitigate culpability in an offense. In a sense, the gamer sociopath may be *too* easy to work up; however, the resulting diagnosis may be inaccurate.

ADD/ADHD patients, to the contrary, are tedious and difficult to work up. They must repeatedly be redirected back to the question at hand because they become easily distracted and confused. In a sense, their ADHD can be "contagious" as the clinician is shifted off track due to the patients' confusion and lack of direction (see Hallowell & Ratey, 1994). On the other hand, the manipulating sociopath is too easy, too likable, and too smooth in helping you to arrive at his "diagnosis." Their acute processing memory and fluid shifting and focus are primary clues into the actual diagnosis in spite of the convincing stories they may relate and symptoms they may convey.

It is critical that the clinician does not share with psychopaths the reasons underlying the actual diagnosis and why the clinician does not believe them to have ADHD. Because psychopaths have such acute perceptions, they may quickly refine their act and attempt to fool a subsequent clinician with a revised set of symptoms. Once again, in contrast, the ADD/ADHD or Tourette's patient, or the learning disabled dyslexic man, struggles with shame and embarrassment. They evince self-loathing and self-anger at being poorly motivated or "dumb" (as they have often been told).

The occasional inmate who fools a clinician into an incorrect diagnosis should not discourage treatment staff from evaluating, diagnosing, and treating this large segment of the population in prison. While effective treatment is difficult, frustrating, and replete with "relapses," psychopathic individuals do respond well to positive rewards and highly structured environments. Some reports indicate that cognitive-behavioral therapy works well in this population.

An Example of True ADD/ADHD

There is tremendous potential for the treatment of ADD and ADHD in prison inmates who are properly diagnosed, and effective treatment can yield some unanticipated gains. "'Andy" is one case in point. His teacher in prison brought this shy and very small 19-year-old man in for an interview. He had been labeled as retarded in the fourth grade. And while he never acted out, he quietly withdrew from the taunts of "retard" from his classmates and even his cousins. Easily led by those whose friendship he longed for, he was rounded up in a theft charge and now was serving his first sentence. It was very difficult to get a history from this withdrawn and retarded man. One of my ADD program graduates, Larry, took note of this victim-prone youngster who barely weighed ninety-five pounds and who had stringy, unkempt, dishwater blond hair hanging in his face. Larry taught him how to read four nights weekly with Garfield comics and hard-bound books. Andy begged him to keep this a secret for fear of being ridiculed.

After a challenging series of evaluations, I decided that Andy had ADD and a primary reading disorder, type uncertain. He was also determined to be mentally dull, primarily due to his poor ability to communicate. In group sessions, he sat quietly with his head down until Larry persuaded him to say a sentence or two. Although we were unaware of his reading lessons, we discovered later that his reading and learning accelerated the day he started a stimulant medication. Andy's cover was subsequently blown when he received two weeks in the "hole" (solitary confinement) for smoking in his cell. When I saw him after his release, I asked how he could stand the solitude. He answered, "It was OK, I read some books!" Asking which one he like the most, he replied "Salem's Lot." It scared the piss out of me at night, doc!" He then related the entire plot with details to my astonishment. Andy was paroled last month with his GED and some vocational training, reading avidly. This so-called illiterate and retarded youngster exhibited remarkable improvements in his fifteen months in prison due to the training and treatment he received.

THE HIDDEN COSTS OF MISSED DIAGNOSES

At the end of 1997, the United States had 1.7 million individuals incarcerated in some type of local or county jail, state or federal prison. Over the past ten years, about 50 percent of the increase was due to drug-associated charges and sentences. New scientific studies are showing that vulnerability to drug abuse may be a result of "reward deficiency syndrome" for many individuals. This syndrome is characterized by genetic and/or biochemical deficiencies that lead to a perceived need to self-medicate. Drugs of abuse may help to assuage the restlessness and emotional and physical discomfort that the syndrome causes. This phenomenon is seen in many genetically based conditions, including many types of attentional deficits, Tourette's syndrome, bipolar tendencies, obsessive-compulsive behavior, and anger or impulse dyscontrol. To describe the burgeoning scientific evidence in this area is beyond the scope of this discussion. Dr. David E. Comings and I (1999) have written a comprehensive book that serves as a manual and treatment guide focusing on attention deficits among offenders and based on scientific research. I am inspired by this significant subgroup of offenders who are highly treatable once their underlying disorder is identified. The provision of such treatment serves the purpose, first and foremost, to protect society. Additional benefits will also be reaped given that ultimately our economy and gross national product cannot bear the burden of so many prisons and so little "correction" of the criminal mind. A unified effort must be applied by every discipline to the understanding, prevention, and treatment of criminal behavior (Laufer & Adler, in press).

The previous imprisonment champion of the so-called advanced western world was South Africa at the peak of apartheid. It reached an imprisonment rate of 3.1 citizens behind bars for each 1,000. Today, the USA has approximately 6.2 per 1,000. We spend over $7 million daily in new prison or jail construction and we will have to staff and pay to run these soon (BJS, 1997). This is a championship I would like to see us forfeit and instead apply all of the resources that placed men on the moon to this challenge of the criminal mind, its workings and its treatment.

References

Abwender, D. A., Como, P.G., Kurlan, R., Parry, K., Fett, K. A., Cui, l., Plumb, S. & Deeley, C. (1996, June). School problems in children with Tourette's syndrome. Archives of Neurology, 53, 509–511.

Blum, K., Noble, E. P. & Comings, D. E. (1997, April) Reward deficiency syndromes. *American Scientist*, 132–145.

Blum, K., Noble, E. P., Sheridan, P. J., Montgomery, A., Ritchie, T., Jagadeeswaran, P., Briggs, A. H. & Cohn, J. B. (1990) Allelic association of human dopamine D2 receptor gene in alcoholism. *Journal of the American Medical Association, 263*, 3156–3160.

Bureau of Justice Statistics (1997, June, December). U.S. Department of Justice reports, Washington, DC: Office of Justice Programs.

Cocores, J., Davies, R. & Mueller, P. (1987). Cocaine abuse and adult attention deficit disorder. *Journal of Clinical Psychiatry,* 4341–4432.

Cocores, J., Patel, M., Gold, M. & Pottash, A. (1987). Cocaine abuse, attention deficit disorder, and bipolar disorder. *Journal of Nervous and Mental Disease, 175,* 376–377.

Comings, D. E. (1998, personal communication), Chief of Human Genetics, Director of Tourette Disorder Clinic, City of Hope National Hospital, Duarte, CA.

Comings, D. E. (1996). *Search for the Tourette syndrome and human behavior genes.* Duarte, CA: Hope Press.

Comings, D. E. & Comings, B. G. (1984). Tourette's syndrome and attention deficit disorder with hyperactivity: Are they genetically related? *Journal of the American Academy of Child Psychiatry, 23,* 138–146.

Comings, D. E. & Comings, B. G. (1987). A controlled study of Tourette syndrome: I, ADD, learning disorders, and school problems. *American Journal of Human Genetics, 41,* 701–741.

Copeland, E. D. (1987). Copeland rating scale for adult ADD. Macon, GA: Macon University. Available via the Southeastern Psychological Insitute, Atlanta.

Eyestone, L. L. & Howell, R. J. (1994). An epidemiological study of attention deficit hyperactivity disorder and major depression in a male prison population. *Bulletin of the American Academy of Psychiatry Law, 22,* 181–193.

Hallowell, E. & Ratey, J. (1994). *Driven to distraction: Recognizing and coping with attention deficit disorder from childhood through adulthood.* New York: Pantheon Books..

Hare, R. D. (1991). *The Hare psychopathy checklist—rev. manual.* Multi-Health Systems, 908 Niagara Falls Blvd, North Tonwanda, NY, 14120-2060 (supplied to qualified users only).

Hare, R. D. (1993). *Without conscience: The disturbing world of the psychopaths among us.* New York: Pocket Books.

Hartmann, T. (1993). *Attention deficit disorder: A different perception (the problem of a hunter in a farmer's world).* Grass Valley, CA: Underwood.

Jeffery, C. R. (in 1998). Criminology and criminal law: Science vs. policy, and the interaction of science and law. In W. S. Laufer & F. Adler. (Eds.), *Advances in criminological theory,* vol. 8. New Brunswick, NJ: Transaction.

McCallon, D. W. & Comings, D. E. (1999). *The treatable criminal mind.* Duarte, CA: Hope Press.

Richardson, W. (1997). *The link between ADD. & addiction.* Colorado Springs, CO: Piñon Press.

Satterfield, J., Hope, C. & Schell, A. (1982). A prospective study of delinquency in 110 adolescent boys with attention deficit disorder and 88 normal adolescent boys. *American Journal of Psychiatry, 139,* 795–798.

Wender, P. H. (1985). The Utah criteria in diagnosing attention deficit disorder. *Psycharmacology Bulletin, 21,* 222–231.

Wender, P. H. (1995). *Attention deficit hyperactivity disorder in adults.* New York: Oxford University Press.

Chapter 18

Criminal Behavior Fueled by Attention Deficit Hyperactivity Disorder and Addiction

by Wendy Richardson, M.A., L.M.F.C.C., C.A.S.

Introduction	18-2
Neurobiological Aspects of Criminal Behavior	18-2
Characterizing ADHD	18-3
Impulse Dyscontrol	18-3
Activity Level	18-4
Enhanced Sensitivity	18-5
Rage and Violence	18-5
Addiction to High Levels of Stimulation	18-5
Acquired ADHD	18-6
Crime in the Blink of an Eye: The Connection Between Crime and ADHD	18-6
The Offender with ADHD	18-7
Formulating an Accurate Diagnosis	18-8
Differentiating Antisocial Personality Disorder From ADHD	18-9
Comprehensive Treatment	18-9
Medication	18-10
Repatterning	18-11
Therapy	18-11
Social Responding	18-11
Anger Management	18-11
ADHD and Co-Occurring Addictions	18-12
Assessment	18-12
Treatment	18-12
Finding Symptoms Dating to Childhood	18-13
Self-Motivation	18-13
Potential Controversy	18-13

Alternative Sentencing 18-14
Conclusion 18-14

INTRODUCTION

It's 5 a.m. Nate takes the blanket from his bed, carefully folds it into a square, and puts it on the concrete floor to protect his bare feet as he begins running in place. Nate wears only prison issue underwear. He runs at a rapid pace in the darkness of his solitary cell until his lunch is delivered. Nate will rest for two hours and then run until dinner. Nate has been in "the hole" for eighty days this time. He will rejoin the general prison population for a week or two. Then he will impulsively provoke another inmate or correctional officer into an argument and return to running in place in the hole. Nate says he prefers the quiet of the hole. "I can't handle it out there. It's too loud. There are too many guys. I can't think right. I can't sit still. I always mess up anyway." Nate has severe attention deficit hyperactivity disorder (ADHD). Prisons and jails in America have adults and juveniles, like Nate, with undiagnosed ADHD.

Due to the restrictions of conducting psychological and biological research in prisons, it has been difficult to ascertain the exact percentage of prisoners with ADHD; however, it is estimated that 50 to 80 percent of prisoners exhibit a significant number of ADHD symptoms (Hallowell & Ratey, 1994). Moreover, ADHD and drug addiction frequently coexist, exacerbating the behavioral difficulties and complicating both the diagnosis and the prognosis for these offenders. ADHD and addiction play a significant role in the criminal and impulsive activities of many offenders. However, it is only recently that contributing neurobiological aspects of criminal behavior have been considered in the sentencing and treatment of offenders and inmates. This chapter addresses the comorbidity of these two conditions by describing their prevalence and significance in a prison environment and providing some insights into their origins and treatment. Recent research and case studies are presented to elucidate how these disorders contribute to criminal offending. This chapter attempts to describe in detail how the symptoms of ADHD are manifested in the prison population, as well as the accurate diagnosis, alternative sentencing, and treatment of these conditions.

NEUROBIOLOGICAL ASPECTS OF CRIMINAL BEHAVIOR

Crime is multifaceted in nature. There is no single reason why one person breaks the law and others do not, or why one person is apprehended while others repeatedly commit crimes virtually undetected. For years, researchers have examined factors such as environment, learned experiences, poverty, education, and addiction in relation to crime and delinquency. This research has been helpful in identifying factors that predispose certain individuals to commit criminal acts and in providing potential explanations for why certain people offend and reoffend. Understanding the myriad factors that contribute to criminal behavior enables researchers to develop prevention, early intervention, and treatment programs for offenders.

The study of genetics and neurobiology is useful for exploring and understanding the causes and correlates of antisocial and criminal behavior. Researchers in these fields seek to determine whether certain individuals have genetic and/or neurochemical conditions that contribute to their criminality. If such factors exist, they can provide a context for understanding why some people do not appear to understand cause and effect, do not learn from consequences, and reoffend. Two conditions possessing a strong relationship with antisocial/criminal behavior, ADHD and drug abuse/addiction, have neurobiological origins and consequences. By understanding how ADHD and drug abuse contribute independently and interactively to criminal activity, we can begin to treat offenders, decrease recidivism, and create prevention and early intervention programs for juveniles and adults with these disorders.

Research in this area has been directed towards understanding how neurotransmitters are affected in ADHD and addiction, and how medications can help to control and ameliorate symptoms. There are two primary neurotransmitter systems associated with ADHD and addiction, serotonin and dopamine. Dopamine is crucial to our ability to feel pleasure and to the regulation of attention and impulses. Low levels of dopamine activity contribute to feelings of anxiety, difficulty focusing attention, impulse control problems, and the lack of a feeling of well-being. Dopamine production and utilization problems are found in people with ADHD, Tourette's syndrome, impulsive, compulsive and addictive disorders, and posttraumatic stress disorder.

Serotonin also plays a role in the development and symptoms of ADHD and addiction. Decreased levels of serotonin are linked to depression, sleep disturbances, and increased sensitivity to pain. Researchers have also linked low levels of serotonin to violent behavior and completed suicides. Åsberg et. al. (1976) found that patients diagnosed with depression who have low serotonin levels are at an increased risk of committing suicide by violent means (e.g., guns, knives, ropes, jumping from high places) than other equally depressed patients with higher levels of serotonin (also see Kotulak, 1996).

Brain imaging studies have provided further insights into the workings of the ADHD brain. Zametkin and his colleagues (1990) used PET (positron emission tomography) scan imaging to examine the metabolism of glucose (with a radioactive tracer) in the brains of adults with and without histories of hyperactivity dating back to childhood. They found that the adults with histories of hyperactivity were slower to metabolize glucose in the prefrontal cortex and superior prefrontal cortex, also referred to as the frontal lobes, than the control group. Through the use of brain imaging technology, we have learned that the frontal lobes of the ADHD brain are slower in their metabolic rate and activity level than a "normal" brain. This finding is reflective of an impairment in frontal lobe functioning, which contributes to difficulties regulating attention, concentration, and impulse control. It also causes problems with information processing, judgment, and the ability to think through the consequences of one's behavior. Since the frontal lobes also interact with other areas of the brain that regulate activity level, other features such as aggression modulation, motor movements, and emotional state are likely to be impaired.

CHARACTERIZING ADHD

Impulse Dyscontrol

ADHD is characterized by loss of control of attention, impulses, and activity level. People with ADHD do not always directly suffer from a deficit of attention. Frequently instead, they cannot consistently control where and how their attention is focused. Some people with ADHD are very distractible and unable to maintain attentional focus for more than a few minutes or seconds. Others have difficulty shifting their attention once it is captured by something stimulating. These people may become interested in an activity and lose track of time. Their attention becomes "hyperfocused" and it becomes difficult or even impossible for them to consciously shift their focus.

Attentional difficulties make it frustrating for the child with untreated ADHD to learn and succeed in school. An estimated 40 to 80 percent of children and adults with ADHD also have related learning disabilities. This inability to succeed in the classroom can cause children to develop a poor self-image, which has a negative impact on their personality development. Without intervention, children with untreated ADHD frequently grow up to be adolescents and adults with poor self-esteem.

Adults with ADHD commonly lack the ability to obtain and maintain gainful and fulfilling employment, even though they may be quite intelligent. They often lack basic skills essential for employment due to their inability to succeed in school. It is also difficult for many to follow or attend to directions, maintain their focus, and complete tasks.

Controlling one's impulses is a combination of biological ability, socialization, and motivation to do so. Until recently, poor impulse control was viewed more as a function of poor socialization and lack of motivation to conform to social norms. However, ADHD is known to be a biologically based dysfunction that interferes with control over impulses; offenders with ADHD have difficulty in refraining from activities with immediate rewards (e.g., stealing, using drugs, committing assaults, and engaging in other crimes). Centers of the brain that regulate "executive functions" (see Giancola, Chapter 11 in this book) are impaired in their ability to assess consequences of actions. Such impairments also lead to difficulties in analyzing situations, evaluating the consequences, and refraining from making damaging statements or suppressing inappropriate behaviors—all functions that occur within milliseconds in the non-ADHD brain. Often people with ADHD are stunned by their behavior and statements. They also often lack insight into why they behaved as they did.

Many offenders with ADHD do not learn from the consequences of their behavior. This can result from an inability to control impulses and think through the consequences of their actions. And while neurological disregulation is not an excuse for crime, awareness of its impact on the individual is an important part of the rehabilitation process. We will not be able to significantly decrease recidivism until we are prepared to treat the neurochemical aspects of poor impulse control.

Activity Level

It is unrealistically limiting to assess ADHD primarily by physical activity level. Not all adults with ADHD exhibit physical or motor hyperactivity. Some people with ADHD have an average activity level, where others may even exhibit very low levels of activity. For many years, professionals have diagnosed ADHD as a disorder defined primarily by hyperactivity. The DSM-IV (*Diagnostic and Statistical Manual of Mental Disorder,* 4th ed., 1994) diagnosis of attention deficit hyperactivity disorder leads many lay people and clinicians to assume that hyperactivity is a key component of ADHD. There are several problems with this assumption. First, not everyone with

ADHD is hyperactive as a child. Second, as stated above, many hyperactive children do not manifest motor or physical hyperactivity as adults. Frequently they will report having a restless or hyperactive brain, even though they are not physically restless. Lastly, ADHD is also characterized by attentional and self-control difficulties that can be misdiagnosed when hyperactivity is the focus of the diagnosis. The DSM-IV subtypes allow for the diagnosis of ADHD primarily inattentive type. A significant subgroup of both men and women who are involved in the criminal justice system suffer from this form of the disorder.

Enhanced Sensitivity

Living with ADHD is like living in a room with window screens with large irregular holes. A window is opened to get some fresh air, but there is little control over what enters the room. Mosquitoes, flies, and even small birds may shatter the serenity. Many people with ADHD experience enhanced sensitivity to visual, auditory, kinesthetic, and emotional stimuli. They can not always focus on what they want to hear and filter out the sound of the television, radio, or discussion in the adjacent restaurant booth.

Rage and Violence

Rage and violence are often life-long problems for people with untreated ADHD. The ADHD brain has difficulties in screening out visual, auditory, kinesthetic, and emotional stimuli, which leads to "stimulus augmentation" (Miller & Blum, 1996). People with this type of stimulus overload are frequently frustrated because they are overwhelmed by internal and external stimuli that they cannot process. Stimulus overload leads to low frustration tolerance and the inability to control spontaneous temper and rage attacks. Many inmates live with continuous stress and frustration from the stimulus augmentation of the prison environment. One way for them to decrease this overload is to break prison rules, which seems to come naturally for inmates with ADHD, and then spend time in solitary confinement.

Many ADHD offenders present with histories of fighting as children, adolescents, and adults. They may report being easily provoked by others, or provoking others with the intent to fight. They may have committed domestic violence, assault and battery, and child abuse. Frequently, ADHD offenders were physically abused as children. This can result from the fact that they were difficult children to manage and elicited harsher parental responses. Chances are that they were raised in a family where one or more parents or siblings also had ADHD and impulsive rage.

Addiction to High Levels of Stimulation

The ADHD brain craves stimulation in a sense to keep it awake and functioning. Seeking out high-risk and stimulating situations becomes a way that some people inadvertently self-medicate their underactive frontal lobes. Criminal behavior can be especially stimulating. Offenders often describe the rush experienced while committing a crime. Some report that they feel alert, focused, and alive when they are shoplifting, robbing a bank, forging checks, or being pursued by the police. This level of high-risk stimulation can be addicting to offenders with ADHD. They will often find themselves committing a crime more for the way it makes them feel than for the financial payoff.

Self-medicating with alcohol and other drugs is another method to temporarily aid in abating the symptoms of ADHD. Specifically, alcohol and other drugs stimulate dopamine production in the brain, thus creating feelings of pleasure and well being. All abusable drugs that are derived from natural sources, such as alcohol from the fermenting process, caffeine from coffee beans, nicotine from tobacco leaves, cocaine from coca leaves, opium from poppy seeds, and THC (tetra hydro cannabinol) from marijuana plants bind to receptor sites in the brain. Abusable synthetic drugs also bind at the receptor sites in the brain. Synthetic drugs and drugs from natural sources have different mechanisms for increasing dopamine levels in the brain, but they all function similarly to reduce or provide a sense of relief from ADHD symptoms. By increasing and effectively using dopamine in this way, a person can enhance his or her dopamine concentration, which provides an internal source of stimulation, thereby quieting the restless ADHD brain and body. Increased dopamine activity in a brain otherwise deprived of its stimulation is also tremendously reinforcing and pleasure-producing.

Unfortunately for the person who chooses to self-medicate their disorder, what initially feels like the solution soon becomes a problem in its own right. Many who self-medicate their ADHD become addicted, and their newly acquired addiction takes on a destructive life of its own. The addicted brain now craves increasingly more dopamine-enhancing drugs to feel normal; the initial high experienced when drugs were first used is gone, and addicts become entangled in what is referred to as the reward deficiency syndrome (RDS) (Miller & Blum, 1996). RDS is characterized by a deficiency in dopamine activity and a consequent reliance on substances to feel pleasure or decrease emotional and physical pain. Sufferers of this syndrome will often do almost anything to increase the amount of dopamine available. People with ADHD who already have dopamine system disturbances are even more susceptible to the effects of RDS.

Acquired ADHD

Although ADHD is considered to be largely a genetic disorder, some individuals acquire ADHD during the birth process or later in life. Closed head injury, especially to the prefrontal lobes, for example, may evoke ADHD symptoms. Individuals with ADHD, especially those with the hyperactive component, are also unusually susceptible to incurring head injuries. Some people with ADHD engage in high-risk sports and other stimulating activities and tend to be accident prone due to their impulsivity and sensation-seeking tendencies. Bicycling, skate boarding, skiing, jumping off roofs or out of trees are common causes of head injury. In some cases, it is difficult to determine whether a head injury or inherited ADHD is the culprit in behavioral disorders because sometimes they co-occur and can contribute to attention deficits, impulsivity, and other ADHD symptoms.

CRIME IN THE BLINK OF AN EYE: THE CONNECTION BETWEEN CRIME AND ADHD

As stated earlier, the ADHD brain is slower to absorb glucose in the prefrontal cortex or executive center and, thus, is actually working more slowly than the non-

ADHD brain. One way to jump start the brain's executive center is through risk-taking or conflict. Highly stimulating behaviors and mood states have the effect of arousing the central nervous system; therefore, some people with ADHD actually provoke or readily respond to conflict-producing situations. They feel alert, stimulated, and engaged when they are arguing, debating, or fighting with others. This drive to keep their "sleepy" executive center awake may lead to a myriad of altercations at home, work, and with the law. Criminal behaviors, which are inherently risky and can provoke high levels of arousal in the perpetrator, can serve the same purpose—to stimulate the underaroused brain. The attentional difficulties, poor employment skills, and low self-esteem that often accompany ADHD can exacerbate these tendencies by reducing the ability to control impulses and make more productive choices. Further contributing to these outcomes is the need for acceptance that ADHD individuals often exhibit. Because the presence of ADHD can limit the extent to which an individual can succeed and function within the bounds of society, sufferers often associate with others who will accept them. A vulnerable subgroup of adolescents with ADHD tend to join gangs to feel accepted and successful. Of course, there are many other significant factors that determine why one person with ADHD commits crimes while others do not. Most people with ADHD are not criminals.

Lack of impulse control that characterizes ADHD can also lead to antisocial behavior. Offenders with ADHD are often shocked by their impulsive behavior or by what they say, and they frequently do not understand their own actions. Offenders with ADHD often commit impulsive crimes such as car theft or jacking, robbery, petty or grand theft, assault, domestic violence, child abuse, and drug related crimes. These crimes are usually not planned, or are planned with little thought as to how to execute them. Rarely is the criminal with ADHD aware of the consequences of his behavior. Nevertheless, many offenders will often acknowledge the unlawful behavior and feel sincere remorse for their actions. They respond differently than the offender with antisocial personality who shows no remorse for his or her actions.

The ADHD brain has problems putting on the brakes and controlling actions; this is called disinhibition. The inhibiting mechanisms of the brain are not working properly. The already disinhibited ADHD brain is further disinhibited by the use and abuse of substances. Alcohol and other drugs impair brain functioning in people without ADHD. In general, individuals under the influence of substances become more impulsive, irrational, violent, highly emotional, and can exhibit compromised judgment. In the ADHD individual, illicit substances even further exacerbate their existing difficulties with controlling impulses, concentration, emotional and environmental sensitivity, and activity level. The combination of an already disinhibited ADHD brain and substance abuse can lead to serious consequences.

THE OFFENDER WITH ADHD

A common theme among offenders with ADHD is that many of them are not successful criminals. Due to their attentional problems and impulsivity, they have a tendency to get caught. And once caught, offenders with ADHD frequently do not respond well to their contact with authority. They oftentimes blurt out insults, make threats, or become assaultive. This is especially true if they are under the influence of alcohol or other drugs.

As a result, it is common among adults and juveniles with untreated ADHD to exacerbate their legal problems. For example, some individuals with ADHD and learning disabilities will have a hard time answering questions when arrested. They may not be able to process the questions or remember the details or sequence of events that led to their crime. They can appear to be withholding, confabulating, or lying. In addition, the ADHD offender has an even more difficult time accessing information when under the type of stress a confrontation with a police officer creates. Sometimes, when arrested, the person with ADHD will impulsively blurt out the details of their crime. Some may even exaggerate the importance of the role they played.

FORMULATING AN ACCURATE DIAGNOSIS

An accurate diagnosis is the key to treatment for offenders with ADHD and/or addiction. People with ADHD often exhibit exaggerations in behaviors that are otherwise considered normal. For example, everyone can be forgetful, have difficulties paying attention, impulsively speak or act, or have high or low activity levels at times. For the person with ADHD, however, problems with attention, impulsivity, and activity level are more severe and often interfere with normal daily functioning. They also have a history of ADHD symptoms that dates back to childhood or adolescence. ADHD does not just suddenly occur in adults; usually there have been pervasive, disruptive symptoms throughout their lives.

Adults with ADHD frequently present with histories of learning difficulties and school failure even though they may be quite intelligent. Many will have problems maintaining intimate relationships. They may have few employment skills and a history of being fired and impulsively quitting jobs. Some will report becoming bored easily and will change jobs, relationships, and geographic locations frequently.

A variety of assessment tools, ranging from self-assessment checklists to brain imaging, are useful in the diagnosis of ADHD. The Copeland Symptom Checklist (1989) for Adults with Attention Deficit Disorder and the Adult ADHD assessment questionnaire are reliable tools. The TOVA (Test of Variables of Attention; Greenberg, 1996) is a computerized visual performance test that measures an individual's ability to press a button when the target symbol appears and to refrain from pressing when a similar symbol appears. The score is derived from errors of omission (missing the target), errors of commission (pressing the button at the wrong target), mean response time, and variability of responses. The TOVA has been criticized because it only tests visual attention, and does not test for auditory attention or for performance under stress. Some people will test well visually and yet have difficulty sustaining auditory attention, especially in noisy or stressful environments.

Brain PET and SPECT (single photon emission computed tomography) imaging techniques take pictures of the brain at work. These tests reveal the brain's rate of metabolizing glucose or blood flow in various areas of the brain, thus showing the areas of the brain that are either high or low in levels of activity.

Assessment screening questionnaires are inexpensive and a good place to start; however, using a questionnaire alone will not always provide an accurate diagnosis. If an individual scores in the ADHD range, it is then important to refer him to someone with specific expertise in diagnosing and treating ADHD. According to Hallowell and Ratey (1994), "It is important to understand this point: the diagnosis of ADHD is based first and foremost on the individual's history or life story. The most important step in determining whether one has ADHD is sitting down and talking to somebody who is knowledgeable in the field" (p. 282). This can be a difficult task to accomplish in the criminal justice and correctional systems, which are bursting at the seams with offenders and overworked staff.

DIFFERENTIATING ANTISOCIAL PERSONALITY DISORDER FROM ADHD

The behaviors exhibited by people with ADHD are similar (and, in some cases identical) to the behaviors of those with antisocial personality disorder (APD). Common symptoms include failure to conform to social norms, impulsivity or failure to plan ahead, irritability and aggressiveness, and consistent irresponsibility, as indicated by repeated failure to sustain work behavior or honor financial obligations, in addition to many others. Due to these similarities, it is easy to misdiagnose APD in adults or conduct disorder in juveniles who have ADHD. And because ADHD in adults is frequently accompanied by other disorders, some offenders will exhibit both ADHD and APD.

There is a clear overlap of behaviors between the antisocial personality and the person with ADHD. Some people with ADHD fail to conform to social norms and frequently break the law. Due to their inability to control impulses, they may disregard their safety as well as the safety of others. Constant irresponsibility can be a life-long pattern for those with untreated ADHD. They may not show up for court dates or probation meetings, and they may neglect to pay their bills or child support. Also, spontaneous rage attacks and aggression may have been a part of the ADHD person's life since childhood.

One clear distinction between ADHD and APD is that most people with ADHD are able to express sincere feelings of remorse. This is especially true once they are properly treated for their ADHD. The true antisocial personality neither feels nor expresses remorse for his actions. The offender with antisocial personality may express remorse about being caught but is unable to empathize with the feelings of their victims. In contrast, the ADHD offender often feels and expresses great shame about who they are and how they have hurt others.

Distinguishing ADHD from APD is imperative. There are very few treatment options for the antisocial personality and the prognosis is usually poor. Frequently, when a child with ADHD is misdiagnosed with conduct disorder, he or she is often automatically diagnosed with antisocial personality disorder as an adult. The judicial system often views an APD offender as beyond help and an unlikely candidate for an alternative sentencing or treatment program.

COMPREHENSIVE TREATMENT

The most important part of a comprehensive treatment plan is an accurate diagnosis of ADHD and any accompanying co-occurring conditions. Accurate diagnosis is the cornerstone of effective treatment. ADHD is a neurochemical disorder that contributes to emotional and behavioral problems. As a result, living with untreated ADHD creates a host of difficulties ranging from poor social and occupational skills to depression, personality disorders, and explosive, violent behavior. All the dimensions of ADHD and co-occurring conditions must be addressed and treated for the best outcome. Treatment components include education about the disorder, medication, behavioral repatterning, emotional healing, shame reduction, social and occupational training, and accommodation strategies. With the acceptance that ADHD is rooted in their neurochemistry and not in the fibers of their moral character, many begin to better deal with their shame and harsh self-judgments.

Medication

Medication is often an essential treatment component for many individuals who have ADHD. Medication is most helpful when used in combination with other treatment modalities and should never be used as the sole treatment for ADHD. Not everyone with ADHD, however, requires medication. It depends on the severity of the disorder and the extent to which the individual's level of functioning is impaired. People with mild ADHD can benefit from understanding their disorder and learning ways to repattern their behavior without the use of medicine.

On the other hand, many people with ADHD who enter the juvenile or adult criminal justice system have moderate to severe ADHD. In these cases, medication can be an essential part of their treatment. Otherwise, they may find it difficult to sustain employment, maintain relationships, and control their impulsive, restless minds. Individuals with untreated ADHD are also more likely to treat themselves through alcohol, drugs, and other addictions, all of which can contribute to criminal behavior.

Psychostimulants are the medications primarily used to treat ADHD in children and adults. Hallowell and Ratey found that for both children and adults who were correctly diagnosed with ADD, certain medications are effective about 80 percent of the time (Hallowell & Ratey, 1994). Barkley states that medication has been found to improve behavior in children over the age of five 70 to 90 percent of the time (Barkley, 1998).

Psychostimulant medications work by increasing dopamine levels in the brain. The exact mechanism of action is slightly different for each medication, which is why one individual may respond well to Ritalin, for example, and another to Adderall. Overall, they work by inhibiting dopamine transporters, decreasing the reuptake of dopamine, and allowing dopamine to bind to the receptor sites on other neurons. This increases the amount of available dopamine to the brain.

Medications known as selective serotonin reuptake inhibitors (SSRI), such as Prozac, Paxil, and Zoloft, are often used in conjunction with psychostimulants. These medications work much like the psychostimulants except that they influence the neurotransmitter serotonin, and not dopamine directly. The use of SSRI's as the sole medical intervention for ADHD is effective for some, but most people experience greater improvements with psychostimulants. Another medication that is proving to be an effective treatment for ADHD is Wellbutrin. Wellbutrin works as a weak blocker of the neuronal uptake of serotonin and norepinephrine, and also inhibits the reuptake of dopamine. It is neither a psychostimulant nor an SSRI.

Finding the right medication and dosage is not an exact science. It is important that the prescribing physician is well versed in adult ADHD and willing to try different medications until the patient's symptoms decrease or abate. There are also the 10 to 30 percent of individuals who will not respond to any medication.

Since ADHD is frequently accompanied by co-occurring conditions, often more than one medication is necessary to treat the various aspects of the individual's disorders. Again, accurate diagnosis is the key to positive treatment outcome, and medication is only one component of a comprehensive treatment program.

Repatterning

Another important component of treatment is behavioral repatterning, or learning new patterns of living and specific behaviors. Repatterning behavior means learning specific strategies to accommodate or compensate for the impact of ADHD. These accommodations may be relatively simple. Some include using organizational systems, practicing listening and communication skills, and avoiding environmental overload. Other types of repatterning are more difficult. Some with ADHD need intensive training to control their impulses to interrupt others, talk incessantly, steal, or explode into rages.

Therapy. Individual therapy that focuses on helping the individual change his or her behavior can be helpful. Group therapy is also beneficial in that people with ADHD see themselves and their behavior in the eyes of others. Group treatment helps break down the sense of isolation and embarrassment that many with ADHD experience. Group treatment is especially helpful for inmates to learn to be aware of their anger and notice internal cues indicating that their anger is about to escalate. They also benefit from learning to disengage from people and situations, and leave situations before they become angry.

Social Responding. People with ADHD require further help to understand and initiate appropriate social responses. Many such individuals frequently interrupt, talk endlessly, become inattentive during conversation, or even become distracted in the middle of a conversation and inadvertently begin to focus, for example, on the television or radio. Skills that are basic and simple for most people can be difficult for those with ADHD. It is necessary for them to become aware of their tendencies, to identify appropriate role models, and to practice their newly acquired skills for them to learn social skills such as knowing when to leave a party, remembering names, and listening attentively during conversations.

Anger Management. Anger control and management is an essential part of treatment for most offenders with ADHD. Uncontrolled rage and anger frequently contribute to arrests and incarceration. The first step in anger management is to help the offender understand the consequences of his anger and rage. For some, the consequences of uncontrolled rage are prison terms, life in prison, and frequent time in isolation. Understanding the cause and effect of one's behavior increases the chances for a positive prognosis.

Inmates are better equipped to benefit from job skills and educational training when their ADHD is treated. Their ability to sustain their attention and to control their impulses and activity level improves, making it possible for many to develop skills they were never able to master before. Inmates who leave prison with the ability to control themselves, and with educational and job skills, have a greater chance of staying out of prison.

ADHD AND CO-OCCURRING ADDICTIONS

Assessment

Accurate diagnosis can be complicated by the complex composition of symptoms and behaviors that many offenders exhibit. It is not uncommon for an offender to have several DSM-IV, Axis I diagnoses. For example, an individual may have ADHD, alcohol abuse, and major depression. All of these disorders must be properly treated to insure recovery and abatement of symptoms.

Many offenders with ADHD are misdiagnosed with an Axis II personality disorder. Clinicians will mistakenly assume the "personality disorder'" has disappeared when an offender undergoes treatment with medication and therapy. Because the symptoms and behaviors were actually a component of ADHD, the symptomatology of ADHD can easily be misinterpreted as characteristic of a personality disorder as well as other disorders such as bipolar, obsessive-compulsive, anxiety, and intermittent explosive disorders.

To further complicate the diagnostic puzzle, many offenders with ADHD have a variety of co-occurring disorders, all of which must be assessed and treated. Children with untreated ADHD will frequently self-medicate with drugs, alcohol, food, and addictive and compulsive behaviors. As these young people reach adulthood, many suffer from chronic depression or anxiety disorders, and engage in stimulation-seeking activities such as gambling or high-risk and compulsive sex. The adrenaline rush these behaviors produce can be quite reinforcing in the presence of an underactive dopamine system.

Treatment

It has been estimated that 25 to 50 percent of individuals with substance abuse disorders have co-occurring ADHD (Richardson, 1997). We also know that a large percentage of people in the criminal justice system have substance abuse and addiction issues. This means there is an even greater need to diagnose and treat ADHD in conjunction with an existing drug addiction in this population. Offenders who are more fortunate may receive treatment for their chemical dependency, but rarely is co-occurring ADHD diagnosed. Treating the addiction without treating the ADHD can often lead to relapse and poor treatment outcome.

It is difficult, if not impossible, for some with ADHD to stay clean and sober when they cannot sustain their attention during treatment. Poor impulse control also contributes to difficulties maintaining and achieving abstinence. Those with restless bodies and brains have a harder time resisting alcohol and other drugs as a means of calming themselves.

There are several criteria that should be met when treating alcoholics and addicts who have ADHD with medication. Again, accurate diagnosis is the first step. Some addicts and alcoholics will appear to have ADHD during the period known as "post acute withdrawal." People in post acute withdrawal are detoxifying from the effects of dopamine enhancing substances; their brains become deprived of dopamine activity and can mimic ADHD symptoms. Their concentration may be poor and they are easily distractible. They may present with psychomotor and emotional restlessness, express impulsive thoughts and actions. These symptoms can last several months into early sobriety even though the physical detoxification is completed.

Finding Symptoms Dating to Childhood. Symptoms that appear to be ADHD-related will gradually disappear as the individual progresses through treatment. There are those, however, who even after months and years of recovery continue to be restless, hyperactive, impulsive, and inattentive. The key to accurately diagnosing ADHD in this population is finding a history of symptoms that date back to childhood. Many individuals with ADHD did poorly in school even though they may be bright. They often report becoming bored easily and engaging in high-risk behavior as children and adolescents. Patterns of frequent job losses, geographic moves, failed relationships, self-medicating, aggressive and compulsive behavior are woven into the fabric of their lives. ADHD does not just appear after a specific event; it is an enduring and pervasive part of the individual.

Once the dual diagnosis is established, treatment for both disorders can begin. Some individuals in addiction recovery benefit from understanding how their ADHD symptoms are affecting them and from practicing strategies to manage these symptoms. Others will need medication to balance their neurochemistry in order to function in a recovery program and learn to manage their ADHD.

Self-Motivation. Individuals must be motivated to work with addiction recovery and ADHD issues. This is not always easy, since denial is a component of both disorders. It is not appropriate to treat addicts with medication who are not actively involved in addiction treatment. The potential for abuse is present when well-meaning physicians give untreated addicts medication for ADHD. People who are actively involved in addiction treatment do not tend to abuse their medication. Medication should be dispensed in small amounts, and the person should be closely monitored by both the prescribing physician and ADHD and addiction specialists. When these criteria are met, abuse of medication is rare. Prisons provide an environment where medication can be closely monitored and controlled.

Potential Controversy

There is much controversy regarding the treatment of alcoholics and addicts with ADHD medication, especially since amphetamine-based medication is usually administered to relieve ADHD symptoms. It is important to remember that the dosage of medication used to treat ADHD is minimal compared to what is used to get "high" or "loaded." The method of administration also makes a significant difference. Medication is taken orally in prescribed doses. It is not smoked, snorted, or injected. The dose and quality of medication is also exact, whereas the potency and quality of street drugs are not. Treating alcoholics and addicts with ADHD medication should be done with caution and supervision as part of a comprehensive treatment program. For some, medical treatment of their ADHD symptoms aids in their ability to maintain recovery, control their behavior, and stay out of the criminal justice system.

ALTERNATIVE SENTENCING

Drug courts are being instituted across the country for the processing of offenders with certain drug- and alcohol-related offenses. These courts evaluate whether an offender is appropriate for sentencing to chemical dependency treatment programs in lieu of incarceration. Each court may have different criteria, but most drug court judges are looking for offenders who have untreated substance abuse and addiction, show some insight into their chemical dependency-related problems, and are motivated to participate in treatment. Alternative sentencing to treatment provides some offenders with the opportunity to recover from their addiction where incarceration would not.

Drawing from the drug court model, similar types of alternative sentencing can be made available for those with untreated ADHD. Some offenders who are sentenced to addiction treatment programs in lieu of jail or prison also require treatment for coexisting ADHD. It is difficult to find treatment programs that treat dual diagnosed ADHD and addiction, but some chemical dependency programs are beginning to understand the importance of treating ADHD as well.

When ADHD is clearly a component of criminal behavior, offenders have been sentenced to ADHD treatment programs. It is critical that the treatment for ADHD is comprehensive and intensive. This usually involves residential treatment with an aftercare component. If an offender is facing a two-year prison term, the alternative sentence to a treatment program should be close to two years in duration. The alternative sentence should be rigorous and compliance should be closely monitored.

In order to request an alternative sentence, offenders must admit their guilt and not use ADHD as an excuse for their behavior. ADHD is a contributing factor that unless treated, increases the likelihood of reoffending. ADHD is not an excuse for breaking the law, but rather provides a context for treatment. Not everyone is a good candidate for alternative sentencing, especially those who are truly antisocial or a danger to others. However, with proper diagnosis for all co-occurring conditions and a good clinical assessment of one's criminal history, it is not difficult to discern who will benefit for treatment versus incarceration.

CONCLUSION

There has been little research on treating offenders who suffer from neurobiological disorders such as ADHD, substance abuse, and addiction. In most cases, such offenders wind up in the general prison population. They usually do not function well because it is difficult if not impossible for them to follow even the basic prison rules without treatment. Their impulsivity can contribute to rage outbursts, assaults, murders, escapes, extensive time in solitary confinement, and protracted periods of incarceration.

Our present model of incarceration without treatment has failed inmates, judicial and prison systems and our society. As science understands more about the neurochemical aspects of human behavior, we are better able to treat disorders that were once believed to be a matter of free will. However, the greatest hurdle for many is to move away from a mind set that people with neurochemical disorders who commit crimes are inherently bad people. It seems to be easier in our culture to view human beings as fundamentally bad and evil rather than to acknowledge that a treatable genetic, biological condition may be contributing to their unacceptable behavior. With greater understanding of the biological components of criminal behavior we can move towards a system of early intervention and treatment of neurochemical disorders. We can also offer humane treatment for the many inmates who are uncontrollably driven by their neurochemistry.

References

American Psychiatric Association (1994). *Diagnostic and statistical manual of mental disorders* (4th ed.). Washington, DC: American Psychiatric Press.

Åsberg, M, Träksman, L. & Thoren, P. (1976). 5-HIAA in the cerebrospinal fluid: A biochemical suicide predictor? *Archives of General Psychiatry, 33,* 1193–1197.

Barkley, R. A. (1998, Sept.). Attention-deficit hyperactivity disorder. *Scientific American,* 69–72.

Copeland Symptom Checklist for Attention Deficit Disorder (1989). Self-administered test available online at *http://www.oberlin.edu/njkapell.*

Greenberg, L. M. (1996). *TOVA (Test of Variables of Attention).* Los Alamitos, CA: Universal Attention Disorders.

Hallowell, E. M. & Ratey, J. R. (1996). *Answers to distraction.* New York: Bantam Books.

Hallowell, E. M. & Ratey, J. (1994). *Driven to distraction: Recognizing and coping with attention deficit disorder from childhood throught adulthood.* New York: Pantheon Books.

Kotulak, R. (1996). *Inside the brain: Revolutionary discoveries of how the mind works.* Kansas City, MO: Andrews McMeel.

Miller, D. & Blum, K. (1996). *Overload: Attention deficit disorder and the addictive brain.* Kansas City, MO: Andrews McMeel.

Nadeau, K. G. (Ed.) (1995). *A comprehensive guide to attention deficit disorder in adults:* Research, diagnosis, treatment. New York: Brunner/Mazel.

Richardson, W. (1997). *The link between ADD & addiction.* Colorado Springs, CO: Piñon Press.

Zametkin, A. J., Nordahl, L. & T. E., Gross, M., King, A. C., Semple, W. E., Rumsey, J., Hamberger, S. & Cohen, R. M. (1990). Cerebral glucose metabolism in adults with hyperactivity of childhood onset. *New England Journal of Medicine, 323,* 1361–1366.

Part 7

Medical Approaches to Understanding and Treating Antisocial Behavior

Pharmacological approaches to treatment intervention, otherwise known as pharmacotherapy, are increasingly used in clinical settings for the modification of behaviors often associated with crime and violence. Several studies provide support for the notion that pharmacotherapy, combined with conventional psychosocial treatments, produces more favorable treatment outcomes than traditional therapies alone or simple incarceration. While no medications are approved by the Food and Drug Administration specifically for criminal or antisocial behavior, several drugs have been approved for use in patients with behavioral and personality disorders related to criminality (e.g., violence, drug abuse, impulsivity, negative affect and angry temperament) with significant success. The medications have improved the disordered behavior of individuals who attract the attention of the criminal justice system. Pharmacologic treatment of certain offenders is predicated on research that finds that violence and aggression, drug addiction, and other excessive and compulsive behaviors are often present in those with underlying disorders of the brain. Medication in these cases may lead to behavioral improvements by stabilizing a neurochemical imbalance or physiological disturbance that would otherwise increase risk for offending behaviors. As a result, the individual becomes more in control of his or her own behavior, minimizing the need for external controls.

Because the chemical correction of antisocial behaviors is multifaceted and controversial, it is critical that several key issues are addressed by both research and public policy experts before pharmacotherapy is incorporated into correctional policies. First, we must identify the underlying mechanisms in certain forms of antisocial behavior that are potentially responsive to chemical corrections; we must identify the individuals or subgroups appropriate for pharmacologic treatments; we must identify the specific medications that alter underlying mechanisms for antisocial behavior; and we must identify the ethical, social, and legal ramifications. The latter issue recognizes the need for further research and regulations prior to implementing policies to incorporate a pharmacologic approach, particularly with respect to voluntary versus coercive treatment.

Until recently, the overwhelming emphasis of studies on the causes of aggressive behavior has been on social and psychological factors, with little more than lip service being paid to the neurological part of the equation. Dr. Frank Elliott, a prominent and reputable neurologist who has published widely on the topic of the neurology of violent behavior, explains in Chapter 19 why this is no longer acceptable. Investigations have disclosed that organic defects are much more common in patients with behavioral disorders than in the general population. Chapter 19 is devoted to an understanding of the various neurological causes of violence and other antisocial behaviors. While it is true that aggressive behavior is often learned from parents and peers, it is equally true that many people brought up in violent surroundings are not violent, and that many who are reared in good homes are. Furthermore, the literature provides many examples of behavioral disorders in individuals who were born of violent parents but were adopted at a very early age into good homes where they could not have learned antisocial behavior or explosive rage from their adoptive parents. Yet, they more closely resemble their biological parents in this respect. Dr. Elliott takes the reader on a trip through the brain where particular regions and their function are implicated in violence that is not strictly learned.

Individuals with persistent violent and antisocial behavior show a much higher prevalence of overt and covert neurologic and neurophysiologic abnormalities than nonviolent control subjects or in the population at large. The increasing awareness of the close connections between recurrent interpersonal violence and anatomic, chemical, and neurological abnormalities calls for more participation by neurologists in the assessment and pharmacological treatment of these individuals, whether they be clinical patients or prison inmates. Their intervention is particularly desirable in forensic cases because the unfortunate reality for those who come into the courts by virtue of their dysfunction is that the underlying causes of their disorder are inaccurately evaluated or simple unattended. Dr. Elliott describes ways in which violent behavior can be treated through an enhanced understanding of its neurological origins.

In Chapter 20, Dr. Fava, a noted expert in the pharmacological treatment of anger attacks in various mental disorders, presents an overview of neurochemical systems involved in aggressive behavior and angry mood state. This discussion sets the stage for an extensive delineation of mental illnesses that are often characterized by intermittent or repeated episodes of hostility and violence, from dementia and mental retardation, to premenstrual mood disorder, to personality disorders. Within each subsection, Dr. Fava discusses the use of medications to control these episodes, including a justification for their use based on the brain systems known to be involved in the disorder, in addition to the effects of the medications on these neural processes and the behavioral results. The literature is amply cited so that the reader can access further information on any given disorder and medication. There is also mention of adverse effects of medications and those that are contraindicated in particular disorders. This chapter is essential to the medical professional treating patients in need of anger management techniques and will also enlighten practitioners who are referring clients to physicians for their aggressiveness so that their clients can be properly monitored and treated.

Over the past decade, we have become increasingly aware of the extent and magnitude of the sexual victimization of children in our society, and considerable efforts have been made to offer help and assistance to these victims. However, to a large extent, their perpetrators have been regarded more as offenders deserving punishment than as persons needing help. Chapter 21, by Dr. Fred Berlin, serves to broaden the base of our knowledge in regard to an adult's sexual attraction to a child and helps us differentiate between the perpetrator and his offense. It is a conceptual work, exploring the nature of pedophilia, its etiology, manifestation, diagnosis, and treatment, which encompasses both clinical and ethical considerations.

Chapter 19

A Neurological Perspective of Violent Behavior

by Frank A. Elliott, M.D., F.A.C.P.; F.R.C.P. London

A Neurological Perspective 19-2
A Neurologic Typology 19-2
    Predatory Violence 19-2
    Adolescent Psychopathy 19-4
Affective Aggression 19-4
    Intermittent Explosive Disorder 19-4
    Single-Episode Rage 19-5
    Over-Controlled Personalities 19-6
    Organic Obsessional Pathologies 19-6
    Sleeping Disorders 19-7
Epilepsy and Violence 19-8
Anatomical and Chemical Substrates of Violence 19-9
    Damage to Structural Inhibitors 19-9
    Neurochemical Activators 19-9
    Testosterone and PMS Syndrome 19-10
    Hypoglycemia 19-10
    Other Variables 19-11
Neurophysiological Correlates of Violent Behavior 19-11
    Age 19-11
    Sex 19-12
    Genetics 19-12
Neuropathological Correlates of Criminal Violence 19-12
The Clinical Evolution of Violence 19-13

Excerpted from a chapter in Elliott, F. A., "Neurologic Perspective," *Handbook of Psychological Approaches to Violent Criminal Offenders*, M. Hersen and V. Van Hasselt eds. Copyright © 1999 by Plenum Press. Adapted with permission.

Neuropathology in Murderers 19-15
Conclusions 19-15

A NEUROLOGICAL PERSPECTIVE

Socioeconomic and environmental causes of criminal violence are so many, and the role of mental disorders so obvious, that they have been allowed to obscure the contributions of organic brain defects. This should no longer be acceptable in the criminal courts or elsewhere. There is abundant evidence, collected over a century of research, that damage to specific structures in the brain can lead to recurrent attacks of destructive aggression in formerly equable individuals, that this and other disinhibited behaviors can also be associated with covert neurodevelopmental defects incurred before or after birth, and that the liability to violence in such individuals is usually increased by childhood exposure to social adversity, emotional deprivation, and physical/mental abuse, and is reinforced by criminal example. On the other hand, worldwide ethnological studies have established that violent crime is relatively low in communities and societies that have retained their cultural tabus and constraints (Goldstein & Segall, 1983; Eibl-Ebesfeldt, 1979).

This chapter is not concerned with collective aggression or with the violent responses of psychotics to their delusions, illusions, and hallucinations or to incidents of violence in the course of medical illness or intoxication (Tardiff, 1992), but focuses largely on the small segment of the population that is responsible for over 60 percent of recurrent criminal violence.

Social and criminologic studies of the past commonly treated violence as a homogeneous entity, which it is not. Homogenization, as in some major studies of large cohorts, can lead to errors of interpretation in individual cases (Moffitt, 1993); what is needed is closer scrutiny of the etiology, pathology, and clinical features of the several types of violent aggression (Eichelman, 1992) as a guide to disposal, treatment, and prognosis.

A NEUROLOGIC TYPOLOGY

Destructive interpersonal violence appears in at least two broad categories, predatory and affective, in both animals and humans. They differ in their modes of expression, provoking stimuli, chemical and anatomical bases, prognosis, and treatment (Reis, 1974; Moyer, 1976; Valzelli, 1981) and each category can be subdivided according to etiology. However, tidy classification is often complicated by the presence of multiple biological and social pathologies.

Predatory Violence

Predatory violence is cold, callous, and casual, and either planned or impulsive. It is carried out for profit—money, goods, power, sex (including the satisfaction of deviant sex), and getting rid of the opposition or of a witness to crime. It is the predominant form of aggression during epidemics of violence, and is found in both apparently normal individuals and in psychopaths (overlapping with antisocial personality disorder). The latter is characterized by retardation of social and emotional development, without intellectual impairment, which was described by Kraepelin (1915) as "circumscribed infantilism," a view supported by modern developmental psychology (Kegan, 1986) and by personal observations of this life-long disorder. Compared with other male criminals, psychopaths commit a disproportionate number of crimes, as well as more violent crimes (Hare & McPherson, 1984), but fortunately, the majority, though troublesome, are not violent. Some achieve political or commercial eminence, for as Prichard (1835) commented: "The power of self-government is lost or greatly impaired in the individual, who is found to be incapable not of talking or reasoning on any subject proposed to him, but of conducting himself in decency and propriety in the business of life."

The full personality profile includes a mask of superficial charm behind which lies inflated ideas of self-worth, incapacity for empathy, lack of remorse, manipulative behavior, a parasitic lifestyle, a need for stimulation, impulsivity, poor self-control, shallow affect, and social irresponsibility, including multiple short-term sexual relationships. Marginal cases do not display the fully fledged mosaic and may present only fragments of the pattern. A particularly malign combination of impulsivity, aggression, lack of empathy, and lack of foresight is not uncommon after severe head injury and encephalitis, and occurs in a subset of those with attention deficit hyperactivity disorder and other neurodevelopmental abnormalities. Cleckley (1982) and others have remarked that the psychopath has what seems to be a profound defect in understanding the meaning of emotionally charged words—evil, cancer, homicide, love, strangle—which in them evoke the same brain wave patterns (cortical electroencephalogram, or EEG, potentials) as neutral words, such as table, life, children, and the like, implying a neurophysiological basis for their absence of guilt and lack of empathy for the disasters of others.

Psychopathy is usually classified as within psychiatric territory but has a neurobiological basis (Ratey, 1995). This is indicated by abnormal responses to neuropsychological tests designed to detect "organicity," nonspecific EEG abnormalities (usually in the form of bilateral theta waves in aggressive cases), a high P300 wave of event-related evoked potentials (Raine & Venables, 1988), resistance to aversive conditioning (and therefore failure to learn by experience) and defective skin conductive responses to significant social cues, which is consistent with bifrontal defect (Damasio et al., 1990). There is also a low level of serotonin metabolites in the spinal fluid and low serotonin in the blood platelets of children with the aggressive conduct disorder, a common precursor of violence in adults (Stoff et al., 1987). Minor neurological abnormalities are often present. Monroe (1978) carried out a detailed neurologic, neuropsychologic, psychiatric, and sociological study of ninety-three incorrigibly violent criminals in a maximum security institution. The personality profile of the group was that of the psychopath. Using a neurologic scale that included birth data, head injury, epileptoid mechanisms, brain insults, congenital minor physical anomalies, photophobia, motor strength, incoordination, and others, there was a correlation at the .001 level between the neurological scale and violent behavior. At the .05 level and beyond, violent behavior was associated with a psychiatric history of overreactive emotional behavior, poor judgment, poor effort to improve, self-defeating actions, lack of responsibility, grandiose illusions, hyperchondriasis, and disassociated states with amnesia. There was also a close correlation of antisocial traits in childhood, and poor peer relations in adolescence.

Adolescent Psychopathy

A second type of predatory behavior includes many of the features of the psychopath, but starts in adolescence rather than childhood, increases rapidly in numbers and severity until the age of about 16 and then declines precipitously until the early twenties as the brain matures (Yakovlev & LeCours, 1967). It appears in epidemic form, like a highly contagious disease, in times of anomie and social change, as in Germany after World War I (Reich, 1974) and the United States since the 1960s (Wishnie & Nevis-Olesen, 1979). And in England between 1950 and 1978, violent interpersonal crime carried out by boys ages 14 to 16 increased twenty-three-fold (Rutter & Giller, 1983). Moffitt (1993) found, from extensive studies in the United States and New Zealand, that in both countries antisocial behavior occurred in two groups of adolescents—those whose violence started early in childhood and persisted into adult life, and a much larger group whose criminal activities were limited to adolescents who temporarily copied the misbehavior of the psychopaths in their midst, which they perceived to be exciting, assertive, and profitable. It is logical to presume that their mimicry will extend to the examples set by television and the movies. A meta-analysis prepared for the National Research Council by Comstock and Paik (1990), covering 188 studies, reported that the vast majority showed that exposure to television violence resulted in increased aggressive behavior both at the time and over time.

Mimicking behaviors (mimicry) observed directly or on television plays a major role in learning and has a neurophysiological basis. Normal in children, it diminishes with maturity, but can return in an exaggerated form in adults with lesions of the frontal lobe who display pathological dependency on environmental cues and a loss of personal autonomy (Lhermitte et al., 1986). Fortunately, mimicry in youth applies not only to antisocial behavior but also to the prosocial influences of role models whose example helps them to resist a criminogenic environment, as illustrated by Werner and Smith (1982) in their study of adolescent Hawaiians, in which some individuals proved to be "vulnerable but invincible."

AFFECTIVE AGGRESSION

Intermittent Explosive Disorder

Intermittent explosive disorder, formerly known as episodic dyscontrol (Menninger & Mayman, 1956), leads to a serious form of violence and often characterizes domestic violence in particular. Its hallmark is recurrent attacks of intense rage, without reflective delay, sometimes accompanied by visible evidence of sympathetic discharge—sweating, piloerection (body hair standing erect), and dilation of the pupils. In the words of an observant witness who escaped an homicidal attack, "his eyes darkened and his mustache bristled." Kaplan (1899) described it thus in his description of attacks in patients with head injury, psychosis, and arteriosclerosis:

> [F]ollowing the most trivial and impersonal causes there is the effect of rage with its motor accompaniments. There may be the most grotesque gesticula-

tions, excessive movements of the face and a sharp explosiveness of speech; there will be cursing and outbreaks of violence which are often directed towards things; there may or may not be amnesia for these events afterwards. The outburst may terminate in an epileptic fit. There is an excessive reaction with inadequate adaptation to the situation, which is so remote from a well considered and purposeful act that it approaches a pure psychic reflex.

The highly charged affect distinguishes it from the cold violence of predatory aggression and the habitual violence practiced as a means of survival in city slums and prisons (Wolfgang & Ferracuti, 1982). It is a cause of unpremeditated homicide and suicide, senseless attacks on strangers, bar fights, criminally aggressive driving, spouse and child abuse, and savage attacks on animals. Sometimes, particularly in women, the aggression is verbal. Its contents are vindictive, profane, and out of character, and are often accompanied by salivation and a feline retraction of the upper lip. It is a form of child abuse, and can lead to criminal violence by provoking fatal retaliation on the part of a male who prefers to hit rather than argue.

Intermittent explosive disorder can exist on its own but usually accompanies psychological or neurological disorders—neuroses, posttraumatic stress disorder, psychoses, borderline disorders, trauma and acquired neurological diseases, neuro-developmental abnormalities including mental retardation and autism, metabolic disorders including hypoglycemia, and exogenous and endogenous intoxications and toxaemias (Tardiff, 1992). It is usually associated with other less alarming forms of impulsive behavior (Monroe, 1978; Bach-y-Rita et al., 1971) and appears to be linked to a failure of the central inhibitory mechanisms that normally control the expression of aggression (Gorenstein & Neuman, 1980).

Single-Episode Rage

A second type of affective violence, less common than the above, resembles the "sham rage" caused in animals by damaging the deep connections between the hypothalamus and the cortex, and occurs as a single episode. The rage "is excessive in degree, unfocused, cannot be interrupted, and does not fatigue" (Poeck, 1969). It can last for hours or days. The usual cause is a severe closed head injury, involving the prefrontal (orbitofrontal) cortex, hippocampus, and anterior cingulate gyrus (Roberts, 1979). It has also resulted from damage to the midbrain by hemorrhage from an aneurysm (Poeck, 1969).

A typical example: a 30-year-old farmer was struck by lightning while riding a tractor. His scalp was badly burned, and his skull and one arm were fractured when he fell to the ground. Pulse and respiration failed but were immediately restored by a bystander. When he emerged from a coma three weeks later, he was delirious and violent, shouting, cursing, attempting to bite attendants, and throwing things. He had to be forcibly restrained and did not respond to medication until he was given propranolol, as an experimental measure, whereupon his violence ceased though he did not appear sedated. The violence returned two days later when the propranolol was temporarily withdrawn (Elliott, 1977).

Clearly, such very sick patients are incapable of focused criminal violence, except by accident. Their significance lies in the demonstration of involvement of early mammalian and reptilian components of the human brain in primitive behavior, extreme examples of which are the cannibalism by some serial murderers (see Ferreira, Chapter 15 in this text) and the biting by patients with rabies.

Over-Controlled Personalities

A third type of affective violence appears in individuals who are not disinhibited, but over-controlled (Megargee, 1982). They put up with intense provocation for a long time but finally explode in an outburst of destructive fury in vengeance for past wrongs, minor or major, real or imagined. Blackburn (1968) examined sixty-three such cases in a maximum security mental institution. Of the thirty-eight most violent cases, only eight had a previous criminal record, and no less than thirty-one out of the thirty-eight were acquainted with their victims. There is no mention of neurological examination. They were intensively examined by neuropsychological tests, the results of which were consistent with a diagnosis of an over-controlled personality. Williams (1969) carried out electroencephalographic tests on 333 violent criminals and found that those guilty of a single major offense had only slightly more EEG abnormalities than the normal population, whereas 65 percent of violent recidivists had abnormal recordings; this has been confirmed by others (Strafford-Clark, 1959).

A well-known example is that of Charles Whitman, who had a good record of self-control—altar-boy, Eagle scout, marine—but at age 25, he became obsessed with thoughts of killing which he recorded in a lengthy diary and reported to a psychiatrist. In it he expressed the hope that his case might help others in the same predicament and explained that he was going to kill his wife and mother to spare them embarrassment from what he proposed to do, which was to ascend the tower on the university campus in Houston and open fire on the public. He did so, killing fourteen people and wounding seventeen before he was shot in the head by a policeman (Moyer, 1987). Autopsy revealed a malignant tumor which from the histological evidence appeared to be from a temporal lobe, a conclusion supported by two other symptoms suggestive of temporal lobe pathology, hypergraphia and obsession with the moral aspects of his behavior. New evidence has recently been supplied by Brown (1994), the psychiatrist in charge of a state-ordered investigation of the massacre, who found that Whitman and his mother had been oppressed and abused by his father who forced him into a joyless and lonely childhood, the effects of which were obvious to his teachers at the time, but gave no warning of what was to come. Once again, nature and nurture both played a role in this crime.

Organic Obsessional Pathologies

In a fourth type of violence, the patient is obsessed with uncontrollable thoughts of death and killing, and may ultimately feel driven to carry them out. There were many such cases in the 1915-1925 epidemic of encephalitis lethargica, in which compulsive movements and bizarre postures were also common. Sporadic cases of encephalitis due to other viruses are not uncommon today in children with cognitive and emotional impairments, occasionally including criminal violence. Thus, a 10-year-old boy had mumps encephalitis, after which his personality was grossly altered, though his intellectual powers were unimpaired. He was given to attacks of rage, and to compulsive letter writing and endless moral introspection, all of which suggested temporal lobe pathology. He also had an obsession about women's breasts, and a compulsion to fondle them, which he yielded to by stalking his victims' homes, breaking in, and raping them.

Obsessive-compulsive features without rituals were present in twenty-one recurrently violent subjects observed by the writer. There was covert evidence of neuropathology in fourteen; neurodevelopmental defects in eight; serious head injuries in three; temporal lobe epileptic attacks in one; encephalitis in one; and excessive temporal lobe slow wave activity in one. Denckla (1989) reported neuropathological findings in forty-four out of fifty-four cases of obsessive-compulsive disorder in children, and they were also present in thirteen of nineteen cases seen by Hollander et al. (1987). Interpersonal violence occurred, but rarely, in these studies. Published reports (Frazier, 1974) suggest that obsessions and compulsions play a role in some serial murderers' behaviors, who feel "driven."

Additional evidence of organic pathology in obsessional personalities has been provided by neuropsychological studies (Cox et al., 1989) and by imaging studies that showed hypermetabolism in the orbital gyrus and caudate nucleus (Baxter et al., 1987) and in the medial frontal cortex (Macklin et al., 1991), and by the fact that clomipramine, which inhibits serotonin reuptake, also has anti-obsessional effects (Rapoport, 1989), and may therefore be expected to reduce compulsive violence. A diminished level of the serotonin metabolite 5-HIAA has been found in the spinal fluid of nonviolent patients with the obsessive-compulsive disorder.

Sleeping Disorders

Sleep-related violence can be responsible for murder, homicide, suicide, assault, and child abuse. It can be neurogenic or psychogenic. The latter embraces dissociative disorders (multiple personality) and malingering, and neurological types include:

1. Disorders of arousal ("drunk with sleep").
2. Rapid-eye movement (REM) sleep disorders in which the normal, active sleep paralysis of muscles is temporarily abrogated, allowing the subject to act-out dreams, violent and otherwise.
3. Sleep-walking (somnambulism) that occurs early in the night, when eye movements are normal and the subject is in a state of automation, without control of his or her behavior.
4. Nocturnal post-epileptic automatism (Mahowald et al., 1990; Broughton et al., 1994).

Somnambulism, often associated with a personal and familial history of sleep disorders, has been responsible for homicides, some of them extremely violent. It can be triggered by alcoholic, soporific (sleep-inducing) medications and street drugs.

Clinical differentiation between REM disorders, somnambulism, psychiatric dissociative states, nocturnal seizure phenomena, and pathological intoxication is often impossible without investigation in a sleep disorder center.

EPILEPSY AND VIOLENCE

It is generally accepted that uncomplicated epileptics are statistically no more liable to crime than the rest of the population, that planned aggression carried out for profit is inconsistent with the epileptic process, and that during post-ictal confusion the patient may violently resist attempts to restrain him or her and thus cause accidental injury. The same is occasionally true of persistent automatism following a temporal lobe seizure, so that from the forensic point of view it is unwise to plead that directed post-ictal aggression cannot occur (Gunn, 1991). In general, inter-ictal violence is not due to the epilepsy per se, but to temporal lobe pathology that may be responsible for both the seizures and the behavioral and emotional disorders (Stevens & Hermann, 1981; Blumer, 1991; Treiman, 1986).

Nevertheless, the proportion of epileptics is greater in prisons and state hospitals than in the population at large. In Broadmoor, a British maximum security hospital for the insane, it was found that 2.7 percent of males and 2 percent of the females were epileptic (Wong et al., 1994), and in Philadelphia, a random computer check disclosed that 3.4 percent of over 4,000 prisoners were receiving Dilantin prescribed by physicians.

There is a link between temporal lobe pathology and sexual dysfunction. Global hyposexuality is common in temporal lobe epileptics (Blumer, 1991) and sexual perversions are not rare; they include transvestitism, voyeurism, fetishism, sadism, masochism, heterosexual and homosexual pederasty, and genital self-mutilation (Bear et al., 1984). Such deviations are apt to be associated with a history of hypoxia or brain damage at or shortly after birth (Kolarsky et al., 1967), and Langevin (1990) has reported a high prevalence of morphologic defects in the temporal lobe, disclosed by computerized tomography, in persons given to deviant sexual practices. Unilateral destruction by stereotaxic surgery of the ventromedial hypothalamic nucleus has been successful in reducing or abolishing pedophilia in a small number of cases (Roeder, 1966; Diekmann & Hassler, 1975).

In many cases of criminal violence the diagnosis, prognosis, and treatment are complicated by multiple pathologies, psychological, sociological, and acquired or developmental neurobiological disorders, many of which are not clinically obvious and are apt to be missed by traditional neurological examination and by IQ tests (Levine, 1995). The following case is illustrative . A 38-year-old man was given two life sentences for sexually assaulting and murdering two 12-year-old boys. Prior offenses included juvenile delinquencies from age 11, attempted rape on a 12-year-old girl, beating to death a 37-year-old aunt, and murder of a 4-year-old boy. Pedophilia and homosexuality dated from age 16 and persisted throughout adult life. The family history was turbulent but not criminal, and a brother was epileptic. The prisoner had convulsions with severe cyanosis shortly after birth and was not expected to live; nocturnal convulsions returned at puberty, and then ceased. EEGs at that time and since have shown an epileptic spike focus in the left temporal lobe. Dilantin was prescribed by a distinguished psychiatrist, but was not given then or later. In addition to epilepsy, he had neurodevelopmental disorders against a background of high intelligence and considerable artistic gifts. The disorders included poor impulse control for both kindly deeds and criminal activities, explosive rage on minor provocation (including sudden loud noises in domestic altercations due to hyperacousis), defective audiomotor coordination, difficulty in spatial perceptions, as in copying plans on paper and painting pictures, and poor attention span. During his confinement he learned to control his temper and his "almost uncontrollable sexual drives" and has led a constructive life as artist, pest control officer and peace maker. But he does not consider that he should be paroled.

ANATOMICAL AND CHEMICAL SUBSTRATES OF VIOLENCE

A century of experimental work with animals and pathological studies in man has shown that the capacity to express and inhibit violence is vested in a genetically ordered network of neural connections that involve structures from the orbitofrontal cortex to the limbic system and midbrain. Some of these structures are excitatory and some inhibitory, while others, like the amygdala and hypothalamus, are both (Volavka, 1995; Brown & Goodwin, 1986). The balance between excitation and inhibition in the normal nervous system is often disturbed in violent behavior. For example, unusually high levels of neuronal excitation can lead to aberrant and socially inappropriate behaviors. Damage to inhibitory systems that normally maintain stability between excitation and inhibition in the brain can also lead to excessive excitability. Secondly, low level sensory stimulation can provoke an unusually intense response in individuals so affected, often exemplified by an explosive rage in response to repeated minimal provocations, like a loud noise, a shove, or other irritant.

Damage to Structural Inhibitors

Structures in the brain that act to inhibit behavior include the orbitofrontal cortex, the septal area, the medial nucleus, of the amygdala, the hippocampus, cingulate gyrus, caudate nucleus and various nuclei of the hypothalamus (Valzelli, 1981; Weiger & Bear, 1988). When these areas are damaged, behavior can be impulsive and unrestrained. There are many more areas of the brain involved in inhibition as compared with excitation, which may help to explain why pathological aggression more often occurs in individuals who have damage to both sides of the brain. Unilateral damage can be compensated for or counterbalanced by the other hemisphere. Bilateral damage can be caused by a tumor, head injury, prenatal insults including drug exposures, encephalitis, alcoholic degeneration, neurodevelopmental disorders, dementias, chronic degenerative diseases, cardio-respiratory failure, and mental retardation. Head injury is the most common origin of organic brain damage among violent offenders.

Neurochemical Activators

While specific locations in the brain regulate particular behavioral patterns and tendencies, neurochemicals are responsible for their activation. Neurotransmitters, chemical messengers in the brain, are distributed throughout these structures and exert differential effects at each site. Neuromodulators, on the other hand, are slower-acting hormones that also have particular relevance to violent behavior. Neurotransmitters chiefly concerned with aggression include dopamine (DA), norepinephrine (NE) and acetylcholine (ACh), which are all excitatory, in addition to serotonin (5-HT) and gamma-aminobutyric acid (GABA), which are inhibitory. NE activates (emotionally driven) affective aggression and reduces predatory violence. ACh and DA activate both types of aggression, and serotonin inhibits both. Low levels of 5-HT in particular have been associated with impulsive behavior and emotionally charged aggression, including suicide and antisocial behavior. Low blood serotonin is found in children suffering from conduct disorder, which is often a precursor of future violence.

NE, 5-HT and DA are metabolized by two enzymes: MAOA and MAOB. Low MAO (monoamine oxidase) activity is associated with disinhibition—impulsivity and aggression—and a point mutation in the structural gene for MAOA has been identified in a kindred of violent males with a history of assaultive behaviors (Brunner et al., 1993). While this genetic defect is believed to be rare, it is possible that subtler forms of defects in MAOA activity may be somewhat more common in the population and may predispose to violence (see Goldman & Fishbein, Chapter 9).

Testosterone and PMS Syndrome

There is clinical evidence indicating an association between elevated levels of testosterone and aggression. The incidence of aggressive behavior often coincides with a tenfold increase of testosterone in boys at puberty, and a dramatic reduction of sex crimes follows castration and administration of antiandrogens (drugs that inhibit testosterone) in man (Moyer, 1976). Hawke (1950) quotes a group of sex offenders whose violence was reduced by castration but returned following the administration of large doses of testosterone. There are also reports of criminal violence carried out by formerly equable individuals who in their pursuit of athletic ambitions injected themselves with anabolic steroids over a considerable period (Volavka, 1995).

In women, the most common hormonal contributor to both verbal and physical aggression is the premenstrual tension syndrome, which can have devastating and permanent effects on children exposed to it from their mothers. It is thought to be due to an abnormally high estrogen-progesterone ratio but is also aggravated by psychosocial factors to a degree that may obscure the hormonal factor (Rutter, 1980).

Hypoglycemia

Hypoglycemia, produced by excessive insulin, was first recorded by Joslin in 1937 and Wilder and his colleagues in 1947 at the Mayo Clinic. They had assembled a formidable list from the world literature of hypoglycemia-related crimes, from theft and arson to homicide and child abuse. It is produced by insulin overdose, pancreatic insulinomas (tumors), an excessive fall of blood sugar after a carbohydrate meal, and an alcoholic hangover caused by the effect of alcohol on glucose metabolism (Kanarek, 1994; Virkkunen, 1986). It is particularly liable to produce violence in intermittent explosive disorder, antisocial personality disorder, and organic brain defects.

A personal case: a respected citizen who was diabetic and had also developed occasional temporal lobe seizures in midlife took an evening dose of insulin but did not eat dinner. While parking his car, he got into an altercation with a policeman, whom he assaulted. He then drove around the parking lot in a pointless manner and attempted to run down another policeman, who shot him in the arm and so brought the chase to an end. When apprehended he was belligerent and confused, and his blood sugar was found to be below 40 mgms%. The confusion was immediately abolished by intravenous glucose; he had no recollection of anything he had done since leaving home.

A diagnosis is often missed if there is no clear-cut time relationship between food intake and hypoglycemia. It depends less on the history than on rigorous laboratory studies of the blood glucose response to fasting and other provocations, and on blood insulin assays; it cannot be accurately diagnosed by a routine three-hour glucose tolerance test. A fall of blood sugar induced under laboratory conditions can fail to induce the violence that occurs under social circumstances; this can have forensic implications.

Other Variables

It is possible that fluctuations in the frequency of violent behavior are related to diurnal, circadian, and seasonal variations in levels of neurotransmitters and neuromodulators. This would help to explain not only the irregular episodicity of personal violence but also the seasonal alterations in rates of homicide and suicide. Chemical systems are not immutable throughout life and are alterable through both environmental and pharmacological means.

Social or psychological pathology can give rise to antisocial behaviors more readily in individuals compromised by neurological dysfunction. On the other hand, a stable social and family background can reduce the impact of neurological handicaps. There is also recent evidence that exposure to neglect, abuse or severe trauma early in life can induce permanent changes in brain function and chemistry to increase the likelihood for abnormal or deviant behavior.

NEUROPHYSIOLOGICAL CORRELATES OF VIOLENT BEHAVIOR

Age

Pathological degrees of violent aggression can begin with the tantrums of infancy or a conduct disorder of childhood, and such aggression may also occur at any age in a previously stable individual following a serious head injury or other brain insult. In males, a tenfold rise of testosterone levels during puberty is often blamed for the usual increase in aggressiveness in adolescence; however, this is not the whole story. Homicidal violence can begin before puberty, and there is evidence in animals that androgens can both influence and be influenced by aggression. The current peak of criminal violence in normal adolescents is reached at about the sixteenth year, after which it falls precipitously over the next few years. It is likely that the process of social maturation that occurs in the late teens and early twenties is related to the completion of myelination (development in the nervous system), which is reached late in the third decade, particularly in brain regions identified for involvement in aggression (Benes et al., 1994; Kaes, 1907; Yakovlev & Lecours, 1967). The question arises as to whether the clumsiness, dyspraxias, and defective bimanual coordination, which are the most common of the covert developmental motor disorders in children, are due to the vulnerability associated with the relatively late maturation of the cerebellar cortex (Zecevic & Rakic, 1976) and the large cerebral commissures (Yakovlev & Lecours, 1966). Complete maturational development differs from system to system, and there is clinical evidence that it can be modified in either direction by biological and environmental influences that can affect different systems and behaviors to an unequal degree (Glaser, 1981). Exposure in infancy and childhood to physical abuse and emotional neglect, for example, can permanently alter brain development, in turn adversely affecting social and emotional development.

Sex

Most normal male individuals from cradle to grave are more prone to physical aggression than are most females, and pathological violence exhibited by individuals in the form of both affective and predatory aggression is far more common in males, who are also more prone to conditions that predispose to it: neurodevelopmental disorders, natal and perinatal injuries, and infections. In Sweden, men with a major mental handicap were 5.5 times more likely than men with no disorder to be registered for a violent act, while women with a mental disorder were 24.8 times more likely than women without a disorder to be guilty of a violent crime (Lindqvist & Allebeck, 1990). Conversely, high intelligence has protective value (Volavka, 1995).

An absolute distinction between the two sexes is the liability of women to the premenstrual dysphoric disorder, which in some individuals is accompanied by attacks of extreme rage and violence: 60 percent of violent crimes committed by women are said to occur in the premenstrual week (Morton et al., 1953; Dalton, 1964).

Genetics

When violence runs in the family—a familiar explanation—it is commonly ascribed to intergenerational transfer of learned responses. This may not be the whole story. Consistently, studies show that the majority of those who experience violence in the home do not themselves become perpetrators (Stacey & Shupe, 1983). Numerous studies do, however, report that aggression and assaultiveness have at least partial roots in genetic contributions (Elliott, 1982). The National Research Council panel on violence, for example, concludes that the data on the heritability of violence applies to important correlates of aggression (impulsivity, conduct disorder, novelty seeking, negative affect) and not to violence itself (Carey, 1994).

NEUROPATHOLOGICAL CORRELATES OF CRIMINAL VIOLENCE

The most convincing evidence of a close link between destructive personal violence and brain damage is provided by the occasional cases in which aggression occurs for the first time in a previously docile individual following damage by a tumor to structures that appear to exert an inhibitory influence on the repression of aggression—the orbitofrontal cortex (Strauss & Keschner, 1936), the anterior cingulate cortex (Elliott, 1982), the hippocampus (Malamud, 1967), the medial amygdala nuclei (Vonderahe, 1944), the anterior temporal lobe, the ventromedial hypothalamus (Reeves & Plum, 1969), the anterior hypothalamus (Alpers, 1937), and, in children, the pons (Cairns, 1950; Lassman & Arjona, 1967). Rarely, lesions of the cerebellum have been followed by attacks of rage. In the majority of tumor cases the subject is too sick to embark on criminal activities; the importance of tumor damage cases lies in the demonstration that a small focal lesion in certain specific areas can give rise to violent behavior on mild provocation.

Severe head injuries are a much more common source of recurrent aggression. Repeated minor trauma to the head, as in jockeys and boxers, can also occasionally result in chronic irritability and attacks of rage on minor provocation. From the forensic point of view it is necessary to remember, since head trauma is often used as an alibi, that the type of injury that can be held responsible for subsequent violence is usually severe enough to produce posttraumatic amnesia for seven days or more and involves hospitalization. Individuals so affected, particularly in childhood, usually develop neurodevelopmental and motor disorders.

Disorders are often covert and easily missed by routine neurological examination and IQ tests (Levine, 1995). The search for neuropathology has to cover conception, pregnancy, birth, infancy, childhood, adolescence, and beyond. The defects are often forgotten, and even more often, denied or regarded as irrelevant (Ratey, 1995). Common ingredients are attention deficit disorder, learning disorders, higher cognitive dysfunctions, poor social perceptions and skills, inability to learn common manual skills, lack of athletic dexterity, disorders of working memory and remote and sequence memory, incapacity to assess time intervals and rhythms, and difficulties with spatial perceptions. The pathological basis for some of these handicaps is known. For example, a physical basis for attention deficit hyperactivity disorder has been reported in a PET (positron emission tomography) that found depressed glucose metabolism in multiple areas of the cortex during an auditory-attention test (Zametkin et al., 1990).

THE CLINICAL EVOLUTION OF VIOLENCE

Longitudinal analyses of aggressive behavior have shown that its appearance in early childhood may predict criminal convictions for violence latter in life. Also, disinhibited violent behavior is usually accompanied by other, less dramatic forms of impulsive behavior and lack of reflective delay in social activities—overdrinking, gambling, traffic offenses, sexual promiscuity, theft, truancy, and pathological lying (Robins, 1966; Farrington, 1983; Bach-y-Rita et al., 1971). The importance of scrutinizing the entire life-history from conception onward was demonstrated in a unique study by Denno (1990) of the records of 987 subjects who were born at the Philadelphia Hospital in Pennsylvania between 1959 and 1962. The subjects were nonwhite and predominantly of low socioeconomic status. The sample (487 males and 500 females) had been followed up from birth until the age of 22 years. It involved examination of the mothers as soon as they started attending the prenatal clinic. Their pregnancies were supervised, as was labor and delivery. Each child was examined immediately after birth and at intervals thereafter. Researchers collected socioeconomic and family data when the mothers registered and at the child's seventh-year examination. School data were available, focusing on academic achievement during ages 13 to 14 and on evidence of learning and behavior disability during school attendance. Police records were collected for children ages 7 to 22. Much information was gathered from frequent home interviews with parents or caretakers. Each child was interviewed sixteen times in all and was given pediatric examinations three times in the first seven years. They all received selective intelligence tests at age 7 and achievement tests at ages 13 and 14. Lead levels were examined at age 7.

This exercise carries with it the authority of facts recorded at the time, thus avoiding the dubious validity of retrospective questionnaires. Of the 987 subjects, 151 became offenders by the age of 18, and nearly one-quarter of these were arrested for violent crimes. Five percent of the male sample were chronic offenders, a figure that jibes with those in the study by Tracey et al. (1990) on a cohort of 10,000 male individuals born in Philadelphia, Pennsyvania in 1945 and with the results of their second study of 27,160 individuals born in 1958, approximately half of whom were male. In Denno's study, the chronic offenders were responsible for 61 percent of the violent offenses. The neurologic differences between them and the control subjects included higher figures for neurodevelopmental disorders (attention deficit disorder, incoordination, articulation), head injury, and serum lead levels at age 7. Denno concluded that "biological and environmental variables exert strong and independent influences on juvenile crime, which appeared to be directly related to familial instability and, most important, a lack of behavioral control associated with central nervous system disorders" (p. 659).

Similar findings were reported by Spreen (1989) in a longitudinal study of 203 children (average age 9) with learning difficulties, compared with fifty-two controls, whom he followed until their mid-twenties. He found that covert and overt neurological abnormalities were common in the learning disabled subjects. Those with learning difficulties but without neurological impairment fared worse than controls. Those with minimal brain dysfunction did worse than those without it. And those with learning disabilities and definite brain damage did worst of all as regards temper outbursts, impulsivity, and fighting.

Another study of fifty-three older delinquent males, ages 11 to 16, 20 percent of whom had been convicted for violent crimes, and fifty-one nondelinquents, was carried out by Levine et al. (1985). Thirty-two areas were covered, including general health, seizures, trauma, neurodevelopmental defects, behavioral history, educational assessments and handicaps, attention, and the Wechsler Intelligence Scale for children. There was no socioeconomic difference between the subjects and the controls. The latter showed vulnerabilities, but the delinquents displayed far more defects in the areas surveyed.

The continuity between birth injuries and subsequent aggression is especially noticeable when it is complicated by maternal neglect in the first year (Towbin, 1971; Lewis et al., 1979). A cohort of 4,269 males in Denmark was assessed for birth injury recorded at the time of delivery, maternal rejection in the first year, and violent crime at 18 years; 4.5 percent with both risk factors were responsible for 18 percent of the violent crime committed by the cohort (Raine et al., 1994).

NEUROPATHOLOGY IN MURDERERS

The chief psychiatrist of the California State Prison at San Quentin wrote, "It has been my experience that organic brain pathology is vastly under-diagnosed in the prison population and plays a much larger part in criminal behavior than we have previously thought" (Hicks, 1988). Studies of violent offenders too numerous to mention here support this observation, showing abnormalities in PET, MRI (magnetic resonance imaging) and CAT (computerized axial tomography) scans, neurodevelopmental defects, organic brain disorders, significant brain damage, EEG abnormalities, and various other forms of neurological impairment (Raine et al., 1994; Frazier, 1974; Bender, 1959; Lewis et al., 1988; Merikangas, 1981; Elliott, 1982; Megargee, 1982; Blackburn, 1968). Nevertheless, most brain-damaged individuals are not violent, and in those that are, there is usually also evidence of psychopathology and/or prolonged exposure to significant social adversity. Thus, compounding these problems is the high incidence of co-occurring family dysfunction, child abuse and neglect, and economic, emotional, and social deprivation.

CONCLUSIONS

Many recent studies of violent criminals—other than professional hit-men—have found neurological or neuropsychological defects. Additional evidence of pathology is being identified by electrophysiological investigation, CT (computerized tomography) scans, PET scans, magnetic imaging, and neurochemical studies. Nevertheless, most brain damaged individuals are not violent, and in those that are, there is usually evidence of psychopathology and/or prolonged exposure to significant social adversity. Thus, criminal violence appears to be a result of the confluence and interaction at a given moment, or over a period of time, of multiple biological and environmental variables, some excitatory and some inhibitory. They include the behavior of the putative victim and the blood levels of alcohol and drugs in both the aggressor and the aggressed.

It has been pointed out that neurological disorders are not obvious in many cases. Many affected people look and sound normal. As Eric Fromm (1973) once remarked, "they don't wear the mark of Cain." The defects are often covert and are missed by cursory neurological and IQ examinations. This is especially true of neurodevelopmental disorders, which are apt to go unrecognized and unaddressed as these subjects pass through schools, medical clinics, social services, and the courts.

Perhaps the most powerful inhibitory influences are prosocial cultural and religious constraints, and social taboos. Historical examples over the centuries have illustrated the disastrous effects when they are weakened during periods of social disruption and anomie, from which may arise widespread erosion of personal integrity, a drying-up of compassion and altruism, uncontrolled material greed, corruption in high places, a lust for cruelty in entertainment, a descent of sexual mores to barnyard levels, and even a recourse to medieval demonology.

It is comforting to recall that through the centuries these epidemics have come to an end (Gurr, 1969). It is also encouraging that much progress has been made by pharmacological research that has provided an impressive array of agents that can not only control specific types of violence (Miczek et al., 1994; Volavka, 1995), but can make recalcitrant juvenile delinquents and criminals more accessible to psychotherapy by reducing their hostility (Eichelman, 1988). An early example is phenytoin, which in 1939 brought a measure of peace to the epileptic wards of state hospitals by controlling inter-ictal violence. Later on, carbamezapine had an even wider sphere of activity, as did antipsychotic agents: lithium for mania and depression; propranolol and other beta blockers for intermittent explosive disorder and violence in all organic cases, regardless of diagnosis (Miczek et al., 1994); serotonergic agents for a variety of conditions, both organic and functional; antiandrogens to reduce the sex drive in sex offenders, and clomipramine to reduce aggressive thoughts (Rapoport, 1989).

Useful as they are for symptomatic control in subjects who can be supervised, whether in hospitals, prisons, clinics or stable households, they cannot reach street criminals. The thrust of social and criminal studies, especially longitudinal investigations, is to reinforce the importance of prophylaxis by multimodal behavior therapies for the children and adolescents who give early evidence of pathological aggression and neurological or neuropsychological deviance.

References

Alpers, B. J. (1937). Relation of the hypothalamus to disorders of personality. Report of a case. *Archives of Neurology and Psychiatry, 38*, 291–303.

Bach-y-Rita, G., Lion, J. R., Climent, C. E.. & Ervin, F. R. (1971). Episodic dyscontrol: A study of 130 violent patients. *American Journal of Psychiatry, 127*, 1473–1478.

Barkley, R. A. (1990). *Attention deficit hyperactivity disorder. A handbook for diagnosis and treatment in psychiatric offenders.* New York: Guilford Press.

Barrett, H. J. & Hyland, H. H. (1952). Tumours involving the brainstem. *Quarterly Journal of Medicine, 21*, 265–284.

Baxter, L. R., Phelps, M. E., Mazziotta, J. C., Guze, B. H., Schwartz, B. & Selin, C. E. (1987). Local cerebral glucose metabolic rates in obsessive-compulsive disorders. *Archives of General Psychiatry, 44*, 211–218.

Bear, D. M., Freeman, R. & Greenberg, M. (1984). Behavioral alterations in temporal lobe epilepsy. In Blumer, D. (Ed.), *Psychiatric aspects of epilepsy*. Washington, DC: American Psychiatric Press.

Bender, L. (1959). Children and adolescents who have killed. *American Journal of Psychiatry, 116*, 510–513.

Benes, F. M., Turtle, M., Khan, Y. & Farol, P. (1994). Myelination of a key relay zone in the hippocampal formation occurring in the human body during childhood, adolescence, and adulthood. *Archives of General Psychiatry, 51*, 477–484.

Blackburn, R. (1968). Personality in relation to extreme aggression in psychiatric offenders. *British Journal of Psychiatry, 114*, 821–828.

Blake, P. Y., Pincus, J. H. & Buckner, C. (1993). Neurologic abnormalities in murderers. *Neurology, 45*, 1641–1647.

Blumer, D. (1991). Epilepsy and disorders of mood. In D. S. Smith, D. M. Treiman & M. Trimble (Eds.), *Advances in neurology*, vol 55. New York: Raven Press, 185–196.

Broughton, R., Billings, R. Cartwright, R., Doucette, J., Edmeads, J., Edwards N., Ervin, F. R., Orchard, B., Hill, R. & Turrell, G. (1994). Homicidal somnambulism: A case report. *Sleep, 17*, 253–964.

Brown, G. L. & Goodwin, F. K. (1986). Human aggression: A biologic perspective. In W. W. Reid, D. Dore, J. Walker & I. W. Bonner (Eds.), *Unmasking the psychopath*. New York: W. W. Norton.

Brown, S. L. (1994, Dec.). Animals at play. *The National Geographic, 186*, 8–12.

Brunner, H. G., Nelen, M. R., Breakefield, X.O., Ropers, H. H. & van Oost, B. A. (1993). Abnormal behavior associated with a point mutation in the structural gene for monoamine oxidase A. *Science, 262,* 578–580.

Cairns, H. (1950). Mental disorders with tumors of the pons. *Folia Psychiatry Neurology* (Netherlands), *53,* 193–203.

Cantwell, D. P. & Baker, L. (1991). *Psychiatric and developmental disorders in children with communication disorders.* Washington, DC: American Psychiatric Press.

Carey, G. (1994). Genetics and violence. In A. J. Reiss, K. A. Miczek & J. A. Roth (Eds.), *Understanding and preventing violence,* vol. 2, *Biobehavioral influences.* Washington, DC: National Academy Press, 21–58.

Cleckley, H. C. (1982). *The mask of sanity.* St. Louis, MO: Harcourt Health Sciences.

Clements, S. D. (1966). *Minimal brain dysfunction in children.* Monograph No. 3, National Institute of Neurology and Blindness. Washington, DC: U.S. Department of Health, Education, and Welfare.

Clements, S. D. & Peters, J. E. (1962). Minimal brain dysfunction in the school-age child. *Archives of General Psychiatry, 6,* 185–197.

Comstock, G. & Paik, H. (1990). The effects of television on aggressive behavior. Unpublished report to the National Academy of Science on Understanding and Control of Violent Behaviors, vol. 1. Washington, DC: National Academy Press.

Cooper, I. S. (1978). *Cerebellar stimulation in man.* New York: Raven Press.

Cox, C. S., Fedio, P. & Rapoport, J. C. (1989). Neuropsychological testing of obsessive-compulsive adolescents. In J. Rapoport (Ed.), *Obsessive compulsive disorders in children and adolescents.* Washington, DC: American Psychiatric Press.

Dalton, K. (1964). *The premenstrual syndrome.* Springfield, IL: Charles C Thomas.

Damasio, A. R., Tramel, D. T. & Damasio, M. (1990). Individuals with sociopathic behavior caused by frontal damage fail to respond automatically to social stimuli. *Behavioral Brain Reseach, 41,* 81–94.

Davenport, D. B. (1915). The feebly inhibited: Violent temper and its inheritance. *Journal of Nervous and Mental Diseases, 42,* 493–528.

Denckla, M. B. (1989). In J. Rapoport (Ed.), *Obsessive compulsive disorders in children and adolescents.* Washington, DC: American Psychiatric Press.

Denno, D. W. (1988). *University of Pennsylvania Law Review, 137,* 659.

Denno, D. W. (1990). *Biology and violence: From birth to adulthood.* New York: Cambridge University Press.

Diekmann, G. & Hassler, R. (1975). Unilateral hypothalamotomy in social delinquents. Report on 6 cases. *Confinia Neurologica, 37,* 177–186.

Eibl-Ebesfeldt, I. (1979). *The biology of peace and war: Men, animals, and aggression.* New York: Viking Press.

Eichelman, B. (1988). Toward a rational pharmacotherapy for aggressive violent behavior. *Hospital and Community Psychiatry, 39,* 31–39.

Eichelman, B. (1992). Aggressive behavior: From laboratory to clinic: Quo vadis? *Archives of General Psychiatry, 49,* 488–492.

Elliott, F. A. (1977). Propranolol for the control of belligerent behavior following acute head injury. *Annals of Neurology, 1,* 489–491.

Elliott, F. A. (1982). Neurological findings in adult minimal brain dysfunction and the dyscontrol syndrome. *Journal Nervous and Mental Diseases, 170,* 680–687.

Elliott, F. A. (1992). Violence. The neurological contribution: an overview. *Archives of Neurology, 49,* 495–603.

Falconer, M. A. & Cavannagh, I. B. (1959). Clinicopathological considerations of temporal lobe epilepsy due to small focal lesions. *Brain, 82,* 483–504.

Farrington, D. P. (1983). Offending from 10 to 20 years of age. In K. Vandusen & S. A. Mednick (Eds.), *Prospective studies of crime and delinquency.* Boston: Kluwer-Nijhoff.

Frazier, S. H. (1974). Murder—single and multiple. In S. H. Frazier (Ed.), *Research publica-*

tions, Association for Research in Nervous and Mental Diseases. Baltimore: Williams & Wilkins.

Fromm, E. (1973). *The anatomy of human destructiveness.* New York: Holt, Rinehart & Winston.

Galaburda, A. M. (1991). Neuropathological correlates of learning difficulties. *Seminars in Neurology, 11,* 20–97.

Glaser, G. H. (1981). Critical periods in brain development related to behavior, especially epilepsies. In J. R. Merikangas (Ed.), *Brain behavior relationships.* Lexington, MA: Lexington Books.

Golden, C. J., Jackson, M. L., Peterson-Rohne, A. & Gontkovsky, S. T. (1996). Neuropsychological correlates of violence and aggression: A review of the clinical literature. *Aggression and Violent Behavior, 1,* 3–25.

Goldstein, A. P. & Segall, M. A. (1982). *Aggression in global perspective.* New York: Pergamon.

Gorenstein, E. E. & Newman, P. (1980). Disinhibitory psychopathology: A new perspective and a model for research. *Psychological Reviews, 87,* 301–315.

Gunn, J. C. (1991). Legal implications of behavioral changes in epilepsy. *Advances in Neurology, 55,* 461–472.

Gurr, T. R. (1976). The history of violent crime in Europe and America. In H. D. Graham & T. R. Gurr (Eds.), *Violence in America: Historical and comparative perspectives.* Newbury Park, CA: Sage.

Hare, R. & McPherson, L. M. (1984). Violent and aggressive behavior by criminal psychopaths. *International Journal of Law and Psychiatry, 7,* 35–50.

Hawke, C. C. (1950). Castration and sex crimes. *American Journal of Medical Deficiency, 55,* 220–296.

Heath, E. G. (1977). Modulation of emotion with a brain pacemaker. *Journal of Nervous and Mental Diseases, 165,* 300–317.

Hicks, P. S. (1988). Preface. In J. Morris & W. T Birnes (Eds.), *Serial killers.* New York: Dolphin Books.

Hollander, E., Shiffman, E. & Liebowitz, M. (1987, May). Neurological soft signs in obsessive-compulsive disorder. Poster presentation presented at the 140th annual meeting of the American Psychiatric Association, Chicago, IL.

Hoslin E. P. (1937). *Treatment of diabetes mellitus.* Philadelphia: Lea & Febiger.

Kaes, T. (1907). *Die grosshirninoe des menschen in ihren wassen und in ihren fassengehalt. Ein Gehirnanatomische Atlas.* Jena, Germany: Fischer.

Kanarek, R. B. (1994). Nutrition and violent behavior. In *Understanding and preventing violence,* vol. 2. Washington, DC: National Academy Press, 515–540.

Kaplan, J. (1899). *Kopftrauma und pschosen. Allg. Psychiatrie, 56,* 292–297.

Kegan, R. G. (1986). Sociopathy, a developmental delay. In W. H. Reid, D. Dorr & J. Walker (Eds.), *The child behind the mask.* New York: W. W. Norton.

Keschner, M., Bender, M. R. & Strauss, I. (1937). Mental symptoms in cases of subtentorial tumor. *Archives of Neurology and Psychiatry, 37,* 1–17.

Kim, S. G. Ugurbil, K. & Strick, P. L. (1994). Activation of cerebellar output nucleus during cognitive processing. *Science, 265,* 949–951.

Kolarski, A., Freund, K., Machek, J. & Polak, O. (1967). Male sexual deviation associated with early temporal lobe damage. *Archives of General Psychiatry, 17,* 735–743.

Kraepelin, E. (1915). *Psychiatrie. Die gesellschafs feiriig (Antisozialem)* (8th ed.), vol. 4. Leipzig: Barth, 1076–2110.

Langevin, R. (1990). Sexual anomalies and the brain. In W. L. Marshall, D. R. Laws & H. L. Barbaree (Ed.), *Handbook of sexual assault: Issues, theories and treatment of the offender.* New York: Plenum Press, 103–113.

Lassman, L. P. & Arjona, V. (1967) Pontine glioma in childhood. *Lancet, 1,* 913–915.

Leiner, H., Leiner, A. L. & Dow, R. S. (1989). Re-appraising the cerebellum. What does the hindbrain contribute to the fore-brain? *Behavioral Neuroscience, 103,* 998–1008.

Levine, M. D. (1995). Childhood neurodevelopmental dysfunctional learning disorders. *Harvard Mental Health Letter, 12,* 5–6.

Levine, M., Karniski, W. M., Palfrey, J. S., Meltzer, L. & Fenton, T. (1985). A study of risk factor complexes in early adolescent delinquency. *American Journal of Diseases of Childhood, 139,* 50–56.

Lewis, D. O., Pincus, J. H., Bard, S., Richardson, E., Pritchep, L. S., Feldman, M. & Yeager, C. (1988). Neuropsychiatric, psycho-educational and family characteristics of 14 juveniles condemned to death in the United States. *American Journal of Psychiatry, 145,* 584–589.

Lewis, D. O., Pincus, J. H. & Glaser, G. H. (1979). Violent juvenile delinquents: Psychiatric, neurological and abuse factors. *American Academy of Psychiatry, 18,* 307–319.

Lhermitte, F., Pillon, B. & Serdaru, M. (1986). Human anatomy and the frontal lobe: Imitation and utilization behavior. A neuro-psychological study of 75 patients. *Annals of Neurology, 19,* 326–334.

Linnoila, M., Virkkunen, M., Scheinen, M., Nuutila, A., Rimon, R. & Goodwin, F. K. (1983). Low cerebrospinal fluid 5-hydroxy indolacetic acid differentiates impulsive from nonimpulsive violent behavior. *Life Sciences, 33,* 2609–2614.

Linqvist, P. & Allebeck, F. (1990). Schizophrenia and crime: A longitudinal follow-up of 644 schizophrenics in Stockholm. *British Journal of Psychiatry, 157,* 345–350.

Macklin, S. R., Harris, G. H., Pearson, G. D., Hohn-Saric, R., Jeffery, P., Camargo, E. (1991). Elevated medial frontal blood flow in obsessive-compulsive patients in a SPECT study. *American Journal of Psychiatry, 148,* 1240–1242.

Mahowald, M. W., Bundlie, S. R., Hurwitz, T. D. & Schenck, C. H. (1990). Sleep violence: Forensic science implications: Polygraphic and video documentation. *Journal of Forensic Science, 35,* 413–430.

Malamud, N. C. (1967). Psychiatric disorders with intra-cranial tumors of the limbic system. *Archives of Psychiatry 17,* 113–123.

Mathieson, G. (1975). Pathology of temporal lobe foci. In J. K. Penry & D. Daly (Eds.), *Advances in Neurology,* vol. 11. New York: Raven.

Mednick, S. A. & Christiansen, K. (1977). *Biological bases of criminal behavior.* New York: Gardner Press.

Megargee, E. I. (1982). Psychological correlates and determinants of criminal behavior. In M. Wolfgang & M. Weiner (Eds.), *Criminal Violence.* Newburg Park, CA: Sage.

Merikangas, J. R. (1981). *Brain-behavior relationships.* Lexington, MA: Lexington Books.

Miczek, K. A., Haney, M., Tidey, J., Jeffrey, L., & Weerts, E. (1994). The neurochemistry and pharmacotherapeutics of aggression and violence. In A. J. Reis, J. Miczek & J. A. Roth (Eds.), *Understanding and preventing violence.* Washington, DC: National Academy Press.

Miczek K. A., Mirsky, A. F., Carey, G., DeBold, J. & Raine, A. (1994). In A. J. Reis, J. Miczek & J. A. Roth (Eds.), *Understanding and preventing violence.* Washington, DC: National Academy Press.

Moffitt, T. E. (1993). Adolescence-limited and life-course persistent antisocial behavior: A developmental taxonomy. *Psychological Review, 100,* 674–701.

Monroe, R. R. (1978). *Brain dysfunction in aggressive criminals.* Lexington, MA: Lexington Books.

Morton, J. H., Additon, H., Addison, R. G., Hunt, L. & Sullivan, H. A. (1953). A clinical study of pre-menstrual tension. *American Journal of Obstetrics and Gynecology, 65,* 1182–1191.

Moruzzi, G. (1958). In R. S. Dow & G. Moruzzi (Eds.), *The physiology and psychology of the cerebellum.* Minneapolis: University of Minnesota Press.

Moyer, K. E. (1976). *The psychohistology of aggression.* New York: Harper.

Poeck, K. (1969). Pathophysiology of emotional disorders associated with brain damage. In P. J. Vinken & G. W. Bruyn (Eds.), *Handbook of clinical neurology,* vol. 3. Amsterdam: North Holland.

Pritchard, J. D. (1835). *Treatise on insanity.* London: Sherwood, Gilbert & Piper.

Raine, A., Bauchsbaum, M., Stanley, J., Lottenberg, S., Abel, M. & Stoddard, J. (1994). Selective reductions in prefrontal glucose metabolism in murderers. *Biological Psychiatry, 36,* 368–373.

Raine, A., Brennan, P. & Mednick, S. A. (1994). Birth complications combined with early maternal rejection at age 1 year predispose to violent crime at age 18 years. *Archives of General Psychiatry, 51,* 984–988.

Raine E. & Venables, P. H. (1988). Enhanced P3 evoked potentials and psychopathy. *International Journal of Psychophysiology, 8,* 1–16.

Rapoport, J. L. (1989). The biology of obsessions and compulsions. *Scientific American, 260,* 83–89.

Ratey, J. J. (Ed.) (1995). *Neuropsychiatry of personality disorders.* Malden, MA: Blackwell.

Reeves, A. G. & Plum, F. (1969). Hyperphagia, rage, and dementia accompanying a ventromedial hypothalamic neoplasm. *Archives of Neurology, 20,* 616–624.

Reich, W. (1974). *The impulsive character and other writings.* New York: Viking.

Reis, D. J. (1974). Central neurotransmitters in aggression. R*esearch Publications of the Association for Research in Nervous and Mental Diseases, 52,* 119–148.

Roberts, A. H. (1979). *Severe accidental head injury. An assessment of long-term prognosis.* London: The Macmillan Press.

Robins, L. N. (1966). *Deviant children grown up.* Baltimore: Williams & Wilkins.

Roeder, F. D. (1966). Stereotactic lesions of the tuber cinerium in sexual deviation. *Confinia Neurologica, 27,* 162–163.

Rutter, M. (1980). *Changing youth in a changing society.* Cambridge, MA: Harvard University Press.

Rutter, M. & Giller, G. (1983). *Juvenile delinquency: Trends and perspectives.* New York, Guilford Press.

Sano, K. (1962). Sedative neurosurgery: With special reference to posterior-medial hypothalamotomy. *Neurol Medico-Chirg, 4,* 112–142.

Scheibel, A. B. (1991). Are complex partial seizures a sequel of temporal lobe dysgenesis? In D. B. Smith, D. M. Treiman & M. R. Trimble (Eds.), *Advances in Neurology,* vol. 55. New York: Raven.

Schmahmann, J. D. (1991). An emerging concept: The cerebellar contribution to higher function. *Archives of Neurology, 48,* 1178–1187.

Sherrington, C. S. (1925). On the nature of reflex excitation and inhibition. *Proceedings of the Royal Society, 97B,* 519–545.

Spreen, O. (1989). The relationship between learning disorders and neuropsychology: Some results and observations. *Journal of Clinical and Experimental Neuropsychology, 11,* 117–140.

Stacey, W. & Shupe, H. (1983). *The family secret.* Boston: Beacon Press.

Stafford-Clark, D. (1959). The foundations of research in psychiatry. *British Medical Journal, 2,* 1199–1204.

Stevens, J. R. & Hermann, B. P. (1981). Temporal lobe epilepsy, psychopathology, and violence: The state of the evidence. *Neurology, 31,* 1127–1132.

Stoff, D. M., Pollock, L., Vitiello, B., Behar, D. & Bridger, W. H. (1987). Reduction of (3H)-imipramine binding sites on platelets of conduct-disordered children. *Neuropsychopharmacology,* 1, 55–62.

Strauss, I. & Keschner, M. (1936). Mental symptoms in tumor of the frontal lobe. *Archives of Neurology and Psychiatry, 35,* 572–596.

Tardiff, K. (1992). The current state of psychiatry in the treatment of violent patients. *Archives of General Psychiatry, 49,* 493–499.

Taylor, D. C. (1993). The roots and role of violence in development. In P. J. Taylor (Ed.), *Violence in Society.* London: Royal College of Physicians.

Thompson, G. M. (1953). *The psychopathic delinquent and criminal.* Springfield, IL: Charles C. Thomas.

Towbin, A. (1971). Organic causes of minimal brain dysfunction: Peri-natal origins of minimal cerebral lesions. *Journal of the American Medical Assocation, 217,* 1207–1214.

Tracy, P. E., Wolfgang, M. E. & Figlio, R. M. (1990). *Delinquency careers in two birth cohorts.* New York: Plenum Press.

Treiman, D. M. (1986). Epilepsy and violence: Medical and legal issues. *Epilepsia, 27,* S77–S104.

Valzelli, L. (1981). *Psychobiology of aggression and violence.* New York: Raven Press.

Virkkunen, M. (1986). Reactive hypoglycemic tendency among habitually violent offenders. *Nutrition Reviews, 44,* 94–103.

Volavka, J. (1995). *Neurobiology of violence.* Washington, DC: American Psychiatric Press.

Vonderahe, A. R. (1944). The anatomic substratum of emotion. *The New Scholasticism, 18,* 79–95.

Weiger, W. A. & Bear, D. M. (1988). An approach to the neurology of aggression. *Journal of Psychiatric Research, 22,* 85–98.

Werner, E. E. & Smith, R. S. (1982). *Vulnerable but invincible. A longitudinal study of resilient children and youth.* New York: McGraw-Hill.

Wilder, S. (1947). Sugar metabolism and its relation to criminology. In R. M. Lindner & R. V. Seliger (Eds.), *Handbook of correctional psychology.* New York: Philosophical Library.

Williams, D. (1969). Neural factors related to habitual aggression: Consideration of differences between those habitual aggressives and others who have committed crimes of violence. *Brain, 92,* 501–520.

Wishnie, H. A. & Nevis-Oleson, J. (1979). *Working with the impulsive person.* New York: Plenum Press.

Wolfgang, M. E. & Ferracuti, F. (1982). *The subculture of violence.* Newbury Park, CA: Sage.

Wong, M. T., Lumsden, S., Fenton, G. W. & Fenwick, P. B. G. (1994). Epilepsy and violence in mentally abnormal offenders in a maximum security mental hospital. *Journal of Epilepsy, 7,* 253–258.

Yakovlev, P. & Lecours, A. R. (1967). The myelogenetic cycle of regional maturation of the brain. In A. Minkowski (Ed.), *Regional development of the brain in early life.* Philadelphia: F. A. Davis, 3–70.

Yudofsky, S. C., Williams, A. D. & Gorman, J. (1981). Propranolol in the treatment of rage and violent behaviors in patients with chronic brain syndromes. *American Journal of Psychiatry, 138,* 218–220.

Zametkin, A. J., Nordahl, T. E., Gross, M., King, A. C., Semple, W. E., Rumsey, J., Hamberger, S. & Cohen, R. M. (1990). Cerebral glucose metabolism in adults with hyperactivity of childhood onset. *New England Journal of Medicine, 323,* 1361–1366.

Zecevic, M. & Rakic, P. (1976). Differentiation of Purkinje cells and their relationship to other components of developing cerebellar cortex in man. *Journal of Comparative Neurology, 167,* 97–48.

Zeman, W. & King, F. A. (1958). Tumor of the septum pellucidum and adjacent structures with abnormal affective behavior: An anterior midbrain structure syndrome. *Journal of Nervous and Mental Disease, 127,* 490–503.

Chapter 20

Drug Treatment of Pathologic Aggression

by Maurizio Fava, M.D.

Introduction	20-2
Assessment Instruments	20-3
Clinician-Rated Instruments	20-3
Self-Report Instruments	20-4
Drug Treatments	20-5
Dementia	20-6
Huntington's Disease	20-8
Brain Injury and Organic Brain Syndrome	20-8
Seizure Disorder	20-9
Mentally Handicapped and Retarded Patients	20-9
Children and Adolescents With Aggressive Conduct Disorder or Attention Deficit Disorder	20-10
Psychostimulants	20-10
Lithium and Neuroleptic Medications	20-11
Anticonvulsants	20-11
Other Agents	20-12
Autism	20-12
Schizophrenia and Other Psychoses	20-12
Antipsychotic Medications	20-12
Anticonvulsants	20-13
Serotonergic Agents	20-13
Psychoactive Substance Intoxication or Withdrawal	20-14
Unipolar Depression	20-14
Bipolar Disorder	20-15
Posttraumatic Stress Disorder	20-15
Premenstrual Dysphoric Disorder	20-15

This chapter is adapted with permission from an article originally published in *The Psychiatric Clinics of North America*, vol. 20, 1997.

Personality Disorders 20-16
    Antisocial Personality 20-16
    Borderline Personality 20-16
Summary 20-17

INTRODUCTION

Pathologic aggression and anger are extremely heterogeneous phenomena present in a variety of psychiatric and neurologic disorders, ranging from brain injury to schizophrenia and major depressive disorder. Several researchers have attempted to link certain forms of pathologic aggression with specific neuropsychiatric conditions. For example, whereas repetitive unprovoked assaultive behaviors have been associated with brain injury (Michals et al., 1993), recurrent inappropriate verbal or physical responses to external stimuli have been considered to be characteristic of mood disorders accompanied by marked irritability (Fava, 1987; Fava et al., 1993b). Pathologic aggression, however, is influenced heavily by many psychological, developmental, and environmental factors in addition to the possible underlying medical condition, so that its manifestations within subjects with the same neuropsychiatric disorder are quite variable and somewhat unpredictable.

A number of neurochemical systems, including those involving GABAergic, serotonergic, noradrenergic, dopaminergic, and glutaminergic neurotransmission, have been implicated in the modulation of aggressive behavior in animal models (Carlini et al., 1977; Eichelman, 1979; Giacalone et al., 1968; Mandel et al., 1979; Siegel & Schubert, 1995). As described by Kavoussi et al. (1997), neurochemical studies in human beings have supported the modulating role in pathologic aggression of several systems of neurotransmitters, in particular serotonin. It is therefore not surprising that investigators have studied the effects of psychotropic drugs both in animal models and human subjects. The effects of specific psychotropic agents, however, do vary across different animal models of affective aggression (Delini-Stula & Vassout, 1979), and in human beings, the same drug, for example methylphenidate, can show antiaggressive effects in certain populations (i.e., adolescents with attention deficit hyperactivity disorder) and precipitate aggressive responses in others (i.e., bipolar patients).

The systematic study of the effects of treatment on pathologic aggression is complicated by the fact that this is typically an intermittent phenomenon whose occurrence and intensity are often unpredictable. An alternative approach to the clinical trial in affected populations would be that of studying the effects of a particular drug in individuals undergoing pharmacologic challenges that recreate in the laboratory setting aggressive responses. Although researchers have developed pharmacologic challenges (e.g., yohimbine and lactate) to induce fear or panic in the laboratory among patients with a history of panic attacks, there is no comparable test to study anger attacks or rage in patients with a history of pathologic aggression. A possible tool for such investigation is m-chlorophenylpiperazine (m-CPP), which was found to induce an anger response in patients with generalized anxiety disorder, although not in patients with other disorders (Germine et al., 1992).

Despite the lack of approval by the Food and Drug Administration (FDA) of any drug specifically for the treatment of aggression, a number of currently available drugs are used for this purpose. The FDA (P. David, personal communication) does recognize that pathologic aggression may be an aspect of certain disorders (e.g., bipolar disorder and schizophrenia) for which specific drug treatments have been approved. In addition, no pharmaceutical company has yet applied for approval of a drug indicated for the treatment of pathologic aggression, suggesting that the lack of FDA-approved uses of certain drugs in the management of aggressive patients may stem from a relative lack of market interest in this field and, perhaps, from the medico-legal risk related to the process leading to such approval. It is not difficult to imagine the degree of concern on the part of the legal departments of pharmaceutical companies conducting placebo-controlled clinical trials in subjects with pathologic aggression.

In spite of these limitations, a number of studies and anecdotal reports have been guiding physicians' decisions concerning the drug treatment of pathologic aggression. The aim of this chapter is, therefore, to review the drug treatment of pathologic aggression. In addition, some of the most frequently used instruments for the assessment of pathologic aggression and anger are reviewed, as the characteristics of the instruments used in the clinical trials may affect outcome.

ASSESSMENT INSTRUMENTS

A number of instruments have been developed for the assessment of pathologic anger and aggression. Some of these instruments may not be suitable for use in clinical trials because of their relative lack of sensitivity. In particular, those instruments measuring trait-anger and trait-aggression are probably the least likely to show marked changes following drug treatment, given the relative stability of such traits. Clinician-rated instruments may reflect the investigators' biases and may fail to distinguish between drug-induced sedation from specific antiaggressive effects. On the other hand, with self-report measures, there is a risk of patients underreporting violent outbursts. Of course, self-report measures cannot be used reliably with children or with psychotic, mentally retarded, and demented patients; they can, however, be used in patients with affective disorders and nonpsychotic adult patients.

Clinician-Rated Instruments

The Overt Aggression Scale (Yudofsky et al., 1986), a widely used clinician-rated instrument in inpatient studies of pathologic aggression, was designed to provide a state measure of specific aspects of aggressive behaviors in four categories: verbal aggression, physical aggression against objects, physical aggression against self, and physical aggression against other people. This scale has the advantages of tracking each incident of aggressive behavior and of being sensitive and valid (Silver & Yudofsky, 1987). Several modified versions of the Overt Aggression Scale have become available including one for outpatients (Coccaro et al., 1990).

Two clinician-rated instruments that offer a fairly descriptive approach to the assessment of aggressive events are the Staff Observation Aggression Scale (Palmstiema & Wistedt, 1987) and the Scale for the Assessment of Aggression and Agitated Behaviors (Brizer et al., 1987). Their sensitivity to detect change following treatment, however, remains to be established. The Nurses' Observation Scale for Inpatient Evaluation (Honigfeld et al., 1965), which is a clinician-rated instrument that evaluates the severity of patient violence, also has only limited sensitivity. The Suicide and Aggression Survey (Kern et al., 1992) is a semistructured interview for the measurement of suicidality and aggression. Because this scale's main goal is that of predicting the possibility of future overaggressive acts, its use in clinical trials of antiaggressive therapies is unlikely. The Social Dysfunction and Aggression Scale (Wistedt et al., 1990) is a twenty-one-item, clinician-rated instrument that assesses irritability, aggressiveness, physical violence, self-mutilation, dysphoric mood, and social withdrawal. Its usefulness in clinical trials remains to be tested.

Some researchers still rely on an adaptation of the Clinical Global Impression Scale (Guy, 1976), where the scores range from 1 ("normal") to 7 ("among the most severely violent and aggressive"). The Brief Psychiatric Rating Scale (Lukoff et al., 1986) is a reliable and sensitive clinician-rated, general measure of various psychopathology symptoms, and it includes the assessment of aggression, suspicion, and hostility. This instrument certainly can be used in clinical trials as a secondary efficacy measure.

Self-Report Instruments

Several self-report measures of aggression are also available. Self-report assessments of aggression, however, do require patient insight and willingness to acknowledge aggressive behavior. Perhaps for this reason, no significant relationship was found between scores on the Buss-Durkee Hostility Inventory and observed aggression (Edmunds & Kendrick, 1980). The Buss-Durkee Hostility Inventory (Buss & Durkee, 1957) is the most widely used self-rated measure of aggression, and it includes seven scales (Assault, Indirect Aggression, Irritability, Negativism, Resentment, Suspicion, and Verbal Aggression). Its sensitivity and language (somewhat obsolete), however, have been questioned. The newer version of this instrument, the Buss-Perry Aggression Questionnaire (Buss & Perry, 1992) includes only four scales (Physical Aggression, Verbal Aggression, Anger, and Hostility), but it appears to be primarily a trait measure of aggression, with items such as "My friends say that I am somewhat argumentative" and "I get into fights a little more than the average person."

Another self-report version of the Buss-Durkee Hostility Inventory is the Anger, Irritability, Aggression Questionnaire, developed by Coccaro and Kavoussi (1991). This instrument uses a Likert-type approach to rating symptoms, and it specifies times (e.g., past week, past month), so that it can be used as a state measure. The State-Trait Anger Scale (Spielberger et al., 1983) is a self-rating scale aimed at assessing the intensity of anger as an emotional state, and individual differences in anger proneness as a personality trait. Spielberger et al. (1985) subsequently developed the Anger Expression Scale, which was then combined with the State-Trait Anger Scale to form the State-Trait Anger Expression Inventory, which measures the experience, expression, and control of anger (Spielberger, 1988). The Barratt Impulsiveness Scale—Version 11 (Patton et al., 1995) is a questionnaire that examines the tendency to think or act impulsively. This scale is mostly a trait measure of impulsiveness, as reflected by items such as "I do things without thinking" and "I act on impulse." Another trait measure of aggression is the Conflict Tactics Scales (Strauss, 1979), which is aimed at measuring verbal aggression and violence within the family. The Cook-Medley Hostility Scale (Cook & Medley, 1954) is derived from the Minnesota Multiphasic Personality Inventory and is another trait measure of different types of hostile and aggressive behavior, with its sensitivity to change being quite limited. The Anger Attacks Questionnaire (Fava et al., 1991) is a state-measure of aggressive behavior and anger outbursts found to show significant changes following drug treatment in mood-disordered patients (Fava et al., 1996; Fava et al., 1997; Fava et al., 1993b). The Symptom Questionnaire (Kellner, 1987) is a highly sensitive state-measure of anger/hostility, as well as depression, somatic symptoms, and anxiety. Because the Symptom Questionnaire does not capture acts of violence, it is probably best to use this instrument as a secondary efficacy measure.

Ideally, treatment studies of pathologic aggression should include, whenever possible, both clinician-rated and self-rated instruments to allow the most comprehensive assessment of changes occurring among patients.

DRUG TREATMENTS

The heterogeneity of the psychiatric conditions associated with pathologic aggression represents a methodologic obstacle to the study of treatments. Table 20.1 lists psychiatric and neurologic disorders that may be accompanied by pathologic anger or assaultive and aggressive behavior. When the pathologic aggression does not appear to be secondary to another psychiatric or medical disorder, the diagnosis of intermittent explosive disorder, according to the DSM-IV (*Diagnostic and Statistical Manual of Mental Disorders*, 4th ed.) classification, should be used to describe a behavioral syndrome characterized by episodes of loss of control of aggressive impulses result-

Table 20.1
Neurologic and Psychiatric Disorders Associated with Pathologic Anger and Aggression

- Dementia
- Huntington's disease
- Brain injury
- Organic brain syndrome
- Korsakoff's psychosis
- Brain tumors or lesions
- Mental retardation
- Autism
- Seizure disorder
- Bipolar disorder
- Major depressive disorder
- Dysthymia
- Psychoactive substance intoxication and withdrawal
- Psychotic disorders
- Premenstrual dysphoric disorder
- Posttraumatic stress disorder
- Panic disorder and generalized anxiety disorder
- Antisocial personality disorder
- Borderline personality disorder
- Other personality disorders
- Attention deficit disorder

ing in serious assaultive acts or destruction of property. On the other hand, if the pathologic aggression appears to be secondary to a neurologic or other medical illness and represents a marked change from the individual's previous characteristic personality pattern, the DSM-IV classifies this as personality change owing to a general medical condition, aggressive type. The first step, therefore, in the treatment of pathologic anger and aggression requires a careful medical and psychiatric assessment of the patient to identify, and wherever possible to treat, the underlying psychiatric or medical disorder. The diagnosis of intermittent explosive disorder then becomes an exclusionary diagnosis.

Given the heterogeneity of the neuropsychiatric disorders associated with pathologic aggression and the diversity of assessment approaches to pathologic aggression, meta-analyses of the published treatment studies in this field may not be feasible because of contrasting approaches to population selection or efficacy assessment. For example, some studies use trait measures of aggressive behavior that tend to remain stable over time and to show minimal changes with treatment, whereas others use state measures of anger and hostility that are more sensitive to change; some researchers use primarily observer-rated instruments whereas others rely on self-report measures. Rather than limiting this review of the existing literature to those studies that use rigorous double-blind, placebo-controlled designs, this chapter also presents the results of some of the uncontrolled studies, as many of them tend to reflect current clinical interests and practices.

Drug treatments studied in pathologic aggression include agents indicated in the treatment of a specific neuropsychiatric condition associated with anger and aggression, or other drugs with possible antiaggressive properties but not otherwise specific to the population treated. An example of the first type of treatment study would be the assessment of efficacy of a neuroleptic agent in psychotic, assaultive patients, whereas an example of the second type would be the study of a beta-blocker in dementia. Although a specifically indicated agent offers a monotherapy approach, the use of nonspecific agents more often will require polypharmacy. In the latter case, concomitant medications may obscure the relative contribution of the study drug to outcome.

Because responsiveness to treatment varies greatly with the diagnosis and the inclusion criteria of each study, this article reviews the studies on the antiaggressive effects of drug treatment in each specific diagnostic group. Certain drugs may be the treatment of choice for specific neurologic or psychiatric conditions associated with aggressiveness and, at the same time, be ineffective in the treatment of aggressive patients with other neuropsychiatric disorders. Most studies report the overall response as a mean group change in efficacy measure score, without providing the actual response rates. This, of course, limits the interpretation of such studies.

DEMENTIA

Violent behavior and verbal outbursts are reported in 30 percent and 24 percent, respectively, of outpatients with Alzheimer's disease (Reisberg et al., 1987). Eimer (1989) reviewed the controlled studies on the efficacy of neuroleptic medications in the management of pathologic aggression in dementia and concluded that these drugs have modest effects, often similar to placebo. Nygaard et al. (1992) carried out a meta-analysis of the data from two double-blind, multicenter studies among nursing home elderly. They found that three antipsychotic drugs (zuclopenthixol, melperone, and a combination of haloperidol and levomepromazine) were comparably effective in the management of agitation and hostility/aggression. A limitation of the data from this meta-analysis is the lack of a placebo comparison, particularly in light of the findings of Eimer's previous meta-analysis (1989).

A similar issue concerns a double-blind study by Carlyle et al. (1993), which found comparable efficacy of the antipsychotic drugs loxapine and haloperidol in the management of pathologic aggression in demented patients. Despite the overall modest efficacy of traditional neuroleptic medications in the treatment of agitation and aggression in dementia (Eimer, 1989), atypical neuroleptic agents (i.e., clozapine, risperidone, and olanzapine) appear to be a promising group of drugs for the management of pathologic aggression in demented patients. For example, Jeanblanc and Davis (1995) reported the usefulness of risperidone (1.5-2.5 mg per day) in reducing agitation or violent behavior among five demented patients who had been refractory to conventional antipsychotic and other commonly used drugs.

Studies on the use of benzodiazepines in populations with poorly defined diagnoses of dementia have shown reductions of agitation and irritability greater than placebo and comparable with neuroleptic agents (Smith & Ferry, 1992). Concerns about excessive sedation and paradoxical disinhibition limit the usefulness of these drugs, with lorazepam and oxazepam being primary choices because they are less likely to accumulate in the elderly (Smith & Ferry, 1992).

The potential usefulness of the anticonvulsant drug valproate in the management of agitation and aggression among demented patients has been suggested by a case series reported by Mellow et al. (1993) and by two open trials (Haas et al., 1997; Kunik, 1998). Similarly, the anticonvulsant drug carbamazepine was found effective in the treatment of aggression among thirteen patients with primary degenerative dementia and a history of refractoriness to previous drug treatments (Patterson, 1988).

Beta-blockers have been used successfully in these populations. In a double-blind study, the sustained release form of the beta-blocker propranolol, up to 520 mg per day, was significantly more effective than placebo in reducing the number of assaults and attempted assaults in nine medication-free patients with severe dementia (Greendyke et al., 1986). In addition, a recent study by Shankle et al. (1995) reported the usefulness of low-dose propranolol (10-80 mg per day) monotherapy in reducing aggression in eight of twelve demented patients.

Drugs that are relatively serotonergic appear to be promising agents. In a multicenter study of ninety-eight demented patients, the relatively selective serotonin reuptake inhibitor (SSRI) citalopram was more effective than placebo in treating emotional disturbances, including irritability in patients with Alzheimer's disease, but not in those with vascular dementia (Nyth & Gottfries, 1990). Another SSRI, fluvoxamine, however, was only marginally more effective than placebo in reducing irritability in forty-six demented patients (Olafsson et al., 1992). Finally, irritability was decreased significantly after treatment with the serotonin 5-HT-2 blocker trazodone, 25 mg three times per day, in an open trial among thirteen patients with Alzheimer's disease (Lebert et al., 1994). In a recent article, Sultzer et al. (1997) found trazodone as effective as haloperidol in treating agitation and aggression among patients with dementia.

HUNTINGTON'S DISEASE

Very little is known about the efficacy of drug treatments in the management of pathologic aggression in patients with Huntington's disease. Anecdotal reports suggest the usefulness of the serotonin 5-HT-1A receptor partial agonist buspirone (Bhandary & Masand, 1997), the beta-blocker propranolol (Stewart et al., 1987), and the SSRI sertraline (Ranen et al., 1996) in the treatment of irritability and pathologic anger and aggression among patients suffering from Huntington's disease.

BRAIN INJURY AND ORGANIC BRAIN SYNDROME

Aggressive and assaultive behaviors are relatively common among patients with brain injuries (Brooke et al., 1992; Rosenbaum & Hoge, 1989) and organic brain syndromes (Greendyke et al., 1986). Yudofsky et al. (1984) reported the usefulness of propranolol in controlling the rage and violent behavior of a patient with Korsakoff's psychosis. Propranolol, in dosages of up to 420 mg per day, was also more effective than placebo in reducing the intensity of agitated and combative behavior in twenty-one subjects with traumatic brain injury, although the number of episodes of agitation was similar in the two groups (Brooke et al., 1992). The beta-blocker, pindolol, in doses up to 100 mg per day, was more effective than placebo in reducing hostility in eleven patients with organic brain syndrome (Greendyke & Kanter, 1986), although a subsequent study by the same group failed to show significant differences between placebo and pindolol in patients with organic brain syndrome and behavioral disturbances (Greendyke et al., 1989). In the latter study, however, six of thirteen patients treated with pindolol showed a decrease in aggressive behavior, an overall reasonable response rate.

Anticonvulsant medications may be helpful in this patient population. For example, valproic acid was found to help treat pathologic aggression in two patients with organic brain syndromes and normal electroencephalogram (EEG) findings (Mature et al., 1992). A double-blind pilot study by Foster et al. (1989) found that patients with frontal lobe damage showed improvements in behavioral measures after carbamazepine treatment. In addition, reports by Glenn et al. (1989) and Williams and Goldstein (1979) on two small samples of brain-injured patients suggested the usefulness of lithium.

The use of psychostimulants in this population also has been investigated. In a study of thirty-eight adults with brain injury-related anger, 30 mg per day of methylphenidate was superior to placebo in treating anger, with greater improvement on all of the general psychopathology outcome measures as well (Mooney & Haas, 1993).

The usefulness of serotonergic agents in this population is suggested by a number of studies. The serotonin 5-HT-1A receptor partial agonist buspirone was reported to be effective in reducing aggression in a retrospective study among hospitalized patients with brain injury (Stanislav et al., 1994), and among seven patients with anger outbursts and suicidal ideation associated with traumatic brain injury (Gualtieri, 1991). The serotonin 5-HT-2 receptor antagonist trazodone, in doses between 150 and 500 mg per day, was effective in three of seven patients with organic mental disorders and physically aggressive behavior (Pinner & Rich, 1988) and in four elderly patients with severe organic brain syndromes and combative behavior unresponsive to neuroleptic medications (Simpson & Foster, 1986). Finally, treatment with the serotonin 5-HT-2 and dopamine receptor antagonist clozapine (in doses ranging from 250-750 mg per day) was followed by mild to marked improvement in aggressive behavior among five of eight brain-injured patients with outbursts of rage and aggression refractory to other medications (Michals et al., 1993).

SEIZURE DISORDER

Patients with a seizure disorder may present with a history of episodic aggression (Lewis & Pincus, 1989), in particular those with complex partial seizures (King & Marsan, 1977). Anticonvulsant drugs are the obvious choice for the treatment of pathologic anger and aggression in these populations (Eadie & Tyrer, 1980). As pointed out in the review of the literature by Yudofsky et al. (1987), the literature does suggest that anticonvulsant agents such as carbamazepine are effective in the treatment of aggression in patients with abnormal EEGs, particularly with temporal lobe foci. However, not all patients with such behavioral problems respond to anticonvulsant treatment. For these reasons, a number of drugs, including lithium (Kligman & Goldberg, 1975), have been studied in the management of aggression among temporal lobe epileptic patients.

MENTALLY HANDICAPPED AND RETARDED PATIENTS

High rates of pathologic aggression and violent behavior have been reported among mentally retarded patients (Reid et al., 1984). Although an earlier double-blind study had shown an increase in aggressive behavior with the antipsychotic drug thioridazine compared with placebo among fifty-one mentally retarded patients (Elie et al., 1980), in a subsequent study on thirty mentally handicapped patients, the antipsychotic drug pipothiazine palmitate was superior to placebo in reducing aggressiveness (Lynch et al., 1985). In two studies of mentally handicapped patients, the antipsychotic drug zuclopenthixol decanoate (Izmeth et al., 1988) and zuclopenthixol dihydrochloride tablets (Singh & Owino, 1992) were superior to placebo in reducing aggressive behavior. The atypical antipsychotic drug clozapine (with serotonin 5-HT-2 and dopamine receptor antagonist activity) also was shown to be helpful in six patients with mental retardation in reducing levels of aggression and self-injurious behavior (Cohen & Underwood, 1994). Finally, the benzodiazepine derivative midazolam was administered successfully to three mentally retarded patients with acute and refractory aggressivity and violence (Bond et al., 1989).

An open study by Ratey et al. (1986) suggested the usefulness of propranolol (mean dose: 120 mg per day) in a sample of nineteen severely mentally retarded patients.

A number of studies have been conducted on the usefulness of lithium in this population. Worrall et al. (1975) conducted a double-blind study of lithium in eight mentally retarded women with frequent aggressive behavior and found that lithium (at serum concentrations of 0.6-1.4 mEq/L) was effective in reducing aggression in 50 percent of the patients who were allowed to continue on concomitant psychotropic medications. Similarly, Tyrer et al. (1984) found lithium (with serum concentrations of 0.5-0.8 mEq/L) more effective than placebo in reducing aggression among twenty-five aggressive mentally handicapped subjects, using a crossover design involving a one-month washout between treatments and allowing other prestudy psychotropic medications to remain unchanged during the study. Finally, lithium (with serum concentrations of 0.7-1.0 mEq/L) also was found to be more effective than placebo in a four-month trial in forty-two mentally handicapped patients, with 73 percent of patients showing a significant reduction in aggression with lithium and 30 percent with placebo (Craft et al., 1987). Prestudy psychotropic drug treatment, including anticonvulsant and neuroleptic medications, however, were continued unchanged during this trial.

Very little is known about the efficacy of anticonvulsant drugs among these patients. In a double-blind, placebo-controlled, crossover trial in profoundly mentally retarded patients, carbamazepine, with serum concentrations between 25-42 µmol/L, was no different from placebo in treating behavioral disturbances (Reid et al., 1991).

Serotonergic agents also have been tested in mentally retarded populations. In a multiple-baseline open trial with a placebo lead-in (Ratey et al., 1991), the serotonin 5-HT-1A receptor partial agonist buspirone, up to 45 mg per day, was reported to be effective in reducing aggression in six mentally retarded adult patients. Eltoprazine, a mixed serotonin 5-HT-1 agonist, was found to be no more effective than placebo in reducing aggression in a large, multicenter study with 160 mentally handicapped patients (de Koning et al., 1994). Efficacy greater than placebo, however, was observed in a subgroup of patients (de Koning et al., 1994) supporting the findings of a previous open trial where eltoprazine had been found to be effective in four of nine mentally retarded patients with self-injurious behavior (Verhoeven et al., 1992) and in six patients with mental retardation (Tiihonen et al., 1993). Markowitz (1992) showed that treatment with the SSRI fluoxetine (20-40 mg per day) was followed by moderate to marked clinical improvement in seventeen of twenty-one severely mentally retarded patients with aggression and self-injurious behavior. In a small open trial among adults primarily with mental retardation, treatment with the SSRI sertraline (25-150 mg per day) was followed by marked improvement in aggression and self-injury (Hellings et al., 1996).

CHILDREN AND ADOLESCENTS WITH AGGRESSIVE CONDUCT DISORDER OR ATTENTION DEFICIT DISORDER

Psychostimulants

Oppositional and conduct disorders in childhood and adolescence are often accompanied by violent and aggressive behavior as well as anger outbursts (McDaniel, 1986). These two disorders frequently are observed among patients with attention deficit disorder (Biederman et al., 1987). Given the efficacy of psychostimulants in the treatment of attention deficit disorder, it is not surprising that many trials in these populations have focused on the possible role of dextroamphetamine and methylphenidate. Dextroamphetamine was found to be significantly more effective than placebo in reducing aggressiveness in a sample of institutionalized male delinquent adolescents (Eisenberg et al., 1963) and among antisocial adolescent outpatients

(Maletzky, 1974). A relatively small, double-blind study in adolescents with aggressive conduct disorder and attention deficit disorder showed a significantly greater reduction in aggressivity with methylphenidate (Kaplan et al., 1990). Similarly, methylphenidate (20-60 mg per day) was superior to placebo in reducing aggression in a double-blind study among conduct disordered children, although in an earlier study this drug was not superior to placebo in aggressive delinquent boys (Conners et al., 1971). In a double-blind, placebo-controlled study of thirty-four prepubescent children with attention deficit hyperactivity disorder and comorbid tic disorder, methylphenidate treatment resulted in marked reductions of disruptive and aggressive behavior, with only a small but statistically significant increase in the frequency of motor tics (Gadow et al., 1995). In a recent study, Klein et al. (1997) found methylphenidate to be superior to placebo in treating patients with conduct disorder. Finally, a study by Simeon et al. (1986) suggested the efficacy of bupropion (up to 150 mg per day) in the management of children with attention deficit disorder and conduct disorder.

Lithium and Neuroleptic Medications

The usefulness of lithium in the management of pathologic aggression in these populations has been studied extensively. Siassi (1982) found that high doses of lithium for three months were accompanied by a substantial reduction in unprovoked aggressive outbursts among fourteen children with conduct problems. Lithium (500-2000 mg per day) and haloperidol (1-6 mg per day) were equally effective and superior to placebo in reducing aggressiveness in sixty-one hospitalized children with conduct disorder (Campbell et al., 1984). In a subsequent double-blind study, Campbell et al. (1995) found that lithium (mean dose: 1248 mg per day; mean serum level: 1.12 mEq/L) was superior to placebo in reducing aggressive behavior among fifty children with conduct disorder who had been hospitalized for treatment-refractory severe aggressiveness.

As pointed out by Campbell et al. (1992) in their review of the literature, neuroleptic medications, in spite of the risk of tardive dyskinesia and the relative paucity of studies supporting their efficacy, are the most commonly used psychotropic drugs in the treatment of aggressive children and adolescents, particularly in those who are hospitalized chronically. A double-blind study by Greenhill et al. (1985) found molindone to be as effective as thioridazine in improving overall behavior among thirty-one aggressive hospitalized children. The lack of a placebo comparison, however, limits the interpretation of these results.

Anticonvulsants

On the other hand, anticonvulsant medications have not been particularly effective in these populations. Diphenylhydantoin was no better than placebo in treating aggressiveness in male juvenile delinquents (Conners et al., 1971; Lefkowitz, 1969) and in children with severe temper tantrums (Looker & Conners, 1970). Similarly, carbamazepine (mean dose: 683 mg per day; serum levels of 5.0-9.1 mcg/mL) was not superior to placebo in reducing aggression among twenty-two children hospitalized for treatment-resistant aggressiveness and who had been diagnosed with conduct disorder (Cueva et al., 1996), despite promising results in a previous open trial with carbamazepine (Kafantaris et al., 1992).

Other Agents

An open study on twenty-two hospitalized children previously unresponsive to other treatments found that thirteen children (67 percent) improved significantly after treatment with the serotonin 5-HT-2 receptor antagonist trazodone, with the benefits being maintained for three to fourteen months in most patients (Zubieta & Alessi, 1992). Another open study found an overall decrease in aggressive behavior among seventeen children with a history of cruel behavior and destruction of property following treatment with (α_2-adrenergic receptor agonist clonidine (Kemph et al., 1993). Finally, the tricyclic antidepressant, amitriptyline, was superior to placebo in reducing aggression in a double-blind study among conduct disordered children (Yepes et al., 1977).

AUTISM

Irritability and aggressive behavior can be present in autism. In a placebo-controlled, double-blind crossover study of eight male children with autistic disorder, only a slightly greater improvement in irritability was reported with clonidine compared with placebo (Jaselskis et al., 1992). On the other hand, a ten-week, double-blind crossover comparison of clomipramine and placebo in twelve autistic children showed that clomipramine was superior to placebo in the treatment of anger. (Gordon et al., 1993). Within the same study, twelve different autistic subjects completed a similar comparison of the tricyclic antidepressants clomipramine and desipramine, with clomipramine being more effective than desipramine in the treatment of anger (Gordon et al., 1993). Given clomipramine's relative selectivity for serotonin reuptake inhibition compared with desipramine, which is relatively more selective for norepinephrine reuptake inhibition, one could interpret these data as suggesting that relative serotonergic selectivity may be particularly effective in this population. In fact, among thirty adults with autism, the SSRI fluvoxamine was found to be more effective than placebo in reducing aggression and maladaptive behaviors (McDougle et al., 1996). An open trial of the 5-HT-1A buspirone partial agonist in dosages ranging from 15-45 mg per day showed a moderate to marked response in irritability among 15–22 children with pervasive developmental disorders (Buitelaar et al., 1998). Finally, the atypical antipsychotic agent risperidone has been shown to be superior to placebo in treating irritability and aggressive behavior in adults with autistic disorder and other pervasive developmental disorders (McDougle et al., 1998).

SCHIZOPHRENIA AND OTHER PSYCHOSES

Antipsychotic Medications

Pathologic aggression can result from psychotic states, particularly when patients have persecutory delusions or mistakenly perceive themselves as being under threat.

The use of antipsychotic medications such as phenothiazines, butyrophenones, thioxanthines, indolics, dibenzoxazepines, and pimozide have, therefore, been reported to be effective in the treatment of pathologic anger and aggression in psychotic patients (Bobon et al., 1970; Casey et al., 1960; Feldman et al., 1969; Holden et al., 1971; Itil et al., 1971; Tuason, 1986).

In some cases, however, the use of these drugs is accompanied by minimal if no improvement in aggressive behavior, even when the psychotic symptoms show good response. The atypical antipsychotic agents may be more effective. In fact, quetiapine was superior to standard antipsychotic agents in treating hostility and aggression among patients with acute schizophrenia, and the atypical antipsychotic clozapine appeared to be useful in the treatment of aggressive schizophrenic patients resistant to standard therapies (Spivak et al., 1997). Clinicians have developed specific adjunctive strategies to the antipsychotic drug treatment, with the goal of increasing the overall antiaggressive effect.

In particular, beta-blockers have been used extensively for this purpose. Sorgi et al. (1986), for example, used nadolol (dose range: 40-160 mg per day) and propranolol (80 mg twice per day) with relative success in seven chronic schizophrenic patients with assaultive behavior. Following the initial positive report by Ritrovato et al. (1989), in addition to the one by Sorgi et al. (1986), on the use of the beta-blocker nadolol in the treatment of aggressive behavior associated with schizophrenia, Ratey et al. (1992) conducted a study on forty-one chronic psychiatric inpatients and found that nadolol in dosages from 40-120 mg per day was superior to placebo in reducing the frequency of aggressive behavior and in hostility scores. A subsequent study on thirty-four acutely aggressive schizophrenic patients by Allan et al. (1996) found nadolol (in dosages ranging from 80-120 mg per day) as effective as placebo as an adjunct to antipsychotic drugs.

Anticonvulsants

Anticonvulsants appear to be quite helpful in the management of assaultive behavior in psychotic patients. In particular, the anticonvulsant carbamazepine has been found to be helpful in the management of pathologic aggression in two small samples of violent schizophrenic patients (Hakola & Laulumaa, 1982; Luchins, 1983). In a double-blind, placebo-controlled study among eleven psychotic patients with nonspecific temporal lobe EEG abnormalities, carbamazepine appeared to be effective in treating aggression (Neppe, 1982). On the other hand, among hospitalized psychiatric patients, the anticonvulsant drug valproate was significantly better than carbamazepine in reducing aggression (Alam et al., 1995).

Serotonergic Agents

In addition, the serotonin precursor tryptophan, up to 6 grams per day, was more effective than placebo in reducing the need for injections of antipsychotic medications and sedatives in aggressive psychiatric inpatients (Volavka et al., 1990). Eltoprazine, a mixed serotonin 5-HT-1 agonist, was found to be effective in reducing aggressive behavior in a subset of violent patients with schizophrenia (Tiihonen et al., 1993). To further support the usefulness of serotonergic agents in the management of pathologic aggression in psychosis, a double-blind study on nineteen violent schizophrenic patients showed that the SSRI citalopram (20-60 mg per day) was superior to placebo as an adjunct to neuroleptic medications in reducing the frequency of aggressive incidents (Vartiainen et al., 1995).

Atypical antipsychotic agents, which combine dopaminergic and serotonergic effects, may be more effective than traditional antipsychotic drugs. A retrospective study by Ratey et al. (1992) among aggressive psychiatric inpatients in a state hospital found that the use of clozapine was followed by a significant reduction in the overall frequency of assaults, and in the use of seclusion and mechanical and chemical restraint, in spite of minimal effects on the psychotic symptoms. Similarly, a retrospective study by Su et al. (1994) on forty-eight inpatients with chronic schizophrenia found that the episodes of aggression were significantly lower with clozapine than on placebo, with the traditional antipsychotic drug fluphenazine having an effect intermediate between clozapine and placebo. Finally, a meta-analysis of multicenter studies showed that the atypical antipsychotic drug olanzapine was superior to placebo in decreasing hostility in both the acute phase and the long-term extension of these studies (data on file, Eli Lilly and Company, Indianapolis, Indiana, 1997).

PSYCHOACTIVE SUBSTANCE INTOXICATION OR WITHDRAWAL

The relationship between pathologic aggression and psychoactive substance intoxication or withdrawal is well established (Fava, 1987). The acutely violent and agitated patient who is either intoxicated or withdrawing from psychoactive substances frequently is treated with injectable droperidol or haloperidol (Clinton et al., 1987; Thomas et al., 1992), although many other sedative and tranquilizing drugs are used as tools for chemical restraint, such as the benzodiazepines and the low-potency antipsychotic agents (Hyman, 1994).

UNIPOLAR DEPRESSION

Depressed inpatients report greater levels of hostility and anger than do normal controls (Riley et al., 1989), and 37 percent of depressed inpatients report moderate to severe outwardly directed irritability (Snaith & Taylor, 1985). The presence of anger attacks also was reported in 44 percent of 126 depressed outpatients, most of whom had attacked others physically or verbally (Fava et al., 1993b). Anger attacks also were present in 28 percent of seventy-four outpatients with dysthymia and in none of thirty-eight normal controls (Fava et al., 1997). After treatment with fluoxetine, 20 mg per day for eight weeks, patients with major depression reported significant reductions in hostility, and anger attacks ceased in most (71 percent) of those who had previously reported them (Fava et al., 1993b). These findings were replicated in a different cohort of depressed outpatients (Fava et al., 1996). Finally, anger attacks subsided in 53 percent and 57 percent of depressed patients treated with sertraline, up to 200 mg per day, and imipramine, up to 300 mg per day, and only in 37 percent of those patients treated with placebo (Fava et al., 1997).

BIPOLAR DISORDER

Irritability, anger outbursts, and impulsive aggression commonly are observed in bipolar patients during their manic/hypomanic/mixed phases. Therefore, clinicians typically approach these issues by using drugs with established mood-stabilizing or antimanic properties such as lithium, carabamazepine, valproate, clonazepam, clonidine, and calcium channel-blockers (Rosenbaum et al., 1995). Certainly, lithium is probably a first-line treatment for bipolar patients with excessive irritability and anger outbursts, as it has been shown to be effective in reducing these symptoms specifically in this population (Corrigan et al., 1993). Similarly, treatment with the antimanic drug valproate has been found to be followed by marked reductions in aggressive behavior among bipolar patients (Wilcox, 1994). When the traditional mood stabilizers fail to control the aggressive behavior and the agitation, benzodiazepines and antipsychotic agents have been used as adjuncts with relative success in the management of pathologic aggression (Lenox et al., 1992; Salzman, 1988).

POSTTRAUMATIC STRESS DISORDER

Research studies have shown associations between posttraumatic stress disorder (PTSD) and anger and aggressive behavior (Reilly et al., 1994). Two of three double-blind studies with tricyclic antidepressants (Davidson et al., 1990; Kosten et al., 1991; Reist, 1989) and one of two double-blind studies with monoamine oxidase inhibitors (Kosten et al., 1991; Shetatsky, 1988) have shown some superiority of these drugs over placebo. Also, two open trials (Davidson et al., 1990; Nagy et al., 1993) and the placebo-controlled trial C (van der Kolk, 1994) found that fluoxetine significantly reduced overall PTSD symptomatology. A limitation of these controlled studies is that state measures of anger, irritability, and aggression were not used so that it is hard to estimate the effect of these treatments on pathological anger and aggression. On the other hand, the usefulness of lithium in the treatment of irritability and angry outbursts is suggested only by case reports (Forster et al., 1995).

PREMENSTRUAL DYSPHORIC DISORDER

Premenstrual dysphoric disorder often includes symptoms such as persistent and marked anger and irritability (Fava & Keefe, 1998). Large, double-blind, placebo-controlled studies in patients with this disorder have shown the efficacy of alprazolam (Freeman et al., 1995) and SSRIs such as fluoxetine (Steiner et al., 1995; Wood et al., 1992), sertraline (Yonkers et al., 1995), paroxetine (Yonkers et al., 1996), and clomipramine (Sundblad et al., 1993; Sundblad et al., 1992). A recent study by Eriksson et al. (1995) also found that the SSRI paroxetine was superior to the norepinephrine reuptake inhibitor maprotiline in reducing irritability among women with premenstrual syndrome, suggesting the importance of using relatively serotonergic drugs in these patients. In support of this idea, Rickels et al. (1989) found the serotonin 5-HT-1 receptor partial agonist buspirone to be superior to placebo in reducing irritability in thirty-four patients with premenstrual syndrome.

PERSONALITY DISORDERS

Antisocial Personality

A number of personality disorders are associated with pathologic aggression and anger. There has been very little research on the efficacy of drug treatments in the management of patients with antisocial personality disorder (Reid, 1985). An open study has suggested, however, the usefulness of lithium in reducing aggression among prison inmates (Tupin et al., 1973), and a subsequent double-blind study has shown the superiority of lithium (with serum levels between 0.6 and 1.0 mEq/L) over placebo in the management of aggression among a prison population (Sheard et al., 1976). A double-blind, placebo-controlled study of phenytoin in aggressive prison inmates has suggested its superiority over placebo (Barratt et al., 1997).

Borderline Personality

On the other hand, several studies have been conducted on the pharmacologic management of aggressiveness among borderline personality disorder patients. In a double-blind study, the antipsychotic agent haloperidol was superior to both amitriptyline and placebo in the management of hostility among borderline patients, with no significant difference between amitriptyline and placebo (Soloff et al., 1989; Soloff et al., 1986). A more recent double-blind, placebo-controlled study of 108 borderline inpatients by Soloff et al. (1993), however, showed modest support for the efficacy of haloperidol in managing overt hostility and aggression, whereas it showed that the monoamine oxidase inhibitor phenelzine was superior to placebo in the management of anger and hostility. This is consistent with the results of a previous double-blind, placebo-controlled study with the monoamine oxidase inhibitor tranylcypromine (Cowdry & Gardner, 1988). An open trial of fifteen patients showed that the atypical antipsychotic agent clozapine was used successfully in the management of patients with borderline personality disorder (Frankenburg, 1993).

A study by Gardner and Cowdry (1986) found carbamazepine to be significantly superior to placebo in decreasing the severity of loss of behavioral control in patients with borderline personality disorder. The usefulness of carbamazepine in the management of behavioral dyscontrol was further supported by a double-blind, crossover trial by Cowdry and Gardner (1988). Another anticonvulsant medication showed promising results in an eight-week open study. In this study, eleven patients with borderline personality disorder were treated with valproate, with blood levels between 50 and 100 mcg/ml and three of the eight completers were responders on change scores for anger and impulsivity (Stein et al., 1995).

Two open studies by Cornelius et al. (1990) and Markovitz et al. (1991) suggested the efficacy of the SSRI fluoxetine in reducing impulsive symptoms among patients with borderline personality disorder. Similarly, open studies by Kavoussi et al. (1994) and Markowitz and Wagner (1995) found that treatment with the SSRIs sertraline and venlafaxine was followed by a significant improvement in irritability and hostility among personality-disordered patients. In a thirteen-week placebo-controlled, double-blind study of patients with mild to moderately severe borderline personality disorder, treatment with the SSRI fluoxetine was followed by a significant improvement in anger, independent from changes in levels of depression (Salzman, 1995). More recently, a double-blind study showed the superiority of fluoxetine over placebo in the management of impulsive aggression among personality-disordered patients (Coccaro & Kavoussi, 1997).

SUMMARY

Several drugs are apparently effective in treating pathologic anger and aggression. Because many of the studies on aggressive populations allowed the use of concomitant medications, it is unclear whether the efficacy of each drug in a particular population is dependent on the presence of other medications, such as antipsychotic agents. Finally, one needs to be circumspect in inferring efficacy of a particular drug in aggressive patients with neuropsychiatric conditions other than the ones in which some efficacy has been established.

Lithium appears to be an effective treatment of aggression among nonepileptic prison inmates, mentally retarded and handicapped patients, and among conduct-disordered children with explosive behavior. Certainly, lithium would be the treatment of choice in bipolar patients with excessive irritability and anger outbursts, and it has been shown to be effective in this population (Corrigan et al., 1993).

Anticonvulsant medications are the treatment of choice for patients with outbursts of rage and abnormal EEG findings. The efficacy of these drugs in patients without a seizure disorder, however, remains to be established, with the exception perhaps of valproate and carbamazepine. In fact, diphenylhydantoin did not appear to be effective in treating aggressive behavior in children with temper tantrums and was found to be effective only in a prison population. There is some evidence for the efficacy of carbamazepine and valproate in treating pathologic aggression in patients with dementia, organic brain syndrome, psychosis, and personality disorders.

As Yudofsky et al. (1987) point out in their review of the literature, although traditional antipsychotic drugs have been used widely to treat aggression, there is little evidence for their effectiveness in treating aggression beyond their sedative effect in agitated patients or their antiaggressive effect among patients whose aggression is related to active psychosis. Antipsychotic agents appear to be effective in treating psychotic aggressive patients, conduct-disordered children, and mentally retarded patients, with only modest effects in the management of pathologic aggression in patients with dementia. Furthermore, in at least in one study (Elie et al., 1980), these drugs were found to be associated with increased aggressiveness in mentally retarded subjects. On the other hand, atypical antipsychotic agents (i.e., clozapine, risperidone, and olanzapine) may be more effective than traditional antipsychotic drugs in aggressive and violent populations, as they have shown efficacy in patients with dementia, brain injury, mental retardation, and personality disorders.

Similarly, benzodiazepines can reduce agitation and irritability in elderly and demented populations, but they also can induce behavioral disinhibition (van der Bijl & Roelofse, 1991). Therefore, one should be careful in using this class of drugs in patients with pathologic aggression.

Beta-blockers appear to be effective in many different neuropsychiatric conditions. These drugs seem effective in reducing violent and assaultive behavior in patients with dementia, brain injury, schizophrenia, mental retardation, and organic brain syndrome. As pointed out by Campbell et al. (1982) in their review of the literature, however, systematic research is lacking, and little is known about the efficacy and safety of beta-blockers in children and adolescents with pathologic aggression. Although widely used in the management of pathologic aggression, the use of this class of drugs has been limited partially by marked hypotension and bradycardia, which are side effects common at the higher doses.

The usefulness of the antihypertensive drug clonidine in the treatment of pathologic aggression has not been assessed adequately, and only marginal benefits were observed with this drug in irritable autistic and conduct-disordered children.

Psychostimulants seem to be effective in reducing aggressiveness in brain-injured patients as well as in violent adolescents with oppositional or conduct disorders, particularly when these patients suffer from attention deficit disorder. These drugs, however, should not be prescribed when there is comorbid substance abuse.

Antidepressants are the treatment of choice of aggressiveness and hostility among patients with unipolar depression and anger attacks. The fact that clomipramine, a tricyclic antidepressant with potent serotonin uptake blocking action, was found to be more effective than desipramine, a primarily noradrenergic agent, in treating anger in autistic children is consistent with the view that SSRIs may be particularly effective in patients with pathologic aggression and anger attacks. SSRIs have been found to be effective in reducing irritability and aggressive behavior in other psychiatric conditions, such as Alzheimer's disease, autism, mental retardation, psychosis, PTSD, premenstrual dysphoric disorder, and personality disorders.

The role of these antidepressants in the treatment of pathologic aggression in non-depressed patients needs further investigation, although Conn and Goldman (1992) have observed that 10.5 percent of patients in long-term care in a geriatric hospital were on antidepressants and that one of the most common reasons for their use was aggression. As Eichelman (1990) points out in his review, the development of more specific drugs affecting the serotonin (5-HT) system offers strong promise of increasingly better treatment of pathologic aggression. In fact, a 5-HT-1A receptor partial agonist, buspirone, may be effective in reducing aggression in mentally retarded and brain-injured patients, as well as among women with premenstrual dysphoric disorder. Trazodone, a serotonin 5-HT-2 receptor antagonist, has shown some efficacy in patients with Alzheimer's disease, organic brain syndrome, and conduct disorder. Finally, a new class of drugs described as "serenics" is under development. These drugs, which are 5-HT-1A/B agonists, appear to be effective in blocking aggressive behavior in various animal models without inducing sedation or impairing motor function (Eichelman, 1990).

Pathologic aggressive behavior is an extremely heterogeneous phenomenon present in a variety of neuropsychiatric disorders, with such diversity being reflected in marked differences in neurochemical substrates and response to treatment. Many different psychotropic drugs appear to be able to reduce irritability and aggressiveness in patients with pathologic aggression. Consistent with the results of animal studies that show that the effects of psychotropic drugs vary across different animal models of affective aggression, some of these drugs may have antiaggressive properties in certain patient populations and not in others. In the author's opinion, the most promising agents overall are those affecting the serotonergic system, which at least in human beings, appears to be involved heavily in disorders with pathologic aggression.

References

Alam, M., Klass, D. & Luchins, D. (1995). *Divalproex sodium, valproic acid and carbamazepine in aggression.* Presented at the 35th Annual New Clinical Drug Evaluation Unit Program meeting, Orlando, FL.

Allan, E. R., Alpert, M., Sison, C. E., Citrome, L., Laury, G. & Berman, I. (1996). Adjunctive nadolol in the treatment of acutely aggressive schizophrenic patients. *Journal of Clinical Psychiatry, 57,* 455–459.

Barratt, E. S., Stanford, M. S., Felthouse, A. R. & Kent, T. A. (1997). The effects of phenytoin on impulsive and premeditated aggression: A controlled study. *Journal of Psychopharmacology, 17,* 341–349.

Bhandary, A. N. & Masand, P. S. (1997). Buspirone in the management of disruptive behaviors due to Huntington's Disease and other neurological disorders. *Psychosomatics, 38,* 389–391.

Biederman, J., Munir, K. & Knee, D. (1987). Conduct and oppositional disorder in clinically referred children with attention deficit disorder: A controlled family study. *Journal of the American Academy of Child and Adolescent Psychiatry, 26,* 724–727.

Bobon, D. P., Plomteux, G., Heusghem, C. & Bobon, J. (1970). Clinical toxicology and efficacy of pimozide. *International Journal of Pharmacopsychiatry, 4,* 194–203.

Bond, W., Mandos, L. & Kurtz, M. (1989). Midazolam for aggressivity and violence in three mentally retarded patients. *American Journal of Psychiatry, 146,* 925–926.

Brizer, D., Convit, A., Krakowski, M. & Volavka, J. (1987). A rating scale for reporting violence on psychiatric wards. *Hospital and Community Psychiatry, 38,* 769–770.

Brooke, M. M., Patterson, D. R., Questad, K. A., Cardenas, D. & Farrel-Roberts, L.(1992). The treatment of agitation during initial hospitalization after traumatic brain injury. *Archives of Physical Medicine and Rehabilitation, 73,* 917–921.

Buitelaar, J. K., van der Gaag, R. J. & van der Hoeven, J. (1998). Buspirone in the management of anxiety and irritability in children with pervasive developmental disorders: Results of an open label study. *Journal of Clinical Psychiatry, 59,* 56–59.

Buss, A. H. & Durkee, A. (1957). An inventory for assessing different kinds of hostility. *Journal of Consulting Psychology, 21,* 343–349.

Buss, A. H. & Perry, M. (1992). The aggression questionnaire. *Journal of Personal and Social Psychology, 63,* 452–459.

Campbell, M., Adams, P. B., Small, A. M., Kafantaris, V., Silva, R. R., Shell, J., Perry, R. & Overall, J. E. (1995). Lithium in hospitalized aggressive children with conduct disorder: A double blind and placebo-controlled study. *Journal of the American Academy of Child and Adolescent Psychiatry, 34,* 445–453.

Campbell, M., Gonzalez, N. M. & Silva, R. R. (1992). The pharmacologic treatment of conduct disorders and rage outbursts. *Psychiatric Clinics of North America, 15,* 69-85.

Campbell, M., Small, A. M., Green, W. H., Jennings, S. J., Perry, R., Bennett, W. G. & Anderson, L. (1984). Behavioral efficacy of haloperidol and lithium carbonate: A comparison in hospitalized aggressive children with conduct disorder. *Archives of General Psychiatry, 41,* 650–656.

Carlini, E. A., Lindsey, C. J. & Tufik, S. (1977). Cannabis, catecholamines, rapid eye movement sleep and aggressive behaviour. *British Journal of Pharmacology, 61,* 371–379.

Carlyle, W., Ancill, R. & Sheldon, L. (1993). Aggression in the demented patient: A double-blind study of loxapine versus haloperidol. *International Journal of Clinical Psychopharmacology, 8,* 103–108.

Casey, J. F., Lasky, J. J., Klett, C. J. & Hollister, L. E. (1960). Treatment of schizophrenic reactions with phenothiazine derivatives. *American Journal of Psychiatry, 117,* 97–105.

Clinton, J., Sterner, S. & Stelmachers, Z. (1987). Haloperidol for sedation of disruptive emergency patients. *Annals of Emergency Medicine, 16,* 319–322.

Coccaro, E., Astill, J., Herbert, J. & Schut, A. G. (1990). Fluoxetine and impulsive aggression in DSM-III-R personality disorder patients. *Journal of Clinical Psychopharmacology, 10,* 373–375.

Coccaro, E. F. & Kavoussi, R. G. (1991). Biological and pharmacological aspects of borderline personality disorder. *Hospital and Community Psychiatry, 42,* 1029–1033.

Coccaro, E. F. & Kavoussi, R. G. (1997). Fluoxetine and impulsive aggressive behavior in personality disordered subjects. *Archives of General Psychiatry, 54,* 1081–1088.

Cohen, S. & Underwood, M. (1994). The use of clozapine in a mentally retarded and aggressive population. *Journal of Clinical Psychiatry, 55,* 440–444.

Conn, D. K. & Goldman, Z. (1992). Pattern of use of antidepressants in long-term care facilities for the elderly. *Journal of Geriatric Psychiatry and Neurology, 5,* 228–232.

Conners, C. K., Kramer, R., Rothschild, G. H., Schwartz, L. & Stone, A. (1971). Treatment of young delinquent boys with diphenylhydantoin sodium and methylphenidate. *Archives of General Psychiatry, 24,* 156–160.

Cook, W. & Medley, D. (1954). Proposed hostility and pharasaic-virtue scales for the MMPI. *Journal of Applied Psychology, 383,* 414–418.

Cornelius, J. R., Soloff, P. H., Perel, J. M. & Ulrich, R. F. (1990). Fluoxetine trial in borderline personality disorder. *Psychopharmacology Bulletin, 26,* 151–154.

Corrigan, P. W., Yudofsky, S. C. & Silver, J. M. (1993). Pharmacological and behavioral treatments for aggressive psychiatric inpatients. *Hospital and Community Psychiatry, 44,* 125–133.

Cowdry, R. & Gardner, D. (1988). Pharmacology of borderline personality disorder. *Archives of General Psychiatry, 45,* 111–119.

Craft, M., Ismail, I. A., Krishnamurti, D., Mathews, J., Regan, A., Seth, R. V. & North, P. M. (1987). Lithium in the treatment of aggression in mentally handicapped patients: A double-blind trial. *British Journal of Psychiatry, 150,* 685–689.

Cueva, J. E., Overall, J. E., Small, A. M., Armenteros, J. L., Perry, R. & Campbell, M. (1996). Carbamazepine in aggressive children with conduct disorder: A double-blind and placebo-controlled study. *Journal of the American Academy of Child and Adolescent Psychiatry, 35,* 480–490.

Davidson, J., Kudler, H., Smith, R., Mahorney, S. L., Lipper, S., Hammett, E., Saunders, W. B. & Cavenar, J. O. Jr. (1990). Treatment of post-traumatic stress disorder with amitriptyline and placebo. *Archives of General Psychiatry, 47,* 259–266.

Davidson, J., Roth, S. & Newman, E. (1991). Treatment of post-traumatic stress disorder with fluoxetine. *Journal of Traumatic Stress, 4,* 419–423.

de Koning, P., Mak, M., de Vries, M. H., Allsopp, L. F., Stevens, R. B., Verbruggen, R., Van den Borre, R., van Peteghem, P., Kohen, D. & Arumainayagam, M. (1994). Eltoprazine in aggressive mentally handicapped patients: A double-blind, placebo- and baseline-controlled multi-centre study. *International Journal of Clinical Psychopharmacology, 14,* 187–194.

Delini-Stula, A. & Vassout, A. (1979). Differential effects of psychoactive drugs on aggressive responses in mice and rats. In M. Sandler (Ed.), *Psychopharmacology of aggression.* New York, Raven, 41–60.

Donlon, P., Hopkin, J. & Tupin, I. (1979). Overview: Efficacy and safety of the rapid neuroleptization method with injectable haloperidol. *American Journal of Psychiatry 136,* 273–278.

Eadie, M. & Tyrer, J. (1980). *Anticonvulsant therapy: Pharmacological basis and practice.* New York: Churchill Livingstone.

Edmunds, G. & Kendrick, D. C. (1980). *The measurement of human aggressiveness.* Chichester, England: Ellis Horwood.

Eichelman, B. S. (1979). Role of biogenic amines in aggressive behavior. In M. Sandler (Ed.), *Psychopharmacology of aggression.* New York: Raven, 61–94.

Eichelman, B. S. (1990). Neurochemical and psychopharmacologic aspects of aggressive behavior. *Annual Review of Medicine, 41,* 149–158.

Eimer, M. (1989). Management of the behavioral symptoms associated with dementia. *Primary Care, 16,* 431–450.

Eisenberg, L., Lachman, R., Moiling, P. A., Lockner, A., Mizelle, J. D. & Conners, C. K. (1963). A psychopharmacologic experiment in a training school for delinquent boys. *American Journal of Orthopsychiatry, 33,* 431–447.

Elie, R., Langlois, Y., Cooper, S. F., Gravel, G. & Albert, J. M. (1980). Comparison of SCH-12679 and thioridazine in aggressive mental retardates. *Candian Journal of Psychiatry, 25,* 484–491.

Eriksson, E., Hedberg, M. A., Andersch, B. & Sundblad, C. (1995). The serotonin reuptake inhibitor paroxetine is superior to the noradrenaline reuptake inhibitor maprotiline in the treatment of premenstrual syndrome. *Neuropsychopharmacology, 12,* 167–176.

Fava, G. A. (1987). Irritable mood and physical illness. *Stress Medicine, 3,* 293–299.

Fava, M., Alpert, J., Nierenberg, A. A., Ghaemi, N., O'Sullivan, R., Tedlow, J. R., Worthington, J. J. & Rosenbaum, J. F. (1996). Fluoxetine treatment of anger attacks: A replication study. *Annals of Clinical Psychiatry, 8,* 7–10.

Fava, M., Anderson, K. & Rosenbaum, J. F. (1993a). Are thymoleptic-responsive "anger attacks" a discrete clinical syndrome? *Psychosomatics, 34,* 350–355.

Fava, M. & Keefe, B. (1998). Approach to the patient with premenstrual mood dysregulation. In T. Stern, J. B. Herman & P. L. Slavin (Eds.), *The MGH guide to psychiatry in primary care.* New York: McGraw-Hill.

Fava, M., Nierenberg, A. A., Quitkin, F. M., Zisook, S., Pearlstein, T., Stone, A. & Rosenbaum, J. F. (1997). A preliminary study on the efficacy of sertraline and imipramine on anger attacks in atypical depression and dysthymia. *Psychopharmacology Bulletin, 33,* 101–103.

Fava, M., Rosenbaum, J. F., McCarthy, M. K., Pava, J. A., Steingard, R. J. & Bless, E. (1991). Anger attacks in depressed outpatients and their response to fluoxetine. *Psychopharmacology Bulletin, 27,* 275–279.

Fava, M., Rosenbaum, J. F., Pava, J. A., McCarthy, M. K., Steingard, R. J. & Bouffides, E. (1993b). Anger attacks in unipolar depression: I. Clinical correlates and response to fluoxetine treatment. *American Journal of Psychiatry, 150,* 1158–1163.

Feldman, P., Bay, A. N. & Baser, A. (1969). Parenteral haloperidol in controlling patient behavior during acute psychotic episodes. *Current Therapeutic Research, Clinical and Experimental, 11,* 362–366.

Forster, P. L., Schoenfeld, F. B., Marmar, C. R. & Lang, A. J. (1995). Lithium for irritability in post-traumatic stress disorder. *Journal of Traumatic Stress, 8,* 143–149.

Foster, M., Hillbrand, M. & Chi, C. (1989). Efficacy of carbamazepine in assaultive patients with frontal lobe dysfunction. *Progress in Neuro-Psychopharmacology and Biological Psychiatry, 23,* 865–874.

Frankenberg, F. R. (1993). Clozapine and bipolar disorder. *Journal of Clinical Psychopharmacology, 13,* 289–290.

Freeman, E. W., Rickels, K., Sondheimer, S. J. & Polansky, M. (1995). A double-blind trial of oral progesterone, alprazolam, and placebo in treatment of severe premenstrual syndrome. *Journal of the American Medical Association, 274,* 51–57.

Gadow, K. D., Nolan, E., Sprafkin, J. & Sverd, J. (1995). School observations of children with attention-deficit hyperactivity disorder and comorbid tic disorder: Effects of methylphenidate treatment. *Journal of Developmental and Behavioral Pediatrics, 16,* 167–176.

Gardner, D. & Cowdry, R. (1986). Positive effects of carbamazepine on behavioral dyscontrol in borderline personality disorder. *American Journal of Psychiatry, 143,* 519–522.

Germine, M., Goddard, A. W., Woods, S. W., Charney, D. S. & Heninger, G. R. (1992). Anger and anxiety responses to m-chlorophenylpiperazine in generalized anxiety disorder. *Biological Psychiatry, 32,* 457–461.

Giacalone, E., Tansella, M., Valzelli, L. & Garattini, S. (1968). Brain serotonin metabolism in isolated aggressive mice. *Biochemical Pharmacology, 17,* 1315–1327.

Glenn, M. B., Wroblewski, B., Parziale, J., Levine, L., Whyte, J. & Rosenthal, M. (1989). Lithium carbonate for aggressive behavior or affective instability on ten brain-injured patients. *American Journal of Physical Medicine and Rehabilitation, 68,* 221–226.

Gordon, C. T., State, R. C., Nelson, J. E., Hamburger, S. D. & Rapoport, J. L. (1993). A double-blind comparison of clomipramine, desipramine, and placebo in the treatment of autistic disorder. *Archives of General Psychiatry, 50,* 441–447.

Greendyke, R. M., Berkner, J. P., Webster, J. C. & Gulya, A. (1989). Treatment of behavioral problems with pindolol. *Psychosomatics, 30,* 161–165.

Greendyke, R. M. & Kanter, D. R. (1986). Therapeutic effects of pindolol on behavioral disturbances associated with organic brain disease: A double-blind study. *Journal of Clinical Psychiatry, 47,* 423–426.

Greendyke, R. M., Kanter, D. R., Schuster, D. B., Verstreate, S. & Wootton, J. (1986). Propranolol treatment of assaultive patients with organic brain disease. *Journal of Nervous and Mental Diseases, 174,* 290–294.

Greenhill, L. L., Solomon, M., Pleak, R. & Ambrosini, P. (1985). Molindone hydrochloride treatment of hospitalized children with conduct disorder. *Journal of Clinical Psychiatry, 46,* 20–25.

Gualtieri, C. (1991). Buspirone for the behavioral problems of patients with organic brain disorders. *Journal of Clinical Psychopharmacology, 11,* 280–281.

Guy, W. (Ed.) (1976). DHEW Publication No. (ADM) 76-338, *ECDEU Assessment Manual for Psychopharmacology* (rev. ed.). Rockville, MD: National Institute of Mental Health.

Haas, S., Vincent, K., Holt, J. & Lippmann, S. (1997). Divalproex: A possible treatment alternative for demented, elderly, aggressive patients. *Annals of Clinical Psychiatry, 9,* 145–147.

Hakola, H. & Laulumaa, V. (1982). Carbamazepine in treatment of violent schizophrenics (letter). *Lancet, 8285,* 1358.

Hellings, J. A., Kelley, L. A., Gabrielli, W. F., Kilgore, E. & Shah, P. (1996). Sertraline response in adults with mental retardation and autistic disorder. *Journal of Clinical Psychiatry, 57,* 333–336.

Holden, J. M., Itil, T. M., Gannon, P. J. & Keskiner, A. (1971). The clinical effects of intramuscular thiothixene and trifluoperazine in chronic schizophrenia: A comparative study. *Current Therapeutic Research, Clinical and Experimental, 13,* 298–310.

Honigfeld, G., Gillis, R. D. & Klett, C. J. (1965). Nurses' observation scale for inpatient evaluation: A new scale for measuring improvement in chronic schizophrenia. *Journal of Clinical Psychology, 21,* 65–71.

Hyman, S. (1994). The violent patient. In S. Hyman & G. Tesar (Ed.), *Manual of psychiatric emergencies* (3d ed.). Boston: Little, Brown.

Itil, T. M., Polvan, N., Ucok, A., Eper, E., Guven, F. & Hsu, W. (1971). Comparison of the clinical and electroencephalographical effects of molindone and trifluoperazine in acute schizophrenic patients. *Behavioral Neuropsychiatry, 3,* 6–13.

Izmeth, M. G., Khan, S. Y., Kumarajeeva, D. I., Shivanathan, S., Veall, R. M. & Wiley, Y. V. (1988). Zuclopenthixol decanoate in the management of behavioural disorders in mentally handicapped patients. *Pharmatherapeutica, 5,* 217–227.

Jaselskis, C. A., Cook, E. H. Jr., Fletcher, K. E. & Leventhal, B. L. (1992). Clonidine treatment of hyperactive and impulsive children with autistic disorder. *Journal of Clinical Psychopharmacology, 12,* 322–327.

Jeanblanc, W. & Davis, Y. (1995). Risperidone for treating dementia-associated aggression. *American Journal of Psychiatry, 152,* 1239.

Kafantaris, V., Campbell, M., Padrone-Gayol, M. V., Small, A. M., Locascio, J. J. & Rosenberg, C. R. (1992). Carbamazepine in hospitalized aggressive conduct disorder children: An open pilot study. *Psychopharmacology Bulletin, 28,* 193–199.

Kaplan, S. L., Busner, J., Kupietz, S., Wassermann, E. & Segal, B. (1990). Effects of methylphenidate on adolescents with aggressive conduct disorder and ADDH: A preliminary report. *Journal of the American Academy of Child and Adolescent Psychiatry, 29,* 719–723.

Kavoussi, R. J., Liu, J. & Coccaro, E. F. (1994). An open trial of sertraline in personality disordered patients with impulsive aggression. *Journal of Clinical Psychiatry, 55,* 137–141.

Kellner, R. A. & Kavoussi, R. J. (1987). A symptom questionnaire. *Journal of Clinical Psychiatry, 48,* 268–274.

Kemph, J. P., DeVane, C. L., Levine, G. M., Jarecke, R. & Miller, R. L. (1993). Treatment of aggressive children with clonidine: Results of an open pilot study. *Journal of the American Academy of Child and Adolescent Psychiatry, 32,* 577–581.

King, D. & Marsan, C. (1977). Clinical features and ictal patterns in epileptic patients with EEG temporal lobe foci. *Annals of Neurology, 2,* 138–147.

Klein, R. G., Abikoff, H., Klass, E., Ganeles, D., Seese, L. M. & Pollack, S. (1997). Clinical efficacy of methylphenidate in conduct disorder with and without attention deficit hyperactivity disorder. *Archives of General Psychiatry, 54,* 1073–1080.

Kligman, D. & Goldberg, D. (1975). Temporal lobe epilepsy and aggression. *Journal of Nervous and Mental Diseases, 160,* 324–341.

Korn, M. L., Botsis, A. J., Kotler, M., Plutchik, R., Conte, H. R., Finkelstein, G., Grosz, D., Kay, S., Brown, S. L. & van Praag, H. M. (1992). The suicide and aggression survey: A semistructured instrument for the measurement of suicidality and aggression. *Comprehensive Psychiatry, 33,* 359–365.

Kosten, T. R., Frank, J. B., Dan, E., McDougle, C. J. & Giller, E. L. Jr. (1991). Pharmacotherapy for posttraumatic stress disorder using phenelzine and imipramine. *Journal of Nervous and Mental Diseases, 179,* 366–370.

Kunik, M. E., Puryear, L., Orengo, C. A., Molinari, V. & Workman, R. H. Jr. (1998). The efficacy and tolerability of divalproex sodium in elderly demented patients with behavioral disturbances. *International Journal of Geriatric Psychiatry, 13,* 29–34.

Lebert, F., Pasquier, F. & Petit, F. (1994). Behavioral effects of trazodone in Alzheimer's disease. *Journal of Psychiatry, 55,* 536–538.

Lefkowitz, M. M. (1969). Effects of diphenylhydantoin on disruptive behavior: Study of male delinquents. *Archives of General Psychiatry, 20,* 643–651.

Lenox, R. H., Newhouse, P. A., Creelman, W. L. & Whitaker, T. M. (1992). Adjunctive treatment of manic agitation with lorazepam versus haloperidol: A double-blind study. *Journal of Clinical Psychiatry, 53,* 47–52.

Lewis, D. O. & Pincus, J. H. (1989). Epilepsy and violence: Evidence for a neuropsychotic-aggressive syndrome. *Journal of Neuropsychiatry, 1,* 413–418.

Looker, A. & Conners, C. K. (1970). Diphenylhydantoin in children with severe temper tantrums. *Archives of General Psychiatry, 23,* 80–89.

Lovett, L. M. & Shaw, D. M. (1987). Outcome in bipolar affective disorder, after stereotactic tractomy. *British Journal of Psychiatry, 151,* 113–116.

Luchins, D. (1983). Carbamazepine for the violent psychiatric patients. *Lancet, I,* 766.

Lukoff, D., Nuechterlein, K. H. & Ventura, I. (1986). Appendix A: Manual for the expanded BPRS. *Schizophrenia Bulletin, 12,* 594–602.

Lynch, D., Eliatamby, C. & Anderson, A. (1985). Pipothiazine palmitate in the management of aggressive mentally handicapped patients. *British Journal of Psychiatry, 146,* 525–529.

Maletzky, B. (1974). d-Amphetamine and delinquency: Hyperkinesis persisting. *Diseases of the Nervous System, 35,* 543–547.

Mandel, P., Mack, G. & Kempf, E. (1979). Molecular basis of some models of aggressive behavior. In M. Sandler (Ed.), *Psychopharmacology of aggression.* New York: Raven, 95–110.

Markovitz, P. J., Calabrese, J. R., Schulz, S. C. & Meltzer, H. Y. (1991). Fluoxetine in the treatment of borderline and schizotypal personality disorders. *American Journal of Psychiatry, 148,* 1064–1067.

Markowitz, P. I. (1992). Effects of fluoxetine on self-injurious behavior in the developmentally disabled: A preliminary study. *Journal of Clinical Psychopharmacology, 12,* 27–31.

Markowitz, P. I. & Wagner, S. (1995). Venlafaxine in the treatment of borderline personality disorder. *Psychopharmology Bulletin, 31,* 773–777.

Mature, C. M., Druss, B. G. & Cellar, J. S. (1992). Valproate treatment of older psychotic patients with organic mental syndromes and behavioral dyscontrol. *Journal of the American Geriatric Society, 10,* 914–916.

McDaniel, K. (1986). Pharmacologic treatment of psychiatric and neurodevelopmental disorders in children and adolescents. *Clinical Pediatrics, 25,* 65–71.

McDougle, C. J., Holmes, J. P., Carlson, D. C., Pelton, G. H., Cohen, D. J. & Price, L. H. (1998). A double-blind, placebo-controlled study of risperidone in adults with autistic disorder and other pervasive developmental disorders. *Archives of General Psychiatry, 55,* 633–641.

McDougle, C. J., Naylor, S. T., Cohen, D. J., Volkmar, F. R., Heninger, G. R. & Price, L. H. (1996). A double-blind, placebo-controlled study of fluvoxamine in adults with autistic disorder. *Archives of General Psychiatry, 53,*1001–1008.

Mellow, A., Solano-Lopez, C. & Davis, S. (1993). Sodium valproate in the treatment of behavioral disturbance in dementia. *Journal of Geriatric Psychiatry and Neurology, 6,* 205–209.

Michals, M. L., Crismor, M. L., Roberts, S. & Childs, A. (1993). Clozapine response and adverse effects in nine brain-injured patients. *Journal of Clinical Psychopharmacology, 13,* 198–203.

Mooney, G. F. & Haas, L. I. (1993). Effect of methylphenidate on brain injury-related anger. *Archives of Physical Medicine and Rehabilitation, 74,* 153–160.

Nagy, L. M., Morgan, C. A., Southwick, S. M. & Charney, D. S. (1993). Open prospective trial of fluoxetine for posttraumatic stress disorder. *Journal of Clinical Psychopharmacology, 13,* 107–113.

Neppe, V. (1982). Carbamazepine in the psychiatric patient. *Lancet, II,* 334.

Nygaard, H. A., Fuglum, E. & Elgen, K. (1992). Zuclopenthixol, melperone and haloperidol/levomepromazine in the elderly: Meta-analysis of two double-blind trials at 15 nursing homes in Norway. *Current Medical Research and Opinion, 12,* 615–622.

Nyth, A.L. & Gottfries, C. G. (1990). The clinical efficacy of citalopram in treatment of emotional disturbances in dementia disorders: A Nordic multicenter study. *British Journal of Psychiatry, 157,* 894–901.

Olafsson, K., Jorgensen, S., Jensen, H. V., Bille, A., Arup, A. & Andersen, J. (1992). Fluvoxamine in the treatment of demented elderly patients: A double-blind, placebo-controlled study. *Acta Psychiatrica Scandinavia, 85,* 453–456.

Palmstiema,T. & Wistedt, B. (1987). Staff observation aggression scale. SOAS: Presentation and evaluation. *Acta Psychiatrica Scandinavica, 76,* 657–663.

Patterson, J. F. (1988). A preliminary study of carbamazepine in the treatment of assaultive patients with dementia. *Journal of Geriatric Psychiatry and Neurology, 1,* 21–23.

Patton, J. H., Stanford, M. S. & Barratt, E. S. (1995). Factor structure of the Barratt impulsiveness scale. *Journal of Clinical Psychiatry, 51,* 768–774.

Pinner, E. & Rich, C. (1988). Effects of trazodone on aggressive behavior in seven patients with organic mental disorders. *American Journal of Psychiatry, 145,* 1295–1296.

Ranen, N. G., Lipsey, J. R., Treisman, G. & Ross, C. A. (1996). Setraline in the treatment of severe aggressiveness in Huntington's disease. *Journal of Neuropsychiatry and Clinical Neuroscience, 8,* 338–340.

Ratey, J. J., Leveroni, C., Kilmer, D., Gutheil, C. & Swartz, B. (1993). The effects of clozapine on severely aggressive psychiatric inpatients on a difficult to manage unit of a state hospital. *Journal of Clinical Psychiatry, 54,* 1–6.

Ratey, J. J., Mikkelsen, E. J., Smith, G. B., Upadhyaya, A., Zuckerman, S., Martell, D. & Busnell, S. (1986). Beta blockers in the severely and profoundly mentally retarded. *Journal of Clinical Psychopharmacology, 6,* 103–107.

Ratey, J. J., Sorgi, P., O'Driscoll, G. A., Sands, S., Daehler, M. L., Fletcher, J. R., Kadish, W., Spruiell, G., Polakoff, S., Lindem, K. L., Bemporad, J. R., Richardson, L. & Rosenfeld, B. (1992). Nadolol to treat aggression and psychiatric symptomatology in chronic psychiatric inpatients: A double-blind, placebo-controlled study. *Journal of Clinical Psychiatry, 53,* 41–46.

Ratey, J. J., Sovner, R., Parks, A. & Rogentina, K. (1991). Buspirone treatment of aggression and anxiety in mentally retarded patients: A multiple-baseline, placebo lead-in study. *Journal of Clinical Psychiatry, 52,* 159–162.

Reid, A. H., Ballinger, B. R., Heather, B. B. & Melvin, S. J. (1984). The natural history of behavioural symptoms among severely and profoundly mentally retarded patients. *British Journal of Psychiatry, 145,* 289–293.

Reid, A. H., Naylor, G. J. & Kay, D. S. (1981). A double-blind, placebo controlled, crossover trial of carbamazepine in overactive, severely mentally handicapped patients. *Psychological Medicine, 11,* 109–113.

Reid, W. (1985). The antisocial personality: A review. *Hospital and Community Psychiatry, 36,* 831–837.

Reilly, P. M., Clark, H. W., Shopshire, M. S., Lewis, E. W. & Sorensen, D. J. (1994). Anger management and temper control: Critical components of posttraumatic stress disorder and substance abuse treatment. *Journal of Psychoactive Drugs, 26,* 401–407.

Reisberg, B., Borenstein, J., Salob, S. P., Ferris, S. H., Franssen, E. & Georgotas, A. (1987). Behavioral symptoms in Alzheimer's disease: Phenomenology and treatment. *Journal of Clinical Psychiatry, 48,* 9–15.

Reist, C., Kaufman, C. & Haler, R. (1989). A controlled trial of desipramine in 18 men with PTSD. *American Journal of Psychiatry, 146,* 513–516.

Rickels, K., Freeman, E. & Sondheimer, S. (1989). Buspirone in the treatment of premenstrual syndrome. *Lancet, 1(8641),* 777.

Riley, W. T., Treiber, F. A. & Woods, M. G. (1989). Anger and hostility in depression. *Journal of Nervous and Mental Diseases, 177,* 668–674.

Ritrovato, C. A., Weber, S. S. & Dufresne, R. L. (1989). Nadolol in the treatment of aggressive behavior associated with schizophrenia. *Clinical Pharmacy, 8,* 132–135.

Rosenbaum, A. & Hoge, S. (1989). Head injury and marital aggression. *American Journal of Psychiatry, 146,* 1048–1051.

Rosenbaum, J. F., Fava, M., Nierenberg, A. A. & Sachs, G. (1995). Treatment resistant mood disorders. In G. Gabbard (Ed.), *Treatment of psychiatric disorders: The DSM-IV edition.* Washington, DC: American Pychiatric Press, 1275–1328.

Salzman, C. (1988). Use of benzodiazepines to control disruptive behavior in inpatients. *Journal of Clinical Psychiatry, 49,* 77–87.

Salzman, C., Wolfson, A. N., Schatzberg, A., Looper, J., Henke, R., Albanese, M., Schwartz, J. & Miyawaki, E. (1995). Effect of fluoxetine on anger in symptomatic volunteers with borderline personality disorder. *Journal of Clinical Psychopharmacology, 15,* 23–29.

Shankle, W., Nielson, K. & Cotman, C. (1995). Low-dose propranolol reduces aggression and agitation resembling that associated with orbitofrontal dysfunction in elderly demented patients. *Alzheimer Disease and Associative Disorders, 9,* 233–237.

Sheard, M. H., Marini, J. L., Bridges, C. I. & Wagner, E. (1976). The effect of lithium on impulsive aggressive behavior in man. *American Journal of Psychiatry, 133,* 1409–1413.

Shetatsky, M., Greenberg, D. & Lerer, B. (1988). A controlled trial of phenelzine in post-traumatic stress disorder. *Psychiatry Research, 24,* 149–155.

Siassi, I. (1982). Lithium treatment of impulsive behavior in children. *Journal of Clinical Psychiatry, 43,* 482–484.

Siegel, A. & Schubert, K. (1995). Neurotransmitters regulating feline aggressive behavior. *Reviews in the Neurosciences, 6,* 47–61.

Silver, F. I. & Yudofsky, S. C. (1987). Documentation of aggression in the assessment of the violent patient. *Psychiatric Annals, 17,* 375–384.

Simeon, J., Ferguson, H. & van Wyck Fleet, J. (1986). Bupropion effects in attention deficit and conduct disorders. *Canadian Journal of Psychiatry, 31,* 581–585.

Simpson, D. & Foster, D. (1986). Improvement in organically disturbed behavior with trazadone treatment. *Journal of Clinical Psychiatry, 47,* 191–193.

Singh, I. & Owino, W. J. (1992). A double-blind comparison of zuclopenthixol tablets with placebo in the treatment of mentally handicapped inpatients with associated behavioral disorders. *Journal of Intellectual Disabilities Research, 36,* 541–549.

Smith, D. A. & Ferry, P. J. (1992). Nonneuroleptic treatment of disruptive behavior in organic mental syndromes. *Annals of Pharmacotherapy, 26,* 1400–1408.

Snaith, R. P. & Taylor, C. M. (1985). Irritability: Definition, assessment and associated factors. *British Journal of Psychiatry, 147,* 127–136.

Soloff, P. H., Cornelius, J., George, A., Nathan, S., Perel, J. M. & Ulrich, R. F. (1993). Efficacy of phenelzine and haloperidol in borderline personality disorder. *Archives of General Psychiatry, 50,* 377–385.

Soloff, P. H., George, A., Nathan, S., Schulz, P. M., Cornelius, J. R., Herring, J. & Perel, J. M. (1989). Amitriptyline versus haloperidol in borderlines: Final outcomes and predictors of response. *Journal of Clinical Psychopharmacology, 9,* 238–246.

Soloff, P. H., George, A., Nathan, S., Schulz, P. M., Ulrich, R. F. & Perel, J. M. (1986). Progress in pharmacotherapy of borderline disorders. *Archives of General Psychiatry, 43,* 691–697.

Sorgi, P., Ratey, J. J. & Polakoff, S. (1986). Beta-adrenergic blockers for the control of aggressive behaviors in patients with chronic schizophrenia. *American Journal of Psychiatry, 143,* 775–776.

Spielberger, C. D. (1988). *Manual for the state-trait anger expression inventory (STAXI).* Psychological Assessment Resources, Odessa, FL.

Spielberger, C. D., Jacobs, G. A., Russell, S. & Crane, R. J. (1983). Assessment of anger: The state-trait anger scale. In J. N. Butcher & C. D. Spielberger (Eds.), *Advances in personality assessment,* vol. 2. Hillsdale, NJ: Erlbaum, 159–187.

Spielberger, C. D., Johnson, E. H., Russell, S., Crane, R. J., Jacobs, G. A. & Worden, T. J. (1985). The experience and expression of anger: Construction and validation of an anger expression scale. In M. A. Chesney & R. H. Rosenman (Eds.), *Anger and hostility in cardiovascular and behavioral disorders.* Washington, DC: Hemisphere, 5–30.

Spivak, B., Mester, R., Wittenberg, N., Maman, Z. & Weizman, A. (1997). Reduction of aggressiveness and impulsiveness during clozapine treatment in chronic neuroleptic-resistant schizophrenic patients. *Clinical Neuropharmacology, 20,* 442–446.

Stanislav, S. W., Fabre, T., Crimson, M. L. & Childs, A. (1994). Buspirone's efficacy in organic-induced aggression. *Journal of Clinical Psychopharmacology, 14,* 126–130.

Stein, D. J., Simeon, D., Frenkel, M., Islam, M. N. & Hollander, E. (1995). An open trial of valproate in borderline personality disorder. *Journal of Clinical Psychiatry, 56,* 506–510.

Steiner, M., Steinberg, S., Stewart, D., Carter, D., Berger, C., Reid, R., Grover, D. & Streiner, D. (1995). Fluoxetine in the treatment of premenstrual dysphoria. *New England Journal of Medicine, 332,* 1529–1534.

Stewart, J. T., Mounts, M. L. & Clark, R. L. Jr. (1987). Aggressive behavior in Huntington's disease: Treatment with propranolol. *Journal of Clinical Psychiatry, 48,* 106–108.

Strauss, S. M. (1979). Measuring intrafamily conflict and violence: The conflict tactics (CT) scales. *Journal of Marriage and the Family, 41,* 75–88.

Su, T., Tuskan, J., Tsao, L. & Pickar, D. (1994). *Aggression during drug-free and antipsychotic treatment in inpatients with chronic schizophrenia, using the overt aggression scale.* Presented at the American College of Neuropsychopharmacology Meeting, San Juan, PR.

Sultzer, D. L., Gray, K. F., Gunay, I., Berisford, M. A. & Mahler, M. E. (1997). A double-blind comparison of trazodone and haloperidol for treatment of agitation in patients with dementia. *American Journal of Geriatric Psychiatry, 5,* 60–69.

Sundblad, C., Hedberg, M. & Eriksson, E. (1993). Clomipramine administered during luteal phase reduces the symptoms of premenstrual syndrome: A placebo-controlled trial. *Neuropsychopharmacology, 9,* 133–145.

Sundblad, C., Modigh, K., Andersch, B. & Eriksson, E. (1992). Clomipramine effectively reduces premenstrual irritability and dysphoria: A placebo-controlled trial. *Acta Psychiatrica Scandinavica, 85,* 39–47.

Thomas, H. I., Schwartz, E. & Petrilli, R. (1992). Droperidol versus haloperidol for chemical restraint of agitated and combative patients. *Annals of Emergency Medicine, 21,* 407–413.

Tiihonen, J., Hakola, P., Paanila, J. & Turtiainen, M. (1993). Eltoprazine for aggression in schizophrenia and mental retardation. *Lancet, 341,* 307.

Tuason, V. (1986). A comparison of parenteral loxapine and haloperidol in hostile and aggressive acutely schizophrenic patients. *Journal of Clinical Psychiatry, 47,* 126–129.

Tupin, J. P., Smith, D. B., Clanon, T. L., Nugent, A. & Groupe, A. (1973). The long-term use of lithium in aggressive prisoners. *Comprehensive Psychiatry, 14,* 311–317.

Tyrer, S. P., Walsh, A., Edwards, D. E., Berney, T. P. & Stephens, D. A. (1984). Factors associated with a good response to lithium in aggressive mentally handicapped subjects. *Progress in Neuro-Psychopharmacology and Biological Psychiatry, 8,* 751–755.

van der Bijl, P. & Roelofse, I. (1991). Disinhibitory reactions to benzodiazepines: A review. *Journal of Oral Maxillofacial Surgery, 49,* 519–523.

van der Kolk, B. A., Dreyfuss, D., Michaels, M., Shera, D., Berkowitz, R., Fisler, R & Saxe, G. (1994). Flouxetine in posttraumatic stress disorder. *Journal of Clinical Psychiatry, 55,* 517–522.

Vartiainen, H., Tiihonen, J., Putkonen, A., Koponen, H., Virkkunen, M., Hakola, P. & Lehto, H. (1995). Citalopram, a selective serotonin reuptake inhibitor, in the treatment of aggression in schizophrenia. *Acta Psychiatrica Scandinavia, 91,* 348–351.

Verhoeven, W. M., Tuinier, S., Sijben, N. A., van den Berg, Y. W., de Witte-van der Schoot, E. P., Pepplinkhuizen, L. & van Nieuwenhuizen, O. (1992). Eltoprazine in mentally retarded self-injuring patients (letter). *Lancet, 340,* 1037–1038.

Volovka, J., Crowner, M., Brizer, D., Convit, A., Van Praag, H. & Suckow, R. F. (1990). Tryptophan treatment of aggressive psychiatric inpatients. *Biological Psychiatry, 28,* 728–732.

Wilcox, J. (1994). Divalproex sodium in the treatment of aggressive behavior. *Annals of Clinical Psychiatry, 6,* 17–20.

Williams, K. & Goldstein, G. (1979). Cognitive and affective responses to lithium in patients with organic brain syndrome. *American Journal of Psychiatry, 136,* 800–803.

Wistedt, B., Rasmussen, A., Pedersen, L., Malm, U., Traksman-Bendz, L., Wakelin, J. & Bech, P. (1990). The development of an observer-scale for measuring social dysfunction and aggression. *Pharmacopsychiatry, 23,* 249–252.

Wood, S. H., Mortola, J. F., Chan, Y. F., Moossazadeh, F. & Yen, S. S. (1992). Treatment of premenstrual syndrome with fluoxetine: A double-blind placebo-controlled, crossover study. *Obstetrics and Gynecology, 80,* 339–344.

Worrall, E. P., Moody, J. P., Naylor, G. J. (1975). Lithium in non-manic depressives: Antiaggressive effect and red blood cell lithium values. *British Journal of Psychiatry, 126,* 461–468.

Yepes, L., Balks, E., Winsberg, B. G. & Bigler, I. (1977). Amitriptyline and methylphenidate treatment of behaviorally disordered children. *Journal of Child Psychology and Psychiatry, 18,* 39–52.

Yonkers, K. A., Gullion, C., Williams, A., Novak, K. & Rush, A. J. (1996). Paroxetine as a treatment for premenstrual dysphoric disorder. *Journal of Clinical Psychopharmacology, 16,* 3–8.

Yonkers, K. A., Halbreich, U., Freeman, E., Brown, C. & Pearlstein, T. (1996). Sertraline in the treatment of premenstrual dysphoric disorder. *Psychopharmacology Bulletin, 32,* 41–46.

Yudofsky, S. C., Silver, J. M., Jackson, W., Endicott, J. & Williams, D. (1986). The overt aggression scale for the objective rating of verbal and physical aggression. *American Journal of Psychiatry, 143,* 35–39.

Yudofsky, S., Silver, J. & Schneider, S. (1987). Pharmacologic treatment of aggression. *Psychiatric Annals, 17,* 397–407.

Yudofsky, S. C., Stevens, L., Silver, J. M., Barsa, J. & Williams, D. (1984). Propranolol in the treatment of rage and violent behavior associated with Korsakoff's psychosis. *American Journal of Psychiatry, 141,* 114–115.

Zubieta, J. K. & Alessi, N. E. (1992). Acute and chronic administration of trazodone in the treatment of disruptive behavior disorders in children. *Journal of Clinical Psychopharmacology, 12,* 346–351.

Chapter 21

The Etiology and Treatment of Sexual Offending

by Fred S. Berlin, Ph.D.

Introduction 21-1
Assessment 21-2
    Paraphilic Disorders Defined 21-3
    Biologically Based Drives 21-5
    Distinguishing Abnormal Sexual Makeup From Bad Behaviors 21-5
Etiology 21-6
    Sexual Orientation and Affectional Interests 21-6
    Childhood Sexual Abuse 21-7
    Biological Abnormalities 21-7
Rationale for Treatment 21-8
Treatment Approaches 21-8
    Craving Disorder Defined 21-8
    Psychotherapy 21-9
    Behavior Therapy 21-9
    Surgery 21-10
    Medication 21-11
    Medication Plus Counseling 21-12
Concluding Comments 21-13
Editor's Note 21-14

INTRODUCTION

In the U.S. criminal justice system, all offenders are effectively treated as though they were the same. As a result, punitive sanctions are applied under the auspices that the offender will learn a lesson and consequently "straighten up." Only under highly unusual circumstances does the system question mental competency, and even then, most mentally disturbed or psychologically disadvantaged defendants are processed through the system as if they were fully intact. Clinical studies have shown that there is a high incidence of mental illness and cognitive deficits among criminal defendants and prison and jail inmates (Teplin, 1994; Krober et al., 1994). One distinctive group of offenders, albeit a minority, have sexual disorders and tend to repeat their crimes. This subgroup poses a particular problem for both the courts and correctional facilities.

Individuals who are sexually oriented towards children and are often diagnosed with pedophilia or a related disorder are the focus of this chapter. Child sexual abuse is a criminal offense and, as such, attracts the attention of the law and criminal justice system. The apprehension of these sexual offenders often leads to their conviction and incarceration. Unfortunately, there is absolutely nothing about being in prison that is going to either erase their attractions or heighten their capacity to successfully resist acting on unacceptable sexual feelings. Instead, a collaborative effort between the criminal justice system and the medical/scientific community should be established to deal with the myriad of issues raised by the criminal processing of offenders with mental disorders.

For practical purposes, the discussion in this chapter is set forth under four main headings, to highlight in a meaningful fashion the concepts presented. The premise for this chapter is that many individuals who commit a sex offense have a mental disorder, and thus the first part of the discussion involves how practitioners and physicians can medically assess and evaluate a sex offender. There are some people who are of sound mind who are simply misbehaving, and we need to attempt to distinguish them from people who have a legitimate psychiatric condition. Consequently, this concept of assessment becomes paramount in order to make these distinctions and prescribe appropriate remediations.

Second, the underlying etiology, or causes, of sexual offending must be better understood. This understanding applies to many of the sexual disorders, although the focus here is on pedophilia. Third, a rationale for treatment is presented. This is a critical issue in an area in which many people believe we are just talking about bad people misbehaving. In reality, there is substantial medical evidence that some sex offenders suffer from mental disorders, oftentimes with biomedical underpinnings. Thus, it is incumbent upon this chapter to make an argument as to why treatment is a valid and necessary response to sexual offending. Fourth, this chapter presents general treatment approaches for conditions such as pedophilia, not the entire spectrum of treatments that are available. If indeed we do begin to understand these disorders as mental conditions, how would we treat them both from the psychological perspective and from the biological perspective?

ASSESSMENT

Conceptually, people behave in various ways for various reasons. An evaluation of a sex offender is critical in identifying some of these reasons. An assessment is conducted to determine: (1) whether the individual suffers from a mental disorder, since there are plenty of sex offenders who certainly do not; and (2) if he does, whether it is one that represents an aberration of his sexual makeup. An example of someone who might commit a sex offense who does not have a psychiatric disorder would be the person who breaks into a home with the intention of stealing money, a television set or other items, finds a woman home alone, and decides to rape her. He is a sex offender by definition, but there is certainly no reason to assume that there is something abnormal about his mental makeup or his sexual makeup other than the fact that he may be lacking a sense of conscience and moral responsibility. His behavior could not be classified as a disease and may instead be an example of somebody misbehaving. There are many such examples of sex offenses that have nothing to do with a sexual disorder.

There is a subgroup of sex offenders who seem to be predisposed to misbehave sexually because there is something fundamentally different about their sexual make-up. The prevailing belief in this country, which is perpetrated by teachings we receive from early childhood, is that everyone is created equal. While everyone should be thought of as having equal moral worth and we should all have equality of opportunity, we are not all equal to the extent that equal means the same, and one of the ways in which we differ from one another is in our sexual makeup. Briefly, there are four ways in which individuals differ from one another sexually: sexually arousing behaviors, sexually attractive partners, intensity of the sex drive, and attitudes about our sexual make-up. Such differences help to explain how those ways account for what is referred to in the fourth edition of the *Diagnostic and Statistical Manual of Mental Disorders* (DSM-IV) as paraphilias or sexual deviation disorders.

People do not decide voluntarily what will arouse them sexually. Rather, in maturing, they discover the nature of their own sexual orientation and interests, which differ in several ways. Thus, the first way in which people differ regards the kinds of behaviors that they either do or do not find to be erotically arousing. The behavioral spectrum ranges dramatically from the conventional (missionary position) to the "deviant" (sado-masochism), as labeled by society-at-large. Second, people differ regarding the kind of partners toward whom they either are or are not attracted. The majority of the population is attracted primarily to adults of the opposite sex; however, many individuals do have homosexual attractions. Only a small percentage is desirous of children. These first two types of variation are qualitative by nature in that they can be classified by type rather than amount. Third, people differ in the degree of sexual drive that they experience. This difference involves an intensity dimension and is characterized by the extent to which their sex drive motivates their behavior and the degree of difficulty that they experience in trying to resist sexual temptations. Finally, although it does not involve the sex drive per se, people differ in their attitudes about their own sexual makeup, how they perceive themselves in terms of physical sexuality and attitudes towards their sexuality. Attitudes about whether such temptations *should* be resisted also vary from individual to individual.

Paraphilic Disorders Defined

When persons experience erotic desires to engage in types of sexual behaviors that could cause themselves or others harm, such as sadistic, coercive, or masochistic sexual involvements, psychiatric help may be needed. This may also be necessary when a person experiences strong erotic attractions towards unacceptable sexual partners, such as children, dead bodies, or animals. The primary definition of a *paraphilic* disorder according to psychiatric textboooks is the experience of intense, recurrent, erotically arousing fantasies and urges that are directed toward (1) nonhuman objects, (2) suffering or humiliation, or (3) children or other nonconsenting persons. *Transvestitic fetish-*

es, for example, is a condition in which people have intense cravings of an erotic nature to cross-dress in the clothing of the opposite gender. While any man is capable of attiring himself in female clothing, the average man will not experience intense, recurrent, erotically arousing fantasies and urges about behaving in that way. A second paraphilic disorder, *exhibitionism*, exemplifies the notion that people differ regarding the kinds of cravings they experience that lead them to behave in unusual ways. Again, the average man is certainly capable of exposing himself publicly, but it would be ludicrous to argue that the average man is afflicted with intense, recurrent, erotically arousing urges and fantasies about exposing himself. Yet in my clinical practice I have seen literally hundreds of men who have exposed themselves thousands of times in response to these abnormal sexual cravings. Again, these are only two examples of how people experience erotic cravings to behave in an unusual fashion.

The second way in which people differ pertains to the kinds of partners that they either do or do not crave sexually. A clear example of that, which is important for teaching purposes but not so much practically, is *zoophilia*, an abnormality in which people are intensely, sexually attracted to animals. For most of us, the last thing that we experience when thinking about or observing animals is a sense of erotic arousal. We most likely feel repulsed, disgusted, and a variety of other negative feelings at the thought of a sexual attraction to animals. The point is that, what for one person may be a very erotically attractive and appealing partner may for the other person be just the opposite, demonstrating just how different we can be from one another regarding the kinds of partners we either are or are not attracted to sexually.

The next example of how people differ regarding partners is *pedophilia*, and this is certainly an important issue not only from the psychiatric perspective, but also from a criminal justice perspective. As stated above, this condition occurs when people's sexual orientation is directed towards children. In the exclusive form of pedophilia, the individual is attracted only to children and not to adults at all. In the nonexclusive form of pedophilia, there is some attraction to adults, but that does not diminish their intense cravings for children as well.

Some psychiatric diagnoses can be made simply by asking cooperative persons about the range of behaviors they find to be erotically appealing and about the difficulty they experience in trying to resist succumbing to such sexual temptations. This line of questioning can identify the person who meets the DSM-IV diagnostic criteria for sexual exhibitionism, sexual sadism, sexual masochism, transvestism, and compulsive voyeurism. Each of these represents an unconventional form of sexual appetite. These men, unlike the average man, often experience great difficulty resisting erotic temptations to repeatedly expose themselves, to repeatedly have themselves beaten, or to repeatedly peep in windows, depending on the nature of their particular sexual compulsion.

In pedophilia specifically, a condition that seems to have been identified almost exclusively in men, some men report that they are attracted sexually to both children and adults, but that when they have a satisfying adult relationship they are sometimes better able to resist the temptation of becoming sexually intimate with a child. During periods of their lives when they do not have a satisfying adult relationship, they may be more at risk of becoming involved sexually with children. Groth (1979) refers to such men who find both adults and children to be erotically appealing as *regressed pedophiles*. There are other men who experience absolutely no erotic attraction whatsoever towards adults but who have a great deal of difficulty resisting the sexual temptations that they experience towards children. Groth refers to these men as *fixated pedophiles*. When the man is attracted sexually only to boys, a diagnosis of *homosexual pedophilia* can be made. As with other appetites and "addictions," the pedophilic appetite craves satiation, with recurrence of hunger an expected event.

Biologically Based Drives

From the perspective of biological research, the question arises as to why it is that those with the nonexclusive form of pedophilia do not simply resist unacceptable temtations when they seem to have a choice available to them. The inability to conform and resist temptation involves biologically based drives, which is fundamentally what fuels the sex drive. Thus, the sex drive is essentially an appetite, and appetites are characterized by varying tastes. For example, an individual may be able to finish a big turkey dinner and not desire any more, but may still have a difficult time resisting the temptation of dessert—that piece of strawberry shortcake. That is similar to the dilemma of the person who has the nonexclusive form of pedophilia. The fact that he is capable of being intimate with an adult doesn't erase the fact that he also has strong cravings of a sexual nature for children and that those cravings need to be dealt with in their own right. In essence, some people are predisposed to commit sexual offenses because there is something fundamentally and biologically different about their sexual makeup.

Distinguishing Abnormal Sexual Makeup From Bad Behaviors

In the performance of a thorough assessment of the sex offender, it is essential that behaviors exhibited in response to an abnormal sexual makeup are distinguished from behaviors that are a reflection of faulty conscience, character, personality, and conditioning. In other words, in assessing the integrity of the sex drive and the orientation of an individual, the diagnosis for the majority of individuals would be "heterosexuality," which would indicate that the individual is attracted to the opposite sex. And after a certain age, the individual has probably acted on those attractions. Such a diagnosis does not, however, indicate whether the individual is kind or cruel, caring or not caring, temperamental or not very temperamental—those characteristics must be examined separately from sexual behaviors and attractions.

This is a central point: that when considering issues that revolve around assessment of the paraphilias, one must recognize that it is not simply an issue of character, of somebody attempting to be in control, or of misusing power. Pedophilia, once again, involves an abnormality in sexual makeup. No matter what the social context or setting, a pedophile would think about a child and become sexually aroused, while a normal heterosexual would think about a member of the opposite sex and become aroused. The central issue is one of sexual desire, not about some abnormality of power or control.

The following is a brief verbatim quote from a man who does not want to be pedophilic but whose sexual orientation can be characterized as fixated and homosexual pedophilic.

What starts a person like myself doing what I do? Why me? Why can't I be normal like everybody else? You know, did God put this as a punishment or something towards me? I am ashamed. Why can't I just go out and have a good time with girls? I feel empty when a female is present. An older "gay" person would turn me off. I have thought about suicide. I think after this long period of time, I have actually seen where I have an illness. It is getting uncontrollable to the point where I can't put up with it anymore. It is a sickness. I know it's a sickness. But as far as society is concerned, you are a criminal and should be punished. Even if I go to jail for twelve or fifteen years, or whatever, I am still going to be the same when I get out.

ETIOLOGY

What is the cause of a disorder such as pedophilia? Three issues are addressed herein that help to elucidate various mechanisms in sexual disorders. The first pertains to what factors do *not* play a role in the onset of a pedophilia. From a traditional criminal justice perspective, sex offending is considered to be volitional; in other words, the criminal justice system most often treats sex offenders as if they made a conscious decision to be sexually deviant. In stark contrast to these views, however, scientific research and clinical experience convincingly show that no one makes a volitional decision about what partners will attract them. These are not conscious choices and decisions to be made. Moreover, scientific studies indicate that sexual orientation and disposition are related to biology and relatively stable, showing directional signs early in life (Bain, 1983; Buhrich et al., 1991; Collaer & Hines, 1995). As a result, individuals "discover" at some point early in puberty what their sexual proclivities are to be. Thus, the man who is attracted exclusively to little boys does not exhibit these tendencies because he was a bad child who weighed his options and decided to be different. Most definitely, no one in their right mind in our society would choose to grow up to be sexually attracted to children. Rather, people discover that they are afflicted with these aberrations of sexual makeup, and this is one of the saddest and most tragic of afflictions, not only for the individual himself, but for others in society as well.

Sexual Orientation and Affectional Interests

How is it then that sexual orientation and affectional interests are acquired? It appears that both life experience and constitution play a role. The role that environment can play was dramatically demonstrated by a tragic case report by Money (1980) in which one of two genetically identical male twins was so severely damaged at the time of circumcision several months after birth that a total penectomy was required. That child was then reared as a girl. The child's chromosomal pattern, obviously, remained unchanged, and she has now reached her teenage years. She has developed breasts by virtue of having been administered estrogens and surgically, an artificial vagina was created. According to Diamond (1982), however, she nevertheless experiences considerable difficulty in adjusting as a female, and she is in some ways ambivalent about her status. Still, at age 19, this twin raised as a female apparently feels herself to be a woman in terms of gender identity and also experiences some level of sexual attraction towards age-appropriate males. Thus, although she is a woman with an XY rather than an XX chromosomal pattern, as a consequence presumably of how she has been raised, she feels herself to be a woman and finds men to be sexually appealing.

Childhood Sexual Abuse

In terms of what contributes to paraphilias, the interaction between nature and nurture must once again be considered. There is clearly evidence that some individuals who are sexually abused or traumatized during childhood become warped in their subsequent sexual development in a way that predisposes them to experience abnormal sorts of sexual cravings (Groth, 1979; Money, 1980). Many men who experience pedophilic erotic urges as adults were sexually involved with adults when they were children. Thus, there is a subgroup of individuals with paraphilic disorders that is characterized by childhood sexual abuse. Although many children who experience abuse appear to be immune or resistant to that particular outcome, others are more susceptible and develop deviations in sexual development. In either event, in treating the pedophile, one is in point of fact often treating a former victim later on in life after the circumstances of his childhood, or the intricacies of his biological constitution, have produced their psychological sequelae.

Biological Abnormalities

On the other hand, biological conditions can also significantly contribute to the paraphilias. Once again, no one becomes interested in sex simply because they read a book and decided that it makes sense. The fact that we experience sexual desires in the first place is very much rooted in biology. Sexual behavior in humans is often a response to subjectively experienced erotic desires and fantasies. Although it appears that specific sexual tastes or preferences may sometimes be modified by virtue of early life experiences, the phenomenon of sexual desire itself is apparently unlearned and rooted in biology.

People who have paraphilic disorders, who are experiencing abnormal sexual cravings, have been compared to people who exhibit conventional sexual interests (Berlin, 1983b). In a significant majority of these patients, a total of sixty-three biological abnormalities were found. These included seven chromosomal anomalies (most frequently Klinefelter's syndrome, an abnormality of the XY chromosomes) as well as abnormalities of hormones related to human sexuality—for example, eighteen abnormal levels of testosterone, eight abnormal levels of follicle stimulating hormone (FSH), and fourteen abnormal levels of luteinizing hormone (LH). There were also seven abnormal CT scans of the brain, four pathological electroencephalograms (EEGs), and five abnormal neurological examinations. Berlin (1983b) concluded that there may indeed be an association between the presence of certain kinds of biological abnormalities and the presence of unconventional kinds of sexual interests such as pedophilia.

More recently, Gaffney and Berlin (1984) documented an abnormal pattern of LH release over time in response to the intravenous administration of LH releasing factor in a group of pedophilic patients. At the Johns Hopkins Hospital Sexual Disorders Clinic, it is unusual to see a man who experiences recurrent pedophilic cravings in the absence of: (1) significant biological abnormality, (2) a past history of sexual involvements with an adult during childhood, or (3) both. That does not imply that the cause of a paraphilic disorder such as pedophilia is due exclusively to biological abnormality any more than studies suggest that it is due exclusively to childhood abuse. Nevertheless, both of those factors, having been abused or having a biological abnormality, are risk factors that heighten the likelihood that someone will have such a disorder.

RATIONALE FOR TREATMENT

The rationale behind treatment for sexual disorders primarily lies in the goal to help patients control their own behavior, rather than relying strictly on external restraints. While some sex offenders may also require intensive supervision, approaches that work best act to increase self-control over otherwise compelling urges. And although this chapter concludes that the individual is not entirely responsible for developing the disorder of pedophilia, clearly it is his responsibility, and the responsibility of clinicians and the system, to seek ways to ameliorate or gain control over the condition. According to the underlying assumptions of the criminal justice system, willpower alone can conform our behavior to the appropriate standards. In the absence of such assumptions, we would have anarchy. Any criminal offender could enter the court and say, "I was overpowered, your Honor, by feelings of greed that were so intense I couldn't control myself. Get me to the Greed Clinic. I need treatment! I'm not really a criminal." Although this example is a bit facetious, the law does have to assume some degree of free will to promote accountability. For a physician or other practitioner, on the other hand, it can become obvious that a person's capacity for free will decision-making is not invariably intact, particularly with behaviors enacted in response to a powerful biological drive. Take overeating, for example—a problem with which millions of Americans suffer. Even after numerous, very expensive and time- consuming attempts to diet, many dieters fail to lose weight, in spite of the fact that for most people, all they have to do is eat less. And yet the hidden, unseen power of a biological drive can be so profound that in spite of their best efforts, many dieters are unable to resist temptations and repeatedly "relapse." The sexual appetite functions in quite similar ways, and those who suffer from sexual compulsions also need help. We have now recognized that as with other kinds of craving disorders (e.g., alcoholism, substance abuse, and compulsive gambling), it is not a person's fault that he or she suffers from the problem. It is that person's responsibility, however, to seek help, and one way to begin that process is with the person's admission of a lack of adequate self-control and a need for proper assistance.

TREATMENT APPROACHES

Craving Disorder Defined

The paraphilias are often considered to be craving disorders and as such, are best treated with modalities used for other similar compulsive disorders. Unlike other disorders, however, all too often a double standard is applied in dealing with compulsive paraphilic types of human sexuality. If a person states that he is trying his best to diet, to stop smoking, or to stop compulsive hand washing, he is often believed and helped. If, however, a person says he needs help in order to be able to resist the urge to have sex with children, his claim is often dismissed. Treatment approaches must take into account these frustrations and pervasive roadblocks.

What is meant by a craving disorder? When an individual needs help in order to be able to resist the urge to have sex with children, to expose himself publicly, or to engage in coercive sexual acts, his claim that he cannot control himself through willpower alone is indicative of a craving disorder. An analogy would be that the child may be perceived to the person with pedophilia in the same way that the bottle of alcohol is perceived to the alcoholic. There are many reasons why people drink, but the final common pathway is that they succumb to their cravings. In the process, they may permanently traumatize or even kill an innocent child and/or destroy their own life.

There are four major modalities proposed for treating the craving disorder of pedophilia, each of which is either psychological or medical in orientation: psychotherapy, behavior therapy, surgery, and medication.

Psychotherapy

Classical psychodynamic theory assumes that all men would ordinarily develop conventional erotic attractions towards age-appropriate partners of the opposite sex, but that this does not occur in some instances due to unhealthy early life experiences that interfere with the normal process of psychological maturation. Therapy uses the process of introspection to try to figure out what went wrong, with the expectation that newly acquired insights will then facilitate the problem being rectified. Unfortunately, it is doubtful that individuals can come to fully understand the basis of their own sexual interests through the process of introspection alone. The average man probably cannot figure out simply by thinking about it why he prefers women rather than men. Similarly, it is not certain that the pedophilic individual can figure out the basis of his own sexuality. Furthermore, even if he could, knowing why one is hungry—be it for food or for children—does not make one any less hungry, nor does it make it any easier for one to resist temptation. Finally, there is little convincing evidence showing that the traditional psychotherapies alone are an effective means for treating pedophilia.

One type of therapeutic approach that has been effective with craving disorders is group therapy. The patient confronts the denial and rationalization that are common with individuals who experience these intense cravings. Group therapy also provides a supportive atmosphere in which patients can speak openly about very private issues, and it allows discussions of establishing a change in lifestyle that will help them to better succeed in resisting unacceptable sexual temptations. In the particular case of pedophilia, group therapy enables the participants to establish an essential support system. Families may not be part of the problem, but they often act as part of the solution.

Behavior Therapy

Behavior therapists tend to be less concerned with the historical antecedents of pedophilia than with the question of what can be done about it. The feature common to most behavioral approaches is an attempt to extinguish erotic feelings associated with children, while simultaneously teaching an individual to become sexually aroused by formerly nonarousing age-appropriate partners. Although in laboratory settings behaviorists have shown that some pedophilic men no longer demonstrate physiological evidence of sexual arousal when looking at pictures of naked children, and that the men can begin to show arousal to age-appropriate stimuli, it has not been well-established that such changes invariably carry over into the non-laboratory situation (Marks, 1981). Most of us can appreciate how difficult it would be to try and stop feeling the sexual attractions we have experienced as natural throughout our lives. There is no reason to believe that it is any easier for the fixated homosexual pedophile to learn to lose his interest in boys and to become sexually aroused by women, than it would be for the average male to lose his interest in women and to instead begin lusting for young boys.

Another type of "behavior therapy" that has been tried is punishment, usually in the form of incarceration. Although society sometimes chooses to punish for reasons other than behavior modification, behavior modification is often one of the intended goals. There is, however, nothing about being in prison that can change the nature of a pedophile's sexual orientation or that can increase his ability to resist acting upon improper sexual temptations.

Surgery

While we do not know enough about the biology of pedophilia to change a fundamental sexual orientation, we do know a great deal about the intensity of the sex drive. Thus, the sexual hunger for children may be medically treatable by diminishing that hunger. Such a medical approach may not be a cure or guarantee, but would make it easier to resist unacceptable temptations. Testosterone is the "male" hormone that fuels the sexual drive. Lowering testosterone diminishes sexual cravings. Testosterone can be lowered either through removal of the testes, which is castration, or through various medications. There is currently evidence to indicate that the medical treatment of sex offenders results in lower rates of recidivism (see Berlin & Krout, 1986), in contrast to traditional treatment approaches.

Two types of surgery have been proposed as a treatment for pedophilia, stereotactic neurosurgery and removal of the testes. Neurosurgery for this purpose is still investigational and will not be discussed here. Its rationale has been explored in a review article by Freund (1980). Removal of the testes (castration) has been suggested as a treatment for pedophilia because the testes are the major source of testosterone production in the body. There has been much confusion about castration, a procedure that does not remove the penis, but instead removes the testes in order to lower testosterone.

As mentioned above, testosterone is an important hormone related to human sexuality and gender differences. If the testes of a male fail to produce adequate amounts during early embryonic life, he will be born with the external anatomical appearance of a female. Thus, testosterone causes external anatomical masculinization of the fetus, and also produces certain changes in the endocrinological functioning of the male brain (Wilson et al., 1981). The marked increase in testosterone production that occurs at the time of puberty in males is associated with the development of increased pubic and facial hair, deepening of the voice, an increase of muscle mass, and a marked increase in sexual libido. The idea of lowering testosterone in the case of the pedophile is to try to decrease the intensity of his sexual cravings, which are for children.

Some critics have argued that castrating the sex offender, which involves removal of the testes and not the penis, is like cutting off the hand of the thief. This is not an accurate analogy. Cutting off the penis, instead, would be analogous to cutting off the hand of the thief. A male animal whose penis has been surgically removed will still try to mount a female in heat, suggesting that the penectomized male is still sexually *motivated*, though unable sexually to perform. A castrated male, on the other hand, whose penis is intact can perform sexually but will ordinarily not attempt to mount a female in heat, suggesting that he is no longer *motivated* to do so.

In animals, lowering testosterone by means of removing the testes usually leads to a total cessation of virtually all sexually motivated behavior, although sometimes this may take as long as two years to occur (Freund, 1980). In humans, the relationship between very low testosterone levels and low sexual libido is also fairly well established. This evidence comes from a variety of sources including studies on hypogonadal men, data from persons with androgenital disorders, studies on drugs that lower testosterone as side effects, and from several well-controlled studies looking at the effects of administering testosterone in an attempt to increase sexual libido (Ellis, 1982; Kwan et al., 1983; Sturup, 1972; Carney et al., 1978).

In an article entitled "Therapeutic Sex Drive Reduction," Freund (1980) reviewed data regarding removal of the testes in humans as a means of trying to help some men gain better control over their sexual behavior. In one study in Denmark, Sturup (1972) reported upon a thirty-year investigation of 900 castrated sex offenders, many of whom were pedophiles, involving over 4,000 follow-up examinations. He documented less than a 3 percent recidivism rate. Others have reported comparable findings (Van Rossum, Kinmark & Oster, and Cornu—see Freund, 1980). The study by Van Rossum involved 237 men with a 1.3 percent recidivism rate. The study by Cornu found a 5.8 percent recidivism rate among 120 men following castration, with a 52 percent recidivism rate in the noncastrated control group. Follow-ups ranged from five to thirty years. Bremer (1959) reported a 58 percent recidivism rate in the five years prior to treatment in a group of men who showed only a 7.3 percent recidivism rate during the five years post-surgery. Thus, the surgical method of lowering testosterone did seem to enable many men to better control their sexual cravings. Furthermore, many of these men did not lose their capacity to perform sexually following castration.

Medication

Today it is no longer necessary to perform castration in order to reduce testosterone levels. This can now be accomplished pharmacologically in a graduated way without the physical or psychological trauma of surgery. In Europe and the Scandinavian countries, cyproterone acetate has been used for this purpose, and there are several "blind" as well as "non-blind" studies supporting its effectiveness (Laschet & Laschet, 1976; Money et al., 1976). In the United States, since Money first began this practice in 1967 for the treatment of pedophilia, the drug most often employed as a pharmacological method for lowering testosterone has been medroxyprogesterone acetate, or Depo-Provera (Money et al., 1976; Berlin & Meinecke, 1981; Berlin & Coyle, 1981; Berlin, 1981; Berlin & Schaerf, 1984).

Medroxyprogesterone acetate (MPA) can be injected intramuscularly once per week. There it binds to the muscle, from where it is then gradually released over the course of several days into the bloodstream. At this time, the initial starting dosage used in the Johns Hopkins Clinic has been 500mg IM (intramuscularly) once per week of the 100mg per cc concentration. No more than 250cc is given into a single injection site.

Major side effects of MPA have been weight gain and, in some cases, hypertension. Mild lethargy, cold sweats, nightmares, hot flashes, and muscle aches have also been reported. The drug, which is not feminizing, may cause an increased incidence of breast cancer in female beagle dogs and of uterine cancer in monkeys. It has been used in over eighty countries of the world as a female contraceptive, supported in its use for this purpose by the World Health Organization. No studies showing an increased risk of cancer in males (either humans or animals) have been reported. Two articles, one in *Science* (Sun, 1982) and the other in the *Journal of the American Medical Association* (Rosenfield et al., 1983), failed to find convincing evidence that MPA is carcinogenic in humans.

There is no doubt that MPA consistently decreases serum testosterone levels significantly. This can be confirmed by means of a simple blood test. The idea of using MPA in the case of the pedophile is to try to decrease the intensity of his sexual cravings, thereby making it easier for him to successfully resist unwanted temptations. The drug cannot change the nature of his sexual orientation.

The optimal MPA dosage has not yet been fully established, nor is it clear yet what the long-term side effects are. Also, it is not known which of the paraphilias will respond most adequately and what the precise long-term recidivism percentages will be. There is little reason to believe, however, that recidivism should be any higher than those low rates documented when surgical removal of the testes was used as a method of lowering testosterone. Of more than seventy men treated at the Johns Hopkins Clinic with MPA over a three-year period for some form of paraphilia (mostly pedophilia and exhibitionism), less than 10 percent have relapsed. In addition, compliance rates have been better than 90 percent.

There has also been some concern about whether MPA should be administered to pedophilic men who are on legal probation. In the author's opinion, if the drug is effective, as it often seems to be, then it is difficult to see why a person should be denied the opportunity to take it just because he is on probation or perhaps even incarcerated. Some incarcerated men report that MPA frees them from intrusive, obsessional sexual preoccupations.

MPA is not a cure. It is not a guarantee. It is not a punishment. Some pedophiles report being unable to successfully resist sexual temptations through willpower alone, even with the assistance of professional counseling. Such individuals should be afforded the opportunity to see whether or not MPA confers upon them an increased capacity for self control.

Medication Plus Counseling

Some critics argue that psychotropic drugs such as MPA may in some ways be "mind controlling." The legitimate medical indications for use of psychotropic drugs are (1) to decrease suffering (as in the case of antidepressants), (2) to restore function (as in the case of antipsychotic medications), or (3) to increase rather than decrease a person's capacity to successfully exercise self-control, which is the rationale for the use of MPA (Berlin, 1983b).

Most pedophiles receiving MPA also attend group counseling sessions. These are similar to the type often used with alcoholics. There, they are expected to acknowledge being tempted to do something improper. They then discuss among themselves strategies intended to help enable them to resist such temptations successfully. This includes discussions of whom to call, what early warning signs to look for, and what situations to avoid. The groups provide both peer pressure and peer support.

When a person desires sex or falls in love, it is often easy to become convinced that the relationship is good and healthy, and not harmful or wrong. Such self-deception may at times be easy for the pedophilic individual in light of the fact that sex with children, though wrong, may not in every instance be obviously damaging (Standfort, 1984). Some children may enjoy certain sexual and nonsexual aspects of their relationships with an adult, thus facilitating self-deception on the part of the adult. Treatment, therefore, may have to involve helping a person to stop rationalizing and to develop strategies for more successfully resisting sexual and affectional temptations.

CONCLUDING COMMENTS

To provide treatment to persons with pedophilic sexual orientations in no way reflects a lack of concern for children. One can treat children and treat pedophiles as well. These are not mutually exclusive choices. In counseling a child, it may help if that child understands that the pedophilic individual may genuinely have cared about him, even though that caring was expressed in an improper and unacceptable way. Preventive treatment cannot be completely accomplished without dealing with the pedophile himself. To the extent that treatment helps the pedophile gain better self-control, both his interests and society's interests are well served.

Although it is not the pedophile's fault that he has the sexual orientation that he has, it is his responsibility to deal with his sexuality in a manner that does not put innocent children at risk. However, in order for him to be able to accomplish this and to be held accountable by society, adequate treatment facilities must be made available; facilities where a person can seek help without fear of stigmatization, ridicule, retaliation, or unwarranted disdain. Only under such circumstances can one expect an individual to talk candidly about the innermost aspects of his own sexuality. This requires trust.

The values that we try to instill in our children are important. Almost two thousand years ago, as an outraged crowd attempted to stone to death a woman whose sexual behavior they considered offensive, one man stepped forward to stop the retribution, speaking against such revenge while espousing values such as compassion, understanding, forgiveness, and reformation. He asked that persons be judged not simply by their behavior, but with some appreciation for their humanity. Perhaps that message still goes unheeded today when it comes to the issue of how we deal with some of those who have sexual and affectional orientations of a sort that frighten us and that differ from our own. While their behavior must not be allowed to continue, an effective and compassionate response should include treatment.

Editor's Note

I have been familiar with Dr. Berlin and his work for fifteen years. His extensive clinical and research experiences with pedophiles have led him to become a leading expert on this disorder. In reading his literature and observing him in court with his patients, I have been struck with the impression of pedophiles not as homicidal maniacs, but as helpless, depressed, and often highly distressed individuals. Many of us think of someone who would sexually molest a child as necessarily violent and vicious. But the overwhelming majority of pedophiles are not violent and do not *intend* to harm their victims. Many are religious, family men whose behavior is a source of tremendous conflict and personal disgust; nevertheless, they have difficulty in controlling their sexual urges. Most likely, these are the reasons why Dr. Berlin argues convincingly for a humane and compassionate response to pedophiles who are badly in need of treatment—for their sake, and for our public safety. Conventional treatments of pedophiles, which pervasively include psychotherapy, punishment, and incarceration within the criminal justice system, have resulted in very high recidivism rates. In viewing sexual offending of this nature as a mental health issue, rather than strictly a criminal justice problem, it becomes important that we make available effective treatments to these offenders so that we can substantially reduce the incidence of child molestation by pedophiles.

References

American Psychiatric Association (1994). *Diagnostic and statistical manual of mental disorders* (4th ed.). Washington, DC: American Psychiatric Press.

Bain, J. (1983). Sexual development, maturation, and behavior. *Comprehensive Therapies, 9,* 21–31.

Berlin, F. S. (1981). Ethical use of antiandrogenic medications (letter). *American Journal of Psychiatry, 138,* 1515–1516.

Berlin, F. S. (1983a). Ethical use of psychiatric diagnosis. *Psychiatric Annals, 13,* 231–331.

Berlin, F. S. (1983b). Sex offenders: A biomedical perspective and a status report on biomedical treatment. In J. C. Greer & I. R. Stuart (Eds.), *The sexual aggressor: Current perspectives on treatment.* New York: Van Nostrand Reinhold.

Berlin, F. S. & Coyle, G. S. (1981). Sexual deviation syndromes (clinical conference). *Johns Hopkins Medical Journal, 149,* 119–125.

Berlin, F. S. & Krout, E. (1986). Pedophilia: Diagnostic concepts, treatment, and ethical considerations. *American Journal of Forensic Psychiatry, 7,* 13–30.

Berlin, F. S. & Meinecke C. F. (1981). Treatment of sex offenders with antiandrogenic medication: conceptualization, review of treatment modalities, and preliminary findings. *American Journal of Psychiatry, 138,* 601–607.

Berlin, F. S. & Schaerf, F. W. (1984). Laboratory assessment of the paraphilias and their treatment with antiandrogenic medication. In R. C. W. Hall & T. P. Beresford (Eds.), *A handbook of psychiatric diagnostic procedures.* New York: Spectrum.

Bremer, J. (1959). *Asexualization: A follow-up study of 244 cases.* New York: Macmillan.

Buhrich, N., Bailey, J. M. & Martin, N. G. (1991). Sexual orientation, sexual identity, and sex-dimorphic behaviors in male twins. *Behavioral Genetics, 21,* 75–96.

Carney, A., Bancroft, J. & Matthews, A. (1978). A combination of hormonal and psychological treatment for female sexual unresponsiveness: A comparative study. *British Journal of Psychiatry, 132,* 339–346.

Collaer, M. L. & Hines, M. (1995). Human behavioral sex differences: a role for gonadal hormones during early development? *Psychological Bulletin, 118,* 55–107.

Diamond, M. (1982). Sexual identity: Monozygotic twins reared in discordant sex roles and a BBC followup. *Archives of Sexual Behavior, 11,* 181–186.

Ellis, L. (1982). Developmental androgen fluctuations and the five dimensions of mammalian sex. *Ethology and Sociobiology, 3,* 171–197.

Freund, K. (1980). Therapeutic sex drive reduction. *Acta Psychiatria Scandinavia, 287,* 1–39.

Gaffney, G. R. & Berlin, F. S. (1984). Is there hypothalamic-pituitary-gonadal dysfunction in paedophilia? A pilot study. *British Journal of Psychiatry, 145,* 657–660.

Groth, A. N. (1979). Sexual trauma in the life histories of rapists and child molesters. *Victimology: An International Journal, 4,* 10–16.

Krober, H. L., Scheurer, H. & Sass, H. (1994). Cerebral dysfunction, neurologic symptoms and recurrent delinquency— I. Review of the literature. *Fortschritte der Neurologie Psychiatrie, 62,* 169–178.

Kwan, M., Greenleaf, W. J., Mann, J., Crapo, L. & Davidson, J. M. (1983). The nature of androgen action on male sexuality: A combined laboratory-self report study on hypogonadal man. *Journal of Clinical Endocrinology and Metabolism, 57,* 557–562.

Laschet, V. & Laschet, L. (1976). Antiandrogens in the treatment of sexual deviation in men. *Journal of Steroid Biochemistry, 16,* 821–826.

Marks, I. M. (1981). Review of behavioral psychotherapy, II: Sexual disorders. *American Journal of Psychiatry, 138,* 750–756.

Money, J. (1980). *Love and love sickness.* Baltimore, MD: Johns Hopkins University Press.

Money, J., Wideling, A. Walker, P. S. & Gain, D. (1976). Combined antiandrogenic and counseling program for treatment of 46 XY and 47 XYY sex offenders. In E. J. Sachar (Ed.), *Hormones, behavior and psychopathology.* New York: Raven Press.

Rosenfield, A., Marne, D., Rochat, R., Shelton, J. & Hatcher, R. A. (1983). The Food and Drug Administration and medroxyprogesterone acetate: What are the issues? *Journal of the American Medical Association, 249,* 2922–2928.

Standfort, T. G. M. (1984). Sex in pedophilic relationships: An empirical investigation among a non-representative group of boys. *Journal of Sexuality Research, 20,* 123–142.

Sturup, G. K. (1972). Castration: The total treatment. In H. P. L. Resnick & M. E. Wolfgang, (Eds.), *Sexual behaviors: Social, clinical, and legal aspects.* Boston: Little, Brown.

Sun, M. (1982). Depo-Provera debate revs up at FDA. *Science, 217,* 424–428.

Teplin, L. A. (1994). Psychiatric and substance abuse disorders among male urban jail detainees. *American Journal of Public Health, 84,* 290–293.

Wilson, J. D., George, F. W. & Griffin, J. E. (1981). The hormonal control of sexual development. *Science, 211,* 1278–1284.

Part 8

Application of the Behavioral Sciences to the Law and Criminal Justice System

Based largely on technological advances in brain imaging and neurochemistry, the knowledge explosion in the neurosciences of the past three decades has yielded major changes in the fundamental paradigms in neuropsychiatry and in scientific psychology. Because of customary paradigm lags between disciplines and even across subspecialties in the same discipline, such massive paradigm shifts have been slow to radiate outward toward adjacent disciplines in the social sciences in general and toward criminology in particular. Although a "biological brain-proneness" toward violence is now widely accepted by neuroscientists, that proposition is still greeted with skepticism among criminologists. In some measure, the communications gap is maintained both by suspicion toward animal models on the part of social scientists and by the failure of neuroscientists to articulate the character of analogic reasoning across species.

To support the proposition that criminology needs to broaden its conceptual bases to include data from the neurosciences, in Chapter 22 Drs. Pallone and Hennessy review various studies over a period of nearly forty years with an aggregate of nearly 2,000 offenders. Collectively, these studies suggest a relative incidence of neuropathology among violent offenders many times in excess of that found in the general population, at ratios ranging from a high of 31:1 in the case of homicide offenders, to 21:1 among "habitual aggressive" offenders, to a low of 4:1 in the case of "one-time aggressives." The authors propose that although such discrepancies do not confirm neuropathology as univariately causative of criminal aggression, neither is it reasonable to believe that they are simple artifacts of chance.

In Chapter 23, Judge Nygaard conveys that for the last seventeen years, he has wrestled with philosophical issues involving criminal behavior, sentencing and punishment, seeking to find something rational in what he was doing with respect to criminal offenders and crime. As a new judge in 1981, he felt that in sending offenders to prison, he was simply shoveling sand against the tide. Then the prison population stood at 283,000; now it stands at 1.5 million+—and he still feels this way. The American criminal justice system[1] seems to have profited little from the philosophical debate about the efficacy of penal methods that has tensed and eased over the centuries. Scholars have mused over the repressive, nondeterministic Hobbsian model at the one end,[2] to the somewhat more centrist theories of Cesarre di Beccaria, Jeremy Bentham and Samuel Romilly,[3] then to the deterministic/rehabilitative Ferrian view on the other end.[4] Without much regard for the merits of the various theories and penal justifications, we Americans maintain essentially a nondeterminist, social world view and penal model. This leaves most persons behaviorally on their own and fully responsible for their actions. Offenses against the law, whatever the actual reasons and causes, are generally viewed as the result of moral flaws and lapses, to which we respond by punishing the offender by our limited form of banishment—prison. The durability of this penal model in American culture results, however, from the ease with which it is explained to the governed and executed by the government—not from its success in countering crime.

The criminal justice system also has profited little from the social, biological, and medical sciences. Within the past decade research in these sciences increasingly points toward genetic, neurological, neurobiological, toxicological, environmental, and traumatic factors as playing significant roles in aberrant behavior. Moreover, the research is also leading us toward help from suitable psychological and pharmacological therapies to intervene between some factors and their potentially disruptive results, but only if we choose to follow. Little of this, unfortunately, has found its way into either the "correction" that is supposed to take place when an offender's crime places him within the state's control or the dialogue of legislators and jurists who must decide the remedial measures to be imposed on offenders. Perhaps it is with penology and prison, as Pascal says about life, "Being unable to cure death, wretchedness and ignorance, men have decided, in order to be happy, not to think about such things."[5] And so, we think but little about our equation of crime = punishment = prison. It simply is a facile and politically acceptable response to the common and base emotions of revulsion and anger that we feel towards the misbehavior of others. This attitude and response, however, leaves us well to the lee of behavioral reality.

Judge Nygaard is convinced that we must develop a better theory than this simplistic, reactive equation, now so thoroughly engrafted upon our penology, politics, and popular culture. He asserts in his chapter that the failures of this equation to deter or prevent crime, or to correct the offenders who commit crimes, require that we take a wholly different approach and embrace a new theory. This new theory must not simply provide society with a medium to express a vengeful response to offending behavior. He fully recognizes that anger is a natural and expected reaction by a fearful public, because fear is a natural predicate of anger. Moreover, it is natural for victims of crimes to be angry. As such, punishment may be necessary both to denounce the act and as a component of correction. A complete penology, however, must do more. It must first and foremost focus on discovering the reasons for offending acts, whatever they are, and on providing pragmatic remedies, whatever they may be. He looks to therapeutic justice to help us meet these requirements.

In Chapter 24, Stephen Dinwiddie discusses how research over the last three decades has firmly established the role of biologically transmissible, presumably genetic factors in the genesis of antisocial behavior. This realization, however, has been slow to spread to the social sciences, and even slower to influence legal theory. While this delay in acceptance has hampered the development of more sophisticated conceptualizations of criminality that might integrate findings from the biological and social sciences, uncritical application of recent advances in behavioral genetics to specific legal issues also has its dangers. It risks commission of the same conceptual errors that have undermined the credibility of psychiatric testimony in the past. In particular, the expert must take care to avoid the conceptual error of attempting to use such scientific advances to address issues that are primarily moral rather than scientific in nature.

Endnotes

[1] The judge hesitates to use the word "system" even loosely, but for want of another, he occasionally uses it anyway. He does not believe, however, that we really have "a" criminal justice system. Instead, we have a confusing patchwork of individual functions, most operating separately; some not coordinating, or even cooperating; or worse, some even competing with coordinate components thereof. Criminal justice in America is like a perversely designed jigsaw puzzle, no two pieces of which fit precisely together, that forms a recognizable image nonetheless.

[2] The determinist says simply that what will be, will be; one's behavior is shaped entirely by non-willed events or by God. The indeterminist believes there is room for some autonomy. The nondeterminist says all events are a consequence of an exercise of free will.

[3] See generally Phillipson and Coleman, *Three Criminal Law Reformers: Beccaria, Bentham, Romilly*. Montclair, NJ: Patterson Smith, 1970.

[4] Kittrie, N. *The Right to Be Different: Deviance and Enforced Therapy*, 29 (1971); cited in Wexler, D., "Therapeutic Justice," 57 *Minn. L.R.* 289 (1972). Enrico Ferri believed that criminal responsibility and moral guilt should be wholly abolished.

[5] Pascal, Blaise (1941). *Pensées* (tr. F. W. Potter). New York: Random House, p. 60.

Chapter 22

Indifferent Communication Between Social Science and Neuroscience—The Case of "Biological Brain-Proneness" for Criminal Aggression

by Nathaniel J. Pallone, Ph.D. and James J. Hennessy, Ph.D.

Introduction 22-1
Knowledge Explosion in the Neurosciences 22-2
    Biological Brain-Proneness to Violence, Meet the Skeptics 22-3
    False Positives, While Big Brother Watches 22-3
Animal Models and Analogical Reasoning 22-4
    ICD-9 and Frontal Lobe Syndrome 22-5
    Brain Damage Among Peaceable Rats 22-5
Correlated Variables: But Which Governs Which? 22-6
    Nonaccidental Correlates 22-7
    Neuropathology—An Important Contributor to Criminal Aggression .. 22-9
Conceptual and Clinical Cross-Fertilization 22-10
    Benefits to the Social Sciences 22-10
    Bridging the Gap 22-11

INTRODUCTION

It is an unexceptionable proposition that paradigm shifts within any single discipline radiate outward toward (as well as inward from) adjacent disciplines rather slowly, at least as those disciplines are represented in the academy and in the trappings of academic structure (scholarly organizations, journals, and the like grounded in each discipline rather than bridging disciplines). Hence, we have come to expect a palpable

---

An earlier, nontechnical version of this chapter appeared in *Society*, 1998, vol. 35, 21–27.

"paradigm lag" between analytic models of behavior anchored in contemporary scientific psychology (or sociology, anthropology, or criminology) and those anchored in the other behavioral or social science disciplines; what remains less clear is the typical duration of such a paradigm lag and its implications for interdisciplinary communication and conceptual cross-fertilization (Pallone & Hennessy, 1995). Quite in contrast, however, as Horowitz (1993) argues in *The Decomposition of Sociology,* the behavioral and social science disciplines, as they are incarnated (or "applied") in the "real world," can ill afford to tolerate indifferent communication among and between themselves if they are to resolve and clarify pressing problems and issues via a concerted effort. Society has a right to expect that these relevant disciplines will play a role in this effort.

KNOWLEDGE EXPLOSION IN THE NEUROSCIENCES

At one end of its spectrum, the focal concerns and methods of inquiry in scientific psychology converge with those of the biological sciences; at the other end, they converge with those of the social sciences. In scientific psychology, an essentially unexceptionable proposition has long held that *all behavior results from the interactive effects of bio-psycho-social engines.* Implicitly, that proposition asserts that in any "unit" of behavior (whether that unit be inflected as cognitive, emotional, physiological, antisocial, or any other such denominator), there are discernible biological, psychological, and social components and antecedents.

The monumental knowledge explosion in the neurosciences in the past three decades has been enabled by massive technological advances that have yielded an alphabet soup of techniques (from BEAM, for brain electrical activity mapping, through the familiar electroencephalogram, or EEG, to SQUID, for superconducting quantum interference device) for studying "events" as they occur in the brain and central nervous system. From hospital patients with disordered neurology that has been medically documented (and is being medically treated) to human or animal laboratory subjects with apparently normal neurology, an explicit corollary assigns primacy in the biological components of behavior to the functioning of the brain and the central nervous system.

According to distinguished neuropsychiatrist Joseph Coyle (1988) of Harvard, the "nearly logarithmic growth in neuroscience research" since the 1960s has yielded a major paradigm shift, producing in the process "new methods for diagnosing psychiatric disorders, clarifying their pathophysiology, and developing more specific and effective therapies." As the eminent Dutch neuropsychiatrist Herman van Praag (1988) put it, the net effect has been to reunite psychiatry and scientific psychology with biology as their governing discipline. In what may prove something of an omen, the department of psychology at Baylor University has recently rechristened itself by adding the phrase "and neurosciences" to its title, and as of this writing, the counterpart department at an eastern university that is a decade older than the republic itself seems bent on rendering itself asunder into, respectively, a department of psychology and a department of behavioral neuroscience.

It is a fair assessment that many social scientists (as indeed even some within the disciplines of psychiatry and psychology) have displayed little warmth toward the wealth of knowledge newly generated by these behavioral sciences. Instead, there lingers an attitude of suspicion toward the application of knowledge from the neurosciences to conceptual models for human behavior, as if that body of exploding knowledge amounted to no more than Lombroso or Kretschmer revisited on their worst days. In some subdisciplines in the social sciences, indifferent communication with the neurosciences yields little more than curiously isolated and compartmentalized knowledge that grows increasingly irrelevant to "real world" issues. For example, some sociology departments include a section on the relevance of biology to human behavior, but this information is not incorporated into their paradigms, nor are biological factors viewed as significant players. Criminology has over the recent past broadened its conceptual foundations, which once rested virtually exclusively in sociology. Walters (1992), Raine (1993), Jeffrey (1990), Hillbrand & Pallone (1994), Volavka (1995) and the present writers (1992, 1993, 1996) have urged that the time is ripe for criminology to broaden its foundations once again to incorporate the burgeoning body of knowledge about both normal and deviant behavior emanating from the neurosciences.

Biological Brain-Proneness to Violence, Meet the Skeptics

Nowhere are the impediments to effective interdisciplinary communication and the consequent barriers to effectively marshaling the aggregate resources of the behavioral and social sciences in the service of real world issues more evident than in the analysis of human aggression. In particular, impediments are most noteworthy in the study of aggressive behaviors that are eventually labeled as formally criminal, whether by an international tribunal or the more customary local venues of criminal jurisdiction.

A report by *Scientific American* staff writer Wayt Gibbs (1995) summarizes the state of the matter from the perspective of the neuroscience community relatively accurately. Stuart Yudofsky, an exceptionally well-known neuropsychiatrist who is the senior editor of the American Psychiatric Association's semi-official *Textbook of Neuropsychiatry* and editor of the *Journal of Neuropsychiatry and Clinical Neurosciences,* is quoted as predicting that within the near term, "we're going to be able to diagnose many people who are biologically brain-prone to violence," creating conditions that yield "the opportunity to prevent tragedies" by screening "people at high risk" for aggressive criminal offending. In Gibbs's account, responses to Yudofsky's assessment vary widely among social scientists. They range from skepticism that the state of the neurosciences is nearly so advanced as to permit the identification of brain-proneness to violence—one surmises, whether by SQUID, squiggle, squirm, or some other new-fangled technology—to disdain predicated on what appears to be a far greater (and in some ways commendable) humanistic concern for the false positive than for the false negative.

False Positives, While Big Brother Watches

To paraphrase John Monahan's (1981) classic formulation, the modal response among social scientists seems to attest to a greater concern for one person's right not to be falsely identified as a prospective aggressor than for another person's right to be accurately identified as a prospective victim of aggression. In its turn, that concern seems to pivot on the conviction that unless watchfully supervised, the pill-pushers, the neurosurgeons, and their acolytes and lackeys (i.e., the behavior therapists) will inevitably wind up doing all sorts of contemptible things to folk who have the right to be left alone, like prescribing Prozac or ordering up brain transplants at the drop of a hat and for the wrong people.

ANIMAL MODELS AND ANALOGICAL REASONING

Derision or dismissal are not unusual responses to that which is little understood. What they reveal in the present case may be imprecise communication, not so much about substance, as about the *methods of inquiry* and *conceptual processing* of data on the basis of which substantive findings are pronounced.

A major impediment to communication between the neurosciences and the social sciences is neuroscience's reliance on evidence from laboratory studies of infra-human species. Social scientists complain, cogently, that the brains and central nervous systems of rats, cats, pigeons, planaria, or what-have-you are substantially simpler than those of humans in fundamental anatomical and physiological terms and that, therefore, "evidence" derived from studies on such species is hardly applicable to humans. Indeed, so far are they from a willingness to attend to inter-species data that Gottfredson & Hirschi (1994) have famously dismissed what they term "laboratory aggression" studies with human subjects as largely irrelevant to the illumination of real-time issues of criminal behavior.

For their part, neurobehavioral researchers are too often content merely to note that research on infra-human species (at least until adoption of the Federal Animal Welfare Act a dozen years ago) permits the experimental induction in the laboratory (and by means of protocols that are simply unthinkable with human subjects) of dysfunctions that are encountered among humans only as the result of massive injury to the brain and/or central nervous system. Too often neuroscience fails to acknowledge that its mode of reasoning when processing evidence from animal studies is essentially *analogical*. The process whereby evidence from animal models comes to be applied to human behavior may start with clinical observation by medical personnel of behavioral anomalies among patients with verifiable and documentable neurological dysfunction, typically as a result of injury (and such injury may well result from criminal violence). Next, in order to isolate those consequences, it is necessary that the behavior of the neurologically disordered be compared and contrasted with that of healthy human subjects. Finally, analogous neurological dysfunctions may be deliberately induced in infra-human subjects to determine whether analogously similar behavioral anomalies arise. If they do, then analogically at least, the neurosciences feel justified in characterizing such dysfunctions as "consequences" and not merely as "correlates."

Hence, the evidence we find most persuasive is that which (1) remains congruent between clinical and laboratory observations within the human species *and* (2) simultaneously congruent *across species*. Put somewhat differently:

- If the clinical observations of neurologists and neuropsychiatrists say that behavior A is related to neurological condition B,
- And if empirical data from human studies seem to corroborate that association in a wide array of subjects (thus seeming to control for the selective perception endemic to clinical observation),

- And if broad-gauged research in comparative behavioral psychobiology yields the finding that a behavior *analogous* to A on the part of laboratory animals is associated with neurological condition B in those animals,
- And if there is evidence of essentially similar neurodevelopment across species, then
- How much skepticism is it reasonable to maintain about an association between A and B that may be constant even *across* species?

ICD-9 and Frontal Lobe Syndrome

Consider the evidence that links damage or dysfunction in the frontal lobes of the brain to impulsive aggression both among humans and in laboratory animals. The frontal lobes in the human brain are generally held to be the seat of such mental functions as cognition, memory, abstraction, concentration, and judgment. Both clinical and empirical evidence linking impulsive violence to frontal lobe dysfunction (whether as the result of injury or of congenital anomaly) among humans is sufficient to warrant the inclusion of "frontal lobe syndrome" as a distinct organic mental disorder in the ninth edition of the World Health Organization's *International Classification of Diseases* (ICD-9).

At least when engendered by an identifiable injury to the brain (so that baseline data can be inspected for purposes of contrast), the principal manifestations of frontal lobe syndrome include impairment in self-control, foresight, creativity, and spontaneity, behaviorally observable "as increased irritability, selfishness, restlessness, and lack of concern for others," and most important, including "a change toward impulsiveness, boastfulness, temper outbursts," even in the absence of "measurable deterioration of intellect or memory." Such a litany is similar to the antecedents to criminal aggression, and many social scientists will recognize in that litany precisely those characteristics that have been held, at least since Cleckley described the "mask of sanity" half a century ago, to be the distinguishing attributes of persons labeled as psychopathically deviant. In consonance with the ICD description, many neuropsychiatrists and neuropsychologists attribute human aggressiveness to dysfunction in the frontal lobes of the brain as a principal cause.

Brain Damage Among Peaceable Rats

Now let's consider some evidence from infra-human species, among whom we do not expect to encounter mental operations that can be characterized as foresight, creativity, cognition, or abstraction. What can the experimental induction of a condition analogous to frontal lobe syndrome in such species reveal or confirm, even by analogy, about human behavior?

The naturally occurring rate of generational maturation in such laboratory species as the white rat, coupled with the wide availability and relatively low cost of videotape equipment, enables animal experimenters to record virtually every moment in the life of a laboratory animal, including the animal's learning history (or, if one insists on anthropomorphism, "pattern of socialization" to reinforcers and contingency conditions of various sorts) from birth onward (or at least until the point of an experimental intervention)—a set of conditions under which the usual academic debate about "nature versus nurture" essentially evaporates. Rather, it is possible to specify with high precision those conditions under which a laboratory animal has been trained or "nurtured" (e.g., to behave either aggressively or peaceably in response to intrusion or attack by another animal). The very character of the laboratory itself enables the investigator to "target" dysfunction in ways that are simply not possible in research on human subjects. Under these conditions, we can determine what happens when we deliberately damage the frontal lobes of the brain in laboratory rats who have been reared to respond peaceably or aggressively.

So, in the classic design, we acquire two hundred laboratory rats from a breeding farm that specializes in robust animals with good memories. We separate the animals randomly into two groups of one hundred each and condition one group to behave peaceably toward intruders, and the other to behave aggressively. We videotape every moment in their lives, a practice that obviates suspicions about "covert" counter-conditioning not in accordance with the formal research protocols. Next, we acquire a surgical instrument that resembles a long, ugly hat pin. With that instrument, we deliberately damage the frontal lobes in half of the peaceably raised and half the aggressively raised rats. We now have

1. Fifty brain-damaged, peaceably nurtured rats,
2. Fifty brain-damaged, aggressively nurtured rats,
3. Fifty peaceably nurtured rats with intact brains, and
4. Fifty aggressively nurtured rats with intact brains.

Now the experiment begins. We introduce another rat into each cage, and this is what happens, according to distinguished neuropsychopharmacologists Robert Feldman and Linda Quenzer (1984): The behavioral consequences of deliberately induced frontal lobe damage are uniform, whether the animals thus damaged have been "socialized" to respond aggressively or nonaggressively to intrusion or attack. Not only do the deliberately brain-damaged animals, regardless of whether they were nurtured peaceably or aggressively, respond with vicious lethal aggression (and seemingly to a greater degree than animals with intact brains who had been nurtured aggressively) when another animal "intrudes" into the experimental space, but they respond with a particularly virulent form of violence, so that "the topography of the killing is different in that . . . [animals] with frontal lobe lesions are particularly vicious and ferocious, biting the [victim] again and again even though the victim is dead (p.248).

There seems to be only a short *analogical* step between that description and a scene-of-the-crime report in a case of sadistic murder with mutilation. It is hardly surprising, then, that Feldman and Quenzer conclude that "each form of aggression has a particular anatomical and endocrine basis" (p.252). Nor is there, in the situation just described, much tolerance for the customary chicken-and-egg discussion about what preceded what or which is the "causative" and which the "resultant" variable.

CORRELATED VARIABLES: BUT WHICH GOVERNS WHICH?

So much for brain-damaged rats, who may behave in very nasty ways but will surely never be convicted of unwarranted, willful aggression. What of human beings?

Clearly (save for that emanating from Germany during the Nazi era or from Russia during the Stalinist era), there is no experimental evidence issuing from laboratory studies in which brain damage in humans has been deliberately induced. Instead, the relevant empirical evidence derives from studies of the incidence of neuropathology among offenders who have been convicted of violent and aggressive crimes. With the exception of a relative handful of Scandinavian studies that have yielded longitudinal data on aggressive behavior in relation to preexisting, medically documented neuropathology (typically, among veterans of the armed services who had sustained brain trauma as young men), indices both of offending and of neuropathology have been gathered *ex post facto*—after the offender has been convicted, and typically after he or she has also been incarcerated.

Nonaccidental Correlates

Such data may at best reveal association or correlation but cannot reveal causation, an issue of perhaps greater concern to social science than to neuroscience. But such relationships as are revealed via correlation should not on that account alone be regarded as merely "accidental." In the familiar example, height and weight are highly correlated, and each is also highly correlated with age (most twenty-one-year-olds are taller and weigh more than most seven-year-olds). While it is clear that height does not "cause" weight, nor does weight cause height, biological scientists (including neuroscientists) typically have less difficulty in labeling "age" a *governing variable*, which, it is not unreasonable to assume, affects both height and weight.

In connection with our work on the conceptual model for human criminal aggression, which we have termed the "tinder-box" (Pallone & Hennessy, 1992, 1993, 1996), we have collated studies of adjudicated offenders reported in the past four decades that permit the nearly precise calculation of the relative incidence (in terms of percentage of cases examined) of neuropathology, whether gauged directly through neurological measures (from the EEG to more advanced brain imaging techniques) or indirectly through neuropsychological measures such as the Luria-Nebraska or the Reitan protocols, now widely accepted as indices of the psychological (primarily cognitive) consequences to neurological dysfunction (Reitan & Wolfson, 1992). We have amalgamated the data from these studies in Table 22.1, which also includes a rather liberal estimate of the relative incidence of neuropathology in the general population and further reports the relative incidence of neuropathology found among victims of child abuse. Virtually by way of footnote, we might stress that the quite generous estimate of the prevalence of neuropathology in the general population we cite (3 percent) includes cases of subclinical severity, or what in the nomenclature of toxicology might be labeled a level of severity "with no observable permanently adverse effects." Many neurologists would argue in a more conservative vein that when such cases are set aside, the prevalence of neuropathology in the general population that rises to the level of clinical severity would not exceed one percent (cf. Hales & Yudofsky, 1987, pp. 179–180; Brown et al., 1994).

In all, nineteen offender groups are represented in Table 22.1, with an aggregate number of subjects approximating 2,000. N varies widely between studies, from a low of 15 (DeWolfe & Ryan, 1984) to a high of 623 (Geiger, 1960), with only an imprecise relationship between number of subjects and such factors as the cost and ease of

Table 22.1
Forty Years of Research Links Brain Dysfunction and Criminal Violence—Relative Incidence of Neuropathology (in % of Cases) Inventoried by Neurological and/or Neuropsychological Measures Among Aggressive Offenders, Juvenile Offenders, Victims of Child Abuse, and in the General Population

Offender Group	Citation (First author, year of publication)	N	Incidence	Relative Ratio (in relation to estimated prevalence in general population
Homicide offenders	Yeudall, 1979	33	94%	47:1
Sex offenders	Galski, 1990	35	77%	39:1
Sex offenders	Yeudall, 1979	24	96%	48:1
Sexual aggressives	Langevin, 1995	41	67%	34:1
Rapists	DeWolfe, 1984	15	86%	43:1
Rapists	Yeudall, 1987	[75]*	77%	39:1
Incest offenders	Langevin, 1995	75	65%	33:1
Incest offenders	Langevin, 1988	91	24%	12:1
Repetitive pedophiles	Pallone, 1998	54	33%	17:1
Assault offenders	Yeudall, 1987	[75]*	77%	39:1
Assault offenders	Yeudall, 1979	37	89%	45:1
Habitual aggressives	Volavka, 1991	180	64%	32:1
Habitual aggressives	Williams, 1969	206	65%	33:1
Persistent violent offenders	Bach-y-Rita, 1971	139	50%	25:1
One-time aggressives	Volavka, 1991	153	12%	6:1
One-time aggressives	Yeudall, 1987	[75]*	25%	12:1
One-time aggressives	Williams, 1969	68	12%	6:1
Juvenile offenders	Yeudall, 1979	99	86%	43:1
Juvenile offenders	Geiger, 1960	623	74%	37:1
Comparative Data				
Victims of child abuse	Ito, 1993		54%	27:1
CDC data on prevalence in the general population	Marino, 1999		2%	1:1

* N in the 1987 study by Yeudall et al. aggregates to 75 across the offender groups represented.
Adapted [and extended] from Pallone & Hennessy, *Tinder-Box Criminal Aggression: Neuropsychology, Demography, Phenomenology.* New Brunswick, NJ: Transaction Books, 1996, pp. 57–62.

administration of the measure of neuropathology used—for example, EEG readings versus CT (computerized tomography), CAT (computerized axial tomography), or PET (positron emission tomography) scan, versus such a familiar psychometric marker toward probable neuropathology as a discrepancy between aggregate Performance and Verbal scores on the Wechsler instruments in excess of two standard errors.

In the main, the prototypical sort of neuropathology uncovered among aggressive offenders can be subsumed under the ICD category for frontal lobe syndrome. Neuropathology is found in very high incidence among those offenders who have committed the most serious of aggressive offenses and among those whose offense histories reveal persistently aggressive patterns. At the extremes, the relative incidence of neuropathology among the homicide offenders in a 1979 report by Yeudall and Fromm (94 percent) exceeds the estimated incidence in the general population (3 percent) at a ratio of nearly 47:1—or, phrased differently, *the incidence of neuropathology among the murderers studied in that investigation exceeds the estimated incidence in the general population by 4700 percent.* Among the habitually aggressive offenders studied by Williams (1969) and by Volavka (1991), the mean incidence of neuropathology exceeds that in the general population by some 3200 percent. Statistical purists may wish to calculate with precision the significance of the difference between such proportions. But the data speak rather loudly for themselves—and argue rather forcefully that the relationship between neuropathology and aggressive criminal offending can hardly be dismissed.

In contrast to other offender groups, the relative incidence (at 6:1) is markedly lower among the one-time aggressives studied by Williams (1969) and by Volavka (1991). One might construe the criminal behavior of these offenders as a function of what Megargee (1966) has termed "over-controlled hostility," a designation that distinguishes persistent patterns of aggressive behavior from what may be regarded as isolated episodes of stimulus-triggered explosiveness. Yet even an incidence of 12 percent exceeds, in relative terms, the incidence estimated in the general population by 600 percent, so that one might even be led to speculate about a linkage between neuropathology and over-controlled hostility.

Let's place such ratios within a different context. Suppose our colleagues in the field of alcoholism were to produce convincing evidence that the incidence of alcohol abuse among young adults whose paternal grandfathers, say, repeatedly lost their jobs as a result of excessive absenteeism lubricated by alcohol use is reliably found to be four times as great as its incidence in the general population. Doubtless there would follow massive public health campaigns seeking to inform the public that such an unfortunate ancestry places those so affected at substantially increased risk for alcoholism. Why are our colleagues who study alcohol use less reluctant to draw implications for social intervention from correlative data than are we who study criminal aggression? Is alcoholism so markedly greater a societal concern than criminal aggression that we are willing to build protocols for intervention on associational data that bear on the one but not on the other?

Neuropathology—An Important Contributor to Criminal Aggression

Nonetheless, we must stress that we do not propose naively that neuropathology constitutes a sole and unitary "cause" of violent criminal aggression. Were that the case, since it is (liberally) estimated that the incidence of neuropathology in the general population approximates 3 percent, and provided that we make the rather questionable assumption of a ratio of 1:1 between neuropathology and criminal aggression that the notion of "causation" implies, we should expect the annual incidence of episodes of violent criminal aggression to approximate at least 7.5 million. But whether one gauges this incidence on the basis of episodes formally reported to law enforcement authorities as reflected in Uniform Crime Report data or includes the (virtually equal number) of episodes estimated on the basis of household victimization surveys to have been committed but not reported, the annual incidence of episodes of criminal violence is no higher than 2.8 million. Moreover, it is quite clear that criminal aggression is not "rationed" on an annual basis per perpetrator, so that the 7.5 million in the general population who evince symptoms of neuropathology might reasonably be expected to behave impulsively many times per day, week, month, or year; and surely some of those episodes of impulsive behavior could be expected to find their way to a formal adjudication as criminal.

Instead of the 1:1 correspondence implied in the notion of unitary causation, then, we argue that neuropathology represents an important contributor to criminal aggression that interacts with other psychological, social, and stimulus determinants. And as a corollary, we assert that efforts to understand, predict, or constrain criminal aggression that ignore the contribution made by neuropathology will in effect remain fragmentary and less than comprehensive.

Many of our colleagues who readily orient themselves to incorporating simple correlative data derived from the social sciences tend to display little regard for the wealth of knowledge on human aggression generated by research in the neurosciences. It is not uncommon that on consideration of such data as presented above, the social scientist resistant to effective communication with the neurosciences will dismissively pose a question such as this: Is it not the case that these proportions are derived from assessments of convicted offenders, which assessments are often conducted long after the crime has been committed and the offender convicted and incarcerated? When we answer in the affirmative, the response is often to the effect that, "if you guys had been incarcerated for any length of time, your brains might look pretty funny, too"—that is, data from the neurosciences are lampooned by asserting that neuropathology *results from* habituation to mind-numbing prison routines *rather than contributes to* the genesis of criminal aggression that yields incarceration in its wake.

CONCEPTUAL AND CLINICAL CROSS-FERTILIZATION

Benefits to the Social Sciences

The interests of the social sciences and those of the neurosciences (or, with particular attention to criminal aggression, those of society) are not served by continued indifference in communication. For the social sciences, conceptual benefits may accrue from an opening in the channels of communication in such manner as to elucidate a fresh set of *governing variables* that explain vexing issues. For example, social scientists are fond of attributing violent behavior in adulthood to victimization in child abuse, with social learning typically cited as the mechanism for intergenerational transmission. The matter of the character and effect of the physical injuries that abused children sustain is rarely of major concern. In what does not appear to be a particularly related set of findings, a half-century of social science research on Wechsler's measures for intelligence has indicated that discrepancies in which nonverbal intelligence significantly exceeds verbal intelligence are reliably associated both with neurological dysfunction in the left hemisphere *and* with aggressive criminal offending, particularly in adolescence. The matter of *how* such dysfunctions may have been generated has received little attention among social scientists. Without input from the neurosciences, such social science data lack a coherent explanatory context; they merely hang in space as interesting curiosities.

Neuroscience data from a study conducted at Harvard Medical School and McLean Hospital by Ito, Teicher, Glod, and their associates (1993) may provide that coherent context. These investigators reported that the injuries sustained in child abuse were *modally* neurological, with a prevalence in electrophysiologically measured brain abnormalities in abused subjects precisely twice as great (54.4 percent versus 26.9 percent) as in nonabused subjects. Such abnormalities are consistent with either or both (1) the genesis of frontal lobe syndrome and (2) abnormalities in the left hemisphere. Since minimally 90 percent of adults are right-handed, injuries to the left hemisphere are consistent with blows to the head of a facing person delivered by a right-handed abuser, whether by fist, open hand, or blunt instrument (e.g., baseball bat, broom handle).

Data from the neurosciences thus point toward a *governing variable* that amplifies social science research both on the intergenerational transmission of patterns of violent behavior and on the genesis of cognitive dysfunction related to persistent aggressivity. Alternately, neuroscience data will hang in space without practical application to societal problems in the absence of broad-gauged *clinical* interventions designed largely on the basis of *social science* knowledge.

Bridging the Gap

The overarching twin goals in medical epidemiology are to determine the means by which the pathogens responsible for physical disease (or illness) are transmitted and to identify those groups who are particularly "at risk" to contract "target" diseases. These goals are most frequently accomplished by contrasting the relative incidence with which the target disease is found in a group differentiated according to demographic (or sometimes behavioral) characteristics and in the population at large. In the first task, medical epidemiology relies on the investigative methods of the biological sciences and, in the second, on those of the social sciences. Once "risk markers" are identified, public health efforts are mounted to control the spread of illness or disease through what is usually called "preventive medicine." In this approach, the knowledge base of the social sciences is brought to the clinical task of convincing those "at risk" to avoid pathogens, contaminants, or other agents that favor the spread of a target disease.

Identification of the neurologic variables associated with biological brain-proneness to violence can do no more than specify "risk markers" at a fundamental, physiological level; what needs to happen next to apply such knowledge to social and personal betterment will be largely the work of the applied social sciences. But the efforts of applied social science to alter patterns of human criminal aggression in the absence of appropriate attention to those neurologic variables associated with aggression, indeed perhaps across species, will necessarily remain fragmentary until the communication gap between the neurosciences and the social sciences is securely bridged.

References

Bach-y-Rita, G., Lion, J. R. & Climent, C. E. & Ervin, F. R. (1971). Episodic dyscontrol: A study of 130 violent patients. *American Journal of Psychiatry, 127,* 1473–1478.

Brown, S. J., Fann, J. R. & Grant, I. (1994). Postconcussional disorder: Time to acknowledge a common source of neurobehavioral morbidity. *Journal of Neuropsychiatry and Clinical Neurosciences, 6,* 15–22.

Coyle, J. T. (1988). Neuroscience and psychiatry. In J. A. Talbott, R. E. Hales & S. C. Yudofsky (Eds.), *American psychiatric press textbook of psychiatry*. Washington, DC: American Psychiatric Press, 3–32.

DeWolfe, A. S. & Ryan, J. J. (1984). PIQ >> VIQ index in a forensic sample: A reconsideration. *Journal of Clinical Psychology, 40,* 291–294.

Feldman, R. S. & Quenzer, L. F. (1984). *Fundamentals of neuropsychopharmacology.* Sunderland, MA: Sinauer.

Galski, T., Thornton, K. E. & Shumsky, D. (1990). Brain dysfunction in sex offenders. *Journal of Offender Rehabilitation, 16,* 65–80.

Geiger, S. G. (1960). Organic factors in delinquency. *Journal of Social Therapy, 6,* 1–16.

Gibbs, W. W. (1995). Trends in behavioral science: Seeking the criminal element. *Scientific American, 272,* 100–107.

Gottfredson, M. R. & Hirschi, T. (1994). Aggression. In T. Hirschi & M. R. Gottfredson (Eds.), *The generality of deviance.* New Brunswick, NJ: Transaction, 23–45.

Hales, R. E. & Yudofsky, S. C. (1987). *The American Psychiatric Press textbook of neuropsychiatry.* Washington, DC: American Psychiatric Press.

Hillbrand, M. & Pallone, N. J. (1994). *The psychobiology of aggression.* New York: Haworth Press.

Horowitz, I. L. (1993). *The decomposition of sociology.* New York: Oxford University Press.

Ito, Y., Teicher, M. H., Glod, C. A., Harper, D., Magnus, E. & Gelbard, H. A. (1993). Increased prevalence of electrophysiological abnormalities in children with psychological, physical, and sexual abuse. *Journal of Neuropsychiatry and Clinical Neurosciences, 5,* 401–408.

Jeffery, C. R. (1990). *Criminology: An interdisciplinary approach.* Englewood Cliffs, NJ: Prentice-Hall.

Langevin, R., Marentette, D. & Rosati, B. (1995). Why therapy fails with some sex offenders: Learning difficulties examined empirically. *Journal of Offender Rehabilitation, 23 ,* 145–157.

Langevin, R., Wortzman, G., Dickey, R., Wright, P. & Handy, L. (1988). Neuropsychological impairment in incest offenders. *Annals of Sex Research, 1,* 401–415.

Marino, M. J. (1999). CDC report shows prevalence of brain injury. *TBI Challenge, 3,* 1, 13.

Megargee, E. I. (1966). Undercontrolled and overcontrolled personality types in extreme antisocial aggression. *Psychological Monographs, 80,* No. 611.

Monahan, J. (1981). *The clinical prediction of violent behavior.* Washington, DC: National Institute of Mental Health.

Pallone, N. J. & Hennessy, J. J. (1992). *Criminal behavior: A process psychology analysis.* New Brunswick, NJ: Transaction.

Pallone, N. J. & Hennessy, J. J. (1993). Tinder-box criminal violence: Neurogenic impulsivity, risk-taking, and the phenomenology of rational choice. In R. V. Clarke & M. Felson (Eds.), *Routine activity and rational choice: Advances in criminological theory*. New Brunswick, NJ: Transaction, 127–158.

Pallone, N. J. & Hennesy, J. J. (1995). *Fraud and fallible judgment: Varieties of deception in the social and behavioral sciences.* New Brunswick, NJ: Transaction.

Pallone, N. J. & Hennessy, J. J. (1996). *Tinder-box criminal aggression: Neuropsychology, phenomenology, demography.* New Brunswick, NJ: Transaction.

Pallone, N. J. & Voelbel, G. T. (1998). Limbic system dysfunction and inventoried psychopathology among incarcerated pedophiles. *Current Psychology*, *17*, 57–74.

Raine, A. (1993). *The psychopathology of crime: Criminal behavior as a clinical disorder.* San Diego, CA: Academic Press.

Reitan, R. M. & Wolfson, D. (1992). *Neuropsychological evaluation of older children.* Tucson, AZ: Neuropsychology Press.

Van Praag, H. M. (1988). Biological psychiatry audited. *Journal of Nervous and Mental Diseases*, *176*, 195–199.

Volavka, J. (1991). Aggression, electroencephalography, and evoked potentials: A critical review. *Neuropsychiatry, Neuropsychology and Behavioral Neurology, 3*, 249–259.

Volavka, J. (1995). *Neurobiology of violence.* Washington, DC: American Psychiatric Press.

Walters, G. D. (1992). *Foundations of criminal science: The development of knowledge.* New York: Praeger.

Williams, D. (1969). Neural factors related to habitual aggression: Consideration of differences between those habitual aggressives and others who have committed crimes of violence. *Brain, 92*, 501–520.

Yeudall, L. T. & Fromm-Auch, D. (1979). Neuropsychological impairments in various psychopathological populations. In J. Gruzelier & P. Flor-Henry (Eds.), *Hemisphere asymmetries of function in psychopathology.* Amsterdam: Elsevier/North Holland Biomedical Press, 401–428.

Yeudall, L. T., Fedora, O. & Fromm, D. (1987). A neuropsychological theory of persistent criminality: Implications for assessment and treatment. *Advances in Forensic Psychology and Psychiatry*, *2*, 119–191.

Chapter 23

The Dawn of Therapeutic Justice

by Richard L. Nygaard, U.S.C.J.

Introduction 23-1
    A Vision for the Criminal Justice System 23-2
    Public Safety Issue 23-3
Kansas v. Hendricks 23-3
    History 23-3
    The Kansas Sexually Violent Predator Act 23-4
    Procedural Issues 23-5
    State's Reversal of Ruling 23-5
    The United States Supreme Court's Reasoning 23-6
        Civil vs. Criminal Commitment 23-6
        A Wider Net for "Mental Illness" 23-7
        Effect on Legislative Branch of Government 23-7
        Summary 23-8
Penal Implications of *Hendricks* Decision 23-9
Therapeutic Justice 23-11
    Culpability 23-12
    Crime as Antisocial Act, Not Pathology 23-13
    "Traditional" Rehabilitation vs. Therapeutic Justice 23-13
    The "War" on Drugs 23-14
Conclusion 23-15

INTRODUCTION

Recently there has been a reduction in violent crime. According to many of us who should know better than to employ post hoc rationalization, it is because we are finally getting tough on criminals. Under current theory, little thought is given to prevention, and none to preemption of crime. Our system is essentially passive, content to wait for a victim to bestir us into a reaction. And our post-offense reaction to a crime is essentially one-dimensional—we incarcerate, as a method of and venue for punishment. Thus, our theory goes, as the severity of the crimes committed increases, we merely increase the duration of the punishment, or perhaps even put the offender to death. One of the ironies of this formula is that many of us—legal professionals and laypersons alike—believe that it fully accounts for (1) *why* we punish generally and (2) the *purpose* behind a decision to punish an offender specifically. But it is not really that simple.

The fact is that most of us do not know why we punish and may have no idea of the purpose a sentence may serve, and none of us really knows why our violent crime statistics are improving. Massive and extensive incarceration does account for some of the improved statistics. We know that empirically and intuitively, recidivists account for substantially more crimes than those for which they are convicted. But a program that calls for long prison terms for all offenders, regardless of reason, is a bit like a "carpet bombing" in which everyone is blasted with the hope that sufficient numbers of the enemy are killed along with the noncombatants. If with a little effort we could determine the offenders who need long incarceration, who need treatment, and who need neither, we could prevent enormous social and fiscal waste. Our penal theory and practice are failing our culture, and the social and economic cost is staggering.

As anyone who has read my essays may know, I have a narrow but deep professional passion outside the duties of my court, that being to reformulate our criminology and penology so that they respond to the needs of society, the victim, *and* the offender. In earlier essays I have argued that American penology is fundamentally flawed, that punishment as a solitary response to crime is largely a failure, and that it makes no sense not to require positive behavioral change from anyone who is ever to be released from prison (Nygaard, 1995). I have attacked the reasoning by which we purport to support offense-based punishment and have argued instead for a criminal justice delivery system that concentrates on the offender's shortcomings in formulating an appropriate and coordinated response (Nygaard, 1996a). I have challenged the concept of prison as a sufficient remedy for doing so (Nygaard, 1996b) and have reviewed the philosophical, psychological, and penological supports for our policy on the death penalty, stating my belief that contemporary notions of capital punishment are philosophically flawed (Nygaard, 1996c). I have looked with some hope to biomedical science and to behavioral genetics and what its discoveries may mean to the future of remedial penology (Nygaard, 1996d). And I have rejected as nonsense the binary, sane/insane option we give jurors who must decide whom the system will treat with compassion and whom it must punish with vengeance (Nygaard, 1996e).

A Vision for the Criminal Justice System

All this, of course, is easier to theorize about than to apply. Admittedly, my suggestion that we bifurcate criminal trials—deciding in the first phase whether the offender did the act, and in the second the reasons why, so that we can develop an appropriate response—had some criminological and constitutional impediments. First, if we continue to insist on using "guilt" and "innocence" as mutually exclusive moral concepts to determine whether we may punish the offender, then scienter (state of mind)[1] is a necessary ingredient of the process (Nygaard, 1996e). Second, if all we want is retribution against offenders to assuage a public's desire to get even, irrespective of whether it leads to positive consequences, then knowing why one performed an offensive act only complicates our vengeful emotion. Nonetheless, I have advocated (and do so now) that we fully revise our thinking and transform our legal codes to comply with Cicero's maxim *"Salas populi suprema lex esto"*—the safety of the public shall be the first law. My vision for the criminal justice system requires that we think about it operating much the same as a health maintenance organization (HMO) in the health care context. Indeed, it is my belief that eventually the criminal justice delivery system will closely resemble an "SMO"—a "safety maintenance organization," if you will—committed to providing preoffense intervention and prevention, incarceration behavioral modification, and postrelease observation and support (Nygaard, 1997). The HMO has been given a target population and the mission, "keep them healthy." An SMO would likewise be given a jurisdiction and the mission, "keep them safe."

Public Safety Issue

I am concerned with rights and individual autonomy, but as a judge, I am also keenly aware of the social costs of irresponsibility and am motivated by public safety as a primary goal of criminal law. Hence, I am concerned with results. We may imprison and punish if it serves a productive purpose, but by all means we must either correct and prepare an offender for release or decide that we are going to contain him humanely. I say "him" because over 90 percent of those convicted of violent offenses are male (see Caplice, 1994). But for everyone's sake, let us do something to stop the offender from coming back time and again, and to stop the offenses by learning something about prevention, preemption, and intervention. The discoveries about behavior in the social, biomedical, and physical sciences are of no value to criminology and penology unless they can become factors in legislative and judicial decision-making and find their way into remedial use in sentencing, treating offenders, and preventing crimes.

In this chapter, I wish to examine how the recent U.S. Supreme Court opinion in *Kansas v. Hendricks* (117 S. Ct. 2072, 1997) may well open the constitutional doors to a positive remedial penology and therapeutic justice. Near the end of the 1997 Court term in an opinion authored by Justice Clarence Thomas, the Court unanimously agreed that a law permitting the civil commitment of persons likely to engage in sexually predatory acts because of mental abnormalities did not offend substantive due process principles.

KANSAS v. HENDRICKS

History

Leroy Hendricks had a history dating from 1955 of sexually molesting children. He was charged with several offenses in 1957 and in 1960, detained in a state mental hospital until 1965, and discharged. Nevertheless, by 1967 he was in prison for molesting an eight-year-old girl and an eleven-year-old boy. He refused to participate in a sex offenders treatment program and remained incarcerated until he was paroled in 1972. While on parole, Hendricks began to abuse his own stepdaughter and stepson. He was diagnosed as a pedophile and entered into a treatment program, which he later abandoned. In 1984, Hendricks was convicted of taking indecent liberties with two thirteen-year-old boys, for which he served nearly ten years.

The Kansas Sexually Violent Predator Act

Just before he was scheduled to be released in 1994, Kansas authorities filed a petition seeking to commit him as a sexually violent predator under the Kansas Sexually Violent Predator Act, a civil statute that permits convicted sex offenders who are scheduled for release from prison to be involuntarily committed for treatment if they have a mental abnormality that makes them likely to engage in predatory acts of sexual violence.

The Kansas legislature, in enacting the statute, noted that there exist sexually violent predators who have no mental disease or defect that would subject them to involuntary commitment under extant general civil commitment statutes. Because these sexually violent predators may also not be amenable to existing mental illness treatments and are likely to continue to engage in sexually violent behavior, the legislature declared that the existing involuntary commitment procedure is inadequate to address the risk such predators pose to society, and that the duration of civil commitments themselves is insufficient for the long-term care and treatment necessary for these offenders. Kansas recognized what most of us intimate with the criminal justice delivery system know, that the prognosis for rehabilitating anyone in the prison setting is extremely poor, especially in the case of a sexually violent predator. Indeed, it is difficult to imagine a more debilitating behavioral system than the American prison. Moreover, any therapeutic commitment, unlike current criminal sentences, must be of a duration that is not likely to be determinable at the outset (i.e., at sentencing) and certainly not by a legislature, which determines mandatory sentences, sentencing ranges, and guidelines long before the crime is even committed. Thus, Kansas found it necessary to establish "a civil commitment procedure for the long-term care and treatment of the sexually violent predator."

> The Act defined a "sexually violent predator" as:
>
> any person who has been convicted of or charged with a sexually violent offense and who suffers from a mental abnormality or personality disorder which makes the person likely to engage in the predatory acts of sexual violence.[2]
>
> A "mental abnormality" is defined, in turn, as a
>
> congenital or acquired condition affecting the emotional or volitional capacity which predisposes the person to commit sexually violent offenses in a degree constituting such person a menace to the health and safety of others.[3]
>
> The Act's civil commitment procedures as pertained to *Hendricks* were:
>
> 1. A presently confined person who, like Hendricks, "has been convicted of a sexually violent offense" and is scheduled for release;
> 2. A person who has been "charged with a sexually violent offense" but has been found incompetent to stand trial;
> 3. A person who has been found "not guilty by reason of insanity of a sexually violent offense"; and

4. A person found "not guilty" of a sexually violent offense because of a mental disease or defect.[4]

Procedural Issues

The initial version of the Act, as it applied to an offender such as Hendricks, was designed to initiate a specific series of procedures. The custodial agency was required to notify the local prosecutor sixty days before the scheduled release date of a person who might meet the Act's criteria.[5] The prosecutor had forty-five days to decide whether to file a petition to involuntarily commit the person.[6] The court would then determine whether "probable cause" existed to support a finding that the offender was a "sexually violent predator" and thus eligible for civil commitment. If the court made that determination, the individual was transferred to a secure facility for professional evaluation.[7] After that evaluation, the offender would be tried, the finder of fact having to determine beyond a reasonable doubt whether the offender was a sexually violent predator. If determined to be a sexually violent predator, the offender would then be transferred to the custody of the Secretary of Social and Rehabilitation Services for "control, care and treatment until such time as the offender's mental abnormality or personality disorder has so changed that the person is safe to be at large."[8]

Once an individual is confined, the Act requires that "[t]he involuntary detention or commitment . . . shall conform to constitutional requirements for care and treatment."[9] Confined persons have three separate avenues of review: First, the committing court is obligated to conduct an annual review to determine whether continued detention is warranted. Second, the Secretary is permitted at any time (1) to decide that the confined individual's condition has so changed that release is appropriate, and then (2) to authorize the person to petition for release. Finally, the confined person may file a release petition at any time.[10] If the court finds that the state can no longer satisfy its burden under the initial commitment standard, the individual will be freed from confinement.

State's Reversal of Ruling

Hendricks's motions to dismiss the petition against him on federal constitutional grounds were unsuccessful because the state court reserved ruling on the Act's constitutionality. The court concluded there was probable cause to believe that Hendricks was a sexually violent predator and ordered him to be evaluated at a state hospital.

Hendricks requested a jury trial during which he admitted his sexual abuse and further acknowledged that he abused children whenever he was not confined. He testified that whenever he got "stressed out," he could not control the urge to molest children. He agreed with the state physician's diagnosis of pedophilia and that he still had the condition, and he expressed his belief that treatment for it was all "bull____." He then despaired that the only way he would be cured was "to die." The jury unanimously found on the standard of proof "beyond a reasonable doubt" (the highest evidentiary standard)[11] that he was a sexually violent predator. The trial court also concluded as a matter of law that pedophilia qualified as a "mental abnormality" under the Act. Hendricks was committed to the custody of the Kansas Secretary of Social and Rehabilitation Services based on the court's conclusion and the jury's finding that he was a sexually violent predator.

Hendricks appealed, raising federal constitutional claims under due process, double jeopardy, and ex post facto clauses. He was partially successful before the Kansas Supreme Court, which held that the Act's definition of "mental abnormality" did not satisfy the U.S. Supreme Court's definition of "mental illness" as a predicate to civil commitment.

The United States Supreme Court's Reasoning

The U.S. Supreme Court reversed the Kansas Supreme Court's judgment. It held that the Sexually Violent Predator Act did meet the threshold requirements of due process and did not transgress either double jeopardy or ex post facto protections. In the past, the Supreme Court has sustained civil commitment statutes when they have coupled proof of dangerousness with the proof of some additional factor, such as a "mental illness" (*Heller v. Doe*, 509 U.S. 312, 314–315, 1993). The Kansas Act is different. As the Supreme Court noted, the Act extends "involuntary civil confinement to those who suffer from a volitional impairment rendering them dangerous beyond their control." Hendricks was diagnosed as a pedophile. Psychiatrists classify his condition as a serious mental disorder. Hendricks himself admitted that his sexual desires were out of his control.

Justice Thomas's opinion first addressed Hendricks's substantive due process claim, recognizing as to the first predicate to commitment under the Act—a finding that a person poses a danger to society—that "[p]revious instances of violent behavior are an important indicator of future violent tendencies." The Kansas Act requires a finding based on the offender's history of sexually violent behavior, and on evidence of a current mental condition, which together support the conclusion that the offender is likely to engage in future acts of predatory violence. Because, however, a finding of dangerousness standing alone is ordinarily not a sufficient ground on which to justify indefinite involuntary commitment, the Kansas Act went further, requiring evidence both (1) of sexually violent acts and (2) a present mental condition that creates a likelihood of repetition if the offender is not incapacitated. The Court said that a statute such as this, which is triggered by acts and requires proof of more than a mere predisposition to violence, does not offend either legally accepted behavioral principles or constitutional due process protections.

Next, the decision refuted double jeopardy and ex post facto arguments by holding that the proceeding under the Act was not a criminal proceeding and that confinement under the Act did not constitute punishment. The Court found it significant that the Kansas legislature labeled the proceedings under the Act as "civil" and that "[n]othing on the face of the statute suggests that the legislature sought to create anything other than a civil commitment scheme designed to protect the public from harm" (*Hendricks*, 117 S. Ct. at 2082). This, the Court indicated, counsels against "reject[ing a] legislature's manifest intent [unless] a party challenging the statute provides 'the clearest proof' that the statutory scheme [is] so punitive either in purpose or effect as to negate [the State's] intention 'to deem it civil'" (*Hendricks*, 117 S. Ct. at 2082).

Civil vs. Criminal Commitment. Justice Thomas also found several other factors significant in distinguishing this Act as civil rather than criminal in nature. First, the Act does not implicate what he considers to be the two principal philosophical supports for criminal punishment: retribution and deterrence. Second, unlike a criminal statute, the Kansas Act does not require a finding of scienter for commitment. Third, although the Act permits a potentially infinite duration of commitment, this in itself does not manifest a punitive purpose because no person can be committed for more than a year without another judicial proceeding. Finally, Kansas's inclusion of procedural safeguards typically associated with criminal trials does not transform the commitment proceedings from civil to criminal.

A Wider Net for "Mental Illness." This opinion muffles some earlier constitutional limitations on involuntary civil commitment by approving language in the Kansas Act that breaks with Supreme Court precedent. Before *Hendricks*, for example in the cases *Foucha v. Louisiana* (504 U.S. 71, 1992, at 75–76) and *Addington v. Texas* (441 U.S. 418, 1979), involuntary commitment proceedings required that two preconditions be established by clear and convincing evidence: (1) that the person was mentally ill and (2) that he posed a danger to himself or to others. In *Hendricks*, the Court opened the mental illness definition to include not only the mentally ill but also the mentally abnormal—those offenders suffering from a "personality disorder," whether congenital or acquired, that creates a "volitional" impairment.

Moreover, the Court simply was not deterred by the lack of an exact calculus of what constitutes "mental illness." First, it deflected the argument that a finding of mental "illness" is a prerequisite for civil commitment, concluding that because a mental abnormality or personality disorder justifying civil commitment is equivalent to what is commonly thought of as a mental illness, the generic, nonscientific terms "mental abnormality" and "personality disorder" would suffice, although they do not describe any specifically identified condition.

Second, the Court called into question the relevance of scientific evidence by psychiatric and psychological professionals, by accepting empirical or behavioral evidence over examination and theory, thus undercutting the value of scientific or other expert opinion. Indeed, the Kansas legislature acknowledged in its preamble to the Act that the definition of "mental abnormality" or "personality disorder" would not rise to the level of "mental disease or defect." Hendricks was diagnosed as suffering from pedophilia, which, because one who molests children is likely to be a pedophile, can be a largely fact-driven diagnosis. Other volitional dysfunctions, however, may not be so patent. Third, building on these two premises, the Court's opinion leaves state legislatures with the discretion to define the mental health concepts that have legal implications. I am skeptical that given the vagaries of politics, we can assume that legislators will rely solely upon scientific data in their determination.

Effect on Legislative Branch of Government. Unfortunately, in criminal sentencing, especially in sentencing sex offenders, correction or therapy is likely to be well down on the list of considerations that compete with a culture's desire for revenge. Thus, the fact that the class of individuals targeted for treatment lacks volitional control and as a result is likely to be dangerous in the future is enough to justify commitment, regardless of whether such individuals "fit precisely with the definitions employed by the medical community." In so saying, the opinion rejects the traditional requirement that tests used to decide whether a behavior arises from a mental abnormality or personality disorder and justifies civil commitment must have some basis in what is generally accepted among professionals as scientific support. This, of course, also gives to the legislatures the authority of determining which offenses may be amenable to treatment rather than punishment, and it places squarely upon the legislative branch of government the responsibility for failure if it does not develop an appropriate response to crime. Unfortunately, this also places the response to crime in the arena of politics and exacerbates the potential that the remedies the legislature prescribes for crime may continue to be driven by popular opinion, whether or not they are scientifically supportable.

Hendricks thus represents a shift in due process analyses since *Addington* (1979), when the Court's approach with respect to due process protection of liberty was built on caution: "Given the lack of certainty and the fallibility of psychiatric diagnosis, there is a serious question as to whether a state could ever prove beyond a reasonable doubt that an individual is both mentally ill and likely to be dangerous" (441 U.S. at 429). Now with the states' legislatures wide discretion in defining mental health and behavioral concepts that have penal implications, the relevance of psychiatric, psychological, and other scientific evidence by experts is depreciated in value, sweeping this "lack of certainty" and "fallibility" aside. Indeed, taken literally, the Court's new standard could potentially permit application of indefinite civil commitment to many offenders, depending on how legislatures define the mental predicates to civil commitment, by juries and judges with no scientific training, and with no clinical guidance about risk assessment. While concurring with the *Hendricks* opinion, Justice Kennedy did however raise a red flag about the future implications of the Court's analysis, saying:

> If the civil system is used simply to impose punishment after the State makes an improvident plea bargain on the criminal side, then it is not performing its proper function . . . [because] incapacitation is a goal common to both the criminal and civil systems of confinement. (*Hendricks*, 117 S. Ct. at 2087)

I find this deference to legislative authority in matters of behavioral and medical science disturbing. Even more disturbing is that a civil commitment is not rendered punitive by the Act's failure to actually require legitimate treatment, or even palliative care. Although punitive containment or incapacitation is a traditional rationale of penology, the opinion states that "incapacitation may [also] be a legitimate end of the civil law," ostensibly, even if it is a defensive detention. Thus, the Act's "overriding concern" for the continued "segregation of sexually violent offenders" is consistent with the Court's definition of civil commitment to include the goal of incapacitation. And more disturbing to me still is the opinion's posture that even if therapy is not being provided, that does not render the commitment punitive. Justice Thomas, relying upon the language of the Act, justified his position by noting that even if providing treatment was not the primary purpose of the Act, it was an ancillary purpose.

Summary. In sum, Justice Thomas concluded that because the Act is civil in nature, commencement of commitment proceedings does not constitute a second prosecution. Because commitment under the Act is not punitive, involuntary confinement does not constitute double jeopardy even when confinement follows a prison term. Finally, the Act does not violate the ex post facto clause, which "forbids the application of any new punitive measure to a crime already consummated," because the Act is not a punitive measure. And because Hendricks suffers from a mental abnormality under the Act, and because the state is free, within the limits of reason, to define the level of mental infirmity required for commitment, Hendricks's confinement under the Act comported with due process.

PENAL IMPLICATIONS OF *HENDRICKS* DECISION

The Supreme Court's decision in *Hendricks* may well have a greater impact on future legal developments in penology and criminology generally rather than for sexual predators like Hendricks specifically, because the expansion of the due process civil commitment standard from mental "illness" to mental "abnormality" eases another of the rigid distinctions that have jurisprudentially separated criminal and civil commitments. That is to say, merely because one has performed a criminal act, that which follows need not be a penal commitment. A civil commitment for treatment or preventive detention, either as an additive or an alternative, is an option for structuring the sentence if the offense was actuated by a mental or perhaps biological flaw rather than a moral lapse. I see little from this opinion to believe civil commitments will not extend to dangerousness to others in contexts of deviance and crime *other than sexually predatory violence*, if the criminal behavior is caused by a person's mental or biological status. The opinion thus steers towards an area the Court avoided in *Foucha* and *Addington*, the jurisprudence of prevention. That is to say, the Court held that in certain circumstances one may be defensively detained to be prevented from committing acts of predatory violence. In doing so, the Court embraced the ideology of therapeutic justice. But I suggest that it seriously erred by doing so without also requiring more scientific certainty and, at minimum, that the commitment be either motivated by some sincere therapeutic effort or driven by research if there is no known treatment for the offender's condition. The implications of this are enormous.

There are, no doubt, myriad behavioral actuators or precipitators that will fall within the label of "abnormalities" and "disorders." Awareness of and acceptance of this fact in itself will be enabling to a system that wants to affect positive change in its offenders. A therapeutic focus may also lighten the adversarial context that is the unseen specter in criminal law decisions. In other words, honest dialogue over the most productive, acceptable remedy may encourage cooperation from offenders and defense attorneys. Offenders who are offered treatment may opt for a therapeutic remedy in lieu of a totally punitive sentence. And an offender who is assured of treatment may be more inclined to admit his wrongdoing and seek help that is offered. Detailed admissions, such as in plea colloquies, could help to overcome the ever-prevalent offender denial. The "presumption of innocence" that is the frame of reference in criminal trials often has a life that lasts beyond findings of guilt and usually conspires against the cognitive restructuring necessary for correction. Structured pleas could include agreements among the offender, victims, families, health care professionals, the court, penal institutions, and probationary supervisors and would permit the court to fashion consensus and corrective remedies for which there is written record and accountability as to the results. A court faced with an offender suffering from a qualifying abnormality could steer offenders toward therapeutic alternatives to prison.

Next, as we begin to think of and focus more on treatment or palliation, the criminal justice delivery system will be forced to look for the *reasons* why a person behaved as he did—not to excuse the behavior, but to discover how to counteract, correct, or otherwise impose a useful sentence to provide a remedy for it. When we begin to concentrate on reasons why a person has erred, and collect offense and offender-specific data, I am certain the resulting knowledge we accumulate will permit more informed sentencing conclusions and advance the criminal justice delivery system's ability to predict recurrent violence or violent propensities, and engage in appropriate remediation. From full accounting by the system for the results of its sentencing decisions will come data to test our hypotheses about the operation of the corrective process and the value of its constituent parts. From this, we can begin to develop a purpose behind each sentence.

Both the Kansas Legislature and the U.S. Supreme Court were addressing "sexually violent behavior" in the context of persons who have been charged with or convicted of sexual crimes. Nevertheless, as I earlier suggested, the argument can be made that if a person has a history of violent and predatory behavior—sexual or nonsexual, and even without a criminal charge or conviction—then that person could be civilly committed, if legislatures are convinced that the offender's present mental condition creates a likelihood that the offender will engage in similar violent behavior again. Some hope lies in the fact of this recognition; that is to say, if we concede the existence of behavioral actuators other than moral, we can begin to speak of *treatment* for shortcomings in addition to or as a replacement for mere *punishment* for misbehavior. Therein lies this opinion's importance to therapeutic justice. This approach does not abandon punishment. As any counselor, parent, or custodian knows, correction often requires it. Dr. Phillip Roche called the criminal law a "child rearing system for grown-ups" (Weihofen, 1956, p. 26). Moreover, the notion of and need for valence between a predatory act and the victim's and society's needs cannot be ignored if the procedure and result are to be cathartic and therapeutic to the most significant presence in criminal sentencing—the general public.

There are a substantial number of offenders who want to lead "normal" lives and would opt for treatment rather than incarceration if they had some confidence they really would be treated, not merely indefinitely warehoused in a different setting. In their classic work on sentencing, Irwin and Austin (1994) state, "[W]hat may be . . . surprising is that a majority of all persons sent to prison, even the high-rate offenders, aspire to a relatively modest conventional life and hope to prepare for that while serving their prison sentences" (p. 61).

I fear, however, that the combination of (1) political overattention to the collective ignorance of society about the efficacy of incarceration and punishment, (2) the reactionary anger towards crimes and offenders, (3) the comparison of direct costs for effective treatment and research, with preventive or preemptive detention, and (4) the popularity of "macho toughness" will groom the path of least resistance for legislatures. The Achille's heel of this case for real therapeutic progress is thus exposed—therapeutically rationalized commitment without therapy, or conversely, therapy without boundaries—and neither will withstand the scrutiny of time.

THERAPEUTIC JUSTICE

I advocate a criminal justice delivery system that (1) views a sentence as a journey, not an end; (2) retains *detention*, not just for punishment, but also as a venue for change; (3) introduces *intervention*, to remove the offender from his milieu, and coordinates and deploys social forces that make crimes more difficult to commit; (4) uses *prevention*, to intercede in past and potential offenders' lives at an earlier stage to thwart offenses; and (5) supports *preemption*, by employing all civic and social forces to make the commission of crimes more difficult, or at least less convenient. Moreover, each of us is becoming professionally more centripetal, driven by the competitive rigors of our own endeavors to concentrate our intellectual energies on an ever-diminishing scholastic locus in quo. We truly need each other to fully comprehend the contours of any situation, discovery, or action.

Towards this end, I would transform sentencing into a meeting of experts from many disciplines—sociologists, education professionals, psychologists, victims and victim support organizations, ministers, priests, rabbis, and even urban planners—who are convened as the court's jury to help it formulate an integrated social and penal response to infractions based on a holistic view of the whole ecology of the crime. The courts and the panels would, where deemed possible, work to develop appropriate remedial sentences that present offenders with *real* obligations and *real* opportunities to change their behavior, to achieve the end goal of correcting the criminal offenders at all points on the continuum between preoffense and postrelease. This would remake criminal justice into an interdisciplinary justice delivery system. And because hindsight is a ruthless critic, each element thereof must be accountable to the others, and the whole criminal justice delivery system must be accountable for the results of its actions to society. I believe that the criminal justice delivery system must, in addition to everything else, become a therapeutic vector and look at sentencing as a behavioral tool, and where indicated, through a mental health prism.

So, what is therapeutic justice? Law, whether we jurists admit it or not, is a significant social force in American culture that will be either socially corrosive or therapeutic. Seldom is it neutral, at least in the criminal law and penal context. It will produce change, positive or negative. Therapeutic jurisprudence, which studies "the extent to which substantive rules, legal procedures, and the roles of lawyers and judges produce therapeutic consequences" (Finkelman & Grisso, 1994 [quoting Wexler & Winick, 1991, p. 981]), began as a mental health approach to law, but in its brief history has attracted significant attention among jurists as a legitimate extension of the legal realism movement. The concept was introduced by Professor David Wexler (1992) and has expanded and quickly emerged as a legitimate branch of legal theory (Wexler & Winick, 1996), although Wexler's critical analysis of the shortcomings of therapeutic justice (1972) differ a bit from my views.

The concept is particularly attractive because it tackles what we jurists recognize as the primary shortcoming of any movement that begins with what "ought" to be—it fails to know what really "is." Therapeutic justice is a descendant of therapeutic jurisprudence, which, however, is at once narrower and broader than therapeutic jurisprudence. Therapeutic justice is narrower because it looks at the therapeutic response as it relates to criminal offenses specifically and not law generally. It is broader because mental health is only one behavioral actuator with which it is concerned. Therapeutic justice as an interdisciplinary approach to solving the problems of crime is concerned with discovering causes of crime generally, segregating offenders who are amenable to treatment, then determining which therapies are indicated for them, in addition to the initial punitive response.

Culpability

It is important to consider what therapeutic justice is not. First, therapeutic justice says nothing about free will and determinism, or good and evil. Philosophically, free will and determinism are just titles for the opposite ends of a continuum upon which, and at different points, each of us lie, with perhaps no one at either polar extreme. Each of us has a different genetic menu that equips us differently for coping with stress, temptation, and other social pressures. Moreover, none of us can escape the fact that our lives, in significant measure, have been shaped by antecedent causes—that is, other people, external events, developmental milieu, which combine in some individualized personal equation with the genes our ancestors gave us. We, unfortunately, are not as Immanuel Kant contended, free and rational sovereigns in the "realm of ends." Moreover, irrespective of genetic, environmental, or educational factors, and depending on the strength of the temptation or provocation, each of us is capable of performing acts that lie somewhere between the good and evil poles of the moral continuum. Where an offender lies on these continua, however, only assists in determining the appropriate remedy.

Thus it follows that therapeutic justice has nothing to say about culpability. That is to say, in determining whether an accused "did it," that the offense was the product of a volitional abnormality has nothing to contribute to the decision (unless, of course, certain offenders become more willing to admit their complicity in an event if they qualify for a sentence that includes treatment, and in a proceeding that has a lower moral stigmata). There may be multiple *reasons* why one performed a criminal act— but none may *excuse* it. The concept of guilt should not be confused with the need to develop an appropriate response to the offender and the offensive act, for the victim specifically and society generally. Hendricks may have committed his crimes because he is a pedophile; but that does not excuse what he did to the children. Therapeutic justice does not expand the concept of conditional or status defenses by putting new "whine" in old bottles; it contracts it so that each offender is held to a scientifically rational and legally appropriate degree of accountability for his actions—to face up to what he has done. Anyone who has performed an illegal act perhaps deserves some remedy; therapeutic justice helps determine it.

Think of these examples. In 1994, Lorena Bobbitt was acquitted of mutilating her husband's genitals because the jury deemed her temporarily insane. Psychologists and psychiatrists testified that she suffered myriad posttrauma disorders as a result of mistreatment by her husband. At about the same time, the Menendez brothers' murder trial ended in a mistrial on a defense that they had suffered mental, sexual, and emotional abuse from their parents whom they had killed. Other *defenses* proffered in other trials, and with varying degrees of success, include insanity, diminished emotional or mental capacity, irresistible impulses, overindulgence in movies and television, junk food, alcohol and drugs, post-partum depression, attention deficit disorder, age, premenstrual syndrome, and most recently genes, an inherited predisposition to violence, to name a few. Some or all may be reasons. Nonetheless, I suggest that they are not and should not be defenses by which one can be excused from accounting to society for an offending act or be declared to some degree as innocent.

Truth *is* stranger than fiction, because in fiction we reform and conform the truth to make it more believable than the reality of what actually exists, but which we may not wish to believe. So too in behavior. The real reasons why one behaves as one does *is* truth, and, as in the adage, stranger than the fiction employed in attempts to obtain an excuse for that behavior. The truth truly may be strange, exceedingly complex, seemingly incomprehensible, and indeed often bizarre. The search for truth about behavior may lead us to nutrition, neurotransmitters, toxins, testosterone levels, brain damage, genes, and a host of other variables, hitherto unexamined, that explain behavior, and hence crime. That is the point: explanation. Under therapeutic theory one is neither absolved of responsibility for one's act, nor found not guilty by reason of some fiction or condition. Therapeutic justice is concerned with what to do, and doing *something* if someone performs an offending act, and with what to do to prevent offending acts from being performed in the first place. It looks for the true reasons why one misbehaved, so that we can understand and provide a systemic response to treat, to counteract, and to prevent future acts of misbehavior.

Crime as Antisocial Act, Not Pathology

Therapeutic justice also does not treat crime as a disease or a pathology. Crime may, of course, be a symptom of both, and each may precipitate aberrant behavior not engaged in by the nondiseased or nonpathological. Some chronic diseases and psychological or biological conditions may be legitimate reasons why one behaves as one does. The crime, however, remains an antisocial act. Whatever an offender's health, mental capacity, or state of normalcy, therapeutic justice recognizes his degree of competency and accords him that extent of autonomy, to which degree he must endure some opprobrium and condemnation and face the consequences of his offense. Research reveals that individuals, wherever they lie upon the intelligence continuum, can think to some extent for themselves and learn lessons to some extent from experience (on the "sheltered workshop" concept for the mentally retarded, see Nygaard, 1996b, discussing G. A. Barber). A study by the Royal Commission on Capital Punishment (1953) regarding the mentally disabled and the law reveals that "the great majority of the patients in mental hospitals, even among the grossly insane [and the psychotic], know what [conduct] is forbidden by the rules [of the hospital] and that ... [breach of these rules may result in the] forfeit[ure of] some privilege" (p 103) and hence, understanding right from wrong, theoretically respond to disapproval. We are all morally responsible for our actions in varying degrees according to our emotional, mental, and biological equipment. To be therapeutic, justice requires that we discover that degree and respond accordingly.

"Traditional" Rehabilitation vs. Therapeutic Justice

Under traditional rehabilitation theory, the purpose of punishing criminal offenders is to modify their behavior, a laudable goal. At one time, some believed that rehabilitation was the future of the criminal justice system. Unfortunately, earlier rehabilitation theory was based on the flawed premise that *we*, whoever we are, could change *them*, whoever they are. Coerced change, however, usually lasts only as long as the pressure to do so remains. Our earlier theory on rehabilitation represents to some extent what happens when the mental health professionals have an insufficient grasp on the reality of sentencing, and the legal theorists have an authority that exceeds the value of their ideas. Those who were called on to execute the rehabilitation scheme had neither a realistic view of the goal nor a firm commitment to the ideal. Nor did either the theorists or the administrators understand either *how* to rehabilitate or *who* was capable of being rehabilitated. Finally, punishment was placed in too shallow a grave, and the idea of rehabilitation was scrapped too soon. Had we been more tenacious, I think that we would have discovered and repaired its flaws.

This paternalistic notion of rehabilitation, however, is not therapeutic theory. Therapeutic justice is all about change, about creating a clinical and penal climate in which transgressors are encouraged to change and, for the offenders who sincerely want to change, about assisting them in their endeavors. Nonetheless, people who are correctable or have treatable conditions bear the ultimate moral responsibility both for the change resulting from treatment and their condition afterwards; this applies whether one has a physical ailment, an addiction disease, a more complex emotional problem, or has committed a crime. The system can help one do what one cannot do for, or by, himself. It can restore hope where despair exists. It can coordinate individual and component efforts. It can intervene. But it cannot rehabilitate. We have learned that lesson. Change is tough. Therapeutic justice is not a soft, easy remedy.

The "War" on Drugs

Follow me through another example: After presiding over hundreds of criminal trials, guilty pleas and sentences, I was asked following a speech, "What is the central feature of crime in America?" I replied that I did not know except that I could not recall the last criminal case I tried that did not in some way implicate the abuse of alcohol or the use of drugs. Most people have read some statistics on drug-related crimes. They are but the tip of the iceberg. In my experience, which is in a relatively peaceful section of the country, statistics are conservative. A substantial number of arrestees test positive for drugs. A substantial number of addicts support their habits by crime. Addiction in its various forms is inextricable from crime.

Nonetheless, I have yet to meet an addict, drug dealer, or drug treatment specialist who believes punishment alone will cure our drug problem. Moreover, the "war" on drugs (or on crime) is a flawed metaphor. The battle concept is a dramatic, catchy slogan but does not describe reality, for we have declared war on no one. We are not shooting down planes that smuggle drugs into the United States; we mine no harbors to sink ships carrying drugs; we do not shoot drug dealers or invade drug-producing countries; indeed we continue to give economic aid to some countries that we know just wink at the drug trade. Moreover, the concept of a war is itself a delusion, for we fail thereby either to prevent crime or to destroy or catch a sufficient number of offenders. It is flawed, too, because in the business of crime or the crime of business, one cannot easily discern who is on which side. It is flawed because when one's mind set is fully for war, the arts of peace, intervention, and prevention are of no use, and peace-makers are ignored.

Traditionally, crimes were committed for one of two reasons, greed or passion. With drugs, a third reason now dominates—need. Aristotle described the need-driven offender in his *Politics* as one who steals of necessity, and then, to eat. Today in America, drugs are a close analog to this; they create crime driven by the need arising not from an empty belly but from an addiction. And experience tells us that you cannot by threat of punishment prevent someone from committing a crime to get something he actually needs, or thinks he needs, to survive. Addiction requires treatment, not war. The concept of a war on drugs is flawed because those who use or accept it forget that in any war both victor and vanquished sustain battle casualties. Pyrrhus said after the costly victory at Asculum that although he won victory after victory, he lost so many troops in each battle that he despaired of winning the war: "Another such victory over the Romans and we are undone" (Plutarch, *Lives*, § 21).

Drugs and alcohol, however, are but two reasons why some persons commit crimes. There are many others. I recall a tearful telephone call from a mother, distraught because her otherwise decent son at times performed bizarre and violent acts. She had nowhere to go and could not attract anyone's attention to get help. She was told that unless her son committed a crime, the authorities had no opportunity to intervene. She was able eventually to get help, but only after her son assaulted a police officer and while in the custody of the courts was discovered to be suffering from schizophrenia. His condition is treatable. He is now taking medicine that controls his condition, and he is a peaceful and productive citizen. This is therapeutic justice in action; but for him and for the police officer, it came a bit late. Perhaps justice to police offices, to victims of crime, and to our culture requires that we try therapy, not to excuse the acts the offenders have performed, but because we will thereby discover how to intervene and to prevent offensive acts and other victims. That is therapeutic justice.

If we are able to diagnose a physical, biological, or emotional condition that may precipitate violent behavior and then to treat it, does it not make sense that we do so? I think so. Is it not the most humane response to crime that we try to prevent the trauma of someone becoming a victim of crime, the trauma of being accused and convicted of crime, or the solitary negative experience of prison? I think so. And if we can do all this while guaranteeing to the individual no fewer rights than those afforded to the criminally accused, should we not do so? Again, I think so. That is therapeutic justice.

CONCLUSION

Criminology is all about behavior, but our criminal law pays little attention to the behavioral sciences. Penology is all about mental health, but our sentencing policy pays little attention to the medical, biological, or social sciences. Correction is all about change, but our penal system is content with punishment. Science has much to tell law, but we are not listening.

Justice Thomas' opinion may represent the first light for including therapeutic concepts as alternatives, complements, or supplements to our criminal justice delivery system. But I fear that it will remain just that—a dawn on the horizon, in sight but always out of reach—unless the criminal justice delivery system advances hand-in-hand with civil responses to misbehavior and deploys remedial measures that advance with the discoveries from research in all the allied sciences. When it comes to behavioral control, punitive criminal incarceration and therapeutic civil commitments are not a "them" (deserving of punishment) versus "us" (deserving of therapy) proposition; the two must operate as parts of a justice delivery system focused on correction.

In my view, Justice Kennedy sets the condition for whether civil commitments for behavioral control will become a permanent fixture in American penology. If the treatment provisions are just a "sham or mere pretext" and the civil commitment procedure is being used for retribution or general deterrence—objectives of criminal statutes—his theory could find them punitive and criminal in nature, subject then to ex post facto or double jeopardy claims, and invalidate them. Even for Justice Kennedy, defensive confinement to protect the public, a common denominator of civil and criminal statutes, is constitutionally acceptable. He warns, however, "against dangers inherent when a civil confinement law is used in conjunction with the criminal process, whether or not the law is given retroactive application" (*Hendricks*, 117 S. Ct. at 2087). I also suggest that although incapacitation is a goal common to civil and criminal confinement, were the criminal justice delivery system willing to set retribution and deterrence aside and reembrace confinement for correction, it too could gain by considering confinement as a tool for correction and treatment.

Justice Kennedy's concurring opinion will have the greatest impact on future civil commitment laws and the durability of therapeutic justice. His caveat is a clear warning that civil commitment/treatment laws cannot be used simply as surrogates for punishment, that civil commitments cannot be a mere pretext for criminal incarceration. He specifically noted that "If . . . civil confinement were to become a mechanism for retribution or general deterrence, or it were shown that mental abnormality is too imprecise a category to offer a solid basis for concluding that civil detention is justified," he could not validate it (*Hendricks*, 117 S. Ct. at 2087). Neither would I. Moreover, he wrote for three other Justices, all of whom would have validated this Act with respect to individuals who committed violent sexual offenses after its enactment, and perhaps with respect to Hendricks if a higher level of treatment were provided. The dissent, written by Justice Breyer, also focused on the punishment. He delineated treatment as the distinguishing characteristic between civil and criminal statutes. Civil therapeutic commitment is here to stay if we offer therapy to the persons so committed and thus effect change in offenders' behavior.

I am constantly amazed that we Americans, who give with unprecedented generosity to charity and count ourselves as a humanitarian conscience among other governments and cultures of the world, are so content with a vengeful and unproductive criminal justice delivery system. We can treat each other with such dignity and respect until someone of us whose legal flaws may have been well-known is declared by charge and verdict to be "guilty"; then we turn our backs. It is my firm belief that the criminal justice delivery system should be an instrument of social harmony rather than discord and should prescribe remedies for offenders that are not socially corrosive. I suggest that we have an obligation to be humane, and that our government, which after all is *all of us*, has an obligation to set a humanitarian standard for our culture to follow, whether in imprisoning the criminally rebellious or in committing the violent and mentally abnormal predacious. In either case, however, I doubt that we can effect change by perpetrating senseless emotional cruelty or indignity upon prisoners. I suggest that we explore a gentler way. We must prepare the incarcerated or committed for a functional life in society. If we fail to do so, if we fail to care for each other and to keep our sights therapeutic and treat the treatable, the dawn of therapeutic justice will not only produce little daylight, but will simply result in another unspectacular sunset.

Endnotes

1 "Scienter" is a Latin adverb meaning "knowingly." Our system shares with most other systems as a prerequisite to culpability for crimes that the offender not only have "done" the act that the law forbids, but that he also have a threshold knowledge, mental capacity, and intention—a "frame of mind" if you will.

2 Kan. Stat. Ann. § 59-29a02(a).

3 Kan. Stat. Ann. § 59-29a02(b).

4 Kan. Stat. Ann. §§ 59-29a03(a), 22-3221 (1995).

5 Kan. Stat. Ann. § 59-29a03.

6 Kan. Stat. Ann. § 59-29a04.

7 Kan. Stat. Ann. § 59-29a05.

8 Kan. Stat. Ann. § 59-29a07(a).

9 Kan. Stat. Ann. § 59-29a09.

10 Kan. Stat. Ann. §§ 59-29a08, 59-29a10, 59-29a11.

11 In criminal trials, the government must prove guilt "beyond a reasonable doubt." For civil trials, a plaintiff must prove his case by a "preponderance of the evidence." Proof by "clear and convincing evidence," an intermediate level, is used for some proceedings.

References

Addington v. Texas, 441 U.S. 418 (1979).

Barber, G. A. (1982). *Sheltered employment work experience program.*(2d rev. ed.) Erie, PA: Barber Center Press.

Caplice, K. S. (1994). The case for public single-sex education. *Harvard Journal of Law and Public Policy, 18*, 277–292.

Finkelman, D. & Grisso, T. (1994). Therapeutic jurisprudence: From idea to application. *New England Journal on Criminal and Civil Confinement, 20*, 243–257

Foucha v. Louisiana, 504 U.S. 71 (1992).

Heller v. Doe, 509 U.S. 312, 113 S. Ct. 2637, 125 L. Ed. 2d 257 (1993).

Irwin, J. & Austin, J. (1994). *It's about time: America's imprisonment binge.* Belmont, CA: Wadsworth.

Kansas v. Hendricks, 117 S. Ct. 2072, 138 L. Ed. 2d 501, 65 USLW 4564 (1997).

Kansas Sexually Violent Predator Act, Kan. Stat. Ann. § 59-29 a01 et seq. (1994).

Kant, Immanuel ([1797]1965). The metaphysical elements of justice (J. Ladd, tr.). New York: Bobbs-Merrill.

Nygaard, R. L. (1995, spring). The myth of punishment: Is American penology ready for the 21st century? *Regent University Law Review, 5*, 1–12.

Nygaard, R. L. (1996a). On the philosophy of sentencing: Or, why punish? *Widener Journal of Public Law, 5*, 237–268.

Nygaard, R. L. (1996b, summer). Is prison an appropriate response to crime? *St. Louis University Law Journal, 40*, 677–697.

Nygaard, R. L. (1996c). On death as punishment. *University of Pittsburgh Law Review, 57,* 825–840.

Nygaard, R. L. (1996d). Freewill, determinism, penology, and the human genome: Where's a new Leibniz when we really need him? *University of Chicago Law School Roundtable, 3,* 417–437.

Nygaard, R. L. (1996e). The insanity of mental defenses and the law. *Villanova University Law Review, 41,* 951–987.

Nygaard, R. L. (1997, summer). The ten commandments of behavioral genetic data and criminology. *The Judges Journal, 36,* 59.

Pascal, Blaise (1941). *Pensées* (F. W. Trotter, tr.). New York: Random House, 60, ¶ 168.

Plutarch (1952). *Lives.* Chicago, IL: Great Books of the Western World, § 21, ¶ 14.

Royal Commission on Capital Punishment (1953). 1949–1953 report. Presented to Parliament by command of Her Majesty, September 1953, Her Majesty's Stationery Office. OCLC: 15113131.

Weihofen, H. (1956). *The urge to punish: New Approaches to the problem of mental irresponsibility for crime.*

Wexler, D. (1992). Putting mental health in mental health law. *Law and Human Behavior, 16,* 27–28.

Wexler, D. (1972). Therapeutic justice. *Minnesota Law Review, 57,* 289–338.

Wexler, D. & Winick, B. (1991). Therapeutic jurisprudence as a new approach to mental health law policy analysis and research. *Miami Review, 45,* 979–1004

Wexler, D. & Winick, B. (Eds.) (1996). *Law in a therapeutic key: Developments in therapeutic jurisprudence.* Durham, NC: Carolina Academic Press.

Chapter 24

Biological Causes of Criminality and Expert Testimony—Some Cautionary Thoughts

by Stephen H. Dinwiddie, M.D.

Introduction: Heritable Factors in Criminality 24-1
    Nature and Nurture 24-1
    Adoption Studies 24-2
    Twin Studies 24-3
Implications for Legal Policy 24-4
    Morality vs. Science 24-4
    The Problem With the Paradigm Shift 24-5
Implications for Experts 24-6
    The Legal System vs. Science 24-6
    Role of the Mental Health Scientist 24-7

INTRODUCTION: HERITABLE FACTORS IN CRIMINALITY

Nature and Nurture

Fundamental advances in brain imaging and neurochemistry have radically changed the way that neuroscientists and many others think about biological factors in violent behavior, and indeed about criminal and antisocial behavior in general. Another revolution, equally fundamental, is occurring in behavioral genetics. The implications of these scientific revolutions are significant, not only for how society views the offender, but for policy-making, the law, and the methods used to process criminal cases in the courtroom.

Evidence that determinants of normal personality as well as psychopathology are substantially heritable cannot be ignored; indeed, support for this position has been accumulating for decades (Dinwiddie, 1994). More recently, reports that specific

---

Prepared for the 35th Annual Meeting, Academy of Criminal Justice Sciences, Albuquerque, NM, March 14, 1998.

genetic loci accounting for substantial portions of the variance in attributes of temperament have been identified and characterized at the molecular level are beginning to emerge (Sullivan et al., 1997), and it seems unlikely that the tale will end there. The proposition that some determinants of behavior, whether antisocial or otherwise, are rooted in transmissible, presumably genetic factors should be seen as an unexceptional statement, no more worthy of comment than the opposite side of that coin—that the manifestation of any specific behavior ultimately depends on unique environmental factors for its occurrence. This observation holds true no less for criminal behavior. Nature and nurture are equally and significantly influential.

On what scientific grounds, in the case of criminality, is this assertion based? The modern era of study of the psychiatric construct most commonly associated with criminal behavior—the antisocial personality disorder—began more than thirty years ago, when Guze and colleagues systematically interviewed relatives of felons, finding elevated rates of specific psychiatric disorders, including Briquet's syndrome (what is now called somatization disorder), alcohol and drug addiction, and, most prominently, sociopathy among first-degree relatives (Guze et al., 1967; Guze et al., 1968). Subsequently, Cloninger, Reich and Guze (1972) again found substantially higher rates of sociopathy among first-degree relatives of felons than among relatives of controls, which provides further evidence that sociopathy runs in families. Intriguingly, rates have been shown to be higher among relatives of *female* felons, suggesting that the genders differ in threshold for expression of the trait, that is, that women must have a greater loading of liability factors than men before exhibiting the disorder, which provides evidence that social factors play a role (Cloninger et al., 1978).

Adoption Studies

Of course, familial transmission does not necessarily imply a genetic basis, as anyone who has inherited money can attest. To disentangle what is biologically inherited from purely environmental factors shared by family members requires some separation of nature from nurture. Classically, that is the adoption study. The premise is simple (though the mechanics of study are complex): If adopted-away children tend to resemble their biological parents in the expression of the trait of interest, in this case criminality or some similar construct, the trait is biologically and presumably genetically based (or at least some part of it is). Conversely, if the children tend to resemble their adoptive parents, the trait is learned.

In fact, adoption studies using Danish, U.S., and Swedish adoptees (Schulsinger, 1972; Crowe, 1974; Cadoret, 1978; Cloninger et al., 1982; Mednick, et al., 1984) all indicate the presence of some heritable liability factors in antisocial and criminal behavior. While difficult to compare due to differences in the way subjects are ascertained and diagnosed, taken as a whole, the adoption literature clearly supports a role for heritable, presumably genetic, factors. Again, as in the case of family studies, there appears to be a difference in manifestation based on gender, with women requiring a higher genetic loading in order to manifest antisocial behavior, and there appears to be a significant interaction with environmental factors (Bohman et al., 1982; Sigvardsson et al., 1982; Baker et al., 1989; Cadoret et al., 1990; Cadoret et al., 1995).

In that regard, Cloninger et al.'s (1982) cross-fostering analysis of a Swedish cohort of adoptees is particularly worthy of mention. Of those with high-risk prenatal backgrounds reared in high-risk environments, 40 percent had criminal registration versus 3 percent of those with neither. Those from high-risk biological backgrounds but lower-risk postnatal environments and vice versa had intermediate risks, 12 percent and 7 percent, respectively.

Interestingly, adoption studies have found better evidence for biological heritability of factors predisposing to property crime rather than violence. While this may be a manifestation of lack of statistical power (because of the relative rarity of violent behavior as opposed to property crimes), it probably also reflects other factors, including the multiplicity of factors predisposing to violence (many of which clearly are not genetic) and the difficulty in ascertaining (particularly from registry databases) episodes of violent behavior, many if not most of which may not reach official notice. Also, those who predominantly commit property crimes tend to commit many more crimes than do those who engage primarily in violent behavior. Thus, property offenders can be more readily characterized by a pattern of criminal behavior, whereas most violent offenders commit many fewer offenses over a shorter period of time. Patterns of criminality over time, or more specifically over the life span, are probably more heritable than isolated behaviors, which are often a function of circumstance and situation. In order to more fully tease out genetic factors in violent crime, subjects with long-lived patterns of violence must be selected for study.

This highlights only one challenge in studying the intergenerational transmission of criminality, which has a number of other methodological difficulties. For example, what constitutes criminal behavior and the likelihood of being caught obviously has in some cases changed dramatically over time. And, of course, there is the uncertainty of ascertaining criminality from arrests—an uncertain guide if one is interested in examining some underlying characteristic that will manifest only erratically as some subset of criminal behaviors that results in arrest, conviction, or registration in some database. Consequently, the use of official source of data to ascertain criminality can be highly misleading and confounding.

Twin Studies

Another means of determining the relative contributions of nature and nurture, which can eliminate at least some of these difficulties, is the twin study. Identical (monozygotic, MZ) twins have identical genomes, while fraternal (dizygotic, DZ) twins on average share 50 percent of their genes identical by descent. Shared environmental factors should be roughly the same in either case. Thus, closer resemblance for antisocial behavior between MZ twins would argue for genetic influence. For example, if IQ levels are 70 percent similar between MZ twins and 30 percent similar between DZ twins, then one can conclude that IQ is substantially heritable.

Early twin studies, because of variations in ascertainment and definition of criminality, are difficult to interpret, but tend on balance to support the significant role of genetic factors (Hurwitz & Christiansen, 1983). There is more support in the later literature for a genetic role when antisocial (not just criminal) behavior is examined, with a substantial part of the variance in liability for antisocial behavior explained by genetic factors in some recent studies (Rowe, 1983; Rowe & Osgood, 1984; Centerwall & Robinette, 1989; Lyons et al., 1995; Slutske et al., 1997), but not all (Thapar & McGuffin, 1996). Dimensions of antisocial behavior are much more valid phenotypes (outward expressions of genetic traits) than criminality, which is a legal abstraction and carries with it many confounds. Nonetheless, even though twins have a natural "partner in crime" increasing the likelihood of overestimating the genetic contribution (Carey, 1992), there is little support for the hypothesis that learned, non-genetic factors alone can account for twin resemblance in antisocial behavior. Conversely, there is evidence that at least in the case of adolescent conduct difficulties, a large part of the liability can be attributed to genetic factors. Thus, the weight of available evidence strongly supports the contention that antisocial behavior aggregates within families, and further that this aggregation cannot be explained solely by the effects of learning or shared environment. Rather, transmissible biological factors appear to play a role in liability to antisocial and criminal behavior.

IMPLICATIONS FOR LEGAL POLICY

Morality vs. Science

In spite of the evidence of genetic transmission, as pointed out by Pallone and Hennessy in Chapter 22 of this book, in the case of brain injury and aggression, there has been a "paradigm lag": allied academic disciplines have been slow to respond to these advances, and further diffusion into the realm of policy has been even slower. Is this solely a problem with the diffusion of knowledge? The proposition seems obvious that an understanding of criminal behavior based on a more complete understanding of neurobiology should influence criminal law. But on further reflection, this does not necessarily follow. We must keep in mind that the law is founded more on principles of morality than science—and one may cite cases (such as the notorious Chaplin paternity suit) to support the contention that legal findings of "fact" may well run contrary to scientific fact.

Rather than aiding the quest for justice, advances in our understanding of the biological foundations of behavior are very likely to worsen the present collision of paradigms. If our very personality is so profoundly influenced by biological factors—by definition beyond our control—how might these developments influence legal opinion about blameworthiness and criminal behavior?

Classically, the law holds that except under unusual circumstances in which it would be unjust to hold the actor accountable (e.g., in cases of coercion, self-defense, sleepwalking, involuntary intoxication, or profound mental disturbance), individuals, even those facing hard choices, should be treated as autonomous agents. In accordance, autonomous agents are not ruled by external forces, but instead are capable of making "free will" decisions.

It also supposes that punishment, for our purposes more or less equivalent to deprivation of freedom, can be justified only if it serves the purpose of deterrence (specific or general), incapacitation, retribution, or rehabilitation. It is obvious that these ends hold the potential for conflict with each other, with justifications for criminal sanctions tracking the swing of the pendulum from an orientation toward rehabilitation to greater emphasis on incapacitation and punishment, and back again.

The Problem With the Paradigm Shift

While it would seem that a better understanding of the biological causes of criminal behavior should lead to a greater interest in rehabilitation, this change in paradigm carries with it several risks.

First, we must keep in mind that scientific models are deterministic (even if they fail to explain most of the variance in outcomes of the phenomena observed by scientists), as are the dominant theories in mental health (Dinwiddie, 1996). While this determinism may be based more on practical considerations than philosophy, there is nonetheless a tendency to equate understanding of cause with negation of moral responsibility, at least among mental health professionals. In the forensic setting, unfortunately, the fact that behavior is so much better explained in retrospect is rarely pointed out. This difference in orientation may lead to a profound conflict, though often not admitted and usually not overtly acknowledged, in the way that behavioral experts and the justice system try to understand wrongful behavior: as a deterministic, scientifically observable event flowing causally from preexisting vulnerability factors—or, as a moral choice justifiably censured by society.

Second, it would seem that understanding of cause should lead to effective treatment, which indeed it often does. But as shown by the lag between the explosion of knowledge in molecular genetics and the advent of gene therapies, there may be a considerable delay before new therapies are perfected and available. Unfortunately, it has long been a tradition in mental health treatment to accept theoretically attractive interventions and testify to their wondrous potential without requiring rigorous proof of effectiveness. Therapeutic optimism is perhaps better suited to those in clinical practice than those charged with meting out justice.

Third, while biological assays (sophisticated neuroimaging today, perhaps biochemical or genetic testing tomorrow) may be developed in clinical samples to identify those at elevated risk for criminal behavior, this does not imply improved prediction when such findings are applied to nonclinical populations. Depending on the base rate of the behavior in the population and the specificity of the test(s), it may well be possible to identify markers associated with antisocial behavior, yet our predictions turn out to be wrong more often than not. For example, assume that in a highly selected sample, some biological attribute—a metabolic difference in brain function, say, or a specific genetic marker—has been shown to be very closely related to risk of violence. Assume further that in the interest of public safety, we wish to apply this test to "screen" for violence risk, and that in the population we are screening, the "base rate" of such risk is 5 percent; that is, 5 percent will behave violently. Finally, let us assume (rather optimistically) that the test has a sensitivity of 90 percent, it will pick up 90 percent of these individuals, and that it is 95 percent specific and will correctly *exclude* those without risk of violence 95 percent of the time.

While such test performance might appear to be quite good, the results are counterintuitive. If we screened 1,000 subjects, the results would appear as shown on Table 24.1. What does it show? Our test has identified forty-five of the fifty who indeed acted violently, and 903 individuals, over 90 percent of the sample, were correctly identified as not at risk of violence. Unfortunately, we also incorrectly labeled forty-seven nonviolent individuals as violent, potentially to great social harm. In terms of "positive predictive value," we were wrong more often than we were right. Perhaps I

Table 24.1
Results of 90% Sensitive/95% Specific Test for Proneness to Violent Behavior

Prediction of violent behavior	Actual violent behavior		Total
	No occurrence	Occurrence	
Not violent	903	5	908
Violent	47	45	92
Total	950	50	

am overly pessimistic in believing that in the course of testimony a jury would be more likely to hear merely that the test is 90 percent accurate in picking up risk of violence rather than an involved explanation of why it is important to consider risks of "false positive" and "false negative" results when interpreting the results.

Fourth, the glamour of high technology seems often to direct attention away from poor reasoning in other areas. An example of this is the use of sophisticated neuroimaging studies to apply a finding uncommon in the general population but common in an affected group, such as presence of dilated cerebral ventricles, to bolster a diagnosis, and then use the diagnosis to explain (and in some minds, excuse) wrongful behavior (Faust & Ziskin, 1988; Ciccone, 1992).

Finally, in the current political climate, rather than supporting an emphasis on treatment and rehabilitation, more accurate prediction, particularly if it appears to be based on "hard science" rather than social science, may lead the justice system instead to impose longer sentences in order to maximize incapacitation with the belief that neither deterrence (specific or general) nor rehabilitation works. A variant of this phenomenon appears to be occurring now for those identified as sexual predators, for whom only the thinnest veneer of "treatment" is required for the justice system to allow indefinite commitment, or incapacitation by another name. This tendency appears to be aggravated by the fact that the cost of error (in terms of adverse publicity) is less when one imposes too great a sentence than when one releases a recidivist.

IMPLICATIONS FOR EXPERTS

The Legal System vs. Science

Advances in our understanding of the interplay between biological and learned factors in the genesis of criminal behavior should lead to more enlightened treatment of the offender and, potentially even more important, application of this new knowledge to public health initiatives. Use of this information in specific legal cases by the mental health expert, however, has its perils.

It is sobering to realize that forty years ago, when the foundations for modern biologically oriented psychiatry were being laid, the then-dominant model in psychiatric thought was felt to hold great promise when applied to legal issues. Stemming from a tradition of healing, the contribution of psychiatry to the legal system would be, first, to help it better understand the pathological thought processes of criminals. As a result, more individualized and just decisions would be promoted and the legal system would evolve to a more humane, rehabilitative perspective, with the invaluable assistance, of course, of those professionals best trained to understand (and interpret to the lay public) the complexities of the human mind and its aberrations. Possibly the consummation of this idealism is to be found in the *Durham* (94 U.S. App. 228, 1954) decision, which held that a criminal defendant should not be held accountable if it could be shown that his wrongful behavior was the "product" of mental disease or defect.

Experience did not, however, justify this optimism. The legal system found that the promises of this brand of forensic psychiatry could not be kept. Subsequent legal decisions tried to limit the scope of psychiatric testimony, but ultimately, in 1973, the entire exercise was abandoned and the "Durham rule" replaced in the court's decision in *United States v. Brawner* (471 F.2d 969 (D.C. Cir 1972).

With nearly half a century's perspective and attendant scientific advance, it seems clear that the promise of psychiatric testimony was destined to fail, primarily because it is a categorical error to expect scientific testimony to answer questions that are in essence moral, not scientific. At best, science can report observations, such as that individuals with brain injuries are many times more likely than those without brain injury to commit acts of violence. We can and should act on that information to reduce its incidence and to treat and rehabilitate the victims. In none of those endeavors is moral responsibility assigned. But the degree to which we find the actions of a brain-injured aggressor blameworthy and subject to legal sanction is traditionally a social, not scientific, judgment.

Second, and more important on practical grounds, the mental health experts that the legal professionals have been looking to for help simply have not delivered. Instead of the informed guidance Judge Bazelon believed psychiatry could offer, testimony revealed profound professional disagreement and confusion, both in how specific cases were diagnosed and prognosticated about and in the extent to which professionals were willing to consider certain conditions as "mental disease" and, hence, not blameworthy (*Washington v. United States*, 129 U.S. App. 29, 1967).

Role of the Mental Health Scientist

We are now in the same position vis-à-vis the legal system, but instead of framing our understanding of wrongful human behavior within psychoanalytic constructs, we have a broader basis, more firmly founded on biological science. How can we avoid making the same mistakes? First of all, we must keep in mind that the legal system is primarily a mechanism for settling disputes, not for ascertaining scientific truth. Scientific accuracy is useful only insofar as it assists in mediation and resolution: recourse to the truth allows greater efficiency and the ability to render decisions that are (presumably) more palatable to the involved parties. Expert testimony should acknowledge the primacy of the legal system and leave advocacy for theories and suppositions for other arenas. The clinician who fails to do so risks, at best, being made irrelevant.

Clinical experts must also keep in mind that like it or not, assignment of moral accountability and blame is the prerogative of the legal system, not of the expert. One of the devastating criticisms leveled at psychiatric testimony under the *Durham* rule (and still applicable today) was that experts occasionally succumbed to the temptation of making their own assessment of blame and slanting their testimony accordingly (*Washington*, 129 U.S. App. 29, 1967). Even "impartial" experts advocate for their opinions. It is vital not to step beyond the limits of what is known in an effort to achieve a "just" decision: the expert's role is to interpret scientific and clinical concepts, not to usurp the role of moral judgment.

On practical grounds, as well, it should be kept in mind that the law has evolved over centuries, and has great inertia. Changes in law and legal procedure may have an immense and, for the most part, unforeseeable social impact.

How, then, can scientific advances influence legal decision-making at the level of individual cases? First, on practical grounds, we must ensure that those qualified by the legal system as experts truly are experts. The concern here is less for the potential damage done by "hired guns" than by well-meaning, sincere, but inadequately prepared clinical experts who may try to interpret a body of knowledge they incompletely grasp to a system more notable for rhetoric and advocacy than for scientific sophistication. This implies that better communication between basic researchers and clinicians is needed—on both sides. Basic researchers must better communicate the *clinical* implications of their work, while clinicians must take responsibility for ensuring that their scientific understanding stays current.

Another implication is that researchers in different disciplines should make an effort to understand the implications of progress in other fields. The example cited by Hennessy and Pallone relating head trauma to the intergenerational transmission of child abuse is an excellent one (see Chapter 22). A simple "billiard ball" model where a single cause (parental child abuse) is seen as adequate in itself to set in motion the events causing the next generation to be abusive is a gross oversimplification of the web of contingent causality, of the complex interaction between promoting and protecting factors leading to such an outcome. The addition of findings from neuroscience markedly enriches the model, suggesting that neurological trauma in the setting of the emotional and social deprivation which is indexed by parental abuse might prove to be a more powerful and complete explanation.

Another example is a recent study of childhood sexual abuse which showed elevated rates of psychopathology among twins discordant for such abuse (Dinwiddie et al., 1999), suggesting that such abuse, in addition to its direct effect on the victim, may be a marker for the presence of deleterious environmental influences even in the absence of overt victimization. Rather than relying on an overly simplistic cause-and-effect model, the ability to account for both genetic and nongenetic vulnerability factors allows for a more precise estimation of the relative contribution of such factors.

Second, clinical experts consulting to the legal system must be more cautious and humble in making assertions about the "cause" of a specific wrongful act. Perhaps, since behaviors are influenced by many factors, it might be better to cite the increase in relative risk conveyed by a given finding rather than providing a blanket "all-or-none" opinion.

Third, if the legal system desires (as it purports to) access to higher-quality science more directly applicable to legal issues, there must be more openness in the law to permit study of and within the system. As it is, fears, often uninformed, of one side or the other gaining legal advantage make such study cumbersome and frequently so difficult that the effort is abandoned.

Finally, the expert has the obligation of learning what the legal system expects of him or her, and communicating that in a clear and useful fashion. Ultimately, the expert's role is to employ his or her scientific and clinical expertise, not to determine the outcome of a legal issue, but rather to educate the finder of fact—the judge or jury—so that they can reach an informed, just decision.

Unless the legal system undergoes tremendous alterations in the near future, there will remain both liabilities and advantages for neuroscientific advances in the courtroom, as this chapter outlines. Nevertheless, there is a substantial, potential role for science in the law and criminal justice system. In an ideal world, evidence of biological involvement in criminal and antisocial behavior would be incorporated into global measures to develop more effective prevention and early intervention programs. Within the courtroom, such evidence could be used on an individual basis to determine culpability and identify and exact the most effective and public safety minded sentence, whether that be treatment or incarceration. Until that time, however, the issues delineated herein must be taken into consideration for science to play a role in the reformation and evolution of our legal system.

References

Baker, L. A., Mack, W., Moffitt, T. E. & Mednick, S. (1989). Sex differences in property crime in a Danish adoption cohort. *Behavior Genetics, 19,* 355–370.

Bohman, M., Cloninger, C. R., Sigvardsson, S. & von Knorring, A. L. (1982). Predisposition to petty criminality in Swedish adoptees: I. Genetic and environmental heterogeneity. *Archives of General Psychiatry, 39,* 1233–1241.

Cadoret, R. J. (1978). Psychopathology in adopted-away offspring of biologic parents with antisocial behavior. *Archives of General Psychiatry, 35,* 176–184.

Cadoret, R. J., Troughton, E., Bagford, J. & Woodworth, G. (1990). Genetic and environmental factors in adoptee antisocial personality. *European Archives of Psychiatry and Neurological Sciences, 239,* 231–240.

Cadoret, R. J., Yates, W. R., Troughton, E., Woodworth, G. & Stewart, M. A. (1995). Genetic-environmental interaction in the genesis of aggressivity and conduct disorders. *Archives of General Psychiatry, 52,* 916–924.

Carey, G. (1992). Twin imitation for antisocial behavior: Implications for genetic and family environment research. *Journal of Abnormal Psychology, 101,* 18–25.

Centerwall, B. S. & Robinette, C. D. (1989). Twin concordance for dishonorable discharge from the military: With a review of the genetics of antisocial behavior. *Comprehensive Psychiatry, 30,* 442–446.

Ciccone, J. R. (1992). Murder, insanity, and medical expert witnesses. *Archives of Neurology, 49,* 608–611.

Cloninger, C. R., Christiansen, K. O., Reich, T. & Gottesman, I. I. (1978). Implication of sex differences in the prevalences of antisocial personality, alcoholism, and criminality for familial transmission. *Archives of General Psychiatry, 35,* 941–951.

Cloninger, C. R., Reich, T. & Guze, S. B. (1975). The multifactorial model of disease III. Familial relationship between sociopathy and hysteria (Briquet's syndrome). *British Journal of Psychiatry, 127,* 23–32.

Cloninger, C. R., Sigvardsson, S., Bohman, M. & von Knorring, A. L. (1982). Predisposition to petty criminality in Swedish adoptees II. Cross-fostering analysis of gene-environment interaction. *Archives of General Psychiatry, 39,* 1242–1247.

Crowe, R. R. (1974). An adoption study of antisocial personality. *Archives of General Psychiatry, 31,* 785–791.

Dinwiddie, S. H. (1994). Psychiatric genetics and forensic psychiatry: A review. *Bulletin of the American Academy of Psychiatry and the Law, 22,* 327–342.

Dinwiddie, S. H. (1996). Genetics, antisocial personality, and criminal responsibility. *Bulletin of the American Academy of Psychiatry and the Law, 24,* 95–108.

Dinwiddie, S. H., Heath, A. C., Dunne, M. P., Bucholz, K. K., Madden, P. A. F., Slutske, W. S., Bierut, L. J., Statham, D. B. & Martin, N. G. (1999, in press). Early sexual abuse and lifetime psychopathology: A cotwin-control study. *Psychological Medicine.*

Durham v. United States, 94 U.S. App. 228, 214 F.2d 862 (D.C. Cir. 1954).

Faust, D. & Ziskin, J. (1988). The expert witness in psychology and psychiatry. *Science, 241,* 31–35.

Guze, S. B., Wolfgram, E. D., McKinney, J. K. & Cantwell, D. P. (1967). Psychiatric illness in the families of convicted criminals: A study of 519 first-degree relatives. *Diseases of the Nervous System, 28,* 651–659.

Guze, S. B., Wolfgram, E. D., McKinney, J. K. & Cantwell, D. P. (1968). Delinquency, social maladjustment, and crime: The role of alcoholism. *Diseases of the Nervous System, 29,* 238–243.

Hurwitz, S. & Christiansen, K. O. (1983). *Criminology.* Boston: Allen & Unwin.

Lyons, M. J., True, W. R., Eisen, S. A., Goldberg, J., Meyer, J. M., Faraone, S. V., Eaves, L. J. & Tsuang, M. T. (1995). Differential heritability of adult and juvenile antisocial traits. *Archives of General Psychiatry, 52,* 906–915.

Mednick, S. A., Gabrielli, W. F. & Hutchings, B. (1984). Genetic influences in criminal convictions: Evidence from an adoption cohort. *Science, 224,* 891–894.

Rowe, D. C. (1983). Biometrical genetic models of self-reported delinquent behavior: A twin study. *Behavior Genetics, 13,* 473–489.

Rowe, D. C. & Osgood, D. W. (1984). Heredity and sociological theories of delinquency: A reconsideration. *American Sociology Review, 49,* 526–540.

Schulsinger, F. (1972). Psychopathy: Heredity and environment. *International Journal of Mental Health, 1,* 190–206.

Sigvardsson, S., Cloninger, C. R., Bohman, M. & von Knorring, A. L. (1982). Predisposition to petty criminality in Swedish adoptees: III. Sex differences and validation of the male typology. *Archives of General Psychiatry, 39,* 1248–1253.

Slutske, W. S., Heath, A. C., Dinwiddie, S. H., Madden, P. A., Bucholz, K. K., Dunne, M. P., Statham, D. J. & Martin, N.G. (1997). Modeling genetic and environmental influences in the etiology of conduct disorder: A study of 2,682 adult twin pairs. *Journal of Abnormal Psychology, 106,* 266–279.

Sullivan, P. F., Fifield, W. H., Kennedy, M. A., Mulder, R. T., Sellman, J. D. & Joyce, P. R. (1997). Novelty seeking and a dopamine transporter gene polymorphism (DAT1). *Biological Psychiatry, 42,* 1070–1072.

Thapar, A. & McGuffin, P. (1996). A twin study of antisocial and neurotic symptoms in childhood. *Psychological Medicine, 26,* 1111–1118.

United States v. Brawner, 471 F.2d 969 (D.C. Cir. 1972).

Washington v. United States, 129 U.S. App. 29, 390 F.2d 444 (D.C. Cir. 1967).

Part 9

Implications for the Prevention and Treatment of Antisocial Behaviors

Behavioral sciences research has convincingly shown that risk factors for drug abuse are neither entirely environmental nor biological; they are a product of their dynamic interaction. While we know a great deal about both the influence of psychoactive drugs on the brain and the effects of socioenvironmental conditions on propensity to use drugs, only recently have discoveries in the field of neuroscience linked brain function with a predisposition for various behavioral outcomes, including drug abuse. Several putative brain functional markers for drug abuse and its related behaviors have been identified and associated with particular behaviors and temperaments that characterize liability for drug abuse. For example, structural differences in genes regulating dopamine function have been related to novelty seeking and attention deficit disorder, both of which are related to drug abuse liability. Results to date suggest that individuals who abuse drugs possess a greater number of particular genetic variations, called polymorphisms, affecting serotonin and dopamine systems than those who do not, although identification of specific genes is still underway. Also, neuropsychological and imaging studies implicate dysfunction of the prefrontal cortex (e.g., orbitofrontal and dorsolateral cortices) in several aspects of vulnerability to drug addiction, including impaired judgment, impulsivity, and compulsive behavioral patterns. Physiological differences reflective of central nervous system arousal levels are consistent with these findings, showing low levels of skin conductance, slowing of the EEG, delays in evoked response potentials, and low heart rates in subjects with traits that often typify drug abusers. In short, there is convincing evidence for a biological basis for features strongly associated with high risk for drug abuse such as impulsivity, sensation-seeking, attention deficits, and childhood aggressiveness that may be amenable to intervention.

There is both a genetic and an environmental component to the neural substrates for antisocial behavior and drug abuse. Social and physical deprivation, poverty, traumatic stress, prenatal drug exposures, and other deleterious childhood experiences and environmental conditions can all have a direct impact on brain function. Conversely, an individual's brain dysfunction can have an impact on environmental or social responses to the individual, compounding the risk for an adverse outcome. Manifestations of these impacts are often measurable in cognitive processes (e.g., attention deficits), behavioral patterns (e.g., conduct disorder), temperamental traits (e.g., impulsivity or sensation-seeking), psychophysiological indices (e.g., EEG or skin conductance) and/or neurochemical aberrations (e.g., serotonin or adrenocorticotropic hormone). Of relevance here is that these indicators of brain function are now known to be at least partially alterable by our environment in ways that may increase or decrease liability for antisocial behaviors. Whether origins of brain functional mechanisms in drug abuse are genetically determined or environmentally induced, their presence can cumulatively alter an individual's developmental trajectory to influence subsequent development and behavioral outcomes. Thus, it is critical that prevention research begins to identify these interactions and explore ways in which prevention programs can redirect this developmental track, as outlined in the first chapter of this part, Chapter 25.

In Chapter 26, issues raised by the prospects of developing both a mental and public health response to antisocial behaviors are discussed. The use of genetic and biological research to inform criminal justice techniques or strategies to control antisocial behavior in general have been controversial. Implications to those unfamiliar with the research include the labeling of children who are at high risk, coerced treatment, widespread use of medications to tranquilize those at risk, or even dissolution of social programs. This chapter addresses those issues, answering those that can be answered and identifying issues that remain unresolved.

Throughout this book, evidence has been introduced for the interactive influences of the environment and our biology on propensity for antisocial behavior. Given this dynamic interaction between a myriad of factors, it is possible to alter or redirect deleterious outcomes through environmental and individual interventions. The American Psychological Association (APA) recommends a comprehensive approach to assessment, treatment, and prevention that incorporates the many perspectives of social workers, psychologists, physicians, teachers, community agencies, and other relevant specialists. In this way, the variety of underlying conditions that commonly contribute to antisocial outcomes can be more directly addressed. Chapter 27 provides a portion of a report released by the APA that focuses particularly on the prevention of family violence through the use of a comprehensive approach, but that also has import to all sorts of antisocial outcomes. Because family violence is so pervasive and contributes so substantially to antisocial behavior among childhood victims, their caregivers, and their future children, it is included in this book to elucidate ways in which violence in our society can be prevented and to recommend policies that can expedite these solutions.

Chapter 25

How Can Neurobiological Research Inform Prevention Strategies?

by Diana H. Fishbein, Ph.D.

Introduction 25-2
Structuring the Environment to Minimize Risk Factors 25-2
    Does Neurobiological Research Assume Behavior Is Predestined? 25-3
    Traumatic Experiences 25-4
The Respective Roles of Genetic and Biological Traits and
Environmental Conditions 25-4
    Concepts Essential to a Prevention Effort 25-4
    A Heuristic Biosocial Model of Antisocial Behavior 25-5
    Examples of the Nature-Nurture Interaction 25-6
        Serotonin Activity 25-6
        Temperament 25-6
        Drugs and Alcohol 25-6
        Cognitive Differences Between Males and Females 25-7
Environmentally Induced Biological Aspects of Antisocial Behaviors 25-7
    "Stress" Defined 25-7
    Prenatal Influences 25-8
        Minor Physical Anomalies 25-8
        Prenatal Drug Exposure 25-9
        Nicotine Exposure 25-10
        Cocaine Effects 25-11
        Social Environment During Pregnancy 25-12
    Perinatal Complications 25-12
    The Social Environment and Its Stressors 25-13
    Environmental Stimulation Needs 25-13
    Caregiver-Child Interactions 25-14
    Child Abuse and Other Traumatic Experiences 25-15
        Abnormal Hormonal Development 25-15

      Brain Cell Death 25-15
      Interactions Between Prenatal Conditions and Parenting 25-16
      Trauma During Adolescence and Adulthood 25-16
      Observing Violence: The Impact of Television Violence 25-17
Implications for Prevention Strategies 25-18
      Neurobiological Processes Affecting Behavior 25-18
      Prevention Techniques to Increase Resiliency and Minimize the
         Impact of Risk Factors 25-19
      Future Research Agenda 25-21

INTRODUCTION

While we know a great deal about the effects of socio-environmental conditions on propensity to certain behavioral disorders, only recently have discoveries in the field of neuroscience linked brain function with a predisposition for various behavioral outcomes, including drug abuse and related antisocial behaviors. Several markers indicative of brain dysfunction have been identified and associated with particular behaviors and temperaments that characterize liability for antisocial behavior and drug abuse. For example, studies suggest that individuals so affected possess a greater number of particular genetic variations or irregularities involving serotonin and dopamine systems than those who do not (see Fishbein, 1998). Also, physiological, neuropsychological, and imaging studies implicate dysfunction of particular brain regions in several aspects of vulnerability to drug addiction and related behaviors, including impaired judgment, sensation-seeking, attention deficits, and impulsivity (see Raine, 1993).

Research has clearly established that the origins of brain and behavioral dysfunction are both genetically determined and environmentally induced (O'Connor et al., 1998b; McGuire et al., 1994; Pike et al., 1996; Reiss et al., 1995); thus, their presence can cumulatively alter an individual's developmental trajectory to influence subsequent development and behavioral outcomes. Because brain function is now known to be at least partially alterable by our environment in ways that may increase or decrease liability for antisocial behavior and drug abuse, it is critical that prevention research begin to identify these interactions and explore ways in which prevention programs can redirect this developmental track.

STRUCTURING THE ENVIRONMENT TO MINIMIZE RISK FACTORS

There is a critical need for research-based prevention programming and supportive social systems. The ability to make rational choices and control one's own destiny relies on decision-making ability, capacity for rational thought, and even more important, the availability of alternative (preferably legal) choices and lifestyles. In order for individuals to rationally choose from a variety of available options, a supportive and responsive social system must exist. Children and adults must be initially presented with legitimate choices and opportunities, and they must have the necessary internal controls to select and sustain a productive path. In the absence of viable resources and options, delinquency or drug use more likely becomes the default option. This is where prevention strategies become paramount; prevention programs provide the choices, support systems, safety nets and opportunities that enable individuals to make productive decisions and avail themselves to legitimate options.

To structure the environment to be more responsive to human needs and to expand the range of available choices, we must identify environmental and biological risks and their interactive effects. This identification process will generate a better understanding not only of how environmental conditions influence brain function, but also how genetic traits and aspects of brain function affect or moderate the social environment. Such information will more fully explain why some individuals are more likely to choose to alter their brain function via drugs, or even engage in risky and antisocial behaviors, than others under certain conditions. While this book concentrates on innate strengths and vulnerabilities that can either increase or decrease propensity for antisocial and drug using behaviors, this particular chapter focuses on the external environment's contribution to these behavioral outcomes through its influence on brain structure and function. And because drug abuse and antisocial behaviors share many features in common, including their "symptoms," related behaviors, and biological and social origins, effective prevention programs can be expected to reduce the incidence of both.

The purposes of examining neurobiological research in the context of prevention approaches are many and varied. In particular, this body of research will help practitioners to identify individual vulnerabilities by virtue of their genetic and biological background, and as a function of prevailing environmental conditions. Second, this research will lead to the consistent identification of environmental conditions that act as triggers, resulting in the expression of vulnerabilities such as antisocial and drug-taking behaviors. Third, neurobiological findings suggest that certain prevention programs under certain conditions will be most effective, including methods for early detection, interventions, treatments, and primary prevention strategies. And fourth, the empirical literature provides support for the argument that public health and medical approaches are superior to simple incarceration, which generates many extraordinary personal, social, and financial costs.

Does Neurobiological Research Assume Behavior Is Predestined?

Although both biological and environmental conditions are powerful predictors of antisocial behavior and drug abuse, they are not "causal" in a deterministic sense—they are probabilistic. The intensity and frequency of exposure to negative environmental conditions, and the number and severity of internal risk factors present, determine the extent to which an individual is liable or vulnerable to behavioral disorders in general. Inherently vulnerable individuals (by virtue of their genetic make-up or biological constitution) who are subsequently exposed to an adverse environment are at imminently greater risk, particularly when adverse external influences are cumulative over time (e.g., prenatal drug exposure, perinatal complications, child abuse or neglect, exposure to racism, social isolation, economic deprivation, dysfunctional family, negative peer influences, witnessing violence, and so forth). The cumulative presence of many of these factors can result in antisocial or drug-taking behaviors by altering brain function, disengaging coping mechanisms, and compromising ability to formulate and act on rational choices.

Traumatic Experiences

Critical to this discussion of implications of neurobiological research for prevention are beliefs that in the absence of pharmacological treatments or genetic engineering, genetic and biological conditions are immutable or unchangeable. This chapter will present empirical findings supportive of the conclusion that genetic and biological conditions are environmentally influenced and can be altered via environmental manipulations. For example, posttraumatic stress disorder (PTSD) is characterized by measurable differences in brain chemistry, in particular a decline in serotonin activity levels (Davis et al., 1997; Fichtner et al., 1995; Graeff et al., 1996; van der Kolk, 1997; Southwick et al., 1997). PTSD is no longer unique to conditions of battle or war. The disorder is becoming more prevalent in inner city residents, especially children, who witness or experience violence in their homes and neighborhoods (Ackerman et al., 1998; Bell et al., 1991; De Zulueta, 1998; Selner-O'Hagan et al., 1998). This finding implies that traumatic experiences directly affect biological traits that can subsequently increase risk for negative behavioral outcomes. One might anticipate, as a result, increases in serotonergic activity levels with an effective intervention. In sum, genetic and biological features can be either suppressed or expressed by environmental inputs. No individual is predestined strictly by virtue of his or her genes or his or her biology to an antisocial orientation; environmental conditions carry significant weight in this equation.

THE RESPECTIVE ROLES OF GENETIC AND BIOLOGICAL TRAITS AND ENVIRONMENTAL CONDITIONS

Concepts Essential to a Prevention Effort

Genetic and biological traits are not synonymous and, consequently, not environmentally influenced in the same way. Genetic traits are inherited from parents for the most part, although genetic mutations or recombinations during embryonic development also contribute to an individual's genotype, or genetic complement. Biological traits, on the other hand, are either inherited or result from the impact on environmental conditions, both in utero or in the external world. Genetic predispositions can be redirected by providing particular experiences, directive training, and opportunities for various alternate modes of behavior; however, they cannot be "reprogrammed"—we cannot readily change the molecular genetic structure to alter outcomes. For example, brain chemistry and its activity levels are genetically designed with respect to the synthesis and metabolism of brain chemicals, the number of receptor sites present, and the activity of competing or regulating enzymes. Nevertheless, environmental inputs and experiences can modify the *expression* of these genetic traits, for better or for worse. Biological predispositions that are not genetically determined, however, can be more directly manipulated without changing the fundamental constitution. For example, sensory deprivation in early childhood reduces the number of neural connections in the brain. Enhancing sensory stimulation, conversely, increases the number of neural connections, resulting in improved brain function, without altering the genetic make-up. Genes establish the framework for brain function while the environment customizes and fine-tunes it. These concepts are essential to a concerted prevention effort.

Genetic and biological factors do not affect antisocial or drug abusing behaviors per se. Rather, they have an influence on the underlying behavioral phenotypes (see Goldman & Fishbein, Chapter 9 in this book, and Comings, Chapter 16) that are strongly associated with the eventual behavioral outcome, such as temperament, personality traits, patterns and orientations of behavior. Those particular phenotypes that are most related to and predictive of antisocial and drug taking behaviors include: impulsivity, cognitive deficits, negative affect, attention deficits, high activity levels, sensation or novelty seeking, inability to empathize, frustration intolerance, hostility, risk imperception, poor conditionability, lack of pain avoidance responses, lack of foresight, abnormal levels of arousal, low learning ability, and certain types of psychopathology (see Fishbein, 1998; Raine, 1993). Prevention strategies will be most effective if they focus on these underlying phenotypes, in conjunction with particular forms of environmental stimulants and supports as indicated by the needs of targeted individuals and neighborhoods.

A Heuristic Biosocial Model of Antisocial Behavior

Adrian Raine and his colleagues (1997) proposed a model to guide investigations into biological and social interactions that has import for the use of neurobiological findings in prevention strategies. In their model, Raine et al. suggest that biological factors play a role along with social risk and protective factors to produce antisocial outcomes. Existing risk and protective factors are a function of both genetic and environmental conditions. These conditions, subsequently, interact in a dynamic and cumulative process to determine risk status. It is this intricate and constantly fluctuating interaction that can act as a direct determinant of violence or drug abuse.

Protective factors exert an influence and can alter this pathway at any point in the developmental process to reduce risk status and improve the outcome. The behavioral outcome can also, in a feedback loop, affect risk and protective conditions to further strengthen or weaken risk status. For example, a child with attention deficit hyperactivity disorder, a disorder considered to be largely genetic, may be easily frustrated and difficult to manage. Parents without proper coping skills may harshly and inconsistently punish the child, further strengthening the child's risk for antisocial behavior (O'Connor et al., 1998a, 1998b). The child may react to such parenting with hostility and defiance, providing further fuel for a negative developmental outcome. The results may be quite different for a learning disabled child in the presence of a supportive home with appropriate intervention.

This integrated model readily applies to the widely accepted drug abuse prevention principles outlined by Hawkins and Catalano (1995). The authors suggest that the most promising route to effective strategies for the prevention of alcohol and other drug problems is through a focus on risk and protective factors, from the individual to the community level. Their framework can easily accommodate biological and genetic factors as they interact with the social and psychological conditions the authors include to formulate a comprehensive and contemporary model for prevention strategies. An understanding of differential vulnerability to social and environmental conditions—that is, of individual differences in resiliency against similar social stressors (Anisman et al., 1998)—would be subsequently enhanced. The resulting more encompassing model implies that prevention programs will be infinitely more effective when they account for both neurobiological and environmental aspects of risk and resiliency factors.

Examples of the Nature-Nurture Interaction

Serotonin Activity. Several examples of how the environment interacts with biological and genetic factors deserve mention. The neurotransmitter serotonin is of particular interest for its role in impulsivity and aggressiveness. An individual's range for synthesis and metabolism of serotonin is largely determined by his genes, although serotonin activity is exquisitely sensitive to changes in the environment. Animal studies show that when the social hierarchy is altered, the loss in status by dominant monkeys results in decreases in serotonin activity and vice versa (Edwards & Kravitz, 1997; Higley et al., 1996a; Raleigh et al., 1991) and they become more impulsive and subordinate. Human studies consistently report lower levels of serotonin in individuals exposed to high and chronic amounts of stress (e.g., PTSD) than individuals not exposed to high levels of stress (Dinan, 1996; Graeff et al., 1996; Petty et al., 1996; Stokes, 1995). Studies further show that poor parenting is associated with low serotonin levels in the child (Pine et al., 1996, 1997) and good parenting techniques can raise serotonin activity levels (Field et al., 1998), subsequently minimizing the impact of other risk factors for negative behavioral outcomes.

Temperament. Temperament is known to be largely heritable and stable across the life span (Plomin & Daniels, 1987). Nevertheless, the behavioral expression of any given temperament is strongly contingent upon environmental circumstances such as stressors, situational factors, opportunities, and learning experiences. Shyness is one form of temperament with biological and genetic origins that can be environmentally altered to influence its behavioral manifestations. Overactivity of the autonomic nervous system (ANS) is in part responsible for behavioral withdrawal in social situations in susceptible individuals (Schmidt & Fox, 1994). Strategies to combat shyness in a child may result in more extroverted behavior and less nervousness in social situations, which is associated with lower reactivity of the ANS (Gunnar et al., 1997; Kagan, 1992; Kagan et al., 1988; Schmidt et al., 1997).

Drugs and Alcohol. Alcoholism, known to be significantly heritable and associated with several genetic markers contributing to its expression (see Goldman & Fishbein, Chapter 9 in this book), is also susceptible to environmental influence. While alcoholism is considered to be in large part a genetic disease state, its expression is significantly dependent on family stability factors (Finney & Moos, 1992; Hussong & Chassin, 1997; Power & Estaugh, 1990). The same may also be true for other forms of drug abuse and addiction in which genetics plays a role, but the environment and learning experiences help to determine their actual expression.

A significant population of children chronically exposed to cocaine prenatally have been characterized as difficult to manage, temperamental, hyperresponsive to environment stimuli (e.g., lights and noises), developmentally delayed, learning disabled, impulsive, and sometimes aggressive. Cocaine can dramatically alter the developing nervous system to increase the likelihood of these behaviors in predictable ways (Azuma & Chasnoff, 1993; Brooke-Gunn et al., 1994; Giacoia, 1990; Mayes et al., 1993; Mott et al., 1993). Because the brain continues to develop for twelve months after birth, however, the provision of supportive therapies and interventions can substantially alter these negative outcomes. Children raised by the "crack" mothers who gave birth to them exhibit significantly worse behavioral and cognitive outcomes than cocaine-exposed children raised in more supportive and nurturing environments (see Hofkosh et al., 1995; Zuckerman & Bresnahan, 1991), suggesting that although prenatal cocaine exposure is a highly preventable cause of behavioral and cognitive disorders, environmental enrichment during the formative years can substantially improve the outcome (Field et al., 1998).

Cognitive Differences Between Males and Females. Similar to other parts of the anatomy, the structure of the developing fetal brain is influenced after the seventh week of pregnancy by the introduction of testosterone, a male hormone, in the presence of a Y chromosome. Subsequent changes in neuroanatomy occur to differentiate the male and female brain, in addition to the development of external genitalia, a larger musculature, and, eventually, facial hair. One result of these differences is distinctive cognitive styles, with males and females performing somewhat differently in various cognitive tasks. Interestingly, however, the gender gap in these cognitive differences has been narrowing in recent decades. Can the environment produce such significant changes in a trait known to be largely genetic?

Researchers believe that differences in the way parents treat their children may contribute to cognitive styles and actually alter brain development in the early years (Bjorklund & Brown, 1998). A few decades ago, psychological studies found that parents were more likely to encourage exploration of the environment and active play in baby boys, while little girls were coddled, comforted and "kept safe" from their environment. In contrast, parents in the 1990s tend to treat male and female babies more equally; a practice that can theoretically lead to a smaller magnitude of gender differences in cognitive abilities by increasing activity levels in baby girls.

ENVIRONMENTALLY INDUCED BIOLOGICAL ASPECTS OF ANTISOCIAL BEHAVIORS

"Stress" Defined

Understanding the dynamics and consequences of stress is key to unraveling etiological mechanisms in antisocial outcomes. Stress is defined as the damage incurred by internal organs as a result of an acute or chronic stressor, the cause or precipitant of stress. Stress is the physical and psychological response to an excess of stimulation compared with an individual's resources for coping. The source of stimulation may be either environmental (e.g., child abuse, family dysfunction, sensory deprivation), biological (e.g., lead poisoning, prenatal drug exposure, head trauma) or an interactive combination. Resources for coping may also be grounded in conditions that are either biological (e.g., I.Q. and executive cognitive skills), social (e.g., parenting techniques), psychological (e.g., self-esteem), or a combination.

Stressful experiences can temporarily or permanently alter brain function and chemistry. An acute stressor occurs in the short term and generally produces only a temporary effect; biological and physiological adjustments in the brain's response to the stressor take place after the stressor terminates. The presence of a chronic or reoccurring stressor, in contrast, more often results in a cumulative effect on biological and physiological responses that can impair coping abilities; this constitutes a formidable risk factor. As a direct consequence of these effects, chronic stress primes the brain for maladaptive responses to the environment, thereby increasing the likelihood of psychopathological or antisocial behavior (Anisman & Zacharko, 1986). Inherent susceptibilities or vulnerabilities help to determine particular behavioral outcomes of that stress (e.g., from schizophrenia to depression to violence), while positive attributes of either the individual or the environment can provide some protection from these outcomes.

Prenatal Influences

Integrity of the internal environment of the developing fetus is strongly predictive of future outcomes in terms of organ function, anatomical features, cognitive ability, intelligence level, psychiatric status, and behavioral patterns (Glover, 1997). The mother's experiences and mental state influence this internal environment and, consequently, play an active role in determining the range of abilities the child will have in interaction with his or her genetic make-up. Her nutritional intake, use of substances and even stress levels directly affect fetal development. Hundreds of studies document the relationship between suboptimal prenatal conditions and later behavioral and psychological disorders. One particular study (Lou et al., 1994) followed 3,021 women through their pregnancy and compared the seventy most stressed with fifty controls from the sample. Both antenatal stress and smoking contributed independently and significantly to lower gestational age, lower birth weight, and small head circumference when corrected for birth weight. Prenatal stress was also significantly associated with poorer scores on the neonatal neurological examination. Further investigations have begun to examine the specific effects of the prenatal environment on various dimensions and risk factors for antisocial behavior, including conduct disorder, hyperactivity, attention deficits, aggressiveness, and propensity for crime and substance abuse.

Minor Physical Anomalies. The presence of minor physical anomalies (MPAs) is indicative of prenatal trauma or disruption. MPAs are congenital abnormalities in the body's structure that reflect impairment in fetal development. They originate in the same embryonic layer that produces the central nervous system; thus, it is reasoned that MPAs are markers of nervous system anomalies (Fogel et al., 1985). Specifically, certain body features develop at particular times during gestation. A disruption to the fetal environment during that period of time will likely affect the development of those particular features, resulting in visible abnormalities in facial or body form. The visible presence of one or more MPAs provides a clue as to when the insult took place and is reflective of possible damage to portions of the central nervous system that are developing simultaneous to those bodily structures. A disruption during the first trimester of pregnancy is perhaps most insidious given that all major organs are forming and that the brain is in a critical and vulnerable phase of development. Table 25.1 provides a list of typical MPAs resulting from prenatal trauma.

Several studies have identified multiple MPAs in behavioral and developmental disorders (Pomeroy et al., 1988) associated with antisocial outcomes. For example, Bell and Waldrop's (1982) review found that high MPA counts in males during the newborn period have shown strong predictive relationships to preschool temperament factors such as short attention span, high activity level, and aggressive-impulsive behavior. For females, high anomaly scores showed relationships to short attention span and to inhibition. Fogel et al. (1985) found high MPA counts to be associated with hyperactive behavior in normal and clinical populations of boys, and with inhibited behavior in normal groups of girls. Kandel et al. (1989) tested the hypothesis that MPAs predict adolescent and adult recidivistic violent criminal behavior. The number of MPAs was measured at eleven to thirteen years of age and police records of criminal behavior were ascertained at twenty to twenty-two years of age. Recidivistic violent offenders evidenced an elevated level of MPAs compared to subjects with one violent offense or subjects with no violent offenses. Mednick & Kandel (1988) further reported that MPAs appear to be strongly related to hyperactivity and later criminal involvement, but only if the offender was reared in an unstable, nonintact family. They concluded that indices of perinatal problems relate to later violent crime, rather than to property crime, and may have as their basis some form of trauma occurring very early in life.

Prenatal Drug Exposure. One of the most profound and also preventable precipitants of behavioral and psychological disorders during pregnancy is prenatal drug exposure. Animal and human studies indicate that repeated prenatal exposure to abusable drugs leads to disruptions in normal neurotransmitter function and may enhance development of tolerance and/or sensitization to later drug use in the offspring (Allan et al., 1998; Battaglia et al., 1995; Henry et al., 1995; Legido, 1997; Howard & Takeda, 1990; Slotkin, 1998). One very profound and direct cause of mental retardation that is entirely preventable is fetal alcohol exposure. Fetal alcohol syndrome (FAS) is easily diagnosable due to the obvious facial deformities and mental retardation that occur in the offspring when alcohol was consumed in large quantities throughout pregnancy. However, subtler forms of FAS can also result from lower or less frequent intake of

Table 25.1
Minor Physical Anomalies (Waldrop & Halverson, 1971)

Head circumference out of normal range	Asymmetrical ears
More than one hair whorl	Soft pliable ears
Fine electric hair	No ear lobes
Epicanthus	High steepled palate
Hypertelorism	Furrowed tongue
Malformed ears	Curved fifth finger
Low-set ears	Single palmar crease
Wide gap between first and second toes	Third toe longer than second
Partial syndactalia of toes	

alcohol, which contributes to less obvious facial deformities, making diagnosis more difficult. Rather than profound mental retardation, these cases may present themselves with cognitive deficits, learning disabilities, hyperactivity, and behavioral problems. Individuals so affected are more vulnerable to antisocial behavior by virtue of the many risk factors they possess (Backon, 1989; Famy et al., 1998; Streissguth et al., 1991).

Damage to the brain from fetal alcohol exposure increases vulnerability to antisocial behavior specifically by affecting executive cognitive functioning and verbal skills. Also, neurobiological research suggests that the activity levels of serotonin in the offspring are lower (Guerri, 1998; Gorio et al., 1992; Tajuddin & Druse, 1988), which can contribute to the development of impulsivity and aggressiveness. Impairments are exhibited in the following forms:

- An inability to calculate the consequences of one's actions
- Difficulty linking cause with effect
- Impaired logic
- Relative lack of remorse
- Memory and learning impairments
- Inappropriate behaviors and impulsivity
- Defects in abstract thought
- Difficulty in following directions

The social consequences of these neuropsychological deficits include:

- Suggestibility, poor judgment, and gullibility
- Increased vulnerability to abuse
- Rejection by peers
- Frustration and hostility
- Tendency to associate with like-peers
- Alienation in school

Each of these traits is associated with antisocial behavior. The impairments suffered by FAS victims last a lifetime and frequently remain undiagnosed.

Nicotine Exposure. Maternal smoking during pregnancy also increases the risk for behavioral problems and cognitive deficits in the offspring, which in turn increases the risk for antisocial outcomes. Prenatal exposure to nicotine is associated with adverse reproductive outcomes, including alterations in neural structure and functioning, cognitive deficits, and behavior problems in the child. Wakschlag et al. (1997) reported that mothers who smoked more than half a pack of cigarettes daily during pregnancy were significantly more likely to have a child with conduct disorder. A significant effect of maternal smoking on externalizing behavior problems (e.g., oppositional, aggressive and/or overactive behaviors) was also reported by Orlebeke et al. (1997). Rantakallio et al. (1992) found an association between maternal smoking in pregnancy and delinquency in the offspring during adolescence and early adulthood, although the nature of causal mechanisms was unclear. Milberger and colleagues (1996) reported an association between maternal smoking during pregnancy and attention deficit hyperactivity disorder in the children they sampled.

The assumption underlying these and other studies is that maternal smoking causes brain damage by reducing oxygen to the fetal brain and by interfering with the development of neurotransmitter and modulator systems. For example, there is evidence that acetylcholine receptor activity is disrupted in fetuses exposed to nicotine (Navarro et al., 1989; Slotkin, 1998; Tizabi et al., 1997), contributing to lower cognitive, psychomotor, language and academic performance, in addition to hyperactivity and attention deficits (Dunn et al., 1997; Milberger et al., 1996, 1997). In combination with a disadvantageous or suboptimal environment (e.g., poor parenting or family dysfunction), the effects of maternal smoking during pregnancy on antisocial behavior are expected to be even stronger.

Cocaine Effects. In some large urban areas, between 10 and 15 percent of all women in their child-bearing years are users of cocaine (Giacoia, 1990). Cocaine readily crosses the placental barrier and rapidly becomes concentrated in fetal brain tissue. Chronic prenatal exposure results in depletion of brain chemicals (e.g., dopamine) and damage to receptors. For example, prenatal cocaine exposure increases release of the adrenergic amines, such as norepinephrine, to initiate the "stress response" (fight/flight mechanism). These chemicals are also involved in basic neuropsychological functions (e.g., attention, activity levels, and regulation of anxiety and other emotional states). Cocaine further affects blood flow, possibly resulting in fetal hypoxemia and decreased nutrient transfer. Mothers who use cocaine are also less likely to obtain prenatal care, follow a proper diet or experience appropriate weight gain. Similarly, most cocaine users also consume alcohol, complicating the isolation of specific effects.

Consequences to the fetus are believed to be many and varied, from cerebral infarction and seizures to disrupted sleep patterns and irritability. Problems with attention regulation, activity levels, and capacity to modulate behavior have been reported, all of which are risk factors for later antisocial behavior and drug use. Neurobiological research shows that receptor activity of serotonin, dopamine, and norepinephrine is disrupted in exposed newborns, resulting in developmental delays that pose a substantial liability to negative outcomes (Battaglia et al., 1995; Legido, 1997; Seidler & Slotkin, 1992; Slotkin, 1998). Also, electroencephalogram (EEG) abnormalities in the newborn exposed to cocaine prenatally suggest cerebral irritation in addition to tremors, irritability, and hypertonicity. Fetal weight tends to be lower, fetal length shorter, and head circumference smaller, but lags in the development of these features become more trivial as the infant matures. There are also indications of:

- Impairments in interactive capabilities, state regulation, and habituation
- Hyperexcitability or depression
- Lowered mental and psychomotor developmental scores
- Deficits in context of free play
- Less representational play
- A high rate of scattering, batting, and picking up and putting down toys rather than sustained play or curious exploration
- Minimal brain dysfunction and learning disabilities
- Difficulty in concentrating, interacting with other children, and playing alone
- Impairment in basic attentional regulation processes

Cognitive effects are strongly dependent on the quality of home environment. The prevailing lifestyle can complicate the outcome for the developing child (Azuma & Chasnoff, 1993; Brooks-Gunn et al., 1994). Conditions that often exist in the homes of children exposed prenatally to cocaine include a chaotic environment, a lack of appropriate stimulation, lack of parenting skills, mother with impaired mental functioning by virtue of her addiction, inappropriate developmental modeling, and abuse and neglect. The presence of these conditions increases the likelihood of further impairments to intellectual capability and social-ethical behavior.

Social Environment During Pregnancy. The social environment of a mother during pregnancy can also alter the prenatal biological environment, subsequently affecting outcomes for the offspring. Exposure to high levels of stress during pregnancy can influence the integrity of physiological, hormonal, and neurotransmitter systems developing in the fetus, subsequently increasing the risk for psychopathology in the child (Benes, 1997; McIntosh et al., 1995; Roughton et al., 1998; van Os & Selten, 1998; Ward, 1991). Recent studies suggest that environmental stress during this period can activate genes linked to various mental problems (Benes, 1997; Kaufer et al., 1998; Smith et al., 1997; Stabenau, 1977; Van Os & Selten, 1998). In particular, the gene called "C-fos" may be turned on in the fetus by exposure to both stress and drugs of abuse experienced by the mother (Kaufer et al., 1998; Senba & Ueyama, 1997). Increased C-fos activity is believed to create abnormal neural connections, causing neurons to fire in the absence of a trigger which may elicit feelings or behaviors that are out of context given environmental conditions. Children who experience high levels of stress, hypothetically either in utero or in early life, may become sensitized to future stressful experiences and exhibit inappropriate emotions associated with mental disorders (Post, 1992).

Perinatal Complications

Perinatal conditions occur between the seventh month of pregnancy to twenty-eight days after birth (Brennan & Mednick, 1997). They include prematurity and delivery complications such as hypoxia, infectious disease, prolapsed cord during delivery, irregular heart beat in the child during delivery, late stage drug use, and other difficulties immediately before, during, or after birth. These conditions are believed to increase the risk for negative outcomes, including impulsive and aggressive behavior, as a function of the fetal brain damage they can cause. Piquero and Tibbetts (1999) provide a thorough overview of research on the relationship between perinatal factors and criminal or antisocial behavior. The predominance of literature they review, in addition to their own research, shows support for the relationship, although there are some discrepancies. More importantly, however, are the studies they cite that suggest a strong interactive relationship between the effects of perinatal complications and the social environment on antisocial outcomes. They conclude from their review that "poor or deficient familial and socioeconomic environments may magnify the effects of pre/perinatal complications." Piquero and Tibbetts surmise that perinatal complications may contribute to neuropsychological deficits that impede the socialization process. In the dual presence of neuropsychological impairment and a poor familial environment, characterized by family dysfunction, neglect or abuse, inconsistent parenting or lack of supervision, the socialization process is further compromised, exponentially increasing risk for an antisocial outcome.

The Social Environment and Its Stressors

The social environment of the mother and her offspring contributes in substantial and necessary ways to brain development and function. Not only does the growing brain of a child require a certain amount of physical stimulation, there are also strong biological needs for positive social interactions, bonding, and protection against traumatic experiences. Even the most basic biological systems depend on the quality of social stimulation early in life. The brain continues to develop neural connections during the first year of life, and approximately 50 percent of all human learned responses are formed by then. Between year one and year three, adaptational responses to the environment are formed, including the essential stage called "basic trust." Through attachments to caregivers, infants and children develop a sense of security, self-efficacy, reassurance about the safety of their environment, and successful experiences with others.

Children who do not develop basic trust often have attachment disorders, aggressiveness, attention deficits, anxiety, emotional disturbances, and withdrawal. It is apparent that early experiences are of the utmost importance in contributing to the integrity of brain function. Most basic biological systems depend on social stimulation early in life. Without it, children lack the foundation to deal with everyday life, let alone trauma and stress. Thus, even in the presence of prenatal trauma or perinatal complications, manipulations of the environment can minimize biological risks or disadvantages to alter outcomes.

Environmental Stimulation Needs

Social and physical stimulation, from mother-child bonds to visual explorations of the environment, are essential to develop and maintain proper brain function. Deprived of adequate sensory experiences, the brain atrophies and neural connections are lost. The brain experiences crucial periods when cells must be stimulated adequately to develop vision, language, smell, muscle control, and reasoning ability. Connections not supported by the external environment shrink and may die; an impoverished environment where sensory stimulation is inadequate can decrease neural connections by 25 percent or more. One of the most extreme examples of such deprivation is in certain orphanages where infants lack routine caregiver interactions, both social and tactile; mental retardation and even physical deformities may result. Also, children who are not provided with the most basic academic skills (e.g., learning colors or how to spell their names) during the first few years may have difficulty once they enter school and become academically disadvantaged even though they may be quite bright. More intense stimulation to cognitive functions may be necessary for these children to advance appropriately. Thus, early experiences are essential determinants of how the brain functions later in life.

Under conditions of sensory deprivation, animals and humans alike tend to seek stimulation the brain requires for proper functioning: "an inactive mind leads to an active body." The reticular activating system (RAS) radiates from the brainstem up through the thalamus in the center of the brain with fibers that connect to higher centers in the cortex. It is the RAS that activates the brain on receipt of information from the environment, enabling the individual to become aware of that input and act on it if necessary. When stimulation from the environment is inadequate, due either to sensory deprived conditions or physiological deficiencies within the RAS, the tendency to seek stimulation elsewhere increases. For a child, stimulation needs are primarily physical; too little stimulation often results in distractibility, constant motion, inability to sit still, and excessive physical contact with others, as seen in hyperactivity. Hypoarousal within the RAS has been associated with hyperactivity, which may help to explain why the administration of a stimulant, Ritalin, helps to calm and focus hyperactive children. Their unusual need for external stimulation is counterbalanced when the RAS is receiving proper amounts of internal stimulation.

As the child matures, however, high stimulation needs may be met in more sophisticated ways by risk-taking activities, thrill or novelty seeking, drug use, criminal activity, and other excessive behaviors. Thus, even in the absence of a genetic or biological deficit in central nervous system (CNS) arousal levels, environmental stimulus deprivation can simulate a condition such as hyperactivity or sensation-seeking by creating a deficiency state and increasing needs for external stimulation. Starting as young as six weeks old, an enriched environment can alter lives of children in deprived environments by improving brain function. There is evidence from animal (Schwartz & Goldman-Rakic, 1990; Passig et al., 1996; Pham et al., 1997), human biological (Meaney et al., 1991; Pham et al., 1997; Weisglas-Kuperus et al., 1993), and neuroimaging (Risch, 1997) studies that changes incurred through environmental enrichment, where complex and intensive inanimate and social stimulation is provided, may endure through adulthood.

Caregiver-Child Interactions

With respect to the need for environmental stimulation, the bond between caregiver and child is critical. Regular tactile and sensory contact is a basic biological need. Premature animals (Meaney et al., 1991; Meaney & Aitken, 1985) and human babies (Kuhn & Schanberg, 1998) who are touched frequently gain more weight, are more active and alert, and show more brain growth. Touch has biological value to maintain normal growth and development. A deficiency in tactile contact is associated with enzyme deficiencies in the brain and body. For example, a syndrome called "psychosocial dwarfism" has been documented whereby a lack of environmental stimulation in an infant leads to a deficiency in stimulation to the hypothalamus, which regulates the release of growth hormone (Albanese et al., 1994; Voss et al., 1998). As a result, growth is stunted and can be permanent if not reversed at an early age. Because the hypothalamus also regulates many aspects of both survival and emotional responses, underactivity in the hypothalamus due to stimulus deprivation can affect behavior and emotionality.

In general, animals and human babies who are stimulus deprived are less responsive to their environments, and if the condition is chronic, learning impairments, a thinner cortex (especially in the occipital portion), inadequate neurotransmitter activity, less dense connections between neurons, and increased incidence of premature aging can occur (Holsboer, 1989; Kempermann et al., 1998; Kuhn & Schanberg, 1998; McEwen, 1997; Stokes, 1995). Coping skills under stressful conditions can also be impaired throughout life in individuals so affected. An extreme example of this condition can be seen in Romanian orphans who experienced extreme sensory deprivation. Many, although genetically normal, became severely mentally and physically retarded. Less extreme, albeit severe, examples may be seen in neglected children throughout the United States who are at risk for behavioral disorders by virtue of sensory and intellectual stimulus deprivation.

Child Abuse and Other Traumatic Experiences

There is no doubt that child abuse plays a distinct and significant role in the risk for behavioral disorders due to the social and psychological trauma (Maxfield & Widom, 1996). What is less well known, however, is the impact of child abuse on the developing brain and its functioning, which may actually mediate the behavioral response. Child abuse has been associated with alterations in neurotransmitter activity (e.g., serotonin) and stress hormone levels, including cortisol and epinephrine (Kaufman et al., 1997; Lemieux & Coe, 1995; Lewis, 1992). Furthermore, fewer neural connections, EEG abnormalities, and aberrant cortical development have been reported in individuals with a history of child abuse (Ito et al., 1993, 1998; Shin et al., 1997; Stein et al., 1997a, 1997b; Teicher et al., 1997). These findings help to explain the higher incidence of developmental delays and behavioral disorders in this population.

Abnormal Hormonal Development. Sexual abuse during childhood has been linked to negative physiological changes that can affect childhood development. In particular, abnormal hormonal, pubertal, and neuroendocrine changes have been noted (Stein et al., 1997a, 1997b; DeBellis et al., 1994). Subgroups of girls sexually abused as children tend to mature earlier, have different hormonal reactions, and possibly develop impaired immune functioning compared to control girls (DeBellis et al., 1994). Higher levels of urinary catecholamines were reported in abused girls relative to controls. Catecholamines are a class of neurotransmitter secreted by the locus ceruleus in the brain and the adrenal glands near the kidneys. Excessive amounts of these transmitters induce stress and hyperarousal throughout the body and brain. As a result, sleep disorders, nervousness, and anxiety can occur. In a related study, responses of the "stress" hormones cortisol and ACTH (adrenocorticotrophic hormone) to the injection of corticotropin releasing hormone (CRH) were abnormal in sexually abused girls compared with controls. This finding indicated that the hypothalamic-pituitary-adrenal axis, which is responsible for the "fight or flight mechanism," was disregulated in these girls and that various other parts of this system were attempting to compensate for the abnormality by keeping cortisol levels down. Such disregulation has been linked to depression in other studies of adults (Dinan, 1996). Another study by these investigators examined the immune system responses of sexually abused girls and controls. The abused girls showed twice the levels of ANA (antinuclear antibody), a measure of immune system overactivity (DeBellis et al., 1994).

Brain Cell Death. Stress from child abuse and other traumatic childhood events can cause an unusual amount of brain cell death (McEwen, 1997; McEwen et al., 1995; Sapolsky, 1996; Smith, 1996; Uno et al., 1994). The increase in glucocorticoid release associated with chronic stress can lead to deficits in learning and memory by the damage "stress" hormones cause in the hippocampus, a brain structure responsible for memory, among other functions. Later in life, the stress associated with traumatic events has been associated with social rank, self-esteem, and competency in animals and humans (De Goeij et al., 1992; Gust et al., 1991; Higley et al., 1991; Kraemer et al., 1989; Oates et al., 1985; Sapolsky, 1989; Sapolsky & Mott, 1987; Virgin & Sapolsky, 1997). Levels of stress and sex hormones, cholesterol, and immune system function have all been linked to previous stress and present social rank. On the other side of the coin, there is speculation that high quality parenting can minimize problems associated with abnormal levels of neurotransmitter and hormonal activity, regardless of whether the deficit was a function of genetics, environment, or a combination thereof.

Interactions Between Prenatal Conditions and Parenting

Babies exposed to prenatal insults or perinatal complications are often more difficult children to care for. While some prenatally disadvantaged babies sleep excessively, others are more volatile and temperamental, cry more frequently, do not develop normal sleep or eating patterns, have colic, and are difficult to soothe. Furthermore, delays in brain development and greater physical needs are often coupled with a lack of appropriate stimulation from caretakers, particularly in cases in which the mother is a drug abuser, a teenager, or unusually stressed or anxious (McIntosh et al., 1995; Ward, 1991)—all conditions associated with improper prenatal care, drug exposure, and pre- and perinatal complications.

As a result, these more "difficult" children commonly elicit harsher responses from their primary caretakers, who may not have the psychological or physical resources to cope with their babies' special problems and needs. Once the relationship between caretaker and child is strained, the risk for abuse and/or neglect is much greater. For example, O'Connor et al. (1998a) found that adopted children who were at genetic risk by virtue of their biological mother's antisocial behavior were more likely to receive negative parenting. Thus in a developmental sense, these children enter the world disadvantaged and subsequently experience harsh, inconsistent, or inadequate parenting (O'Connor et al., 1998a, 1998b). On entering school, their difficulties are compounded and risk for antisocial outcomes heightened when they exhibit learning disabilities, failure in school, social isolation, and further parental rejection (Moffitt, 1993).

Trauma During Adolescence and Adulthood

Severe and/or chronic traumatic experiences throughout the lifespan can alter brain function. Studies consistently report disruptions in neurotransmitter activity and metabolism as a consequence of trauma. For example, separation from the mother and social isolation have been shown to increase vulnerability to drug abuse in the affected individual (or animal), with abnormalities in DNA synthesis, hormone responses, and neurotransmitter systems as the mediator of this effect (Kuhn & Schanberg, 1998; Phillips et al., 1997; Piazza & Le Moal, 1996, 1998). Posttraumatic stress disorder, associated not only with conditions of battle, but with conditions in many inner cities, is also linked to low levels of serotonin activity and other neurotransmitters (Beckham et al., 1997; Fitchner et al., 1995; Kaufer et al., 1998). There is further evidence that severe stress during adolescence can damage coping responses by disrupting neurotransmitter responses (Gerra, et al., 1998; Ryan, 1998). Parental divorce, for example, has been associated with neuroendocrine changes in adolescents (Gerra et al., 1993). It is widely recognized that parental divorce can have serious psychological and behavioral consequences during childhood, and these impairments include problems in peer relationships and a high incidence of aggressive behavior and alcohol consumption. These studies suggest that these impairments may be due to changes in the secretion patterns of neurohormones induced by the stress of the parental divorce, thereby reducing adaptation to stress in the adolescent. Fortunately, several factors offer some protection from these deleterious conditions, including quality of the home life, relationships with others, and intimate bonds.

Evidently, exposure to highly stressful and/or novel situations can alter sensitivity of the mesolimbic dopamine reward system, the same system that mediates the rewarding effects of drugs of abuse (Bardo et al., 1996; Cools & Gingras, 1998; Horger & Roth, 1996). Recent studies shed light on individual differences in drug-seeking behavior by demonstrating that heightened sensitivity of this system, due to environmental stress or novelty, may increase susceptibility to abuse and addiction (Phillips et al., 1997; Piazza & Le Moal, 1996, 1998). Stress can also switch genes on or off at the "wrong" times, leading to the development of abnormal networks of brain cell connections that can result in, for example, excessive secretion of stress hormones (e.g., glucocorticoids).

When levels of stress hormones are excessive, their presence increases sensitivity of mesolimbic dopamine neurons to drugs, further exacerbating the risk for drug abuse. Stress can also damage key brain structures, producing irregularities in brain function that are similar to those associated with propensity to both drug abuse and impulsive-aggressive behavior. Accordingly, consequences may include learning deficits, mood disturbances, drug abuse, tension, depression, and an inability to cope with external stressors, each of which is associated with antisocial outcomes.

Bardo et al. (1996) persuasively advocate that prevention programs selectively target individuals with the trait of sensation seeking, given research that implicates this trait in propensity to use drugs and engage in antisocial behavior. Because high sensation seekers are "biologically prepared to attend to novel information more than low sensation seekers" (p. 36), prevention strategies should incorporate messages that attract individuals with this biological predisposition. Donohew et al. (1994) (see also Lorch et al., 1994; Palmgreen et al., 1994) have implemented interventions that convey anti-drug messages using highly sensational program content with high-risk teens. Significant changes in attitudes towards drugs were incurred. A lesson learned from this research is that programs that simply attempt to extinguish drug abuse may not be sufficient in high-risk populations; instead, treatment and prevention strategies should replace drug-seeking behaviors with new behaviors that are inconsistent with drug use (Bardo et al., 1996).

Observing Violence: The Impact of Television Violence

The frequency and severity of violent incidences depicted on television have increased in recent years and generated some controversy about whether children exposed to violence on television are at increased risk for "acting out" or externalizing behaviors. While the predominant literature views this relationship as a result of modeling and social learning, there is also evidence that observations of violence alter physiological responses related to aggression. Heightened emotional reactions of children to violence on television, as measured by galvanic skin response, stress hormones, heart rate and aggressive behaviors, have been reported (Carruthers & Taggart, 1973; Osborn & Endsley, 1971). Significant increases in heart rate have also been associated with viewing violence on television (Groer & Howell, 1990). A stronger electrodermal response to violent shows was found irrespective of whether the violence was implicit or actual (Kalamas & Gruber, 1998). Bushman and Geen (1990) reported that highly violent videotapes elicited more aggressive cognitions than did a less violent tape. In a second experiment, these investigators found that aggressive cognitions increased with the level of violence in the videotape, and physical assaultiveness moderated that effect. Also, hostility and systolic blood pressure were higher in response to the most violent video. These findings and others indicate that stress and emotional systems have been activated in response to viewing television violence. Activation of these systems likely elicits more externalizing behaviors in children with preexisting vulnerability to aggressive behaviors by virtue of their arousability than more "prosocial" children.

IMPLICATIONS FOR PREVENTION STRATEGIES

Findings from research in neurobiology show how critical it is that bridges be built to link the neurosciences with prevention science. On an individual level, neurobiological findings have demonstrated that individuals vary considerably with respect to their biological strengths (protective factors) and weaknesses (risks). Biological weaknesses or vulnerabilities are influential in an individual's risk for antisocial behavior. Rather than acting alone, however, this body of research suggests that these biological features operate by setting the stage for how adaptively an individual will respond to personal stressors.

A stressful environment is more likely to contribute to some form of psychopathology when it is received by a biological system that is somehow compromised. Thus, although the probability of a pathological response is a function of the number of these individual risk factors present, the probability is even greater in the presence of an adverse environment with severe stressors. Thus, prevention programs that incorporate findings linking environmental stressors to neurobiological impacts and vice versa are likely to produce improvements in integrity of both psychosocial and biological mechanisms. Once communication and exchange between these disciplines occur, investigators will be able to identify: (1) which interventions will work best, (2) during which developmental stages, (3) with which risk factors, and (4) in which populations.

Neurobiological Processes Affecting Behavior

So far, neurobiological research shows that stress, both internally and externally induced, affects neurological processes and behavioral outcomes during particular phases of development for better or for worse. The environment can contribute to changes in behavior by altering:

- Neurotransmitter responses
- CNS and behavioral activity levels
- Blood flow and glucose metabolic rates in the brain
- Development of neuronal connections over time
- Psychoneuroimmunological responses
- Density of autoreceptors affecting regulatory capabilities
- Hormonal responses
- Physiological responses and tone

All of these biological processes underlie many forms of psychopathology. Measurable differences and changes in biological processes that are associated with behavioral and mood state have both genetic and environmental origins. Thus, an individual's developmental trajectory is determined by both genotype and environmental experiences.

Prevention Techniques to Increase Resiliency and Minimize the Impact of Risk Factors

Approaches to prevention that promise to reduce vulnerability to antisocial behavior are too numerous to delineate herein. Nevertheless, it is important to note that interventions shown to be effective in reducing the incidence of behavioral disorders (see especially Botvin et al., 1995; Eggert et al., 1994; Olds et al., 1998; Spoth et al., 1998; Thompson et al., 1997; Webster-Stratton & Hammond, 1997) most likely also enhance integrity of brain function, although further research is necessary to document specific changes over time. Two characteristics of preventive interventions clearly have potential to yield the highest gains: (1) a stress reduction component and (2) early interventions, from prenatal to preschool stages, to exert an influence before problems become magnified across the lifespan. The National Academy of Sciences (Reiss & Roth, 1993) recommends that the following interventions may prove most effective given the known risk factors:

- Prenatal, perinatal, and postnatal health care
- Cognitive-behavioral interventions
- Minimizing the effects of television violence
- Social skills training
- Parent training
- School-based interventions (intellectual enrichment, social relations, anti-bullying programs)

Additional programs that focus on reducing the number of individual risk factors and minimizing the impact of environmental stressors include:

- Neuropsychological enhancements
- Cognitive remediation
- Problem-solving training program
- "Low tech," small group interventions within an intensive behavioral rehabilitation program

- Psychoeducational programs
- Speech and language therapy
- Environmental enrichment
- Computer games for sensory and motor rehabilitation
- Alternative activities
- Functional and integrative training
- Interdisciplinary consultation

Findings reported in this chapter suggest that universal manipulations of the environment also hold the potential to significantly improve behavioral self-regulation via their impact on brain systems. Global prevention and intervention programs can be implemented to increase resiliency to prevailing risk factors in a population. Building safety nets, providing recourse for those without options, increasing availability of alternative modes of behavior, revitalizing neighborhoods, assembling multidisciplinary teams to intervene, and enhancing community involvement could have an immediate impact on the problem by providing insulation to those who are particularly "vulnerable." Several examples of prevention programs and policies that logically flow from the findings reported herein are presented below.

1. *Environmental stimulation.* Recognition that a deprived environment can induce below normal levels of nervous system arousal may enhance understanding of why some individuals under these circumstances develop an unusual need for stimulation, often expressed as risk-taking behaviors in the absence of more constructive alternatives. Programs that educate parents, caretakers, teachers, and policy-makers on the essential need for adequate environmental stimulation may result in the provision of more optimal forms of interaction and activities that ultimately influence brain function and subsequent behaviors in affected children.

2. *Abuse outcome education.* Reports that child abuse may compromise integrity of neuroendocrine systems over time, impairing effective coping strategies and leading to various forms of psychopathology, provide support for standard parenting classes within the school curriculum, in conjunction with early detection and intervention strategies, and a better equipped child welfare system.

3. *Stress management and prevention.* Evidence that chronic or high levels of environmental stress at any point during the life span may lower serotonin activity levels suggest that stress prevention, management, and reduction programs may alter negative outcomes. Also, given that perceptions of "helplessness" are associated with low serotonin, social programs that empower and increase self-control may produce improvements (e.g., employment, spousal abuse, drug addiction, and self-efficacy programs).

4. *Reduced maternal drug use.* Associations between fetal drug exposure and later behavioral and cognitive disorders provide ample fuel for educational campaigns and policies to reduce maternal drug use.

5. *Enhanced home environment.* Findings that the home environment may mitigate the effects of fetal drug exposure and other both genetic and acquired biological disadvantages strongly suggests that parent training, postnatal home visitation, and family therapy are warranted in high-risk populations.

6. *Early identification of high-risk children.* Because a significant amount of brain development is known to continue through the first year of life, early identification of high-risk children and the provision of a stimulating and nurturing environment with strong social bonds can substantially improve later outcomes.

7. *Good prenatal care.* Research establishing a relationship between prenatal and perinatal complications and later conduct problems in the offspring suggests that the provision of adequate prenatal care to high-risk populations would reduce our reliance on the criminal justice system.

8. *Reduced exposure to television violence.* Physiological and hormonal responses to television violence suggest that observing violent behavior can activate the body's stress response in some children, increasing the expression of aggressive behaviors and feelings of agitation. Policies designed to minimize exposure of children to violence on television and other media are likely to substantially reduce the incidence of learned aggression and the eventuality of desensitization to violence.

Manipulations of the social environment, therefore, may profoundly alter an individual's biological stamina, possibly improving impulse control and coping strategies.

Future Research Agenda

Although research has consistently shown that certain social and environmental conditions alter brain function, the mechanisms for that change are not well understood. Scientific examinations are needed to isolate the neurological effects of these factors, providing greater insight into specific brain-environment interactions. Furthermore, there is a need for human research, since many of the most intriguing bits of evidence are generated from animal research that cannot be easily extrapolated. Armed with knowledge based on human research, prevention scientists can design programs that directly target such neurologic effects to reverse or attenuate negative outcomes. For example, the effects of prenatal drug exposure on cognitive function and related behaviors have yet to be fully delineated, and thus remain controversial. Some investigators report evidence for both gross and subtle deficits as a result of prenatal cocaine exposure, while others do not. Identification of drug effects on the growing fetus and child will lead to a better understanding of prenatal exposures and their possible influence on liability to drug abuse. The prevention implications for such studies are substantial.

Future research questions pertaining to potential linkages between neurobiology and prevention sciences are many and varied, and include the following:

1. How can we assess environmental-neurobiological influences and then design interventions that impact at critical points in an individual's developmental trajectory to alter risk status?
2. If the genotype and neurobiological environment set the stage for responses to environmental input, can environmental interventions change the behavioral outcome?
3. Can the environment be altered to produce a trend toward normalization in the brain?
4. And will the behavioral outcome of this impact be sufficiently measurable?

One example of an integrated research design is the examination of changes in brain function during drug abuse treatment. The use of a combination of neuropsychological, imaging (e.g., PET or fMRI), and behavioral measures before, during, and after an intervention will, hypothetically, demonstrate a trend toward normalization over time. Thus, the biological impact of prevention approaches can be determined by combining assessment techniques to discern change in both brain function and related behaviors.

Research in neurobiology suggests that a sole focus on the social contributions to behavioral disturbances is insufficient. Nor is it adequate to simply examine biological influences. Individual vulnerability factors differentially interact with and are altered by environmental conditions to either heighten or minimize risk for antisocial and drug-taking behaviors. In accordance, a more comprehensive and effective approach to the science, treatment, and prevention of antisocial behaviors includes an estimation of relative and interactive biological *and* social contributions. As a result of the ineffective, unidimensional approaches of the past, we are now defaulting to the criminal justice system with troubled individuals. Rather than ignoring the warning signs in childhood and waiting until adulthood to put into motion the criminal justice or mental health system, spending billions for legal remedies that do not produce favorable outcomes, the provision of sorely needed services and interventions to high-risk individuals can yield far greater benefits to this country and its citizenry.

References

Ackerman, P. T., Newton, J. E., McPherson, W. B., Jones, J. G. & Dykman, R. A. (1998). Prevalence of post traumatic stress disorder and other psychiatric diagnoses in three groups of abused children. *Child Abuse and Neglect, 22,* 759–774.

Albanese, A., Hamill, G., Jones, J., Skuse, D., Matthews, D. R. & Stanhope, R. (1994). Reversibility of physiological growth hormone secretion in children with psychosocial dwarfism. *Clinical Endocrinology, 40,* 687–692

Allan, A. M., Wu, H., Paxton, L. L. & Savage, D. D. (1998). Prenatal ethanol exposure alters the modulation of the gamma-aminobutyric acid A1 receptor-gated chloride ion channel in adult rat offspring. *Journal of Pharmacology and Experimental Therapeutics, 284,* 250–257.

Anisman, H., Zacharia, M. D., Meaney, M. J. & Merali, Z. (1998). Do early-life events permanently alter behavioral and hormonal responses to stressors? *International Journal of Developments in Neuroscience, 16,* 149–164.

Anisman, H. & Zacharko, R. M. (1986). Behavioral and neurochemical consequences associated with stressors. *Annals of the New York Academy of Sciences, 467,* 205–225.

Azuma, S. D. & Chasnoff, I. J. (1993). Outcome of children prenatally exposed to cocaine and other drugs: A path analysis of three-year data. *Pediatrics, 92,* 396–402.

Backon, J. (1989). Etiology of alcoholism: Relevance of prenatal hormonal influences on the brain, anomalous dominance, and neurochemical and pharmacological brain asymmetry. *Medical Hypotheses, 29,* 59–63.

Bardo, M. T., Donohew, R. L. & Harrington, N. G. (1996). Psychobiology of novelty seeking and drug seeking behavior. *Brain and Behavior Research, 77,* 23–43.

Battaglia, G., Cabrera, T. M. & Van de Kar, L. D. (1995). Prenatal cocaine produces biochemical and functional changes in brain serotonin systems in rat progeny. National Institute on Drug Abuse Research Monograph No. 158, 115–148.

Beckham, J. C., Feldman, M. E., Kirby, A. C., Hertzberg, M. A. & Moore, S. D. (1997) Interpersonal violence and its correlates in Vietnam veterans with chronic posttraumatic stress disorder. *Journal of Clinical Psychology, 53,* 859–869.

Bell, C. C. & Jenkins, E. N. (1991). Traumatic stress and children. *Journal of Health Care for the Poor and Underserved, 2,* 175–185.

Bell, R. Q. & Waldrop, M. F. (1982). Temperament and minor physical anomalies. *Ciba Foundation Symposium, 89,* 206–220.

Benes, F. M. (1997). The role of stress and dopamine-GABA interactions in the vulnerability for schizophrenia. *Journal of Psychiatric Research, 31,* 257–275.

Bjorklund, D. F. & Brown, R. D. (1998). Physical play and cognitive development: Integrating activity, cognition and education. *Child Development, 69,* 604–606.

Botvin, G. J., Baker, E., Dusenbury, L., Botvin, E. M. & Diaz, T. (1995). Long-term follow-up results of a randomized drug abuse prevention trial in a white middle-class population. *Journal of the American Medical Association, 273,* 1106–1112.

Brennan, P. & Mednick, S. (1997). Medical histories of antisocial individuals. In D. Stoff, J. Breiling & J. Maser (Eds.), *Handbook of antisocial behavior.* New York: John Wiley & Sons.

Brooks-Gunn, J., McCarton, C. & Hawley, T. (1994). Effects of in utero drug exposure on children's development: Review and recommendations. *Archives of Pediatric and Adolescent Medicine, 148,* 33–39.

Bushman, B. J. & Geen, R. G. (1990). Role of cognitive-emotional mediators and individual differences in the effects of media violence on aggression. *Journal of Personality and Social Psychology, 58,* 156–163.

Carruthers, M. & Taggart, P. (1973). Vagotonicity of violence: Biochemical and cardiac responses to violent films and television programmes. *British Medical Journal, 3,* 384–389.

Cools, A. R. & Gingras, M. A. (1998). Nijmegen high and low responders to novelty: A new tool in the search after the neurobiology of drug abuse liability. *Pharmacology and Biochemistry of Behavior, 60,* 151–159.

Davis, L. L., Suris, A., Lambert, M. T., Heimberg, C. & Petty, F. (1997). Post-traumatic stress disorder and serotonin: New directions for research and treatment. *Journal of Psychiatry Neuroscience, 22,* 318–326.

De Bellis, M. D., Chrousos, G. P., Dorn, L. D., Burke, L., Helmers, K., Kling, M. A., Trickett, P. K. & Putnam, F. W. (1994). Hypothalamic-pituitary-adrenal axis dysregulation in sexually abused girls. *Journal of Clinical Endocrinology and Metabolism, 78,* 249–255.

De Goeij, D. C., Dijkstra, H. & Tilders, F. J. (1992). Chronic psychosocial stress enhances vasopressin, but not corticotropin-releasing factor, in the external zone of the median eminence of male rats: Relationship to subordinate status. *Endocrinology, 131,* 847–853.

De Zulueta, F. I. (1998). Human violence: A treatable epidemic. *Medical Conflict Survivors, 14,* 46–55.

Dinan, T. G. (1996). Serotonin: Current understanding and the way forward. *International Clinical Psychopharmacology, 11,* 19–21.

Donohew, L., Palmgreen, P. & Lorch, E. P. (1994). Attention, need for sensation and health communication campaigns. *American Behavioral Scientist, 38,* 310–322.

Dunn, H. G., McBurney, A. K., Ingram, S. & Hunter, C. M. (1977). Maternal cigarette smoking during pregnancy and the child's subsequent development: II. Neurological and intellectual maturation to the age of 6 1/2 years. *Canadian Journal of Public Health, 68,* 43–50.

Edwards, D. H. & Kravitz, E. A. (1997). Serotonin, social status and aggression. *Current Opinions in Neurobiology, 7,* 812–819.

Eggert, L. L., Thompson, E. A., Herting, J. R., Nicholas, L. J. & Dicker, B. G. (1994). Preventing adolescent drug abuse and high school dropout through an intensive school-based social network development program. *American Journal of Health Promotion, 8,* 202–215.

Famy, C., Streissguth, A. P. & Unis. A. S. (1998). Mental illness in adults with fetal alcohol syndrome or fetal alcohol effects. *American Journal of Psychiatry, 155,* 552–554.

Fichtner, C. G., O'Connor, F. L., Yeoh, H. C., Arora, R. C. & Crayton, J. W. (1995). Hypodensity of platelet serotonin uptake sites in posttraumatic stress disorder: Associated clinical features. *Life Sciences, 57,* PL37–PL44.

Field, T. M., Scafidi, F., Pickens, J., Prodromidis, M., Pelaez-Nogueras, M., Torquati, J., Wilcox, H., Malphurs, J., Schanberg, S. & Kuhn, C. (1998). Polydrug-using adolescent mothers and their infants receiving early intervention. *Adolescence, 33,* 117–143.

Finney, J. W. & Moos, R. H. (1992). The long-term course of treated alcoholism: II. Predictors and correlates of 10-year functioning and mortality. *Journal of Studies on Alcohol, 53,* 142–153.

Fishbein, D. H. (1998). Differential susceptibility to comorbid drug abuse and violence. *Journal of Drug Issues, 28,* 859–890.

Fogel C. A., Mednick, A. & Michelsen, N. (1985). Hyperactive behavior and minor physical anomalies. *Acta Psychiatrica Scandinavia, 72,* 551–556.

Gerra, G., Caccavari, R., Delsignore, R., Passeri, M., Fertonani-Affini, G., Maestri, D., Monica, C. & Brambilla, F. (1993). Parental divorce and neuroendocrine changes in adolescents. *Acta Psychiatrica Scandinavia, 87,* 350–354.

Gerra, G., Zaimovic, A., Giucastro, G., Folli, F., Maestri, D., Tessoni, A., Avanzini, P., Caccavari, R., Bernasconi, S. & Brambilla, F. (1998). Neurotransmitter-hormonal responses to psychological stress in peripubertal subjects: Relationship to aggressive behavior. *Life Sciences, 62,* 617–625.

Giacoia, G. P. (1990). Cocaine in the cradle: A hidden epidemic. *Southern Medical Journal, 83,* 947–951.

Glover, V. (1997). Maternal stress or anxiety in pregnancy and emotional development of the child. *British Journal of Psychiatry, 171,* 105–106.

Gorio, A., Germani, E., Mantegazza, P., Di Giulio, A. M. & Bertelli, A. (1992). Perinatal exposure to ethanol affects postnatal degeneration and regeneration of serotonergic pathways in the spinal cord. *Drugs in Experimental and Clinical Research, 18,* 461–464.

Graeff, F. G., Guimaraes, F. S., De Andrade, T. G. & Deakin, J. F. (1996). Role of 5-HT in stress, anxiety, and depression. *Pharmacology and Biochemistry of Behavior, 54,* 129–141.

Groer, M. & Howell, M. (1990). Autonomic and cardiovascular responses of preschool children to television programs. *Journal of Child and Adolescent Psychiatry and Mental Health Nursing, 3,* 134–138.

Guerri, C. (1998). Neuroanatomical and neurophysiological mechanisms involved in central nervous system dysfunctions induced by prenatal alcohol exposure. *Alcohol Clinical and Experimental Research, 22,* 304–312.

Gunnar, M. R., Tout, K., de Haan, M., Pierce, S. & Stansbury, K. (1997). Temperament, social competence, and adrenocortical activity in preschoolers. *Developmental Psychobiology, 31,* 65–85.

Gust, D. A., Gordon, T. P., Wilson, M. E., Ahmed-Ansari, A., Brodie, A. R. & McClure, H. M. (1991). Formation of a new social group of unfamiliar female rhesus monkeys affects the immune and pituitary adrenocortical systems. *Brain Behavioral Immunology, 5,* 296–307.

Hawkins, D. & Catalano, R. (1995). Preventing substance abuse. In M. Tonry & D. Farrington (Eds.), *Crime and justice: A review of research,* vol. 19. Chicago: University of Chicago Press.

Henry, C., Guegant, G., Cador, M., Arnauld, E., Arsaut, J., LeMoal, M. & Demotes-Mainard, J. (1995). Prenatal stress in rats facilitates amphetamine-induced sensitization and induces long-lasting changes in dopamine receptors in the nucleus accumbens. *Brain Research, 685,* 179–186.

Higley, J. D. & Linnoila, M. (1997). Low central nervous system serotonergic activity is traitlike and correlates with impulsive behavior. A nonhuman primate model investigating genetic and environmental influences on neurotransmission. *Annals of the New York Academy of Sciences, 836,* 39–56.

Higley, J. D., Mehlman, P. T., Poland, R. E., Taub, D. M., Vickers, J. H., Suomi, S. J. & Linnoila, M. (1996). CFS testosterone and 5-HIAA correlate with different types of aggressive behaviors. *Biological Psychiatry, 40,* 1067–1082.

Higley, J. D., Suomi, S. J. & Linnoila, M. (1991). CSF monoamine metabolite concentrations vary according to age, rearing, and sex, and are influenced by the stressor of social separation in rhesus monkeys. *Psychopharmacology, 103,* 551–556.

Hofkosh, D., Pringle, J. L., Wald, H. P., Switala, J., Hinderliter, S. A. & Hamel, S. C. (1995). Early interactions between drug-involved mothers and infants: Within-group differences. *Archives of Pediatric and Adolescent Medicine, 149,* 665–672.

Holsboer, F. (1989). Psychiatric implications of altered limbic-hypothalamic-pituitary adrenocortical activity. *European Archives of Psychiatry and Neurological Science, 238,* 302–322.

Horger, B. A. & Roth, R. H. (1996). The role of mesoprefrontal dopamine neurons in stress. *Critical Reviews in Neurobiology, 10,* 395–418.

Howard, S. G. & Takeda, H. (1990). Effect of prenatal exposure to phencyclidine on the postnatal development of the cholinergic system in the rat. *Developmental Neuroscience, 12,* 204–209.

Hussong, A. M. & Chassin, L. (1997). Substance use initiation among adolescent children of alcoholics: Testing protective factors. *Journal of Studies on Alcohol, 58,* 272–279.

Ito, Y., Teicher, M. H., Glod, C. A. & Ackerman, E. (1998). Preliminary evidence for aberrant cortical development in abused children: A quantitative EEG study. *Journal of Neuropsychiatry and Clinical Neuroscience, 10,* 298–307.

Ito, Y., Teicher, M. H., Glod, C. A., Harper, D., Magnus, E. & Gelbard, H. A. (1993). Increased prevalence of electrophysiological abnormalities in children with psychological, physical, and sexual abuse. *Journal of Neuropsychiatry and Clinical Neuroscience, 5,* 401–408.

Kagan, J. (1992). Behavior, biology, and the meanings of temperamental constructs. *Pediatrics, 3,* 510–513.

Kagan, J., Reznick, J. S. & Snidman, N. (1988). Biological bases of childhood shyness. *Science, 240,* 167–171.

Kalamas, A. D. & Gruber, M. L. (1998). Electrodermal responses to implied versus actual violence on television. *Journal of General Psychology, 125,* 31–37.

Kandel, E. S., Brennan, P. A., Mednick, S. A. & Michelson, N. M. (1989). Minor physical anomalies and recidivistic adult violent criminal behavior. *Acta Psychiatrica Scandinavia, 79,* 103–107.

Kaufer, D., Friedman, A., Seidman, S. & Soreq, H. (1998). Acute stress facilitates long-lasting changes in cholinergic gene expression. *Nature, 393,* 373–377.

Kaufman, J., Birmaher, B., Perel, J., Dahl, R. E., Moreci, P., Nelson, B., Wells, W. & Ryan, N. D. (1997). The corticotropin-releasing hormone challenge in depressed abused, depressed nonabused, and normal control children. *Biological Psychiatry, 42,* 669–679.

Kempermann, G., Brandon, E. P. & Gage, F. H. (1998). Environmental stimulation of 129/SvJ mice causes increased cell proliferation and neurogenesis in the adult dentate gyrus. *Current Trends in Biology, 8,* 939–942.

Kraemer, G. W., Ebert, M. H., Schmidt, D. E. & McKinney, W. T. (1989). A longitudinal study of the effect of different social rearing conditions on cerebrospinal fluid norepinephrine and biogenic amine metabolites in rhesus monkeys. *Neuropsychopharmacology, 2,* 175–189.

Kuhn, C. M. & Schanberg, S. M. (1998). Responses to maternal separation: Mechanisms and mediators. *International Journal of Developmental Neuroscience, 16,* 261–270.

Legido, A. (1997). Intrauterine exposure to drugs. *Reviews in Neurology, 25,* 691–702.

Lemieux, A. M. & Coe, C. L. (1995). Abuse-related posttraumatic stress disorder: Evidence for chronic neuroendocrine activation in women. *Psychosomatic Medicine, 57,* 105–115.

Lewis, D. O. (1992). From abuse to violence: Psychophysiological consequences of maltreatment. *Journal of the American Academy of Child and Adolescent Psychiatry, 31,* 383–391.

Lorch, E. P., Palmgreen, P., Donohew, R. L., Helm, D., Baer, S. & D'Silva, M. (1994). Program context, sensation seeking and attention to televised anti-drug public service announcements. *Human Communication Research, 20,* 390–412.

Lou, H. C., Hansen, D., Nordenfoft, M., Pryds, D., Jensen, F., Nim, J. & Hemmingsen, R. (1994). Prenatal stressors of human life affect fetal brain development. *Developmental Medicine and Child Neurology, 36,* 826–832.

Maxfield, M. G. & Widom, C. S. (1996). The cycle of violence. Revisited 6 years later. *Archives of Pediatric and Adolescent Medicine, 150,* 390–395.

Mayes, L. C., Granger, R. H., Frank, M. A., Schottenfeld, R. & Bornstein, M. H. (1993). Neurobehavioral profiles of neonates exposed to cocaine prenatally. *Pediatrics, 91,* 778–783.

McEwen, B. S. (1997). Possible mechanisms for atrophy of the human hippocampus. *Molecular Psychiatry, 2,* 255–262.

McEwen, B. S., Albeck, D., Cameron, H., Chao, H. M., Gould, E., Hastings, N., Kuroda, Y., Luine, V., Magarinos, A. M. & McKittrick, C. R. (1995). Stress and the brain: A paradoxical role for adrenal steroids. *Vitamins and Hormones, 51,* 371–402.

McIntosh, D. E., Mulkins, R. S. & Dean, R. S. (1995). Utilization of maternal perinatal risk indicators in the differential diagnosis of ADHD and UADD children. *International Journal of Neuroscience, 81,* 35–46.

McGuire, S., Neiderhiser, J. M., Reiss, D., Hetherington, J. E. M. & Plomin, R. (1994). Genetic and environmental influences on perceptions of self-worth and competence in adolescence: A study of twins, full siblings, and step-siblings. *Child Development, 65,* 785–799.

Meaney, M. J. & Aitken, D. H. (1985). The effects of early postnatal handling on hippocampal glucocorticoid receptor concentrations: Temporal parameters. *Brain Research, 354,* 301–304.

Meaney, M. J., Mitchell, J. B., Aitken, D. H., Bhatnagar, S., Bodnoff, S. R., Iny, L. J. & Sarrieau, A. (1991). The effects of neonatal handling on the development of the adrenocortical response to stress: Implications for neuropathology and cognitive deficits in later life. *Psychoneuroendocrinology, 16,* 85–103.

Mednick, S. A. & Kandel, E. S. (1988). Congenital determinants of violence. *Bulletin of the American Academy of Psychiatry and Law, 16,* 101–109.

Milberger, S., Biederman, J., Faraone, S. V., Chen, L. & Jones, J. (1996). Is maternal smoking during pregnancy a risk factor for attention deficit hyperactivity disorder in children? *American Journal of Psychiatry, 153,* 1138–1142.

Milberger, S., Biederman, J., Faraone, S. V., Chen, L. & Jones, J. (1997) Further evidence of an association between attention-deficit/hyperactivity disorder and cigarette smoking. Findings from a high-risk sample of siblings. *American Journal of Addiction, 6,* 205–217.

Moffitt, T. E. (1993). Adolescence-limited and life-course-persistent antisocial behavior: A developmental taxonomy. *Psychological Review, 100,* 674–701.

Mott, S. H., Packer, R. J. & Soldin, S. J. (1993). Neurologic manifestations of cocaine exposure in childhood. *Pediatrics, 92,* 557–560.

Navarro, H. A., Seidler, F. J., Eylers, J. P., Baker, F. E., Dobbins, S. S., Lappi, S. E., Slotkin, T. A. (1989). Effects of prenatal nicotine exposure on development of central and peripheral cholinergic neurotransmitter systems. Evidence for cholinergic trophic influences in developing brain. *Journal of Pharmacology and Experimental Therapeutics, 251,* 894–900.

Oates, R. K., Forrest, D. & Peacock, A. (1985). Self-esteem of abused children. *Child Abuse and Neglect, 9,* 159-163.

O'Connor, T. G., Deater-Deckard, K., Fulker, D., Rutter, M. & Plomin, R. (1998a). Genotype-environment correlations in late childhood and early adolescence: Antisocial behavioral problems and coercive parenting. *Developmental Psychology, 34,* 970-981.

O'Connor, T. G., Reiss, D., McGuire, S. & Hetherington, E. M. (1998b). Co-occurrence of depressive symptoms and antisocial behavior in adolescence: A Common genetic liability. *Journal of Abnormal Psychology, 107,* 27–37.

Olds, D., Henderson, C. R., Cole, R., Eckenrode, J., Kitzman, H., Luckey, D., Pettitt, L., Sidora, K., Morris, P. & Powers, J. (1998). Long-term effects of nurse home visitation on children's criminal and antisocial behavior: 15-year follow-up of a randomized controlled trial. *Journal of the American Medical Association, 280,* 1238–1244.

Orlebeke, J. F., Knol, D. L. & Verhulst, F. C. (1997). Increase in child behavior problems resulting from maternal smoking during pregnancy. *Archives of Environmental Health, 52,* 317–321.

Osborn, D. K. & Endsley, R. C. (1971). Emotional reactions of young children to TV violence. *Child Development, 42,* 321–331.

Palmgreen, P., Lorch, E. P., Donohew, L., Harrington, N. G., D'Silva, M. & Helm, D. (1994). Reaching at-risk populations in a mass media drug abuse prevention campaign: Sensation seeking as a targeting variable. *Drugs and Society, 8,* 29–45.

Passig, C., Pinto-Hamuy, T., Moreno, J. P., Rodriquez, C., Rojas, C. & Rosas, R. (1996). Persistence of the cognitive effects of early stimulation assessed with an animal model. *Reviews of Medicine in Chile, 124,* 409–416.

Petty, F., Davis, L. L., Kabel, D., Kramer, G. L. (1996). Serotonin dysfunction disorders: A behavioral neurochemistry perspective. *Journal of Clinical Psychiatry, 57,* 11–16.

Pham, T. M., Soderstrom, S., Henriksson, B. G. & Mohammed, A. H. (1997). Effects of neonatal stimulation on later cognitive function and hippocampal nerve growth factor. *Behavioral Brain Research, 86,* 113–120.

Phillips, T. J., Roberts, A. J. & Lessov, C. N. (1997). Behavioral sensitization to ethanol: Genetics and the effects of stress. *Pharmacology and Biochemistry of Behavior, 57,* 487–493.

Pike, A., Hetherington, E. M., Reiss, D. & Plomin, R. (1996). Using MZ differences in the search for nonshared environmental effects. *Journal of Child Psychology and Psychiatry, 37,* 695–704.

Piazza, P. V. & Le Moal, M. L. (1996). Pathophysiological basis of vulnerability to drug abuse: Role of an interaction between stress, glucocorticoids and dopaminergic neurons. *Annual Reviews in Pharmacology and Toxicology, 36,* 359–378.

Piazza, P. V. & Le Moal, M. L. (1998). The role of stress in drug self-administration. *Trends in the Pharmacological Sciences, 19,* 67–74.

Pine, D. S., Coplan, J. D., Wasserman, G. A., Miller, L. S., Fried, J. E., Davies, M., Cooper, T. B., Greenhill, L., Shaffer, D. & Parsons, B. (1997). Neuroendocrine response to d,lfenfluramine challenge in boys. Associations with aggressive behavior and adverse rearing. *Archives of General Psychiatry, 54,* 839–846.

Pine, D. S., Wasserman, G. A., Coplan, J., Fried, J. E., Huang, Y. Y., Kassir, S., Greenhill, L., Shaffer, D. & Parsons, B. (1996). Platelet serotonin 2A (5-HT2A) receptor characteristics and parenting factors for boys at risk for delinquency: A preliminary report. *American Journal of Psychiatry, 153,* 538–544.

Piquero, A. & Tibbetts, S.G. (1999). The impact of pre/perinatal disturbances and disadvantaged familial environment in predicting criminal offending. *Studies on Crime and Crime Prevention, 7.*

Plomin, R. & Daniels D. (1987). Why are children in the same family so different from one another? *Behavioral and Brain Sciences, 10,* 1–16.

Pomeroy, J. C., Sprafkin, J. & Gadow, K. D. (1988). Minor physical anomalies as a biologic marker for behavior disorders. *Journal of the American Academy of Child and Adolescent Psychiatry, 27,* 466–473.

Post, R. M. (1992). Transduction of psychosocial stress into the neurobiology of recurrent affective disorder. *American Journal of Psychiatry, 149,* 999–1010.

Potts, R., Huston, A. C. & Wright, J. C. (1986). The effects of television form and violent content on boys' attention and social behavior. *Journal of Experimental Child Psychology, 41,* 1–17.

Power, C. & Estaugh, V. (1990). The role of family formation and dissolution in shaping drinking behaviour in early adulthood. *British Journal on Addiction, 85,* 521–530.

Raine, A. (1993). *The psychopathology of crime: Criminal behavior as a clinical disorder.* San Diego, CA: Academic Press.

Raine, A., Brennan, P. & Farrington, D. P. (1993). Biosocial bases of violence: Conceptual and theoretical issues. In A. Raine, P. Brennan, D. P. Farrington & S. A. Mednick (Eds.), *Biosocial bases of violence.* New York: Plenum Press, 1–20.

Raine, A., Brennan, P., Farrington, D. P. & Mednick, S. A. (1997). *Biosocial bases of violence.* New York: Plenum Press.

Raleigh, M. J., McGuire, M. T., Brammer, G. L., Pollack, D. B. & Yuwiler, A. (1991). Serotonergic mechanisms promote dominance acquisition in adult male vervet monkeys. *Brain Research, 559,* 181–190.

Rantakallio, P., Laara, E., Isohanni, M. & Moilanen, I. (1992). Maternal smoking during pregnancy and delinquency of the offspring: An association without causation? *International Journal of Epidemiology, 21,* 1106–1113.

Reiss, A. J. & Roth, J. A. (Eds.) (1993). *Understanding and preventing violence.* Washington, DC: National Academy Press.

Reiss, D., Hetherington, E. M., Plomin, R., Howe, G. W., Simmens, S. J., Henderson, S. H., O'Connor, T. J., Bussell, D. A., Anderson, E. R. & Law, T. (1995). Genetic questions for environmental studies: Differential parenting and psychopathology in adolescence. *Archives of General Psychiatry, 52,* 925–936.

Risch, S. C. (1997). Recent advances in depression research: From stress to molecular biology and brain imaging. *Journal of Clinical Psychiatry, 58,* 3–6.

Roughton, E. C., Schneider, M. L., Bromley, L. J. & Coe, C. L. (1998). Maternal endocrine activation during pregnancy alters neurobehavioral state in primate infants. *American Journal of Occupational Therapy, 52,* 90–98.

Ryan, N. D. (1998). Psychoneuroendocrinology of children and adolescents. *Psychiatric Clinics of North America, 21,* 435–441.

Sapolsky, R. M. (1989). Hypercortisolism among socially subordinate wild baboons originates at the CNS level. *Archives of General Psychiatry, 46,* 1047–1051.

Sapolsky, R. M. (1996). Why stress is bad for your brain. *Science, 273,* 749–750.

Sapolsky, R. M. & Mott, G. E. (1987). Social subordinance in wild baboons is associated with suppressed high density lipoprotein-cholesterol concentrations: The possible role of chronic social stress. *Endocrinology, 121,* 1605–1610.

Schmidt, L. A & Fox, N. A. (1994). Patterns of cortical electrophysiology and autonomic activity in adults' shyness and sociability. *Biological Psychology, 38,* 183–198.

Schmidt, L. A., Fox, N. A., Rubin, K. H., Sternberg, E. M., Gold, P. W., Smith, C. C. & Schulkin, J. (1997). Behavioral and neuroendocrine responses in shy children. *Developmental Psychobiology, 30,* 127–140.

Schwartz, M. L. & Goldman-Rakic, P. (1990). Development and plasticity of the primate cerebral cortex. *Clinical Perinatology, 17,* 83–102.

Seidler, F. J. & Slotkin, T. A. (1992). Fetal cocaine exposure causes persistent noradrenergic hyperactivity in rat brain regions: Effects on neurotransmitter turnover and receptors. *Journal of Pharmacology and Experimental Therapeutics, 263,* 413–421.

Selner-O'Hagan, M. B., Kindlon, D. J., Buka, S. L., Raudenbush, S. W. & Earls, F. J. (1998). Assessing exposure to violence in urban youth. *Journal of Child Psychology and Psychiatry, 39,* 215–224.

Senba, E. & Ueyama, T. (1997). Stress-induced expression of immediate early genes in the brain and peripheral organs of the rat. *Neuroscience Research, 29,* 183–207.

Shin, L. M., McNally, R. J., Kosslyn, S. M., Thompson, W. L., Rauch, S. L., Alpert, N. M., Metzger, L. J., Lasko, N. B., Orr, S. P. & Pitman, R. K. (1997). A positron emission tomographic study of symptom provocation in PTSD. *Annals of the New York Academy of Sciences, 821,* 521–523.

Slotkin, T. A. (1998). Fetal nicotine or cocaine exposure: Which one is worse? *Journal of Pharmacology and Experimental Therapeutics, 285,* 931–945.

Smith, M. A. (1996). Hippocampal vulnerability to stress and aging: possible role of neurotrophic factors. *Behavioral Brain Research, 78,* 25–36.

Southwick, S. M., Krystal, J. H., Bremmer, J. D., Morgan, C. A., 3d, Nicholaou, A. L., Nagy, L. M., Johnson, D. R., Heninger, G. R. & Chorney, D. S. (1997). Noradrenergic and serotonergic function in posttraumatic stress disorder. *Archives of General Psychiatry, 54,* 749–758.

Spoth, R., Redmond, C. & Shin, C. (1998). Direct and indirect latent-variable parenting outcomes of two universal family-focused preventive interventions: Extending a public health-oriented research base. *Journal of Consulting and Clinical Psychology, 66,* 385–399.

Stein, M. B., Koverola, C., Hanna, C., Torchia, M. G. & McClarty, B. (1997a). Hippocampal volume in women victimized by childhood sexual abuse. *Psychological Medicine, 27,* 951–959.

Stein, M. B., Yehuda, R., Koverola, C. & Hanna, R. (1997b). Enhanced dexamethasone suppression of plasma cortisol in adult women traumatized by childhood sexual abuse. *Biological Psychiatry, 42,* 680–686.

Stokes, P. E. (1995). The potential role of excessive cortisol induced by HPA hyperfunction in the pathogenesis of depression. *European Neuropsychopharmacology, 5,* 77–82.

Streissguth, A. P., Aase, J. M., Clarren, S. K., Randels, S. P., LaDue, R. A. & Smith, D. F. (1991). Fetal alcohol syndrome in adolescents and adults. *Journal of the American Medical Association, 265,* 1961–1967.

Tajuddin, N. & Druse, J. J. (1988). Chronic maternal ethanol consumption results in decreased serotonergic 5-HT1 sites in cerebral cortical regions from offspring. *Alcohol, 5,* 465–470.

Teicher, M. H., Ito, Y., Glod, C. A., Andersen, S. L., Dumont, N. & Ackerman, E. (1997). Preliminary evidence for abnormal cortical development in physically and sexually abused children using EEG coherence and MRI. *Annals of the New York Academy of Sciences, 821,* 160–175.

Thompson, R. J., Jr., Gustafson, K. E., Oehler, J. M., Catlett, A. T., Brazy, J. E. & Goldstein, R. F. (1997). Developmental outcome of very low birth weight infants at four years of age as a function of biological risk and psychosocial risk. *Journal of Development and Behavior in Pediatrics, 18,* 91–96.

Tizabi, Y., Popke, E. J., Rahman, M. A., Nespor, S. M. & Grunberg, N. E. (1997). Hyperactivity induced by prenatal nicotine exposure is associated with an increase in cortical nicotinic receptors. *Pharmacology and Biochemistry of Behavior, 58,* 141–146.

Uno, H., Eisele, S., Sakai, A., Shelton, S., Baker, E., DeJesus, O. & Holden, J. (1994). Neurotoxicity of glucocorticoids in the primate brain. *Hormones and Behavior, 28,* 336–348.

van der Kolk, B. A. (1997). The psychobiology of posttraumatic stress disorder. *Journal of Clinical Psychiatry, 58,* 16–24.

van Os, J. & Selten, J. P. (1998). Prenatal exposure to maternal stress and subsequent schizophrenia. The May 1940 invasion of The Netherlands. *British Journal of Psychiatry, 172,* 324–326.

Virgin, C. E., Jr. & Sapolsky, R. M. (1997). Styles of male social behavior and their endocrine correlates among low-ranking baboons. *American Journal of Primatology, 42,* 25–39.

Voss, L. D., Mulligan, J. & Betts, P. R. (1998). Short stature at school entry—an index of social deprivation? (The Wessex Growth Study). *Child Care and Health Development, 24,* 145–156.

Wakschlag, L. S., Lahey, B. B., Loeber, R., Green, S. M., Gordon, J. R. A. & Leventhal, B. L. (1997). Maternal smoking during pregnancy and the risk of conduct disorder in boys. *Archives of General Psychiatry, 54,* 670–676.

Waldrop, M. F. & Halverson, C. F., Jr. (1971). Minor physical anomalies relate to hyperactive behavior in young children. In J. Hellmuth (Ed.), *Exceptional infant.* New York: Brunner/Mazel, 341–361.

Ward, A. J. (1991). Prenatal stress and childhood psychopathology. *Child Psychiatry and Human Development, 22,* 97–110.

Webster-Stratton, C. & Hammond, M. (1997). Treating children with early-onset conduct problems: A comparison of child and parent training interventions. *Journal of Consulting and Clinical Psychology, 65,* 93–109.

Weisglas-Kuperus, M. N., Baerts, W., Smrkovsky, M. & Sauer, P. J. (1993). Effects of biological and social factors on the cognitive development of very low birth weight children. *Pediatrics, 92,* 658-665.

Zuckerman, B. & Bresnahan, K. (1991). Developmental and behavioral consequences of prenatal drug and alcohol exposure. *Pediatric Clinics of North America, 38,* 1387–1407.

Chapter 26

Prospects for a Public Health Model to Prevent and Treat Antisocial Behaviors

by Diana H. Fishbein, Ph.D.

Assessing the Relevance and Significance of Research 26-1
    Estimate the Risk Factors in the Offender Population 26-2
    Identify the Environmental Risk Factors 26-2
    Assess the Dynamic Relationship of Scientific and
        Environmental Factors 26-3
    Determine Whether Intervention Actually Changes Behavior 26-4
Prospective Applications 26-4
    Drug Abuse and Addiction 26-4
    Legal Considerations 26-5
    Public Health Approach 26-5
    Civil Liberty Issues 26-6
Conclusion 26-7

ASSESSING THE RELEVANCE AND SIGNIFICANCE OF RESEARCH

While biological and genetic research is widely recognized for its scientific and practical value in the human behavioral sciences, the implications of its newfound focus on antisocial behavior for the fields of criminology and criminal justice, or for social policy, remain unchartered territory. Historically, the study of antisocial behavior has been the purview of criminology and criminal justice fields, which differ somewhat from other behavioral sciences in that policy generated from their findings may result in large-scale behavioral controls. Thus, despite the relative prematurity of

---

This chapter was first published in *Politics and the Life Sciences*, March 1996. Adapted with permission.

biological and genetic research on antisocial behavior, the possibility that findings could substantially impact criminal justice proceedings and result in global prevention policies is an impetus for discourse about the future of this research to begin now, prior to conclusive findings.

In the absence of information, there is likely to be a continuation of public fear or misconception that this research is inherently racist, or worse, that it justifies racist policies. Public education is a powerful way of dispelling myths and quelling discriminatory attitudes. Moreover, informing the public and policy-makers of findings, interpretations, and limitations will reduce the likelihood that abusive or discriminatory practices will result. Statutory regulations over the research and its potential application may also be needed to tangibly avoid abuse and provide guidelines. Unfortunately, the majority of criminologists have either rejected or remained unfamiliar with biological and genetic approaches despite their suitability to judge the social, legal, and ethical implications of this research. At a minimum, it is critical that criminologists and legal scholars familiarize themselves with biological and genetic research on antisocial behavior to provide scrutiny and statutory recommendations. Given that the research will continue whether or not the public or social scientists recognize or accept its role in the study of antisocial behavior, it is proposed that relevant issues be examined by multidisciplinary teams to determine its value in anticipation of its utility.

Estimate the Risk Factors in the Offender Population

In order to assess the relevance and significance of biological and genetic findings for crime and violence treatment and prevention, several tasks must first be undertaken. Initially, the incidence of biologically and genetically based proclivities, risk factors, or disorders among offender or antisocial populations must be estimated. Numerous studies and reports show a high incidence of psychopathology within offender populations, particularly among violent offenders (Raine, 1993). Nevertheless, the extent of genetic involvement remains unknown; psychopathology can result from many diverse influences. Once prevalence rates are known for biologically and genetically influenced forms of psychopathology in relevant populations, we can better determine how substantially a prevention strategy that incorporates biological and genetic findings may influence the problems generated by antisocial conduct. At a minimum, however, indications that a significant number of criminal offenders and troubled youth may suffer from some type of psychopathology suggest the need for early identification and intervention.

Identify the Environmental Risk Factors

A second task is to identify biological and genetic etiologic mechanisms that influence an individual's risk status in combination with environmental factors. So far, correlations between antisocial behavior and particular personality, neurochemical, and physiological traits that have a genetic base are significant in many studies (see, e.g., Fishbein, 1990; Mednick et al., 1987; Raine, 1993; Reiss et al., 1994). Similarly, twin, adoption, and molecular genetic studies are revealing significant genetic effects on antisocial behavior including aggressiveness and substance abuse (Cadoret et al.,

1986; Carey, 1992; Cloninger et al., 1982; Mednick et al., 1987; Rowe, 1986; see also Goldman & Fishbein, Chapter 9, and Comings, Chapter 16, in this book). These studies, however, are not able to discern mechanisms by which "high risk" traits may be inherited or to demonstrate precisely which biological systems are being affected by such genetic transmission. The markers for antisocial behavior relate to biological functions that may or may not be due to gene expression; they are also strongly influenced by environmental conditions. Recent work in neurobiology and molecular genetics will likely generate a more rigorous understanding of the mechanisms involved.

Proceedings within the criminal justice system require a more reliable identification of causal relationships than we are now able to provide using any known set of standards. Bail, release on recognizance, determination of competency, determination of guilt, sentencing options, probation, and parole decisions all pertain to the ability to establish the (1) commission of a crime, (2) mental state or mens rea indicative of intent, and (3) proclivity to recidivate. There are stringent guidelines for admissibility of various types of evidence that speak to these conditions, particularly with regard to biological and genetic measures that are pervasively unfamiliar to the criminal justice profession. Similar to other forms of evidence, the state of biological and genetic research must be adequately scientifically tested, reliable, and consensually agreed upon in order to meet criteria to establish causality in a courtroom. The inclusion of both social and biological variables in research and eventually in individual assessments will enhance the ability to make these determinations given the substantially increased potential to know both sides of the equation—nature plus nurture—rather than only half.

Assess the Dynamic Relationship of Scientific and Environmental Factors

A third prerequisite is the assessment of dynamic relationships between biological, genetic, and socioenvironmental factors—their interactions and relative contributions to antisocial behavior. To establish the role of biology and genetics in the study of antisocial behavior, inclusion of these variables in a sociological data set should facilitate the isolation of significant predictors and enhance explanatory power. There is strong evidence that more of the variance in incidence of antisocial behavior can be explained with an integrated approach (Brizer & Crowner, 1989). For example, Virkkunen et al. (1989) found that the inclusion of both behavioral and psychobiological variables significantly increased prediction of recidivism. Denno (1990), in a comprehensive study of environmental and biological variables on criminal behavior, juvenile delinquency, and disciplinary problems, reported that family instability and central nervous system disorders in combination were strongly related to a lack of behavioral control.

While these studies did not directly assess the role of genetics, there is expectation that both biological and genetic research will help to explain individual variation within a social context. Theoretically, while biological and genetic vulnerabilities and defects cross all social boundaries, an adverse environment increases the likelihood of a vulnerability becoming manifest (Tarter & Edwards, 1987). In other words, individuals with biological and genetic disadvantages or risk traits may be more likely to exhibit violent or antisocial behavior in a "criminogenic" environment than others under similar circumstances. Biological and genetic research may eventually answer such questions as:

- Why don't all children who are abused become victimizers?
- Why don't *most* inner city residents engage in crime? and
- Why do some in protective, middle class homes engage in crime?

Those exposed to powerful social risks (e.g., child abuse) who do not become antisocial may be equipped with genetic "insulators" such as high I.Q. or adequate impulse control. The answers, putatively, lie in individual vulnerabilities and resiliencies that may in part be genetically influenced.

Determine Whether Intervention Actually Changes Behavior

Finally, a determination must be made of whether behavioral improvements follow large-scale interventions that target individuals or populations considered to be at biological or genetic risk. Can antisocial behavior be manipulated and controlled via so-called biological or genetic approaches? Because the research is in its infancy, not many biological or genetic approaches have yet been conceived (but see, e.g., Comings, Chapter 16). Nevertheless, it is clear that genes code for biological functions with behavioral consequences that can be altered not only via so-called genetic techniques. Manipulations of behavioral disorders (e.g., depression, anxiety, alcoholism, and psychosis) have been accomplished using biological and environmental techniques (medications or changes in environmental design) in clinical settings that target traits with genetic origins. Trials in the fields of psychology, psychiatry, and drug abuse suggest that behavioral, psychotherapeutic, and medicinal regimens work best when used in conjunction with one another.

PROSPECTIVE APPLICATIONS

Clinical approaches based on the medical or mental health models hold the most promise for the eventual application of whatever treatments result from biological and genetic research, given that they are, for the most part, individualized and consensual. Unfortunately, however, only those who are economically and opportunistically privileged in our society have access to clinical services. Those who are less privileged are denied access due to a variety of systemic conditions and are often relegated to the criminal justice system instead. Although the criminal justice system has a notorious reputation for doling out tranquilizers and mood stabilizers, these medications have custodial, not therapeutic, purposes. Cases with biomedical involvement, possibly genetic in origin, could instead be managed by the mental health system, possibly within secure facilities for those deemed dangerous.

Drug Abuse and Addiction

This approach is particularly appropriate for use in drug abuse and addiction. A majority of offenders in our correctional facilities are nonviolent, petty drug users. In other words, while serious and violent offenders threaten society, create disorder, and victimize individuals, *most* substance abusers and addicts threaten only themselves. Rather than incarceration, which costs billions of dollars and usurps precious space, drug addicts could receive compassionate treatment, sensitive to the needs of the individual, with strong benefits to the offender, the family, and the greater society. Recovery can be achieved if effective treatment is available. Still, 75 percent of our federal and state funds for drug abuse are provided to law enforcement, recognized by experts to be an inadequate remedy.

Clinicians may eventually be able to identify individuals at risk in accordance with knowledge of social, biological, and genetic traits that increase risk. If this comes to fruition, more effective interventions, earlier in developmental stages, can be provided. Children will be better equipped to overcome disadvantages, social or genetic, and reach their potential. Adults will be better equipped to maintain control over their own behavior rather than requiring external restraints. Consistent findings indicate that far fewer crimes are committed when individuals are actively in treatment (see Fishbein, 1991; Fishbein & Pease, 1996). For drug users in particular, the length of treatment is negatively related to crime and drug use. If treatments or alternatives remain unavailable and ineffective, individuals at risk will likely continue to fall through the cracks and engage in crime and drug abuse.

Legal Considerations

Prior to the application of a clinical approach that focuses on biological and genetic vulnerabilities in antisocial behavior, legal professionals should be charged with the responsibility of scrutinizing the research and creating statutes to guide its application. The likelihood of abuse is greater if such research is not made public and regulated. Consent and compliance are also pertinent issues, and related questions must be answered by legal scholars and ethicists before research influences policy. Can we enforce compliance with treatment? Will coercive treatments be effective? Many argue that treatment is much more humane than techniques we currently resort to, including incarceration, solitary confinement, capital punishment, or even neglect for underlying precursors. We do not presently require consent for punishment or even execution. To what extent do we require consent for treatment?

Public Health Approach

In contrast to the medical approach is the public health model, which orchestrates global primary prevention programs aimed at populations at risk. Based on the notion that interpersonal violence is a public health problem (Rosenberg & Mercy, 1986), widescale manipulations may be implemented to prevent the development of a problem and lessen the toll in illness, death, and quality of life without stigmatization. "The key to prevention may lie in greater understanding of the behavioral components that contribute to violence" (Spivak et al., 1988, p. 1341). For example, there is convincing evidence that later behavioral problems are associated with perinatal complications (Piquero & Tibbetts, 1999; Mednick & Kandel, 1988; Raine et al., 1994). An appropriate public health approach would be to provide readily available prenatal care, particularly to populations without ready access to medical care. A public health approach strives to insulate vulnerable individuals from the effects of a criminogenic environment, increasing resiliency by building safety nets and resources in a community. Such strategies are proposed to work regardless of the origins of behavior. Contrary to popular belief, biological and genetic traits are not immutable; they are alterable in a social environment. Thus, theoretically at least, large-scale social programs can lead to behavioral improvements even in cases in which the propensities are genetically influenced, by minimizing the impact of an environment conducive to antisocial behavior.

Educational, social, economic, and behavioral programs all minimize the impact of an environment and a biological constitution conducive to antisocial behavior. As described by Tarter and Vanyukov in Chapter 2 of this book, adverse interactions in the home such as physical abuse, parental absenteeism, and poor discipline practices exacerbate a child's innate liability to behavioral disorders. Also, association with peers promoting antisocial behavior is related to the combined influence of an innate negative affect and deficient parental monitoring. These findings indicate how, among high-risk individuals, adverse interactions with the social environment can orient the child toward enhanced risk for a negative outcome. The quality of interaction between the person with a particular biological disposition and the social environment that determines his or her behavior response patterns and emotional reactions should be the focus of intervention. Universal programs that target these risk factors to minimize their impact particularly on vulnerable, high-risk individuals (also outlined in Chapter 25) include:

- Proper prenatal care
- Postnatal home visitation
- Rehabilitation for pregnant drug abusers
- Educational campaigns and enrichment programs
- Teacher training and parenting education
- Antibullying programs
- School-based conflict resolution and skill building
- After-school programs
- Reduction of television and other media violence
- Gun control
- Identification and treatment of learning disabilities
- Drug and alcohol treatment

Civil Liberty Issues

While the potential benefits are apparent, the public health approach also raises civil liberties issues pertaining to rights to privacy, freedom from unwanted disclosures, and ethical considerations concerning widescale medical and social surveillance of select populations (Rosenfeld & Decker, 1993). Such interventions may extend services to those who do not want them, have potential to further victimize underprivileged classes, and may compromise personal freedoms (Hawkins, 1989; Kittrie, 1971; Marx, 1985). Adverse consequences must be minimized by providing necessary safeguards for personal rights and liberties. On the other hand, however, "what rights and liberties [do the] beneficiaries of violence prevention programs currently enjoy [?]." Many of those "... who would be directly affected by the interventions" cannot safely walk the streets and have already had many basic legal rights curtailed because they are under control of the criminal justice system. The issue . . . then, may not be whether their freedom will be endangered by violence prevention programs, but how such programs might improve their lives while they are under custody and reduce their risk for violence after they are released." (Rosenfeld & Decker, 1993, pp. 31-32)

CONCLUSION

Biological and genetic research highlights the important role of the environment in modulating both social and genetic instigators and can inform us of the value of primary prevention strategies to curb antisocial behavior and violence. Interventions that are primarily social and educational can be employed to enhance environmental and biological insulators, as listed above. It is not necessary to wait for biological and genetic research to demonstrate definitive causal influences. We have known for decades which social forces are protective against both social and genetic risks and have neglected to adequately fund programs that will provide insulation.

Conducting biological and genetic research does not excuse us from supporting social programs, particularly given the ability of social approaches to positively affect behavior no matter what the origins. Nevertheless, interdisciplinary research is crucial if we are ever to provide needed services and treatments for individuals with compelling biological and genetic disadvantages. Studies suggest that a subgroup of our population suffers from biological and genetic vulnerabilities that overwhelm the influence of any environment. Not only do these individuals stand to greatly benefit from the research, but the public may eventually give way to more tolerance of behavioral aberrations, understanding that behavior is not entirely volitional at all times in all individuals. Instead of waiting until a vulnerable child becomes old enough to incarcerate, perhaps early assistance will enable us to avoid the personal and financial expense of criminal justice system involvement. There is little evidence that present tactics are effective; thus, we need to move forward into an era of early intervention and compassionate treatment that genetic research may advance.

References

Brizer, D. A. & Crowner, M. (1989). *Current approaches to the prediction of violence.* Washington, DC: American Psychiatric Press.

Cadoret, R. J., Troughton, E., O'Gormon, T. W. & Heywood, E. (1986). An adoption study of genetic and environmental factors in drug abuse. *Archives of General Psychiatry 43,* 1131–1136.

Carey, G. (1992). Twin imitation for antisocial behavior: Implications for genetic and family environment research. *Journal of Abnormal Psychology 101,* 18–25.

Cloninger, C. R., Sigvardsson, S., Bohman, M. & von Knorring, A. L. (1982). Predisposition to petty criminality in Swedish adoptees: II. Cross-fostering analysis of gene-environment interaction. *Archives of General Psychiatry 39,* 1242–1247.

Denno, D. W. (1990). *Biology and violence: From birth to adulthood.* New York: Cambridge University Press.

Fishbein, D. H. (1990). Biological perspectives in criminology. *Criminology 28,* 27–72.

Fishbein, D. H. (1991). Medicalizing the drug war. *Behavioral Sciences and the Law 9,* 323–344.

Fishbein, D. H. & Pease, S. (1996). *The dynamics of drug abuse.* Needham, MA: Allyn & Bacon, Inc.

Hawkins, D. (1989). Intentional injury: Are there no solutions? *Law, Medicine and Health Care, 17,* 32–41.

Kittrie, N. (1971). *The right to be different: Deviance and enforced therapy.* Baltimore, MD: Johns Hopkins University Press.

Marx, G. (1985, winter). I'll be watching you. *Dissent,* 6–34.

Mednick, S. A. & Kandel, E. (1987). Genetic and perinetal factors in violence. In S. A. Mednick & T. Moffitt (Eds.), *Biological contributions to crime causation.* Dordrecht, Holland: Martinus Nijhoff, 121–134.

Mednick, S. A., Moffitt, T. E. & Stack, S. A. (Eds.) (1988). *The causes of crime: New biological approaches.* New York: Cambridge University Press.

Piquero, A. & Tibbetts, S. G. (1999). The impact of pre/perinatal disturbances and disadvantaged familial environment in predicting criminal offending. *Studies on Crime and Prevention, 7.*

Raine, A. (1993). *The psychopathology of crime: Criminal behavior as a clinical disorder.* San Diego, CA: Academic Press.

Raine, A., Brennan, P. & Mednick, S. A. (1994). Birth complications combined with early maternal rejection at age 1 year predispose to violent crime at age 18 years. *Archives of General Psychiatry, 51,* 984–988.

Reiss, A. J., Miczek, K. A. & Roth, J. A. (Eds.) (1994). *Understanding and preventing violence,* vol. 2. *Biobehavioral influences.* Washington, DC: National Academy Press.

Rosenberg, M. & Mercy, J. (1986). Homicide: Epidemiologic analysis at the national level. *Bulletin of the New York Academy of Medicine 62,* 376–399.

Rosenfeld, R. & Decker, S. (1993). Where public health and law enforcement meet: Monitoring and preventing youth violence. *American Journal of Police 12,* 11–57.

Rowe, D. C. (1986). Genetic and environmental components of antisocial behavior: A study of 265 twin pairs. *Criminology 24,* 513–532.

Spivak, H., Prothrow-Stith, D. & Hausman, A. (1988). Dying is no accident: Adolescents, violence, and intentional injury. *The Pediatric Clinics of North America 35,* 1339–1347.

Tarter R. E. & Edwards K. (1987). Vulnerability to alcohol and drug abuse: A behavior-genetic view. *Psychological Bulletin 102,* 204–218.

Virkkunen, M., De Jong, J., Barko, J., Goodwin, F. K. & Linnoila, M. (1989). Relationship of psychobiological variables to recidivism in violent offenders and impulsive fire setters. *Archives of General Psychiatry 46,* 600–603.

Chapter 27

Violence and the Family—Promoting Violence-Free Families

Past and Present Approaches to Family Violence 27-2
What Is Needed to Stop the Violence? 27-3
Developing Effective Prevention Programs 27-3
    An Epidemiological Perspective 27-3
    The Identification of Risk and Protection Factors 27-3
    Attention to Developmental Processes 27-4
    Environmental Context 27-4
The Effects of Gender Role Socialization 27-4
Developmental Processes and Risk Factors 27-5
The Promise of Empowerment 27-5
The Role of Health Promotion Programs in Preventing
   Violence 27-6
Universal Interventions 27-6
    Interventions for Changing the Social Conditions That Breed
       Violence 27-6
    Interventions for Changing the Attitudes and Behaviors of a
       Whole Population 27-6
    Interventions for Changing the Attitudes and Behaviors of a
       Specific Class of People 27-6
Targeted Interventions—For Changing the Attitudes and Behavior of
   Special At-Risk Groups 27-7
Advantages and Potential Limitations of Universal and Targeted
   Interventions 27-7
    Universal Interventions—Advantage 27-7
    Universal Interventions—Potential Limitations 27-8

Excerpted from the Report of the American Psychological Association Presidential Task Force on Violence and the Family, Washington, DC: APA 1996.

Targeted Interventions—Advantages 27-8
Targeted Interventions–Potential Limitations 27-8
Promising Approaches to Prevention 27-9
The Importance of Community-Wide Efforts 27-10
The Economic Benefits of Violence Prevention 27-11
What Can Communities and Psychologists Do Together? 27-11
Building Bridges: Mental Health Professionals and Family Violence
 Advocates 27-12
Key Points 27-14
Recommendations 27-14
Recommendations for Public Policy and Intervention 27-15
Recommendation for Prevention and Public Education 27-18

PAST AND PRESENT APPROACHES TO FAMILY VIOLENCE

The offender-specific treatment approach most commonly used today has been developed from the punishment and deterrence model used in the criminal justice system. Based on the assumption that batterers and other chronically aggressive individuals are violent because no one stops them, this approach advocates early, swift, and certain punishment (such as arrest and prosecution for a first offense) to intensify the negative consequences of violence and thereby make violence less attractive as a behavioral choice. Some people who believe in this approach suggest that it deters other perpetrators through example, but there are no data to support this view.

A new approach that is just receiving recognition by some researchers, the neuropsychological approach, stresses biological or neuropsychological factors as they relate to battering in relationships and other violent situations. This approach suggests that violence in relationships is similar to other forms of human aggression, and that biological processes in the brain (i.e., neuropsychological and physiological factors) may play a role in the ways some violent individuals respond to stress (internal or external). Thus, brain functioning must be evaluated to determine whether impairment that is due to phenomena such as head injury, biochemical imbalances, illness, learning disabilities, or attention deficit disorder may be combining with psychosocial factors to increase violent behavior. In such cases, treatment would include medication and cognitive and neurological rehabilitation in conjunction with the other approaches.

Research data suggest that an eclectic and comprehensive combination of the theoretical perspectives probably is the most effective. Current data do not indicate that one particular theoretical approach is the best or is appropriate for all violent individuals. Therefore, having a variety of options for different situations and different offenders is the best recommendation.

Although many advocates believe that short-term psychoeducational programs are important to help stop physical violence immediately, recent studies suggest another promising approach: assigning different batterers to different types of short- and long-term programs, depending on their specific needs. Ideally, a community should have a number of different types of short- and long-term offender-specific treatment programs, including psychotherapy, for individuals, groups, and families.

WHAT IS NEEDED TO STOP THE VIOLENCE?

Society has an urgent need to find ways to prevent family violence and its negative consequences on individuals, families, and communities. Psychologists play an important role in helping to promote violence-free families.

Promoting healthy, violence-free families requires prevention efforts to reduce the likelihood that any one family member will abuse another. Such prevention requires identification of the major factors that put people at risk for behaving violently, knowledge about how the factors interact, and concerted efforts to eliminate those factors. Work in these areas already has begun:

- Psychologists, with other social scientists, have identified risk factors for violent behavior.
- Research on child and adult development has demonstrated the importance of early experiences and socialization in later life.
- Clinical observations and research have confirmed the far-reaching negative effects of violence throughout the life span.

DEVELOPING EFFECTIVE PREVENTION PROGRAMS

Prevention of family violence requires a society's commitment to make available theory- based, carefully researched, and thoroughly evaluated prevention programs tailored to reach everyone who is at risk for violence. Current prevention theory takes into account four overlapping themes that are critical in the development of violence-prevention programs: an epidemiological perspective, the identification of risk and protective factors, attention to developmental processes, and environmental context. Although the themes are intertwined, they are separated here for clarity and emphasis.

An Epidemiological Perspective

This theme focuses prevention efforts on populations rather than individuals. Populations are addressed across the demographics of gender, age, ethnicity, ability status, sexual orientation, economic and social class, or geographic region. For example, communities often design prevention programs to educate all of their members.

The Identification of Risk and Protection Factors

A number of risk factors associated with violence have been identified, although the causes of family violence are not known definitely. Members of the general population with these risk factors—which may be psychological, social, or biological—have a higher probability of becoming offenders or victims of family violence than do members of the general population. Even less is known about the factors that protect against the development of violent behavior, although current research is expanding knowledge in this area as well. Prevention programs are designed to reduce the risk factors associated with the development of violent behavior, and to strengthen the factors that protect against its development.

Attention to Developmental Processes

This theme emphasizes the importance of looking at the full life span in planning prevention programs. Young children and senior citizens, in addition to young and mid-life adults, can be victims of violence as well as perpetrators. For example, a critical risk in the development of violent behavior is exposure to family violence and abuse in childhood. Children model behavior they observe and experience in their homes. Although further study is needed to understand the ways in which developmental processes interact with risk and protective factors to produce or prevent violent behavior, enough is known to prompt the creation of prevention efforts to protect children from exposure to family violence and abuse whenever possible.

Environmental Context

Risk and protective factors emerge and fade across the stages of the life span, interacting with the social, physical, and cultural environment to shape human behavior. The beliefs and myths common to a culture, the norms dictating gender-based behavior, situational factors, and features of the physical environment—street lights, shelters, and availability of guns—all affect the level of violence in a community. The depiction of violence in the media contributes to the level of violence in our society, especially among children and youth. Prevention programs are designed to change the environmental factors that contribute to violent behavior.

Three principles that emerge from the extensive body of psychological knowledge form the basis for programs that will effectively promote violence-free families:

- What people learn about and adopt regarding gender roles plays an important part in the development and continuation of violent behavior.
- There are factors that put people at risk for violence throughout the life span.
- Only by empowering men and women to live violence-free lives will we as a society break the cycle of violence.

THE EFFECTS OF GENDER ROLE SOCIALIZATION

Gender role socialization is a term for the life experiences that encourage people to behave according to preset expectations based on whether they are male or female. Many young children are taught that men and women behave differently, according to social stereotypes that restrict their behavior and limit their options. Gender roles play an important part in how boys and girls and men and women learn to accept and use violence. Historically, men were expected to be dominant, active, and in control. Women were expected to be submissive, passive, and dependent. In recent decades, however, women's decreasing dependence on men for economic support, along with women's increasing independence, especially as heads of single-parent families, has changed many of those assumptions.

Many of these gender-role stereotypes have a negative effect on a person's behavior and emotional well-being. Men, for example, receive the false message that they have a right and a mandate to control the women and children in their families. That belief contributes significantly to men's continued use of violence to maintain power and control. Individuals, families, and society are damaged when such behavior is tolerated as being normal.

Violence-free families encourage members to choose their own behaviors without the limitations of traditional expectations for their gender. To stop violence and prevent its recurrence, a social consensus must arise that encourages choices for men and women.

DEVELOPMENTAL PROCESSES AND RISK FACTORS

Children are not born violent. They model their own behavior on the behavior they observe and experience in their homes and communities. A critical risk factor in the development of violent behavior is exposure to family violence and abuse in childhood. For boys and girls, such exposure interacts with the messages they receive about appropriate roles and behavior for men and for women, setting the stage for boys and men to become abusers and for girls and women to become victims of abuse. Children, particularly boys, who are exposed to violence in their homes are at high risk to commit violence themselves.

Programs that stop and prevent children's exposure to violence at home can break the cycle. Because many of the social, psychological, and biological risk factors associated with family violence have been identified, health promotion and prevention programs can be designed to reduce the risk factors associated with the development of violent behavior. To prevent the violence from occurring, more programs based on the best available research are needed; such programs should be scientifically evaluated to determine which programs are most effective for specific populations. Models for boys to develop into men need to be changed to nonviolent models.

Education can help reduce and stop violence. Violence is the result of abusers' misuse of power and control within a social milieu that condones and even encourages such controlling behavior. Education can help to change public opinion about power and violence.

THE PROMISE OF EMPOWERMENT

Many interventions today can empower men and women with the tools they need to live violence-free lives. These tools range from methods of resolving conflict to ways of enhancing self-esteem. These efforts also include enrolling young single mothers in psychoeducational programs and retraining highly aggressive boys and men to manage their anger and their impulses. Grassroots women's groups have developed interventions to increase women's sense of individual autonomy, independence, and power to control their own destiny. Religious and community programs designed to strengthen healthy families, to end the isolation of high-risk families, and to improve positive interactions also help potential victims resist, avoid, or end abuse. Schools that encourage both girls and boys to participate in science, sports, and parenting classes can reduce the destructive effects of gender role stereotypes that promote abuse.

THE ROLE OF HEALTH PROMOTION PROGRAMS IN PREVENTING VIOLENCE

Universal interventions and targeted interventions are the two important types of health promotion programs in any campaign to end family violence. Universal interventions are designed to change social conditions or the attitudes and behaviors of the general population or of an entire group of people, such as all high school students. Targeted interventions are designed to change the attitudes and behaviors of special groups of individuals who have been identified as being at high risk for becoming abusers—such as boys and men with histories of childhood abuse, and people at high risk for becoming victims—such as young, single mothers. Examples of both types of interventions are listed in the following tables.

UNIVERSAL INTERVENTIONS

Interventions for Changing the Social Conditions That Breed Violence

- Media efforts that educate about the connection between gender role expectations and family violence
- Programs that reduce unemployment and poverty, which are strongly associated with increased rates of family violence
- Enforcement of existing handgun laws; creation of handgun laws where none exist
- Change laws to criminalize family violence
- Advocate for community agency support
- Change the physical structure of schools to reduce opportunities for expression of highly aggressive behavior
- Media efforts to deglamorize violence and more accurately portray its consequences

Interventions for Changing the Attitudes and Behaviors of a Whole Population

- School-based programs to teach conflict-management, problem-solving, and anger-management skills to all children
- School programs to counter traditional gender role stereotypes and expectations
- Alcohol and drug abuse prevention programs
- Parenting education programs
- Documentaries about family violence shown on network television

Interventions for Changing the Attitudes and Behaviors of a Specific Class of People

- Sex abuse prevention programs such as "good touch, bad touch" for young children

- Training legal, medical, and mental health professionals to better understand the dynamics of family violence
- Sermons delivered by religious leaders declaring family violence immoral
- Community-based activities, such as clean-up and beautification projects or midnight basketball, that bring people—particularly adolescents or young adult men—together in productive activities

TARGETED INTERVENTIONS—FOR CHANGING THE ATTITUDES AND BEHAVIOR OF SPECIAL AT-RISK GROUPS

- Volunteer visits to high-risk homes to prevent families' isolation
- Empowerment training for girls and women who have been exposed to violence in their childhood homes
- Interventions for boys and men who have been exposed to physical or sexual abuse or maltreatment as children
- Social and community support for isolated, young, single mothers and for families with many children or with one or more children with disabilities
- Respite care for caretakers of those with physical disabilities and the elderly
- Interventions for boys who repeatedly use bullying behavior on the playground or unusually high levels of aggressive behavior in the home, school, or community
- Psychoeducational programs for children at battered women shelters or through a domestic violence court
- Psychoeducational programs on changes in gender role expectations for groups of men
- Community-based recreation and care programs for the elderly
- Restriction of possession of firearms for anyone who has been convicted of any violence or who has domestic violence charges or restraining orders pending
- Group discussion and support programs for recent immigrants conducted in their own language to reduce isolation
- Attention to adolescents who are being victimized by family members and schoolmates
- Safety programs for elderly battered women whose partners are diagnosed with deteriorating physical conditions that are associated with a high risk of battering behavior

ADVANTAGES AND POTENTIAL LIMITATIONS OF UNIVERSAL AND TARGETED INTERVENTIONS

Universal Interventions—Advantages

Universal interventions reach the entire population without stigmatizing any group of people. They are most effective for changing behavior at the societal level if the costs and risks are acceptable. Also, it is easier to target an entire population than to locate people who may be at risk of using violence or becoming victims.

Examples:

Recent television programs alerting the general population to the reality of violence behind the closed doors of the family have been successful in creating a widespread awareness of family violence.

School programs that encourage sports activities for girls as well as boys strengthen girls' physical capabilities and self-esteem.

Universal Interventions—Potential Limitations

Universal interventions that have not been developed with care and have not been thoroughly evaluated have the potential for creating unforeseen negative consequences that can affect large segments of the society.

Examples:

A universal intervention that used television programs to educate youth to avoid the dangers of suicidal behavior actually increased the suicidal thoughts and attempts in teenagers, at least initially.

A drug education program that was introduced in the public schools during the 1970s without emphasizing proper training of the teachers actually increased rather than decreased teenagers' use of drugs and made it more difficult for the teenagers to trust talking with supportive adults.

Targeted Interventions—Advantages

Targeted interventions are specially designed to address particular risks and risk groups, and they can more readily be tailored to the sensitivities of different cultures and individual needs. They also may be less expensive than programs that reach the entire population.

Targeted Interventions—Potential Limitations

Identifying children or adults as being at risk can stigmatize them. It also may have the effect of a self-fulfilling prophecy, encouraging rather than discouraging aggressive behavior.

Although researchers have identified risk factors for family violence, it still is difficult to identify precisely those who may need preventive interventions or those who are likely to benefit from other specific types of interventions. Therefore, universal interventions that promote healthy interactions among family members may be effective for the largest number of people.

Family violence has a profound effect on society, putting individuals at risk for further family violence, criminal behavior, suicide, and health problems in the future. Intervention of appropriate scope, duration, and focus is key to diminishing those risks.

Early treatment of victims of child abuse and maltreatment may be one of the most important ways to prevent the later expression of violence in adult relationships. Men who are exposed to violence or experience abuse as children are at greatest risk to abuse their partners. Creating more positive interaction opportunities has been shown to reverse the aggressive behavior often demonstrated by these children.

PROMISING APPROACHES TO PREVENTION

A universal prevention program can, at nominal cost, reduce the risks associated with patterns that assign roles of power and action to men and of submission and passivity to women. For example, programs for children and adolescents in schools and religious institutions can teach ways to resolve conflicts by other than physical means. These programs can strengthen youths' problem-solving skills and can stress to boys and girls that they have equal power and shared responsibilities in human relationships and conflicts. Such programs can be used to provide community education and can have a widespread effect.

A major prevention effort, which has been led by grassroots women's groups, empowers potential victims to learn how to avoid or resist abuse or to find safer refuge from abuse. Universal prevention programs support the empowerment of all women and children to resist harm if they are exposed to or subjected to violence. They work to reduce the risk that violence will occur. Targeted programs, which have included community programs sponsored by battered women's shelters and task forces, have focused on children who were exposed to family violence and therefore are at high risk for being abused or becoming abusive. Programs that teach high-risk populations to avoid or resist abuse can also target women and children who have grown up in homes in which they were abused, people who witnessed their mothers being battered, people who were raised in poverty, and women who are dependent on a man to support them financially.

Prevention programs can inoculate people who are at high risk for being abused. Risk can be reduced and resiliency increased when people are helped to develop personal competency and strength and to increase their autonomy, independence, and power to control their own lives. Developing these skills may reduce the effects of family violence, such as learned helplessness, or other psychological effects of the trauma. Such prevention programs also may include special components that are offered to a whole class of people at risk—adolescents who are beginning to date, for example—without identifying specific at-risk individuals.

Efforts that change the environment that supports family violence are important ways to prevent and stop family violence and abuse. Much within the environment either raises or lowers the risk of family violence. Appropriate strategies to lower the risk include instilling greater sensitivity to gender inequities in the workplace or other institutions, passing new legislation that attempts to protect women and children from repeated violence, training medical personnel to be more attentive to the signs of abuse, opening shelters for children or women who are abused, and providing more effective training for police to protect victims.

When church and community programs strengthen and empower healthy families, they also change the environment to prevent family violence. Recent legislation to control access to handguns is an example of a measure that prevents family violence by changing the (local, state, or national) government's message about violence.

Grassroots women's organizations have tried to change the environment at public agencies so that these agencies offer better support to victims of family violence; this kind of fundamental change will uncover the true extent of family violence as well as prevent further violence by breaking the cycle.

Efforts to teach families to have more positive interactions with each other can prevent the spread of violent behavior. That is the one consistent research finding that has emerged from the study of family violence. Fostering an optimistic approach to life that is based on a belief in everyone's good will rather than on the inevitability of continual power struggles, has been shown to change the cycle of violence in families that spend more time in negative interactions.

Few programs in any area of family violence have received rigorous evaluation of their effects on the levels of violence committed. However, many existing programs (such as shelters for women in crisis or school-based programs that teach children to recognize "good touch" and "bad touch") have been accepted by their communities as effectively serving the function for which they were created.

THE IMPORTANCE OF COMMUNITY-WIDE EFFORTS

Psychologists agree that comprehensive, community-based health promotion, prevention, and treatment programs are more effective than fragmented efforts that reach only a portion of the population. Although the issues involved in family violence are more complicated than those of drunk driving, the drunk driving campaign is a model of a successful community-based promotion. Through interactive efforts in prevention, intervention, and treatment, drunk driving arrests and automobile crashes have been reduced by more than 30 percent in a decade, with an even higher percentage reduction in the rate of drunk driving among teenagers. Alcohol and drug prevention and treatment programs, which target the limited population of users, had existed for decades. However, drunk driving did not decline until local groups orchestrated a strong, nationwide prevention campaign, spearheaded by Mothers Against Drunk Driving, that changed community attitudes about drinking and driving and that won legislative changes.

Comprehensive community programs can help create violence-free families. Each health promotion effort will reach only a percentage of the population; therefore, to foster a violence-free community, a variety of programs needs to be adopted according to a comprehensive plan. These programs should be widely inclusive of the members of the community, and they should be free of discrimination and bias. For example, programs that foster community pride and facilitate communication among community segments, programs that foster violence-free relationships, psychoeducational and psychotherapy treatment programs, jail and prison sentences, and programs that train people in conflict-resolution and problem-solving skills all can help create a community of violence-free families.

A community Family Violence Coordinating Council in every community—rural, suburban, or urban—can bring together different groups to develop complementary programs for health promotion and violence-free families. In communities where such councils already coordinate legal advocacy, shelters, intervention, and treatment, a prevention component should be added so that schools, religious groups, community councils, and media can participate with mental health specialists in the field of health promotion.

THE ECONOMIC BENEFITS OF VIOLENCE PREVENTION

When evaluating the economics of health promotion, communities need to compare the resources spent on prevention with those spent to stop the violence after it begins. For example, communities spend significant funds to build new prisons to incarcerate perpetrators, many of whom are youthful and might have grown up to be violence-free had they been identified earlier in their lives and placed in a program to prevent or mediate the effects of the family violence. Prison programs deter further violence in the community for as long as someone is incarcerated. However, experience shows that violence only continues or worsens unless the root causes of the violence are addressed. Spending additional funds now to promote violence-free families, including for treatment of the current prison population, may be an important way to curtail the costs of incarcerating violent offenders in the future.

Proper assessment of a prevention program's effectiveness takes into account the program's effect over the long term. For example, when a program targets a specific group, the number of new cases identified may actually increase initially, because closer scrutiny is given to that group. However, those new cases may be discovered at an earlier stage than might otherwise have occurred; therefore, intervention may actually have more benefit over a longer period of time.

Those conducting cost-benefit analyses of prevention programs should consider how many potential perpetrators will become violence-free. If one prevention program reduces violence by 25 percent to 35 percent (the usual number who are affected by any one particular health promotion program), the implications for future financial savings are enormous. A good example is working with youngsters who are at high risk to commit more violence over their lifetime. Many of the children of men and women currently incarcerated for crimes of violence have been exposed to violence in their families; they need such a prevention program now if we are to help them remain violence-free.

The current legislative priority of punishing violent offenders more often and more severely, without also including intervention, treatment, and health promotion programs to teach violence-free living, needs to be seriously questioned. Making it easier to assign the death penalty to violent offenders does not deter violence; sentencing a person to death only prevents further violence by that person. Although increasingly popular punishments such as boot camps for teenage offenders may help young people learn discipline, some of the programs perpetuate hostile attitudes and behaviors and do not foster positive attitudes and nonviolent behaviors.

The data are unequivocal: Without active prevention and intervention, violence begets more violence!

WHAT CAN COMMUNITIES AND PSYCHOLOGISTS DO TOGETHER?

Psychologists have been involved in helping communities develop a variety of programs that prevent family violence from occurring and that reduce the risk of its recurrence. Many of these programs are based on principles of health promotion. Although individual skill-building programs are particularly popular, psychologists are also involved in the design of community programs with a more universal prevention approach. In other universal prevention efforts, psychologists have served as consultants to the media in the production of documentaries, movies, and even talk shows that deal with issues of family violence. Psychological knowledge is also brought to bear in the development of legislation and social policies.

Psychology must lead the effort to resolve tensions that hamper collaboration among various advocates and limit psychologists' effectiveness in treating perpetrators and victims of family violence. Some of the divisive issues arise from competition for funding and other resources; other issues arise from philosophical differences. Different advocates focus on different members of the family or on different aspects of family violence. These differing approaches can sometimes lead to conflicting responses to the same phenomena. For example:

- Child abuse advocates sometimes appear to blame the mother, who may also be a victim of abuse.
- Battered women advocates may appear to ignore a child's needs and to focus exclusively on a woman's issues.
- People who work with perpetrators often do not take enough care in protecting the victims from potential harm.
- Family preservation advocates often treat the family unit without having sufficient concern for the safety of the victims.
- Child custody evaluators and courts often make recommendations that downplay the seriousness of domestic violence, placing children in dangerous situations.

BUILDING BRIDGES: MENTAL HEALTH PROFESSIONALS AND FAMILY VIOLENCE ADVOCATES

To promote their common goals of preventing family violence and ameliorating its effects, mental health professionals and family violence advocates are beginning to seek ways to work together. This new interest in finding common ground is an important step toward overcoming the past distrust between the professions. That distrust was based in part on the limited knowledge about family violence and on the different knowledge bases: Mental health professionals were more familiar with clinical experience and psychological research; advocates were more familiar with the experience of violence. Efforts now are under way to collaborate by sharing knowledge to gain a more complete picture of the complex dynamics of family violence.

Many factions and systems must work together and share a commitment to operate fairly and effectively—even when they represent different groups and perspectives—if family violence is to be defined, measured, addressed, and prevented. Because these factions seem adversarial at times, only concerted effort will enable them to move together toward the common goal of violence-free families. The following are ways in which the interests of various factions can be coordinated:

- Mental health professionals need systematic access to research information and continued training to appropriately evaluate and treat confirmed and alleged perpetrators and victims of abuse.

- Accused perpetrators of child abuse need representation and protection of their rights, particularly when there remain reasonable doubts about claims.
- Mental health licensing and grievance boards and insurers need to be able to evaluate accurately the actions of licensed professionals and the complaints of clients and others, even when the complex, emotionally charged issues of family violence are raised.
- The press needs accurate, up-to-date information about family violence so it can inform the public accurately about the prevalence, causes, prevention, and treatment of family violence.
- Legislators need to craft laws that protect individuals from violence and from unfair prosecution while protecting the society from the far-reaching effects of family violence. Lawmakers also need to improve access to effective prevention and treatment services.

Together, the various groups can improve the systems to enable each player to take a role in preventing and stopping family violence and in promoting violence-free families. Psychology can play a leadership role in finding solutions to the problems that prevent such cooperation:

- Facilitating the free flow of information among health, mental health, and social service professionals; advocates; community leaders; and the legal community
- Encouraging grassroots organizations to share scarce resources while they build coalitions to obtain greater funding and resources
- Promoting and providing careful, competent investigations of accusations of past and present abuse while discouraging scare tactics and rushed judgments before investigations are complete
- Training licensing and grievance boards to understand family violence better
- Suggesting limitations on the powers of these boards and methods of review so that the boards can fairly and competently promote the good practices that will stop family violence and prevent future violence

Psychology can also improve its own ability to prevent and stop family violence and promote violence-free families. Following the task force's recommendations on interdisciplinary training should help prevent the polarization that can occur when different perspectives are not understood and information is not shared among groups and disciplines. Psychology's own efforts to deal with the diversity within our profession should be an asset to this task.

Violence within the family is used as a method of social control, tending to keep both women and men within rigidly-defined social roles.

Social institutions that are in a position to influence the development and maintenance of attitudes and behaviors that tolerate such use of violence need to be educated about the consequences of violence and made aware of their institutional roles in perpetuating and shaping it.

Individuals and institutions that have a responsibility for not perpetuating violence include parents, teachers, church leaders, health service providers, police officers, judges, sports figures, military personnel, and members of the news media and entertainment industries.

KEY POINTS

- The best way to promote violence-free families is to stop the development of abusive behavior, especially in boys and men; to strengthen and empower potential victims to resist or avoid victimization; and to change the environment that promotes the use of violence.
- Although the many prevention programs use a variety of methods to reach specific population groups, universal prevention programs—those applied to an entire population—are the most effective for changing behavior at a societal level, assuming that the costs and risks are acceptable.
- Because family violence has been a discrete area of study for a relatively short time, there are still gaps in the knowledge about ways to prevent family violence. There is general agreement, however: prevention efforts are needed to address the societal conditions that contribute to family violence, and intervention and treatment efforts must take place in every community if family violence is going to be reduced or eliminated.
- Psychology has a key role to play in building the community-based coalitions that can prevent and treat family violence.

RECOMMENDATIONS

Violence is primarily a learned behavior, and the family provides the most fertile ground for teaching violence. Family violence is linked to other forms of violence and to a range of problems such as substance abuse, emotional disorders, poor achievement in school, aggressive behavior, serious injuries, health problems, suicide attempts, separation and divorce, and physical and mental disabilities.

Only in the last few decades have the horrors of child abuse, woman and partner battering, and elder abuse been brought out of the shadows of private behavior into the light of public awareness and scientific research. Because families are made up of individuals who are entangled in a web of cultural, social, and community influences, efforts to stop family violence cannot address only the violent individuals themselves or the members of their households. Interventions must take into account individual characteristics, community norms and expectations, the role of mass media, institutional processes, and public policies.

Psychology has contributed a great deal to the study of family violence, but solutions must involve the efforts of people from many disciplines. Such solutions require the coordinated efforts of advocates, professionals from many disciplines, business and political leaders, and representatives of community and government agencies. Psychologists frequently look to child welfare advocates and advocates for battered women when designing their research or training programs or working with victims or abusers in their clinical practices. Furthermore, psychologists frequently work collaboratively with advocates and professionals in other disciplines to share knowledge, to help each other maintain safety, and to address professionals' emotional and psychological reactions to working in the field of family violence.

With dedicated, collaborative efforts, there is hope that victims of family violence can find safety, help, and healing, and that abusers can receive the education and treatment they need to stop their violent behavior.

To address the complexities of violence and the family, to improve the scope and quality of research in the field, to enhance the training of clinicians, and to increase the effectiveness of treatment for victims and abusers, the American Psychological Association's Presidential Task Force on Violence in the Family recommends actions in the following broad areas: public policy and intervention, prevention and public education, clinical services, training, and psychological research.

Recommendations for Public Policy and Intervention

1. We recommend that every community develop multidisciplinary Family Violence Coordinating Councils with full participation of community service agencies, residents of the area served, and behavioral scientists. The function of such councils will be to organize a comprehensive response to violence in the community and to coordinate the work of relevant agencies to plan, develop, and implement intervention programs that can restore healthy functioning to individuals and families. Effective programs require collaboration among and regular meetings of service providers and community agencies, including law enforcement personnel; courts; medical, psychological, and mental health services; social services; religious institutions; business and political leaders; child welfare agencies; educational institutions; and survivors of family violence. Attention to characteristics of the community (e.g., rural, suburban, urban, impoverished, affluent, and immigrant) and to issues of diversity (e.g., gender, race, class, family structure, and sexual orientation) is crucial for community agencies to provide effective services for victims and perpetrators.

1.1 We recommend that under the leadership of these Family Violence Coordinating Councils, communities develop Model Comprehensive Service Programs based on behavioral and social science theories and research findings. Coordinating efforts of health, social service, and criminal justice agencies, these programs should include a minimum of seven kinds of services: consultation, education, prevention, treatment and support services, legal services, residential services, and advocacy. Some of the key components of the core services in model community programs might include shelter, counseling, and therapy for children and adults, both victims and perpetrators; substance abuse prevention and treatment; service programs designed for specific groups, including home visits for high-risk families; support groups for victims; education and counseling for perpetrators; advocacy and legal services; and victim compensation programs.

1.2 We recommend that intervention programs be developed that strengthen the bond between mothers and children who have been exposed to violence. Studies show that children who have a strong relationship with their mothers are most able to heal quickly from abuse; such studies suggest the need for greater experimentation with such models.

1.3 We recommend that communities develop evaluation protocols to measure the effectiveness of all intervention programs.

1.4 We recommend that psychologists and other researchers collaborate with grassroots organizations to establish better data collection systems and to help design and conduct much-needed evaluation programs on the efficacy of treatment services, in a manner that safeguards victims and their families. These grassroots organizations have provided much of the treatment for women and children victimized by violence in their families, and most of these organizations have struggled to survive. Funds recently authorized through the Violence Against Women Act, which was enacted as part of the Violent Crime Control and Law Enforcement Act of 1994, offer many of these organizations resources to continue to expand and to develop more knowledge about family violence services.

2. We recommend that community intervention programs be established to help victims find safety and heal from their trauma, to stop offenders' abusive behavior, and to prevent recurrence of the violence. Such a coordinated approach includes assessing the potential for lethal violence within a violent family situation, providing for the safety of the victims, and involving the perpetrator in appropriate legal and rehabilitative processes. Although services and intervention programs are already available in many communities for victims and perpetrators of family violence, the work of such programs must be more closely coordinated to build on what exists and to make the best use of available resources.

3. We recommend the development of regional centers, preferably university-based, for multidisciplinary professional training in family violence intervention. Regional training centers should be linked to programs of basic and clinical research so that new knowledge is continually integrated into training curricula and practice experiences. The educational program should focus on graduate and postgraduate training of community professionals who provide services to family violence victims and perpetrators in the community. Program professionals should design new and innovative approaches to intervention and should assess their effectiveness through an ongoing program of applied research and program evaluation. Multidisciplinary centers should include faculty and trainees from psychology, law, social work, medicine, nursing, and allied health services; battered women and child advocacy groups; criminology; law enforcement; journalism and communications; and public administration. In addition to training professionals and providing services to the community, such centers could also be used to evaluate the impact of laws pertaining to family violence and to develop communication strategies for public education about family violence.

4. We recommend that presentence assessment be mandated for everyone convicted of violence against a family member, whether the conviction is a misdemeanor or a felony. Approximately 80 percent of all cases of family violence are filed as misdemeanors; consequently, in the majority of family violence convictions, the court must proceed with limited information to determine sentencing and treatment conditions. This presentence assessment should be conducted independently, should include psychological assessment, and should be reported directly to the court.

5. We recommend that treatment be mandated for people convicted of violence against a family member. Mandated treatment should be in addition to, not a substitute for, other sentencing conditions. Such treatment programs should take into account the research data available concerning perpetrators. New studies have identified several types of batterers, including those who abuse just one person, those who abuse all family members, those who have serious mental health and substance abuse problems in addition to violent behavior, those who show other types of violent and antisocial behavior, and those who continue to harass and stalk their partners after separation.

5.1 We recommend further research on the varieties of offender-specific programs that deal with stopping the violent behavior as well as with correcting the dysfunctional thinking that perpetuates the violence. Models to be assessed include brief therapy with probation, long-term therapy, cognitive behavioral treatment, education and attitude readjustment, anger management, resocialization, and anti-stalking therapy.

5.2 We recommend further research on the efficacy of various treatment modalities in stopping violence and preventing its recurrence. Among the variables to be evaluated are the group size and characteristics of facilitators. Many treatment programs for batterers occur in small groups with at least one facilitator who is a clinician, although some programs, particularly those that stress reeducation and gender resocialization, use nonprofessionals or paraprofessionals as facilitators.

5.3 We recommend gathering information about the optimum length of time a batterer should be in treatment as well as standards and guidelines for measuring temporary and permanent changes.

5.4 We recommend that programs be developed and implemented in jails and prisons by mental health professionals for incarcerated abuse victims and perpetrators.

6. We support policies that deny possession of firearms and ammunition as a condition of bail before trial to people arrested for battering an intimate partner. We recommend denying possession of firearms and ammunition as a condition of sentencing for people convicted of battering an intimate partner. The presence of a firearm in a home increases manyfold the chances of someone in that home becoming a victim of homicide or suicide. In murders of an intimate partner, the most common deadly weapon is a firearm.

6.1 We recommend that families, communities, and schools move to restrict guns from youth and, furthermore, that families be educated about the need for safety measures if guns are in the home.

7. We recommend systematic evaluation of the impact of community policing programs on the reduction and control of family violence. Community policing is an approach to law enforcement directed toward crime prevention, early intervention in problems that set the scene for crime, and creation of safer communities. Encouraged at the highest levels of government, community policing is being implemented in cities throughout the nation. Basic principles underlying this new approach to law enforcement are consonant with a preventive approach to family violence.

8. We recommend that victims of family abuse be eligible for victim compensation programs. These funds are provided as grants to the state government, which distributes them to individuals as compensation for being a victim of a violent crime. Assessment and psychotherapy to treat the effects of family violence could be paid for through these funds.

9. We recommend new efforts and programs within the public schools to detect and intervene in family violence and abuse. The effects of family violence often are manifested in schools through children's academic failure, behavior problems, emotional disturbances, truancy, early dropout, and other troublesome indicators. Teachers may be the first to notice children who are showing symptoms that may signal the effects of family violence. Most school systems have psychologists and counselors who can assist in the assessment of such problems and in the development of appropriate referrals and services for children who suffer from trauma.

> **9.1** We recommend pre- and in-service training for all teachers and school administrators about family violence and community resources for dealing with it. Such programs should include information about gender role socialization and expectations that facilitate family violence, as well as about the impact of trauma on child development and mental health.
>
> **9.2** We recommend the development and assessment of school-based programs to teach children and adolescents how to recognize problems and seek help when they witness or experience family violence.
>
> **9.3** We recommend that schools create services for the earliest possible identification and referral of children who show emotional and behavioral problems related to unusually high levels of aggression and provide these children with appropriate educational experiences and psychological interventions.

Recommendations for Prevention and Public Education

10. We recommend a focus on the development of primary prevention strategies to keep family violence from occurring. The prevention of family violence involves changing attitudes, norms, and expectations for behavior. Primary prevention programs should be grounded in theory and take into account data from empirical findings, clinical experience, developmental knowledge, epidemiological research, and crime reports. Such programs should be long-term, should involve multiple community institutions and culturally appropriate approaches, and should be implemented through different venues within the community, including schools, healthcare systems, communications media, welfare systems, religious organizations, and other institutions and agencies.

10.1 We recommend that resources for public mental health services be reallocated so that more services are available for prevention programs and for early treatment of children and families with problems of aggression and violence.

10.2 We recommend that schools and parents teach children skills for critically viewing television and other media, to temper the effects of violence in the media and to help children benefit from the many positive educational aspects of television and other media. More than fifty years of research has shown that heavy viewing of violence on television is associated with an increase in violent behavior. But research also has shown that these harmful effects can be ameliorated by programs designed to enhance children's critical viewing skills.

10.3 We recommend that radio, television, and other electronic multimedia producers review all productions for the potential impact of any violent content on families. We believe that manufacturers and producers should take responsibility for the content of the programs they develop. This may include hiring staff or consultants to assist with using research or clinical materials to understand potential risks to children and adults.

10.4 We encourage community, school, family, and media involvement in prevention and treatment programs that focus on the links between substance abuse and violence.

10.5 We recommend that television producers develop shows that present constructive alternatives to violence in conflict situations and in family relationships.

11. We recommend the development of programs within the public schools to prevent family violence and abuse. Schools are an important venue for such prevention efforts because they have continuous contact with young families in the community and can be influential agents to alter the culture of violence prevalent in American society.

11.1 We encourage schools to take the long view of violence prevention, ensuring that their curricula, administrative practices, and interactions with students aim toward preventing the development of violent behaviors. Implementation of such an approach would involve teachers, school administrators and staff, students, and parents. It would foster nonviolent conflict resolution, creative problem-solving, constructive gender role socialization, and respect for all people.

11.2 We recommend that schools and parents teach both girls and boys to respect the skills and capacities of all children so that they grow up valuing achievement and nurturance in themselves and others, free of the prejudice and bias that comes from stereotyped gender roles, as well as from racism, homophobia, and discrimination that is based on differing physical and mental abilities.

11.3 We recommend that schools integrate material into their curricula targeted to problem-solving and conflict resolution, with a focus on nonviolent means of resolution.

12. We recommend the development of a public-private-media partnership for national education on family violence. Using the knowledge base that psychology has developed through scientific research and clinical experience, such a partnership should include an information campaign to educate the public about ways to prevent family violence and to seek help as early as possible if violence occurs. It also should include the development of coordinated interdisciplinary training and educational materials for psychologists and others involved in the field of family violence.

12.1 We recommend that corporations, businesses, and other places of work provide public education programs to increase the recognition that physical abuse is not acceptable, that violence at home is a crime, and that services are available to help families troubled by violence. A number of public education campaigns on battering and child abuse currently exist, and it is important to work with other professional groups to coordinate these efforts. The media has the potential to contribute to the escalating level of family violence or to seek new and innovative ways to curtail it. The advent of the information superhighway, with its potential increase in programming capacity, makes it more important than ever to eliminate excessive, gratuitous violence in the media. The information superhighway and developing technologies also will provide an unprecedented opportunity for public education programming.

13. We recommend that corporations, businesses, and institutions develop policies that address family violence. The effects of family violence are costly for employers when they are evidenced in absenteeism, poor performance, disruptive behavior, injuries requiring medical attention, or violent incidents in the workplace. Employers can work in their own economic interest and in the public interest to educate managers and staff about family violence, to facilitate referrals through employee assistance programs or community agencies for victims or perpetrators of family violence, to assist with workplace security concerns as necessary for victims, and to support violence prevention programs in the workplace and the community.

14. We recommend the development of programs to help families meet their own responsibilities in preventing violence at home and in coping with its conse-

quences in their communities. Families themselves bear the ultimate responsibility for reducing family violence in their own homes. However, the intensity and level of danger involved in the violence as well as the complexities involved in stopping the violence often make it difficult for family members to meet this responsibility without assistance. Various community institutions can be employed to educate and support families in parenting, nonviolent problem-solving, tolerance for diversity, discipline without physical punishment, and balanced power relationships.

15. We recommend that human service organizations, churches, parent-teacher associations, and other groups attempt to involve isolated families in community activities; to provide educational programs on family communication, conflict resolution, and power and control; and to disseminate information on the prevention and treatment of family abuse.

> **15.1** We recommend the provision of early and prompt treatment for alcohol and drug abuse problems as an important aspect of reducing family violence. Alcohol use is associated with more than half of fights and assaults in the home and with nearly two-thirds of all homicides.

16. We recommend that routine screening for a history of victimization be included in standard medical and psychological examinations and be considered in the development of individual treatment plans. The psychological trauma associated with violence among family members should become widely recognized by all health care providers, and referrals should be made to appropriate specialists for treatment. When the psychological reaction to violence is severe, it often meets criteria for a clinical diagnosis, termed a disorder. The most common disorders associated with family violence include conduct disorders among children, aggressive behaviors, attention deficit disorder, dissociative disorders, PTSD, anxiety disorders, depression, and other affective disorders. However, in the face of such symptoms, too often health care practitioners, educators, and other service providers or community leaders do not recognize the probability that such disorders are the direct result of exposure to violence; nor do they realize that they should be taken as an indicator that abuse may have occurred in the home and may be an underlying factor in the disorder. Validation of the experience of assault as a trauma is an important first step in the recovery process of victims, and they need reassurance that they can be helped to recover from the traumatic experience.

> **16.1** We recommend training for all health professionals, especially staff in hospital emergency rooms, on crisis hotlines, in mental health centers, and in substance abuse treatment programs, in how to recognize symptoms of abuse, how to query patients effectively, how to assess danger, how to make safety plans, and how to make appropriate referrals to local community resources.
>
> **16.2** We recommend that psychologists and other clinicians be specially trained and be available to provide psychotherapy and other clinical and support services as needed to help victims heal from the effects of trauma. Such ser-

vices should be available to victims of all ages and should include assessment and treatment for trauma-related mental health problems such as neuropsychological, affective, anxiety, and behavioral disorders.

16.3 We recommend the development and dissemination of new models of clinical intervention that address the vast numbers of victims, without pathologizing the victims, in settings that are easily accessible and affordable.

17. We recommend that standards and guidelines be established by each professional discipline that is concerned with family violence identified in a clinical setting. These standards and guidelines should focus on evaluation and treatment of woman and partner battering, child abuse and maltreatment, and elder abuse. We recommend that the APA take the lead and establish such standards and guidelines for the discipline of psychology. Professionals in criminal justice, law, health care and allied fields, psychology and mental health, social service, and education should have guidelines for recognizing, evaluating, and treating such cases. Each profession also should work to establish uniform standards of education and training for those who work with family violence cases, and to develop policies about collaboration with other disciplines and advocacy organizations.

17.1 We recommend that clinical guidelines be established for evaluating and treating adults who report or recover traumatic memories of childhood abuse. These guidelines should encompass constructive interviewing techniques that reduce the likelihood of suggestibility by the clinician at the same time they respect the possibility that traumatic memories can be dissociated and later recalled during psychotherapy.

17.2 We recommend that the APA and appropriate governmental, legal, and regulatory bodies act swiftly to address the ethical, legal, and practical concerns growing out of recent legal actions against psychotherapists working in the area of interpersonal violence. Clinicians have raised new concerns about their professional and legal vulnerability in providing services to victims. In recent years, harassment of therapists who work with victims of abuse has escalated. An organized campaign to undermine the practice of psychotherapy is under way with the introduction of a misleadingly titled "Mental Health Consumer Protection Act" in state legislatures. Other efforts have centered on state licensure and grievance procedures and legal malpractice actions. The absence of professional guidelines for psychotherapists working with victims of interpersonal violence contributes to the vulnerability of therapists. Similarly, psychotherapists working in the area of interpersonal violence almost always must interact with the courts, although few have been formally trained in how to deal with the legal system. The increase in ethics charges and legal cases against therapists, and the ease with which unfounded charges may be pursued at great personal cost and expense to the therapist who is ultimately exonerated, has a chilling effect that in time could discourage the provision of mental health services in instances of family violence, and this may jeopardize the public interest.

18. We recommend that the next revisions of the *Diagnostic and Statistical Manual* include a separate category for trauma reactions covering the symptoms that occur when someone is subjected to long-term severe physical, sexual, and emotional abuse within the family. The *Diagnostic and Statistical Manual* (DSM-IV) does not yet have a special category for trauma reactions, although a range of reactions is covered within the PTSD category and within the new Acute Stress Reaction category that describes trauma reactions lasting less than a month. A separate trauma disorder category would facilitate more precision in diagnosis by mental health service providers. Research is needed to more clearly define the criteria to be included in such a category.

19. We recommend the development of psychology curricula, graduate training, practicum experiences, internships, and residencies in the area of family violence and other forms of trauma. Each year, large numbers of families who are victimized by violence seek help at a time of critical need, and they often are unable to locate professionals with specific training to help them take steps to stop violence at home and heal from their trauma. This situation is, in part, a consequence of the presently fragmented and irregular nature of professional education and training in family violence interventions. A great deal of family violence intervention training is conducted by individual practitioners without institutional support; university programs for training and research in these specialized interventions are rare. There is a pressing need for stable institutional resources with a critical mass of expertise to test promising new interventions, to train newcomers to the field, and to disseminate information about successful intervention models to practitioners in several professions. It is important to begin teaching about family violence in undergraduate psychology curricula and to integrate studies of trauma and violence throughout all levels of psychology education.

20. We recommend specialized training for therapists working with perpetrators and victims of family violence. Training programs should incorporate the extensive knowledge acquired in recent years about how to diagnose and treat victims of family violence who experience PTSD and other trauma-related disorders and how to use the law and support systems to assist these victims. Issues around the training of therapists and about their professional role are assuming increased importance as the nature of family violence grows more complex. Graduate preparation and continuing education curricula should include treatment of both victims and perpetrators of family violence, as well as instruction on how to interact with the legal and judicial systems, including how to be an expert witness and how to interact with the advocacy community.

    20.1 We recommend consideration of creating a specialization in family violence research methods and clinical interventions.

    20.2 We recommend that all mental health professionals performing evaluations in child custody cases be trained in domestic violence issues.

21. We recommend that allocations for research funds in the area of family violence should be commensurate with the magnitude of the problem and the

seriousness of the impact of such violence. **More resources should be devoted to the study of family violence, and such resources should be made available immediately.** There is a critical need to expand and refine our knowledge about the frequency, etiology, and course of violence in family settings and to evaluate and refine intervention strategies aimed at prevention, treatment, and rehabilitation, as well as to evaluate and refine social service, law enforcement, and legal approaches to perpetrators and victims.

22. We recommend the initiation of a long-term, comprehensive, prospective program of epidemiologic research on violence in the family. Such a research program initially could clarify the extent and nature of family violence by establishing rates by age, gender, sexual orientation, and marital status, as well as by socioeconomic and ethnic differences in rates of each type of abuse. At the same time, such a program of research could identify risk and resiliency factors and answer questions such as the extent to which child abuse or neglect is a precursor to involvement in abuse during adulthood, either as victim or as perpetrator. The inclusion of nonclinical populations outside the criminal justice system can advance scientific understanding of the multiple pathways to and outcomes of family violence, as well as the context in which such violence occurs. Follow-up studies could provide information on changes over time in violent behaviors and on the long-term physical and psychological outcomes of experiencing violence in the family setting.

23. We recommend that research on the social contexts in which family violence occurs include ecologic and ethnographic research on communities, neighborhoods, and social networks. The role of community institutions such as churches and schools in preventing, sustaining, and ameliorating violence should be explored. Too often, the social context in which violence occurs has been ignored. The structure of a society, prevailing attitudes, and gender expectations all have been implicated in fostering violence, but few studies of family violence have taken into account the social factors that impinge on perpetrators and victims.

24. We recommend that public and private research funding agencies convene groups of experts to develop a lexicon of terms and definitions recommended for use in research studies and data gathering on family violence. These standard definitions should also be implemented through guidelines in other systems that apply the research findings—for example, clinical services, education, law enforcement, and social services—and respond to family violence. Inconsistencies in terminology make it difficult to establish large epidemiological studies. Furthermore, these inconsistencies confound the interpretation of findings across studies, and limit communication across professions and academic disciplines that conduct and evaluate research on family violence. In interpreting research findings, therefore, it is necessary to pay close attention to definitions of basic terms before making comparisons of statistics among various studies.

25. We recommend improved data collection and analysis to answer many scientific and policy questions. The importance of such data warrants a concerted effort to coordinate and meld findings from data collected through health, legal,

social service, education, and law enforcement agencies in order to understand patterns of family violence and its aftermath in communities and societal institutions.

25.1 We recommend continued monitoring and refinement of the Department of Justice National Crime Victimization Survey and the Uniform Crime Reporting Program to improve means of tracking the prevalence of family violence.

25.2 We recommend that the Congress mandate and fund a federally supported national survey to determine the full extent and character of violence in families. Increased attention should be paid to groups of individuals neglected in existing studies, including adolescents, single adult women, incarcerated and institutionalized people, the homeless, people with physical disabilities, ethnic minorities, and the elderly.

26. We recommend a review and evaluation of existing instruments for measuring family violence and its aftermath with an eye toward developing and testing new instruments and methodologies that not only quantify violent acts but also take into account their provocation, context, intentionality, and consequences. Empirical research on family violence is hampered by a dearth of appropriate assessment instruments.

26.1 We recommend the development of gender-sensitive and culturally sensitive measures that take into account the differences in men's and women's use of and response to violence as well as the differences in cultural norms regarding violence. We recommend psychological tests and assessment instruments that improve prediction of violence and responses to treatment and that assess adequately the multitude of abusive encounters that an individual may have experienced, as well as the emotional aftermath. Such instruments should be developed through the use of behavioral assessment strategies that are appropriate to adults and children, perpetrators and victims; norms should be established on ethnic and other minority groups.

Appendix 1

Selected Excerpts From the Diagnostic and Statistical Manual of Mental Disorders, Fourth Edition

American Psychiatric Association
Washington, D.C.

[*Editor's Note:* Several pertinent diagnostic categories, primarily from the Axis II portion of the DSM-IV, are selected for reproduction herein. Included are the criteria, agreed upon by professionals contributing to this volume, that are used to identify individuals with particular psychiatric disorders. The diagnostic categories included are substance abuse and dependence disorders, along with various behavioral and personality disorders that are often predictive of eventual drug abuse and dependence, and relevant dimensions of antisocial behavior and aggressiveness.]

Criteria for Substance Dependence

A maladaptive pattern of substance use, leading to clinically significant impairment or distress, as manifested by three (or more) of the following, occurring at any time in the same 12-month period:

(1) tolerance, as defined by either of the following:

   (a) a need for markedly increased amounts of the substance to achieve intoxication or desired effect

   (b) markedly diminished effect with continued use of the same amount of the substance

(2) withdrawal, as manifested by either of the following:

   (a) the characteristic withdrawal syndrome for the substance

   (b) the same (or closely related) substance is taken to relieve or avoid withdrawal symptoms

(3) the substance is often taken in larger amounts or over a longer period than was intended

(4) there is a persistent desire or unsuccessful efforts to cut down or control substance use

(5) a great deal of time is spent in activities necessary to obtain the substance (e.g., visiting multiple doctors or driving long distances), use the substance (e.g., chain-smoking), or recover from its effects

(6) important social, occupational, or recreational activities are given up or reduced because of substance use

(7) the substance use is continued despite knowledge of having a persistent or recurrent physical or psychological problem that is likely to have been caused or exacerbated by the substance (e.g., current cocaine use despite recognition of cocaine-induced depression, or continued drinking despite recognition that an ulcer was made worse by alcohol consumption)

Criteria for Substance Abuse

A. A maladaptive pattern of substance use leading to clinically significant impairment or distress, as manifested by one (or more) of the following, occurring within a 12-month period:

  (1) recurrent substance use resulting in a failure to fulfill major role obligations at work, school, or home (e.g., repeated absences or poor work performance related to substance use; substance-related absences, suspensions, or expulsions from school; neglect of children or household)

  (2) recurrent substance use in situations in which it is physically hazardous (e.g., driving an automobile or operating a machine when impaired by substance use)

  (3) recurrent substance-related legal problems (e.g., arrests for substance-related disorderly conduct)

  (4) continued substance use despite having persistent or recurrent social or interpersonal problems caused or exacerbated by the effects of the substance (e.g., arguments with spouse about consequences of intoxication, physical fights)

B. The symptoms have never met the criteria for Substance Dependence for this class of substance.

Diagnostic Criteria for Antisocial Personality Disorder

A. There is a pervasive pattern of disregard for and violation of the rights of others occurring since age 15 years, as indicated by three (or more) of the following:

  (1) failure to conform to social norms with respect to lawful behaviors as indicated by repeatedly performing acts that are grounds for arrest

  (2) deceitfulness, as indicated by repeated lying, use of aliases, or conning others for personal profit or pleasure

  (3) impulsivity or failure to plan ahead

  (4) irritability and aggressiveness, as indicated by repeated physical fights or assaults

  (5) reckless disregard for safety of self or others

  (6) consistent irresponsibility, as indicated by repeated failure to sustain consistent work behavior or honor financial obligations

  (7) lack of remorse, as indicated by being indifferent to or rationalizing having hurt, mistreated, or stolen from another

B. The individual is at least age 18 years.

C. There is evidence of Conduct Disorder with onset before age 15 years.

D. The occurrence of antisocial behavior is not exclusively during the course of Schizophrenia or Manic Episode.

Diagnostic Criteria for Intermittent Explosive Disorder

A. Several discrete episodes of failure to resist aggressive impulses that results in serious assaultive acts or destruction of property.

B. The degree of aggressiveness expressed during the episodes is grossly out of proportion to any precipitating psychosocial stressors.

C. The aggressive episodes are not better accounted for by another mental disorder (e.g., Antisocial Personality Disorder, Borderline Personality Disorder, a Psychotic Disorder, a Manic Episode, Conduct Disorder, or Attention-Deficit/Hyperactivity Disorder) and are not due to the direct physiological effects of a substance (e.g., a drug of abuse, a medication) or a general medical condition (e.g., head trauma, Alzheimer's disease).

Diagnostic Criteria for Attention-Deficit Hyperactivity Disorder

A. Either (1) or (2):

 (1) six (or more) of the following symptoms of inattention have persisted for at least 6 months to a degree that is maladaptive and inconsistent with developmental level:

 Inattention

 (a) often fails to give close attention to details or makes careless mistakes in schoolwork, work, or other activities

 (b) often has difficulty sustaining attention in tasks or play activities

 (c) often does not seem to listen when spoken to directly

 (d) often does not follow through on instructions and fails to finish school work, chores, or duties in the workplace (not due to oppositional behavior or failure to understand instructions)

 (e) often has difficulty organizing tasks and activities

 (f) often avoids, dislikes, or is reluctant to engage in tasks that require sustained mental effort (such as schoolwork or homework)

 (g) often loses things necessary for tasks or activities (e.g., toys, school assignments, pencils, books, or tools)

 (h) is often easily distracted by extraneous stimuli

 (i) is often forgetful in daily activities

 (2) six (or more) of the following symptoms of **hyperactivity-impulsivity** have persisted for at least 6 months to a degree that is maladaptive and inconsistent with developmental level:

 Hyperactivity

 (a) often fidgets with hands or feet or squirms in seat

 (b) often leaves seat in classroom or in other situations in which remaining seated is expected

 (c) often runs about or climbs excessively in situations in which it is inappropriate (in adolescents or adults, may be limited to subjective feelings of restlessness)

 (d) often has difficulty playing or engaging in leisure activities quietly

 (e) is often "on the go" or often acts as if "driven by a motor"

 (f) often talks excessively

 Impulsivity

 (g) often blurts out answers before questions have been completed

(h) often has difficulty awaiting turn

(i) often interrupts or intrudes on others (e.g., butts into conversations or games)

B. Some hyperactive-impulsive or inattentive symptoms that caused impairment were present before age 7 years.

C. Some impairment from the symptoms is present in two or more settings (e.g., at school [or work] and at home).

D. There must be clear evidence of clinically significant impairment in social, academic, or occupational functioning.

E. The symptoms do not occur exclusively during the course of a Pervasive Developmental Disorder, Schizophrenia, or other Psychotic Disorder and are not better accounted for by another mental disorder (e.g., Mood Disorder, Anxiety Disorder, Dissociative Disorder, or a Personality Disorder).

Diagnostic Criteria for Conduct Disorder

A. A repetitive and persistent pattern of behavior in which the basic rights of others or major age-appropriate societal norms or rules are violated, as manifested by the presence of three or more of the following criteria in the past 12 months, with at least one criterion present in the past 6 months:

Aggression to People and Animals

(1) often bullies, threatens, or intimidates others

(2) often initiates physical fights

(3) has used a weapon that can cause serious physical harm to others (e.g., a bat, brick, broken bottle, knife, gun)

(4) has been physically cruel to people

(5) has been physically cruel to animals

(6) has stolen while confronting a victim (e.g., mugging, purse snatching, extortion, armed robbery)

(7) has forced someone into sexual activity

Destruction of Property

(8) has deliberately engaged in fire setting with the intention of causing serious damage

(9) has deliberately destroyed others' property (other than by fire setting)

Deceitfulness or Theft

(10) has broken into someone else's house, building, or car

(11) often lies to obtain goods or favors or to avoid obligations (i.e., "cons" others)

(12) has stolen items of nontrivial value without confronting a victim (e.g., shoplifting, but without breaking and entering; forgery)

Serious Violations of Rules

(13) often stays out at night despite parental prohibitions, beginning before age 13 years

(14) has run away from home overnight at least twice while living in parental or parental surrogate home (or once without returning for a lengthy period)

(15) is often truant from school, beginning before age 13 years

B. The disturbance in behavior causes clinically significant impairment in social, academic, or occupational functioning.

C. If the individual is age 18 years or older, criteria are not met for Antisocial Personality Disorder.

Specify type based on age at onset:

Childhood-Onset Type: onset of at least one criterion characteristic of Conduct Disorder prior to age 10 years

Adolescent-Onset Type: absence of any criteria characteristic of Conduct Disorder prior to age 10 years

Specify severity:

Mild: few if any conduct problems in excess of those required to make the diagnosis and conduct problems cause only minor harm to others

Moderate: number of conduct problems and effect on others intermediate between "mild" and "severe"

Severe: many conduct problems in excess of those required to make the diagnosis or conduct problems cause considerable harm to others

Diagnostic Criteria for Oppositional Defiant Disorder

A. A pattern of negativistic, hostile, and defiant behavior lasting at least 6 months, during which four or more of the following are present:

(1) often loses temper

(2) often argues with adults

(3) often actively defies or refuses to comply with adults' requests or rules

(4) often deliberately annoys people

(5) often blames others for his or her mistakes or misbehavior

(6) is often touchy or easily annoyed by others

(7) is often angry and resentful

(8) is often spiteful or vindictive

Note: consider a criterion met only if the behavior occurs more frequently than is typically observed in individuals of comparable age and developmental level.

B. The disturbance in behavior causes clinically significant impairment in social, academic, or occupational functioning.

C. The behaviors do not occur exclusively during the course of a Psychotic or Mood Disorder.

D. Criteria are not met for Conduct Disorder, and, if the individual is 18 years or older, criteria are not met for Antisocial Personality Disorder.

Appendix 2

Glossary

Acetylcholine (ACh)—An excitatory neurotransmitter partially responsible for memory and intelligence.

Adaptation—Adjustments made to accommodate prevailing conditions in the immediate environment.

Adoption studies—A method of study that assesses biological heritability of a trait by comparing the incidence of that trait between adopted children and their biological versus their adoptive parents; evidence for a genetic contribution is found when children are more similar to their biological parents than their adoptive parents.

ADHD—Attention deficit hyperactivity disorder.

Allele—One of a set of genetic variants at a given gene.

Anhedonia—The inability to experience pleasure.

Anxiolytic medications—Drugs used to treat anxiety disorders.

Anticonvulsant medications—Drugs used for therapeutic purposes that operate to raise the seizural threshold by reducing electrical activity in the brain in particular regions; often used to treat impulsive aggressiveness and intermittent explosive disorders.

Antidepressant medications—Drugs used to treat depression and related disorders by altering neurotransmitter activity in the brain.

Antipsychotic medications—Drugs used to treat psychotic disorders such as schizophrenia that act on neurotransmitters in the brain believed to be involved in the disorder.

Antisocial behavior—Socially inappropriate behavior that harms others.

Association studies—A method to study how a behavior varies as a function of different combinations of genes at one or more specific locations, called candidate genes, that are suspected to influence the phenotype.

Assortative mating—Pairing and reproducing with a partner with similar traits that are often subsequently passed on to offspring.

Autonomic nervous system—A portion of the peripheral nervous system that is responsible for functions not generally under conscious control (e.g., heart rate, blood pressure, respiration).

Bipolar disorder—Previously called manic-depression.

Biogenetic—Biological traits with genetic origins.

Brainstem—The most primitive part of the brain responsible for vital functions, balance, breathing, and motor functions.

Candidate gene—A specific gene thought to play a role in a given behavior.

Cerebrospinal fluid—The fluid within the ventricles of the brain that circulate and distribute various substances.

Clinical sample or population—A group of individuals with some form of psychopathology.

Cloning—Duplicating DNA, which is usually necessary to identify the location, functional significance, and genetic variation of specific genes.

Cognition—Information processing in the brain.

Cognitive rehabilitation or intervention—Techniques used to strengthen executive cognitive functioning in individuals with deficits or dysfunction.

Compulsion—Excessive need to repeat certain behaviors despite their negative consequences, often interrupting normal, daily activities.

Comorbid—Two or more psychological and behavioral disorders that coexist in a single individual.

Conduct disorder—A behavioral disorder that generally develops in childhood associated with belligerence, physical and verbal hostility, aggression, defiance, and poor impulse control.

Contextual factors—Societal or communitywide conditions that influence individual behavior.

Cortex—The gray matter covering the brain that is responsible for higher intellectual functioning.

Controls or control subjects—Participants in research who do not have the characteristic under study in the target or experimental group.

Criminogenic—Influences or conditions that contribute to criminal behavior.

Criterion measures—Factors that measure various criteria or correlates of a behavior that are used to define and study it (i.e., measures of attributes of a behavior under study).

Disaggregation—Sorting people or things into homogeneous groups or types.

Disinhibition—Lack of inhibition; can be either neurological or behavioral.

Disregulation (neurological)—Instability within the central nervous system that contributes to unstable and disinhibited behaviors.

Dopamine (DA)—A neurotransmitter involved in movement, emotion, and reward.

Downregulation—Lowered activity in physiological or chemical systems.

Drug abuse—The use or misuse of a drug for recreational or medicinal purposes to the detriment of the user or others with whom the user comes into contact.

Drug addiction—A state of periodic or chronic intoxication produced by repeated consumption of a drug; to include an overpowering desire or compulsion to continue taking the drug and to obtain it by any means, the tendency to increase the dose, and a psychological and/or physical dependence on the drug's effects.

Dizygotic twins—Fraternal twins who share 50 percent of their genetic complement.

Dysphoria—Psychological discomfort or pain.

EEG (Electroencephalogram)—A method to measure the electrical activity of the brain.

Electrophysiology—The study of physiological processes via electrical activity (e.g., EEG, skin conductance, and evoked potentials).

Endocrinology or endocrine system—The internal system of glands that produce hormones to exert an effect elsewhere in the body (e.g., sex hormones, prolactin, cortisol, or adrenocorticotropic hormone).

Epidemiology—The study of phenomena on a populationwide basis.

Epilepsy—Irregular and excessive electrical activity in portions of the brain that are often associated with seizures.

Epinephrine (adrenalin)—An excitatory adrenal hormone.

Epigenesis—The developmental process that occurs over the course of a life, in which various innate characteristics interact with external influences to produce a behavioral or phenotypical outcome.

Epistasis—Interactions between several locations on a chromosome in which the genetic effect on a phenotype occurs in a manner other than the sum of individual genes' influence on the phenotype.

Etiology—The study of the causes of a phenomenon.

Executive cognitive functions—Higher order activities subserved by the frontal cortex that involve goal-directed behaviors, forethought, impulse control, assessment of consequences, social skills, and the like.

Exon—Portion of the gene that is translated into an amino acid sequence.

Familial—Traits that occur within families.

Fenfluramine—A drug that stimulates serotonin activity that is sometimes used in research to assess serotonin function by measuring neuroendocrine outputs.

Fetal alcohol syndrome (FAS)—The exposure to alcohol during fetal development, which produces many abnormalities and defects in the offspring.

First-degree relatives—Biologically related nuclear family members (e.g., parents and their children).

GABA (gamma-aminobutyric acid)—An inhibitory neurotransmitter that has a calming effect.

Genetic markers—Defects or irregularities in genes that may be associated with a trait or disorder, but may not themselves be functional genes; they may co-occur with genes directly involved in the trait or disorder.

Genetic variants—Irregularities or defects in genes.

Genome—The genetic complement for an entire population.

Genotype—The genetic complement of an individual inherited from parents.

Knockout—An animal lacking a specific gene.

Heritability—The estimate of the minimum extent to which interindividual variation in a trait within a particular human population is genetically determined.

Homogeneous subgroup—A group of individuals who are similar in particular traits under study.

Hypoglycemia—Low blood sugar.

Hypomania—Nearly manic behavior.

Ictal—Referring to a brain seizure (e.g., inter-ictal is during a seizure, post-ictal is after one).

Impersonal cognitions—The processing of information and stimuli from the physical world, including intelligence.

Impulsivity—Acting without deliberation or forethought.

Inhibition—Depression of neurological processes or behaviors.

Interpersonal cognition (social cognition)—Deals with understanding people and social interactions.

Intergenerational—The occurrence of a characteristic across generations within families.

Intermittent explosive disorder—Frequent outbursts of temper, often associated with uncontrollable verbal or physical violence.

Interventions—Programs that attempt to intervene in the development of antisocial or problematic behaviors and outcomes.

Latent class analysis—A research technique to compare groups by subclassifying subjects into relatively homogeneous groups with respect to a given set of characteristics.

Limbic system—A primitive part of the brain responsible for emotions, moods, memories, impulses, and drives.

Linkage analysis—Studies to detect behaviorally significant genetic variation, regardless of whether the gene has been previously identified or even if the structural variation is not located in the coding region of a candidate gene.

Lithium—A drug used commonly to treat manic-depression (bipolar depression) and sometimes aggressiveness.

MAO (monoamine oxidase)—An enzyme that degrades norepinephrine and dopamine.

Meta analysis—Analyzing the combination of primary results and their effect sizes from several studies in a single analysis to formulate a global conclusion.

Minor physical anomalies (MPAs)—Congenital abnormalities in the body's structure that reflect impairment in fetal development.

Monozygotic twins—Identical twins who share 100 percent of their genetic complement.

Narcissistic personality disorder—A chronic and pervasive pattern of grandiose self-importance, exaggeration of achievements, feelings of entitlement, need for recognition and admiration, lack of empathy, and inability to sustain stable interpersonal relationships.

Neurobiology—The study of brain chemistry.

Neurodevelopmental abnormalities—Delays in the development of certain neurological processes that lead to behavioral, psychological, and/or intellectual disorders.

Neuropsychology—The study of brain-behavior relations with respect to the manner in which changes or deviations in brain functioning affect behavior.

Neuroscience—The study of brain function.

Neuroendocrine—Systems of glands in the brain that produce hormones that act elsewhere in the brain and body.

Neurotransmitter—A brain chemical involved in the communication between neurons.

Noradrenergic blockers (beta blockers)—Drugs that block the activity of the adrenal gland to reduce the activity of epinephrine (adrenalin) often used to treat hypertension, irregular heart rhythms, and aggressiveness.

Norepinephrine (NE)—A neurotransmitter that especially plays a role in arousal and is considered to be the brain's "fuel."

Nosology—The science of the classification of diseases or disorders.

Nucleotide—The building blocks of DNA: guanine, adinine, cytosine, and thymidine.

Obsession—Repetitive and consuming thoughts, thought to result from the need to reduce anxiety.

Ontogenetic—Processes and influences that occur from conception throughout life.

Operationalization or operationalized—To dissect a variable into its many components for each to be measured for research purposes.

Opioids—Synthetic narcotics.

Orbitofrontal cortex—A portion of the prefrontal cortex responsible for social skills, impulse control, and aspects of cognition.

Paradigm—A model by which the world or a phenomenon is viewed or understood.

Paraphilias—Sexual deviance disorders.

Pathognomonic—Characteristic or distinction of a disease or disorder, enabling its recognition and differentiation from others.

Pedophilias—Sexual attraction to children.

Perinatal conditions—Events that occur between the seventh month of pregnancy to twenty-eight days after birth.

Personality traits—Relatively stable, longstanding, and predictable psychological characteristics of individuals that are usually consistent with their behavioral patterns and orientations.

P.E.T. (positron emission tomography)—An imaging technique.

Pharmaco-challenge studies (psychopharmacologic)—The administration of an active drug to produce an expected response by the brain's neuroendocrine system to study differences in neurotransmitter function.

Pharmacology—A field of scientific inquiry that studies the effects of drugs on the brain and behavior.

Phenotype—The measurable or observable result of the interaction between genetic traits and environmental experiences.

Placebo—An inactive substance believed to be a drug.

Polygenetic—Traits that result from the expression of many genes.

Polymorphism—A genetic variant present in more than one percent of the general population.

Precursor—An event, substance, or experience that occurs before and causes some outcome (e.g., amino acids are precursors to neurotransmitters; they are necessary for neurotransmitter synthesis).

Predictors—Factors related to an eventual outcome (e.g., risk factors that significantly predict the occurrence of aggression in a population).

Predisposition—Preexisting tendency to behave or respond to situations within a certain range or pattern.

Prefrontal cortex—The anterior portion of the brain that modulates executive cognitive function and other intellectual processes.

Prevention—Implementation of programs that target various risk and resiliency factors to intervene early in an individual's life, with a goal towards reducing the likelihood of eventual behavioral, social, psychological, medical, or health problems.

Proband—The individual or index case who is the starting point of a family pedigree or genealogical chart.

Protective factors—Traits or conditions that reduce the impact of risks and "protect" against negative outcomes.

Psychometric measures—Standardized tests of personality and behavioral characteristics.

Psychopathology—Includes a wide spectrum of psychological and behavioral disorders.

Psychopathy—A personality disorder that is generally associated with antisocial behavior, lack of remorse, inability to feel intimacy, high pain threshold, pathological lying and other syndromes; also associated with low levels of autonomic nervous system activity.

Psychostimulants—Drugs that stimulate the central nervous system, largely via stimulation of dopamine activity, to remediate a behavioral disorder such as hyperactivity.

Psychotropic medications—Drugs used to treat psychiatric disorders by restoring or altering the brain's chemistry.

PTSD—Posttraumatic stress disorder.

r—Correlation coefficient, a measure of the degree that two variables are correlated.

Receptors—Proteins, usually located on the cell membrane and oriented toward the extracellular world, which specifically bind particular neurotransmitters and hormones.

Recidivism—Repeated commission of crimes.

Relapse—Reverting to drug abuse or another form of psychopathology after a treatment episode.

Repatterning—Learning new patterns of behavior and lifestyle.

Repeat sequence—A sequence of two, three, or more nucleotides that is tandomly repeated; these sequences are often polymorphic.

Reward deficiency syndrome—A deficiency in dopamine activity and a consequent reliance on substances or highly stimulating activities to feel pleasure or to decrease emotional and physical pain.

Reward pathways—A system of brain regions that when stimulated induces pleasurable effects; centrally involves the neurotransmitter dopamine and structures within the limbic system.

Risk factors—Conditions, from the genetic to the environmental, that increase the likelihood of a negative outcome.

Sensation or stimulation seeking—The unusual tendency to seek out highly stimulating, exciting, or risky activities and situations.

Sequelae—Abnormal conditions, or complications, following a disease or disorder that are directly or indirectly dependent on the disorder.

Serial killers—Individuals who methodically kill several individuals using the same methods each time.

Serotonin (5-HIAA)—A neurotransmitter that especially plays a role in mood, aggression, impulsivity, and anger and is considered to be the brain's "brakes."

Skin conductance—Galvanic skin response or electrodermal rate.

Somatic—Pertaining to the body.

SSRI (selective serotonin reuptake inhibitor)—Medication that acts on serotonin systems in the brain to increase its activity, used often for depression, anxiety, and aggressiveness.

Stimulant medications—Drugs used for therapeutic purposes that increase activity in the central nervous system; often used to treat hyperactivity and attention deficits.

Strains—Animals with the same lineage or ancestry that are engineered to have particular characteristics.

Stress—The response of the body and its organs (including the brain) to an excess of stimulation relative to coping skills.

Stressor—The precipitant or cause of stress.

Structural variant—Irregularities in a gene that influences the metabolism and activity of chemicals in the brain.

Subcortical—Structures and areas in the brain below the cortex.

Symptomology—A cluster of symptoms that makes up a disorder.

Temperament—The mixture of physical, intellectual, emotional, and moral qualities that make up a person's personality, attitudes, and behavioral responses to varying life situations; considered to be largely genetic.

Testosterone—A male hormone sometimes associated with aggressiveness.

Therapeutic jurisprudence or justice—The extent to which substantive rules, legal procedures, and the roles of lawyers and judges produce therapeutic consequences; a mental health approach to law.

Tourette's syndrome—A disorder characterized by facial tics, grunting, uncontrolled vocal noises, eye blinking and other symptoms, and known to involve the neurotransmitters dopamine and serotonin in particular.

Transgenerational—The transmission (either social or genetic) of a trait from generation to generation within the same family.

Transporter—Proteins present on the surface of presynaptic neurons that are responsible for transporting a given substance across the membrane.

Tryptophan—The amino acid precursor that helps to synthesize serotonin in the brain.

Twin studies—A method to estimate genetic influences on a trait or behavior by comparing its incidence between identical and fraternal twins.

Variance—The percentage of a behavior that can be explained by a given variable. In statistical terms, variance = r^2.

Vulnerability—To be at high risk for the development of some disorder or dysfunction.

Appendix 3

Bibliography

Abrahamsen, D. (1944). *Crime and the human mind.* New York: Columbia University Press.

Abwender, D. A., Como, P.G., Kurlan, R., Parry, K., Fett, K. A., Cui, l., Plumb, S. & Deeley, C. (1996, June). School problems in children with Tourette's syndrome. *Archives of Neurology, 53,* 509–511.

Achenbach, T. M. (1991). *Manual for the youth self-report and 1991 profile.* Burlington, VT: Department of Psychiatry, University of Vermont.

Achenbach, T. M. & Edelbrock, C. (1983). *Manual for the child behavior checklist and revised child behavior profile.* Burlington VT: University of Vermont.

Achenbach, T. M., Edelbrock, C. & Howell, C. (1987). Empirically-based assessment of the behavioral/emotional problems of 2-3 year old children. *Journal of Abnormal Child Psychology, 15,* 629–650.

Ackerman, P. T., Newton, J. E., McPherson, W. B., Jones, J. G. & Dykman, R. A. (1998). Prevalence of posttraumatic stress disorder and other psychiatric diagnoses in three groups of abused children. *Child Abuse and Neglect, 22,* 759–774.

Agnew, R. (1985). Social control theory and delinquency: A longitudinal test. *Criminology, 23,* 47-62.

Agnew, R. (1992). Foundations for a general strain theory of crime and delinquency. *Criminology, 30,* 47–87.

Agren, H., Mefford, I. N., Rudorfer, M. V., Linnoila, M. & Potter, W. Z. (1986). Interacting neurotransmitter systems: A non-experimental approach to the 5-HIAA-HVA correlation in human CSF. *Journal of Psychiatry Research, 20,* 175-193.

Ainslie, G. (1975). Specious reward: A behavioral theory of impulsiveness and impulse control. *Psychological Bulletin, 82,* 463–496.

Akers, R. L. (1990). Rational choice, deterrence, and social learning theory in criminology: The path not taken. *The Journal of Criminal Law & Criminology, 81,* 653–676.

Akers, R. L., Krohn, M. D., Lanza-Kaduce, L. & Radosevich, M. (1979). Social learning and deviant behavior: A specific test of a general theory. *American Sociological Review, 44,* 636–655.

Alam, M., Klass, D. & Luchins, D. (1995). *Divalproex sodium, valproic acid and carbamazepine in aggression.* Presented at the 35th Annual New Clinical Drug Evaluation Unit Program meeting, Orlando, FL.

Albanese, A., Hamill, G., Jones, J., Skuse, D., Matthews, D. R. & Stanhope, R. (1994). Reversibility of physiological growth hormone secretion in children with psychosocial dwarfism. *Clinical Endocrinology, 40,* 687–692

Allan, A. M., Wu, H., Paxton, L. L. & Savage, D. D. (1998). Prenatal ethanol exposure alters the modulation of the gamma-aminobutyric acid A1 receptor-gated chloride ion channel in adult rat offspring. *Journal of Pharmacology and Experimental Therapeutics, 284,* 250–257.

Allan, E. R., Alpert, M., Sison, C. E., Citrome, L., Laury, G. & Berman, I. (1996). Adjunctive nadolol in the treatment of acutely aggressive schizophrenic patients. *Journal of Clinical Psychiatry, 57,* 455–459.

Allen, G., Harvald, B. & Shields, J. (1967). Measures of twin concordance. *Acta Genetica et Statistica Medica, 17,* 475–481.

Allgulander, C., Nowak, J. & Rice, J. P. (1991). Psychopathology and treatment of 30,344 twins in Sweden. II. Heritability estimates of psychiatric diagnosis and treatment in 12,884 twin pairs. *Acta Psychiatrica Scandinavia, 83,* 12–14.

Allport, G. (1961). *Pattern and growth in personality.* New York: Holt, Rinehart & Winston.

Alpers, B. J. (1937). Relation of the hypothalamus to disorders of personality. Report of a case. *Archives of Neurology and Psychiatry, 38,* 291–303.

Alterman, A. & Tarter, R. (1983). The transmission of psychological vulnerability. Implications for alcoholism etiology. *Journal of Nervous and Mental Disease, 171,* 147–154.

Alterman, A., Tarter, R., Petrarulo, E. & Baughman, T. (1984). Evidence for impersistence in young male alcoholics. *Alcoholism: Clinical and Experimental Research, 8,* 448–450.

American Psychiatric Association (1987). *Diagnostic and statistical manual of mental disorders* (3d ed. rev.). Washington, DC: American Psychiatric Press.

American Psychiatric Association (1994). *Diagnostic and statistical manual of mental disorders* (4th ed.). Washington, DC: American Psychiatric Press.

Anastopoulos, A. D., DuPaul, G. J. & Barkley, R. A. (1991). Stimulant medication and parent training therapies for attention deficit-hyperactivity disorder. *Journal of Learning Disabilities, 24,* 210–217.

Andrew, J. (1974). Violent crime indices among community-retained delinquents. *Criminal Justice Behavior, 1,* 123–130.

Andrews, D. A., Zinger, I., Hoge, R. D., Bonta, J., Gendreau, P. & Cullen, F. T. (1990). Does correctional treatment work? A clinically relevant and psychologically informed meta-analysis. *Criminology, 28,* 369–404.

Anisman, H., Zacharia, M. D., Meaney, M. J. & Merali, Z. (1998). Do early-life events permanently alter behavioral and hormonal responses to stressors? *International Journal of Developments in Neuroscience, 16,* 149–164.

Anisman, H. & Zacharko, R. M. (1986). Behavioral and neurochemical consequences associated with stressors. *Annals of the New York Academy of Sciences, 467,* 205–225.

Anthony, J. C., Arria, A. M. & Johnson, E. O. (1995). Epidemiological and public health issues for tobacco, alcohol, and other drugs. In J. M. Oldham & M. B. Riba (Eds.), *American Psychiatric Press review of psychiatry,* vol. 14. Washington, DC: American Psychiatric Press, 15–49.

Appellof, E. & Augustine, E. (1985). Prefrontal functions in juvenile delinquents. *Journal of Clinical and Experimental Neuropsychology, 7,* 604.

Archer, J. (1991). The influence of testosterone on human aggression. *British Journal of Psychology, 82,* 1–28.

Arellano, C. M. (1996). Child maltreatment and substance use: A review of the literature. *Substance Use and Misuse, 31,* 927–935.

Arnsten, A. F. (1997). Catecholamine regulation of the prefrontal cortex. *Journal of Psychopharmacology, 11,* 151–162.

Arnsten, A. F. & Goldman-Rakic, P. S. (1986). Reversal of stress-induced delayed response deficits in rhesus monkeys by clonidine and naloxone. *Society of Neuroscience Abstacts, 12,* 1464.

Arnsten, A. F., Steere, J. C. & Hunt, R. D. (1996). The contribution of a2-noradrenergic mechanism to prefrontal cortical cognitive function. Potential significance for attention-deficit hyperactivity disorder. *Archives of General Psychiatry, 53,* 448–455.

Åsberg, M., Schalling, D., Traskman-Bendz, L. & Wagner, A. (1987). Psychobiology of suicide, impulsivity and related phenomena. In H. Y. Meltzer (Ed.), *Psychopharmacology: The third generation of progress.* New York: Raven, 655–668.

Åsberg, M, Träksman, L. & Thoren, P. (1976). 5-HIAA in the cerebrospinal fluid: A biochemical suicide predictor? *Archives of General Psychiatry, 33,* 1193–1197.

Asghari, V., Sanyal, S., Buchwaldt, S., Paterson, A., Jovanovic, V. & Van Tol, H. H. M. (1995). Modulation of interacellular cyclic AMP levels by different human dopamine D4 receptor variants. *Journal of Neurochemistry, 65,* 1157–1165.

August, G. J., Stewart, M. A. & Holmes, C. S. (1983). A four-year follow-up of hyperactive boys with and without conduct disorder. *British Journal of Psychiatry, 143,* 192–198.

Azuma, S. D. & Chasnoff, I. J. (1993). Outcome of children prenatally exposed to cocaine and other drugs: A path analysis of three-year data. *Pediatrics, 92,* 396–402.

Baars, B. J. (1986). *The cognitive revolution in psychology.* New York: Guilford Press.

Bach-y-Rita, G., Lion, J. R. & Climent, C. E. & Ervin, F. R. (1971). Episodic dyscontrol: A study of 130 violent patients. *American Journal of Psychiatry, 127,* 1473–1478.

Backon, J. (1989). Etiology of alcoholism: Relevance of prenatal hormonal influences on the brain, anomalous dominance, and neurochemical and pharmacological brain asymmetry. *Medical Hypotheses, 29,* 59–63.

Baer, D. & Corrado, J. J. (1974). Heroin addicts' relationships with parents during childhood and early adolescent years. *Journal of Genetic Psychology, 124,* 99–103.

Bain, J. (1983). Sexual development, maturation, and behavior. *Comprehensive Therapies, 9,* 21–31.

Baker, L. A., Mack, W., Moffitt, T. E. & Mednick, S. (1989). Sex differences in property crime in a Danish adoption cohort. *Behavior Genetics, 19,* 355–370.

Ballenger, J. C., Goodwin, F. K., Major, L. F. & Brown, G. L. (1979). Alcohol and central serotonin metabolism in man. *Archives of General Psychiatry, 36,* 224–227.

Bandura, A. (1969). *Principles of behavior modification.* New York: Holt, Rinehart & Winston.

Bandura, A. (1973). *Aggression: A social learning analysis.* Englewood Cliffs, NJ: Prentice-Hall.

Bandura, A., Ross, D. & Ross, S. (1963). Imitation of film-mediated aggressive models. *Journal of Abnormal and Social Psychology, 66,* 3–11.

Barber, G. A. (1982). *Sheltered employment work experience program.*(2d rev. ed.) Erie, PA: Barber Center Press.

Bardo, M. T., Donohew, R. L. & Harrington, N. G. (1996). Psychobiology of novelty seeking and drug seeking behavior. *Brain and Behavior Research, 77,* 23–43.

Barkley, R. A. (1981). *Hyperactive children: A handbook for diagnosis and treatment.* New York: Guilford Press.

Barkley, R. A. (1990). *Attention deficit hyperactivity disorder. A handbook for diagnosis and treatment in psychiatric offenders.* New York: Guilford Press.

Barkley, R. A. (1997). Behavioral inhibition, sustained attention, and executive functions: Constructing a unifying theory of ADHD. *Psychological Bulletin, 121,* 65–94.

Barkley, R. A. (1998, Sept.). Attention-deficit hyperactivity disorder. *Scientific American,* 69–72.

Barnes, G. (1983). Clinical and prealcoholic personality characteristics. In B. Kissin & H. Begleiter (Eds.), *The pathogenesis of alcoholism,* vol. 6. New York: Plenum Press, 113–195.

Baron, R. A. & Richardson, D. R. (1994). *Human aggression* (2d ed). New York: Plenum Press.

Barratt, E. S. (1963). Behavioral variability related to stimulation of the cat's amygdala. *Journal of the American Medical Association, 186,* 773–775.

Barratt, E. S. (1967). The effects of thiazesim, LSD-25, and bilateral lesions of the amygdalae on the release of a suppressed response. *Recent Advances in Biological Psychiatry, 9,* 229–240.

Barratt, E. S. (1972). Impulsiveness and anxiety: toward a neuropsychological model. In C. Spielberger (Ed.), *Anxiety: current trends in theory and research.* New York: Academic Press, 195–222.

Barratt, E. S. (1983). The biological basis of impulsiveness: The significance of timing and rhythm disorders. *Personality Individual Differences, 4,* 387–391.

Barratt, E. S. (1991). Measuring and predicting aggression within the context of a personality theory. *Journal of Neuropsychiatry and Clinical Neuroscience, 3,* S35–S39.

Barratt, E. S., Kent, T. A., Bryant, S. G. & Felthous, A. R. (1991). A controlled trial of phenytoin in impulsive aggression. *Journal of Clinical Psychopharmacology, 11,* 388–389.

Barratt, E. S. & Patton, J. H. (1983). Impulsivity: Cognitive, behavioral, and psychophysiological correlates. In M. Zuckerman (Ed.), *Biological bases of sensation seeking, impulsivity and anxiety.* Hillsdale, NJ: Erlbaum, 77–116.

Barratt, E. S., Patton, J., Olsson, N. G. & Zuker, G. (1981). Impulsivity and paced tapping. *Journal of Motor Behavior, 13,* 286–300.

Barratt, E. S., & Pray, S. L. (1954). Effect of a chemically depressed amygdala on the behavioral manifestations produced in cats by LSD-25. *Experimental Neurology, 12,* 173–178.

Barratt, E. S. & Slaughter, L. (1998). Defining, measuring, and predicting impulsive aggression: A heuristic model. *Behavioral Sciences & the Law, 16,* 285–302.

Barratt, E. S., Stanford, M. S., Dowdy, L., Liebman, M. J. & Kent, T. A. (in press). Impulsive and premeditated aggression: A factor analysis of self-reported acts. *Psychiatry Research.*

Barratt, E. S., Stanford, M. S., Felthouse, A. R. & Kent, T. A. (1997). The effects of phenytoin on impulsive and premeditated aggression: A controlled study. *Journal of Psychopharmacology, 17,* 341–349.

Barratt, E. S., Stanford, M. S., Kent, T. A. & Felthous, A. (1997). Neuropsychological and cognitive psychophysical substrates of impulsive aggression. *Biological Psychiatry, 41,* 1045–1061.

Barrett, H. J. & Hyland, H. H. (1952). Tumours involving the brainstem. *Quarterly Journal of Medicine, 21,* 265–284.

Barrett, J. A., Edinger, H. & Siegel, A. (1990). Intrahypothalamic injections of norepinephrine facilitate feline affective aggression via alpha-2 adrenoceptors. *Brain Research, 525,* 285–293.

Bates, H. E. (1980). The concept of difficult temperament. *Merrill-Palmer Quarterly, 26,* 299–319.

Battaglia, G., Cabrera, T. M. & Van de Kar, L. D. (1995). Prenatal cocaine produces biochemical and functional changes in brain serotonin systems in rat progeny. *National Institute on Drug Abuse Research Monograph No. 158,* 115–148.

Bauman, P. S. & Dougherty, F. E. (1983). Drug-addicted mothers' parenting and their children's development. *International Journal of the Addictions, 18,* 291–302.

Bauman, P. S. & Levine, S. A. (1986). The development of children of drug addicts. *International Journal of the Addictions, 21,* 849–863.

Baxter, L. R., Phelps, M. E., Mazziotta, J. C., Guze, B. H., Schwartz, B. & Selin, C. E. (1987). Local cerebral glucose metabolic rates in obsessive-compulsive disorders. *Archives of General Psychiatry, 44,* 211–218.

Bear, D. M., Freeman, R. & Greenberg, M. (1984). Behavioral alterations in temporal lobe epilepsy. In Blumer, D. (Ed.), *Psychiatric aspects of epilepsy.* Washington, DC: American Psychiatric Press.

Beck, P. & Mak, M. (1995). Measurements of impulsivity and aggression. In E. Hollander & D. Stein (Eds.), *Impulsivity and aggression.* New York: John Wiley & Sons.

Becker, J., Alpert, J. L., BigFoot, D. S., Bonner, B. L., Geddie, L. F., Henggeler, S. W., Kaufman, K. L. & Walker, C. E. (1995). Empirical research on child abuse treatment: Report by the Child Abuse and Neglect Treatment Working Group, APA. *Journal of Clinical Child Psychology, 24,* 23–26.

Beckham, J. C., Feldman, M. E., Kirby, A. C., Hertzberg, M. A. & Moore, S. D. (1997). Interpersonal violence and its correlates in Vietnam veterans with chronic posttraumatic stress disorder. *Journal of Clinical Psychology, 53,* 859–869.

Begleiter, H., Porjesz, B. & Kissin, B. (1984). Event-related brain potentials in children at risk for alcoholism. *Science, 225,* 1493–1495.

Beitchman, J. H., Zucker, K. J., Hood, J. E., daCosta, G. A., Akman, D. & Cassavia, E. (1992). A review of the long-term effects of child sexual abuse. *Child Abuse and Neglect, 16,* 101–118.

Bell, C. C. & Jenkins, E. N. (1991). Traumatic stress and children. *Journal of Health Care for the Poor and Underserved, 2,* 175–185.

Bell, R. Q. (1986). Age specific manifestations in changing psychosocial risk. In D. C. Farren & J. D. McKinney (Eds.), *The concept of risk in intellectual and psychosocial development.* New York: Academic Press.

Bell, R. Q. & Harper, L. V (1977). *Child effects on adults.* Hillsdale, NJ: Erlbaum.

Bell, R. Q. & Waldrop, M. F. (1982). Temperament and minor physical anomalies. *Ciba Foundation Symposium, 89,* 206–220.

Belsky, J. (1981). Child maltreatment: An ecological integration. *American Psychologist, 35,* 320–335.

Bender, B. G., Linden, M. G. & Robinson, A. (1987). Environment and developmental risk in children with sex chromosome abnormalities. *Journal of the American Academy of Child and Adolescent Psychiatry, 26,* 499–503.

Bender, L. (1959). Children and adolescents who have killed. *American Journal of Psychiatry, 116,* 510–513.

Benes, F. M. (1997). The role of stress and dopamine-GABA interactions in the vulnerability for schizophrenia. *Journal of Psychiatric Research, 31,* 257–275.

Benes, F. M., Turtle, M., Khan, Y. & Farol, P. (1994). Myelination of a key relay zone in the hippocampal formation occurring in the human body during childhood, adolescence, and adulthood. *Archives of General Psychiatry, 51,* 477–484.

Benjamin, J., Li, L., Paterson, C., Greenberg, B., Murphy, D. L. & Hamer, D. (1996). Population and familial association between the D4 dopamine receptor gene and measures of novelty seeking. *Nature Genetics, 12,* 81–84.

Benkelfat, C., Murphy, D. L., Hill, J. L., George, D. T., Nutt, D. & Linnoila, M. (1991). Ethanol-like properties of the serotonergic partial agonists meta-chlorophenylpiperazine in chronic alcoholic patients. *Archives of General Psychiatry, 48,* 383.

Benton, A. & Hamsher, K. (1983). *Multilingual aphasia examination.* Iowa City: AJA Associates.

Benward, J. & Densen-Gerber, J. (1975). Incest as

a causative factor in anti-social behavior: An exploratory study. *Contemporary Drug Problems, 4,* 32–55.

Bergman, B. & Brismar, B. (1994). Characteristics of violent alcoholics. *Alcohol and Alcoholism, 29,* 451-457.

Berlin, F. S. (1981). Ethical use of antiandrogenic medications (letter). *American Journal of Psychiatry, 138,* 1515–1516.

Berlin, F. S. (1983). Ethical use of psychiatric diagnosis. *Psychiatric Annals, 13,* 231–331.

Berlin, F. S. (1983). Sex offenders: A biomedical perspective and a status report on biomedical treatment. In J. C. Greer & I. R. Stuart (Eds.), *The sexual aggressor: Current perspectives on treatment.* New York: Van Nostrand Reinhold.

Berlin, F. S. & Coyle, G. S. (1981). Sexual deviation syndromes (clinical conference). *Johns Hopkins Medical Journal, 149,* 119–125.

Berlin, F. S. & Krout, E. (1986). Pedophilia: Diagnostic concepts, treatment, and ethical considerations. *American Journal of Forensic Psychiatry, 7,* 13–30.

Berlin, F. S. & Meinecke C. F. (1981). Treatment of sex offenders with antiandrogenic medication: conceptualization, review of treatment modalities, and preliminary findings. *American Journal of Psychiatry, 138,* 601–607.

Berlin, F. S. & Schaerf, F. W. (1984). Laboratory assessment of the paraphilias and their treatment with antiandrogenic medication. In R. C. W. Hall & T. P. Bereseford (Eds.), *A handbook of psychiatric diagnostic procedures.* New York: Spectrum.

Berrettini, W. H., Goldin, L. R., Nurnberger, J. I. Jr. & Gershon, E. S. (1984). Genetic factors in affective illness. *Journal of Psychiatry Research, 18,* 329–350.

Berrueta-Clement, J. R., Schweinhart, L. J., Barnett, W. S., Epstein, A. S. & Weikart, D. P. (1984). Changed lives: The effects of the Perry preschool programs on youths through age 19. Ypsilanti, MI: High/Scope Press.

Berrueta-Clement, J. R., Schweinhart, L. J., Barnett, W. S., Epstein, A. S. & Weikart, D. P. (1987). The effect of early educational interventions on crime and delinquency in adolescence and early adulthood. In J. D. Burchard & S. N. Burchard (Eds.), *Primary prevention of psychopathology,* vol. 10, *Prevention of delinquent behavior.* Newbury Park, CA: Sage, 220–240.

Bhandary, A. N. & Masand, P. S. (1997). Buspirone in the management of disruptive behaviors due to Huntington's Disease and other neurological disorders. *Psychosomatics, 38,* 389–391.

Biederman, J., Faraone, S. V., Keenan, K., Benjamin, J., Krifcher, B., Moore, C., Sprich-Buckminster, S., Ugaglia, K., Jellinek, M. S., Steingard, R., Spencer, T., Norman, D., Kolodny, R., Kraus, I., Perrin, J., Keller, M. B. & Tsuang, M. T. (1992). Further evidence for family-genetic risk factors in attention deficit hyperactivity disorder. *Archives of General Psychiatry, 49,* 728–738.

Biederman, J., Munir, K. & Knee, D. (1987). Conduct and oppositional disorder in clinically referred children with attention deficit disorder: A controlled family study. *Journal of the American Academy of Child and Adolescent Psychiatry, 26,* 724–727.

Biederman, J., Munir, K., Knee, D., Habelow, W., Armentano, M., Autor, S., Hoge, S. K. & Waternaux, C. (1986). A family study of patients with attention deficit disorder and normal controls. *Journal of Psychiatric Research, 20,* 263–274.

Biederman, J., Newcorn, J. & Sprich, S. (1991). Comorbidity of attention deficit hyperactivity disorder with conduct, depressive, anxiety, and other disorders. *American Journal of Psychiatry, 148,* 564–577.

Biederman, J., Wilens, T., Mick, E., Faraone, S.V., Weber, W., Curtis, S., Thornell, A., Pfister, K., Jetton, J. G. & Soriano, J. (1997). Is ADHD a risk factor for psychoactive substance use disorders? Findings from a four-year prospective follow-up study. *Journal of the American Academy of Child and Adolescent Psychiatry, 36,* 21–29.

Binion, V. J. (1980). A descriptive comparison of the families of origin of women heroin users and abusers. In *Addicted women: Family dynamics, self-perceptions and support systems.* DHEW Publication No. ADM 80-762, National Institute on Drug Abuse, Rockville, MD.

Bioulac, B., Benezech, M., Renaud, B., Noel, B. & Roche, D. (1980). Serotonergic dysfunction in the 47,XYY syndrome. *Biological Psychiatry, 15,* 917–923.

Bishop, D. M. (1984). Legal and extralegal barriers to delinquency: A panel analysis. *Criminology, 22,* 403–419.

Bjork, J. M., Dougherty, D. M., Moeller, F. G., Cherek, D. R. & Swann, A. C. (1999). The effects of tryptophan depletion and loading on laboratory aggression in men: Time course and a food restricted control. *Psychopharmacology, 142,* 24–30.

Bjorklund, D. F. & Brown, R. D. (1998). Physical play and cognitive development: Integrating activity, cognition and education. *Child Development, 69,* 604–606.

Blackburn, R. (1968). Personality in relation to extreme aggression in psychiatric offenders. *British Journal of Psychiatry, 114,* 821–828.

Blackson, R., Tarter, R., Martin, C. & Moss, H. (1993). Temperament mediates the effects of family history of substance abuse on externalizing and internalizing child behavior. *American Journal of Orthopsychiatry, 64,* 280–292.

Blake, P. Y., Pincus, J. H. & Buckner, C. (1993). Neurologic abnormalities in murderers. *Neurology, 45,* 1641–1647.

Blanchard, D., Shepherd, J. K., Rodgers & R. J. Blanchard, R. J. (1988). Evidence for differential effects of 8-OH-DPAT on male and female rats in the anxiety/defense test battery. *Psychopharmacology Series (Berl), 106,* 531–539.

Blanchard, G. (1995). Sexually addicted lust murderers. *Sexual Addiction and Compulsivity, 2,* 62–71.

Blood, L. & Cornwall, A. (1996). Childhood sexual victimization as a factor in the treatment of substance abusing adolescents. *Substance Use and Misuse, 31,* 1015–1039.

Bloom, F. E. (1996). Neurotransmission and the central nervous system. In L. S. Goodman & L. E. Limbird (Eds.), *Goodman and Gilman's the pharmacological basis of therapeutics* (9th ed.). New York: McGraw-Hill, 267–293.

Blum, K., Noble, E. P. & Comings, D. E. (1997, April) Reward deficiency syndromes. *American Scientist,* 132–135.

Blum, K., Noble, E. P., Sheridan, P. J., Montgomery, A., Ritchie, T., Jagadeeswaran, P., Nogami, H., Briggs, A. H. & Cohn, J. B. (1990). Allelic association of human dopamine D2 receptor gene in alcoholism. *Journal of the American Medical Association, 163,* 2055–2060.

Blum, K., Noble, E. P., Sheridan, P. J., Montgomery, A., Ritchie, T., Jagadeeswaran, P., Briggs, A. H. & Cohn, J. B. (1990). Allelic association of human dopamine D2 receptor gene in alcoholism. *Journal of the American Medical Association, 263,* 3156–3160.

Blumer, D. (1991). Epilepsy and disorders of mood. In D. S. Smith, D. M. Treiman & M. Trimble (Eds.), *Advances in neurology,* vol 55. New York: Raven Press, 185–196.

Bobon, D. P., Plomteux, G., Heusghem, C. & Bobon, J. (1970). Clinical toxicology and efficacy of pimozide. *International Journal of Pharmacopsychiatry, 4,* 194–203.

Bohman, M. (1978). Some genetic aspects of alcoholism and criminality. A population of adoptees. *Archives of General Psychiatry, 35,* 269–276.

Bohman, M. (1983). Alcoholism and crime: Studies of adoptees. *Substance and alcohol actions/misuse, 4,* 137–147.

Bohman, M. (1996). Predisposition to criminality: Swedish adoption studies in retrospect. In G. R. Bock & J. A. Goode (Eds.), *Genetics of criminal and antisocial behavior.* West Sussex, England: John Wiley & Sons, 99–114.

Bohman, M., Cloninger, C. R., Sigvardsson, S. & von Knorring, A. L. (1982). Predisposition to petty criminality in Swedish adoptees: I. Genetic and environmental heterogeneity. *Archives of General Psychiatry, 39,* 1233–1241.

Bohman, M., Sigvardsson, S. & Cloninger, C. R. (1981). Maternal inheritance of alcohol abuse: Cross-fostering analysis of adopted women. *Archives of General Psychiatry, 38,* 965–969.

Bond, W., Mandos, L. & Kurtz, M. (1989). Midazolam for aggressivity and violence in three mentally retarded patients. *American Journal of Psychiatry, 146,* 925–926.

Boomsma, D. I. & Molenaar, P. C. M. (1987). The genetic analysis of repeated measures. I. Simplex models. *Behavior Genetics, 17,* 111–123.

Booth, R. E., Watters, J. K. & Chitwood, D. D. (1993). HIV risk-related sex behaviors among injection drug users, crack smokers, and injection drug users who smoke crack. *American Journal of Public Health, 83,* 1144–1148.

Botvin, G. J., Baker, E., Dusenbury, L., Botvin, E. M. & Diaz, T. (1995). Long-term follow-up results of a randomized drug abuse prevention trial in a white middle-class population. *Journal of the American Medical Association, 273,* 1106–1112.

Bouchard, T. H., Jr. & Propping, P. (Eds.) (1993). *Twins as a tool of behavioral genetics.* New York: John Wiley & Sons.

Bowlby, J. (1944). Forty-four juvenile thieves. *International Journal of Psychoanalysis, 25,* 107–128.

Bowlby, J. (1951). *Maternal care and mental health.* Geneva: World Health Organization.

Begleiter, H., Porjesz, B. & Kissin, B. (1984). Event-related brain potentials in children at risk for alcoholism. *Science, 225,* 1493–1495.

Brain, P. F., Mainardi, D. & Parmigiani, S. (1989). *House mouse aggression: A model for understanding the evolution of social behavior.* London: Harwood Academic Publishers.

Bremer, J. (1959). *Asexualization: A follow-up study of 244 cases.* New York: Macmillan.

Brennan, P. & Mednick, S. (1997). Medical histories of antisocial individuals. In D. Stoff, J. Breiling & J. Maser (Eds.), *Handbook of antisocial behavior.* New York: John Wiley & Sons.

Briere, J. (1989). *Therapy for adults molested as children: Beyond survival.* New York: Springer.

Briere, J. & Runtz, M. (1988). Symptomatology associated with childhood sexual victimization in a non-clinical adult sample. *Child Abuse and Neglect, 12,* 51–59.

Brizer, D. A. (1988). Psychopharmacology and the management of violent patients. *Psychiatric Clinics of North America, 11,* 551–568.

Brizer, D., Convit, A., Krakowski, M. & Volavka, J. (1987). A rating scale for reporting violence on psychiatric wards. *Hospital and Community Psychiatry, 38,* 769–770.

Brizer, D. A. & Crowner, M. (1989). *Current approaches to the prediction of violence.* Washington, DC: American Psychiatric Press.

Brody, J. F. Jr. (1970). Behavioral effects of serotonin depletion and of p-chlorophenylanlanine (a serotonin depletor) in rats. *Psychopharmacologia, 17,* 14–33.

Bronfenbrenner, U. (1977). Toward an experimental ecology of human development. *American Psychologist, 32,* 513–531.

Brook, J. S., Whiteman, M., Finch, S. J. & Cohen, P. (1996). Young adult drug use and delinquency: Childhood antecedents and adolescent mediators. *Journal of American Academy of Child and Adolescent Psychiatry, 35,* 1584–1592.

Brooke, M. M., Patterson, D. R., Questad, K. A., Cardenas, D. & Farrel-Roberts, L.(1992). The treatment of agitation during initial hospitalization after traumatic brain injury. *Archives of Physical Medicine and Rehabilitation, 73,* 917–921.

Brooks-Gunn, J., McCarton, C. & Hawley, T. (1994). Effects of in utero drug exposure on children's development: Review and recommendations. *Archives of Pediatric and Adolescent Medicine, 148,* 33–39.

Brooner, R. K., Greenfield, L., Schmidt, C. W. & Bigelow, G. E. (1993). Antisocial personality disorder and HIV infection among intravenous drug abusers. *American Journal of Psychiatry, 150,* 53–58.

Brooner, R. K., King, V. L., Kidorf, M., Schmidt, C. W. & Bigelow, G. E. (1997). Psychiatric and substance use comorbidity among treatment-seeking opioid abusers. *Archives of General Psychiatry, 54,* 71–80.

Brooner, R. K., Schmidt, C. W., Felch, L. J. & Bigelow, G. E. (1992). Antisocial behavior of intravenous drug abusers: Implications for diagnosis of antisocial personality disorder. *American Journal of Psychiatry, 149,* 482–487.

Broughton, R., Billings, R. Cartwright, R., Doucette, J., Edmeads, J., Edwards N., Ervin, F. R., Orchard, B., Hill, R. & Turrell, G. (1994). Homicidal somnambulism: A case report. *Sleep, 17,* 253–964.

Brown, G. L., Ebert, M. H., Goyer, P. F., Jimerson, D. C., Klein, W. F., Bunney, W. E. & Goodwin, F. K. (1982). Aggression, suicide and serotonin: Relationships to CSF amine metabolites. *American Journal of Psychiatry, 139,* 741–746.

Brown, G. L. & Goodwin, F. K. (1986). Human aggression: A biologic perspective. In W. W. Reid, D. Dore, J. Walker & I. W. Bonner (Eds.), *Unmasking the psychopath.* New York: W. W. Norton.

Brown, G. L., Goodwin, F. K., Ballenger, J. C., Goyer, P. F. & Major, L. F. (1979). Aggression in humans correlates with cerebrospinal fluid amine metabolites. *Psychiatry Research, 1,* 131–139.

Brown, G. L., Kline, W. J., Goyer, P. F., Minichiello, M. D., Kruesi, M. J. P. & Goodwin, F. K. (1985). Relationship of childhood characteristics to cerebrospinal fluid 5-hydroxyindoleacetic acid in aggressive adults. In C. Chagass (Ed.), *Biological psychiatry.* New York: Elsevier, 177–179.

Brown, S. J., Fann, J. R. & Grant, I. (1994). Postconcussional disorder: Time to acknowledge a common source of neurobehavioral morbidity. *Journal of Neuropsychiatry and Clinical Neurosciences, 6,* 15–22.

Brown, S. L. (1994, Dec.). Animals at play. *The National Geographic, 186,* 8–12.

Browne, A. & Finkelhor, D. (1986). Impact of child sexual abuse: A review of the research. *Psychological Bulletin, 99,* 66–77.

Brunner, H. G. (1996). MAOA deficiency and abnormal behaviour: Perspectives on an association. In Ciba Foundation Symposium, *Genetics of Criminal and Antisocial Behaviour,* Chichester: John Wiley & Sons.

Brunner, H. G., Nelen, M. R., Breakefield, X.O., Ropers, H. H. & van Oost, B. A. (1993). Abnormal behavior associated with a point mutation in the structural gene for monoamine oxidase A. *Science, 262,* 578–580.

Brunner, H. G., Nelen, M. R., van Zandvoort, P., Abeling, N. G., van Gennip, A. H., Wolters, E. C., Kuiper, M. A., Ropers, H. H. & van Oost, B. A. (1993). X-linked borderline mental retardation with prominent behavioral disturbance: Phenotype, genetic localization & evidence for disturbed monoamine metabolism. *American Journal of Human Genetics, 52,* 1032–1039.

Bry, B. H., McKeon, P. & Pandina, R. J. (1982). Extent of drug use as a function of number of risk factors. *Journal of Abnormal Psychology, 91,* 273–279.

Bryant, E., Scott, M., Tori, C. & Golden, C. (1984). Neuropsychological deficits, learning disability, and violent behavior. *Journal of Consulting and Clinical Psychology, 52,* 323–324.

Buchsbaum, M. S., Coursey, R.D. & Murphy, D. (1976). The biochemical high-risk paradigm: Behavioral and familial correlates of low platelet monoamine oxidase activity. *Science, 194,* 339–341.

Buckley, P., Bartell, J., Donenwirth, K., Lee, S., Torigoe, F. & Schulz, S. C. (1995). Violence and schizophrenia: Clozapine as a specific antiaggressive agent. *Bulletin of the American Academy of Psychiatry & the Law, 23,* 607–611.

Buhrich, N., Bailey, J. M. & Martin, N. G. (1991). Sexual orientation, sexual identity, and sex-dimorphic behaviors in male twins. *Behavioral Genetics, 21,* 75–96.

Buitelaar, J. K., van der Gaag, R. J. & van der Hoeven, J. (1998). Buspirone in the management of anxiety and irritability in children with pervasive developmental disorders: Results of an open label study. *Journal of Clinical Psychiatry, 59,* 56–59.

Bureau of Justice Statistics (BJS) (1988). *Criminal victimization in the United States: Trends.* Washington, DC: U.S. Department of Justice reports.

Bureau of Justice Statistics (1997, June, December). U.S. Department of Justice reports, Washington, DC: Office of Justice Programs.

Burnam, M. A., Stein, J. A., Golding, J. M., Siegel, J. M., Sorenson, S. B., Forsythe, A. B. & Telles, C. A. (1988). Sexual assault and mental disorders in a community population. *Journal of Consulting Clinical Psychology, 56,* 843–850.

Bushman, B. J. & Geen, R. G. (1990). Role of cognitive-emotional mediators and individual differences in the effects of media violence on aggression. *Journal of Personality and Social Psychology, 58,* 156–163.

Buss, A. H. (1961). *The psychology of aggression.* New York: John Wiley & Sons.

Buss, A. H. & Durkee, A. (1957). An inventory for assessing different kinds of hostility. *Journal of Consulting Psychology, 21,* 343–349.

Buss, A. H. & Perry, M. (1992). The aggression questionnaire. *Journal of Personal and Social Psychology, 63,* 452–459.

Buss, A. H. & Plomin, R. (1975). *A temperament theory of personality development.* New York: John Wiley & Sons.

Buss, A. H. & Plomin, R. (1984). *Temperament: Early developing personality traits.* Hillsdale, NJ: Erlbaum.

Buydens-Branchey, L., Noumair, D. & Lieber, C. S. (1989). Age of alcohol onset: Relationship to susceptibility to serotonin precursor availability. *Archives of General Psychiatry, 46,* 231–236.

Buzzell, T. (1992). Using law-related education to foster social development: Towards a cognitive/structural intervention. Report prepared for the Juvenile Justice Initiative of the National Training and Dissemination Project for Law-Related Education, Office of Juvenile Justice and Delinquency Prevention, U.S. Dept. of Justice.

Cacciola, J. S., Rutherford, M. J., Alterman, A. I. & Snider, E. C. (1994). An examination of the diagnostic criteria for antisocial personality disorder in substance abusers. *Journal of Nervous and Mental Disease, 182,* 517–523.

Cadoret, R. J. (1978). Psychopathology in adopted-away offspring of biologic parents with antisocial behavior. *Archives of General Psychiatry, 35,* 176–184.

Cadoret, R. J. (1982). Genotype-environment

interaction in antisocial behaviour. *Psychological Medicine, 12,* 235–239.

Cadoret, R. J. (1985). Genes, environment and their interaction in the development of psychopathology. In T. Sakai & T. Tsuboi (Eds.), *Genetic aspects of human behavior.* Tokyo, Japan: Igaku-Shoin.

Cadoret, R. J., O'Gorman, T. W., Troughton, E. & Heywood, E. (1985). Alcoholism and antisocial personality: Interrelationships, genetic and environmental factors. *Archives of General Psychiatry, 42,* 161–167.

Cadoret, R. J. & Stewart, M. A. (1991). An adoption study of attention deficit/ hyperactivity/ aggression and their relationship to adult antisocial personality. *Comprehensive Psychiatry, 32,* 73–82.

Cadoret, R. J., Troughton, E., Bagford, J. & Woodworth, G. (1990). Genetic and environmental factors in adoptee antisocial personality. *European Archives of Psychiatry and Neurological Sciences, 239,* 231–240.

Cadoret, R. J., Troughton, E. & O'Gorman, T. W. (1987). Genetic and environmental factors in alcohol abuse and antisocial personality. *Journal of Studies on Alcohol, 48,* 1–8.

Cadoret, R. J., Troughton, E., O'Gorman, T. W. & Heywood, E. (1986). An adoption study of genetic and environmental factors in drug abuse. *Archives of General Psychiatry, 43,* 1131–1136.

Cadoret, R. J., Yates, W. R., Troughton, E., Woodworth, G. & Stewart, M. A. (1995). Adoption study demonstrating two genetic pathways to drug abuse. *Archives of General Psychiatry, 52,* 42–52.

Cadoret, R. J., Yates, W. R., Troughton, E., Woodworth, G. & Stewart, M. A. (1995). Genetic-environmental interaction in the genesis of aggressivity and conduct disorders. *Archives of General Psychiatry, 52,* 916–924.

Cadoret, R.J., Yates, W. R., Troughton, E., Woodworth, G. & Stewart, M.A. (1996). An adoption study of drug abuse/dependence in females. *Comprehensive Psychiatry, 37,* 88–94.

Cairns, H. (1950). Mental disorders with tumors of the pons. *Folia Psychiatry Neurology* (Netherlands), *53,* 193–203.

Caldwell, C. B. & Gottesman, I. I. (1991). Sex differences in the risk for alcoholism: A twin study. Paper presented at Behavior Genetics Association meeting, St. Louis, MO.

Campbell, A. & Gibbs, J. J. (Eds.) (1986). *Violent transactions.* Oxford, UK: Blackwell.

Campbell, M., Adams, P. B., Small, A. M., Kafantaris, V., Silva, R. R., Shell, J., Perry, R. & Overall, J. E. (1995). Lithium in hospitalized aggressive children with conduct disorder: A double blind and placebo-controlled study. *Journal of the American Academy of Child and Adolescent Psychiatry, 34,* 445–453.

Campbell, M., Gonzalez, N. M. & Silva, R. R. (1992). The pharmacologic treatment of conduct disorders and rage outbursts. *Psychiatric Clinics of North America, 15,* 69-85.

Campbell, M., Small, A. M., Green, W. H., Jennings, S. J., Perry, R., Bennett, W. G. & Anderson, L. (1984). Behavioral efficacy of haloperidol and lithium carbonate: A comparison in hospitalized aggressive children with conduct disorder. *Archives of General Psychiatry, 41,* 650–656.

Cantwell, D. P. (1972). Psychiatric illness in the families of hyperactive children. *Archives of General Psychiatry, 27,* 414–417.

Cantwell, D. P. & Baker, L. (1991). *Psychiatric and developmental disorders in children with communication disorders.* Washington, DC: American Psychiatric Press.

Caplice, K. S. (1994). The case for public single-sex education. *Harvard Journal of Law and Public Policy, 18,* 277–292.

Caprara, G., Cinanni, V., D'Imperio, G., Passerini, S., Renzi, P. & Travaglia, G. (1985). Indicators of impulsive aggression: Present status of research on irritability and emotional susceptibility scales. *Personality and Individual Differences, 6,* 655–674.

Cantwell, D. P. (1972). Psychiatric illness in the families of hyperactive children. *Archives of General Psychiatry, 27,* 414–417.

Carey, G. (1986). Sibling imitation and contrast effects. *Behavior Genetics, 16,* 319–341.

Carey, G. (1992). Twin imitation for antisocial behavior: Implications for genetic and family environment research. *Journal of Abnormal Psychology, 101,* 18–25.

Carey, G. (1994). Genetics and violence. In A. J. Reiss, Jr., K. A. Miczek & J. A. Roth (Eds.), *Understanding and preventing violence,* vol. 2, *Biobehavioral influences.* Washington, DC: National Academy Press, 21–58.

Carey, G. (1996). Family and genetic epidemiology of aggressive and antisocial behavior. In D. M. Stoff & R. B. Cairns (Eds.), Aggression and violence: *Genetic, neurobiological and biosical perspectives.* Hillsdale, NJ: Erlbaum, 3–21.

Cargill, M., Altshuler, D., Ireland, J., Sklar, P., Ardlie, K., Patil, N., Lane, C. R. Lim, E. P., Kalyanaraman, N., Nemesh, J., Ziagura, L., Friedland, L., Rolfe, A., Warrington, J., Lipshutz, R., Daley, G. Q. & Landers, E. S. (1999). Characterization of single-nucleotide polymorphisms in coding regions of human genes. *Nature Genetics, 22,* 231–238.

Carlini, E. A., Lindsey, C. J. & Tufik, S. (1977). Cannabis, catecholamines, rapid eye movement sleep and aggressive behaviour. *British Journal of Pharmacology, 61,* 371–379.

Carlisle, A. (1993). The divided self: Toward an understanding of the dark side of the serial killer. *American Journal of Criminal Justice, 17,* 23–36.

Carlson, N. R. (1991). *Physiology of behavior* (4th ed). Boston: Allyn & Bacon.

Carlyle, W., Ancill, R. & Sheldon, L. (1993). Aggression in the demented patient: A double-blind study of loxapine versus haloperidol. *International Journal of Clinical Psychopharmacology, 8,* 103–108.

Carney, A., Bancroft, J. & Matthews, A. (1978). A combination of hormonal and psychological treatment for female sexual unresponsiveness: A comparative study. *British Journal of Psychiatry, 132,* 339–346.

Caron, M. (1996). A mouse knockout. *American Journal of Psychiatry, 153,* 1387.

Carroll, K. M., Gall, S. A. & Rounsaville, B. J. (1993). A comparison of alternate systems for diagnosing antisocial personality disorder in cocaine abusers. *Journal of Nervous and Mental Disease, 181,* 436–443.

Carruthers, M. & Taggart, P. (1973). Vagotonicity of violence: Biochemical and cardiac responses to violent films and television programmes. *British Medical Journal, 3,* 384–389.

Carson, D. K., Council, J. R. & Volk, M. A. (1988). Temperament, adjustment, and alcoholism in adult female incest victims. *Violence Victims, 3,* 205–216.

Cases, O., Seif, I., Grimsby, J., Gaspar, P., Chen, K., Pournin, S., Muller, U., Aguet, M., Babinet, C., Shih, J. C. & DeMaeyer, E. (1995). Aggressive behavior and altered amounts of brain serotonin and norepinephrine in mice lacking MAOA. *Science, 268,* 1763–1766.

Casey, J. F., Lasky, J. J., Klett, C. J. & Hollister, L. E. (1960). Treatment of schizophrenic reactions with phenothiazine derivatives. *American Journal of Psychiatry, 117,* 97–105.

Centerwall, B. S. & Robinette, C. D. (1989). Twin concordance for dishonorable discharge from the military: With a review of the genetics of antisocial behavior. *Comprehensive Psychiatry, 30,* 442–446.

Chalmers, J. B. & Townsend, M. (1990). The effects of training in social perspective taking on socially maladjusted girls. *Child Development, 61,* 178–190.

Chamberlain, N. L., Driver, E. D. & Miesdeld, R. L. (1994). The length and location of CAG trinucleotide repeats in the androgen receptor N-terminal domain affect transactivation function. *Nucleic Acids Research, 22,* 3181–3186.

Chandler, M. J. (1973). Egocentric and antisocial behavior: The assessment and training of social perspective-taking skills. *Developmental Psychology, 9,* 326–332.

Chassin, L., Pillow, D., Curran, P., Molina, B. & Barrera, M. (1993). Relation of parental alcoholism to early adolescent substance use: A test of three mediating mechanisms. *Journal of Abnormal Psychology, 102,* 3–19.

Chassin, L., Rogush, F. & Barrera, M. (1991). Substance use and symptomatology among adolescent children of alcoholics. *Journal of Abnormal Psychology, 100,* 449–463.

Chen, C., Rainnie, D. G., Greene, R. W. & Tonegawa, S. (1994). Abnormal fear response and aggressive behavior in mutant mice deficient for alpha-calcium-calmodulin kinase II. *Science, 266,* 291–294.

Cherek, D. R. (1981). Effects of smoking different doses of nicotine on human aggressive behavior. *Psychopharmacology, 75,* 339–349.

Cherek, D. R. & Lane, S. D. (in press). Laboratory and psychometric measurements of impulsivity among female parolees with violent or nonviolent histories. *Biological Psychiatry.*

Cherek, D. R., Lane, S. D. & White, S. (in press). Laboratory and self-report measures of aggression among female parolees with violent or nonviolent histories. *Aggressive Behavior.*

Cherek, D. R., Moeller, F. G., Schnapp, W. & Dougherty, D. M. (1997). Studies of violent and nonviolent male parolees I. Laboratory and psychometric measurements of aggression. *Biological Psychiatry, 41,* 514–522.

Cherek, D. R., Schnapp, W., Moeller, F. G. & Dougherty, D.M. (1996). Laboratory measures of aggressive responding in male parolees with violent and nonviolent histories. *Aggressive Behavior, 22,* 27–36.

Cherek, D. R., Spiga, R. Bennett, R. H. & Graboski, J. (1991). Human aggression and escape responding: Effects of provocation frequency. *Psychological Record, 41,* 3–17.

Cherek, D. R., Steinberg, J. L. & Manno, B. R. (1985). Effects of alcohol on human aggressive behavior. *Journal of Studies on Alcohol, 46,* 321–328.

Christiansen, K. O. (1977). A review of studies of criminality among twins. In S. A. Mednick & K. O. Christiansen (Eds.), *Biosocial bases of criminal behavior.* New York: Gardner Press, 45–88.

Cicchetti, D. & Lynch, M. (1993). Toward an ecological/transactional model of community violence and child maltreatment: Consequences for children's development. *Psychiatry: Interpersonal & Biological Processes, 56,* 96–118.

Ciccone, J. R. (1992). Murder, insanity, and medical expert witnesses. *Archives of Neurology, 49,* 608–611.

Cleare, A. J. & Bond, A. J. (1995). The effect of tryptophan depletion and enhancement on subjective and behavioural aggression in normal male subjects. *Psychopharmacology, 118,* 72–81.

Cleckley, H. C. (1982). *The mask of sanity.* St. Louis, MO: Harcourt Health Sciences.

Clements, S. D. (1966). *Minimal brain dysfunction in children.* Monograph No. 3, National Institute of Neurology and Blindness. Washington, DC: U.S. Department of Health, Education, and Welfare.

Clements, S. D. & Peters, J. E. (1962). Minimal brain dysfunction in the school-age child. *Archives of General Psychiatry, 6,* 185–197.

Clinton, J., Sterner, S. & Stelmachers, Z. (1987). Haloperidol for sedation of disruptive emergency patients. *Annals of Emergency Medicine, 16,* 319–322.

Cloninger, C. R. (1987). A systematic method for clinical description and classification of personality variants: A proposal. *Archives of General Psychiatry, 44,* 573–588.

Cloninger, C. R. (1987). Neurogenetic adaptive mechanisms in alcoholism. *Science, 236,* 410–416.

Cloninger, C., Bohman, M. & Sigvardssen, S. (1981). Inheritance of alcohol abuse: Cross fostering analyses of adopted men. *Archives of General Psychiatry, 38,* 861–868.

Cloninger, C. R., Bohman, M., Sigvardsson, S. & von Knorring, A. L. (1985). Psychopathology in adopted-out children of alcoholics. The Stockholm adoption study. *Recent Developments in Alcoholism, 3,* 37–51.

Cloninger, C. R., Christiansen, K. O., Reich, T. & Gottesman, I. I. (1978). Implications of sex differences in the prevalences of antisocial personality, alcoholism and criminality for familial transmission. *Archives of General Psychiatry, 35,* 941–951.

Cloninger, C. R. & Gottesman, I. I. (1987). Genetic and environmental factors in antisocial behavior disorders. In S. A. Mednick, T. E. Moffitt & S. A. Stack (Eds.), *The causes of crime: New biological approaches.* New York: Cambridge University Press, 92–109.

Cloninger, C. R., Reich, T. & Guze, S. B. (1975). The multifactorial model of disease transmission: II. Sex differences in the familial transmission of sociopathy (antisocial personality). *British Journal of Psychiatry, 127,* 11–22.

Cloninger, C. R., Reich, T. & Guze, S. B. (1975). The multifactorial model of disease transmission: III. Familial relationship between sociopathy and hysteria (Briquet's syndrome). *British Journal of Psychiatry, 127,* 23–32.

Cloninger, C. R., Sigvardsson, S., Bohman, M. & von Knorring, A. L. (1982). Predisposition to petty criminality in Swedish adoptees: II. Cross-fostering analysis of gene-environment interaction. *Archives of General Psychiatry 39,* 1242–1247.

Cloward, R. A. & Ohlin, L. E. (1960). *Delinquency and opportunity.* Glencoe, IL: Free Press.

Coccaro, E. F. (1989). Central serotonin and impulsive aggression. *British Journal of Psychiatry, 155,* 52–62.

Coccaro, E. F. (1998). [Unpublished data.] Clinical Neuroscience Research Unit, Department of Psychiatry, MCP at Hanemann School of Medicine, Philadelphia.

Coccaro, E. F. & Astill, J. (1990). Central serotonergic function in parasuicide. *Progress in Neuro-Psychopharmacology and Biological Psychiatry, 14,* 663–674.

Coccaro, E., Astill, J., Herbert, J. & Schut, A. G. (1990). Fluoxetine and impulsive aggression in DSM-III-R personality disorder patients. *Journal of Clinical Psychopharmacology, 10,* 373–375.

Coccaro, E. F., Bergeman, C. S. & McClearn, G. E. (1993). Heritability of irritable impulsiveness: A study of twins reared together and apart. *Psychiatry Research, 48,* 229–242.

Coccaro, E. F., Berman, M. E. & Kavoussi, R. J. (1997). Assessment of life-history of aggression: Development and psychometric characteristics. *Psychiatry Research, 73,* 147–157.

Coccaro, E. F. & Kavoussi, R. J. (1991). Biological and pharmacological aspects of borderline personality disorder. *Hospital and Community Psychiatry, 42,* 1029–1033.

Coccaro, E. F. & Kavoussi, R. J. (1994). The neuropsychopharmacologic challenge in biological psychiatry. *Clinical Chemistry, 40,* 319–327.

Coccaro, E. F. & Kavoussi, R. J. (1997). Fluoxetine and impulsive aggressive behavior in personality disordered subjects. *Archives of General Psychiatry, 54,* 1081–1088.

Coccaro, E. F., Kavoussi, R. J., Cooper, T. B. & Hauger, R. L. (1996). Hormonal responses to d- and d,l-fenfluramine in healthy human subjects. *Neuropsychopharmacology, 15,* 595–607.

Coccaro, E. F., Kavoussi, R. J., Cooper, T. E. & Hauger, R. L. (1997). Central serotonin activity and aggression: Inverse relationship with prolactin response to d-fenfluramine, but not CSF 5-HIAA concentration, in human subjects. *American Journal of Psychiatry, 154,* 1430–1435.

Coccaro, E. F., Kavoussi, R. J. & Hauger, R. L. (1995). Physiological responses to d-fenfluramine and ipsapirone challenge correlate with indices of aggression in males with personality disorder. *International Clinical Psychopharmacology, 10,* 177–179.

Coccaro, E. F., Kavoussi, R. J., Hauger, R. L., Cooper, T. B. & Ferris, C. F. (1998). CSF vasopressin: Correlates with indices of aggression and serotonin function in personality-disordered subjects. *Archives of General Psychiatry, 55,* 708–714.

Coccaro, E. F., Kavoussi, R. J., Sheline, Y. I., Lish, J. D. & Csernansky, J. G. (1996). Impulsive aggression in personality disorder: Correlates with H-paroxetine binding in the platelet. *Archives of General Psychiatry, 53,* 531–536.

Coccaro, E. F., Lawrence, T., Trestman, R., Gabriel, S., Klar, H. M. & Siever, L. J. (1991). Growth hormone responses to intravenous clonidine challenge correlates with behavioral irritability in psychiatric patients and in healthy volunteers. *Psychiatry Research, 39,* 129–139.

Coccaro, E. F. & Murphy, D. L. (1991). *Serotonin in major psychiatric disorders.* Washington, D. C.: American Psychiatric Press.

Coccaro, E. F., Siever, L. J., Klar, H. M., Mourer, G., Cochrane, K. Cooper, T. B., Mohs, R. C. & Davis, K. L. (1989). Serotonergic studies in patients with affective and personality disorders. *Archives of General Psychiatry, 46,* 587–599.

Cocores, J., Davies, R. & Mueller, P. (1987). Cocaine abuse and adult attention deficit disorder. *Journal of Clinical Psychiatry,* 4341–4432.

Cocores, J., Patel, M., Gold, M. & Pottash, A. (1987). Cocaine abuse, attention deficit disorder, and bipolar disorder. *Journal of Nervous and Mental Disease, 175,* 376–377.

Cohen, A. K. (1955). *Delinquent boys: The Culture of the gang.* Glencoe, IL: Free Press.

Cohen, J. (1977). *Statistical power analysis for the behavioral sciences.* New York: Academic Press.

Cohen, S. & Underwood, M. (1994). The use of clozapine in a mentally retarded and aggressive population. *Journal of Clinical Psychiatry, 55,* 440–444.

Cohn, E. S. & White, S. O. (1986). Cognitive developmental versus social learning approaches to studying legal socialization. *Basic and Applied Social Psychology, 7,* 195–209.

Cohn, E. S. & White, S. O. (1990). *Legal socialization: A study of norms and rules.* New York: Springer-Verlag.

Coid, B., Lewis, S. W. & Reveley, A. M. (1993). A twin study of psychosis and criminality. *British Journal of Psychiatry, 162,* 87–92.

Coie, J. D. & Dodge, K. A. (1983). Continuities and changes in children's social status: A five-year longitudinal study. *Merrill-Palmer Quarterly, 29,* 261–281.

Coie, J. D. (1990). Toward a theory of peer rejection. In S. R. Asher & J. D. Coie (Eds.), *Peer rejection in childhood.* New York: Cambridge University Press.

Cole, E. & Kumchy, C. I. (1981). The CPI battery: Identification of depression in a juvenile delinquent population. *Journal of Clinical Psychology, 37,* 880–884.

Collaer, M. L. & Hines, M. (1995). Human behavioral sex differences: a role for gonadal hormones during early development? *Psychological Bulletin, 118,* 55–107.

Comer, R. (1996). *Fundamentals of abnormal psychology.* New York: W. H. Freeman.

Comings, D. E. (1990), *Tourette syndrome and human behavior.* Duarte, CA: Hope Press.

Comings, D. E. (1995). The role of genetic factors in conduct disorder based on studies of Tourette syndrome and ADHD probands and their relatives. *Journal of Developmental and Behavioral Pediatrics, 16,* 142–157.

Comings, D. E. (1996). *The gene bomb.* Duarte, CA: Hope Press.

Comings, D. E. (1996). Genetic mechanisms in neuropsychiatric disorders. In K. Blum, E. P. Noble, R. S. Sparks & P. J. Sheridan (Eds.), *Handbook of psychoneurogenetics.* Boca Raton, FL: CRC Press, Inc.

Comings, D. E. (1996). *Search for the Tourette syndrome and human behavior genes.* Duarte, CA: Hope Press.

Comings, D. E. (1998). Why different rules are required for polygenic inheritance: Lessons from studies of the DRD2 gene. *Alcohol, 16,* 1–10.

Comings, D. E. (1998, personal communication) Chief of Human Genetics, Director of Tourette Disorder Clinic, City of Hope National Hospital, Duarte, CA.

Comings, D. E. & Comings, B. G. (1984). Tourette's syndrome and attention deficit disorder with hyperactivity: Are they genetically related? *Journal of the American Academy of Child Psychiatry, 23,* 138–146.

Comings, D. E. & Comings, B. G. (1987). A controlled study of Tourette syndrome: I. ADD, learning disorders, and school problems. *American Journal of Human Genetics, 41,* 701–741.

Comings, D. E. & Comings, B. G. (1987). A controlled study of Tourette syndrome. II. Conduct. *American Journal of Human Genetics, 41,* 742–760.

Comings, D. E., Comings, B. G., Muhleman, D., Dietz, G., Shahbahrami, B., Tast, D., Knell, E., Kocsis, P., Baumgarten, R., Kovacs, B. W., Levy, D. L., Smith, M., Kane, J. M., Lieberman, J.A., Klein, D. N., MacMurray, J., Tosk, J., Sverd, J., Gysin, R. & Flanagan, S. (1991). The dopamine D2 receptor locus as a modifying gene in neuropsychiatric disorders. *Journal of the American Medical Association, 266,* 1793–1800.

Comings, D. E., Comings, B. G., Tacket, T. & Li, S. (1990). The clonidine patch and behavioral problems. *Journal of the American Academy of Child and Adolescent Psychiatry, 29,* 667–668.

Comings, D. E., Ferry, L., Bradshaw-Robinson, S., Burchette, R., Chiu, C. & Muhleman, D. (1996). The dopamine D2 receptor (DRD2) gene: A genetic risk factor in smoking. *Pharmacogenetics, 6,* 73-79.

Comings, D. E., Gade, R., Gonzalez, N., Blake, H., Wu, S. & MacMurray, J. P. (1998). Additive effect of three adrenergic genes (ADRA2A, ADRA2C, DBH) on ADHD in subjects with Tourette syndrome with and without learning disabilities. *Journal of the American Academy of Child and Adolescent Psychiatry,* (submitted).

Comings, D.E., Gade, R., Gonzalez, N., Wu, S., Muhleman, D., Chen, C., Farwell, K., Blake, H., Dietz, G., Saucier, G. & MacMurray, J .P. (1998). A multiple additive associations technique for the identification of genes in polygenic disorders: Results for ADHD and comorbid disorders.

Comings, D. E., Gade, R., Wu, S., Chiu, C., Dietz, G., Muhleman, D., Saucier, G., Ferry, L., Burchete, R., Johnson, P., Verde, R. & MacMurray, J. P. (1997). Studies of the potential role of the dopamine D1 receptor gene in addictive behaviors. *Molecular Psychiatry, 2,* 44–56.

Comings, D. E., Muhleman, D., Ahn, C., Gysin, R. & Glanagan, S. (1994). The dopamine D2 receptor gene: A genetic risk factor in substance abuse. *Drug and Alcohol Dependence, 34,* 1–16.

Comings, D. E., Muhleman, D., Dietz, G., Sherman, M. & Forest, G. (1995). Sequence of human tryptophan 2,3-dioxygenase: Presence of a glucocorticoid response-like element composed of a GTT repeat and an intronic CCCCT repeat. *Genomics, 29,* 390–396.

Comings, D. E., Muhleman, D., Gade, R., Chiu, C., Wu, H., Dietz, G., Winn-Dean, E., Ferry, L., Rosenthal, R. J., Lesieur, H. R., Rugle, L., Sverd, J., Johnson, P. & MacMurray, J. P. (1996). Exon and intron mutations in the human tryptophan 2,3-dioxygenase gene and their potential association with Tourette syndrome, substance abuse and other psychiatric disorders. *Pharmacogenetics, 6,* 307–318.

Comings, D. E., Muhleman, D. & Gysin, R. (1996). The dopamine D2 receptor (DRD2) gene in posttraumatic stress disorder: A study and replication. *Biological Psychiatry, 40,* 368–372.

Comings, D. E., Rosenthal, R. J., Lesieur, H. R., Rugle, L., Muhleman, D., Chiu, C., Dietz, G. & Gade, R. (1996a). A study of the dopamine D2 receptor gene in pathological gambling. *Pharmacogenetics, 6,* 223–234.

Comings, D. E., Wu, H., Chiu, C., Ring, R. H., Dietz, G. & Muhleman, D. (1996b). Polygenic inheritance of Tourette syndrome, stuttering, ADHD, conduct and oppositional defiant disorder: The additive and subtractive effect of the three dopaminergic genes—DRD2, DbH and DAT1. *American Journal of Medical Genetics (Neuropsychiatric Genetics), 67,* 264–288.

Compton, W. M., Cottler, L. B., Shillington, A. M. & Price, R. K. (1995). Is antisocial personality disorder associated with increased HIV risk behaviors in cocaine users? *Drug and Alcohol Dependence, 37,* 37–44.

Comstock, G. & Paik, H. (1990). The effects of television on aggressive behavior. Unpublished report to the National Academy of Science on Understanding and Control of Violent Behaviors, vol. 1. Washington, DC: National Academy Press.

Conklin, J. E. (1972). *Robbery and the criminal justice system.* Philadelphia: Lippincott.

Conn, D. K. & Goldman, Z. (1992). Pattern of use of antidepressants in long-term care facilities for the elderly. *Journal of Geriatric Psychiatry and Neurology, 5,* 228–232.

Conners, C. K., Kramer, R., Rothschild, G. H., Schwartz, L. & Stone, A. (1971). Treatment of young delinquent boys with diphenylhydantoin sodium and methylphenidate. *Archives of General Psychiatry, 24,* 156–160.

Cook, E. H., Fletcher, K. E., Wainwright, M., Marks, N., Yan, S.Y. & Levanthal, B. L. (1994). Primary structure of the human platelet serotonin 5-HT-2a receptor: Identity with frontal cortex serotonin 5-HT-2a receptor. *Journal of Neurochemistry, 63,* 465–469.

Cook, E. H. Jr., Stein, M. A., Krasowski, M. D., Cox, N. J., Olkon, D. M., Kieffer, J. E., Leventhal, B. L. (1995). Association of attention-deficit disorder and the dopamine transporter gene. *American Journal of Human Genetics, 56,* 993–998.

Cook, W. & Medley, D. (1954). Proposed hostility and pharasaic-virtue scales for the MMPI. *Journal of Applied Psychology, 383,* 414–418.

Cools, A. R. & Gingras, M. A. (1998). Nijmegen high and low responders to novelty: A new tool in the search after the neurobiology of drug abuse liability. *Pharmacology and Biochemistry of Behavior, 60,* 151–159.

Cooper, I. S. (1978). *Cerebellar stimulation in man.* New York: Raven Press.

Copeland Symptom Checklist for Attention Deficit Disorder (1989). Self-administered test available online at *http://www.oberlin.edu/njkapell.*

Copeland, E. D. (1987). Copeland rating scale for adult ADD. Macon, GA: Macon University. Available via the Southeastern Psychological Insitute, Atlanta.

Copeland, J. & Hall, W. (1992). A comparison of women seeking drug and alcohol treatment in a specialist women's and two traditional mixed-sex treatment services. *British Journal of Addiction, 87,* 65–74.

Corcoran, K. & Fischer, J. (1987). *Measures for clinical practice: A sourcebook.* New York: The Free Press.

Cornelius, J. R., Soloff, P. H., Perel, J. M. & Ulrich, R. F. (1990). Fluoxetine trial in borderline personality disorder. *Psychopharmacology Bulletin, 26,* 151–154.

Corrigan, M., Garbutt, J. C., Ekstrom, D. & Golden, R. N. (1992) Serotonergic function in trauma victims. *Biological Psychiatry, 31,* 12.Cairns, R. B. (1979). *Social development: The origins and plasticity of interactions.* San Francisco: Freeman.

Corrigan, P. W., Yudofsky, S. C. & Silver, J. M. (1993). Pharmacological and behavioral treatments for aggressive psychiatric inpatients. *Hospital and Community Psychiatry, 44,* 125–133.

Cottler, L. B., Compton, W. C., Price, R. K., Shillington, A. M., Claverie, D. J., Works, J. E., Mager, D. E., Sharma, D. & Miller, O. (1993). St. Louis' efforts to reduce the spread of AIDS. In J. A. Inciardi, F. Tims & B. Fletcher (Eds.), *Innovative approaches to the treatment of drug abuse, program models and strategies.* Westport, CT: Greenwood Press, 205–218.

Cowdry, R. & Gardner, D. (1988). Pharmacology of borderline personality disorder. *Archives of General Psychiatry, 45,* 111–119.

Cox, C. S., Fedio, P. & Rapoport, J. C. (1989). Neuropsychological testing of obsessive-compulsive adolescents. In J. Rapoport (Ed.), *Obsessive compulsive disorders in children and adolescents.* Washington, DC: American Psychiatric Press.

Coyle, J. T. (1988). Neuroscience and psychiatry. In J. A. Talbott, R. E. Hales & S. C. Yudofsky (Eds.), *American psychiatric press textbook of psychiatry.* Washington, DC: American Psychiatric Press, 3–32.

Craft, M., Ismail, I. A., Krishnamurti, D.,

Mathews, J., Regan, A., Seth, R. V. & North, P. M. (1987). Lithium in the treatment of aggression in mentally handicapped patients: A double-blind trial. *British Journal of Psychiatry, 150,* 685–689.

Crowe, R. R. (1974). An adoption study of antisocial personality. *Archives of General Psychiatry, 31,* 785–79.

Cueva, J. E., Overall, J. E., Small, A. M., Armenteros, J. L., Perry, R. & Campbell, M. (1996). Carbamazepine in aggressive children with conduct disorder: A double-blind and placebo-controlled study. *Journal of the American Academy of Child and Adolescent Psychiatry, 35,* 480–490.

Cunningham, L., Cadoret, R. J., Loftus, R. & Edwards, J. E. (1975). Studies of adoptees from psychiatrically disturbed biological parents: Psychiatric conditions in childhood and adolescence. *British Journal of Psychiatry, 126,* 534–549.

Cyphers, L., Phillips, K., Fulker, D. & Mrazek, D. (1990). Twin temperament during the transition from infancy to early childhood. *Journal of the American Academy of Child Psychiatry, 29,* 392–397.

Dalgard, O. S. & Kringlen, E. (1976). A Norwegian twin study of criminality. *British Journal of Criminology, 16,* 213–232.

Dalton, K. (1964). *The premenstrual syndrome.* Springfield, IL: Charles C Thomas.

Daly, M. & Wilson, M. (1988). *Homicide.* Hawthorne, NY: Aldine de Gruyter.

Damasio, A. R., Tramel, D. T. & Damasio, M. (1990). Individuals with sociopathic behavior caused by frontal damage fail to respond automatically to social stimuli. *Behavioral Brain Reseach, 41,* 81–94.

Davenport, D. B. (1915). The feebly inhibited: Violent temper and its inheritance. *Journal of Nervous and Mental Diseases, 42,* 493–528.

Davidson, J., Kudler, H., Smith, R., Mahorney, S. L., Lipper, S., Hammett, E., Saunders, W. B. & Cavenar, J. O. Jr. (1990). Treatment of post-traumatic stress disorder with amitriptyline and placebo. *Archives of General Psychiatry, 47,* 259–266.

Davidson, J., Roth, S. & Newman, E. (1991). Treatment of post-traumatic stress disorder with fluoxetine. *Journal of Traumatic Stress, 4,* 419–423.

Davies, W. (1982). Violence in prison. In P. Feldman (Ed.), *Developments in the study of criminal behavior.* London: Violence.

Davis, L. L., Suris, A., Lambert, M. T., Heimberg, C. & Petty, F. (1997). Post-traumatic stress disorder and serotonin: New directions for research and treatment. *Journal of Psychiatry Neuroscience, 22,* 318–326.

Dawes, M. A., Tarter, R. E. & Kirisci, L. (1997). Behavioral self-regulation: Correlates and 2 year follow-ups for boys at risk for substance abuse. *Drug and Alcohol Dependence, 45,* 165–176.

De Bellis, M. D., Chrousos, G. P., Dorn, L. D., Burke, L., Helmers, K., Kling, M. A., Trickett, P. K. & Putnam, F. W. (1994). Hypothalamic-pituitary-adrenal axis dysregulation in sexually abused girls. *Journal of Clinical Endocrinology and Metabolism, 78,* 249–255.

DeFelipe, C., Herrero, J. F., O'Brien, J. A., Palmer, J. A., Doyle, C. A., Smith, A. J. H., Laird, J. M., Belmonte, C., Cervero, F. & Hunt, S. P. (1998). Altered nociception, analgesia and aggression in mice lacking the receptor for substance P. *Nature, 392,* 394–397.

De Goeij, D. C., Dijkstra, H. & Tilders, F. J. (1992). Chronic psychosocial stress enhances vasopressin, but not corticotropin-releasing factor, in the external zone of the median eminence of male rats: Relationship to subordinate status. *Endocrinology, 131,* 847–853.

DeHart, D. & Mahoney, J. (1994). The serial murderer's motivations: An interdisciplinary review. *Omega, 29,* 29–45.

de Koning, P., Mak, M., de Vries, M. H., Allsopp, L. F., Stevens, R. B., Verbruggen, R., Van den Borre, R., van Peteghem, P., Kohen, D. & Arumainayagam, M. (1994). Eltoprazine in aggressive mentally handicapped patients: A double-blind, placebo- and baseline-controlled multicentre study. *International Journal of Clinical Psychopharmacology, 14,* 187–194.

Delini-Stula, A. & Vassout, A. (1979). Differential effects of psychoactive drugs on aggressive responses in mice and rats. In M. Sandler (Ed.), *Psychopharmacology of aggression.* New York, Raven, 41–60.

Delva, N. J., Matthews, D. R. & Cowen, P. (1996). Brain serotonin (5-HT) neuroendocrine function in patients taking cholesterol-lowering drugs. *Biological Psychiatry, 39,* 100–106.

Dembo, R., Dertke, M., LaVoie, L., Borders, S., Washburn, M. & Schmeidler, J. (1987). Physical abuse, sexual victimization and illicit drug use: A structural analysis among high risk adolescents. *Journal of Adolescence, 10,* 13–33.

DeMore, S. W., Fisher, J. D. & Baron, R. M. (1988). The equity-control model as a predictor of vandalism among college students. *Journal of Applied Social Psychology, 18,* 80–91.

Denckla, M. B. (1989). In J. Rapoport (Ed.), *Obsessive compulsive disorders in children and adolescents.* Washington, DC: American Psychiatric Press.

Denno, D. W. (1988). *University of Pennsylvania Law Review, 137,* 659.

Denno, D. W. (1990). *Biology and violence: From birth to adulthood.* New York: Cambridge University Press.

Derogatis, L. R., Lipman, R. S., Rickels, K., Uhlenhuth, E. H. & Covi, L. (1974). The Hopkins Symptom Checklist (HSCL): A measure of primary symptom dimensions. In P. Pichot (Ed.), *Psychological measurements in psychopharmacology.* Basel, Switzerland: Karger.

Des Jarlais, D. C. & Friedman, S. R. (1988). Intravenous cocaine, crack, and HIV infection. *Journal of the American Medical Association, 259,* 1945–1946.

Devor, E. J., Cloninger, C. R., Hoffman, P. L. & Tabakoff, B. (1994). Association of monoamine oxidase (MAO) activity with alcoholism and alcoholic subtypes. *American Journal of Medical Genetics, 48,* 209–213.

DeVries, A. C., Young, W. S. & Nelson, R. J. (1997). Reduced aggressive behaviour in mice with targeted disruption of the oxytocin gene. *Journal of Neuroendocrinology, 9,* 363–368.

DeWolfe, A. S. & Ryan, J. J. (1984). PIQ >> VIQ index in a forensic sample: A reconsideration. *Journal of Clinical Psychology, 40,* 291–294.

De Zulueta, F. I. (1998). Human violence: A treatable epidemic. *Medical Conflict Survivors, 14,* 46–55.

Diamond, M. (1982). Sexual identity: Monozygotic twins reared in discordant sex roles and a BBC followup. *Archives of Sexual Behavior, 11,* 181–186.

Dickman, S. J. (1990). Functional and dysfunctional impulsivity: Personality and cognitive correlates. *Journal of Personality and Social Psychology, 58,* 95–102.

Diekmann, G. & Hassler, R. (1975). Unilateral hypothalamotomy in social delinquents. Report on 6 cases. *Confinia Neurologica, 37,* 177–186.

DiLalla, L. F. & Gottesman, I. I. (1989). Heterogeneity of causes for delinquency and criminality: Lifespan perspectives. *Development and Psychopathology, 1,* 339–349.

Dinan, T. G. (1996). Serotonin: Current understanding and the way forward. *International Clinical Psychopharmacology, 11,* 19-21.

Dinwiddie, S. H. (1994). Psychiatric genetics and forensic psychiatry: A review. *Bulletin of the American Academy of Psychiatry and the Law, 22,* 327–342.

Dinwiddie, S. H. (1996). Genetics, antisocial personality, and criminal responsibility. *Bulletin of the American Academy of Psychiatry and the Law, 24,* 95–108.

Dinwiddie, S. H. (1997). Characteristics of injecting drug users derived from a large family study of alcoholism. *Comprehensive Psychiatry, 38,* 218–229.

Dinwiddie, S. H., Ben Abdallah, A., Compton, W. & Cottler, L. (1998). Subtypes of injecting drug users: A latent class analysis. Paper presented at the Thirty-fifth Annual Meeting of the Academy of Criminal Justice Sciences, Albuquerque, NM.

Dinwiddie, S. H. & Cloninger, C. R. (1991). Family and adoption studies in alcoholism and drug addiction. *Psychiatric Annals, 21,* 206–214.

Dinwiddie, S. H., Cottler, L., Compton, W. & Ben Abdallah, A. (1996). Psychopathology and HIV risk behaviors among injection drug users in and out of treatment. *Drug and Alcohol Dependence 43,* 1–11.

Dinwiddie, S. H. & Daw, E. W. (1998). Temporal stability of antisocial personality disorder: Blind follow-up study at eight years. *Comprehensive Psychiatry, 39,* 28–34.

Dinwiddie, S. H., Heath, A. C., Dunne, M. P., Bucholz, K. K., Madden, P. A. F., Slutske, W. S., Bierut, L. J., Statham, D. B. & Martin, N. G. (1999, in press). Early sexual abuse and lifetime psychopathology: A cotwin-control study. *Psychological Medicine.*

Dinwiddie, S. H. & Reich, T. (1993). Attribution of antisocial symptoms in coexistent antisocial personality disorder and substance abuse. *Comprehensive Psychiatry, 34,* 235–242.

Dinwiddie, S. H., Reich, T. & Cloninger, C. R. (1992). Lifetime complications of drug use in intravenous drug users. *Journal of Substance Abuse, 4,* 13–18.

Dinwiddie, S. H., Reich, T. & Cloninger, C. R.

(1992). Patterns of lifetime drug use among intravenous drug users. *Journal of Substance Abuse, 4,* 1–11.

Dinwiddie, S. H., Reich, T. & Cloninger, C. R. (1992). Prediction of intravenous drug use. *Comprehensive Psychiatry 33,* 173–179.

Dinwiddie, S. H., Reich, T. & Cloninger, C. R. (1992). Psychiatric comorbidity and suicidality among intravenous drug users. *Journal of Clinical Psychiatry, 53,* 364–369.

Dishion, T. J., Loeber, R., Stouthamer-Loeber, M. & Patterson, G. R. (1984). Skill deficits and male adolescent delinquency. *Journal of Abnormal Child Psychology, 12,* 37-53.

Dodge, K. A. (1980). Social cognition and children's aggressive behavior. *Child Development, 51,* 162–170.

Dodge, K. A., Bates, J. E. & Pettit, G. S. (1990). Mechanisms in the cycle of violence. *Science, 250,* 1678–1683.

Dodge, K. A. & Schwartz, D. (1997). Social information processing mechanisms in aggressive behavior. In D. M. Stoff, J. Breiling & J. D. Maser (Eds.), *Handbook of Antisocial Behavior.* New York: John Wiley & Sons.

Donlon, P., Hopkin, J. & Tupin, I. (1979). Overview: Efficacy and safety of the rapid neuroleptization method with injectable haloperidol. *American Journal of Psychiatry 136,* 273–278.

Donohew, L., Palmgreen, P. & Lorch, E. P. (1994). Attention, need for sensation and health communication campaigns. *American Behavioral Scientist, 38,* 310–322.

Donzinger, S. R. (1997). *The real war on crime.* New York: HarperCollins.

Douglas, V. (1972). Stop, look, and listen: The problem of sustained attention and impulse control in hyperactive and normal children. *Canadian Journal of Behavioral Science, 4,* 259–282.

Draucker, C. B. (1995). A coping model for adult survivors of childhood sexual abuse. *Journal of Interpersonal Violence, 10,* 159–175.

Drukteinis, A. (1992). Serial murder: The heart of darkness. *Psychiatric Annals, 22,* 532–538.

Duckett, J. H. (1988). The prediction of violence. *South African Journal of Psychology, 18,* 10–18.

Duke, M. P. & Fenhagen, E. (1975). Self-parental alienation and locus of control in delinquent girls. *Journal of Genetic Psychology, 127,* 103–107.

Dulcan, M. K., Bregman, J. D., Weller, E. B. & Weller, R. A. (1995). Treatment of childhood and adolescent disorders. In C. Nemeroff (Ed.), *The American Psychiatric Association textbook of psychopharmacology.* Washington, DC: American Psychiatric Press.

Dunn, H. G., McBurney, A. K., Ingram, S. & Hunter, C. M. (1977). Maternal cigarette smoking during pregnancy and the child's subsequent development: II. Neurological and intellectual maturation to the age of 6 1/2 years. *Canadian Journal of Public Health, 68,* 43–50.

Eadie, M. & Tyrer, J. (1980). *Anticonvulsant therapy: Pharmacological basis and practice.* New York: Churchill Livingstone.

Earls, F., Reich, W., Jung, C. G. & Cloninger, C. R. (1988). Psychopathology in children of alcoholic and antisocial parents. *Alcoholism: Clinical and experimental research, 12,* 481–487.

Eaves, L. J. (1976). A model for sibling effects in man. *Heredity, 36,* 205–214.

Eaves, L. J., Silberg, J. L., Meyer, J. M., Maes, H. H., Simonoff, E., Pickles, A., Rutter, M., Neale, M. C., Reynolds, C. A., Erikson, M. T., Heath, A. C., Loeber, R., Truett, K. R., Hewitt, J. K. (1997). Genetics and developmental psychopathology: 2. The main effects of genes and environment on behavioral problems in the Virginia twin study of adolescent behavioral development. *Journal of Child Psychology and Psychiatry, 38,* 965–980.

Ebstein, R. P., Novick, O., Umansky, R., Priel, B., Osher, Y., Blaine, D., Bennett, E.R., Nemanov, L., Katz, M. & Belmaker, R. H. (1996). Dopamine D4 receptor (D4DR) exon III polymorphism asociated with the human personality trait of novelty seeking. *Nature Genetics, 12,* 78–80.

Edmunds, G. & Kendrick, D. C. (1980). *The measurement of human aggressiveness.* Chichester, England: Ellis Horwood.

Edwall, G. E., Hoffman, N. G. & Harrison, P. A. (1989). Psychological correlates of sexual abuse in adolescent girls in chemical dependency treatment. *Adolescence, 26,* 279–288.

Edwards, D. H. & Kravitz, E. A. (1997). Serotonin, social status and aggression. *Current Opinions in Neurobiology, 7,* 812–819.

Egeland, B., Jacobvitz, D. & Papatola, K. (1987). Intergenerational continuity of abuse. In R. J. Gelles & J. B. Lancaster (Eds.), *Child abuse and neglect: Biosocial dimensions.* New York: Aldine de Gruyter.

Egger, S. (1998). *The killers among us.* Englewood Cliffs, NJ: Prentice Hall.

Eggert, L. L., Thompson, E. A., Herting, J. R., Nicholas, L. J. & Dicker, B. G. (1994). Preventing adolescent drug abuse and high school dropout through an intensive school-based social network development program. *American Journal of Health Promotion, 8,* 202–215.

Eibl-Ebesfeldt, I. (1979). *The biology of peace and war: Men, animals, and aggression.* New York: Viking Press.

Eichelman, B. S. (1979). Role of biogenic amines in aggressive behavior. In M. Sandler (Ed.), *Psychopharmacology of aggression.* NewYork: Raven, 61–94.

Eichelman, B. (1988). Toward a rational pharmacotherapy for aggressive violent behavior. *Hospital and Community Psychiatry, 39,* 31–39.

Eichelman, B. S. (1990). Neurochemical and psychopharmacologic aspects of aggressive behavior. *Annual Review of Medicine, 41,* 149–158.

Eichelman, B. (1992). Aggressive behavior: From laboratory to clinic: Quo vadis? *Archives of General Psychiatry, 49,* 488–492.

Eimer, M. (1989). Management of the behavioral symptoms associated with dementia. *Primary Care, 16,* 431–450.

Eisenberg, L., Lachman, R., Moiling, P. A., Lockner, A., Mizelle, J. D. & Conners, C. K. (1963). A psychopharmacologic experiment in a training school for delinquent boys. *American Journal of Orthopsychiatry, 33,* 431–447.

Eldred, C., Brown, B. & Mahabir, C. (1974). Heroin addict clients' description of their families of origin. *International Journal of the Addictions, 9,* 315–320.

Elie, R., Langlois, Y., Cooper, S. F., Gravel, G. & Albert, J. M. (1980). Comparison of SCH-12679 and thioridazine in aggressive mental retardates. *Candian Journal of Psychiatry, 25,* 484–491.

Ellen, P., Wilson, A. S. & Powell, E.W. (1964). Septal inhibition and timing behavior in the rat. *Journal of Comparative Neurology, 10,* 120–132.

Elliott, D. E. & Briere, J. (1992). Sexual abuse trauma among professional women: Validating the Trauma Symptom Checklist (TSC-40). *Child Abuse and Neglect, 16,* 391–398.

Elliott, F. A. (1977). Propranolol for the control of belligerent behavior following acute head injury. *Annals of Neurology, 1,* 489–491.

Elliott, F. A. (1982). Neurological findings in adult minimal brain dysfunction and the dyscontrol syndrome. *Journal Nervous and Mental Diseases, 170,* 680–687.

Elliott, F. A. (1992). Violence. The neurological contribution: an overview. *Archives of Neurology, 49,* 495–603.

Ellis, A. & Harper, R. A. (1976). *A new guide to rational living.* North Hollywood, CA: Wilshire Book Co.

Ellis, L. (1982). Developmental androgen fluctuations and the five dimensions of mammalian sex. *Ethology and Sociobiology, 3,* 171–197.

Ellis, P. L. (1982). Empathy: A factor in antisocial behavior. *Journal of Abnormal Child Psychology, 10,* 123–133.

Emmelkamp, P. & Heeres, H. (1988). Drug addiction and parental rearing style: A controlled study. *International Journal of the Addictions, 23,* 207–216.

Epstein, N. B., Baldwin, L. M. & Bishop, D. S. (1983). The McMaster family assessment device. *Journal of Marital and Family Therapy, 9,* 171–180.

Eriksson, E., Hedberg, M. A., Andersch, B. & Sundblad, C. (1995). The serotonin reuptake inhibitor paroxetine is superior to the noradrenaline reuptake inhibitor maprotiline in the treatment of premenstrual syndrome. *Neuropsychopharmacology, 12,* 167–176.

Evans, T. D., Cullen, F. T., Burton, Jr., V. S., Dunaway, R. G. & Benson, M. S. (1997). The social consequences of self-control: Testing the general theory of crime. *Criminology, 35,* 475–504.

Evenden, J. L. & Ryan, C. N. (1996). The pharmacology of impulsive behavior in rats: The effects of drugs on response choice with varying delays of reinforcement. *Psychopharmacology, 128,* 161–170.

Eyestone, L. L. & Howell, R. J. (1994). An epidemiological study of attention deficit hyperactivity disorder and major depression in a male prison population. *Bulletin of the American Academy of Psychiatry Law, 22,* 181–193.

Eysenck, H. J. & Eysenck, S. B. (1975). *Eysenck personality questionnaire (junior) manual.* San Diego, CA: Educational & Industrial Testing Service.

Eysenck, S. G. B. & Eysenk, H. J. (1978). Impulsiveness and venturesomeness: Their position in a dimensional system of personality description. *Psychological Reports, 43,* 1247–1255.

Eysenck, S. G. B., Pearson, P. R., Easting, G. & Allsopp, J. F. (1985). Age norms for impulsiveness, venturesomeness and empathy in adults. *Personality & Individual Differences, 6,* 613–619.

Fagan J., Piper E. & Moore, M. (1986). Violent delinquents and urban youths. *Criminology, 24,* 439–471.

Falconer, D. (1965). The inheritance of liability to certain diseases estimated from the incidence among relatives. *Annals of Human Genetics, 29,* 51–86.

Falconer, D. S. & Mackay, T. F. C. (1996). *Introduction to quantitative genetics.* Essex, England: Longman.

Falconer, M. A. & Cavannagh, I. B. (1959). Clinicopathological considerations of temporal lobe epilepsy due to small focal lesions. *Brain, 82,* 483–504.

Famy, C., Streissguth, A. P. & Unis, A. S. (1998). Mental illness in adults with fetal alcohol syndrome or fetal alcohol effects. *American Journal of Psychiatry, 155,* 552–554.

Faraone, S. V., Biederman, J., Chen, W. J., Milberger, S., Warburton, R. & Tsuang, M. T. (1995). Genetic heterogeneity in attention-deficit hyperactivity disorder (ADHD): Gender, psychiatric comorbidity, and maternal ADHD. *Journal of Abnormal Psychology, 104,* 334–345.

Faraone, S. V., Biederman, J., Keenan, K. & Tsuang, M. T. (1991). A family-genetic study of girls with DSM-III attention deficit disorder. *American Journal of Psychiatry, 148,* 112–117.

Farnworth, M., Schweinhart, L. J. & Berrueta-Clement, J. R. (1985). Preschool intervention, school success and delinquency in a high-risk sample of youth. *American Educational Research Journal, 22,* 445–464.

Farrington, D. P. (1983). Offending from 10 to 20 years of age. In K. Vandusen & S. A. Mednick (Eds.), *Prospective studies of crime and delinquency.* Boston: Kluwer-Nijhoff.

Farrington, D. P. (1987). Predicting individual crime rates. In D. M. Gottfredson & M. Tonry (Eds.), *Crime and justice,* vol. 3, *Prediction and classification.* Chicago: University of Chicago Press, 53–101.

Farrington, D. P. (1989). Early predictors of adolescent aggression and adult violence. *Violence and Victims, 4,* 79–100.

Farrington, D. P. (1991). Antisocial personality from childhood to adulthood. *The Psychologist, 4,* 389–394.

Farrington, D. P. (1991). Childhood aggression and adult violence: Early precursors and later life outcomes. In D. J. Pepler & K. H. Rubin (Eds.), *The development and treatment of childhood aggression.* Hillsdale, NJ: Erlbaum, 2–29.

Farrington, D. P. (1993). Interactions between individual and contextual factors in the development of offending. In R. Silbereisen & E. Todt (Eds.), *Adolescence in context.* New York: Springer-Verlag, 366–389.

Farrington, D. P. (1995). The development of offending and antisocial behavior from childhood: Key findings from the Cambridge study in delinquency development. *Journal of Child Psycholology and Psychiatry, 360,* 929–964.

Farrington, D. P., Gallagher, B., Morley, L., St. Ledger, R. J. & West, D. J. (1988). Are there any successful men from criminogenic backgrounds? *Psychiatry, 51,* 116–130.

Farrington, D. P., Loeber, R. & Van Kammen, W. B. (1990). Long-term criminal outcomes of hyperactivity-impulsivity-attention deficit and conduct problems in childhood. In L. N. Robins & M. Rutter (Eds.), *Straight and devious pathways from childhood to adulthood.* New York: Cambridge University Press, 62–81.

Farrington, D. P., Ohlin, L. E. & Wilson, J. Q. (1986). *Understanding and controlling crime.* New York: Springer-Verlag.

Faust, D. & Ziskin, J. (1988). The expert witness in psychology and psychiatry. *Science, 241,* 31–35.

Fava, G. A. (1987). Irritable mood and physical illness. *Stress Medicine, 3,* 293–299.

Fava, M., Alpert, J., Nierenberg, A. A., Ghaemi, N., O'Sullivan, R., Tedlow, J. R., Worthington, J. J. & Rosenbaum, J. F. (1996). Fluoxetine treatment of anger attacks: A replication study. *Annals of Clinical Psychiatry, 8,* 7–10.

Fava, M., Anderson, K. & Rosenbaum, J. F. (1993). Are thymoleptic-responsive "anger attacks" a discrete clinical syndrome? *Psychosomatics, 34,* 350–355.

Fava, M. & Keefe, B. (1998). Approach to the patient with premenstrual mood dysregulation. In T. Stern, J. B. Herman & P. L. Slavin (Eds.), *The MGH guide to psychiatry in primary care.* New York: McGraw-Hill.

Fava, M., Nierenberg, A. A., Quitkin, F. M., Zisook, S., Pearlstein, T., Stone, A. & Rosenbaum, J. F. (1997). A preliminary study on the efficacy of sertraline and imipramine on anger attacks in atypical depression and dysthymia. *Psychopharmacology Bulletin, 33,* 101–103.

Fava, M., Rosenbaum, J. F., McCarthy, M. K., Pava, J. A., Steingard, R. J. & Bless, E. (1991). Anger attacks in depressed outpatients and their response to fluoxetine. *Psychopharmacology Bulletin, 27,* 275–279.

Fava, M., Rosenbaum, J. F., Pava, J. A., McCarthy, M. K., Steingard, R. J. & Bouffides, E. (1993). Anger attacks in unipolar depression: I. Clinical correlates and response to fluoxetine treatment. *American Journal of Psychiatry, 150,* 1158–1163.

Favarino, B. J. (1988). The frequency of depression and attention deficit-hyperactivity disorder in inmates of a county jail. Master's thesis, Brigham Young University.

Feighner, J. P., Robins, E., Guze, S. B., Woodruff, R. A., Winokur, G., and Munoz, R. (1972). Diagnostic criteria for use in psychiatric research. *Archives of General Psychiatry, 26,* 57–63.

Feldman, P., Bay, A. N. & Baser, A. (1969). Parenteral haloperidol in controlling patient behavior during acute psychotic episodes. *Current Therapeutic Research, Clinical and Experimental, 11,* 362–366.

Feldman, R. A., Caplinger, T. E., Wodarski, J. S. (1983). *The St. Louis conundrum: The effective treatment of antisocial youths.* Englewood Cliffs, NJ: Prentice-Hall.

Feldman, R. S. & Quenzer, L. F. (1984). *Fundamentals of neuropsychopharmacology.* Sunderland, MA: Sinauer.

Fernstrom, J. D. (1993). Role of precursor availability in control of monoamine biosynthesis in the brain. *Physiological Reviews, 63,* 484–546.

Ferrero-Lombroso, C. (1911). *Criminal man, according to the classification of Cesare Lombroso.* New York: Putnam's Sons.

Ferris, C. F. & Delville, Y. (1994). Vasopressin and serotonin interactions in the control of agonistic behavior. *Psychoneuroendocrinology, 19,* 593–601.

Feshbach, S. (1980). Child abuse and the dynamics of human aggression and violence. In J. Gerbner, C. J. Ross & E. Zigler (Eds.), *Child abuse: An agenda for action.* New York: Oxford University Press.

Fichtner, C. G., O'Connor, F. L., Yeoh, H. C., Arora, R. C. & Crayton, J. W. (1995). Hypodensity of platelet serotonin uptake sites in posttraumatic stress disorder: Associated clinical features. *Life Sciences, 57,* PL37–PL44.

Field, T. M., Scafidi, F., Pickens, J., Prodromidis, M., Pelaez-Nogueras, M., Torquati, J., Wilcox, H., Malphurs, J., Schanberg, S. & Kuhn, C. (1998). Polydrug-using adolescent mothers and their infants receiving early intervention. *Adolescence, 33,* 117–143.

Fiks, K. B., Johnson, H. L. & Rosen, T. S. (1985). Methadone-maintained mothers: Three year follow-up of parental functioning. *International Journal of the Addictions, 20,* 651–660.

Finkelhor, D. (1979). *Sexually victimized children.* New York: The Free Press.

Finkelhor, D. & Browne, A. (1985). The traumatic impact of child sexual abuse: A conceptualization. *American Journal of Orthopsychiatry, 55,* 530–541.

Finkelman, D. & Grisso, T. (1994). Therapeutic jurisprudence: From idea to application. *New England Journal on Criminal and Civil Confinement, 20,* 243–xxx.

Finn, P., Zeitouni, N. & Pihl, R. (1990). Effects of alcohol on psychophysiological hyperactivity to nonaversive and aversive stimuli in men at high risk for alcoholism. *Journal of Abnormal Psychology, 99,* 79–85.

Finney, J. W. & Moos, R. H. (1992). The long-term course of treated alcoholism: II. Predictors and correlates of 10-year functioning and mortality. *Journal of Studies on Alcohol, 53,* 142–153.

Fishbein, D. H. (1990). Biological perspectives in criminology. *Criminology, 28,* 27–72.

Fishbein, D. H. (1991). Medicalizing the drug war. *Behavioral Sciences and the Law 9,* 323–344.

Fishbein, D. H. (1998). Differential susceptibility to comorbid drug abuse and violence. *Journal of Drug Issues, 28,* 859–890.

Fishbein, D. H., Lozovsky, D. & Jaffe, J. H. (1989). Impulsivity, aggression, and neuroendocrine responses to serotonergic stimulation in substance users. *Biological Psychiatry, 25,* 1049–1066.

Fishbein, D. H. & Pease, S. (1996). *The dynamics of drug abuse.* Needham, MA: Allyn & Bacon.

Fishbein, D. H. & Thatcher, R. W. (1982). Nutritional and electrophysiological indices of maladaptive behavior. Paper presented at the MIT Conference on Research Strategies for Assessing the Behavioral Effects and Nutrients. Cambridge, MA.

Flor-Henry, P. (1976). Lateralized temporal-limbic dysfunction and psychopathology. *Annals of the New York Academy of Science, 280,* 777–795.

Fogel C. A., Mednick, A. & Michelsen, N. (1985). Hyperactive behavior and minor physical anomalies. *Acta Psychiatrica Scandinavia, 72,* 551–556.

Foglia, W. D. (1995). Thinking and experiencing: Adding cognition to a social learning model to enhance understanding of self-reported delinquency among urban youth. Paper presented at the 1995 Annual Meeting of the American Society of Criminology, Boston, MA.

Foglia, W. D. (1996). Exploring the interaction of cognitive and social learning influences to enhance understanding of self-reported delinquency among inner-city youths. Unpublished dissertation, Department of Criminology, University of Pennsylvania, Philadelphia, PA.

Forsberg, L. & Goldman, M. (1987). Experience-dependent recovery of visuospatial functioning in older alcoholic person. *Journal of Abnormal Psychology, 94,* 519–529.

Forster, P. L., Schoenfeld, F. B., Marmar, C. R. & Lang, A. J. (1995). Lithium for irritability in post-traumatic stress disorder. *Journal of Traumatic Stress, 8,* 143–149.

Foster, M., Hillbrand, M. & Chi, C. (1989). Efficacy of carbamazepine in assaultive patients with frontal lobe dysfunction. *Progress in Neuro-Psychopharmacology and Biological Psychiatry, 23,* 865–874.

Frankenberg, F. R. (1993). Clozapine and bipolar disorder. *Journal of Clinical Psychopharmacology, 13,* 289–290.

Frazier, S. H. (1974). Murder—Single and multiple. In S. H. Frazier (Ed.), *Research publications, Association for Research in Nervous and Mental Diseases.* Baltimore: Williams & Wilkins.

Freedman, B. J., Rosenthal, L., Donahoe, Jr., C. P., Schlundt, D. G. & McFall, R. M. (1978). A social-behavioral analysis of skill deficits in delinquent and nondelinquent adolescent boys. *Journal of Consulting and Clinical Psychology, 46,* 1448–1462.

Freeman, E. W., Rickels, K., Sondheimer, S. J. & Polansky, M. (1995). A double-blind trial of oral progesterone, alprazolam, and placebo in treatment of severe premenstrual syndrome. *Journal of the American Medical Association, 274,* 51–57.

Freud, S. A. (1946). Some character-types met with in psycho-analytic work. In *Collected papers,* vol. 4. London: Hogarth, 318–344.

Freund, K. (1980). Therapeutic sex drive reduction. *Acta Psychiatria Scandinavia, 287,* 1–39.

Frick, P. J., Lahey, B. B., Loeber, R., Stouthamer-Loeber, M., Christ, M. A. G. & Hanson, K. (1992). Familial risk factors to oppositional defiant disorder and conduct disorder: Parental psychopathology and maternal parenting. *Journal of Consulting and Clinical Psychology, 60,* 49–55.

Friedrick-Cofer, L., & Huston, A. C. (1986). Television violence and aggression: The debate continues. *Psychological Bulletin, 100,* 364–371.

Fromm, E. (1973). *The anatomy of human destructiveness.* New York: Holt, Rinehart & Winston.

Fuller, R. W. (1996). The influence of fluoxetine on aggressive behavior. *Neuropsychopharmacology, 14,* 77–81.

Gabel, S., Stadler, J., Bjorn, J., Shindledecker, R. & Bowden, C. (1993). Dopamine-beta-hydroxylase in behaviorally disturbed youth. *Biological Psychiatry, 34,* 434–442.

Gabel, S., Stadler, J., Bjorn, J., Shindledecker, R. & Bowen, C. J. (1995). Homovanillic acid and monoamine oxidase in sons of substance-abusing fathers: Relationship to conduct disorders. *Journal of Studies on Alcohol, 56,* 135–139.

Gade, R., Blake, H., MacMurray, J., Muhleman, D., Johnson, J., Verde, R. & Comings, D. E. (1996). Relationship of the GABRB3 gene to adult ADHD and personality traits in Caucasian and African-American samples. *Psychiatric Genetics, 6,* 164–165.

Gade, R., Muhleman, D., MacMurray, J. & Comings, D. E. (1998). Correlation of length of VNTR alleles at the X-linked MAOA gene and phenotypic effect in Tourette syndrome and drug abuse. *Molecular Psychiatry, 3,* 50–60.

Gadow, K. D., Nolan, E., Sprafkin, J. & Sverd, J. (1995). School observations of children with attention-deficit hyperactivity disorder and comorbid tic disorder: Effects of methylphenidate treatment. *Journal of Developmental and Behavioral Pediatrics, 16,* 167–176.

Gaffney, G. R. & Berlin, F. S. (1984). Is there hypothalamic-pituitary-gonadal dysfunction in paedophilia? A pilot study. *British Journal of Psychiatry, 145,* 657–660.

Galaburda, A. M. (1991). Neuropathological correlates of learning difficulties. *Seminars in Neurology, 11,* 20–97.

Galski, T., Thornton, K. E. & Shumsky, D. (1990). Brain dysfunction in sex offenders. *Journal of Offender Rehabilitation, 16,* 65–80.

Gandour, M. (1989). Activity level as a dimension of temperament in toddlers: Its relevance for the organismic specificity hypothesis. *Child Development, 60,* 1092–1098.

Gardner, D. & Cowdry, R. (1986). Positive effects of carbamazepine on behavioral dyscontrol in borderline personality disorder. *American Journal of Psychiatry, 143,* 519–522.

Garmezy, N. (1981). Children under stress: Perspectives on antecedents and correlates of vulnerability and resistance to psychopathology. In A. J. Rabin, J. Aronoff, A. M. Barclay, & R. A. Zucker (Eds.), *Further explorations in personality.* New York: John Wiley & Sons, 196–269.

Garmezy, N. & Rutter, M. (1983). *Stress, coping and development in children.* New York: McGraw-Hill.

Garrett, C. J. (1985). Effects of residential treatment on adjudicated delinquents: A meta-analysis. *Journal of Research in Crime and Delinquency, 22,* 287–308.

Gau, J. S., Silberg, J. L., Erickson, M. T. & Hewitt, J. K. (1992). Childhood behavior problems: A comparison of twin and non-twin samples. *Acta Geneticae Medicae et Gemellologiae, 41,* 53–63.

Geiger, S. G. (1960). Organic factors in delinquency. *Journal of Social Therapy, 6,* 1–16.

Gejman, P. V., Ram, A., Gelernter, J., Friedman, E., Cao, Q., Pickar, D., Blum, K., Noble, E. P., Kranzler, H. R. & O'Malley, S. (1994). No structural mutation in the dopamine D2 receptor gene in alcoholism or schizophrenia: Analysis using denaturing gradient gel electrophoresis. *Journal of the American Medical Association, 271,* 204–208.

Gelernter, J., Kranzler, H., Coccaro, E., Siever, L., New, A. & Mulgrew, C. L. (1997). D4 dopamine-receptor (DRD4) alleles and novelty seeking in substance-dependent, personality-disorder, and control subjects. *American Journal of Medical Genetics, 61,* 1144–1152.

Gendreau, P. & Ross, R. R. (1987). Revivification of rehabilitation: Evidence from the 1980s. *Justice Quarterly, 4,* 349–408.

George, D. T., Benkelfat, C., Rawlings, R. R. Eckardt, M. J., Phillips, M. J., Nutt, D. J., Wynne, D., Murphy, D. L. & Linnoila, M. (1997). Behavioral and neuroendocrine responses to m-chlorophenylpiperazine in subtypes of alcoholics and in healthy comparison subjects. *American Journal of Psychiatry, 154,* 81–87.

Germine, M., Goddard, A. W., Woods, S. W., Charney, D. S. & Heninger, G. R. (1992). Anger and anxiety responses to m-chlorophenylpiperazine in generalized anxiety disorder. *Biological Psychiatry, 32,* 457–461.

Gerra, G., Caccavari, R., Delsignore, R., Passeri, M., Fertonani-Affini, G., Maestri, D., Monica, C. & Brambilla, F. (1993). Parental divorce and neuroendocrine changes in adolescents. *Acta Psychiatrica Scandinavia, 87,* 350–354.

Gerra, G., Zaimovic, A., Giucastro, G., Folli, F., Maestri, D., Tessoni, A., Avanzini, P., Caccavari, R., Bernasconi, S. & Brambilla, F. (1998). Neurotransmitter-hormonal responses to psychological stress in peripubertal subjects: Relationship to aggressive behavior. *Life Sciences, 62,* 617–625.

Gerstley, L. J., Alterman, A. I., McLellan, A. T. & Woody, G. E. (1990). Antisocial personality disorder in patients with substance abuse disorders: A problematic diagnosis? *American Journal of Psychiatry, 147,* 173–178.

Ghodsian-Carpey, J. & Baker, L. A. (1987). Genetic and environmental influences on aggression in 4- to 7-year-old twins. *Aggressive Behavior, 13,* 173–186.

Giacalone, E., Tansella, M., Valzelli, L. & Garattini, S. (1968). Brain serotonin metabolism in isolated aggressive mice. *Biochemical Pharmacology, 17,* 1315–1327.

Giacoia, G. P. (1990). Cocaine in the cradle: A hidden epidemic. *Southern Medical Journal, 83,* 947–951.

Giancola, P. (1995). Evidence for dorsolateral and orbital prefrontal cortical involvement in the expression of aggressive behavior. *Aggressive Behavior, 21,* 431–450.

Giancola, P. R. & Chermack, S. T. (1998). Construct validity of laboratory aggression paradigms: A response to Tedeschi and Quigley (1996). *Aggression and Violent Behavior, 3,* 237–253.

Giancola, P., Martin, C., Tarter, R., Pelham, W. & Moss, H. (1996). Executive cognitive functioning and aggressive behavior in preadolescent boys at high risk for substance abuse/dependence. *Journal of Studies on Alcohol, 57,* 352–359.

Giancola, P., Mezzich, A. & Tarter, R. (1998). Executive cognitive functioning mediates the relation between language competence and antisocial behavior in conduct disordered adolescent females. Submitted for publication.

Giancola, P., Mezzich, A. & Tarter, R. (in press). Disruptive, delinquent, and aggressive behavior in adolescent female substance abusers: Relation to executive cognitive functioning. *Journal of Studies on Alcohol, 59,* 560–567.

Giancola, P., Mezzich, A. & Tarter, R. (in press). Executive cognitive functioning, temperament, and antisocial behavior in conduct disordered adolescent females. *Journal of Abnormal Psychology.*

Giancola, P. & Moss, H. (in press). Executive cognitive functioning in alcohol use disorders. In M. Galanter (Ed.), *Recent developments in alcoholism, vol. XIV: The consequences of alcoholism.* New York: Plenum Press.

Giancola, P. & Mezzich, A. (1998). Executive cognitive functioning, temperament, and antisocial behavior in conduct disordered adolescent females. *Journal of Abnormal Psychology, 107,* 629–641.

Giancola, P. & Mezzich, A. (in press). Executive cognitive functioning mediates the relation between language competence and antisocial behavior in conduct disordered females. *Aggressive Behavior.*

Giancola, P., Mezzich, A. & Tarter, R. (1998). Disruptive, delinquent, and aggressive behavior in adolescent female substance abusers: Relation to executive cognitive functioning. *Journal of Studies on Alcohol, 59,* 560–567.

Giancola, P. & Moss, H. (1998). Executive cognitive functioning in alcohol use disorders. In M. Galanter (Ed.), *Recent developments in alcoholism,* vol. 14, *The consequences of alcoholism.* New York: Plenum Press, 227–251.

Giancola, P., Moss, H., Martin, C., Kirisci, L. & Tarter, R. (1996). Executive cognitive functioning predicts reactive aggression in boys at high risk for substance dependence: A prospective study. *Alcoholism: Clinical and Experimenetal Research, 20,* 740–744.

Giancola, P. & Zeichner, A. (1994). Neuropsychological performance on tests of frontal-lobe functioning and aggression in human males. *Journal of Abnormal Psychology, 103,* 832–835.

Giancola, P. R. & Zeichner, A. (1995). Construct validity of a competitive reaction time aggression paradigm. *Aggressive Behavior, 21,* 199–204.

Giancola, P. R. & Zeichner, A. (1995). An investigation of gender differences in alcohol-related aggression. *Journal of Studies on Alcohol, 56,* 573–579.

Gibbons, J. L., Barr, G. A. & Bridger, W. H. (1978). Effects of *para*-chlorophenylalanine and 5-hydroxytryptophan on mouse killing behavior in killer rats. *Pharmacology, Biochemistry & Behavior, 9,* 91–98.

Gibbs, W. W. (1995). Trends in behavioral science: Seeking the criminal element. *Scientific American, 272,* 100–107.

Gill, K., Nolimal, D. & Crowley, T. (1992). Antisocial personality disorder, HIV risk behavior and retention in methadone maintenance therapy. *Drug and Alcohol Dependence, 30,* 247–252.

Gill, M., Daly, G., Heron, S., Hawi, Z. & Fitzgerald, M. (1997). Confirmation of association between attention deficit disorder and a dopamine transporter polymorphism. *Molecular Psychiatry, 2,* 311–313.

Gillis, J. J., Gigler, J. W., Pennington, B. F. & DeFries, J. C. (1992). Attention deficit disorder in reading-disabled twins: evidence for a genetic etiology. *Journal of Abnormal and Child Psychology, 20,* 343–348.

Gillstrom, B. J. & Hare, R. D. (1988). Language related hand gestures in psychopaths. *Journal of Personality Disorders, 2,* 21–27.

Giros, B., el Mestikawy, S. & et al. (1992). *Molecular Pharmacology, 42,* 383–390.

Giros, B., el Mestikawy, S. R., Wightman, R. M. & Caron, M. G. (1996). Hyperlocomotion and indifference to cocaine and amphetamine in mice lacking dopamine transporter. *Nature, 379,* 606–612.

Glaser, G. H. (1981). Critical periods in brain development related to behavior, especially epilepsies. In J. R. Merikangas (Ed.), *Brain behavior relationships.* Lexington, MA: Lexington Books.

Glenn, M. B., Wroblewski, B., Parziale, J., Levine, L., Whyte, J. & Rosenthal, M. (1989). Lithium carbonate for aggressive behavior or affective instability on ten brain-injured patients.

American Journal of Physical Medicine and Rehabilitation, 68, 221–226.

Glennon, R. A., Dukat, M., Ploom, F. E. & Kupfer, D. J. (1995). Serotonin receptor subtypes. In *Psychopharmacology: The fourth generation.* New York: Raven Press, 415–429.

Glover, V. (1997). Maternal stress or anxiety in pregnancy and emotional development of the child. *British Journal of Psychiatry, 171,* 105–106.

Glueck, S. & Glueck, E. (1950). *Unraveling juvenile delinquency.* New York: The Commonwealth Fund.

Golden, C. J., Jackson, M. L., Peterson-Rohne, A. & Gontkovsky, S. T. (1996). Neuropsychological correlates of violence and aggression: A review of the clinical literature. *Aggression and Violent Behavior, 1,* 3–25.

Goldman, D. (1993). Alcoholism: Genetic transmission. *Recent Developments in Alcoholism, 11,* 231–248.

Goldman, D. (1995). Candidate genes in alcoholism. *Clinical Neuroscience, 3,* 174–181.

Goldman, D. (1996). The search for genetic alleles contributing to self-destructive and aggressive behaviors. In D. M. Stoff & R. B. Cairns (Eds.), *Aggression and violence: Genetic, neurobiological, and biological perspectives.* Hillsdale, NJ: Erlbaum, 23–40.

Goldman, D., Dean, M., Brown, G. L., Bolos, A. M., Tokola, R., Virkkunen, M. & Linnoila, M. (1992). D2 dopamine receptor genotype and cerebrospinal fluid homovanillic acid, 5 hydroxyindoleacetic acid and 3-methoxy-4-hydroxyphenylglycol in alcoholics in Finland and the United States. *Acta Psychiatrica Scandinavia, 86,* 351–357.

Goldman, M., Klisz, D. & Williams, D. (1985). Experience-dependent recovery of cognitive functioning in young alcoholics. *Addictive Behaviors, 10,* 169–176.

Goldstein, A. P. & Segall, M. A. (1982). *Aggression in global perspective.* New York: Pergamon.

Gomberg, E. (1982). The young male alcoholic: A pilot study. *Journal of Studies on Alcohol, 43,* 683–701.

Goodwin, D. W., Schulsinger, F., Hermansen, L., Guze, S. B. & Winokur, G. (1973). Alcohol problems in adoptees raised apart from alcoholic biological parents. *Archives of General Psychiatry, 28,* 238–243.

Goodwin, D. W., Schulsinger, F., Hermansen, L., Guze, S. B. & Winokur, G. (1975). Alcoholism and the hyperactive child syndrome. *Journal of Nervous and Mental Disease, 160,* 349–353.

Goodwin, D. W., Schulsinger, F., Knop, J., Mednick, S. & Guze, S. B. (1977). Alcoholism and depression in adopted-out daughters of alcoholics. *Archives of General Psychiatry, 34,* 751–755.

Gorenstein, E. (1987). Cognitive-perceptual deficit in an alcoholism spectrum disorder. *Journal of Studies on Alcohol, 48,* 310–318.

Gorenstein, E. E. & Newman, P. (1980). Disinhibitory psychopathology: A new perspective and a model for research. *Psychological Reviews, 87,* 301–315.

Gordian Group (1991). *Drug Use Screening Inventory,* P.O. Box 1587, Hartsville, SC 29550.

Gordon, C. T., State, R. C., Nelson, J. E., Hamburger, S. D. & Rapoport, J. L. (1993). A double-blind comparison of clomipramine, desipramine, and placebo in the treatment of autistic disorder. *Archives of General Psychiatry, 50,* 441–447.

Gorio, A., Germani, E., Mantegazza, P., Di Giulio, A. M. & Bertelli, A. (1992). Perinatal exposure to ethanol affects postnatal degeneration and regeneration of serotonergic pathways in the spinal cord. *Drugs Experimental and Clinical Research, 18,* 461–464.

Gottesman, I. I. (1966). Genetic variance in adaptive personality traits. *Journal of Child Psychology and Psychiatry, 7,* 199–208.

Gottesman, I. I. (1991). *Schizophrenia genesis: The origins of madness.* New York: W. H. Freeman.

Gottesman, I. I. & Goldsmith, H. H. (1994). Developmental psychopathology of antisocial behavior: Inserting genes into its ontogenesis and epigenesis. In C. A. Nelson (Ed.), *Threats to optimal development: integrating biological, psychological, and social risk factors.* Hillsdale, NJ: Erlbaum, 69–104.

Gottesman, I. I. & Shields, J. (1972). *Schizophrenia and genetics: A twin study vantage point.* New York: Academic Press.

Gottesman, I. I. & Shields, J. (1982). *The epigenetic puzzle.* Cambridge: Cambridge University Press.

Gottfredson, M. R. & Hirschi, T. (1990). *A gen-*

eral theory of crime. Palo Alto, CA: Stanford University Press.

Gottfredson, M. R. & Hirschi, T. (1994). Aggression. In T. Hirschi & M. R. Gottfredson (Eds.), *The generality of deviance.* New Brunswick, NJ: Transaction, 23–45.

Gottfries, C. G., Oreland, L., Wiberg, A. & Winblad, B. (1975). Lowered monoamine oxidase activity in brains from alcoholic suicides. *Journal of Neurochemistry, 25,* 667–673.

Gough, H. G. (1987). *California Psychological Inventory (Administrator's Guide).* Palo Alto, CA: Consulting Psychologists Press.

Graeff, F. G., Guimaraes, F. S., De Andrade, T. G. & Deakin, J. F. (1996). Role of 5-HT in stress, anxiety, and depression. *Pharmacology and Biochemistry of Behavior, 54,* 129–141.

Graham, K. R. (1993). Toward a better understanding and treatment of sex offenders. *International Journal of Offender Therapy & Comparative Criminology, 37,* 41–57.

Grasmick, H. G., Tittle, C. R., Bursik, Jr., R. J. & Arneklev, B. J. (1993). Testing the core empirical implications of Gottfredson and Hirschi's general theory of crime. *Journal of Research in Crime and Delinquency, 30,* 5–29.

Greenberg, L. M. (1996). *TOVA (Test of Variables of Attention).* Los Alamitos, CA: Universal Attention Disorders.

Greendyke, R. M., Berkner, J. P., Webster, J. C. & Gulya, A. (1989). Treatment of behavioral problems with pindolol. *Psychosomatics, 30,* 161–165.

Greendyke, R. M. & Kanter, D. R. (1986). Therapeutic effects of pindolol on behavioral disturbances associated with organic brain disease: A double-blind study. *Journal of Clinical Psychiatry, 47,* 423–426.

Greendyke, R. M., Kanter, D. R., Schuster, D. B., Verstreate, S. & Wootton, J. (1986). Propranolol treatment of assaultive patients with organic brain disease. *Journal of Nervous and Mental Diseases, 174,* 290–294.

Greenfield, S. A. (1996). *The human mind explained.* New York: Henry Holt & Co.

Greenhill, L. L., Solomon, M., Pleak, R. & Ambrosini, P. (1985). Molindone hydrochloride treatment of hospitalized children with conduct disorder. *Journal of Clinical Psychiatry, 46,* 20–25.

Grice, D. E., Leckman, J. F., Pauls, D. L., Kurlan, R., Kidd, K. K., Pakstis, A. J., Chang, F. M., Buxbaum, J. D., Cohen, D. J. & Gelernter, J. (1996). Linkage disequilibrium of an allele at the dopamine D4 receptor locus with Tourette's syndrome by TDT. *American Journal of Human Genetics, 59,* 644–652.

Groer, M. & Howell, M. (1990). Autonomic and cardiovascular responses of preschool children to television programs. *Journal of Child and Adolescent Psychiatry and Mental Health Nursing, 3,* 134–138.

Groth, A. N. (1979). *Men who rape: The psychology of the offender.* New York: Plenum Press.

Groth, A. N. (1979). Sexual trauma in the life histories of rapists and child molesters. *Victimology: An International Journal, 4,* 10–16.

Grove, W. M., Eckert, E. D., Heston, L., Bouchard, T. J. Jr., Segal, N. & Lykken, D. T. (1990). Heritability of substance abuse and antisocial behavior: A study of monozygotic twins reared apart. *Biological Psychiatry, 27,* 1293–1304.

Gualtieri, C. (1991). Buspirone for the behavioral problems of patients with organic brain disorders. *Journal of Clinical Psychopharmacology, 11,* 280–281.

Guerri, C. (1998). Neuroanatomical and neurophysiological mechanisms involved in central nervous system dysfunctions induced by prenatal alcohol exposure. *Alcohol Clinical and Experimental Research, 22,* 304–312.

Guerra, N. G. (1989). Consequential thinking and self-reported delinquency in high-school youth. *Criminal Justice and Behavior, 16,* 440–454.

Gunn, J. C. (1991). Legal implications of behavioral changes in epilepsy. *Advances in Neurology, 55,* 461–472.

Gunnar, M. R., Tout, K., de Haan, M., Pierce, S. & Stansbury, K. (1997). Temperament, social competence, and adrenocortical activity in preschoolers. *Developmental Psychobiology, 31,* 65–85.

Gurling, H. M. D., Oppenheim, B. E. & Murray, R. M. (1984). Depression, criminality & psychopathology associated with alcoholism: Evidence from a twin study. *Acta Geneticae Medicae et Gemellogiae, 33,* 333–339.

Gurr, T. R. (1976). The history of violent crime in Europe and America. In H. D. Graham & T. R. Gurr (Eds.), *Violence in America: Historical and comparative perspectives.* Newbury Park, CA: Sage.

Gust, D. A., Gordon, T. P., Wilson, M. E., Ahmed-Ansari, A., Brodie, A. R. & McClure, H. M. (1991). Formation of a new social group of unfamiliar female rhesus monkeys affects the immune and pituitary adrenocortical systems. *Brain Behavioral Immunology, 5,* 296–307.

Guy, W. (Ed.) (1976). DHEW Publication No. (ADM) 76-338, *ECDEU Assessment Manual for Psychopharmacology* (rev. ed.). Rockville, MD: National Institute of Mental Health.

Guze, S. B., Wolfgram, E. D., McKinney, J. K. & Cantwell, D. P. (1967). Psychiatric illness in the families of convicted criminals: A study of 519 first-degree relatives. *Diseases of the Nervous System, 28,* 651–659.

Guze, S. B., Wolfgram, E. D., McKinney, J. K. & Cantwell, D. P. (1968). Delinquency, social maladjustment, and crime: The role of alcoholism. *Diseases of the Nervous System, 29,* 238–243.

Gynther, L. M., Carey, G., Gottesman, I. I. & Vogler, G. P. (1995). A twin study of non-alcohol substance abuse. *Psychiatry Research, 56,* 213–220.

Haas, S., Vincent, K., Holt, J. & Lippmann, S. (1997). Divalproex: A possible treatment alternative for demented, elderly, aggressive patients. *Annals of Clinical Psychiatry, 9,* 145–147.

Haber, G. B., Heaton, K. W. & Murphy, D. (1977). Depletion and disruption of dietary fiber: Effects on society, plasma, glucose and serum insulin. *Lancet, 2,* 679–689.

Hains, A. A. & Herrman, L. P. (1989). Social cognitive skills and behavioral adjustment of delinquent adolescents in treatment. *Journal of Adolescence, 12,* 323–328.

Hakola, H. & Laulumaa, V. (1982). Carbamazepine in treatment of violent schizophrenics (letter). *Lancet, 8285,* 1358.

Hale, R. (1993). The application of learning theory to serial murder. *American Journal of Criminal Justice, 17,* 37–45.

Hale, R. (1994). The role of humiliation and embarrassment in serial murder. *Psychology: A Journal of Human Behavior, 31,* 17–23.

Hales, R. E. & Yudofsky, S. C. (1987). *The American Psychiatric Press textbook of neuropsychiatry.* Washington, DC: American Psychiatric Press.

Hall, R. L., Hesselbrock, V. M. & Stabenau, J. R. (1983). Familial distribution of alcohol use: I. Assortative mating in the parents of alcoholics. *Behavior Genetics, 13,* 361–372.

Hall, R. L., Hesselbrock, V. M. & Stabenau, J. R. (1983). Familial distribution of alcohol use: II. Assortative mating of alcoholic probands. *Behavior Genetics, 13,* 373–382.

Hallowell, E. M. & Ratey, J. R. (1994). *Driven to distraction: Recognizing and coping with attention deficit disorder from childhood through adulthood.* New York: Pantheon Books.

Hallowell, E. M. & Ratey, J. R. (1996). *Answers to distraction.* New York: Bantam Books.

Halperin, J. M., Newcorn, J. H., Koda, V. H., Pick, L., McKay, K. E. & Knott, P. (1997). Noradrenergic mechanisms in ADHD children with and without reading disabilities: A replication and extension. *Journal of the American Academy of Child and Adolescent Psychiatry, 36,* 1688–1696.

Halperin, J. M., Newcorn, J. H., Schwartz, S. T., McKay, K. E., Bedi, G. & Sharma, V. (1993). Plasma catecholamine metabolites in ADHD boys with and without reading disabilities. *Journal of Clinical and Child Psychology, 22,* 219–225.

Halperin, J. M., Newcorn, J. H., Schwartz, S. T., Sharma, V., Siever, L. J., Koda, V. H. & Gabriel, S. (1997). Age-related changes in the association between serotonergic function and aggression in boys with ADHD. *Biological Psychiatry, 41,* 682-689.

Halperin, J. M., Sharma, V., Siever, L. J., Schwartz, S. T., Matier, K., Wornell, G. & Newcorn, J. H. (1994). Serotonergic function in aggressive and nonaggressive boys with attention deficit hyperactivity disorder. *American Journal of Psychiatry, 151,* 243-248.

Halpern, A. (1991). The insanity defense in the 21st century. *International Journal of Offender Therapy and Comparative Criminology, 35,* 187–189.

Hanley, C. (1961). The gauging of criminal predispositions. In H. Toch (Ed.), *Legal and criminal psychology.* New York: Holt, Rinehart & Winston, 213–242.

Hare, R. D. (1984). Performance of psychopaths on cognitive tasks related to frontal lobe function. *Journal of Abnormal Psychology, 93,* 133–140.

Hare, R. D. (1991). *The Hare psychopathy checklist—rev. manual.* Multi-Health Systems, 908 Niagara Falls Blvd, North Tonwanda, NY, 14120-2060 (supplied to qualified users only).

Hare, R. D. (1993). *Without conscience: The dis-*

turbing world of the psychopaths among us. New York: Pocket Books.

Hare, R. D. & McPherson, L. M. (1984). Violent and aggressive behavior by criminal psychopaths. *International Journal of Law and Psychiatry, 7,* 35–50.

Harlow, J. M. (1848). Passage of an iron rod through the head. *Boston Medical and Surgical Journal, 39,* 389–393.

Harmon-Jones, E., Barratt, E. S. & Wigg, C. (1997). Impulsiveness, aggression, reading, and the P300 of the event related potential. *Personality and Individual Differences, 22,* 439–445.

Harrison, J. M. (1991). Stimulus control. In I. H. Iversen & K. A. Lattal (Eds.), *Experimental analysis of behavior.* Amsterdam: Elsevier.

Hartmann, T. (1993). *Attention deficit disorder: A different perception (the problem of a hunter in a farmer's world).* Grass Valley, CA: Underwood.

Hasin, D., Grant, B. & Endicott, J. (1990). The natural history of alcohol abuse: Implications for definitions of alcohol use disorders. *American Journal of Psychiatry,* 147, 1537–1541.

Hauser, P., Zametkin, A. J., Martinez, P., Vitiello, B., Matochik, J. A., Mixson, A. J. & Weintraub, B. D. (1993) Attention deficit-hyperactivity disorder in people with generalized resistance to thyroid hormone. *New England Journal of Medicine, 328,* 997–1001.

Haverkos H. W. & Lange, W .R. (1990). Serious infections other than human immunodeficiency virus among intravenous drug abusers. *Journal of Infectious Disease, 161,* 894–902.

Hawke, C. C. (1950). Castration and sex crimes. *American Journal of Medical Deficiency, 55,* 220–296.

Hawkins, D. (1989). Intentional injury: Are there no solutions? *Law, Medicine and Health Care, 17,* 32–41.

Hawkins, D. & Catalano, R. (1995). Preventing substance abuse. In M. Tonry & D. Farrington (Eds.), *Crime and justice: A review of research,* vol. 19. Chicago: University of Chicago Press.

Hawkins, J. D. (1996). *Delinquency and crime: Current theories.* New York: Cambridge University Press.

Hawkins, J. D. & Lam, T. (1987). Teacher practices, social development and delinquency. In J. D. Burchard & S. N. Burchard (Eds.), *Primary prevention of psychopathology,* vol. 10, *The prevention of delinquent behavior.* Newbury Park, CA: Sage, 241–274.

Hawkins, J. D., Lishner, D. M., Catalano, R. F. & Howard, M. O. (1986). Childhood predictors of adolescent substance abuse: Toward an empirically grounded theory. *Journal of Children in Contemporary Society, 18,* 1–65.

Hawkins, J. D. & Weis, J. C. (1985). The social development model: An integrated approach to delinquency prevention. *Journal of Primary Preventions, 6,* 73–97.

Hay, D. A., O'Brien, P. J., Johnston, C. J. & Prior, M. (1984). The high incidence of reading disability in twin boys and its implication for genetic analysis. *Acta Geneticae Medicae et Gemellogiae, 33,* 223–236.

Hayashi, S. (1967). A study of juvenile delinquency in twins. In H. Mitsuda (Ed.), *Clinical genetics in psychiatry.* Tokyo, Japan: Iqaku Shoin, 153–172.

Haynes, N. M., Comer, J. P. & Hamilton-Lee, M. (1988). Gender and achievement status differences on learning factors among black high school students. *Journal of Educational Research, 81,* 233–237.

Heath, A., Meyer, J., Jardine, R. & Martin, N. (1991). The inheritance of alcohol consumption in a general population twin study: II. Determinants of consumption frequency and quantity consumed. *Journal of Studies on Alcohol, 52,* 425–433.

Heath, A. C. (April 20, 1998). Personal communication.

Heath, A. C. & Madden, P. A. F. (1995). Genetic influences on smoking behavior. In J. R. Turner, L. R. Cardon & J. K. Hewitt (Eds.), *Behavior genetic approaches in behavioral medicine.* New York: Plenum Press, 45–66.

Heath, E. G. (1977). Modulation of emotion with a brain pacemaker. *Journal of Nervous and Mental Diseases, 165,* 300–317.

Heaton, R. (1981). *Wisconsin card sorting test manual.* Odessa, FL: Psychological Assessment Resources.

Heilbrun, A. B. Jr. (1982). Cognitive models of criminal violence based upon intelligence and psychopathy levels. *Journal of Consulting and Clinical Psychology, 50,* 546–557.

Hellings, J. A., Kelley, L. A., Gabrielli, W. F., Kilgore, E. & Shah, P. (1996). Sertraline response in adults with mental retardation and autistic disorder. *Journal of Clinical Psychiatry, 57,* 333–336.

Helzer, J., Burman, A. & McEvoy, L. (1991). Alcohol abuse dependence. In L. Robins & D. Regier (Eds.), *Psychiatric disorders in America,* New York, Free Press, 81–115.

Henry, C., Guegant, G., Cador, M., Arnauld, E., Arsaut, J., LeMoal, M. & Demotes-Mainard, J. (1995). Prenatal stress in rats facilitates amphetamine-induced sensitization and induces long-lasting changes in dopamine receptors in the nucleus accumbens. *Brain Research, 685,* 179–186.

Heppner, P. P. & Petersen, C. H. (1982). The development and implications of a personal problem-solving inventory. *Journal of Counseling Psychology, 29,* 66-75.

Hesselbrock, M. N., Hesselbrock, V. M., Babor, T. F., Stabenau, J. R., Meyer, R. E., Weidenman, M., Van Dusen, K. T. & Mednick, S. A. (1984). Antisocial behavior, psychopathology and problem drinking in the natural history of alcoholism. In D. Goodwin (Ed.), *Longitudinal research in alcoholism.* Boston: Kluwer-Nijhoff Publishing Co., 197–214.

Hesselbrock, V. M. & Hesselbrock, M. N. (1994). Alcoholism and subtypes of antisocial personality disorder. *Alcohol and Alcoholism, Supp. 2,* 479–484.

Hickey, E. (1991). *Serial murderers and their victims.* Belmont, CA: Wadsworth Publishing.

Hickey, E. (1997). *Serial murderers and their victims* (2d ed.). Belmont, CA: Wadsworth Publishing.

Hicks, P. S. (1988). Preface. In J. Morris & W. T Birnes (Eds.), *Serial killers.* New York: Dolphin Books.

Hiester, M., Ogawa, J. R., Ostoja, E., Susman, A. R. & Weinfield, N. S. (1994). The role of biological and psychosocial risk factors in development: Commentary on Kopp, Musick, and Aber. In C.A. Nelson (Ed.), *Threats to optimal development: Integrating biological, psychological, and social risk factors.* Hillsdale, NJ: Erlbaum, 273–284.

Higgens, J. P. & Thies, A. P. (1981). Social effectiveness and problem-solving thinking of reformatory inmates. *Journal of Offender Counseling Services & Rehabilitation, 5,* 93–98.

Higgins, A., Power, C. & Kohlberg, L. (1984). The relationship of moral atmosphere to judgments of responsibility. In W. M. Kurtines & J. L. Gewirtz (Eds.), *Morality, moral behavior, and moral development.* New York: John Wiley & Sons.

Higley, J. D. & Linnoila, M. (1997). Low central nervous system serotonergic activity is traitlike and correlates with impulsive behavior. A nonhuman primate model investigating genetic and environmental influences on neurotransmission. *Annals of the New York Academy of Sciences, 836,* 39–56.

Higley, J. D., Mehlman, P. T., Poland, R. E., Taub, D. M., Vickers, J. H., Suomi, S. J. & Linnoila, M. (1996). CFS testosterone and 5-HIAA correlate with different types of aggressive behaviors. *Biological Psychiatry, 40,* 1067–1082.

Higley, J. D., Mehlman, P. T., Taub, D. M., Higley, S. B., Suomi, S. J., Vickers, J. H. & Linnoila, M. (1992). Cerebrospinal fluid monoamine and adrenal correlates of aggression in free-ranging rhesus monkeys. *Archives of General Psychiatry,* 49, 436–441.

Higley, J. D., Suomi, S. J. & Linnoila, M. (1991). CSF monoamine metabolite concentrations vary according to age, rearing and sex, and are influenced by the stressor of social separation in rhesus monkeys. *Psychopharmacology, 103,* 551–556.

Higley, J. D., Thompson, W. W., Champoux, M., Goldman, D., Hasert, M. F., Kraemer, G. W., Scanlan, J. M., Suomi, S. J. & Linnoila, M. (1993). Paternal and maternal genetic contributions to cerebrospinal fluid monoamine metabolites in rhesus monkeys (Macaca Mulatta). *Archives of General Psychiatry, 50,* 615–623.

Higley, J. D., et al. (1996). Nonhuman primate model of type II alcoholism? Part 2. Diminished social competence and excessive aggression correlates with low cerebrospinal fluid 5-hydroxyindoleacetic acid concentrations. *Alcoholism Clinical and Experimental Research, 20,* 643–650.

Hillbrand, M. & Pallone, N. J. (1994). *The psychobiology of aggression.* New York: Haworth Press.

Hirschi, T. (1969). *Causes of delinquency.* Berkeley, CA: University of California Press.

Hirschi, T. (1983). Crime and the family. In James Q. Wilson (Ed.), *Crime and public policy.* San Francisco: Institute for Contemporary Studies.

Hirschi, T. & Hindelang, A. (1977). Intelligence and delinquency: A revisionist review. *American Sociological Review, 42,* 371–387.

Hoaken, P., Assaad, J. & Pihl, R. (1998).

Cognitive functioning and the inhibition of alcohol-induced aggression. *Journal of Studies on Alcohol, 59,* 599–607.

Hodgins, S., Mednick, S. A., Brennan, P. A., Schulsinger, F., & Engberg, M. (1996). Mental disorder and crime. *Archives of General Psychiatry, 53,* 489–496.

Hoffman, J., Hall, R. & Bartsch, T. (1987). On the relative importance of "psychopathic" personality and alcoholism on neuropsychological measures of frontal lobe dysfunction. *Journal of Abnormal Psychology, 96,* 158–160.

Hofkosh, D., Pringle, J. L., Wald, H. P., Switala, J., Hinderliter, S. A. & Hamel, S. C. (1995). Early interactions between drug-involved mothers and infants: Within-group differences. *Archives of Pediatric and Adolescent Medicine, 149,* 665–672.

Hogan, R. T. (1969). Development of an empathy scale. *Journal of Consulting & Clinical Psychology, 33,* 307–316.

Holden, J. M., Itil, T. M., Gannon, P. J. & Keskiner, A. (1971). The clinical effects of intramuscular thiothixene and trifluoperazine in chronic schizophrenia: A comparative study. *Current Therapeutic Research, Clinical and Experimental, 13,* 298–310.

Hollander, E., Shiffman, E. & Liebowitz, M. (1987, May). Neurological soft signs in obsessive-compulsive disorder. Poster presentation presented at the 140th annual meeting of the American Psychiatric Association, Chicago, IL.

Hollin, C. R. (1989). *Psychology and crime: An introduction to criminological psychology.* London: Routledge.

Hollin, C. R. (1990). *Cognitive-behavioral interventions with young offenders.* Elmsford, NY: Pergamon.

Holmes, C. B. (1992). *Recognizing brain dysfunction.* Brandon, VT: Clinical Psychology Publishing.

Holmes, R. & DeBurger, J. (1990). *Serial murder.* Newbury Park, CA: Sage.

Holsboer, F. (1989). Psychiatric implications of altered limbic-hypothalamic-pituitary adrenocortical activity. *European Archives of Psychiatry and Neurological Science, 238,* 302–322.

Honigfeld, G., Gillis, R. D. & Klett, C. J. (1965). Nurses' observation scale for inpatient evaluation: A new scale for measuring improvement in chronic schizophrenia. *Journal of Clinical Psychology, 21,* 65–71.

Horger, B. A. & Roth, R. H. (1996). The role of mesoprefrontal dopamine neurons in stress. *Critical Reviews in Neurobiology, 10,* 395–418.

Horowitz, I. L. (1993). *The decomposition of sociology.* New York: Oxford University Press.

Hoslin E. P. (1937). *Treatment of diabetes mellitus.* Philadelphia: Lea & Febiger.

Howard, S. G. & Takeda, H. (1990). Effect of prenatal exposure to phencyclidine on the postnatal development of the cholinergic system in the rat. *Developmental Neuroscience, 12,* 204–209.

Hrubec, Z. (1973). The effect of diagnostic ascertainment in twins on the assessment of the genetic factor in disease etiology. *American Journal of Human Genetics, 25,* 15–28.

Hrubec, Z. & Omenn, G. S. (1981). Evidence of genetic predisposition to alcoholic cirrhosis and psychosis: Twin concordances for alcoholism and its biological endpoints by zygosity among male veterans. *Alcoholism: Clinical and Experimental Research, 5,* 207–212.

Hsu, Y. P., Powell, J. F., Sims, K.B. & Breakefield, X. O. (1989). Molecular genetics of the monoamine oxidases. *Journal of Neurochemistry, 53, 12*–18.

Hudziak, J. J., Heath, A. C., Madden, P. A. F., Reich, W., Bucholz, K. K., Slutske, W., Bierut, L. J., Neuman, R. & Todd, R. D. (1998). The latent class and factor analysis of DSM-IV ADHD: A study of female adolescents. *Journal of the American Academy of Child and Adolescent Psychiatry.*

Huesmann, L. R., Eron, L. D., Lefkowitz, M. M. & Walder, L. O. (1984). Stability of aggression over time and generations. *Journal of Abnormal Psychology, 20,* 1120–1134.

Hunt, R. D. (1987). Treatment effects of oral and transdermal clonidine in relation to methylphenidate: An open pilot study in ADD-H. *Psychopharmacology Bulletin, 23,* 111–114.

Hunt, R. D., Minderaa, R. B. & Cohen, D. J. (1985). Clonidine benefits children with attention deficit disorder and hyperactivity: Report of a double-blind placebo-crossover therapeutic trial. *Journal of the American Academy of Child Psychiatry, 24,* 617–629.

Hurwitz, S. & Christiansen, K. O. (1983). *Criminology.* Boston: Allen & Unwin.

Hussong, A. M. & Chassin, L. (1997). Substance

use initiation among adolescent children of alcoholics: Testing protective factors. *Journal of Studies on Alcohol, 58,* 272–279.

Hyman, S. (1994). The violent patient. In S. Hyman & G. Tesar (Ed.), *Manual of psychiatric emergencies* (3d ed.). Boston: Little, Brown.

Irvine, R. A., Yu, M. C., Ross, R. K. & Coetzee, G. A. (1995). The CAG and GGC microsatellites of the androgen receptor gene are in linkage disequilibrium in men with prostate cancer. *Cancer Research, 55,* 1937–1940.

Irwin, J. & Austin, J. (1994). *It's about time: America's imprisonment binge.* Belmont, CA: Wadsworth.

Itil, T. M., Polvan, N., Ucok, A., Eper, E., Guven, F. & Hsu, W. (1971). Comparison of the clinical and electroencephalographical effects of molindone and trifluoperazine in acute schizophrenic patients. *Behavioral Neuropsychiatry, 3,* 6–13.

Ito, Y., Teicher, M. H., Glod, C. A. & Ackerman, E. (1998). Preliminary evidence for aberrant cortical development in abused children: A quantitative EEG study. *Journal of Neuropsychiatry and Clinical Neuroscience, 10,* 298–307.

Ito, Y., Teicher, M. H., Glod, C. A., Harper, D., Magnus, E. & Gelbard, H. A. (1993). Increased prevalence of electrophysiological abnormalities in children with psychological, physical, and sexual abuse. *Journal of Neuropsychiatry and Clinical Neuroscience, 5,* 401–408.

Itokawa, M., Arinami, T., Futamura, N., Hamaguchi, H. & Toru, M. (1993). A structural polymorphism of human dopamine receptor D2 (Ser311-Cys). *Biochemical and Biophysiology Research Community, 196,* 1369–1375.

Izmeth, M. G., Khan, S. Y., Kumarajeeva, D. I., Shivanathan, S., Veall, R. M. & Wiley, Y. V. (1988). Zuclopenthixol decanoate in the management of behavioural disorders in mentally handicapped patients. *Pharmatherapeutica, 5,* 217–227.

Izzo, R. L. & Ross, R. R. (1990). Meta-analysis of rehabiliatation programs for juvenile delinquents. *Criminal Justice and Behavior: An International Journal, 17,* 134–142.

Jacobs, B. L. & Azmitia, E. C. (1992). Structure and function of the brain serotonin system. *Physiological Reviews, 72,* 165–229.

Jang, K. L., Livesley, W. J. & Vernon, P. A. (1995). Alcohol and drug problems: A multivariate behavioural genetic analysis of co-morbidity. *Addiction, 90,* 1213–1221.

Jarvis, T. J. & Copeland, J. (1997). Child sexual abuse as a predictor of psychiatric co-morbidity and its implications for drug and alcohol treatment. *Drug and Alcohol Dependence, 49,* 61–69.

Jaselskis, C. A., Cook, E. H. Jr., Fletcher, K. E. & Leventhal, B. L. (1992). Clonidine treatment of hyperactive and impulsive children with autistic disorder. *Journal of Clinical Psychopharmacology, 12,* 322–327.

Jeanblanc, W. & Davis, Y. (1995). Risperidone for treating dementia-associated aggression. *American Journal of Psychiatry, 152,* 1239.

Jeffery, C. R. (1990). *Criminology: An interdisciplinary approach.* Englewood Cliffs, NJ: Prentice-Hall.

Jeffery, C. R. (1998). Criminology and criminal law: Science versus policy and the interaction of science and law. In W. Laufer & F. Adler (Eds.), *Advances in criminological theory,* vol. 8. New Brunswick, NJ: Transaction.

Jeffery, C. R. (1998). The prevention of juvenile violence. Paper presented at the thirty-fifth annual conference of the Academy of Criminal Justice Sciences, Albuquerque, NM.

Jenkins, R. L. (1966). Psychiatric syndromes in children and their relations to family background. *American Journal of Orthopsychiatry, 36,* 450–457.

Jennings, W. S., Kilkenny, R. & Kohlberg, L. (1983). Moral-development theory and practice for youthful and adult offenders. In W. S. Laufer & J. M. Day (Eds.), *Personality theory, moral development, and criminal behavior.* Lexington, MA: Lexington Books.

Jessor, R., Donovan, J. & Costa, F. (1991). *Beyond adolescence. Problem behavior and young adult development.* New York: Cambridge University Press.

Johnson, G. (1992). Evaluation of the specialized drug offender program for the Colorado Judicial Department. Boulder, CO: Action Research Project, University of Colorado.

Johnson, G. & Hunter, R. M. (1987). Using school-based programs to improve students' citizenship in Colorado. Boulder, CO: Action Research Project, University of Colorado.

Johnson, G. & Hunter, R. M. (1992). Evaluation of the specialized drug offender program for the Colorado Judicial Department. Boulder, CO: Action Research Project, University of Colorado.

Jones, M. (1968). Personality correlates and

antecedents of drinking patterns in adult males. *Journal of Consulting and Clinical Psychiatry, 32,* 2–12.

Jumper, S. A. (1995). A meta-analysis of the relationship of child sexual abuse to adult psychological adjustment. *Child Abuse and Neglect, 19,* 715–728.

Kaes, T. (1907). Die grosshirninoe des menschen in ihren wassen und in ihren fassengehalt. *Ein Gehirnanatomische Atlas.* Jena, Germany: Fischer.

Kafantaris, V., Campbell, M., Padrone-Gayol, M. V., Small, A. M., Locascio, J. J. & Rosenberg, C. R. (1992). Carbamazepine in hospitalized aggressive conduct disorder children: An open pilot study. *Psychopharmacology Bulletin, 28,* 193–199.

Kagan, J. (1992). Behavior, biology, and the meanings of temperamental constructs. *Pediatrics, 3,* 510–513.

Kagan, J., Reznick, J. S. & Snidman, N. (1988). Biological bases of childhood shyness. *Science, 240,* 167–171.

Kagan, J. & Saidman, N. (1991). Infarct predictors of inhibited and uninhibited profiles. *Psychological Science, 2,* 40–44.

Kaij, L. (1960). *Studies on the etiology and sequels of abuse of alcohol.* Lund, Sweden: Almqvist & Wiksell Int'l.

Kalamas, A. D. & Gruber, M. L. (1998). Electrodermal responses to implied versus actual violence on television. *Journal of General Psychology, 125,* 31–37.

Kalmuss, D. (1984). The intergenerational transmission of marital aggression. *Journal of Marriage and the Family, 46,* 11–19.

Kanarek, R. B. (1994). Nutrition and violent behavior. In *Understanding and preventing violence,* vol. 2. Washington, DC: National Academy Press, 515–540.

Kandel, D., Davies, M. & Baydar, N. (1990). The creation of interpersonal contexts: Homophily in dyadic relationships in adolescence and young adulthood. In L. Robins & M. Rutter (Eds.), *Straight and devious pathways from childhood to adulthood.* New York: Cambridge University Press, 221–241.

Kandel, E. S., Brennan, P. A., Mednick, S. A. & Michelson, N. M. (1989). Minor physical anomalies and recidivistic adult violent criminal behavior. *Acta Psychiatrica Scandinavia, 79,* 103–107.

Kandel, E. & Mednick, S.A. (1991). Perinatal complications predict violent offending. *Criminology, 29,* 519–530.

Kant, Immanuel ([1797]1965). The metaphysical elements of justice (J. Ladd, tr.). New York: Bobbs-Merrill.

Kantak, K. M., Hegstrand, L. R. & Eichelman, B. (1981). Dietary tryptophan reversal of septal lesions and 5,7-DHT lesion elicited shock-induced fighting. *Pharamcology, Biochemistry & Behavior, 15,* 343–350.

Kaplan, H. & Sadock, B. (1985). *Comprehensive textbook of psychiatry.* Baltimore: Williams & Wilkins.

Kaplan, J. (1899). *Kopftrauma und pschosen. Allgemein Psychiatrie, 56,* 292–297.

Kaplan, J. R., Shively, C. A., Fontenot, M. B., Morgan, T. M., Howell, S. M., Manuck, S. B., Muldoon, M. F. & Mann, J. J. (1994). Demonstration of an association among dietary cholesterol, central serotonergic activity, and social behavior in monkeys. *Psychosomatic Medicine, 56,* 479–484.

Kaplan, P. J. & Arbuthnot, J. (1985). Affective empathy and cognitive role-taking in delinquent and nondelinquent youth. *Adolescence, 20,* 323–333.

Kaplan, S. L., Busner, J., Kupietz, S., Wassermann, E. & Segal, B. (1990). Effects of methylphenidate on adolescents with aggressive conduct disorder and ADDH: A preliminary report. *Journal of the American Academy of Child and Adolescent Psychiatry, 29,* 719–723.

Kaufer, D., Friedman, A., Seidman, S. & Soreq, H. (1998). Acute stress facilitates long-lasting changes in cholinergic gene expression. *Nature, 393,* 373–377.

Kaufman, E. (1981). Family structures of narcotic addicts. *International Journal of the Addictions, 16,* 93–112.

Kaufman, J., Birmaher, B., Perel, J., Dahl, R. E., Moreci, P., Nelson, B., Wells, W. & Ryan, N. D. (1997). The corticotropin-releasing hormone challenge in depressed abused, depressed nonabused, and normal control children. *Biological Psychiatry, 42,* 669–679.

Kavoussi, R. J., Liu, J. & Coccaro, E. F. (1994). An open trial of sertraline in personality disordered patients with impulsive aggression. *Journal of Clinical Psychiatry, 55,* 137–141.

Kazdin, A. (1988). *Child psychotherapy:*

Developing and identifying effective treatments. Oxford, England: Pergamon Press.

Kazdin, A., Rodgers, A., Colbus, D. & Siegel, T. (1987). Children's hostility inventory: Measurement of aggression and hostility in psychiatric inpatient children. *Journal of Clinical Child Psychology, 16,* 320–328.

Kegan, R. G. (1986). Sociopathy, a developmental delay. In W. H. Reid, D. Dorr & J. Walker (Eds.), *The child behind the mask.* New York: W. W. Norton.

Kellam, S., Ersminger, M. & Simon, M. (1980). Mental health in first grade and teenage drug, alcohol, and cigarette use. *Drug and Alcohol Dependence, 5,* 273–304.

Kelley, T. (1997). An integrated systems approach to screening for brain dysfunction in delinquent offenders. Master's thesis. Florida State University, Tallahassee, FL.

Kellner, R. A. & Kavoussi, R. J. (1987). A symptom questionnaire. *Journal of Clinical Psychiatry, 48,* 268–274.

Kellogg, R. T. (1995). *Cognitive psychology.* Newbury Park, CA: Sage.

Kempermann, G., Brandon, E. P. & Gage, F. H. (1998). Environmental stimulation of 129/SvJ mice causes increased cell proliferation and neurogenesis in the adult dentate gyrus. *Current Trends in Biology, 8,* 939–942.

Kemph, J. P., DeVane, C. L., Levine, G. M., Jarecke, R. & Miller, R. L. (1993). Treatment of aggressive children with clonidine: Results of an open pilot study. *Journal of the American Academy of Child and Adolescent Psychiatry, 32,* 577–581.

Kendler, K. S. (1993). Twin studies of psychiatric illness: Current status and future directions. *Archives of General Psychiatry, 50,* 905–915.

Kendler, K. S. & Eaves, L. J. (1986). Models for the joint effects of genotype and environment on liability to psychiatric illness. *American Journal of Psychiatry, 143,* 279–289.

Kendler, K. S., Heath, A. C., Neale, M. C., Kessler, R. C. & Eaves, L. J. (1992). A population-based twin study of alcoholism in women. *Journal of the American Medical Associaton, 268,* 1877–1882.

Kendler, K. S., Neale, M. C., Kessler, R. C., Heath, A. C. & Eaves, L. J. (1993). A test of the equal-environment assumption in twin studies of psychiatric illness. *Behavior Genetics, 23,* 21–27.

Kern, M., Botsis, A., Kotler, M., et al. (1992). The suicide and aggression survey: A semistructured instrument for the measurement of suicidality and aggression. *Comprehensive Psychiatry, 33,* 359–365.

Kernberg, O. (1992). *Severe personality disorders.* New Haven: Yale University Press.

Keschner, M., Bender, M. R. & Strauss, I. (1937). Mental symptoms in cases of subtentorial tumor. *Archives of Neurology and Psychiatry, 37,* 1–17.

Kessler, R. C., McGonagle, K. A., Zhao, S., Nelson, C. B., Hughes, M., Eshleman, S., Wittchen, H.-U. & Kendler, K. S. (1994). Lifetime and 12-month prevalence of DSM-III-R psychiatric disorders in the United States. *Archives of General Psychiatry, 51,* 8–19.

Kessler, R. C., Nelson, C. B., McGonagle, K. A., Edlund, M. J., Frank, R. G. & Leaf, P. J. (1996). The epidemiology of co-occurring addictive and mental disorders: Implications for prevention and service utilization. *American Journal of Orthopsychiatry, 66,* 17–31.

Kilby, M. D., Govind, A. & O'Brien, P. M. (1994). Outcome of twin pregnancies complicated by a single intrauterine death: A comparison with viable twin pregnancies. *Obstetrics and Gynecology, 84,* 107–109.

Kim, S. G. Ugurbil, K. & Strick, P. L. (1994). Activation of cerebellar output nucleus during cognitive processing. *Science, 265,* 949–951.

King, D. & Marsan, C. (1977). Clinical features and ictal patterns in epileptic patients with EEG temporal lobe foci. *Annals of Neurology, 2,* 138–147.

Kittrie, N. (1971). *The right to be different: Deviance and enforced therapy.* Baltimore, MD: Johns Hopkins University Press.

Klein, R. G., Abikoff, H., Klass, E., Ganeles, D., Seese, L. M. & Pollack, S. (1997). Clinical efficacy of methylphenidate in conduct disorder with and without attention deficit hyperactivity disorder. *Archives of General Psychiatry, 54,* 1073–1080.

Kligman, D. & Goldberg, D. (1975). Temporal lobe epilepsy and aggression. *Journal of Nervous and Mental Diseases, 160,* 324–341.

Kohlberg, L. (1969). Stage and sequence: The cognitive-developmental approach to socialization. In D. A. Goslin (Ed.), *Handbook of socialization theory.* Chicago: Rand McNally.

Kohlberg, L. E., Scharf, P. & Hickey, J. (1972). The justice structure of the prison: A theory and intervention. *Prison Journal, 51,* 3-14.

Kolarski, A., Freund, K., Machek, J. & Polak, O. (1967). Male sexual deviation associated with early temporal lobe damage. *Archives of General Psychiatry, 17,* 735–743.

Kolvin, I., Miller, F. J. W., Fleeting, M. & Kolvin, P. A. (1988). Social and parenting factors affecting criminal-offence rates: Findings from the Newcastle Thousand Family Study (1947–1980). *British Journal of Psychiatry, 152,* 80–90.

Konig, M., Zimmer, A. M., Steiner, H., Holmes, P. V., Crawley, J. N., Brownstein, M. J. & Zimmer, A. (1996). Pain responses, anxiety and aggression in mice deficient in pre-proenkephalin. *Nature, 383,* 535–538.

Koop, C. E. & Lundberg, G. D. (1992). Violence in America: A public health emergency. Time to bite the bullet back. *Journal of the American Medical Association, 267,* 3048–3053.

Korn, M. L., Botsis, A. J., Kotler, M., Plutchik, R., Conte, H. R., Finkelstein, G., Grosz, D., Kay, S., Brown, S. L. & van Praag, H. M. (1992). The suicide and aggression survey: A semistructured instrument for the measurement of suicidality and aggression. *Comprehensive Psychiatry, 33,* 359–365.

Kosten, T. R., Frank, J. B., Dan, E., McDougle, C. J. & Giller, E. L. Jr. (1991). Pharmacotherapy for posttraumatic stress disorder using phenelzine and imipramine. *Journal of Nervous and Mental Diseases, 179,* 366–370.

Kosten, T. R., Kosten, T. A. & Rounsaville, B. J. (1991). Alcoholism and depressive disorders in opioid addicts and their family members. *Comprehensive Psychiatry, 32,* 521–527.

Kotulak, R. (1996). *Inside the brain: Revolutionary discoveries of how the mind works.* Kansas City, MO: Andrews McMeel.

Kraemer, G. W., Ebert, M. H., Schmidt, D. E. & McKinney, W. T. (1989). A longitudinal study of the effect of different social rearing conditions on cerebrospinal fluid norepinephrine and biogenic amine metabolites in rhesus monkeys. *Neuropsychopharmacology, 2,* 175–189.

Kraepelin, E. (1915). *Psychiatrie. Die gesellschafsfeiriig (Antisozialem)* (8th ed.), vol. 4. Leipzig: Barth, 1076–2110.

Kramer, T. H., Ottomanelli, G. & Bihari, B. (1992). IV versus non-IV drug use and selected patient variables related to AIDS risk behaviors. *International Journal of the Addictions, 27,* 477–485.

Kristiansson, M. (1995). Incurable psychopaths? *Bulletin of the American Academy of Psychiatry and Law, 23,* 555–562.

Krober, H. L., Scheurer, H. & Sass, H. (1994). Cerebral dysfunction, neurologic symptoms and recurrent delinquency—I. Review of the literature. *Fortschritte der Neurologie Psychiatrie, 62,* 169–178.

Kuhn, C. M. & Schanberg, S. M. (1998). Responses to maternal separation: Mechanisms and mediators. *International Journal of Developmental Neuroscience, 16,* 261–270.

Kuhne, M., Schachar, R. & Tannock, R. (1997). Impact of comorbid oppositional or conduct problems on attention-deficit hyperactivity disorder. *Journal of the American Academy of Child and Adolescent Psychiatry, 36,* 1715–1724.

Kumchy, C. I., & Sayer, L. A. (1980). Locus of control in a delinquent adolescent population. *Psychological Reports, 46,* 1307–1310.

Kumpfer, K. (1987). Special populations: Etiology and prevention of vulnerability to chemical dependency in children of substance abusers. In B. S. Brown & A. R. Mills (Eds.), *Youth at risk for substance abuse.* Washington, DC: U.S. Government Printing Office.

Kunik, M. E., Puryear, L., Orengo, C. A., Molinari, V. & Workman, R. H. Jr. (1998). The efficacy and tolerability of divalproex sodium in elderly demented patients with behavioral disturbances. *International Journal of Geriatric Psychiatry, 13,* 29–34.

Kurtines, W. & Hogan, R. (1972). Sources of conformity in unsocialized college students. *Journal of Abnormal Psychology, 80,* 49–51.

Kurtz, R. R. & Grummon, D. L. (1972). Different approaches to the measurement of therapist empathy and their relationship to therapy outcome. *Journal of Consulting and Clinical Psychology, 39,* 105–115.

Kwan, M., Greenleaf, W. J., Mann, J., Crapo, L. & Davidson, J. M. (1983). The nature of androgen action on male sexuality: A combined laboratory-self report study on hypogonadal man. *Journal of Clinical Endocrinology and Metabolism, 57,* 557–562.

Labouvie, E., Pandina, R. & Johnson, V. (1991). Developmental trajectories of substance use in adolescence. Difference and predictors. *International Journal of Behavioral Development, 14,* 305–328.

LaBuda, M. C., Svikis, D. S. & Pickens, R. W. (1997). Twin closeness and co-twin risk for substance use disorders: Assessing the impact of the equal environment assumption. *Psychiatry Research, 70,* 155–164.

Lahey, B. B., Piacentini, J. C., McBurnett, K., Stone, P., Hartdagen, S. & Hynd, G. (1988). Psychopathology in the parents of children with conduct disorder and hyperactivity. *Journal of the American Academy of Child and Adolescent Psychiatry, 27,* 163–170.

Lahoste, G. J., Swanson, J. M., Wigal, S. B., Glabe, C., Wigal, T., King, N. & Kennedy, J. L. (1996). Dopamine D4 receptor gene polymorphism is associated with attention deficit hyperactivity disorder. *Molecular Psychiatry, 1,* 121–124.

Lane, S. D., Cherek, D. R., Dougherty, D. M. & Moeller, F. G. (1998). Laboratory measurement of adaptive behavior change in humans with a history of substance dependence. *Drug and Alcohol Dependence, 51,* 239–252.

Lange, J. (1931). *Crime as destiny* (trans. C. Haldene). London: Allen & Unwin.

Langevin, R. (1990). Sexual anomalies and the brain. In W. L. Marshall, D. R. Laws & H. L. Barbaree (Ed.), *Handbook of sexual assault: Issues, theories and treatment of the offender.* New York: Plenum Press, 103–113.

Langevin, R., Marentette, D. & Rosati, B. (1995). Why therapy fails with some sex offenders: Learning difficulties examined empirically. *Journal of Offender Rehabilitation, 23,* 145–157.

Langevin, R., Wortzman, G., Dickey, R., Wright, P. & Handy, L. (1988). Neuropsychological impairment in incest offenders. *Annals of Sex Research, 1,* 401–415.

Lappalainen, J., Dean, M., Charbonneau, L., Virkkunen, M., Linnoila, M. & Goldman, D. (1995). Mapping of the serotonin 5-HT1Db autoreceptor gene on chromosome 6 and direct analysis for sequence variants. *American Journal of Medical Genetics (Neuropsychiatric Genetics), 60,* 157–161.

Lappalainen, J., Long, J. C., Eggert, M., Ozaki, N., Robin, R. W., Brown, G. L., Naukkarinen, H., Virkkunen, M., Linnoila, M. & Goldman, D. (1998). Linkage of antisocial alcoholism to the serotonin 5-HT1B receptor gene in 2 populations. *Archives of General Psychiatry, 55,* 989–994.

Laschet, V. & Laschet, L. (1976). Antiandrogens in the treatment of sexual deviation in men. *Journal of Steroid Biochemistry, 16,* 821–826.

Lassman, L. P. & Arjona, V. (1967). Pontine glioma in childhood. *Lancet, 1,* 913–915.

Lau, M. & Pihl, R. (1996). Cognitive performance, monetary incentive, and aggression. *Aggressive Behavior, 22,* 417–430.

Lau, M., Pihl, R. & Peterson, J. (1995). Provocation, acute alcohol intoxication, cognitive performance, and aggression. *Journal of Abnormal Psychology, 104,* 150–155.

Lau, S. & Leung, K. (1992). Self-concept, delinquency, relations with parents and school and Chinese adolescents' perception of personal control. *Personality & Individual Differences, 13,* 615–622.

Laufer, W. S., Skoog, D. K. & Day, J. M. (1982). Personality and criminality: A review of the California psychological inventory. *Journal of Clinical Psychology, 38,* 562–573.

Lazarus, A. & Launier, R. (1978). Stress-related transactions between person and environment. In L. A. Pervin & M. Lewis (Eds.), *Perspectives in interactional psychology.* New York: Plenum Press.

Lebert, F., Pasquier, F. & Petit, F. (1994). Behavioral effects of trazodone in Alzheimer's disease. *Journal of Psychiatry, 55,* 536–538.

Lederer, J. M., Kielhofner, G. & Watts, J. H. (1985). Values, personal causation and skills of delinquents and nondelinquents. *Occupational Therapy in Mental Health, 5,* 59–77.

Lee, M. & Prentice, N. M. (1988). Interrelations of empathy, cognition, and moral reasoning with dimensions of juvenile delinquency. *Journal of Abnormal Child Psychology, 16,* 127–139.

Lefcourt, H. M. (1976). *Locus of control: Current trends in theory and research.* Hillsdale, NJ: Erlbaum.

Lefcourt, H. M. (1991). Locus of control. In J. P. Robinson, P. R. Shaver & L. S. Wrightsman (Eds.), *Measures of personality and social psychological attitudes.* New York: Academic Press.

Lefcourt, H. M. & Ludwig, G. W. (1965). The American Negro: A problem in expectancies. *Journal of Personality and Social Psychology, 1,* 377–380.

Lefkowitz, M. M. (1969). Effects of diphenylhydantoin on disruptive behavior: Study of male delinquents. *Archives of General Psychiatry, 20,* 643–651.

Lefkowitz, M. M., Eron, L. D., Walder, L. D. & Huesmann, L. R. (1972). Television violence and child aggression: A follow-up study. In G. A. Comstock & E. A. Rubinstein (Eds.), *Television and social behavior,* vol. 3. Washington, DC: U.S. Government Printing Office, 35–135.

Legido, A. (1997). Intrauterine exposure to drugs. *Reviews in Neurology, 25,* 691–702.

Leiner, H., Leiner, A. L. & Dow, R. S. (1989). Re-appraising the cerebellum. What does the hind-brain contribute to the fore-brain? *Behavioral Neuroscience, 103,* 998–1008.

Lemieux, A. M. & Coe, C. L. (1995). Abuse-related posttraumatic stress disorder: Evidence for chronic neuroendocrine activation in women. *Psychosomatic Medicine, 57,* 105–115.

Lenox, R. H., Newhouse, P. A., Creelman, W. L. & Whitaker, T. M. (1992). Adjunctive treatment of manic agitation with lorazepam versus haloperidol: A double-blind study. *Journal of Clinical Psychiatry, 53,* 47–52.

Lerner, J. & Vicary, J. (1984). Difficult temperament and drug use: Analysis from the New York Longitudinal Study. *Journal of Drug Education, 14,* 1–8.

Lesch, K.-P., Wolozin, B. L., Murphy, D. L. & Reiderer, P. (1993). Primary structure of the human platelet serotonin uptake site: Identity with the brain serotonin transporter. *Journal of Neurochemistry, 60,* 2319–2322.

Levenson, H. (1974). Multidimensional locus of control in prison inmates. *Personality & Social Psychology Bulletin, 1,* 354–356.

Levine, M. D. (1995). Childhood neurodevelopmental dysfunctional learning disorders. *Harvard Mental Health Letter, 12,* 5–6.

Levine, M., Karniski, W. M., Palfrey, J. S., Meltzer, L. & Fenton, T. (1985). A study of risk factor complexes in early adolescent delinquency. *American Journal of Diseases of Childhood, 139,* 50–56.

Lewis, C. E., Rice, J. & Helzer, J. E. (1983). Diagnostic interactions: Alcoholism and antisocial personality. *Journal of Nervous and Mental Disease, 171,* 105–113.

Lewis, D.O. (1976). Delinquency, psychomotor epileptic symptoms, and paranoid ideation: a triad. *American Journal of Psychiatry, 133,* 1395–1398.

Lewis, D. O. (1992). From abuse to violence: Psychophysiological consequences of maltreatment. *Journal of the American Academy of Child and Adolescent Psychiatry, 31,* 383–391.

Lewis, D. O. & Pincus, J. H. (1989). Epilepsy and violence: Evidence for a neuropsychotic-aggressive syndrome. *Journal of Neuropsychiatry, 1,* 413–418.

Lewis, D. O., Pincus, J. H., Bard, S., Richardson, E., Pritchep, L. S., Feldman, M. & Yeager, C. (1988). Neuropsychiatric, psycho-educational and family characteristics of 14 juveniles condemned to death in the United States. *American Journal of Psychiatry, 145,* 584–589.

Lewis, D. O., Pincus, J. H. & Glaser, G. H. (1979). Violent juvenile delinquents: Psychiatric, neurological and abuse factors. *American Academy of Psychiatry, 18,* 307–319.

Lewis, D. O., Pincus, J. H., Shanok, S. & et al. (1982). Psychomotor epilepsy and violence in a group of incarcerated adolescent boys. *American Journal of Psychiatry, 139,* 882–887.

Lezak, M. (1995). *Neuropsychological assessment* (3d ed.). New York: Oxford University Press.

Lhermitte, F., Pillon, B. & Serdaru, M. (1986). Human anatomy and the frontal lobe: Imitation and utilization behavior. A neuro-psychological study of 75 patients. *Annals of Neurology, 19,* 326–334.

Lichter, J. B., Barr, C. L., Kennedy, J. L., Van Tol, H. H. M., Kidd, K. K. & Livak, K. J. (1993). A hypervariable segment in the human dopamine receptor (DRD4) gene. *Human Molecular Genetics, 2,* 767–773.

Lidberg, L., Modin, I., Oreland, L., Tuck, J. R. & Gillner, A. (1985). Platelet monoamine oxidase activity and psychopathy. *Psychiatry Research, 16,* 339–343.

Lidberg, L., Tuck, J. R., Åsberg, M., Scalia-Tomba, G. P. & Bertilsson, L. (1985). Homocide, suicide and CSF 5-HIAA. *Acta Psychiatrica Scandinavia, 71,* 230–236.

Liebert, J. (1985). Contributions to psychiatric consultation in the investigation of serial murder. *International Journal of Offender Therapy and Comparative Criminology, 29,* 187–200.

Limson, R., Goldman, D., Roy, A., Lamparski, D., Ravitz, B., Adwoff, B. & Linnoila, M. (1991). Personality and cerebrospinal fluid monoamine metabolites in alcoholics and controls. *Archives of General Psychiatry, 48,* 437–441.

Lindberg, L., Asberg, M. & Sundqvist-Stensman, U. B. (1984). 5-hydroxyindole acetic acid levels in attempted suicides who have killed their children. *Lancet, 2,* 928.

Lindquist, P. & Allebeck, P. (1990). Schizophrenia and crime: A longitudinal follow-up of 644 schizophrenics in Stockholm. *British Journal of Psychiatry, 157,* 345–350.

Linnoila, M. & Virkkunen, M. (1992). Biologic correlates of suicidal risk and aggressive behavioral traits. *Journal of Clinical Psychiatry, 12,* S19–S20.

Linnoila, M., Virkkunen, M., Eckardt, M., Higley, J. D., Nielsen, D. & Goldman, D. (1994). Serotonin, violent behavior and alcohol. *EXS, 71,* 155–163.

Linnoila, M., Virkkunen, M., Scheinin, M., Nuutila, A., Rimon, R. & Goodwin, F. K. (1983). Low cerebrospinal fluid 5-hydroxyindolacetic acid concentration differentiates impulsive from nonimpulsive violent behavior. *Life Sciences, 33,* 2609–2614.

Linqvist, P. & Allebeck, F. (1990). Schizophrenia and crime: A longitudinal follow-up of 644 schizophrenics in Stockholm. *British Journal of Psychiatry, 157,* 345–350.

Lipsitz, J. D., Williams, J. B. W., Rabkin, J. G., Remien, R. H., Bradbury, M., el Sadr, W., Goetz, R., Sorrell, S. & Gorman, J. M. (1994). Psychopathology in male and female intravenous drug users with and without HIV infection. *American Journal of Psychiatry, 151,* 1662–1668.

Little, V. L. & Kendall, P. C. (1979). Cognitive-behavioral interventions with delinquents: Problem solving, role-taking, and self-control. In P. C. Kendall & S. D. Holton (Eds.), *Cognitive-behavioral interventions: Theory, research, and procedures.* New York: Academic Press.

Livesley, W. J. & Jackson, D. N. (1995). *Manual for the dimensional assessment of personality pathology.* Port Huron, MI: Research Psychologists Press.

Loeber, R. (1990). Development and risk factors of juvenile antisocial behavior and delinquency. *Clinical Psychology Review, 10,* 1–41.

Loeber, R. (1991). Questions and advances in the study of developmental pathways. In D. Cicchetti & S. Toth (Eds.), *Models and integration: Rochester symposium on developmental psychopathology.* Rochester, NY: University of Rochester Press, 97–115.

Loeber, R. & Dishion, T. (1983). Early predictors of male delinquency: A review. *Psychological Bulletin, 94,* 68–99.

Loeber, R. & Hay, D. (1997). Key issues in the development of aggression and violence from childhood to early adulthood. *Annual Review of Psychology, 48,* 371–410.

Loeber, R. & LeBlanc, M. (1990). Toward a developmental criminology. In M. Tonry & N. Morris (Eds.), *Crime and justice: An annual review,* vol. 12. Chicago: University of Chicago Press, 375–473.

Loeber, R. & Stouthammer-Loeber, M. (1986). Family factors as correlates and predictors of juvenile conduct problems and delinquency. In A. Morris & M. Tonry (Eds.), *Crime and justice: An annual review of research,* vol. 7. Chicago: University of Chicago Press.

Loeber, R. & Stouthamer-Loeber, M. (1998). Development of juvenile aggression and violence: Some common misconceptions and controversies. *American Psychologist, 53,* 242–259.

Loehlin, J. C. & Nichols, R. C. (1976). *Heredity, environment and personality: A study of 850 sets of twins.* Austin, TX: University of Texas Press.

Loehlin, J. C., Willerman, L. & Horn, J. M. (1985). Personality resemblances in adoptive families when the children are late-adolescent or adult. *Journal of Personality and Social Psychology, 48,* 376–392.

Loehlin, J. C., Willerman, L. & Horn, J. M. (1987). Personality resemblances in adoptive families: A 10-year follow-up. *Journal of Personality and Social Psychology, 53,* 961–969.

Loehlin, J. C. Willerman, L. & Horn, J. M. (1988). Human behavior genetics. *Annual Review of Psychology, 39,* 101–233.

Loevinger, J. (1966). The meaning and measurement of ego-development. *American Psychologist, 21,* 195–206.

Logue, A. W. (1995). *Self-control.* Englewood Cliffs, NJ: Prentice-Hall.

Loney, J. & Milich, R. (1982). Hyperactivity, inattention, and aggression in clinical practice. *Advances in Developmental and Behavioral Pediatrics, 3,* 113–147.

Long, J. C., Knowler, W. C., Hanson, R. L., Robin, R. W., Urbanek, M., Moore, E., Bennett, P. H. & Goldman, D. (1998). Evidence for genetic linkage to alcohol dependence on chromosomes 4 and 11 from an autosome-wide scan in an American Indian population. *Neuropsychiatric Genetics, 81,* 216–221.

Longshore, D., Turner, S. & Stein, J. A. (1996). Self-control in a criminal sample: An examination of construct validity. *Criminology, 34,* 209–228.

Looker, A. & Conners, C. K. (1970). Diphenylhydantoin in children with severe temper tantrums. *Archives of General Psychiatry, 23,* 80–89.

Lorch, E. P., Palmgreen, P., Donohew, R. L., Helm, D., Baer, S. & D'Silva, M. (1994). Program context, sensation seeking and attention to televised anti-drug public service announcements. *Human Communication Research, 20,* 390–412.

Lou, H. C., Hansen, D., Nordenfoft, M., Pryds, D., Jensen, F., Nim, J. & Hemmingsen, R. (1994). Prenatal stressors of human life affect fetal brain development. *Developmental Medicine and Child Neurology, 36,* 826–832.

Lovett, L. M. & Shaw, D. M. (1987). Outcome in bipolar affective disorder, after stereotactic tractomy. *British Journal of Psychiatry, 151,* 113–116.

Luchins, D. (1983). Carbamazepine for the violent psychiatric patients. *Lancet, I,* 766.

Lukoff, D., Nuechterlein, K. H. & Ventura, I. (1986). Appendix A: Manual for the expanded BPRS. *Schizophrenia Bulletin, 12,* 594–602.

Luria, A. (1961). The role of speech in the regulation of normal and abnormal behavior. New York: Basic Books.

Luria, A. R. (1973). *The working brain: An introduction to neuropsychology.* New York: Basic Books.

Luria, A. (1980). Higher cortical functions in man. New York: Basic Books.

Lynch, D., Eliatamby, C. & Anderson, A. (1985). Pipothiazine palmitate in the management of aggressive mentally handicapped patients. *British Journal of Psychiatry, 146,* 525–529.

Lynskey, M. T. & Fergusson, D. M. (1997). Factors protecting against the development of adjustment difficulties in young adults exposed to childhood sexual abuse. *Child Abuse and Neglect, 21,* 1177–1190.

Lyons, M. J. (1996). A twin study of self-reported criminal behavior. In G. R. Bock & J. A. Goode (Eds.), *Genetics of criminal and antisocial behavior.* West Sussex, England: John Wiley & Sons, 61–75.

Lyons, M. J., True, W. R., Eisen, S. A., Goldberg, J., Meyer, J. M., Faraone, S. V., Eaves, L. J. & Tsuang, M. T. (1995). Differential heritability of adult and juvenile antisocial traits. *Archives of General Psychiatry, 52,* 906–915.

Lytton, H. (1990). Child and parent effects in boys' conduct disorder: A reinterpretation. *Developmental Psychology, 26,* 683–697.

Maccoby, M. (1972). Emotional attitudes and political choice. *Politics and Society,* 209–239.

MacDonnell, M. F. & Flynn, J. P. (1966). Control of sensory fields by stimulation of hypothalamus. *Science, 152,* 1406–1408.

Macklin, S. R., Harris, G. H., Pearson, G. D., Hohn-Saric, R., Jeffery, P., Camargo, E. (1991). Elevated medial frontal blood flow in obsessive-compulsive patients in a SPECT study. *American Journal of Psychiatry, 148,* 1240–1242.

MacLeod, C. (1991). Half a century of research on the Stroop effect: An integrative review. *Psychological Bulletin, 109,* 163–203.

Mahowald, M. W., Bundlie, S. R., Hurwitz, T. D. & Schenck, C. H. (1990). Sleep violence: Forensic science implications: Polygraphic and video documentation. *Journal of Forensic Science, 35,* 413–430.

Mak, A. S. (1990). Testing a psychosocial control theory of delinquency. *Criminal Justice and Behavior, 17,* 215–230.

Mak, A. S. (1991). Psychosocial control characteristics of delinquents and nondelinquents. *Criminal Justice and Behavior, 18,* 287–303.

Malamud, N. C. (1967). Psychiatric disorders with intra-cranial tumors of the limbic system. *Archives of Psychiatry 17,* 113–123.

Maletzky, B. (1974). d-Amphetamine and delinquency: Hyperkinesis persistin. *Diseases of the Nervous System, 35,* 543–547.

Malhotra, A. K., Virkkunen, M., Rooney, W., Eggert, M., Linnoila, M. & Goldman, D. (1996). The association between the dopamine D4 receptor (DRD4) 16 amino acid repeat polymorphisms and novelty seeking. *Molecular Psychiatry, 1,* 388–391.

Mallouh, C. (1996). The effects of dual diagnosis on pregnancy and parenting. *Journal of Psychoactive Drugs, 28,* 367–380.

Mandel, P., Mack, G. & Kempf, E. (1979). Molecular basis of some models of aggressive behavior. In M. Sandler (Ed.), *Psychopharmacology of aggression.* New York: Raven, 95–110.

Mannuzza, S., Klein, R. G., Konig, P. H. & Giampino, T. L. (1989). Hyperactive boys almost grown up. IV. Criminality and its relationship to psychistric status. *Archives of General Psychiatry, 46,* 1073–1091.

Marek, G. J., Li, A. A. & Seiden, L. S. (1990). Evidence for involvement of 5-hydroxytryptamine[1] receptors in antidepressant-like drug effects on differential reinforcement of low-rate 72-second schedule. *Journal of Pharmacology & Experimental Therapeutics, 250,* 60–71.

Marino, M. J. (1999). CDC report shows prevalence of brain injury. *TBI Challenge, 3,* 1, 13.

Mark, V. H. & Ervin, J. F. R. (1970). *Violence and the brain.* New York: Harper & Row.

Markovitz, P. J., Calabrese, J. R., Schulz, S. C. & Meltzer, H. Y. (1991). Fluoxetine in the treatment of borderline and schizotypal personality disorders. *American Journal of Psychiatry, 148,* 1064–1067.

Markovitz, P. & Wagner, S. (1995). Venlafaxine in the treatment of borderline personality disorder. *Psychopharmology Bulletin, 31,* 773–777.

Markowitz, P. I. (1992). Effects of fluoxetine on self-injurious behavior in the developmentally disabled: A preliminary study. *Journal of Clinical Psychopharmacology, 12,* 27–31.

Markowitz, P. I. & Wagner, S. (1995). Venlafaxine in the treatment of borderline personality disorder. *Psychopharmology Bulletin, 31,* 773–777.

Marks, I. M. (1981). Review of behavioral psychotherapy, II: Sexual disorders. *American Journal of Psychiatry, 138,* 750–756.

Marks, V. (1981). The regulation of blood glucose. In V. Maker & F.C. Rose (Eds.), *Hypoglycemia.* Oxford, England: Blackwell.

Marlowe, M., Stellern, J., Moon, C. & Errera, J. (1985). Main and interaction effects of metallic toxins on aggressive classroom behavior. *Aggressive Behavior, 11,* 41–48.

Marsh, D. T. (1982). The development of interpersonal problem-solving among elementary-school children. *Journal of Genetic Psychology, 140,* 107–118.

Martin, C. S., Earleywine, M., Blackson, T. C., Vanyukov, M. M., Moss, H. B. & Tarter, R. E. (1994). Aggression, inattention, hyperactivity, and impulsivity in boys at high and low risk for substance abuse. *Journal of Abnormal Child Psychology, 22,* 177–203.

Martinson, R. (1974). "What works? Questions and answers about prison reform." *Public Interest,* 35, 22–54.

Marx, G. (1985, winter). I'll be watching you. *Dissent,* 6–34.

Mason, S. T. (1980). Noradrenaline and selective attention: A review of the model and the evidence. *Life Sciences, 27,* 617–631.

Masters, R. (1997). Environmental pollution, neurotoxicity, and criminal violence. In J. Rose (Ed.), *Environmental toxicity.* New York: Gordon & Breach, 1–61.

Mathieson, G. (1975). Pathology of temporal lobe foci. In J. K. Penry & D. Daly (Eds.), *Advances in Neurology,* vol. 11. New York: Raven.

Matsueda, R. L. (1982). Testing control theory and differential association: A causal modeling approach. *American Sociological Review, 47,* 489–504.

Mattes, J. A. (1980). The role of frontal lobe dysfunction in childhood hyperkinesis. *Comprehensive Psychiatry, 21,* 358–369.

Mattes, J. A. (1986). Propranolol for adults with temper outbursts and residual attention deficit disorder. *Journal of Clinical Psychopharmacology, 6,* 299–302.

Mature, C. M., Druss, B. G. & Cellar, J. S. (1992). Valproate treatment of older psychotic patients with organic mental syndromes and behavioral dyscontrol. *Journal of the American Geriatric Society, 10,* 914–916.

Maxfield, M. G. & Widom, C. S. (1996). The cycle of violence. Revisited 6 years later. *Archives of Pediatric and Adolescent Medicine, 150,* 390–395.

Maxson, S. C. (1990). Methodological issues in genetic analyses of an agonistic behavior (offense) in male mice. In D. Goldowitz, R. E. Wimer & D. Wahlsten (Eds.), *Techniques for the genetic analysis of brain and behavior.* Amsterdam: Elsevier Science Publishers.

Maxson, S. C. (1992). Potential genetic models of aggression and violence in males. In P. Driscoll (Ed.), *Genetically defined animal models of neurobehavioral dysfunctions.* Boston, MA: Birkhauser, 174–188.

Maxson, S. C. (1996). Issues in the search for candidate genes in mice as potential animal models of human aggression. In *Genetics of criminal and antisocial behavior.* New York: John Wiley & Sons, 21–35.

Mayes, L. C., Granger, R. H., Frank, M. A., Schottenfeld, R. & Bornstein, M. H. (1993). Neurobehavioral profiles of neonates exposed to cocaine prenatally. *Pediatrics, 91,* 778–783.

Maziade, M., Caron, C., Cote, R., Merrette, C., Bernier, H., Laplante, B., Boutin, P. & Thivierge, J. (1990). Psychiatric status of adolescents who had extreme temperaments at age 7. *American Journal of Psychiatry, 147,* 1531–1537.

McBurnett, K., Harris, S., Swanson, J., Pfiffner, L., Tamm, L. & Freeland, D. (1993). Neuropsychological and psychophysiological differentiation of inattention/overactivity and aggression/defiance symptom groups. *Journal of Clinical Child Psychology, 22,* 165–171.

McCallon, D. W. & Comings, D. E. (2000). *The treatable criminal mind.* Duarte, CA: Hope Press.

McCarney, K., Harris, M. J. & Bernieri, F. (1990). Growing up and growing apart: A developmental meta-analysis of twin studies. *Psychological Bulletin, 107,* 226–237.

McClearn, G., Plomin, R., Gora-Maslak, G. & Crabbe, J. (1991). The gene chase in behavioral science. *Psychiatry and Science, 2,* 222–229.

McCleary, R. A. (1966). Response modulating function of the limbic system: Initiation and suppression. In E. Stellar & J. M. Sprague (Eds.), *Progress in physiological psychology*, vol. 1. San Diego, CA: Academic Press, 209–271.

McCord, J. (1972). Etiological factors in alcoholism: Family and personal characteristics. *Quarterly Journal of Studies on Alcohol, 33,* 1020–1027.

McCord, J. (1983). A forty year perspective on effects of child abuse and neglect. *Child Abuse and Neglect, 7,* 265–270.

McCord, J. & McCord, W. (1958). The effects of parental role model on criminality. *Journal of Social Issues, 14,* 66–75.

McCord, W. & McCord, J. (1960). *Origins of alcoholism.* Palo Alto, CA: Stanford University Press.

McCracken, J. T. (1991). A two-part model of stimulant action on attention-deficit hyperactivity disorder in children. *Journal of Neuropsychiatry, 3,* 201–209.

McDaniel, K. (1986). Pharmacologic treatment of psychiatric and neurodevelopmental disorders in children and adolescents. *Clinical Pediatrics, 25,* 65–71.

McDougle, C. J., Holmes, J. P., Carlson, D. C., Pelton, G. H., Cohen, D. J. & Price, L. H. (1998). A double-blind, placebo-controlled study of risperidone in adults with autistic disorder and other pervasive developmental disorders. *Archives of General Psychiatry, 55,* 633–641.

McDougle, C. J., Naylor, S. T., Cohen, D. J., Volkmar, F. R., Heninger, G. R. & Price, L. H. (1996). A double-blind, placebo-controlled study of fluvoxamine in adults with autistic disorder. *Archives of General Psychiatry, 53,* 1001–1008.

McElroy, S. L., Keck, P. E., Pope, H. G. & Hudson, J. I. (1989). Pharmacological treatment of kleptomania and bulimia nervosa. *Journal of Clinical Psychopharmacology, 9,* 358–360.

McEwen, B. S. (1997). Possible mechanisms for atrophy of the human hippocampus. *Molecular Psychiatry, 2,* 255–262.

McEwen, B. S., Albeck, D., Cameron, H., Chao, H. M., Gould, E., Hastings, N., Kuroda, Y., Luine, V., Magarinos, A. M. & McKittrick, C. R. (1995). Stress and the brain: A paradoxical role for adrenal steroids. *Vitamins and Hormones, 51,* 371–402.

McGee, R., Williams, S. & Silva, P. A. (1984). Behavioral and developmental characteristics of aggressive, hyperactive and aggressive-hyperactive boys. *Journal of the American Academy of Child Psychiatry, 23,* 270–279.

McGue, M. (1994). Genes, Environment & the Etiology of Alcoholism. National Institute on Alcohol Abuse and Alcoholism, Research Monograph 26. Washington, DC: U.S. Government Printing Office, 1–40.

McGue, M., Pickens, R. W. & Svikis, D. S. (1992). Sex and age effects on the inheritance of alcohol problems: A twin study. *Journal of Abnormal Psychology, 101,* 3–17.

McGuire, M. T. & Raleigh, M. J. (1987). Serotonin, social behavior, and aggression in vervet monkeys. In B. Oliver, J. Mos & P. F. Brain (Eds.), *Ethopharmacology of agonistic behavior in animals and humans.* Boston: Martinus Nijhoff, 207–222.

McGuire, S., Neiderhiser, J. M., Reiss, D., Hetherington, J. E. M. & Plomin, R. (1994). Genetic and environmental influences on perceptions of self-worth and competence in adolescence: A study of twins, full siblings, and stepsiblings. *Child Development, 65,* 785–799.

McIntosh, D. E., Mulkins, R. S. & Dean, R. S. (1995). Utilization of maternal perinatal risk indicators in the differential diagnosis of ADHD and UADD children. *International Journal of Neuroscience, 81,* 35–46.

McKenna, T. & Pickens, R. (1981). Alcoholic children of alcoholics. *Journal of Studies on Alcohol, 42,* 1021–1029.

McKenzie, C. (1995). A study of serial murder.

International Journal of Offender Therapy and Comparative Criminology, 39, 3–10.

McLoyd, V .C. (1990). The impact of economic hardship on black families and children: psychological distress, parenting, and socio-economic development. *Child Development, 61,* 311–346.

McNeil, T. F., Cantor-Graae, E., Torrey, E. F., Sjostrom, K., Bowler, A., Taylor, E., Rawlings, R. & Higgins, E. S. (1994). Obstetric complications in histories of monozygotic twins discordant and concordant for schizophrenia. *Acta Psychiatrica Scandinavia, 89,* 196–204.

Mealey, L. (1995). The sociobiology of sociopathy: An integrated evolutionary model. *Behavioral & Brain Sciences, 18,* 523–599.

Meaney, M. J. & Aitken, D. H. (1985). The effects of early postnatal handling on hippocampal glucocorticoid receptor concentrations: Temporal parameters. *Brain Research, 354,* 301–304.

Meaney, M. J., Mitchell, J. B., Aitken, D. H., Bhatnagar, S., Bodnoff, S. R., Iny, L. J. & Sarrieau, A. (1991). The effects of neonatal handling on the development of the adrenocortical response to stress: Implications for neuropathology and cognitive deficits in later life. *Psychoneuroendocrinology, 16,* 85–103.

Mednick, S. A. & Christiansen, K. (1977). *Biological bases of criminal behavior.* New York: Gardner Press.

Mednick, S. A., Gabrielli, W. F. & Hutchings, B. (1984). Genetic influences in criminal convictions: Evidence from an adoption cohort. *Science, 224,* 891–894.

Mednick, S. A., Gabrielli, W. F. & Hutchings, B. (1987). Genetic factors in the etiology of criminal behavior. In S. A. Mednick, T. E. Moffitt & S. A. Stack (Eds.), *The causes of crime: New biological approaches.* New York: Cambridge University Press, 74–91.

Mednick, S. A. & Kandel, E. (1987). Genetic and perinetal factors in violence. In S. A. Mednick & T. Moffitt (Eds.), *Biological contributions to crime causation.* Dordrecht, Holland: Martinus Nijhoff, 121–134.

Mednick, S. A. & Kandel, E. S. (1988). Congenital determinants of violence. *Bulletin of the American Academy of Psychiatry and Law, 16,* 101–109.

Mednick, S. A., Moffitt, T. E. & Stack, S. A. (Eds.) (1988). *The causes of crime: New biological approaches.* New York: Cambridge University Press.

Meehl, P. (1954). *Clinical versus statistical prediction: A theoretical analysis and review of the evidence.* Minneapolis: University of Minnesota Press.

Megargee, E. I. (1966). Undercontrolled and overcontrolled personality types in extreme antisocial aggression. *Psychological Monographs, 80,* No. 611.

Megargee, E. I. (1972). *The California Psychological Inventory handbook.* San Francisco: Jossey-Bass.

Megargee, E. I. (1982). Psychological correlates and determinants of criminal behavior. In M. Wolfgang & M. Weiner (Eds.), *Criminal Violence.* Newburg Park, CA: Sage.

Megargee, E. I. (1995). Assessment research in correctional settings: Methodological issues and practical problems. *Psychological Assessment, 7,* 359–366.

Mehlman, P. T., Higley, J. D., Faucher, I., Lilly, A. A., Taub, D. M., Vickers, J., Suomi, S. J. & Linnoila, M. (1994). Low CSF 5-HIAA concentrations and severe aggression and impaired impulse control in nonhuman primates. *American Journal of Psychiatry, 151,* 1485–1491.

Meier, R. F. & Johnson, W. T. (1977). Deterrence as social control: The legal and extra-legal production of conformity. *American Sociological Review, 42,* 292–304.

Mellow, A., Solano-Lopez, C. & Davis, S. (1993). Sodium valproate in the treatment of behavioral disturbance in dementia. *Journal of Geriatric Psychiatry and Neurology, 6,* 205–209.

Meltzer, H. M. & Arora, R. C. (1988). Genetic control of serotonin uptake in blood platelets: A twin study. *Psychiatry Research 24,* 263–269.

Meltzer, L. J., Roditi, B. N. & Fenton, T. (1986). Cognitive and learning profiles of delinquent and learning-disabled adolescents. *Adolescence, 83,* 581–591.

Menard, S. & Morse, B. J. (1984). A structuralist critique of the IQ-delinquency hypothesis: Theory and evidence. *American Journal of Sociology, 89,* 1347–1378.

Merikangas, J. R. (1981). *Brain-behavior relationships.* Lexington, MA: Lexington Books.

Merikangas, K. R. (1990). The genetic epidemiology of alcoholism. *Psychology in Medicine, 20,* 11–22.

Merton, R. K. (1938). Social structures and

anomie. *American Sociological Review, 3,* 672-682.

Mezzich, A., Tarter, R., Kirisci, L., Clark, D., Bukstein, O. & Martin, C. (1993). Subtypes of early age onset alcoholism. *Alcoholism in Clinical and Experimental Research, 17,* 767–770.

Mezzich, A., Tarter, R., Moss, H. & Hsieh, Y. *Substance abuse vulnerability in three groups of prepubertal children of substance abusing fathers.* Unpublished manuscript, University of Pittsburgh, Department of Psychiatry.

Michals, M. L., Crismor, M. L., Roberts, S. & Childs, A. (1993). Clozapine response and adverse effects in nine brain-injured patients. *Journal of Clinical Psychopharmacology, 13,* 198–203.

Michard-Vanhee, C. (1988). Aggressive behavior induced in female mice by an early single dose of testosterone is genotype dependent. *Behavior Genetics, 18,* 1–12.

Michelson, J. B., Robin, H. S. & Nozik, R. A. (1986). Nonocular manifestations of parental drug abuse. *Survey of Ophthalmology, 30,* 314–320.

Miczek, K. A., Haney, M., Tidey, J., Jeffrey, L., & Weerts, E. (1994). The neurochemistry and pharmacotherapeutics of aggression and violence. In A. J. Reis, J. Miczek & J. A. Roth (Eds.), *Understanding and preventing violence.* Washington, DC: National Academy Press.

Miczek K. A., Mirsky, A. F., Carey, G., DeBold, J. & Raine, A. (1994). In A. J. Reis, J. Miczek & J. A. Roth (Eds.), *Understanding and preventing violence.* Washington, DC: National Academy Press.

Milberger, S., Biederman, J., Faraone, S. V., Chen, L. & Jones, J. (1996). Is maternal smoking during pregnancy a risk factor for attention deficit hyperactivity disorder in children? *American Journal of Psychiatry, 153,* 1138–1142.

Milberger, S., Biederman, J., Faraone, S. V., Chen, L. & Jones, J. (1997). Further evidence of an association between attention-deficit/hyperactivity disorder and cigarette smoking. Findings from a high-risk sample of siblings. *American Journal of Addiction, 6,* 205–217.

Miller, B. A. (1990). The interrelationships between alcohol and drugs and family violence. In *Drugs and violence: Causes, correlates, and consequences.* Research Monograph No. 103. Rockville, MD: National Institute on Drug Abuse.

Miller, D. & Blum, K. (1996). *Overload: Attention deficit disorder and the addictive brain.* Kansas City, MO: Andrews McMeel.

Miller, J. G. (1978). *The living system.* New York: McGraw Hill.

Miller, L. (1987). Neuropsychology of the aggressive psychopath: An integrative review. *Aggressive Behavior, 13,* 119–140.

Miller, L. (1990). Major syndromes of aggressive behavior following head injury: An introduction to evaluation and treatment. *Cognitive Rehabilitation, 8,* 14–19.

Miller, L., Kramer, R., Warner, V., Wickramaratne, P. & Weissman, M. (1997). Intergenerational transmission of parental bonding among women. *Journal of the American Academy of Child and Adolescent Psychiatry, 36,* 1134–1139.

Milner, B. (1995). Aspects of human frontal lobe function. In H. Jasper, S. Riggio & P. Goldman-Rakic (Eds.), *Epilepsy and the functional anatomy of the frontal lobe.* New York: Raven Press, 67–84.

Milner, B. & Petrides, M. (Nov. 1984). Behavioural effects of frontal-lobe lesions in man. Trends in *Neurosciences,* 403–407.

Mirin, S. M., Weiss, R. D., Griffin, M. L. & Michael, J. L. (1991). Psychopathology in drug abusers and their families. *Comprehensive Psychiatry, 32,* 36–51.

Mischel, W., Shoda, Y. & Rodriguez, M. L. (1989). Delay of gratification in children. *Science, 244,* 933–938.

Mitchell, S. & Rosa, P. (1981). Boyhood behavior problems as precursors of criminality: A fifteen-year follow-up study. *Journal of Child Psychology and Psychiatry, 22,* 19–33.

Modai, I., Apter, A., Meltzer, M., Tyano, S., Walevski, A. & Jerushalmy, Z. (1989). Serotonin uptake by platelets of suicidal and aggressive adolescent psychiatric inpatients. *Neuropsychobiology, 21,* 9–13.

Moeller, F. G., Dougherty, D. M., Lane, S. D. & Cherek, D. R. (1998). Antisocial personality disorder and alcohol induced aggression. *Alcoholism: Clinical and Experimental Research, 22,* 1898–1902.

Moeller, F. G., Dougherty, D. M., Swann, A. C.,

Collins, D., Davis, C. M. & Cherek, D. R. (1996). Tryptophan depletion and aggressive responding in healthy males. *Psychopharmacology, 126,* 97–103.

Moffitt, T. E. (1993). Adolescence-limited and life-course-persistent antisocial behavior: A developmental taxonomy. *Psychological Review, 100,* 674–701.

Moffitt, T. E. (1993). The neuropsychology of conduct disorder. *Development and Psychopathology, 5,* 135–151.

Moffitt, T. E., Gabrielli, W. F., Mednick, S. A. & Schulsinger, F. (1981). Socioeconomic status, IQ, and delinquency. *Journal of Abnormal Psychology, 90,* 152–156.

Monahan, J. (1981). *The clinical prediction of violent behavior.* Washington, DC: National Institute of Mental Health.

Monahan, J. (1992). Mental disorder and violent behavior: Perceptions and evidence. *American Psychologist, 47,* 511–521.

Monahan, J. & Splane, S. (1980). Psychological approaches to criminal behavior. In E. Bittner & S. L. Messinger (Eds.), *Criminology review yearbook,* vol. 2. Newbury Park, CA: Sage, 17–47.

Money, J. (1980). *Love and love sickness.* Baltimore, MD: Johns Hopkins University Press.

Money, J., Wideling, A. Walker, P. S. & Gain, D. (1976). Combined antiandrogenic and counseling program for treatment of 46 XY and 47 XYY sex offenders. In E. J. Sachar (Ed.), *Hormones, behavior and psychopathology.* New York: Raven Press.

Monroe, R. R. (1978). *Brain dysfunction in aggressive criminals.* Lexington, MA: Lexington Books.

Mooney, G. F. & Haas, L. I. (1993). Effect of methylphenidate on brain injury-related anger. *Archives of Physical Medicine and Rehabilitation, 74,* 153–160.

Moore, M. (1995). Public health and criminal justice approaches to prevention. In M. Tonry & D. Farrington (Eds.), *Building a safer society.* Chicago: University of Chicago Press, 237–262.

Morrison, J. R. & Stewart, M. A. (1971). A family study of the hyperactive child syndrome. *Biological Psychiatry, 3,* 189–195.

Morris-Yates, A., Andrew, G., Howie, P. & Henderson, S. (1990). Twins: A test of the equal environments assumption. *Acta Psychiatrica Scandinavia, 8,* 322–326.

Morse, W. H. (1966). Intermittent reinforcement. In W. K. Honig (Ed.), *Operant behavior: Areas of research and application.* New York: Appleton-Century-Crofts, 52–108.

Morton, J. H., Additon, H., Addison, R. G., Hunt, L. & Sullivan, H. A. (1953). A clinical study of pre-menstrual tension. *American Journal of Obstetrics and Gynecology, 65,* 1182–1191.

Moruzzi, G. (1958). In R. S. Dow & G. Moruzzi (Eds.), *The physiology and psychology of the cerebellum.* Minneapolis: University of Minnesota Press.

Moss, H., Blackson,T., Martin, C. & Tarter, R. (1992). Heightened motor activity level in male offspring of substance abusing fathers: Association with temperament, behavior, and psychiatric diagnosis. *Biological Psychiatry, 32,* 1135–1147.

Moss, H. B., Yao, J. K. & Panzak, G. L. (1990). Serotonergic responsivity and behavioral dimensions in antisocial personality disorder with substance abuse. *Biological Psychiatry, 28,* 325–328.

Mott, S. H., Packer, R. J. & Soldin, S. J. (1993). Neurologic manifestations of cocaine exposure in childhood. *Pediatrics, 92,* 557–560.

Moyer, K. E. (1976). *The psychohistology of aggression.* New York: Harper.

Muehrer, P. & Koretz, D. S. (1992). Issues in preventive intervention research. *Current Directions in Psychological Sciences, 1,* 109–112.McGue, M., Pickens, R. & Svikis, D. (1992). Sex and age effects on the inheritance of alcohol problems: A twin study. *Journal of Abnormal Psychology, 101,* 3–17.

Muhlbauer, H. D. (1985). Human aggression and the role of central serotonin. *Pharmacopsychiatry, 18,* 218–221.

Mullen, P. E., Martin, J. L., Anderson, J. C., Romans, S. E. & Herbison, P. G. (1993). Childhood sexual abuse and mental health in adult life. *British Journal of Psychiatry, 163,* 721–732.

Mulvey, E. P., Arthur, M. W. & Reppucci, N. D. (1993). The prevention and treatment of juvenile delinquency: A review of the research. *Clinical Psychology Review, 13,* 133–167.

Muntaner, C., Walter, D., Nagoshi, C., Fishbein, D., Haertzen, C. A. & Jaffe, J. (1990). Self-report vs. laboratory measures of aggression as predictors of substance abuse. *Drug and Alcohol Dependence, 25,* 1–11.

Murray, H. (1938). *Explorations in personality.* New York: Oxford University Press.

Myers, W. (1995, Fall). Addictive sexual behavior. *American Journal of Psychotherapy, 49,* 473–483.

Myers, W., Burket, R. & Harris, E. (1995). Adolescent psychopathy in relation to delinquent behaviors, conduct disorder and personality disorders. *Journal of Forensic Sciences, 40,* 436–440.

Nadeau, K. G. (Ed.) (1995). *A comprehensive guide to attention deficit disorder in adults: Research, diagnosis, treatment.* New York: Brunner/Mazel.

Nagin, D. S. Farrington, D. P. & Moffitt, T. E. (1995). Life-course trajectories of different types of offenders. *Criminology, 33,* 111–139.

Nagin, D. S. & Land, K. C. (1993). Age, criminal careers, and population heterogeneity: Specification and estimation of a nonparametric, mixed poisson model. *Criminology, 31,* 327–362.

Nagy, L. M., Morgan, C. A., Southwick, S. M. & Charney, D. S. (1993). Open prospective trial of fluoxetine for posttraumatic stress disorder. *Journal of Clinical Psychopharmacology, 13,* 107–113.

Nakhai, B., Nielsen, D. & Goldman, D. (1995). Two naturally occurring amino acid substitutions in the human 5HT1A receptor: 5HT1A-22>Ser and 5HT1A-28>Val. *Biochemistry and Biophysiology Research Community, 210,* 530–536.

Nash, M. R., Hulsey, T. L., Sexton, M. D., Harralson, T. L. & Lambert, W. (1993). Perceived family environment, psychopathology, and dissociation. *Journal of Consulting and Clinical Psychology, 61,* 276–283.

Navarro, H. A., Seidler, F. J., Eylers, J. P., Baker, F. E., Dobbins, S. S., Lappi, S. E., Slotkin, T. A. (1989). Effects of prenatal nicotine exposure on development of central and peripheral cholinergic neurotransmitter systems. Evidence for cholinergic trophic influences in developing brain. *Journal of Pharmacology and Experimental Therapeutics, 251,* 894–900.

Neale, M. C. & Cardon, L. R. (1992). *Methodology for genetic studies of twins and families.* Dordrecht, Netherlands: Kluwer.

Nebert, D. W. (1997). Polymorphisms in drug-metabolizing enzymes: What is their clinical relevance and why do they exist? *American Journal of Human Genetics, 60,* 265–271.

Needleman, H. & Gatsonis, C. (1990). Low-level lead exposure and the IQ of children. *Journal of the American Medical Association, 263,* 673–678.

Needleman, H., Gunnoe, C., Leviton, A., Reed, P., Peresie, H., Maher, C. & Barrett, P. (1979). Deficits in psychologic and classroom performance of children with elevated dentine lead levels. *New England Journal of Medicine, 300,* 689–695.

Needleman, H., Schell, A., Bellinger, D., Leviton, A. & Alred, E. (1990). The long-term effects of exposure to low doses of lead in children. *New England Journal of Medicine, 322,* 83–88.

Nelson, R. J., Demas, G. E., Huang, P. L., Fishman, M. C., Dawson, V. L., Dawson, T. M. & Snyder, S. H. (1995). Behavioral abnormalities in male mice lacking neuronal nitric oxide synthase. *Nature, 378,* 383–386.

Nemeroff, C. (Ed.) (1995). *The American Psychiatric Association textbook of psychopharmacology.* Washington, DC: American Psychiatric Press.

Neppe, V. (1982). Carbamazepine in the psychiatric patient. *Lancet, II,* 334.

Nestor, P. G. (1992). Neuropsychological and clinical correlates of murder and other forms of extreme violence in a forensic psychiatric population. *Journal of Nervous and Mental Diseases, 180,* 418 423.

Newby, R. F., Fischer, M. & Roman, M. A. (1991). Parent training for families of children with ADHD. *School Psychology Review, 20,* 252–265.

Newman, J. P., Gorenstein, E. E. & Kelsey, J. E. (1983). Failure to delay gratification following septal lesions in rats: Implications for an animal model of disinhibitory psychopathology. *Personality and Individual Differences, 4,* 147–156.

Newman, J. P., Kosson, D. S. & Patterson, C. M. (1992). Delay of gratification in psychopathic and nonpsychopathic offenders. *Journal of Abnormal Psychology, 101,* 630–636.

Newman, J. P., Patterson, C. M., Howland, E. W. & Nichols, S. L. (1990). Passive avoidance in psychopaths: The effects of reward. *Personality and Individual Differences, 11,* 1101–1114.

Nicholi, A. (Ed.) (1988). *The new Harvard guide to psychiatry.* Cambridge, MA: Harvard University Press.

Nielsen, D. A., Goldman, D., Virkkunen M.,

Tokola, R., Rawlings, R. & Linnoila, M. (1994). Suicidality and 5-hydroxyindoleacetic acid concentration associated with a tryptophan hydroxylase polymorphism. *Archives of General Psychiatry, 51,* 34–38.

Nielsen, D. A., Lappalainen, J., Eggert, M., Virkkunen, M., Brown, G., Goldman, D. & Linnoila, M. (1998). Alcoholism and suicidality are linked to and associated with tryptophan hydroxylase in Finns. *Archives of General Psychiatry, 55,* 593–602.

Niskanen, P. & Achte, K.A. (1972). The course and prognoses of schizophrenic psychoses in Helsinki: A comparative study of first admissions in 1950, 1960 and 1965. Monograph of Psychiatric Clinics in Helsinki, University Central Hospital.

Noble, E. P., Blum, K., Khalsa, E., Ritchie, T., Montgomery, A., Wood, R. C., Fitch, R. J., Ozkaragoz, T., Sheridan, P. J., Anglin, M. D., Paredes, A., Treiman, L. J. & Sparkes, R. S. (1993). Allelic association of the D2 dopamine receptor gene with cocaine dependence. *Drug and Alcohol Dependence, 33,* 271–285.

Norris, J. (1988). *Sexual killers.* New York: Doubleday.

Novick, O., Ebstein, R., Umansky, R., Priel, B., Osher, Y. & Belmaker, R. H. (1995). D-4 receptor polymorphism associated with personality variation in normals. *Psychiatric Genetics, 5,* S36.

Nowicki, S., Jr. & Strickland, B. R. (1973). A locus of control scale for children. *Journal of Consulting and Clinical Psychology, 40,* 148–154.

Nunnally, J. C. (1978). *Psychometric theory* (2nd ed.). New York: McGraw-Hill.

Nurco, D. N., Blatchley, R. J., Hanlon, T. E., O'Grady, K. E. & McCarren, M. (1998). The family experiences of narcotic addicts and their subsequent parenting practices. *American Journal of Drug and Alcohol Abuse, 24,* 37–59.

Nygaard, H. A., Fuglum, E. & Elgen, K. (1992). Zuclopenthixol, melperone and haloperidol/levomepromazine in the elderly: Meta-analysis of two double-blind trials at 15 nursing homes in Norway. *Current Medical Research and Opinion, 12,* 615–622.

Nygaard, R. L. (1995, spring). The myth of punishment: Is American penology ready for the 21st century? *Regent University Law Review, 5,* 1–12.

Nygaard, R. L. (1996). Freewill, determinism, penology, and the human genome: Where's a new Leibniz when we really need him? *University of Chicago Law School Roundtable, 3,* 417–437.

Nygaard, R. L. (1996). The insanity of mental defenses and the law. *Villanova University Law Review, 41,* 951–987.

Nygaard, R. L. (1996, summer). Is prison an appropriate response to crime? *St. Louis University Law Journal, 40,* 677–697.

Nygaard, R. L. (1996). On death as punishment. *University of Pittsburg Law Review, 57,* 825–840.

Nygaard, R. L. (1996). On the philosophy of sentencing: Or, why punish? *Widener Journal of Public Law, 5,* 237–268.

Nygaard, R. L. (1997, summer). The ten commandments of behavioral genetic data and criminology. *The Judges Journal, 36,* 59.

Nyth, A.L. & Gottfries, C. G. (1990). The clinical efficacy of citalopram in treatment of emotional disturbances in dementia disorders: A Nordic multicenter study. *British Journal of Psychiatry, 157,* 894–901.

Oates, R. K., Forrest, D. & Peacock, A. (1985). Self-esteem of abused children. *Child Abuse and Neglect, 9,* 159-163.

O'Connor, P. G., Samet, J. H. & Stein, M. D. (1994). Management of hospitalized intravenous drug users: Role of the internist. *American Journal of Medicine, 96,* 551–558.

O'Connor, T. G., Deater-Deckard, K., Fulker, D., Rutter, M. & Plomin, R. (1998). Genotype-environment correlations in late childhood and early adolescence: Antisocial behavioral problems and coercive parenting. *Developmental Psychology, 34,* 970-981.

O'Connor, T. G., Reiss, D., McGuire, S. & Hetherington, E. M. (1998). Co-occurrence of depressive symptoms and antisocial behavior in adolescence: A Common genetic liability. *Journal of Abnormal Psychology, 107,* 27–37.

Offord, D., Boyle, M., Szatmari, P., Rae-Grant, N., Links, P., Cadman, D., Byles, J., Crawford, J., Blum, H., Byrne, C., Thomas, H. & Woodward, C. (1987). Ontario Child Health Study. II. Six-month prevalence of disorder rates of service utilization. *Archives of General Psychiatry, 44,* 832–836.

Ogawa, S., Lubahn, D. B., Korach, K. S. & Pfaff, D. W. (1996). Aggressive behaviors of transgenic estrogen-receptor knockout male mice. *Annals of the New York Academy of Science, 794,* 384–385.

O'Keane, V., Moloney, E., O'Neill, H., O'Connor

A., Smith, C. & Dinan, T. (1992). Blunted prolactin response to d-fenfluramine in sociopathy. Evidence for subsensitivity of central serotonergic function. *British Journal of Psychiatry, 160,* 643–646.

O'Keefe, S. & Marks, V. (1977). Lunch time gin and tonic a cause of reactive hypoglycemia. *Lancet, 1,* 1286–1288.

Olafsson, K., Jorgensen, S., Jensen, H. V., Bille, A., Arup, A. & Andersen, J. (1992). Fluvoxamine in the treatment of demented elderly patients: A double-blind, placebo-controlled study. *Acta Psychiatrica Scandinavia, 85,* 453–456.

Olds, D., Henderson, C. R., Cole, R., Eckenrode, J., Kitzman, H., Luckey, D., Pettitt, L., Sidora, K., Morris, P. & Powers, J. (1998). Long-term effects of nurse home visitation on children's criminal and antisocial behavior: 15-year follow-up of a randomized controlled trial. *Journal of the American Medical Association, 280,* 1238–1244.

Olweus, D. (1980). Financial and temperamental determinants of aggressive behavior in adolescent boys: A causal analysis. *Developmental Psychology, 16,* 644–660.

Orlebeke, J. F., Knol, D. L. & Verhulst, F. C. (1997). Increase in child behavior problems resulting from maternal smoking during pregnancy. *Archives of Environmental Health, 52,* 317–321.

Osborn, D. K. & Endsley, R. C. (1971). Emotional reactions of young children to TV violence. *Child Development, 42,* 321–331.

Ott, J. (1991). *Analysis of human genetic linkage.* Baltimore: Johns Hopkins University Press.

Palermo, G. & Knudten, R. (1994). The insanity plea in the case of a serial killer. *International Journal of Offender Therapy and Comparative Criminology, 38,* 3–16.

Pallone, N. J. (1991). *Mental disorders among prisoners.* New Brunswick, NJ: Transaction.

Pallone, N. J., & Hennessy, J. J. (1992). *Criminal behavior: A process psychology analysis.* New Brunswick, NJ: Transaction.

Pallone, N. J. & Hennessy, J. J. (1993). Tinder-box criminal violence: Neurogenic impulsivity, risk-taking, and the phenomenology of rational choice. In R. V. Clarke & M. Felson (Eds.), *Routine activity and rational choice: Advances in criminological theory.* New Brunswick, NJ: Transaction, 127–158.

Pallone, N. J. & Hennessy, J. J. (1995). *Fraud and fallible judgment: Varieties of deception in the social and behavioral sciences.* New Brunswick, NJ: Transaction.

Pallone, N. J. & Hennessy, J. J. (1996). *Tinder-box criminal aggression: Neuropsychology, phenomenology, demography.* New Brunswick, NJ: Transaction.

Pallone, N. J. & Voelbel, G. T. (1998). Limbic system dysfunction and inventoried psychopathology among incarcerated pedophiles. *Current Psychology, 17,* 57–74.

Palmer, T. (1995). Programmatic and nonprogrammatic aspects of successful intervention: New directions for research. *Crime & Delinquency, 41,* 100–131.

Palmgreen, P., Lorch, E. P., Donohew, L., Harrington, N. G., D'Silva, M. & Helm, D. (1994). Reaching at-risk populations in a mass media drug abuse prevention campaign: Sensation seeking as a targeting variable. *Drugs and Society, 8,* 29–45.

Palmstiema, T. & Wistedt, B. (1987). Staff observation aggression scale. SOAS: Presentation and evaluation. *Acta Psychiatrica Scandinavia, 76,* 657–663.

Parrott, C. A. & Strongman, K. T. (1984). Locus of control and delinquency. *Adolescence, 19,* 459–471.

Parsian, A., Todd, R. D., Devor, E. J., O'Malley, K. L., Suarez, B. K., Reich, T. & Cloninger, C. R. (1991). Alcoholism and alleles of the human D2 dopamine receptor locus. *Archives of General Psychiatry, 48,* 655–663.

Pascal, Blaise (1941). *Pensées* (F. W. Trotter, tr.). New York: Random House, 60, ¶ 168.

Passig, C., Pinto-Hamuy, T., Moreno, J. P., Rodriquez, C., Rojas, C. & Rosas, R. (1996). Persistence of the cognitive effects of early stimulation assessed with an animal model. *Reviews of Medicine in Chile, 124,* 409–416.

Paternoster, R. (1989). Decisions to participate in and desist from four types of common delinquency: Deterrence and the rational choice perspective. *Law & Society Review, 23,* 7–40.

Patterson, C. M. & Newman, J. P. (1993). Reflectivity and learning from aversive events: Toward a psychological mechanism for the syndromes of disinhibition. *Psychological Review, 100,* 716–736.

Patterson, G. R., Capaldi, D. & Bank, L. (1991). The development and treatment of childhood aggression. In D. Pepler & R. K. Rubin (Eds.), *The development and treatment of childhood aggression.* Hillsdale, NJ: Erlbaum, 139–168.

Patterson, G. R., Crosby, L. & Vuchinish, S. (1992). Predicting risk for early police arrest. *Journal of Quantititative Criminology, 8,* 335–355.

Patterson, G. R., DeBaryshe, B. D. & Ramsey, E. (1989). A developmental perspective on antisocial behavior. *American Psychologist, 44,* 329–335.

Patterson, J. F. (1988). A preliminary study of carbamazepine in the treatment of assaultive patients with dementia. *Journal of Geriatric Psychiatry and Neurology, 1,* 21–23.

Patton, J. H., Stanford, M. S. & Barratt, E. S. (1995). Factor structure of the Barratt impulsiveness scale. *Journal of Clinical Psychiatry, 51,* 768–774.

Pearson, K. (1901). Mathematical contributions to the theory of evolution, VII: On the correlation of characters not quantitatively measureable. *Philosophical Transactions of the Royal Society of London, Series A 1901, 195,* 1–47.

Pedersen, N. (1981). Twin similarity for usage of common drugs. *Progress in Clinical Biological Research, 69,* 53–59.

Pelham, W., Lang, A., Atkeson, B., Murphy, D., Gnagy, E. & Greiner, A. *Stress induced alcohol consumption in parents interacting with confederate children: Effects of child behavior, offspring psychopathology, and family history of alcohol problems.* Unpublished manuscript, University of Pittsburgh, Department of Psychiatry.

Pelham, W., Milich, R., Cummings, E., Murphy, D., Schaughency, E. & Greiner, A. (1991). Effects of background anger, provocation, and methylphenidate on emotional arousal and aggressive responding in attention-deficit hyperactivity disordered boys with and without concurrent aggressiveness. *Journal of Abnormal Child Psychology, 19,* 407–426.

Pennington, B. & Ozonoff, S. (1996). Executive functions and developmental psychopathology. *Journal of Child Psychology and Psychiatry, 37,* 51–87.

Perlman, D. & Cozby, P. C. (1983). *Social psychology.* New York: Holt, Rinehart & Winston.

Peters, S. D. (1988). Child sexual abuse and later psychological problems. In G. E. Wyatt & G. J. Powell (Eds.), *Lasting effects of child sexual abuse.* Newbury Park, CA: Sage, 101–117.

Petty, F., Davis, L. L., Kabel, D., Kramer, G. L. (1996). Serotonin dysfunction disorders: A behavioral neurochemistry perspective. *Journal of Clinical Psychiatry, 57,* 11–16.

Pham, T. M., Soderstrom, S., Henriksson, B. G. & Mohammed, A. H. (1997). Effects of neonatal stimulation on later cognitive function and hippocampal nerve growth factor. *Behavioral Brain Research, 86,* 113–120.

Phillips, T. J., Roberts, A. J. & Lessov, C. N. (1997). Behavioral sensitization to ethanol: Genetics and the effects of stress. *Pharmacology and Biochemistry of Behavior, 57,* 487–493.

Pianta, R. C. & Egeland, B. (1990). Life stress and parenting outcomes in a disadvantaged sample: Results of mother-child interaction project. *Journal of Clinical Child Psychology, 19,* 329–336.

Piazza, P. V. & Le Moal, M. L. (1996). Pathophysiological basis of vulnerability to drug abuse: Role of an interaction between stress, glucocorticoids and dopaminergic neurons. *Annual Reviews in Pharmacology and Toxicology, 36,* 359–378.

Piazza, P. V. & Le Moal, M. L. (1998). The role of stress in drug self-administration. *Trends in the Pharmacological Sciences, 19,* 67–74.

Pickens, R. W., Elmer, G. I., LaBuda, M. C. & Uhl, G. R. (1996). Research in the study of drug action and addiction. In C. R. Schuster & M. J. Kuhar (Eds.), *Pharmacological aspects of drug dependence: Towards an integrated neurobehavioral approach.* Berlin: Springer-Verlag, 3–52.

Pickens, R. W. & Svikis, D. S. (1995). Vulnerability as cause of substance abuse: An overview. In J. H. Jaffe, J. C. Anthony, C. Johanson, M. J. Kuhar, M. H. Moore & E. M. Sellers (Eds.), *Encyclopedia of drugs and alcohol.* New York: Macmillan Library Reference, 1246–1252.

Pickens, R. W., Svikis, D. S., McGue, M. & LaBuda, M. C. (1995). Common genetic mechanisms in alcohol, drug, and mental disorder comorbidity. *Drug and Alcohol Dependence, 39,* 129–138.

Pickens, R. W., Svikis, D. S., McGue, M., Lykken, D. T., Heston, L. & Clayton, P. J. (1991). Heterogeneity in the inheritance of alcoholism: A study of male and female twins. *Archives of General Psychiatry, 48,* 19–28.

Pihl, R., Peterson, J. & Finn, P. (1990). Inherited predisposition to alcoholism: Characteristics of sons of male alcoholics. *Journal of Abnormal Psychology, 99,* 291–301.

Pihl, R. O., Young, S. N., Harden, P., Plotnik, S., Chamberlain, B. & Ervin, F. R. (1995). Acute effect of altered tryptophan levels and alcohol on aggression in normal human males. *Psychopharmacology, 119,* 353–360.

Pike, A., Hetherington, E. M., Reiss, D. & Plomin, R. (1996). Using MZ differences in the search for nonshared environmental effects. *Journal of Child Psychology and Psychiatry, 37,* 695–704.

Pine, D. S., Coplan, J. D., Wasserman, G. A., Miller, L. S., Fried, J. E., Davies, M., Cooper, T. B., Greenhill, L., Shaffer, D. & Parsons, B. (1997). Neuroendocrine response to d,l-fenfluramine challenge in boys. Associations with aggressive behavior and adverse rearing. *Archives of General Psychiatry, 54,* 839–846.

Pine, D. S., Wasserman, G. A., Coplan, J., Fried, J. E., Huang, Y. Y., Kassir, S., Greenhill, L., Shaffer, D. & Parsons, B. (1996). Platelet serotonin 2A (5-HT2A) receptor characteristics and parenting factors for boys at risk for delinquency: A preliminary report. *American Journal of Psychiatry, 153,* 538–544.

Pinner, E. & Rich, C. (1988). Effects of trazodone on aggressive behavior in seven patients with organic mental disorders. *American Journal of Psychiatry, 145,* 1295–1296.

Piquero, A. & Tibbetts, S.G. (1999). The impact of pre/perinatal disturbances and disadvantaged familial environment in predicting criminal offending. *Studies on Crime and Crime Prevention, 7.*

Platt, J. J., Scura, W. & Hannon, J. R. (1973). Problem-solving thinking of youthful incarcerated heroin addicts. *Journal of Community Psychology, 1,* 278–281.

Platt, J. J., Spivack, G., Altman, N., Altman, D. & Peizer, S. B. (1974). Adolescent problem-solving thinking. *Journal of Consulting and Clinical Psychology, 42,* 787–793.

Pliszka, S. R., McCracken, J. T. & Maas, J. W. (1996). Catecholamines in attention-deficit hyperactivity disorder: Current perspectives. *Journal of the American Academy of Child and Adolescent Psychiatry, 35,* 264–272.

Plomin, R. (1990). The role of inheritance in behavior. *Science, 248,* 183–188.

Plomin, R. & Daniels D. (1987). Why are children in the same family so different from one another? *Behavioral and Brain Sciences, 10,* 1–16.

Plomin, R. & DeFries, J. C. (1983). The Colorado adoption project. *Child Development, 54,* 276–289.

Plomin, R., DeFries, J. C. & Loehlin, J. C. (1977). Genotype-environment interaction and correlation in the analysis of human behavior. *Psychological Bulletin, 84,* 309–322.

Plomin, R., DeFries, J. C., McClearn, G. E. & Rutter, M. (1997). *Behavior genetics* (3d ed.). New York: Freeman & Co.

Plomin, R., Foch, T. T. & Rowe, D. C. (1981). Bobo clown aggression in childhood: Environment, not genes. *Journal of Research in Personality, 15,* 331–342.

Plutarch (1952). *Lives.* Chicago, IL: Great Books of the Western World, § 21, ¶ 14.

Plutchik, R. & Kellerman, H. (1974). Manual of the Emotions Profile Index. Los Angeles: Western Psychological Services.

Plutchik, R. & Van Praag, H. M. (1989). The measurement of suicidality, aggresivity and impulsivity. *Progress in Neuro-psychopharmacology & Biological Psychiatry, 13,* 523–534.

Plutchik, R. & Van Praag, H. M. (1995). The nature of impulsivity: Definitions, ontology, genetics, and relations to aggression. In E. Hollander & D. Stein (Eds.), *Impulsivity and aggression.* New York: John Wiley & Sons, 7–24.

Plutchik, R., Van Praag, H. M., Conte, H. R. & Picard, S. (1989). Correlates of suicide and violence risk: I. The suicide risk measure. *Comprehensive Psychiatry, 30,* 296–302.

Poeck, K. (1969). Pathophysiology of emotional disorders associated with brain damage. In P. J. Vinken, & G. W. Bruyn (Eds.), *Handbook of clinical neurology,* vol. 3. Amsterdam: North Holland.

Pollock, P. (1995). A case of spree serial murder with suggested diagnostic opinions. *International Journal of Offender Therapy and Comparative Criminology, 39,* 258–268.

Pollock, V. E., Briere, J., Schneider, L., Knop, J., Mednick, S. A. & Goodwin, D. W. (1990). Childhood antecedents of antisocial behavior: Parental alcoholism and physical abusiveness. *American Journal of Psychiatry, 147,* 1290–1293.

Pomeroy, J. C., Sprafkin, J. & Gadow, K. D. (1988). Minor physical anomalies as a biologic marker for behavior disorders. *Journal of the*

American Academy of Child and Adolescent Psychiatry, 27, 466–473.

Pontius, A. A. (1973). Dysfunction patterns analogous to frontal lobe system and caudate nucleus syndrome in some groups of minimal brain dysfunction. *Journal of the American Medical Women's Association, 26,* 285–292.

Popova, N. K., Kulikov, A. V., Nikulina, E. M., Kozlachkova, E. Y. & Maslova, G. B. (1991). Serotonin metabolism and serotonergic receptors in Norway rats selected for low aggressiveness towards man. *Aggressive Behavior, 17,* 207–213.

Porteus, S. (1965). *Porteus maze test: Fifty years' application.* Palo Alto, CA: Pacific Books.

Posner, M. I. & Peterson, S. E. (1990). The attention system of the human brain. *Annual Review of Neuroscience, 13,* 25–42.

Post, R. M. (1992). Transduction of psychosocial stress into the neurobiology of recurrent affective disorder. *American Journal of Psychiatry, 149,* 999–1010.

Potts, R., Huston, A. C. & Wright, J. C. (1986). The effects of television form and violent content on boys' attention and social behavior. *Journal of Experimental Child Psychology, 41,* 1–17.

Power, C. & Estaugh, V. (1990). The role of family formation and dissolution in shaping drinking behaviour in early adulthood. *British Journal on Addiction, 85,* 521–530.

Prentice, N. M. & Kelly, F. J. (1963). Intelligence and delinquency: A reconsideration. *Journal of Social Psychology, 60,* 327–337.

Prentky, R., Cohen, M. & Seghorn, T. (1985). Development of a rational taxonomy for the classification of rapists: The Massachusetts Treatment Center system. *Bulletin of the American Academy of Psychiatry and Law, 13,* 39–70.

Pribor, E. F. & Dinwiddie, S. H. (1992). Psychiatric correlates of incest in childhood. *American Journal of Psychiatry, 149,* 52–56.

Price, R. H., Cowen, E. L., Lorion, R. P. & Ramos-McKay, J. (Eds.) (1988). *Fourteen ounces of prevention: A casebook for practitioners.* Washington, DC: American Psychological Association.

Pritchard, J. D. (1835). *Treatise on insanity.* London: Sherwood, Gilbert & Piper.

Pulkkinen, L. (1983). Search for alternatives to aggression in Finland. In A. P. Goldstein & M. Segal (Eds.), Aggression in global perspective. Elmsford, NY: Pergamon, 104–144.

Rabinowitz, J., Avnon, M. & Rosenberg, V. (1996). Effect of clozapine on physical and verbal aggression. *Schizophrenia Research, 22,* 249–255.

Rachlin, H. & Green, L. (1972). Commitment, choice and self-control. *Journal of the Experimental Analysis of Behavior, 17,* 15–22.

Raine, A. (1993). *The psychopathology of crime: Criminal behavior as a clinical disorder.* San Diego, CA: Academic Press.

Raine, A., Bauchsbaum, M., Stanley, J., Lottenberg, S., Abel, M. & Stoddard, J. (1994). Selective reductions in prefrontal glucose metabolism in murderers. *Biological Psychiatry, 36,* 368–373.

Raine, A., Brennan, P. & Farrington, D. P. (1993). Biosocial bases of violence: Conceptual and theoretical issues. In A. Raine, P. Brennan, D. P. Farrington & S. A. Mednick (Eds.), *Biosocial bases of violence.* New York: Plenum Press, 1–20.

Raine, A., Brennan, P., Farrington, D. P. & Mednick, S. A. (1997). *Biosocial bases of violence.* New York: Plenum Press.

Raine, A., Brennan, P. & Mednick, S. A. (1994). Birth complications combined with early maternal rejection at age 1 year predispose to violent crime at age 18 years. *Archives of General Psychiatry, 51,* 984–988.

Raine, A., Roger, D. & Venables, P. H. (1982). Locus of control and socialization. *Journal of Research and Personality, 16,* 147–156.

Raine E. & Venables, P. H. (1988). Enhanced P3 evoked potentials and psychopathy. *International Journal of Psychophysiology, 8,* 1–16.

Raleigh, M. J., McGuire, M. T., Brammer, G. L., Pollack, D. B. & Yuwiler, A. (1991). Serotonergic mechanisms promote dominance acquisition in adult male vervet monkeys. *Brain Research, 559,* 181–190.

Raleigh, M. J., McGuire, M. T., Brammer, G. L. & Yuwiler, A. (1984). Social and environmental influences on blood serotonin concentrations in monkeys. *Archives of General Psychiatry, 41,* 405–410.

Ramboz, S., Saudou, F., Amara, D. A., Belzung, C., Segu, L., Misslin, R., Buhot, M. C. & Hen, R. (1996). 5-HT1B receptor knock out—behavioral consequences. *Behavioral Brain Research, 73,* 305–312.

Randrup, A. & Scheel-Kruger, J. (1966). Diethyldithiocarbamate and sterotyped behavior. *Journal of Pharm Pharmacol, 18,* 752.

Ranen, N. G., Lipsey, J. R., Treisman, G. & Ross, C. A. (1996). Setraline in the treatment of severe aggressiveness in Huntington's disease. *Journal of Neuropsychiatry and Clinical Neuroscience, 8,* 338–340.

Rantakallio, P., Laara, E., Isohanni, M. & Moilanen, I. (1992). Maternal smoking during pregnancy and delinquency of the offspring: An association without causation? *International Journal of Epidemiology, 21,* 1106–1113.

Ranen, N., Lipsey, J., Treisman, G., et al. (1996). Semaline in the treatment of severe aggressiveness in Huntington's disease. *Journal of Neuropsychiatry and Clinical Neuroscience, 8,* 338–340.

Rantakallio, P., Laara, E., Isohanni, M. & Moilanen, I. (1992). Maternal smoking during pregnancy and delinquency of the offspring: An association without causation? *International Journal of Epidemiology, 21,* 1106–1113.

Rapoport, J. L. (1989). The biology of obsessions and compulsions. *Scientific American, 260,* 83–89.

Ratey, J. J. (Ed.) (1995). *Neuropsychiatry of personality disorders.* Malden, MA: Blackwell.

Ratey, J. & Gordon, A. (1993). The psychopharmacology of aggression: Toward a new day. *Psychopharmacology Bulletin, 29,* 65–73.

Ratey, J., Greenberg, M. S. & Lindem, K. J. (1991). Combination of treatments for attention deficit hyperactivity disorder in adults. *Journal of Nervous and Mental Disorders, 179,* 699–701.

Ratey, J. J., Leveroni, C., Kilmer, D., Gutheil, C. & Swartz, B. (1993). The effects of clozapine on severely aggressive psychiatric inpatients on a difficult to manage unit of a state hospital. *Journal of Clinical Psychiatry, 54,* 1–6.

Ratey, J. J., Mikkelsen, E. J., Smith, G. B., Upadhyaya, A., Zuckerman, S., Martell, D. & Busnell, S. (1986). Beta blockers in the severely and profoundly mentally retarded. *Journal of Clinical Psychopharmacology, 6,* 103–107.

Ratey, J. J., Sorgi, P., O'Driscoll, G. A., Sands, S., Daehler, M. L., Fletcher, J. R., Kadish, W., Spruiell, G., Polakoff, S., Lindem, K. L., Bemporad, J. R., Richardson, L. & Rosenfeld, B. (1992). Nadolol to treat aggression and psychiatric symptomatology in chronic psychiatric inpatients: A double-blind, placebo-controlled study. *Journal of Clinical Psychiatry, 53,* 41–46.

Ratey, J. J., Sovner, R., Parks, A. & Rogentina, K. (1991). Buspirone treatment of aggression and anxiety in mentally retarded patients: A multiple-baseline, placebo lead-in study. *Journal of Clinical Psychiatry, 52,* 159–162.

Reckless, W. C. (1967). *The crime problem.* New York: Appleton-Century-Crofts. (from ch. 10)

Reeves, A. G. & Plum, F. (1969). Hyperphagia, rage, and dementia accompanying a ventromedial hypothalmic neoplasm. *Archives of Neurology, 20,* 616–624.

Regier, D. A., Farmer, M. E., Rae, D. S., Locke, B. Z., Keith, S. J., Judd, L. L. & Goodwin, F. K. (1990). Comorbidity of mental disorders with alcohol and other drug abuse. *Journal of the American Medical Association, 264,* 2511–2518.

Reich, J. (1986). The relationship between early life events and DSM-III personality disorders. *Hillside Journal of Clinical Psychiatry, 8,* 164–173.

Reich, T., Cloninger, C. R., Lewis, C. & Rice, J. (1981). Some recent findings in the study of genotype-environment interaction in alcoholism. National Institute on Alcohol Abuse and Alcoholism, Research Monograph 5. Washington, DC: U.S. Government Printing Office, 145–165.

Reich, T., Rice, J., Cloninger, C. R., Wette, R. & James, J. (1979). The use of multiple thresholds and segregation analysis in analyzing the phenotypic heterogeneity of multifactorial traits. *Annals of Human Genetics, 42,* 371–389.

Reich, W. (1974). *The impulsive character and other writings.* New York: Viking.

Reid, A. H., Ballinger, B. R., Heather, B. B. & Melvin, S. J. (1984). The natural history of behavioural symptoms among severely and profoundly mentally retarded patients. *British Journal of Psychiatry, 145,* 289–293.

Reid, A. H., Naylor, G. J. & Kay, D. S. (1981). A double-blind, placebo controlled, crossover trial of carbamazepine in overactive, severely mentally handicapped patients. *Psychological Medicine, 11,* 109–113.

Reid, J. B. & Patterson, G. R. (1989). The development of antisocial behavior patterns in childhood and adolescence. *European Journal of Personality, 3,* 107–109.

Reid, W. (1985). The antisocial personality: A review. *Hospital and Community Psychiatry, 36,* 831–837.

Reilly, P. M., Clark, H. W., Shopshire, M. S., Lewis, E. W. & Sorensen, D. J. (1994). Anger management and temper control: Critical components of posttraumatic stress disorder and substance abuse treatment. *Journal of Psychoactive Drugs, 26,* 401–407.

Reis, D. J. (1974). Central neurotransmitters in aggression. R*esearch Publications of the Association for Research in Nervous and Mental Diseases, 52,* 119–148.

Reisberg, B., Borenstein, J., Salob, S. P., Ferris, S. H., Franssen, E. & Georgotas, A. (1987). Behavioral symptoms in Alzheimer's disease: Phenomenology and treatment. *Journal of Clinical Psychiatry, 48,* 9–15.

Reiss, A. J., Jr. (1951). Delinquency as the failure of personal and social controls. *American Sociological Review, 16,* 196–207.

Reiss, A. J., Miczek, K. A. & Roth, J. A. (Eds.) (1994). *Understanding and preventing violence,* vol. 2. *Biobehavioral influences.* Washington, DC: National Academy Press.

Reiss, A. J., Jr. & Roth, J. A. (Eds.) (1993). *Understanding and preventing violence.* Washington, DC: National Academy Press.

Reiss, D., Hetherington, E. M., Plomin, R., Howe, G. W., Simmens, S. J., Henderson, S. H., O'Connor, T. J., Bussell, D. A., Anderson, E. R. & Law, T. (1995). Genetic questions for environmental studies: Differential parenting and psychopathology in adolescence. *Archives of General Psychiatry, 52,* 925–936.

Reiss, D., Plomin, R. & Hetherington, M. (1991). Genetics and psychiatry: An unheralded window on the environment. *American Journal of Psychiatry, 148,* 283–291.

Reist, C., Kaufman, C. & Haler, R. (1989). A controlled trial of desipramine in 18 men with PTSD. *American Journal of Psychiatry, 146,* 513–516.

Ressler, R. (1985). Violent crimes. *FBI Law Enforcement Bulletin, 54,* 1–31.

Ressler, R., Burgess, A. & Douglas, J. (1988). *Sexual homicide.* Lexington, MA: Lexington Books.

Rice, M. E. (1997). Violent offender research and implications for the criminal justice system. *American Psychologist, 52,* 414–423.

Richardson, D. R., Vandenberg, R. J. & Humphries, S. A. (1986). Effect of power to harm on retaliatory aggression among males and females. *Journal of Research in Personality, 20,* 402–419.

Richardson, W. (1997). *The link between ADD & addiction.* Colorado Springs, CO: Piñon Press.

Rickels, K., Freeman, E. & Sondheimer, S. (1989). Buspirone in the treatment of premenstrual syndrome. *Lancet, 1(8641),* 777.

Ridenour, T. A. & Heath, A. C. (in press). A note on issues in meta-analysis for behavioral genetic studies of non-randomly ascertained samples. *Behavior Genetics.*

Rietschel, M., Nothen, M. M., Lannfelt, L., Sokoloff, P., Schwartz, J. C., Lanczik, M., Fritze, J., Cichon, S., Fimmers, R. & Korner, J. (1993). A serine to glycine substitution at position 9 in the extracellular N-terminal part of the doapmine D3 receptor protein: No role in the genetic predisposition to bipolar affect disorder. *Psychiatry Research, 46,* 253–259.

Riley, W. T., Treiber, F. A. & Woods, M. G. (1989). Anger and hostility in depression. *Journal of Nervous and Mental Diseases, 177,* 668–674.

Risch, S. C. (1997). Recent advances in depression research: From stress to molecular biology and brain imaging. *Journal of Clinical Psychiatry, 58,* 3–6.

Ritrovato, C. A., Weber, S. S. & Dufresne, R. L. (1989). Nadolol in the treatment of aggressive behavior associated with schizophrenia. *Clinical Pharmacy, 8,* 132–135.

Robbins, L. E. (1995). The epidemiology of aggression. In E. Hollander & D. Stein (Eds.), *Impulsivity and aggression.* New York: John Wiley & Sons, 43–58.

Roberts, A. H. (1979). *Severe accidental head injury. An assessment of long-term prognosis.* London: The Macmillan Press.

Robins, L. N. (1966). *Deviant children grown up: A sociological and psychiatric study of sociopathic personality.* Baltimore: Williams & Wilkins.

Robins, L. N. (1986). The consequence of conduct disorder in girls. In D. Olweus, J. Block & M. Radke-Yarrow (Eds.), *Development of antisocial and prosocial behavior: Research, theories, and issues.* Orlando, FL: Academic Press, 82–414.

Robins, L. N. (1991). Conduct disorder. *Journal of Child Psychology and Psychiatry, 32,* 193–212.

Robins, L. N., Helzer, J. E., Croughan, J. & Ratcliff, K. (1981). National Institute of Mental Health diagnostic interview schedule: Its history, characteristics and validity. *Archives of General Psychiatry, 38,* 381–389.

Robins, L. N., Helzer, J., Weissman, M. N., Orvascel, H, Gruenberg, E., Burke, J. D. &

Reiger, D. A. (1984). Lifetime prevalence of specific psychiatric disorders in three sites. *Archives of General Psychiatry, 41,* 949–958.

Robins, L. N. & Rutter, M. (1990). *Straight and devious pathways from childhood to adulthood.* New York: Cambridge University Press.

Robins, L. N., Tipp, J. & Przybeck, T. R. (1991). Antisocial personality. In L. N. Robins & D. A. Regier (Eds.), *Psychiatric disorders in America: The epidemiologic catchment area study.* New York: The Free Press, 258–290.

Robinson, M. B. (1998). The theoretical development of crime prevention through environmental design. In W. Laufer & F. Adler (Eds.), *Advances in criminological theory,* vol. 8. New Brunswick, NJ: Transaction.

Roe, A. (1944). The adult adjustment of children of alcoholic parents raised in foster homes. *Journal of Studies on Alcohol, 5,* 378–393.

Roeder, F. D. (1966). Stereotactic lesions of the tuber cinerium in sexual deviation. *Confinia Neurologica, 27,* 162–163.

Rogeness, G. A., Hernandez, J. M., Macedo, C. A., Mitchell, E. L., Amrung, S. A. & Harris, W. R. (1984). Clinical characteristics of emotionally disturbed boys with very low activities of dopamine ß-hydroxylase. *Journal of the American Academy of Child and Adolescent Psychiatry, 23,* 203–208.

Rogeness, G. A., Hernandez, J. M., Macedo, C. A., Amrung, S. A. & Hoppe, S. K. (1986). Near-zero plasma dopamine-b-hydroxylase and conduct disorder in emotionally disturbed boys. *Journal of the American Academy of Child Psychiatry, 25,* 521–527.

Rogeness, G. A., Maas, J. W., Javors, M. A., Macedo, C. A., Fischer, C. & Harris, W. R. (1989). Attention deficit disorder symptoms and urine catecholamines. *Psychiatry Research, 27,* 241–251.

Rosanoff, A. J., Handy, L. M. & Plesset, I. R. (1941). The etiology of child behavior difficulties, juvenile delinquency and adult criminality with special reference to their occurrence in twins. State of California Department of Institutions Psychiatric Monographs, Serial No. 187.

Rose, R. J. (1988). Genetic and environmental variance in content dimensions of the MMPI. *Journal of Personality and Social Psychology, 55,* 302–311.

Rosenbaum, A. & Hoge, S. (1989). Head injury and marital aggression. *American Journal of Psychiatry, 146,* 1048–1051.

Rosenbaum, A. & O'Leary, K. D. (1981). Children: The unintended victims of mental violence. *American Journal of Orthopsychiatry, 51,* 692–699.

Rosenbaum, J. F., Fava, M., Nierenberg, A. A. & Sachs, G. (1995). Treatment resistant mood disorders. In G. Gabbard (Ed.), *Treatment of psychiatric disorders: The DSM-IV edition.* Washington, DC: American Pychiatric Press, 1275–1328.

Rosenberg, M. & Mercy, J. (1986). Homicide: Epidemiologic analysis at the national level. *Bulletin of the New York Academy of Medicine 62,* 376–399.

Rosenfeld, R. & Decker, S. (1993). Where public health and law enforcement meet: Monitoring and preventing youth violence. *American Journal of Police 12,* 11–57.

Rosenfield, A., Marne, D., Rochat, R., Shelton, J. & Hatcher, R. A. (1983). The Food and Drug Administration and medroxyprogesterone acetate: What are the issues? *Journal of the American Medical Association, 249,* 2922–2928.

Rosman, J. & Resnick, P. (1989). Sexual attraction to corpses: A psychiatric review of necrophilia. *Bulletin of the American Academy of Psychiatry Law, 17,* 153–161.

Ross, R. R. (1980). *Socio-cognitive development in the offender: An external evaluation of the UVIC program at Matsgui Penitentiary.* Ottawa, Canada: Report of the Office of the Solicitor-General.

Ross, R. R. (1992). *Time to think: A cognitive model of delinquency prevention and offender rehabilitation summary.* Ottawa, Canada: University of Ottawa Research Press.

Ross, R. R. & Fabiano, E. A. (1985). *Time to think: A cognitive model of delinquency prevention and offender rehabilitation.* Johnson, TN: Institute of Social Sciences and Arts.

Ross, R. R., Fabiano, E. A. & Ross, R. D. (1988). (Re)Habilitation through education: A cognitive model for corrections. *Journal of Correctional Education, 39,* 44–47.

Rotenberg, M. (1974). Conceptual and methodological notes on affective and cognitive role taking (sympathy and empathy): An illustrative experiment with delinquent and nondelinquent boys. *The Journal of Genetic Psychology, 125,* 177–185.

Rotter, J. B. (1954). Social learning and clinical psychology. Englewood Cliffs, NJ: Prentice-Hall.

Rotter, J. B. (1966). Generalized expectancies for internal versus external control of reinforcement. *Psychological Monographs 80,* No. 609.

Rotter, M. & Goodman, W. (1993). The relationship between insight and control in obsessive-compulsive disorder: Implications for the insanity defense. *Bulletin of the American Academy of Psychiatry Law, 21,* 245–252.

Roughton, E. C., Schneider, M. L., Bromley, L. J. & Coe, C. L. (1998). Maternal endocrine activation during pregnancy alters neurobehavioral state in primate infants. *American Journal of Occupational Therapy, 52,* 90–98.

Rounsaville, B. J., Kosten, T. R., Weissman, M. M., Prusoff, B., Pauls, D., Anton, S. F. & Merikangas, K. (1991). Psychiatric disorders in relatives of probands with opiate addiction. *Archives of General Psychiatry, 48,* 33–42.

Rowe, D. C. (1983). Biometrical genetic models of self-reported delinquent behavior: A twin study. *Behavior Genetics, 13,* 473–489.

Rowe, D. C. (1985). Sibling interaction and self-reported delinquent behavior: A study of 265 twin pairs. *Criminology, 23,* 223–241.

Rowe, D. C. (1986). Genetic and environmental components of antisocial behaivor: A study of 265 twin pairs. *Criminology, 24,* 513–532.

Rowe, D. C. & Osgood, D. W. (1984). Heredity and sociological theories of delinquency: A reconsideration. *American Sociology Review, 49,* 526–540.

Rowe, D. & Plomin, R. (1977). Temperament in early childhood. *Journal of Personality Assessment, 41,* 150–156.

Rowland, N. E. & Carlton, J. (1986). Neurobiology of an anorectic drug: fenfluramine. *Progress in Neurobiology, 27,* 13–62.

Roy, A., Virkkunen, M., Guthrie, S., Poland, R. & Linnoila, M. (1986). Monamines, glucose metabolism, suicidal and aggressive behaviors. *Psychopharmacology Bulletin, 22,* 661–665.

Roy, A., Virkkunen, M. & Linnoila, M. (1987). Reduced central serotonin turnover in a subgroup of alcoholics. *Progress in Neuropsychopharmacology and Biological Psychiatry, 11,* 173–177.

Royal Commission on Capital Punishment (1953). 1949–1953 report. Presented to Parliament by command of Her Majesty, September 1953, Her Majesty's Stationery Office. OCLC: 15113131.

Rushton, J. P., Fulker, D. W., Neale, M. C., Nias, N. K. B. & Eysenck, H. J. (1986). Altruism and aggression: The heritability of individual differences. *Journal of Personality and Social Psychology, 50,* 1192–1198.

Russell, G. C., Barratt, E. S., Deaton, J. M. & Taylor, R. R. (1968). Evoked responses in the putamen and globus pallidus following stimulation of the basolateral amygdala. *Brain Research, 7,* 459–462.

Rutter, M. (1980). *Changing youth in a changing society.* Cambridge, MA: Harvard University Press.

Rutter, M. (1997). Nature-nurture integration: The example of antisocial behavior. *American Psychologist, 52,* 390–398.

Rutter, M. & Giller, H. (1983). *Juvenile delinquency: Trends and perspectives.* New York: Guilford Press.

Ryan, N. D. (1998). Psychoneuroendocrinology of children and adolescents. *Psychiatric Clinics of North America, 21,* 435–441.

Rydelius, P. A. (1983). Alcohol-abusing teenage boys: Testing a hypothesis on the relationship between alcohol abuse and social background factors, criminality and personality in teenage boys. *Acta Psychiatrica Scandinavia, 68,* 368–380.

Rydelius, P. A. (1983). Alcohol-abusing teenage boys: Testing a hypothesis on alcohol abuse and personality factors using a personality inventory. *Acta Psychiatrica Scandinavia, 68,* 381–385.

Salzman, C. (1988). Use of benzodiazepines to control disruptive behavior in inpatients. *Journal of Clinical Psychiatry, 49,* 77–87.

Salzman, C., Wolfson, A. N., Schatzberg, A., Looper, J., Henke, R., Albanese, M., Schwartz, J. & Miyawaki, E. (1995). Effect of fluoxetine on anger in symptomatic volunteers with borderline personality disorder. *Journal of Clinical Psychopharmacology, 15,* 23–29.

Sameroff, A. J. (1991). Transactional risk factors and prevention. In J. A. Steinberg & M. M. Silverman (Eds.), *Preventing mental disorders.* Rockville, MD: U.S. Department of Health and Human Services, 74–89.

Sampson, R. J. & Laub, J. H. (1993). *Crime in the making: Pathways and turning points through life.* Cambridge, MA: Harvard University Press.

Sampson, R. J. & Lauritsen, J. (1994). In A. J. Reiss, Jr. & J. Roth (Eds.), *Understanding and preventing violence: Social influences.* Washington, DC: National Academy Press, 1–114.

Sampson, R. J., Raudenbush, S. W. & Earls, F. (1997). Neighborhoods and violent crime: A multilevel study of collective efficacy. *Science, 277,* 918–924.

Sano, K. (1962). Sedative neurosurgery: With special reference to posterior-medial hypothalamotomy. *Neurol Medico-Chirg, 4,* 112–142.

Santilla, P. & Haapasalo, J. (1997). Neurological and psychological risk factors among young homicidal, violent, and non-violent offenders in Finland. *Homicide, 1,* 1–20.

Sapolsky, R. M. (1989). Hypercortisolism among socially subordinate wild baboons originates at the CNS level. *Archives of General Psychiatry, 46,* 1047–1051.

Sapolsky, R. M. (1996). Why stress is bad for your brain. *Science, 273,* 749–750.

Sapolsky, R. M. & Mott, G. E. (1987). Social subordinance in wild baboons is associated with suppressed high density lipoprotein-cholesterol concentrations: The possible role of chronic social stress. *Endocrinology, 121,* 1605–1610.

Satterfield, J., Hope, C. & Schell, A. (1982). A prospective study of delinquency in 110 adolescent boys with attention deficit disorder and 88 normal adolescent boys. *American Journal of Psychiatry, 139,* 795–798.

Satterfield, J. H. & Schell, A. (1997). A prospective study of hyperactive boys with conduct problems and normal boys: Adolescent and adult criminality. *Journal of the American Academy of Child and Adolescent Psychiatry, 36,* 1726–1735.

Satterfield, J. H., Swanson, J., Schell, A. M. & Lee, F. (1994). Prediction of antisocial behavior in attention-deficit hyperactivity disorder boys from aggression deficit scores. *Journal of the American Academy of Child and Adolescent Psychiatry, 33,* 185–190.

Saudou, F., Amara, D. A., Dierich, A., LeMeur, M., Ramboz, S., Segu, L., Buhot, M. C. & Hen, R. (1994). Enhanced aggressive behavior in mice lacking 5-HT1B receptor. *Science, 265,* 1875–1878.

Saunders, B. E., Villeponteaux, L. A., Lipovsky, J. A., Kilpatrick, D. G. & Veronen, L. J. (1992). Child sexual assault as a risk factor for mental disorders among women: A community survey. *Journal of Interpersonal Violence, 7,* 189–204.

Scarr, S. (1966). The origins of individual differences in adjective check list scores. *Journal of Consulting Psychology, 30,* 354–357.

Schachter, S. C. (1995). Review of the mechanisms of action of antiepileptic drugs. *Central Nervous System Drugs, 4,* 469–477.

Schalling, D., Åsberg, M., Edman, G. & Oreland, L. (1987). Markers for vulnerability to psychopathology—Temperament traits associated with platelet MAO activity associated with impulsivity and aggressivity. *Acta Psychiatrica Scandinavia, 76,* 172–182.

Scheibel, A. B. (1991). Are complex partial seizures a sequel of temporal lobe dysgenesis? In D. B. Smith, D. M. Treiman & M. R. Trimble (Eds.), *Advances in Neurology,* vol. 55. New York: Raven.

Schmahmann, J. D. (1991). An emerging concept: The cerebellar contribution to higher function. *Archives of Neurology, 48,* 1178–1187.

Schmidt, L. A. & Fox, N. A. (1994). Patterns of cortical electrophysiology and autonomic activity in adults' shyness and sociability. *Biological Psychology, 38,* 183–198.

Schmidt, L. A., Fox, N. A., Rubin, K. H., Sternberg, E. M., Gold, P. W., Smith, C. C. & Schulkin, J. (1997). Behavioral and neuroendocrine responses in shy children. *Developmental Psychobiology, 30,* 127–140.

Schneider, J. & Irons, R. (1996). Differential diagnosis of Addictive sexual disorders using the DSM-IV. *Sexual Addictions and Compulsivity, 3,* 7–21.

Schnittman, S. M. & Fauci, A. S. (1994). Human immunodeficiency virus and acquired immunodeficiency syndrome: An update. *Advances in Internal Medicine, 39,* 305–355.

Schoenthaler, S. J. (1982). The effect of sugar on the treatment and control of antisocial behavior: A double-blind study of an incarcerated juvenile population. *International Journal of Biosocial Research, 3,* 1–9.

Schooler, C., Zahn, T. P., Murphy, D. L. & Buchsbaum, M. S. (1978). Psychological correlates of monoamine oxidase acivity in normals. *Journal of Nervous and Mental Diseases, 166,* 177–186.

Schuckit, M. A. (1973). Alcoholism and sociopathy—diagnostic confusion. *Journal of Studies on Alcohol, 34,* 157–164.

Schuckit, M. A. (1985). The clinical implications

of primary diagnostic groups among alcoholics. *Archives of General Psychiatry, 42,* 1043–1049.

Schuckit, M. A., Goodwin, D. W. & Winokur, G. (1972). A study of alcoholism in half siblings. *American Journal of Psychiatry, 128,* 1132–1136.

Schuckit, M. A. & Hesselbrock, V. (1994). Alcohol dependence and anxiety disorders: What is the relationship? *American Journal of Psychiatry, 151,* 1723–1734.

Schuessler, K. E. & Cressey, D. R. (1950). Personality characteristics of criminals. *American Journal of Sociology, 55,* 476–484.

Schulsinger, F. (1972). Psychopathy: Heredity and environment. *International Journal of Mental Health, 1,* 190–206.

Schwartz, M. L. & Goldman-Rakic, P. (1990). Development and plasticity of the primate cerebral cortex. *Clinical Perinatology, 17,* 83–102.

Schweinhart, L. J. & Weikart, D. B. (1988). The High/Scope Perry Preschool Program. In R. H. Price, E. L Cowen, R. P. Lorion & J. Ramos-McKay (Eds.), *Fourteen ounces of prevention: A casebook for practitioners.* Washington, DC: American Psychological Association, 53-65.

Scott, J. P. (1989). *The evolution of social systems.* New York: Gordon & Breach.

Seguin, J., Pihl, R., Harden, P., Tremblay, R., Boulerice, B. (1995). Cognitive and neuropsychological characteristics of physically aggressive boys. *Journal of Abnormal Psychology, 104,* 614–624.

Seidler, F. J. & Slotkin, T. A. (1992). Fetal cocaine exposure causes persistent noradrenergic hyperactivity in rat brain regions: Effects on neurotransmitter turnover and receptors. *Journal of Pharmacology and Experimental Therapeutics, 263,* 413–421.

Seitz, B., Rosenbaum, L. K. & Apfel, N. H. (1985). Effects of family support intervention: A ten-year follow-up. *Child Development, 56,* 376–391.

Seligman, M. E. P. (1975). *Helplessness: On depression, development, and death.* San Francisco, CA: Freeman.

Selner-O'Hagan, M. B., Kindlon, D. J., Buka, S. L., Raudenbush, S. W. & Earls, F. J. (1998). Assessing exposure to violence in urban youth. *Journal of Child Psychology and Psychiatry, 39,* 215–224.

Senba, E. & Ueyama, T. (1997). Stress-induced expression of immediate early genes in the brain and peripheral organs of the rat. *Neuroscience Research, 29,* 183–207.

Shankle, W., Nielson, K. & Cotman, C. (1995). Low-dose propranolol reduces aggression and agitation resembling that associated with orbitofrontal dysfunction in elderly demented patients. *Alzheimer Disease and Associative Disorders, 9,* 233–237.

Shantz, C. U. (1975). The development of social cognition. In E. M. Hetherington (Ed.), *Review of child development research,* vol. 5. Chicago: University of Chicago Press.

Shaw, D. S. & Bell, R. Q. (1992). Developmental theories of parental contributors to antisocial behavior. Presented at the Conference for Life History Research, Coercion and Punishment in Long-Term Perspectives, Philadelphia, PA.

Sheard, M. H., Marini, J. L., Bridges, C. I. & Wagner, E. (1976). The effect of lithium on impulsive aggressive behavior in man. *American Journal of Psychiatry, 133,* 1409–1413.

Shekim, W. O., Bylund, D. B., Frankel, F., Alexson, J., Jones, S. B., Blue, L. O., Kirby, J. & Corchoran, C. (1989). Platelet MAO activity and personality variations in normals. *Psychiatry Research, 27,* 81–88.

Shekim, W. O., Davis, L. G, Bylund, D. B., Brunngraber, E., Fikes, L. & Lanham, J. (1982). Platelet MAO in children with attention deficit disorder and hyperactivty: A pilot study. *American Journal of Psychiatry, 139,* 936–938.

Shekim, W. O., Dekirmenjian, H. & Chapel, J. L. (1997). Urinary MHPG excretion in minimal brain dsyfunction and its modification by d-amphetamine. *American Journal of Psychiatry, 136,* 667–671. Sheldon, W. H. (1949). *Varieties of delinquent youth: An introduction to constitutional psychiatry.* New York: Harper.

Sher, K. & Levenson, R. (1982). Risk for alcoholism and individual differences in the stress-response-dampening effect of alcohol. *Journal of Abnormal Psychology, 19,* 350–367.

Sher, K., Walitzer, K., Wood, P. & Brent, E. (1991). Characteristics of children of alcoholics: Putative risk factors, substance use and abuse, and psychopathology. *Journal of Abnormal Psychology, 100,* 427–488.

Sheridan, M. J. (1995). A proposed intergenerational model of substance abuse, family functioning, and abuse/neglect. *Child Abuse and Neglect, 19,* 519–530.

Sherman, D. K., Iacono, W. G. & McGue, M. K. (1997). Attention-deficit hyperactivity disorder dimensions: A twin study of inattention and impulsivity-hyperactivity. *Journal of the American Academy of Child and Adolescent Psychiatry, 36,* 745–753.

Sherman, D. K., McGure, M. K. & Iacono, W. G. (1997). Twin concordance for attention deficit hyperactivity disorder: a comparison of teachers' and mothers' reports. *American Journal of Psychiatry, 154,* 532–535.

Sherrington, C. S. (1925). On the nature of reflex excitation and inhibition. *Proceedings of the Royal Society, 97B,* 519–545.

Shetatsky, M., Greenberg, D. & Lerer, B. (1988). A controlled trial of phenelzine in post-traumatic stress disorder. *Psychiatry Research, 24,* 149–155.

Shin, L. M., McNally, R. J., Kosslyn, S. M., Thompson, W. L., Rauch, S. L., Alpert, N. M., Metzger, L. J., Lasko, N. B., Orr, S. P. & Pitman, R. K. (1997). A positron emission tomographic study of symptom provocation in PTSD. *Annals of the New York Academy of Sciences, 821,* 521–523.

Shure, M. B., Spivack, G. & Jaeger, M. A. (1971). Problem-solving thinking and adjustment among disadvantaged preschool children. *Child Development, 42,* 1791–1803.

Siassi, I. (1982). Lithium treatment of impulsive behavior in children. *Journal of Clinical Psychiatry, 43,* 482–484.

Siegel, A. & Schubert, K. (1995). Neurotransmitters regulating feline aggressive behavior. *Reviews in the Neurosciences, 6,* 47–61.

Siegel, S. (1956). *Nonparametric statistics for the behavioral sciences.* New York: McGraw Hill.

Siever, L. & Trestman, R. L. (1993). The serotonin system and aggressive personality disorder. *International Clinical Psychopharmacology, 8 (Suppl. 2),* 33–39.

Sigvardsson, S., Cloninger, C. R., Bohman, M. & von Knorring, A. L. (1982). Predisposition to petty criminality in Swedish adoptees. III. Sex differences and validation of the male typology. *Archives of General Psychiatry, 39,* 1248–1253.

Silberg, J., Meyer, J., Pickles, A., Simonoff, E., Eaves, L., Hewitt, J., Maes, H. & Rutter, M. (1996). Heterogeneity among juvenile antisocial behaviours: Findings from the Virginia Twin Study of Adolescent Behavioural Development. In G. R. Bock & J. A. Goode (Eds.), *Genetics of criminal and antisocial behavior.* West Sussex, England: John Wiley & Sons, 76–85.

Silver, F. I. & Yudofsky, S. C. (1987). Documentation of aggression in the assessment of the violent patient. *Psychiatric Annals, 17,* 375–384.

Simeon, J., Ferguson, H. & van Wyck Fleet, J. (1986). Bupropion effects in attention deficit and conduct disorders. *Canadian Journal of Psychiatry, 31,* 581–585.

Simmons, R. & Blyth, D. (1987). *Moving into adolescence: The impact of pubertal change and school context.* Hawthorne, New York: Aldine de Gruyter.

Simonoff, E. (1992). A comparison of twins and singletons with child psychiatric disorders: An item sheet study. *Journal of Child Psychology and Psychiatry, 33,* 1319–1332.

Simpson, D. & Foster, D. (1986). Improvement in organically disturbed behavior with trazadone treatment. *Journal of Clinical Psychiatry, 47,* 191–193.

Singer, A. (1974). Mothering practices and heroin addiction. *American Journal of Nursing, 74,* 77–82.

Singer, J. L. (1955). Delayed gratification and ego-development: Implications for clinical and experimental research. *Journal of Consulting Psychology, 19,* 259–266.

Singh, I. & Owino, W. J. (1992). A double-blind comparison of zuclopenthixol tablets with placebo in the treatment of mentally handicapped inpatients with associated behavioral disorders. *Journal of Intellectual Disabilities Research, 36,* 541–549.

Skinner, B. F. (1938). *The behavior of organisms: An experimental analysis.* New York: Appleton-Century-Crofts.

Slaby, R. G. & Guerra, N. G. (1988). Cognitive mediators of aggression in adolescent offenders: 1. Assessment. *Developmental Psychology, 24,* 580–588.

Slater, E. & Cowie, V. (1971). *The genetics of mental disorder.* London: Oxford University Press.

Sleddens, H. F., Oostra, B. A., Brinkman, A. O. & Trapman, J. (1993). Trinucleotide (GGN) repeat polymorphism in the human androgen receptor (AR) gene. *Human Molecular Genetics, 2,* 493.

Slotkin, T. A. (1998). Fetal nicotine or cocaine

exposure: Which one is worse? *Journal of Pharmacology and Experimental Therapeutics, 285,* 931–945.

Slutske, W. S., Heath, A. C., Dinwiddie, S. H., Madden, P. A., Bucholz, K. K., Dunne, M. P., Statham, D. J. & Martin, N. G. (1997). Modeling genetic and environmental influences in the etiology of conduct disorder: A study of 2,682 adult twin pairs. *Journal of Abnormal Psychology, 106,* 266–279.

Slutske, W. S., Heath, A. C., Dinwiddie, S. H., Madden, P. A. F., Bucholz, K. K., Dunne, M. P., Statham, D. J. & Martin, N. G. (1998). Common genetic risk factors for conduct disorder and alcohol dependence. *Journal of Abnormal Psychology, 107,* 363–374.

Smith, C. (1974). Concordance in twins: Methods and interpretation. *American Journal of Human Genetics, 26,* 454–466.

Smith, D. A. & Ferry, P. J. (1992). Nonneuroleptic treatment of disruptive behavior in organic mental syndromes. *Annals of Pharmacotherapy, 26,* 1400–1408.

Smith, M. A. (1996). Hippocampal vulnerability to stress and aging: possible role of neurotrophic factors. *Behavioral Brain Research, 78,* 25–36.

Smith, S., Arnett, P. & Newman, J. (1992). Neuropsychological differentiation of psychopathic and nonpsychopathic criminal offenders. *Personality and Individual Differences, 13,* 1233–1243.

Smith, S., Pihl, R. O., Young, S. N. & Ervin, F. R. (1987). A test of possible cognitive and environmental influences on the mood lowering effect of tryptophan depletion in normal males. *Psychopharmacology, 91,* 451–457.

Snaith, R. P. & Taylor, C. M. (1985). Irritability: Definition, assessment and associated factors. *British Journal of Psychiatry, 147,* 127–136.

Soloff, P. H., Cornelius, J., George, A., Nathan, S., Perel, J. M. & Ulrich, R. F. (1993). Efficacy of phenelzine and haloperidol in borderline personality disorder. *Archives of General Psychiatry, 50,* 377–385.

Soloff, P. H., George, A., Nathan, S., Schulz, P. M., Cornelius, J. R., Herring, J. & Perel, J. M. (1989). Amitriptyline versus haloperidol in borderlines: Final outcomes and predictors of response. *Journal of Clinical Psychopharmacology, 9,* 238–246.

Soloff, P. H., George, A., Nathan, S., Schulz, P. M., Ulrich, R. F. & Perel, J. M. (1986). Progress in pharmacotherapy of borderline disorders. *Archives of General Psychiatry, 43,* 691–697.

Sorgi, P., Ratey, J. J., Knoedler, D. W., Markert, R. J. & Reichman, M. (1991). Rating aggression in the clinical setting: A retrospective adaptation of the overt aggression scale. Journal of *Neuropsychiatry and Clinical Neurosciences, 3,* S52–S56.

Sorgi, P., Ratey, J. J. & Polakoff, S. (1986). Beta-adrenergic blockers for the control of aggressive behaviors in patients with chronic schizophrenia. *American Journal of Psychiatry, 143,* 775–776.

Soubrie, P. (1986). Reconciling the role of central serotonin neurons in human and animal behavior. *Behavior and Brain Sciences, 9,* 319–364.

Southwick, S. M., Krystal, J. H., Bremmer, J. D., Morgan, C. A., 3d, Nicholaou, A. L., Nagy, L. M., Johnson, D. R., Heninger, G. R. & Chorney, D. S. (1997). Noradrenergic and serotonergic function in posttraumatic stress disorder. *Archives of General Psychiatry, 54,* 749–758.

Sowder, B. J. & Burt, M. R. (1980). *Children of heroin addicts: An assessment of health, learning, behavioral, and adjustment problems.* Praeger studies in issues and research in substance abuse. New York: Praeger.

Sperry, R. W. (1993). The promise and impact of the cognitive revolution. *American Psychologist, 48,* 878–885.

Spielberger, C. D. (1988). *Manual for the state-trait anger expression inventory (STAXI).* Psychological Assessment Resources. Odessa, FL.

Spielberger, C. D., Jacobs, G., Russell, S. & Crane, R. S. (1983). Assessment of anger: The state-trait anger scale. In J. N. Butcher & C. D. Spielberger (Eds.), *Advances in personality assessment,* vol. 2. Hillsdale, NJ: Erlbaum, 159–187.

Spielberger, C. D., Johnson, E. H., Russell, S., Crane, R. J., Jacobs, G. A. & Worden, T. J. (1985). The experience and expression of anger: Construction and validation of an anger expression scale. In M. A. Chesney & R. H. Rosenman (Eds.), *Anger and hostility in cardiovascular and behavioral disorders.* Washington, DC: Hemisphere, 5–30.

Spielman, R. S., McGinnis, R. E. & Ewens, W. J. (1993). Transmission test for linkage disequilibirum: the insulin gene region and insulin-dependent diabetes mellitus (IDDM). *American Journal of Human Genetics, 52,* 506–516.

Spivak, B., Mester, R., Wittenberg, N., Maman, Z.

& Weizman, A. (1997). Reduction of aggressiveness and impulsiveness during clozapine treatment in chronic neuroleptic-resistant schizophrenic patients. *Clinical Neuropharmacology, 20,* 442–446.

Spivack, G., Platt, J. J. & Shure, M. B. (1976). *The problem-solving approach to adjustment: A guide to research and intervention.* San Francisco: Jossey-Bass.

Spivak, H., Prothrow-Stith, D. & Hausman, A. (1988). Dying is no accident: Adolescents, violence, and intentional injury. *The Pediatric Clinics of North America 35,* 1339–1347.

Spoth, R., Redmond, C. & Shin, C. (1998). Direct and indirect latent-variable parenting outcomes of two universal family-focused preventive interventions: Extending a public health-oriented research base. *Journal of Consulting and Clinical Psychology, 66,* 385–399.

Spreen, O. (1989). The relationship between learning disorders and neuropsychology: Some results and observations. *Journal of Clinical and Experimental Neuropsychology, 11,* 117–140.

Spreen, O. & Strauss, E. (1991). *A compendium of neuropsychological tests: Administration, norms, and commentary.* New York: Oxford University Press.

Sroufe, L. A. (1983). Infant-caregiver attachment and patterns of adaptation in preschool: The roots of maladaptation and competence. In M. Perlmutter (Ed.), *Minnesota symposium in child psychology,* vol. 16. Hillsdale, NJ: Erlbaum, 41–81.

Sroufe, L. A. & Rutter, M. (1984). The domains of developmental psychology. *Child Development, 55,* 17–29.

Stabenau, J. R. & Hesselbrock, V. M. (1994). *Substance abuse and psychopathology.* Washington, DC: American Psychiatric Association.

Stacey, W. & Shupe, H. (1983). *The family secret.* Boston: Beacon Press.

Stafford-Clark, D. (1959). The foundations of research in psychiatry. *British Medical Journal, 2,* 1199–1204.

Standfort, T. G. M. (1984). Sex in pedophilic relationships: An empirical investigation among a nonrepresentative group of boys. *Journal of Sexuality Research, 20,* 123–142.

Stanislav, S. W., Fabre, T., Crimson, M. L. & Childs, A. (1994). Buspirone's efficacy in organic-induced aggression. *Journal of Clinical Psychopharmacology, 14,* 126–130.

Stanley, M. & Mann, J. (1983). Increased serotonin-2 binding sites in frontal cortex of suicide victims. *Lancet, 1,* 214–216.

Stanton, M. D. & Todd, T. C. (1982). *The family therapy of drug abuse and addiction.* New York: Guilford Press.

Starke, K., Montel, H., Gayk, W. & Marker, R. (1974). Comparision of the effects of clonidine on pre-and postsynaptic adrenoceptors in the rabbit pulmonary artery. *Naunyn-Schmiedeberg's Archives of Pharmacology, 285,* 133–150.

Starkstein, S. & Robinson, R. (1991). The role of the frontal lobes in affective disorder following stroke. In H. Levin, H. Eisenberg & L. Benton (Eds.), *Frontal lobe function and dysfunction.* New York: Oxford University Press, 288–303.

Stattin, H. & Magnusson, D. (1989). The role of early aggressive behavior in the frequency, seriousness and types of later crime. *Journal of Consulting and Clinical Psychology, 30,* 23–51.

Steadman, H. & Cocozza, J. J. (1978). Selective reporting and the public's misconceptions of the criminally insane. *Public Opinion Quarterly, 41,* 523–533.

Steadman, H., Cocozza, J. J. & Melick, M. E. (1978). Explaining the increased arrest rate among mental patients: The changing clientele of state hospitals. *American Journal of Psychiatry, 135,* 816–820.

Stein, D. J., Simeon, D., Frenkel, M., Islam, M. N. & Hollander, E. (1995). An open trial of valproate in borderline personality disorder. *Journal of Clinical Psychiatry, 56,* 506–510.

Stein, D. J., Hollander, E. & Liebowitz, M. R. (1993). Neurobiology of impulsivity and the impulse control disorders. *Journal of Neuropsychiatry and Clinical Neuroscience, 5,* 9–17.

Stein, D. J., Trestman, R. L., Mitropoulou, V. & Coccaro, E. F. (1996). Impulsivity and serotonergic function in compulsive personality disorder. *Journal of Neuropsychiatry & Clinical Neurosciences, 8,* 393–398.

Stein, M. B., Koverola, C., Hanna, C., Torchia, M. G. & McClarty, B. (1997). Hippocampal volume in women victimized by childhood sexual abuse. *Psychological Medicine, 27,* 951–959.

Stein, M. B., Yehuda, R., Koverola, C. & Hanna, R. (1997). Enhanced dexamethasone suppression of plasma cortisol in adult women traumatized by childhood sexual abuse. *Biological Psychiatry, 42,* 680–686.

Stein, M. D. (1990). Medical complications of intravenous drug use. *Journal of General Internal Medicine, 5,* 249–257.

Steiner, M., Steinberg, S., Stewart, D., Carter, D., Berger, C., Reid, R., Grover, D. & Streiner, D. (1995). Fluoxetine in the treatment of premenstrual dysphoria. *New England Journal of Medicine, 332,* 1529–1534.

Stenbacka, M., Allegeck, P., Brandt, L. & Romelsjo, A. (1992). Intravenous drug abuse in young men: Risk factors assessed in a longitudinal perspective. *Scandanavian Journal of Social Medicine, 20,* 94–101.

Stevens, J. R. & Hermann, B. P. (1981). Temporal lobe epilepsy, psychopathology, and violence: The state of the evidence. *Neurology, 31,* 1127–1132.

Stevenson, J. (1992). Evidence for a genetic etiology in hyperactivity. *Behavioral Genetics, 22,* 337–344.

Stevenson, J. & Graham, P. (1988). Behavioral deviance in 13-year-old twins: An item analysis. *Journal of the American Academy of Child and Adolescent Psychiatry, 27,* 791–797.

Stewart, J. T., Mounts, M. L. & Clark, R. L. Jr. (1987). Aggressive behavior in Huntington's disease: Treatment with propranolol. *Journal of Clinical Psychiatry, 48,* 106–108.

Stewart, M. A., Cummings, C., Singer, S. & Deblois, C. S. (1981). The overlap between hyperactive and unsocialized aggressive children. *Journal of Child Psychology and Psychiatry, 22,* 35–45.

Stewart, M. A., deBlois, C. S. & Cummings, C. (1980). Psychiatric disorder in the parents of hyperactive boys and those with conduct disorder. *Journal of Child Psychology and Psychiatry, 21,* 283–292.

Stoff, D. M., Pastiempo, A. P., Yeung, J. H., Cooper, T. B., Bridger, W. H. & Rabinovich, H. (1992). Neuroendocrine responses to challenge with d,l-fenfluramine and aggression in disruptive behavior disorders of children and adolescents. *Psychiatry Research, 43,* 263–276.

Stoff, D. M., Pollock, L., Vitiello, B., Behar, D. & Bridger, W. H. (1987). Reduction of ^{3}H-imipramine binding sites on platelets of conduct disordered children. *Neuropsychopharmacology, 1,* 55–62.

Stokes, P. E. (1995). The potential role of excessive cortisol induced by HPA hyperfunction in the pathogenesis of depression. *European Neuropsychopharmacology, 5,* 77–82.

Stone, M. (1989). Murder. *Psychiatric Clinics of North America, 12,* 643–651.

Strain, E. C., Brooner, R. K. & Bigelow, G. E. (1991). Clustering of multiple substance use and psychiatric diagnoses in opiate addicts. *Drug and Alcohol Dependence, 27,* 127–134.

Straus, M. (1979). Measuring intrafamily conflict and violence: The conflict tactics (CT) scales. *Journal of Marriage and the Family, 41,* 75–88.

Straus, M. & Gelles, R. J. (Eds.) (1990). *Physical violence in American families: Risk factors and adaptations to violence in 8145 families.* New Brunswick, NJ: Transaction Books.

Straus, M., Gelles, R. J. & Steinmetz, S. A. (1980). *Behind closed doors.* Garden City, NY: Anchor/Doubleday.

Strauss, I. & Keschner, M. (1936). Mental symptoms in tumor of the frontal lobe. *Archives of Neurology and Psychiatry, 35,* 572–596.

Strauss, S. M. (1979). Measuring intrafamily conflict and violence: The conflict tactics (CT) scales. *Journal of Marriage and the Family, 41,* 75–88.

Streissguth, A. P., Aase, J. M., Clarren, S. K., Randels, S. P., LaDue, R. A. & Smith, D. F. (1991). Fetal alcohol syndrome in adolescents and adults. *Journal of the American Medical Association, 265,* 1961–1967.

Sturup, G. K. (1972). Castration: The total treatment. In H. P. L. Resnick & M. D. Wolfgang, (Eds.), *Sexual behaviors: Social, clinical, and legal aspects.* Boston: Little, Brown.

Stuss, D. & Benson, D. (1984). Neuropsychological studies of the frontal lobes. *Psychological Bulletin, 95,* 3–28.

Stuss, D., Gow, C. & Hetherington, C. (1992). "No longer Gage": Frontal lobe dysfunction and emotional changes. *Journal of Consulting and Clinical Psychology, 60,* 349–359.

Su, T., Tuskan, J., Tsao, L. & Pickar, D. (1994). *Aggression during drug-free and antipsychotic treatment in inpatients with chronic schizophrenia, using the overt aggression scale.* Presented at the American College of Neuropsychopharmacology Meeting, San Juan, PR.

Sullivan, P. F., Fifield, W. H., Kennedy, M. A.,

Mulder, R. T., Sellman, J. D. & Joyce, P. R. (1997). Novelty seeking and a dopamine transporter gene polymorphism (DAT1). *Biological Psychiatry, 42,* 1070–1072.

Sultzer, D. L., Gray, K. F., Gunay, I., Berisford, M. A. & Mahler, M. E. (1997). A double-blind comparison of trazodone and haloperidol for treatment of agitation in patients with dementia. *American Journal of Geriatric Psychiatry, 5,* 60–69.

Sun, M. (1982). Depo-Provera debate revs up at FDA. *Science, 217,* 424–428.

Sundblad, C., Hedberg, M. & Eriksson, E. (1993). Clomipramine administered during luteal phase reduces the symptoms of premenstrual syndrome: A placebo-controlled trial. *Neuropsychopharmacology, 9,* 133–145.

Sundblad, C., Modigh, K., Andersch, B. & Eriksson, E. (1992). Clomipramine effectively reduces premenstrual irritability and dysphoria: A placebo-controlled trial. *Acta Psychiatrica Scandinavica, 85,* 39–47.

Sutker, P. & Allain, A. (1987). Cognitive abstraction, shifting, and control: Clinical sample comparisons of psychopaths and nonpsychopaths. *Journal of Abnormal Psychology, 96,* 73–75.

Svikis, D. S., Valez, M. & Pickens, R. W. (1994). Genetic aspects of alcohol use and dependence in women. *Alcohol, Health and Research World, 18,* 192–196. Schweinhart, L. J. (1987). Can preschool programs help prevent delinquency? In J. Q. Wilson & G. C. Loury (Eds.), *From children to citizens,* vol. 3, *Families, schools, and delinquency prevention.* New York: Springer-Verlag, 135–153.

Swanson, J., Holzer, C., Ganju, V. & Jono, R. (1990). Violence and psychiatric disorder in the community: Evidence from the epidemiologic catchment area surveys. *Hospital and Community Psychiatry, 41,* 761–770.

Swanson, J. M., Sunohara, G. A., Kennedy, J. L., Regino, R., Fineberg, E., Wigal, T., Lerner, M., Williams, L., Lahoste, G. J. & Wigal, S. (1998). Association of the dopamine receptor D4 (DRD4) gene with a refined phenotype of attention deficit hyperactivity disorder (ADHD): A family based approach. *Molecular Psychiatry, 3,* 38–41.

Szatmari, P., Reitsma-Street, M. & Offord, D. (1986). Pregnancy and birth complications in antisocial adolescents and their siblings. *Canadian Journal of Psychiatry, 31,* 513–516.

Tajuddin, N. & Druse, J. J. (1988). Chronic maternal ethanol consumption results in decreased serotonergic 5-HT1 sites in cerebral cortical regions from offspring. *Alcohol, 5,* 465–470.

Tallal, P., Miller, S., Bedi, G., Byma, G., Wang, X., Nagarajan, S., Schreiner, C., Jenkins, W. & Merzenich, M. (1996). Language comprehension in language-learning impaired children improved with acoustically modified speech. *Science, 271,* 81–84.

Tardiff, K. (1992). The current state of psychiatry in the treatment of violent patients. *Archives of General Psychiatry, 49,* 493–499.

Tarter, R. (1988). Are there inherited behavioral traits which predispose to substance abuse? *Journal of Consulting and Clinical Psychology, 56,* 189–196.

Tarter, R. (1990). Evaluation and treatment of adolescent substance abuse: A decision tree method. *American Journal of Drug and Alcohol Abuse, 61,* 1–46.

Tarter, R., Alterman, A. & Edwards, K. (1985). Vulnerability to alcoholism in men. A behavior-genetic perspective. *Journal of Studies on Alcohol, 46,* 329–356.

Tarter, R., Arria, A., Moss, H., Edwards, K. & Van Thiel, D. (1987). DSM-III criteria for alcohol abuse. Association with alcohol consumption behavior. *Alcoholism: Clinical and Experimental Research, 11,* 541–543.

Tarter, R., Blackson, T., Martin, C., Loeber, R. & Moss, H. (1993). Characteristics and correlates of child discipline practices in substance abuse and normal families. *American Journal on Addiction, 2,* 18–25.

Tarter, R., Blackson, T., Martin, C., Seilhamer, R., Pelham, W. & Loeber, R. (1993). Mutual dissatisfaction between mother and son in substance abuse and normal families. Association with child behavior problems. *American Journal on Addiction, 2,* 1–10.

Tarter R. E. & Edwards K. (1987). Vulnerability to alcohol and drug abuse: A behavior-genetic view. *Psychological Bulletin 102,* 204–218.

Tarter, R. & Edwards, K., (1988). Psychological factors associated with the risk for alcoholism. *Alcoholism: Clinical and Experimental Research, 12,* 471–480.

Tarter, R. & Hegedus, A. (1992). The drug use screening inventory. Its application in the evaluation and treatment of alcohol and drug abuse. *Alcohol, Health and Research World, 15,* 65–75.

Tarter, R., Hegedus, A., Goldstein, G., Shelly, C. & Alterman, A. (1984). Adolescent sons of alcoholics: Neuropsychological and personality characteristics. *Alcoholism: Clinical and Experimental Research, 8,* 216–222.

Tarter, R., Kabene, M., Escallier, E., Laird, S. & Jacob, T. (1990). Temperament deviation and risk for alcoholism. *Alcoholism: Clinical and Experimental Research, 14,* 380–382.

Tarter, R., Kirisci, L., Hegedus, A., Mezzich, A. & Vanyukov, M. (1994). Heterogeneity of adolescent alcoholism. *Annals of the New York Academy of Science, 708,* 102–107.

Tarter, R., McBride, H., Buonpane, N. & Schneider, D. (1977). Differentiation of alcoholics: Childhood history of minimal brain dysfunction, family history, and drinking pattern. *Archives of General Psychiatry, 34,* 761–768.

Tarter, R., Moss, H., Arria, A. & Mezzich, A. (1992). Psychiatric diagnosis of alcoholism: Critique and reformulation. *Alcoholism: Clinical and Experimental Research, 16,* 106–116.

Tarter, R., Moss, H. & Vanyukov, M. (1995). Behavior-genetic perspective of alcoholism etiology. In H. Begleiter & B. Kissin (Eds.), *Alcohol and alcoholism.* New York: Oxford University Press.

Taylor, D. C. (1993). The roots and role of violence in development. In P. J. Taylor (Ed.), *Violence in Society.* London: Royal College of Physicians.

Taylor, J., McGue, M., Iacono, W. G. & Lykken, D. T. (1997). A twin family study of delinquency. Paper presented at the Annual Meeting of the Behavior Genetics Association, Toronto.

Taylor, S. (1993). Experimental investigation of alcohol-induced aggression in humans. *Alcohol Health and Research World, 17,* 108–112.

Taylor, S. E. (1983). Adjustment to threatening events: A theory of cognitive adaption. *American Psychologist, 38,* 1161–1173.

Taylor, S. P. (1967). Aggressive behavior and physiological arousal as a function of provocation and the tendency to inhibit aggression. *Journal of Personality, 35,* 297–310.

Taylor, S. P. & Gammon, C. (1975). Effects of type and dose of alcohol on human physical aggression. *Journal of Personality & Social Psychology, 32,* 169–175.

Teicher, M. H., Ito, Y., Glod, C. A., Andersen, S. L., Dumont, N. & Ackerman, E. (1997). Preliminary evidence for abnormal cortical development in physically and sexually abused children using EEG coherence and MRI. *Annals of the New York Academy of Sciences, 821,* 160–175.

Tellegen, A. (1982). Brief manual for the differential personality questionnaire. Unpublished manuscript. Minneapolis, MN: University of Minnesota.

Tellegen, A., Lykken, D. T., Bouchard, T. J., Jr., Wilcox, K. J., Segal, N. L. & Rich, S. (1988). Personality similarity in twins reared apart and together. *Journal of Personality and Social Psychology, 54,* 1031–1039.

Tennenbaum, D. J. (1977). Personality and criminality: A summary and implications of the literature. *Journal of Criminal Justice, 5,* 225–235.

Teplin, L. (1984). Criminalizing mental disorder: The comparative arrest rate of the mentally ill. *American Psychologist, 39,* 794–803.

Teplin, L. (1990). The prevalence of severe mental disorder among male urban jail detainees: Comparison with the epidemiologic catchment area program. *American Journal of Public Health, 80,* 663–669.

Teplin, L. A. (1994). Psychiatric and substance abuse disorders among male urban jail detainees. *American Journal of Public Health, 84,* 290–293.

Terao, T., Yoshimura, R., Ohmorl, O., Takano, T., Takahashi, N., Iwata, N., Suzuki, T. & Abe, K. (1997). Effect of serum cholesterol levels on meta-chlorophenylpiperazine neuroendocrine responses in healthy subjects. *Biological Psychiatry, 41,* 974–978.

Thapar, A. & McGuffin, P. (1996). A twin study of antisocial and neurotic symptoms in childhood. *Psychological Medicine, 26,* 1111–1118.

Thomas, A. & Chess, S. (1977). *Temperament and development.* New York: Brunner/Mazel.

Thomas, A. & Chess, S. (1984). Genesis and evolution of behavioral disorders: From infancy to early adult life. *American Journal of Psychiatry, 141,* 1–9.

Thomas, H. I., Schwartz, E. & Petrilli, R. (1992). Droperidol versus haloperidol for chemical restraint of agitated and combative patients. *Annals of Emergency Medicine, 21,* 407–413.

Thompson, G. M. (1953). *The psychopathic delinquent and criminal.* Springfield, IL: Charles C. Thomas.

Thompson, R. J., Jr., Gustafson, K. E., Oehler, J. M.,

Catlett, A. T., Brazy, J. E. & Goldstein, R. F. (1997). Developmental outcome of very low birth weight infants at four years of age as a function of biological risk and psychosocial risk. *Journal of Development and Behavior in Pediatrics, 18,* 91–96.

Thornberry, T. P. (1987). Toward an interactional theory of delinquency. *Criminology, 25,* 863–891.

Thornberry, T. P., Lizotte, A. J., Krohn, M. D., Farnworth, M. & Sung, J. J. (1994). Delinquent peers, beliefs, and delinquent behavior: A longitudinal test of interactional theory. *Criminology, 32,* 47-83.

Tidey, J. W. & Miczek, K. A. (1996). Social defeat stress selectively alters mesocorticolimbic dopamine release: An in vivo microdialysis study. *Brain Research, 721,* 140–149.

Tienari, P. (1963). Psychiatric illnesses in identical twins. *Acta Psychiatrica Scandinavia, 39,* 140–142.

Tiihonen, J., Hakola, P., Paanila, J. & Turtiainen, M. (1993). Eltoprazine for aggression in schizophrenia and mental retardation. *Lancet, 341,* 307.

Tiihonen, J., Kuikka, J., Hakola, P., Paanila, J., Airaksinen, J., Eronen, M. & Hallikainen, T. (1994). Acute ethanol-induced changes in cerebral blood flow. *American Journal of Psychiatry, 151,* 1505–1508.

Time Life Editors (1992). *Mass murderers.* New York: Time Life Books.

Tittle, C. R. (1980). *Sanctions and social deviance.* New York: Praeger.

Tizabi, Y., Popke, E. J., Rahman, M. A., Nespor, S. M. & Grunberg, N. E. (1997). Hyperactivity induced by prenatal nicotine exposure is associated with an increase in cortical nicotinic receptors. *Pharmacology and Biochemistry of Behavior, 58,* 141–146.

Toch, H. (1992). *Violent men: An inquiry into the psychology of violence.* Washington, DC: American Psychological Association.

Toch, H. & Adams, K. (1989). *The disturbed violent offender.* New Haven, CT: Yale University Press.

Toch, H., Adams, K. & Grant, J. D. (1989). *Coping: Maladaptation in prisons.* New Brunswick, NJ: Transaction Books.

Tomas, J. M., Vlahov, D. & Anthony, J. C. (1990). Association between intravenous drug use and early misbehavior. *Drug and Alcohol Dependence, 25,* 79–89.

Tonry, M. & Farrington, D. (1995). *Building a safer society.* Chicago: University of Chicago Press.

Tonry, M., Ohlin, L. E. & Farrington, D. P. (1991). *Human development and criminal behavior.* New York: Springer-Verlag.

Towbin, A. (1971). Organic causes of minimal brain dysfunction: Peri-natal origins of minimal cerebral lesions. *Journal of the American Medical Assocation, 217,* 1207–1214.

Tracy, P. E., Wolfgang, M. E. & Figlio, R. M. (1990). *Delinquency careers in two birth cohorts.* New York: Plenum Press.

Treiman, D. M. (1986). Epilepsy and violence: Medical and legal issues. *Epilepsia, 27,* S77–S104.

Tremblay, R. E., Masse, B., Perron, D., LeBlanc, M., Schwartzman, A. E. & Ledingham, J. E. (1992). Early disruptive behavior, poor school achievement, delinquent behavior and delinquent personality: Longitudinal analyses. *Journal of Consulting and Clinical Psychology, 60,* 64–72.

Tsuang, M. T. (1983). Risk of suicide in relatives of schizophrenics, manic depressives and controls. *Journal of Clinical Psychiatry, 44,* 396–400.

Tsuang, M. T., Lyons, M. J., Eisen, S. A., Goldberg, J., True, W. R., Lin, N., Meyer, J. M., Toomey, R., Faraone, S. V. & Eaves, L. J. (1996). Genetic influences on DSM-III-R drug abuse and dependence: A study of 3372 twin pairs. *American Journal of Medical Genetics, 67,* 473–477.

Tuason, V. (1986). A comparison of parenteral loxapine and haloperidol in hostile and aggressive acutely schizophrenic patients. *Journal of Clinical Psychiatry, 47,* 126–129.

Tupin, J. P., Smith, D. B., Clanon, T. L., Nugent, A. & Groupe, A. (1973). The long-term use of lithium in aggressive prisoners. *Comprehensive Psychiatry, 14,* 311–317.

Turner, C. F., Ku, L., Rogers, S. M., Lindberg, L. D., Pleck, J. H. & Sonenstein, F. L. (1998). Adolescent sexual behavior, drug use, and violence: Increased reporting with computer survey technology. *Science, 280,* 867–873.

Turner, W. J. (1967). The usefulness of diphenylhydantoin in treatment of non-epileptic emotional disorders. *International Journal of Neuropsychiatry, 3,* S8–S20.

Tyrer, S. P., Walsh, A., Edwards, D. E., Berney, T.

P. & Stephens, D. A. (1984). Factors associated with a good response to lithium in aggressive mentally handicapped subjects. *Progress in Neuro-Psychopharmacology and Biological Psychiatry, 8,* 751–755.

Uno, H., Eisele, S., Sakai, A., Shelton, S., Baker, E., DeJesus, O. & Holden, J. (1994). Neurotoxicity of glucocorticoids in the primate brain. *Hormones and Behavior, 28,* 336–348.

Vaillant, G. (1983). *The natural history of alcoholism.* Cambridge, MA: Harvard University Press.

Valliant, P. M., Asu, M. E. & Howitt, R. (1983). Cognitive styles of Caucasian and Native Indian juvenile offenders. *Psychological Reports, 52,* 87-92.

Valzelli, L. (1981). *Psychobiology of aggression and violence.* New York: Raven Press.

Vandenbergh, D. J., Persico, A. M., Hawkins, A. L., Griffin, C. A., Li, X., Jabs, E. W. & Uhl, G. R. (1992). Human dopamine transporter gene (DAT1) maps to chromosome 5p15.3 and displays a VNTR. *Genomics, 14,* 1866–1868.

Vandenbergh, D. J., Persico, A. M. & Uhl, G. R. (1992). A human dopamine transporter cDNA predicts reduced glycosylation, displays a novel repetitive element and provides racially-dimorphic Taq I RFLPs. *Molecular Brain Research, 15,* 161–166.

Van den Bree, M. B. M., Johnson, E. O., Neale, M. C. & Pickens, R. W. (1998). Genetic and environmental influences on drug use and abuse/dependence in male and female twins. *Drug and Alcohol Dependence, 52,* 231–241.

van der Bijl, P. & Roelofse, I. (1991). Disinhibitory reactions to benzodiazepines: A review. *Journal of Oral Maxillofacial Surgery, 49,* 519–523.

van der Kolk, B. A. (1997). The psychobiology of posttraumatic stress disorder. *Journal of Clinical Psychiatry, 58,* 16–24.

van der Kolk, B. A., Dreyfuss, D., Michaels, M., Shera, D., Berkowitz, R., Fisler, R & Saxe, G. (1994). Flouxetine in posttraumatic stress disorder. *Journal of Clinical Psychiatry, 55,* 517–522.

Van Dusen, K. T., Mednick, S. A., Gabrielli, W. F., Jr. & Hutchings, B. (1983). Social class and crime in an adoption cohort. *Journal of Criminal Law and Criminology, 74,* 249–269.

Van Oortmerssen, G. A. & Bakker, T. C. (1981). Artificial selection for short and long attack latencies in wild Mus musculus domesticus. *Behavior Genetics, 11,* 115–126.

van Os, J. & Selten, J. P. (1998). Prenatal exposure to maternal stress and subsequent schizophrenia. The May 1940 invasion of The Netherlands. *British Journal of Psychiatry, 172,* 324–326.

Van Praag, H. M. (1988). Biological psychiatry audited. *Journal of Nervous and Mental Diseases, 176,* 195–199.

Van Praag, H. M. (1991). Serotonergic dysfunction and aggression control. *Psychological Medicine, 21,* 15–19.

Van Praag, H. M., Kahn, R. S., Asnis, G. M., Wetzler, S., Brown, S. L., Bleich, A. & Korn, M. L. (1987). Denosologization of biological psychiatry or the specificity of 5-HT disturbances in psychiatric disorders. *Journal of Affective Disorders, 13,* 1–8.

Van Tol, H. H. M., Wu, C. M., Guan, H-C., Ohara, K., Bunzow, J. R., Civelli, O., Kennedy, J., Seeman, P., Niznik, H. B. & Javanovic, V. (1992). Multiple dopamine D4 receptor variants in human population. *Nature, 358,* 149–152.

Van Voorhis, P. (1987, Mar.). Correctional effectiveness: The high cost of ignoring success. *Federal Probation,* 56–62.

Vanyukov, M., Moss, H., Plail, J., Blackson, T., Mezzich, A. & Tarter, R. (1993). Antisocial symptoms in preadolescent boys and their parents: Association with cortisol. *Psychiatric Research, 46,* 9–17.

Vanyukov, M. M., Moss, H. B. & Tarter, R. E. (1994). Assortment for the liability to substance abuse and personality traits. *Annals of the New York Academy of Science, 708,* 102–107.

Vanyukov, M. M., Neale, M. C., Moss, H. B. & Tarter, R. E. (1996). Mating assortment and the liability to substance abuse. *Drug and Alcohol Dependence, 42,* 1–10.

Vartiainen, H., Tiihonen, J., Putkonen, A., Koponen, H., Virkkunen, M., Hakola, P. & Lehto, H. (1995). Citalopram, a selective serotonin reuptake inhibitor, in the treatment of aggression in schizophrenia. *Acta Psychiatrica Scandinavia, 91,* 348–351.

Verhoeven, W. M., Tuinier, S., Sijben, N. A., van den Berg, Y. W., de Witte-van der Schoot, E. P., Pepplinkhuizen, L. & van Nieuwenhuizen, O. (1992). Eltoprazine in mentally retarded self-injuring patients (letter). *Lancet, 340,* 1037–1038.

Virgin, C. E., Jr. & Sapolsky, R. M. (1997). Styles of male social behavior and their endocrine correlates among low-ranking baboons. *American Journal of Primatology, 42,* 25–39.

Virkkunen M. (1979). Serum cholesterol in antisocial personality. *Neuropsychobiology, 5,* 27–30.

Virkkunen, M. (1983). Serum cholesterol levels in homicidal offenders: A low cholesterol level is connected with a habitually violent tendency under the influence of alcohol. *Neuropsychobiology, 10,* 65–69.

Virkkunen, M. (1986). Reactive hypoglycemic tendency among habitually violent offenders. *Nutrition Reviews, 44,* 94–103.

Virkkunen, M., De Jong, J., Bartko, J., Goodwin, F. K. & Linnoila, M. (1989). Relationship of psychobiological variables to recidivism in violent offenders and impulsive fire setters. *Archives of General Psychiatry, 46,* 600–603.

Virkkunen, M., DeJong, J., Bartko, J. & Linnoila, M. (1989). Psychobiological concomitants of history of suicide attempts among violent offenders and impulsive fire setters. *Archives of General Psychiatry, 46,* 604–606.

Virkkunen, M., Eggert, M., Rawlins, R. & Linnoila, M. (1996). A prospective follow-up study of alcoholic violent offenders and fire setters. *Archives of General Psychiatry, 53,* 523–529.

Virkkunen, M., Goldman, D. & Linnoila, M. (1995). Serotonin in alcoholic violent offenders. In *Genetics of criminal and antisocial behavior.* Chichester, England: John Wiley & Sons, 168–171.

Virkkunen, M. & Huttunen, M. O. (1982). Evidence for abnormal glucose tolerance test among violent offenders. *Neuropsychobiology, 8,* 30–34.

Virkkunen, M. & Linnoila., M. (1990). Serotonin in early onset, male alcoholics with violent behaviour. *Annals of Medicine, 22,* 327–331.

Virkkunen, M. & Narvanen, S. (1987). Plasma insulin, tryptophan and serotonin levels during the glucose tolerance test among habitually violent and impulsive offenders. *Neuropsychobiology, 17,* 19–23.

Virkkunen, M., Nuutila, A., Goodwin, F. K. & Linnoila, M. (1987). Cerebrospinal fluid monoamine metabolite levels in male arsonists. *Archives of General Psychiatry, 44,* 241–247.

Virkkunen, M., Rawlings, R., Tokola, R., Poland, R. E., Guidotti, A., Nemeroff, C., Bissette, G., Kalogeras, K., Karonen, S. L. & Linnoila, M. (1994). CSF biochemistries, glucose metabolism & diurnal activity rhythms in alcoholic, violent offenders, fire setters and healthy volunteers. *Archives of General Psychiatry, 51,* 20–27.

Volavka, J. (1991). Aggression, electroencephalography, and evoked potentials: A critical review. *Neuropsychiatry, Neuropsychology and Behavioral Neurology, 3,* 249–259.

Volavka, J. (1995). *Neurobiology of violence.* Washington, DC: American Psychiatric Press.

Volovka, J., Crowner, M., Brizer, D., Convit, A., Van Praag, H. & Suckow, R. F. (1990). Tryptophan treatment of aggressive psychiatric inpatients. *Biological Psychiatry, 28,* 728–732.

Vonderahe, A. R. (1944). The anatomic substratum of emotion. *The New Scholasticism, 18,* 79–95.

von Knorring, A. L., Hallmann, J., Vonknorring, L. & Oreland, L. (1991). Platelet monoamine oxidase activity in Type-1 and Type-2 alcoholism. *Alcohol, 26,* 409–416.

von Knorring, L., Oreland, L. & Winblad, B. (1984). Personality traits reated to monoamine oxidase activity in platelets. *Psychiatry Research, 12,* 11–26.

von Knorring, L., von Knorring, A-L., Smigan, L., Lindberg, U. & Edholm, M. (1987). Personality traits in subtypes of alcoholics. *Journal of Studies on Alcohol, 48,* 523–527.

Voss, L. D., Mulligan, J. & Betts, P. R. (1998). Short stature at school entry—an index of social deprivation? (The Wessex Growth Study). *Child Care and Health Development, 24,* 145–156.

Wachs, T. & Gandour, M. (1983). Temperament, environment, and six-month cognitive-intellectual development: A test of the organismic specificity hypothesis. *International Journal of Behavioral Development, 6,* 135–152.

Wakschlag, L. S., Lahey, B. B., Loeber, R., Green, S. M., Gordon, J. R. A. & Leventhal, B. L. (1997). Maternal smoking during pregnancy and the risk of conduct disorder in boys. *Archives of General Psychiatry, 54,* 670–676.

Waldrop, M. F. & Halverson, C. F., Jr. (1971). Minor physical anomalies relate to hyperactive behavior in young children. In J. Hellmuth (Ed.), *Exceptional infant.* New York: Brunner/Mazel, 341–361.

Walters, G. D. (1992). *Foundations of criminal*

science: The development of knowledge. New York: Praeger.

Wang, S., Detera-Wadleigh, S. D., Coon, H., Sun, C. E., Goldin, L. R., Duffy, D. L., Byerley, W. F., Gershon, E. S. & Diehl, S. R. (1996). Evidence of linkage disequilibrium between schizophrenia and the SCa1 CAG repeat on chromosome 6p23 [letter]. *American Journal of Human Genetics, 59,* 731–736.

Ward, A. J. (1991). Prenatal stress and childhood psychopathology. *Child Psychiatry and Human Development, 22,* 97–110.

Ward, M. F., Wender, P. H. & Reimherr, F. W. (1993). The Wender Utah rating scale: An aid in the retrospective diagnosis of childhood attention deficit hyperactivity disorder. *American Journal of Psychiatry, 150,* 885–890.

Warr, M. & Stafford, M. (1991). The influence of delinquent peers: What they think or what they do? *Criminology, 29,* 851–865.

Watkins, K. E., Metzger, D., Woody, G. & McLellan, A. T. (1992). High-risk sexual behaviors of intravenous drug users in- and out-of-treatment: Implications for the spread of HIV infection. *American Journal of Drug and Alcohol Abuse, 18,* 389-398.

Webster, C. D. & Jackson, M. A. (1997). *Impulsivity: Theory assessment and treatment.* New York: Guilford Press.

Webster-Stratton, C. & Eyberg, S. (1982). Child temperament: Relationship with child behavior problems and parent-child interactions. *Journal of Clinical Child Psychology, 11,* 123.

Webster-Stratton, C. & Hammond, M. (1997). Treating children with early-onset conduct problems: A comparison of child and parent training interventions. *Journal of Consulting and Clinical Psychology, 65,* 93–109.

Weiger, W. A. & Bear, D. M. (1988). An approach to the neurology of aggression. *Journal of Psychiatric Research, 22,* 85–98.

Weihofen, H. (1956). *The urge to punish: New Approaches to the problem of mental irresponsibility for crime.*

Weisglas-Kuperus, M. N., Baerts, W., Smrkovsky, M. & Sauer, P. J. (1993). Effects of biological and social factors on the cognitive development of very low birth weight children. *Pediatrics, 92,* 658-665.

Welsh, M., Pennington, B., Ozonoff, S., Rouse, B. & McCabe, E. (1990). Neuropsychology of early-treated phenylketonuria: Specific executive function deficits. *Child Development, 61,* 1697–1713.

Wender, P. H. (1985). The Utah criteria in diagnosing attention deficit disorder. *Psycharmacology Bulletin, 21,* 222–231.

Wender, P. H. (1995). *Attention deficit hyperactivity disorder in adults.* New York: Oxford University Press.

Werner, E. (1983). Vulnerability and resiliency among children at risk for delinquency. Presented at the annual meeting of the American Society of Criminology, Denver, CO.

Werner, E. (1987). Vulnerability and resiliency among children at risk for delinquency: A longitudinal study from birth to young adulthood. In J. D. Burchard & S. N. Burchard (Eds.)., *Primary prevention of psychopathology,* vol. 10, *Prevention of delinquent behavior.* Newbury Park, CA: Sage, 6–43.

Werner, E. E. & Smith, R. S. (1982). *Vulnerable but invincible: A longitudinal study of resilient children and youth.* New York: McGraw-Hill.

West, D. J. & Farrington, D. P. (1973). *Who becomes delinquent?* London: Heinemann.

Wexler, D. (1972). Therapeutic justice. *Minnesota Law Review, 57,* 289–338.

Wexler, D. (1992). Putting mental health in mental health law. *Law and Human Behavior, 16,* 27–28.

Wexler, D. & Winick, B. (1991). Therapeutic jurisprudence as a new approach to mental health law policy analysis and research. *Miami Review, 45,* 979–1004.

Wexler, D. & Winick, B. (Eds.) (1996). *Law in a therapeutic key: Developments in therapeutic jurisprudence.* Durham, NC: Carolina Academic Press.

Whalen, C. K. & Henker, B. (1991). Therapies for hyperactive children: Comparisons, combinations, and compromises. *Journal of Consulting and Clinical Psychology, 59,* 126–137.

White, J. L., Moffitt, T. E., Caspi, A., Bartusch, D. J., Needles, D. J. & Stouthamer-Loeber, M. (1994). Measuring impulsivity and examining its relationship to delinquency. *Journal of Abnormal Psychology, 103,* 192–205.

Wiberg, A., Gottfries, C. G. & Oreland, L. (1977). Low platelet monoamine oxidase activity in human alcoholics. *Medical Biology, 55,* 181–186.

Widom, C. S. (1989). The cycle of violence. *Science, 244,* 160–166.

Widom, C. S. (1989). Does violence beget violence? A critical examination of the literature. *Psychological Bulletin, 106,* 3–28.

Widom, C. S. (1991). Avoidance of criminality in abused and neglected children. *Psychiatry, 54,* 62–74.

Wiig, E. & Secord, W. (1989). *Test of language competence* (expanded edition). Psychological Corporation. New York: Harcourt Brace.

Wilcox, J. (1994). Divalproex sodium in the treatment of aggressive behavior. *Annals of Clinical Psychiatry, 6,* 17–20.

Wilcox, R. E. & Gonzales, R. A. (1995). Introduction to neurotransmitters, receptors, signal transduction, and second messengers. In A. F. Schatzberg & C. B. Nemeroff (Eds.), *Textbook of psychopharmacology.* Washington, DC: American Psychiatric Press, 3–29.

Wilder, S. (1947). Sugar metabolism and its relation to criminology. In R. M. Lindner & R. V. Seliger (Eds.), *Handbook of correctional psychology.* New York: Philosophical Library.

Willerman, L., Loehlin, J. C. & Horn, J. M. (1992). An adoption and a cross-fostering study of the Minnesota Multiphasic Personality Inventory (MMPI) Psychopathic Deviate Scale. *Behavior Genetics, 22,* 515–529.

Williams, D. (1969). Neural factors related to habitual aggression: Consideration of differences between those habitual aggressives and others who have committed crimes of violence. *Brain, 92,* 501–520. (from ch. 19, 22)

Williams, K. & Goldstein, G. (1979). Cognitive and affective responses to lithium in patients with organic brain syndrome. *American Journal of Psychiatry, 136,* 800–803.

Wills, T. (1990). Multiple networks and substance use. *Journal of Social and Clinical Psychology, 9,* 78–90.

Wilson, J. D., George, F. W. & Griffin, J. E. (1981). The hormonal control of sexual development. *Science, 211,* 1278–1284.

Wilson, J. Q. & Herrnstein, R. (1985). *Crime and human nature.* New York: Simon & Schuster.

Wind, T. W. & Silvern, L. (1994). Parenting and family stress as mediators of the long-term effects of child abuse. *Child Abuse and Neglect, 18,* 439–453.

Windle, M. (1990). Temperament and personality attributes of children of alcoholics. In M. Windle & J. Searles (Eds.), *Children of alcoholics: A critical review of the literature.* New York: Guilford Press, 129–167.

Windle, M. (1991). The difficult temperament in adolescence: Associations with substance use, family support, and problem behaviors. *Journal of Clinical Psychology, 47,* 310–315.

Windle, M. & Lerner, R. (1986). Reassessing the dimensions of temperamental individuality across the life span: The revised dimensions of temperament survey (DOTS-R). *Journal of Adolescent Research, 1,* 213–230.

Winokur, G., Reich, T., Rimmer, J. & Pitts, F. N. (1970). Alcoholism III. Diagnosis and familial psychiatric illness in 259 alcoholic probands. *Archives of General Psychiatry, 23,* 104–111.

Wishnie, H. A. & Nevis-Oleson, J. (1979). *Working with the impulsive person.* New York: Plenum Press.

Wistedt, B., Rasmussen, A., Pedersen, L., Malm, U., Traksman-Bendz, L., Wakelin, J. & Bech, P. (1990). The development of an observer-scale for measuring social dysfunction and aggression. *Pharmacopsychiatry, 23,* 249–252.

Wolfe, D. A. (1991). *Preventing physical and emotional abuse of children.* New York: Guilford Press.

Wolfe, D. A., Jaffe, P., Wilson, S. K. & Zak, L. (1985). Children of battered women: The relation of child behavior to family violence and maternal stress. *Journal of Consulting and Clinical Psychology, 53,* 657–665.

Wolfgang, M. E. & Ferracuti, F. (1982). *The subculture of violence.* Newbury Park, CA: Sage.

Wong, M. T., Lumsden, S., Fenton, G. W. & Fenwick, P. B. G. (1994). Epilepsy and violence in mentally abnormal offenders in a maximum security mental hospital. *Journal of Epilepsy, 7,* 253–258.

Wood, D., Wender, P. & Reimherr, F. (1983). The prevalence of attention deficit disorder, residual type, or minimal brain dysfunction in a population of male alcoholic patients. *American Journal of Psychiatry, 140,* 95–98.

Wood, S. H., Mortola, J. F., Chan, Y. F., Moossazadeh, F. & Yen, S. S. (1992). Treatment of premenstrual syndrome with fluoxetine: A double-blind placebo-controlled, crossover study. *Obstetrics and Gynecology, 80,* 339–344.

Woody, G. E., McLellan, A. T., Luborsky, L. & O'Brien, C. P. (1985). Sociopathy and psychotherapy outcome. *Archives of General Psychiatry, 42,* 1081–1086.

Worrall, E. P., Moody, J. P., Naylor, G. J. (1975). Lithium in non-manic depressives: Antiaggressive effect and red blood cell lithium values. *British Journal of Psychiatry, 126,* 461–468.

Wurtman, R. J. (1982). Nutrients that modify brain function. *Scientific American, 246,* 50–59.

Wurtman, R. J. (1983). Behavioral effects of nutrients. *Lancet, 1*(8334), 1145–1147.

Wurtman, R. J., Hefti, F. & Melamed, E. (1981). Precursor control of neurotransmitter synthesis. *Pharmacology Review, 32,* 315–335.

Yaari, Y., Selzer, M. E. & Pincus, J. H. (1986). Phenytoin: Mechanisms of its anticonvulsant action. *Annals of Neurology, 20,* 171–184.

Yakovlev, P. & Lecours, A. R. (1967). The myelogenetic cycle of regional maturation of the brain. In A. Minkowski (Ed.), *Regional development of the brain in early life.* Philadelphia: F. A. Davis, 3–70.

Yepes, L., Balks, E., Winsberg, B. G. & Bigler, I. (1977). Amitriptyline and methylphenidate treatment of behaviorally disordered children. *Journal of Child Psychology and Psychiatry, 18,* 39–52.

Yeudall, L. T. (1977). Neuropsychological assessments in forensic disorders. *Canada's Mental Health, 25,* 7–14.

Yeudall, L. T., Fedora, O. & Fromm, D. (1987). A neuropsychological theory of persistent criminality: Implications for assessment and treatment. *Advances in Forensic Psychology and Psychiatry, 2,* 119–191.

Yeudall, L. T. & Fromm-Auch, D. (1979). Neuropsychological impairments in various psychopathological populations. In J. Gruzelier & P. Flor-Henry (Eds.), *Hemisphere asymmetries of function in psychopathology.* Amsterdam: Elsevier/North Holland Biomedical Press, 401–428.

Yochelson, S. &. Samenow, S. E. (1976). *The criminal personality: A profile for change,* vol. 1. New York: Jason Aronson.

Yonkers, K. A., Gullion, C., Williams, A., Novak, K. & Rush, A. J. (1996). Paroxetine as a treatment for premenstrual dysphoric disorder. *Journal of Clinical Psychopharmacology, 16,* 3–8.

Yonkers, K. A., Halbreich, U., Freeman, E., Brown, C. & Pearlstein, T. (1996). Sertraline in the treatment of premenstrual dysphoric disorder. *Psychopharmacology Bulletin, 32,* 41–46.

Young, E. B. (1990). The role of incest issues in relapse. *Journal of Psychoctive Drugs, 22,* 249–258.

Young, S. N., Pihl, R. O. & Ervin, F. R. (1988). The effect of altered tryptophan levels on mood and behavior in normal human males. *Clinical Neuropharmacology, 11,* S207–S215.

Young, S. N., Smith, S. E., Pihl, R. O. & Ervin, F. R. (1985). Tryptophan depletion causes a rapid lowering of mood in normal males. *Psychopharmacology, 87,* 173–177.

Yu-cum, S. & Yu-feng, W. (1984). Urinary 3-methoxy-4 hydroxyphenylglycol sulfate excretion in seventy-three schoolchildren with minimal brain dysfunction syndrome. *Biological Psychiatry, 19,* 861–868.

Yudofsky, S. C., Silver, J. M., Jackson, W., Endicott, J. & Williams, D. (1986). The overt aggression scale for the objective of verbal and physical aggression. *American Journal of Psychiatry, 143,* 35–39.

Yudofsky, S., Silver, J. & Schneider, S. (1987). Pharmacologic treatment of aggression. *Psychiatric Annals, 17,* 397–407.

Yudofsky, S. C., Stevens, L., Silver, J. M., Barsa, J. & Williams, D. (1984). Propranolol in the treatment of rage and violent behavior associated with Korsakoff's psychosis. *American Journal of Psychiatry, 141,* 114–115.

Yudofsky, S. C., Williams, A. D. & Gorman, J. (1981). Propranolol in the treatment of rage and violent behaviors in patients with chronic brain syndromes. *American Journal of Psychiatry, 138,* 218–220.

Zametkin, A. J., Nordahl, T. E., Gross, M., King, A. C., Semple, W. E., Rumsey, J., Hamberger, S. & Cohen, R. M. (1990). Cerebral glucose metabolism in adults with hyperactivity of childhood onset. *New England Journal of Medicine, 323,* 1361–1366.

Zecevic, M. & Rakic, P. (1976). Differentiation of Purkinje cells and their relationship to other components of developing cerebellar cortex in man. *Journal of Comparative Neurology, 167,* 97–48.

Zeman, W. & King, F. A. (1958). Tumor of the septum pellucidum and adjacent structures with abnormal affective behavior: An anterior midbrain structure syndrome. *Journal of Nervous and Mental Disease, 127,* 490–503.

Zigler, E., Taussig, C. & Black, K. (1992). Early childhood intervention: A promising preventative for juvenile delinquency. *American Psychologist, 47,* 997–1006.

Zimrin, H. (1986). A profile of survival. *Child Abuse and Neglect, 10,* 339–349.

Zubieta, J. K. & Alessi, N. E. (1992). Acute and chronic administration of trazodone in the treatment of disruptive behavior disorders in children. *Journal of Clinical Psychopharmacology, 12,* 346–351.

Zubieta, J. K. & Alessi, N. E. (1993). Is there a role of serotonin in the disruptive behavior disorders? A literature review. *Journal of Child & Adolescent Psychopharmacology, 3,* 11–35.

Zuckerman, B. & Bresnahan, K. (1991). Developmental and behavioral consequences of prenatal drug and alcohol exposure. *Pediatric Clinics of North America, 38,* 1387–1407.

Zuckerman, M. (1972). Drug usage as one manifestation of a "sensation seeking" trait. In E. Keup (Ed.), *Drug abuse: Current concepts and research.* Springfield, IL: C. C. Thomas, 154.

Zur Nieden, M. (1951). The influence of constitution and environment upon the development of adopted children. *The Journal of Psychology, 31,* 91–95.

Table of Acronyms

5-HIAA	5-hydroxyindolacetic acid
5-HT	5-hydroxytryptamine (serotonin)
AAQ	Aggressive Acts Questionnaire
ABE	Adult basic education
ACh	Acetylcholine
ACTH	Adrenocorticotrophic hormone
ADD	Attention deficit disorder
AIDS	Acquired immunodeficiency syndrome
ANA	Antinuclear antibody
ANS	Autonomic nervous system
APD	Antisocial personality disorder
API	Adolescent Problems Inventory
AR	Affective responsiveness (MFAD subscale)
BC	Behavior control (MFAD subscale)
BDHI	Buss-Durkee Hostility Inventory
BEAM	Brain electrical activity mapping
BHVQ	Brown History of Violence Questionnaire
BIS 11	Barratt Impulsiveness Scale, 11th ed.
BPAQ	Buss-Perry Aggression Questionnaire
CAT scan	Computerized axial tomography scan
CD	Conduct disorder
CD+	Conduct disorder, psychiatric criteria met for
CM	Communication (MFAD subscale)
COGA	Collaborative Study on the Genetics of Alcoholism
CO-	Conduct disorder, control group for test
COMT	Catechol-o-methyl-transferase
CPI	California Psychological Inventory
CRH	Corticotropin releasing hormone
CSA	Childhood sexual abuse
CSF	Cerebrospinal fluid
CT scan	Computerized tomography scan
Cz	Vertex (electrodes)
c^2	Common environmental influences
d,l	Dextro, levo (refers to a configuration or its mirror image of fenfluramine
DßH	Dopamine ß-hydroxylase
D1-D5	Dopamine receptors D1 through D5
DA	Dopamine
DAPP-DQ	Dimensional Assessment of Personality Pathology—Differential Questionnaire
DAT1	Dopamine transporter 1 (gene)
DHEW	Department of Health, Education & Welfare (now DHHS)
DHHS	Department of Health and Human Services

DHT	Dihydroxytriptamine
DLO	Direct lawful orders (from an officer, in prison)
DOTS-R	Dimensions of Temperament Survey—Revised
DRD4	D4 dopamine receptor
DRL	Differential reinforcement of low rate
DUI	Driving under the influence
DUSI	Drug Use Screening Inventory
DZ	Dizygotic (twins, fraternal)
ECF	Executive cognitive functioning
EEG	Electroencephalogram
EIVQ	Eysenck Impulsivity and Venturesomeness Questionnaire
EPQ-Jr.	Junior Eysenck Personality Questionnaire
ERP	Event-related potential
e^2	Unique environmental influences
FAS	Fetal alcohol syndrome
FDA	Food and Drug Administration
FEN	Fenfluramine
FH	Family history
FSH	Follicle stimulating hormone
Fz	Frontal (electrodes)
GABA	Gamma-amino butyric acid
GED	Graduate equivalency degree
GF	General functioning (MFAD subscale)
HIV	Human immunodeficiency virus
HMO	Health maintenance organization
HSCL	Hopkins Symptom Checklist
h^2	Heritability
ICD-9	*International Classification of Diseases,* 9th ed.
IDDM	Insulin-dependent diabetes mellitus
IDU	Injecting drug use
IED	Intermittent explosive disorder
IEP	Individualized education plan
IM	Intramuscularly
IPA	Interpersonal Problem-Solving Analysis
IQ	Intelligence quotient
LCA	Latent class analysis
LD	Learning disorder
LH	Luteinizing hormone
LHA	Life History of Aggression Scale
MAA	Multiple addictive associations
MAO	Monoamine oxidase
MAOA	Monoamine oxidase (form A)
MAOB	Monoamine oxidase (form B)
MAPS	Means End Problem-Solving technique
mCPP	m-chlorophenylpiperazine
MDE	Major depressive episode
MFAD	McMaster Family Assessment Device

MHPG	3 methy-4 hydroxy phenylglycol (major dopamine byproduct)
MMPI	Minnesota Multiphasic Personality Inventory
MPA	Medroxyprogesterone acetate
MPAs	Minor physical anomalies
MRI	Magnetic resonance imaging
MZ	Monozygotic (twins, identical)
NE	Norepinephrine
NIAAA	National Institute on Alcohol Abuse and Alcoholism
NIDA	National Institute on Drug Abuse
NIH	National Institute of Health
NIMH	National Institute of Mental Health
NRC	National Research Council
NT	Norepinephrine transporter
OCD	Obsessive-compulsive disorder
ODD	Oppositional defiant disorder
PCP/Psyche	Phencyclidine/psychedelics
PCR	Polymerase chain reaction
PET	Positron emission tomography
PRL	Prolactin response
PRL (*d,l*-FEN)	Prolactin response to fenfluramine
PSAP	Point Subtraction Aggression Paradigm
PS	Problem-solving (MFAD subscale)
PSI	Problem-solving inventory
PTSD	Posttraumatic stress disorder
Pz	Parietal (electrodes)
QTI	Quantitative trait loci
RAS	Reticular activating system
RDS	Reward deficiency syndrome
REM	Rapid eye movement
RL	Roles (MFAD subscale)
SCL	Symptom Check List
SES	Socioeconomic status
SMO	Safety maintenance organization
SO-CPI	Sociability Subscale of the California Psychological Inventory
SPECT	Single photon emission computer tomography
SQUID	Superconducting quantum interference device
SSRIs	Selective serotonin reuptake inhibitors
STAXI	State-Trait Anger Expression Inventory
SUD	Substance use disorder
TAP	Taylor Aggression Paradigm
TDO	Tryptophan dioxygenase
THC	Tetra hydro cannibanol
TOVA	Test of Variables of Attention
TPH	Tryptophan hydroxylase
TSC-4	Trauma Symptom Checklist

UCR	Uniform Crime Report
UTMB	University of Texas Medical Branch
WURS	Wender Utah Rating Scale
YO	Youthful offender

Index

[References are to pages.]

A

AAQ. *See* Aggressive Acts Questionnaire
Accountability, for antisocial behavior, 1-6, 1-7
Acetylcholine, 19-10
Acquired immunodeficiency syndrome (AIDS), 13-3
ACTH. *See* Adrenocorticotropic hormone
Acting out, 25-18
ADD. *See* Attention deficit disorder
Adderal, 7-11, 7-12
Addiction
    course of, 14-4, 14-5
    dopamine and, 18-3
    drug. *See* Substance abuse/addiction
    DSM-IV criteria, 13-1, 13-2
    to high stimulation, in attention deficit hyperactivity disorder, 18-5, 18-6
    sexual, 15-14
    treatment of, 23-15
Addington v. Texas, 23-7
ADHD. *See* Attention deficit hyperactivity disorder
Adolescent Problems Inventory (API), 10-9
Adolescents
    delinquents. *See* Delinquency
    disorders of. *See specific adolescent disorders*
    female, executive cognitive functioniong and, 11-6, 11-10
    psychopathy of, 19-4
    traumatic experiences, 25-16, 25-17
    violence and, 19-11, 19-12
Adoption studies
    antisocial personality disorder
        comorbidity with SUD, 8-10, 8-11
        genetic influences on, 7-6, 7-11, 8-6, 8-8
    concordance rates, 9-5
    of criminality, 24-2, 24-3
    epidemiological estimations, 7-6, 7-8
    goals of, 9-5
    methodology, 8-3, 8-4
    rationale for, 7-5, 7-6
    substance use disorder, 8-5
    vs. twin studies, 7-15, 7-16
ADRA2A gene, 16-10, 16-11
ADRA2C gene, 16-10, 16-11
Adrenergic genes, 16-10, 16-11
Adrenocorticotropic hormone, 25-15
Affective aggression, 19-4, 19-7
Affective empathy, 10-7, 10-8
Age
    assessments, for twin vs. adoption studies, 7-15
    violence and, 19-11, 19-12
Aggression
    affective, 19-4, 19-7
    animal models
        analogical reasoning and, 22-4, 22-5
        studies with, 7-3
    biological studies, 5-4, 5-9
        current, 5-7, 5-9
        serotonin, 5-4, 5-6
        tryptophan manipulation, 5-6, 5-7
    biological vulnerability, treatment implications of, 6-10, 6-11
    brain dysfunction and, P4-1, P4-2
    classification, 4-9, 6-2
        exploratory studies of, 4-10, 4-11
        in general population, 4-12, 4-14
        in inmate population, 4-9, 4-12
        outpatient studies of, 4-11, 4-12
        phenytoin use and, 4-9, 4-10
        selection process for, 4-10, 4-11
    cognitive deficits and, P4-1, P4-2
    criminal, factors in, 6-2
    criterion measures, 4-2, 4-4, 4-9, 4-15
        biological predictor measures and, 4-5, 4-7, 4-9
        family measures and, 4-6, 4-7
        interrelationships of, 4-5, 4-6
        personality measures and, 4-5
        personality traits and, 4-7
        social predictor measures and, 4-4, 4-6, 4-7
    defensive, 6-3
    definition of, 5-2
    dopamine and, 9-8, 9-9
    environmental factors, 5-15, 6-13
    facilitation, norepinephrine and, 6-7
    forms of, 6-2, 6-3
    genetic factors, 5-14, 6-13, 9-3
    from humiliation, 15-4
    impulsive
        See also Impulsivity
        biological mediators, 6-8, 6-9
        case study of, 6-11, 6-13
        definition of, 6-3
        dopamine receptor sensitivity and, 6-7, 6-8
        facilitation, norepinephrine and, 6-7
        genetic vulnerabilities, 6-9, 6-10
        serotonin in, 6-3, 6-4
    measurement
        laboratory, 5-2, 5-4
        rating scales for, 5-2

[References are to pages.]

Aggression *(continued)*
  molecular genetics, 16-5, 16-6
    dopamine genes and, 16-6, 16-9
    serotonin genes and, 16-9, 16-10
  neuropathology and, 22-9, 22-10
  pathological, 20-2
    in antisocial personality disorder, 20-16
    assessment instruments for, 20-3, 20-5
    in autism, 20-12
    in bipolar disorder, 20-15
    in borderline personality disorder, 20-16, 20-17
    in brain injury, 20-8, 20-9
    in dementia, 20-6, 20-7
    in Huntington's disease, 20-8
    in mental retardation, 20-9, 20-10
    in mentally handicapped patients, 20-9, 20-10
    neurochemical systems in, 20-2
    in organic brain syndrome, 20-8, 20-9
    pharmacotherapy for, 20-2, 20-3, 20-5, 20-6, 20-17, 20-18
    in posttraumatic stress disorder, 20-15
    in premenstrual dysphoric disorder, 20-15
    in psychoactive substance intoxication/withdrawal, 20-14
    in schizophrenia, 20-12, 20-14
    in seizure disorder, 20-9
    treatment of, 20-2
  pharmacotherapy, 4-15, 4-16, 5-15, 5-16
  premeditated, vs. impulsivity, 4-12, 4-14, 4-15
  prenatal drug exposure and, 25-10
  in psychopathology, 5-1, 5-2
  reactive, executive cognitive functioning and, 11-4, 11-6
  repeated, 5-2
  serotonin and, 5-14
  stability, 3-7
  victim rights, vs. aggressor rights, 22-3, 22-4
Aggressive Acts Questionnaire (AAQ), 4-12, 4-13
Aggressive responses, definition of, 5-3
AIDS. *See* Acquired immunodeficiency syndrome
Alcohol abuse
  See also Alcoholism
  in attention deficit hyperactivity disorder, 18-6, 18-7
  criminality and, 7-14
  dependent. *See* Alcoholism
  necrophilia and, 15-8
  progression to illicit drug use, 13-14
Alcoholism, P1-1, P1-2
  adoption studies, 8-5
  antisocial behavior and, 2-4
  antisocial personality prevalence in, 8-1
  with attention deficit hyperactivity disorder
    assessment of, 18-12
    treatment controversy, 18-13, 18-14
    crime control strategies and, 7-16, 7-17
  developmental trajectory
    description of, 2-3, 2-4
    environmental effects on, 2-11, 2-14
    DRD2 gene and, 16-6, 16-7
    of drug injectors, 13-7, 13-8
    environmental factors, 25-6
    epigenesis process in, 2-2, 2-3
  etiology, 2-2, 2-3, 2-10
  developmental disorders and, 2-4, 2-5
  developmental-behavior-genetic perspective, 2-16
  epigenetic model of, 2-14, 2-16
  genetic factors, 25-6
  impulsive/aggressive behavior and, 9-6, 9-9
  inheritance, 2-2, 2-3, 8-10, 8-11
  intervention programs, 2-11, 2-17, 2-18
  liability, 2-2, 2-3, 2-5, 2-6
  linkage analysis, 9-7
  phenotype, 2-5, 2-6
    defining, importance of, 2-10
    end-point, 2-11
    environmental effects on, 2-11, 2-14
    heterogeneity of, 2-10, 2-11
  prevention, 2-16, 2-17
  risk, behavioral genetics and, 2-9, 2-10
  suicidal behavior and, 9-9
  temperament associated with, 2-6, 2-9
  treatment, 2-17, 2-18
  twin studies, 8-5, 8-6
  type II, 9-10
Alienation, serial murder and, 15-13, 15-14
Alleles, 9-5
Alpha blockers, 17-12
Alternative sentencing, 18-14
Aluminum toxicity, 12-7
a-Mannosidosis, 7-3
Amitriptyline, 20-16
Ammunition possession, family violence offenders and, 27-17
Amphetamine
  combined salts of, 7-11, 7-12
  d-Amphetamine (Dexedrine), 16-9
  dependence, of drug injectors, 13-7, 13-8
ANA. *See* Antinuclear antibody
Anafranil, for obsessive-compulsive behavior, 17-13
Analogical reasoning, animal models of aggression and, 22-4, 22-5
Androgen receptor gene, 16-12
Anger Attacks Questionnaire, 20-5
Anger Expression Scale, 20-4
Anger management therapy, for ADHD, 18-11, 18-12
Animal models
  of aggression, 22-4, 22-5
  brain damage in, 22-5, 22-6
Anticonvulsants, for aggression, 4-9, 4-10, 4-15, 4-16, 20-17
  in conduct disorder, 20-11, 20-12
  in dementia, 20-7
  in mental retardation, 20-10
  in organic brain syndrome, 20-8
  in schizophrenia, 20-13
  in seizure disorder, 20-9
Antidepressants, for aggression, 20-18
Antinuclear antibody (ANA), 25-15
Antipsychotics, for aggression, 20-17
  in dementia, 20-7
  in mental retardation, 20-9
  in schizophrenia, 20-12–20-14
Antisocial behavior
  alcoholism and, 2-4, 2-5

[References are to pages.]

biological aspects, environmentally induced, 25-7, 25-18
    caregiver-child interactions, 25-13, 25-14
    perinatal complications, 25-12, 25-13
    prenatal, 25-8, 25-12
    social environment, 25-13
    stress, 25-7, 25-8
biological factors, P2-1, P2-3
consequences of, 11-1, 11-2
developmental precursors, 3-7
dopamine and, 9-9
early- vs. late-starter pathways, 3-5, 3-6
executive cognitive functioning and, 11-3
    in female adolescents, 11-6, 11-7
    hypothetical explanation of, 11-11
    implications for prevention, 11-12, 11-13
    laboratory studies of, 11-10, 11-11
    in preadolescent boys, 11-3, 11-5
gender differences, 24-2
genetic factors, 9-2, 9-14
heuristic biosocial model of, 25-5, 25-6
inheritance, 7-3, 7-4
neuropsychological perspective, 11-2
neutral interdisciplinary model of, 1-4, 1-5
pathologic. *See* Antisocial personality disorder
predicting
    early behavior problems and, 3-7
    family factors in, 3-7, 3-8
prevention, P9-1, P9-2
risk factors, low executive cognitive functioning as, 11-13
treatment, P9-1, P9-2
twin studies, 24-3, 24-4
vulnerability, 1-3
Antisocial personality disorder (APD)
    aggression in, 20-16
    vs. attention deficit hyperactivity disorder, 18-9
    behavior patterns in, 8-2
    comorbidity
        illicit drug use, 13-4, 13-6, 13-6, 13-7
        with SUD. *See* Substance use disorder, with antisocial personality disorder
    differential diagnosis, 17-17, 17-18
    of drug injectors, 13-7, 13-8
    DSM-IV criteria, A-2
    etiology, 8-2, 8-3
    genetic influences, 8-6
        adoption studies, 8-6, 8-8
        ethical issues and, 16-18, 16-19
        twin studies, 8-8, 8-9
    impulsivity and, 5-10, 5-11
    lifetime prevalance
        in general population, 8-1
        in substance abusers, 8-1, 8-2
    molecular genetics of, 16-5, 16-6
    prediction of
        attention deficit hyperactivity disorder and, 16-4, 16-5
        conduct disorder and, 16-4, 16-5
    serial killers and, 15-6
    serial murder and, 15-9, 15-10
    serotonin levels in, 5-6

Anxiety
    of drug injectors, 13-7, 13-8
    obsessive-compulsive disorder and, 15-12
APD. *See* Antisocial personality disorder
API. *See* Adolescent Problems Inventory
Arsenic toxicity, 12-7
Assessment instruments, for pathological aggression, 20-3, 20-5
Association studies, of genotype-behavior relationships, 7-4
Attachment, 3-15 n.1, 10-14
Attachment theory of criminality, 3-6
Attention deficit disorder (ADD)
    See also Attention deficit hyperactivity disorder
    aggressive, psychostimulants for, 20-10, 20-11
    alcoholism and, 2-8, 2-9
    case example, 17-18, 17-19
    missed diagnosis, hidden costs of, 17-19, 17-20
    in prison, medications for, 17-11, 17-12
Attention deficit hyperactivity disorder (ADHD)
    acquired, 18-6
    adult antisocial behavior prediction and, 16-47, 16-5
    alternative sentencing and, 18-14
    antisocial behavior and, 7-14, P6-1, P6-2
    vs. attention deficit hyperactivity disorder, 18-9
    brain imaging, 18-3
    case example, 17-18, 17-19
    clinical manifestations, 16-3
        activity level, 18-4, 18-5
        addiction to high stimulation levels, 18-5, 18-6
        in adult, 17-2, 17-3
        enhanced sensitivity, 18-5
        gender differences in, 17-2
        impulse dyscontrol, 18-3, 18-4
        of inmate, 18-2
        rage/violence, 18-5
    comorbidity
        with addiction, 18-12, 18-14
        with conduct disorder, 16-3
        criminal behavior and, 18-6, 18-7
    diagnosis
        accurate, formulation of, 18-8, 18-9
        missed, hidden costs of, 17-19, 17-20
    differential diagnoses, 17-16, 17-18
    DSM-IV criteria, A-3, A-4
    executive cognitive functioning and, 11-3
    as genetic disorder, 16-3
    molecular genetics, 16-12, 16-13
        adrenergic genes, 16-10, 16-11
        androgen receptor gene, 16-12
        DRD2 gene and, 16-6, 16-7
        DRD4 gene and, 16-7, 16-8
        DRD5 gene and, 16-8, 16-9
        GABA genes, 16-12
        monoamine oxidase genes and, 16-11, 16-12
    neurobiological basis, P6-2
    offender with, 18-7, 18-8, 18-14, 18-15
    pharmacotherapy, site of action for, 16-9
    polygenetic inheritance, 16-13, 16-15
        multivariate analysis of associations of, 16-13, 16-17
        relevance to treatment, 16-17, 16-19
    in prison inmates, P6-2, P6-3

[References are to pages.]

Attention deficit hyperactivity disorder *(continued)*
    ritalin therapy, for adult, 17-3
    self-help/educational books/articles, 17-6
    symptoms, in childhood, 18-13
    treatment, 18-9, 18-10
        behavioral repatterning for, 18-11, 18-12
        medications for, 18-10, 18-11
        prison, before, 16-17
        prison, in, 16-17, 16-18
Attention difficulties, in attention deficit hyperactivity disorder, 18-4
Attention span-persistence, alcoholism and, 2-8, 2-9
Autism
    aggression in, 20-12
    DRD2 gene and, 16-6, 16-7

B

Barratt Impulsiveness Scale (BIS-11), 4-5, 5-10
BDHI. *See* Buss-Durkee Hostility Inventory
Behavior
    activity level
        alcoholism and, 2-7
        high, alcoholism and, 2-12, 2-13
        measurement, 2-7
    analytic models, 22-1–22-3
    antisocial. *See* Antisocial behavior
    bad, vs. abnormal sexual makeup, 21-5, 21-6
    brain dysfunction and, 25-2
    brain structure and, 12-2
    catecholamine neurotransmitters and, 6-6, 6-7
    criminal. *See* Criminal behavior
    in criminology explanations, 10-3, 10-4
    delinquent. *See* Delinquency
    dysfunction, causes of, 25-2
    externalized, 25-18
    heritable, impact of environment on, 9-13
    inhibition, brain structures and, 19-9
    intervention-related changes, evaluation of, 26-4
    neuroscientific models, 22-3
    outcomes, genetic traits and, 9-2, 9-3
    predestination of, 25-3, 25-4
    problems, 3-15 n.2
        early, in predicting criminal behavior, 3-7
        genetic basis for, 17-10
        medical treatment, justification for, 17-10
        minor physical anomalies in, 25-8, 25-9
        polygenetic inheritance, 17-10
    repatterning, for attention deficit hyperactivity disorder, 18-11, 18-12
    toward family violence, intervention focus on, 27-6, 27-7
    transactional model of, 3-7, 3-8
    truth about, search for, 23-14
Behavior theory of criminal behavior, 3-3, 3-4
Behavior therapy, for sexual deviation disorders, 21-9, 21-10
Behavioral disorders. *See* Behavior, problems
Behavioral genetics
    of alcoholism risk, 2-9, 2-10
    of APD and SUD comorbidity, 8-13
Behavioral sciences
    criminal justice system applications, P8-1, P8-3
    legal applications, P8-1, P8-3

Benzodiazepines, for aggression, 20-7, 20-17
Beta-blockers
    See also specific beta-blockers
    for aggression, 6-11, 20-17, 20-18
    in dementia, 20-7
    in schizophrenia, 20-13
BHVQ. *See* Brown History of Violence Questionnaire
Biological factors
    in antisocial outcome, 25-5
    in paraphilia development, 21-7, 21-8
    risk, dynamic relationships of, 26-3, 26-4
    television violence effects on, 25-18
    traits
        prevention and, 25-4, 25-5
        traumatic experiences and, 25-4
    vulnerability, 1-3
Biological measures
    aggression criterion measures and, 4-7, 4-9
    data replication in, 1-7
    predictive, 4-5
Bipolar disorder
    aggression in, 20-15
    differential diagnosis, 17-16
    medications for, 17-13, 17-14
Birth complications
    brain dysfunction from, 12-7, 12-8
    of twins, 7-14, 7-15
BIS-11. *See* Barratt Impulsiveness Scale
Borderline personality disorder, impulsive/aggressive behavior in, 9-6, 20-16, 20-17
BPAQ. *See* Buss-Perry Aggression Questionnaire
Brain
    cellular death, from child abuse/trauma, 25-15, 25-16
    chemical alterations, antisocial behavior and
    damage/dysfunction
        aggression and, P4-1, P4-2, 22-6, 22-7
        in animal model, 22-5, 22-6
        behavior/temperament and, 25-2
        from birth complications, 12-7, 12-8
        criminal violence and, 19-12, 19-13
        from dietary conditions, 12-6, 12-7
        from environmental toxins, 12-7
        from head injuries, 12-5
        from maternal drug use, 12-7, 12-8
        in murderers, 19-15
        nonaccidental correlates, 22-7, 22-9
        with pathological aggression, pharmacotherapy for, 20-8, 20-9
        from prenatal nicotine exposure, 25-10, 25-11
        prevention of, 12-15, 12-16
        violent behavior and, 12-3, 12-5
    development, testosterone and, 25-7
    imaging, for ADHD diagnosis, 18-3, 18-8
    proneness, to violence, 22-3
    stress effects on, 25-7, 25-8
    structure
        behavior and, 12-2
        behavioral inhibition and, 19-9
Brain-behavior relationship research
    objectives for, 12-2
    premises, 12-2
    primary purpose of, 12-3

[References are to pages.]

Brawner, United States v., 24-7
Brief Psychiatric Rating Scale, 20-4
Briquet's syndrome, 24-2
Brown History of Violence Questionnaire (BHVQ), 5-2, 5-4
Bupropion (Wellbutrin)
  for aggression
    in ADD, 20-11
    in conduct disorder, 20-11
  for attention deficit hyperactivity disorder, 18-10
  for emotional leveling, 17-12, 17-13
  site of action, 16-9
Businesses, role in family violence prevention, 27-20
Buspirone
  for aggression, 20-18
  in autism, 20-12
  in Huntington's disease, 20-8
  in mental retardation, 20-10
  in organic brain syndrome, 20-8
  prolactin release and, 5-7, 5-8
  serotonin function and, 5-5
Buss-Durkee Hostility Inventory (BDHI), 5-2, 20-4
Buss-Perry Aggression Questionnaire (BPQ), 4-4, 5-2, 20-4
Buss's Aggression Machine Paradigm, 5-3

C

Cadmium toxicity, 12-7
California Personality Inventory (CPI), 10-7
Candidate genes, 7-4, 9-7
Cannabis
  dependence, of drug injectors, 13-7, 13-8
  progression to illicit drug use, 13-14
Carbamazepine (Tegretol)
  for aggression in dementia, 20-7
  for borderline personality disorder, 20-16
  for emotional leveling, 17-13
  for schizophrenia, 20-13
  for seizure disorder, 20-9
Career criminals, 7-16
Caregiver-child interaction, 25-13, 25-14
Castration, for sexual deviation disorders, 21-10, 21-11
Catecholamines, 25-15
Cerebrospinal fluid 5-HIAA. *See* 5-Hydroxyindolacetic acid, CSF
C-fos gene, 25-12
Character, definition of, 6-2
Chemical dependency treatment programs, sentencing for, 18-14
Child physical abuse
  behavioral disorder risk and, 25-15, 25-16
  differential diagnosis, 17-17
  head injuries, neurological dysfunction from, 12-5
Child sex abuse
  adult psychological symptoms and, 14-10, 14-11
  developmental impact of, 14-2
  disorders associated with, 14-3
  of female addicts, 14-2, 14-3
    background for current study, 14-4
    data analysis, 14-3, 14-4
    methodology for studying, 14-3
    statistical analyses, findings of, 14-4, 14-8
    treatment/prevention approaches, 14-12, 14-13

home atmosphere and, 14-11, 14-12
later drug abuse risk, P5-1, P5-2
paraphilia development and, 21-7
parental substance abuse and, 14-10
parenting and, 14-11
Children
  abuse of. *See* Child physical abuse; Child sex abuse
  aggressive, adult criminal violence and, 19-13, 19-14
  of alcoholics, emotionality and, 2-8
  difficult, discipline for, 25-16
Cholesterol, in impulsive aggression, 6-9
Chromosomal abnormalities, paraphilia development and, 21-7
Churches, role in family violence prevention, 27-21
Circadian rhythms, violence and, 19-11
Circumscribed infantilism, 19-3
Citalopram, for aggression, 20-7, 20-14
Civil commitment, 23-9
  vs. criminal commitment, 23-6, 23-7
  procedures, 23-4, 23-5
Civil liberty, public health model and, 26-6, 26-7
Clinical Global Impression Scale, 20-4
Clinician-rated instruments, for assessment of pathological aggression, 20-3, 20-4
Clomipramine, for aggression, 20-12, 20-18
Clonidine
  for aggression, 20-12, 20-18
  for attention deficit hyperactivity disorder, 16-10, 16-11
  for conduct disorder, 16-10, 16-11, 20-12
  for emotional leveling, 17-12
  for obsessive-compulsive behavior, 17-13
  for Tourette's syndrome, 17-12
Cloning, 9-5
Clozapine, for aggression
  in borderline personality disorder, 20-16
  in mental retardation, 20-9
  in organic brain syndrome, 20-9
  in schizophrenia, 20-14
Cocaine
  addiction, aggressiveness and, 9-9
  dependence, of drug injectors, 13-7, 13-8
  prenatal exposure, 25-6, 25-7, 25-10, 25-11
  use, prevalence of, 13-3
COGA. *See* Collaborative Study on the Genetics of Alcoholism
Cognition
  cocaine-exposed infants and, 25-12
  in correctional interventions, 10-18, 10-19
  crime and, 10-5, 10-12
  in criminology theory
    implicit role of, 10-12, 10-16
    integration of, 10-16, 10-18
  deficits
    aggression and, P4-1, P4-2
    violence and, 12-4, 12-5
  definition of, 10-4
  effect on criminal/delinquent behavior, 3-10
  focus, in criminology, 10-19, 10-20
  gender differences in, 25-7
  impersonal
    deficits of, 10-5, 10-6

[References are to pages.]

Cognition *(continued)*
    definition of, 10-5
    interpersonal or social
        deficits of, 10-5, 10-6
        definition of, 10-5
    interrelatedness of, 10-16, 10-17
    lack of emphasis on, in criminological theory, 10-3, 10-5
    locus of control, 10-10, 10-12
    problem-solving ability, 10-8, 10-10
    social perspective-taking, 10-6, 10-8
Cognitive intervention modalities, 10-18, 10-19
Cognitive psychology, 10-2
Cognitive social learning, of criminality, 3-5, 3-6
Cognitive tests, 11-2
"Cogntive revolution," 10-2
Collaborative Study on the Genetics of Alcoholism (COGA), 13-5, 13-6
Community programs, for family violence prevention, 27-10
    multidisciplinary approach for, 27-15, 27-16
    psychologist role in, 27-11, 27-12
Competitive Reaction Time Task, 5-3, 5-4
Computer game interventions, for cognitive skills training, 11-12, 11-13
Conditional free will, 1-5, 1-6
Conduct disorder
    adult antisocial behavior prediction and, 16-4, 16-5
    aggressive
        anticonvulsants for, 20-11, 20-12
        lithium for, 20-11
        neuroleptics for, 20-11
        psychostimulants for, 20-10, 20-11
    antisocial behavior and, 7-14
    clonidine for, 16-10, 16-11
    comorbidity
        with attention deficit hyperactivity disorder, 16-3
        with illicit drug use, 13-4, 13-5
    difficult temperament and, 11-7, 11-9
    dopamine and, 9-8
    DSM-IV criteria, A-4, A-5
    executive cognitive functioning and, 11-3, 11-7, 11-9
    as genetic disorder, 16-3, 16-4
    inheritance, polygenic, 16-13, 16-15
    molecular genetics, 16-5, 16-6
        androgen receptor gene, 16-12
        dopamine genes and, 16-6, 16-9
        serotonin genes and, 16-9, 16-10
    norepinephrine in, 16-10, 16-11
Conflict Tactics Scales, 20-5
Continuous traits, 8-4
Control
    in obsessive-compulsive disorder, 15-12
    in serial murder, 15-3
Cook Medley Hostility Scale, 20-5
Copeland Symptom Checklist, 18-8
Corporations, role in family violence prevention, 27-20
Correctional programming
    cognitive, effectiveness of, 10-18, 10-19
    effective/adequate, 12-14, 12-15

Corrections officers, ADD/ADHD education of, 17-14, 17-15
Corticotropin releasing hormone (CRH), 25-15
Cortisol, 25-15
CPI. *See* California Personality Inventory
Craving disorders, paraphilias as, 21-8, 21-9
CRH. *See* Corticotropin releasing hormone
Crime
    as antisocial act, 23-14
    commission, reasons for, 23-15
    control strategies, genetic epidemiologic research implications, 7-16, 7-18
    general theory of, 10-15
Criminal behavior
    alcohol abuse and, 7-14
    alcoholism and, 8-11
    attachment theory of, 3-6
    attention deficit hyperactivity disorder and, 18-6, 18-7
    cognition and, 3-10
    diagnosis, accuracy of, 16-2
    female, 7-14
    genetic identification, ethical issues in, 16-18, 16-19
    heritable factors in
        adoption studies and, 24-2, 24-3
        nature-nurture controversy and, 24-1, 24-2
        twin studies and, 24-3, 24-4
    intergenerational transmission, study of, 24-3
    mental disorders
        classification and, 3-14
        disaggregation and, 3-13, 3-14
        monoamine oxidase and, 9-11, 9-12
        motivation and, 3-10
    neurobiology of
        legal policy and, 24-4, 24-6
        research on, 18-2, 18-3
    neurological perspective, 19-2
    protective factors, 3-8, 3-9
    psychological theories of, 3-2, 3-3
        behavioral, 3-3, 3-4
        cognitive social learning, 3-5, 3-6
    social control, 3-6, 3-7
    social learning, 3-4, 3-5
    self-control and, 10-15
    twin study data, 7-6, 7-10
    violent
        neuropathologic correlates of, 19-12, 19-13
        neuropathology and, 19-15
        pharmacotherapy for, 19-15, 19-16
Criminal commitment, vs. civil commitment, 23-6, 23-7
Criminal justice system
    accountability in, 1-6, 1-7
    behavioral science applications, P8-1, P8-3
    components, 23-11
    courses, psychology role in, 3-2, 3-3
    education, psychology in, 3-14, 3-15
    familiarity with psychiatric diagnoses, 3-12, 3-13
    as health maintenance organization, 23-3
    heritability/molecular genetic studies and, 9-12, 9-13
    identification of causal relationships, 26-3
    integrating services in, 2-19

[References are to pages.]

medications, custodial, 26-4
practices
    current effectiveness of, 1-5, 1-6
    in past, 1-1, 1-2
    public safety and, 23-3
    as safety maintenance organization, 23-2, 23-4
    scientific basis for, 1-1
Criminality
    paradigm shift, 24-5, 24-6
Criminology education, psychology role in, 3-2, 3-3
Criminology theory
    cognitive approach, 10-3, 10-5
        methodological problems and, 10-4, 10-5
        sociological/behavioral explanations and, 10-3, 10-4
    integration of cognition in, 10-16, 10-18
Cross-fostering analyses, 7-12, 7-14
CSF 5-HIAA. *See* 5-Hydroxyindolacetic acid, CSF
Cycle of violence, 3-4, 3-5
Cylert (pemoline), 7-11, 16-9
Cyproterone acetate, for sexual deviation disorders, 21-11

D

Dahmer, Jeffrey, 15-1, 15-2, 15-6, 15-7
DAT1 gene, 16-9
DBH gene, 16-10
Deafness-hypogonadism syndrome, 7-3
Defenses, 23-12, 23-14
Degradation of partner, serial murder and, 15-8
Dehumanization, in serial murder, 15-8, 15-13
Delinquency
    aggressive, dextroamphetamine for, 20-10, 20-11
    behavior theory of, 3-3, 3-4
    cognition and, 10-4, 10-5
    cognitive variables in, 10-16
    early, in predicting criminal behavior, 3-7
    impulsivity and, 5-10, 5-11
    intervention programs, multidimensional, 3-11, 3-12
    prevention, early childhood intervention for, 3-10, 3-12
    protective factors, 3-8, 3-9, 3-11
    rates, in twin studies, 7-6, 7-8
    risk, 3-11
    social egocentricism and, 10-7
Delusions, differential diagnosis, 17-17
Depakote. *See* Valproate
Depo-Provera (medroxyprogesterone acetate), 21-11, 21-13
Depression
    bipolar. *See* Bipolar disorder
    comorbidity
        with attention deficit hyperactivity disorder, 18-12
        with illicit drug use, 13-6–13-8
    pathological aggression in, 20-14
    polygenic inheritance, 16-13, 16-15
Desipramine, 20-12
Developmental disorders
    alcoholism etiology and, 2-4, 2-5
    minor physical anomalies in, 25-8, 25-9

Dexedrine (d-amphetamine), 16-9
Dextroamphetamine, 20-10, 20-11
Diagnostic and Statistical Manual of Mental Disorders
    diagnostic criteria for mental disorders, 3-13
    DSM-IV criteria
        addiction, 13-1, 13-2
        antisocial personality disorder, A-2
        attention deficit hyperactivity disorder, 17-4, 18-4, A-3, A-4
        Axis I disorders, 15-5
        Axis II disorders, 15-5, 15-6
        conduct disorder, A-4, A5
        intermittent disorder, A-2, A-3
        mental disorders, 15-5, 15-7
        obsessive-compulsive personality disorder, 15-11, 15-12
        oppositional defiant disorder, A-5
        paraphilias, 21-3
        pathological aggression, 20-5, 20-6
        sexual addiction, 15-14
        substance abuse, A-2
        substance dependence, A-1, A-2
        substance use disorder, 8-2
    future considerations for trauma reactions, 27-23
    validity of, 2-11
Dietary conditions, causing brain dysfunction, 12-6, 12-7
Differential reinforcement of low rate reinforcement schedule, 5-10
Diphenylhydantoin, for aggression, 20-11, 20-12, 20-17
Disaggregation, 3-13, 3-14
Disinhibition, alcoholism and, 2-9
Disruptive behavioral disorders, childhood, 16-17
Dissociation, of serial killer, 15-3
Diurnal rhythms, violence and, 19-11
Dizygotic twins. *See* Twin studies
DNA cloning, 9-5
DNA sequence scanning, 9-7, 9-8
Doe, Heller v., 23-6
Domestic violence. *See* Family violence
Dominance, 7-4
Dopamine
    addiction and, 18-3
    aggression and, 9-8, 9-9
    attention deficit hyperactivity disorder and, 18-3
    behavioral effects, 19-10
    reward pathways, 9-8, 9-9
Dopamine b-hydroxylase, 16-10
Dopamine genes, 16-6, 16-9
Dopamine receptor sensitivity, impulsive aggression and, 6-7, 6-8
Dopamine reward system, stress and, 25-17
Dopamine transporter gene, 16-9
DRD1 gene, 16-9
DRD2 gene, 16-6, 16-7
DRD5 gene, 16-8, 16-9
Drug abuse/addiction. *See* Substance abuse/addiction; Substance use disorder
Drug injectors, subclassification, 13-7, 13-9
Drug Use Screening Inventory (DUSI), 2-11, 2-18
Drugs, prescription. *See* Medications
Due process, 23-8
DUSI. *See* Drug Use Screening Inventory

[References are to pages.]

E

ECF. *See* Executive cognitive functioning
Education
    in cognitive intervention modalities, 10-19
    of corrections officers on ADD/ADHD, 17-14, 17-15
    criminology, psychology role in, 3-2, 3-3
    on family violence
        professional, 27-23
        public, 26-2, 27-18, 27-25
EIVQ. *See* Eysenck Impulsivity and Venturesomeness Scale
Electroencephalography (EEG)
    for attention deficit hyperactivity disorder diagnosis, 17-16, 17-17
    of neonate exposed to cocaine, 25-11
    in psychopathy, 19-3
Eltoprazine, for aggression, 20-10, 20-13
Emotional disorders, nonepileptic, phenytoin for, 4-10
Emotional leveling, medications for, 17-12, 17-13
Emotionality, alcoholism and, 2-8
Emotions Profile Index, 5-10
Empathy, 10-6, 10-8
Empowerment, for family violence prevention, 27-5, 27-9
Encephalopathy, differential diagnosis, 17-17
Environment
    aggression and, 5-15, 6-13
    alcoholism and, 2-11, 2-14
    in antisocial personality disorder, 8-3
    in antisocial personality disorder with substance abuse, 8-12
    behavioral dysfunction and, 25-2
    context, for family violence prevention, 27-4
    home
        adoptive, adverse, 7-13
        alcoholism development and, 2-5, 2-13, 2-14
        child sexual abuse and, 14-11, 14-12
        female narcotics addicts and, 14-7, 14-8
    impulsivity and, 5-15
    influences
        on heritable behaviors, 9-13
        twin studies on, 7-8, 7-10, 7-12
    interaction
        with genetic factors, 25-6, 25-7
        with temperament, alcoholism and, 2-15
    risk factors
        dynamic relationships of, 26-3, 26-4
        identification of, 26-2, 26-3
    social. *See* Social environment
    stimulation, from mother-child bond, 25-13, 25-14
    stressors, interaction with genetic risks, 7-17, 7-18
    structuring, to minimize risk factors, 25-2, 25-4
Enzymes, 9-4
Epidemiology, genetic
    adoption studies, 7-5, 7-6
    twin studies, 7-4, 7-5
Epigenesis, in alcoholism, 2-2, 2-3
Epilepsy, violence and, 19-8, 19-9
Episodic dyscontrol. *See* Intermittent explosive disorder
EPQ-Jr. *See* Junior Eysenck Personality Questionnaire
Ethical issues, genetic identification of criminal/antisocial behavior risk, 16-18, 16-19
Event related potentials (ERPs), 4-5, 4-8
Executive cognitive functioning (ECF), 11-2
    antisocial behavior and, 11-3
        explanation, hypothetical, 11-11
        prevention, implications for, 11-12, 11-13
    development of
        computer games, use of, 11-12, 11-13
        interactive intervention, 11-13
    difficult temperament and, 11-7, 11-9
    early skills development, 11-12
    female adolescents and, 11-6, 11-10
    language skills and, 11-9, 11-10
    measurement of, 11-2
    reactive aggression and, 11-4, 11-6
    social disadvantage and, 11-4
Exhibitionism, 21-4
Expert opinion, on mental illness, 23-7
Eysenck Extroversion Scale, 5-10
Eysenck Impulsivity and Venturesomeness Scale (EIVQ), 5-10

F

Facilitators, for serial murder, 15-3
Familial aggregation, 7-2
Family
    factors, in predicting antisocial behavior, 3-7, 3-8
    of female addicts, 14-5, 14-6
    responsibility in preventing violence, 27-20, 27-21
    studies, of genetic influences, 8-3
    violence in. *See* Family violence
Family predictor measures, aggression criterion measures and, 4-6, 4-7
Family violence
    advocates, mental health professionals and, 27-12, 27-14
    attitudes, intervention focus on, 27-6, 27-7
    developmental processes and, 27-5
    empowerment and, 27-5
    gender role socialization and, 27-4, 27-5
    interventions
        past/present approaches, 27-2
        professional training for, 27-16
        public policy and, 27-15, 27-18
        in public schools, 27-18
        targeted, 27-7, 27-9
        universal, 27-6, 27-8
    measurement instruments, 27-25
    offenders
        firearm/ammunition possession and, 27-17
        treatment programs for, 27-17
    presentence assessment, 27-16, 27-17
    prevention
        collaborative efforts for, 27-14, 27-15
        community-wide efforts for, 27-10
        developmental process focus for, 27-4
        economic benefits of, 27-11
        environmental context for, 27-4
        epidemiological perspective for, 27-3
        health promotion programs in, 27-6
        primary, strategies for, 27-18, 27-19
        program development for, 27-3, 27-4
        promising approaches for, 27-9, 27-10
        public education and, 27-18, 27-25

[References are to pages.]

public policy and, 27-15, 27-18
public school programs for, 27-19, 27-20
requirements for, 27-3
standards/guidelines for, 27-22
protection factors, identification of, 27-3
reduction, by community policing programs, 27-18
research
    data collection for, 27-24, 27-25
    epidemiologic, 27-24
    funding of, 27-23, 27-24
    on social context, 27-24
risk factors, 27-3, 27-5
training/education
    professional, 27-23
    for therapists, 27-23
victimization
    compensation for, 27-18
    history of, screening for, 27-21, 27-13
    individual treatment plans for, 27-21, 27-13
Famiy Violence Coordinating Councils, 27-10, 27-15
Fantasies, serial murder and, 15-3, 15-4
FAS. *See* Fetal alcohol syndrome
Fenfluramine
    for impulsivity, 5-11, 5-12
    pharmaco-challenge studies of impulsive aggression, 6-5, 6-6
    serotonin function and, 5-5, 5-7, 5-9
Fetal alcohol syndrome (FAS), 25-9, 25-10
Fetishes. *See* Transvestitic fetishes
Firearm possession, family violence offenders and, 27-17
5-HT. *See* Serotonin
5-Hydroxyindolacetic acid, CSF
    aggressive behavior and, 5-6
    impulsive aggression and, 6-3, 6-4, 6-7, 6-8
    impulsivity and, 5-11, 5-12, 9-9
    suicide and, 6-3, 6-4
5-Hydroxytryptamine. *See* Serotonin
Fixated pedophilia, 21-5
Fluoxetine (Prozac)
    for aggression, 4-16, 6-10, 6-11
    in borderline personality disorder, 20-16
    for emotional leveling, 17-13
    in mental retardation, 20-10
    for obsessive-compulsive behavior, 17-13
Fluphenazine, 20-14
Fluvoxamine, for aggression, 20-7, 20-12
Follicle-stimulating hormone (FSH), 21-7
Food intake, hypoglycemia and, 19-11
Foucha v. Louisiana, 23-7
Fragile X syndrome, 7-3
Free will, 15-14, 15-15, 24-4
Frontal lobe syndrome, 12-3, 12-4, 22-5
FSH. *See* Follicle-stimulating hormone

G

GABA. *See* Gamma-aminobutyric acid
GABRB3 receptor gene, 16-12
Gage, Phineas, 12-3, 12-4
Gamma-aminobutyric acid (GABA), 19-10
Gamma-aminobutyric acid genes, 16-12
Gender differences
    in antisocial personality disorder, 8-9, 24-2

in cognition, 25-7
in criminality, adoption studies of, 24-2, 24-3
in violent behavior, 19-12
Gender role socialization, family violence and, 27-4, 27-5
Gene-behavior relationships, dopamine and, 9-8
Gene-environment interactions
    mechanisms, 9-4, 9-5
    terminology, 9-3, 9-4
General strain theory, 10-14, 10-15
Genetic disorders, antisocial behavior risk in, 7-3, 7-4
Genetic epidemiology
    adoption studies, 7-5, 7-6
    implications for crime control, 7-16, 7-18
    twin studies, 7-4, 7-5
Genetic factors, 7-2
    aggression, 5-14, 6-13
    assessment/evaluation of, 9-6, 9-7
        by DNA sequence scanning, 9-7, 9-8
        by linkage analysis, 9-7
    in impulsive aggression, 6-9, 6-10
    impulsivity, 5-14
    interaction with environmental factors, 25-6, 25-7
    markers, 9-3
    risk, dynamic relationships of, 26-3, 26-4
    traits
        environmental impact on, 25-4, 25-5
        transmission, measuring extent of, 9-5, 9-6
Genetic influences, P3-1, P3-2
    adoption studies, 8-3, 8-4
    in antisocial personality disorder
        adoption studies, 8-6, 8-8
        twin studies, 8-8, 8-9
    family studies, 8-3
    in substance use disorder, 8-4, 8-5
        adoption studies, 8-5
        twin studies, 8-5, 8-6
    twin studies, 8-4
Genetics
    of attention deficit hyperactivity disorder, 16-3
    of conduct disorder, 16-3, 16-4
    violence and, 19-12
Genotype, 9-3, 9-12, 9-13
Genotype-behavior relationships
    animal studies, 7-2, 7-3
    association studies, 7-4
    linkage studies, 7-4
Genotype-environment correlation, 7-12, 7-13
Genotype-environment interaction, 7-12–7-14
Glucocorticoid release, in stress, 25-15, 25-16
Glucose, in impulsive aggression, 6-8
"Go, no-go" task, 5-10
Governing variables, 22-10
Group therapy, for attention deficit hyperactivity disorder, 18-11
Growth hormone, 25-14
Guanfacine (Tenex), 17-12

H

Hallucinations, differential diagnosis, 17-17
Hallucinogen dependence, of drug injectors, 13-7, 13-8
Haloperidol, for aggression, 20-7, 20-16

[References are to pages.]

Head injuries
  criminal violence and, 19-13
  differential diagnosis, 17-17
  neurological dysfunction from, 12-5
Health promotion programs, in family violence prevention, 27-6
Heller v. Doe, 23-6
Hendricks decision. *See Kansas v. Hendricks*
Heritability
  of behavior, legal impact of, 9-12
  definition of, 8-4
  of emperament, 2-6
  estimations, 9-5
  of impulsive behavioral disorders, 9-6
  serotonin, 9-10
Heroin use, by injection, 13-3, 13-4
High-risk behavior
  in attention deficit hyperactivity disorder, 18-5, 18-6
  of drug injectors, 13-7, 13-9
HIV. *See* Human immunodeficiency virus
Home atmosphere. *See* Environment, home
Homosexual pedophilia, 21-5
Homovanillic acid (HVA), 6-7, 6-8
Hormones
  See also specific hormones
  abnormalities
    childhood sex abuse and, 25-15
    paraphilia development and, 21-7, 21-8
  brain effects, 9-4
Hostility, over-controlled, 22-9
HTR1B gene, 16-9
HTR1DA gene, 16-10
HTR2B gene, 16-9, 16-10
Human immunodeficiency virus (HIV), 13-3
Human service organizations, role in family violence prevention, 27-21
Humiliation
  aggresssion from, 15-4
  serial murder and, 15-8, 15-13, 15-14
Huntington's disease, 20-8
HVA. *See* Homovanillic acid
Hyperactivity
  in attention deficit hyperactivity disorder, 18-4, 18-5
  in Tourette's syndrome, 17-12
Hypoglycemia
  brain dysfunction and, 12-6, 12-7
  violent behavior and, 19-10, 19-11
Hyposexuality, temporal lobe pathology and, 19-8
Hypothalamus, underactivity, 25-14

I

IDU. *See* Injecting drug use
Imipramine, 20-14
Impulse control disorder, case study of, 6-11, 6-13
Impulse Control Scale, 5-10
Impulsivity
  alcoholism, suicidal behavior and, 9-9
  in attention deficit hyperactivity disorder, 18-3, 18-4
  biological studies, 5-11, 5-14
  with laboratory-measured data, 5-12, 5-14
  serotonin, 5-11, 5-12
  crime control strategies and, 7-17
  definition of, 5-9
  delinquent behavior and, 5-10, 5-11
  environmental factors, 5-15
  fluoxetine for, 4-16
  genetic factors, 5-14, 9-14
  genetic studies, 9-3
  heritability of, 9-6
  measurement
    laboratory, 5-10, 5-11, 5-12, 5-14
    rating scales for, 5-9, 5-10
  personal controls for, 10-7
  pharmacotherapy, 5-15, 5-16
  vs. premeditated aggression, 4-12, 4-14, 4-15
  prenatal drug exposure and, 25-10
  in prison, medications for, 17-11, 17-12
  in psychopathology, 5-1, 5-2
  repeated, 5-2
  serotonin and, 5-14, 9-9, 9-11
  sub-seizure states and, 4-9, 4-10
Injecting drug use (IDU), P5-1
  classifying, 13-1, 13-2
  comorbidity, 13-9
    antisocial personality, 13-4, 13-6, 13-7
    depression, 13-6
  substance use/dependence, 13-3, 13-4
    health consequences, 13-3
    injectors, subclassification of, 13-7, 13-9
    prognosis, 13-2, 13-3
    treatment, 13-2, 13-3
Inmates
  aggression classification
    exploratory studies of, 4-10, 4-11
    outpatient studies of, 4-11, 4-12
    phenytoin use and, 4-9, 4-10
    selection process for, 4-10, 4-11
  with attention deficit hyperactivity disorder, ritalin therapy for, 17-3
  epileptic, 19-8
  mental disorder prevalence of, 3-12
  recidivism of, 16-2
Insanity, legal definition of, 15-5
Insight, in obsessive-compulsive disorder, 15-12
Institutions, role in family violence prevention, 27-20
Intelligence, protective influence of, 3-8, 3-9
Interdisciplinary perspective, P1-1
  neutral model of, 1-4, 1-5
  public health implications, 1-7
Interdisciplinary research, in future, 1-7, 1-8
Intermittent explosive disorder, 19-4, 19-5
  case study of, 6-11, 6-13
  CSF 5-HIAA and, 5-11
  DSM-IV criteria, A-2, A-3
Intermittent explosive rage disorder, 17-4, 17-5
International Classification of Diseases (ICD-9), frontal lobe syndrome and, 22-5
Interpersonal Problem Solving (IPA), 10-10
Isolation, serial murder and, 15-13, 15-14

J

Jail population. *See* Inmates

[References are to pages.]

Junior Eysenck Personality Questionnaire (EPQ-Jr), 4-5, 4-7
Juvenile delinquency. *See* Delinquency
Juvenile justice system, alcoholism treatment and, 2-18, 2-19

K

Kansas Sexually Violent Predator Act, 23-4, 23-5, 23-8, 23-9
Kansas v. Hendricks
   history, 23-3
   Kansas Sexually Violent Predator Act and, 23-4, 23-5
   penal implications, 23-9, 23-10
   state's reversal of ruling, 23-5, 23-6
   Supreme Court ruling, 23-6, 23-9
Kelley Form, 12-3, 12-16, 12-18
   correlates of neurological dysfunction, 12-9
   findings/interpretations, 12-10, 12-14
   research methodology, 12-8, 12-10
Klinefelter's syndrome, 21-7
Knockout mutations, 7-2

L

Laboratory aggression, 22-4
   See also Animal models, of aggression
Laboratory studies
   of antisocial behavior, executive cognitive functioning and, 11-10, 11-11
   measurement
      of aggression, 5-2, 5-4
      of impulsivity, 5-10–5-12, 5-14
Language skills
   executive cognitive functioning and, 11-9, 11-10
   temporal lobe dysfunction and, 12-4
Law
   behavioral science applications, P8-1, P8-3
   neurobiology of criminal behavior and, 24-4, 24-6
Lead toxicity, 12-7
Learned helplessness, 10-12
Learning disabilities, with Tourette's syndrome, 16-10
Learning disorders, 16-12
Legal system
   considerations, for treatment models, 26-5
   vs. science, 24-6, 24-7
Legislative branch of government, punishment/treatment authority, 23-7, 23-9
Lesch-Nyhan syndrome, 9-6
LH. *See* Luteinizing hormone
Life History of Aggression Interview, 4-4
Life History of Aggression Scale, 5-2
Linkage analysis, 7-4, 9-7
Lipoid proteinosis of Urbach and Wiethe, 7-3
Lithium, for aggression, 6-11, 20-17
   in antisocial personality disorder, 20-16
   in attention deficit disorder, 20-11
   in conduct disorder, 20-11
   in mental retardation, 20-9, 20-10
Locus of control
   development, 10-12
   external, 10-10, 10-11
   internal, 10-10
   measuring, 10-11, 10-12

Louisiana, Foucha v., 23-7
Loxapine, 20-7
Lust killers, 15-11
   See also Serial murder, killers
Luteinizing hormone (LH), 21-7

M

MAA. *See* Multivariate analysis of associations
Males
   preadolescent, executive cognitive functioning in, 11-3, 11-5
   precocious puberty in, 7-3
Malignant narcissism, 15-10, 15-11, 15-14
Manic-depressive illness. *See* Bipolar disorder
a-Mannosidosis, 7-3
MAO. *See* Monoamine oxidase
Maternal drug use, brain dysfunction from, 12-7, 12-8
m-Chlorophenylpiperazine (m-CPP), 20-2
McMaster Family Assessment Device (MFAD), 4-4
Means Ends Problem Solving (MEPS), 10-9
Medications, P7-1, P7-2
   for antisocial behavior, P7-1, P7-3
   for attention deficit hyperactivity disorder, 18-10, 18-11
      administration to inmates, 17-11
      for inmates, 17-10, 17-11
   for attention deficit hyperactivity disorder, DAT1 gene and, 16-9
   for bipolar disorder, 17-13, 17-14
   for criminal violence, 19-15, 19-16
   for obsessive-compulsive behavior, 17-13
   for pathological aggression, 20-5, 20-6
   in prison, selling, 17-11
   in prison, using. *See* Prison, medications used in
Medroxyprogesterone acetate (MPA; Depo-Provera), 21-11, 21-13
Mental abnormality, definition of, 23-4, 23-7
Mental disorders
   See also specific mental disorders
   crime/violence and
      classification and, 3-14
      disaggregation and, 3-13, 3-14
   definition, broadening of, 23-7
   diagnostic classifications, 15-5, 15-7
   expert opinion, relevance of, 23-7
   temporal distribution, 3-13
   violence and, 3-12, 3-13
Mental health professionals
   experts, implications for, 24-6, 24-9
   family violence advocates and, 27-12, 27-14
Mental health scientist, role of, 24-7, 24-9
Mental illness. *See* Mental disorders
Mental retardation, pathological aggression in, 20-9, 20-10
Mentally handicapped patients, pathological aggression in, 20-9, 20-10
MEPS. *See* Means Ends Problem Solving
Mercury toxicity, 12-7
Methylphenidate (Ritalin), 16-9
   for aggression
      in ADD/ADHD, 20-11
      in conduct disorder, 20-11
   for attention deficit hyperactivity disorder, 7-11

[References are to pages.]

Methylphenidate *(continued)*
    in adult, 17-3
    in inmate, 17-11
    for impulsivity, 7-11
    for Tourette's syndrome, 7-11, 17-12
MFAD. *See* McMaster Family Assessment Device
Mimicry, adolescent psychopathy and, 19-4
Minnesota Multiphasic Personality Inventory (MMPI), 7-10, 10-7
Minor physical anomalies (MPA), 25-8, 25-9
Monoamine oxidase (MAO), 9-11, 9-12
Monoamine oxidase genes, 16-11, 16-12
Monozygotic twins. *See* Twin studies
Moral development theory, criminology and, 10-3
Morality, vs. scientific models, 24-4
Motivation
    effect on criminal/delinquent behavior, 3-10
    for serial murder, 15-4
MPA. *See* Medroxyprogesterone acetate
Multidisciplinary perspective. *See* Interdisciplinary perspective
Multivariate analysis of associations (MAA), 16-13, 16-17
Murderers
    neuropathology in, 19-15
    serial. *See* Serial murder, killers in

N

Nadolol, for aggression, 6-11, 20-13
Narcissism, malignant, 15-10, 15-11
Narcissistic personality disorder, 15-11, 15-12
National Comorbidity Survey, 13-3
Nature-nurture controversy, criminality and, 24-1, 24-2, 25-6, 25-7
Necrophilia
    definition of, 15-7
    etiology, 15-7, 15-8
Neurobiology
    of criminal behavior, legal policy and, 24-4, 24-6
    research, behavioral predestination and, 25-3, 25-4
Neurochemical systems
    activators, 19-9, 19-10
    in pathological aggression, 20-2
Neurologic disorders/deficits. *See* Neuropathology
Neuromodulators, 19-9
Neuronal synthesis, diet and, 12-6
Neuropathology
    correlates of, 12-9
    criminal aggression and, 22-9, 22-10
    in murderers, 19-15
    with pathological anger/aggression, 20-5
    sources, head injuries, 12-5
    violence and, 12-4, 12-5
Neuropsychology
    abnormal, violence and, 12-4, 12-5
    cognitive tests, 11-2
    definition of, 11-2
    research, social consequences of, 25-10
    specialists, executive cognitive skills interventions and, 11-12, 11-13
Neurosciences, knowledge explosion in, 22-2, 22-3
Neurotransmitters, 9-3, 9-4
    See also specific neurotransmitters
    behavioral effects, 19-9, 19-10
    child abuse and, 25-15
    criminal behavior and, 18-3
Nicotine
    See also Tobacco dependence
    prenatal exposure, 25-10, 25-11
Norepinephrine
    in attention deficit hyperactivity disorder, 16-10, 16-11
    behavioral effects, 19-10
    facilitation of aggression, 6-7
Norm of reaction, for phenotype change, 2-2, 2-4
Nowicki-Strickland Locus of Control Scale (N-SLCS), 10-11, 10-12
Nurses' Observation Scale for Inpatient Evaluation, 20-4

O

Obsessive-compulsive disorder (OCD)
    diagnostic criteria, 15-11, 15-12
    dopamine and, 9-8
    medications for, 17-13
    in serial murder, 15-11, 15-12, 15-16
Offenders
    ADD/ADHD missed diagnosis, hidden costs of, 17-19, 17-20
    with attention deficit hyperactivity disorder, 18-7, 18-8
    cognitive processes, lack of emphasis on, 10-3, 10-5
    family violence, treatment programs for, 27-17
    impulsive, CSF 5-HIAA in, 6-4
    mental illness of, 21-1, 21-2
    in prison. *See* Inmates; Prison
    psychopathology risk factors in, 26-2
    sexual assessment of, 21-2, 21-3
    sexually violent. *See* Sexually violent predator
Opioid dependence, of drug injectors, 13-7, 13-8
Oppositional defiant disorder
    DSM-IV criteria, A-5
    inheritance, polygenic, 16-13, 16-15
    molecular genetics, androgen receptor gene, 16-12
Organic brain disorder
    differential diagnosis, 17-17
    in murderers, 19-15
    pathological aggression in, pharmacotherapy for, 20-8, 20-9
Organic obsessional pathologies, 19-6, 19-7
Organismic specificity hypothesis, 2-12
Over-controlled personalities, 19-6
Overt Aggression Scale, 20-3
Oxazepam, 20-7

P

Pairwise concordance, 8-4
Paraphilias
    biological basis for, 21-7, 21-8
    biologically based drives and, 21-6
    classification of, 21-3
    as craving disorders, 21-8, 21-9
    definition of, 15-7, 21-3, 21-4
    etiology, 15-7, 15-8, 21-6, 21-8
    psychiatric diagnosis of, 21-4

[References are to pages.]

treatment
    behavioral, 21-9, 21-10
    pharmacologic, 21-11, 21-12
    psychotherapy, 21-9
    rationale for, 21-8
    surgical, 21-10, 21-11
Parent-child relationship
    alcoholism development and, 2-5, 2-13, 2-14
    bidirectionality of influences in, 3-7, 3-8
Parenting
    by female addicts, 14-6, 14-7
    interaction with prenatal conditions, 25-16
    intergenerational transmission, 14-11
Parents
    adoptive, criminal history, effect on child, 7-13
    biological, criminal history, effect on child, 7-13
    of female addicts, 14-5, 14-6
Parent-teacher associations, role in family violence prevention, 27-21
Paroxetine (Paxil), 20-15
Paxil (paroxetine), 17-13
Pedophilia, 21-4, 21-5
    development, affectional interests and, 21-6, 21-7
    fixated, 21-5
    homosexual, 21-5
    nonexclusive form of, 21-5
    regressed, 21-4, 21-5
Peer groups, alcoholism and, 2-5
Pemoline (Cylert), 7-11, 16-9
Perception of skills, vs. skill, 10-10
Perinatal complications, impulsivity/aggression and, 25-12, 25-13
Perry Preschool Project, 3-11, 3-12
Personality, heuristic model of, 4-3
Personality disorders
    aggression in, 20-16, 20-17
    antisocial. *See* Antisocial personality disorder
    definition of, 23-7
    DSM-IV classification, 15-5, 15-6
    intermittent explosive. *See* Intermittent explosive disorder
    narcissistic, 15-11, 15-12
    necrophilia and, 15-7, 15-8
    obsessive-compulsive. *See* Obsessive-compulsive disorder
Personality factors
    heritability of, 9-2
    traits, aggression criterion measures and, 4-7
Personality measures, 4-5
Pharmacotherapy. *See* Medications; specific medications
Phencyclidine dependence, of drug injectors, 13-7, 13-8
Phenocopies, 7-16
Phenothiazines, for Tourette's syndrome, 17-12
Phenotype, 9-4
Phenotypic variance, genetic-environment interaction and, 7-15, 7-16
Phenytoin, for aggression, 4-9, 4-10, 4-15, 4-16
Physical anomalies, minor, 25-8, 25-9
Pindolol, 20-8
PMS syndrome, testosterone and, 19-10
Point Subtraction Aggression Paradigm (PSAP), 5-3, 5-4

Post acute withdrawal, 18-13
Posttraumatic stress disorder (PTSD), 25-16, 25-17
    aggression in, 20-15
    brain biochemistry, 25-4
    dopamine and, 9-8
    DRD2 gene and, 16-6, 16-7
Power, serial murder and, 15-3
Precocious puberty, male, 7-3
Predatory violence, 19-2, 19-3
Pregnancy
    smoking during, 25-10, 25-11
    social environment during, 25-12
Premature aging, 25-14, 25-15
Premeditated aggression, vs. impulsivity, 4-12, 4-14, 4-15
Premenstrual dysphoric disorder, aggression in, 20-15
Prenatal conditions
    drug exposure, 25-9, 25-10
    interaction with parenting, 25-16
Prevention, of antisocial behaviors
    of delinquency, early childhood intervention for, 3-10, 3-12
    essential concepts for, 25-4, 25-5
    neurobiological research implications, 25-18, 25-22
Preventive medicine, 22-11
Prison
    ADD/ADHD missed diagnosis, hidden costs of, 17-19, 17-20
    attention deficit hyperactivity disorder treatment program, 16-17, 16-18
    certificate of completion, 17-7
    challenge for prison medicine, 17-15, 17-16
    education of corrections officers and, 17-14, 17-15
    evolution of, 17-3
    follow-up for, 17-4, 17-5
    group training methods, 17-7, 17-9
    initial interview for, 17-3, 17-4
    justification for medical therapy, 17-10
    medication use concerns, 17-10, 17-11
    relation to corrections program, 17-5
    results, 17-9, 17-10
    self-help/educational books/articles, 17-6
    training group, 17-5, 17-7
    medications used in
        for attention deficit, 17-11, 17-12
        for bipolar disorder, 17-13, 17-14
        for emotional leveling, 17-12, 17-13
        for impulsive distractibility, 17-11, 17-12
        for obsessive-compulsive behavior, 17-13
    offenders in. *See* Inmates
Probation officers, brain dysfunction identification by. *See* Kelley Form
Problem-solving ability, measuring, 10-9, 10-10
Problem-Solving Inventory (PSI), 10-10
Professional education/training, in family violence, 27-23
Prolactin release
    buspirone and, 5-7, 5-8
    impulsivity and, 5-12, 5-14

[References are to pages.]

Propranolol, for aggression, 6-11
   in dementia, 20-7
   in Huntington's disease, 20-8
   in mental retardation, 20-9
   in organic brain syndrome, 20-8
Protective factors
   for abused/neglected children, 3-8, 3-9
   in antisocial outcome, 25-5
   for family violence, identification of, 27-3
   temperament as, 3-9, 3-10
Prozac. *See* Fluoxetine
PSAP. *See* Point Subtraction Aggression Paradigm
PSI. *See* Problem-Solving Inventory
Psychiatric disorders, with pathological anger/
    aggression, 20-5
Psychiatric testimony, 24-7, 24-8
Psychiatry, contributions to legal system, 24-6,
   24-7
Psychoactive substance intoxication/withdrawal,
   aggression in, 20-14
Psychological theories, of criminality
   attachment, 3-6
   cognitive social learning, 3-5, 3-6
   social control, 3-6, 3-7
Psychologists, role in community family violence
   prevention programs, 27-11, 27-12
Psychology
   in criminal justice education, 3-14, 3-15
   in criminology/criminal justice education, 3-2,
   3-3
Psychopathy
   See also specific psychopathological disorders
   adolescent, 19-4
   classification, 19-3
   differential diagnosis, 17-17, 17-18
   impulsivity/aggression in, 5-1, 5-2
   low executive cognitive functioning and, 11-3
   risk factors, in offender population, 26-2
Psychosis, dopamine and, 9-8
Psychosocial dwarfism, 25-14
Psychostimulants
   for aggression, 20-8, 20-18
   for attention deficit hyperactivity disorder,
   18-10
Psychotherapy, for sexual deviation disorders,
   21-9
PTSD. *See* Posttraumatic stress disorder
Public education
   for family violence prevention, 27-18, 27-25
   importance of, 26-2
Public health
   interdisciplinary research implications, 1-7
   model
     civil liberty and, 26-6, 26-7
     description of, 26-5, 26-6
   policy
     for family violence prevention, 27-15,
     27-18
     genetic research impact on, 9-13, 9-14
Public safety, criminal justice system and, 23-3
Public schools. *See* School
Punishment
   for crime, 23-1, 23-2
   for drug problem, 23-14

Q
Quantitative trait loci (QTL), 2-16

R
Rage
   in attention deficit hyperactivity disorder, 18-5
   single-episode, 19-5, 19-6
RAS. *See* reticular activating system
Receptors, 9-4, 9-5
Regressed pedophilia, 21-4, 21-5
Rehabilitation, traditional vs. therapeutic justice, 23-13,
   23-14
Rejection, as trauma event for serial killer, 15-3
Responsibility, free will and, 15-14, 15-15
Reticular activating system (RAS), 25-13, 25-14
Retrospective Overt Aggression Scale, 5-2
Reward deficiency syndrome, 17-19
Reward pathways, in dopamine system, 9-8, 9-9
Risk markers, for brain-proneness to violence, 22-11,
   22-12
Risperidone, for aggression in dementia, 20-7
Ritalin. *See* Methylphenidate
Role-taking, 10-6, 10-8

S
Sanity
   of serial killers, 15-7, 15-8
   serial murder and, 15-4, 15-7
Scale for the Assessment of Aggression and Agitated
   Behaviors, 20-3, 20-4
Schizophrenia
   impulsive/aggressive behavior in, 9-6
   pathological aggression in, 20-12, 20-14
School
   family violence interventions, 27-18
   family violence prevention programs, 27-19, 27-20
   performance, protective influence of, 3-9
Science, vs. legal system, 24-6, 24-7
Scientific models, vs. morality, 24-4
Seasonal variations, violence and, 19-11
Sedative-hypnotic dependence, of drug injectors, 13-7,
   13-8
Seizure disorders
   atypical, differential diagnosis of, 17-16
   pathological aggression in, 20-9
Selective serotonin reuptake inhibitors (SSRIs).
   See also specific serotonin reuptake inhibitors
   for aggression, 6-10, 6-11, 20-18
     in autism, 20-12
     in dementia, 20-7
     in mental retardation, 20-10
   for attention deficit hyperactivity disorder,
   18-10
Self-control, criminal behavior and, 10-15
Self-esteem, of serial killer, 15-3
Self-medication behavior, in ADHD, 18-6
Self-motivation, for addiction recovery in ADHD,
   18-13
Self-report instruments, for assessing pathological
   aggression, 20-4, 20-5
Sensation-seeking, 25-14, 25-17
Sensitivity, in attention deficit hyperactivity disorder,
   18-5
Sensory deprivation, 25-13, 25-14

[References are to pages.]

Sentencing, multidisciplinary approach, 23-11
Serial murder, 15-15, 15-16, P5-2
   alienation and, 15-13, 15-14
   as compulsion
      factors in, 15-11, 5-14
      free will and, 15-14, 15-15
   conceptual models, 15-2, 15-4
   drug addiction and, 15-16, 15-17
   fantasies and, 15-3, 15-4
   insanity defense for, 15-4, 15-5
   isolation and, 15-13, 15-14
   killers in, 15-2
      antisocial personality disorder and, 15-6
      characteristics of, 15-2, 15-3, 15-8
      circumstantial traits of, 15-9, 15-10
      definition of, 15-2
      dissociation of, 15-3
      nonpsychotic, 15-13
      predispositional factors of, 15-3
      psychological traits of, 15-9, 15-10
      psychotic, 15-6
      sadistic, 15-11
      sanity of, 15-7, 15-8
      self-esteem of, 15-3
   motivation for, 15-4
   obsessive-compulsive disorder and, 15-16
   of sexual nature, 15-2
   sexual sadism and, 15-8
   terminology, 15-2
Serotonergic agents, for aggression
   in mental retardation, 20-10
   in schizophrenia, 20-13, 20-14
Serotonin
   addiction and, 18-3
   in aggression, 5-4, 5-6, 5-14
      pharmaco-challenge studies, 6-5, 6-6
      treatment implications of, 6-10, 6-11
   alcohol-induced behaviors and, 9-10, 9-11
   attention deficit hyperactivity disorder and, 18-3
   behavioral effects, 19-10
   cholesterol and, 6-9
   genetic variants, 9-11
   heritability, 9-10
   in impulsive aggression, 6-3, 66-4
   impulsivity and, 5-11, 5-12, 5-14, 9-9, 9-11
   nature-nuture interaction and, 25-6
   overexpression, early, 6-5, 6-6
   in psychopathy, 19-3
   stress levels and, 25-6
   synapse, abnormalities in, 6-4, 6-5
   transmission functions, 5-4
   tryptophan manipulation and, 5-6, 5-7
Serotonin genes, 16-9, 16-10
Sertraline (Zoloft)
   for aggression
      in Huntington's disease, 20-8
      in mental retardation, 20-10
   for emotional leveling, 17-13
   for obsessive-compulsive behavior, 17-13
Sex differences. *See* Gender differences
Sex offender
   assessment of, 21-2, 21-3
   violent. *See* Sexually violent predator
Sexual addiction, 15-14

Sexual deviation disorders
   See also Paraphilias; Pedophilia
   vs. bad behaviors, 21-5
   biological basis for, 21-5, 21-7, 8
   as mental health issue, 21-2, 21-3, 21-14
   treatment, 21-8, 21-9
      behavioral, 21-9, 21-10
      pharmacologic, 21-11, 21-12
      pharmacologic with counseling, 21-12, 21-13
      psychotherapy, 21-9
      rationale for, 21-8
      surgical, 21-10, 21-11
Sexual dysfunction, temporal lobe pathology and, 19-8
Sexual makeup
   abnormal, vs. bad behavior, 21-5, 21-6
   biologically based drives and, 21-5
Sexual orientation, pedophilia development and, 21-6, 21-7
Sexual perversion, temporal lobe pathology and, 19-8
Sexual sadism, serial murder and, 15-8
Sexually violent predators
   definition of, 23-4
   probable cause, 23-5
   segregation of, 23-8
Skill, vs. perception of skills, 10-10
Sleeping disorders, 19-7
Smoking
   See also Tobacco dependence
   during pregnancy, 25-10, 25-11
Sociability, alcoholism and, 2-9
Sociability Subscale of California Psychological Inventory (SO-CPI), 4-4
Social bonding theory, 10-14, 10-17
Social control, delinquency and, 10-17
Social control theory, 3-15 n.2
Social disadvantage, executive cognitive functioning and, 11-4
Social Dysfunction and Aggression Scale, 20-4
Social environment
   for aggression, 5-3
   brain development/function and, 25-13
   breeding violence, interventions for changing, 27-6
   during pregnancy, 25-12
Social factors, criminal justice practices and, 1-2
Social learning theory, 3-4, 3-5, 10-13, 10-14
Social perspective-taking, 10-6, 10-8
Social predictor measures
   aggression criterion measures and, 4-6, 4-7
   description, 4-4
Social responding, for attention deficit hyperactivity disorder, 18-11
Social risk factors, in antisocial outcome, 25-5
Social sciences, governing variables and, 22-10, 22-10
Socioenvironmental risk factors, dynamic relationships of, 26-3, 26-4
Sociological explanations, for criminology, 10-3, 10-4
Somatization disorder, 24-2
Somnambulism, 19-7
Soothability, alcoholism and, 2-8
Speech processes, in violent offenders, 12-4
SSRIs. *See* Selective serotonin reuptake inhibitors
Staff Observation Aggression Scale, 20-3, 20-4

[References are to pages.]

State-Trait Anger Expression Inventory, 20-4
State-Trait Anger Scale, 5-2, 20-4
Stimulants, for Tourette's syndrome, 17-12
Stimulation level, in attention deficit hyperactivity disorder, 18-5, 18-6
Stress
   definition of, 25-7, 25-8
   prenatal, 25-8
Stress hormones, child abuse/trauma and, 25-15–25-17
Stress-diathesis model of schizophrenia, 7-17
Stressors, social environment, 25-13
Substance abuse/addiction
   See also Alcohol abuse; Alcoholism; Substance use disorder
   antisocial personality prevalence in, 8-1
   in attention deficit hyperactivity disorder, 18-6
      crime and, 18-7
      treatment controversy for, 18-13, 18-14
   cocaine, aggressiveness and, 9-9
   dependence, DSM-IV criteria, A-1, A-2
   differential diagnosis, 17-17
   difficult temperament and, 2-15
   dopamine and, 9-8
   DRD2 gene and, 16-6–16-8
   DSM-IV criteria, A-2
   environmental factors, 25-6, 25-7
   female addicts
      addiction careers and, 14-10
      child sex abuse of, 14-2, 14-3
      course of addiction, 14-5, 14-6
      family dynamics, 14-5, 14-6
      general impressions on, 14-8, 14-9
      home atmosphere ratings, 14-7, 14-8
      parental substance use and, 14-10
      parenting behaviors of, 14-6, 14-7
      parents of, 14-5, 14-6
      psychological status of, 14-7, 14-8
      psychological symptoms and, 14-10, 14-11
      treatment/prevention approaches, 14-12, 14-13
   genetic factors, 25-6
   inheritance, APD and, 8-11
   necrophilia and, 15-8
   parental, 2-15, 14-10
   prenatal drug exposure and, 25-9, 25-10
   reward deficiency syndrome and, 17-19
   risk, child sexual abuse and, P5-1, P5-2
   serial murder and, 15-16, 15-17
   serotonin levels in, 5-6
   treatment for, 26-4, 26-5
   war on drugs and, 23-14, 23-15
Substance use disorder (SUD)
   See also Alcoholism; Substance abuse/addiction
   with antisocial personality disorder, 8-2
      adoption studies, 8-10, 8-11
      behavioral genetics of, 8-13
      diagnostic problems, 8-12, 8-13
      etiology and, 8-2, 8-3, 8-12
      familial risk and, 8-10
      familial transmission and, 8-12
      future studies of, 8-13, 8-14
      prevalence of, 8-1, 8-2

      shared environmental influences, 8-12
      twin studies, 8-10–8-12
   executive cognitive functioning and, 11-3
   family history, executive cognitive functioning and, 11-3, 11-5
   genetic influences, 8-4, 8-5
      adoption studies, 8-5
      twin studies, 8-5–8-7
   with illicit drug use, 13-3, 13-4
   subclassification, 13-2
Substantive due process, 23-6
Suicidal behavior
   alcoholism, impulsivity and, 9-9
   depression and, 9-6, 13-6
   low CSF 5-HIAA and, 6-3, 6-4
   serotonin levels and, 9-9
   serotonin synapse abnormalities and, 6-4, 6-5
Suicide and Aggression Survey, 20-4
Symptom Questionnaire, 20-5

T

Tactile contact, deficiency in, 25-14
Taylor Aggression Paradigm (TAP), 11-11
Taylor's Competitive Reaction Time Task, 5-3, 5-4
TDO (trypthophan 2,3-dioxygenase), 16-10
TD02A gene, 16-10
Tegretol. *See* Carbamazepine
Television violence, 25-17, 25-18
Temperament
   aggression and, 6-2
   alcoholism liability and, 2-2, 2-3, 2-6, 2-9
   brain dysfunction and, 25-2
   definition of, 2-6
   difficult
      alcoholism risk and, 2-14, 2-15
      behavior problems and, 2-13
   executive cognitive functioning and, 11-7, 11-9
   heritibility of, 2-6
   nature-nuture interaction and, 25-6
   protective effects of, 3-9, 3-10
   substance abuse and, 2-15
Temporal lobe pathology
   sexual dysfunction and, 19-8
   violence and, 12-3, 12-4
Tenex (guanfacine), 17-12
Test of Variables of Attention (TOVA), 18-8
Testosterone
   brain development and, 25-7
   in impulsive aggression, 6-8
   lowering, to diminish sexual cravings, 21-10, 21-11
   PMS syndrome and, 19-10
Texas, Addington v., 23-7
Therapeutic jurisprudence, 23-11
Therapeutic justice, 23-15, 23-17
   culpability and, 23-12, 23-14
   definition of, 23-11, 23-12
   vs. therapeutic jurisprudence, 23-11
   vs. traditional rehabilitation, 23-13, 23-14
   view of crime and, 23-14
Therapists, family violence training for, 27-23
Tobacco dependence

[References are to pages.]

of drug injectors, 13-7, 13-8
twin studies, 8-6
Tourette's syndrome
  with ADHD, pharmacotherapy for, 17-5
  aggression in, 7-3
  conduct disorder and, 16-3
  DBH gene and, 16-10
  dopamine and, 9-8
  dopamine genes and, 16-8, 16-9
  DRD2 gene and, 16-6, 16-7
  hyperactivity/tics in, 17-12
  learning disabilities with, 16-10
  methylphenidate for, 7-11
  monoamine oxidase genes in, 16-12
  stimulant usage in, 17-12
TOVA. *See* Test of Variables of Attention
TPH gene (tryptophan hydroxylase), 9-11
Transvestitic fetishes, 21-3, 21-4
Tranylcypromine, 20-16
Trauma Control Model for Serial Murder, 15-2–15-4
Traumatic experience
  adolescent, 25-16, 25-17
  adult, 25-16, 25-17
  behavioral disorder risk and, 25-15, 25-16
  biologial traits and, 25-4
  specific event, for serial killer, 15-3
Trazodone, for aggression, 20-18
  in conduct disorder, 20-12
  in dementia, 20-7
  in organic brain syndrome, 20-8
Tricyclic antidepressants, 20-12
Tridimensional Personality Profile, 5-10
Trypthophan 2,3-dioxygenase (TDO), 16-10
Tryptophan
  aggression and, 5-6, 5-7
  for aggression in schizophrenia, 20-13
  depletion, 5-6, 5-7
  serotonin system and, 5-5
Tryptophan hydroxylase gene (TPH), 9-11
Twin studies
  vs. adoption studies, 7-15, 7-16
  antisocial personality disorder, 8-8, 8-9
  birth complication risks and, 7-14, 7-15
  comorbidity with SUD, 8-10, 8-11, 8-12
  criminal behavior data, 7-6, 7-10
  of criminality, 24-3, 24-4
  environmental influences, 7-8, 7-10, 7-12
  genetic influences on, 7-6, 7-8
  epidemiological estimations, 7-6, 7-8
  methodology, 8-4
  rationale for, 7-4, 7-5

substance use disorder, 8-5, 8-6, 8-7

U

United States, Washington v., 24-7
United States v. Brawner, 24-7
Urban stress syndrome, 1-7
Urokinase deficiency, 7-3

V

Valproate (Depakote)
  for aggression, 20-17
  in borderline personality disorder, 20-16
  in dementia, 20-7
  for emotional leveling, 17-13
Vasopressin, in impulsive aggression, 6-8, 6-9
Violence
  in adolescent psychopathy, 19-4
  anatomical substrates, 19-9
  in attention deficit hyperactivity disorder, 18-5
  biological brain-proneness, 22-3, 22-11, 22-22
  brain dysfunction and, 12-3, 12-5
  chemical substrates, 19-9, 19-11
  clinical evolution of, 19-13, 19-14
  criminal. *See* Criminal behavior
  cycle of, 3-4, 3-5
  epilepsy and, 19-8, 19-9
  family. *See* Family violence
  mental disorders and, 3-12, 3-13
    classification and, 3-14
    disaggregation and, 3-13, 3-14
  neurologic typology of, 19-2, 19-4
  neuropathology and, 19-15
  neurophysiological correlates, 19-11, 19-12
  pharmacotherapy for, 19-15, 19-16
  predatory, 19-2, 19-3
  as sickness, perceptions of, 15-15
  sleeping-related, 19-7
  television, 25-17, 25-18
Vulnerability
  to antisocial behavior, P1, P2, 1-3, 9-2
  levels of, 9-5, 9-6

W

Washington v. United States, 24-7
Wellbutrin. *See* Bupropion
Wender Utah Rating Scale, 5-10
Women's groups, family violence prevention and, 27-9, 27-10

Z

Zoloft. *See* Sertraline
Zoophilia, 21-4
Zuclopenthixol, 20-9